Transportation
Noise
Reference
Book

Transportation Noise Reference Book

Edited by
P. M. Nelson, BSc, PhD, FIOA

With specialist contributors

Butterworths
London · Boston · Durban · Singapore
Sydney · Toronto · Wellington

First published, 1987

© **Butterworth & Co. (Publishers) Ltd., 1987**

British Library Cataloguing in Publication Data

Transportation noise reference book
    1. Transportation Noise
    I. Nelson, P.M.
    363.7′43   TD893.6.T7
    ISBN 0–408–01446–6

Library of Congress Cataloging in Publication Data

Transportation noise reference book.
    Includes bibliographies
    1. Transportation noise—Handbooks, manuals, etc.
    2. Noise control—Handbooks, manuals, etc.
    I. Nelson, P.M.
    TD893.6.T7T73   1987   363.7′41   86–29944
    ISBN 0–408–01446–6

Photoset by Latimer Trend & Company Ltd, Plymouth
Printed in Great Britain at the University Press, Cambridge

Preface

This book was commissioned to provide a comprehensive and up-to-date review of transportation noise and vibration, its impact on man and structures, and the methods of control that are available. As a Reference book it aims to provide the reader with a balanced and unbiased presentation of the essential facts and interpretations that have emerged from research and other areas of development and, in addition, to provide directions for further information. The book is intended to be used by both students and teachers in universities and colleges and, as a research and consultancy aid, by the wide range of vocational groups who work in this field.

The book comprises 24 chapters arranged in six parts. In grouping the chapters, I have attempted to account for the need to divide the subject into easily managed component parts whilst retaining sufficient flexibility for a full coverage of each topic. Part 1 gives a general introduction to transportation noise covering the basic acoustics and the scales, indices and ratings that are used frequently in the book. Also included is a general overview of the subject area, an examination of the extent of the problem on a worldwide basis and the trends in exposure expected in the future. Part 2 deals with the effects of noise on man. The chapters include a review of community effects, which include summaries of activity disturbance, task performance and annoyance. Possible links between noise, physiological change and health outcomes are examined as is the particularly important problem of the effects of transport noise on sleep. Parts 3, 4 and 5 deal in turn with the three principal transport modes. Each of these parts is structured in a similar way, beginning with a description of the sources of noise on the transport vehicle and the engineering processes which can be invoked to control emission, through to the wider issues associated with transport systems and their operation. Here a full coverage is given of the noise generation and propagation characteristics, methods of prediction, and noise and vibration control procedures. In addition, chapters have been included which justify special attention. For example in Part 3, which deals with road traffic noise, there is a chapter devoted entirely to vehicle noise emission legislation and type approval test methods. This reflects the considerable activity that has oc- curred on this topic in recent years worldwide and the particular importance that recent developments have had on the Com- munity countries of Western Europe. The final part of the book describes the methods that have been devised to allow the noise impacts resulting from transport development to be considered alongside other economic and social factors. The case for putting money values to noise impacts in order to influence decisions about transport development and the use of fiscal incentives in the form of taxes and compensation are presented.

The SI system of units is used throughout the book although some relaxations have been allowed and where necessary imper- ial equivalents are also given where these are still in common use. An appendix at the end of the book lists some of the more important conversion factors. Other appendices include a gloss- ary of acoustical terms, a collation of standards and standard authorities and some addresses which appear frequently in the text.

I have greatly enjoyed planning, editing and writing contribu- tions for the Transportation Noise Reference Book. The project provided me with the opportunity and challenge of bringing together in a single publication, the results of a vast library of research and development on a broadly based range of topics covering a wide range of disciplines. I am, of course, greatly indebted to all the authors for the very worthwhile chapters they have contributed, for the hard work that they all have put in, and for their patience and sustained interest during the lengthy development of this project. I am also grateful for the support and encouragement given to me by Don Goodsell of Butter- worths who originally agreed to commission the work and more recently by Anne Smith at Butterworths who guided the book through the various stages of production and checking. Finally I would like to thank the Director of the Transport and Road Research Laboratory who originally gave his permission for me to undertake this project.

Paul M. Nelson
Transport and Road Research Laboratory
Crowthorne
Berkshire
England.

Basic Definitions and Symbology Conventions

Definitions

The terms 'level', 'scale', 'index' and 'rating' occur frequently within the literature, often without distinction, and this can be confusing. In this book it has been the intention to adopt the following convention throughout:

'*Level*' is the instantaneous auditory magnitude of the sound, e.g. the A-weighted sound level, L_A.

'*Noise scale*' refers to a combination of the physical variables which contribute to peoples' overall response to noise, such as sound pressure, time etc., e.g. the noise level exceeded for 10% of the time, L_{10}.

'*Noise index*' or '*noise rating*' refers to the numerical description of noise in which other factors are superimposed on the scale numbers describing the physical properties of the noise. These may include corrections for type of neighbourhood, number of noisy events, corrections for time of day or season etc. For example, the noise and number index, NNI.

Symbology

Whenever possible, all levels and scales used in formulae and mathematical expressions in this book will be symbolized by the letter 'L' with an appropriate suffix. In some cases this will distinguish the symbology used from the definition and description of the level or scale in the text which will, preferably, use the acronymic abbreviation.

For example: the scale of the perceived noise level will be described in the text by its acronym, PNL, but will appear in mathematical expressions as L_{PN}.

Exceptions to the convention will occur for some noise scales which are regarded as having a generally accepted form in the literature. For example, the equivalent continuous noise level will appear as L_{eq} whether it is referred to as part of the text or as part of a mathematical expression.

Contents

Contents

List of Contributors

A ALEXANDRE, PhD
Organisation for Economic Co-operation and Development,
2 rue Andre Pascale, Paris 16, France

Ariel Alexandre is a doctor in Social Psychology (Sorbonne
University). Until 1968 he participated in various research
studies on housing and neighbourhood adaptation to human
needs with the Paris Laboratory of Applied Anthropology.
Since then he has been an international civil servant working
with the OECD Environment Directorate where he is responsible for programmes on noise and transport and for various
projects aimed at improving the urban environment. He is the
co-author with Jean Philippe Barde of several books and articles
on noise. He has also published various articles on transport
and urban affairs.

J-PH BARDE, PhD
Organisation for Economic Co-operation and Development, 2
rue Andre Pascal, Paris 16, France

Jean-Philippe Barde has a PhD in economics and is in charge of
economic analysis of environmental policies at the Organisation
for Economic Co-operation and Development (OECD) in Paris.
As such he has been involved in the work on Noise Abatement
Policies. He is member of the French Scientific Committee on
Noise and Vibration and is teaching Environmental Economics
at Paris University. He has published one book and several
articles in environmental economics and is co-author with Ariel
Alexandre of several books and articles on noise.

C J BAUGHAN, BSc, MSc, MErgS
Transport and Road Research Laboratory, Crowthorne, Berkshire, UK

Chris Baughan is head of Environmental Appraisal Section at
the Transport and Road Research Laboratory. His current
research interests include developing methods of forecasting
perceived nuisance from roads and traffic, and the measurement
of water spray from lorries. He has published work on nuisance
from road construction operations, public attitudes to alternative sizes of lorry, a national survey of lorry nuisance, and the
nature and forecasting of traffic vibration nuisance. He holds
degrees in Mechanical Engineering and in Applied Psychology
and is a Registered Member of the Ergonomics Society.

C R BRAGDON, PhD, AICP
Professor, City Planning Director, Continuing Education,
Georgia Institute of Technology, Atlanta, Georgia, USA

Clifford Bragdon is a professor of City Planning and Associate
Vice President of Education Extension at the Georgia Institute
of Technology. He has been at the University since 1972. Prior
to his present position, he was the Assistant Dean, College of
Architecture.

Professor Bragdon's specialty is the field of environmental
planning, in which he has published four books as well as over
40 articles. He has lectured widely on this general subject
throughout the United States besides performing consultative
services for approximately 200 clients in government and in
business. Dr Bragdon is a Fellow, Acoustical Society of America, and serves on several national and international committees.

He holds a Masters in City Planning from Michigan State
University and a PhD in the same field from the University of
Pennsylvania.

B BUNA BSc, PhD, MIOA
Head of Research Department, Institute for Transport Sciences,
H-1502 Budapest, P O Box 107, Hungary

Bela Buna graduated in traffic engineering and later in electrical
engineering from University of Technology Budapest. He joined
the Institute for Transport Sciences, Budapest, in 1967 and has
been the head of the Department for Environment Protection
since 1982. He completed his PhD in mechanics in 1972. He
participates in the work of professional working groups in both
Hungary and abroad.

M BURGESS BSc, MSc, MAAS
School of Architecture, University of New South Wales, PO
Box 1, Kensington, NSW 2033, Australia

Marion Burgess graduated with honours in Physics from Sydney
University and spent some years working in the Acoustics
Laboratory at the Experimental Building Station. She obtained
a MSc in Acoustics and has been teaching in the School of
Architecture at the University of New South Wales since 1974.
Her research interests have included the measurement and
prediction of road traffic noise and the methods for reducing its
transmission into buildings.

B M FAVRE, IngDiplENSMP, ENSPM, PhD
Renault–DR, 9–11, Avenue du 18 Juin 1940, 92500 Rueil-
Malmaison, France

Bernard Favre studied civil and mechanical engineering at the
Ecole Nationale Superieure des Mines de Paris then at the
Ecole Nationale Superieure du Petrole et des Moteurs. He then
joined Institut de Recherche des Transports in 1973, where he
worked on the development of road traffic noise computation
methods and concluded a Doctorat d'Etat thesis in applied
acoustics. He has contributed to research in the field of road
vehicle noise emission, propagation, computer simulation, noise
screens assessment, low frequency noise and vibration; he has
been in charge of quiet road vehicle development technical
assessment and has been an expert attached to the French and
EEC administrations. He headed at IRT/CERNE the Physics
and Acoustics Section involved in transportation noise and

vibration, tyre/road and wheel/rail contact research, and general physics related to vehicle comfort, driving conditions, nuisance. He joined the Renault Company in 1985 where he heads the Acoustics and Ergonomics Research Group.

J M FIELDS, BA, PhD
United States General Accounting Office, 441 G Street NW Washington, DC 20548, USA

Jim Fields is a research sociologist. He conducts noise research on community residents' reactions to environmental noise. He received a PhD in sociology from the University of Michigan in 1971. His involvement in social surveys on a range of topics has included over 15 community noise surveys in 7 countries. At the Institute of Sound and Vibration Research he conducted a social survey of community reaction to railway noise in Great Britain. He has established a community noise survey archive. His research at the National Aeronautics and Space Administration Langley Research Center in Hampton, Virginia, has focussed on the effects of numbers of noise events, on the impact of noise at different times of day, and on methodological requirements for combined social survey/noise measurement studies.

R D FORD, BSc(Eng), PhD, FIOA
Department of Applied Acoustics, University of Salford, Salford, M5 4WT, UK

Roy Ford is a Reader in Acoustics at the University of Salford. He first became interested in acoustics while studying for his doctorate and subsequently in the aircraft industry. He is now engaged in the teaching of acoustics and in research into building acoustics and the environment impact of transportation noise. He was educated at the University of Southampton where he received his BSc(Eng) in 1959 and PhD in 1962. He is a fellow of the Institute of Acoustics and a member of the Acoustical Society of America and of the Audio Engineering Society.

F L HALL, BA, MS, PhD
McMaster University, Department of Geography, 1280 Main Street West, Hamilton, Ontario, Canada L8S 4K1

Fred Hall is a professor in the Department of Civil Engineering and in the Department of Geography, and is Associate Dean of Graduate Studies. He received a BA degree in mathematics from Amherst College in 1965, an MSc from the Sloan School of Management at MIT in 1967, and a PhD in Geography from the University of Chicago in 1972. Since 1975 he has been involved in studies aimed at predicting the effects of transportation noise in residential areas. He chaired an American National Standards Institute (ANSI) working group on community response to noise.

B HEMSWORTH, BSc, MRAeS, CEng
British Railways Board, Research Division, Railway Technical Centre, London Road, Derby DE2 8UP, UK

Brian Hemsworth is Deputy Head of the Acoustics Unit of British Railways Research Division. He obtained a BSc in Aeronautical Engineering from Southampton University in 1965 and worked initially for Hawker Siddely Aviation Ltd. In 1972 he joined British Railways to work primarily on a research project associated with the generation of wheel/rail noise. Since that time he has been involved additionally with a variety of railway noise projects including propagation of noise, locomotive noise, ground vibration studies and the development of train noise prediction schemes.

Mr Hemsworth is a Member of the Royal Aeronautical Society, a Chartered Engineer and is currently British Railway's representative on an ORE Committee dealing with railway noise.

M E HOUSE, BSc(Eng), FIOA
Wolfson Unit, The Institute of Sound and Vibration Research, University of Southampton, Southampton, Hants, UK

Michael House is currently Manager, Wolfson Unit for Noise and Vibration Control, a consultancy group operating within the Institute of Sound and Vibration at the University of Southampton. He graduated from the University of Bristol, UK in 1958 with a BSc in Aeronautical Engineering. Following a graduate traineeship at the Aero Engine Division of Rolls Royce Ltd, joined the then Noise Research and Development Department at the Company's Hucknall Flight Test Establishment near Nottingham. Although in his current occupation Mr House specializes in airport noise studies and aviation noise control, he has also been active in many of the Wolfson Unit's other areas of technology, including building vibrations, medical acoustics, industrial noise control, spacecraft vibroacoustics, signal data processing and micro-computer software development.

L G KURZWEIL, BS, MS, PhD
US Department of Transportation, Transportation Systems Center, Kendall Square, Cambridge, Massachusetts, USA

Leonard Kurzweil has been a senior consultant and program manager at the Transportation Systems Center from 1971 to 1977 and again since 1985. He has performed research in the areas of rail system noise and vibration and railroad track design, and managed the US Department of Transportation's Urban Rail Noise Abatement Program. His current activities include aircraft noise modelling and information system development. Between 1979 and 1985, Dr Kurzweil was a senior consultant with Bolt Beranek and Newman Inc., where he specialized in noise and vibration control for rail systems. His research and consulting activities in this area have included groundborne noise and vibration control, airborne noise propagation, wheel/rail noise control, and propulsion system noise control. Dr Kurzweil received his BS degree in mechanical engineering from Cooper Union in 1964, his MS in mechanical engineering from Northwestern University in 1966 and his PhD in mechanical engineering from the Massachusetts Institute of Technology in 1971.

M G LEVENTHALL, MSc, PhD, FINSTP, FIOA
Head of Acoustics, Atkins Research and Development, Woodcote Grove, Epsom, Surrey KT18 5BW, UK

Geoff Leventhall is Head of Acoustics at Atkins Research and Development, a member of the WS Atkins Group of Consultants. The company has a strong interest in Transportation Engineering, the noise assessment and control aspects of which are developed in the Acoustics Department. Before joining Atkins in 1982, Geoff Leventhall was Reader in Acoustics at the University of London where one of his research specialisms was low frequency noise, its occurrence, assessment and effects. He and his postgraduate students have many publications in the area of low frequency noise. He is currently editor of the *Journal of Low Frequency Noise and Vibration* and is a past President of the UK Institute of Acoustics.

D MORRISON, BTech, CEng, MI MechE
Ricardo Consulting Engineers, Shoreham by Sea, Sussex

David Morrison graduated in Mechanical Engineering from Loughborough University in 1968. He spent two years in West Pakistan under the auspices of Voluntary Service Overseas, where he was responsible for teaching engineering subjects at a military cadet college. He then worked for London Transport for a year in their Technical Investigation Department, before joining Ricardo in 1971 as a Development Engineer working on advanced Rankine cycle engines. He was transferred to the Noise Department in 1977 and has since been responsible for many wide-ranging engine and vehicle noise reduction and research projects. He was appointed Section Leader of the Department in 1980 and Departmental Manager in June 1984. Mr Morrison has written and presented papers on noise at several international conferences and was co-author of a chapter on automotive engine noise published in Lilly's *Diesel Engine Reference Book*.

P M NELSON, BSc, PhD, FIOA
Transport and Road Research Laboratory, Crowthorne, Berkshire, UK

Paul Nelson obtained his PhD from London University in 1972. He joined the Noise Section of the Transport and Road Research Laboratory (TRRL) in 1971 and was made Head of Section in 1976. He was elected Fellow of the Institute of Acoustics in 1981 and was temporarily transferred to Head the Assessment Division at TRRL in 1985. He has specialized in road vehicle and traffic noise generation and control and, in particular, has worked on the development of computer prediction techniques for traffic noise and vehicle noise quietening studies. He has published over 30 papers and articles on vehicle and traffic noise and vibration and has been a regular contributor at both national and international meetings and conferences. He has represented the Department of Transport on both British and International Standards Committees.

P J REMINGTON, BS, MS, PhD
BBN Laboratories, Inc., 10 Moulton Street, Cambridge, Massachusetts, USA

Paul Remington joined BBN Laboratories Inc. in 1969 where he is currently a principal engineer. In the field of rail transportation noise and vibration his research activities have included studies of transit car interior noise and vibration, propulsion system noise, elevated structure noise, locomotive noise, and the mechanisms underlying the generation of wheel/rail noise. He was educated at the Massachusetts Institute of Technology and received his BS and MS degrees in 1966 and a PhD in 1970. He is a fellow of the Acoustical Society of America, the associate editor for Mechanical Vibration and Shock for the *Journal of the Acoustical Society of America* and a member of the American Society of Mechanical Engineers.

M J T SMITH, MA
Head of Noise Technology, Rolls Royce Ltd, PO Box 31, Derby, DE2 8BJ, UK

Mike Smith joined Rolls-Royce Ltd. in 1956, specializing in aircraft noise matters from 1958. He is currently Corporate Chief of Noise Technology, where he controls R & D activities and the implementation of findings into the product line. Since graduating from Cambridge University, he has been closely concerned with all aspects of the aircraft noise issue, including activity in several international spheres. These include representation of international industry at ICAO, participation on Society of Automotive Engineers committees and in advisory groups to both government and industry. In 1972 he was awarded the British Acoustical Society's Rayleigh Medal for work on the RB211 series of engines.

C G STANWORTH, BSc
British Railways Board, Research Division, Railway Technical Centre, London Road, Derby DE2 8UP, UK

Colin Stanworth was awarded an honours degree in Physics by the University of Birmingham and held research appointments with the Scientific Civil Service and the United Steel Companies Ltd before joining the Research Division of British Railways in 1969. Since taking up his appointment with the railway, he has concentrated largely on noise and vibration and is now head of the Acoustics Section which undertakes a full range of railway and engineering noise and vibration problems. He has worked on railway noise for some overseas administrations, whilst with BR, and his international work includes collaboration within the research wing of the Union Internationale des Chemins de Fer, the Office de Recherche et d'Essais, as well as being a member of the British delegation at railway noise discussions within the European Economic Community.

S M TAYLOR, BA, MA, PhD, MCAA
Department of Geography, McMaster University, 1280 Main Street West, Hamilton, Ontario, Canada

Martin Taylor has a BA from Bristol University and an MA and PhD from the University of British Columbia. He has been on faculty at McMaster University since 1974 where he holds the position of Full Professor of Geography. He was a Visiting Scholar in the Institute of Sound and Vibration Research at Southampton University, 1980–1981. His current research topics are transportation noise impacts, community mental health care, and the behavioural determinants of health. He has published papers in the *Journal of Sound and Vibration, Journal of the Acoustical Society of America, Canadian Acoustics* and *Noise Control Engineering*. He is a member of the Canadian Acoustical Association.

D A TOWERS, BS, MS
Harris Miller Miller and Hanson Inc, 429 Marrett Road, Lexington, Massachusetts 02173, USA

David A Towers is a senior consultant with the acoustical consulting firm of Harris Miller Miller and Hanson Inc., specializing in noise and vibration control for surface transportation projects and for microelectronics and other sensitive facilities. From 1974 until 1986, Mr Towers was a consulting engineer with Bolt Beranek and Newman Inc., working on projects in a variety of areas including architectural, industrial and community noise and vibration control. Mr Towers received his BS degree in mechanical engineering from Columbia University in 1972. He began his work in acoustics at Purdue University where he received his MS degree in mechanical engineering in 1973. He is presently a member of the Institute of Noise Control Engineering, an associate member of the American Society of Mechanical Engineers and a registered professional engineer in California, Florida and Massachusetts (USA)

J W TYLER, FIHT, FIOA, DipStats, HonRCM
Pooh Corner, Chalkhouse Green, Reading, RG4 9AG, UK

John Tyler joined the Road Research Laboratory in 1947 after an early career as a research and development physicist in industrial instrumentation. From then until 1982 he carried out research on a wide range of subjects including vehicle safety and economics, traffic and transportation engineering and reduction of vehicle noise. From 1972 to 1979 as Principal Scientific Officer, he was responsible for the TRRL Quiet Heavy Vehicle Project. Following this he headed a research team studying the environmental effects of heavy goods vehicles. Since leaving the Laboratory he has been involved in road transport consultancy. At present he is a consultant to TRRL working as Project

Manager for the government's QHV **90** Project, which is designed to assist the UK commercial vehicle industry meet the forthcoming EEC noise regulations. Mr Tyler is a Fellow of the Institution of Highways and Transportation and of the Institute of Acoustics.

M VALLET, PhD
Institut National de Recherche Sur Les Transports et Leur Securite, 109 Avenue Salvador Allende, 69675 Bron, France

Michel Vallet is a Director of Research at the Institut National de Recherche Sur Les Transports et Leur Securité, formally the Institut de Recherche des Transport. He was awarded his PhD in 1972 from the University of Lyon for a study on sleep disturbance *in situ* and has since carried out several major research projects in this field. He has published his work widely and has been a member of international committees including participation in the European Commissions' acoustical environmental programme between 1976 and 1983. He is currently a member of the French Research Committee on noise and vibration.

C H E WARREN, MA, FRAeS, FIMA, FCASI
19 Rectory Road, Farnborough, GU14 7BU, UK

Hugh Warren formerly Head of Dynamics Division, Royal Aircraft Establishment, Farnborough, graduated in mathematics from Trinity College Cambridge, prior to joining the Royal Aircraft Establishment. He has been associated with the development of the theory of sonic booms and studies of their effects since their inception around 1952. He is the author of many papers on sonic booms and has presented papers at international conferences. He was a member of the Sonic Boom Panel of the International Civil Aviation Organisation, whose report on the phenomenon was published in 1970, and subsequently of its Sonic Boom Committee.

P A WILKINS, B Mech Eng, MSc, PhD, MAAS, MIOA
Department of Occupational Health, Safety and Welfare, PO Box 194, West Perth, Western Australia 6005

Peter Wilkins has conducted a variety of research and consultancy work at the Institute of Sound and Vibration Research, Southampton in the areas of occupational deafness, hearing conservation, auditory communications, and noise measurement and control. In his current position he is Head of the Noise Control Branch of the Department of Occupational Health, Safety and Welfare of Western Australia which is responsible for the administration of the State's Hearing Conservation Regulations, and supporting advisory, technical and policy activities. He serves on a State Advisory Committee and a National Working Party on occupational noise.

J WILLIAMS, BSc MSc, PhD, FRAEeS, CEng
'Grovelands', Metcombe, Ottery St Mary, Devon, UK

John Williams has had over 40 years research experience on aircraft flutter, aerodynamics and aeroacoustics at the National Physical Laboratory, the Royal Aircraft Establishment, Princeton University and Southampton University. His noise research at the RAE, as a Deputy Chief Scientific Officer from 1971 to 1982, included jet, fan, propeller, rotor and airframe considerations; also developments in theoretical, windtunnel and flight-testing techniques. Currently, he is visiting Professor (part-time) in the Aeronautics and Astronautics Department of Southampton University, where he is involved with noise research on propeller aircraft and helicopters, as well as teaching aircraft performance and aeroacoustics.

S L WOLFE, MS
Wilson, Ihrig and Associates, Inc. 5776 Broadway, Oakland, California, USA

Steven Wolfe graduated in engineering from the Harvey Mudd College, Claremont, California, in 1972. He then joined the Bechtel Corporation and worked on environmental impact statements and research in industrial and construction noise control. He gained his Master of Science degree in Mechanical Engineering from the University of California, Berkeley, in 1974. He is currently a principal consultant with Wilson Ihrig and Associates where projects have included the measurement and evaluation of noise and vibration from high speed transit systems and railways, determination of criteria for design and planning of transit systems and the control of noise propagated into surrounding communities from industrial and transportation facilities.

Part 1

Introduction and Physical Assessment

1

Introduction to Transport Noise

P. M. Nelson BSc, PhD, FIOA
Transport and Road Research Laboratory,
Crowthorne,
UK

Contents

1.1 Introduction

No one can deny that mechanized transport has greatly affected the development of modern society. Its seemingly unrelenting growth has been instrumental in reshaping the landscape to such a marked extent that few people can justly claim that their mode of living remains untouched by the influence of transport and transportation systems. We have, in fact, engineered a transport-dominated society which has led, over a relatively short period of time, to a dispersal of land use and to the increased opportunity for the separate development of residential and industrial areas. Our desire for increased mobility has therefore become a necessity, and like any addictive process we have become dependent on the support provided by transport in order to maintain the higher living standards that, ironically, transportation has helped to provide.

Although the development of transport systems has, in the main, produced both economic and social benefits to large numbers of people, transport can also pollute the environment in which it is constrained to such an extent that, on balance, the quality of life to those exposed to these disbenefits can be worsened rather than improved. Of the environmental factors that are commonly associated with pollution from transport, noise is, perhaps, the most commonly cited of all. The reasons are obvious; noise from transport is ubiquitous and is easily detected by the human hearing system. Its effects can be cumulative and it influences many aspects of our daily lives. It penetrates the work environment, causing disturbance and interruption in concentration and vigilance. It also disturbs us at home and during our leisure periods. Sleep provides no real escape, because even if we are fortunate enough to be able to sleep seemingly undisturbed by external noise, its presence may well reduce the quality of sleep without the subject being consciously aware of the fact. To the city dweller, transport noise has become such an everyday occurrence that ultimately it has a desensitizing effect and becomes more acceptable as a result, with a concomitant acceptance that the quality of life has also deteriorated.

The problem is not confined by political or social frontiers. Vehicles manufactured in one country may be exported along with their noise to another. It affects the rich who may live in a fashionable quiet suburb but who must make full use of transport to maintain their affluent existence, as well as the less fortunate who must live close to a major road, an elevated railway line, or an airport flight path.

The control of transport noise is not straightforward. We are presented with great difficulties, of a social and technological nature, which are themselves in conflict. Who cannot claim, for example, to have stood in a once quiet and tranquil part of the countryside only to be disturbed by the distant sounds made by a major road or a high-flying aeroplane? It is tempting to forget, under these circumstances, that it was a car or train or aeroplane that enabled us to travel in the first place.

The technical development of quiet transport requires a great deal of ingenuity. The energy developed by modern power plants may be very much greater than the energy wasted or emitted as noise, and yet only a small amount of noise energy can be very intrusive. For example, a heavy-duty truck diesel engine may develop over 200 kW of useable power and yet only 10 W of acoustic power emitted as a by-product would be regarded by the listener as painfully loud. A second major problem of noise control occurs because large reductions in acoustic power are needed before the human detector system recognizes the fact that a benefit has been achieved. For instance, a reduction of 50% in the acoustic energy would be barely noticeable to the average listener in a transportation context, and the net result would be a reduction of only 3 dB. A

reduction of 10 dB would be instantly recognized as a major reduction in noise, equivalent to an approximate halving subjectively in the loudness of the sound, but to achieve this desirable result at least 90% of the initial acoustic energy must be removed.

1.2 Trends in transport noise exposure

While noise from transport is not a new phenomena—there are, for example, documented cases of noise control ordinances dating back to the Romans—it was not until more modern times that environmental factors were considered formally in any major transport planning decisions. Indeed, it was not until the early 1960s and 1970s that the environmental qualities of transport were recognized as a powerful force affecting the course of new development. In fact, the environmental lobby became so powerful at that time that almost all new transport development was labelled as environmentally undesirable and the more traditional engineering and economic arguments supporting new development were pushed seemingly into the background of what was, essentially, a political arena. This remarkable environmental revolution did not come about solely as a result of public reaction to environmental pollution in all its forms, but rather as a result of a combination of increased public awareness of the need to conserve environmental quality, conditioned by the rapid growth occurring at that time in transport, transportation systems and urbanization. Road traffic, for example, increased three-fold between 1960 and 1980 in OECD countries while air traffic doubled over the same period. The urban populations of these countries increased by 50% and the number of towns with more than a million inhabitants doubled. In addition large numbers of motorways, airports and other large-scale transport facilities were constructed.

With this degree of growth both in mobility and in urbanization it is not surprising to find that the quality of the noise environment has steadily deteriorated. For example, in the 5 years from 1973 to 1978 the percentage of the population of the United States exposed to road traffic noise greater than 65 dB(A)* almost doubled.[1] By the mid-1970s about 15% of the population (about 100 million people in the OECD area as a whole) were exposed to traffic noise levels of over 65 dB(A). The figure was much higher in larger cities, where it often exceeded 50%.

The exposure to the noise from various transport modes has also been studied in many countries. For example, *Table 1.1* shows the percentage of the population exposed to the noise of road and air traffic in various countries in the mid-1970s. It can be seen that while there are substantial variations between countries there are, generally, far fewer people exposed to aircraft noise than exposed to road traffic noise. The most obvious example is Japan where over 30% of the population were exposed to traffic noise levels greater than 65 dB(A) whereas less than 1% were exposed to similar levels of aircraft noise. In the United States, however, the problem is more evenly distributed with about 6% exposed to traffic noise in excess of 65 dB(A) and 2% exposed to aircraft noise at the same levels. The impact of railways is generally similar to the impact caused by aircraft with approximately 1–2% of the population of most developed countries exposed to 65 dB(A) or more from trains. The exception is Switzerland where it is estimated that 4% of the population are exposed to such a level.

Since the late 1970s, largely as a result of measures concerning the regulation of noise emission from individual vehicles and

* The level of 65 dB(A) is often regarded as an absolute upper acceptable limit, and in several cases is used as the basis for regulations concerning sound insulation compensation (*see* Chapter 11). In this case the level refers to an *Leq* averaged over 24 hours measured in front of an exposed wall of the building.

Table 1.1 Population exposed to road traffic and aircraft noise in selected countries

Noise level measured outside at building façade (Leq dB/A)	Road traffic noise (% of national population exposed to given noise levels)[a]												Aircraft noise (% national population exposed to given levels)[b]				
	United States[b]	Japan[f]	Belgium[f]	Denmark[f]	France[f]	Germany[f]	Netherlands[f]	Norway[b]	Spain[f]	Sweden[b]	Switzerland[f]	United Kingdom[g]	United States[c]	Canada[d]	Japan[f]	Europe[e]
≥55 Sleep can be disturbed if windows are open	40	80	68	50	47	72	—	22	74	38	66	50	13	2	3	3
≥60 Sleep and conversation can be disturbed if windows are open	18	58	39	—	32	46	30	12	50	24	28	27	5	1	1	1
≥65 Sleep and conversation can be disturbed even if windows are closed	6.4 (7)	31 (31)	12 (12)	20 (12)	14 (13)	18 (8)	7.4 (5)	5 (5)	23 (23)	11 (11)	12 (11)	11	2	1	0.5	0.2
≥70 Sleep and conversation disturbance; possible complaints	1.8	10	1	—	4	4	1.6	2	7	4	1	4	0.6	0.3	0.2	0.05

Figures in brackets refer to a survey conducted in 1984.
Source: The State of the Environment, OECD, Paris (1979).[1]

[a] Data refers to various years in the early seventies for different countries. Since many measurements and surveys do not give results in *Leq*, equations relating *Leq* and other indices have been used.
[b] Expressed as *Leq* over 24 hours.
[c] For all airports.
[d] For 5 major airports.
[e] For 34 airports.
[f] Expressed in *Leq* over the period 0600–2200 hrs.
[g] Expressed in *Leq* over the period 0600–2400 hrs, England only.

aircraft, and partly as a result of improved design of roads and insulation of buildings, the previous level of transport noise has tended to stabilize. In consequence, the situation at time of writing is roughly comparable with that experienced during the late 1970s. *Table 1.1* includes the results of a more recent survey of OECD countries.[2] The percentages of the populations exposed to road traffic noise of 65 dB(A) or more in 1984 are given in brackets in the table. Taking all sources together it has been estimated that in the early 1980s some 17% of the inhabitants of the 12 nations listed were exposed to noise levels exceeding 65 dB(A). Fifteen per cent were exposed to traffic noise, with approximately 1% exposed to aircraft noise and 1% exposed to noise from railways. Taking this estimate and applying it to all OECD countries, a total population of nearly 800 million people, we find that currently about 135 million are exposed to transport noise which is judged, by most authorities, to be unacceptably high.

Expected trends in the noise levels over the next few years suggest that some improvements will be made. In the European Community, road vehicles will be subject to progressively more stringent noise emission regulations which by the 1990s should produce substantial benefits, particularly to those sections of the population exposed to heavy lorry noise (*see* Chapter 9). In addition, some countries have introduced improved design standards for new road development and have enacted legislation giving people whose homes are affected by high traffic-noise levels the right to have fitted additional sound insulation treatments (*see* Chapter 11).

In France by the year 2000, it has been estimated that the numbers of urban dwellers exposed to 65 dB(A) or more will be reduced to 13% (5.6M) which compares with the figure noted in 1975 of 16% (6.5M). This represents a small, but nevertheless, significant reduction.

Further considerable improvements are forecast should more stringent actions be taken in reducing vehicle noise at source. A target regulation level of 80 dB(A) for heavy lorries was recommended as long ago as 1971 when the United Kingdom Quiet Heavy Vehicle Project was started (*see* Chapters 7 and 8). Even though this project demonstrated that current technology could achieve the degree of noise reduction required and would be commercially acceptable, there still remains technical and political problems in achieving the necessary legislation to enforce this particular design standard. If a policy of this kind were introduced it has been estimated that the numbers of people exposed to 65 dB(A) or more would be substantially reduced. For example, in Switzerland the numbers would be expected to reduce by 30%, in Denmark by 60%, in France by 50% and in Norway by 55%.[2]

Regarding commercial aircraft noise, most studies forecast a reduction in exposure to noise over the long term. Two main reasons are given: First, the new generation of aircraft will be less noisy; and secondly, all older aircraft types which do not comply with current noise limitations will be phased out by the end of this decade. The rate of improvement will, of course, depend upon many factors, principally the rate at which aircraft are replaced with new-generation types and the degree of offset caused by the expected increase in general aviation and the use of helicopters. Taking these factors into account, OECD forecasts indicate that in the United States there will ultimately be a reduction in the numbers of people exposed to 65 dB(A) of about 50–70%. In Denmark the reduction in numbers exposed to 65 dB(A) is expected to be 35% and in France, a reduction of 75% of the area exposed to aircraft noise is estimated for the five main airports. While the numbers of people benefiting by these measures are small in relation to the substantially larger numbers exposed to high traffic noise levels, this nevertheless represents a significant step forward.

Exposure to railway noise has in most countries remained fairly static and is expected to remain in this state for the foreseeable future. However, there are locations where noise from trains is a major source of annoyance, and the recent introduction of high-speed trains and rapid transit systems have tended to expose new problem areas. The comfort of people living in the vicinity of railways can be improved if serious attempts are made to reduce noise (*see* Chapter 17).

1.3 Summary of the effects of noise on man

The effects of noise on people are various and often interrelated. For example, speech interference can result in annoyance and tiredness, and, in turn, tiredness may exacerbate annoyance. There are also interrelationships between the general state of health of individuals and the various effects of noise. Stress may be introduced by the presence of noise, and stress may then induce physiological changes in the body and a general decline in health and well being. For convenience, the various effects of noise on man can be considered to comprise of three categories:

1. Health effects.
2. Activity effects, including sleep disturbance.
3. Annoyance.

1.3.1 Health effects (*see* Chapter 4)

There are many definitions of health, but perhaps the most appropriate is that used by the World Health Organisation:

> 'Health is a state of complete physical, mental and social well-being, and not merely an absence of disease and infirmity.'

For the most part, people's well-being is diminished by noise, so in this sense of the term there is no doubt that noise affects health. Very loud sounds are clearly highly injurious to man as well as animals. A 20 kHz siren emitting 160–165 dB will cause flies and larvae to die even when exposed only for a short period of time. With these exposures human beings become dizzy and tired, they may experience facial pain and the skin may become burnt. These unambiguous effects decrease as the sound pressure is lowered and at sound pressure levels of approximately 120 dB the reactions to the sounds becomes ambiguous. At the levels of exposure normally associated with transport, individual reactions will vary over considerable ranges.

It is well known that long-term exposure to high noise levels can result in permanent hearing loss. This effect has been associated mainly with occupational noise such as might exist in certain manufacturing plants and, in some cases, for drivers operating noisy vehicles. It is generally accepted that permanent deafness will occur if the ear is exposed to 90 dB(A) *Leq* for 8 hours per day over more than 20 years. However, further studies have indicated that noise levels commonly experienced in the daily environment may cause, in the long term, loss of auditory acuity (partial hearing loss). As a result, in the United States, the Environmental Protection Agency has concluded that there is a risk of permanent hearing damage after 40 years of exposure to a steady daily noise level of 75 dB(A) *Leq* for 8 hours per day. This statement clearly changes the emphasis on noise-related hearing loss, from the work place, where few people are affected and where protective measures are generally either available on request or enforced by the employer, to the general environment where large numbers of people may be at risk and where there may be no obvious remedial action. It is estimated, for example, that 13 million Americans are exposed to an *Leq* of 75 dB(A) or greater in transportation and recreational vehicles and OECD estimates suggest that up to 1% of the population are exposed to daily noise levels above 75 dB(A).

Nevertheless, despite these genuine concerns by some authorities there is little evidence to suggest that the general public are suffering hearing loss as a result of sustained exposure to transport noise. It seems, therefore, that transportation noise control in the community cannot be justified on grounds of hearing protection alone.

Noise and its effects on other aspects on human physiology has been the subject of a number of studies and these are reviewed in Chapter 4. It is clear that noise can induce a range of physiological response reactions such as increases in blood pressure, heart rate and breathing and that these reactions are not confined to high noise levels and sudden noise events, but are also true for noise levels commonly experienced in noisy environments such as busy streets. However, there is no strong evidence that noise alone has a direct causal effect on such health outcomes as cardiovascular disease, reproductive abnormality or psychiatric disorders, although noise may be in some way involved as part of a multi-causal process leading to these disorders. Further epidemiological studies may yield more definitive connections; however, the inherent difficulty of isolating the health effects of a low dose level, such as transportation noise, operating within a complex aetiological system, will remain.

1.3.2 Effects on sleep (see Chapter 5)

Of all the effects on noise on man, interference with sleep is probably the least tolerated. Sleep deprivation may at the same time produce physiological effects, disturb an essential activity and, as an indirect effect, reduce performance during the day and create a feeling of annoyance. Such impacts depend mainly upon the type and level of noise and on the time during the sleep period when the noise is produced, since sleep is not a continuum but is composed of various stages organized in repetitive cycles during the night. Studies carried out on sleeping people have shown that noise can affect sleep in a number of ways. It may shorten the length of the sleeping period and increase the number or frequency of awakenings, but equally important it may affect the duration of the various stages of sleep. For example, subjects exposed to noise invariably have a reduced period of deep sleep compared with subjects sleeping in a quiet environment.

The question of adaptation to noise during sleep has been widely studied. Some apparent habituation seems to occur for exposure to low intensity levels; however, there seems to be very little or no adaptation to noise levels above 60 dB(A) indoors.

1.3.3 Effects on communication (see Chapter 3)

One of the most readily understood effects of noise on man is communication because, at a fairly well-defined level, noise will mask the sound communicated. The level which interferes with the communication, contrary to annoyance or sleep disturbance, does not vary greatly from person to person and does not have a subjective dimension since the process of communication interference by noise is a straightforward matter of physical objective masking of desired sounds.

If communication is impaired, i.e. if a part of the sound is lost or if special efforts have to be made to overcome the interference, then this may create both annoyance and a loss of information. Loss of information caused by noise interference may also be dangerous in cases where it masks auditory warnings, the malfunction of equipment or the approach of vehicles. It can also reduce the quality of teaching and affect the ability of children to learn.

1.3.4 Effects on performance (see Chapter 3)

Knowledge relating the effects of noise to human task perfor-

mance tends to be both slight and contradictory. Noise can distract a person involved in a specific task or change the state of alertness. However, this may increase or decrease efficiency depending largely on the type of noise and on the psychophysiological state of the person. Nevertheless, tasks involving high concentration, vigilance, mental activity and high complexity are undoubtedly affected by intruding noise.

1.3.5 Annoyance effects (see Chapter 3)

In addition to the direct effects of noise on sleep, communication and performance there are also indirect effects of annoyance or disturbance which are related to the way a person feels about the noise. Unfortunately, although it is a simple matter to define noise annoyance, e.g. the World Health Organisation definition is, 'A feeling of displeasure evoked by the noise,' in practice it proves to be a most difficult attribute of human behaviour to quantify. Attempts to measure annoyance usually take the form of a questionnaire administered to a representative sample of the population. These surveys attempt to relate annoyance expressed by the people interviewed with some physical measurement of the noise causing the annoyance. Generally, each person is assigned an annoyance score which varies according to the disturbance felt. The annoyance scale so defined must be designed so as to allow testing of the coherence of the replies concerning any noise, to assign a variable weight to each reply, and to rank the replies. Clearly, the design of the questionnaire is vitally important if these objectives are to be achieved.

Using these techniques, it is found, not surprisingly, that people's individual annoyance scores vary over a considerable range for a given noise exposure, and it is quite clear that in most cases people's feelings about noise are not precisely conditioned by the intensity of the sound or by any other physical descriptor of the noise. In essence, the noise sensation appears to acquire associations beyond its natural meaning. For example, one person listening to a piece of music may find the experience pleasant even exhilarating if it is associated with some fond memory, whereas another person may find the same piece depressing for the converse reasons. Surveys of the effects of traffic or aircraft noise have revealed, on occasions, that the people complaining most about the noise were in fact more concerned about their personal safety or in the difficulty in parking their cars owing to the presence of the other traffic, etc. Clearly, a large number of factors can influence individual opinions or feelings about noise. These include, an individual's personality, social habits, psychological state or just simply prejudice.

In all this, noises are no different from other sensory stimuli. For while there may be individual preferences and dislikes for a particular view, or taste, or sound, which may themselves be conditioned by psychological effects and social factors, generally speaking most people agree broadly on what is considered unpleasant or unwanted. Consequently, for practical reasons it becomes necessary to abandon the ideal of explaining individual attitudes or annoyance with noise and instead adopt the concept of an average or community annoyance rating for each noise level. While these averages do not reflect the feelings of each individual, they do reflect, nevertheless, what on average is felt by the population in a given area. It is on this basis that it has become common practice to base noise policy decisions or remedial actions on the cumulative percentages of people who describe their noise exposure as either annoying or highly annoying.

The use of the questionnaire survey in this context has been instrumental in establishing a large number of noise scales which are then used by the scientist or engineer to, for example, formulate prediction models or construct new designs which reduce the level on the scale and which, by implication, reduce the annoyance caused. Some of the more important and commonly used scales are described in the following chapter.

Although it is not really recommended to generalize from the large number of surveys that have been carried out and the numerous scales that have evolved, it is perhaps useful in this introduction to point out that very few people are found to be highly annoyed from transport noise below a level of about 45 dB(A) *Leq*. However, as the outdoor level rises above 60 dB(A) *Leq*, the proportion increases sharply and, generally speaking, it is expected that at 65 dB(A) *Leq* about 25% of the population will be highly annoyed.

1.4 Summary of transportation noise control techniques

In general, transport noise control methods can be classified in three categories:

1. Noise reduction at the source, including the removal of vehicles and re-routing.
2. Noise control of the transmission path.
3. The use of noise protective measures at the receiver.

Which method, or which combination of methods is employed depends to a large extent on the degree and nature of the noise reduction required and upon the influence of both economical and operational constraints.

Any attempt to control noise must start from an understanding of the sources of that noise. However, although there are substantial similarities, the sources are sufficiently different for the three types of transport considered in this book, i.e. road, rail and aircraft, for them to be considered separately. The book is therefore divided into separate parts which deal in turn with the description of sources and methods of control for each transport mode. The chapters provide a comprehensive coverage and, consequently, only a brief review of some of the main points will be given here.

1.4.1 Road transport

There can be little doubt that of the three primary transport modes, road transport produces the greatest noise intrusion. The Final Report of the Committee on the Problem of Noise (The Wilson Report) published in 1963[3] concluded that, 'In London, road traffic is, at the present time, the predominant source of annoyance and no other single noise source is of comparable importance.' It is clear that the problems of London's traffic, graphically described in the Wilson Report, is as relevant today as it was in the early 1960s, a feature that is broadly true of all other major cities throughout the world. Furthermore, it is only necessary to examine the statistics given in Table 1.1 to see that traffic noise exposure extends far beyond the city boundaries, where it affects large numbers of people living both in urban and in suburban settings.

1.4.1.1 Vehicle noise control (see *Chapter 7*)

The noise produced by vehicles running on roads form the components of traffic stream noise. Generally, the heaviest vehicles produce the most noise and passenger cars are the quietest. At low road speeds, and high engine speeds, the power unit is usually the main noise source, while at higher speeds and reduced engine speed and power, tyre–surface interaction noise may become important. If the road surface is uneven, then suspension noise and load and body rattle may predominate.

On the complete vehicle it is often very difficult to determine the relative importance of the various noise sources. Therefore, an understanding of how the noise output of these sources changes with vehicle operating conditions can provide valuable

information if the vehicle is to be quietened. Because of the importance of a number of sources on the vehicle, attempts have been made to obtain information on the behaviour of each of these in isolation so that the most practical methods of reducing noise from each can be determined and the most economic method of reducing the total noise of the vehicle can be prescribed.

Engine noise The two primary sources of engine noise are combustion-induced and noise due to mechanical impacts. Combustion noise is that emanating from the pressure change characteristics in the combustion chamber, and mainly results from gas loads applied to the engine structure, whilst mechanical noise is that resulting from a collection of discrete sources which are broadly mechanical in nature, e.g. piston slap, timing drive noise, bearing noise, valve train noise, fuel injection pump, injection needle closing impacts, etc. Combustion noise is usually a more important source in diesel than in petrol engines because of the higher gas loads that result during the combustion. The rate of change of noise level with engine speed and the effect of load on noise emission also show important differences for the two combustion processes. In petrol engines, noise levels can change by over 10 dB with load whereas the change does not normally exceed 1–2 dB for diesel engines. The engine surfaces and components which are usually significant noise radiators are the crankcase, cylinder head, sump, rocker cover, front timing cover, fuel injection pump, gearbox and intake and exhaust manifolds. The noise generated by these components depends, to a large extent, upon their stiffness and mass, and upon the radiation efficiency of the surface.

Methods of controlling engine noise include:

1. Controlling combustion noise by smoothing the pressure rise in the cylinders. This may include staged fuel injection, ignition retardation and turbocharging.
2. Reduction of mechanical forces, e.g. improved piston design to reduce piston slap, attention to gear tooth profiles, repositioning the timing gears to provide a smoother drive, replacement of chain drives with toothed belts.
3. Reducing the magnitude of vibration of the outer surfaces of the engine structure by redesign. Techniques involve structural optimization, stiffening panels to change the natural frequency, using damped panels or laminated panels to reduce surface vibration, and isolation of engine structures using resilient mounts and gaskets.
4. Use of covers or shields fitted over the engine compartment. (Enclosures may, however, severely degrade engine cooling and make access for maintenance difficult as well as increasing vehicle weight (*see* Chapter 7).)

Gas and fan noise The unsilenced exhaust of the internal combustion engine is probably the noisiest single source on a vehicle. For example, noise levels of 90–110 dB(A) at 7.5 m are possible from a large diesel engine. Generally, the lowest frequency component, which occurs at the fundamental firing frequency of the engine, is the most difficult to silence, the difficulty increasing with a decrease in firing frequency. Exhaust noise is dependent mainly upon engine load and speed but considerable deviations occur between different engine and silencer combinations due mainly to silencer system resonances, and, therefore, achieving a satisfactory degree of noise attenuation over a wide speed range can be a very difficult problem.

Improvements in exhaust noise can be obtained by careful consideration of silencer design and by attention to the control of cylinder pressure at the point where the exhaust valve opens. Generally, the latter effect can be improved by modification to the valve geometry and to the lift and closing characteristics determined by the cam profile. The basic problem with silencer design is to achieve adequate noise reduction over the important range of frequencies at the tail pipe with minimum restriction to the outflow gases and with the silencer volume as small as possible.

The cooling fan is an important noise source, particularly on commercial vehicles which have powerful engines requiring large airflows through the radiator matrix to stabilize engine temperatures. The noise generated by the cooling fan is caused by a combination of effects which include air turbulence caused by the airstream, the rotation of the fan and the blades past fixed objects, and mechanical noise caused by vibration of the fan and cowling. Fan noise increases with fan power and blade-tip speed and so noise control methods include techniques to reduce fan speed whilst maintaining sufficient duty to cool the engine. Additional improvements can be obtained by attention to the dimensions of the fan blades and to the symmetry of the blade layout.

Transmission Although there has so far been little evidence of external problems caused by the transmission system, there is little doubt that this noise source will need to be studied in greater detail as the noise from other major sources is reduced. The principal source of noise from transmission systems occurs from the meshing of gear teeth which produce both torsional and lateral vibrations. These vibrations are then transmitted to either the transmission housing or, via the mountings, to vehicle panels where they are radiated as sound. The main factors that affect gear vibration and noise are tooth profile errors and drive shaft deflections. Methods of controlling these sources of noise include modifications to the tooth profiles, for example the use of overlapping helical gears, better control of drive shaft alignment and damping radiating surfaces.

Tyre–surface interaction The noise generated by the action of tyres rolling on road surfaces can have a considerable influence on the total noise levels emitted by moving vehicles. The noise level from this source increases at the rate of 30–40 dB(A) per tenfold increase in speed for most tyre patterns and road surface textures which means that at a vehicle speed of about 100 km/h, tyre noise becomes dominant for most vehicles.

The factors affecting tyre noise are mainly vehicle speed or, more precisely, the rotational speed of the tyre, and also the texture pattern applied to the road surface. The tyre pattern and construction of the tyre have a significant but smaller effect. For example, changing the tyre pattern from a smooth or bald tyre to a deeply patterned traction tyre will, generally, only increase the noise by 2–3 dB(A) on most surfaces, whereas changing the road surface texture from a smooth polished surface to a deeply textured motorway surface can increase tyre noise by 8–10 dB(A). For this reason it is generally considered that there are greater opportunities to control tyre/surface noise by changing the road surface texture rather than by re-design of the tyre. This feature of tyre surface noise is, perhaps, underlined by the performance of certain types of open-textured road surfaces which provide high acoustic absorption and, as a result, substantial improvements in tyre–surface noise. Other methods of achieving some control of tyre surface noise include:

1. Using tyre patterns with circumferential rather than regular transverse patterns and randomizing the road surface texture—this helps to minimize the generation of annoying tonal effects.
2. Using radial ply tyres with steel belts rather than cross-ply braced tyres. This type of construction helps to minimize the degree of tyre slip in the contact area which is largely responsible for the vibration excitation imparted to the tyre, and the steel bracing helps to maximize damping in the tyre structure.

Other sources Noises from the vehicle body and suspension and from movement of the load carried can be very objectionable, but these aspects are not easily dealt with and it has been suggested that some form of legislative action is needed in order to control this form of noise. It follows that good road maintenance is a prime requirement for reduced load and body noise (*see* Chapter 9).

Aerodynamic noise refers to the noise generated in the boundary layer as air flows over a surface. This noise has a random type spectrum including frequency components throughout the audible range and into the ultrasonic range. The sound pressures developed depend upon the speed of the air flow over the surface, being roughly proportional to the square of the velocity, and on the aerodynamic shape of the surface. For road vehicles the speeds generated during normal driving are not, at present, sufficient to give rise to a significant contribution from aerodynamic sources.

Other wind effects arise from edge tones and the shedding of vortices. Edge tones are discrete frequencies which arise from the unsteady flow in the region of a sharp edge. Similarly vortex shedding from blunt objects such as door posts can also give rise to tonal effects. However, neither of these sources currently produce significant contributions to total vehicle noise at normal passing speeds.

Wind flutter is a low-frequency disturbance which is heard inside a car when one of the front windows is partially or totally open and the air stream is free to impinge upon the rear edge of the window frame. The frequencies involved are generally in the 10–20 Hz range and are generated by a Helmholtz resonator action in which the area of the neck is the open window, the length of the neck is the thickness of the door and window frame, and the volume is that of the entire cab of the vehicle. Control can be achieved by attention to the aerodynamics so that air is deflected past the open window.

Brake squeal is the most important aspect of brake noise and can cause considerable annoyance particularly in the case of public service vehicles. Vibration of the brake drum appears to be a contributory factor in the production of audible brake squeal; however, very little appears to be known about the fundamental mechanisms. Some improvements can be obtained by applied damping on the brake drum.

1.4.1.2 Noise control external to the vehicle (see Chapter 11)

While controlling road-traffic noise by treatments at source is to be encouraged as the principal method of control, measures which attempt to limit the spread of noise, once generated, are also of considerable value. The techniques include road design and alignment, the management of traffic flows, the use of screens and barriers, and general consideration given the allocation of land use in the vicinity of major transport routes. A further technique, which applies to all transport modes, is the improved design and insulation of property to minimize disturbance within buildings.

Road design and alignment The noise radiated by traffic can be influenced by both the vertical and horizontal alignment of the road. Generally, the steeper the longitudinal gradient the greater the resulting noise.

One of the main methods of control is to use distance of the road from the area to be protected. Generally speaking, doubling the distance will lead to a reduction in *Leq* from a given traffic flow of between 3 and 5 dB(A) depending upon the absorbing qualities of the ground between the road surface and the reception point. In areas where distance cannot be utilized to produce a desired effect the road may be placed in a cutting, where the sides of the cutting act to screen the sensitive area, or, where a higher degree of noise attenuation is required, the use of covers, enclosures or tunnels can be considered. However, the high cost of these constructions generally precludes their use in most situations.

A possibly more cost effective method is to erect a barrier or screen alongside the road. The main requirement is that the barrier should be sufficiently high and long enough to provide a reasonable vertical and horizontal overlap with the line of sight of the road from the reception point. When the buildings to be screened are close to heavily trafficked roads, appreciable reductions in noise level can be achieved in the order of 5–10 dB(A). However, at greater distances the screening potential may be substantially lower. There is now a considerable experience in the design and location of noise barriers and comprehensive prediction and design methods are available (*see* Chapters 2 and 10).

Vehicle noise in the vicinity of road junctions can often be higher than alongside road sections where the traffic flows smoothly. Consequently, junction designs that help to smooth the flow of traffic can also provide noise benefits. For example, some noise reduction can be expected from the use of linked or demand-controlled traffic light systems as these systems are designed to smooth traffic flow and increase throughput in congested urban areas. The disadvantage is that, in many situations, the improved flow tends to generate an increase in capacity which is then rapidly taken up by locally generated traffic. Alternatively, an increase in traffic speed may result with a corresponding increase in noise. In general, roundabouts tend to produce fewer noise problems than signalized intersections.

Traffic management Concentrating urban traffic on a few main routes, thus reducing noise levels over the remaining area can provide considerable benefits to large numbers of people. For example, halving the traffic flow on a lightly trafficked residential street may reduce noise by 3 dB(A) and yet the number of vehicles that are redirected could be quite small and easily absorbed in neighbouring roads purpose built to take higher traffic flows. Other techniques include restricting access both in terms of type of vehicle, (e.g. lorry bans or preferred lorry routes), and in terms of time of day. For instance, night bans have been imposed in some areas. The use of by-passes can provide substantial benefits by taking traffic away from populated areas. Reductions in journey times and accidents are also benefits to result from by-pass construction.

Land use planning Noise impact control can be achieved by appropriate management of the land adjoining a major transport route. Appropriate techniques include:

1. Placing noise compatible activities such as car parks, shopping areas and commercial facilities between the noise source and the noise-sensitive areas.
2. Using the natural land form and planting to act as screens or barriers to sensitive areas.
3. The adoption of cluster development concepts for housing as opposed to more conventional grid patterns or 'ribbon' development where the first row of houses tends to take the full impact of the noise.

Building design and insulation (see Chapter 11) The use of single aspect housing with the living rooms and bedrooms facing in the opposite direction to the noise source can provide noise benefits to sensitive areas indoors. Other building layouts can also be used to minimize noise disturbance.

Improvements to the acoustic insulation of buildings can be considered both for new buildings where layout and insulation can be considered as part of the overall design objectives as well as existing buildings where some form of retrofit may be needed.

Doors and windows provide the most obvious components of low sound insulation in a building and generally, the quality of these components dictate the degree of insulation achieved by the building as a whole. For example, if an external wall has an opening or gap of about 1% of its area, the overall noise reduction will only be about 20 dB(A) even if the rest of the wall is such to provide high insulation, (e.g. 40–50 dB(A)). If the opening is 10% (a value typical for windows) an overall reduction of not more than 10 dB(A) is to be expected. However, good quality double windows with at least a 100 mm separation between panes can achieve a sound insulation of approximately 35 dB when closed; solid well-fitting doors, with good quality gaskets and rebated sills, can achieve a sound insulation of 25–30 dB in typical residential installations.

It should be noted, however, that tightly closed or sealed windows cannot be used for natural ventilation, and a mechanical ventilation system or air conditioning system must be provided. It follows that the associated air vents and inlets should be located away from the roadside facade or should have baffles so that they do not provide paths for the transmission of sound.

1.4.2 Trains

In contrast to the growth of road and air traffic, railways have not developed in the same way. Indeed, in many countries the railway system has been in a state of decline. This has been due largely to the rapid development of the commercial airlines and to the growth in the road network and road traffic. Recently, however, there have been indications that railways will assume a new role. Following the success of high-speed trains in Japan and France, many countries have decided to increase the speed and numbers of their passenger services and have plans to operate trains running at speeds up to 300–400 km/h, thereby providing a more competitive service with air travel. In addition, many new rail links have been built and are planned in the form of 'rapid transit' schemes specifically designed to move people rapidly and efficiently within urban areas. Consequently, as rail traffic increases both in volume and in speed of travel, both of which will tend to result in increased noise levels, environmental problems are bound to occur. Such situations have already arisen in Japan where a wave of public protest occurred against high-speed train noise following the opening of the Sanyo extension to the existing high-speed Shinkansen network. As a result of this adverse reaction, the Japanese National Railway delayed the construction of new rail links to the Tokyo Airport at Narita and, in addition, announced ambitious plans for reducing wayside noise levels along the Shinkansen route.

In this volume the main body of information of train noise sources and their control is contained in Chapters 13–17. The following gives a brief review.

1.4.2.1 Train noise sources (see Chapters 13 and 14)

The sources of train noise and the factors that affect their generation and propagation are numerous. Additionally these factors are complicated by the wide variety of train types and operating conditions since trains can operate in a subway at grade or on elevated structures.

The generation of way-side noise depends largely upon the type of locomotive propulsion system, the auxiliary equipment such as compressors, motor generators, brakes etc., the interaction of the wheels and rails, the noise radiated by vibrating structures such as steel bridges, the speed of train and its length, and for high-speed operations (i.e. >250 km/h) aerodynamic noise may also become important. In addition to the airborne noise radiated into the community, there is also groundborne noise and vibration which travels through the track and support structure and the intervening soil to nearby buildings, where it is often perceived as a low frequency rumbling noise or as a perceptible vibration of the building.

Power unit noise (diesel traction) Of the various power units in use, the diesel locomotive usually represents the most common noticeable noise source on a modern railway. Engine powers range from a few hundred kilowatts to several megawatts and they may have from 4 to upwards of 16 cylinders arranged in a variety of configurations. The larger engines are usually turbocharged and both 4-stroke and 2-stroke engines are in use. With large engines, noise from the inlet side of the engine can be very important producing, via the turbo-charger, the characteristic whine which is a familiar feature of the noise emission. Control of this form of noise can be achieved using inlet silencers but often space restrictions within the locomotive envelope and air flow constraints preclude the optimization of this form of treatment.

Similar problems occur on the exhaust side of the engine where large exhaust silencer volumes are often needed in order to deal effectively with the low-frequency noise components of the exhaust. Typically, maximum engine speeds lie in the range 750–1500 rpm producing, as a result, low-frequency noise with a fundamental firing frequency in the range 6–12 Hz.

With the smaller locomotives used primarily for shunting, the diesel engines are normally aspirated and the problems of inlet and exhaust noise are consequently less severe.

Other sources on the engine are related to vibration radiated from the engine block and crankcase and to the whole locomotive body. Techniques to control this form of noise are generally aimed at improvements to the locomotive casing, primarily to reduce panel vibration and to screen the casing from the noisier parts of the engine. Structural optimization techniques of the engine itself are not considered cost effective at present. Reductions in the noise radiated by the locomotive structure can sometimes be achieved by isolating the engine from its surroundings using appropriate engine mounts. However, the frequency response characteristic of the mounts can be critical and it is often necessary to match the mount characteristics with the particular aspect of vibration isolation required.

Other sources of noise on a diesel engine are associated with engine cooling, the noise of traction motor blowers and air compressors which service the trains brakes. Methods of control of these noise sources include the use of modern fan designs to reduce cooling fan and blower noise and decoupling the brake compressor motors from the locomotive frame to reduce structure-borne vibration radiation.

Power unit noise (electric traction) Electric motors are extensively used for rail rapid transit as well as in diesel–electric locomotives. Compared with the diesel locomotive, the electric locomotive is much quieter. The worst problems are those provided by cooling fans for the electrical control equipment and for the traction motors together with the compressors used for a variety of both locomotive and train services.

Methods of control for these sources are similar to those employed on diesel locomotives. However, in general, most modern electric-powered railway vehicles are designed so that at maximum speed the propulsion system noise is roughly equivalent to the wheel and rail system noise. Consequently, over the range of lower speeds, wheel rail noise tends to dominate all other sources.

Rail wheel noise The major element of rail and vehicle suspension system noise is that caused by the interaction of the steel wheels and the steel rails. The interaction generates sound by the vibration of wheels, rails and vehicle structure, track support

system and ground. Both wheel and rails are capable of being excited into resonant response.

The following vibration generating mechanisms may be considered to occur as a result of rail–wheel interactions.

1. The impact of the wheel on a rail joint—a mechanism that is not present in the case of continuously welded rail.
2. The impact of wheel flanges against the rail.
3. The motions caused by track and wheel irregularities. This can take the form of corrugations in the rail and flats on the wheel as well as smaller scale roughness in both rail and wheel and can raise the noise level from passing trains by between 10 and 20 dB(A).
4. Sliding contact of wheel flanges resulting in flange squeal.
5. Vibration of the supporting structure.

Methods of controlling rail/wheel noise generally follow two directions. First, it may be possible to reduce or control the roughness both of wheels and of rails and to reduce the formation of wheel flats and rail corrugations. For example, it has been found that both wheel flats and rail corrugations may be substantially reduced by employing disc brakes rather than the more conventional wheel tread braking, as disc brakes provide a more efficient braking action and reduce sliding of the wheel over the rail. Additionally, rail corrugations can be controlled by remedial action involving the routine grinding of the rail head by a specially equipped train.

The second method of control is to reduce the response of the radiating members. The most obvious way is to add damping to the wheels and various forms of acoustic wheel have been used (*see* Chapters 16 and 17). Some designs incorporate rubber spacers between the hub and the rim assemblies to accomplish damping in the wheel and to provide vibration isolation between the tread and hub. The reductions are most marked in reducing flange squeal noise on curved track where up to 10 dB(A) reduction in way-side levels can be achieved, reaching 20–30 dB reductions at squeal frequencies. As an extension of the acoustically quiet wheel—elastomeric coatings both on tyre and on rail head—have been used, with limited success, as well as pneumatic tyres which run on a concrete guideway, as on sections of the Paris Metro.

Other methods of control include the use of bogie skirts, railside noise barriers, reducing the number of wheels per unit length of the train and the employment of rail isolation techniques. These include the use of resilient rail fasteners to aid damping in the rail and to decouple the rail from the support structure, and the use of ballast mats on bridge decks to limit vibration coupling through the ballast to the bridge structure (*see* Chapter 17).

1.4.2.2 Ground-borne noise and vibration (see Chapter 16)

All trains generate vibrations in the ground as they pass by. The effect is usually significant only at distances close to the track; however, in cases where these vibrations are transmitted to property, considerable annoyance can be caused. Vibrations may be perceived either as a result of mechanical vibration of the structure (and, therefore, felt as a tactile sensation), or as a result of noise generated by the mechanical vibration. This latter effect is often described as a low-frequency rumble although other higher frequency sound may be generated by the rattling of ornaments and windows etc. Besides annoyance, vibrations from trains can have other types of effects. For example, even at very low levels, the vibrations can disrupt the operation of sensitive equipment and, in severe cases, damage may occur in sensitive buildings.

The prediction of vibration effects from trains is very difficult mainly because of the highly complex nature of the various stages involved. For example, even if the vibration waveform can be determined at the track side, the effects on propagation of variations in the soil or rock structure along the propagation path are often impossible to assess with accuracy. In addition, the coupling of vibrations into buildings can prove to be equally difficult to predict. Building floors, walls and ceilings are often subject to significant amplifications of vibration relative to the vibration at the foundations, for example. The result is that for a given vibration excitation occurring at the track-side it proves to be very difficult to estimate what vibration characteristics will develop at various points in an adjacent building.

Despite the difficulties of assessing the risk of vibration in a building, a variety of methods of control are available. These include treatment at the source, such as removing and controlling wheel flats and rail corrugations, reducing the primary stiffness of the vehicle suspension, using resilient rail fasteners or floated slabs and ballast mats to isolate the track bed from the soil, and reducing the speed of the train. Treatments along the propagation path include the use of trenches either open or backfilled with a low-impedance material and the isolation of the building itself from the soil. This may be achieved using either isolation pads inserted beneath the foundations or by constructing an inner building which is isolated from the outer building.

For trains running in tunnels, attention to tunnel design can be beneficial. For example, increasing the mass of the tunnel structure can be expected to reduce transmitted vibration in light soils.

1.4.3 Aircraft

The problem of disturbance due to noise from aircraft became widespread with the introduction of the jet engine into civil aviation towards the end of the 1950s. Since then the numbers both of commercial and of private jet aircraft have increased with currently over 7000 of both types in regular service. In contrast, the propeller-powered sector of the civil fleet has remained essentially constant at around 2000 operating commercial aircraft. Helicopters are few in numbers at present but their numbers are increasing, primarily in the inner city areas.

Over this period the problem of noise control has received substantial attention and, as a result, some major successes have been achieved. The methods of alleviating the problem can be divided into three main areas. First, and perhaps most important, is the investigation of the sources of noise and, in particular, the development of quieter power units. Secondly, there is the regulation and control of aircraft operation in the vicinity of airports; and, finally, there are non-operational controls which include the appropriate management of land use both within the airport and in the surrounding community and the insulation of property exposed to high noise levels.

The detailed information on subsonic aircraft noise and its control is contained in Chapters 18–20 and the particular problems created by the introduction of supersonic aircraft and sonic boom effects are discussed in Chapter 21. This brief review will be confined to subsonic aircraft noise control.

1.4.3.1 Jet aircraft noise control (see Chapter 18)

The major source of noise from a jet aircraft on landing and take off is the aircraft power plant, although aerodynamic noise caused by air flow over the air frame can influence the overall noise signature during the approach to land.

Jet engines effect propulsion by accelerating the mass of air through them. In the earlier turbo-jet engines, air is compressed in a mechanical compressor, heated in a combustion chamber and then accelerated by expansion through the jet nozzle. The expanding gas also drives a turbine which, in turn, drives the compressor. These processes produce three types of noise: (1)

inlet noise radiated from the air intake, primarily as a result of compressor noise plus aerodynamic noise; (2) vibrations resulting from the body of the engine, which are generally of minor importance; and (3) exhaust noise which may include a mixture of internally generated noise from the compressor and turbine and high-velocity jet mixing noise generally termed aerodynamic jet noise. For the turbo-jet engine, aerodynamic jet noise is by far the most important noise source and it is only at very low engine powers that other sources become predominant.

With the development of turbofan engines which employ high by-pass air flow concepts, i.e. with only about 20–30% of the intake air being used in the gas producing process, the rank ordering of noise sources radically changes. A modern high by-pass ratio turbofan engine uses, typically, 3 or 4 times as much air per unit of developed thrust compared with the 'pure' turbo-jet engine and, as a result, produces a substantially lower hot jet velocity with concomitant reductions in aerodynamic jet noise. The result is that for a range of turbofan designs, the fan and compressor noise tends to dominate the noise signature.

Fan and compressor noise These noise sources are characterized by both broad band and tonal features. The broad band sources are associated with turbulence generated in the air flow mainly in the vicinity of the compressor ducting and are influenced by the interaction of the tips of the rotating blades of the compressor fan and the turbulent boundary layer located close to the wall of the duct. Methods of controlling this source of noise are generally directed towards the optimization of compressor blade incidence angle to the direction of air flow. It is known, for example, that 1 degree of divergence from optimum incidence angle can increase noise levels by up to 3 dB. Discrete tones are produced by a variety of complex mechanisms which have been the subject of considerable study (*see* Chapter 18). The frequencies generated depend upon the rotational speed of the compressor and the numbers of compressor blades and the stationary blades at the compressor inlet. Discrete frequencies are produced at the blade passing frequency and its harmonics and are noticeable at engine power settings used for take-off where supersonic tip-speed conditions exist. At these high tip speeds, blade distortion produces additional harmonics which combine with the fundamental characteristic to produce the familiar buzz-saw noise associated with modern turbofan jet engined aircraft.

Methods of controlling fan and compressor noise include:

1. Attention to blade design so that there is good aero mechanical similarity between fan blades. This helps to minimize 'buzz' noise at high tip speeds.
2. Reducing tip speed to minimize airflow velocities as far as is practical.
3. Optimization of rotor and stator blade numbers. In addition, acoustically absorbent material can be incorporated in the walls of the intake and by-pass ducts.

Combustion noise This arises from the turbulence generated both by the compressor stage and the burning process of the fuel/air mixture in the combustion chamber. This produces an intense broad band signal. However, the radiation of this noise source to the far-field is often less of a problem than either compressor fan noise or jet mixing noise. No specific control methods are, therefore, applied. However, analysis of combustion noise is often used as a diagnostic tool to identify potential problems with the operation of the engine.

Turbine noise Sources of turbine noise are similar to those generated by the compressor fan, but the propagation is different. Since the outflow velocities in the combustion chamber are supersonic, all the turbine noise energy is directed downstream where it passes out of the rear of the engine to interact with the turbulent jet exhaust. Turbine noise contains the same basic broad band and tonal characteristics as compressor noise but the tonal element is more dominant. Nevertheless, turbine noise is, generally , less of a problem in the far field than compressor noise. This is partly related to the fact that the tone frequencies are higher because the turbine blade numbers are high and, as a result, many tones are outside the audible range. In addition, higher frequencies are absorbed more readily in the atmosphere than lower frequencies.

Jet mixing noise This is the most important source in the exhaust of the engine. However, with high by-pass ratio jet engines it is normally significant only during take-off. The source originates in the turbulent mixing between the jet and the atmosphere and, in the case of by-pass jets, in the mixing between the hot and cold streams. It is heavily dependent on jet velocity and, therefore, the reduction of jet velocity is the most important jet noise control tool. The success of the turbofan engine is evidence of this type of control.

Other methods of control utilize nozzles located on the jet orifice which help to 'compact' the jet and to change the frequency character by reducing the low-frequency component and increasing the higher frequencies. Control is achieved through the atmosphere's natural ability to absorb higher frequencies rather better than lower frequencies.

Improvements to mixed flow jet noise can be achieved by arranging the mixing of fan and core flows to be either partially or completely within the engine so that it is expelled as a single jet through a single nozzle.

1.4.3.2 Propeller aircraft noise control (see Chapter 18)

The noise from propeller driven aeroplanes is a combination of two main sound sources—the propeller and the power plant. For most practical conditions, propeller noise is the more important noise source. However, with modern turbo-prop designs, turbine engine whine, combustion noise and transmission/gearbox vibration can become important at low blade rotation speeds.

The rotating propeller can produce sound by three different mechanisms. The first is given by bending vibrations of the propeller blade which is generally a low order effect, and is kept to a minimum in practice by the necessity of keeping propeller vibration to the minimum. The second, and most important mechanism, is the propeller rotation noise generated by the pressure field which surrounds each blade and which rotates with the rotating propeller blade. This noise is generally subdivided into noise due to torque and thrust, dictated by blade angle and camber, and noise due to blade thickness. The third mechanism relates to the noise produced by vortices in the propeller wake which are shed by the blades during rotation. At low propeller speeds the vortex noise can be greater than the rotation noise, whereas at higher tip speeds the vortex noise appears only in the higher frequency range of the propeller spectrum.

Reductions of propeller noise at source can be achieved by minimizing the blade tip speed although in such cases the blade area will have to be increased to maintain propeller thrust. Alternatively, co-axial pairs of contra-rotating propellers may be employed to provide high thrust with lower tip speeds and smaller diameters than required by simple rotating propellers. Complementary methods of reducing propeller noise can include increases in blade number, which tends to increase the solidity of the propeller disk producing appreciable reductions in the sound pressure level of the fundamental tone and its harmonics, and improving the uniformity of blade loading,

offloading the blade tips, reducing the blade tip volume and incorporating greater blade tip sweep angles.

1.4.3.3 Helicopter noise control

Helicopter noise sources are similar in many respects to the sources on a propeller aircraft. Present generation helicopters generally have power plants which are acoustically well designed incorporating advanced noise reduction treatments. Consequently, the contributions to external noise from the engine, transmission and gearbox are usually of secondary importance to the noise generated by the helicopter rotors.

Rotor noise is essentially impulsive in nature and, typically, in flight the peak-to-overall RMS level ranges between 10 and 15 dB. On some helicopters a loud 'banging' noise is generated by the main rotor and this is termed blade slap. On a helicopter subjected to severe blade slap the peak-to-RMS value can be as high as 25 dB. Blade slap occurs at the main rotor blade passing frequency which is typically in the region of 15–20 Hz. In addition to the distinctive main rotor noise, tail rotor rotational noise is radiated as a whine and is often the most pronounced noise on a helicopter during cruise flight. Other well-defined noise sources of a helicopter are main rotor rotational noise, main rotor broadband noise and engine and transmission noise.

Control methods are aimed mainly at reducing the rotor tip speed although, for a given aerodynamic design, the blade area would have to be enlarged to maintain rotor aerodynamic performance. This could be achieved either by increasing the blade chord or span or by increasing the number of blades. However, both treatments will tend to lead to an increase in weight either directly by increases in the rotor configuration, or indirectly, by the necessity to fit a larger gearbox and transmission to deal with the rise in rotor torque. Reducing blade tip speed can, therefore, lead to changes in the operational efficiency of the helicopter.

1.4.3.4 Aircraft operational controls (see Chapters 19 and 20)

The exposure of points on the ground to the noise from any particular aeroplane is closely related to the manner in which the aeroplane is operated. Consequently, the noise in airport communities can vary considerably depending upon the particular climb-out or landing approach profiles that are in use. In addition, ground operations can influence airport noise impact.

In-flight operations Aircraft have to use high or full power at take off and are then at their noisiest. At some airports, they will have climbed to a sufficient height before crossing any residential area for noise not to be specially serious, but action will be necessary where residential and other sensitive communities exist close to the runway. At London's Heathrow, for example, advantage is taken to reduce power once a safe height of about 300 m (1000 ft) has been reached and thereafter to climb gradually under the reduced power. Control of climb-out is achieved at most major airports using monitoring stations located under each departure route which establish, by virtue of the noise emitted, whether the climb profile and engine power settings have been adhered to.

People living under an approach route to an airport are similarly subject to aircraft noise although, on approach, the power plants are operating at much lower settings than at takeoff. The rate of descent is a critical factor but this must be kept within safe limits. At Heathrow the rate of descent for the last 11 km (7 miles) of approach is 3 degrees from an initial height of 600 m (2000 ft).

Time of day restriction It is generally accepted that aircraft noise is more annoying at night than during the day. Consequently, most major airports have some form of restricted operation of aircraft movements during the night hours. Washington National, for example, has no jet operations at night in certain specified areas and Heathrow has substantially restricted the number of take-offs during the period 11 pm–6 am. In a region with more than one jet airport, a night curfew can be a feasible proposition.

Ground operations Aircraft ground operations can also cause noise nuisance to communities living close to airports. The sources of ground operation noise include engine testing and run up prior to taxiing including the start of roll point, standing aircraft noise on apron and terminal stands, and cargo and maintenance area noise.

Methods of modifying the impacts caused by these operations include, for run-up, reorientating the aircraft, relocating the aircraft more remotely from noise-sensitive areas and/or the use of run-up suppressors and barriers. The control of other sources of ground operations include the use of space to separate noisy operations, such as start of roll, from sensitive areas, and the use of buildings and screens to contain the noise within the airport boundary. With modern turbo fan powered aircraft, taxiing can be achieved entirely at minimum ground idle power whereas other aircraft types may need an initial higher engine power setting to get the aircraft rolling before reducing the power to the minimum.

1.4.3.5 Non-operational controls *(see Chapter 20)*

Even with significant reductions in aircraft noise exposure have been accomplished through operational procedures, additional methods of control are often required. Non-operational controls primarily include the management of land use in the vicinity of an airport and the sound insulation of property as well as other forms of subsidy and compensation.

Land use management Airport noise like any other noise is not a problem if no-one is bothered by it, and good planning of the land use, by securing adequate spacial separation of noise sources and noise-sensitive area, can contain the size of existing noise problems and minimize their further spread. Unfortunately, land possessing the characteristics that make possible the siting of new airports is becoming relatively scarce and is usually found only at some distance from the cities. For example, Milan's airport is some 85 km from the city centre. The airport at Montreal is at a similar distance from the centre but it also represents one of the first examples of the siting of a new airport where the total area of the land purchased includes the area to be impacted by noise; in this case approximately 300 km^2.

Where noise problems occur as a result of an existing airport and/or where space cannot be used to effect a satisfactory solution, other land use management options can be employed. These include:

1. Land zoning, to provide separate areas for commercial, recreational and residential development which are compatible with the noise exposure.
2. Negotiated and compulsory acquisition of land and property by the airport authority. This permits the proprietor to develop the land with a more noise compatible use.
3. Financial compensation where the property owner receives payment in return for permitting the over-flight of aircraft.

Insulation of property Around many of the larger airports, domestic dwellings that are seriously affected by noise are eligible for a grant for acoustic insulation to reduce the internal noise levels. The methods of sound insulation primarily involve improvements to the insulation of windows and doors in a

similar manner to traffic noise insulation requirements (*see* Chapter 11). However, roof insulation and the blocking of chimney flues may also be required for aircraft noise. As with traffic noise, insulation against the provision of fixed or double windows will often require additional ventilation by fans.

1.5 Decision making and transport noise control (*See* Chapters 22–24)

The technologically based solutions to noise problems described in the previous sections will, of course, feature strongly in any planning decisions regarding transport, particularly if the costs can be kept at a low level in relation to the total investment in the scheme. However, noise abatement measures do have a finite cost, and how much money should be spent is often a key issue in any transport development decision. In other words, the decision maker will need to know whether the costs of the noise control methods envisaged will be worth the benefits obtained in terms of reduced noise. The difficulty here is that economic costs and social benefits are not assessed on the same common scale and so, in the absence of further guidance, the balancing of costs and benefits ultimately requires some form of judgement by the decision maker. The planning decision is often further complicated by the fact that noise, while being a major pollutant associated with transport, is rarely the only environmental factor of concern. A new road may introduce noise into a once quiet area but it may also affect other factors such as severance, visual intrusion, air pollution and perceived danger, which are not necessarily related to noise impact. In addition, some noise control measures may adversely affect other environmental considerations. For example, the erection of a noise barrier to contain the spread of noise from a major road may further reduce the quality of the visual scene and add to the difficulty in crossing the road. The decision maker must, therefore, consider the environmental impact of transport schemes in its entirety and must be able to 'weight' the importance of impacts with each other to arrive at an assessment of the impacts and benefits.

A further, and, perhaps, more intractable aspect of the decision making process is the difficulty in balancing the gains and losses provided to the transport user with the gains and losses such as environmental effects felt by others. In the example of a new road scheme, the costs of construction and maintenance of the road will need to be balanced against the benefits to the motorist in terms of reduced accidents and journey times, together with gains and losses affecting communities impacted environmentally. Again, these elements of the problem do not sum naturally, and unless there is some way of combining the various factors to give them an acceptable weight, the decision made about any particular transport plan will not necessarily achieve its primary objective which, simply stated, is to maximize benefit. The following paragraphs very briefly outline the methods that have been developed to assist or coerce the decision maker to accept and then to account for the costs and benefits 'felt' environmentally as a result of transport development. The detailed descriptions are contained in Chapters 22–24.

1.5.1 Environmental appraisal (*see* Chapter 22)

The objective of environmental appraisal is to allow judgements to be reached about the environmental consequences of development plans. A variety of methods have been developed ranging from informal guidance which leaves the user of the appraisal method with a completely 'free hand' as to what impacts to assess and what interpretation to give, to the other extreme where all impacts are listed and methods are given for their assessment and interpretation. Intermediate approaches have been suggested which incorporate both a detailed formal and analytical phase, whilst leaving the final interpretation and decision or judgement to the decision maker. Such a method has been in operation in the UK as a means of assessing the impact caused by new road development. The method, known as the 'framework approach' allows the economic aspects of plans to be considered alongside environmental effects and is used at all stages of trunk road route selection. Its main purposes are to assist highway designers to produce plans that are likely to be acceptable environmentally, and to inform the public in an easy to understand way, what impacts have been considered, what were the outcomes, and what are the feasible options or alternatives.

In the United States the environmental appraisal process leads to the preparation of an Environmental Impact Statement (EIS) which applies to all Federal schemes which 'affect the quality of the human environment'. The European Community has also adopted a directive which gives guidance on the assessment of the environmental impact caused by roads, airports and long distance railways as well as ports and inland waterways.

1.5.2 Cost-benefit analysis (*see* Chapters 22 and 23)

In its simplest form cost–benefit analysis, values, in monetary terms, all the consequences of a plan. It then sums the benefits and costs to arrive at a net value for the scheme. Potentially it is an attractive solution to the appraisal problem since it overcomes the basic problem of comparing costs and benefits. By providing a common scale for both aspects expressed in a familiar unit they can then be combined as a single index of economic performance for the scheme as a whole.

The problems with this approach lie both with the placing of money values on environmental impacts (*see* Chapter 23) and with the methods of combining these impacts to form an overall assessment (*see* Chapter 22).

1.5.3 Economic incentives (*see* Chapter 24)

Environmental appraisal methods and the particular method of cost benefit analysis are examples of decision making tools which enable authorities that have the responsibility for planning the development of transport systems, the opportunity to exercise appropriate control over noise and other environmental impacts which result from the scheme. In this case the responsibility for control is clearly with the authority and not with the transport user. Invariably the transport user only 'sees' the benefits provided by the transport facility and does not 'feel' the environmental 'costs' created by its use.

An alternative approach is to leave the decision making power with the users or operators of the transport system, but, in addition, to force them through monetary incentives to see the impacts they create as costs instead of externalities. In practice this can be achieved by levying a tax which, ideally, would be equal to the cost to society of the impact caused. This

is often referred to as the 'polluter pays principle' and it is intended to cause the producer to reduce environmental impacts to an optimum level while at the same time compensating society for the impacts that are produced. However, its success depends, amongst other things, on being able to assess the correct amount of tax to levy. Some of the schemes that adopt this philosophy of approach are:

1. Aircraft landing charges. A noise tax can be incorporated into the landing fee to encourage operators to use quieter aircraft with reduced operational costs.
2. Motor vehicle noise charges. Here the incentive is to encourage manufacturers to design quieter vehicles and therefore to make their products more competitive, and buyers to exercise choice by achieving benefits from the reduced taxes on offer for quieter vehicles.

References

1 *Proceedings of The Conference on Noise Abatement Policies*, OECD, Paris, May 1980.
2 Environment Committee, *Noise Abatement: Present Situation and Future Outlook*, OECD, Paris, January 1985.
3 WILSON, A. *Noise (Final Report)*, Her Majesty's Stationery Office, London (1963).

Further reading

A summary of major reference books and reviews, recommended for further reading, are listed below.

1 WHITE, R. G. and WALKER, J. G. (Eds) *Noise and Vibration*, Ellis Horwood (1982).
2 SCHULTZ, E. *Community Noise Ratings*, 2nd edn., Applied Science (1982)
3 BURNS, W. *Noise and Man*, 2nd edn., John Murray, London (1973).
4. KRYTER, K. D. *Physiological, Psychological and Social Effects of Noise*, NASA, Washington DC (1984).
5 BERANEK, L. L. *Noise and Vibration Control*, McGraw Hill, New York (1971).
6 HOTHERSALL, D. G. and SALTER R. G. *Transport and the Environment*, Granada, London (1977).
7 HARRIS, C. M. *Handbook of Noise Control*, 2nd edn., McGraw Hill, New York (1979).
8 SMITH, B. J., PETERS R. J. and OWEN, S. *Acoustics and Noise Control*, Longman (1982).
9 LYON, R. H. *Lectures in Transportation Noise*, Grazier Publishing (1972).
10 STEFFANS, R. J. *Structural Vibration and Damage*, HMSO, London (1974).
11 LILLY, L. R. C. (Ed) *Diesel Engine Reference Book*, Butterworths, London (1984).
12 WATKINS, L. H. *Environmental Impact of Roads and Traffic*, Applied Science, London (1981).
13 BUGLIARELLO, G., ALEXANDRE, A., BURNES, J. and WAKESTEIN, C. *The Impact of Noise Pollution: a Socio-Technological Introduction*, Pergamon Press, New York (1976).

2

Physical Assessment of Transportation Noise

R. D. Ford BSc (Eng), PhD, FIOA
Department of Applied Acoustics,
University of Salford,
UK

Contents

2.1 Introduction

This chapter is concerned with the physical aspects of noise and is in three parts—(1) basic acoustics; (2) levels, scales and ratings; and (3) measurement.

Basic acoustics describes the terminology and physical parameters that provide the foundation for the remainder of the book. The broad principles of outdoor propagation are laid down but the details are left to the relevant chapters because different aspects of propagation assume special importance for the various types of transport that will be considered. Indeed the precise details of outdoor propagation—particularly in relation to ground attenuation, meteorological influences and topography—are only just becoming available. Consequently researchers have developed, and are still updating, their own empirical methods for calculating noise levels at some distance from the source.

Noise levels, scales and ratings all appear in the literature and are related in the sense that all are concerned with the human assessment of noise. The distinction is that level refers to the instantaneous value of sound while scale combines level with variation in time or frequency of occurrence. Ratings additionally bring into account the specific time of day and, perhaps, the season. The more important levels, scales and ratings are described in this chapter but the preferences which have emerged are covered in later chapters.

The last part discusses some of the problems of measuring noise from transport. In practice the only two factors which the user need worry about are the behaviour and positioning of the microphone. Once the pressure has been converted into an electrical signal there are a wide variety of instruments available, often incorporating microprocessors, which will calculate any desired result.

2.2 Basic acoustics

2.2.1 The speed of sound

Noise, often defined as unwanted sound, consists of tiny pressure fluctuations which propagate through the air at the local speed of sound. The magnitude of the fluctuation is very small, generally in the range from 2×10^{-5} Pa to 20 Pa* (0–120 dB) as compared with the standard atmospheric pressure of 101 325 Pa. The ear cancels out the steady pressure, responding only to the fluctuation.

The speed of sound, c, is given by the expression

$$c = (\gamma R T / M)^{\frac{1}{2}} \qquad (2.1)$$

where γ is the ratio of specific heats ($= 1.4$ for air), R is the gas constant ($= 8.31 \times 10^3$ Jkmol^{-1}K^{-1}), T is the absolute temperature and M is the molecular weight in kg ($= 28.8$ kg for air).

At 20°C and standard atmospheric pressure, the speed of sound is taken to be 344 ms^{-1}.

The significant parameter in equation 2.1 is the temperature. Temperature gradients in the atmosphere lead to ray curvature which can seriously affect propagation over long distances. This aspect will be discussed in Section 2.2.15.

Equation 2.1 implies that the speed of sound is independent of the magnitude of the pressure fluctuation. Within the pressure range quoted above, this is true but if the pressure fluctuations are much in excess of 20 Pa (120 dB), then some deviation from the assumed linear behaviour occurs. For very loud sounds, which would be painful to the ear and would necessitate the

wearing of hearing defenders, non-linear distortion causes the frequency content of the sound to change as it propagates.[1] So far as the recipient is concerned this fact is probably not very important but the engineer attempting to calculate the noise level at a distant location from a high-power source may have to make allowances. The application is, however, rather specialized and will not be dealt with in this chapter.

2.2.2 Frequency and wavelength

The frequency range of human hearing is usually said to be between 20 and 20 000 Hz. The upper limit generally decreases with age and every individual has an upper frequency limit above which he hears nothing. The lower limit is also rather uncertain in that it really represents a transition between hearing and whole body feeling. Hearing sensitivity decreases quite markedly as frequency decreases below about 250 Hz and eventually, with large pressure fluctuations at very low frequencies, the whole body responds to the pulsating pressure. Infrasonics is the name which has been given to the study of human reaction to frequencies below 20 Hz and it has been shown to be a factor contributing to passenger comfort inside some vehicles.[2]

The wavelength of sound, λ, is related to the speed of sound and the frequency, f, through the expression

$$c = f\lambda \qquad (2.2)$$

Typically the wavelength ranges from 17.2 m at 20 Hz to 17.2 mm at 20 000 Hz which is a very large variation. The wavelength is significant in diffraction and it will be seen in Section 2.2.16 that low-frequency waves bend around corners and over barriers while a shadow zone for high-frequency sound can be produced quite easily.

2.2.3 Doppler shift

If either source or receiver is moving, as is usually the case with transport, then the frequency of the sound perceived may differ from that which is emitted. In the general case illustrated in *Figure 2.1* it can be shown that the perceived frequency, f', is related to the emitted frequency, f, through the expression (2.3).

$$f' = \frac{c + u_1 \cos \theta_1}{c + u_2 \cos \theta_2} f \qquad 2.3$$

Figure 2.1 Moving source or receiver in a stationary medium give rise to Doppler shift

If the relative motion of the source and receiver is such that they are moving closer together then the net effect is a rise in frequency while if they are moving apart the frequency is reduced.

This is consistent with the obvious physical fact that in front of a moving source the wavefronts are pushed closer together whilst behind they are stretched farther apart. Similarly, a receiver moving towards the source encounters the wavefronts more frequently than when it is moving away.

2.2.4 Root mean square pressures

The typical range of pressure fluctuation amplitudes has already

---

*Pa denotes Pascal. Acoustical pressures are measured in Pascals where 1 Pa = 1 N m^{-2}.

been mentioned but, except at very low frequencies, the brain does not respond to the instantaneous pressure. Rather it behaves like an integrator, perceiving a signal which depends upon what has happened just previously. An equivalent signal can be realized mathematically by squaring and integrating the instantaneous pressure fluctuation, dividing by the integration time and then taking the square root. The result is known as the root mean square (rms) value and is defined as follows:

$$\bar{p} = \left[\frac{1}{T}\int_{t-T}^{t} p^2(\tau)d\tau\right]^{\frac{1}{2}}$$

(2.4)

In fact equation 2.4 represents a 'linear' averaging process in which the squared signal has been averaged over the time T immediately prior to the actual time t. Equal weighting is given to all parts of the signal that fall within the period T, and T can be chosen at will to suit the occasion. For the simple case of a continuous sinusoidal signal, T would be one period and the rms pressure would be 0.707 times the pressure amplitude. For more complicated signals T should be selected to provide the information required. For example, it might be sufficient to choose a value of 0.25, 0.5 or 1.0 s to obtain an average which still allows the variation in time to be observed, e.g. for an aircraft fly-over. Alternatively the signal could be averaged over a much longer time period, e.g. 1, 8 or even 24 hours to obtain what is usually referred to as the 'equivalent' level over the defined time period (*see* Section 2.3.7).

A 'linear' average refers to a time period with a clearly defined beginning and end. With a short averaging time this may necessitate breaking an event down into a sequence of discrete intervals. Human hearing, however, calculates a running average in which the instantaneous perceived level depends more upon the present and less upon the past pressure fluctuations. 'Exponential' averaging is a suitable mathematical representation of this process. In this case the rms pressure is given by:

$$\bar{p} = \left[\frac{1}{RC}\int_{-\infty}^{t} p^2(\tau)e^{(\tau-t)/RC}d\tau\right]^{\frac{1}{2}}$$

(2.5)

Theoretically, equation 2.5 includes all fluctuations up to time t. In practice the exponential weighting attaches greatest significance to the most recent fluctuations. *Figure 2.2* compares linear and exponential averaging. RC is the time constant of the averaging circuit.

The time constant of human hearing is uncertain but is said to be between 30 and 300 ms.[5] Sound level meters usually have fast and slow detector circuits with time constants of 125 ms and 1000 ms respectively.[6] Because of the different types of time weighting in equations 2.4 and 2.5 there can be no absolute equivalence between linear and exponential averaging. If it is

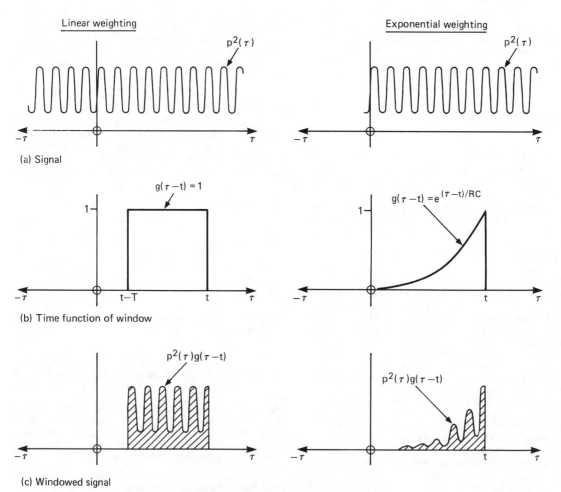

(a) Signal

(b) Time function of window

(c) Windowed signal

Figure 2.2   Linear and exponential time averaging of signal (After reference 4.)

necessary to compare the two processes then it has been shown that approximate equivalence is obtained by taking $T \simeq 2RC$.[7]

2.2.5 Decibels

Although pressure is measured in Pascals it is customary to specify sound level in decibels. This is a logarithmic scale well suited to human hearing which is logarithmic rather than linear in its behaviour. Consequently a change of sound level of, say, 5 dB results in roughly the same change in hearing sensation at any level, except near threshold, whereas a change of sound pressure of, say, 0.01 Pa would be equivalent to a very large subjective change at low levels while being hardly noticeable at high levels.

In order to provide a convenient scale, the actual rms acoustic pressure is divided by the reference pressure of 2×10^{-5} Pa before the logarithm is taken. Since the reference pressure is approximately equal to the minimum audible pressure at 1 kHz, the ratio for an audible sound is generally greater than unity and the sound pressure level, in dB, is positive. 0 dB corresponds closely to the threshold of hearing at 1 kHz and the scale extends upwards, typically to 120 dB before the sound becomes so loud that it starts to hurt. The word 'level' is always included when the decibel scale is used, and the sound pressure level (SPL) is defined as

$$SPL = 20 \log_{10} \left(\frac{\bar{p}}{2 \times 10^{-5}} \right) \text{dB} \tag{2.6}$$

The factor of 20 appears because decibels were originally defined for power ratios. Acoustic power is proportional to the square of the pressure and, in equation 2.6, a factor of two has been taken outside the logarithm.

Decibels have a wider use than within the strict definition of equation 2.6. Intensity level and power level are both used in acoustics and more will be said of them later. More generally, any ratio can be written in decibels. 40 dB, for example, is always equivalent to a ratio of 10 000 in power or 100 in pressure. A wall which transmits 1/100 of the incident sound power (1/10 of the incident sound pressure) is said to have a sound reduction index of 20 dB and the transmitted level is always 20 dB less than the incident level whatever the absolute values of SPL may be. In many instances the use of decibels turns a multiplicative process into a simple addition or subtraction.

2.2.6 Intensity and power

With a sound wave propagating away from the source in free space there is a simple relationship between the pressure and the intensity of the sound wave, i.e.:

$$I = \bar{p}^2 / \rho c \tag{2.7}$$

where $\bar{p}^2$ is the mean square pressure, ρ is the density of air (1.2 kgm^{-3} at standard atmospheric pressure) and c is the speed of sound (344 ms^{-1} at 20°C). ρc is sometimes referred to as the characteristic impedance of air (413 Pam^{-1}s). Although the human ear responds to pressure, the concept of intensity is useful because it can be related to acoustic power and calculations can often be carried out quite easily on a power flow basis.

Intensity is defined as the rate of flow of energy per unit area. Integrating the intensity over a notional surface area gives the total power flowing through that surface. The method only works satisfactorily if the direction of power flow is clearly defined. In an enclosed space there are multiple reflections of the sound waves and the actual net intensity through any notional surface may be very small even though the acoustic pressure fluctuations are large. Under those conditions equation 2.7 is not applicable. It can be used whenever it is reasonable to say

that the energy is travelling in a specific direction although it is not limited to just one dimension. A noise source outdoors on the ground radiates into a solid angle of 2π and all of the power must be distributed over a notional hemispherical surface of any chosen radius. If the source power is known and it exhibits no particular directivity, it is simple to calculate the intensity at any given distance and then use equation 2.7 to find the rms pressure.

Conversely the source power could be found by initially measuring the rms pressure at a large number of points on the notional hemisphere. Equation 2.7 is used to find the intensity at each point, which is then integrated over the surface area.

Since the SPL in decibels is used in preference to the acoustic pressure in Pa it is logical also to use decibel scales for intensity and power. Intensity level is defined as:

$$L_I = 10 \log_{10} \left(\frac{I}{10^{-12}} \right) \text{dB} \tag{2.8}$$

By choosing the reference intensity to be 10^{-12} Wm^{-2} the numerical values for the SPL and IL of any particular sound wave in air only differ by 0.16 dB. This small difference can generally be ignored and so SPL and IL can be regarded, for many applications, as being interchangeable.

To conform with intensity level the power level is defined as:

$$L_W = 10 \log_{10} \left(\frac{W}{10^{-12}} \right) \text{dB} \tag{2.9}$$

where 10^{-12} W is the reference acoustic power.

2.2.7 Frequency spectra

The simplest sound wave is a continuous pure tone of fixed single frequency. This is shown in *Figure 2.3(a)* but rarely occurs outside the laboratory. Even musical instruments create a sound wave consisting of many harmonics superimposed on the fundamental. More complicated repetitive waveforms are illustrated in *Figures 2.3(b)* and *2.3(c)*, in which the actual waveform can be constructed from a Fourier series of harmonically related sinusoids, each with the appropriate relative phase. A noise signal, illustrated in *Figure 2.3(d)*, is not repetitive and, if analysed, is found to contain all possible frequencies in a given range. If any one frequency could be filtered out and studied its amplitude would be found to vary randomly with time. The only way to describe the frequency content of such a signal is to break the full frequency range down into a series of contiguous bands and to measure the signal level in each band over a sufficiently long time to obtain a meaningful average. The resulting frequency information is known as a spectrum.

2.2.8 Octave and 1/3 octave frequency bands

Grouping the frequencies into octave bands provides a crude form of analysis suited to broad-band sounds which do not contain any dominant frequencies. The reference frequency in any acoustic work is always 1000 Hz and this is the centre frequency of the 1000 Hz octave band.[9] Other octave band centre frequencies are related to 1000 Hz by the factor $10^{\pm 0.3 N}$, where N is a positive integer. The band limiting frequencies are related to the centre frequency by the factor $10^{\pm 0.15}$. The actual centre frequencies are rounded slightly to make them into the preferred frequencies which are listed in *Table 2.1*. More detail is obtained by using 1/3 octave bands. The centre frequencies of these are related to 1000 Hz by the factor $10^{\pm 0.1 N}$ and the band limiting frequencies are related to the centre frequency by the factor $10^{\pm 0.05}$. These also are listed in *Table 2.1*.

It is worth noting that it is the mean square pressure which is distributed among the various frequency bands, so if the bands

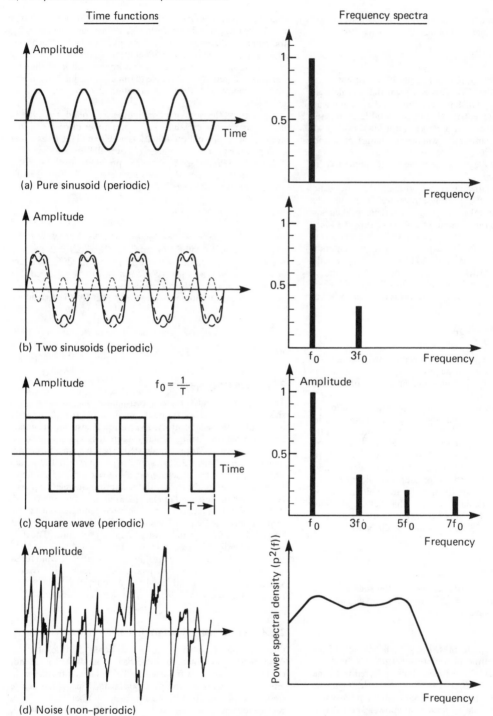

Figure 2.3 Sound waveforms and their spectra (After reference 8.)

Table 2.1 Octave and 1/3 octave band centre and limiting frequencies in Hz

Lower limiting frequency	Preferred centre frequency	Upper limiting frequency
* 22.4	25	28.2
28.2	* 31.5	35.5
35.5	40	* 44.7
* 44.7	50	56.2
56.2	* 63	70.8
70.8	80	* 89.1
* 89.1	100	112.2
112.2	* 125	141.3
141.3	160	* 177.8
* 177.8	200	223.9
223.9	* 250	281.8
281.8	315	* 354.8
* 354.8	400	446.7
446.7	* 500	562.3
562.3	630	* 707.9
* 707.9	800	891.3
891.3	* 1 000	1 122
1 122	1 250	* 1 413
* 1 413	1 600	1 778
1 778	* 2 000	2 239
2 239	2 500	* 2 818
* 2 818	3 150	3 548
3 548	* 4 000	4 467
4 467	5 000	* 5 623
* 5 623	6 300	7 079
7 079	* 8 000	8 913
8 913	10 000	* 11 220
* 11 220	12 500	14 125
14 125	* 16 000	17 783
17 783	20 000	* 22 387

*Octave band values.

were to be recombined the total mean square pressure would be equal to the sum of the mean square pressures in all of the frequency bands, i.e.:

$$\bar{p}^2 = \sum_{i=1}^{n} \bar{p}_i^2 \qquad (2.10)$$

where $\bar{p}_i^2$ is the mean square pressure in band i. If, as is likely, it is the level in decibels in each frequency band which is to be recombined to obtain the total level, then each one has to be raised to the power of 10 before summing. The formula is:

$$L_T = 10 \log_{10} \left(\sum_{i=1}^{n} 10^{L_i/10} \right) \text{dB} \qquad (2.11)$$

where

$$L_i = 20 \log_{10} \left(\frac{\bar{p}_i}{2 \times 10^{-5}} \right) \text{dB}$$

2.2.9 Narrow bands

Very fine detail can be obtained using narrow band analysis which may be necessary if a sound contains a discrete frequency, perhaps buried in noise. Although the bandwidth can be varied to suit the analysis, the result should be presented as the spectral density, i.e. the mean square pressure per Hz, $\bar{p}^2(f)$. The total mean square pressure is given by:

$$\bar{p}^2 = \int_0^\infty \bar{p}^2(f) \mathrm{d}f \qquad (2.12)$$

Obviously the spectral density of, say, an octave band is found by dividing the mean square pressure in that band by the bandwidth, but the spectral density is then implicitly constant and no further frequency detail is actually obtained.

2.2.10 Contributions from separate sources

The idea of adding together separate frequency components to give the total mean square pressure can be extended to adding contributions from separate sources. In general the total mean square pressure is the sum of the individual mean square pressure contributions, except in the special case of two or more sources emitting precisely the same frequency. Then it is essential to go back to first principles and to add two signals of the same frequency as phasor quantities, i.e.:

$$p = p_1 \cos (\omega t + \varphi_1) + p_2 \cos (\omega t + \varphi_2) \qquad (2.13)$$

where φ_1 and φ_2 represent the phases of the two pressure waves of amplitude p_1 and p_2. Squaring and averaging equation 2.13 to obtain the mean square pressure leads to the expression:

$$\bar{p}^2 = \frac{1}{2} \left\{ p_1^2 + p_2^2 + 2p_1 p_2 \overline{\cos(\varphi_1 - \varphi_2)} \right\} \qquad (2.14)$$

If the two signals are coherent, i.e. the waveforms are identical in shape although they may be displaced in time, the phase difference $(\varphi_1 - \varphi_2)$ is constant and equation 2.14 can be used to calculate the mean square pressure. If the phase difference varies randomly then the time average of $\cos(\varphi_1 - \varphi_2)$ is zero and again the total mean square pressure is the sum of the component mean square pressures. Coherent sources are not common in acoustics. They are restricted to sources which are connected in some way such as loudspeakers driven from the same source, synchronized engines on a multi-engined vehicle or a single source with its image reflected in a plane. Separate vehicles, although ostensibly the same, never operate in an absolutely identical manner and it is sufficient to add the mean square pressures, ignoring the possibilities of constructive or destructive interference, using equations 2.10 or 2.11 as appropriate.

2.2.11 Geometric spreading of sound

In the open it is self-evident that sound level diminishes as the distance from the source increases owing to the geometric dispersion of the sound power. In a still atmosphere of uniform temperature with no barriers or other obstructions and neglecting the possibility of air absorption, the total source power must pass through any notional surface surrounding that source. In the simplest case of a source in free space radiating equally in all directions the intensity at distance r is:

$$I = W/4\pi r^2 \qquad (2.15)$$

or, in logarithmic form:

$$SPL \simeq L_I = L_w - 11 - 20 \log_{10} r \text{ dB} \qquad (2.16)$$

The final term in Equation 2.16 represents the inverse square law in acoustics. It can be seen that the level decreases by 6 dB every time that the distance is doubled.

If the source is directional then the intensity is not distributed evenly over the notional surface. Directional behaviour may be specified by the directivity factor, DF, which is defined as the ratio of the actual intensity in a given direction to the intensity of an omni-directional source of the same power output. If the DF is greater than unity in some directions then it must be less in other directions so that the value of DF averaged over the complete sphere is unity. The directivity index, DI, is the logarithmic form of the DF. Equation 2.16 is modified as follows.

$$SPL \simeq L_I = L_w - 11 + DI - 20 \log_{10} r \text{ dB} \tag{2.17}$$

In the particular case of a source on a flat reflective surface radiating equally in all directions into a hemisphere rather than a sphere the DF is 2 everywhere on the hemisphere and the DI is 3 dB. Usually sources do have some directivity and then DI should be specified as a function of direction.

The other type of source which is of interest is a line of length L on a hard flat surface. If the line source can be regarded as a distributed set of elements, dx, of source strength Wdx, which are each omni-directional and incoherent, then the integration to find the total intensity at a given point is relatively easy. The arrangement, in plan, is shown in *Figure 2.4*. The intensity at d is given by:

$$I = \int_{-L/2}^{L/2} \frac{Wdx}{2\pi r^2} = \frac{W}{2\pi d} \int_{-a}^{a} d\theta$$

$$= \frac{W}{2\pi d} 2 \tan^{-1}\left(\frac{L}{2d}\right) \tag{2.18}$$

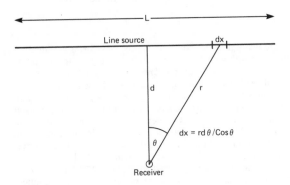

Figure 2.4 Representation of a continuous line array of incoherent sources

In logarithmic form this would be:

$$L_I = L_w - 8 - 10 \log_{10} d$$

$$+ 10 \log_{10}\left[2 \tan^{-1}\left(\frac{L}{2d}\right)\right] \text{dB} \tag{2.19}$$

The last term is illustrated in *Figure 2.5*. Close to the source the total reduction is asymptotic to 3 dB/doubling of distance, while far from the source it becomes asymptotic to 6 dB/doubling of distance. This case might be applicable to a line of moving vehicles, although it has been assumed that the acoustic power is distributed uniformly along the line, i.e. all vehicles would have to be identical. Further information on the mathematical de-

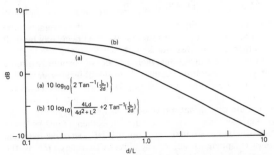

Figure 2.5 Variation of sound level with distance from a line array of incoherent sources which are (a) monopoles and (b) dipoles

scription of both point and line sources in relation to traffic noise modelling is given in Chapter 10. For rail/wheel interaction noise from a train, a $3\cos^2\theta$ term must be included in the integral in equation 2.18, because the wheels radiate as incoherent dipoles[10]. Equation 2.19 is then modified to:

$$L_I = L_w - 6 - 10 \log_{10} d$$

$$+ 10 \log_{10}\left[\frac{4Ld}{L^2 + 4d^2} + 2\tan^{-1}\left(\frac{L}{2d}\right)\right] \text{dB} \tag{2.20}$$

The last term in equation 2.20 is also plotted in *Figure 2.5*. A description of rail-wheel interaction noise is given in Chapter 15 and further information on the mathematical modelling of train noise is given in Chapter 16.

2.2.12 Sound energy from a moving source

The sources considered in the previous section were treated as if they were stationary, but transport moves. It is of some interest, therefore, to calculate the total sound energy received at a given point as a simple omni-directional point source moves past at a constant velocity V. The geometrical situation is shown in *Figure 2.6*.

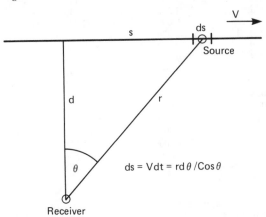

Figure 2.6 Geometry for calculating the sound energy received from a moving source

The energy received in time dt is given by:

$$dE = I dt$$

$$= \frac{W}{4\pi r^2} dt$$

This assumes spherical spreading of sound with no directivity but the following argument would be equally valid if the source were placed on a hard reflecting plane with a DF of 2 ($DI = 3$ dB).

Changing variables and integrating gives the total energy:

$$E = \frac{W}{4\pi r d} \int_{-\pi/2}^{\pi/2} d\theta$$

$$= \frac{W}{4\pi d^2} \frac{Kd}{V} \tag{2.21}$$

where

$$K = \pi$$

In Section 2.3.8 L_{AX} will be defined as the level of the total sound energy of an event. So, dividing by $10^{-12}\,\mathrm{Wm^{-2}}$ and taking logarithms leads to the expression:

$$L_{AX} = L_{Amax} + 10\log_{10}\left(\frac{Kd}{V}\right)\;\mathrm{dB} \tag{2.22}$$

where L_{max} is the instantaneous level when the source is at its nearest position and K has a maximum value of π.

In reality K may be less than π, either because of source directivity or possibly because of air absorption (*see* Section 2.2.13). For aircraft noise an empirical value of 1.83 has been suggested.[11] The directivity of noise radiated from diesel locomotives is said to be proportional to $\cos\theta$,[12] which then appears in the integral in equation 2.21 leading to a maximum value of 2 for K.

The line source of length L on a hard surface can be regarded as a set of omnidirectional sources each of length dx and power Wdx. The contribution of each source to the total energy is, from equation 2.21:

$$dE = \frac{Wdx}{2\pi d^2}\frac{\pi d}{V}$$

So:

$$E = \frac{W}{2\pi}\cdot\frac{\pi L}{Vd} \tag{2.23}$$

Substituting the value of I_{max} from equation 2.18 gives.

$$E = I_{max}\cdot\frac{\pi L}{V}\cdot\frac{1}{\tan^{-1}\left(\dfrac{\pi L}{v}\right)}$$

Dividing by the reference value and taking logarithms gives:

$$L_{AX} = L_{Amax} + 10\log_{10}\left(\frac{\pi L}{V}\right)$$
$$-10\log_{10}\left[2\tan^{-1}\left(\frac{L}{2d}\right)\right]\;\mathrm{dB} \tag{2.24}$$

For trains, the dipole directivity associated with radiation from the wheels modifies the integrals and equation 2.24 becomes:

$$L_{AX} = L_{Amax} + 10\log_{10}\left(\frac{\pi L}{V}\right)$$
$$-10\log_{10}\left[\frac{4Ld}{L^2+4d^2}+2\tan^{-1}\left(\frac{L}{2d}\right)\right]\;\mathrm{dB} \tag{2.25}$$

2.2.13 Air absorption

The geometric spread considered in the previous sections assumed that the total acoustic power remains undiminished as it travels away from the source. In fact a proportion of the sound energy is converted into heat as it travels through the air although it is usually only significant at high frequencies or over large distances. The 'classical' absorption is due to the viscosity and heat conduction of air but both of these are negligible when compared with the 'molecular' absorption. The presence of water vapour in the air facilitates the excitation, by the sound wave, of resonant vibrations of the oxygen and nitrogen molecules. The amount of energy transferred by this mechanism depends significantly upon frequency and relative humidity and to a lesser extent upon temperature. *Figure 2.7* shows typical frequency domains in which the different mechanisms assume major importance. Absorption values at 20°C are shown in *Table 2.2*.[13] Further details are given in Chapter 19 on aircraft noise propagation.

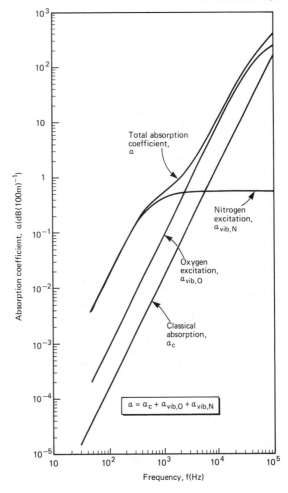

Figure 2.7 Air absorption at 20°C and 70% RH (After reference 13.)

2.2.14 Ground attenuation

When both source and receiver are close to the ground, interference between the direct and reflected waves produces some curious effects. The simplest case to consider is that of a still atmosphere of uniform temperature, and consequently no velocity gradient, over flat ground. Measurements suggest that most ground surfaces can be regarded as locally reacting, i.e. a pressure at one point on the surface does not give rise to ground motion at some other point on the surface. This would not be true over water where the physical situation is rather more complicated.

Figure 2.8 shows the simple geometry of a source and receiver above a flat ground plane. The reflected wave appears to come from an image source. Assuming that the ground is locally reacting, the total complex pressure at the receiver is given by[14]:

$$p = p_0 e^{j(wt-kr_1)}\left\{1+\left[R_p + (1-R_p)F\right]\frac{r_1}{r_2}e^{-jk(r_2-r_1)}\right\} \tag{2.26}$$

where p_0 is the pressure amplitude in the absence of the reflective plane. The first term represents the direct wave from the source. The second term represents the reflection of a plane wave and R_p is the plane wave reflection coefficient given by:

Table 2.2 Air absorption (dB/100 m) at 20°C

Frequency (Hz)	Relative humidity (%)									
	10	15	20	30	40	50	60	70	80	100
50	0.02	0.02	0.01	0.01	0.01	0.01	0.01	0.00	0.00	0.00
63	0.03	0.03	0.02	0.02	0.01	0.01	0.01	0.01	0.01	0.01
80	0.05	0.04	0.03	0.02	0.02	0.02	0.01	0.01	0.01	0.01
100	0.06	0.06	0.05	0.04	0.03	0.02	0.02	0.02	0.02	0.02
125	0.08	0.07	0.07	0.05	0.04	0.04	0.03	0.03	0.02	0.02
160	0.10	0.10	0.09	0.08	0.07	0.06	0.05	0.04	0.04	0.03
200	0.12	0.12	0.12	0.11	0.10	0.08	0.07	0.07	0.06	0.05
250	0.15	0.14	0.15	0.14	0.13	0.12	0.11	0.10	0.09	0.07
315	0.20	0.18	0.18	0.18	0.18	0.17	0.16	0.14	0.13	0.11
400	0.27	0.22	0.22	0.22	0.23	0.22	0.22	0.21	0.19	0.17
500	0.38	0.29	0.27	0.27	0.28	0.28	0.28	0.27	0.27	0.24
630	0.55	0.39	0.34	0.33	0.34	0.35	0.36	0.36	0.35	0.34
800	0.82	0.55	0.45	0.40	0.41	0.42	0.44	0.45	0.45	0.45
1 000	1.21	0.79	0.62	0.51	0.49	0.50	0.52	0.54	0.55	0.57
1 250	1.80	1.15	0.87	0.66	0.61	0.61	0.62	0.64	0.66	0.69
1 600	2.78	1.77	1.31	0.94	0.81	0.77	0.77	0.78	0.80	0.84
2 000	4.05	2.65	1.94	1.32	1.09	1.00	0.96	0.96	0.97	1.01
2 500	5.79	3.95	2.89	1.92	1.53	1.34	1.25	1.21	1.20	1.22
3 150	8.09	5.91	4.40	2.89	2.23	1.90	1.71	1.61	1.56	1.52
4 000	10.93	8.80	6.75	4.45	3.37	2.80	2.47	2.26	2.13	2.00
5 000	13.82	12.40	9.93	6.69	5.05	4.13	3.57	3.21	2.97	2.70
6 300	16.80	17.03	14.52	10.18	7.71	6.27	5.36	4.75	4.33	3.82
8 000	19.65	22.54	20.79	15.54	11.96	9.73	8.27	7.28	6.57	5.65
10 000	22.05	27.97	27.98	22.65	17.91	14.69	12.50	10.96	9.84	8.35

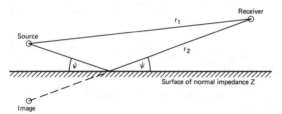

Figure 2.8 Geometry for a source and a receiver in the vicinity of a reflecting ground plane

$$R_p = \frac{\text{Sin } \psi - \rho c/Z}{\text{Sin } \psi + \rho c/Z} \qquad (2.27)$$

where ρc is the characteristic impedance of air and Z is the normal impedance of the surface. Several attempts have been made to measure the impedance of different ground surfaces. One set of data for grass-covered flat ground[15] is shown in *Figure 2.9*. Suitable empirical equations are:

$$R/\rho c = 1 + 9.08 (f/\sigma)^{-0.75}$$
$$X/\rho c = -11.9 (f/\sigma)^{-0.73} \qquad (2.28)$$

where σ is given the numerical value of 300 cgs units. For other types of ground cover the same equations could be used but with different values of σ.

The third term arises because the outgoing wave is actually spherical rather than plane and it contains the so-called 'ground' and 'surface' waves. F is a complicated function given by:

$$F = 1 + j(\pi W)^{\frac{1}{2}} e^{-w} erfc(-j\sqrt{w}) \qquad (2.29)$$

where:

$$w = -(jkr_2/2)(\text{Sin } \psi + \rho c/Z)^2 \qquad (2.30)$$

Enumerating F is difficult although recognized series expansions are available.[15,16]

When w is small, i.e. at small distances or at low frequencies, F tends to unity and equation 2.26 becomes:

$$p = p_0 \left\{ 1 + \frac{r_1}{r_2} e^{-jk(r_2 - r_1)} \right\} e^{j(wt - kr_1)} \qquad (2.31)$$

The ground impedance is unimportant and, for small path differences, the free-field pressure is approximately doubled.

When w is large, i.e. at large distances or at high frequencies, F tends to zero and equation 2.26 becomes:

$$p = p_0 \left\{ 1 + R_p \frac{r_1}{r_2} e^{-jk(r_2 - r_1)} \right\} e^{j(wt - kr_1)} \qquad (2.32)$$

Interference patterns emerge depending upon the values of R_p and the path difference.

At intermediate values of w, equation 2.26 must be evaluated in its entirety, generally giving rise to a pattern similar to that shown in *Figure 2.10*. For sound at shallow angles of incidence to the ground, destructive interference occurs in a frequency band somewhere in the range 200 to 600 Hz. The actual frequency and the magnitude of the attenuation depend upon the ground impedance and the path difference. Although the calculation procedure is complicated, the results can be significant when predicting a noise environment or when relating the noise power of a source to a set of measurements.

A simplified procedure[17] suggests that, for propagation over soft flat ground, the frequency of maximum attenuation can be calculated from the formula:

$$f_{max} = \frac{1500}{h \log_{10}(r/0.3)} \qquad (2.33)$$

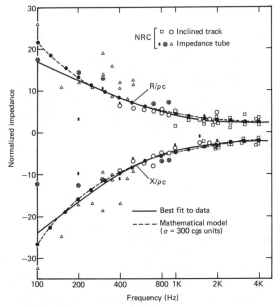

Figure 2.9 The normal impedance of grass-covered soil (After reference 15.)

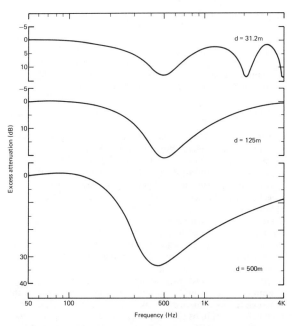

Figure 2.10 Ground attenuation for propagation over mown grass; source height is 1.8 m, receiver height is 1.5 m (After reference 14.)

where h is the mean path height and r is the distance from source to receiver. The attenuation in the octave band containing f_{max} is then calculated from

$$A_g = 15 \log_{10}(0.065r/h) \, \text{dB} \qquad (2.34)$$

A_g is never less than zero and the attentuation in each adjacent octave band is taken to be $A_g/2$.

2.2.15 Wind and temperature gradients

So far it has been assumed that the air is still and that the speed of sound is constant throughout the atmosphere. In reality the wind gives rise to a moving medium and the local wind vector must be added to the speed of sound in order to obtain the speed relative to fixed ground coordinates. If the wind were constant that would not be important but the wind speed usually

increases with height above the ground. Consequently, in the downwind direction, the top side of the wavefront is pushed forward and the sound rays curve down towards the ground. Upwind, however, the top side of the wavefront is retarded and the rays curve upward away from the ground creating a shadow zone. These situations are illustrated in *Figure 2.11*.

Temperature gradients produce a similar effect because, to a first approximation, the rate of change of speed of sound with height is proportional to the temperature gradient. Consequently, in lapse temperature conditions, which generally occur during the day when the ground is warmest, the speed of sound decreases with height and the sound rays curve upwards. This creates a shadow zone all around the source unlike that arising from a wind gradient. In inversion conditions, which tend to occur in the late evening when skies are clear and the ground has

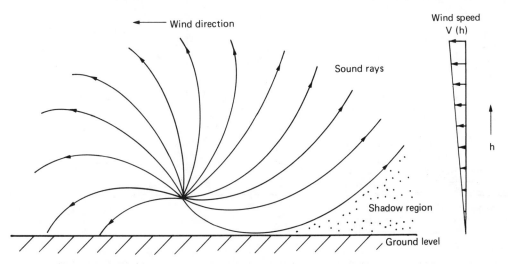

Figure 2.11 Sound ray curvature with a wind gradient (After reference 8.)

cooled rapidly, there is a region above ground where the air temperature, and therefore the speed of sound, increases with height and the rays bend down towards the ground, so enhancing the sound level. These cases are illustrated in *Figure 2.12*

In the simple case of a uniform velocity gradient, i.e. the speed of sound changes linearly with height, the rays follow the arc of a circle and the radius, R, is given by[18]:

$$R = \frac{-c}{g \cos \psi} \qquad (2.35)$$

where c is the local speed of sound, g is the velocity gradient and ψ is the angle of inclination to the horizontal. At heights of more than 10 m or so above ground a uniform gradient may be a reasonable approximation to reality but in the boundary layer below 10 m both wind and temperature display a variation with height which is nearer logarithmic than linear and the ray path, although curved, is not a simple arc.

Nevertheless, given sufficient meteorological data, it is feasible to compute ray paths with reasonable confidence. It should then be possible theoretically to calculate the enhancement or reduction of sound pressure, as compared with that expected from the simple inverse square law, from the relative concentration of the sound rays at any particular point. So far, quantitative calculations of that type have not proved successful although the location of a focus corresponding to an unusually high concentration of rays has been predicted with some success.[19] The difficulties arise from inadequate meteorological data and the interference of other factors such as ground attenuation and the topography of the intervening terrain.

In the absence of good predictive methods, several attempts have been made to produce empirical charts demonstrating the dependence of sound level on wind speed, direction and distance.[14,20] These are inevitably crude, based as they are on insufficient data, and offer little more information than that levels are enhanced downwind and reduced upwind. It can, of course, be argued that long-term average levels are independent of meteorological conditions and that wind and temperature effects can be ignored for predictive purposes. The danger in that approach is that occasionally wind or temperature may produce unusually high noise levels in a particular area which would give rise to complaints. Consequently, a safety factor may need to be built in to the estimate.

2.2.16 Barriers

The attenuation obtainable from a sharp-edged barrier in still air and constant temperature conditions is well understood.[21] It is a classical diffraction problem and, as would be expected, high frequencies are attenuated more easily than low frequencies. First, it should be appreciated that the noise must not be able to pass through the barrier. Consequently the barrier must be impervious and have a superficial mass of at least 15kgm^{-2}

The attenuation of sound from a point source by an infinitely long thin barrier can be approximately determined from the formula[22]:

$$A = 10 \log_{10}(3 + 20N) \, \text{dB} \qquad (2.36)$$

where:

$$N = \pm \frac{2}{\lambda}(a + b - d)$$

and a, b and d are defined in *Figure 2.13*. $N = 0$ corresponds to minimum line of sight across the top of the barrier when the attenuation is approximately 5 dB. Positive values of N are obtained when the receiver is in the shadow zone. Negative values of N are obtained when the receiver is in the illuminated or bright zone but still receives some attenuation. N cannot be less than -0.1. It is found that the attenuation provided by barriers never exceeds about 25 dB, probably as a result of the limitation imposed by scattering due to atmospheric turbulence.

A barrier of finite length gives a reduced attenuation as a result of noise diffracting around the ends. The combined attenuation can be found by calculating A_1, A_2 and A_3 from equation 2.36 as if the three possible routes, over the top and

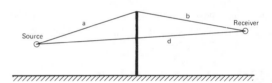

Figure 2.13 Source and receiver in relation to an infinitely long barrier

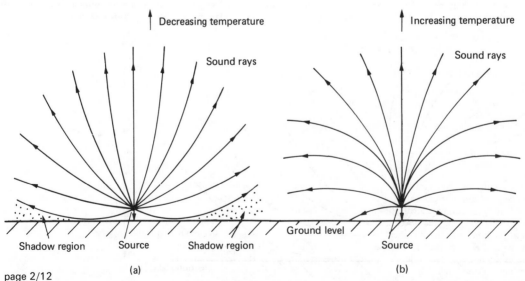

(a)   (b)

Figure 2.12 Sound ray curvature with (*a*) a normal temperature lapse rate and (*b*) an inverted temperature lapse rate (After reference 8.)

around both ends, were all around infinite barriers and then combining them according to the expression:

$$A_T = -10 \log_{10}(10^{-A_1/10} + 10^{-A_2/10} + 10^{-A_3/10}) \, \text{dB} \qquad (2.37)$$

Equation 2.36 is for a thin barrier, in which the thickness is less than the wavelength of sound. For a thicker barrier, such as a building, it is suggested that the actual barrier is replaced by a notional thin barrier as illustrated in *Figure 2.14*.

It is stressed[17] that if there is a barrier between source and receiver then the ground attenuation, described in Section 2.2.14, is precluded. This can lead to situations where a barrier gives little or no net gain over the ground attenuation which would otherwise occur. In such cases it is usually advised that calculations of both barrier and ground attenuation should be made and the greater attenuation taken.[23]

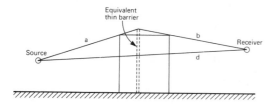

Figure 2.14 Representation of a thick barrier

Transport noise usually comes from a moving or extended source rather than the stationary source to which the previous analysis refers. Then the effective barrier attenuation may be slightly less than that calculated for when the source is at its closest point. The degree of lost attenuation depends on the rating being used for assessing the noise. Clearly the maximum attenuation would be appropriate to a rating utilizing the peak noise levels, whereas the average attenuation would be appropriate to a rating linked to the average level. Even then equation 2.36 will give a reasonably good indication of the performance of a long barrier.

One final point concerning barriers is that the predicted attenuation is for still air conditions. If the barrier is downwind of the source the noise can be carried over the top by the ray curving process described in Section 2.2.15.[24] Then the attenuation predicted for the barrier is not achieved, because it is no longer in the path of the direct rays from source to receiver. A similar condition arises with temperature inversion.

2.3 Levels, scales and ratings

Assessing noise in terms of probable subjective reaction requires three steps, each of which should be validated by subjective experimentation. The first is to isolate the noise from other influencing factors and devise a measurement of level which correlates with noisiness. The measurement should emulate the ear's variation of sensitivity with frequency and, possibly, take masking into account. At this stage time is not included so the level is a function of time. The 'A', 'B', 'C' and 'D' weighted levels together with perceived noise level and tone corrected perceived noise level fall into this category.

The second step is to combine level with time in some way to give a scale. This may be the level exceeded for a given proportion of the time as in the statistical level or it may be an integration of level with respect to duration as in equivalent level, single event noise exposure level, disturbance index or effective perceived noise level.

The rating or index goes one step further in that the time period is clearly specified. A scale may become a rating simply

by defining the time period, or the rating may be an aggregate of different scales applied to daytime and night-time. The object is to produce an evaluation for a particular type of noise in particular circumstances. Day/night level, community noise equivalent level, total noise load, noise exposure forecast and weighted equivalent continuous perceived noise level are all 24-hour ratings while the isopsophic index is defined separately for day and night and the noise and number index is defined for daytime only.

In this section the more popular levels, scales and ratings will be described. It is beyond the scope of this chapter to designate preferences for the assessment of different noise sources. These aspects will be dealt with in later chapters. A further discussion of noise scales and ratings is covered by Schultz.[25]

2.3.1 'A' weighted sound pressure level, L_A

Human hearing is not equally sensitive to all frequencies. This is illustrated in *Figure 2.15*. A further complication is that the variation with frequency is a function of level, the variation being less for very loud sounds than near the hearing threshold. The 'A' weighting corresponds most nearly to the 30 phon curve, i.e. the equal loudness contour which passes through 30 dB at 1000 Hz. The specification for the 'A' weighting is shown in *Table 2.3*.[6] A sound level meter has an electronic filter, meeting these specifications within acceptable tolerances, interposed between the microphone and the display. So, in principle, the meter has a frequency characteristic approximating, for low-level sounds, to that of the human ear. Logically the characteristic should be slightly different for medium or high-level sounds, because the shape of the equal loudness contour changes, and for that reason the 'B' and 'C' weightings were also proposed (*see* Sections 2.3.2 and 2.3.3).

In fact the 'A' weighting is now used for all levels of noise and a measurement so made is given in units of dB(A). Since the 'A' weighting was introduced there have been several surveys correlating subjective reaction with objective measurements, but no weighting was proved to be significantly better than the 'A' weighting, which is why it has now been almost universally adopted for the measurement of transport noise.

2.3.2 'B' weighted sound pressure level, L_B

The 'B' weighting is similar to the 'A' weighting in concept, corresponding roughly with the 70 phon equal loudness contour. Its specification is given in *Table 2.3*. In practice it is seldom used because it offers no positive advantages over the 'A' weighting. The sound levels obtained using the 'B' weighting are quoted in dB(B).

2.3.3 'C' weighted sound pressure level, L_C

The 'C' weighting corresponds roughly with the 100 phon equal loudness contour and is defined in *Table 2.3*. In fact it differs little from a flat weighting over the audio frequency range, being just a few dB down at both extremes. Like the 'B' weighting it offers little advantage over the 'A' weighting and is rarely used.

The exception might be for impulsive noises such as sonic boom. In the past it has been customary to measure the peak unweighted or 'C' weighted overpressure which is then expressed in dB(C). A typical waveform is illustrated in *Figure 2.16*. In practice little correlation has been found between the peak overpressure in dB(C) and subjective reaction, but it has proved useful for predicting the likelihood of damage to buildings. Chapter 21 covers sonic boom in some detail.

Whether or not the 'C' weighting is desirable is conjectural.

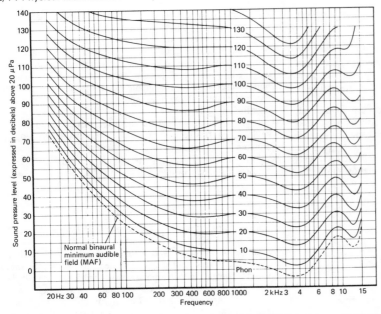

Figure 2.15 Equal loudness contours for human hearing in free field listening conditions (After reference 26.)

Table 2.3 A, B, C and D weightings

Centre frequency	Correction (dB)			
(Hz)	A	B	C	D
20	− 50.5	− 24.2	− 6.2	− 20.6
25	− 44.7	− 20.4	− 4.4	− 18.7
31.5	− 39.4	− 17.1	− 3.0	− 16.7
40	− 34.6	− 14.2	− 2.0	− 14.7
50	− 30.2	− 11.6	− 1.3	− 12.8
63	− 26.2	− 9.3	− 0.8	− 10.9
80	− 22.5	− 7.4	− 0.5	− 9.0
100	− 19.1	− 5.6	− 0.3	− 7.2
125	− 16.1	− 4.2	− 0.2	− 5.5
160	− 13.4	− 3.0	− 0.1	− 4.0
200	− 10.9	− 2.0	0.0	− 2.6
250	− 8.6	− 1.3	0.0	− 1.6
315	− 6.6	− 0.8	0.0	− 0.8
400	− 4.8	− 0.5	0.0	− 0.4
500	− 3.2	− 0.3	0.0	− 0.3
630	− 1.9	− 0.1	0.0	− 0.5
800	− 0.8	0.0	0.0	− 0.6
1 000	0.0	0.0	0.0	0.0
1 250	0.6	0.0	0.0	2.0
1 600	1.0	0.0	− 0.1	4.9
2 000	1.2	− 0.1	− 0.2	7.9
2 500	1.3	− 0.2	− 0.3	10.4
3 150	1.2	− 0.4	− 0.5	11.6
4 000	1.0	− 0.7	− 0.8	11.1
5 000	0.5	− 1.2	− 1.3	9.6
6 300	− 0.1	− 1.9	− 2.0	7.6
8 000	− 1.1	− 2.9	− 3.0	5.5
10 000	− 2.5	− 4.3	− 4.4	3.4
12 500	− 4.3	− 6.1	− 6.2	1.4
16 000	− 6.6	− 8.4	− 8.5	− 0.7
20 000	− 9.3	− 11.1	− 11.2	− 2.7

The justification for its use is that it is defined. The alternative would be to use the unweighted overall sound pressure level which is undefined and depends entirely on the performance of the chosen microphone and its associated electronics.

2.3.4 'D' weighted sound pressure level, L_D

The 'D' weighting was introduced solely for the purpose of measuring aircraft noise. Its specification is given in *Table 2.3*.[27] The preferred method is to compute the perceived noise level (*see* Section 2.3.5) but that requires more than a simple sound level meter. An alternative is to use a sound level meter equipped with the 'D' weighting which measures in dB(D).

Table 2.3 shows that the 'D' weighting attributes far more significance to the 1000 to 10 000 Hz frequency region than do the others. This is consistent with equal noisiness contours for aircraft, which are discussed in the next section.

2.3.5 Perceived noise level, *PNL*

The concept of perceived noise level was developed in the 1960s specifically to account for the noisiness or annoyance of jet aircraft. Although it has since been argued that it can be used for other noises, there is actually little application outside aircraft certification and, perhaps, airport planning because the process of calculating the *PNL* is so complicated.

The method is based on the equal noisiness contours shown in *Figure 2.17*.[28] They were developed to take into account the high-pitched whine associated with jet engine noise. During a fly-over the noise is monitored and the full 1/3 octave band spectrum is determined at intervals of 0.5 s. For each time interval, each frequency band is converted to a noy value using the data contained in *Figure 2.17*. The set of noy values is then summed according to the formula:

$$N = N_{max} + 0.15 \left[\sum_{i=1}^{n} N_i - N_{max} \right] \quad (2.38)$$

where N_i is the noy value in band i and N_{max} is the maximum noy

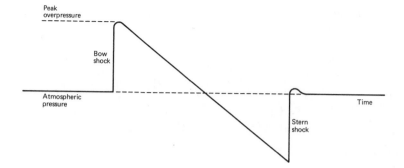

Figure 2.16 Idealized sonic boom waveform

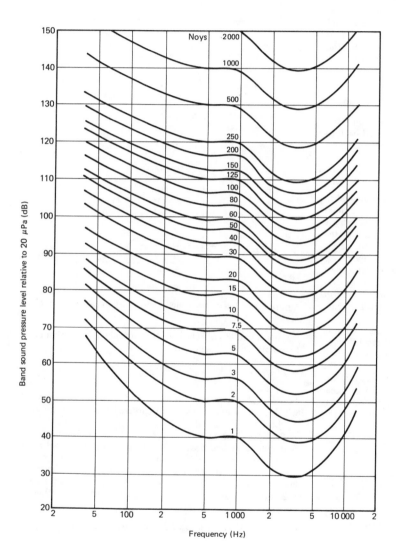

Figure 2.17 Contours of perceived noisiness
(After reference 28.)

value of any band. The total noy value, N, is changed back to *PNL* through the relationship:

$$L_{PN} = 40 + 33.3 \log_{10} N \text{ PNdB} \qquad (2.39)$$

A further refinement is to correct each value of *PNL* for any strong tonal content. This involves going through the 1/3 octave band spectrum to identify any relatively large peaks and making a correction according to the rules laid down in the standard.[28]

The correction can be as much as 6.7 dB in the worst case. The result is known as the tone-corrected perceived noise level, *PNLT*.

An alternative method of arriving at the *PNL* is to use either the 'A' weighting, described in Section 2.3.1, or the 'D' weighting, described in Section 2.3.4. These give direct readings of level as a function of time and so avoid the computations involved in using *Figure 2.17* and equations 2.38 and 2.39. Unfortunately, there are numerical differences between the 'A' and 'D' weighted levels and the corresponding perceived noise level, so the following empirical relationship must be used:

$$L_{PN} \simeq L_A + 13 \quad \text{PNdB} \tag{2.40}$$

$$L_{PN} \simeq L_D + 7 \quad \text{PNdB} \tag{2.41}$$

Equation 2.40 is said to be accurate to within about 3 dB while equation 2.41 should be slightly better. This method is not suited to calculating the tone-corrected perceived noise level, *PNLT*.

Another simplified method[29] of obtaining the maximum value of the perceived noise level during a fly-over, *PNL*, may be used as an intermediate step in calculating the noise and number index (*see* Section 2.3.16). During the fly-over the noise is analysed into octave bands and the maximum level in each band is recorded irrespective of when it occurs. The single set of octave band values is then converted into noy values using the data shown in *Figure 2.17*. The noy values are summed according to the formula:

$$N = N_{max} + 0.3 \left[\sum_{i=1}^{n} N_i - N_{max} \right] \tag{2.42}$$

where N_i is the noy value in band i and N_{max} is the maximum noy value of any band. The total noy value, N, is changed back to *PNL* using equation 2.39. No tone correction can be made.

2.3.6 Statistical level, L_N

A time-varying noise, measured in dB(A), can be described in terms of its cumulative distribution.[30] An example is illustrated in *Figure 2.18(b)*. This type of chart can be used to determine the level which is exceeded for a particular percentage of the total time. Popular values are L_{10}, L_{50} and L_{90}, the levels exceeded for 10%, 50% and 90% of the time respectively. L_{10} gives an indication of the top end of the level range although it can still be substantially less than the occasional peak. L_{90} corresponds to the background noise level in the absence of nearby noise sources. These features are illustrated in *Figure 2.18(a)*.

The statistical level is suited to any stationary random noise, although in the context of transport, it is only freely flowing traffic that falls neatly into that category. The time over which the measurement is made should be long enough for the statistical sampling to be meaningful but not so long that the noise cannot be regarded as stationary. Typically for the measurement of L_{10} for traffic noise the measurement period would be 5–15 min. One recommendation[23] is that the minimum sampling time should be:

$$t_{min} = \left(\frac{4000}{q} + \frac{120}{s} \right) \text{min} \tag{2.43}$$

where q is the vehicle flow rate in vehicles/hour and s is the sampling rate in samples/min. There is a proviso that t_{min} should not be less than 5 or greater than 55 min.

L_{eq} is often an alternative measure of traffic noise and, for freely flowing traffic, an empirical relationship between L_{10} and L_{eq} has been found[31]:

$$L_{10} \simeq L_{eq} + 3 \text{ dB(A)} \tag{2.44}$$

This equation, however, does not hold for vehicle flows of less than about 100 vehicles per hour.

2.3.7 Equivalent continuous sound level, L_{eq}

The equivalent continuous sound level contains the same quantity of sound energy over a defined time period as the actual time

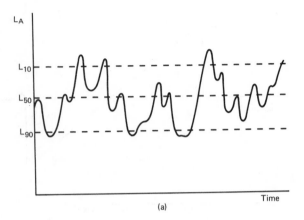

(a)

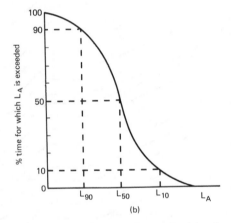

(b)

Figure 2.18 Typical traffic noise time variation (*a*) and cumulative distribution (*b*)

varying sound level.[32] The level is invariably 'A' weighted prior to the averaging process, i.e.:

$$L_{eq} = 10 \log_{10} \left[\frac{1}{T} \int_0^T 10^{L_A/10} dt \right] \text{dB(A)} \tag{2.45}$$

Equation 2.45 is actually a logarithmic form of equation 2.4 which gives the linear rms value of a signal over a time period T. L_{eq}, however, is normally defined over a relatively long time, e.g. 1, 8, 12 or 24 hours. As a measure of noise nuisance it is frequently criticized because it de-emphasizes occasional noisy events. The energy in a short burst of high-level noise is 'spread' into the quieter parts by the time averaging process. Nevertheless, L_{eq}, and derivatives of L_{eq} which will be discussed later, have been accepted as a means of assessing a variety of different noises.

2.3.8 Single event noise exposure level, *SENEL*, *SEL* or L_{AX}

This is defined[32] as the continuous sound level which, when maintained for 1 s, contains the same quantity of sound energy as the actual time varying level of one noise event. (This may be referred to in some texts as L_{AE} where the value is estimated rather than measured using an integrating sound level meter.) Like L_{eq} the level is 'A' weighted prior to integration, i.e.:

$$L_{AX} = 10 \log_{10} \left[\int_{-\infty}^{\infty} 10^{L_A/10} dt \right] \text{dB(A)} \tag{2.46}$$

In practice the integration is limited to the time during which the actual noise level is within 10 dB(A) of the maximum, i.e.:

$$L_{AX} = 10 \log_{10} \left[\int_{t_1}^{t_2} 10^{L_A/10} \mathrm{d}t \right] \mathrm{dB}(A) \tag{2.47}$$

where t_i and t_2 denote the beginning and end, respectively, of the single event.

Since most noise events, other than impulses, last for more than 1 s, the value of L_{AX} is usually higher than the maximum value of L_A during the event. Consequently the direct quotation of an L_{AX} value is intrinsically misleading unless it is supported by further information or explanation. Its real use is as an aid to calculating L_{eq} over a given time period because L_{AX} defines the energy contribution of the single event. The value of L_{eq} over the period T from a number of single events is given by the formula:

$$L_{eq} = 10 \log_{10} \left[\frac{1}{T} \sum_{i=1}^{n} 10^{L_{AXi}/10} \right] \mathrm{dB}(A) \tag{2.48}$$

2.3.9 Disturbance index, Q

The disturbance index[33] originated in Germany and is another variation on L_{eq} (*see also Table 19.1*). The general formula is written:

$$Q = 13.3 \log_{10} \left[\frac{1}{T} \int_0^t 10^{L/13.3} \mathrm{d}t \right] \mathrm{dB} \tag{2.49}$$

By choosing 13.3 as the factor outside the logarithm, less significance is attached to high-level short-duration noises than in the formula for L_{eq} which uses the factor 10. This means that the trade-off between level and time is 4 dB per doubling of time in Q compared with 3 dB per doubling in L_{eq}.

In Germany the disturbance index was originally derived for assessing aircraft noise. The level used in the formula is the perceived noise level, PNL, and the time period is over the six busiest months. Additionally a night-time penalty of 5PN dB is added during the period 2200–0600 hours.

In Austria the index has been used for traffic noise situations.[34] Then the level is the 'A' weighted level, L_A, and the time is appropriate to the situation. Some care must be exercised when applying the index because the value will be of the order of 13 dB less with L_A than with PNL.

2.3.10 Effective perceived noise level, *EPNL*

The effective perceived noise level, EPNL, is calculated by integrating the energy over the time period during which the tone-corrected perceived noise level is within 10 PN dB of the maximum value and normalising with respect to a reference time of 10 s[28]. *Figure 2.19* shows the variation of $PNLT$ for a typical fly-over in which the integration period is shown as t_1 to t_2. The EPNL is defined as:

$$L_{EPN} = 10 \log_{10} \left[\frac{1}{10} \int_{t_1}^{t_2} 10^{L_{PNT}/10} \mathrm{d}t \right] \mathrm{PN\ dB} \tag{2.50}$$

where L_{PNT} is tone corrected perceived noise level. In practice, the integration would be carried out as a summation, and if the values of PNLT are available at 0.5 s intervals, equation 2.50 becomes

$$L_{EPN} = 10 \log_{10} \left[\frac{0.5}{10} \sum_{i=1}^{n} 10^{L_{PNTi}/10} \right]$$

$$= 10 \log_{10} \left[\sum_{i=1}^{n} 10^{L_{PNLT}/10} \right] - 13 \ \mathrm{PN\ dB} \tag{2.51}$$

The idea of normalizing to 10 s is to penalize those aircraft that make a lot of noise for a long time. 10 s is thought to be a reasonable time for a typical fly-past.

A short-cut method is to estimate *EPNL* from PNL_{max} and the duration. PNL_{max} may be obtained by any of the simplified methods described in Section 2.3.5. Then it is assumed that the total energy under the actual curve can be represented by the energy contained within the rectangle of level PNL_{max} and time T, shown in *Figure 2.20*. Equation 2.50 can be written:

$$L_{EPN} = 10 \log_{10} \left[\frac{T}{10} 10^{\ L_{PN_{max}}/10} \right]$$

$$= L_{PN_{max}} + 10 \log_{10}(T/10) \ \mathrm{PN\ dB} \Big\} \tag{2.52}$$

If it is further assumed that T is approximately equal to one half of the actual time interval, $t_2 - t_1$, then:

$$L_{EPN} = L_{PN_{max}} + 10 \log_{10} \left(\frac{t_2 - t_1}{20} \right) \ \mathrm{PN\ dB} \tag{2.53}$$

The factor of 2 is rather arbitrary and clearly incurs some error. It should also be remembered that no tone correction has been made and so any result obtained by this method will be less than the tone-corrected value. Clearly the approximate method would not be acceptable for aircraft certification but it can be acceptable for planning purposes or community noise assessment where lack of maximum precision will not affect planning judgements or community ratings (NB PNL_{max} and PN_{max} may also be written as *PNLM* and *PNM* in the text.)

2.3.11 Day/night equivalent sound level, *DNL*

This is a rating based on L_{eq} which originated in the USA.[35] The energy is averaged over 24 hours but the noise level during the night-time period, 2200 to 0700 hours, is penalized by the addition of 10 dB(A), i.e.:

$$L_{DN} = 10 \log_{10} \left[\frac{1}{24} \int_{7}^{22} 10^{L_A/10} \mathrm{d}t \right.$$

$$\left. + \int_{22}^{1} 10^{(L_A + 10)/10} \mathrm{d}t \right] \mathrm{dB}(A) \tag{2.54}$$

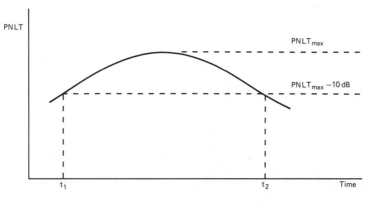

PNLT

PNLT$_{max}$

PNLT$_{max}$ −10 dB

t_1 t_2 Time

Figure 2.19 Typical PNLT history

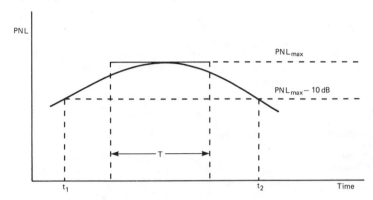

Figure 2.20 Typical PNL history

The concept of penalizing night-time noise by 10 dB(A) was probably based more on common sense than experimental evidence. Nevertheless, DNL has found widespread acceptance in the USA for community noise assessment including the impact of aircraft and traffic noise. It can be criticized for not making any allowance for either tonal or impulsive content of noises but the same is true of the majority of scales and ratings.

2.3.12 Community noise equivalent level, *CNEL*

This is a small variation on the day/night level originating in the USA[36] and subsequently adopted by Denmark. It was intended for use in assessing aircraft noise, but, like DNL, makes use of the 'A' weighted sound level uncorrected for tonal content. It differs from DNL in that it also includes an evening period, from 1900 to 2200 hours, in which all noise levels are penalized by the addition of 5 dB(A), i.e.:

$$L_{CNE} = 10 \log_{10} \left[\frac{1}{24} \left\{ \int_{7}^{19} 10^{L_A/10} dt \right. \right.$$
$$\left. \left. + \int_{19}^{22} 10^{(L_A+5)/10} dt + \int_{22}^{7} 10^{(L_A+10)/10} dt \right\} \right] dB(A) \quad (2.55)$$

The numerical difference between *DNL* and *CNEL* is usually very small. (NB also referred to as the day, evening, night level *DENL* and symbolized as L_{DEN}.)

2.3.13 Total noise load, *B*

This is a Dutch rating developed for assessing aircraft noise. (*See also Table 19.1*).[37] The formula is written as a summation rather than an integral because the maximum 'A' weighted level, $L_{A_{max}}$, of each event is used, no account being taken of its duration. The formula is:

$$B = 20 \log_{10} \left[\sum_{i=1}^{n} w_i 10^{L_{Amaxi}/15} \right] - C \text{ dB(A)} \quad (2.56)$$

where the constant C is 157 for a time period of one year or 106 for one day, L_{Amaxi} is the maximum 'A' weighted level of event *i*, *n* is the number of events and w_i is a weighting factor depending on the time of day (10 from 2300 to 0600 hours, 8 from 0600 to 0700 hours, 4 from 0700 to 0800 hours, 1 from 0800 to 1800 hours, 2 from 1800 to 1900 hours, 3 from 1900 to 2000 hours, 4 from 2000 to 2100 hours, 6 from 2100 to 2200 hours, 8 from 2200 to 2300 hours).

2.3.14 Noise exposure forecast, *NEF*

The noise exposure forecast was developed in the USA for assessing the effect of noise from civil aircraft.[38] It is based on the effective perceived noise level, *EPNL*, (*see* Section 2.3.10)

and the number of events. For one particular class of aircraft *i* on flight path *j* producing $EPNL_{ij}$, the contribution to the *NEF* is:

$$NEF_{ij} = L_{EPN_{ij}} + 10 \log_{10} \left[n_{Dij} + 16 \cdot 67 n_{Nij} \right] - 88 \quad (2.57)$$

where n_{Dij} is the number of daytime flights (0700–2200 hours) and n_{Nij} is the number of night-time flights (2200–0700 hours). The total *NEF* is then given by:

$$NEF = 10 \log_{10} \left[\sum_i \sum_j 10^{NEF_{ij}/10} \right] \text{PN dB} \quad (2.58)$$

The weighting against night flights as compared with day flights is 16.67, which is quite a severe penalty. The constant 88 is arbitrary and serves to confine *NEF* values to a range similar to other ratings.

2.3.15 Weighted equivalent continuous perceived noise level, *WECPNL* (2)

This may be regarded as an international hybrid of the *EPNL*, which is tone and duration corrected, and a day/night energy average together with a seasonal correction based on temperature.[39]

The equivalent continuous perceived noise level, *ECPNL*, is calculated for each separate time period, i.e.:

$$L_{ECPN} = 10 \log_{10} \left[\frac{10}{T} \sum_{i=1}^{n} 10^{L_{EPN_i}/10} \right] \text{PN dB} \quad (2.59)$$

where *n* represents the number of aircraft movements in time *T* and the 10 adjusts to the actual time from each 10 s *EPNL*. The weighted *ECPNL* is then obtained from the appropriate day and night values of *ECPNL* according to the expression:

$$L_{WECPN} = 10 \log_{10} \left[\frac{15}{24} 10^{(L_{ECPN})_D/10} \right.$$
$$\left. + \frac{9}{24} 10^{(L_{ECPN})_N + 10)/10} \right] + S \text{ PN dB} \quad (2.60)$$

where $(L_{ECPN})_D$ is the daytime value from 0700 to 2200 hours and $(L_{ECPN})_N$ is the night-time value from 2200 to 0700 hours. *S* depends on the outdoor temperature (−5 when <100 hours per month above 20°C, 5 when >100 hours per month above 25.6°C, 0 otherwise). The seasonal correction reflects the likelihood of windows being open.

2.3.16 Noise and number index, *NNI*

The noise and number index is of British origin and is relatively unsophisticated.[40] It combines the maximum perceived noise level of each aircraft, not corrected for tone or duration, with the number of aircraft movements according to the formula:

$$NNI = 10 \log_{10} \left[\frac{1}{n} \sum_{i=1}^{n} 10^{L_{PN_{maxi}}/10} \right]$$
$$+ 15 \log_{10} n - 80 \, \text{PN dB} \qquad (2.61)$$

An event is only included if it creates a maximum level of 80 PN dB or more and the period to be taken is from 0600 to 1800 hours GMT. In principle the *NNI* could also be evaluated for the night-time period and a more stringent criterion set. The constant is subtracted because 80 PN dB is said to correspond to zero nuisance.

2.3.17 Isopsophic index, *I*

This is a French scheme[41] similar in concept to the *NNI* (*see* Section 2.3.16). It began as two separate expressions, one for day and the other for night, but has now evolved into a single expression for the 24 hours with night-time events weighted by 10 dB. It is used specifically for assessing aircraft noise. The index is defined as:

$$I = 10 \log_{10} \left[\sum_{i=1}^{n_D} 10^{L_{PN_{maxi}}/10} + \right.$$
$$\left. \sum_{j=1}^{n_N} 10^{(L_{PN_{maxj}} + 10)/10} \right] - 32 \, \text{PN dB} \qquad (2.62)$$

where n_D is the number of day-time events (0600–2200 hours) and n_N is the number of night-time events (2200–0600 hours).

2.4 Measurement

Several different companies manufacture high-quality electronic equipment for measuring and analysing noise. The more sophisticated versions are capable of calculating the most complicated scales and ratings and new models appear at frequent intervals. Consequently there is little point in describing the equipment available at the present time because such a list would rapidly become obsolete. The one item, however, on which all instrumentation depends is the microphone. Therefore, this section will concentrate on the behaviour and limitations of a typical instrumentation microphone and on the influence of nearby reflecting surfaces on the sound field which it measures. Finally some of the conditions laid down in various International Standards will be briefly mentioned.

2.4.1 The instrumentation microphone

The metal-diaphragm air-capacitor microphone has established its premier position because it has a wide dynamic range coupled with an excellent amplitude response with respect to frequency, because it has good long-term stability and because of the extraordinary amount of technical information which is readily available. The only real disadvantages are the catastrophic, but temporary, effects of high humidity and the fragility of the diaphragm.

The construction and operation of a typical capacitor microphone is adequately described by its manufacturers[42] and is not considered in this Handbook. What is important is a knowledge of the range of microphones available and some understanding of the merits of each.

Each microphone capsule screws directly onto a pre-amplifier, as is illustrated in *Figure 2.21*, or onto a sound level meter, perhaps with a short extension tube, as shown in *Figure 2.22*. There are four different sizes ranging from 1″ diameter to $\frac{1}{8}$″

diameter, although the $\frac{1}{2}$″ is probably the most commonly used because it provides the best compromise between frequency range, directivity and sensitivity. The 1″ capsule becomes significantly directional at too low a frequency while the $\frac{1}{4}$″ and $\frac{1}{8}$″ capsules are too insensitive for normal applications.

At low and medium frequencies all of the microphones may be regarded as omni-directional, i.e. the sensitivity is independent of the microphone orientation within the sound field. Disturbance of the sound field by the physical presence of the microphone is negligible and the microphone measures the free-field sound pressure, i.e. the acoustic pressure fluctuation which occurs in the absence of the microphone.

At higher frequencies, when the dimensions of the microphone on its mounting become comparable with the wavelength of sound then diffraction takes place and the sound field is disturbed by the presence of the microphone. This is illustrated in *Figure 2.23*. The actual pressure at the diaphragm is different from the free-field pressure and that difference depends on the angle of incidence, so causing a directional effect. For a $\frac{1}{2}$″ microphone the pressure level at the diaphragm relative to the free-field, undisturbed, pressure level is shown in *Figure 2.24*. So, even for this size of microphone, variations in excess of 1 dB occur at frequencies as low as 4 kHz. The random incidence line refers to the response in a diffuse sound field and is relevant to indoor measurements.

To cater for differing requirements, some manufacturers supply two different versions of their microphones, which are referred to as 'pressure' and 'free-field'. The pressure version is designed so that the ratio of the output voltage to the actual pressure acting on the diaphragm is independent of frequency. If a $\frac{1}{2}$″ pressure microphone is placed in a plane wave the pressure on the diaphragm is altered from the free-field value by the amount shown in *Figure 2.24*. There are, of course, similar families of curves for microphones of other sizes. At the higher frequencies, at 0° incidence, the pressure is increased by the presence of the microphone. The output signal is correspondingly increased so the ratio of output voltage to free-field pressure is not independent of frequency. The free-field version of the microphone has its high frequency sensitivity reduced compared with the pressure version to compensate for the pressure increase arising from diffraction so that its free-field response at 0° incidence is substantially independent of frequency. Frequency response curves for pressure and free-field microphones are illustrated in *Figures 2.25* and *2.26*.

Figures 2.25 and *2.26* indicate broadly that as the size of the microphone decreases the sensitivity also decreases while the frequency range increases. The exceptions are the $\frac{1}{2}$″ microphones, types 4165 and 4166, manufactured by B & K which are made more sensitive at the expense of frequency range, presumably by reducing the diaphragm tension slightly.

Increased sensitivity makes it easier to measure low noise levels because the lower limit of a microphone's dynamic range occurs when the microphone signal can no longer be distinguished from electronic noise generated in the pre-amplifier. The dynamic range of the various B & K microphones is shown in *Figure 2.27*. It can be seen that the standard $\frac{1}{2}$″ microphones, types 4133, 4134 and 4149, are capable of measuring down to about 26 dB(A) while the high sensitivity $\frac{1}{2}$″ microphones, types 4165 and 4166, can go down to about 17 dB(A).

2.4.2 Environmental effects

The greatest enemy of air capacitor microphones is high humidity. The microphone capsule must be internally vented to atmosphere in order to allow for static pressure variations. Consequently, if moisture finds its way inside it can condense into the gap between the diaphragm and the electrode and

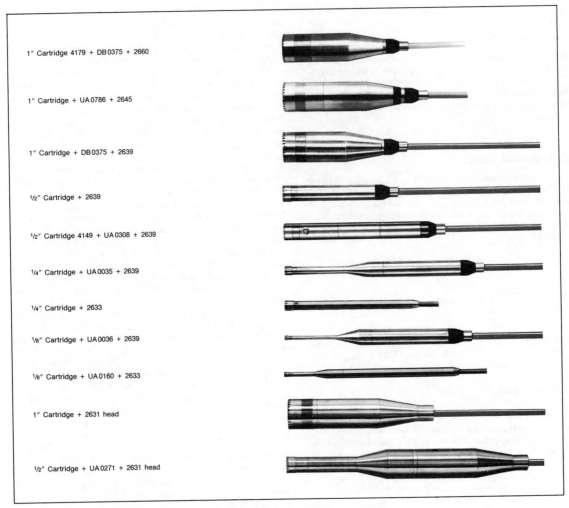

1" Cartridge 4179 + DB0375 + 2660

1" Cartridge + UA0786 + 2645

1" Cartridge + DB0375 + 2639

½" Cartridge + 2639

½" Cartridge 4149 + UA0308 + 2639

¼" Cartridge + UA0035 + 2639

¼" Cartridge + 2633

⅛" Cartridge + UA0036 + 2639

⅛" Cartridge + UA0160 + 2633

1" Cartridge + 2631 head

½" Cartridge + UA0271 + 2631 head

Figure 2.21 Range of B & K microphones mounted on preamplifiers (After reference 42.)

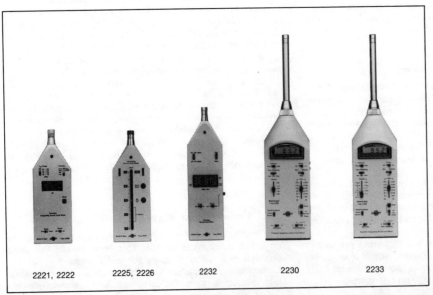

2221, 2222   2225, 2226   2232   2230   2233

Figure 2.22 Range of B & K sound level meters (After reference 42.)

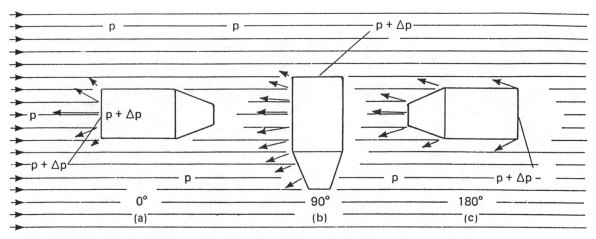

Figure 2.23 Pressure increase at the microphone diaphragm when it is placed in a free field (After reference 43.)

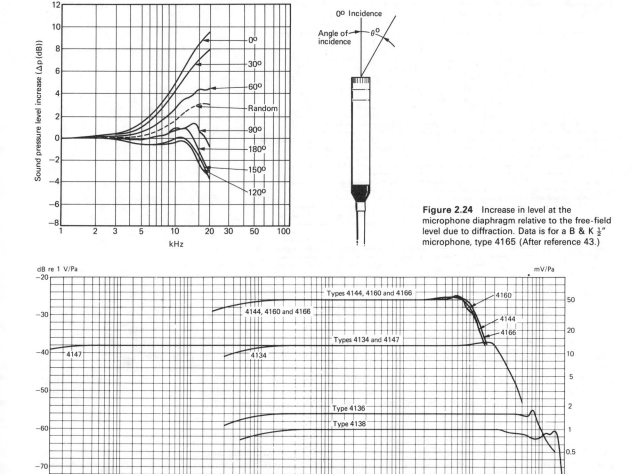

Figure 2.24 Increase in level at the microphone diaphragm relative to the free-field level due to diffraction. Data is for a B & K $\frac{1}{2}$" microphone, type 4165 (After reference 43.)

Figure 2.25 Typical pressure response of various B & K pressure microphones. Types 4144 and 4160 are 1"; types 4134, 4147 and 4166 are $\frac{1}{2}$"; type 4136 is $\frac{1}{4}$"; type 4138 is $\frac{1}{8}$" (After reference 42.)

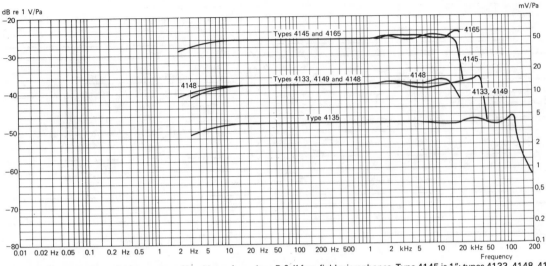

Figure 2.26 Typical free-field response at 0° incidence for various B & K free-field microphones. Type 4145 is 1″; types 4133, 4148, 4149 and 4165 are $\frac{1}{2}$″; type 4135 is $\frac{1}{4}$″ (After reference 42.)

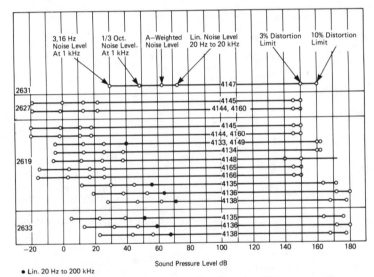

• Lin. 20 Hz to 200 kHz

Figure 2.27 The dynamic range of various B & K microphones and preamplifiers (After reference 42.)

prevent the microphone from functioning as it should. This condensation can be dried out but if the moisture contains impurities these are left in the microphone to its long-term detriment. For a permanent outdoor installation it is essential to use a system which vents the microphone through a dehumidifier. For short-term outdoor measurements such a system is not essential, provided that proper care is taken.

The other problem encountered outdoors is the pseudo-noise associated with wind-induced turbulence. This can be reduced, but not eliminated, by using a windshield on the microphone. A permanent outdoor windscreen together with a rain cover is illustrated in *Figure 2.28*. The reduction in wind noise afforded by this shield is about 15 dB(A) and is shown in *Figure 2.29*.

A 90 mm diameter sphere of porous polyurethane foam provides a much simpler alternative suitable for short-term outdoor use. The wind noise is also shown in *Figure 2.29* and it is in fact slightly superior to the all-weather model previously described.

Whichever form of windshield is used it must be stressed that the residual wind noise should be 10 dB or more below the level of noise to be measured, otherwise the reading will be incorrect. It is, in any event, unwise to carry out measurements in anything but a low wind speed because of the meteorological effects described in Section 2.2.15.

2.4.3 Choice of microphone

For outdoor measurement of transportation noise the $\frac{1}{2}$″ standard sensitivity microphones are the most likely choice, because of their wide frequency range. If humidity could be a problem then back-venting through a dehumidifier is obviously worth considering. The most difficult question to answer is whether the pressure or free-field version should be chosen. If the noise source were stationary the free-field microphone could be used at 0° incidence. Because the source moves, however, this orientation can only be correct at one particular instant. This might

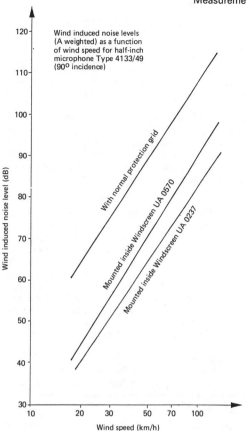

Figure 2.29 'A' weighted wind noise for B & K ½" microphones with and without windscreens (After reference 42.)

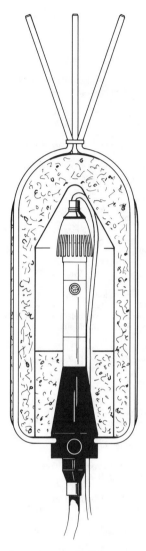

Figure 2.28 B & K ½" microphone fitted with rain-cover and permanent windshield (After reference 42.)

be satisfactory if only the maximum noise level is required but could pose some problems if the level must be measured as a function of time. The better alternative might be to use the pressure version orientated so that its diaphragm is in the plane of the noise source. Then the sound wave will always be at 90°, which, according to *Figure 2.24*, means that the frequency response is reasonably constant. Unfortunately, as will be seen in later sections, some International Standards appear to specify the use of a free-field microphone when a pressure microphone might be better.

2.4.4 Reflections from nearby surfaces

Free-field measurements either require or imply that there are no nearby buildings or other large reflective surfaces to influence the sound level at the microphone. There is, of course, always ground attenuation which was discussed in Section 2.2.14; but, although that may have a marked influence on the

spectrum shape, the effect on the 'A' weighted level may be less serious.

The sound level in the vicinity of a building facade is a composite of both the direct and the reflected sound waves. Right at the surface, both waves are completely in phase and an increase of 6 dB above the free-field value should be expected. Away from the surface the increase is less, probably becoming negligible at distances in excess of about 10 m. For traffic noise it is estimated that the increase in level at a distance of 1 m is 2.5 dB(A).[23]

2.4.5 Measuring traffic noise

The International Standard[44] for measuring the noise emitted by individual vehicles is really intended for type testing. The measurement should take place on a hard flat surface of at least 50 m radius and there should be no obstructions or nearby reflecting surfaces. The microphone is placed at a height of 1.2 m above ground and 7.5 m from the centre line of the vehicle. A free-field microphone should be used at 0° incidence, i.e. with the diaphragm vertical.

The method can be adapted for measuring traffic noise on a site adjacent to an existing road. The microphone would then be located at a height and distance commensurate with the purpose of the measurement.

In Great Britain the measurement procedure for general traffic noise is well defined.[23] If the building exists then the microphone should be located at the appropriate height and at a distance of 1 m from the facade. The microphone diaphragm should be horizontal, i.e. the noise should arrive at near grazing incidence, and, by implication, a pressure microphone should be used. The building facade creates a reflection which is also measured by the microphone and it is estimated that the effective increase over the free-field level is 2.5 dB(A). If the building does not exist then the same procedure would be adopted except that 2.5 dB(A) is added to the measured level in order to obtain the level at a distance of 1 m from a notional building facade.

The wind speed should, preferably, be less than 2 ms^{-1}. If, however, the dominant component of the wind vector is from the source towards the receiver then the wind speed may be as great as 10 ms^{-1}, provided that the noise to be measured is 10 dB(A) or more above the wind noise. Finally, measurements should only be made when the road surface is dry.

2.4.6 Measuring railway noise

The International Standard[45] is primarily intended for type testing of rail vehicles. The microphone should be located at a height of 1.2–1.5 m above the rails and at a distance of 7.5 m from the centre-line of the rails. Alternative distances of 25, 50 or 100 m may be used, although ground attenuation and meteorological effects could then be quite marked. The surrounding area should be flat for a radius of at least 50 m and should be free of obstructions or reflecting surfaces. The microphone should be of the free-field type and used at 0° incidence, i.e. with the diaphragm vertical. Wind speed should be less than 5 ms^{-1}

Clearly this method can be modified by moving the microphone to any desired position, e.g. outside an existing building or to the site of a proposed building development. It is, of course, necessary to remember that an adjacent building will give rise to an increase in the measured level.

2.4.7 Measuring aircraft noise

The International Standard[28] is applicable to measuring noise either from aircraft on the ground or from aircraft in flight (see also Chapter 19). If on the ground the intervening ground should be flat and hard, i.e. concrete or tarmac, and free from obstructions. If in the air the intervening ground should be flat and a hard concrete base at least 6 m square should be provided for the microphone. In both cases the microphone should be mounted at a height of 1.2 m above ground level. A pressure microphone should be used with its diaphragm in the plane containing the path of the aircraft, i.e. the noise should arrive at grazing incidence. The wind speed should be less than 5 ms^{-1} at a height of 10 m above ground. Other meteorological conditions must be met if the measurement is for aircraft certification purposes.

2.4.8 Measuring sonic boom

The International Standard[47] states that the microphone should be mounted with its diaphragm flush with the surface of a hard plane baffle, at least 1.5 m in diameter, set into the ground. The surrounding area should be free from obstructions. The microphone should be of the pressure type and be capable of measuring down to 0.1 Hz. A special recording system would be required. Further details are given in Chapter 21.

References

1 PIERCE, A. D. *Acoustics; An Introduction to its Physical Principles*, McGraw-Hill, New York, Chapter 11 (1981).
2 TEMPEST, W. (Ed.) *Infrasound and Low Frequency Vibration*, Academic Press, New York (1976).
3 FREY, A. R., KINSLER, L. E., *et al. Fundamentals of Acoustics*, 3rd edn., Wiley, Chichester, p. 415 (1982).
4 *Application of Bruel and Kjaer Equipment to Frequency Analysis*, Bruel and Kjaer, Denmark (1977).
5 *Acoustic Noise Measurement*, Bruel and Kjaer, Denmark, p. 28 (1973).
6 *Specifications for Sound Level Meters*, BS5969:1981, IEC651:1979.
7 *Application of Bruel and Kjaer Equipment to Frequency Analysis*, Bruel and Kjaer, Denmark, p. 66 (1977).
8 *Acoustic Noise Measurement*, Bruel and Kjaer, Denmark (1973).
9 *Preferred Frequencies for Acoustical Measurement*, BS3593:1963, ISO R266.
10 PETERS, S. The prediction of railway noise profiles. *J. Sound Vib.*, **32**, 87–99 (1974).
11 Noise Advisory Council. *A Guide to Measurement and Prediction of The Equivalent Continuous Sound Level*, HMSO, London, p. 28 (1978).
12 *Railway Noise and The Environment—A Summary*, British Railways Technical Board, Research and Development Division, Technical note TN4, Revised edn. (1977).
13 *Method for the Calculation of the Absorption of Sound by the Atmosphere*, American National Bureau of Standards, Washington, D.C. ANSI S126 (1978).
14 PIERCY, J. E., EMBLETON, T. F. W. and SUTHERLAND, L. C. Review of noise propagation in the atmosphere. *J. Acoust. Soc. Am.*, **61**, 1403–18 (1977).
15 CHESSELL, C. I. Propagation of noise along a finite impedance boundary. *J. Acoust. Soc. Am.*, **62**, 825–34 (1977).
16 SOROKA, W. W. and CHIEN, C. F. A note on the calculation of sound propagation along an impedance surface. *J. Sound Vib.*, **69**, 340–343 (1980).
17 Noise Advisory Council. *A Guide to Measurement and Prediction of The Equivalent Continuous Sound Level*, HMSO, London, p. 45 (1978).
18 FREY, A. R., KINSLER, L. E., *et al. Fundamentals of Acoustics*. 3rd edn., Wiley, Chichester, p. 402 (1982).
19 SILLS, A. G. The prediction of sound intensity from an explosive source. *J. App. Acoust.*, **15**, 231–40 (1982).
20 BERANEK, L. L. (Ed.) *Noise and Vibration Control*, McGraw-Hill, New York, pp. 164–193 (1971).
21 MAEKAWA, Z. Noise reduction by screens. *J. App. Acoust.*, **1**, 157–73 (1968).
22 Noise Advisory Council. *A Guide to Measurement and Prediction of The Equivalent Continuous Sound Level*, HMSO, London, p. 44 (1978).
23 *Calculation of Road Traffic Noise*, HMSO, London (1975).
24 KURZE, U. J. Noise reduction by barriers. *J. Acoust. Soc. Am.*, **55**, 504–18 (1974).
25 SCHULTZ, T. J. *Community Noise Rating*, 2nd edn., Applied Science (1982).
26 *Normal Equal Loudness Contours for Pure Tones and Normal Threshold of Hearing Under Free-field Listening Conditions*. British Standards Institution, London. BS3383:1961, ISO R226-1961.
27 *Specification for Frequency Weighting for the Measurement of Aircraft Noise*. British Standards Institution, London. BS5721:1979, IEC537:1976.
28 *Procedure for Describing Aircraft Noise Heard on the Ground*. British Standards Institution, London. ISO 3891-1978.
29 KRYTER, K. D. Scaling human reactions to the sound from aircraft. *J. Acoust. Soc. Am.*, **31**, 1415–29 (1959).
30 PARKING, P. H., PURKIS, H. J., *et al. London Noise Survey. Building Research Station Report SO67-266*, HMSO, London (1968).
31 ALEXANDRE, A., BARDE, J-Ph. *et al.*, *Road Traffic Noise*, Applied Science, p. 104 (1975).
32 Noise Advisory Council. *A Guide to Measurement and Prediction of The Equivalent Continuous Sound Level*, HMSO, London, p. 4 (1978).
33 BURCK, W., GRUTZMACHER, M. *et al. Aircraft Noise: Its Measurement and Evaluation, Its Significance for Community Planning, and Measures for its Abatement*, Report for the German Federal Ministry of Health, Gottingen (1965).
34 LANG, J. Measurement and presentation of traffic noise, Paper F-35, Presented at *The Fifth International Congress on Acoustics*, Liege (1965).
35 *Information on Levels of Environmental Noise Requisite to Protect Public Health and Welfare with an Adequate Margin of Safety*,

Report No. 550/9-74-004, USEPA, Office of noise abatement and control, Washington, D.C. (1974).

36 California Department of Aeronautics, *Noise Standards*, California administrative code, Register 70, No. 48, Chapter 9 (1970).

37 SCHULTZ, T. J. *Community Noise Rating*, 2nd edn., Applied Science, p. 152 (1982).

38 *Analysis of Community and Airport Relationship; Noise Abatement*, Bolt, Beranek and Newman, Report Nos. 1093 and 1254 (1964 and 1965).

39 ICAO, *Aircraft Noise*, Annex 16, Vol. 1, Aircraft Noise, 1st edn. (1981).

40 WILSON, A. (Chairman). *Noise. Final Report of the Committee on the Problem of Noise*, Cmnd. 2056, HMSO, London (1963).

41 ALEXANDRE, A. Prediction of annoyance due to noise around airports and speculation on the means of controlling it. *Anthropol. Appl.*, Doc. AA28/70 (1970).

42 *Condenser Microphones and Microphone Preamplifiers for Acoustic Measurements*, Bruel and Kjaer, Denmark (1982).

43 BRUEL, P. V. Sound level meters—the Atlantic divide. *Noise Control Eng.*, **March–April**, 64–75 (1983).

44 *Measurement of Noise Emitted by Vehicles*. International Standards Organization, Geneva. ISO R362-1964.

45 *Measurement of Noise Emitted by Railbound Vehicles*. International Standards Organization, Geneva. ISO 3095-1975.

46 *Measurement of Noise Emitted by Vessels on Inland Waterways and Harbours*. International Standards Organization, Geneva. ISO 2922-1975.

47 *Description and Measurement of Physical Properties of Sonic Booms*. International Standards Organization, Geneva. ISO 2249-1973.

Further reading

ALEXANDRE, A., BARDE, J-Ph. *et al. Road Traffic Noise*, Applied Science (1975).

BERANEK, L. L. (Ed.) *Noise and Vibration Control*, McGraw-Hill, New York (1971).

HOTHERSALL, D. G. and SALTER, R. J. *Transport and The Environment*, Granada, London (1977).

KINSLER, L. E., FREY, A. R., *et al. Fundamentals of Acoustics*, 3rd edn., Wiley, Chichester (1982).

PIERCE, A. D. *Acoustics; An Introduction to Its Physical Principles*, McGraw-Hill, New York (1981).

SCHULTZ, T. J. *Community Noise Rating*, 2nd edn., Applied Science (1982).

WHITE, R. G. and WALKER, J. G. *Noise and Vibration*, Ellis Horwood (1982).

Acoustic Noise Measurement, Bruel and Kjaer, Denmark (1973).

Application of Bruel and Kjaer Equipment to Frequency Analysis, Bruel and Kjaer, Denmark (1977).

Condenser Microphones and Microphone Pre-amplifiers for Acoustic Measurements, Bruel and Kjaer, Denmark (1982).

Handbook of Noise Measurement, General Radio, USA (1978).

Noise Advisory Council, *A Guide to Measurement and Prediction of the Equivalent Continuous Sound Level*, HMSO, London (1978).

Part 2

The Effects of
Transportation
Noise on Man

3

Community Effects of Noise

James M. Fields PhD
United States General Accounting Office,
Washington DC,
USA

and

Frederick L. Hall BA, MS, PhD
Department of Geography,
McMaster University,
Hamilton, Ontario,
Canada

Contents

3.1 Introduction

Research has consistently shown that transportation noise not only affects the users of transportation systems but also affects the quality of life and activities of people when they are passive observers of the transportation process. By comparing the reactions of people living in different types of noise environments it is found that high transportation noise levels are associated with adverse affects on communities. However, in spite of this consistency in the average impact of noise on aggregates of people, it is important to realize that the relationship between measured noise level and the effect of that noise is not a simple, deterministic relationship which can be applied to undifferentiated objects of study. Instead, the objects of study are physically and psychologically differentiated human beings who experience noise in the context of particular personal and community settings. Even the standard definition of noise as unwanted sound implies that there is a subjective component in the evaluation of the degree of the 'unwantedness' of the sound. As might be expected, research shows that the effects of transportation noise are modified, but not eliminated, by a variety of community and personal characteristics. The final result is that individuals' responses to the same sound vary considerably even though the averages of these responses are systematically related to noise level.

Figure 3.1 presents a general model of the most important relationships between physical noise levels, the social context and the effects of that noise. Noise is seen to directly cause some 'immediate' reactions as well as some possibly more delayed 'annoyance' reactions. The absence of connections between the personal characteristics or community context and the immediate effects indicates that the immediate effects are relatively automatic, at least relative to the annoyance or other effects in the figure. These immediate effects include physiological effects, startle responses and activity disturbances to communication, sleep or concentration. Such direct interferences are one of the causes of the more subjective and more consciously considered 'annoyance' effects in *Figure 3.1*. The direct linkage between the noise level and annoyance suggests that the level or character of a noise may lead to negative emotional or cognitive reactions even if the noise has not been responsible for activity interference. The personal characteristics of individuals are also seen to directly influence the extent to which sounds are felt to be annoying. A person may either suffer or enjoy a sound without any outward manifestation of the noise effect. The model presented in the figure suggests, however, that these subjective feelings can also lead to visible, identifiable behavioural reactions to the noise. Some of these are behavioural modifications which are attempts to adapt to the existing noise environment through changes within the home such as closing windows, altering the configuration of the house or changing the location or timing of activities.

The model implies that such behaviours are influenced by both the individual's characteristics and the extent to which the constraints in the physical layout of the home permit flexibility in locating activities such as conversing, eating, or sleeping. Other behaviours in response to noise are 'public actions' directed towards changing rather than adapting to the noise environment. Such actions include complaining to authorities, joining organized community action groups and engaging in lawsuits. Such public action is a function both of the degree of annoyance and of personal characteristics which enable or lead a person to perform publicly. In addition, the incidence of such public behaviours is strongly affected by community characteristics which facilitate or inhibit the formation of organized public response.

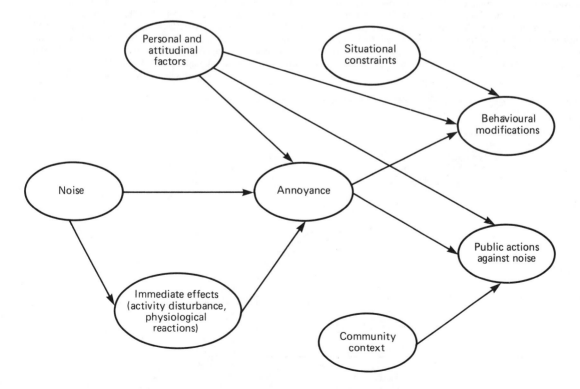

Figure 3.1 Relation between noise and noise effects in community settings

Two types of study methods provide most of the evidence about the effects of noise on people and the characteristics which mediate those effects. In laboratory studies people react to controlled presentations of sounds in a rating situation. In field studies people report feelings that have formed from years of exposure to noise in their everyday home setting.

Evidence about the effects of detailed acoustical characteristics has come almost exclusively from laboratory studies which can closely manipulate and control the characteristics of the acoustical environment. Thus laboratory studies provide most of the information about the effects of tones, different frequency weighting networks, and the duration of sound events.

Field studies are the chief source of information about the effects of noise on people in the community. Over two hundred social surveys of community response to noise have been performed. (A list has been compiled by Fields.[1]) Such studies consist of two main parts: a social survey in which residents answer questions about their reactions to the noise in their neighbourhoods and a physical noise survey in which that noise is measured. The basically subjective nature of the interview response and the possibility that interview responses might be biased has led to carefully designed and tested social survey research procedures for community noise studies. The strengths and weaknesses of these surveys will be assessed in this chapter.

The discussion in this chapter considers the major themes implicit in the model presented in *Figure 3.1*. The relatively immediate responses, especially speech interference, are discussed in Section 3.2. The bulk of the chapter consists of a discussion of the annoyance response and the factors that affect that response. The nature of the annoyance response, characteristics of the noise/annoyance relationship and the validity of the annoyance measures are discussed in Section 3.3. The mediating effects of acoustical, personal, and community factors are the subjects of Sections 3.4 and 3.5. The behavioural modifications that provide objective, verifiable indicators of noise effects are described in Section 3.6. Factors that affect public actions toward noise are discussed in Section 3.7. Section 3.8 provides some information about reactions to noise in non-residential settings: schools, hospitals and recreational areas. The role of social surveys in a noise assessment program is discussed in Section 3.9.

3.2 Immediate effects: activity disturbance

The primary focus of this section is on disturbances to various on-going activities. Automatic, reflexive reactions such as startle responses are only briefly discussed since such physiological effects are primarily the subject of Chapter 4. Three principal categories of activities are subject to disturbance by noise. These are sleep, mental concentration (e.g. task performance), and aural communications (e.g. speech or listening to radio or television). The effects of noise on sleep are discussed in Chapter 5. The findings from laboratory studies of speech interference and task interference are presented before turning to findings from people's reports about activity disturbance in the home environment.

3.2.1 Laboratory studies of speech interference

Laboratory studies provide extensive information about the acoustical and situational characteristics that affect speech interference. Early laboratory studies examined problems in communication via electrical devices (e.g. telephones) in the presence of constant noise levels. The studies led to several noise metrics which weight the characteristics of the noise so as to best predict speech interference.

The first of these, the Articulation Index (AI), dates from 1947[2] and has since been included in a standard (ANSI S3.5).[3] It is calculated from measures of the relative sound levels of speech and noise within octave or 1/3-octave bands. All 1/3-octave bands from 200–5000 Hz are included, but the bands from 1250 to 3150 HZ are given the most weight in the calculation procedure. The Articulation Index was developed on the basis of the intelligibility of single words. Attempts to validate it with normal sentences have been unconvincing.[4]

A metric which is designed to predict sentence intelligibility is SIL (Speech Interference Level). SIL is based on the average of the levels in the 500, 1000, 2000 and 4000 Hz octave bands (ANSI S3.14).[5] In *Figure 3.2* SIL is related to 'just reliable communication', a measure of intelligibility which is defined as monosyllabic word intelligibility of 70% or sentence intelligibility of 95%.[6] In the figure intelligibility is seen to be related not

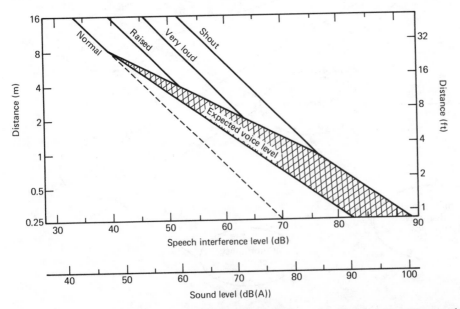

Figure 3.2 Speaker-to-listener distance for just reliable communication in free-field conditions (Source: reference 5.)

only to the noise level but also to the distance between speaker and listener and to the speaker's voice level. For example, in a steady noise environment of 40 dB, two people could communicate in a normal voice as far apart as 8 m. In noisier environments, people tend to raise their voice level to compensate, but they would also have to move closer together in order to maintain 'just reliable communication' (e.g. to about 1 m separation at an SIL of 65 dB).

Other factors have also been found to affect speech interference. Communication is better than indicated in *Figure 3.2* for rooms in typical residences, but communication can be much worse when rooms are highly reverberant.[7] Communication is better when there is a limited vocabulary,[3] the message content is relatively predictable,[6] or when the communicators know beforehand that they will be communicating in a standard format.[8] Communication can be much worse than indicated in *Figure 3.2* if the listeners do not concentrate or if they suffer from certain types of hearing deficiencies.[9]

The superior value of the specialized speech interference indices over the more generally used noise metrics has only been demonstrated under highly controlled laboratory conditions in the presence of steady noise levels. Results from studies in which the noise levels are allowed to vary over time have been inconclusive. A recent Working Group of the National Academy of Sciences concluded that it is not possible to recommend 'specific functions that relate loss of intelligibility of speech to levels of time-varying noise'.[10] They found that when used in conjunction with speech levels, A-weighted sound level and perceived noise level (PNL) also did reasonably well at predicting speech interference. Consequently there appears to be little justification for replacing standard environmental noise metrics with specialized speech interference metrics as descriptors of the complex noise environments found in residential settings in which people communicate under varying conditions.

3.2.2 Laboratory studies of task interference

Tasks that include verbal communication can clearly be disrupted by noise which leads to speech interference. Some auditory signals that carry strong, clear meanings such as danger can also obviously disrupt task performance. The major question for studies of task interference has been whether less meaningful types of noise can interrupt non-auditory activities. This question has received very little attention in natural field settings because of the methodological difficulties posed by the effects of other motivational and environmental variables on work performance. Laboratory studies of task performance have, however, been extensive. The resulting body of literature has been the subject of several detailed reviews.[11–13]

No simple, consistent relationship has been found between increasing noise level and the various descriptors of task interference. As a result various complex theories have been proposed which would relate task performance to the interactions between noise and other variables. However, there is not a consensus as to which theories are supported by current research. Furthermore, the previously cited publications provide conflicting assessments of the meaning of the existing research. Consequently, the discussion here is confined to the identification of the variables which are considered in emerging theories.

Three general theories are suggested for the ways in which noise can affect task performance.[14] Noise has traditionally been thought to affect the state of arousal, either by stimulating people with loud noise or by decreasing arousal with possibly monotonous ambient noise. If people have optimal states of arousal for performing particular tasks then whether noise leads to improved or degraded task performance will depend upon the person's pre-existing level of arousal and the effect of noise on that state. A second general theory hypothesizes that the loudness of noise is inherently annoying or distracting. A third theory hypothesizes that noise interferes with physiological mechanisms which are needed for cognition and task performance.

Many other variables are considered in the existing experiments but the findings from one study cannot often be replicated in further studies. It is suggested that unfamiliar noise may be more distracting than familiar noise. It has also been suggested that noise may only affect people with certain types of learning or performance strategies. Others have suggested that noise may not affect the primary task being performed but may impact a secondary task which a subject is not asked to directly attend to. Memory experiments vary according to whether it is hypothesized that performance is affected by noise occurring before, during or after the memorization task. Considerable debate has focused on the issue as to whether noise interferes with some type of internal speech pattern which may be linked to memory. Considerable attention has been focused on the features of the task itself which might determine whether a task would be sensitive to task interference. Broadbent even suggests that one task only showed a noise effect when the response was recorded with 'the person's fingers resting on the contacts rather than needing a large hand movement'.[15]

With the lack of consistent findings, considerable controversy has arisen regarding the study methods. It has been suggested and energetically contested that many of the early experiments were invalid because subtle, but useful, auditory cues were emitted by the testing equipment used in the experiments.[16,17] Kryter suggests that other findings may be artefacts of the demand characteristics of the experimental situation.[18]

The new theories and new variables which are being considered in task interference experiments may lead to firmer conclusions about task interference in the future. At the present time, however, the effects of noise on task interference have not been clearly identified.

3.2.3 Activity disturbance in the residential context

The different types of activity disturbances have been studied in natural, community settings by asking questions in interview surveys rather than by directly observing instances of activity interference as is done in the laboratory setting. (The only exceptions are a small number of in-home sleep disturbance studies which measure sleep directly—*see* Chapter 5.) Respondents are asked a series of questions such as the following questions from the 1967 Heathrow survey:[19]

Do the aircraft ever:
1. Wake you up?
2. Interfere with listening to Radio or TV?
3. Interfere with conversation?

After ascertaining whether there is any disturbance, the questions often determine how annoying the person finds the disturbance to be (e.g. 'very, moderately, or a little annoying') or how often this disturbance occurs in terms of a general verbal descriptor (e.g. 'very often, fairly often, occasionally'). In spite of the diverse exposure conditions found in natural setting and the use of self-reports rather than laboratory observations, the social surveys consistently show that these self-reports of activity interference increase with increasing noise level. For example, the results from a 1972 social survey[20] around the Geneva, Switzerland airport (*Figure 3.3*) show that increasing noise levels lead to increasing reports of four types of immediate effects: aural communications interference, sleep interruption, startle reactions and concentration (work) interruption. Within those four broad categories, surveys have provided examples of specific activities which are interfered with by noise: telephoning, conversing, listening to music, getting to sleep, waking up, getting back to sleep, sleeping during the day, resting, relaxing (both indoors and outdoors), enjoying recreational activities, reading, thinking, studying, enjoying a meal together, entertaining guests, and being startled. Similar survey questions show that experiences of vibration (*see* Chapter 12) and fear (*see* Section 3.5.1) are related to noise level.[21-23]

In *Figure 3.3* the sleep and speech disturbances are more often mentioned than concentration related disturbances. This same pattern has been replicated for Amsterdam airport[24] and Yokota airbase,[25] Osaka airport and Chitose airport in Japan.[26] This is consistent with the laboratory finding that sleep and speech interference are more closely related to noise level than is task interference. The frequency of reporting involuntary 'startle' reactions has been found to be similar to that of sleep interferences in studies around Heathrow airport in England,[27] around four French airports[28] and near high-speed railway lines in Japan.[29]

The two speech interference measures in *Figure 3.3* are more sensitive to noise level than the sleep measures in two respects. Firstly, speech interference increases more rapidly with noise level (a 90% increase from 0 to 90% for conversation in contrast to the 30% increase from 10 to 40% for sleep). Secondly, speech interference is more prevalent than sleep interference at moderate and high noise levels. These same general patterns have been found in other airport and railway surveys.[30-38] Road traffic surveys do not, however, consistently display this pattern. For example, in some road traffic surveys it is found that sleep disturbance is more prevalent and increases more rapidly with noise level than speech interference.[39-42]

Activity disturbance may differ by noise source because the noise environments which are equivalent when measured in 24-hour *Leq* may differ in other respects. An aircraft noise environment will typically consist of intermittent, relatively infrequent events with quite high peak noise levels. A traffic noise environment is likely to have an almost continuous occurrence of events with lower peak levels. For the aircraft, the unpredictable, high peak levels could be responsible for the relatively greater speech interference. The infrequent occurrences of the aircraft events could also mean that people could often go to sleep without being aware of an aircraft noise event. All these studies relate the different types of activity interferences to the overall 24 hour noise levels. The same pattern might not be found if sleep interference were related to night-time noise levels and speech interference to daytime levels.

Reports of speech interference in social surveys depend upon situational factors in ways which are consistent with the findings in laboratory studies. For example, the results from the British railway study in *Figure 3.4* show that there is greater reported speech interference outside than inside the home and for open than for closed window conditions. These results are similar to those from social surveys of traffic noise in Austria,[43] railway noise in France[44] and road traffic in London.[45]

The amount of activity interference reported at different noise levels is often reported but varies widely between surveys.[46] The levels of activity interference found in different surveys cannot be simply combined into a single dose–response relationship because the surveys use different types of questions to measure activity interferences. Using speech interference as an example, even the comparatively subtle distinctions between two ways of asking about television disturbance in *Figure 3.4* yield quite different numbers of disturbed people at high noise levels. In *Figure 3.4*, 20% fewer people at 75 dB *Leq* report that train noise interferes with 'listening to the radio or TV' than report that the noise 'made it hard to hear ... TV ... when the windows are open'. Consequently, any attempt to summarize results across studies, or to compare interference results from different studies needs to take into account the specific question asked in the survey.

The field study results are generally consistent with the laboratory studies. Both methods show that there is considerable activity interference due to noise in residential settings. This shows that there is a basis for human dissatisfaction with high environmental noise levels which is independent of any feelings which community residents may have about the noise source or the pleasant or unpleasant nature of the sound itself.

The very direct impact of noise on communication is certainly one of the reasons that noise evokes such negative reactions from people. However, it seems unlikely that the general negative reaction to noise is due only to communication interference. Laboratory experiments have compared reactions to noise with and without verbal communication activities.[47] For television viewing, when it was not possible to overcome the masking effects of sound by changing the volume, it was found that there was an increase in general annoyance (equivalent to about a 10 dB increase in noise level) over the no communication test condition. However, for a conversation test condition when it was possible to communicate with increased vocal effort, it was found that there was only a small increase or no increase at all

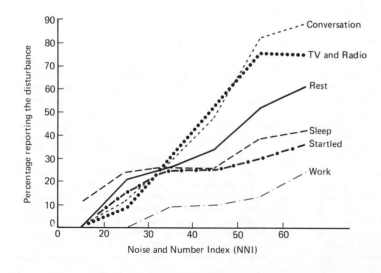

Figure 3.3 Relationship between activity interference and noise level
(Source: reference 20, p. 551.)

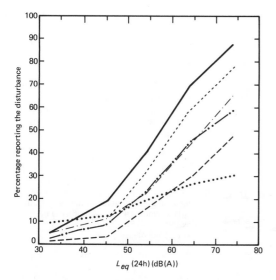

Figure 3.4 Percentage of respondents reporting different types of activity interference from train noise. ——, Q21 . . .', Stop talking or pause or speak louder . . . in the back garden'; – – – –, Q19f, g, h '. . . made it hard to hear . . . TV . . . when the windows are open'; — · —, Q20e, f, g '. . . make you stop talking, pause or speak louder . . . when the windows are open'; — · · —, Q18a (iii) '. . . interfere with listening to radio or TV'; — —, Q18a (v) '. . . interfere with conversation', · · · · ·, Q18a (ii, vii) '. . . wake up . . . or . . . interfere with sleep' (Source: reference 22, p. 185.)

over the no communication test condition. Regardless of the activity disturbance, people were annoyed by the noise. Standard community surveys cannot provide any real information about the independent effect of communication interference on more generalized annoyance, because such surveys do not obtain objective measures of speech interference by an independent observer.[48] As a result, the often noted high correlation between respondents' self-reports of activity disturbance and self-reports of general annoyance[49] could be due either to correlated errors in reporting disturbance or to a single relatively undifferentiated annoyance response. There is not convincing evidence that removing communication interference eliminates noise annoyance in residential setting.[50] In the same way that people dislike visually unattractive environments people can dislike noisy environments for reasons other than the speech or sleep disturbance which the noise causes.

3.3 Definition and assessment of annoyance

The previous section of this chapter has documented the discrete, objective effects noise has on activities. How people feel about the total of such effects is usually summarized by their overall annoyance with noise.

The most widely accepted formal definition of annoyance is 'a feeling of displeasure associated with any agent or condition believed to affect adversely an individual or a group'.[51] This concept of annoyance can be distinguished from other subjective reactions to noise.

The subjective experience with noise can be conceptualized along a number of different dimensions which vary in the extent to which they emphasize feelings and the emotional aspects of

the reaction to the noise. A number of laboratory studies have shown that the rating of the 'loudness' of a sound ('the aspect of the noise that is changed by turning the volume knob on a radio set') is distinct from a rating of a quality of the sound referred to as 'noisiness'.[52,53] At least two other concepts can be clearly distinguished. These are the cognitive evaluations of sounds and the emotional reactions caused by the sounds.[54] In theory, at least, the first concept refers to a judgement about whether the noise environment meets some abstract standard of environmental quality while the second concept actually measures whether the sound has some impact on the person's emotions, causing something like mild anger. The annoyance reactions discussed in this section contain at least some information about the impact of the sound on such feelings and emotions.

The discussion of annoyance in this section first considers the extent of the noise annoyance problem and then turns to the main topic, the relationship between annoyance and measured noise levels. The last part of the section provides information about the validity and reliability of annoyance measures which partially explains the variability in the measured reactions of people to noise.

3.3.1 The extent of the noise annoyance problem

Large numbers of people in nationally representative surveys have reported that they are annoyed by noise. In France 93% of the population reported that they were bothered by noise in their neighbourhood ('quartier').[55] Some 46% reported that it occurred 'very often' (other alternatives were 'rather often' and 'sometimes'). An annual national housing survey in the United States found that about 18% of the population were bothered by traffic noise in their neighbourhoods and about 8% were bothered by aircraft noise.[56] The results in *Figure 3.5* from a representative sample survey of England also show that road traffic is the biggest noise problem. Aircraft noise is the second most widely heard source even though it is not as often rated as annoying as are the noises from children or animals. Noises from trains, factories and construction affect a much smaller proportion of the population. Road traffic noise is clearly the most widespread noise problem.

Noise surveys typically begin with questions about all neighbourhood problems before noise is specifically identified. The surveys usually find that noises and 'road traffic' are the most often mentioned problems.[57,58] In an annual national housing survey in the United States respondents rated a list of 18 neighbourhood problems which included such well-publicized problems as 'Neighbourhood crime', 'Streets in need of repair', and 'Schools'. 'Street (highway) noise' was the most often identified problem[59] and was also most often rated with the most severe of the five ratings ('bothers so much I would like to move'). These surveys thus show that noise is felt to be a severe problem by the population. While these national statistics are based on Western industrialized urban societies, other surveys show that noise is a problem in at least the urban environment in other societies including Japan[60] and India.[61]

3.3.2 The relationship between annoyance and noise level

Social surveys measure annoyance by inquiring about 'annoyance' or 'disturbance' in particular questions. Since the respondents hear only these questions and are not subjected to a philosophical discussion about the 'true' meaning of annoyance, the annoyance which is measured in the surveys is nothing more than whatever dimensions are tapped by the particular wording of the survey questions. Questions which have been used in surveys include the following:

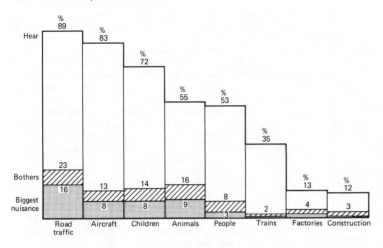

Figure 3.5 Percentage of the population of England who hear and are bothered by eight noise sources (Source: reference 23, p. 33.) (Note: percentages are cumulative.)

Please look at this scale and tell me how much the noise of the aircraft bothers or annoys you:
  Very much
  Moderately
  A little
  Not at all

(This question has been used in surveys around Heathrow and several other British airports:[62])

I want to ask you how you feel about traffic noise here where you live. Looking at this card would you tell me which number best represents how you feel?

  Definitely satisfactory   1
                             2
                             3
                             4
                             5
                             6
  Definitely unsatisfactory 7

(Used in several English road traffic surveys:[63])

Assume this is a thermometer with which you could measure how much traffic noise bothers you at home. The 10 mark means that traffic noise in your home is almost unbearable; the 0 mark that it doesn't bother you at all. Where would you personally grade traffic noise on this thermometer?

Unbearably disturbing   10
                         9
                         8
                         7
                         6
                         5
                         4
                         3
                         2
                         1
Not at all disturbing   0

(Used in Swiss road traffic survey:[64] The labels for the scale in German are *Stört unerträglich* and *Stört kein bisschen*.)

The questions are usually used by themselves to rate the noise, but are sometimes combined into indices. Some of the best-known early surveys used a Guttman scaling technique to combine activity disturbance questions. Though the technique is still occasionally defended,[65] most investigators, including even one of the first investigators to apply the Guttman technique to noise surveys, acknowledge that any of a number of scaling techniques are equally useful.[66] When indices are used now the results from factor analyses have led to the current practice of combining large numbers of different types of annoyance questions (not just activity interference questions) into annoyance indices.[67-70]

Research on annoyance responses has shown that annoyance responses can best be thought of as being ranked along an underlying continuous scale which does not have discrete points of discontinuity. The way in which responses at different points along this annoyance continuum vary with noise level can be illustrated by graphing the different degrees of annoyance at each noise level.[71] One example of these findings is illustrated with data from a Western Ontario traffic noise survey in *Figure 3.6*.

Several other patterns are evident in *Figure 3.6* which are characteristic of the noise/annoyance relationship in many studies. Annoyance increases with noise level, regardless of the annoyance cutting point. At moderate annoyance levels, the relationship between noise level and annoyance is generally linear over a large part of the range of noise levels. The type of departure from a linear relationship depends upon the cutting point: a low annoyance cutting point generates a line that has its steepest slope at the lower noise levels (e.g. top line in *Figure 3.6*) while a severe annoyance cutting point generates a line that has its steepest slope at higher noise levels. Whatever annoyance measure is used, many surveys have shown that there is not the type of sharp discontinuity at high noise levels which could be used to identify extreme noise levels for regulatory purposes.[72,73] At low noise levels, on the other hand, a sufficiently severe measure of annoyance does provide a point of discontinuity at which there are no severe annoyance responses. In *Figure 3.6*, for example, none of the respondents gave a more severe annoyance response than 4 (moderately) at the lowest noise level (below 45 dB *Leq*).

Survey reports often provide information about a range of annoyance responses. The major attempt to combine the results from a large number of surveys, however, has been made by dichotomizing the annoyance scale only at a relatively high level

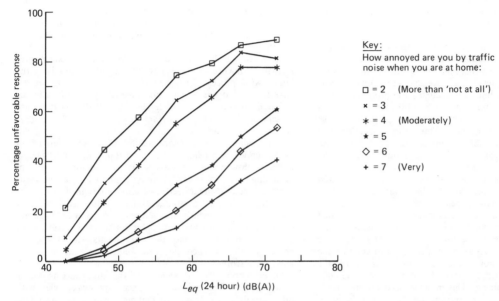

Figure 3.6 Percentages expressing annoyance for six divisions of an annoyance scale (Source: Western Ontario traffic noise survey data obtained from ESRC Data Archive, University of Essex, England.[187])

of annoyance.[46] The people thus identified are said to be 'highly annoyed'. Schultz's article on the subject introduced a curve (reproduced in *Figure 3.7*) which has become the most widely accepted description of the relationship between annoyance and noise level. The curve is the average resulting from dichotomizing a diverse set of activity interference and annoyance scales taken from 11 surveys. The difficult choices of where to dichotomize each of the scales were based on the author's belief that 'a sensible person ought to be able to locate with useful accuracy the points on *all* the scales corresponding to the same degree of annoyance'.[74]

By relating the curve in *Figure 3.7* to the distribution of the population across different noise levels, an estimate may therefore be formed of the number of people who Schultz would classify as 'highly annoyed'. (A formal method for doing this is presented in one report.[75]) The number of people who are counted as being affected by noise using such a severe annoyance cutting point is of course much less than would be counted if a more moderate annoyance cutting point had been used.

While there is widespread usage of a high annoyance cutting point, there is no strong *scientific* reason for choosing a particular dichotomization of the annoyance scale. Some arguments for a high annoyance cutting point prejudge the issue as to what noise levels are important (e.g. arguments that high annoyance measures are best because they do not show annoyance at the median noise levels found in a developed country, or arguments that it is easy to measure noise only in high noise environments). Other arguments imply that a 'high' annoyance response should be less influenced by personal characteristics and more closely related to noise level. The only empirical data that compare different annoyance cutting points show that the high annoyance dichotomization is no more closely related to noise level than are less severe dichotomizations.[76] The choice of a cutting point is a value judgement which cannot be made on scientific grounds. Any slight differences that might exist in the ability of the annoyance scales to locate one point more reliably

than another on the annoyance continuum will not be important enough to outweigh the policy implications that follow from the clear change in the numbers of people who are counted as being affected by noise.

For aircraft noise and to a lesser extent for road traffic noise, a much greater number of people live at low or moderate than at high noise levels. This means that the large numbers of people with moderate annoyance reactions are not counted when a 'highly annoyed' definition is used. However, the numbers of people at the highest noise levels are so small that, even for a

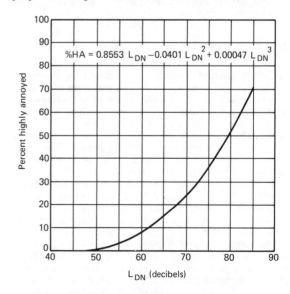

$$\%HA = 0.8553\ L_{DN} - 0.0401\ L_{DN}^2 + 0.00047\ L_{DN}^3$$

Figure 3.7 Relationship between noise level and annoyance averaged over 11 surveys (Source: reference 46, p. 382.)

'highly annoyed' definition of annoyance, the people at high noise levels are only a small proportion of the total number of impacted people.[77]

When the findings from a particular previous survey may not be applied to a new situation then the curve in *Figure 3.7* provides a basis for estimating the relationship between annoyance and noise level. The fact that other investigators have disagreed with Schultz's particular cutting points[78] shows that relating divergent annoyance scales to the word 'highly' (a word not used in any of the study questionnaires) involves large elements of subjective judgement. Thus other researchers can come to different conclusions about the location of the curve. Disagreement could also arise about the amount of dispersion of the surveys around the central tendency curve.

The strength of the relationship between noise level and annoyance is commonly measured by the square of the Pearson product moment correlation coefficient which is interpreted as the percentage of the variation in annoyance which is associated with noise level. The correlations between noise level and individual annoyance scores seldom exceed $r = 0.60$ (36% of the variation explained).[76,79] However, it is common to find that the correlation between noise level and the average of the annoyance scores in a neighbourhood is over $r = 0.90$ (over 80% of the variation explained). This indicates that the individual non-noise differences tend to average out. Noise level is thus a good predictor of the quantity that is of most interest for public policy, the average of the annoyance responses in communities.

Two additional qualifications should be considered in evaluating the shape and strength of the annoyance/noise level relationship. Inaccuracies in specifying the long-term noise level to which people are actually exposed lead to some amount of underestimation of the steepness of the slope relating annoyance to noise level.[80] With perfect information about noise exposure, there would be a somewhat closer relationship between noise level and annoyance. On the other hand, the fact that other transportation-related environmental nuisances (dirt, fumes, severance, visual intrusion, danger) are correlated with the transportation noise levels may mean that some of the annoyance which is evoked in a discussion of noise is intensified by the presence of the other nuisances.[81] To the extent that this is the case, the effect of noise tends to be over-estimated rather than underestimated.

3.3.3 Assessing the annoyance response: validity and reliability

In order to interpret correctly the meaning of the annoyance measurements from social surveys it is important to consider both the validity and the reliability of the annoyance measurements. Validity is defined as the extent to which a question actually measures some 'true' underlying annoyance. The reliability is the extent to which repeated measures of the same individual's annoyance are consistent. An understanding of the causes of less than perfect reliability will provide a basis for realistically applying the results from social surveys.

Confidence in the validity of the measurement of annoyance depends partly upon the quality of the social survey measurement process. Since the annoyance construct is a subjective one, measurement of annoyance follows guidelines that eliminate as many sources of potential bias as possible. Some standard practices are as follows. Surveys conceal the focus of the questionnaire from the respondent as long as possible by being presented as studies of general environmental problems. The primary annoyance questions are presented early in the questionnaire in the context of a list of other environmental disturbances. Interviewers are carefully trained to ask all questions exactly as printed in the questionnaire so that the interviewer will not bias the respondents' answers. Questions, such as the ones reprinted above, are stated in a simple, unbiased manner. The selection of respondents is based on sampling techniques which ensure that interviewer's feelings cannot bias the selection of respondents.

Methodological studies of the annoyance measures give further confidence that they are not biased by details of the interviewing process. British road traffic and railway surveys have found that answers are not affected by variations in the order of questions or the order in which the alternatives are presented.[45,82] A survey in Hamburg, Germany found that annoyance responses were not distorted by the length of the questionnaire or several methodological characteristics of the interviewer.[83] In post-interview debriefings it has been found that most people did not know about the subject of the questionnaire before beginning the interviews.[84,85] A study around Roissy airport near Paris included a standardized scale which is designed to measure the extent to which a person generally tries to falsify results by choosing answers which are perceived to be socially acceptable.[86] No evidence was found for an upward distortion of annoyance ratings. In fact the respondents who scored the highest on the so-called 'lie' scale were those with the lowest annoyance scores.

Other support for the validity of the annoyance measures comes from the fact that the annoyance responses correlate with other variables in a meaningful manner.[87] Annoyance responses are highly correlated with one another as well as with the somewhat more objective activity interferences, private behaviour and public complaint reports. Annoyance is, of course, also related to noise level.

The available research, therefore, indicates that social survey annoyance scales are valid, unbiased measures of annoyance. However, the measured annoyance scores have two other characteristics which are inevitable in social science inquiries but which would indicate serious methodological errors in most physical science inquiries. Firstly, the annoyance responses to any single noise environment are highly variable and, secondly, the annoyance responses are affected by some aspects of the question wording.

The amount of random variation in the answers to the questions is measured in terms of the reliability of the measures, i.e. the extent to which repeated measures of the same concept are correlated. Measures of the reliability of annoyance indices consisting of several questionnaire items have generally been found to meet or exceed the standard, accepted social science criteria of $r = 0.80$.[88,89] Even though standard reliability criteria are met there is still a great deal of variability. When the same individuals have been asked about their (unchanged) noise environments at intervals of from a month[90] to a year[91] only about 35% of the variance in response ratings can be explained by their answers on the previous questionnaire.

This level of reliability is not surprising if two aspects of the respondent's task are considered. The first task is to consolidate immediately all of his diverse experiences and feelings about noise onto a single dimension. Without the opportunity to consider the problem carefully it is understandable that a purely random set of associations during the course of an interview could recall different experiences and feelings which lead to considerable random variation in the location that any one individual places himself on an annoyance scale. Even if the respondent is certain about his feeling there is still an equally difficult second task; the respondent must make a somewhat arbitrary choice between the words or numbers which the interviewer has offered. There are no objective rules that a respondent can draw on to determine whether the subjective feeling should be described as 'very' or 'moderately' annoyed or as '4' or '6' on an annoyance scale.

Given these difficulties in measuring annoyance, it is to be expected that there will be considerable variation in the annoyance scores at any particular noise level. Just such variation is shown in the relation between road traffic noise annoyance and measured noise levels in *Figure 3.8*. The solid regression line shows that there is a clear central tendency for annoyance to increase with noise level but the individual annoyance scores vary widely around that central tendency. Of course the variation around the central tendency could also be

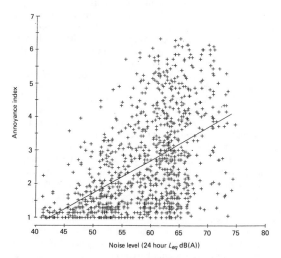

Figure 3.8 Individual responses to noise (1150 interviews) (Source: Western Ontario traffic noise survey data obtained from the ESRC Data Archive, University of Essex, England[187].)

due to differences in the individual 'true' feelings as well as to some of the factors that will be discussed in the following two sections.

The difficulties that respondents face in relating their complex feelings to a previously unseen survey scale explain the second important characteristic of the measurement of annoyance in the social surveys. That is, the number of people who are rated as 'annoyed' depends very much on the form of the annoyance question. Since many people have difficulty in quickly organizing all of their thoughts on an open question early in a questionnaire, fewer people indicate that they are annoyed by noise when asked to name any 'things which bother you around here' than when they are specifically asked about an item (such as 'road traffic noise') later in the questionnaire.[92,23] The number of annoyance categories included in an annoyance question will affect answers because respondents use not only the words but also cues from the length of a scale to classify themselves. As a result the interpretations of the meaning of particular labels on annoyance questions must be made cautiously.

3.4 Acoustical and situational factors affecting annoyance

A larger number of hypotheses have been proposed as explanations for the scatter of the individual annoyance responses around the central tendency illustrated in *Figure 3.8*. This section examines characteristics of acoustical environments and neighbourhood situations which may affect annoyance. The following section will consider characteristics of individuals.

Any evaluation of the effects of these characteristics must

take into account two facts. First acoustical and neighbourhood environments are complex, and secondly the acoustical and neighbourhood characteristics are often correlated with one another. The possibility of characteristics being correlated is heightened by the normal practice of using a number of study areas which is small in relation to the number of uncontrolled variables. To deal with these problems all of the findings reported in this section come from analyses in which multivariate statistical techniques have been used to try to isolate the effects of the characteristics. In a further attempt to guard partially against the problem of correlated variables, findings are reported only if the effect of noise level has been removed in the analysis and if the findings have been reported in at least two studies.

3.4.1 Numbers of noise events

The relative importance of the noise level of individual noise events and the numbers of those events has been a major issue in aircraft noise evaluation. The weighting of number of events is expressed as the number of decibels which is equivalent to a ten-fold increase in the number of events (i.e. a one unit change in the logarithm of the number of events).[95] Under the equivalent energy hypothesis implicit in Leq or DNL, the numerical value is 10; for the British Noise and Number Index (NNI) the value is 15. The 1961 study at Heathrow airport estimated that this weight should be either 24 (regression analysis of individual data) or 15 (a rough graphical analysis).[96,97] The later 1967 Heathrow study was designed to estimate the number weighting and reported a value of 4.[98] A recent review and analysis of available survey data concluded that the balance of the evidence suggests that the weighting is no greater than, and perhaps less than, the weighting of 10 which is implicit in equivalent energy indices such as Leq.[99]

The effect of numbers of noise events and the duration of noise events means that equivalent energy indices summarize many of the factors that affect responses to transportation noise environments. When the transportation noise is relatively continuous (e.g. noise from busy streets) then the simple statistical indices such as L_{10} or L_{50} provides a very similar summary of the noise environment.

3.4.2 Time of day at which noise occurs

In residential areas, equivalent noise levels might be assumed to cause more annoyance in the evening and night because of either the prevalence of noise sensitive activities (sleep at night, and communication activities in the evening), the large numbers of residents who are at home, or the increased intrusiveness of noises against the lowered night-time ambient noise levels. It has been found that people rate their daytime and night-time environments as being equally annoying even though the night-time noise is in fact at a lower level.[100-102] These results show that night-time noise is an important problem which cannot be neglected even though the noise levels may be lower than at other times of the day. Information is not available about reactions in unusual locations where night-time noise levels may exceed the daytime noise levels (e.g. dock traffic or freight handling facilities). The early night-time and early morning hours are often reported to be more annoying than other parts of the sleep period.[103,104] However, the noise levels are also higher during these periods. Several attempts to control roughly for the noise level differences during the parts of the night-time period do not find evidence for greater sensitivity to similar noise levels at any particular time.[105,106]

Though night-time noise is a problem, an important research question is whether control of night-time noise could have a greater impact on annoyance than control of daytime noise.

One important study did not find that people are sensitive to changes in night-time noise levels. A study conducted around Los Angeles International Airport before and after an almost total elimination of night-time flights found that people did not report a reduction in their night-time annoyance.[107] Good numerical estimates of the relative importance of daytime and night-time noise are not available.[108] In fact, analyses of single annoyance ratings of the entire 24-hour period have not consistently found evidence that night-time levels have more effect on annoyance than would be expected from the physically measured noise levels.[69,109–112] While some studies find that the most widely accepted of the night-time indices (DNL) is more closely related to annoyance than a simply unweighted 24 hours Leq measure, other studies find the reverse, i.e. 24 hour Leq is more closely related.

Other studies that have found that annoyance is greater in evening time periods have led to the suggestion that intermittent noise events may cause more annoyance in the evening when they lead to an unavoidable communication interruption than the same noise would at night when they might go unnoticed by much of the sleeping population. The lack of consistency in the survey results may well be due to high correlations between the daytime and night-time noise levels in the studies' designs. The relative importance of daytime, evening, and night-time noise for residential populations has not been established. The support for relatively more severe night-time noise regulations is based more on the physiological importance of sleep disturbance than on field data concerning the annoyance potential of different levels of night-time noise.

3.4.3 Ambient noise and reactions to multiple noise sources

Most high-noise exposure residential environments are dominated by only one type of transportation noise. In cases where several types of noise are of importance, two issues arise which are addressed in this sub-section:

1. Is the annoyance with a single noise source affected by the ambient noise environment in which it occurs?
2. Is the annoyance with a total noise environment sensitive to the extent to which it consists of noises from several important sources?

The reaction to a specified noise source in the presence of ambient noise has been addressed with two alternative hypotheses. It is most often assumed that annoyance with a specific noise would be greater when experienced against a low ambient background because the noise would be more intrusive. However, it has also been hypothesized that as long as a sound is audible, annoyance with an intrusive sound might be greater in a high ambient noise environment because people have been sensitized to noise generally.[113]

Laboratory studies have been conducted in which road traffic provides the background noise and aircraft the intrusive noise. These studies have generally found that annoyance ratings of aircraft noise events increase when the aircraft noise becomes more intrusive relative to the ambient level.[114–117] Most of the early attempts to investigate the topic using community surveys were hindered by inadequate ambient noise level data,[118,19] unacceptably small numbers of study sites (e.g. a single site for each type of noise environment[119]), or analyses which did not take into account the noise levels from both sources.[44] The findings from these surveys were not consistent with one another. Other surveys that provide better information do not find a consistent tendency for annoyance judgements to vary with ambient noise level. The only large-scale survey specifically designed to study ambient noise effects found that aircraft noise annoyance was not affected when road traffic

noise was also present.[120] Road traffic noise did not affect judgements of railway noise in a British survey[121] and did not have a consistent effect in a Dutch survey.[122] Road traffic annoyance was found to be unaffected by aircraft noise in a Swiss survey, but the findings were unclear about whether aircraft noise annoyance was affected by road traffic noise levels.[123]

These studies thus suggest that the population's absolute level of annoyance will not be affected by the presence of other noise sources. That is, people will be just as likely to be, for example, 'very annoyed' by aircraft noise in a quiet location as in a noisy road traffic noise environment. This observation is consistent with the frequently reported findings about quite a different concept, the relative level of annoyance with two sources which are present in the same environment. A railway study in Britain[124] and the Swiss survey[125] found that if people are asked about the most important neighbourhood problems or are asked to rank order the problems, the relative ranking of two noise sources will be affected by their relative noise levels. This finding about the effects of ambient noise on relative rankings has occasionally been misinterpreted as support for the effects on absolute ratings (e.g. in a report on the Swiss survey).[126]

The second mixed noise source evaluation issue is whether annoyance with a total noise environment is affected by the extent to which the environment consists of noises from several important sources. Several models have been suggested to explain how people combine the varying degrees of annoyance which they feel with each of the individual noise sources in order to arrive at an overall evaluation of the total noise environment. In a laboratory study Powell[127] found that the overall evaluation was best explained by a model based on the summation of the perceived magnitudes of the two sounds when the perceived magnitudes of each of the individual sounds take into account the presence of the competing sound. Taylor[128] used social survey data to examine five alternative models for evaluating annoyance reactions in mixed noise environments. The analysis indicated that the reactions were more accurately predicted by any of the complex models than by the simple measurement of the value of Leq for the total noise environment. Though no particular model could be identified as the correct model, the findings do suggest that it may ultimately be possible to identify a model that is better than the simple equivalent energy model.

A different perspective on the ambient noise issue is provided by noise indices which include terms which represent the degree of variation in noise levels during the day.[129] The two best known of these indices are the Traffic Noise Index (TNI)[130] and Noise Pollution Level (NPL).[131] Neither of these indices have proved to be better correlated with annoyance than simpler indices (e.g. Leq) in either laboratory studies[132,133] or field studies.[45,109] This is consistent with the conclusion that ambient noise level does not affect annoyance reactions.

3.4.4 Variations in reactions to different noise sources

Aircraft, road traffic and railway noise have quite different acoustical characteristics. These transportation modes also have quite different economic, emotional and social consequences for individuals and communities. A basis thus exists for hypothesizing that reactions could differ by noise sources even when the noise levels are equal for a physical noise index such as 24 hour Leq.

Estimates of noise source differences cannot be established by comparing the results from road traffic, aircraft, and railway surveys which have been conducted in different countries with different annoyance questions and different noise measurement procedures. The types of variables outlined by Fields and Walker[134] are sufficiently important that attempts to compare such surveys have led Kryter[78] and Schultz[46,72] to quite different conclusions about the same sets of survey data. Evidence about reactions to different sources must instead come from specially designed field surveys and laboratory studies.

Two studies provide the evidence that aircraft noise is more annoying than road traffic noise. Hall et al.[135] provided the most highly controlled comparison of reactions to aircraft and road traffic by studying a sample of people exposed to noise from both sources around Toronto International Airport. The results reproduced in *Figure 3.9* show that aircraft noise was more annoying. Fields and Walker[134] also concluded that aircraft noise was more annoying than road traffic noise on the basis of a planned comparison between a British railway survey and six previous British surveys of road traffic and aircraft noise.

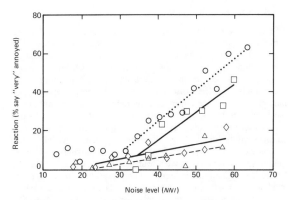

Figure 3.10 Percentage 'very' annoyed in a British railway survey and the 1967 and 1976 Heathrow surveys ○ ···· ○ =Aircraft, 1967 Heathrow; □—□ = aircraft, 1976 Heathrow; ◇–◇=railway (middle correction); △– – △ = railway (low correction) (Source: Reference 134, p. 61.)

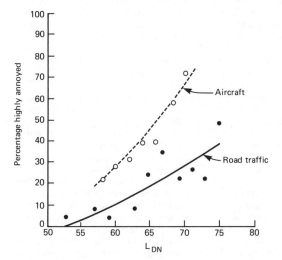

Figure 3.9 Percentage highly annoyed by road traffic and aircraft noise (Source: reference 135, p. 1695.)

Evidence that railway traffic is less annoying than road traffic at the same noise level comes from a comparison of a railway survey with other surveys of traffic in Britain (*Figure 3.10*)[134] and from two specially designed German surveys, each of which contained both railway and road traffic study areas.[136,137] The two German surveys as well as a Dutch survey[138] suggest that while the overall annoyance with railway noise may be less and sleep interference may be less, speech interference is at least equal for railway noise.

Though these studies indicate a difference in reactions to different sources, the strength and nature of that difference has not been established. The studies comparing railway noise differ in whether the difference is only important at high noise levels[137] or is actually greater at lower noise levels.[136] Railways are generally found to have scores on noise annoyance questions that are lower than those for other noise sources by the equivalent of roughly 5–10 dB. The difficulties in making precise comparisons are illustrated in *Figure 3.10*, where the ambiguities in the comparison between surveys has lead to two alternative representations of the railway survey data (middle correction and low correction lines). Other less adequately documented studies raise the possibility that the difference in reactions may not hold in all countries (e.g. Japan[139] or the Netherlands[138]).

A lack of agreement between controlled laboratory listening experiments shows that there is not some simple, invariate acoustical characteristic of noise from different sources which

leads to a difference in reactions. Rice[133] and Large[140] find that road traffic is more annoying than aircraft; but Powell[115] used quite similar procedures and found aircraft to be more annoying. Ohrstrom et al.[141] found that train noise was less annoying than aircraft at 55 dB(A) (Leq) but not at 64 dB(A). (The noise level (Leq) is the average level for the period of exposure; in this case, an experiment judging session.)

Other attempts to explain the differences in reactions to different sources have included an examination of differences in peak noise levels,[142] standard deviations of noise levels,[143] and preventability or fear attitudes.[144] Only one of these attempts, examination of attitudes, explained even a small amount of the difference in the reactions to different noise sources. Since a simple acoustical basis is not apparent, there is a strong possibility that there are complex acoustical characteristics which may vary within as well as between sources. If differences in reactions are due to differences in attitude towards the source, then there is the possibility of differences in reactions to the same broadly defined types of noise source in different countries.

Findings on the differences between different classes of operations are often contradictory. Comparisons of reactions to free-flow and congested road traffic in two similarly designed British surveys led to different conclusions.[45,109] A study in Australia found that noise annoyance around a military airfield was similar or less than that at civilian airfields[145] but a Dutch study concluded that noise annoyance around military airfields in the Netherlands was probably greater than around civilian airports at the same noise levels.[146] Studies around general aviation airports have found that general aviation noise does cause annoyance but that reactions vary considerably between airports.[147-149] However, it is not known whether similar noise levels will lead to different levels of annoyance at general aviation as opposed to commercial airports. In a German survey general aviation noise was reported to be more annoying,[150] but a comparison of a commercial and a general aviation airport in Canada found that the annoyance differentials varied between questions in ways that might be explained by differences in the acoustical environments and timings of operations at the two airports.[151] Without a clearer understanding of the mechanisms that sometimes create differences in reactions to different sources, the extent to which the individual studies' findings can be extrapolated to other acoustical environments and community settings is at present unclear.

3.4.5 Exterior noise barriers

The use of noise barrier walls along urban expressways and motorways has been evaluated in a number of studies. The barriers have been found to reduce noise annoyance in studies in the United States,[152] Canada,[153] England,[154] Germany[155] and France.[156] The respondents in these surveys had all experienced the reduction in the noise level due to the newly constructed barrier. In all but the German study the reduction in annoyance has been found to be at least as much as would be expected from the reduction in noise level. It is not known whether such changes will be long lasting. All of the present surveys have been conducted within 2 years of the barriers' construction. Consequently, there is no evidence about whether new residents in the future who will not have directly experienced the change in noise level would react equally favourably. Barriers change several other characteristics of the neighbourhood in addition to the noise environment. It is not clear whether the overall effect of these other changes should lead to overestimates or to underestimates of the value of the decrease in noise levels: while the reduction in dust and fumes is viewed positively, the change in the visual appearance often evokes strong negative reactions as well as positive reactions.[152,156]

3.4.6 Reactions to changes in noise environments

Almost all of the published data on dose/response curves refers to essentially static situations in which people evaluate noise environments which have been largely unchanged for at least several years. When a noise environment changes, however, reactions to the change might differ from those predicted from the static data. In the previous section the findings from most studies about short-term reactions to newly placed barriers suggested that a reduction in noise level would lead to at least as much of an improvement in reactions as would be predicted from the reactions to static noise environments. On the other hand, a study which found no change in reactions after a severe reduction in the night-time noise environment at Los Angeles International Airport suggested that people might be totally insensitive to changes.[107]

Three studies have been specially designed to investigate the effects of changes in noise environments. Two of the studies examined reactions shortly after changes. A British town bypass study found that reductions in noise environments brought about improvements in reactions which were greater than those that would have been predicted from static data.[155] A Burbank, California study of reactions to temporary changes in noise levels at an airport found that reactions followed the changes in noise levels so that 2 months after the final change, reactions were similar to those predicted from the originally collected static data.[157] The only study of reactions long after the change in noise environment found that the relations between noise level and annoyance 1 and 4 years after the opening of Charles de Gaulle airport were consistent with each other and with the relationships observed in a static noise situation earlier around Orly airport.[158] The studies reviewed in this section, therefore, suggest that changes in noise level do lead to changes in annoyance which, at least after a period of time, would be predicted from static data.

3.4.7 Variations in individualized exposures

Most noise regulations and social surveys are based on the noise level measured at a point outside of the dwelling. However, any particular resident's exposure to that noise at home is a complex function of the amount of time spent at home, amount of time spent outside on the property, the exterior noise levels at different positions (front and back of house), window opening behaviour, type and maintenance of double glazing, location of indoor activities relative to noise levels outside particular windows, timing of activities relative to timing of noise events, and masking by other indoor noises. The major question is whether people simply react to the known outdoor noise levels or whether they react to an integration of the transportation noise which has been experienced at their own ear. Only a few of the aspects of individualized exposure have been investigated. The available evidence shows that at least some of these variations in exposure affect annoyance.

People spending less time at home have sometimes been found to be less annoyed by neighbourhood environmental noise,[159-161] but this effect is often difficult to detect and presumably small. Most of the cited studies find a statistically significant effect for only some, not all, of the annoyance measures. One study even found that while most annoyance responses were unaffected by the amount of time spent at home, one annoyance response (reading interruption) was greater for those spending less time at home.[162] If the amount of time spent at home affects annoyance, the effect is weak enough that there is usually no detectable difference for such imprecise time-at-home indicators as sex or employment status.

With respect to the relative importance of indoors or out-of-doors noise levels, the laboratory study findings about 'perceptual constancy' have provided some support for the importance of exterior noise levels. These studies find a tendency for people to respond to the noise levels that they believe are present on the basis of visual or subtle acoustical cues, rather than to respond to the actually measured noise level at the ear.[163-165]

Social survey research provides instances in which responses are affected by noise levels at other points than those measured at the noisiest point outside. The installation of double glazing was found to reduce but not eliminate noise annoyance in a Dutch study.[166] Several studies find that sleeping is less disturbed by traffic noise in rooms at the back of houses.[162,167] Other studies find that general noise annoyance is less if bedrooms and/or the main living rooms are at the rear[168,169] or if a larger proportion of the rooms are on the low noise exposure side of a dwelling.[170-172] When the size of these annoyance effects were equated to decibel values in the last three studies cited, they were found to be small, ranging from 2 to 5 dB.

Definitive studies of the effects of all aspects of individualized noise exposure cannot be expected because it is impossible to obtain a measurement at the ear of all the noise from only a single source. The most complex study of the effect of localized noise levels found that none of the nine indoor or outdoor noise measurements was consistently any more closely relate to annoyance than was the simplest noise indicator, the noise level at the highest point outdoors on the property.[173]

On balance, it is clear that localized noise exposure does affect annoyance, but it is also clear that localized indoor noise control will not eliminate noise annoyance. Good estimates are not yet available as to the relative effect of a decibel reduction at source as opposed to the same decibel reduction achieved through localized sound attenuation.

3.4.8 Other current hypotheses

A large number of other situational factors have been hypothesized to affect annoyance. Studies of these factors have raised additional issues to consider but have not provided definitive answers.

Since the climate and season of the year affect both window opening patterns and the amount of outdoor activity around the home, climate must also affect the individualized noise exposure. Most surveys that have addressed possible climatic effects have been hindered either by correlated variables[174] or a small range in climate differences.[175] One Dutch study did report an annoyance difference which was the equivalent of 3 dB from a comparison of responses to aircraft noise around Marssum air base during a hot summer and a cool, wet autumn.[176] The effect of seasonal differences in some countries is complicated by the fact that in the warmest months of the year many homes are air-conditioned and thus have tightly closed windows while other houses in the community are not air-conditioned and are thus especially likely to be open during the same period.

Although publicly expressed concern with environmental issues has increased greatly over the last 20 years it is not clear that individual annoyance reactions have changed. A comparison between two Amsterdam airport surveys conducted 12 years apart (1963 and 1975) found no change in the annoyance/noise level relationship.[177] A comparison of three surveys covering 15 years (1961–1976) around Heathrow found some 'mixed evidence for a reduction in annoyance'.[178] Another review of the earlier two of these surveys together with a 1972 Heathrow survey could find no evidence for a change over the 11 years.[179] However, a series of Swiss surveys covering only a 4-year time span (1974–1978) found some evidence for a slight increase in annoyance.[180]

There is some discussion but almost no research about the effect of the spacing of noise events over time. Road traffic is, for example, virtually continuous on heavily used streets but intermittent on lesser used streets. Airports differ considerably in the extent to which the aircraft noise is concentrated over the day. Some airports with multiple runways and flexible operating conditions have the ability either to spread flights evenly through the day over all areas or to move heavy concentrations of flights periodically. A social survey was conducted around JFK airport (New York) to assess the impact of a flight control scheme which timed aircraft noise events so that any one neighbourhood would not experience extended periods of closely spaced aircraft noise events.[181] A weak study design meant that definitive conclusions could not be drawn, though there was some weak evidence to support the efficacy of the noise control scheme.

Many studies find that there are unexplained differences between the reactions found in different study areas.[182] These are sometimes assumed to be due to differences between reactions of people in different countries[183] or different cities.[30,182] The explanation for such differences is not known. The possibility clearly exists that there are other important acoustical or situational variables which have not yet been investigated. Given the presence of correlated neighbourhood characteristics in complex residential and acoustical environments, knowledge about the effects of these variables is not likely to be obtained except through large-scale, carefully designed surveys which include large numbers of fully described study areas.

3.5 Attitudinal and personal factors associated with annoyance

The large amount of variance in annoyance which is unexplained by the various acoustical factors has led to a number of hypotheses about personal and other attitudinal factors which might be associated with noise annoyance responses. Most studies cited in this chapter provide some evidence about the effects of only a few selected personal and attitudinal factors, but a few studies discuss a wide range of variables.[27,70,174,184–186]

3.5.1 Attitudes related to annoyance

Noise annoyance has been hypothesized to be influenced by many attitudes. However, the six most consistently reported are fearfulness, preventability, noise sensitivity, perceived neighbourhood quality, health effects, and non-noise impacts of the source. The findings reported here are all based on analyses in which the effects of noise level have been held constant. Annoyance is generally higher for people who are fearful that some danger to themselves or other people in the local area may be associated with the transportation activities which they can hear. This 'fearfulness' attitude has proved to be important for aircraft, road traffic and railway noise.[19,22,187]

A second attitude which is related to annoyance is the belief that there are reasonable actions which it would be feasible for authorities to take to reduce the noise levels. Different researchers' empirical measurements of the concept vary in the extent to which they stress the noise reduction possibilities ('Preventability'[27] or the motivations of the responsible authorities ('misfeasance'[49]).

The third consistently identified variable is 'noise sensitivity'. The reported sensitivity to other noises or to noise in general is associated with increased annoyance with a particular noise source.[27,188] These measures of sensitivity to noise in general have never been found to be related to environmental noise levels. This suggests that people are not choosing their residences on the basis of noise level.

The fourth important attitude is 'neighbourhood evaluation'. Increased noise annoyance is associated with a generally more negative evaluation of the other neighbourhood characteristics. This seems to be related more to the evaluations of the neighbourhood environment and of the neighbours than to evaluations of the quality of the public services.[189] There is evidence that it is not the actual presence of other neighbourhood environmental problems, but only the subjective, perceived belief that the problems exist which is related to annoyance.[190]

A fifth finding is that those few people who believe that their health is affected by noise from the particular source are also likely to be annoyed by the source. (The relationship between noise and actual health effects, not perceived health effects, is discussed in Chapter 4.)

The last finding is that people's ratings of other aspects of the noise source's intrusion in the area (dirt, dust, lights, odours, visual intrusion, loss of privacy, severance by a right-of-way) are related to their evaluations of the noise in the area. (As always these effects are found after the noise level is held constant in the analysis.)

It is sometimes argued that the above findings show that annoyance is actually caused by these attitudes.[191,49] However, the difficulties in providing firm evidence for the nature of the causal relationships between such variables lead other investigators to state that though the variables are interrelated, conclusions cannot be drawn about the direction of causation.[73,192] While attitudes directed towards the non-noise impacts of the noise source in the neighbourhood are related to annoyance, more general attitudes towards the noise source (its importance or knowledge about it) are not consistently found to be related to annoyance.[22,27,193–195] Similarly, direct economic connections or employment with the noise source industry or use of the particular transportation mode is not consistently found to affect annoyance reactions.[196,197] Very specific attitudes relative to particular classes of noise events can, however, be important: the Heathrow Concorde survey found that patriotic attitudes about Concorde were associated with low levels of annoyance with Concorde noise.[198]

A number of other attitudes have been suggested but not repeatedly tested. General public issue orientations might be important, such as attitudes towards technological progress or awareness of environmental problems on a society-wide basis. Perhaps some personal orientations are also important, such as the level of strain in a person's life or an ability to cope with noise.[83]

The relationship between annoyance, noise level and the attitudes described above is illustrated with the results from one survey in *Figure 3.11*. While a particular attitude is associated with increased annoyance (i.e. the belief that noise could be reduced in *Figure 3.11*), noise level continues to affect annoyance in all attitude groups. This pattern of the continued importance of noise level even when attitudes are considered is found in virtually all surveys. A second pattern in *Figure 3.11* was also observed in the Munich aircraft survey.[199] It is the group of people who have the most unfavourable attitude (i.e. consider the noise most preventable in *Figure 3.11*) which has the most differentiated response (steepest slope) to noise level. This pattern was found for some but not all variables in the Heathrow Concorde study.[198] No consistent pattern was established in a London road traffic survey.[200]

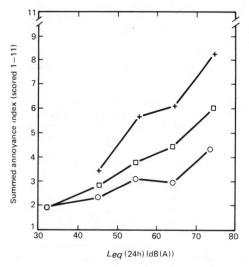

Figure 3.11 Relationship between annoyance and noise level for three attitudes about the preventability of the noise + - + = noise could be reduced here; □ — □ = intermediate preventability attitude; ○-○ = no one can do anything about the noise.[22]

There is some limited evidence that the attitudes of a population can be manipulated so as to reduce expressed annoyance. A study around a Swedish military air base found that a control group at the same noise level was more annoyed by noise than an experimental group which had received favourable information about the air base and a 'positively worded account' of the results from the earlier noise survey in their community.[201] It is not known whether such effects could be obtained for other noise sources or whether such effects would be long lasting (the time between the 'favourable information' and the survey was less than 2 months).

Interpretations of findings about attitudes and noise annoyance should be guided by four important cautions. First, if the attitude is correlated with noise level (fear and evaluations of non-noise impacts of the source usually are) then part of the relationship of the attitude with noise annoyance may be caused by the noise level effect.[202,203] A second caution is necessary because the meaning of a measured attitude can be determined only from reading the actual questionnaire item and *not* from the label (name of the attitude) which the investigator uses in a

report. Two investigators may use the same label to describe questions which measure quite different concepts. The third caution is that the attitudinal variable must be operationalized with a question which is clearly distinct from a noise annoyance question. This requirement is often violated with measurements of 'adaptability' to noise. Most adaptability questions include a restatement of the annoyance question because they ask, at least by implication, whether the respondent is (still) annoyed with noise. A fourth caution is that at least part of the high correlation between annoyance and these attitudes should be discounted because both are measured at the same time in a single questionnaire under similar conditions and thus may be subject to such correlated errors in measurement as 'response set' (the tendency for people to give answers that follow the form rather than the content of the question).

3.5.2 Demographic characteristics

Many studies have examined the standard demographic variables of sex, marital status, size of household, education, social status, income, age, length of residence, type of dwelling and type of tenure (owner or renter).[159,204-207] While studies do occasionally report effects of one variable or another, none of the variables have consistently been found to be associated with noise annoyance. (The relationships with public complaint behaviour will be discussed later.) Hearing loss is sometimes cited as a reason that older people might be expected to be less sensitive to noise, but it could just as well be argued that partial hearing loss would lead to greater sensitivity due to greater difficulties in communicating in the presence of noise.

The lack of a relation with length of residence is often reported.[208,209] Though this seems to be contrary to the perception that people adapt to noise, it may well be that any adaptation occurs in a much shorter time than the surveys could measure (surveys have virtually no information about changes in attitudes within the first 6 months of residence) and that there is a counter-balancing tendency for people who have lived in an area longer to be aware of increases in noise levels over the years. The absence of a relationship with housing tenure or type of structure has been well documented with aircraft,[210] road traffic[211,212] and railway noise.[213] Though it is often hypothesized that owners would be more likely to be concerned because they have more of a long-term interest in their property, it could just as well be theorized that ownership creates a commitment to the property such that owners cannot allow themselves to evaluate objectively the weak points, including the environmental quality, of their property.

3.6 Reactions to noise: modifications in behaviour

Individuals who experience interference due to noise and who find noise disturbing can either react privately to reduce the effects of noise in their own home or react publicly, often politically, to try to modify the conditions that generate the noise. Public actions will be discussed in Section 3.7. The private actions described in this section fall into three main categories:

1. Reducing noise levels near the receiver.
2. Escaping from high-noise locations.
3. Mitigating the effects of noise through medication

All behavioural actions incur financial or other costs. These costs vary from one individual or situation to another. Consequently, as shown in *Figure 3.1*, any behavioural effects must be discussed in the context of the relevant personal characteristics and situational constraints.

Information about behavioural reactions comes almost exclusively from questions asked in social surveys. Two particular surveys provide information about an especially large range of behavioural reactions and therefore provide much of the basis for the following discussion. These are a survey around three airports in Switzerland[123] and a French survey around apartment complexes in 15 locations near roads in Lyon and Marseilles.[79] Interview questions used to measure behavioural effects are less standardized than annoyance and activity interference questions and are, therefore, even harder to compare. The Swiss questionnaire, for example, asks the respondent to report behaviours by 'you or your family' (even for such individual behaviours as taking medication) while most other surveys only ask the respondent to report his or her own behaviours.

The most frequently mentioned behavioural modifications are those that would reduce noise levels in the home. *Figure 3.12* shows that over 80% of the respondents at the highest noise level ($Leq = 75$ dB(A)) reported closing windows for conversational purposes. Window closing was also found to be the most frequent behaviour in the Swiss airport survey (55% at over 60 NNI)[214] and in a British railway survey (35% at a 24 hr Leq of 75 dB(A)).[215] Window or door closing has been reported during both daytime and night-time periods in at least two other surveys; a survey of road traffic noise in England[216] and a Swiss road traffic survey (over 40% at an 8 hr night-time Leq value of 65).[217] Closing doors or windows is likely to have a more severe penalty for comfort in a warm climate. For example, the French traffic survey found that, at least for noise levels below 72 dB(A) (Leq), people are less likely to close their windows in Southern France (Marseilles) than in Lyon.[218]

The installation of double glazing or other more specialized sound-proofing devices is reported in the French traffic survey, a road traffic noise survey in England,[219] a railway survey in Great Britain (about 5% report double glazing at least partly to reduce railway noise at 75 Leq)[220] and an aircraft noise survey around Heathrow.[221] The reported incidence of double glazing varies greatly between surveys. The actual incidence of double glazing may be highly sensitive to the availability of sound-proofing grants and the occupant's concern about insulating the house against heat loss. The surveys differ according to whether all instances of double glazing are tabulated or only those instances in which the owner reports that the double glazing was installed for noise-reduction purposes. The incidence of sound-proofing, especially double glazing, has been found to be affected by a number of factors. The French survey found that noise level was the most important factor but that sound proofing was also more often obtained by people with higher incomes (at least below 65 dB Leq), people who owned rather than rented their homes and people who had lived in their apartments longer.

The Swiss survey reported that the use of ear plugs increases with noise level. It was found that at least one person in about 20% of the households at the highest noise levels (60–70 NNI) was reported to use some type of ear plug at night.[222]

Residents could in theory reduce the effects of noise by staying indoors, moving indoor activities away from rooms on the noisier sides of houses, spending less time at home, or by moving to a new residential location entirely. The Swiss survey found that the percentages who reported staying outside less than they would want to because of aircraft noise increased from less than 1% at the lowest aircraft noise level (below 20 NNI) to over 30% at the highest level (above 60 NNI).[223] *Figure 3.12* shows that there was a similar tendency in the French survey for noise level to restrict the use of a balcony for conversation.

Several studies have investigated the possibility that people might locate their activities within their home away from the noisiest rooms so as to minimize the effects of noise. In an English road traffic survey, 6% of the general population reported that traffic noise affected the way they used their rooms.[224] However, the French survey found that this almost never happened. The explanation appears to be that physical constraints in the design of the apartments permit very little choice of rooms for such activities as sleeping, eating, or television viewing. In fact, the French survey reports that only reading and work of an intellectual nature were moved to quieter rooms. These activities—unlike television listening, conversing with friends, or eating—are most easily transferred between rooms. It may well be that the differences between the surveys reflect a greater flexibility for locating within the typical English single-family dwellings than in the apartments included in the French survey. The French survey could find no evidence that noise levels affect the amount of time spent listening to record players, radio or television even though their use could be interrupted by noise. Avoiding noise by spending less time at home is reported in the Swiss survey for as many as 15% of the households at the highest noise levels[225] but no evidence for this pattern was found in the French survey.[226]

The last and most costly of the avoidance responses is to move to another location. Many investigations find that noise level is related to 'wanting' to move.[227,228] However, no study has reported that actual moving plans can be related to noise level. A study around Munich airport which found there was no relation between noise level and reported moving plans even examined actual pre-survey and post-survey migration patterns and could not find a relationship between moving and noise level.[229] In general, it appears that other factors determining residential mobility are too strong for noise level to have a detectable or systematic effect.

The use of medication for sleep has been found to be related to noise levels in the French survey (*Figure 3.12*) as well as in the

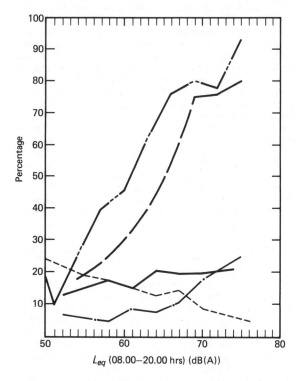

Figure 3.12 Modifications in behaviour by noise level — — — = closing windows for watching TV; — —=closing windows for conversation; ——=use sleeping tablets; — · — · =soundproof dwelling; ——–—=use balconies: (Source: reference 79, p. 165.)

Swiss aircraft noise survey (20% at the highest noise level of over 60 NNI),[230] and Swiss road traffic surveys (about 10% for an 8 hr night-time *Leq* of 65).[102] The Swiss aircraft survey also reports a higher use of tranquillizers at higher noise levels even though the questions did not mention aircraft as a reason for usage.[231]

This section has established that noise level affects a clearly identifiable aspect of individuals in residential areas—their behaviour. The objective, verifiable nature of a behavioural modification has led many commentators to expect that behavioural measures would be more closely related to noise level than the subjective annoyance measures. The French survey was designed with this expectation but found that it was the respondents' reports of annoyance, not of behavioural modifications, that were most closely related to noise level.

3.7 Individual and group actions against noise

Overt, public actions to convince transportation operators and public officials to reduce noise in the environment are taken by either individual residents or residents acting together in community groups. Individual actions can include highly formalized and publicized lawsuits and letters to the editors of newspapers, but more generally they take the form of telephoned or written complaints to various public authorities. Group actions include public meetings, circulation of petitions, presentations at public inquiries, demonstrations, direct participation in the political process and even the type of violent confrontation which accompanied the opening of the new airport near Tokyo, Japan. These individual and group actions against noise are important both because they directly affect the transportation process and because, in the absence of social surveys, they are indicators of noise effects which are likely to be used by public authorities. In order to determine whether such public actions are adequate indicators of noise impact, it is necessary to understand the conditions which affect the amount of community action against noise and to determine whether individual complaints are good indicators of noise impact.

3.7.1 Conditions that affect the amount of public action

The social surveys have provided information about the conditions which are necessary for the emergence of individualized complaints. Social theories of collective behaviour would suggest that similar conditions are necessary for the emergence of group action as well.

The first condition is that there is a basic underlying dissatisfaction with the existing noise situation. The consistent relationship between average annoyance and noise level shows that this condition is met in virtually all high-noise areas. Such dissatisfaction is not, however, sufficient by itself. The second requirement is that there is an identifiable object or authority that is recognized as being in some respect responsible for the noise or the control of the noise. The highly visible and centralized authority of an airport partially explains why airport noise, which was seen in a previous section to affect many fewer people than road-traffic noise, has been the focus of a large amount of public attention. A third requirement is that there is a belief that group or individual action can lead to a change in the noise situation. This requirement is often not fulfilled. In a survey in Sydney, Australia, some 31% of those respondents who were aware that they could complain by telephone, had not done so because they thought it would be a waste of time and would not result in a change.[232] Similarly, beliefs about the preventability

of aircraft noise have even more effect on complaints than on annoyance.[233] The fourth condition is that people must be aware of a means for contacting the appropriate authority. In the Sydney survey, 21% reported that they had not made a complaint because they did not know how. It has been noticed in the United States and in Germany that when the availability of a telephone complaint service is publicized the number of complaints rises.[234] A fifth condition which can substantially increase the amount of action is the introduction of a new focal point for action. The introduction of the supersonic transport, Concorde, or proposals for even small changes in existing transportation systems can lead to considerable public action because they provide a focus and basis for legitimizing pre-existing concerns about noise. The sixth requirement, especially for group actions, is about the social structural characteristics of the area and of the society as a whole facilitate public actions. On a community level, there is a greater likelihood of action if the community members interact with each other and there is a commitment to the community. On a societal level it is obvious that complaints and group action about noise are much more likely to occur in democratic societies which encourage interest group formation than in totalitarian societies.

3.7.2 Characteristics of complaints as noise effect indicators

Centrally collected reports of complaint activity seem to have some superficially attractive characteristics for monitoring responses to noise. For example, they can be obtained cheaply. Furthermore, they seem to indicate an important type of disturbance since the complainant usually must go to some trouble to make the complaint. The surveys have found that in some respects complainants are not unusual members of the population. A survey around Heathrow, for example, could find no evidence that complainants have unusual psychological traits such as neuroticism.[235] An analysis of transcriptions of telephone complaints in Germany could find no evidence that complainants were unusual with respect to physical condition or being under strong psychic stress.[236] Though complainants are more annoyed than the average member of the population with the particular noise source, there is no indication that they are a tiny hypersensitive minority.

Around Heathrow it was found that there are many more equally annoyed members of the population who do not complain. Both the Heathrow survey and a survey around United States airports found that the complainants are no more likely than the population in general to be sensitive to noise sources other than the aircraft about which they were complaining.[237] The United States aircraft noise survey also found that complaints were related to noise level, but not as strongly as were annoyance responses.[238] In spite of the fact that complaints seem to be genuine expressions of annoyance, the accumulated body of research has led to the firm conclusion that complaint records are misleading indicators of the extent or causes of noise effects in populations.[239,240]

Official complaint records seriously underestimate the extent of noise effects. Surveys consistently show that many more people are disturbed by noise than complain: in a sample around Heathrow in which 62% were annoyed by noise, 15% being 'very much' annoyed, only 1% reported making a complaint.[27] Similarly, many more people report that they want to complain than actually complain. In a London road traffic survey, for example, it is reported that about a third of those who had 'felt like complaining' actually had made a complaint.[241]

Complainants differ from the rest of the impacted population in several important respects. Complainants are typically from the more articulate sections of the population who have a greater confidence that they can deal with the authorities. Consequently, unlike the annoyance response, the complaint action is affected by such indicators of social class as occupation, education, income and value of property.[242,243] Complaints, unlike annoyance, are also found to be consistently and strongly affected by the individual's attitude toward the source.[244,245]

The findings in the previous subsection about conditions that affect public action also imply that complaints are inadequate indicators of the sources or timing of noise problems. On the basis of the complaint records, the Sydney study found that there would be expected to be 25 people impacted by factories or industry for every 10 impacted by road traffic, whereas the actual survey results found exactly the opposite was true. For example, there were only about two people annoyed by factories or industry for every 10 impacted by road traffic.[246] Similarly, it is frequently observed that it is the more affluent neighbourhoods which complain about aircraft noise.

Part of the inadequacy of complaint data arises from the fact that these data are collected by authorities for non-research purposes. Reports on complaints that could not be effectively dealt with by the public authorities were not completely recorded by the Environmental Telephone Service in Germany[247] or the State Pullution Control Commission workers in Sydney.[248] The incidence of recorded complaints could depend heavily on the procedures that such disparate agencies as police departments, local governments and airports use for recording, categorizing, tabulating and reporting complaints. Most authorities are well aware of another aspect of complaint data: there are usually fewer individuals who complain than there are numbers of complaints. A few individuals may be the source of a substantial proportion of the complaints.

The above discussion shows how many of the misconceptions about noise impact have arisen. There is a basis for the public authority's perceptions that noise bothers only 'well-to-do' people who are hostile to the noise source and that noise impact varies wildly in ways that are only loosely related to noise level. The basis is experiences with complainants, not with more representative cross-sections of the population. From this discussion it is clear that complaints are an inadequate and inappropriate measure of noise impact.

3.8 Other environments

Almost all of this chapter has dealt with the effects of noise in residential environments. There are, however, other types of areas which constitute part of the larger social environment and in which noise has the potential for causing problems. This section deals briefly with three of these. The first is schools, and the effect of transportation noise on activities within schools. The second environment to be discussed is that in hospitals, which are often thought to require a particularly quiet setting. The third is recreational or resort areas, where again quiet has a special connotation.

3.8.1 Noise in schools

A number of studies suggest that noise, both in the home environment and in the school, may have an effect on some of the academic skills children are expected to acquire. There is one major study currently in progress in California by Lukas and Swing but only preliminary results have yet been published. Those results show 'clearly that the students in the noisier schools attain lower reading achievement scores than students in quieter schools in the three grades tested' (grades 2, 3, and 6).[249] Alternate explanations for this difference were also tested, but were not accepted. Not all studies have shown such a clear result, however. Another study in Los Angeles showed no

differences between pupils from noisy and quiet schools in scores on standard reading and mathematics tests, although there were differences in performance on a cognitive (puzzle-solving) task.[250] This finding was replicated in a follow-up study a year later by the same group.[251] Thus there appears to be some evidence for a potential effect of noise on achievement, but not consistent evidence, nor a consistent result as to which cognitive abilities are affected by noise.

Several mechanisms have been proposed to explain this potential effect. The explanation most often proposed is that the external transportation noise interrupts communication, particularly by the teacher, with the result that either members of the class do not hear what is said, or the teacher is simply not able to cover as much material in the noisy classroom. Crook and Langdon, for example, report that teachers paused during at least one aircraft flyover in four, and that they paused more frequently with increasing noise levels.[252] Ko also reports that the disruption of verbal communication, as reported by the teachers, correlates well with noise level, as measured by NNI.[253] Pearson et al. have also studied communication in the classroom, focusing on the teachers' voice levels in response to changing levels of intrusive noise.[254] Their finding was that teachers were able to maintain a fairly constant speech to noise ratio, up to speech level of about 78 dB(A) (normalized to a 1 m distance). Obviously, this response is capable of maintaining adequate communication only up to certain levels of intrusive noise.

A related explanation has to do with younger students learning to communicate; in essence, learning the language. Several studies have reported that children who live in noisy home environments do not do as well in school as those with quieter homes.[255,256]

The second mechanism proposed has to do with hearing damage to the pupil. The Lukas and Swing study is the only one to have found an effect, in terms of the proportions of pupils with sensorineural hearing losses. This effect was not found by Cohen et al.[250] who found essentially the same proportions of children in the noisy and quiet schools to have hearing problems.

The third mechanism has to do with behaviour and attentiveness in the classroom. Lehmann and Gratiot-Alphandery[257] found that insulating a schoolroom to reduce outdoor noise improved pupils behaviour, and their social contact, and it is assumed their accomplishments in school. Cohen et al.[250] suggest that students in noisy classrooms develop a selective inattentiveness because of the noise, but that after some time (a few years) this is abandoned in favour of a feeling of helplessness in the presence of the noise.

Taken together, then, these studies suggest that noise may be a problem in the school, but more work needs to be done to quantify the effect precisely, and to understand the mechanism better.

3.8.2 Hospital environments

Only a small amount of work has been done on the effects of external noises on people in hospitals. Two studies that have been reported both show very little annoyance at external noise for hospital patients. In a Swiss study, it was found that the relationship between noise level and annoyance was weaker for hospital patients than for housewives in residential areas surveyed in a comparable study. The results of that study led to the conclusion 'that no reason can be derived from patients' questionnaires for particularly severe limits on noise around hospitals'.[258] This is consistent with Dutch results which assert that 'for hospitalized patients, annoyance does not come from noise sources in the environment, but from inside the hospitals'.[259]

Walker[260] also comments on the problems of internally generated noises in hospitals.

Despite this apparent consistency of results, however, some caution is necessary. First, there are few studies. Second, the noise levels experienced in those studies were probably not very high, if the hospitals were in relatively quiet locations. In the Swiss survey, for example, only one of the nine hospitals studied had an exterior 24-hour *Leq* exceeding 61 dB, and that was only 65 dB. The levels were not reported for the Dutch hospitals. Third, to say that the response is not particularly different from that for residential areas is to say that at levels much above 65 dB, many people will be annoyed. Finally, one of the primary reasons for reducing noise around hospitals is not based on annoyance, but on the sleep disturbance noise can cause, which is particularly important for ill or recuperating patients.

Perhaps equally important, noise can have adverse effects on the hospital staff. A survey by Walker and Morgan[261] of two hospitals near Heathrow Airport found that speech interference due to aircraft noise was a major complaint among staff, especially as it affected consultations with patients. Other studies have focused on the interference of external noises with the use of stethoscopes.[262,263] For several reasons, then, it is probably a good idea to encourage quietness for hospitals.

3.8.3 Recreation and natural areas

Recreational activities in natural and other areas differ in important ways from those conducted in everyday residential settings. People value their experiences in many of these areas precisely because they cannot hear the noises of an industrialized society. Guski, for example, has shown that the term quietness is closely associated with recreational activities.[264] No field surveys have been published which described the effects of measured noise levels in such settings. It is plausible that in some natural areas the fact that a noise is distinctly audible and identified as a transportation noise is enough to make it disturbing for some users.

3.9 Designing social surveys for noise effect assessment

Combined social surveys and noise measurement programmes have provided most of the available information about residents' responses to environmental noise. Many of the strengths and weaknesses of surveys as a method have been discussed in the previous sections of this chapter. At this point some guidance will be offered for planning such studies and for determining whether a new survey is likely to make a valuable contribution towards a transportation noise assessment programme.

The most fundamental requirements for a successful community study are that there be a good estimate of the physical noise exposure for each study unit and that there be a good measurement of the reaction to that noise. The general principles for conducting satisfactory social surveys and a guide to detailed procedures can be found in social survey textbooks.[265] The physical noise measurement programmes must not only accurately measure the noise during the measurement period but also satisfactorily sample the noise environment so as to estimate the long-term (often 1 year) noise environment. The most detailed guide to the design and analysis of community noise response surveys is the one prepared for the US Environmental Protection Agency.[266,267] The principles and details of conducting such studies are too numerous to be discussed here. It should only be pointed out that the satisfactory completion of such studies requires considerable expertise both in the social survey and in physical noise survey areas.

While the basic principles of social and noise surveys are important, there are some additional problems that can often be ignored in other types of research surveys but which are especially critical for the combined surveys. Noise surveys generally are rightly concerned with providing high-quality measurements of the noise during the noise measurement period. In order to be useful for the social survey, however, the additional problem must be faced of providing an estimate of the noise exposure for a much longer period than can be directly measured. The provision of this estimate requires that the programme to specify the noise environment will necessarily be based on temporal and spatial sampling strategies which will require special statistical sampling expertise. If the chief interest of the study is in precisely determining the relationship between noise level and response, then knowledge about the standard errors of the noise level estimates are critical.

In addition to the common social survey concerns, the social surveys also face the problem that a highly clustered sample is used in a situation in which the chief dependent variable (noise annoyance) is an evaluation of a characteristic of those clusters (the noise level). Most of the relevant policy variables are also sample cluster characteristics. Any errors in determining values of the independent variable (noise level) are also correlated with the sample cluster. The clustered sample thus requires that sampling errors be computed so as to reflect the cluster sample structure and that the possibility of correlated cluster level variables be considered at all stages of the study design and analysis.[268]

Before any study programme is embarked upon there should be a careful assessment of whether a combined noise and social survey is actually needed for the specific noise assessment purposes. In many instances the only real question is 'Does a transportation noise problem exist in this community?' In such instances either reference to some of the previous 200 noise surveys[1] or a simple sample survey with only a modest noise measurement programme can establish the range of noise levels present and can estimate the numbers of people who are affected in particular ways. If the need is to establish a dose–response relationship for noise annoyance in relation to noise level and other community noise characteristics, then the assessment can be based either on an assessment of existing publications or on a very extensive, expensive research project. Low-investment research programmes are not likely to provide any more useful information about the dose–response relationship than is available in existing research publications. A more extensive discussion of the principles involved in designing surveys for noise policy purposes has been previously published.[190]

3.10 Conclusions about community effects

The research in this chapter shows that transportation noise can have a direct, immediate effect on people's behaviours and on communication activities in the home. Noise can also lead to negative attitudes, including annoyance. It has also been shown that many people do not passively accept noise, but instead move to take individual or group actions directed at reducing the noise.

The research reviewed in this chapter has also shown that there is enormous individual variability in the measured reactions at any one noise level. While much of this variability may be due to random measurement errors, much can also be associated with acoustical, situational, attitudinal and personal factors. In spite of the impact of these non-noise factors, there are three important respects in which noise level has a greater influence on annoyance than any other factor. First, noise level is the only variable that can completely eliminate noise annoyance. For example, at the lowest, but still audible, noise levels in *Figures 3.7* and *3.8* any indication of extreme annoyance is completely eliminated. Second, noise level affects the degree of annoyance within every subcategory of the population, even if the category is defined on the basis of strong attitudinal variables. No factor has been found that consistently identifies types of people who have the same annoyance regardless of noise level. Third, extreme differences in noise levels (30 dB separation) have more effect on noise annoyance (lead to a greater difference in annoyance scores) than do extreme differences on any other measured variable.

As a practical matter, noise level is the only variable that policy makers can ever hope to control on a large-scale basis in order to reduce annoyance levels over long periods of time. Though a variety of steps may enable the policy maker to reduce public *complaints* against noise, the noise annoyance research has not discovered any step that might be taken to reduce the privately felt annoyance with persistent transportation noise sources except that of reducing noise levels.

References

1   FIELDS, J. M. *A Catalog of Social Surveys of Residents' Reactions to Environmental Noise (1943–1980)*. Technical Memorandum-83187. National Aeronautics and Space Administration, Washington, D.C. (1981).

2   FRENCH, N. R. and STEINBERG, J. C. Factors governing the intelligibility of speech sounds. *J. Acoust. Soc. A.*, **19**, 90–119 (1947).

3   American National Standards Institute. *American National Standard Methods for the Calculation of the Articulation Index*. ANSI S3.5–1969, ANSI (1969).

4   SHEPHERD, W. T. and GUNN, W. J. Speech interference assessment: a condensed view of important considerations and a global model of acceptability. *J. Auditory Res.*, **17**, 117–38. (*see* especially p. 128) (1977).

5   American National Standard Institute. *American National Standard for Rating Noise With Respect to Speech Interference*, ANSI S3.14, ANSI (1977).

6   PEARSONS, K. S. Communication in noise: research after the 1973 congress on noise as a public health problem. In *Proceedings of the Third International Congress On Noise As A Public Health Problem*, ASHA Report 10, American Speech–Language–Hearing Association, Rockville, Md., pp. 165–171 (1980).

7   HOUTGAST, T. Indoor speech intelligibility and indoor noise level criteria. In *Proceedings of the Third International Congress On Noise As A Public Health Problem*, ASHA Report 10, American Speech–Language–Hearing Association, Rockville Md., 172–83 (1980).

8   POLLACK, I. Message procedures for unfavorable communication conditions. *J. Acoust. Soc. Am.*, **30**, 196–201 (1958).

9   SUTER, A. H. Hearing level and speech discrimination in noise. In *Proceedings of the Third International Congress on Noise as a Public Health Problem*, Report 10, American Speech–Language–Hearing Association, Rockville, Md. 203–209 (1980).

10 Committee on Hearing, Bioacoustics, and Biomechanics; Assembly of Behavioral and Social Sciences; National Research Council: *The Effects of Time-Varying Noise on Speech Intelligibility Indoors: Report of Working Group 83*, National Academy of Sciences, Washington, D.C. (1981).

11 LOEB, M. Noise and performance: do we know more now? In *Proceedings of the Third International Congress on Noise As A Public Health Problem*, ASHA Report 10, American Speech–Language–Hearing Association, Rockville, Md., pp. 303–21 (1980).

12 BROADBENT, D. E. Recent advances in understanding performance in noise. In *Proceedings of the Fourth International Congress on Noise As A Public Health Problem*, Centro Ricerche E Studi Amplifon, Milan, Italy, pp. 719–38 (1983).

13 KRYTER, K. D. *Physiological, Psychological, and Social Effects of Noise*. Reference Publication–1115, NASA, Washington, D.C. (1984).

14 KRYTER, K. D. *Physiological, Psychological, and Social Effects of Noise*. Reference Publication–1115, NASA, Washington, D.C. p. 344 (1984).

15 BROADBENT, D. Recent advances in understanding performance in noise. In *Proceedings of The Fourth International Congress on Noise As A Public Health Program*, Centro Ricerche E Studii Amplifon, Milan, Italy, p. 720 (1983).

16 POULTON, E. C. Psychology of the scientist: XLI. Continuous noise can degrade performance when using badly designed equipment: a case history. *Percept. Mot. Skills*, **50**, 319–30 (1980).

17 BROADBENT, D. E. The current state of noise research: reply to Poulton. *Psychol. Bull.*, **85**, 1052–67 (1978).

18 KRYTER, K. D. *Physiological, Psychological, and Social Effects of Noise*. Reference Publication–1115, NASA, Washington, D.C. p. 347 (1984).

19 MIL Research. *Second Survey of Aircraft Noise Annoyance Around London (Heathrow) Airport*. HMSO, London, *see* p. 102 (1971).

20 GRANDJEAN, E., GRAF, P. LAUBER, A., MEIER, H. P. and MUELLER, R. *A Survey of Aircraft in Switzerland. Proceedings of the International Congress on Noise as a Public Health Problem*, Dubrovnik, Yugoslavia, May 13–18, US Environmental Protection Agency, Washington, D.C. USEPA 550–9–73–008, pp. 645–59 (1973).

21 MCKENNELL, A. C. Methodological problems in a survey of aircraft noise annoyance. *The Statistician*, **19**, 1–19 (*see* especially pp. 3, 19) (1969).

22 FIELDS, J. M. and WALKER, J. G. The response to railway noise in residential areas in Great Britain. *J. Sound Vib.*, **85**, 177–255 (*see* especially p. 241) (1982).

23 MORTON-WILLIAMS, J., HEDGES, B. and FERNANDO, E. *Road Traffic and the Environment*, Social and Community Planning Research, London, p. 42 (1978).

24 KOSTEN, C. W., DE ZWAAN, G. W., STEENBERGEN, M. H., FALKENHAGEN, C. A. F., DE JONGE, J. A. C. and VAN OS, G. J. *Geluidhinder door Vliegtuigen*, T.N.O., Delft, Netherlands, p. III–14 (1967). Translation available as: *Aircraft Noise Abatement*, NASA TT–F–12,093 (1969). NASA, Washington, D.C.

25 KODAMA, H. *Psychological Effect of Aircraft Noise Upon Inhabitants of an Airport Neighborhood. 17th International Congress of Applied Psychology*. Liège Belgium, June, 1971, The Medical Association of Akishima, Japan, p. 32 (1971).

26 OSADA, Y. Koshu eiseiin Kenkyu Hokoku. *Bull. Inst. Publ. Hlth.* (*Tokyo*), **20**, 119–127 (*see* especially p. 125) (1971). Translation available as: *Community Reactions to Aircraft Noise in the Vicinity of Airports: A Comparative Study of the Social Surveys Using Interview Methods*, NASA TM–75439 (1980).

27 MCKENNELL, A. C. *Aircraft Noise Annoyance Around London (Heathrow) Airport*. Central Office of Information, S.S.337, Government Social Survey, p. 2.1 (1963).

28 Centre Scientifique et Technique du Bâtiment *La Gêne Causée Par le Bruit Atour des Aéroports: Rapport de Fin D'Etude*. C.S.T.B., Paris, p. 91 (1968). Translation available as: *The Annoyance Caused by Noise Around Airports: Final Report*, NASA TM–75784 (1980). NASA, Washington, D.C.

29 NIMURA, T., SONE, T. and KONO, S. *Some Consideration on Noise Problems of High-Speed Railways in Japan*, Internoise 73, Copenhagen, p. 304 (1973).

30 OLLERHEAD, J. B. *A Comparison of Annoyance Caused by Aircraft Noise Near London, Manchester and Liverpool Airports*. TT–7706, Loughborough University of Technology, England, p. 50 (1977).

31 KOSTEN, C. W., DE ZWAAN, G. W., STEENBERGEN, M. H., FALKENHAGEN, C. A. F., DE JONGE, J. A. C. and VAN OS, G. J. *Geluidhinder door Vliegtuigen*, T.N.O., Delft, Netherlands, pp. 111–14 (1967). Translation available as *Aircraft Noise Abatement*, NASA TT–F–12,093 (1969). NASA, Washington, D.C.

32 RYLANDER, R., BJORKMAN, M., AHRLIN, U., SORENSEN, S. and BERGLUND, K. Aircraft noise annoyance contours: importance of overflight frequency and noise level. *J. Sound Vib.*, **69**, 586 (1980).

33 OSADA, Y. Koshu eiseiin kenkyu Hokoku. *Bull Inst. Publ. Hlth.* (*Tokyo*), **20**, 125 (1971). Translation available as: *Community Reactions to Aircraft Noise in The Vicinity of Airports: A Comparative Study of The Social Surveys Using Interview Methods*, NASA–TM–75439 (1982). NASA, Washington D.C.

34 NIMURA, T., SONE, T. and KONO, S. *Some Consideration on Noise*

Problems of High-Speed Railways in Japan, Internoise 73, Copenhagen, p. 304 (1973).

35 Centre Scientifique et Technique du Bâtiment. *La Gêne Causée Par le Bruit Atour des Aéroports: Rapport de Fin D'Etude.* C.S.T.B., Paris, p. 91 (1968). Translation available as: *The Annoyance Caused by Noise Around Airports: Final Report*, NASA TM-75784 (1980). NASA, Washington D.C.

36 FIELDS, J. M. and WALKER, J. G. The response to railway noise in residential areas in Great Britain. *J. Sound Vib.*, **85**, 185 (1982).

37 BOTTOM, C. G. and WALTERS, D. M. *A Survey into the Annoyance Caused by Aircraft Noise and Road Traffic Noise*, TT-7204, Loughborough University of Technology, England, p. 27 (1971).

38 Centre Scientifique et Technique du Bâtiment. *La Gêne Causée Par le Bruit Atour des Aéroports: Rapport de Fin D'Etude.* C.S.T.B., Paris, p. 91 (1968). Translation available as: *The Annoyance Caused by Noise Around Airports: Final Report*, NASA TM-75784 (1980). NASA, Washington D.C.

39 SMALL, A. M., JENKINS, A. and PAHL, J. *Community Response to Freeway Noise in Los Angeles County*. Internoise 74, pp. 445–48, especially p. 447 (1974).

40 SHIBUYA, A., TANNO, S., SONE, T. and NIMURA, T. *Road Traffic Noise and Community Response in Sendai City*. Internoise 75, pp. 425–28, especially p. 428 (1975).

41 FIDELL, S. *The Urban Noise Survey.* USEPA 550–9–77–100, August, p. 56 (1977).

42 GRANDJEAN, E., GRAF, P., LAUBER, A., MEIER, H. P. and MUELLER, R. *A Survey of Aircraft in Switzerland. Proceedings of The International Congress on Noise as A Public Health Problem*, Dubrovnick, Yugoslavia, May 13–18, USEPA 550–9–73–008, p. 652 (1973).

43 BRUCKMAYER, F. and LANG, J. Störung der Bevölkerung durch Verkehrslärm (Annoyance of People by Traffic Noise). *Österreichische Ingenieur-Zeitschrift*, **10**, 302–306, 338–344, 376–385 (*see* especially p. 305) (1967).

44 AUBREE, D. *La Gêne due au Bruit des Trains (Annoyance Due to Train Noise)*. CSTB, Nantes, EN–SH–75.2, pp. 59–61 (1975).

45 LANGDON, F. J. Noise nuisance caused by road traffic in residential areas, Parts I, II. *J. Sound Vib.*, **47**, 243–282 (*see* especially p. 253) (1976).

46 SCHULTZ, T. J. Synthesis of social surveys on noise annoyance. *J. Acoust. Soc. Am.*, **64**, 377–405 (1978).

47. WILLSHIRE, K. F. and POWELL, C. A. *Effects of Activity Interference on Annoyance Due to Aircraft Noise.* Technical Paper–1938. NASA Washington, D.C. (1981).

48 FIDELL, S. Nationwide urban noise survey, *J. Acoust. Soc. Am.*, **64**, 198–206. (*see* especially p. 204) (1978).

49 Tracor, Inc. *Community Reaction to Airport Noise*, Vol. I, NASA CR–1761; Vol. II, NASA CR–111316, (*see* especially p. 76) (1971).

50 HALL, F. L., TAYLOR, S. M. and BIRNIE, S. E. *Community Response to Road Traffic Noise*. Department of Geography, McMaster University, Canada, p. 65 (1977).

51. LINDVALL, T. and RADFORD, E. P. Measurement of annoyance due to exposure to environmental factors. *Env. Res.*, **6**, 1–36 (*see* especially p. 3) (1973).

52 BERGLUND, B., BERGLUND, U. and LINDVALL, T. Scaling loudness, noisiness, and annoyance of aircraft noise. *J. Acoust. Soc. Am.*, **57**, 930–934 (*see* especially p. 931) (1975).

53 KRYTER, K. D. *Physiological, Psychological, and Social Effects of Noise.* Reference Publication–1119. NASA, Washington, D.C. p. 125 (1984).

54 WEINSTEIN, N. D. Human evaluations of environmental noise. In *Perceiving Environmental Quality: Research and Applications.* (K. H. Craik and E. H. Zube, eds) Plenum Press, New York, pp. 229–52 (*see* especially p. 234) (1976).

55 FRANCOIS, J. *Aircraft Noise, Annoyance, and Personal Characteristics. Noise as a Public Health Problem, Proceedings of the Third International Congress*, Report 10, American Speech-Language-Hearing Association, Rockville, Md., pp. 594–99 (*see* especially p. 596) (1980).

56 U.S. Department of Commerce. *Annual Housing Survey.* U.S. Department of Housing and Urban Development: Office of Policy Development, U.S. Department of Commerce: Bureau of the Census, Washington, D.C. pp. 41–42 (1977).

57 MORTON-WILLIAMS, J., HEDGES, B. and FERNANDO, E. *Road Traffic and The Environment*, Social and Community Planning Research, London, p. 98 (1978).

58 Peat, Marwick and Parners *Data Base of the Results of a National Household Survey of Noise Exposure*. Peat, Marwick and Partners for Road and Motor Vehicle Traffic Safety Branch of the Department of Transport, Canada, p. 24.

59 U.S. Department of Commerce. *Annual Housing Survey.* U.S. Department of Housing and Urban Development: Office of Policy Development, U.S. Department of Commerce: Bureau of the Census, Washington, D.C., pp. 41–42 (1977).

60 SHIBUYA, A., TANNO, S., SONE, T. and NIMURA, T. *Road Traffic Noise and Community Response in Sendai City*. Internoise 75, pp. 425–28 (1979).

61 PRABHU, B. T. S. and MUNI-CHAKRABORTY, R. L. *A Planning Study of Urban Noise in Calcutta*. Internoise 79, pp. 815–18 (1979).

62 MIL Research. *Second Survey of Aircraft Noise Annoyance Around London (Heathrow) Airport.* HMSO, London, p. 100 (1971).

63 LANGDON, F. J. Noise nuisance caused by road traffic in residential areas, Parts I, II. *J. Sound Vib.*, **47**, 243–282 (1976).

64 WANNER, H. U., WEHRLI, B., BAKKE, P., NEMECEK, J., TURRIAN, V. and GRANDJEAN, E. *Effects of Road Traffic Noise on Residents.* Internoise 77, pp. B698–B702 (1977).

65 BREMOND, J. Evaluation de la gêne due au bruit des avions par les enquêtes d'opinion. *Médecine Aéronautique et Spatiale, Médecine Subaquatique et Hyperbare*, **18**, 269–274 (1979). Translation available as: *Evaluation of the Disturbance Caused by Aircraft Noise by Opinion Surveys. Technical Memorandum–76579.* NASA, Washington, D.C. (1981).

66 MCKENNELL, A. C. Methodological problems in a survey of aircraft noise annoyance. *The Statistician*, **19**, 6 (1969).

67 FIELDS, J. M. and WALKER, J. G. The response to railway noise in residential areas in Great Britain. *J. Sound Vib.*, **85**, 250 (1982).

68 BRADLEY, J. S. and JONAH, B. A. The effects of site selected variables on human responses to traffic noise, Part I: type of housing by traffic noise level. *J. Sound Vib.*, **66**, 589–604. (*see* especially p. 593).

69 BULLEN, R. B. and HEDE, A. J. Time of day corrections in measures of aircraft noise exposure. *J. Acoust. Soc. Am.*, **73**, 1624–1630 (*see* especially p. 1626) (1983).

70 Deutsche Forschungsgemeinschaft *DFG-Forschungsbericht Fluglärmwirkungen: Eine Interdisziplinäre Untersuchung über die Auswirkungen des Fluglärms auf den Menschen (DFG-Research-Report Aircraft Noise: An Interdisciplinary Investigation of the Effect of Aircraft Noise on People)*. Harald Boldt Verlag KG, Boppard, p. 176 (1967).

71 FIELDS, J. M. and WALKER, J. G. The response to railway noise in residential areas in Great Britain. *J. Sound Vib.*, **85**, 187 (1982).

72 SCHULTZ, T. J. Comments on K. D. Kryter's paper, Community Annoyance from Aircraft and Ground Vehicle Noise. *J. Acoust. Soc. Am.*, **72**, 1243–1252 (1982).

73 ALEXANDRE, A. An assessment of certain causal models used in surveys on aircraft noise annoyance. *J. Sound Vib.*, **44**, 119–125 (1976).

74 SCHULTZ, T. J. Synthesis of social surveys on noise annoyance. *J. Acoust. Soc. Am.*, **64**, 377 (1978).

75 Committee on Hearing, Bioacoustics, and Biomechanics; Assembly of Behavioral and Social Sciences; National Research Council. *Guidelines for Preparing Environmental Impact Statements on Noise: Report of Working Group 69.* National Academy of Sciences, Washington D.C. (1977).

76 FIELDS, J. M. *A Program to Support the Full Utilization of Data from Existing Social Surveys of Environmental Noise.* Internoise 80. pp. 937–940 (*see* especially p. 939) (1980).

77 FINKE, H. O., MARTIN, R., GUSKI, R., ROHRMANN, B., SCHUMER, R. and SCHUMER-KOHRS, A. Effects of aircraft noise on man. *J. Sound Vib.*, **43**, 335–349 (*see* especially p. 348) (1975).

78 KRYTER, K. D. Community annoyance from aircraft and ground vehicle noise. *J. Acoust. Soc. Am.*, **72**, 1222–1242 (*see* especially p. 1232) (1982).

79 LAMBERT, J., SIMONNET, F. and VALLET, M. Patterns of behavior in dwellings exposed to road traffic noise. *J. Sound Vib.*, **92**, 159–172 (1984).

80 FIELDS, J. M. *Effects of Errors in Specifying Noise Environments on Results from Community Response Surveys.* Internoise 82, pp. 609–612 (*see* especially p. 610) (1982).

81 WANNER, H. U., WEHRLI, B., NEMECEK, J. and TURRIAN, V. I Die Belästigung der Anwohner verkehrsreicher Strassen durch Lärm und Luftverunreinigungen. *Sozial Präventivmedizin*, **22**, 108–115

(*see* especially p. 114) (1977). Translation available as: *Annoyance Due to Noise and Air Pollution to the Residents of Heavily Frequented Streets*, NASA TM–75496 (1980). NASA, Washington, D.C.

82 FIELDS, J. M. and WALKER, J. G. The response to railway noise in residential areas in Great Britain. *J. Sound Vib.*, **85**, 250 (1982).

83 GUSKI, I. R., WICHMANN, U., ROHRMANN, B. and FINKE, H. C. Konstruktion und Anwendung eines Fragebogens zur socialwissenschaftlichen Untersuchung der Auswirkung von Umweltlärm. *Zeitschrift für Socialpsychologie*, **9**, 50–65 (1978). Translation available as: *Construction and Application of a Questionnaire for the Social Scientific Investigation of Environmental Noise Effects*. NASA TM–75492 (1980). NASA, Washington, D.C.

84 FIELDS, J. M. and WALKER, J. G. The response to railway noise in residential areas in Great Britain. *J. Sound Vib.*, **85**, 250 (1982).

85 MCKENNELL, A. C. *Aircraft Noise Annoyance Around London (Heathrow) Airport*. Central Office of Information, S.S. 337, Government Social Survey, Appendix F. (1963).

86 FRANCOIS, J. *Les Répercussions Du Bruit Des Avions Sur L'Équilibre Des Riverains Des Aéroports: Etude Longitudinal Autour De Roissy, 3éme Phase (Effects of Aircraft Noise on The Equilibrium of Airport Residents: Longitudinal Study Around Roissy, Phase 3)*. IFOP/ETMAR, Paris, p. 36 (1979). Translation available as: *Effect of Aircraft Noise on The Equilibrium of Airport Residents: Longitudinal Study Around Roissy Phase III*, NASA, TM–75906 (1981). NASA, Washington, D.C.

87 MCKENNELL, A. C. Methodological problems in a survey of aircraft noise annoyance. *The Statistician*, **19**, 11 (1969).

88 BULLEN, R. B. and HEDE, A. J. Time of day corrections in measures of aircraft noise exposure. *J. Acoust. Soc. Am.*, **73**, 1625 (1983).

89 HALL, F. L. and TAYLOR, S. M. Reliability of social survey data on noise effects. *J. Acoust. Soc. Am.*, **72**, 1212–1221. (see especially p. 1217) (1982).

90 GRIFFITHS, I. D., LANGDON, F. J. and SWAN, M. A. Subjective effects of traffic noise exposure: reliability and seasonal effects. *J. Sound Vib.*, **71**, 227–240 (see especially p. 234) (1980).

91 HALL, F. L. and TAYLOR, S. M. Reliability of social survey data on noise effects. *J. Acoust. Soc. Am.*, **72**, 1220 (1982).

92 MCKENNELL, A. C. *Aircraft Noise Annoyance Around London (Heathrow) Airport*. Central Office of Information, s.s. 337, Government Social Survey, Appendix F. (1963).

93 KRYTER, K. D and PEARSONS, K. S. Some effects of spectral content and duration on perceived noise level. *J. Acoust. Soc. Am.*, **35**, 866–883. (1963).

94 OLLERHEAD, J. B. *An Evaluation of Methods for Scaling Aircraft Noise Perception*. Contractor Report–1883. NASA Washington, D.C. (1971).

95 MIL Research. *Second Survey of Aircraft Noise Annoyance Around London (Heathrow) Airport*. HMSO, London, p. 36 (1971).

96 MCKENNELL, A. C. *Aircraft Noise Annoyance Around London (Heathrow) Airport*. Central Office of Information, s.s. 337, Government Social Survey, Appendix K. (1963).

97 WILSON, A. *Noise: Final Report*. Cmnd. 2056, HMSO, London, p. 209 (1963).

98 MIL Research. *Second Survey of Aircraft Noise Annoyance Around London (Heathrow) Airport*. HMSO, London, p. 37 (1971).

99 FIELDS, J. M. The effect of numbers of noise events on people's reactions to noise: An analysis of existing survey data. *J. Acoust. Soc. Am.*, **75**, 447–467 (1984).

100 WILSON, A. *Noise: Final Report*. Cmnd. 2056, HMSO, London, p. 215 (1963).

101 BRADLEY, J. S. *Predictors of Adverse Human Responses to Traffic Noise. ASTM Special Technical Publication 692* (R. J. Peppin and C. W. Rodman, eds.), American Society For Testing and Materials, Philadelphia, Pa., pp. 108–123. (see especially p. 120) (1979).

102 WEHRLI, B., NEMECEK, J., TURRIAN, V., HOFMANN, R. and WANNER, H. U. Auswirkungen des Strassenverkehrslärm in der Nacht. *Kampf dem Lärm*, **25**, 138–149 (see especially p. 142) (1978). Translation available as: *Effects of Street Traffic Noise in the Night*, NASA, TM–75495.

103 NEMECEK, J., WEHRLI, B. and TURRIAN, V. Effects of the noise of street traffic in Switzerland, a review of four surveys. *J. Sound Vib.*, **78**, 223–234 (see especially p. 228) (1981).

104 WEHRLI, B., NEMECEK, J., TURRIAN, V., HOFMANN, R. and WANNER, H. U. Auswirkungen des Strassenverkehrslärm in der Nacht. *Kampf dem Lärm*, **25**, 143 (1978). Translation available as: *Effects of Street Traffic Noise in The Night*, NASA TM–75495 (1980). NASA, Washington, D.C.

105 FRANCOIS, J. *Le Prise en Compte de la Gêne Nocturne dans le Calcul de l'indice psyophique (Taking Account of Night-time Annoyance in the Calculation of N)*. IFOP/ETMAR, Paris, p. 10 (1977). Translation available as: *Taking Into Account Nighttime Annoyance in the Calculation of the Psophic Index*, NASA TM–76580. (1981). NASA, Washington, D.C.

106 LANGDON, F. J. and BULLER, I. B. Road traffic noise and disturbance to sleep. *J. Sound Vib.*, **50**, 13–28 (see especially p. 17) (1977).

107 FIDELL, S. and JONES, G. Effects of cessation of late-night flights on an airport community. *J. Sound Vib.*, **42**, 441–427 (1975).

108 FIELDS, J. M. *Research on the Effect of Noise at Different Times of Day: Models, Methods and Findings*. Contractor Report Number 3888. NASA, Washington, D.C. (1985).

109 YEOWART, N. S., WILCOX, D. J. and ROSSALL, A. W. Community reactions to noise from freely flowing traffic, motorway traffic and congested traffic flow. *J. Sound Vib.*, **53**, 127–145 (see especially p. 135) (1977).

110 BRADLEY, J. S. and JONAH, B. A. The effects of site selected variables on human responses to traffic noise, Part I: type of housing by traffic noise level. *J. Sound Vib.*, **66**, 595 (1979).

111 BRADLEY, J. S. and JONAH, B. A. The effects of site selected variables on human response to traffic noise, Part II: community size by socio-economic status by traffic noise level. *J. Sound Vib.*, **67**, 395–407 (see especially p. 398) (1979).

112 BRADLEY, J. S. and JONAH, B. A. The effects of site selected variables on human response to traffic noise, Part III: community size by socio-economic status by traffic noise level. *J. Sound Vib.*, **67**, 409–423. (see especially p. 412) (1979).

113 SCHULTZ, T. J. Social surveys on noise annoyance—further considerations. In *Proceedings of the Third International Congress on Noise As A Public Health Problem*, ASHA Report 10, American Speech–Language–Hearing Association, Rockville, Md., pp. 529–540 (see especially p. 537) (1980).

114 POWELL, C. A. and RICE, C. G. Judgments of aircraft noise in a traffic noise background. *J. Sound Vib.*, **38**, 39–50 (1975).

115 POWELL, C. A. *Laboratory Study of Annoyance to Combined Airplane and Road-Traffic Noise*. Technical Paper–1478. NASA, Washington, D.C. (1979).

116 JOHNSTON, G. W. and HAASZ, A. A. Traffic background level and signal duration effects on aircraft noise judgment. *J. Sound Vib.*, **63**, 543–560 (1979).

117 RICE, C. G. and IZUMI, K. Annoyance due to combinations of noises. In *Proceedings of the Institute of Acoustics*, April, 1984, pp. 287–294 (1984).

118 WALTERS, D. Annoyance due to railway noise in residential areas. In *Architectural Psychology* (D. V. Center, ed.), R.J.B.A. Publication, Ltd., England (1970).

119 BOTTOM, C. G. A social survey into annoyance caused by the interaction of aircraft noise and traffic noise. *J. Sound Vib.*, **19**, 473–476 (1971).

120 TAYLOR, S. M., HALL, F. L. and BIRNIE, S. E. Effect of background levels on community responses to aircraft noise. *J. Sound Vib.*, **71**, 261–270 (1980).

121 FIELDS, J. M. and WALKER, J. G. The response to railway noise in residential areas in Great Britain. *J. Sound Vib.* **85**, 197 (1982).

122 DE JONG, R. G. Some developments in community response research since the second international workshop on railway and tracked transit system noise in 1978. *J. Sound Vib.*, **87**, 297–309 (see especially p. 300) (1983).

123 GRAF, P., MULLER, R. and MEIER, H. P. *Sozio-psychologische Fluglärmuntersuchung im Gebiet der drei Schweizer Flughäfen, Zürich, Genf, Basel*, pp. 142–144 (1974). Translation available as: *Sociopsychological Investigation of Airport Noise in The Vicinities of Three Swiss Airports, Zurich, Geneva, Basel*. NASA, TM—75787, September (1980). NASA, Washington, D.C.

124 FIELDS, J. M. and WALKER, J. G. The response to railway noise in residential areas in Great Britain. *J. Sound Vib.*, **85**, 198 (1982).

125 GRAP, P., MULLER, R. and MEIER, H. P. *Sozio-psychologische Fluglärmuntersuchung im Gebiet der drei Schweizer Flughäfen, Zurich, Genf, Basel* pp. 142–144 (1974). Translation available as: *Sociopsychological Investigation of Airport Noise in The Vicinities*

of Three Swiss Airports, Zurich, Geneva, Basel. NASA, TM-75787, September (1980). NASA, Washington, D.C.

126 SCHULTZ, T. J. Synthesis of social surveys on noise annoyance. *J. Acoust. Soc. Am.*, **64**, 384 (1978).

127 POWELL, C. A. *A Summation and Inhibition Model of Annoyance Response to Multiple Community Noise Sources*. Technical Paper–1479. NASA, (1979).

128 TAYLOR, S. M. A comparison of models to predict annoyance reactions to noise from mixed sources. *J. Sound Vib.*, **81**, 123–128 (1982).

129 YANIV, S. L. and BAUER, J. W. Effects of time-varying noise on human response: what is known and what is not. In *Proceedings of the Third International Congress on Noise As A Public Health Problem*, ASHA Report 10, American Speech–Language–Hearing Association, Rockville, Md., pp. 511–521 (1980).

130 GRIFFITHS, I. D. and LANGDON, F. J. Subjective responses to road traffic noise. *J. Sound Vib.*, **8**, 16–32 (1968).

131 ROBINSON, D. W. Towards a unified system of noise assessment. *J. Sound Vib.*, **14**, 279–298 (1971).

132 POWELL, C. A. *Annoyance Due to Multiple Airplane Noise Exposure*. Technical Paper–1706. NASA, Washington, D.C., p. 26 (1980).

133 RICE, C. G. Development of cumulative noise measure for the prediction of general annoyance in an average population. *J. Sound Vib.*, **52**, 345–364 (*see* especially p. 355) (1977).

134 FIELDS, J. M. and WALKER, J. G. Comparing the relationships between noise level and annoyance in different surveys: A railway noise *vs*. aircraft and road traffic comparison. *J. Sound Vib.*, **81**, 51–80 (1982).

135 HALL, F. L., BIRNIE, S. E. TAYLOR, S. M. and PALMER, J. E. Direct comparison of community response to road traffic noise and to aircraft noise. *J. Acoust. Soc. Am.*, **70**, 1690–1698 (1981).

136 HEIMERL, G. and HOLZMANN, E. *Ermittlung der Belästingung durch Verkehrslärm in Abhangigkeit von Verkehrsmittel und Verkehrsdichte in einem Ballungsgebiet (Strassen-und Eissenbahnverkehr)*. Verkehrswissenschaftliches Institute an der Universität Stuttgart (1978). Summary of this work is translated as: *Determination of Traffic Nuisance as a Function of Traffic Type and Density in a Heavily Populated Area*, NASA TM–75414 (1979). NASA, Washington, D.C.

137 KNALL, V. I. and SCHUEMER, R. The differing annoyance levels of rail and road traffic noise. *J. Sound Vib.*, **87**, 321–326 (1983).

138 DE JONG, R. G. Some developments in community response research since the second international workshop on railway and tracked transit system noise in 1978. *J. Sound Vib.*, **87**, 305–306 (1983).

139 FIELDS, J. M. Railway noise annoyance in residential areas: current findings and suggestions for future research. *J. Sound Vib.*, **51**, 343–351 (1977).

140 LARGE, J. B. *Stansted Airport—London Future Development: Laboratory Study of Airborne Aircraft, Airport Ground and Road Traffic Noise*. BAA Report 183, British Airports Authority, (1981).

141 OHRSTROM, E., BJORKMAN, M. and RYLANDER, R. Laboratory annoyance and different traffic noise sources. *J. Sound Vib.*, **70**, 333–341 (*see* especially p. 338) (1980).

142 HEIMERL, G and HOLZMAN, E. *Ermittlung der Belästingung durch Verkehrslärm in Abhangigkeit von Verkehrsmittel und Verkehrsdichte in einem Ballungsgebiet (Strassen-und Eisenbahnverkehr)*. Verkehrswissenschaftliches Institute an der Universität Stuttgart, p. 80 (1978). Summary of this work is translated as: *Determinatin of Traffic Noise Nuisance as a Function of Traffic Type and Density in a Heavily Populated Area*, NASA, TM–75414 (1979). NASA, Washington, D.C.

143 RICE, C. G. Development of cumulative noise measure for the prediction of general annoyance in an average population. *J. Sound Vib*, **52**, 354–355 (1977).

144 FIELDS, J. M. and WALKER, J. G. Comparing the relationships between noise level and annoyance in different surveys: A railway noise *vs*. aircraft and road traffic comparison. *J. Sound Vib.*, **81**, 72–73 (1982).

145 HEDE, A. J. and BULLEN, R. B. *Aircraft Noise in Australia: A Survey of Community Reaction*. NAL Report 88, National Acoustic Laboratories, Commonwealth Department of Health, Canberra, Australia, p. 85 (1982).

146 DE JONG, R. G. *Community Response Surveys and the Dutch Noise*

Abatement. Internoise 1980, pp. 787–92 (*see* especially p. 790) (1981).

147 Institute für praxisorientierte Sozialforschung. *Störwirkungen durch den Lärm der Kleinaviatik*. Bundesamt für Umweltschutz, Berne (1980). Translation available as: *Annoyance Caused by Light Aircraft Noise*. NASA TM–76533. NASA, Washington, D.C.

148 CERPAIR and ARC. *La Gêne Causée Par L'Aviation Légère Enquête Effectuée Autour de Quatre Aérodromes de la Région Parisienne. CERPAIR, St.-Cyr-L'École; and ARC, Paris (1978)*. Translation available as: *Annoyance from Light Aircraft Investigation Carried Out Around Four Airports Near Paris*, NASA TM–75823 (1980). *Nuisance Caused by Light Aviation: Enquiry Conducted Around Four Aerodromes of The Parisian District:* Appendix to the main report, NASA TM–76532 (1981). NASA, Washington, D.C.

149 ROHRMANN, B. *Die Gestörtheit Der Bevölkerung Durch Den Flugbetrieb Auf Landeplätzen (The Disturbance of the Population by Aircraft Operations at Airports)*. Prepared for Bundesministeriums des Innern, Bonn, (Unpublished Report) (1975). Translation available as: *Disturbance to the Population due to Flight Operations at Landing Fields*. NASA TM–76531 (1981). NASA, Washington, D.C.

150 ROHRMANN, B. *Community Reaction on Non-commercial and Sporting Aviation*. Internoise 76, pp. 427–430. (*see* especially p. 430) (1976).

151 BIRNIE, S. E., HALL, F. L. and TAYLOR, S. M. Community response to noise from a general aviation airport. *Noise Control Eng.*, **15**, 37–45 (1980).

152 ORLICH, G. P. *Community Attitudes, Before and After Barrier Construction*. Minnesota Department of Transportation DOT–FH–11–9490 (1979).

153 HALL, F. L., BIRNIE, S. E. and TAYLOR, S. M. The effectiveness of shielding in reducing the adverse impacts of highway traffic noise. *Transportation Res. Rec.* **686**, 33–37 (1979).

154 SCHOLES, W. E. *The Physical and Subjective Evaluation of Roadside Barriers*. Internoise 77, pp. A144–A153 (1977).

155 LANGDON, F. J. and GRIFFITHS, I. D. Subjective effects of traffic noise exposure, II: Comparison of noise indices, response scales, and the effects of change in noise levels. *J. Sound Vib.*, **82**, 171–180 (1982).

156 VALLET, M., ABRAMOVITCH, J. M. and LAMBERT, J. *Impact of Noise Barrier on People Annoyance: Case Study at L'Hay Les Roses-France*. Internoise 79, pp. 865–868, Warsaw (1979).

157 FIDELL, S., HORONJEFF, R., TEFFETELLER, S. and PEARSONS, K. *Community Sensitivity to Changes in Aircraft Noise Exposure*. NASA CR-3490, March, p. 26 (1981).

158 FRANCOIS, J. *Les Répercussions Du Bruit Des Avions Sur L'Équilibre Des Riverains Des Aéroports: Etude Longitudinal Autour De Roissy, 3éme Phase (Effects of Aircraft Noise on The Equilibrium of Airport Residents: Longitudinal Study Around Roissy, Phase 3)* IFOP/ETMAR, Paris, p. 52 (1979). Translation available as: *Effect of Aircraft Noise on The Equilibrium of Airport Residents: Longitudinal Study Around Roissy—Phase 3*, NASA, TM–75906 (1981). NASA, Washington, D.C.

159 TAYLOR, S. M. and HALL, F. L. Factors affecting response to road noise. *Environment and Planning A*, **9**, 585–597 (*see* especially p. 594) (1977).

160 WEHRLI, B., NEMECEK, J., TURRIAN, V., HOFMANN, R. and WANNER, H. U. Auswirkungen der Strassenwerkehrslärm in der Nacht. *Kampf dem Lärm*, **25**, 146 (1978). Translation available as: *Effects of Street Traffic Noise in the Night*, NASA, TM–75495 (1980). NASA, Washington, D.C.

161 SORENSEN, S., BERGLUND, K. and RYLANDER, R. *Reaction Patterns in Annoyance Response to Aircraft Noise*. Proceedings of the International Congress on Noise as a Public Health Problem, Dubrovnik, Yugoslavia, p. 671 (1973).

162 AUBREE, D., AUZOU, J. and RAPIN, M. *Étude de la Gêne due au Trafic Automobile Urbain: Compte Rendu Scientifique (Study of Annoyance due to Urban Automobile Traffic: Scientific Report)*. CSTB, Paris, D.G.R.S.T. No. 68–01–389, June, p. 43 (1971).

163 AYLOR, D. E. and MARKS, L. E. Perception of noise transmitted through barriers. *J. Acoust. Soc. Am.*, **59**, 397–400 (1976).

164 FLINDELL, I. H. *A Laboratory Study of the Perceived Benefit of Additional Noise Attenuation by Houses*. TM–85647 (1983).

165 BOWSHER, J. M., JOHNSON, D. R. and ROBINSON, D. W. A further

experiment of judging the noisiness of aircraft in flight. *Acustica,* **17,** 245–267 (1966).

166 VAN DONGEN, J. E. F. *Evaluation of Noise Abatement Measures. Internoise 81,* pp. 813–16 (1981).

167 LANGDON, F. J. and BULLER, I. B. Road traffic noise and disturbance to sleep. *J. Sound Vib.,* **50,** 27 (1977).

168 WEHRLI, B., NEMECEK, J., TURRIAN, V., HOFFMANN, R. and WANNER, H. U. Auswirkungen der Strassenverkehrslärm in der Nacht. *Kampf dem Lärm,* **25,** 112 (1978). Translation available as *Effects of Street Traffic Noise in The Night,* NASA, TM–79495 (1980).

169 RELSTER, E. *Traffic Noise Annoyance, The Psychological Effect of Traffic Noise in Housing Areas.* Polyteknisk Forlag, Lyngby, Denmark (*see* especially p. 69) (1975).

170 AUBREE, D., AUZOU, J. and RAPIN, M. *Étude de la Gêne due au Trafic Automobile Urbain: Compte Rendu Scientifique (Study of Annoyance due to Urban Automobile Traffic: Scientific Report).* (STB, Paris, D.G.R.S.T. No. 68–01–389, June, p. 67 (1971).)

171 AUBREE, D. *La Gêne due au Bruit des Trains (Annoyance Due to Train Noise).* CSTB, Nantes, EN–SH–75.2, p. 44 (1975).

172 LAMURE, C. and BACELON, M. *La Gêne due au Bruit de la Circulation Automobile: Une Enquête Auprès de Riverians d'Autoroutes.* Cahiers du Centre Scientifique et Technique du Batiment, no. 88, C.S.T.B., Paris (1967). Translation available as: *The Nuisance Due to the Noise of Automobile Traffic: An Investigation in the Neighbourhoods of Freeways.* NASA, TM–75812 (1980). NASA, Washington, D.C.

173 DE JONG, R. G. Some developments in community response research since the second international workshop on railway and tracked transit system noise in 1978. *J. Sound Vib.,* **87,** 298–299 (1983).

174 CONNOR, W. K. and PATTERSON, H. P. *Community Reaction to Aircraft Noise Around Smaller City Airports.* NASA CR–2104 (1972).

175 GRIFFITHS, I. D., LANGDON, F. J. and SWAN, M. A. Subjective effects of traffic noise exposure: reliability and seasonal effects. *J. Sound Vib.,* **71,** 232–236 (1980).

176 DE JONG, R. G. *Some Highlights from the Dutch Aircraft Noise Studies.* Publication No. 765, TNO Research Institute for Environmental Hygiene, Delft, Netherlands (*see* especially p. 8) (1981).

177 BITTER, C. *Beleving van Geluidwerende Voorzieningen Tegen Vliegtuiglawaai in de Woonsituatie—de enquête Vóór Het Aanbrengen Van de Geluidwerende Voorzieningen. Band 1: Tekstgedeelte, and Band 2 Tabellen (Experience of Noise Abatement Measures against Aircraft Noise on Residences—The Survey Before the Noise Abatement Measures. Part 1: Text, Part 2: Tables).* Report D44, March, 1980, IMG–TNO, Delft, Netherlands (1980).

178 FIELDS, J. M. and WALKER, J. G. Comparing the relationships between noise levels and annoyance in different surveys: A railway noise *vs.* aircraft and road traffic comparison. *J. Sound Vib.,* **81,** 69 (1982).

179 OLLERHEAD, J. B. *Variation in Community Noise Sensitivity with Time of Day.* Internoise 77, pp. B642–B697 (*see* especially p. B694).

180 NEMECEK, J., WEHRLI, B. and TURRIAN, V. Effects of the noise of street traffic in Switzerland. A review of four surveys. *J. Sound Vib.,* **78,** 226 (1981).

181 PATTERSON, H. P., EDMISTON, R. P. and CONNOR, W. K. *Preliminary Evaluation of the Effect of a Dynamic Preferential Runway System Upon Community Noise Disturbance.* NASA CR–125821 (1972).

182 FIELDS, J. M. *Variability in Individuals' Responses to Noise: Community Differences.* Proceedings of Internoise 1983, pp. 965–68 (1983).

183 JONSSON, E., KAJLAND, A., PACCAGNELLA, B. and SORENSEN, S. Annoyance reactions to traffic noise in Italy and Sweden. *Arch. Environ. Hlth.* **19,** 692–699 (1969).

184 GRAF, P., MULLER, R. and MEIER, H. P. *Sozio-psychologische Fluglärmuntersuchung im Gebiet der drei Schweizer Flughäfen, Zürich, Genf, Basel,* p. 142 (1974). Translation available as: *Sociopsychological Investigation of Airport Noise in The Vicinities of Three Swiss Airports, Zurich, Geneva, Basel.* NASA, TM–75787 (1980). NASA, Washington, D.C.

185 ROHRMANN, B., FINKE, H., GUSKI, R., SCHÜMER, R., and SCHÜMER-KOHRS, A. *Fluglärm und seine Wirkung auf den Menschen: Methoden und Ergebnisse der Forschung, Consequenzen für den Umweltschutz. (Aircraft Noise and its Effects on Man: Methods and Results of Research, Consequences for Environmental Protection).* Hans Huber, Bern (1978).

186 FIELDS, J. M. and WALKER, J. G. The response to railway noise in residential areas in Great Britain. *J. Sound Vib.,* **85,** 217 (1982).

187 BRADLEY, J. S. and JONAH, B. A. *A Field Study of Human Response to Traffic Noise.* SV–77–2, Faculty of Engineering Science, University of Western Ontario (1977).

188 LANGDON, F. J. Noise nuisance caused by road traffic in residential areas, Parts I, II. *J. Sound Vib.,* **47,** 257, 271 (1976).

189 LANGDON, F. J. Noise nuisance caused by road traffic in residential areas, Parts I, II. *J. Sound Vib.,* **47,** 255 (1976).

190 FIELDS, J. M. *Designing Community Surveys to Provide a Basis for Noise Policy,* TM–80110. NASA, Washington, D.C., p. 8 (1980).

191 LEONARD, S. and BORSKY, P. N. A causal model for relating noise exposure, psychosocial variables and aircraft noise annoyance. In *Proceedings of The International Congress on Noise as a Public Health Problem, Dubrovnik, Yugoslavia,* USEPA 550–9–008, pp. 691–705 US Environmental Protection Agency, Washington, D.C. (1973).

192 FIELDS, J. M. and WALKER, J. G. The response to railway noise in residential areas in Great Britain. *J. Sound Vib.,* **85,** 235 (1976).

193 RYLANDER, R., SORENSEN, S. and KAJLAND, A. Annoyance reaction from aircraft noise exposure. *J. Sound Vib.,* **24,** 419–444 (*see* especially p. 432) (1972).

194 GRAF, P., MULLER, R. and MEIER, H. P. *Sozio-psychologische Fluglärmuntersuchung im Gebiet der drei Schweizer Flughäfen, Zürich, Genf, Basel,* p. 291 (1974). Translation available as: *Sociopsychological Investigation of Airport Noise in The Vicinities of Three Swiss Airports, Zurich, Geneva, Basel,* NASA, TM–75787 (1980). NASA, Washington, D.C.

195 and 196 NEMECEK, J., WEHRLI, B. and TURRIAN, V. Effects of the noise of street traffic in Switzerland, a review of four surveys. *J. Sound Vib.,* **78,** 231 (1981).

197 AUBREE, D., AUZOU, J. and RAPIN, M. *Étude de la Gêne due au Trafic Automobile Urbain: Compte Rendu Scientifique (Study of Annoyance due to Urban Automobile Traffic: Scientific Report).* C.S.T.B, Paris, D.G.R.S.T. No. 68–01–389, June, p. 42 (1971).

198 MCKENNELL, A. C. *Reactions to Concorde Flights by Heathrow Residents.* Internoise 78, San Francisco, pp. 573–78 (1978).

199 Deutsche Forschungsgemeinschaft. *DFG-Forschungsbericht Fluglärmwirkungen: Eine Interdisziplinäre Untersuchung über die Auswirkungen des Fluglärms auf den Menschen (DFG Research Report on Aircraft Noise: An Interdisciplinary Investigation of The Effect of Aircraft Noise on People).* Harald Boldt Verlag KG, Boppard, p. 225 (1974).

200 LANGDON, F. J. Noise nuisance caused by road traffic in residential areas, Parts I, II. *J. Sound Vib.,* **47,** 257 (1976).

201 CEDERLOF, R., JONSSON, E. and SORENSEN, S. On the influence of attitudes to the source on annoyance reactions to noise: a field experiment. *Nordisk Hygienisk Tidskrift,* **48,** 46–55 (1967).

202 Deutsche Forschungsgemeinschaft. *DFG-Forschungsbericht Fluglärmwirkungen: Eine Interdisziplinäre Untersuchung über die Auswirkungen des Fluglärms auf den Menschen (DFG Research Report Aircraft Noise: An Interdisciplinary Investigation of The Effect of Aircraft Noise on People).* Harald Boldt Verlag KG, Boppard, p. 181 (1974).

203 LEONARD, S. and BORSKY, P. A causal model for relating noise exposure, psycho-social variables and aircraft noise annoyance. In *Proceedings of The International Congress on Noise as a Public Health Problem, Dubrovnik, Yugoslavia, May 13–18* USEPA 550–9–008, p. 698 US Environmental Protection Agency, Washington, D.C. (1973).

204 AUBREE, D., AUZOU, J. and RAPIN, M. *Étude de la Gêne due au Trafic Automobile Urbain: Compte Rendu Scientifique (Study of Annoyance due to Urban Automobile Traffic: Scientific Report).* CSTB, Paris, D.G.R.S.T. No. 68–01–389, June, p. 42 (1971).

205 NEMECEK, J., WEHRLI, B. and TURIAN, V. Effects of the noise of street traffic in Switzerland, a review of four surveys. *J. Sound Vib.,* **78,** 231 (1981).

206 LEONARD, S. and BORSKY, P. A causal model for relating noise exposure, psycho-social variables and aircraft noise annoyance. In *Proceedings of The International Congress on Noise as a Public Health Problem, Dubrovnik, Yugoslavia, May 13–18,* USEPA 550–9–008, US Environmental Protection Agency, Washington, D.C. p. 697 (1973).

207 MCKENNELL, A. C. *Aircraft Noise Annoyance Around London (Heathrow) Airport*. Central Office of Information, S.S. 337, Government Social Survey, p. 6–5 (1963).

208 AUBREE, D., AUZOU, J. and RAPIN, M. *Étude de la Gêne due au Trafic Automobile Urbain: Compte Rendu Scientifique (Study of Annoyance due to Urban Automobile Traffic: Scientific Report)*. CSTB, Paris, D.G.R.S.T. No. 68–01–389, June, p. 42 (1971).

209 NEMECEK, J., WEHRLI, B. and TURIAN, V. Effects of the noise of street traffic in Switzerland, a review of four surveys. *J Sound Vib.*, **78**, 231 (1981).

210 Deutsche Forschungsgemeinschaft. *DFG-Forschungsbericht Fluglärmwirkungen: Eine Interdisziplinäre Untersuchung über die Auswirkungen des Fluglärms auf den Menschen (DFG Research Report on Aircraft Noise: An Interdisciplinary Investigation of The Effect of Aircraft Noise on People)*. Harald Boldt Verlag KG, Boppard, p. 499 (1974).

211 TAYLOR, S. M., BIRNIE, S. E. and HALL, F. L. Housing type and tenure effects on reactions to road traffic noise. *Environment and Planning A*, **10**, 1377–1386 (1978).

212 BRADLEY, J. S. and JONAH, B. A. The effects of site selected variables on human responses to traffic noise, Part I: type of housing by traffic noise level. *J Sound Vib.*, **66**, 603 (1979).

213 FIELDS, J. M. and WALKER, J. G. The response to railway noise in residential areas in Great Britain. *J. Sound Vib.*, **85**, 223 (1982).

214 GRAF, P., MULLER, R., and MEIER, H. P. *Sozio-psychologische Fluglärmuntersuchung im Gebiet der drei Schweizer Flughäfen, Zürich, Genf, Basel*, p. 80. (1974). Translation available as: *Sociopsychological Investigation of Airport Noise in The Vicinities of Three Swiss Airports, Zurich, Geneva, Basel*. NASA TM–75787 (1980). NASA, Washington, D.C.

215 FIELDS, J. M. and WALKER, J. G. The response to railway noise in Great Britain. *J. Sound Vib.*, **85**, 186 (1982).

216 MORTON-WILLIAMS, J., HEDGES, B. and FERNANDO, E. *Road Traffic and The Environment*, Social and Community Planning Research, London, p. 40 (1978).

217 NEMECEK, J., WEHRLI, B. and TURRIAN, V. Effects of the noise of street traffic in Switzerland, a review of four surveys. *J. Sound Vib.*, **78**, 228 (1981).

218 LAMBERT, J., SIMONNET, F. and VALLET, M. Patterns of behaviour in dwellings exposed to road traffic noise. *J. Sound Vib.*, **92**, 164 (1984).

219 MORTON-WILLIAMS, J., HEDGES, B. and FERNANDO, E. *Road Traffic and The Environment*, Social and Community Planning Research, London, p. 40 (1978).

220 FIELDS, J. M. and WALKER, J. G. The response to railway noise in residential areas in Great Britain. *J. Sound Vib.*, **85**, 186 (1982).

221 MIL Research. *Second Survey of Aircraft Noise Annoyance Around London (Heathrow) Airport*. HMSO, London, p. 53 (1971).

222 and 223 GRAF, P., MULLER, R. and MEIER, H. P. *Socio-psychologische Fluglärmuntersuchung im Gebiet der drei Schwiezer Flughäfen Zurich, Genf, Basel*, Appendix 3, pp. 80, 81 (1974). Translation available as: *Sociopsychological Investigation of Airport Noise in The Vicinity of Three Swiss Airports, Zurich, Geneva, Basel*. NASA, TM–75787 (1980).

224 MORTON-WILLIAMS, J., HEDGES, B. and FERNANDO, E. *Road Traffic and The Environment*, Social and Community Planning Research, London, p. 38 (1978).

225 GRAF, P., MULLER, R. and MEIER, H. P. *Socio-psychologische Fluglärmuntersuchung im Gebiet der drei Schweizer Flughäfen, Zürich, Genf. Basel*, Appendix 3, p. 41 (1974). Translation available as: *Sociopsychological Investigation of Airport Noise in The Vicinity of Three Swiss Airports, Zurich, Geneva, Basel*. NASA, TM–75787 (1980). NASA, Washington, D.C.

226 LAMBERT, J., SIMONNET, F. and VALLET, M. Patterns of behaviour in dwellings exposed to road traffic noise. *J. Sound Vib.*, **92**, 164 (1984).

227 NEMECEK, J., WEHRLI, B. and TURRIAN, V. Effects of the noise of street traffic in Switzerland, a review of four surveys. *J. Sound Vib.*, **78**, 228 (1981).

228 MCKENNELL, A. C. Methodological problems in a survey of aircraft noise annoyance *The Statistician*, **19**, 10 (1969).

229 Deutsche Forschungsgemeinschaft. *DFG-Forschungsbericht. Fluglärmwirkungen: Eine Interdisziplinare Untersuchung uber die Auswirkungen des Fluglärms auf den Menschen (DFG Research Report Aircraft Noise: An Interdisciplinary Investigation of The*

Effect of Aircraft Noise on People). Harald Boldt Verlag KG, Boppard, p. 189 (1974).

230 GRAF, P., MULLER, R. and MEIER, H. P. *Socio-psychologische Fluglärmuntersuchung im Gebeit der drei Schwiezer Flughäfen, Zurich, Genf, Basel*, Appendix 3, p. 79 (1974). Translation available as: *Sociopsychological Investigation of Airport Noise in The Vicinity of Three Swiss Airports, Zurich, Geneva Basel*. NASA, TM–75787 (1980). NASA, Washington, D.C.

231 GRAF, P., MULLER, R. and MEIER, H. P. *Socio-psychologische Fluglärmuntersuchung im Gebeit der drei Schweizer Flughäfen, Zurich, Genf, Basel*, p. 239 (1974). Translation available as: *Sociopsychological Investigation of Airport Noise in The Vicinity of Three Swiss Airports, Zurich, Geneva, Basel*. NASA, TM–75787 (1980). NASA, Washington, D.C.

232 AVERY, G. C. Comparison of telephone complaints and survey measures of noise annoyance. *J. Sound Vib.*, **82**, 215–225 (*see* especially p. 221) (1982).

233 MCKENNELL, A. C. *Aircraft Noise Annoyance Around London (Heathrow) Airport*. Central Office of Information, S.S. 337, Government Social Survey, p. 3–7 (1963).

234 GUSKI, R. An analysis of spontaneous noise complaints. *Env. Res.*, **13**, 229–236 (*see* especially p. 233) (1977).

235 MCKENNELL, A. C. *Aircraft Noise Annoyance Around London (Heathrow) Airport*. Central Office of Information, S.S. 337, Government Social Survey, p. 3–7 (1963).

236 GUSKI, R. An analysis of spontaneous noise complaints. *Env. Res.*, **13**, 234 (1977).

237 Tracor, Inc. *Community Reaction to Airport Noise*, Vol. I, NASA CR–1761; Vol.II, NASA CR–111316, p. 25 (1971).

238 Tracor, Inc. *Community Reaction to Airport Noise*. Vol. I, NASA CR–1761; Vol. II, NASA CR–111316, p. 67 (1971).

239 LINDVALL, T. and RADFORD, E. P. Measurement of annoyance due to exposure to environmental factors. *Env. Res.*, **6**, 15 (1973).

240 BORSKY, P. N. Review of community response to noise. In *Proceedings of The Third International Congress on Noise as a Public Health Problem*, ASHA Report 10, American Speech–Language–Hearing Association, Rockville, Md., pp. 453–74 (*see* especially p. 470) (1980).

241 LANGDON, F. J. Noise nuisance caused by road traffic in residential areas, Parts I, II. *J. Sound Vib.*, **47**, 249 (1976).

242 Tracor, Inc. *Community Reaction to Airport Noise*. (K. H. Craik and E. H. Zube, eds) Vol. I, NASA CR–1761; Vol. II, NASA CR–111316, p. 25 (1971).

243 MCKENNELL, A. C. *Aircraft Noise Annoyance Around London (Heathrow) Airport*. Central Office of Information, S.S. 337, Government Social Survey, p. 7–2 (1963).

244 GUSKI, R. An analysis of spontaneous noise complaints. *Env. Res.*, **13**, 233 (1977).

245 Tracor, Inc. *Community Reaction to Airport Noise*. Vol. I, NASA CR–1761; Vol. II, NASA CR–111316, p. 25 (1971).

246 AVERY, G. C. Comparison of telephone complaints and survey measures of noise annoyance. *J. Sound Vib.*, **82**, 224 (1982).

247 GUSKI, R. An Analysis on spontaneous noise complaints. *Env. Res.*, **13**, 234 (1977).

248 AVERY, G. C. Comparison of telephone complaints and survey measures of noise annoyance. *J. Sound Vib.*, **82**, 224 (1982).

249 LUKAS, J. S. and SWING J. W. Effects of freeway noise on hearing levels and academic achievement of children—Preview of a study. In *Internoise 78*, pp. 549–554 (*see* especially p. 551) (1978).

250 COHEN, S., EVANS, G. W., KRANTZ, D. S and STOKOLS, D. Physiological, motivational and cognitive effects of aircraft noise on children: moving from the laboratory to the field. *Am. Psychol.* **35**, 231–243 (1980).

251 COHEN, S., EVANS, G. W., KRANTZ, D. S., STOKOLS, D. and KELLY, S. Aircraft noise and children: longitudinal and cross-sectional evidence on adaptation to noise and the effectiveness of noise abatement. *J. Personality Soc. Psychol.*, **40**, 331–345 (1981).

252 CROOK, M. A. and LANGDON, F. J. The effects of aircraft noise in schools around London airport. *J. Sound Vib.*, **34**, 221–232 (1974).

253 KO, N. W. M. Responses of teachers to aircraft noise. *J. Sound Vib.*, **62**, 277–292 (1979).

254 PEARSONS, K. S., BENNETT, R. L. and FIDELL, S. *Speech Levels in Various Environments*. EPA–600/1–77–025. US Environmental Protection Agency, Washington. D.C. (1977).

255 COHEN, S., GLASS, D. C. and SINGER, J. E. Apartment noise,

auditory discrimination, and reading ability in children. *J. Exp. Soc. Psychol.* **9**, 407–422 (1973).

256 BRONZAFT, A. L. and MCCARTHY, D. P. The effect of elevated train noise on reading ability. *Env. Behav.*, **7**, 517–527 (1975).

257 LEHMANN, A. and GRATIOT ALPHANDERY, H. Effect of Noise on children at School. In *Proceedings of the Fourth International Congress On Noise As A Public Health Problem.* Milano, Italy,: Centro Ricerche E Studi Amplifon, pp. 859–62 (1983).

258 BAKKE, P., GRANDJEAN, E. and LAUBER, A. Der Verkehrslärm und seine Störwirkungen auf Spitalpatienten (Traffic noise and its annoying effects on hospital patients). *Kämpf dem Lärm*, **25**, 35–39 (1978). Translation available as: *Traffic Noise and its Annoying Effects on Hospital Patients*, NASA TM–75813, (1980). (Quote from p. 11.) NASA, Washington, D.C.

259 DE JONG, R. G. *Community Response Surveys and The Dutch Noise Abatement. Internoise 81*, p. 790 (1981).

260 WALKER, J. G. Noise in hospitals. In *Handbook of Noise Assessment* (D. N. May ed.), Van Nostrand Reinhold, New York, pp. 185–194 (1978).

261 WALKER, J. G. and MORGAN, P. A. *Effect of Aircraft Noise in Hospitals. Consultation Report 1323*, Wolfson Unit, I.S.V.R., Southampton, University (1970).

262 GROOM, D. and CHARLESTON, S. C. The effect of background noise on cardiac auscultation. *Am. Heart J.,* **52,** 781–790 (1956).

263 RICHARDS, E. J., CROOME, D. J. and MATTHEWS, D. *Acceptable Noise Levels in Doctors' Consulting Rooms. Proceedings of The 7th ICA*, Budapest, pp. 725–28 (1971).

264 GUSKI, R. *First Steps Toward the Concept of Quietness and its Psychological and Acoustical Determinants. Internoise 83*, pp. 843–46 (1983). International Congress on Acoustics.

265 For example, MOSER, C. and KALTON, G. *Survey Methods in Social Investigation* (2nd Edn.), Heinemann Educational Books, London (1971).

266 Wyle Research *Community Noise Assessment Manual: Social Survey Workbook.* El Segundo, Cal. (1981).

267 Wyle Research *Community Noise Assessment Manual: Acoustical Survey of a Community.* El Segundo, Cal. (1981).

268 FIELDS, J. M. The effect of numbers of noise events on people's reactions to noise: An analysis of existing survey data. *J. Acoust. Soc. Am.*, **75**, 463 (1984).

Further reading

FIELDS, J. M. and WALKER, J. G. The response to railway noise in residential areas in Great Britain. *J. Sound Vib.*, **85**, 177–255 (1982).

LAMBERT, J., SIMONNET, F. and VALLET, M. Patterns of Behavior in dwellings exposed to road traffic noise. *J. Sound Vib.*, **92**, 159–172 (1984).

MOSER, C. and KALTON, G. *Survey Methods in Social Investigation* (2nd Edn.), Heinemann Educational Books, London (1971).

SCHULTZ T. J. Synthesis of social surveys on noise annoyance. *J. Acoust. Soc. Am.*, **64**, 377–405 (1978).

TAYLOR, S. M. A comparison of models to predict annoyance reactions to noise from mixed sources. *J. Sound Vib.*, **81**, 123–128 (1982).

WEINSTEIN, N. D. Human evaluations of environmental noise. In *Perceiving Environmental Quality: Research and Applications*, (K. H. Craik and E. H. Zube, eds) Plenum Press, New York, pp. 229–52 (1976).

WILSON, A. *Noise: Final Report.* Cmnd. 2056, HMSO, London (1963).

4

Health Effects

S. Martin Taylor PhD
Department of Geography,
McMaster University,
Hamilton, Ontario,
Canada

Peter A. Wilkins PhD
Occupational Health Branch,
Health Department of Western Australia,
Perth,
Australia

Contents

4.1 Introduction

The possibility that noise has a detrimental effect on human health has been a strong impetus for research and a major argument for noise control. The deleterious effects on the auditory system of prolonged exposure to high levels of noise in industrial settings is well established. In contrast, the causal link between community noise, including transportation noise, and both auditory and non-auditory health outcomes remains uncertain and controversial. There are several reasons for this uncertainty including ambiguous definitions of health, the inherent complexity of disease causation and variability in research design and methodological rigour. Some elaboration of these issues is a necessary prelude to a review of the literature.

The question of what constitutes health, and therefore a health effect of noise, is fundamental but not easily resolved. The World Health Organization definition has gained wide acceptance. Health is regarded as more than the absence of disease; it is seen to encompass total physical and psychological well-being. In this context, the annoyance discussed in Chapter 3 would be considered to be a health effect. In the noise literature the term 'health effect' has been used more broadly than the WHO definition implies. It frequently refers to any measurable effect of noise on a body system (e.g. auditory, cardiovascular) whether or not the effect is known to be detrimental to well-being. The focus of this chapter will be on those possible effects of noise that are potentially detrimental. This means that the large volume of literature dealing with physiological effects with largely unknown consequences for well-being will receive little attention. Within the scope of this one chapter, this restriction is deemed both necessary and appropriate.

The emphasis in this chapter is on evaluating the strength of the evidence for a causal relationship between noise exposure and human health. The primary focus will be on exposure to transportation noise. As already implied, there is a logical basis for separating auditory and non-auditory effects, while recognizing that the two are not entirely unconnected.

The chapter is organized as follows. The next section briefly identifies the hypotheses linking noise and health which are implicit in the literature. Distinguishing between these different hypotheses has important implications in determining the effect of noise on human health status. The third section examines the analytical problems involved in assessing the determinants of health and especially the role of environmental factors. Recognizing these problems emphasizes the inherent difficulty of establishing the aetiological significance of environmental factors such as noise. Criteria for evaluating the evidence on noise and health are then presented. One set of criteria relate to methodological rigour and a second set comprises diagnostic tests of causation. The next two sections present assessments of the non-auditory and auditory effects of transportation noise. These lead to the summary and conclusions in the final section.

4.2 Hypotheses linking noise and health

Three hypotheses linking noise and health can be identified. The first proposes a direct causal link between noise exposure and ill health. This is the hypothesis underlying the effects of noise on the auditory system. In this case, there is a demonstrable biological mechanism to support the assertion that noise is the cause of detrimental health outcomes, for example, temporary or permanent hearing loss. This is the most straightforward hypothesis, the one most easily tested and the one leading to the strongest inferences about the causal effects of noise on health. It is not surprising, therefore, that the conclusions about the detrimental effects of high noise exposure on hearing are the most strongly substantiated.

The second hypothesis proposes an indirect effect of noise on health by means of some intervening process. The most common expression of this is the 'stress hypothesis'. The argument is that noise causes stress which, in turn, has a detrimental effect on health. This argument is more complicated and inherently weaker as a basis for causal inference than that for the first hypothesis. A fundamental problem is the definition of stress which cannot be defined or measured precisely. Vagueness in definition introduces ambiguity in the selection of stress indicators. Furthermore, apart from this fundamental problem, there remains the need to demonstrate that noise directly affects the stress indicator and that an increase in stress is directly linked to a reduction in health status. These complications inherent in the stress hypothesis lead to important questions about its value as a direction for research. A logical argument for avoiding the difficulties is that if noise is a 'stressor', and if stressors have detrimental effects on health, it should be possible to measure differences in health status directly in populations exposed and not exposed to high levels of noise. This approach avoids the problems of finding a definition for stress, of validating stress indicators, and of providing good evidence for a causal relationship between the indicators and health outcomes. Clearly the apparent simplicity of the stress hypothesis can be misleading and care should be taken when considering the evidence linking noise, stress and health that the inferential problems outlined above are not ignored.

The third hypothesis proposes that noise has a detrimental effect on those with certain existing disorders. This hypothesis underlies the suggestion that some populations are especially susceptible to exposure to high noise levels, for example people suffering hypertension or those with a history of psychiatric illness. In this sense, the role of noise is one of promoting rather than initiating a deterioration in health status. The biological mechanism is not as clear here as for the first hypothesis with the result that causal connections are harder to establish. The concept of stress is sometimes introduced as part of this hypothesis in which case the complications previously described occur.

In short, the link between noise and health can be conceptualized in different ways as expressed by these three hypotheses. It is important to distinguish them in attempting to establish the role of noise as a variable affecting human health.

4.3 Analytical problems

Several analytical problems beset the investigation of the health effects of transportation noise. Three of these are fundamental to all assessments of health risk and deserve brief elaboration. The first is the multiple causation of disease. A socio-ecological model of disease causation is gaining increasing acceptance in the health sciences.[1] In contrast to the conventional biomedical model, this approach assumes that disease outcomes are the result of a number of interacting biological, environmental and socio-demographic variables. Seldom, it is suggested, is it possible to ascribe causality to a single factor. A consequence of this approach is that it is difficult to isolate the magnitude of the causal effect on health of any one variable.

In the case of transportation noise, this difficulty is accentuated by a second problem. Outside of the workplace, exposure to high levels of noise over a prolonged period is exceptional. For the purpose of assessing health risk, therefore, transportation noise can best be regarded as an environmental agent of low toxicity. An implication of the relatively low level and intermittent exposure to noise in residential environments is that the effect of noise on health among other possible causal factors is both comparatively small and easily masked.

The third problem involves the long latency period of several of the diseases to which noise has been linked. The fact that diagnosis may occur at a time when an individual is exposed to high noise levels is not in itself strong evidence of a causal effect. In many instances the onset of disease precedes diagnosis by a lengthy period. Therefore, exposure levels months or even years before diagnosis may be the more salient consideration. This concern is especially important when examining health outcomes for a population that is residentially mobile and therefore potentially moving from one type of noise environment to another.

These three analytical complications apply most clearly to the effects of noise on non-auditory health outcomes where as already suggested the hypotheses linking noise and health are more complex. Recognition of these issues has led to more conservative assessments of the causal role of noise in recent reviews[2,3] together with appropriate words of caution about interpreting the dramatic claims of some earlier statements.

4.4 Evaluating studies on noise and health

The observation that the health effects of noise are not easily detected implies that very carefully designed studies are required to provide reliable evidence on the existence or non-existence of such effects. The continuing controversy in the literature is in part an outgrowth of the lack of rigorous studies such that a wide range of opinions can be supported. To establish the validity of statements linking noise and health requires evaluating the studies from which supporting evidence is drawn. For this purpose two sets of criteria are proposed. The first set comprises ten criteria for judging methodological rigour in research design, analysis and reporting. These are used to identify rigorous studies as the basis for assessing the strength of the evidence for a causal association between noise and health. The second set of criteria drawn from the epidemiological literature consists of nine diagnostic tests of causation.

The methodological criteria are:

1. *Health outcomes*: Does the outcome measure deal with ill health (e.g. cardiovascular disease) or with physiological changes of unknown consequences for well-being?
2. *Problem statement*: Is the research problem clearly stated and are the hypotheses explicit?
3. *Research setting*: Was the study conducted in a laboratory or field setting?
4. *Sample design*: Is the sample design explicit? Was the health status of subjects recorded prior to noise exposure? Is the sample size adequate to avoid small sample bias? Are response rates and other possible sources of bias reported? Was a control group used?
5. *Noise measure*: Are full details given about the frequency intensity and duration characteristics of the exposure?
6. *Compliance*: Where appropriate, was degree of compliance with intervention strategies (e.g. wearing hearing protection) reported?
7. *Confounding factors*: Are factors which might confound outcome measures acknowledged (e.g. physiological changes which are experimental artefacts)?
8. *Outcome measurement*: Are the outcome measures valid, sensitive and reliable?
9. *Analysis*: Are the analysis procedures replicable and valid?
10. *Interpretation*: Are the study conclusions justified by the research methodology and analytical results?

Studies judged to be rigorous by these criteria can be subse-

quently assessed using the diagnostic tests of causation[4] listed in descending order of importance:

1. *Study design*; Randomized control trials involving human subjects provide the strongest evidence for causation. Successively weaker evidence comes from cohort studies (in which the health status of a population is studied over time), case controls, field surveys and laboratory experiments.
2. *Strength of association*: Satisfied when significant differences in outcomes exist between exposed and non-exposed groups.
3. *Consistency*: Satisfied when independent studies yield the same conclusions about causal association.
4. *Temporality*: Satisfied when the health outcome post-dates exposure to the hypothesized cause.
5. *Gradient*: Satisfied when there is a direct relationship between the degree of exposure and the severity of the outcome.
6. *Epidemiologic sense*: Satisfied when the hypothesized cause–effect link is consistent with the known distribution of the health outcome in the general population.
7. *Biologic sense*: Satisfied when the cause–effect link is consistent with biologic mechanisms observed in animal studies.
8. *Specificity*: Satisfied in those few cases where the outcome is due to a single cause (e.g. hearing loss caused by industrial noise exposure).
9. *Analogy*: Satisfied when the cause–effect link is analogous to a causal association already confirmed by research evidence.

Notice that the diagnostic tests are not mutually exclusive. In particular, the study design influences to a considerable extent the strength of evidence determined from the other tests.

These two sets of criteria were used in recent reviews of the literature by one of the authors.[5,6] Similar criteria were applied in an assessment of studies on the effects of noise on the cardiovascular system.[7] These previous reviews are principal sources for the following section dealing with the non-auditory effects of transportation noise.

4.5 Assessment of non-auditory effects of transportation noise

This section begins with a brief description of the extent of the literature on the non-auditory effects of transportation noise. The major types of effect are identified under the headings of cardiovascular, reproductive and mental health. A synopsis of the conclusions for each of these is presented. Specific consideration is given to the strength of the evidence for a causal link between transportation noise exposure and health outcomes as well as the range of opinion present in the literature.

4.5.1 Extent of the literature

Transportation noise is generally at a lower level and more intermittent than noise from other environmental sources, especially industrial and construction noise. For this reason, the possible health effects of transportation noise have not been as extensively studied. None the less, a substantial volume of literature exists. The review by Taylor *et al.*[5] covered 1038 studies and included 495 references to non-auditory health effects of which 99 involved some form of transportation noise. The most frequently occurring effects were cardiovascular (25), neurological (12), reproductive (11), endocrine (10), non-specific (10) and mental health (9). Limiting attention to those studies which on the basis of methodological rigour provided the strongest evidence for human health effects reduced the main categories to cardiovascular, reproductive and mental health. The most frequently occurring sources were aircraft (64), road traffic (15) and rail (8). The predominance of studies involving aircraft noise is consistent with the comparatively higher levels of exposure at sites affected by aircraft and therefore the higher *a priori* expectation of the incidence of adverse effects on health.

A subsequent update review by the same authors[6] listed an additional 30 studies reporting non-auditory outcomes of which only five involved transportation noise. Of these, two dealt with general health indicators (e.g. drug use) in relation to aircraft noise, one with cardiovascular effects of road traffic noise, one with reproductive effects of aircraft noise and one with mental health effects of aircraft noise.

The review by Thompson[7] deals exclusively with cardiovascular outcomes. 83 studies are included. The large majority 62 involves industrial noise; 16 refer to transportation noise.

4.5.2 Cardiovascular outcomes

The relative emphasis on cardiovascular outcomes is easily explained. The prevalence of cardiovascular disease in the developed world is one reason. A second is the intuitive plausibility of a link between noise exposure and changes in the cardiovascular function. The latter is linked to the stress hypothesis previously discussed. Simply stated, the argument is that noise as a stressor can have detrimental physiological effects, including the promotion of hypertension, which in turn increase the risk of cardiovascular disease. The problems involved by invoking the stress concept have been considered. They remain essentially hypothetical as long as studies examine the direct link between noise exposure and cardiovascular function. There are several studies of this sort.[7]

The principal indicator of adverse cardiovascular effects is hypertension, normally defined as blood pressure above 160/100 mm Hg. Other indicators are pulse rate, respiratory rate, ECG, self-reported symptoms and cardiovascular morbidity and mortality rates. Hypertension is used in 10 of the 16 studies cited by Thompson. Six studies report greater incidence of hypertension in groups with high-noise exposure.[8-13] Four studies conclude no relationship between hypertension and exposure level.[14-17]

The most dramatic claim for cardiovascular effects comes from a study of mortality rates in areas exposed to different levels of aircraft noise in proximity to Los Angeles International Airport.[18] The researchers conclude that mortality due to stroke is significantly higher in the area exposed to aircraft noise in excess of 90 dB(A) (maximum level). Doubts about the methodological rigour of the study led to a re-analysis of the data with appropriate adjustments for age, race and sex differences.[19] The conclusion of this more rigorous analysis was that there were no significant differences in mortality.

This example underlines the importance of evaluating studies in terms of methodological criteria before making any inferences about causation. Application of the ten criteria previously described drastically reduces the number of studies for consideration. Only 10 studies linking transportation noise and non-auditory outcomes were judged methodologically rigorous in the evaluation by Taylor et al.[5] Only one of these, Frerichs et al.[19] dealt with cardiovascular effects and, as indicated, concluded no effect. The same conclusion is reported in a study by Knipschild and Salle[16], judged to be rigorous in the update review.[6]

The lack of rigorous studies precludes definitive conclusions about the link between noise and cardiovascular dysfunction. Further investigation employing stronger study designs and analytical procedures is needed. For example, Thompson[7] makes specific recommendations regarding the design of epidemiological studies to provide a data base for strong inference about the causal effect of noise on cardiovascular disease.

4.5.3 Reproductive outcomes

The hypothesis that exposure of the mother and foetus to high noise levels can have a detrimental effect has been examined in several studies. The health outcomes considered include prematurity, birth weight, birth defects and post-natal adaptability.

These possible reproductive effects gained recognition partly as a result of a series of studies by Ando and Hattori,[20-23] in which outcomes were compared between groups exposed to different levels of aircraft noise. In each study the authors reported significant differences leading to the conclusion that in high-noise areas there is a higher probability of prematurity, low birth weight and abnormal reaction to noise in infancy. However, several methodological problems[5]—including sample bias, confounding variables not accounted for and insufficient or inappropriate statistical tests—weaken the conclusions.

Jones and Tauscher[24] reported higher rates of birth defects in high-noise areas near Los Angeles airport. They presented data separately for blacks and whites but did not adjust for differences in age of mothers or for socio-economic class. As Bader[25] observes, these adjustments could quite possibly alter the conclusions. This highlights a fundamental difficulty in using cross-sectional field survey data; several plausible causal factors (e.g. age, race, socio-economic status) are likely to co-vary with noise exposure and distinguishing their separate effects may be very difficult to achieve.

Inconclusive results also emerge from one of the more recent studies around Schipol Airport, Amsterdam.[26] Birth records revealed a higher proportion of birth weights less than 3000 g in high-noise areas. The meaning of this finding is uncertain, however, since the WHO defines prematurity as a birth weight less than 2500 g. An examination of the data shows that the incidence of prematurity is almost identical between the two areas.

Possibly the most rigorous study to date is that by Edmonds et al.[27] Using data from the Metropolitan Atlanta Congenital Defects Program, they reported no difference between rates of birth defects in high- and low-noise areas. The data did indicate a higher, though still small, incidence of spina bifida in the high-noise areas but the results of a subsequent case–control study failed to confirm this difference.

As with cardiovascular disease, there are few rigorous studies on which to base a conclusion about the effects of transportation noise on reproductive outcomes. The strongest study concludes that there is no effect but not all outcomes are considered. Other studies suggest significant effects but the findings are weakened by methodological problems in design or analysis.

4.5.4 Mental health outcomes

Increased risk of psychiatric disorder is prima facie the most plausible non-auditory effect of exposure to transportation noise. The annoyance or disturbance induced by noise is well documented (*see* Chapter 3) and it is intuitively reasonable to suppose that among those especially sensitive, annoyance could lead to psychiatric symptoms.

The strongest claim for noise-induced mental illness is made by Meecham and Smith.[28] They used mental hospital admissions data from areas near Los Angeles Airport and concluded that admissions are 29% higher from areas exposed to high noise levels. However, there are methodological problems similar to those noted for the parallel study on cardiovascular mortality. Confounders such as age, sex and race are not adjusted for and the conclusions are therefore in question.

A series of studies around London's Heathrow Airport provide a stronger basis for inference. The first[29] involved a retrospective survey of psychiatric hospital admissions from two areas with different exposures to aircraft noise. Rates of first and overall admissions were significantly higher in the higher noise area. Those most affected were female, older and more prone to neurotic or organic mental illness. No claim is made that aircraft noise itself causes mental illness especially as several potential biases in the data are acknowledged.

Gattoni and Tarnopolsky[30] analysed an additional 2 years of data for the same hospital. They used a more precise method of identifying the population at risk and redefined the limit of the maximum noise area as 50 rather than 55 NNI. There was no significant difference in admission rates between the low and high noise areas, although the trends in the data were the same as those reported in the earlier Heathrow study.

A General Health Questionnaire was used to screen for psychiatric disorders in a pilot study involving 200 respondents.[31] Again, no significant difference was found between the high- and low-noise areas. The group at greatest risk was identified as female, younger and of higher educational and occupational status. The study concluded that the relationship between noise and psychiatric morbidity is complex and that factors such as annoyance and sensitivity need to be considered together with social and demographic variables.

In a more recent study, admissions to three psychiatric hospitals over a 4-year period were examined.[32] No consistent relationship between admissions and noise exposure was found leading the authors to conclude that any effect of noise is probably limited to a weak influence on more immediate causal factors.

Taken together, these findings provide no strong evidence that aircraft noise, and transportation noise generally, affects psychiatric morbidity. At the same time, much of the research has been hypothesis generating as much as hypothesis testing. The possibility remains that subsequent research may reveal that noise plays a contributory role in the complex aetiology of mental illness.

4.5.5 Other outcomes

Several studies have examined general indicators of morbidity. Fiedler and Fiedler[33] in a rigorous community survey found no association between residence in areas of high aircraft noise and self-reports of physical or mental effects. Similarly, Graeven[34] found no relation between noise exposure and self-reported health problems in a California survey of communities with different levels of aircraft noise. Data from the General Health Questionnaire administered around London Heathrow Airport include 27 acute and chronic health symptoms.[35] Chronic symptoms were more prevalent in low-noise areas and acute symptoms in high-noise areas but the authors concluded that there is no evidence that noise is a stressor with detrimental effects on health. Using the same data set, Watkins et al.[36] examined the use of drugs and medication, the use of psychotropic drugs, visits to a G.P. or out-patient clinic, in-patient status, and use of community health and welfare services. There was no consistent relationship with noise level for any of the six indicators.

Considerable debate has surrounded the possibility that low-frequency sound, including infrasound, has a detrimental effect on well-being. The frequency range of interest is generally below 100 Hz. Levels of 75–95 dB are commonly experienced by people living or working near to busy transportation routes, while levels up to 120 dB may be produced by road vehicles fitted with poor-quality silencers. Vehicle operators (e.g. locomotive engineers) are especially exposed to low-frequency sound and have been the subject for study.

Early papers examining the effects of low-frequency sound tended to be alarmist. Gavreau[37] warned of 'profound effects on both men and buildings'. Bryan and Tempest[38] gained considerable publicity for their paper, 'Does Infrasound Make Drivers Drunk?'. They claimed that infrasound within motor vehicles could be the cause of many unexplained highway accidents. However, little or no scientific data are reported to support these claims. Using experimental data, Evans and Tempest[39] reported significant effects of infrasound on visual nystagmus (involuntary eye movement) and reaction time, although the exposure levels (130–146 dB) were above those normally found in vehicles. Subsequent work,[40-41] however, does not support these conclusions.

The current balance of opinion,[42,43] based primarily on North American research, is that infrasound effects are found only at high noise levels which can be artificially created (i.e. in laboratory experiments) but rarely, if ever, occur in real world environments. The early reports of dramatic effects appear to be exaggerated. It must be remembered, however, that the research evidence applies to specific, short-term exposures. The effects of low-frequency sound of long duration have not been quantified. In this regard, the possible effects on vehicle operators, for example, justify further investigation.

4.6 Assessment of auditory effects of transportation noise

This section commences with brief reviews of the hearing process, the assessment of hearing and general causes of hearing loss. Noise damage to the ear is then considered and related to noise exposure. Specific evidence relating transportation noise to auditory effects is reviewed and the implications are discussed.

4.6.1 Auditory system

Hearing occurs through a process of transduction. The energy associated with the propagation of the sound waves is transduced to mechanical energy at the ear drum; this mechanical energy is transmitted via the three tiny bones of the middle ear to the fluid-filled chambers of the inner ear; here in the cochlea the energy of the wave motion in the fluids is transduced to electrical signals in the neural pathways.[44,45] The process of transduction in the cochlea is only partly understood, but it appears to involve the mechanical properties of the membranes in the cochlea and sensor cells known as 'hair cells'. The functioning of these hair cells is of considerable research interest because one of the key properties of hearing, its ability to separate and distinguish sounds of different frequencies, appears to depend crucially on the processing at this stage. It is also at this stage, where a form of mechanical energy becomes electrical energy, that the hearing process is most vulnerable.

The ultimate perception of a sound depends on a recognition of its meaning and a wide-ranging judgement of its quality and significance. This final process is less well understood, but involves the decoding of the neural signals at the auditory cortex, the extraction of particular features of the sound and possibly some matching of the patterns involved against a dictionary of such patterns.

4.6.2 Assessment of hearing

Hearing is used in the perception of speech and other environmental and recreational sounds and the judgement of the direction and distance of a sound source. These abilities, and their relative absence in terms of disabilities, can be measured in

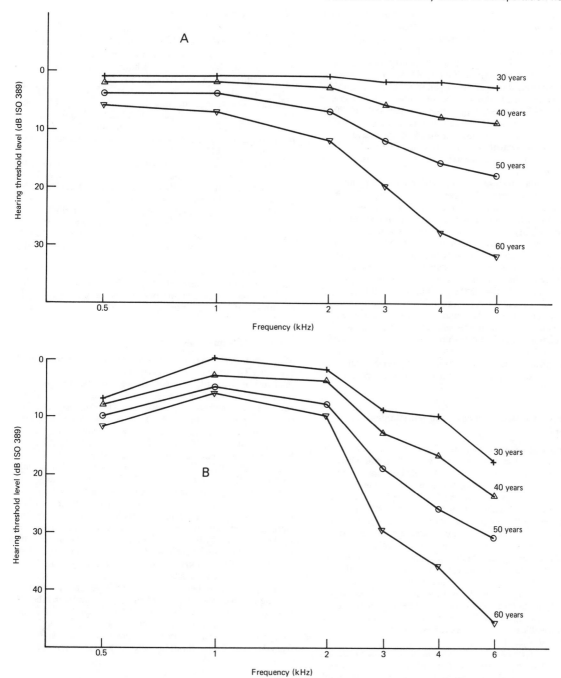

Figure 4.1 Median hearing threshold levels for males as a function of age.
(*a*) An otologically normal population ('highly screened').
(*b*) Typical unscreened population.
(Based on Annexes to ISO DIS 1999.)

tests of auditory task performance. More commonly, the assessment of hearing uses measures of impairment which test more abstract aspects of auditory perception. The most common of these is a test of the ability to hear faint sounds, the threshold of hearing. Other tests assess frequency resolution, temporal resolution and judgements of loudness and pitch.

The measure of hearing most widely used in relation to damage due to noise is the audiogram, which is made up of the thresholds of hearing at several different discrete frequencies. Pure tones are presented via an earphone, and the threshold is determined by varying the intensity of the discrete presentations so as to repeatedly cross from presentations which are not heard to those which are heard. The general format of an audiogram is shown in *Figure 4.1*. The various discrete frequencies are shown on the horizontal axis, and the threshold values are displayed on the vertical axis in terms of the Hearing Threshold Level (HTL) in dB. A Hearing Level of 0 dB has been established through international standardization (ISO R389:1975)[46] to represent the modal threshold of hearing for young adults free of all signs and symptoms of ear disease and of undue noise exposure. Hearing Threshold Levels larger than approximately 10–20 dB are indicative of hearing loss relative to this datum of normality. An impairment may also be determined by successive audiograms on one individual, with increases larger than 10–20 dB at a single frequency being taken as indicative of a deterioration in hearing sensitivity.

Pure-tone audiometry is the first, and often the only measure taken to assess hearing because of the relative simplicity, reliability and repeatability of the test. However, it must be recognized that the audiogram is only a very limited descriptor of hearing ability.[47] It is therefore not surprising that only limited success has been obtained in attempting to relate indices derived from the audiogram with measures of speech perception.[48] More recent attempts to establish a predictive relationship between a battery of tests of impairment and speech perception has provided at best a marginal improvement,[49] which is indicative of the complex auditory analysis involved in speech perception and the failure to incorporate measures related to the cognitive processes involved. Nevertheless, the search for this kind of relationship continues in the hope that better correlations can be obtained between appropriate measures of impairment and measures of conversational listening ability, and ultimately of the handicap experienced by the individual.[50]

4.6.3 Presbyacusis, sociocusis and pathological disorders

It has been observed in many studies that hearing sensitivity deteriorates with increasing age, though it is less clear whether it is age *per se* that is the cause of this deterioration. Various studies have shown a reasonably consistent pattern for this deterioration, and values of the age-related threshold level (ARTL) are provided in an annex to ISO DIS 1999 ratio 1982.[51] Median hearing threshold levels as a function of age are shown in *Figure 4.1(a)* for groups free of evidence of ear disease and undue noise exposure. It is evident that the decline in hearing sensitivity occurs more rapidly at higher frequencies, and although the data are not presented it should be noted that the decline is more severe for men than for women. The decline in hearing sensitivity is termed 'presbyacusis'. It has been argued that presbyacusis is due to a mixture of the effects of ageing and the loss in hearing due to the typical every-day sounds to which nearly the whole population are exposed (the latter effect having been termed 'sociocusis').[52]

Hearing defects can arise from a variety of causes including hereditary factors, disease, infection and accidents. These may affect the sound conducting pathways of the outer and middle ear, the sensori-neural processes which occur in the inner ear and along the auditory nerve, and the nerve pathways and perceptive processes in the brain. When dealing with populations that have not been screened for otological abnormalities, these pathologies will contribute to the overall hearing losses observed. There is only limited evidence of the incidence of hearing disorders in the general population,[53] and no standardized values exist. An example data base of a typical unscreened population is provided in an annex to ISO DIS 1999,[51] and this is illustrated in *Figure 4.1(b)*. The values of median hearing threshold level shown are anywhere between 0 and 14 dB higher than for the highly screened population.

4.6.4 Noise damage to the ear

Exposure to high levels of sounds causes a temporary loss of hearing sensitivity, a noise-induced temporary threshold shift (NITTS). There is a recovery from this in quiet conditions, the major part of which occurs in 24 hours but the recovery has been recorded over a period of up to 72 hours.

Repeated exposure to noises capable of producing NITTS eventually results in a measurable permanent loss of hearing sensitivity, a noise-induced permanent threshold shift (NIPTS). This loss is greatest at frequencies in the range 3–6 kHz which has resulted in audiograms associated with NIPTS being characterized by a '4 kHz notch'.

Prolonged exposure to high levels of noise destroys the hair cells in the inner ear. This damage is irreversible, and the progressive elimination of these cells reduces the ability of the ear to detect faint sounds. In addition, frequency selectivity and the ability to integrate sound energy over time deteriorate, and the ability to perceive speech in the presence of noise is reduced.[54] The damage is often accompanied by tinnitus, which is a spurious sensation of sounds also described as 'ringing in the ears'.

A different mechanism of damage to the ear can be caused by short duration exposures to very high noise levels. In this context, overriding maximum peak sound pressure level limits of 140–150 dB(lin) have been set.[55,56]

4.6.5 NIPTS and noise exposure

The degree of NIPTS is related to the noise level and duration of exposure. There is widespread acceptance that the best available predictor of hearing loss for continuous, variable and impulsive noises is the sound energy, as measured in the A-weighted equivalent continuous sound level, L_{eq}. The principal variation from this approach is the use by O.S.H.A. of a 5 dB trading rule, as distinct from the 3 dB rule implicit in the equal energy concept.[57] Starting with an exposure limit of 85 dB(A) for 8 hours, the energy concept permits as equivalents 88 dB(A) for 4 hours, 91 dB(A) for 2 hours etc., whereas the O.S.H.A. rule permits 90 dB(A) for 4 hours, 95 dB(A) for 2 hours, etc.

There is a large variation between individuals in their susceptibility to NIPTS, so that it is not possible to make accurate predictions for an individual. However, predictions of the statistical distributions of hearing losses for groups can be made, and ISO DIS 1999 provides formulae and tabulated data for this purpose. As an example, *Figure 4.2* shows the growth in median NIPTS at 4 kHz with years of exposure for four different noise exposure levels.

The relationship between noise exposure and permanent hearing loss has been established through a limited number of retrospective studies which determined threshold shifts and noise exposure levels and durations, for a sufficient number of subjects where the noise exposure did not vary substantially from day to day over durations ranging from several months to the full working lifetime.

4.6.6 NIPTS and low levels of noise exposure

The formulations in ISO DIS 1999 provide noise exposure cut-off levels as a function of frequency for which the calculated median NIPTS is zero. The lowest such cut-off is 75 dB(A) for NIPTS at 4 kHz. However, the data that contributed to this standard are likely to be less reliable for noise levels below approximately 85 dB(A) where unreported occupational and other noise exposures are likely to have a proportionally greater effect on the measured hearing thresholds.

On the basis of the available data, the Environmental Protection Agency (E.P.A.) in the United States has recommended the

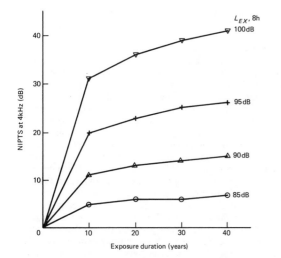

Figure 4.2 Median NIPTS at 4 kHz as a function of years of noise exposure and daily noise exposure level L_{EX} (8 h) (ISO DIS 1999). (NB L_{EX} (8h) is the cumulative sound energy exposure level over a continous 8 hour period.)

equivalent of 75 dB(A) over 8 hours as the limit for noise exposure in order to prevent any measurable hearing loss over a 40 year period.[58] Whilst this may appear to be over-protective in the context of proposed legislative limits for industrial noise of 85–90 dB(A),[56,59] it is appropriate in the context of the stated criteria and the data presented in ISO DIS 1999 which indicate that for daily noise exposures of 90, 85, 80 and 75 dB(A) over a 40-year period the resultant NIPTS at 4 kHz for the more sensitive 10th percentile drops through 20, 9, 2 to 0 dB.

4.6.7 Prevalence of NIPTS associated with transportation noise

The literature review by Taylor *et al.*[5] discussed in Sections 4.4 and 4.5 identified 12 papers considered justified and associated with transportation noise, and two of these were concerned with auditory effects. One of these two studies found a temporary threshold shift in highway patrolmen after patrol.[60] NIPTS is not accepted as a health-related auditory effect in the context of this review, although the authors refer to it as a health effect in the sense that, 'at the conclusion of a high-speed pursuit his life may depend on the ability to detect surreptitious sounds'. The other study used audiometric data on 3322 elementary school-children near Logan International Airport, Boston.[61] The authors found that the average sensori-neural gap, a measure of high-tone hearing loss, was not significantly related to the degree or duration of exposure to aircraft noise, when comparing children living under the flight path with those farther away.

The update review by Taylor *et al.*[6] identified one further paper which related NIPTS and transportation noise for ambulance paramedics.[62] The hearing threshold levels for the screened group were significantly greater than normative data for non-noise exposed populations cited from other studies at all but one test frequency, with the largest effects at 6 and 8 kHz.

Studies such as the two based on NIPTS described above add nothing to the existing knowledge relating noise exposure to hearing loss. They can assist in identifying situations in which hearing damage may be occurring, but to some extent the same information could be obtained by appropriate noise measurements and reference to ISO DIS 1999.

In principle, given a suitable noise survey the predictive

relationships referred to in Section 4.6.5 can be used to determine the NIPTS due to exposure to transportation noise. In cases where the noise exposures are less than 85 dB(A), as noted in Section 4.6.6 less confidence should be placed on the predictions obtained.

Information on noise exposures associated with transportation is not readily available. Illustrative noise levels are provided by Kryter,[52] which suggest the following typical levels for those on board the vehicle:

Motor cars[63]	65–85 dB(A)
Buses, trains	75–95 dB(A)
Trucks	80–90 dB(A)
Passenger aircraft	80–95 dB(A)

Whilst similar levels might be experienced by those near to but outside the vehicles, typical noise levels inside the home provided by Kryter cover the range 34–72 dB(A), with the highest level being associated with a jet aircraft overhead.

Any NIPTS associated with such noise levels would be dependent on the duration of exposure. In this context, Burns[64] speculated that for those living near to major airports there could be a significant risk of hearing loss. In particular, he noted that a noise exposure level of 85 dB(A) would be produced by 30 take-offs of level 110 dB(A), each having an effective duration of 3 s.

In cases where there is a strong predominance of low-frequency noise e.g. inside a motor car, there is some uncertainty about the validity of A-weighted measures for the determination of risk to hearing. This type of spectrum was not included in the extensive survey of Burns and Robinson[65] and so the relationships derived by them should not be extrapolated thoughtlessly to such cases. Conversely, there is not, however, any evidence of significant variations from the predictions based on A-weighted noise measures. Furthermore, Robinson[66] argues that such second-order effects are unlikely to be quantified reliably without rigorous surveys involving several hundred subjects.

4.6.8 The relationship of NIPTS to disability and handicap

When establishing statutory limits for noise exposure, the resultant impairment measured in terms of the NIPTS is difficult to interpret without some indication of the resultant disability or handicap. To this end, the British Standard 5330: 1976 sets a criterion for the minimum hearing level at which hearing handicap is considered to begin. According to this standard, a handicap is deemed to exist when the average hearing threshold level at 1, 2 and 3 kHz is equal to or greater than 30 dB, and the relationship between the percentage of noise-exposed persons deemed to have a handicap and their lifetime noise exposure is as shown in *Figure 4.3*. More recent data have, however, suggested that this criterion may not be sufficiently stringent, and that a criterion value of approximately 15 dB might be more appropriate.[67,68]

The disability associated with a noise-induced hearing impairment may first be manifest when trying to listen to a talker in a noisy environment such as a bar or a party, or when listening to distorted speech in a reverberant environment as occurs with a public address system in a large railway station. The impairment may also affect listening habits, such that the sound output of the television is turned up or the person sits nearer the speaker at a meeting. Whether a particular disability limits the individual's role fulfilment and therefore represents a handicap will depend on their life style and personality. In this sense handicap needs to be assessed through questionnaires, observation of behaviour in the social environment and the reporting of family, colleagues and friends.

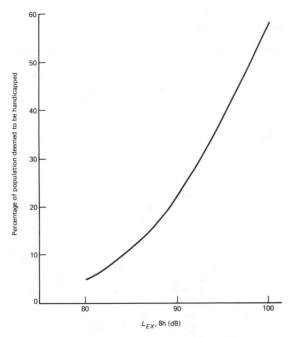

Figure 4.3 Percentage of noise-exposed persons deemed to be handicapped at the end of a nominal working life-time as a function of daily noise exposure level L_{EX} (8 h). The criterion of handicap (the average hearing threshold level at 1, 2 and 3 kHz is equal to or exceeds 30 dB) and data are from BS5330 and the values are derived on the basis of a working lifetime from ages 20–65 years.

4.6.9 Legislation and relevant standards

There are currently no known regulations or standards which deal specifically with the auditory effects of transportation noise. The various legislation and government proposals for occupational noise would apply to those employed persons exposed to the transportation noise. However, passengers and more generally those not at work, e.g. at home or involved in recreational activities would not be covered.

To answer whether there is a need for any legislation to protect the hearing of this latter group would require extensive surveys of the noise exposures related to transportation, and use of the available information relating noise exposure to hearing impairment. It is, however, likely that noise limits set to reduce annoyance would, if adequately enforced, also protect the hearing of those exposed to even the most stringent 75 dB(A) limit recommended by the E.P.A.

4.7 Conclusions

The distinction is drawn in epidemiology between the burden of proof and the burden of prudence. Both terms apply to the weight of evidence to support interventions designed to control or prevent disease; for example, the weight of evidence to justify banning the use of certain food additives or the television advertising of cigarettes. The distinction between them is the relative weight of evidence. The detrimental health effects of smoking are now generally accepted as proved and there is therefore the burden of proof to support interventions to reduce cigarette consumption. On the other hand, the evidence is not definitive regarding the effects of some additives, for example

saccharine, with the result that the burden of proof is lacking, but some jurisdictions may still justify intervention on grounds of the burden of prudence.

These two concepts can be applied in summarizing the balance of evidence on the health effects of noise and, specifically, transportation noise. The Environmental Protection Agency in the United States published a report in 1978 which argued that 'noise is more than just a nuisance. It constitutes a real and present danger to people's health'.[69] The same report concludes by quoting a former Surgeon General whose words speak directly to the proof/prudence issue: 'Must we wait until we prove every link in the chain of causation? ... In protecting health, absolute proof comes late. To wait for it is to invite disaster or to prolong suffering unnecessarily.' These emotive remarks are used to support the conclusion of the report that the burden of prudence justifies noise control measures.

There is no question that this conclusion is justified in relation to the detrimental effects of high noise exposure on hearing. In fact, in this case, the evidence provides the burden of proof. However, the evidence relates almost entirely to industrial noise exposure. As this review indicates, very few studies address the question of hearing loss due to exposure to transportation noise. Those most at risk are personnel in the transportation industry, especially airport ground staff. Beyond this group, it is unlikely that the general public will be exposed to sustained high levels of transportation noise sufficient to result in hearing loss. Transportation noise control in the community can therefore not be justified on grounds of hearing protection.

The evidence on the non-auditory effects of transportation noise is more ambiguous, leading to differences of opinion regarding the burden of prudence for noise control. There is no strong evidence that noise has a direct causal effect on such health outcomes as cardiovascular disease, reproductive abnormality or psychiatric disorder. At the same time, the evidence is not strong enough to reject the hypothesis that noise is in some way involved in the multi-causal process leading to these disorders. The implications of the research on the physiological effects of noise, where the cause and effect link appears stronger, are uncertain because the consequences of the physiological changes for well-being are largely unknown. Future epidemiological studies may yield more definitive results, particularly if more rigorous research designs are used. More precise measurement of noise exposure over extended time periods should be a priority design consideration so that the estimation of dose–response functions for health outcomes is possible. But even with necessary improvements in study design, the inherent difficulty of isolating the effect of a low dose agent such as transportation noise within a complex aetiological system will remain.

It seems unlikely, therefore, that research in the near future will yield findings which are definitive in either a positive or negative direction. Consequently, arguments for transportation noise control will probably continue to be based primarily on welfare criteria such as annoyance and activity disturbance. The question of whether transportation noise is more than just a nuisance will remain open. The possibility of detrimental health effects therefore constitutes additional, although only weak, support for noise control.

References

1   WHITE, N. F. (ed.) *The Health Conundrum: Explorations in Health Studies* (Chapters 1 and 6), Ontario Educational Communications Authority, Toronto, Ontario (1981).

2   KRYTER, K. D. Physiological Acoustics and Health. *Journal of the Acoustical Society of America*, **68**, 10–14 (1980).

3   STREAM, R. W. Effects of Industrial and Community Noise on

Health. In Trieff, N. M. (ed.) *Environment and Health*, Ann Arbor Science Publishers, Ann Arbor, Mi., pp. 331–66 (1980).

4 Department of Clinical Epidemiology and Biostatistics, McMaster University. How to read clinical journals IV: to determine etiology or causation. *Canadian Medical Association Journal*, **124**, 985–990 (1981).

5 TAYLOR, S. M., YOUNG, P. J., BIRNIE, S. E. and HALL, F. L. *Health Effects of Noise: A Review of Existing Evidence*, Research Report, Department of Geography, McMaster University, Hamilton, Ontario (1980).

6 TAYLOR, S. M., BIRNIE, S. E. and HALL, F.L. *Health Effects of Noise: Literature Survey Update*, Research Report, Department of Geography, McMaster University, Hamilton, Ontario (1982).

7 THOMPSON, S. J. *Epidemiology Feasibility Study: Effects of Noise on the Cardiovascular System*, Research Report, Department of Epidemiology and Biostatistics, University of South Carolina, Columbia, South Carolina 29208 (1981).

8 COHEN, S., EVANS, G. W., KRANTZ, D. S. and STOKOLS, D. Physiological, motivational and cognitive effects of aircraft noise on children. *American Psychologist*, **35**, 231–243 (1980).

9 COHEN, S., KRANTZ, D. S., EVANS, G. W., STOKOLS, D. and KELLY, S. Aircraft noise and children: Longitudinal and cross-sectional evidence on adaptation to noise and the effectiveness of noise abatement. *Journal of Personality and Social Psychology*, **40**, 331–345 (1981).

10 DI CANTOGNO, L. V., DALLERBA, R., TEAGNO, P. S. and COCOLA, L. Urban Traffic Noise, Cardiocirculatory Activity and Coronary Risk Factors. *Acta Otolaryngology Supplement*, **339**, 55–63 (1976).

11 KNIPSCHILD, P. Medical effects of aircraft noise: community cardiovascular survey. *International Archives of Occupational and Environmental Health*, **40**, 185–190 (1977).

12 MOSSKOV, J. I. and ETTEMA, J. H. Extra-auditory effects in short-term exposure to aircraft and traffic noise. *International Archives of Occupational and Environmental Health*, **40**, 165–173 (1977).

13 von EIFF, A. W. and NEUS, H. Traffic noise and hypertensive risk. *Munchen medizin wochenschrift*, **122**, 894–896 (1980).

14 DRETTNER, B., HEDSTRAND, H., KLOCKHOFF, I. and SVEDBERG, A. Cardiovascular risk factors and hearing loss: A study of 1000 fifty-year-old men. *Acta Otolaryngologica*, **79**, 366–371 (1975).

15 HEDSTRAND, H., DRETTNER, B., KLOCKHOFF, I. and SVEDBERG, A. Noise and blood pressure. *Lancet*, **ii**, 1291 (1977).

16 KNIPSCHILD, P. and SALLE, H. Road traffic noise and cardiovascular disease: a population study in the Netherlands. *International Archives of Occupational and Environmental Health*, **44**, 55–59 (1979).

17 TAKALA, J., VARKE, S., VAHERI, E. and SIEVERS, K. Noise and blood pressure. *Lancet*, **ii**, 974–975 (1977).

18 MEECHAM, W. C. and SHAW, N. Effects of jet noise on mortality rates. *British Journal of Audiology*, **13**, 77–80 (1979).

19 FRERICHS, R. R., BEEMAN, B. L. and COULSON, A. H. Los Angeles Airport noise and mortality: faulty analysis and public policy. *American Journal of Public Health*, **70**, 357–362 (1980).

20 ANDO, Y. and HATTORI, H. Effects of intense noise during fetal life upon postnatal adaptability. *Journal of the Acoustical Society of America*, **47**, 1128–1130 (1970).

21 ANDO, Y. and HATTORI, H. Statistical Studies on the Effects of Intense Noise during Human Fetal Life. *Journal of Sound and Vibration*, **27**, 101–110 (1973).

22 ANDO, Y. and HATTORI, H. Effects of noise on human placental lactogen levels in maternal plasma. *British Journal of Obstetrics and Gynaecology*, **84**, 115–118 (1977).

23 ANDO, Y. and HATTORI, H. Effects of noise on sleep and babies. *Journal of the Acoustical Society of America*, **62**, 199–204 (1977).

24 JONES, F. N. and TAUSCHER, J. Residence under an airport landing pattern as a factor in teratism. *Archives of Environmental Health*, **33**, 10–12 (1978).

25 BADER, M. Residence under an airport landing pattern as a factor in teratism (Letter). *Archives of Environmental Health*, **33**, 214 (1978).

26 KNIPSCHILD, P., MEIJER, H. and SALLE, H. Aircraft noise and birth weight. *International Archives of Occupational and Environmental Health*, **48**, 131–136 (1981).

27 EDMONDS, L. D., LAYDE, P. M. and ERICKSON, J. D. Airport noise and teratogenesis. *Archives of Environmental Health*, **34**, 243–247 (1979).

28 MEECHAM, W. C. and SMITH, H. G. Effects of jet aircraft noise on mental hsopital admissions. *British Journal of Audiology*, **ii**, 81–85 (1977).

29 ABEY-WICKRAMA, I., A'BROOK, M. F., GATTONI, F. E. and HERRIDGE, C. F. Mental hospital admissions and aircraft noise. *Lancet*, **ii**, 1274–1277 (1969).

30 GATTONI, F. E. and TARNOPOLSKY, A. Aircraft noise and psychiatric morbidity. *Psychological Medicine*, **1**, 516–520 (1973).

31 TARNOPOLSKY, A., BARKER, S. M., WIGGINS, R. D. and MCLEAN, E. K. The effect of aircraft noise on the mental health of a community sample: A pilot study. *Psychological Medicine*, **8**, 219–233 (1978).

32 JENKINS, L., TRANOPOLSKY, A. and HAND, D. Psychiatric admissions and aircraft noise from London airport: four year, three hospitals' study. *Psychological Medicine*, **11**, 765–782 (1981).

33 FIEDLER, F. E. and FIEDLER, J. Port noise complaints: verbal and behavioural reactions to airport-related noise. *Journal of Applied Psychology*, **60**, 498–506 (1975).

34 GRAEVEN, D. B. The effects of airplane noise on health: an examination of three hypotheses. *Journal of Health and Social Behaviour*, **15**, 336–343 (1974).

35 TARNOPOLSKY, A., WATKINS, G. and HAND, D. J. Aircraft noise and mental health: I. Prevalence of individual symptoms. *Psychological Medicine*, **10**, 683–698 (1980).

36 WATKINS, G., TARNOPOLSKY, A. and JENKINS, L. M. Aircraft noise and mental health: II. Use of medicines and health care services. *Psychological Medicine*, **11**, 155–168 (1981).

37 GAVREAU, V. Infrasound. *Science Journal*, **4**, 33–37 (1968).

38 BRYAN, M. and TEMPEST, W. Does infrasound make drivers drunk? *New Scientist*, **53**, 584–586 (1972).

39 EVANS, M. J. and TEMPEST, W. Some effects of infrasonic noise in transportation. *Journal of Sound and Vibration*, **22**, 19–24 (1972).

40 HARRIS, C. S., SOMMER, H. C. and JOHNSON, D. L. Review of the effects of Infrasound on Man. *Aviation Space Environment Medicine*, **47**, 430–434 (1976).

41 von GIERKE, H. E. and PARKER, D. E. Infrasound. *Handbook of Sensory Physiology*, **5**, 585–624 (1976).

42 JOHNSON, D. L. *The Effects of High Level Infrasound*, Research Report, Aerospace Medical Research Laboratory, Wright-Patterson AFB, Ohio (1980).

43 BIRNIE, S. E., HALL, F. L. and TAYLOR, S. M. The effects of infrasound on human health. *Canadian Acoustics*, **11**, 46–55 (1983).

44 MOORE, B. C. J. *An Introduction to the Psychology of Hearing* (2nd edn.), Academic Press, London (1982).

45 PICKLES, J. O. *An Introduction to the Psychology of Hearing*, Academic Press, London (1982).

46 International Standards Organization. *ISO 389–1975: Standard Reference Zero for the Calibration of Pure-Tone Audiometers*, ISO, Geneva (1975).

47 NOBLE, W. E. *Assessment of Impaired Hearing*, Academic Press, New York (1978).

48 NOBLE, W. G. Pure tone acuity, speech–hearing disability and deafness in acoustic trauma. *Audiology*, **12**, 291–315 (1973).

49 FESTEN, J. M. and PLOMP, R. Relations between auditory functions in impaired hearing. *Journal of the Acoustical Society of America*, **73**, 652–662 (1983).

50 WILKINS, P. A. and ROBINSON, D. W. The onset of handicap due to noise-induced hearing loss. In *Proceedings of the 11th International Congress on Acoustics*, (M.R.-O. Prudhomme, ed.) Vol. 3, pp. 265–268 Galp, Paris (1983).

51 International Standards Organization, *ISO/DIS 1999–1982: Assessment of Occupational Noise for Hearing Conservation Purposes*, ISO, Geneva (1982).

52 KRYTER, K. D. *The Effects of Noise on Man*, Academic Press, New York (1970).

53 DAVIS, A. C. Hearing disorders in the population: first phase findings of the MRC national study of hearing. In Lutman, M. E. and Haggard, M. P. (eds), *Hearing Science and Hearing Disorders*, Academic Press (1982).

54 TYLER, R. S., FERNANDES, M. and WOOD, E. J. Frequency resolution and hearing loss. *British Journal of Audiology*, **16**, 45–63 (1982).

55 Noise Abatement (Hearing Conservation in Workplaces) Regulations 1983. Government Printer, Perth, Western Australia (1983).

56 Health and Safety Commission. *Protection of Hearing at Work*, HMSO, London (1981).

57 SALMON, V., MILLS, J. S. and PETERSON, A. C. *Industrial Noise Control*

Manual, U.S. Department of Health, Education and Welfare (NIOSH), Washington, D.C. (1975).

58 Occupational Noise Exposure: Hearing Conservation Amendment. *Federal Register*, **46**, 4078–4179 (1981).

59 Commission of The European Communities. Proposal for a Council Directive on the protection of workers from the risks related to exposure to chemical/physical and biological agents at work: Noise. *Official Journal of the European Commission*, C289/1–6 (1982).

60 PIERSON, W. R. and MAHÉ, J. E. Noise and highway patrolmen. *Journal of Occupational Medicine*, **15**, 892–893 (1973).

61 ANDRUS, W. S., KERRIGAN, M. E. and BIRD, K. T. Hearing and para-airport children. *Aviation and Space Environmental Medicine*, **46**, 740–742 (1975).

62 JOHNSON, D. W., HAMMOND, R. J. and SHERMAN, R. E. Hearing in an ambulance paramedic population. *Annals of Emergency Medicine*, **9**, 557–561.

63 LEMKE, M. and WILLUMEIT, H. P. Measurements of interior noise in vehicles in the infrasound and hearing range. In *Proceedings of The 6th Symposium of Dynamics of Vehicles on Roads and Tracks*, pp. 211–22 (1980).

64 BURNS, W. *Noise and Man* (2nd edn.), John Murray, London (1973).

65 BURNS, W. and ROBINSON, D. W. *Hearing and Noise in Industry*, HMSO, London (1970).

66 ROBINSON, D. W. The spectral factor in noise-induced hearing loss: A case for retaining the A-weighting. *Journal of Sound and Vibration*, **90**, 103–127 (1983).

67 SUTER, A. *The Ability of Mildly Hearing-impaired Individuals to Discriminate Speech in Noise*, EPA.550/9-78-100 (AMRL-TR-4) (1978).

68 SMOORENBURG, G. F., de LATT, J. A. P. M. and PLOMP, R. The effect of noise-induced hearing loss on the intelligibility of speech in noise. *AGARD Conference Proceedings*, No. 311 11-1 to 11-7 (1981).

69 United States Environmental Protection Agency. *Noise: A Health Problem*, Office of Noise Abatement and Control, U.S. Environmental Protection Agency, Washington, D.C., 20460 (1978).

Further reading

BURNS, W. *Noise and Man* (2nd edn.), John Murray, London (1973).

KRYTER, K. D. *The Effects of Noise on Man*, Academic Press, London (1970).

KRYTER, K. D. *Physiological, Psychological and Social Effects of Noise*, NASA, Washington, D.C. (1984).

THIESSEN, G. J. *Effects of Noise on Man*, Research Report, National Research Council, Ottawa, Ontario (1976).

TOBIAS, J. V., JANSEN, G. and WARD, W. D. (eds), *Noise as a Public Health Problem: Proceedings of the Third International Congress*, American Speech and Hearing Association Reports No. 10 (1980).

United States Environmental Protection Agency. *Public Health and Welfare Criteria for Noise*, U.S. Government Printing Office, Washington, D.C. (1973).

United States Environmental Protection Agency. *Information on Levels of Noise Requisite to Protect Public Health and Welfare with an Adequate Margin of Safety*, U.S. Government Printing Office, Washington, D.C. (1974).

WELCH, B. L. and WELCH, A. S. *Physiological Effects of Noise*, Plenum Press, New York (1970).

5

Sleep Disturbance

Michel Vallet PhD
**Institut National de Recherche Sur Les
Transports et Leur Sécurité,
Bron, France**

Contents

5.1 Introduction

People living in the vicinity of major roads, airports and other sources of noise maintain that their sleep is disturbed, that communications are impaired, that they are obliged to close their windows when listening to the radio or television and that the noise can give rise to psychological disturbances. Chapter 3 contains a general overview of this research.

Various psycho-sociological inquiries concerned with noise have been conducted with a view to evaluating the different kinds of sleep disturbance and the frequency of its occurrence. The results of recent studies[1,2] have shown how noise can effect the consumption of medicaments, particularly sleeping pills. Some inquiries have been concerned solely with sleeping difficulties.[3-7]

Another way of evaluating sleep disturbance is to study the physiological changes induced by noise. For example, observations of sleeping subjects have been carried out both under laboratory and field conditions using electroencephalogram and electrocardiogram (EEG and ECG) recordings. The investigators were interested first of all in isolated changes in the EEG and ECG recordings associated with individual noises and then more recently with changes in the sleep structure itself in relation to the noise energy. The advantage of conducting physiological tests *in situ* is that the conditions that apply are more realistic in comparison with what can be reproduced in the laboratory despite the fact that the attachment of electrodes to the scalp while asleep is somewhat unnatural. It is also possible to observe the effects of exposure to noise over very long periods of time, e.g. several years, whereas tests carried out in the laboratory are necessarily of limited duration. A study of the long-term effects of noise is of fundamental importance since, as in the case of sociological inquiries or those concerned with epidemics, this allows the determination of the way in which the sleeping subjects adapt to the exposure by changing their behaviour (e.g. closing windows, changes in sleeping periods), by modifying their dwellings (e.g. sound proofing of the facades of buildings and changes in the arrangement and uses of rooms) or as a result of physiological adjustments, which result in decreasing responses to the noise stimulus.

In this chapter, a review is given of research which describes the nature and purpose of sleep, the techniques used for the evaluation and description of sleep and the effects of transport noise in both its structure and quality. The aspects of adaptation to sleep disturbance, the use of medicaments to aid sleep and the use of physical indices to describe night-time noise are included.

5.2 Nature and structure of sleep

5.2.1 Sleep characteristics

There are three main states of existence which can be described as wakefulness (W), classic deep sleep (made up of four different stages labelled I to IV) and paradoxical sleep (PS).

These different states or stages can be identified by observing several physiological changes occurring during sleep. These have been identified by Rechtschaffen and Kales[8] and also adopted as an international standard.

As a minimum, the following three parameters need to be recorded:

1. Electroencephalographic (EEG) activity as detected by an occipital electrode.
2. Chin muscle or electromyographic (EMG) activity.
3. Ocular-motor or EOG activity as given by the difference in electrical potential between the cornea and retina of the eye.

Other important parameters can also be considered such as heart and breathing rates, blood pressure and sweat gland excretion, etc. but this is not essential to an identification of the different sleep stages.

Sleep is made up of a succession of cycles involving the different stages described in *Table 5.1*.

5.2.1.1 Night sleep structure in the case of a young, normal adult

Certain rules need to have been respected for a night's sleep to be considered normal. In particular, paradoxical sleep should never occur immediately after wakefulness or either stage III or

Table 5.1 Main characteristics of the different stages of sleep

Stage	Electro-physiological data	Description	Percentage of total sleep (young adult)*
PS–REM	Fast waves and muscular slackness (low amplitude EMG)	Paradoxical stage; rapid eye movement (REM) dream stage	20
IV	High-amplitude δ rhythm for more than 50% of the recording	Deep, slow, delta sleep	19
III	Bursts of δ rhythm (2–3 Hz) for between 30 and 50% of the recording		
II	Appearance of δ rhythm (3 Hz). Complex K, vertex peaks on a θ rhythm base		55
I	Decreasing a rhythm (8–12 Hz) Appearance of θ rhythm (5–7 Hz)		
—	Low-amplitude fast waves. Alpha rhythm (8–12 Hz) on closing eyes	Wakefulness	6

*A young adult is taken to be in the age group 20–45 years.

IV sleep. Furthermore, after falling to sleep, the delay following the first occurrence of paradoxical sleep should not have been less than 60–90 minutes.

A subject on going to sleep passes through the sleep stages I, II, III and IV then, following a brief return to stage II, experiences a first period of paradoxical sleep. Four or five periods of PS occur in a similar way during the course of sleeping period, the duration of each one generally increasing progressively from the first to the third occurrence. The interval between the beginning of one period of paradoxical sleep and the next remains essentially the same for a given individual (e.g. 90–93 minutes). Stages III and IV can appear between the first and second period of paradoxical sleep but the occurrence of these stages at the end of the sleeping period is regarded as abnormal, indicating possible pathological disorders.

The sleep structure as a whole is such that paradoxical sleep can be regarded as being predominant at the end of the night, given the fixed interval between successive occurrences of PS and the increasing duration of each period. Stages III and IV occur mainly at the beginning of sleep where there is usually a more uniform distribution of stage II sleep.

5.2.2 Physiological factors affecting sleep structure

Apart from quantitative and qualitative variations associated with the age of the subjects it should be noted that there are types of sleep that will have been inherited or established at a very early age. A number of studies have resulted in subjects being classified as short sleepers (sleep durations of less than 6 hours) or long sleepers (sleep durations of more than 9 hours). The subjects concerned need to have slept for the applicable period of time for them to have the impression that they have had a sufficient or good night's sleep. These differences are also associated with variations in the relative proportions of the different stages with respect to the total amount of sleep. The variations arising here must be regarded as sources of possible errors in cases of studies involving non-uniform samples of subjects.

In the case of an adult the average sleep duration amount to approximately 8 hours and can vary from 6 to 10 hours or sometimes more.

For a newly born subject, wakefulness and sleep alternate during the 24 hour period. The total duration of sleep amounts to 15 to 18 hours.

Between 2 and 5 years, depending on the individual child, the monophase structure is acquired, (i.e. awake during the day, asleep at night). The duration of sleep progressively decreases: 14–15 hours at 1 month, 11–12 hours at 1 year and 9–10 hours at 10 years.

In the case of old people (i.e. above the age of about 70) the duration of sleep is of the order of 6 hours, and it will be noted how there are periods of somnolence during the day and of wakefulness during the night.

5.2.3 Sleeping difficulties and normal variations in sleep

A brief reference to sleeping difficulties due to different circumstances needs to be made here in order to be able to make a distinction in considering those due to noise. These difficulties are concerned in particular with the sleep structure. Insomnia is very common and regarded by the medical profession not as a sickness in itself but as a symptom. The different types of insomnia can be distinguished according to when it occurs: difficulties in getting to sleep, waking up during the night or waking up too early. The general effect is a reduction in the amount of sleep.

Insomnia is a symptom of most mental disorders. Mouret[9] has pointed out how the characteristic features of sleeping difficulties associated with a uni-directional depression is a reduction in the time preceding the appearance of paradoxical sleep and in the duration of slow sleep and/or frequent awakening.

In the case of shift work, Lille[10] on studying the diurnal sleep of subjects accustomed to working at night has shown that there is:

'a minimum sleep duration during the day of 6 hours 4 minutes and less deep sleep, as indicated by the number of body movements, and a higher percentage of stage I sleep than applies in the case of night sleep. The duration of sleep during the day decreases from the beginning to the end of the week which suggests that there is an accumulated sleep debt.'

In the case of diurnal sleep the duration of successive phases of paradoxical sleep remains the same whereas it increases in the case of night sleep.

In studying the irregular working of train drivers, Foret[11] has shown how there is practically a complete absence of any physiological adaptation. Sleep during the morning (on going to bed at 05.00 hours) includes a great deal of paradoxical sleep at the expense of deep sleep and this sleep is more like that normally occurring at the end of the night, i.e. large proportions of paradoxical sleep, than recuperative or deep sleep.

Some of the factors affecting sleep parameters are peculiar to the individuals concerned. Physical exercise taken before sleep generally provokes longer periods of deep sleep (stages III and IV). This demonstrates that this type of sleep is important to the metabolic restoration of the human system. Morgan[12] has also shown how people suffering from cardiovascular disorders are more likely to have their sleep disturbed. It has also been shown that sensory deprivation during the evening leads to an increase in paradoxical sleep during the following night, and Baekeland[13] has suggested that the human organism needs to experience a certain amount of external stimulation.

Anxiety, waiting for the occurrence of some event or a new sleep situation, can give rise to:

1. An increase in the time in getting to sleep and in the time that elapses before the onset of the first period of paradoxical sleep.
2. A reduction in the duration of paradoxical sleep.
3. An increase in the number of times of waking up and in the time of remaining awake.

Some investigators[14] have even observed changes in stage IV sleep in the case of normal people who have been subjected to some stress during the day preceding their night's sleep.

The disturbance to sleep differs according to the type of mental disorder concerned. For example, Kleitman[15] noted that there was a reduction in the duration of sleep in the case of latent or acute psychoses, neurasthenia, depression or a high degree of anxiety. Conversely, there was an increase in the duration of sleep in the case of a low level of anxiety, internal conflicts or chronic schizophrenia.

Gresham[16] and Oswald[17] noted how depressed psychotics, who said that they did not sleep very well, in fact experienced a significant reduction in the duration of stage IV and paradoxical sleep.

Clearly, different types of sleeping difficulty can arise and, therefore, in order to compare the sleeping difficulties attributed to noise it is first necessary to establish whether there are other causes that may affect sleep quality.

5.3 Techniques employed in evaluating the quality of sleep

5.3.1 Questionnaire inquiries

All inquiries into the general effects of noise involve questions concerning sleep. Borsky,[18] in a survey in Oklahoma, found that 42% of the people questioned referred to disturbed sleep due to noise. This was supported in a similar and more recent survey carried out by Lambert.[2]

Questionnaire surveys concerned specifically with sleep disturbances due to traffic noise have been carried out by Langdon[3] and Page,[4] the latter being concerned with sleeping difficulties before and after the opening of a motorway. François[6] attempted to determine the effect of noise from airports on sleep while Fidell[5] evaluated the effects on sleep of cancelling night flights at Los Angeles airport.

Some psychosociological inquiries have been concerned both with questionnaires and with observations of sleep behaviour. For example, Rylander[19] studied body movements in relation to sonic booms of a sub-sample of subjects from a larger population that had been involved in a previous inquiry.

5.3.2 Recordings made during sleep

It is much simpler to carry out recording procedures in the laboratory than in people's homes. However, the recording of body movements can be a useful way of studying sleep quality without the need for intrusive equipment.[21] For example, Rylander[19] has used this technique to carry out tests on sleeping subjects in their homes when studying the effects on sleep of sonic booms.

The multichannel recording techniques that are employed are those that have been developed in hospitals for use in studying the sleep of sick people. The way in which the recordings are interpreted in order to identify the different stages of sleep was standardized in 1968.[8] The different reactions that can be detected on taking account of this standardization include:

1. Changes in the EEG recordings (*see Table 5.1*).
   (a) Appearance or momentary disappearance of a standard electrical activity or momentary disappearance of delta waves.
   (b) Appearance of a transient activity phase associated or not associated with a change in the stage of sleep (any change being in the direction of wakefulness).
   (c) Occurrence of a more or less prolonged period wakefulness.
2. Cardiovascular changes usually in the form of changes in the heart rate or peripheral vasoconstrictions.
3. Electrodermal reactions.
4. Muscular reactions ranging from a slight body movement to a change in body position.
5. Changes in breathing rate or amplitude.

The recordings can be made either in the laboratory (Lukas,[22] Muzet[23]) or in the home (Globus,[24] Vallet[25]). Working in this way it is possible to compare the sleep stages in a number of different noise situations and with a standard *reference sleep structure*, i.e. duration and rhythm of the different sleep stages in the subjects.

The investigators also consider *isolated changes* in sleep due in most cases to noise from particular sources such as trains, aircraft and lorries. This is a matter of transitory activities, changes in the depth of sleep stages and of periods of wakefulness. In these cases it is necessary to relate the number of sleep stage changes to their duration. Therefore, in considering the number of changes from stage III or IV sleep to earlier stages it is necessary to check that the durations of the stages are about the same in the two test situations (usually one quiet and one noisy). In the case of high noise levels (e.g. dense road traffic) it is found that there is a pronounced reduction in the duration of stages III and IV. The number of changes of stage also decreases although the most plausible hypothesis is that this number should increase in a noisy situation.

Given the most recent analytical and data processing techniques it is possible to carry out a fairly detailed and automatic analysis of changes in EEG recordings. Wilkinson[26] and Jurriens[27] have attempted to correlate sleep changes (bursts of a (8–12 Hz), sleep spindle (12–15 Hz) and in particular deep δ waves (0.5–2.5 Hz) with the noise levels.

5.3.3 Morning questionnaires on sleep

Questionnaires have been employed in the case of laboratory tests where noise levels are varied during sleep and where the subjects are asked to give their impressions of their night's sleep on awakening. Depending on the nature of the experiment, subjects have been asked either to give a single indication of their sleep or to complete a questionnaire.[20] The most well-known scale employed here is the Stanford Sleepiness Scale (SSS). The questionnaires in addition to being concerned with the general impressions of the subjects, are aimed at obtaining information that can be related to their physiological activities. The recollections of the subjects with regard to the time taken to get to sleep, the number of times that they awoke and the number of dreams are compared with the indications given by multi-channel recordings that will have been made.

5.3.4 Morning performance and vigilance tests

In some cases the use of morning questionnaires is associated with fairly short duration psychomotor performance tests and sometimes with longer duration tests aimed at determining the vigilance during the course of the day on the assumption that disturbance to sleep due to noise will affect the performance and alertness of the subjects. Wilkinson[26] submitted his subjects to the following four performance tests on the morning after their night's sleep:

1 *Simple reaction time*: the subject responds as quickly as possible to the random appearance of a three-figure number which starting from zero immediately increases until the subject stops the process on pressing a button. The reaction time is then displayed in milliseconds. The next presentation appears after a delay of between 1 and 11 seconds (duration of test: 10 minutes).

2 *Time of reaction to four choices*: the subject presses one of four buttons which light up in a random manner. The response to the stimulus results in the appearance of the next signal and so on (duration of test: 10 minutes).

3 *Short-term auditive memory*: the subject is presented orally with a list of 8 numbers which he has to write down (duration of test: 10 minutes).

4. *Vigilance test*: the subject listens for 1 hour to sounds of a half second duration and must detect a sound of slightly less duration.

The results of these tests give a quantitative indication of the effects of sleeping difficulties experienced during the preceding night.

The availability of techniques making it possible to carry out recordings in the home led Muzet[21] to compare the advantages and disadvantages of each method.

The advantages of carrying out recordings in the laboratory are that it is possible to exercise complete control over the noise levels and the number of and intervals of time between successive occurrences of noise and to submit a sample of subjects to identical test procedures and conditions.

In carrying out tests in the home it is possible to study the reaction of subjects in their normal environment. At home, the noise is real whereas in the laboratory there is always a degree of distortion (rise time, frequency spectrum and reverberation) but it is not possible at home to eliminate parasitic noise coming from sources other than from transport.

The decisive advantage of carrying out tests in the home is that it is possible to observe the effects of exposing subjects to noise over long periods of time (Eberhardt,[28] Vallet,[25] Vernet[29]).

A comparison of the two methods has also been made by Coates[30] and Labiale[31] who took recordings of subjects both in the laboratory and in their homes. They noted that EEG recordings were essentially identical for subjects at home and in the laboratory. There were, however, some other observed differences. For example, more time was spent in getting to sleep and stage II sleep was of longer duration in the home than in the laboratory. The variability in the time of getting to sleep and in the duration of paradoxical sleep, both between and for individual subjects, was greater in the home. Replies to questionnaires showed, however, that the subjects recollection of sleep was the same in both cases except for the time taken in getting to sleep which was estimated more accurately for the home environment.

5.4 Effects of noise on the structure of sleep

Tables 5.2 and 5.3 summarize main recent investigations into the effects of noise changes on sleep. These studies show that noise from traffic and aircraft can be responsible for significant changes in sleep structures.

5.4.1 Psycho-physiological reactions to an increase in noise level

Table 5.2 shows that, generally, an increase in the noise level during the night is associated with changes in the structure of sleep.

Griefahn[32] noted that after a moderate increase in the noise level during the night there was a slight change in sleep while Ehrenstein[33] observed that there was first a reduction in the amount of δ sleep followed by a decrease in the amount of paradoxical sleep. The results of a study carried out in peoples' homes by Vallet and Blanchet[34] has shown that in real conditions the intrusion of noise leads to a reduction in the time preceding the appearance of the first period of paradoxical sleep and in the duration of δ sleep and an increase in the number of awakenings during the night. It also appears that irregular noise leads to more pronounced changes of stage than noise that appears after a uni-directional increase in noise level (Ohrström[40]) (see Table 5.5). There is a reduction both in the subjective appreciation of sleep and in psychomotor performance on awakening following exposure to noise at night.[26,38] Results obtained by Metz and Muzet[37] show how, under laboratory conditions, subjects soon became accustomed to repetitive noise. It was found that their subjective reactions and certain recorded physiological changes showed a degree of adaptation while at the same time the subjects cardiovascular reactions continued without showing signs of adaptation to the increased noise. Similarly, the results of some of the investigations referred to in Table 5.2 are particularly interesting in that they show how there was generally a lack of agreement between the way in which subjects became accustomed to variations in noise level. In these cases, the subjects impressions of sleep quality indicated they were becoming accustomed to the noise whereas other physiological measures of sleep structure and, in particular, cardiovascular reactions did not indicate adaptation.[37,38]

5.4.2 Psycho-physiological reactions following a reduction in noise level

Table 5.3 shows that, whatever tests are organized, statistically significant changes arise in both the duration of the sleep stages and the responses to isolated noises following moderate reductions (of 6–14 dB(A) L_{eq}) in the level of noise during sleep.

The results of three investigations[26,36,39] also show that there is a positive correlation between noise level (L_{eq} averaged over 1 minute) and heart rate whatever stage of sleep is involved. A reduction in noise level is usually followed by an increase in the duration of paradoxical and/or of δ sleep, the latter being little affected by isolated noises[41] (as indicated in Table 5.5), and a reduction in the number of awakenings. Friedmann[42] investigating the effects of a reduction in noise level found that following a long period of exposure, the maximum rebound or increase in δ sleep occurred a week after the noise level was first reduced and steadied off after 1 month. Interestingly, a quieter night-time environment results in an increase in the amount of paradoxical sleep of old people and an improvement in the δ sleep of the youngest subjects. In addition to the EEG improvements the sleep has an improved subjective quality and the subjects have a better morning performance.

This indicates that there is no physiological adaptation to night noise in the long term.

5.4.3 Accumulated sleep debt

A light sleep deficit each night provokes an accumulated sleep debt, and when the conditions of sleep change a clear increase in the deep sleep stages occurs. This acts as a counter-balance to sleep debt and is often called a rebound effect.

A number of investigations have been carried out where the sleep structure of subjects was recorded first of all in a normal noisy environment, then in a quiet one, and again in a noisy environment. Wilkinson[26] noted that there were differences in the sleep structure recorded during the two noisy periods, the subjects being less disturbed in the second noisy period, N2, than they were in the first noisy period, N1. This was true for the total duration of sleep, for the light sleep stages I and II and for the deep sleep stages III and IV. Table 5.4 summarizes the results obtained.

These results suggest that the quiet period results in a certain recuperation with a complete or partial elimination of the accumulated loss of sleep, the sleep in the N2 period being generally of a better quality than that in the N1 period. This supposition is, however, based on a limited amount of data and further experimental verification is required.

5.4.4 Factors affecting the assessment of sleep structure in response to noise

It should be noted at this point that measurements of sleep structure or physiological change are subject to considerable variation for a number of reasons. Generally, there are two main types of variation that need to be considered. These are related to individual subject variability and variations in the recording conditions between different investigations.

Two major parameters, age and sex of the subjects, affect the reactions to noise. Young subjects (21–27 years) who are moved

Table 5.2 Summary of studies on the effects of increasing noise levels on sleep

Authors	Laboratory or at home	Noise sources description	Noise levels background and noise level variation	Assessment criteria	No. of subjects Age & Sex No. of nights	Summary of physiological and psychological results after increasing noise
Jurriens[38]	Lab	Recorded traffic noise	Background: 34 dB(A) L_{eq} Noise 40–60 dB(A)	Sleep stage duration Subjective sleep quality Reaction time test	6 males 18–30 years 10 nights 'quiet' 20 nights 'noisy'	Decreasing delta sleep time, lower sleep subjective quality, no clear alteration of reaction time (RT)
Ehrenstein Muller-Limmroth[33]	Lab	Recorded urban traffic noise + pile driver and air hammers	Background: 38 dB(A) L_{eq} Noise 50–70 dB(A) L_{eq}, 76–86 dB(A) from pile driver	Sleep stages duration + Mood scale + Heart rate + Hormones + Performance	6 males 19–23 years 8 consecutive nights	Decreasing δ sleep time during the first 2 nights with noise. Decreasing REM sleep (nights 3 to 8), worsening of mood.
Muzet[37]	Lab	Simulated noise, 160 trucks noises for each 2 hour period, 10 or 20 sec duration for each noise	Background: 40 dB(A) L_{eq} Peak levels: 80, 65, 55, 40 dB(A)	Sleep stages shifts no. of movements. Cardiovascular, questionnaire, performance	18 males 19–27 years 5 consecutive nights	Increases in stage shifts subjective quality. } nights 1 and 2 Persisting cardiovascular reaction
Ohrström[35]	Lab	Recorded noise Continuous noise	51dB(A) L_{eq}	No. of movements, performance	6 subjects 2 F, 4 M	Increasing no. of movements (+16%)
Vallet & Blanchet[34]	At home (telemetry)	Road traffic noise before/after new expressway	before $L_{eq} \simeq 30$ dB(A) after $L_{eq} = 45$ dB(A) peak 55.6 dB(A)	Sleep stages duration, questionnaire	12 males 27 to 50 years 9 nights = 3 before, 6 after	Decreasing δ sleep (28 min) 6% TST, shorter REM latency
Griefahn & Gros[32]	At home	Road traffic noise; opening the windows	$L_{eq} = 35$–48 dB(A) mean $\varDelta$ $L_{eq} = 6.8$ dB(A) peak (L_1) 41 to 56, dB(A) $\varDelta$ peak (L_1) 9,5 dB(A)	Sleep stages duration. Questionnaire. reaction time (4 choices)	10 (5 couples) 25 to 63 years 12 consecutive nights	Slight modification of sleep stages, poorer sleep quality, increased tiredness in the morning

Table 5.3 Summary of studies on the effect of decreasing noise levels on sleep

Authors	Laboratory or at home	Noise sources description	Noise levels Background and noise level variation	Assessment criteria	No. of subjects Age & Sex No. of nights	Summary of physiological and psychological after-effects of noise reduction
Friedmann & Globus[34]	At home (telemetry)	Years of exposure to aircraft noise Cessation of late flights (Los Angeles)	external noise L_{eq} before 77, after 51 dB(A) inside peak levels 52 before, 39 dB(A) after	sleep stages duration	12 (couples) 45 years ±7 3 blocks of week duration	All sleep stages increase, especially δ sleep maximum 1 week after noise reduction
Wilkinson & Campbell[26]	At home	Years of exposure to traffic noise Reduction of noise by double glazing	mean L_{eq} —47 dB(A) mean L_{eq} after: 41 dB(A) $\Delta = 6$ dB(A)	sleep stages duration, heart rate (HR), questionnaire, reaction time	12 (couples) 1 group <45 years 1 group >45 years 20 nights in 2 blocks	Increasing δ sleep, increasing REM latency. Heart rate positively correlates with noise; better sleep quality reported; simple reaction time improved
Vallet & Gagneux[39]	At home (telemetry)	Years of exposure to traffic noise. Reduction of levels by moving the bed to a quiet room	Noisy L_{eq}: 52–42 dB(A) 'Quiet' L_{eq} 42–27 dB(A)	Sleep stages duration, heart rate questionnaire, reaction time	26 (10 couples) 4 <30 years 10 <50 years 12 >50 years 11 consecutive nights	Increasing REM sleep. Decreasing no awakenings. Correlation between noise levels and heart rate. Improved sleep quality. Shorter reaction the next day
Jurriens & Kumar[36]	At home	Years of exposure to traffic noise Double glazing	'Noisy' L_{eq}: 52–41 'Quiet' L_{eq}: 42–37 dB(A)	Sleep stages duration, heart rate, questionnaire, reaction time	12 (4 couples): age 20–40 years 20 nights in two blocks 20, 30, 50 years 20 nights in two blocks	Increasing REM sleep time, decreasing δ sleep, decreasing awakenings. Correlation between noise and heart rate. Better subjective quality of sleep
Griefahn & Gros[32]	At home	Years of exposure to traffic noise Change by earplugs	L_{eq} 48–35 dB(A) Δ 9 dB(A) peak (L_i)* 56–41	Sleep stages duration, questionnaire, reaction time	10 (5 couples) age 25–65 12 consecutive nights	Increasing δ sleep, decreasing sleep latency. Better performance (less errors)
Eberhardt[28]	At home (telemetry)	Years of exposure to traffic noise temporary double glazing	L_{eq} 38 dB(A)ΔL_{eq}: 6–11 dB(A) peak levels: 50–55 dB(A)	Sleep stages duration, body movements, single events effects	13 males 1 group 63–73 years 1 group 21–27 years 7 nights non-consecutive	Increasing δ sleep for the young subjects Increasing REM sleep Decreasing time spent awake } for the aged group

*L_i: Noise level exceeded for 1% of time.

Table 5.4 Duration of sleep in different noise environments[26]

Type of sleep	Sleeping times in different noise environments (minutes)		
	N1	Quiet	N2
Total sleep	420	432	427
Light sleep stages I and II	225	228	228
Deep sleep stages III and IV	86	95	89

to a quieter room get to sleep on average in a shorter time, and experience a longer deep sleep, whereas older subjects (63–73 years), for whom deep sleep is physiologically shorter, experience a longer paradoxical sleep. The reduction in body movements is, however, the same for both age groups.[28] Women are more sensitive to noise than men.[35] This latter difference will be considered in more detail in the case of isolated noise (aircraft and lorries) in Section 5.5.1.

It should be noted that no account has yet been taken of the two classes of subjects, namely short duration and long duration sleepers (*see* Section 5.2.2), which is another and very important cause of variation in sleep structure.

Regarding the recording conditions, these clearly have some effect on the results of investigations. For example, the criteria employed in carrying out an objective evaluation of alterations in sleep include changes in the frequency of EEG recordings,[43] the reported number of awakenings,[43] changes in heart rate[44] and body movements.[40] The way in which EEG recordings are examined can vary from one investigation to another, the traces being read either visually or automatically. The recordings are analysed with respect to time bases that can vary from 20 seconds to 1 minute. It should also be noted how certain difficulties have been experienced in coding paradoxical sleep and the recorded duration of such sleep can depend on the technique employed.[45] The way in which tests are organized can also vary from one investigation to another. For example, in the laboratory it is possible to conduct a series of tests made up of a given sequence of noisy and quiet nights whereas in the case of tests carried out in the home it is necessary to take advantage, for example, of the opening of a motorway.

Alternatively, the investigator is obliged to make use of various techniques such as the installation of double glazing, moving subjects to another room or asking subjects to wear ear plugs, etc. It should also be noted that the time elapsed between noisy and quiet situations are not the same (varying from 1 day to 2 weeks), and this can give rise to further variations in the test results.[46] There are also significant differences between the characteristics of the different noise signals that are employed, e.g. frequency, level, recorded and reconstituted noise, etc.

Finally, it is worth noting that Mouret in 1978[47] indicated that the noise dose received by subjects during the day could have an effect on the quality of sleep at night. It is surprising to note that this important source of variation has not, as yet, been considered in studies of noise and sleep structure.

Despite the various sources of interference with the sleep structure it should be recognized how noise can give rise to changes (distributed according to individual reactions) to the following sleep stages: deep (sleep stages III and IV), paradoxical sleep (length of time before the appearance of the first period and duration of each period) and periods of wakefulness (length of time before first getting to sleep and duration of wakeful period during the night).

The major problem remains that of interpreting the test results. When there are clearly distinguishable physiological changes resulting from noise exposure, it is not possible to disregard the possibility that noise is a hazard to health given our poor understanding of biological functions of sleep and our inability to attach any clear functional significance to change in the EEG signals.

In conclusion, transport noise clearly disturbs the natural sleep process, and the consequent physiological disturbances are associated with a great deal of annoyance. Associated cardio-vascular responses and otherwise unecessary changes in certain physiological functions could lead to health problems, after very long term exposure to noise; however, there is as yet, no clear indication that transport noise exposures are harmful to health in normal community settings.

5.5 Transitory disturbances to sleep due to isolated occurrences of noise

This section is concerned with isolated occurrences of noise due to aircraft, trains and road vehicles whose peak noise rises well above the background, e.g. noise of lorries in moderate or low flows of traffic.

5.5.1 Analysis of EEG recordings made in the laboratory

Two reviews of the literature concerned with work carried out up to 1975 and 1977 have been made by Lukas[48] and Griefahn.[49] Among the criteria that can be employed in assessing disturbances to sleep described by Williams,[50] two more important ones—namely, awakenings and changes of stage—are considered here.

The main external factor that needs to be taken into account with regard to immediate disturbance to sleep is the peak noise level. Tests carried out by Berry,[51] Collins,[52] Ludlow[53] Lukas,[22,54-55,56,57] Muzet,[58] and Thiessen[59] illustrated the effects of noise on 118 subjects aged from 1 month to 75 years who were exposed to over 8000 occurrences of noise, mainly from overflying aircraft, for a total of 769 nights. A summary of the results obtained is given in *Figure 5.1*. The coefficient of correlation between the percentage awakening with respect to the number of occurrences of noise and the noise levels, was r=0.826 the peak level accounting, therefore, for about 68% of the variance in awakening reaction.[49] It can be seen that there were no awakenings for peak noise levels of less than 60 dB(A). However, awakening can occur below this level particularly for old people or when the noise occurs during light sleep towards the end of the night sleeping period.

The relation between the absence of any changes of stage in the depth of sleep due to noise (zero reaction) and the level of noise is another indication of disturbance to sleep whose use is strongly recommended by Lukas.[48] For the relation between the 'zero reaction' and the aircraft peak noise level L_A, the coefficient of correlation was r = -0.57. The data indicate that there are no changes of sleep indicated for peak noise levels of less than 37 dB(A) but the proportion of subjects for whom there was no such change falls to 44% for peak noise levels of 87 dB(A).

Consequently, by limiting peak noise within bedrooms to 37 dB(A) most sleeping subjects will not exhibit any significant change in EEG reactions. However, controlling transport noise to such low levels is, at present, not a practical proposition.

A laboratory investigation made by Osada[60] revealed that the time taken in getting to sleep increased with the level of train noise. For example, it was found that it takes 2–3 times longer

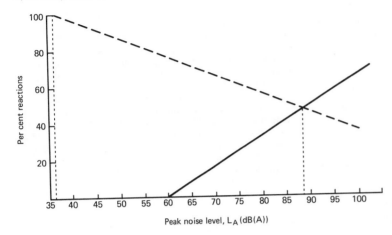

Figure 5.1 Number of awakenings (——) and zero reaction (aircraft noise, – – –) as a function of peak noise level

for a person to get to sleep with peak noise levels of 60 dB(A) due to passing trains than it does in the case of a background noise level of 40 dB(A). Osada also found that the threshold noise level resulting in a person waking up amounts to 60 dB(A), and that the subject is kept awake for a longer period and the disturbance is regarded as more severe as the noise level increases above this threshold value. Finally, he found that the subject sometimes returns to a lighter level of sleep for peak noise levels above 40 dB(A) and very frequently does so for peak noise levels greater than 50 dB(A).

Lukas[48] reported that sleep arousal thresholds are lower in women than in men. This was found to be independent of sleep stage or the type of noise stimulus (i.e. simulated sonic booms or flyover noise).

5.5.2 Recent investigations

In more recent investigations (*Table 5.5*) it has been possible to prolong the period of observation in the laboratory and to make use of indications other than changes in EEG recordings. Muzet[44] has recorded variations in heart rates and peripheral vasoconstrictions. In carrying out tests in the home it has been possible to relate the rates of reaction to different levels of noise over long periods of time. Thiessen[61] has demonstrated how sleep responses to noise (7 occurrences at a level of 65 dB(A) each night) changed over a period of 24 nights (*Figure 5.2*). The number of awakenings decreased significantly during the period of exposure while a change of stage generally appeared for each occurrence of noise.

Vallet[39] has shown how this same distinction between awakenings and stage change frequencies seems to disappear after several years exposure to noise (*Figure 5.3*).

Jansen[62] has shown that noise levels of 55 dB(A) did not wake up his subjects although there were sleep changes and vasoconstrictions that were related to changes in the depth of sleep.

Muzet *et al.*[44] studied the effects of the noise of individual vehicles on 26 subjects in the laboratory, with peak noises ranging from 40 to 65 dB(A) and 90 occurrences of noise per hour. It has shown that heart rate and vasoconstriction varied

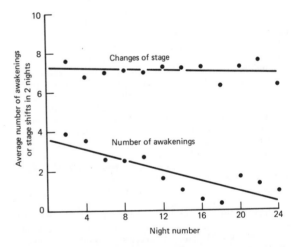

Figure 5.2 Number of awakenings and changes in sleep stages in response to occurrences of noise over a period of 24 nights[61]

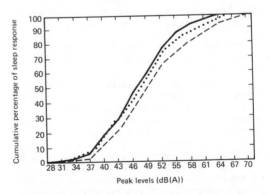

Figure 5.3 Cumulative distribution of sleep responses to peak traffic noise levels after several years exposure.[39] (——) transient effects, (...) sleep stage shift, (– – –) awakening

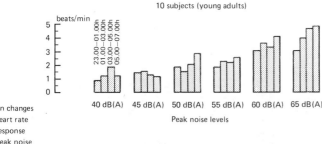

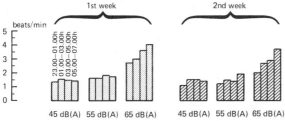

Mean changes in heart rate as response to peak noise level

Figure 5.4 Mean changes in heart-rate responses to noise, for 2-hour periods[43,44]

according to the peak noise level particularly when the levels were between 60 and 65 dB(A). The tests involved three age groups. *Figure 5.4* shows the distribution of average increase in heart rate with peak noise level, for a group of young adults (19–28 years). Examination of the responses for each 2 hour period showed that the subjects did not become accustomed to the noise during the course of the night. The results given at the bottom half of *Figure 5.4* show how there was no significant habituation during 14 nights exposure to the noise. The tests also revealed that the cardiac and vasomotor responses were less pronounced in the case of old people. Regarding noise thresholds, it was found that responses began to appear for levels exceeding 50 dB(A) for children, 55 dB(A) for old people and 60 dB(A) for young adults.

Alternatively, Rice[63] has shown in a study of the effects of sonic booms on sleep disturbance that children were relatively unaffected when the peak external over-pressure was in the range 25–300 N/m² whereas 30% of the middle-aged population woke up as a result of disturbances of this magnitude.

Levere[41] studied the effect of a 15 dB(A) reduction (80 to 65 dB(A)), in the peak noise level of aircraft. He found that there was less disturbance, particularly to sleep stages I and II, and a very slight effect on δ sleep (deep sleep). However, the subjects' impressions of sleep quality indicated no significant improvement.

Vernet[29] has studied isolated disturbances to sleep due to the noise of trains and compared *in situ* effects of train noise and that due to road traffic for levels of 70 L_{eq} dB(A). It was found that the total number of individual disturbances was three times greater for lorries than for trains. *Figure 5.5* shows that for trains there were no awakenings for peak noise levels of less than approximately 50 dB(A) and even for peak noise levels of more than 70 dB(A) there was only a 2.5% probability of an awakening or a stage change.

Peak noise level is not the only noise parameter which can be related to sleep disturbance caused by an individual noise event. Griefahn[64] has studied the effects on disturbance of the time interval between successive occurrences of noise. It was found that there was a maximum probability of an EEG effect when the interval between noise events was 40 minutes. This result is of practical importance in connection with the possible schedul-

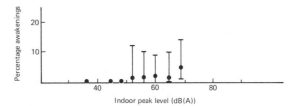

Figure 5.5 Variations in the percentage of awakenings with peak noise levels of trains[29]

ing of night-time air or rail traffic. For example, it would be preferable to group the aircraft occurrences together provided safety considerations allow rather than spread them out. Muzet[37] demonstrated that an average passing frequency of 1.8 vehicles per minute (cars and lorries) gives rise proportionally to a greater EEG effect than a higher frequency of 4.3 vehicles per minute. Vallet[25] considered the number of occurrences of aircraft noises per night and the average noise energy level. The minimum EEG reaction to the flight of an aircraft occurred for an average L_{eq} of 35 dB(A) and for 11–15 flights per night. For an L_{eq} of 40 dB(A) the number of flights did not have any effect on the rate of reaction.

Vernet[65] has found for relatively quiet environments the rise time of a noisy event is an important factor affecting sleep quality, but in noisy environments peak level and duration of noise tend to have the greatest effect on sleep. Kumar[66] has similarly shown how changes in heart rate are related more to the slope of the increase in noise during an event rather than the peak level that is attained.

Ohrström[40] has also studied the effects on sleep of noise level fluctuations. It was found that subjects in the laboratory where there was an overall noise level of 51.4 dB(A), were more sensitive to intermittent noise than to steady state noise. It was found, for example, that the percentage of body movements amounted to 16% for steady state noise compared with 22% for irregular noise.

The type of environment where the noise is generated and the

Table 5.5 Effects of peak noise levels on sleep quality

Authors	Laboratory or at home	Noise sources / No. of noise events	Noise levels (background and noise level variation)	Assessment criteria	No. of subjects Age & Sex No. of nights	Summary of physiological and psychological after-effects of noise reduction
Levere & David[40]	Lab	Recorded aircraft noise. 15 events of 20 s per night	80 dB(A) and 65 dB(A)	EEG desynchronization, questionnaire	12 males 18–23 years 4 nights	Less sleep disruption only during stages I & II little effect on δ sleep no subjective improvement
Thiessen[60]	Lab	Recorded truck noise. 7 events presented each night	Peak level at 65 dB(A) max. Ambient noise: 35–32 dB(A)	EEG awakening, change in depth of sleep	35 subjects Young 8 M, 5 F Middle 7 M, 5F Old 11 M 24 nights	Probability of sleep disturbance begin at 35 dB(A) for awakenings and 40 dB(A) for sleep shifts
Muzet[43]	Lab	Recorded vehicle noise. 90 vehicle/hour	Peak levels at 45, 55, 60, 65 dB(A)	Change in heart rate, vasoconstriction	26 subjects 3 age groups (children, middle, old) 2 weeks	Reactions begin at: 50 dB(A) for children 55 dB(A) for old people 60 dB(A) for young adult
Ohrström[44]	Lab	Recorded traffic noise: Continuous intermittent (trucks)	Ambient noise: $L_{eq} = 34 \rightarrow 51$ dB(A) 37 events 80 dB(A) at peak	Body movements, performance mood	12, 9M, 3F 18.30 years average 6 nights	No. of movements (+22%) poorer subjective sleep quality in intermittent noise condition

personality characterisation of the population can apparently affect sleep disturbance in some instances. For example, Rylander[19] established how a military population was much more tolerant of sonic booms occurring during the night than was the civilian population. Some 10% of the former said that the noise woke them up compared with 56% of the other inhabitants.

Research conducted by Thiessen, Rice and Muzet have shown how the age of the subjects can affect the extent to which their sleep is disturbed by noise. All these different factors are taken into account in what Fidell,[67] Horonjeff[68] and Teffeteler[69] refer to as the detectability concept. Each of the factors can affect the possibility of detecting a noise (where we are referring of course to a clearly identifiable noise and not noise due to continuous, dense traffic). The vulnerability of sleep is very dependent on these different factors.

5.6 Adaptation of sleep to noise: physiological habituation

A number of changes occur with continued exposure to noise. First of all there is physiological habituation in terms of a decrease or even the disappearance of the reactions of the human organism to the noise occurring during sleep. In the case of aircraft noise, it has been shown[25] that the duration of exposure to noise plays an important role in the degree of sleep disturbance. It has been found, for example, that number of awakenings and changes of stage decrease with the number of nights of exposure to noise. *Figure 5.6* shows that after a year's exposure, the sleep of the subjects becomes less disturbed and the peak noise level is no longer such a determining factor given the way in which the rate of reactions remains fairly constant with increases in PNdB.

It is considered that the sensitivity to noise is affected at a very early stage, i.e. by the noise experienced by the unborn child. Ando and Hattori[66] have demonstrated that children born to women who were exposed to the noise from an airport during the beginning of their pregnancy subsequently woke up less frequently than did those born to women who were exposed to the same noise only during the second half of their pregnancy.

Muzet has noted[43] how, during the course of time, differences arise between the subjective appreciation of sleep which soon increases following the beginning of exposure to the noise, the EEG responses which decrease only slightly and the cardiovascular responses which remain fairly pronounced. These differences become even greater in the case of very long periods of exposure to the noise. Fidell,[5] as a result of conducting an inquiry using questionnaires, found that people living in the vicinity of an airport were not aware of any improvement in their sleep despite the fact that night flying had ceased, while Friedmann[42] on recording the physiological responses of subjects in the same area at the same period of time found that there had been a definite improvement in the quality of sleep. For example, it was found that the amount of deep sleep had increased from 12 to 17% 1 week after the cessation of night flying. The same difference was reported by Vallet and François,[70] who concluded that physiological changes in sleep quickly follow changes in noise level while changes in the degree of annoyance follow much more slowly. This both demonstrates and confirms that the degree of annoyance expressed with regard to noise depends largely on factors other than the noise itself. In addition to this it is known that about 20% of the population say that they sleep badly for reasons other than exposure to noise.[3]

5.7 Noise and consumption of medicaments to aid sleep

If it is accepted that an individual in good health has no need of medicaments then the consumption of medicaments by the population exposed to noise can represent a quantifiable effect of this nuisance. For example, recent studies carried out in Ontario[71] and the Netherlands[72] showed that there was a significant increase in the issue of medical prescriptions for people

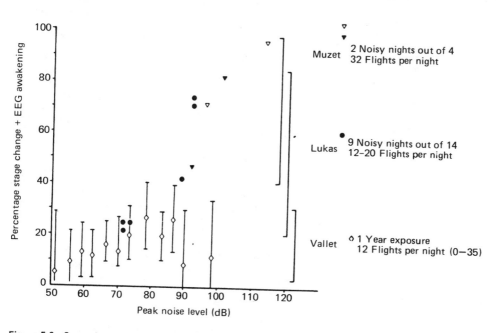

Figure 5.6 Comparison of the reaction to noise for a range of aircraft noise exposures

living in noisy areas when compared with a control group living in a quieter area. The total purchases of medicaments for high blood pressure per year increased for people living in the vicinity of Amsterdam airport and in proportion to the activity of the airport whereas there was no such change in the case of a reference group of people who were not exposed to the noise.

With regard to sleeping difficulties associated with the noise of motor vehicles in urban areas, it has been found difficult to disassociate noise effects from those due to age, anxiety , pain and insomnia. According to Langdon[3] noise was not considered as a major factor in the consumption of medicaments such as sleeping tablets. Alternatively, Lambert[2] suggests that there is a low correlation between the consumption of sleeping pills and traffic noise.

The use of ear plugs is not considered in these studies, although Wehrli[1] found that the proportion of people making use of some form of ear plug varied from 0 to 14% compared with 0–4% for the consumption of sleeping pills. The higher proportions of people using ear plugs was associated with the higher noise exposures in the range considered.

Finally, the results of a recent survey carried out by Relster[73] in Denmark show that in areas where the L_{eq} levels are high, 69–78 dB(A), some 19% of the population compared with 12% in a reference area where the levels are lower, claim to have consulted a psychiatrist or a psychologist during the past 5 years. It was further established that 4% of these cases were referred to a psychiatric hospital whereas only 2% were referred from the quieter area. It is also claimed that 25% of the population exposed to high noise levels regularly took tranquillizers whereas only 17% took this form of medication from the control group.

5.8 Sleep disturbance and performance the following day

It has been shown that sleep adaptation can arise during the course of successive nights of exposure to noise. However, even if there is a certain reduction in the indications of physiological disturbance the performance of subjects during the day following a night's exposure to noise is still affected. Statistically significant increases in motor reaction times were noted by Vallet[39] and more particularly by Wilkinson.[26] The latter found that the unprepared reaction time to a single stimulus and in the case of a multiple choice test was shorter following relatively quiet nights. However, performance involving the short-term memory were not affected by changes in the noise environment.

The test results as a whole confirm the common observation that people sleep badly in the presence of noise and it is, therefore, necessary to consider the possibilities of establishing noise indices which can be used to determine criteria for the protection of sleep.

5.9 Night noise indices and sleep disturbance criteria

Only very rarely do countries make use of noise indices concerned specifically with evening or night noise. Certain countries, however, take account of such periods by making use of a composite index where the noise energy received during the evening and the morning is combined after appropriate weighting with that received during the day. The use of such an index can be considered to be unsatisfactory since in practice it is very insensitive to the characteristics of the night noise that interfere with sleep.

However, it must be realized that the development of noise indices that do not cater for both sleep disturbances and general annoyance require a much better understanding of the parameters of the transport system that cause the noise characteristics that affect sleep. Lamure[74] has reviewed the problems associated with developing noise indices related to sleep disturbances.

Reports issued by various international organizations have shown that there is a considerable interest in the subject of protecting sleep and the process of recovering from physical and nervous fatigue as a result of sleep:

1. *The European Communities Commission*[75] considers that a night-time L_{eq} level of 30–35 dB(A) or below within buildings and peaks of 45 dB(A) or less do not affect sleep.
2. *The Organisation for Economic Cooperation and Development*[76] provisionally recommends adoption of the following L_{eq} levels in member countries: 35 dB(A) during the period of getting to sleep, 45 dB(A) in the case of light sleep and 50 dB(A) for deep sleep.
3. *The World Health Organisation*[77] recommends an internal level of about 35 dB(A) during the night.

However, this last recommendation, based on the results of tests carried out in the laboratory, was considered to be 'unduly strict' by Large[78] and Rice.[79]

The difficulty of determining the amount of traffic and consequent noise that can arise during the night again poses the question as to whether limiting the noise that can occur during the day will not automatically result in a suitable reduction in that occurring during the night.

It is generally accepted that the difference between L_{eq} levels for noise occurring during the day and night in the vicinity of major road traffic routes is of the order of 10 dB(A). This implies that the application of a limit of $L_{eq} = 65$ dB(A) for the period 08.00 to 20.00 hours will automatically result in a limit of $L_{eq} = 55$ dB(A) for the period midnight to 05.00 hours. This would appear to be sufficient to protect the general structural quality of sleep, except in the case of isolated occurrences of noise.

Maurin,[80] however, has shown how the difference between day and night noise levels is of a rather variable nature. It was found that for a sample of about 75 (24-hour periods) the difference between the L_{eq} value for midnight to 05.00 hours and that for 08.00 to 20.00 hours varied from 8.2 to 13.5 dB(A). Differences between day and night levels for average noise profiles in the case of different classes of road are also found to vary over wide limits. This feature is demonstrated in *Table 5.6*. Particular noise profiles for which the day–night difference in levels amounts to less than 6 dB(A) are generally associated with minor, class F, roads. Small differences in these levels are to be expected in extreme cases of heavily trafficked roads and if the difference becomes less than 6.8 dB(A) then the protection provided against exposure to daytime noise will not be sufficient to ensure protection against exposure to that occurring at night.

A similar problem arises in the case of physiological responses. Mouret[47] and Frusthorfer[81] have shown that noise experienced during the day can result in disturbances to the sleep structure the following night. This finding would appear to give support to the adoption of noise indices that are not solely related to particular night-time periods such as the day/night level DNL or L_{10} (18-hour) (the 18-hour period is from 06.00 to 24.00 hours).

Several indices have been developed which include special weighting factors that are applied to night-time noise levels. For example, the day/night index referred to above is given by the formula:

$$L_{DN} = 10 \log 1.24 \ (15.10^{\ L_D/10} + 9.10^{\ (L_N + 10)/10})$$

where $L_D = L_{eq}$ for the period 07.00–22.00 hours
$L_N = L_{eq}$ for the period 22.00–07.00 hours

Table 5.6 L_{eq} noise levels in dB(A) for different periods of time and different classes of road[2]

L_{eq} parameter	Class of road						
	A	B	C	D	E	F	All classes
(1) L_{eq} 08.00–20.00 hrs	55.0	61.7	65.1	69.6	71.9	77.1	68.2
(2) L_{eq} 20.00–08.00 hrs	50.4	55.2	59.8	64.1	67.6	72.2	63.2
(1)–(2)	4.6	6.5	5.3	5.5	4.3	4.9	5.0
(3) L_{eq} 20.00–24.00 hrs	48.9	56.0	60.5	64.6	68.1	72.7	63.6
(1)–(3)	6.1	5.7	4.6	5.0	3.8	4.4	4.6
(4) L_{eq} 00.00–05.00 hrs	43.5	48.2	53.0	58.3	63.7	67.6	57.7
(1)–(4)	11.5	13.5	12.1	11.3	8.2	9.5	10.5
(5) L_{eq} 05.00–08.00 hrs	54.6	57.9	62.6	67.1	70.0	74.8	65.9
(1)–(5)	0.4	3.8	2.5	2.5	1.9	2.3	2.3

Other weighted indices in common use are the CNEL index (community noise equivalent level) which includes a 5 dB evening weighting for the period 19.00–22.00 hours, the German L_{tan} index[82] which is similar to CNEL but extends the period covered from 07.00–22.00 to 06.00–24.00, the French E index[91] and the British NNI (noise and number index). In the last case the acceptable values of NNI differ for the day (50) and the night (30).[83] Further descriptions of noise indices are given in Chapter 2.

Ollerhead[84] and Rice[85] support the use of CNEL since it takes account of the noise during the period of the evening for which there is often the maximum amount of annoyance.

Two recent surveys[86,87] have supported the use of L_{eq} averaged over the period 11.00 pm to 07.00 am. In particular, Brooker[86] shows that total sleep disturbance increases slightly at higher L_{eq} levels. Walker and Diamond[87] discuss the influence of background noise levels at night.

Proposals for a threshold or criteria value for sleep disturbance have been made by referring to individual sleep response to noise, or to a percentage of the population affected by noise-related sleep disturbance. Langdon[3] noted that 20% of the population experienced sleeping difficulties that were not due to noise, and this led Rice[79] to suggest that a minimum of 25% of the population should be treated as a limiting value when assessing sleep disturbances associated with noise sources.

Schultz[88] has compared the disturbance to sleep reported by a variety of surveys of different sources of transport noise. *Figure 5.7* shows that the average L_{DN} level which appears to disturb about 25% of the population is approximately 68 dB(A). If it is assumed that the difference between day and night values of L_{eq} amounts to between 5 and 10 dB(A) then this would suggest that a night-time L_{eq} of 61–62 dB(A) at building facades would be roughly equivalent to 68 dB(A) during the day. This level represents a much higher level than those recommended by the EEC, OECD and the WHO and clearly reflects the difference between criteria based on sleep structure reactivity or physiological change and criteria based on people's subjective opinion of sleep quality.

Rucker,[89] Katska,[90] Holzmann[91] and Finke[92] also reported the results of studies of disturbances to sleep based on subjective surveys. *Figure 5.8* shows a summary of the results of these studies. The figure does not give any clear indication of an acceptable limiting noise level. According to the regression line drawn through the data points, however, the sleep of 25% of the population is disturbed when the external L_{eq} level (22.00–06.00

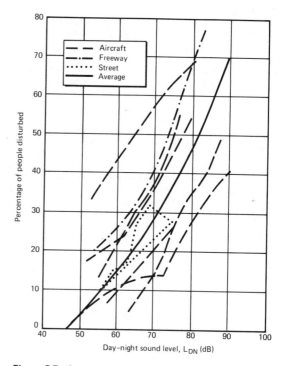

Figure 5.7 Summary of interference with sleep due to noise[88]

hours) is 54 dB(A) which is substantially lower than that indicated by *Figure 5.7* but nevertheless again indicates a higher external level than that recommended by the EEC, OECD and WHO.

It is more difficult to postulate noise level criteria for sleep disturbance when the noise stimulus contains isolated occurrences. However, in certain situations, the use of one L_{eq} value for a particular period of time dispenses with the need to consider the relevance of peak noise levels. For example, for road traffic noise, the existence of a high vehicle flow at a moderate or long distance from the reception point will not generate significant peaks in the noise level time history and,

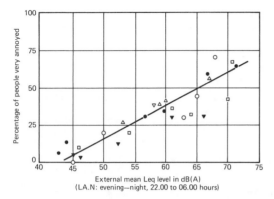

Figure 5.8 Graph summarizing the results of German studies of night annoyance and disturbance due to road traffic noise

Table 5.7 Suggested noise level criteria for sleep disturbance

Noise source	L_{eq} (dB (A))	Peak noise level (dB(A))
Continuous road traffic	35	50
Aircraft	40	52–55
Trains	40	50–55

consequently, the use of an index based on the scale of L_{eq} is probably sufficient to characterize the risk of sleep disturbance.

In other circumstances, e.g. low traffic flows, a reference to peak noise levels is needed although peak levels alone do not adequately explain sleep reactions. For example, for traffic noise exposures in quiet conditions, the average peak noise level causing an EEG effect may vary from about 42–44 dB(A) while that causing the same effect in a noisy situation typically ranges from 50 to 53 dB(A).

It can be concluded that the peak level of an isolated noise is not sufficient to take into account time dependent sleep reactions and consequently, it is necessary to include some measure of the general ambient level in addition to the peak levels.

This general noise level, to which background noise makes an important contribution, may come from sources other than transport and is hardly ever taken into account in studying the noise from aircraft and trains. In laboratory tests Lukas[48] considered that the critical noise level for awakening as indicated by EEG responses amounted to 60 dB(A) while Muzet[44] observed how there was a definite cardiovascular response for noise levels of 50 dB(A) or more. In the case of *in-situ* tests concerned with train noise Vernet[29] found that there was no awakening for peak noise levels of 50 dB(A) but that changes of stage occurred for noise levels of 45 dB(A). Vallet[93] found that people who had been exposed to aircraft noise for 5 years did not wake up for peak noise levels of less than 55 dB(A) and that there were no changes of stage for internal noise levels of 52 dB(A).

Ideally, as indicated above, a noise level criterion for sleep disturbance should incorporate both an energy index, to characterize the ambient levels, together with a peak level. The results of research on various transportation sources suggest that a reasonable comparison between perceived sleep disturbance— i.e. that related to sleeping difficulties and awakening effects— and minimum EEG and physiological responses, can be achieved using the noise level criteria listed in *Table 5.7*.

The value of 50 dB(A) for the peak noise level due to trains takes account of the probable effect of the duration of the noise on changes of sleep stages. For this type of noise it is advisable to make use of short duration L_{eq} or L_{AX} values. In general in considering this noise it is necessary to allow for the correspondence between the energy of an isolated occurrence of aircraft or train noise and the L_{eq} limit in order to determine the maximum number of occurrences of such noise that can be accepted.

It is no easier to decide on the night-time period to be taken into account than it is to decide on the noise scale or index to be employed. It is known, however, that on average people need to have at least 6 hours 30 minutes sleep per night and given the times at which people go to bed and get up in the morning then periods of 22.00 to 06.00 or 07.00 hours associated with currently employed scales or indices would seem to be appropriate.

In all these problems concerning noise and sleep there is an external factor that is never taken into account and which could prove to be of great importance. Investigators studying sleep disturbance generally refer to internal noise levels measured 'near to the head of the sleeping subject' whereas noise limiting regulations are generally concerned with the noise at the external facades of buildings. External levels are, of course, independent of whether the windows in the building are opened or closed or whether the windows are double glazed. It is obvious, therefore, that sleep disturbance criteria based on external levels are inappropriate since the facade insulation can vary over very wide limits. It is necessary, therefore, in determining an acceptable noise criteria to postulate external noise levels which seek to minimize sleep disturbance taking into account the least effective facade insulation condition. The low facade levels that are required in order to achieve this goal indicate that sleep disturbance will continue to occur for a large number of the world's population who are exposed to transport noise at night.

References

1 WEHRLI, B. and WANNER, H. U. Auswirkungen des Strassenwerkehrslärms. *Kampf dem Lärm*, **25**, 138–149 (1978).
2 LAMBERT, J., SIMONNET, F. and VALLET, M. Patterns of behaviour in dwellings exposed to road traffic noise. *Journal of Sound and Vibration*, **92**, 159–172 (1984).
3 LANGDON, J. and BULLER, B. Road traffic and disturbance to sleep. *Journal of Sound and Vibration*, **50**, 13–28 (1977).
4 PAGE, M.A. An extended inquiry on disturbance to sleep due to road traffic noise. *Recherche Environnement—La Documentation Francaise*, Vol. 3, pp. 11–43, Paris (1976).
5 FIDELL, S. and JONES, G. Effects of cessation of late night flights on an airport community. *Journal of Sound and Vibration*, **42**, 422–437 (1975).
6 FRANCOIS, J. *Effects of Aircraft Noise on the Wellbeing of People Living in The Vicinity of Airports. Extended Study in the Vicinity of Roissy Airport*; 3rd phase. IFOP (Institut Francais d'Opinion Publique) report No. BV 77.333 to the Ministry of the Environment, Paris (1979).
7 DORA. *Aircraft Noise and Sleep Deprivation*. Civil Aviation Authority report No. 8008, London (1980).
8 RECHTSCHAFFEN, A. and KALES, A. *A Manual of Standardised Terminology Techniques and Scoring System for Sleep Stages of Human Subjects*. U.S. Government Print Office, Washington D.C. (1968).
9 MOURET, J. Biological principles of sleep deprivation in the treatment of depression. *L'Encéphale*, **VIII**, 229–250 (1982).
10 LILLE, F., FORET, J. and BENOIT, O. Normal sleep; sleep and the psysiological aspects of work. *Vie Médicale*, **53**, 5–16 (1972).
11 FORET, J. *Sleep and Irregular Working Hours*. Thesis, Lille University (1973).
12 MORGAN, P. A. *Effects of Noise Upon Sleep*. Institute for Sound and Vibration Research, report No. 40, Southampton (1970).

13 BAEKELAND, F. Laboratory studies of effects of presleep events on sleep and dreams. In *Sleep and Dreaming* (ed. E. Hartmann), Little, Brown, Boston (1970).

14 LESTER, B. K., BURCH, N. R. and DOSSER, R. C. Nocturnal EEG-G5R profiles: the influence of presleep states. *Psychophysiology*, **3**, 238–245 (1967).

15 KLEITMAN, N. *Sleep and Wakefulness.* Chicago (1963).

16 GRESHAM, S. C., AGNEW, H. W. and WILLIAMS, R. L. The sleep of depressed patients. *Psychiatry*, **13**, 503–509 (1965).

17 OSWALD, I., BERGER, R. *et al.* Melancholia and barbiturates. Controlled EEG, body and eye movement study of sleep. *British Journal of Psychiatry*, **109**, 66–72 (1963).

18 BORSKY, P. *Community Reactions to Sonic Booms in the Oklahoma City Area.* Aerospace Medical Research Laboratory report TR 65-37, National Opinion Research Centre (1962).

19 RYLANDER, R., SORENSEN, S. and BERGLUND, K. Sonic boom effects on sleep—a field experiment on military and civilian populations. Journal of Sound and Vibration, **24**, 41–50 (1972).

20 SCHNEIDER, N. *Subjective Evaluation of Normal Sleep or of That Disturbed by Noise— Relations with Certain Physiological Indications and Personality Traits.* Thesis, Strasbourg University (1973).

21 MUZET, J. and NAITOH, P. Sleep and noise. *Confrontations Psychiatriques*, **15**, 215–235 (1977).

22 LUKAS, J. and KRYTER, K. *Awakening Effects of Simulated Sonic Booms and Subsonic Aircraft Noise.* NASA report 1.17892 (1969).

23 MUZET, A., SCHEIBER, J. P., OLIVIER-MARTIN, N., EHRART, J. and METZ, B. Relationship between subjective and physiological assessments of noise-disturbed sleep. *Proceedings of the 2nd International Congress on Noise as a Health Problem, Dubrovnik*, Report 550/9.73 008, US Environmental Protection Agency, Washington, D.C. pp. 575–85 (1973).

24 GLOBUS, G., FRIEDMANN, J. and COHEN, H. Effects of aircraft noise on sleep as recorded in the home. *Sleep Research*, **2**, 116–122 (1973).

25 VALLET, M., GAGNEUX, J. M. and SIMONNET, F. Effects of aircraft noise on sleep: an in-situ experiment. *Congress on Noise as a Public Health Problem*, ASHA report 10, pp. 391–96 (1980).

26 WILKINSON, R. T. and CAMPBELL, K. Traffic noise at night: effects upon physiology of sleep; subjective report and performance the next day. *Journal of the Acoustics Society of America*, **75**, 468–475 (1984).

27 JURRIENS, B., KUMAR, A., HOFMANN, N. and VAN DIEST, R. Sleeping at home with different sound insulation. *Proceedings Inter-Noise Amsterdam*, Delft, pp.783–86 (1981).

28 EBERHARDT, J. L. and AKSELSON, K. Disturbance by road traffic noise of the sleep of young and elderly males as recorded in the home. In *Sleep 1982. Proceedings of the European Congress of Sleep Research*, Karger, Basle, pp. 298–300 (1983).

29 VERNET, M. Effects of train noise on sleep for people living in houses bordering the railway line. *Journal of Sound and Vibration*, **3**, 66–74 (1979).

30 COATES, T., ROSEKING, M. R., *et al.* Sleep recording in the laboratory and at home: a comparative analysis. *Psychophysiology*, **16**, 339–346 (1979).

31 LABIALE, G. and VALLET, M. Comparative study of sleep disturbances due to noise in the laboratory and in the home. *Travail Humain*, **47.2**, 143–153 (1984).

32 GRIEFAHN, B. and GROS, E. Disturbances of sleep. Interaction between noise, personal and psychological variables. In *Congress on Noise as a Public Health Problem*, Amplifon Tecniche Edizioni Milan, pp. 895–904 (1983).

33 EHRENSTEIN, W. and MÜLLER-LIMMROTH, W. Laboratory investigations into the effects of noise on human sleep. In *Congress on Noise as a Public Health Problem, Freiburg*, Report 10, ASHA, Rockville, Md., pp. 433–441 (1980).

34 VALLET M., BLANCHET, V., BRUYERE, J.C. and THALABARD, J. C. Disturbance to sleep due to road traffic noise—in-situ study. *La Documentation Francaise*, Paris, **3**, 183–212 (1977).

35 OHRSTRÖM, E. and RYLANDER, R. Sleep disturbance effects of traffic noise. A laboratory study of after effects. *Journal of Sound and Vibration*, **84**, 87–104 (1982).

36 KUMAR, A., CAMPBELL, K., HOFMANN, W., VALLET, M., JURRIENS, A. A. and VAN DIEST, P. Evaluation and validation of automatic and visual methods of sleep stage classification of human sleep recordings done at home. In *Proceedings of the International Conference on Cybernetics and Society*, pp. 516–20 (1981).

37 METZ, B. and MUZET, A. Direct effects and interactions of increases in noise levels and ambient temperatures on sleep. In *Noise and Sleep. Collection Recherche et l'Environnement.* Vol. 3, La Documentation Francaise, Paris, pp. 81–160 (1977).

38 JURRIENS, A. Sleeping twenty nights with traffic noise: results of laboratory experiments. In *Congress on Noise as a Public Health Problem*. ASHA, Rockville, Md., Report 10, pp. 413–24 (1980).

39 VALLET, M., GAGNEUX, J. M., BLANCHET, V., FAVRE, B. and LABIALE, G. Long term sleep disturbance due to traffic noise. *Journal of Sound and Vibration*, **90**, 173–191 (1983).

40 OHRSTRÖM, E. and BJORKMAN, M. Sleep disturbance before and after traffic noise attenuation in an apartment building. *Journal of the Acoustic Society of America*, **73**, 877–879 (1983).

41 LEVERE, T. E. and DAVIS, N. Arousal from sleep: the physiological and subjective effects of a 15 dB(A) reduction in aircraft flyover noise. *Aviation Space Environmental Medicine*, **48**, 607–611 (1977).

42 FRIEDMANN, J. and GLOBUS, G. *Effects of The Cessation of Late Night Landing Noise on Sleep Electrophysiology in The Home.* NASA case report 132 543, Washington D.C. (1974).

43 THIESSEN, G. J. Disturbance of sleep by noise. *Journal of the Acoustic Society of America*, **64**, 216–222 (1978).

44 MUZET, A. *Vegetative Changes Due to Noise Occurring During Sleep.* CEB-CNRS report 76-22 for the Ministry of the Environment, Strasbourg (1980).

45 KUMAR, A., CAMPBELL, K., HOFMANN, W., VALLET, M., JURRIENS, A. A. and VAN DIEST, P. Evaluation and validation of automatic and visual methods of sleep stage classification of human sleep recordings done at home. In *Proceedings of the International Conference on Cybernetics and Society*, pp. 516–20 (1981).

46 JURRIENS, A. Noise and sleep in the home: effects on sleep stages. In *Sleep 1984. Proceedings of the European Congress on Sleep Research*, Karger, Basle, pp. 217–20 (1981).

47 BLOIS, R., DEBILLY, G. and MOURET, J. Daytime noise and its subsequent sleep effects. *Congress on Noise as a Public Health Problem, Freiburg 1978. Proceeding of the American Speech–Language Hearing Association*, Report 10, Rockville, pp. 425–432 (1980).

48 LUKAS, J. S. Noise and sleep: a literature review and a proposed criterion for assessing effects. *Journal of the Acoustic Society of America*, **58**, 1232–1242 (1975).

49 GRIEFAHN, B. *Research on Noise Induced Sleep Disturbance Since 1973.* ASHA Report 10, pp. 377–390 (1980).

50 WILLIAMS, H. Effects of noise on sleep: a review. Dubrovnik, 1973. *Proceedings of the International Congress on Noise as a Public Health Problem*, US Environmental Protection Agency, Washington D.C., pp. 501–11 (1973).

51 BERRY, B. and THIESSEN, G. J. *The Effects of Impulsive Noise on Sleep.* National Research Council of Canada publication NRC 11.

52 COLLINS, W. E. and IAMPIETRO, P. F. *Simulated Sonic Booms and Sleep: Effects of Repeated Booms of 1.0 psf.* FAA Office of Aviation Medicine report OAM 72.35 (1972).

53 LUDLOW, J. E. and MORGAN, P. A. Behavioural awakening and subjective reactions to indoor sonic booms. *Journal of Sound and Vibration*, **25**, 479–495 (1972).

54 LUKAS, J. S. and KRYTER, K. D. *Awakening Effects of Simulated Sonic Booms and Subsonic Aircraft Noise on Six Subjects From 7 to 72 Years of Age.* NASA case report 1599, Washington, D.C. (1970).

55 LUKAS, J. S. Awakening effects of simulated sonic booms and aircraft noise on men and women. *Journal of Sound and Vibration*, **20**, 457–466 (1972).

56 LUKAS, J. S., PEELER, D. J. and DAVIS, J. E. *Effects on Sleep of Noise from Two Proposed S.T.O.L. Aircraft.* NASA report CR 132 564 (1975).

57 LUKAS, J. S., PEELER, D. J. and DOBBS, M. E. *Arousal From Sleep by Aircraft Noise on Six Subjects From 7 to 72 Years of Age.* NASA report CR 2279 (1973).

58 MUZET, A., SCHEIBER, J. P., OLIVIER-MARTIN, N., EHRHARDT, J. and METZ, B. Relationship between subjective and physiological assessments of noise-disturbed sleep. In *Proceedings of the 2nd International Congress on Noise as a Health Problem, Dubrovnik*, (W. D. Ward, ed.), US Environmental Protection Agency, Washington D.C. (1973).

59 THIESSEN, G. J. *Truck Noise, Sleep and Habituation.* ASA Meeting, Los Angeles (1973).

60 OSADA, Y., OGAWA, S., OHKUBO C., MIYAZAKI, K. Study on sleep interference by train noise. *Bull. Inst. Public Health*, **23**, 1974.

61 THIESSEN, G. J. Habituation of behavioural awakening and EEG measures of response to noise. *Congress on Noise as a Public Health Problem, Freiburg, 1978. Proceedings of the American Speech-Language Hearing Association.* Report 10, Rockville, pp. 397–400 (1980).

62 JANSEN, G. *Effects of Noise on Physiological State. Noise as a Public Health Hazard.* ASHA Report 4, pp. 89–98 (1969).

63 RICE, C. Sonic boom exposure effects: sleep effects. *Journal of Sound and Vibration*, **22**, 511–517 (1972).

64 GRIEFAHN, B. Long term exposure to noise. Aspects of adaptation, habituation and compensation. *Waking Sleeping*, **1**, 383–386 (1977).

65 VERNET, M. Comparison between train noise and road noise annoyance during sleep. *Journ. Sound Vib.* (1983) 87(2), 331–335.

66 ANDO, Y. and HATTORI, H. Effects of intense noise during fetal life upon postnatal adaptability. *Journal of The Acoustic Society of America*, **47**, 1128–1130 (1970).

67 FIDELL, S., HORONJEFF, R., TEFFETELLER, S. and PEARSONS, K. Adaptation to changes in aircraft noise exposure. Presented at *The 99th Meeting of Acoustical Society of America.* Atlanta (1980).

68 HORONJEFF, R. D., BENNETT, R. L. and TEFFETELLER, S. R. EPRI Report EA-1240, Vol. 2. *Sleep Interference. Initial Study on The Effects of Transformer and Transmission Line Noise on People.* (1979).

69 HORONJEFF, R. D., FIDELL, S., TEFFETELLER, S. R. and GREEN, D. M. Behavioural awakening as functions of duration and detectability of noise intrusions in the home. *Journal of Sound and Vibration*, **84**, 327–336. (1982).

70 VALLET, M. and FRANCOIS, J. Evaluation physiologique et psychosociologique de l'effet du bruit d'avion sur le sommeil. *Travail Humain*, **45**, 155–168 (1982).

71 HEMINGWAY, J. R., DICKINSON, P. J. Report on environmental noise in Ontario with reference to health related effects. Ontario Ministry of Environment, Toronto (1981).

72 KNIPSCHILD, P. Medical effects of aircraft noise. *Int. Archs. occup. envir. Hlth*, **40**, pp. 185–204 (1977).

73 RELSTER, J. *Effects of Traffic Noise on Psychical Health.* National Danish Road Laboratory (1981).

74 LAMURE, C. *et al.* Le problème de l'indice de bruit nocturne pour les riverains de voies de circulation. *Revue d'Acoustique*, **62**, 180–186 (1982).

75 CEC. *EUR Report 5398e—Damage and Annoyance Caused by Noise* (1975).

76 OECD. *Report—Reducing Noise in OECD Countries.* OECD, Paris (1978).

77 WHO. *Environmental Health Criteria 12—Noise.* WHO, Geneva (1980).

78 LARGE, J. Airport noise standards. *New Scientist*, **Dec.**, 651 (1981).

79 RICE, C. G. *A Synthesis of Studies on Noise Induced Sleep Disturbance.* Institute of Sound and Vibration Research, Southampton. Report 623 (1982).

80 MAURIN, M. *Recherche d'un indice Acoustique Nocturne.* Rapport IRT-CERNE au CETUR 1980.

81 FRUSTHORFER, B., *et al.* Daytime noise stress and subsequent night sleep: interference with sleep patterns, endocrine functions and serotoninergic system. *Presented at The 4th International Congress on Noise as a Public Health Problem.* In Rossi, J. (ed.) Amplifon, Torino, pp.00–00 (1983).

82 LIENARD, P. Décibels et iondices de bruit—MASSON—Paris 1978.

83 *Noise. Final Report,* Committee on the problem of noise—Hill. HMSO, London Report SS337 (1963).

84 OLLERHEAD, J. B. *Noise Control Engineering,* **11**, 68–78 Variation of community responses to aircraft noise with time of day. (1978).

85 RICE, C. G. *Time of Day Corrections to Aircraft Noise Metrics.* FAA/NASE Workshop NASA CP 2135/FAA-EE-80-3 (1980).

86 Civil Aviation Authority—DORA Report 8008. Aircraft Noise and Sleep Disturbance: Final Report, London, 1980.

87 DIAMOND, I.A., WALKER, J. G. An interim study of the influence of residual noise on community disturbance due to aircraft noise. *Internoise 86.*

88 SCHULTZ, T. J. Synthesis of social surveys on noise annoyance. *Journal of The Acoustic Society of America*, **64**, 377–405 (1978).

89 RUCKER, A. Strassenverkehrslärm in Wolhgebieten. *Kampf dem Lärm*, **22**, 72–81 (1975).

90 KASTKA, J. and BUCHTA, E. Zum Inhalt der Belästigungsreaktion auf StraBenverkehrslärm. *Kampf dem Lärm*, **24**, 158–165 (1977).

91 HOLZMANN, X. X. In *Beeinträchtigung des Schlafes durch Lärm; Lärmbekämpfung*, Vol. 29, pp. 13–16 (1982).

92 FINKE, H. O., GUSKI, R. and ROHRMANN, B. *Betroffenheit einer Stadt durch Lärm.* UBA-Forschungsbericht 80-105 01 301, Berlin (1980).

93 VALLET, M., GAGNEUX, J. M. and CLAIRET, J. M. *Effects à long terme du bruit d'avion sur le sommeil.* Contrat Ministère de l'Environnement GBV 80-281 (1983).

Further reading

KRYTER, K. D. *The Effects of Noise on Man.* 2nd edn. Academic Press, New York (1985).

GRIEFAHN, B., JANSEN, G. and KLOSTERKÖTTER, W. *Zur Problematik lärmbedingter Schlafstörungen—Eine Auswertung von Schlafliteratur.* Umwelt Bundes amt, Berlin (1976).

JANSEN, G. and GROS, E. *Study to Determine the Critical Groups and the Size of the Population to be Considered for Noise.* Document 4379/1/76e, Commission of the European Communities (1976).

LANGDON, F. J. The problem of measuring the effects of noise. In Alexandre, A., Barde, J. PH., Lamure, C., Langdon, F. J. (eds) *Road Traffic Noise*, London, S. 27 (1975).

GRIFFITHS, I. D. Review of community response to noise. In Rossi, G. (ed.) *Proceedings of The 4th International Congress on Noise*, Edizioni Tecniche Amplifon, Milano (1983).

PACHIAUDI, G., VERNET, M. *et al.* Le bruit des trains: Note d'information 33 de l'Institut de Recherche des Transports, ISBN 2.85782.129.8 Décembre (1984).

STRUMZA, M. V. Influence des bruits intermittents d'avion sur le sommeil. *Medecine Aeronautique et Spatiale, Medecine Subaquatique et Hyperbare*, **17**, 344 (1978).

Part 3

Road Traffic Noise

6

Some Characteristics of Noise From Single Vehicles

B. Buna BSc, PhD, MIOA
Institute for Transport Sciences, Budapest, Hungary

Contents

6.1 Introduction

Traffic noise results from the collective contribution of the noise produced by individual motor vehicles. These vehicles vary enormously depending upon their type and mode of operation. Cars form the largest group and the vast majority of this group are powered by water-cooled diesel or petrol engines with engine capacities ranging typically between 1 and 2 l. Heavy commercial vehicles are generally powered by diesel engines developing engine powers in the range 50–250 kW. These vehicles are designed for freight haulage operations with maximum carrying capacities typically ranging between 3.5 tonnes to 38 tonnes although higher gross vehicles weights are allowed in some countries. Between these two groups there exists a less well-defined range of vehicles which are composed mainly of light commercial vehicles in which petrol and diesel power units are equally common. Motorcycles generally form the smallest of the main groups.

The noise generated by single vehicles depends primarily upon:

1. Type and class of vehicle (e.g. cars, trucks, buses, motor cycles etc.).
2. The quantity and quality of noise control measures used in the vehicle design.
3. The mechanical condition of in-service vehicles (e.g. wearing of components, condition of exhaust silencer, engine tuning, etc.).
4. The mode of operation of the vehicle (e.g. steady speed, acceleration/deceleration, gear setting).
5. The condition of the road surface.
6. The propagation conditions (e.g. reflecting obstacles, screening).

In view of the large number of variables, two main methods have been developed to quantify systematically the peak levels generated by passing vehicles. The first is the standard acceleration test as described in ISO Recommendation ISO R 362 and in BS 3425 (*see* Chapter 9 for a detailed description of the test methods). This requires the use of an open test area which has been standardized specifically for rating vehicle noise. The second method makes use of roadside measurements where a wider grouping of vehicles is used and peak noise levels of individual vehicles are measured in real traffic situations.

6.2 Noise emission characteristics of individual vehicles

An example of vehicle noise data collected using roadside measurement is given in *Figure 6.1*[1]. The figure gives cumulative distributions of noise levels generated by various categories of vehicles in urban conditions. The measurements were carried out at several different locations in Aachen (FRG) and cover a wide range of traffic situations. The distributions were determined from over 22 000 vehicle pass-by events.

The recorded A-weighted maximum noise levels ranged between 57 and 93 dB(A). The quietest vehicles were found to be cars fitted with petrol engines with about 45% having a noise emission level in urban traffic of less than 70 dB(A). The loudest vehicles were heavy trucks with engine powers exceeding 150 kW. Their noise level was found to exceed the noise emission for the car group by 15 dB(A) on average, at similar urban locations. A comparison of the noise output of various categories of road vehicles is given in *Table 6.1*.

The table also shows that trucks form the noisiest group in

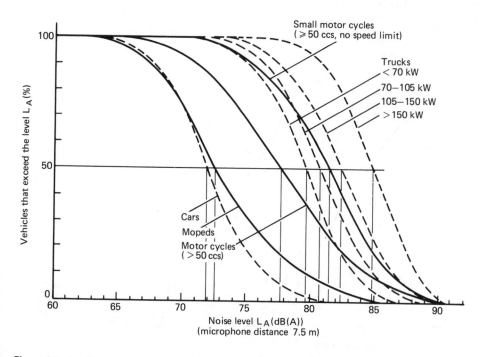

Figure 6.1 Distribution of peak noise levels of various groups of vehicles taken from vehicles operating in urban traffic conditions

Table 6.1 Median and L_5 noise levels of different classes of vehicles (urban conditions—reference distance 7.5 m)

Vehicle category	L_{50} (dB(A))	L_5 (dB(A))
Mopeds	73	82
Small motor cycles	82	88
Motor cycles (general classification)	78	87
Cars:		
With gasoline engines	70.5	77
With diesel engines	72	78
Pick-up vehicles:		
With gasoline engines	72.5	79
With diesel engines	75	80.5
Buses	80	86
Trucks with engines:		
$\leqslant 105\,\text{kW}$	79.5	85.5
$\leqslant 150\,\text{kW}$	82.5	88.5
$> 150\,\text{kW}$	85	90.5

L_5 is the noise level exceeded by 5% of the sample and L_{50} is the level exceeded by 50%.

traffic with buses and some motor cycles next and cars are the quietest. Cars and pick-up vehicles fitted with diesel engines were found to be noisier by some 1–2 dB(A) than those fitted with gasoline engines.

This acoustic classification or ranking of vehicle types does not radically change when comparing the maximum noise output generated during the standard acceleration test procedure. (Details of the acceleration test are given in Chapter 9.) For example, *Figure 6.2* shows distributions of type approval test results[2] obtained in Sweden in 1978–79.

By comparing *Figures 6.1* and *6.2* it can be seen that the L_{50} levels differ by an almost constant amount, 4–7 dB(A) depending upon the class of vehicle. The systematic difference arises because of the higher noise generated during acceleration; however, the rank order remains the same for both cases.

The absolute noise levels of different vehicle classes also depends upon the year of type approval of vehicles. Owing to improvements in vehicle design and to a general tightening of the maximum noise limits of new vehicles in recent years, generally vehicle noise levels have reduced slightly over the past decade. For example, during the 1970s the average noise level of in-service cars reduced by approximately 1.5 dB(A).[2,3]

Typical octave band noise spectra of heavy and light vehicles moving under freely flowing conditions are given in *Figure 6.3*.[4] (Heavy vehicles are classified as having an unladen weight greater than 1525 kg.) The shapes of the spectra are similar; the levels in the 100–200 Hz region are higher than in the mid-frequency range. The A-weighted levels are therefore largely controlled both by the low- and the mid-frequency noise. The scatter within each group is about 10 dB and the differences in levels between groups are 8–10 dB which is similar to the median differences indicated in *Figure 6.1*. Typical one-third octave spectra for heavy and light vehicles are shown in *Figures 7.2–7.5*.

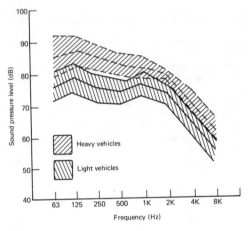

Figure 6.3 Typical noise spectra of vehicles moving under freely flowing conditions

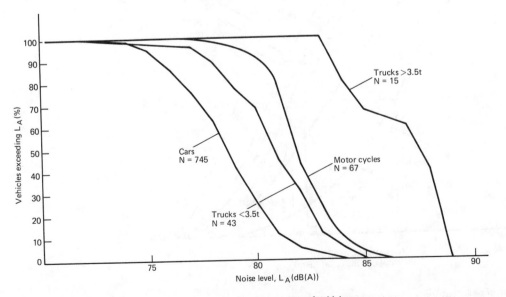

Figure 6.2 Distribution of type approval test results of various groups of vehicles

6.2.1 Cars

Despite the fact that the noise generated by cars is lower than most other vehicle groups they contribute greatly to the overall traffic noise emission characteristics because of their large numbers. In general terms, cars account for about 80% of total travel on roads. *Figure 6.4* compares type approval levels of cars obtained in different countries.[2-9] The levels were taken at the standard distance of 7.5 m except in the USA where the reference distance is 50 ft. In this case the US data has been adjusted to the 7.5 m distance to enable a direct comparison to be made. It can be seen that the average exterior noise of cars manufactured at the beginning of the eighties ranges between 77 and 81 dB(A). Of the data compared, the quietest car group overall is located in Switzerland which although not having a manufacturing base for automobiles has introduced stringent noise emission requirements for vehicles imported into the country. The range of noise levels for the whole group is about 12 dB(A).

Further details of the German and UK surveys[5,9] are given in *Table 6.2*.

6.2.2 Trucks

Some information about the noise levels emitted by commercial vehicles has already been given in *Figures 6.1–6.3*. These vehicles are generally powered by diesel engines although petrol engines are also widely used for light commercial vehicle operation. An important feature differentiating between the two combustion processes in terms of noise is the engine speed range, which is always lower for heavy duty diesel engines and which can give rise, as a result, to a greater degree of low-frequency noise emission. Another feature is the compression ratio, which is substantially higher for diesels leading to greater pressure fluctuations in cylinder pressure and, as a result, generally higher noise levels generated by both mechanical and combustion related sources. Chapter 7 gives a full description of diesel engine noise and other vehicle sources.

Some typical noise levels obtained from trucks at 7.5 m are given in *Table 6.3*.

The table also contains the noise levels, achieved by complete on-the-vehicle encapsulation of the engine and gearbox. Further

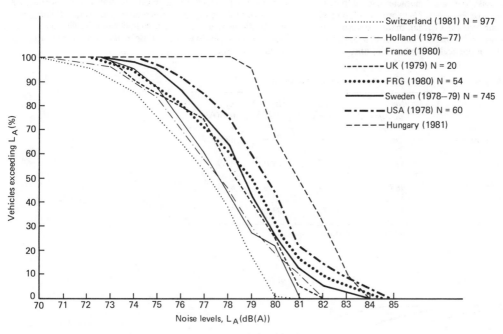

Figure 6.4 Distribution of car type approval test results

Table 6.2 Some typical car drive-by noise test results and vehicle parameters[5,9]—reference distance 7.5 m

Engine type	Power/weight ratio (HP/tonne)	Stroke volume (cm³)	Power (HP)	No. of forward ratios	Maximum engine speed (rpm)	No. of cylinders	Noise level (dB(A))
Gasoline	77	1577	85	Automatic 3	5600	4	77.5
Gasoline	116	2119	135	4	5700	5	82
Gasoline	121	2717	177	Automatic 4	6000	6	74
Gasoline	39	589	23	4	4700	2	80
Gasoline	98	1981	112	5	5600	4	77.5
Diesel	54	2304	71	4	4500	4	81.5
Gasoline	84	1985	102	4	5500	4	79
Diesel	50	2053	60	4	4400	4	82
Gasoline	75	1187	60	4	5400	4	80.5

Note: 1 Hp = 0.746 kW.

Table 6.3 Some truck drive-by noise test results and vehicle parameters—reference distance 7.5 m

Vehicle type	Engine type	Power (kW)	No. of cylinders	No. of forward ratios	Gross weight (tonne)	Stroke volume (cm³)	Max. engine speed (rev/min)	Noise level (dB(A))	
								Standard vehicle	Quietened vehicle
Delivery truck	Diesel	96	6	5	7.49	6 128	2800	90	77
Construction-site truck	Diesel	188	V8	8	26	12 763	2500	88	76
Delivery truck	Diesel	63	4	5	5–6	3 782	2800	87	77
Artic. tractor	Diesel	255	6	12	38	12 950	2100	91	79
Rigid (long distance)	Diesel	255	V10	8	16	15 950	2500	90	80

information on this topic and other vehicle noise quietening programmes are given in Chapter 8.

6.2.3 Buses and coaches

A summary of the noise emission characteristic of buses is contained in *Figure 6.5* and *Table 6.4*. These are based on results taken from 17 different types of German-made urban or long-distance buses and coaches.[10] Further details of bus noise levels is given in Chapter 12, in particular, *Figures 12.5* and *12.6*.

6.2.4 Motor cycles

The noise levels of motor cycles vary over a very substantial range reflecting the diverse nature of the vehicle class. Changes in motor-cycle design over recent years have led to a wide range of engine capacities with a similar large range in vehicle power to weight ratio. High revving multi-cylinder two-stroke engines and large multi-cylinder four-stroke machines fitted with gearboxes with up to six ratios have been developed. The sale of trail bikes with low gearing for road use provides a further variation within the class.

Table 6.4 Typical bus noise levels in urban conditions—reference distance 7.5 m

Traffic condition	No. of measurements	L_{95} (dB(A))	L_{50} (dB(A))	L_5 (dB(A))
Starting (acceleration from rest)	94	70.2	76.9	84.2
Steady speed $V = 40$–50 km/h	493	77.3	81.0	87.9
acceleration $V = 30$–40 km/h	983	74.6	82.6	87.4
high-speed operation (urban freeway)	176	79.7	83.9	87.6

*L_{95}, L_{50} and L_5 are the noise levels exceeded by 95%, 50% and 5% of the sample respectively.

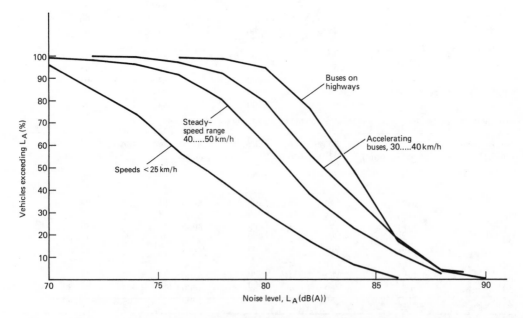

Figure 6.5 Generalized distribution of pass-by noise levels for buses moving under different flow conditions. Reference distance 7.5 m

Table 6.5 lists the results of tests carried out on 37 different motor cycles covering the range of types currently in use. The noise levels quoted are both the EEC 1015 test noise level which is based on a full throttle acceleration in low gear (Chapter 9 gives details of this test) and also the noise level generated at maximum power. A further survey of motor-cycle noise has been carried out by Sandberg *et al.*[12] It can be seen that in many cases the noise levels generated by motor cycles during normal acceleration can exceed the levels generated by heavy diesel engined trucks even though the maximum power capabilities of motor cycles are very much less. It is for this reason and because motor cycles can be ridden in a noisy fashion in sensitive areas

that has led to this category of vehicle being judged the most disturbing in noise terms.[13]

The noise spectra of motor cycles generally have a similar shape as other vehicles; however, because of the high-revving nature of the motor-cycle engine, the fundamental firing frequencies and the higher order harmonics are generally higher than petrol-engined cars and substantially higher than the spectra for heavy-duty diesel engines used in commercial vehicles.

The data collected by Waters[14] suggest that there are three broad classes of motor cycle with different noise characteristics. The divisions were based on engine size rather than engine type,

Table 6.5 Motor cycle description and noise levels

Age (years)	Mileage (km 10³)	Engine description					Noise level* (dB(A))	
		Capacity (cc)	Stroke (2 or 4)	Cylinders (No.)	Max. power (bhp)	Max. power speed (rev/min)	EEC 1015	Max. power
1	8.8	49	2	1	2.9	7 200	72	76
2	2.4	49	2	1	3.1	6 500	72	73
4	5.9	49	2	1	2.2	NA	76	77
3	26.9	89	4	1	7.5	8 000	80	80
1	5.1	99	2	1	11	8 500	80	83
1	5.1	124	2	1	15	8 500	78	88
1	16.2	124	4	2	16.5	9 000	77	90
1	5.3	123	2	1	13.5	8 000	77	90
1	14.9	183	2	1	17.8	8 000	83	86
3	32.0	194	4	2	16	9 000	84	89
1	7.4	195	2	2	20	9 000	81	89
2	6.0	246	4	2	27	10 000	76	83
3	7.2	247	2	2	30	8 000	85	89
1	9.4	248	4	2	27	9 000	87	91
1	2.6	248	4	1	20	7 500	85	91
1	16.8	248	4	2	26	10 000	77	89
1	4.5	249	4	2	27	10 000	81	92
<1	0.1	343	2	2	28	5 250	87	90
3	44.2	371	2	3	27	8 000	87	90
2	14.7	395	4	2	40	9 500	84	91
1	8.5	423	4	2	40	8 500	85	88
2	7.0	496	4	2	50	9 000	90	95
3	20.0	499	4	1	32	7 000	87	93
3	48.3	549	4	4	54	9 500	82	92
<1	15.5	626	4	4	63	9 500	84	91
<1	1.1	649	4	2	50	7 250	85	92
2	6.5	652	4	4	64	8 500	81	87
3	1.8	744	4	2	54	NA	85	90
3	33.3	747	4	3	68	7 500	85	96
3	33.0	748	4	4	79	9 000	82	90
3	28.8	748	4	4	68	9 200	84	93
3	17.4	864	4	2	68	8 000	99	104
<1	5.1	980	4	2	70	7 000	90	96
<1	1.0	980	4	2	70	7 000	91	96
<1	13.6	997	4	4	90	8 500	87	92
1	7.8	1047	4	6	100	9 000	83	93
2	36.8	1102	4	4	95	8 500	85	92

*EEC 1015: Values obtained according to the EEC/1015 test—*see* Chapter 9.

Max. power: Values obtained by extrapolating steady speed results to maximum power speed.

that is on cubic capacity and not according to whether the engine was two- or four-stroke.

Figure 6.6 illustrates the shape of the spectra of the three groups. The upper figure shows the spectra of three motorcycles with engines of more than 350 cc. The high/low frequency content can be seen as a steady decrease in level across the spectrum. These spectra have similar characteristics to light petrol-engined vehicles, and Waters reports that subjectively they had an acceptable character. The spectra of two motor cycles of capacity between 50 cc and 350 cc are shown in *Figure 6.6 (b)*. These have a much flatter shape with a higher ratio of high to low frequency content. The final group in *Figure 6.6 (c)*

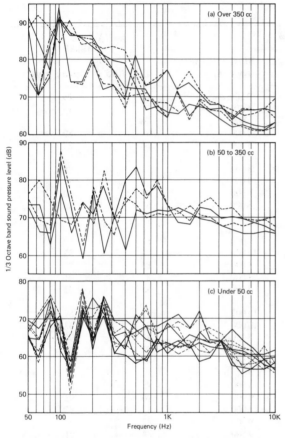

Figure 6.6 One third octave spectra of motor cycle noise (obtained under BS 3425: 1966 test conditions)

are the spectra for five motor cycles or mopeds of under 50 cc capacity. The spectrum of this class of machine is almost flat and the higher proportion of high frequency noise results in a harsher noise which is judged to be subjectively more annoying than the other two classes.

6.2.5 Trams and trolley-buses

The noise levels generated by trams are similar to the levels generated by trucks and are often higher than those of similar railway vehicles. A brief summary of noise levels measured at constant speed from trams are given in *Table 6.6*.[15] The data given in the table are taken from a survey of urban tram noise which included 30 vehicles and 17 different sites.[15] The average

noise level for trams operating at a typical speed of 40 km/h was found to be 78 dB(A) with values ranging between 73 and 84 dB(A) depending upon the type of track and vehicle.

Table 6.6 Tram noise levels taken at the distance of 7.5 m from track centreline

No.	Track	Noise at 40 km/h, (dB(A))	Noise at 60 km/h, (dB(A))
1	Ballast and concrete tie	73	78
2	Concrete slab	72	78
3	Ballast and wood tie	75	81
4	Ballast and concrete tie	76	85
5	Ballast and wood tie	82	86
6	Ballast and grooved rail	77	80
7	Ballast and steel tie	74	81

During the period 1970–1978 the average noise levels from trams operating in the city of Cologne were reduced by about 3 dB(A) due to general improvements in vehicle and track design. The distribution of open site noise levels from trams running on ballasted track is given in *Figure 6.7*. These results are in good agreement with measurements taken of tram noise in the USA which are summarized in *Figure 6.8*.[16]

Figure 6.9 shows typical ⅓rd octave noise spectra for trams operating between the steady speeds of 40 km/h and 60 km/h.[15] The figure shows that apart from an expected shift in the general frequency distribution as the speed increases, the spectra are fairly flat over the mid-frequency range, i.e. from about 200 Hz to 2 kHz. Tram noise does not contain substantial components of low-frequency noise because the main source of noise is rolling noise and not the propulsion system. Individual noise peaks are sometimes found at wheel resonance frequencies.

The noise levels generated by trolley-buses are generally between the levels generated by buses and trams. The rolling noise from trolley buses is, however, less than for trams due to the use of rubber tyred wheels but their electric propulsion noise often exceeds the rolling noise component.

6.3 Vehicle noise and mode of operation

Apart from vehicle class or category, the noise generated by individual vehicles depends upon the mode of operation and, in particular, the speed of the engine and the applied load. These parameters are, in turn, affected by the operating speed of the vehicle, the gear selected, and whether or not the vehicle is accelerating/decelerating or running at constant speed. A further factor that requires consideration is the style of driving adopted by the operator.

Figure 6.10 illustrates, for a medium-capacity saloon car, typical steady speed noise levels as a function of vehicle speed and gear selected. It is clear that when the vehicle is operating in 1st and 2nd gear the overall levels of vehicle noise are controlled mainly by the power unit whereas for vehicle operations in 3rd and, particularly, top gear where the road speed is high, the overall noise levels are strongly influenced by the noise generated from the vehicle tyres rolling on the road surface. Vehicle rolling noise depends upon a number of factors involving both the design of the tyre and the road surface but as a close

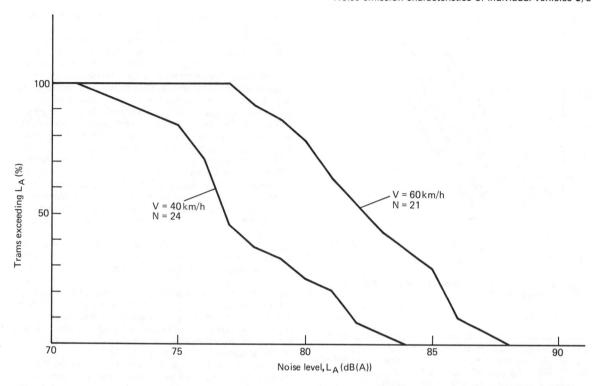

Figure 6.7 Distribution of open site noise levels from trams moving on ballasted track.[15] Reference distance 7.5 m from track centreline

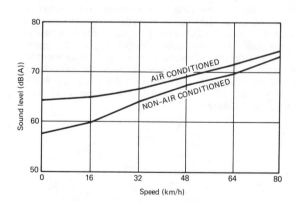

Figure 6.8 Tram noise levels at different speeds[16] measured at 15 m from the track centreline (ballast and tie track)

approximation rolling noise can be considered to depend on vehicle speed increasing by about 9 dB(A) for each doubling of speed within the operating range.

This aspect is clearly demonstrated in *Figure 6.11* which shows regression relations constructed for six different categories of road vehicles.[19] The data were taken from a large number of vehicle noise level and speed observations using vehicles operating in traffic. The figure shows that above about 50 km/h, where rolling noise starts to become important, the noise level increases by about 9 dB(A) per doubling of speed for each vehicle category. For low speeds typical of urban driving the characteristics exhibit a zero dependence on vehicle speed which reflects the mode of operation (gear changing) and the fact that

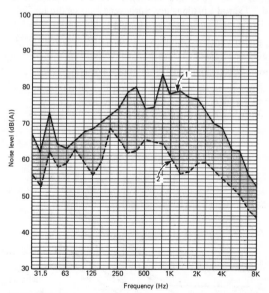

Figure 6.9 Noise spectra for trams moving at constant speed. 1 = Loudest tram–site combination at 60 km/h. 2 = Quietest tram–site combination at 40 km/h.

the power train is the dominant noise source. It is worth noting that for low-speed operation the heaviest trucks were found to be 17 dB(A) noisier than the car group whereas under free-speed operation the trucks were only 9 dB(A) noisier. Further information on vehicle noise level–speed relations can be obtained from *Figures 6.5, 6.7* and *6.9* and *Tables 6.4* and *6.6* of this

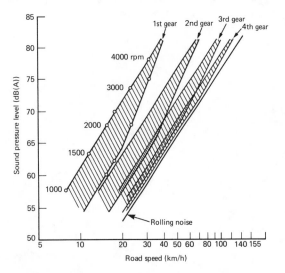

Figure 6.10 Drive-past noise levels of a medium capacity car for a range of vehicle speeds

chapter as well as from Chapter 7 which gives a detailed examination of vehicle noise sources and their control.

When the road speed changes, the drive past noise level will depend upon the rate of change of vehicle speed, i.e. the acceleration/deceleration and the original velocity of the vehicle. Regression equations have been determined which describe the variation in noise level as a function of acceleration and vehicle speed.[20] Typical equations are reproduced below both for light vehicles (i.e. $\leqslant 1525$ kg unladen weight) and for heavy vehicles:

$$L_A \text{ (light)} = 33.2 + 23.8 \log_{10} V + 10.6a - 0.08a^2 - 5.73a \log_{10} V$$
$$L_A \text{ (heavy)} = 48.5 + 18.9 \log_{10} V + 7.5a - 0.11a^2 - 4.29a \log_{10} V$$

where $a =$ acceleration and $V =$ original velocity.

These functions are presented in three-dimensional graphical form in *Figure 6.12* for both groups of vehicles.

A further illustration of the differences in noise levels gener-

ated by vehicles accelerating compared with steady speed operation is given in *Figure 6.13*.[21] The graph shows the results of a large number of vehicle noise tests carried out on cars travelling both at constant speed and accelerating according to the ISO acceleration test. The results are plotted as cumulative distributions of the differences between the two test conditions for three different steady speed vehicle speeds. The full lines were obtained with the vehicles operating in top gear for the steady speed test and the broken line was obtained when the vehicle was operated at 50 km/h in 2nd gear. It can be seen that, in general, the differences are positive, indicating that the acceleration condition produces greater noise levels than steady speed operation even at the highest steady speeds recorded. Some negative differences were observed, particularly for small-capacity and low power to weight cars which were operating close to rated speed at the highest steady speeds. For some large-capacity or high power to weight vehicles operating at low steady speeds the acceleration noise levels exceeded the steady state noise levels by 10–15 dB(A).

Figure 6.14 illustrates how the rate of acceleration can influence vehicle noise for two typical cars powered by petrol and diesel engines respectively.[9] In general, the diesel-powered vehicles generated a smaller increase in noise over the steady state condition than the petrol-powered equivalent. This result is typical of small diesel-powered cars which generally exhibit less dependence of noise on acceleration than larger petrol engines. The non-linear behaviour of the upper curve was due, in this particular example, to the presence of exhaust resonances at critical points in the engine speed range.

Clearly, the mode of operation can have a marked effect on the noise levels generated by vehicles, particularly petrol-powered vehicles with high power to weight performance. A further factor that influences actual noise levels generated by in-service vehicles is the driving style adopted by the operator. *Figure 6.15* compares the drive-by noise levels recorded from a medium-capacity saloon car (1.8 l, 66 kW) when the drivers were asked to drive aggressively (wild), normally (average) and in a passive manner (mild). The distributions clearly show that the aggressive style of driving substantially increased the noise emitted. For example, the median difference between the noisiest and quietest driving style was of the order of 5 dB(A) although at the higher fractiles of the distribution the difference reached approximately 7 dB(A).

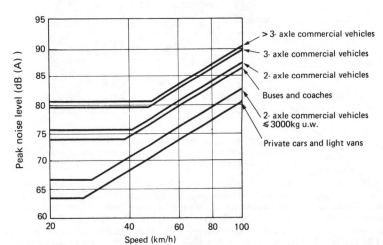

Figure 6.11 Generalized sound level/speed characteristics for different vehicle categories

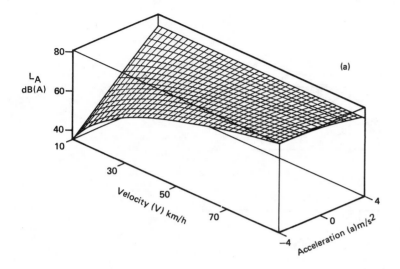

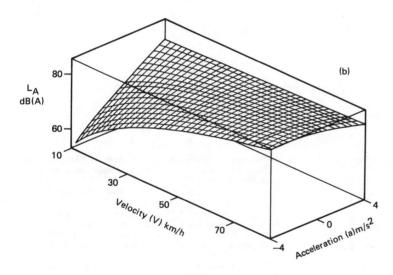

Figure 6.12 Three-dimensional representation of A-weighted sound pressure level functions for (*a*) light vehicles (⩽1525 kg unladen weight) and (*b*) heavy vehicles

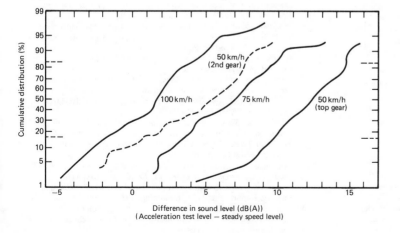

Figure 6.13 Cumulative distributions of the differences in maximum noise levels between ISO acceleration test and constant speed pass by

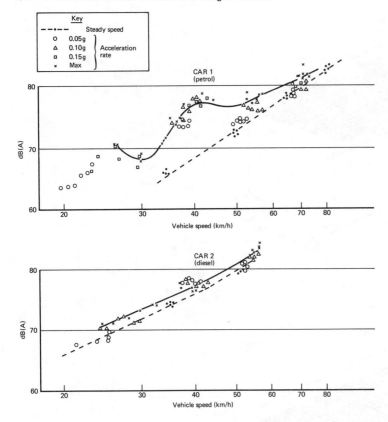

Figure 6.14 Effect of acceleration rate on car noise

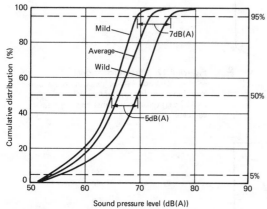

Figure 6.15 Effect of driving style on drive-past noise for a medium capacity car

References

1 STEVEN, H. Geräuschemission von Kraftfahrzeugen im realen Verkehr. *VDI-Berichte*, **499**, 9 (1983).

2 LIEDHOLM, B-L. and ZETTERLING, T. Noise from road vehicles and traffic. *The National Swedish Environment Protection Board, Stockholm*, Report No. 1320 (1980) (in Swedish).

3 ENTHOVEN, M. E. E. and NOORT, R. B. J. C. *Road Traffic and the Noise Abatement Act*. Association of the Dutch motor and cycle trade industry (1977).

4 LEWIS, P. T. The noise generated by single vehicles in freely flowing traffic. *Journal of Sound and Vibration*, **30**, 191, 1973.

5 BETZL, W. *Untersuchungen über das Geräuschverhalten von Kraftfahrzeugen*. Deutsche Kraftfahrtforschung und Strassenverkehrstechnik, 267, VDI-Verlag, Düsseldorf (1980).

6 Light Vehicle Noise. *Wyle Research Report*, Vol. II, WR 78-13 (1978).

7 *Publication Concernant les Émissions des Véhicules*, Office Fédéral de la Police Suisse (1981).

8 LAMBERT, J. *Statistiques de Parcs et Niveaux Sonores des Véhicules Routiers, IRT-CERNE*, Internal Report (1981).

9 MORRISON, D. and CHALLEN, B. J. A survey of passenger car noise levels. In *Diesel Engine Noise Conference*, Society of Automotive Engineers, Warrendale, Paper 790442, p. 80 (1979).

10 STEVEN, H. *Vorbeifahrtgeräuschmessungen an Kraftfahrzeugen*, FIGE Report, Aachen (1980).

11 NELSON, P. M. and ROSS, N. F. *Some Aspects of Motor-cycle Noise Emission. Department of The Environment, Department of Transport TRRL Report SR 795*. Transport and Road Research Laboratory, Crowthorne (1983).

12 NELSON, P. M. *Some Notes on the Noise Disturbance Caused by Motor cycles. Department of The Environment, Department of Transport TRRL Report SR 569*. Crowthorne, Transport and Road Research Laboratory (1980).

13 SANDBERG, U., STAHL, P., BARRET, T. J. and MILD, R. *A Comparative Study of Measurement Standards for Regulating Maximum Motorcycle Noise Emission*, National Road and Traffic Research Institute Report, No. 243A, Linköping (1982).

14 WATERS, P. E. *The Origins and Characteristics of Motor cycle Noise*. Institution of Mechanical Engineering Conference. Vehicle noise and vibration, C144/84 (1984).

15 GROSS, K. and BLENNEMANN, F. *Lärmmessungen bei neuen Schienenfahrzeugen des Stadtverkehrs.* STUVA Report, Köln (1978).

16 SPENCER, R. H. Noise control of the standard light rail vehicle. *Noise Control Engineering*, **10**, 4 (1978).

17 BUNA, B., VERÉB, L. and UJSÁGHY, G. Comparison of the specific noise generation of the passenger transport means, XII. In *Proceedings of the AICB-Congress, Vienna*, p. 251 (1982).

18 STEVEN, H. Einfluss der Fahrweise auf die Gerauschemission eines Kraftfahrzeuges. *Zeitschrift für Larmbekampfung*, **30**, 67 (1983).

19 NELSON, P. M. *Classifying Road Vehicles for The Prediction of Road Traffic Noise.* Department of the Environment, Department of Transport. TRRL Laboratory Report LR752. Transport and Road Research Laboratory, Crowthorne (1977).

20 JONES, R. R. K. and HOTHERSALL, D. C. Effect of operating parameters on noise emission from individual road vehicles. *Applied Acoustics*, **13**, 121 (1980).

21 RATHE, E. J., *et al.* Survey of the exterior noise of some passenger cars. *Journal of Sound and Vibration*, **29**, 483 (1973).

Further reading

WATKINS, L. H. *Environmental Impact of Roads and Traffic*, Applied Science Publishers, London (1981).

ALEXANDRE, A., *et al. Road Traffic Noise*, Applied Science Publishers, London (1975).

BUNA, B. *Transportation Noise Control*, Technical Publisher, Budapest (1982) (in Hungarian, to be published at Springer Verlag, Berlin, in German.)

FASOLD, W. *et al. Taschenbuch Akustik*, Verlag Technik, Berlin (1984).

HECKL, M. and MÜLLER, H. A. *Taschenbuch der Technischen Akustik*, Springer-Verlag, Berlin (1975).

Le Bruit des Vehicules Routiers, Part I, Technica, No. 399 (1977), Part II, No. 401 (1978), L'Association des Anciens Éléves de L'École Centrale de Lyon.

Le Bruit des Vehicules. Ingenieurs de L'Automobile, 6 (1978).

OLSON, N. *Statistical Study of Traffic Noise*, National Research Council of Canada, Report, APS-476, Ottawa (1970).

7

Sources of Vehicle Noise

John W. Tyler FIHT, FIOA, Dip Stats, Hon RCM, Consultant
Transport and Road Research Laboratory, Crowthorne, UK

Contents

7.1 Noise sources and their relative importance

The sources of vehicle noise have been identified as the power unit (engine, air inlet and exhaust), cooling fan, transmission (gearbox and rear axle), rolling noise (aerodynamic and tyre/road surface), brakes, body rattles and load.[1] In general, sources related to the power unit and transmission up to the layshaft are referred to as power train noise and all other sources are termed rolling noise or coasting noise.

The relative importance of these sources depends on the type of vehicle and the operating conditions. With light vehicles the engine is dominant at low road speeds in low gears; at higher road speeds in top gear tyre rolling noise is likely to be of the same order or higher than power train noise. However, with heavy diesel-engined lorries the engine, exhaust and cooling fan noise are the dominant sources under most operating conditions although the noise of the tyres rolling on the road surface can be noticeable at high speeds, particularly with tyres having pronounced transverse ribs (traction tyres).

Internal cab noise is also a problem with the commercial vehicle and much effort has been directed, in recent years, by the manufacturers to reduce this as, of course, for the driver the cab is his place of work.

Because the separate noise sources combine logarithmically to produce overall vehicle noise, it is imperative that all main sources are reduced together since little or no noticeable improvement is made if, for example, exhaust noise is reduced by half when the engine noise is left untreated. Consequently, any workable programme of vehicle noise reduction has to take into account every important noise source.

This chapter will concentrate on the causes and possible solutions to the noise from the power train and the vehicle rolling on the road. Body rattles and load noise are largely a matter of maintenance and operational procedures and as such are not particularly amenable to research solutions.

7.1.1 Comparison of power train noise and rolling noise

A comparison between power train noise and rolling (coasting) noise at various speeds for typical light vehicles ($\leqslant 1.5$ tonnes) and heavy vehicles is shown in *Figure 7.1*. For both vehicle categories rolling noise increases at a rate of about 9 dB(A) per doubling of speed. At higher speeds power train noise, and hence total noise, increases at a similar rate, resulting in the contribution of rolling noise remaining approximately the same. At lower speeds in urban areas where lower gears are used, power train noise tends to be independent of road speed and hence rolling noise becomes less important as speed falls. These effects are usefully summarized in *Table 7.1*, where power train noise, rolling noise and total noise are given for the two vehicle classes and at a low and a high speed.

7.1.2 Vehicle noise spectra

Typical frequency spectra for commercial vehicles and large and small cars are illustrated in *Figures 7.2–7.5*. The principal impression to be gained at this stage from these spectra is that vehicle noise covers a substantial part of the audible range of frequencies and there are certain fairly well defined peaks in amplitude, for example air inlet, exhaust and body resonances around 40–100 Hz (mainly on the heavier goods vehicles), diesel 'knock' at between 1 and 3 kHz, and on cars, exhaust and body resonances in the region of 100–150 Hz. For most vehicles the level above 3 kHz decays at around 20 dB per decade of frequency. More detailed treatments of each vehicle source are given later in the chapter.

Table 7.1 Comparison of rolling and power train noise levels

Road speed (km/h)	Vehicle class	Rolling noise (dB(A))	Power train noise (dB(A))	Total noise (dB(A))
20	Heavy*	61	78	78
	Light	58	64	65
80	Heavy	79	85	86
	Light	76	74	78

*Heavy vehicles are > 1525 kg unladen weight.

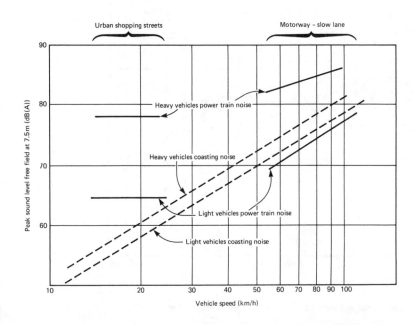

Figure 7.1 Vehicle power train noise and coasting noise (Tyre/road surface and aerodynamic noise.)

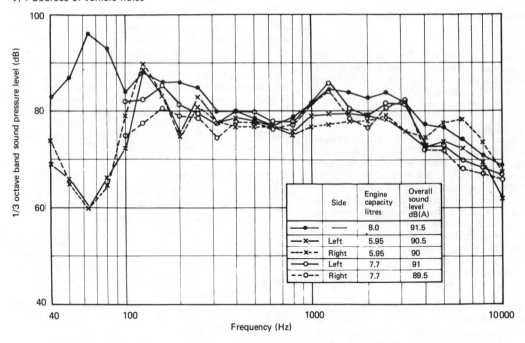

Figure 7.2   Spectrum of noise emitted by medium capacity commercial vehicles. Values taken at 7.5 m

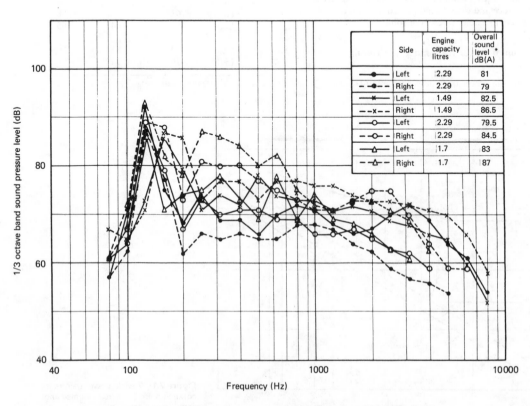

Figure 7.3   Spectrum of noise emitted by light commercial and passenger vehicles. Values taken at 7.5 m

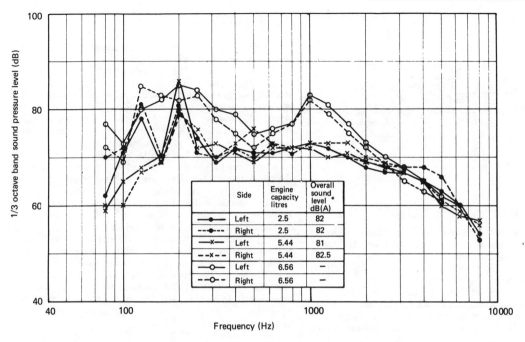

Figure 7.4 Spectrum of noise emitted by large cars. Values taken at 7.5 m

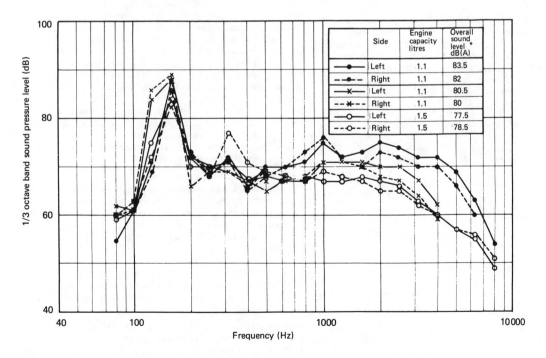

Figure 7.5 Spectrum of noise emitted by small cars. Values taken at 7.5 m

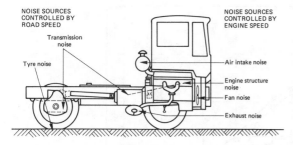

Figure 7.6 Sources of vehicle noise

7.1.3 Rank order of vehicle noise sources

Figure 7.6 illustrates the location of the various sources of noise for a typical diesel engined goods vehicle tractor unit and *Table 7.2* gives an example of the relative magnitude of the noise from the separate sources for a vehicle of this type operating in top gear at a steady speed of approximately 50 km/h.

A similar distribution for a passenger car is given in *Table 7.3*. When assembled into a complete vehicle the rank order of these sources and the combined noise level can change due to the screening effects of the vehicle body and reflections from the road surface. For example, in the case of the goods vehicle in *Table 7.2* the logarithmically combined noise sources give a total of 91 dB(A) whereas the measured noise level at 7.5 m was 89 dB(A). This effect is particularly marked in the case of passenger cars, light vans and buses where the body provides considerable shielding of the engine and transmission. Again in the example given in *Table 7.3* the calculated total noise level of the car components was 85 dB(A) but the measured level was only 79 dB(A).

7.1.4 Cab noise

The internal noise in a commercial vehicle cab has been reduced over the last decade from values typically 90–95 dB(A) to currently around 75 dB(A). This noise is caused by airborne noise and structure-borne vibration from the engine and tyre–road surface interaction and, therefore, is both road and engine speed dependent. Further information on driver comfort and cab noise levels is given in Chapter 8.

Table 7.2 Typical noise levels of sources (dB(A) at 7.5 m) (commercial tractor unit)

Exhaust	Engine and transmission*	Cooling fan	Inlet	Rolling
82	90	78	70	70

*Transmission about 70 dB(A).

Table 7.3 Typical noise levels of sources (dB(A) at 7.5 m) (passenger car)

Exhaust	Engine and transmission*	Cooling fan	Inlet	Rolling
74	84	65	65	68

*Transmission about 65 dB(A).

7.2 Engine noise

Comprehensive reference works on the design and characteristics of engines, both gasoline and diesel, are contained in references 2, 3 and 4. The history of the four-stroke internal combustion engine goes back as far as 1862 when Beu de Rochas[5] put forward the fundamental principles underlying the economical operation of the engine. This was followed 14 years later in 1876 when Dr Nicholas Otto built an engine which operated on the four-stroke principle. At that time the fuel (gas) was ignited electrically in a similar way to gasoline engines today but in 1892 Dr Rudolph Diesel, another German engineer, proposed the ignition of the fuel by compressing the air in the cylinder until a sufficiently high temperature was reached to ignite the fuel at the end of the compression stroke.

In the internal combustion engine, either spark or compression ignition, the duration of the applied force on the piston resulting from combustion in a cylinder is relatively short, typically about 1/50th of the total cycle time, and this transient nature of the force gives rise to the vibration and noise which are familiar characteristics of the internal combustion engine.

In this section the separate sources of engine noise will be identified and discussed first, followed by descriptions of the measurement techniques used. Finally, the noise control methods for each source will be described together with typical values of noise attenuation.

Priede,[6] Russell,[7,8] and Challen *et al.*[9-11] established the principal sources of engine noise. These are illustrated in *Figure 7.7.*[7] The two primary sources of engine noise are combustion-induced noise and noise due to mechanical impacts.

Since all the noise generated from either mechanical or combustion processes within the engine is radiated by the external surfaces of the engine, it might be thought impossible to separate the primary sources. In fact, however, it is possible to do so to a certain extent and is very necessary if a comprehensive and optimum programme of engine quietening is to be accomplished. Noise is produced by the gas loads applied to the engine structure by the combustion process; this is known as 'combustion noise'. Vibration applied to the structure by the impacts from the pistons (piston slap), by the timing gears driving the camshaft and fuel pump, by the bearings and valve gear is classed under the general heading of *mechanical noise*. Methods used to attempt to separate combustion from mechanical noise are discussed later but the general aim is to tackle the problem by controlling both sources. In addition, diesel-engine noise can be controlled by modifying the structure itself so that vibration levels and sound radiation efficiency are reduced and by quietening the auxiliary components attached externally to the engine, for example, fuel injector pump, air pump, alternator, etc.

It will be useful here to identify the main classes of engine that will be covered in this chapter. These are:

1. *Petrol or gasoline engines.* These engines are almost exclusively used for passenger cars and light vans and in general do not constitute the most serious noise problems. However, their characteristics are used in this chapter to compare with those of diesel engines.
2. *Direct injection (DI) diesel engines.* In this engine the fuel is injected directly into the combustion space. *Figure 7.8(a)* illustrates this process.
3. *Indirect injection (IDI), naturally aspirated diesel engine.* Here fuel is injected into a prechamber which communicates with the cylinder through a narrow passage (*see Figure 7.8(b)* and *7.8(c)*).

Both the above diesel engines can be turbocharged, where air is forced into the intake at pressures higher than atmospheric. Turbocharging affects the noise generated as well as the power output.

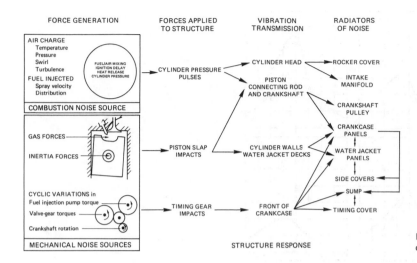

Figure 7.7 Noise generation processes in diesel engines (After Russell, SAE 820238.)

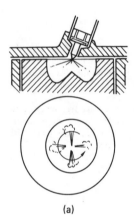

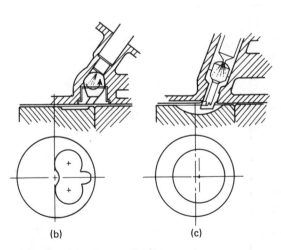

Figure 7.8 Diagram of combustion chamber types. (*a*) Direct injection deep bowl chamber with swirl (as used in DI vehicle engines). (*b*) Compression swirl separate chambers. (*c*) Pre-chamber type as

Direct injection engines are usually manufactured to deliver engine powers in the medium to high range and are, therefore, primarily used in the larger trucks and buses. Indirect injection is preferred for the smaller commercial vehicles and passenger cars because of its ability to run up to higher speeds (5000–6000 rev/min), because it only needs low injection pressures thus making injection problems easier to solve and because it is inherently quieter. Development work is in progress to utilize the DI combustion chamber for small engines with the aim of combining economy with low noise.

7.2.1 Combustion noise

The foundation of the present understanding of noise generation by the combustion process was established by Austen and Priede[6,12] between 1958 and 1966 and much further work has been done since then by other investigators (*see* Further reading). Combustion noise as a major source is primarily restricted to diesel engines although some petrol engines, with the present design objectives of lean mix, advanced ignition timing, and higher compression ratios to achieve high power output with economy, display noticeable combustion noise. The diesel engine achieves its high thermal efficiency by operating unthrottled at lean mixture strengths and high compression ratios. This means that high pressures are reached in the combustion chambers in very short times, the resulting steep pressure wave fronts causing the impacts which are transmitted through the piston, connecting rod, cylinder head and wall and crankcase to reach the outside air as noise. A description of the generation of combustion noise is given by Russell.[7,8] In summary, fuel is injected into the cylinder near the top of the compression stroke and when mixed with the air at a high enough temperature and pressure, the mixture ignites. The period between the start of injection and ignition is known as 'ignition delay period' and this quantity has an important bearing on combustion noise. After ignition the injected fuel burns very rapidly causing a large and sudden release of heat and rise in combustion chamber pressure. Typical cylinder pressure versus crankshaft angle diagrams are shown in *Figure 7.9* for various combustion systems. The steep rise in cylinder pressure near top dead centre (TDC) can be seen. This is particularly marked in the case of the direct injection naturally aspirated engine with its generally long ignition delay period. The rate of pressure rise is, typically, 8 bar per degree of crankshaft rotation. The turbocharged DI engine

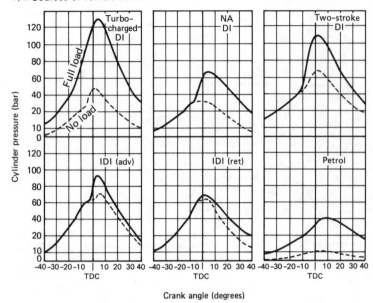

Figure 7.9 Typical pressure diagrams of various combustion systems (NB. 1 bar=10⁵ N m⁻²)

has a shorter delay period with a more gradual rise in pressure (2–3 bar/degree) resulting in lower combustion noise. The naturally aspirated (NA) IDI engine has an intermediate value of 3–4 bar/degree.

A more useful guide to the noise producing potential of combustion pressure pulses is their frequency spectrum. As the engine runs, the piston and cylinder head are subjected to repeated pressure pulses with a steep wave front and many harmonic frequencies. A frequency analysis of the combustion

pressure diagram reveals a lot more about the nature of the combustion process than just the plot of cylinder pressure against time. For example *Figure 7.10* shows the effect of engine speed on combustion noise. The spectra exhibit a shift to higher frequencies proportional to speed.

The general shape of the cylinder pressure frequency spectrum is a decreasing level with increasing frequency. Challen[9] gives typical rates of decay of cylinder pressure level with frequency for different combustion systems:

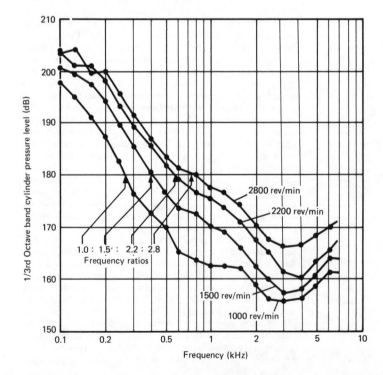

Figure 7.10 Effect of engine speed on cylinder pressure spectra with the engine pulling full load. Note that spectra show shift to right proportional to speed. After Russell[8]

NA-DI	— 25–30 dB/decade*
Turbocharged DI	— 40–50 dB/decade
NA-IDI	— 40–50 dB/decade
Gasoline (petrol)	— 50–60 dB/decade

(*Decade means a change of frequency of one tenth, e.g. 2 kHz–200 Hz).

The part of the spectrum from 1–4 kHz, emphasized in the case of the NA-DI engine in *Figure 7.10*, is responsible for the characteristic diesel 'knock'. The increase in noise at higher frequencies (> 5 kHz) is due to gas oscillation in the cylinder. However, this characteristic of combustion noise generation does not usually show up in the external noise spectra of an engine.

The injection timing of the engine affects the combustion noise. In general, the more retarded the timing the lower the noise. This cannot, of course, be taken to extremes as other aspects of engine performance are adversely affected by retarding, for example, power output and emissions. The effect can be seen in *Figure 7.11* which shows that an ignition retard in a DI engine can reduce the rate of pressure rise and the level of the frequency spectrum to values similar to an IDI engine. In contrast, advancing the timing of an IDI engine can have the effect of making the engine display the combustion characteristics of a DI engine. The cylinder pressure is at a maximum at low frequencies, around 10–30 Hz, of the firing frequency of the particular cylinder being measured. Although these frequencies do not affect the A-weighted noise levels they are important in determining piston loading and hence mechanical noise.

7.2.2 Mechanical noise

The causes and effects of mechanical noise are covered in some detail by Russell,[7,8,13] Priede,[6] Anderton et al.,[14] Challen and Croker[11] and others listed in the Further reading.

Mechanical noise can originate from many different sources on an engine and can be much more difficult to locate and quantify than combustion noise. As Challen[9] points out there are situations where combustion noise and mechanical noise interact. For example, piston slap and loading where the mechanical impact and side force are directly attributable to the cylinder pressure but where the actual mechanism of noise generation may be considered as mechanical. For simplicity therefore it is necessary to consider combustion noise as that emanating from the pressure change characteristics in the combustion chamber, and mechanical noise as that originating from a collection of discrete sources with individual characteristics. As illustrated in *Figure 7.7* the most common sources of mechanical noise are:

1. *Piston slap.* Impacts between piston and cylinder wall as the piston moves from side to side during the engine cycle. References 15–20 describe work on piston slap done by several groups of research workers.
2. *Timing drive noise.* Impacts occur between the teeth of gears in the timing gear train as backlash is taken up in either direction. The reversals of direction occur as a result of crankshaft torsional vibration and the fluctuating torque requirements of the camshaft and the fuel injection equipment. These noises are also referred to as timing gear rattle.[7] The effect is mainly restricted to heavy duty automotive diesel engines which have to use gear drives because of the power transmission requirements. Light duty engines use chain or belt drives which are quieter as shown in *Figure 7.12*.
3. *Bearing forces and rotation.* The clearances between journal and bearing are periodically taken up as the forces reverse in the course of the operating cycle with resulting impacts and vibration generation.
4. *Others.* These include valve train impacts and fuel injection pump and injector needle closing impacts. These sources can produce some additional vibration depending on design but generally are of a lower order than the others mentioned above.

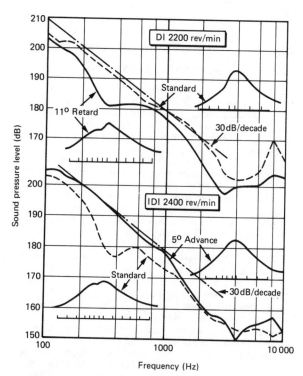

Figure 7.11 Comparison of DI and IDI cylinder pressure diagrams at various timings. After Challen[9]

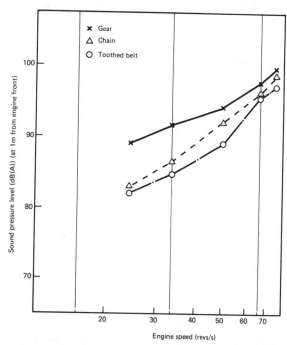

Figure 7.12 Timing drive noise characteristics. After Challen and Croker[11]

7.2.3 Speed and load effects on engine noise

7.2.3.1 Engine speed

Priede[21] has derived general relationships between engine speed and noise for groups of engines of different powers. These are illustrated in *Figure 7.13*.

For a given engine speed the figure shows that, in general, the lower the power output the lower the overall noise, with the gasoline engine being the quietest of all. However, when the engines are run at rated speed the differences are much less. The lower-powered diesel engines and the gasoline engines have rated speeds in the 4000–6000 rev/min range compared with 1200–2500 rev/min for the higher powered engines and this tends to remove some of the difference in noise between the types of engine. *Figure 7.14* shows the differences in slope of speed versus noise curves for four engines of the same size having different combustion systems.[22] For the two engines with quieter combustion characteristics, i.e. the IDI and gasoline engines, the slope of the curve changes at approximately

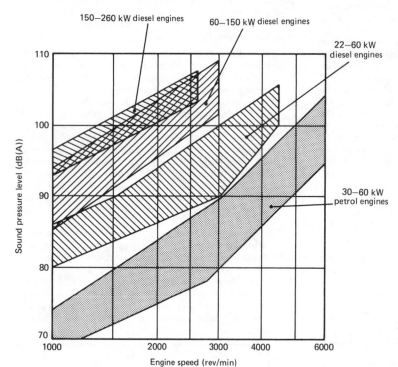

Figure 7.13 Noise of engines in various size groups showing characteristic noise ranges. After Priede[21]

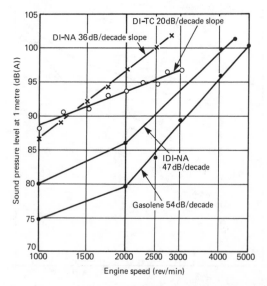

Figure 7.14 Typical noise versus speed curves for engines of 100 mm bore with different combustion systems. After Priede[22]

2000 rev/min whereas with the DI engines the slope is substantially constant although lower for the turbocharged engine. In the former case the change in slope is usually due to the mechanical noise becoming predominant at the change of slope and generally controlling the rate of rise.

With the DI naturally aspirated engines the noise is usually combustion controlled owing to the long ignition delay period and high rate of rise of cylinder pressure although this can be modified by the influence of particularly severe mechanical noise sources such as piston slap. Therefore, with these engines the slope of the curve is in the region of 30–40 dB(A) per decade. The turbocharged DI engine has a lower slope (about 20–30 dB(A) per decade) owing to the combination of smooth combustion at high speeds (and load) and the more abrupt combustion with higher mechanical noise at low speeds (due to the higher peak cylinder pressures arising from turbocharging). There are considerable variations between engines having the same combustion system, and the exact relationship between the two sources of noise, combustion and mechanical, is still not fully understood in spite of the large amount of theoretical and analytical work that has been carried out.

According to Challen[9] typical values for the speed/noise slope for a light duty (Comet V) engine would be 20 dB(A) per decade at speeds up to 1200–1800 rev/min increasing to 50 dB(A) per decade at speeds approaching 4500 rev/min. They give as the possible reasons for this effect that at low speeds the noise is dominated by piston slap, inertia loading being low and gas loading relatively high and piston/cylinder clearances being large at the lower temperature of low-speed running. At high speeds, however, the inertia loading may approach that of the gas load and this, together with the reduced piston/cylinder clearances due to the higher operating temperature, leads to a reduction in the impulsive force excitation and corresponding increase in slope. The noise at high speed is still regarded as mechanical in nature, however, but less impulsive than bearing noise which leads to the increase in slope.

7.2.3.2 Effect of load

The effect of load on engine noise depends on the engine size, rotational speed and method of injection and aspiration. For a high-speed, light-duty diesel engine and small gasoline engine the radiated noise is generally little affected by load, being mainly controlled by mechanical sources. The difference between full load and no load noise levels over the speed range is typically 1–2 dB(A). In the case of gasoline engines the no load noise can be higher than at full load since the cooler combustion chamber may produce a sharper rise in cylinder pressure. For larger normally aspirated DI engines the reduction of noise with load is of the order of 4–6 dB(A) over the speed range whereas with similar turbocharged DI engines the effect of change of load can be very small or 4–5 dB(A) depending on the degree of mechanical noise generated by the increased piston loading due to turbocharging. *Figure 7.15* gives a typical breakdown of combustion and mechanical noise for a 14 litre turbocharged DI engine over the load range.

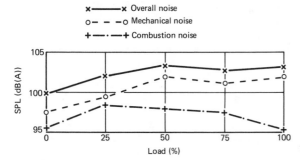

Figure 7.15 Source analysis over the load range of a turbocharged diesel truck engine. After Challen[11]

7.2.3.3 Engine noise prediction

Over the years several workers including Priede[6] and Challen[9] have gathered information on a large number of engines and have produced general empirical relationships which enable the noise of a particular type of engine to be predicted with reasonable accuracy. *Figure 7.16* shows the relationship found by Priede[6] between noise and engine cylinder bore diameter, and *Figure 7.17* gives families of curves established at Ricardo by Challen[11,9] and others, relating engine noise, speed and cylinder bore diameter.

7.2.4 Noise radiated from the engine surfaces and components

The surfaces and components which are usually significant noise sources on a typical automotive diesel engine are crankcase, cylinder head, sump, rocker cover, front timing cover, fuel injection pump, crankshaft front pulley and damper, gearbox,

intake and exhaust manifolds. The rank order of noise levels from these sources varies for different engines but the most prominent sources are usually the crankcase, sump and front timing cover. As an example the Rolls Royce Eagle engine used in the UK Quiet Heavy Vehicle Project described in Chapter 8 had the following rank order for the noise sources:

1. Engine crankcase—cylinder block.
2. Oil sump.
3. Front timing cover.
4. Gearbox.
5. Inlet and exhaust manifolds.

Depending on location some sources can produce different noise levels on the two sides of an engine as shown by Challen and Croker[11] in *Figure 7.18*.

The main sources of surface radiated noise will now be considered in turn.

7.2.4.1 Crankcase/cylinder block

These components exhibit modes of vibration of frequency dependent on engine speed and load and structural factors. The noise generated by these vibration modes depends on their frequency and the radiation efficiency of the surface, which in turn depends on the size of the radiator in relation to the wavelength of the sound. With large engines the fundamental bending mode can be of the order of 200 Hz. *Figure 7.19* illustrates the outline of the structure of a 12 litre 6-cylinder in-line engine with the location of the accelerometers used to measure the amplitude of the vibration. One bending mode at 200 Hz of the crankcase sidewall is shown in *Figure 7.20*. For this engine there were basic beam bending modes at 200 Hz and 500 Hz, and *Figure 7.21* compares these with the theoretical free beam bending modes. The crankcase also exhibits panel modes of vibration at frequencies in the region of 800 Hz to 5 kHz. The radiation efficiency of the structure surface is highest, and therefore produces most noise, in the frequency range 800 Hz to 2000 kHz.

More advanced techniques for studying the vibrational behaviour of engine structures and their noise radiation efficiency are now being developed. These use finite element modelling[11,23-26] and acoustic intensity measurements which have been revolutionized in recent years by the rapid advances made in digital signal processing and the development of two-channel Fast Fourier Transform Analysers.

7.2.4.2 Oil sump

The sump is often made of pressed sheet steel which is attached to the bottom edge of the crankcase where the vibration amplitudes are high. The sump often has a large radiating area, which tends to have natural vibration frequencies around 1 kHz which coincides with the most sensitive part of the A-weighted spectrum. An example of a frequency spectrum of the noise contribution of the sump of a large automotive diesel engine can be seen in *Figure 7.22*. The sump-radiated noise was exposed using a lead covering technique which will be described later.

7.2.4.3 Front timing cover and rocker cover

Similar to the sump, these components are attached to parts of the cylinder block where the vibration levels are generally high and can be significant noise radiators in the 1–5 kHz region particularly when they are made of thin sheet steel. *Figure 7.23* shows the spectrum of noise from the rocker cover of a large turbocharged DI engine.

Again lead covering techniques were used to expose the rocker cover noise contribution.

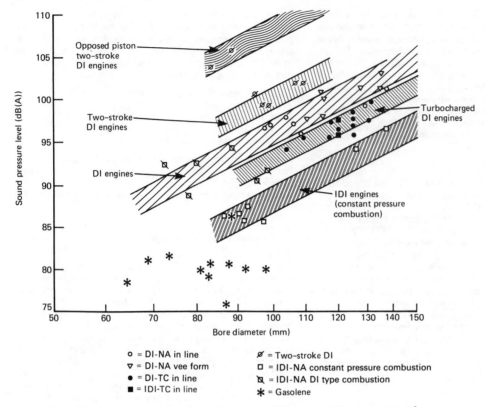

Figure 7.16 Relation between overall noise and bore size at 2000 rev/min full load. After Priede[6]

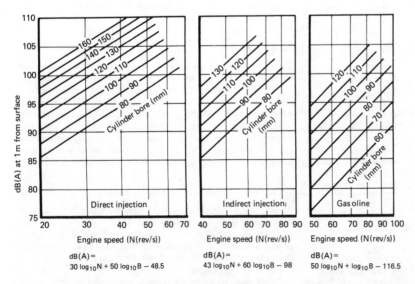

Figure 7.17 Engine noise prediction curves. After Challen and Croker[11] (B=cylinder head bore diameter)

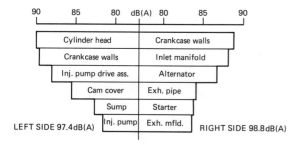

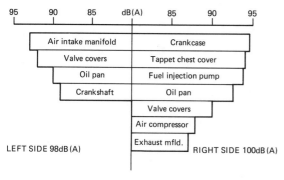

Figure 7.18 Typical surface noise source distributions for a car and truck engine. After Challen and Croker[11]

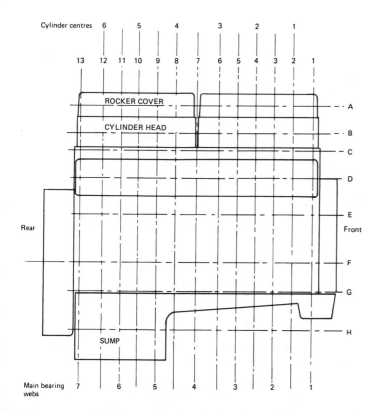

Figure 7.19 Diagram of a 6 cylinder, 12 litre, in line engine showing grid of accelerometer positions. After Tyler[44, 46]

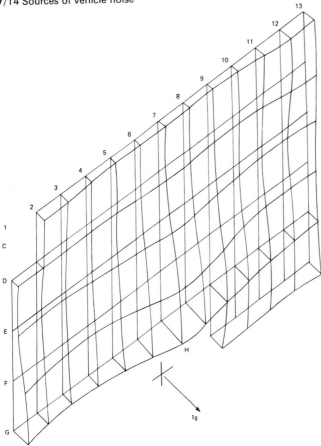

Figure 7.20 Typical surface vibration pattern on side of the crankcase of a large D1 engine (200 Hz)

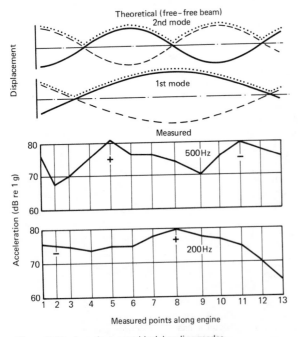

Figure 7.21 Low-frequency block bending modes

7.2.4.4 Fuel injection pump

This component generates high mechanical loading as a result of the injection of fuel at high pressure and can produce noticeable noise at high frequencies. The noise is generated by the sudden changes of hydraulic pressure within the pump and by impacts between the working parts producing a torque reaction on the pump mounting and pump drive. The pump mounting can also transmit engine vibration to the body of the pump which is then radiated as noise.[29]

7.2.4.5 Crankshaft front pulley and damper

The crankshaft experiences torsional vibration and this is transmitted to the air via the front pulley and torsional vibration damper which acts in a similar fashion to a loudspeaker diaphragm. The frequency spectrum of a typical component is shown in *Figure 7.24* together with the effect of engine load. This source principally affects the noise measured at the front of the engine.

7.2.4.6 Gearbox

As the gearbox is usually attached directly to the engine it can act as a radiator of engine noise as well as making its own contribution. The noise from the gearbox is caused by tooth-meshing frequencies and, in idling conditions, impacts due to tolerances in the meshing being taken up in alternate directions.

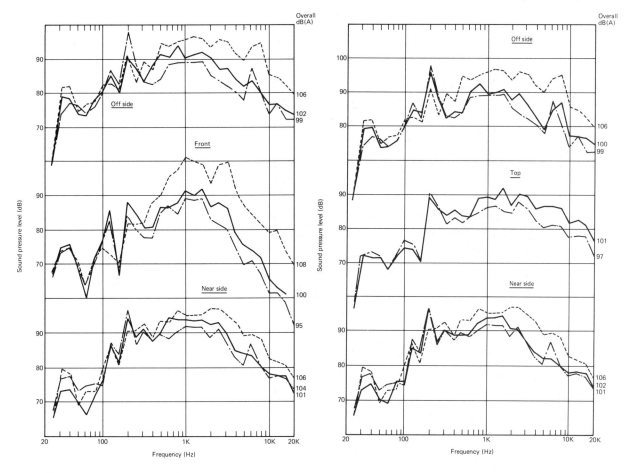

Figure 7.22 Noise contribution from the sump of a large DI engine (at 2100 rev/min under full load) ———=sump exposed; ----=engine standard; — · —=engine fully covered. After Tyler[44, 46]

Figure 7.23 Noise contribution from the rocker covers of a large DI engine (at 2100 rev/min under full load). ———=rocker covers exposed; ----=standard; — · —=all lead covered. After Tyler[44, 46]

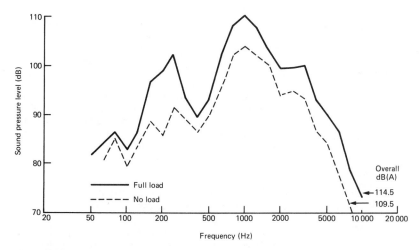

Figure 7.24 Noise from tortional vibration damper (large DI engine at 1500 rev/min) (Microphone ½″ from inertia ring.) After Tyler[44, 46]

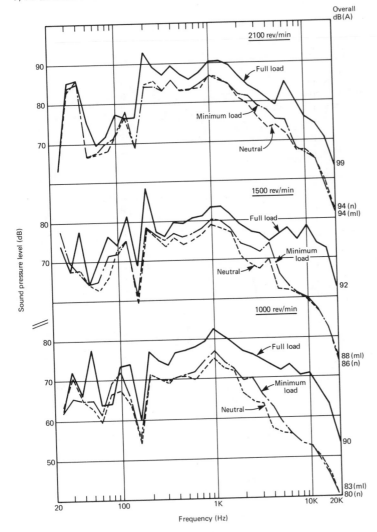

Figure 7.25 Gearbox noise (heavy goods vehicle). Microphone: gearbox—off side. Engine fully covered n=neutral; ml=minimum load. After Tyler[44, 46]

Figure 7.25 compares the noise spectra from the two components of a heavy-duty vehicle gearbox at minimum and full load. In this case the engine was covered to expose the gearbox noise.

7.2.4.7 Inlet and exhaust manifolds

These components are usually bolted directly on to the cylinder head and can be excited via transmission of cylinder head and block vibration. The frequency spectra of the inlet manifold noise for a 285 kW diesel engine both naturally aspirated and turbocharged is shown in *Figure 7.26*. The measurements were taken inside the inlet manifold. The turbine blade passing frequency peaks and high frequency flow noise can be seen in the region 2–20 kHz on the upper graph. The flow noise is much less with the naturally aspirated (NA) engine without the forcing effect of pressure charging. For this example, the external noise levels at 1 m would be in the range 95–100 dB(A). A typical 1 m external noise spectrum for the inlet of an engine similar to the above is shown in *Figure 7.27*.

Exhaust manifold noise is usually similar or higher than inlet noise and has a frequency spectrum of comparable shape.[9]

7.2.5 Idling noise

This aspect of engine noise is subjectively more noticeable and hence annoying with diesel engines than with petrol engines. The differences are most pronounced for passenger cars. The main reason for the characteristic noise at idle is the fact that the diesel engine is unthrottled at idle and has a much higher compression ratio than a gasoline engine leading to high piston loading and piston slap. The combustion of diesel fuel also leads to greater rates of pressure rise in the cylinders. These effects give the noise its characteristic and impulsive nature which is the principal cause of annoyance. *Figure 7.28* shows several sound pressure level spectra from light diesel engines with one from a gasoline engine for comparison.

7.3 Techniques for locating and measuring engine noise sources

Before considering the nature and application of engine noise control measures, the way in which the major sources are identified and ranked is of value in appreciating the remedial measures.

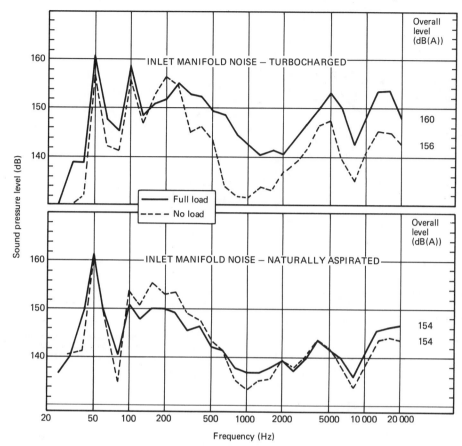

Figure 7.26 Inlet manifold noise (large D1 engine, 2100 rev/min). ——=full load; ———=no load. After Tyler[44, 46]

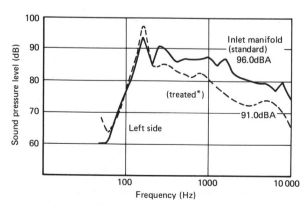

Figure 7.27 Inlet noise spectra at 1 m (remainder of engine lead covered)* Inlet manifold isolated from the cylinder head using neoprene rubber (*see* section 7.4.3). After Challen and Morrison[9]

7.3.1 Combustion and mechanical noise

Austen and Priede[12] and Challen[9] among others have developed methods for separating these sources of noise. The most direct way is to remove combustion noise by driving the engine with an electric motor and measuring the mechanical noise remaining. The disadvantage of this method is that it is difficult to simulate the effect of gas forces on piston slap and to control the temperature of the pistons, oil, and cylinder walls which must all be done to simulate the running engine. A better estimate of mechanical noise can be made by reducing the combustion noise element using ignition improvers and retarded timing to reduce ignition delay and hence combustion noise.

Russell *et al.*[13] have developed a method based on an idea pioneered by Priede[30] for finding the separate contributions to engine noise by the combustion process and mechanical sources. The method is based on the fact that if the fuel injection timing is advanced in stages until each subsequent advance produces the same increase in the spectra of the external noise of the engine as occurs in the cylinder pressure spectrum, then the combustion noise is then dominant. In this condition the transfer function between cylinder pressure and engine noise describes the noise attenuating and radiation properties of the engine structure. The difference between the spectra expressed as decibels is known as the 'structure attenuation'. This concept is illustrated in *Figure 7.29*. The structure attenuation is assumed to be a constant for the particular engine so that the

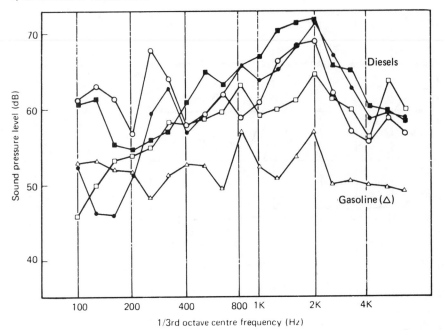

Speed (rev/min)	Type	dB(A)	dB	Symbol
11	Comet V	78.8	79.6	■
12	Comet V	76.6	87.0	○
11	Swirl chamber	72.8	74.2	□
10	Comet V	76.8	80.8	●
13	Gasoline	64.0	71.6	△

Figure 7.28 Comparison of sound pressure level spectra for various light duty diesel and gasoline engines at hot idle. After Challen and Morrison[9]

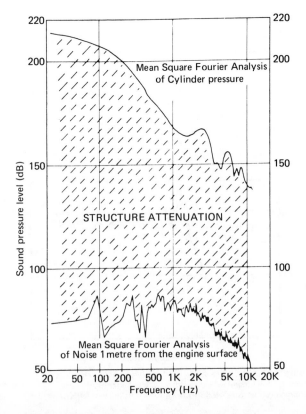

Figure 7.29 Structure attenuation of cylinder block/crankcase. After Russell[13]

combustion contribution at any other engine operating condition may be found by measuring the cylinder pressure spectrum and subtracting from it the structure attenuation value. The difference between this estimated combustion noise spectrum and the total external noise spectrum is assumed to be the contribution from mechanical sources.

Because of the difficulty with some engines in advancing the injection timing sufficiently to enable the combustion noise to dominate the mechanical noise without damaging the engine, more refined methods have been developed[31,32] which enable the desired structure attenuation to be obtained with more restricted injection timing swings. Again the assumption is made that, particularly for small timing adjustments (e.g. 3–5 degrees crank angle from standard), the mechanical noise remains constant and also the structure attenuation of the combustion noise remains constant. As in the methods described earlier the cylinder pressure levels and external noise levels are measured at each timing setting. Then these parameters are equated through four simultaneous equations as below.[31]

$$(L_p)_1 = CN_1 + MN \tag{7.1}$$
$$(L_p)_2 = CN_2 + MN \tag{7.2}$$
$$CN_1 = (L_{cp})_1 - SA \tag{7.3}$$
$$CN_2 = (L_{cp})_2 - SA \tag{7.4}$$

Where

L_p = sound pressure level at given timing.
CN = combustion noise at given timing.
L_{cp} = cylinder pressure level.
MN = mechanical noise.
SA = structure attenuation.

In calculating the above results, logarithmic addition or subtraction is used where appropriate and one-third octave levels are used, usually in the range 400 Hz to 4 kHz. The results, processed by computer, generate spectra for the mechanical and combustion noise as well as overall levels.

7.3.2 Identification and ranking of individual sources on the engine surface

It is important to establish a ranking of noise sources before considering noise reduction measures so that the noisiest sources will be given the highest priority and costs of noise control can be optimized. Dealing with a source which is substantially below the general noise level of the engine would have little effect on the overall noise level due to the effect of logarithmic addition of noise sources.

7.3.2.1 Lead covering

The traditional method for identifying the locations and strengths of the principal sources on an engine is to cover the whole engine with lead sheeting lined with mineral wool or plastic foam and then to expose each part or component in turn and measure the noise level at each stage. The sources which can be identified and ranked in this way include: water jacket panels, crankcase panels, timing cover, sump, side covers, rocker cover, intake and exhaust manifolds, fuel injection pump, turbocharger, bell housing and gearbox, and engine auxiliaries such as alternator and air pump. This can only be an approximate method for measuring absolute values of component noise as a completely covered engine is usually only 10 dB(A) approximately below the untreated engine and so the noise measured at each stage will always include some noise from the rest of the engine. However, as a method of ranking components for noise it has the advantage of simplicity. A major disadvantage is the time taken to cover the engine and to uncover portions in turn.

If this has to be done for several builds of an engine the method can be very time consuming.

Russell[8] has described an alternative method which involves measuring the vibration of all the thin section areas of the engine and comparing the mean square vibration levels of the panels. This analysis allows radiation efficiencies of the more important surfaces, and the locations of peak vibration levels at particular frequencies, to be determined and helps with the design of noise control treatments for the surface areas.

7.3.2.2 Acoustic intensity method

This is a comparatively new technique based on well-established principles and made possible technically as a result of modern high-speed digital processing and the associated hardware. Basically the method uses two closely spaced microphones to measure the acoustic intensity vector close in to the engine by a cross-spectrum method. Chung et al.,[28,33] Croker[27] and others have described the method in some detail. Its main advantage is that no covering of the engine is required as the measurement of the acoustic intensity vector is made in the presence of other noises including background noise. An example of the resolution given by the method can be seen in Figure 7.30 which shows intensity levels measured at various points near to the front of an engine.

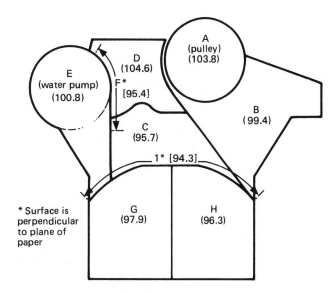

Figure 7.30 A-weighted sound intensity levels for various regions at the front of the engine. After Chung[33]

7.3.2.3 Other methods

These include laser holography used, for example, in modal analysis of the vibration of engine components (Miura and Suzuki[34]) and finite element techniques described by Croker et al.,[27,35] Challen[11] and others listed in the Further reading.

7.4 Engine noise control techniques

Noise from the structure of an engine results from the vibration of the outer surfaces including the attached components. It arises from a system of forces acting from within the engine which are transmitted through the structure and cause it to vibrate in a series of complex mode shapes. Consequently there are a number of ways in which noise reduction may be achieved. Briefly, these are:

1. Reduce the magnitude of the combustion and mechanical forces in the acoustically important frequency range.
2. Modify the transmission paths of these forces by introducing additional damping or stiffness into the engine structure.
3. Reduce the magnitude of vibration of the outer surfaces of the structure by redesign.
4. Further reduce the noise emitted by the outer surfaces by reducing radiation efficiency or by means of covers and shields.
5. Fit quieter components, e.g. injection pump, alternator, air pump, etc.
6. Ultimately, with the engine *in situ* in the vehicle, shield or enclose the engine.

Depending on the final vehicle noise required not all of these measures will be necessary to achieve the desired target level.

7.4.1 Combustion forces

The reduction of combustion noise cannot be allowed to have a significant effect on the efficiency of an engine as a power generator. A lot of work has been carried out on the optimization of combustion chamber shape and control of fuel injection. In the latter case, for example, pilot injection—where a small pilot charge of fuel is injected into the cylinder before the main charge—can reduce the rate of pressure rise. However, problems of emissions and particulates can occur with this method. Fumigation, the aspiration of a fuel/air mix combined with normal injection, can also give improvements but also with the risk of emissions and smoke.

A more reliable and straightforward method of reducing combustion noise is to retard the start of injection. *Figure 7.31* shows the effect on the different types of diesel engine of timing retard. The DI naturally aspirated engine, being dominated by combustion noise, responds best to this treatment (a typical response being 6 dB(A) reduction per 10 degree retard) but IDI and turbocharged DI are less affected. The reason for this is that the combustion is already controlled, in the former case by the type of injection and in the latter by the pressure charging. The noise from the Rolls Royce Eagle engine in the QHV described in Chapter 8, was reduced by 1 dB(A) per 4 degrees of injection retard. However, the degree of retard permissible depends on balancing noise reduction, emissions and power output.

As mentioned above, turbocharging is a means of obtaining greater timing retard without sacrificing performance and economy because the increased temperature and pressure of the air charge tends to reduce ignition delay times.

7.4.2 Mechanical forces

An important source of mechanical noise in both diesel and gasoline engines is associated with piston slap due to the clearances between the piston and cylinder walls; this is particularly evident when the engine is started from cold. Methods of controlling piston slap include a positively injected oil film to cushion the impact, additional scraper rings, Teflon inserts,

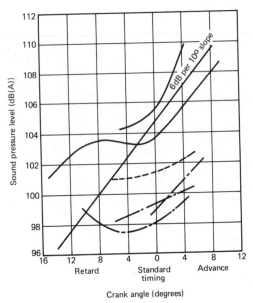

Figure 7.31 Effect of injection timing on noise. ——=direct injection; ————=DI turbocharged; ————=indirect injection. After Challen and Morrison[9]

differential expansion of piston and cylinder bore material and offset gudgeon pins. Noise from the timing drive is usually a significant source. Timing gears are noisier than chain or belt drive but are necessary for the more powerful engines.

A major engine redesign which places the gear train at the rear of the engine instead of the front has been shown to reduce noise at the front of the engine by some 12 dB(A). The reasons for this are that the rear of the crankshaft provides a lower exciting force than the front and the gears are screened by the mass of the engine and the bodywork of the vehicle. Gear noise reduction may also be achieved by attention to gear tooth profile and accuracy of manufacture, surface finish and bearing clearances. However, these processes will almost certainly increase manufacturing costs. For lighter duty engines the use of toothed belts instead of chain drive results in significant improvement (*see Figure 7.12*).

7.4.3 Engine surface noise sources

7.4.3.1 Crankcase/cylinder block restructuring

The aim here is to reduce the level of vibration on the surface of the structure so that noise emission is reduced and the excitation of attached covers is minimized. In Section 7.2.4 it was shown that the principal noise radiation was in the frequency range 800–2000 Hz. For small engines these frequencies are generated by the beam bending modes of the crankcase as well as the panel modes of the thin panels between the main bearing bulkheads. With large engines the bending modes occur at too low a frequency to radiate much noise due to the low radiation efficiency at low frequencies. The noise from these engines comes mainly from the thinner panels between the bulkheads. The use of substantial ribbing on the crankcase panels has been shown to be effective on large and small engines (*Figure 7.32*).

The cylinder block/crankcase structure can be strengthened to reduce vibration levels. This was done on the 12 litre diesel engine used in the QHV described in Chapter 8. The original and revised structures are illustrated in *Figure 8.7*. The basic

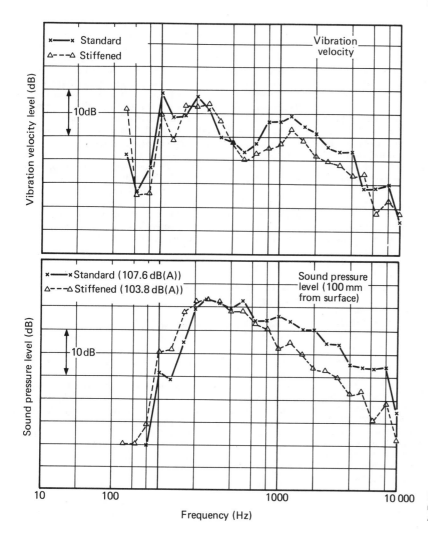

Figure 7.32 Effect of crankcase panel ribbing on vibration and noise radiation. After Challen and Croker[11]

differences between the structures are the splitting of the new crankcase at the crankshaft centre line, fitting a ladder type bedplate containing the lower halves of the bearing saddles and extending the outer walls of the crankcase down to the sump flange, the intention being to provide a greatly stiffened crankcase. The bottom deck of the cylinder block was moved down to the lower end of the cylinders to form a rigid section at this point to reduce flexing of the cylinder block walls caused by distortion of the crankcase. The crankcase was also provided with flat sides to enable close-fitting damped panels to be attached thus providing further reduction of radiated noise. The revised structure produced a noise reduction of about 3 dB(A) at 1 m and the damped panels a further 1.5 dB(A). The work just described was done in a largely empirical manner with the necessity of building prototypes to measure the effect of the changes. The techniques of finite element modelling provide a way of reaching an optimum design on paper with a minimum of engine builds.[23,24,27,35]

7.4.3.2 Covers

The rocker/cam cover, front timing cover and oil sump tend to have natural frequencies in the middle of the A-weighted frequency range and this fact combined with their usually high efficiency as noise radiators means that they are important sources of noise from engines.

The more common remedies for noise from these sources is the use of a laminated steel/polyester sheet to damp vibration, the isolation of the covers from the main structure of the engine by de-coupling mountings and mass loading of the larger surfaces by the attachment of high mass pads. *Figure 7.33* shows several methods of isolating rocker covers. Various problems can arise in the use of laminated sheets such as limitation of use due to temperature sensitivity and the fact that the moulding of the required shapes introduces increased stiffness with a resulting reduction in efficiency. There is considerable ongoing research into the means of predicting cover vibration and noise and optimizing the design of components.

7.4.3.3 Intake and exhaust manifolds

The intake and exhaust manifolds can radiate considerable noise from the engine as they are usually rigidly clamped to the cylinder head. Inlet manifolds can be isolated from the cylinder head by neoprene rubber, and Challen and Morrison[9] have shown that such a modification can give a reduction of 5 dB(A) on the inlet manifold side of the engine.

In the case of exhaust manifolds the high temperatures preclude isolation by resilient compounds and shielding is a more practical solution. Metal shields placed close to the manifold can be a very effective solution. Challen and Morrison[9] have demonstrated that approximately 6 dB(A) reduction in exhaust manifold noise can be obtained using an exhaust shield.

7.4.4 Enclosures and shields

Close-fitting shields made of sheet material may be fitted close to the engine surface or component (10–20 mm spacing) mounted resiliently and sealed as closely as possible to the noise source surface by means of, for example, a rubber strip. They can be used to reduce noise levels from crankcase walls, fuel injection pumps, front timing drive, rocker covers and other significant noise sources.

An alternative, or additional approach to overall engine noise reduction is to use partial or complete enclosures. Complete encapsulation of the engine can be very effective in reducing external noise levels. For example, Thien,[36,37] demonstrated that 10–15 dB(A) reduction was possible. Total encapsulation, however, increases the problems of cooling the engine surfaces and auxiliary components and creates problems of accessibility for maintenance. A more often used alternative to complete encapsulation is to construct what is known as a tunnel enclosure. This type of enclosure is open at both the front and rear of the engine compartment to allow a continual stream of cooling air from the fan and radiator at the front through to the exit at the rear. Careful design can ensure that engine surface temperatures and auxiliaries temperatures do not exceed critical values. The gearbox can be included in the tunnel and noise reductions of 6–10 dB(A) can be achieved.

The duty required of the cooling fan to drive the air through the enclosure is increased owing to increase in pressure drop and special attention has to be given to fan design to ensure that fan noise is not unduly increased. An example of a successful tunnel enclosure design is illustrated in *Figure 8.12*. The noise reduction due to this design of tunnel enclosure was about 6 dB(A).

7.4.5 The effect of diesel fuel quality on engine noise

It is usual to express fuel ignition quality in terms of the equivalent blend of standardized high and low ignition quality reference fuels which gives the same ignition delay as the sample fuel when tested under controlled engine conditions. The two fuels that are universally used as standards are *n*-cetane and *a*-methyl-naphthylamine which are pure hydrocarbons of high and low ignition quality, respectively. The spread of quality bounded by these fuels is large enough to ensure that any commercially available fuel falls within the band. Any particular blend of reference fuels that matches the fuel under test is identified by a cetane number which is the percentage of the *n*-cetane in the mixture. For example a mixture of 48% *n*-cetane and 52% *a*-methyl-naphthalamine is said to have a cetane number of 48. The tests are done by a universally accepted method which has been standardized by the American Society for Testing and Materials as ASTM-613 and is also adopted by the International Standards Organisation as ISO 5165. A standard test engine is used.

While cetane number does not entirely explain the difference in engine behaviour with different fuel qualities it does provide a practical method of rating fuels. In general the lower the cetane number of the fuel the noisier is the resultant combustion process in an engine. Anderton and Waters[38] have shown that the overall noise level in dB(A) at 1 m from a 6 litre DI engine decreased with increasing cetane number at about 1.7 dB(A) per 10 cetane number, although significant variations occur for individual fuels. For a 3.5 litre IDI engine the effect was less at about 0.7 dB(A) per 10 cetane number, while for a turbocharged engine there was no definite trend but a maximum variation of 1.5 dB(A) over the cetane range tested (32–54).

Chan *et al.*[32] using a 3.86 litre DI engine gave values of 0.5 dB(A) increase for a decrease in cetane number of 10, while Russell,[39] for a 6 litre DI engine, quoted increases of 2–3 dB(A) for the same change in cetane number.

Future fuel quality is likely to exhibit cetane numbers in the lower 40s compared with the current 50s which means that engine and vehicle manufacturers must expect to have their noise reduction task increased by 1.5–2 dB(A).

7.5 Inlet and exhaust noise, mechanism and control

The gas exchange processes in the IC engine in which gas columns in both inlet and exhaust systems vibrate at high-pressure amplitudes, are efficient noise producers and the air inlet and exhaust outlets in an unsilenced state would dominate engine noise.[21,40–43]

An unsilenced exhaust outlet would be some 10–15 dB(A) above general engine noise and air inlet about 5 dB(A). Fortunately, these sources can be effectively attenuated by silencers which can still leave exhaust noise comparable with engine noise but in general takes inlet noise some 10 dB(A) or more below the other sources.

7.5.1 Inlet noise

Inlet noise has been shown to result from both the opening and closing of the inlet valve[40] and is also affected by the flow properties of the exhaust valve and exhaust system due to valve overlap. For this reason air inlet noise may increase when an exhaust brake is fitted.

When the inlet valve opens, the pressure in the cylinder is above atmospheric pressure and a sharp positive pulse sets the air in the inlet passage into oscillation at the natural frequency of the column. This oscillation is rapidly damped by the change of volume enclosed by the piston and cylinder caused by the downward movement of the piston. High-frequency noise, around 1 kHz, is generated by the high-velocity air flow across the valve seat. The closing of the air inlet valve produces a similar oscillation which continues for a longer time.

When the inlet manifold and silencers, which are combined with the air filters, are fitted the frequency of the noise impulses are reduced from about 1 kHz down to 80–150 Hz in the engine firing frequency range. *Figure 7.34* shows that the silencing system reduces the dB(A) level of inlet noise but does not appreciably change the slope of the noise/engine speed characteristic.

The design of inlet air cleaner/silencers is generally straightforward, the main considerations being to establish a balance between the need to maximize the length of filter the air has to pass through, thus maximizing the damping effect on the vibrating air column, and the opposing need to minimize the air flow resistance, which requires generously dimensioned air cleaners.

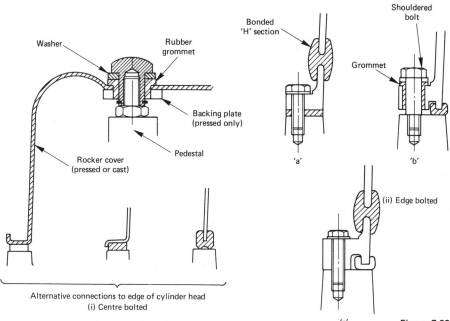

Figure 7.33 Valve cover isolation designs. After Challen and Croker[11]

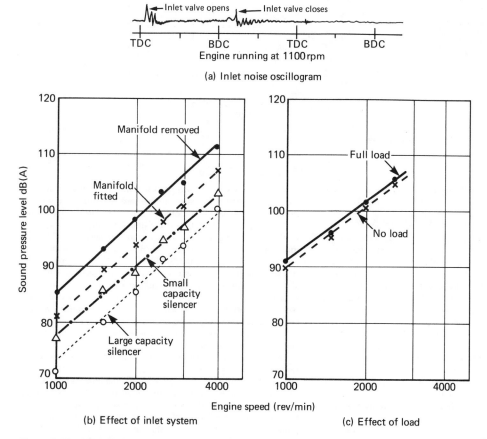

(a) Inlet noise oscillogram

(b) Effect of inlet system

(c) Effect of load

Figure 7.34 Characteristics of air intake noise. After Priede[21]

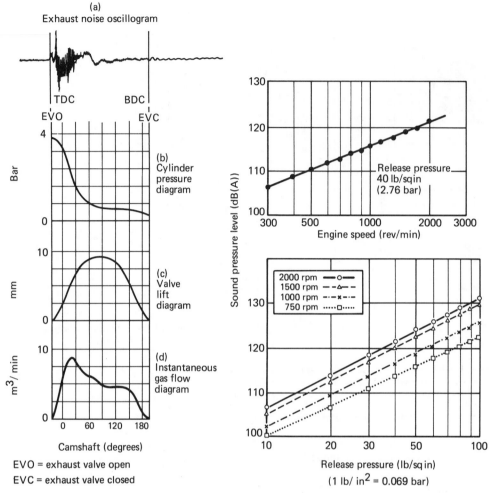

(a)
Exhaust noise oscillogram

Figure 7.35 Characteristics of exhaust noise. After Priede[21]

EVO = exhaust valve open
EVC = exhaust valve closed

7.5.2 Exhaust noise

Exhaust noise is produced by the sudden release of gas into the exhaust system when the exhaust valve opens. *Figure 7.35*[21] shows the noise trace, the pressure–time diagram in the engine cylinder during the exhaust stroke, the valve lift diagram and the instantaneous gas flow. Oscillations are induced in the exhaust passage by the valve both opening and closing as the valve movement near to its seat acts as a piston generating a pressure wave in the passage.

Following the initial pulse generated by the valve motion, a low-frequency wave can be seen in the figure resulting from variations in velocity of the gas flow. Superimposed on the low-frequency wave is a random high-frequency jet type noise. The main factors that determine the level of exhaust noise are the release pressure (cylinder pressure at the time of initial opening), the valve diameter and its lift and closing characteristics determined by the cam profile.

The typical characteristics of exhaust noise are shown by *Figure 7.36*.[21] The effect of engine load can be seen to be appreciable (10–15 dB(A)) since the release pressure is primarily affected by load. The rate of increase of noise with speed generally reduces with load from 30–45 dB(A) per decade to about 20–25 dB(A) per decade depending on engine size and type of combustion.

7.5.3 Exhaust silencers

The design of exhaust silencers is as much empirical as analytical although computer-aided design methods and analytical test procedures are slowly becoming available. The TRRL Quiet Heavy Vehicle Project[44-47] contributed to these new design methods and the new QHV90 Project,[48] designed to assist industry to meet the challenge of the new EEC vehicle noise regulations for the 1990s (84/424/EEC), has, as part of the research programme, further work on this subject (*see also* Chapter 8). This work includes computer modelling, experimental and analytical system development and gas flow noise and back pressure. The aim is to enable manufacturers to understand more fully the behaviour of silencers and to reach optimum designs by the quickest and cheapest route, using a computer-based design package.

The basic problem in silencer design is to achieve adequate noise reduction over the important range of frequencies at the tail pipe with minimum restriction of outflowing gases, and with the silencer volume as small as possible. It is also important to avoid noise generation by the flow of the gases through the pipes connecting the exhaust manifold to the silencer boxes and by the physical features of the boxes themselves. For example, vortex shedding at a sharp edge of pipe within the box can produce substantial noise in the A-weighted range.[49] Vibration of the

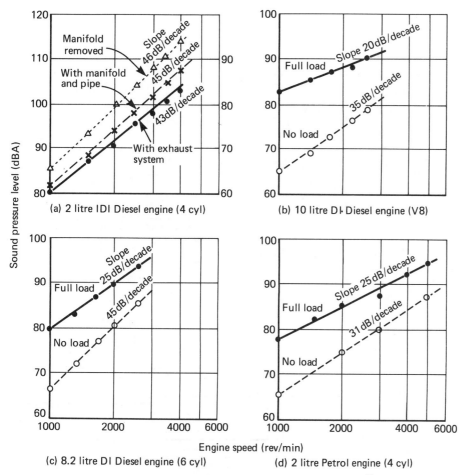

Figure 7.36 Effect of speed, load and silencing system on exhaust noise. After Priede[21]

panels in the silencer boxes must also be minimized.

The task of the silencer designer can be made easier if the open pipe exhaust signature (spectrum) at the engine itself is minimized. By attention to cam profiles which control the timing rate and duration of valve opening the noise at the exhaust manifold, and hence at the input to the exhaust system, can be reduced. For example, in the TRRL QHV[44] which used a 238 kW turbocharged engine, initial treatment of cam profiles using reduced valve clearances together with a change of turbocharger characteristics reduced open pipe exhaust noise by 9 dB(A). *Figure 7.37* shows the reduction in noise achieved over the audible frequency range.

There are various internal design features used by manufacturers, and each company favours particular groups of elements. Very little published information has been found detailing designs presumably because of commercial confidentiality. However, Haynes and Kell,[41] Davies and Alfredson[50] and Inagawa and Nakamura[51] give detailed consideration to various elements of silencer design.

Figure 7.38 illustrates some basic silencer elements. Practical designs comprise combinations of these either in the same box or in two or more boxes connected by rigid or flexible pipes.

The elements used in the TRRL QHV are illustrated as an example in *Figure 7.39* with the attenuation in noise over the

audible frequency range. The design consisted of combinations of perforated tube within expansion chambers having extended inlet and outlet pipes. The use of perforates is essential to reduce gas flow noise and they considerably increase the attenuation above 2 kHz.

To minimize flow noise the finest holed perforate practicable was used and care was taken to avoid sharp edges at the junctions between perforate and pipe to avoid vortex shedding. There was a lower limit to the size of perforate hole that would not clog up the exhaust contaminants during service.

For the attenuation of low frequencies, engine firing components at 30–120 Hz, large enclosed volumes are required. Although these frequencies do not affect the A-weighted noise levels, and as such do not feature in the EEC drive-by test (*see also* Chapter 9), there is concern that they contribute to vibration in people's homes due to airborne transmission (*see* Chapter 12). The basic laws of physics demand that substantial attenuation of low-frequency components of exhaust noise requires large enclosed volumes and this raises serious problems of space on certain types of vehicle. The silencer boxes on the TRRL QHV were about twice the volume of current commercial silencers but had a much better performance at low frequencies. This fact contributed to the favourable subjective impression given by this vehicle.

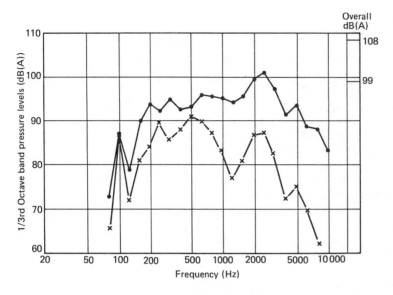

Figure 7.37 One-third octave spectra of engine open pipe exhaust noise at 60 degrees incidence to, and 7.5 m from exhaust orifice. •——• = as delivered; ×——× = with new valve gear, modified camshaft and turbocharger. Engine at 2000 revs/min; full load. After Tyler[44, 46]

(a) Simple expansion chamber

(b) Folded chamber

(c) Extended inlet and outlet

(d) With perforated section

(e) Perforated section with separator

Figure 7.38 Some basic silencer elements

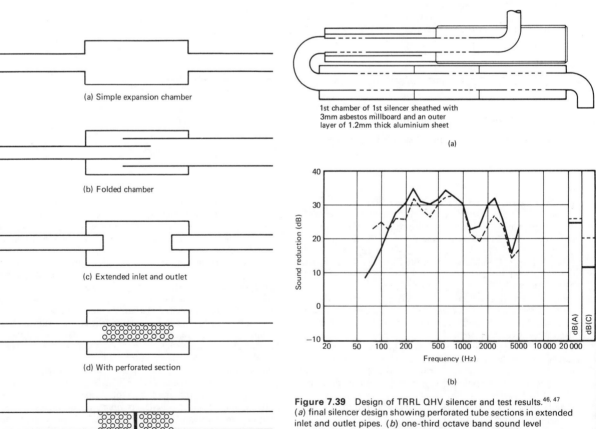

1st chamber of 1st silencer sheathed with 3mm asbestos millboard and an outer layer of 1.2mm thick aluminium sheet

(a)

(b)

Figure 7.39 Design of TRRL QHV silencer and test results.[46, 47] (a) final silencer design showing perforated tube sections in extended inlet and outlet pipes. (b) one-third octave band sound level reductions obtained from measurements with and without silencers on test at 60 degrees incidence to the tailpipe axis. ——=reduction averaged over range of speeds (full throttle, dynamometer controlled) and free acceleration; – – –=reduction at maximum power

7.6 Noise from vehicle cooling systems: effect of fan design

Although most current vehicle designs include engine cooling fans that are thermostatically controlled and hence operate according to the cooling demands of the engine for a comparatively small percentage of the vehicle journey time, fan noise when it occurs can be an important source of vehicle noise. This is particularly so with heavy goods vehicles which have powerful engines requiring large air flows through the radiator matrix to stabilize engine temperatures. The cooling fan is only one component of the cooling system, and a design for a particular vehicle and engine has to take into account many factors. The heat exchanger (radiator) has to be chosen to fit into the available space. The rate of cooling airflow through the heat exchanger, over the engine and through any engine enclosure will determine air temperature and density. This in turn determines the resistance to air flow that the fan has to overcome and hence the fan duty requirements. Given the fan duty, the type of fan can be selected and its design aimed at minimizing noise output.

The latter is still a difficult task as the designed fan noise performance can be degraded by the conditions the fan experiences when installed in the vehicle. For example, the prediction of fan performance (and noise) assumes good aerodynamic flow conditions. In a typical vehicle this is not the case with the fan inlet mounted close to the radiator and the fan discharge close to the engine block. Research has been done on this problem as part of the TRRL QHV project,[44-47] and is reported in detail in a paper by Bolton et al.[52] The QHV 90 project[48] will include further work on cooling systems.

The noise generated by the cooling fan can be classified in the following way:

1. *Broad band noise*—caused by vortices and air turbulance.
2. *Tonal noise*—caused by rotation of the fan and the passing of the blades past fixed objects. The frequency depends on the number of blades, the rotational speed and the blade pitch angle.
3. *Mechanical noise*—caused by vibration of the fan, fan cowling and the radiator.

There are three types of fan likely to be used in vehicle cooling systems. These basic types are illustrated in *Figure 7.40*. The mixed flow fan can produce any desired pressure/volume relationship, being capable of handling the large volumes of axial fans and high pressures of centrifugal fans.

With present-day vehicles the axial fan is almost universal because of its simplicity and its modest space requirements. Designs have reached an advanced state of performance and low cost but with the advent of engine enclosure with correspondingly increased air pressure drop and fan duty, more complex fan designs may have to be used.

Fan noise increases with fan power and fan-tip speed and so for lowest noise output, fans should be run at the lowest speed consistent with the duty required. This has been achieved to a certain extent by using large diameter low speed axial fans,[53] but the space restrictions on a vehicle generally limit the degree of fan noise reduction that can be obtained by this method.

Bolton et al.[52] gives relationships which enable the assessment of the type, size and rotational speed of fans to achieve given duties and to estimate the radiated noise. The fan most suited for any duty is indicated by the value of the non-dimensional specific speed, N_s which is given by:

$$N_s = \frac{\omega Q^{\frac{1}{2}}}{(gH)^{\frac{3}{4}}} \tag{7.5}$$

Where ω is the angular velocity (rad/s), Q is the flow rate (m³/s), g is the acceleration due to gravity (m/s²) and H is the head rise (m).

For centrifugal fans, N_s is less than 2, for mixed flow fans $N_s > 1.5$ but < 3.5, and for axial fans $N_s \geqslant 2.5$. For a mixed or axial fan the relationship between diameter and rotational speed may be approximated by:

$$D = 2 \left(\frac{gHQ}{\omega^3 K_L} \right)^{0.2} \tag{7.6}$$

where K_L is a non-dimensional loading parameter. With careful design, the loading parameter can attain values of 0.1 for an axial fan and 0.15 for a mixed flow fan. These equations define the size and speed of possible fans. The sound power levels (PWL) can be estimated from the relation[54]:

$$L_W = 10 \log_{10}(\rho.Q.g.H.) + 22 \log_{10} \left(\frac{\omega D}{2} \right) + 26 \tag{7.7}$$

where ρ is the air density.

Typical sound power levels from each design of fan and the effect of the rate of air flow on noise are shown in *Figure 7.41* (Deeprose[54]). It can be seen that axial flow fans are 15–20 dB(A) noisier when stalling than at the design flow. This effect is much less marked with the centrifugal and mixed flow fans. The frequency spectrum generated by the fan will depend primarily upon the dimensions of the fan blades, the rate of revolution, the number of blades and the symmetry of the blade layout. Discrete tonal effects can be generated if the blades are evenly spaced, the preferred frequencies depending upong the rate of rotation and the number of blades passing a fixed object per second. By incorporating slight asymmetries in the fan design, the same acoustical energy generated at blade-passing frequencies can be dissipated over a larger frequency range thereby achieving a more acceptable broader band noise characteristic. *Figure 7.42* illustrates the effect of asymmetric pitching of fan blades on frequency spectrum.[54]

The main thrust of recent work on cooling systems has been the development of the package concept where the fan design is considered part of the whole system including the radiator and cowling, the engine and possibly an engine enclosure. This is because, as has been mentioned earlier, fan performance is affected by the proximity of these other components and little is known quantitatively about the causes and magnitude of these installation effects. Also if the total cooling system can be made more efficient thermodynamically, the required fan duty would be less with consequent easing of the fan noise problem.

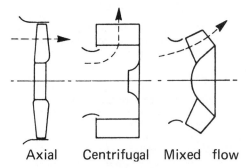

Axial   Centrifugal   Mixed flow

Figure 7.40 The three basic types of cooling fan

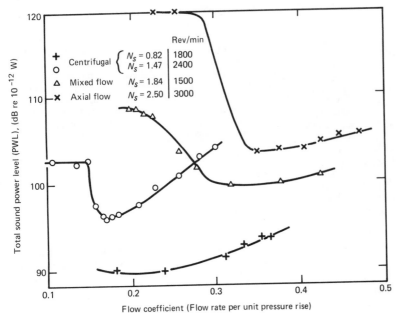

Figure 7.41 Effect of flow rate on total sound power level for four fans. After Deeprose[54]

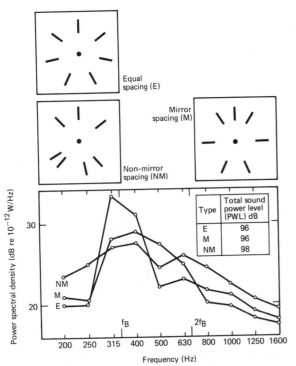

Figure 7.42 Effect of asymmetric pitching of blades on frequency spectra. F_B=Blade passing frequency for fan type E. After Deeprose[54]

7.7 Transmission noise

As components in a vehicle, gearboxes, drive shafts and rear axles have been minimal contributors to total vehicle noise, but as other components become quieter transmission noise will become more apparent. Current levels of noise from transmissions as a whole, or from components, range from 68 to 78 dB(A) at 7.5 m.

The principal source of noise from these components is generated by the meshing of gear teeth. These vibrations create noise in three ways:

1. The torsional vibrations resulting from the gear meshing are carried to the vehicle panels by the driveline and vehicle structure and radiated as sound.
2. Lateral vibrations are transmitted by the mountings to the vehicle panels and radiated as sound.
3. Gear meshing vibrations (both torsional and lateral) are transmitted to the transmission housing to be directly converted to airborne sound.

There is also evidence to show that the transmission can channel and transmit vibration (and hence noise) originating in the engine.

It is generally agreed by researchers that gear vibration and noise is the result of imperfect transmission of motion and forces between gear teeth. Factors that contribute to imperfect gear action include tooth and shaft deflections, tooth profile errors and gear system dynamics. These factors are often grouped together under the term 'transmission error'. Daly and Smith[55] and Welbourn[56] define transmission error as the difference between the actual position of the output shaft of the gear drive and the position it would occupy if the gear drive were perfect, i.e. with no error or deflections. Munro[57] shows how gear errors affect the transmission error of a drive. *Figure 7.43* illustrates the influence of tooth profile error on noise[58]

Work has been done to reduce the excitation forces caused by gear teeth, such as modification of tooth profiles, use of overlapping helical gears and the use of counter-phased planetary gearing where, by choosing the proper timing relationship between multiple planetary pinion meshes, noise level reductions averaged 7 dB(A).[59] Hera[60] describes work to reduce the airborne noise that radiates directly from the transmission housing. He used a photographic technique employing lasers, called 'double pulsed holography'. This method offers a unique means of visualizing housing surface vibrations so that critical areas of the housing that generate most noise can be identified and modified to reduce their ability to radiate sound. *Figure 7.44* shows noise and vibration spectra taken from a transmission casing using this technique. By using a constrained layer of

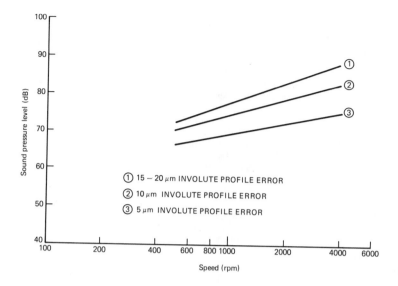

Figure 7.43 Influence of profile error on gear noise. After Houser[61]

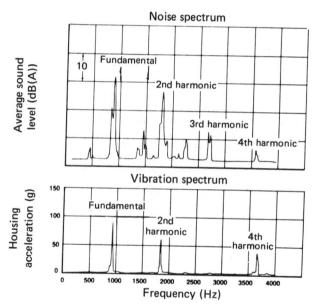

Figure 7.44 Noise and vibration spectra at 1300 rpm. After Hera[60]

damping material as treatment for this particular transmission housing, a reduction of 8 dB(A) was obtained at an engine speed of 1300 rev/min.

Houser[61] of the Gear Dynamics and Gear Noise Research Laboratory, Ohio State University, is engaged in several research projects related to gear design and analysis. His paper discusses projects related to the analysis and prediction of spur and helical gear transmission errors, gear load distribution analysis, gear tooth finite element analysis, force transmission through gearbox bearings and acoustic intensity measurements from operating gearboxes.

One subjectively annoying aspect of gearbox noise is gear rattle at low torques, i.e. at idle. Sakai et al.[62] carried out a computer-simulated analysis and experimental study of this noise source and discovered that by optimizing the torsional characteristics of the clutch plate the noise levels could be reduced to an acceptable value.

7.8 Tyre noise

The noise generated by the action of tyres rolling on road surfaces can have a considerable influence on the total noise levels emitted by moving vehicles. Harland[63] showed that at speeds above 100 km/h on dry roads tyre-road surface noise becomes the dominant source for all but the heaviest diesel-engined goods vehicles. On wet roads, speeds can be much lower to give the same degree of tyre noise. With the reduction of noise from the mechanical sources on a vehicle as a result of new legislation, tyre noise will become more important over a wider range of operating conditions.

The subject of tyre noise has been widely studied by Harland,[63] Hayden,[64] Corcoran,[65] Underwood,[66] Nelson,[67] Nilsson[68] and others[69, 70] both to determine the parameters that affect the noise level and its frequency spectrum and also to try to isolate the generating mechanisms.

7.8.1 Parameters affecting tyre noise

The main parameters affecting lorry tyre noise have been established by Harland[63] and Nelson.[67] The main parameters are described briefly below.

7.8.1.1 Speed of the vehicle

It has been demonstrated that the peak noise in dB(A) of a coasting vehicle measured at 7.5 m along the normal to the centre line of the vehicle path is related to the vehicle speed by an equation of the form[63]:

$$L_A = m\log_{10} V + \text{constant} \tag{7.8}$$

where L_A is the peak noise level, V is the vehicle speed (km/h) and m is a constant. Tests carried out with various tyre and road surface combinations gave values of m ranging between 29 and 43 indicating that noise increases by between 9 dB(A) and 13 dB(A) per doubling of speed approximately depending on the tyre characteristics and surface texture.[66] A high slope coefficient tended to be associated with regular features in the tyre tread and in the road surface. For example, vehicles running with smooth tyres on a regular transverse grooved concrete surface produced a slope coefficient m = 42.8.

7.8.1.2 Weight of the vehicle (tyre loading)[67]

The effect of changing the wheel load has been studied by Leasure[71] and by Underwood.[66] Generally, an increase in wheel load causes an increase in the tyre/surface noise level. For example, by increasing the total gross vehicle weight of a two-axle rigid lorry from 7.65 Mg (tonne) to 13.23 Mg, the levels of tyre noise were found to increase over the range 0.5–6.5 dB(A) at a passing speed of 100 km/h depending upon the tyre–road surface combination employed. The greatest increases were found when the lorry was fitted with traction tyres. The average increase was 2.4 dB(A). Leasure also found that tyre noise levels increased by 6–8 dB(A) for traction tyres for a similar load increase.[71]

7.8.1.3 Tread pattern

In general variations in tread pattern have small effects on the overall levels of tyre noise. However, tyres with regular transverse features are systematically noisier than tyres with predominantly circumferential patterns. For example, it has been shown that traction tyres are about 1 dB(A) noisier on average than the equivalent ribbed patterned tyres.[67] The frequency spectra generated by the vehicles tyres generally have a broadband characteristic with no distinct tonal features. However, tyres with regular transverse features such as traction block patterns can generate tonal characteristics associated with the impact of the block pattern on the road surface. *Figure 7.45* shows narrow band frequency spectra obtained for smooth and tractioned tyres running on a rolled asphalt surface, i.e. the extremes of tread pattern. The spectra are substantially similar and the only marked difference is the peak in the traction tyre response at 400 Hz due to the regular transverse blocks. Even this does not effect the dB(A) level although it might be subjectively noticeable.

7.8.1.4 Tyre structure[67]

The two main kinds of tyre construction are cross ply and radial ply. Briefly, the cross- or bias-ply construction has several layers of rayon or nylon cords laid diagonally so that they cross the circumferential centre-line at an angle of about 40 degrees. With the radial or belted tyre, the cord angle is greatly reduced and the cords form a rigid and almost inextensible belt. On most road surfaces radial ply tyres are about 1–2 dB(A) quieter than cross ply tyres.[67] Other workers have reported similar differences; Allen[72] recorded differences up to 3 dB(A) for lorry tyres while Volmer[73] found 2–3 dB(A) differences between radial and cross ply tyres on an asphalt surface. It has been shown[74,75] that increasing the number of plies increases the stiffness of the structure thus reducing the damping of tyre vibration. This increases tyre noise slightly.

Different ply materials have been tested by Bolt, Beranek and Newman[74] Zeoppritz[76] and Ullrich.[77] They reported that the noise from coasting vehicles with nylon ply tyres was 2 dB(A) greater than tyres with rayon plies and these in turn were 3 dB(A) noisier than steel-belted tyres.

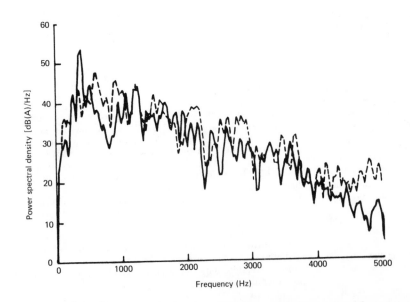

Figure 7.45 Narrow band frequency spectra for traction and smooth tyres on motorway surface at 96 km/h. After Nelson et al.[67] ——— =traction; – – – =smooth

7.8.1.5 Tread materials

In general different rubber compositions have little effect on tyre noise but it has been shown that a high-hysteresis rubber compound gave slightly higher noise levels than natural rubber tyres.[67] However, normal commercial variations in tread materials currently have little effect on the overall levels on tyre noise.

7.8.1.6 Tyre wear

As the tyre wears the depth of tread pattern changes as does the thickness of cross-section. This might be expected to change tyre noise and in general this appears to be the case. Nelson[67] found that noise was greater for part worn tyres by amounts varying from 1 to 5 dB(A). Other workers[64,71,78] have observed increase in noise with tyre wear, the maximum increase being reached when the tyre is worn by 50–75%.

7.8.1.7 Road surface texture

The principal road surface characteristics that effect tyre noise generation are surface pattern, the presence of surface water and the acoustical absorption characteristics of the surface material. It was shown earlier that both tyre tread pattern and road surface pattern affect the functional form of the noise versus vehicle speed relation. Whilst the general speed-level relation may have a slope coefficient lying between 29 and 43, regular features in the road surface such as transverse grooves or brush marks tend to produce a greater noise/speed dependence than randomized surface finishes.[67]

Road surfaces are provided with a macrotexture or pattern in order to enhance tyre–road surface contact at high speeds on wet roads. This helps to reduce the risk of skidding by ensuring good frictional adhesion in the contact area, and to cause the tyre to deform or 'flex' as it passes over the surface asperities. This action helps to further dissipate the energy of braking by hysteresis losses in the tyre.

The manner in which skidding resistance varies with speed of a vehicle is a somewhat controversial topic and depends largely upon the technique used. In the UK it has been established that the risk of accidents involving skidding is related to the skidding resistance measured by the change in braking force coefficient, denoted ΔBFC, between the standard measurement speeds of 50 km/h and 130 km/h.[79] Attempts have been made to relate the ΔBFC variable to the noise of passing vehicles.[80] It was found that at speeds of 70 km/h and 90 km/h the peak noise of 'light' vehicles, i.e. with an unladen weight less than 1.5 Mg (tonne), and 'heavy' vehicles, was linearly related to the logarithm of the ΔBFC. Similar results have been obtained using a lorry coasting over different surfaces.[80] *Figure 7.46* shows the data obtained when the lorry was coasted at 70 km/h. Although the number of data points is small the figure shows the expected separation between the traction tyres and the rib patterned tyres, i.e. about 1–2 dB(A), and the correlation between peak noise level and the skidding resistance of the surface. The relative importance of tyre tread pattern and road surface pattern is also clearly indicated in the figure. The range of noise levels for the different surfaces is considerably greater than the small differences resulting from the changes in tread pattern.

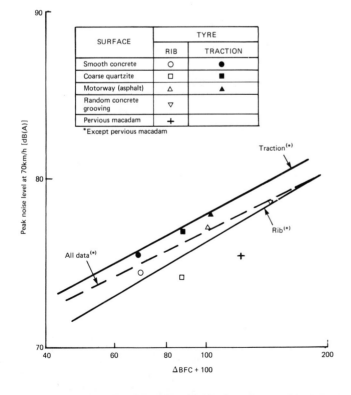

Figure 7.46 Relation between peak noise level and skidding resistance, ΔBFC

This is one of the reasons why it is generally considered that there is greater scope for reducing tyre/surface noise by re-design of the road surface than by design of the tyre (*see also* Chapter 11).

Finally, it is worth noting that the pervious macadam surface has not been included in the regression analysis as it does not appear to conform to the general pattern of behaviour illustrated by the other non-porous surfaces studied. The pervious macadam appears to offer the distinct advantages of good high-speed skidding resistance and low tyre/surface noise emission. This aspect of surface performance is considered later in this chapter and also in Chapter 11 as a technique for controlling traffic noise.

7.8.1.8 Surface water

It is usually assumed that surface water increases tyre noise levels chiefly because of 'splash' created at the tyre/road surface interface. Clearly, however, the amount of water on the road surface is important. A thin film of water may, in certain circumstances, reduce the adhesion forces between the tyre and the road surface without causing any noticeable 'splash' noise. Under these circumstances the presence of surface water may reduce tyre noise levels. In general, however, when puddles form on the road surface, the tyre noise levels increase dramatically, the increase ranging between 1 and 10 dB(A) depending upon the tyre and road surface pattern employed[66] and the vehicle speed. Generally, the main increase in noise due to surface water occurs in the high frequency bands above 2000 Hz. *Figure 7.47* demonstrates this aspect of tyre/surface noise generation.

Bergman has investigated further the mechanism governing splash noise.[81] By modelling the acceleration of water droplets from the contact patch it was shown that the acceleration follows the same velocity–power law as tyre noise on wet roads. It was suggested that wet road noise is due to the acceleration of the water droplets. By using assumed values of droplet size, number and velocity, good agreement was obtained with the measured data (*Figure 7.48*).

7.8.1.9 Road surfaces with high acoustical absorption

It was shown in the previous paragraph that the presence of a surface layer of water can give rise to greatly enhanced tyre noise levels. The presence of surface water can have other very serious disadvantages since the risk of skidding and aqua-

planing at high vehicle speeds is greatly increased and the spray generated, particularly by lorries, can seriously limit visibility for other road users. It was for this latter reason that the Transport and Road Research Laboratory in the UK developed an open textured road surface which allowed water to drain rapidly through the surface matrix to an impervious sub-base. This type of road surface, known as open textured pervious macadam, greatly reduces the formation of spray during wet weather but because of its open texture it has also been found to offer advantages for noise suppression. For example, *Figure 7.46* shows that pervious macadam gives about 3 dB(A) less noise than the non-porous surfaces studied when adjusted to the same *Δ*BFC value.

One possible explanation of this anomalous behaviour is that the pervious surface acts as a good absorber of the acoustic signals radiated by the tyre. *Figure 7.49* compares the absorption coefficients for pervious macadam for a range of one-third octave frequency bands with the coefficients obtained for a smooth concrete and a conventional motorway surface. The measurements were taken on core samples extracted from the test sites and the absorption coefficients were measured at normal incidence in a standing wave tube. ā is defined as the ratio of the absorbed acoustic energy to the incident sound energy.

Over the frequency range 630–1000 Hz the values of ā obtained for the pervious surface were significantly greater than those recorded for the other surfaces, the maximum absorption occurring at about 800 Hz.

Bennerhult[82] has also measured the acoustic absorption of road surfaces using an impedance tube on the road site itself, again at normal incidence to the test surface. However, the

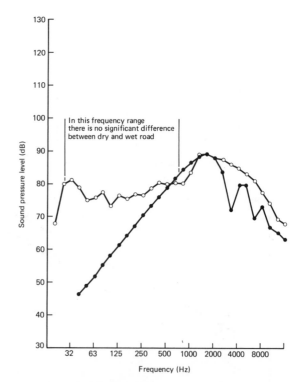

Figure 7.48 Comparison of measured and predicted noise for a car rolling on a wet road surface. After Bergman.[81] ○——○ = rolling noise of a car on a wet road; ●——● = theoretical values for acceleration noise of water droplets

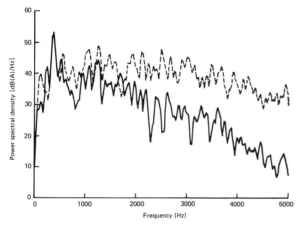

Figure 7.47 Narrow band frequency spectra for traction tyres rolling on dry and wet motorway surface at 96 km/h. After Underwood.[66] ——— = dry; - - - = wet

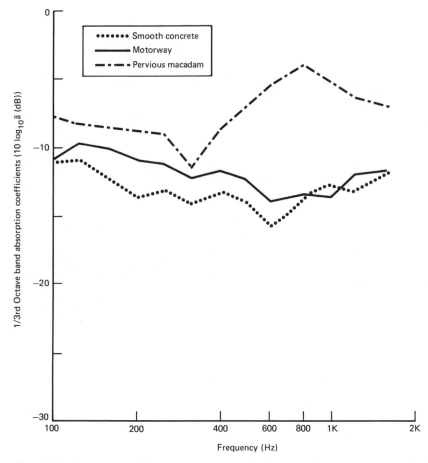

Figure 7.49 Absorption coefficients obtained for normal incidence on different road surfaces. After Nelson[67]

absorption coefficients at 10% to grazing incidence have also been calculated. It is claimed that small angles of incidence relate more closely to the situation when tyre noise is measured. For this condition the surface absorption was found to be much higher than for normal incidence.

7.8.2 Sources of tyre noise

The many workers in this field have reported several possible sources of tyre noise.[64,68,83-86] These include aerodynamic noise from the rotation of the wheel and tyre,[64,85,86] noise from the vibration of the tyre surface,[68] and pressure fluctuations caused by pumping of air in the tread grooves in the contact patch.[64,84]

7.8.2.1 Aerodynamic noise

Even a freely spinning wheel, i.e. not rolling on a surface, generates sound because of a vortex shedding and the generation of turbulance in the surrounding air. Wilken et al.[85] investigated this noise source using a trailer fitted with a smooth tyre. The vortex shedding and turbulence were largely eliminated by the use of splitter boards and side shields but the measured noise level did not drop appreciably. It may be concluded, therefore, that at road vehicle speeds the noise due to air movement in the region of the tyre is not an important source.

7.8.2.2 Air pumping

Air pumping is the process by which air is trapped in the section of the tread groove in contact with the road surface and is then released as the tread elements emerge at the rear of the contact patch. The pressure fluctuations caused by 'air pumping' has been suggested as a possible major cause of tyre noise (Hayden,[64] Plotkin[84]). Nelson[67] and Nilsson[87] both tested this hypothesis by filling tyre grooves with acoustic foam material to restrict the flow of air through the grooves. Coasting noise was measured with and without the foam using a microphone mounted on a boom close to the tyre. The effect on noise level of adding the foam material was less than 1 dB(A). It has also been argued that since tyre noise does not decrease substantially for a smooth tyre running on a smooth surface when, presumably, there are no enclosed air pockets, then air pumping cannot be a major cause of tyre noise. Nevertheless some workers in this field maintain support for the air pumping theory, for example Samuels[88] who obtained results by running tyres on a smooth drum roller in an anechoic chamber.

7.8.2.3 Tyre vibration

Nelson and Underwood[67] studied tyre vibration by attaching accelerometers to the side wall, shoulder and in a tread groove of a tyre fitted to a lorry. Figure 7.50 shows the positioning of the instrumentation on the tyre. The vehicle was coasted over surfaces of smooth concrete, coarse quartzite and rolled asphalt. *Figure 7.51* shows typical oscillograms of vibration amplitude recorded in the tread, shoulder and side wall for about 2 revolutions of the tyre when the vehicle was travelling at 64 km/h. An examination of the excitation frequencies exhibited by different parts of the tyre are shown in *Figure 7.52*. It is shown that the principal frequency bands were in the range 400–1000 Hz for both the tread and side-wall. The higher frequencies excited were generally more localized around the contact region than the lower frequencies.

In order to investigate the possibility that tyre vibration can give rise to substantial levels of tyre noise Nelson[67] compared frequency spectra obtained at the track side microphone with the vibration levels recorded in the tyre. *Figure 7.53* shows this comparison at a speed of 81 km/h on the rolled asphalt surface. Each one-third octave band level was the maximum vibration level recorded at the three transducer positions, i.e. tyre tread, shoulder and side-wall. It can be seen that the sound level spectra and the tyre acceleration level spectra had similar shapes, both spectra were broad band with a peak level occurring at approximately 800 Hz. The increase in vibration level at low frequencies, due mainly to tyre tread vibrations was not, however, reproduced in the sound level spectra.

Nelson[67] used a vibrating sphere model to produce theoretical levels of sound pressure which were close to the observed track-side levels particularly at frequencies below 1000 Hz. This result

taken together with the observed similarity between tyre vibration and track-side sound level spectra gives additional support to the view that tyre vibration is the principal factor controlling the overall levels of tyre noise emission.

From the work of Nelson and Underwood[67] and others it is possible to recommend certain basic rules governing the design of tyres and road surfaces to minimize tyre noise radiation. These are briefly:

1. Tyres should have a random circumferential rib style tread pattern as this allows drainage of water from the contact patch, but does not allow the tyre to vibrate at passing frequencies related to tread pattern.
2. The road surface should have a random pattern to avoid the effects at tyre rotation frequencies.
3. The tyre should be of radial ply construction with steel belts in order to reduce the amount of slip in the contact area and to maximize damping in the tyre structure.
4. The tyre size and inflation pressure should be maximized consistent with safety as this will minimize the deformation of the tyre in the contact region and reduce tyre vibration.
5. If the road surface can be porous, as for example pervious macadam, there will be an additional advantage of the removal of surface water with the reduction of tyre splash noise in wet conditions. This also reduces noise in dry conditions by acoustic absorption in the surface voids.

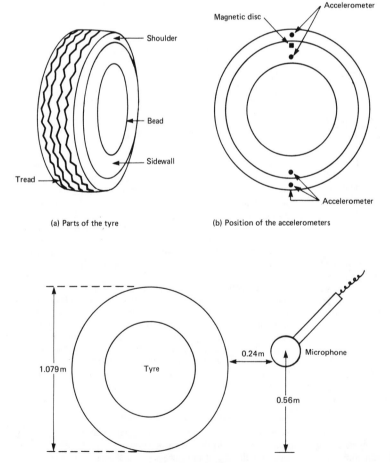

(a) Parts of the tyre

(b) Position of the accelerometers

(c) Position of microphone

Figure 7.50 The location of the transducers around the tyre. After Nelson[67]

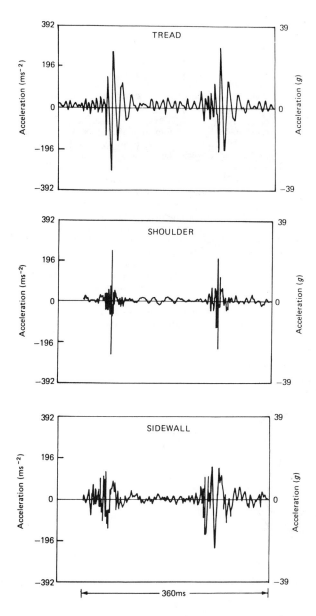

Figure 7.51 Oscillograms of typical tyre surface vibration signals (vehicle speed=64 km/h). After Nelson[67]

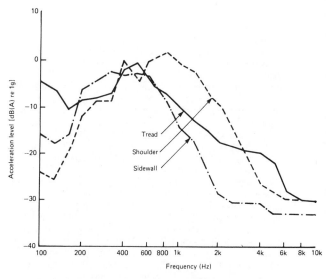

Figure 7.52 Comparison of one-third octave spectra for tread, shoulder and side-wall vibration on the motorway surface at 81 km/h. After Nelson[67]

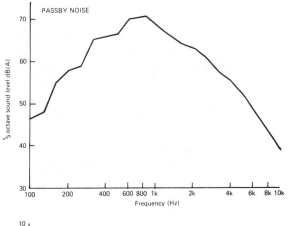

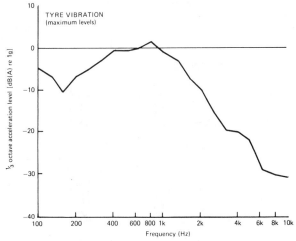

Figure 7.53 One-third octave band tyre vibration levels and passby noise. After Nelson[67]

7.9 Motor-cycle noise

Motor cycles account for less than 3% of total traffic so their contribution to overall noise levels is generally small. However, individual machines can be extremely noisy and cause a great deal of annoyance. The noise of motor cycles as manufactured is not the only problem in reducing the nuisance of motor-cycle noise. Many riders replace the original equipment exhaust silencers with cheap replacements which can bring the machine's noise emission above the legislative limits. As a result of cooperation between the manufacturers and users organizations a British Standard for replacement motor cycle and moped exhaust systems (BSAU 193: 1983 (8)) has been prepared and embodied in UK legislation.

Current noise limits for motor cycles as required by EEC Directive 78/1015/EEC, range from 78 dB(A) for machines having engines less than 80 cc to 86 dB(A) for machines over 500 cc engine capacity.

Figure 7.54 shows the principal sources of motor-cycle noise. The earliest published work on motor-cycle noise appears to be that by Cave-Brown-Cave[89] who, in 1934, improved the silencing of a then current machine by empirical means. Other work carried out before the second world war included that by Dadson, and Fogg[90] and Kaye and Dadson[91] in 1940 and 1939,

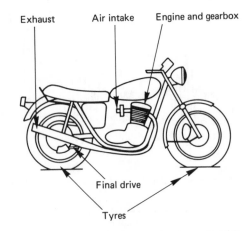

Figure 7.54 Sources of motor-cycle noise

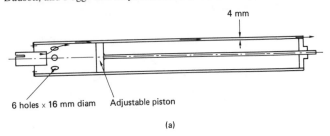

6 holes × 16 mm diam   Adjustable piston

(a)

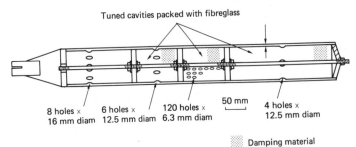

Tuned cavities packed with fibreglass

8 holes × 16 mm diam   6 holes × 12.5 mm diam   120 holes × 6.3 mm diam   50 mm   4 holes × 12.5 mm diam

▨ Damping material

(b)

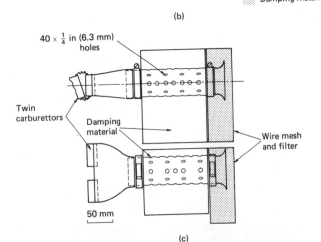

40 × ¼ in (6.3 mm) holes

Twin carburettors

Damping material

Wire mesh and filter

50 mm

(c)

Figure 7.55 Experimental (*a*) and prototype (*b*) exhaust silencers and induction silencer (*c*) for 750 cc motor cycle (1973) (Roe)

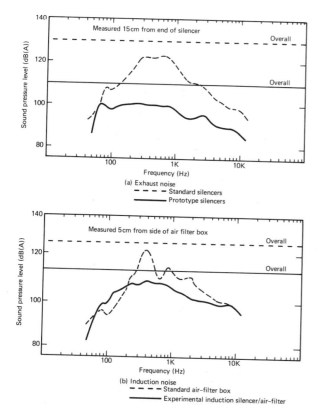

(a) Exhaust noise
- - - Standard silencers
—— Prototype silencers

(b) Induction noise
- - - Standard air-filter box
—— Experimental induction silencer/air-filter

Figure 7.56 Exhaust and inlet noise reduction spectra for 750 cc motor cycle (Roe) (a) measured 6 in (15.2 cm) from end of silencer. (b) measured 2 in (5.1 cm) from end of silencer

knowledge of the characteristics of motor-cycle noise enabled the UK government to assist in the formulation of the current EEC directive on motor-cycle noise (78/1015/EEC). (*See* Chapter 9).

More recent work at the Transport and Road Research Laboratory of the UK Department of Transport[94] has brought the earlier work up to date. Some aspects of this work are also reviewed in Chapter 6.

7.10 General conclusions

It can be judged from the evidence in this chapter that the most efficient methods of vehicle noise reduction are to be achieved in the early stages of vehicle design and during prototype development of the vehicles and engines. It becomes increasingly difficult to achieve cost effective noise reductions using retro-fit techniques as the degree of noise control required increases.

Because of the way in which noise sources combine to produce overall noise, it is important to consider all major sources on a vehicle and to determine a comprehensive appraisal of noise quietening targets which together produce the overall target for the vehicle. While the redesign of noisier engines can produce substantial reductions in noise without the necessity of incurring weight and power penalties, some engine encapsulation for future generation vehicles is likely. For these vehicles the problem of fan noise is likely to be a greater problem as higher duties will be required to achieve efficient engine cooling.

The design of exhaust silencers will improve greatly over the next few years as computer design methods are developed. However, the control of low-frequency noise will continue to provide problems for exhaust silencers owing to the large volumes required and the space limitations on most vehicles.

Tyre noise can be reduced from present-generation levels but only at the expense of safety. It appears likely, therefore, that the noise from future vehicles will be limited by the noise generated by the tyre/road surface interaction. Further improvements in tyre-surface noise are more likely to arise from improvements in the design of the road surface.

respectively. In 1972 Roe[92] reduced the noise level of a 750 cc motor cycle to 86 dB(A) from 98 dB(A) by redesign of the silencer and the provision of a more sophisticated inlet silencer. *Figure 7.55(a)* and *(b)* illustrate the experimental and prototype exhaust silencer designs while *Figure 7.55(c)* shows the design of the induction silencer. The spectra of induction and exhaust noise are shown in *Figure 7.56* where the large reduction in overall noise and the smoothing of the spectra can be seen.

Roe states that the levels of exhaust and induction noise were lower than the mechanical noise of the engine, gearbox and final drive and so mechanical noises would have to be reduced to reduce machine noise further.

In the decade since Roe did this work motor cycles as manufactured have become much quieter to conform with the requirements of legislation. However, because of the way some motor cycles are used, i.e. at high engine revolutions in quiet residential neighbourhoods, they cause more subjective nuisance than their measured noise levels would suggest. This has caused the UK government to take a fresh look at motor-cycle noise and to regard it as a problem in some ways different from other traffic noise problems.

Consequently in 1977 the UK Department of Transport carried out some test work on a range of new and used machines of capacity varying from 50 cc to 650 cc.[93]

Although improving the understanding of motor-cycle noise as a whole this work was not primarily directed at finding ways of reducing noise of individual machine types as there is virtually no motor-cycle industry in the UK to support. However, a

References

1   *A Review of Road Traffic Noise*. Road Research Laboratory Report, LR 357, Crowthorne England (1970).
2   LILLY, L. R. C. (Ed.) *Diesel Engine Reference Book*, Butterworths, London (1984).
3   BENSON, R. S. and WHITEHOUSE, N. D. *Internal Combustion Engines* Vols 1 and 2, Pergamon Press, Oxford (1979).
4   RICARDO, H. R. and HEMPSON, J. G. G. *The High Speed Internal Combustion Engine* (5th edn.), Blackie, Oxford (1968).
5   BEU DE ROCHAS. *Nouvelles Recherches sur les Conditions Pratiques de l'utilisation de la Chaleur er en General de la Force Motrice. Avec Application au chemin de feu et a la Navigation*. E. Lacroix, Paris (1862).
6   PRIEDE, T. In *Search of Origins of Engine Noise—an Historical Review*. Society of Automotive Engineers Congress, Detroit, Paper No. 800534 (1980).
7   RUSSELL, M. F. *Diesel Engine Noise: Control at Source* S.A.E. paper 820238, Society of Automotive Engineers Congress, Detroit (1982).
8   RUSSELL, M. F. *Automotive Diesel Engine Noise Analysis, Diagnosis and Control—Lucas Engineering Review*, Vol. 7, No. 4 (1979).
9   CHALLEN, B. J. and MORRISON, D. Automotive engine noise. In Lilly, L. R. C. (ed.) *Diesel Engine Reference Book*, Butterworths, London (1984).
10   CHALLEN, B. J., ATKINS, K. A. and CROKER, M. D. *Transient and Steady Noise in Automotive Diesel Engines*. Institute of Acoustics, Proceedings of Conference at Loughborough University (1980).
11   CHALLEN, B. J. and CROKER, M. D. *A Review of Recent Progress in Diesel Engine Noise Reduction*. S.A.E. International Congress, Detroit, Paper No. 820517 (1982).

12 AUSTEN, A. E. W. and PRIEDE, T. *Noise of Automotive Diesel Engines: Its Causes and Reduction. SAE Transactions*, Vol. 74, paper 650165 (1966).

13 RUSSELL, M. F., PALMER, D. C. and YOUNG, C. D. *Measuring Diesel Noise at Source with a View to its Control*. Institution of Mechanical Engineers, Paper C142/84, Vehicle Noise and Vibration Conference (1984).

14 ANDERTON, D., GROVER, E. C., LALOR, N. and PRIEDE, T. *The Automotive Diesel Engine—Its Combustion, Noise and Design*. Institute of Mechanical Engineers Conference, Land Transport Engines, Paper No. C14/77 (1977).

15 HAYES, P. A., SEYBERT, A. F. and HAMILTON, J. F. *A Coherence Model for Piston Impact Generated Noise*, SAE Paper No. 790274 in P80 Society of Automotive Engineers Congress, Detroit (1979).

16 HADDAD, S. D. and PULLEN, H. L. Piston slap as a source of noise and vibration in diesel engines. *Journal of Sound and Vibration*, **34**, 249–260 (1974).

17 MUNRO, R. and PARKER, A. *Transverse Movement Analysis and its Influence on Diesel Piston Design*, SAE Paper 750800 in SP397, Society of Automotive Engineers Diesel Engine Noise Conference, Milwaukee (1975).

18 ROHRLE, M. D. *Affecting Diesel Engine Noise by the Piston*, SAE Paper 750799 in SP397, Society of Automotive Engineers Diesel Engine Noise Conference, Milwaukee (1975).

19 UNGAR, E. E. and ROSS, D. *Piston Slap as a Source of Engine Noise* ASME Paper 65-OGP-10, American Society of Mechanical Engineers (1965).

20 FAWCETT, J. N. and BURDESS, J. S. Controlling piston slap. *Engineering Materials and Design*, **March**, 17–19 (1973).

21 PRIEDE, T. *Effect of Operating Parameters on Sources of Vehicle Noise. Symposium on Noise in Transportation*, Section II, University of Southampton (1974).

22 PRIEDE, T. *Problems and Developments in Automotive Engine Noise Research*, SAE Proceedings of Diesel Noise Conference, Detroit, Paper 790205 (1979).

23 CROKER, D. M., LALOR, N. and PETIT, M. *The Use of Finite Element Techniques for the Prediction of Engine Noise*, Institute of Mechanical Engineers Conference, Paper No. C146/79 (1979).

24 TURNER, G. L., MILSTEAD, M. G. and HANKS, P. *Vibration Characteristics of an In-Line Engine Structure*, Institute of Mechanical Engineers Conference, Paper No. C138/84 (1984).

25 HAYES, P. A. and QUANTZ, C. A. *Determining Vibration, Radiation Efficiency and Noise Characteristics of Structural Design Using Analytical Techniques*, SAE International Congress, Detroit, Paper 820440 (1982).

26 FORD, D. M., HAYES, P. A. and SMITH, S. K. *Engine Noise Reduction by Structural Design Using Advanced Experimental and Finite Element Methods*, SAE Diesel Engine Noise Conference, Detroit, Paper 790366 (1979).

27 CROKER, M. D. *Digital Processing Revitalises Old Techniques*, SAE International Congress, Detroit, Paper 820366 (1982).

28 CHUNG, J. Y., POPE, J. and FELDMAIER, D. A. *Application of Acoustic Intensity Measurement to Engine Noise Evaluation*. SAE Diesel Engine Noise Conference, Detroit, Paper 790502 (1979).

29 RUSSELL, M. F. and PULLEN, H. L. *The Influence of Mountings on Injection Pump Noise*, SAE Diesel Engine Noise Conference, Detroit, Paper 790273 (1979).

30 PRIEDE, T. *Relation Between Form of Cylinder Pressure Diagram and Noise*. Institute of Mechanical Engineers, Diesel Engines Proceedings, Auto Division, No. 1, pp. 63–77 (1960–61).

31 ATKINS, K. A. and CHALLEN, B. J. *A Practical Approach to Truck Noise Reduction*, Institute of Mechanical Engineers, C131/79 (1979).

32 CHAN, C. M. P., MONCRIEFF, I. D. AND PETTIT, R. A. *Diesel Engine Combustion Noise with Alternative Fuels*, SAE Conference, Detroit, Paper 820236 (1982).

33 CHUNG, J. Y. and POPE, J. Practical measurements of acoustic intensity—the two microphone cross-spectral method. *Proceedings of International Conference on Noise Control Engineering*, Internoise, San Francisco (1978).

34 MIURA, Y. and SUZUKI, T. *Vibration Modal Analysis of Engine Components Using Double Pulsed Laser Holography*. Institute of Mechanical Engineers Conference. Paper C155/84 (1984).

35 CROKER, M. D., LALOR, N. and PETYT, M. *The Use of Finite Element Techniques for the Prediction of Engine Noise*. Institute of Mechanical Engineers Conference Paper C146/79 (1979).

36 THIEN, G. E. *A Review of Basic Design Principles for Low Noise Diesel Engines*. SAE Paper 790506, Detroit (1979).

37 THIEN, G. E., *et al. Cars with Closed Engine Compartment—Effect on Exterior Noise and Passenger Comfort*. Institute of Mechanical Engineers, Paper C133/84 (1984).

38 ANDERTON, D. and WATERS, P. E. *Effect of Fuel Composition on Diesel Engine Noise and Performance*. SAE International Congress, Detroit. Paper 820235 (1982).

39 RUSSELL, M. F. *Recent CAV Research into Noise Emissions and Fuel Economy of Diesel Engines*. SAE, USA, Paper 770257 (1977).

40 AUSTEN, A. E. W. and PRIEDE, T. *Origins of Diesel Engine Noise*. Symposium on Engine Noise and Noise Suppression. Institute of Mechanical Engineers, London (1958).

41 HAYNES, C. D. and KELL, E. L. *Engine Exhaust Silencing (3 reports)* M.I.R.A. Report Nos 1964/3, 1965/2/12, 1965. Motor Industry Research Association.

42 Air intake silencing. *Automobile Engineer*, **59 (II)**, 398–400 (1969).

43 Exhaust systems. *Automobile Engineer*, **59 (II)**, 400–402 (1969).

44 TYLER, J. W. *TRRL Quiet Vehicle Programme, Quiet Heavy Vehicle (QHV) Project*. Department of the Environment, Department of Transport, TRRL Report SR 521, Crowthorne (Transport and Road Research Laboratory) (1980).

45 TYLER, J. W. and COLLINS, J. F. *TRRL Quiet Heavy Vehicle Project: Development of Foden/Rolls Royce Demonstration Vehicle*. Department of the Environment, Department of Transport, TRRL Report LR 1067 (Transport and Road Research Laboratory), Crowthorne (1983).

46 TYLER, J. W. *The TRRL Quiet Heavy Vehicle Project. Institute of Mechanical Engineers, Automobile Division Proceedings*, Vol. 193, No. 23 (1979).

47 CAWTHORNE, A. R. and TYLER, J. W. The Transport and Road Research Laboratory Quiet Heavy Vehicle Project. SAE Technical Paper 790542, February 1979. *SAE Journal, Feb.*, 315–341 (1979).

48 MITCHELL, C. G. B. *Quiet Heavy Vehicles for 1990—The QHV 90 Programme*. SAE Technical Paper, Surface Vehicle Noise and Vibration Conference, Michigan, May (1985).

49 BROWN, G. B. The vortex motions covering edge tones. *Journal of the Physics Society*, **49**, 493–521 (1937).

50 DAVIES, P. O. A. L. and ALFREDSON, R. J. *Design of Silencers for Internal Combustion Engine Exhaust Systems. Proceedings Institute of Mechanical Engineers, Vibration and Noise in Motor Vehicles*, Vol. 156 (1971).

51 INAGAWA, M. and NAKAMURA, K. Reducing exhaust system noise in heavy truck design. *International Journal of Vehicle Design*, **2**, 127–144.

52 BOLTON, A. N., FARRANT, P. E., MCEWAN, D., MOORE, A. and WILSON, G. *QHV: The NEL Contribution*. Institute of Mechanical Engineers, Automotive Engineer, June/July (1979).

53 TAKEDA, K. Reduction of cooling system noise in heavy duty truck design. *International Journal of Vehicle Design*, **2** (1981).

54 DEEPROSE, W. M. *Fan Noise Generation and its Control*, Institution of Mechanical Engineers, CME (1974).

55 DALY, K. J. and SMITH, J. D. Using gratings in drive line noise problems. In *Institute of Mechanical Engineers Conference, Noise and Vibrations of Engines and Transmissions*, pp. 15–20 (1979).

56 WELBORN, D. B. Fundamental knowledge of gear noise—A survey. In *Proceedings of Institute of Mechanical Engineers Conference, Noise and Vibrations of Engines and Transmissions* (1979).

57 MUNRO, R. G. Effect of geometrical errors on the transmission of motion between gears. *Proceedings of Institute of Mechanical Engineers*, **184**, 79–84 (1969/70).

58 MITCHELL, L. D. and DAWS, J. W. A basic approach to gear noise prediction. Society of Automotive Engineers, International Off-Highway Meeting and Exposition, Wisconsin, Paper No. 821065 (1982).

59 PALMER, W. E. and FUEHRER, R. R. *Noise Control in Planetary Transmissions*, SAE Earthmoving Industry Conference, Illinois, Paper 770561 (1977).

60 HERA, R. W. *Transmission Noise Reduction using Holographic Source Identification and Constrained Layer Damping*. SAE Conference, Paper 790363 (1979).

61 HOUSER, D. R. *Research in the Gear Dynamics and Gear Noise Research Laboratory*, Society of Automotive Engineers, International Off-Highway Meeting and Exposition, Wisconsin, Paper No. 821066 (1982).

62 SAKAI, T., DOI, Y., YAMAMOTO, K., OGASAWARA, T. and NARITA, M.

Theoretical and Experimental Analysis of Rattling Noise of Automotive Gearbox. SAE Paper No. 810773, Passenger car meeting (1981).

63 HARLAND, D. G. *Rolling Noise and Vehicle Noise.* Department of Environment, TRRL Report LR 652, Transport and Road Research Laboratory, Crowthorne (1974).

64 HAYDEN, R. E. Roadside noise from the interaction of rolling tyres with the road surface. In *Proceedings Purdue Noise Control Conference*, Purdue University, pp. 62–67 (1971).

65 CORCORAN, D. A. *Effects of Operating Parameters on Truck Tyre Sounds.* SAE Technical Paper 720925, Society of Automotive Engineers, USA.

66 UNDERWOOD, M. C. P. *A Preliminary Investigation into Lorry Tyre Noise.* Department of Environment, TRRL Paper LR 601, Transport and Road Research Laboratory, Crowthorne (1973).

67 NELSON, P. M. and UNDERWOOD, M. C. P. *Lorry Tyre Noise.* Institute of Mechanical Engineers, Paper C139/84, Vehicle Noise and Vibration Conference, London (1984).

68 NILSSON, N. A., *et al. Radiation of Airborne Sound from a Rolling Tyre due to Contact Patch Excited Vibration. Presentation to Swedish Board for Technical Development*, Institutet for Miljoteknit FM Akustikbyran AB (1975).

69 Society of Automotive Engineers, USA. *SAE Highway Tyre Noise Symposium*, San Francisco, USA 10–12 November, 1976.

70 Society of Automotive Engineers, USA. *International Tyre Noise Conference*, Stockholm, Sweden, 28–31 August 1979.

71 LEASURE, W. A., *et al. Truck Noise—1 Peak A-Weighted Sound Levels due to Truck Tyres.* National Bureau of Standards, Building Research Division, Report UST/TST—72—1, Washington (1972).

72 ALLEN, R. M. *The Pros and Cons of Radial Truck Tyres.* SAE 741134 Truck Tyre Meeting, Michigan (1976).

73 VOLLMER, H. P. Tyre Use in a Common Carrier Fleet. In *Proceedings of The SAE Highway Truck Tyre Noise Symposium*, p. 70 (1976).

74 *Tyre Noise Problems, I, II, III*, Bolt Beranek & Newman, Report, 458, 523, 597, (1958).

75 YURKOUSKI, B., ASTROV, W. A. and IVANTEEV, A. V. The influences of design parameters on the shock-absorbing capacity, road holding and noise levels of car tyres. *Kauchuck i Rezina* **2615**, 30–33 (1967). (In Russian).

76 ZOEPPRITZ, N. P. Moglichkeiten und Grenzen der Verminderung des Reifer—Ablavfgerausches. *ATZ*, **74**, 13–16 (1972).

77 ULLRICH, S. Comparison of free-field and chassis dynamometer measurements of car rolling noise. *ATZ*, **76**, 254–258 (1974).

78 Rubber Manufacturers Association. *Presentation to the Office of Noise Abatement and Control of the Environmental Protection Hearing*, Washington (1971).

79 GILES, C. G. and LANDER, F. T. The Skid Resistance Properties of Wet Surfaces at High Speeds: Exploratory Measurements with a Small Braking–Force Trailer. *Journal of The Royal Aeronautical Society*, **60**, 83–94 (1956).

80 FRANKLIN, R. E., HARLAND, D. G. and NELSON, P. M. *Road Surfaces and Traffic Noise.* Department of the Environment, Department of Transport, TRRL Report LR 896. Crowthorne (Transport and Road Research Laboratory) (1979).

81 BERGMAN, M. *Gerauschent-stehung beim rollen auf Benetzten Oberflachen*, Dissertation, TU, Berlin (1979).

82 BENNERHULT. O., Acoustical and mechanical impedances of road surfaces and the influence on tyre noise. In *Proceedings of International Tyre Noise Conference, Sweden*, pp. 185–195 (1979).

83 RICHARDS, M. G. Automotive tyre noise—a comprehensive study. *Sound and Vibration*, **May,** 42–47 (1974).

84 PLOTKIN, K. J., **et al**. *Identification of tyre Noise Generation Mechanisms using a Roadwheel Facility.* SAE Paper 800281 (SAE SP 80/456), S.A.E. (1980).

85 WILKEN, I. D., OSWALD, L. J. and HICKLING, R. Research on Individual Noise Source Mechanisms of Truck Tyres. Aeroacoustic Sources SAE Paper 762022. *SAE Noise Symposium Proceedings*, p. 70 (1976).

86. HECKL, M. Tyre noise generating mechanisms—state of the art report. Institute fur Technische Akustik de TV Berlin. Paper Presented to *International Tyre Noise Conference, Sweden* (1979).

87 NILSSON, N. A. *Generating Mechanisms of External Tyre Noise.* TR 3.709.14, IFM Akustikbyron, Stockholm (1975).

88 SAMUELS, S. Recent Australian Tyre/Road Noise Research. *Proceedings of International Tyre Noise Conference*, pp. 111–124 (1979).

89 CAVE-BROWN-CAVE, T. R. The reduction of exhaust noise of motorcycles. *Engineering*, **138**, 316–318 (1934).

90 DADSON, R. S. and FOGG, H., *Motorcycle Silencing*, Institution of Automobile Engineers Research Report No 9194B (1940).

91 KAYE, G. W. C. and DADSON, R. S. Noise measurement and analysis in relation to motor vehicles. *Proceedings of The Institution of Automobile Engineers*, **33**, 714 (1939).

92 ROE, G. E. The silencing of a high performance motorcycle. *Journal of Sound and Vibration*, **33**, 29–39 (1974).

93 WATERS, P. E. The origins and characteristics of motorcycle noise. *Institution of Mechanical Engineers Conference on Vehicle Noise and Vibration*, C144/84 (1984).

94 NELSON, P. M. and ROSS, N.F. *Some aspects of Motorcycle Noise Emission.* Department of the Environment, Department of Transport. TRRL Report SR 795, Crowthorne (Transport and Road Research Laboratory) (1983).

Further reading

LILLY, L. R. C. (Ed.). *Diesel Engine Reference Book*, Butterworths, London (1984).

BENSON, R. S. and WHITEHOUSE, N. D. International Combustion Engines, Volumes 1 and 2, Pergamon Press, Oxford (1979).

PRIEDE, T. and ANDERTON, D. *Likely Advances in Mechanics, Cooling Vibration and Noise of Automotive Engines.* Institute of Mechanical Engineers, Proceedings Vol. 7 (1984).

NORTH, M. P. The application of acoustic intensity measurement to engine noise reduction. In *Proceedings International Congress on Recent Developments in Acoustic Intensity Measurement*, Senlis (1981).

BATHE, K. J. and WILSON, E. L. *Numerical Methods in Finite Element Analysis*, Prentice Hall (1976).

LALOR, N. *Finite Element Optimisation Techniques of Diesel Engine Structures*, Society of Automotive Engineers, Paper 820437 (1982).

8

Quiet Vehicle Development

Bernard M. Favre
Ingenieur diplômé ENSPM, ENSMP,
Docteur d'Etat ès Sciences,
Renault-Dast, Rueil-Malmaison, France

J. Tyler FIHT, FIOA, Dip Stats, Hon RCM
Consultant, Transport and Road Research
Laboratory, Crowthorne, UK

Contents

Since the early 1970s, several countries have initiated research and development programmes aimed at producing future generation vehicles and components with substantially reduced noise levels.

In general, the objectives of these projects have been:

1. To determine the technical feasibility of vehicle quietening by providing noise control engineering solutions for individual vehicle types.
2. To gauge the influence of vehicle noise control on other vehicle design goals, e.g. production economics, fuel utilization, engine efficiency and in-use reliability and serviceability.

The previous chapter gives specific information on vehicle noise sources and the methods used to reduce noise emission through improved engineering and design. This chapter is concerned with the practical application of these techniques which lead to the development of both research and production prototype quietened vehicles. The chapter reviews the progress that has been made in different countries to achieve these goals and discusses the interrelationship between quiet vehicle technology and other desirable vehicle design objectives.

8.1 Quiet vehicle engineering projects

A review of the prospects for reducing vehicle noise for future years has been carried out by Favre and Lambert.[1] A summary of the major projects covered by this review is given in this section. Unless otherwise stated, the noise levels quoted were obtained according to the procedure detailed in ISO R 362.[2] This test method and other vehicle noise tests are discussed in more detail in the following chapter.

8.1.1 Federal Republic of Germany (FRG)

Several short- and medium-term vehicle noise reduction programmes have been undertaken in the FRG as well as a more comprehensive long-term programme which includes studies of fuel efficiency and gaseous pollution control. The shorter programmes were carried out between 1978 and 1983 by the Umweltbundesamt (UBA—Berlin Environmental Agency) and the Federal Ministry of the Interior.[3] Further details of the types of vehicles developed, engine powers and target noise levels are given in *Table 8.1*. Some of the vehicles produced have been put into service to evaluate field performance. For example, 50 modified air-cooled 130 M8FL Magirus delivery lorries (77 dB(A)) have been operated by the German Federal Post Office Administration,[4] and similarly 20 encapsulated 240 D Mercedes Benz taxi cars (originally 80 dB(A) reduced to 74 dB(A)) have been put in service in the city of Bad Reichenhall.[5] These programmes are currently being evaluated. German government aid to the UBA programme amounted to approximately DM 8 million.

Longer term research and development has concentrated on the design, construction and testing of new car types which are intended for operation by the year 2000. This has become known as the 'Auto 2000' Project and was initiated in 1978 by the Bundesministerium für Forschung und Technologie (BMFT—Ministry of Research and Technology).[6] The project brought together the principal car manufacturers (Audi-VW, BMW, Porsche, Daimler-Benz) and a working group from four University Institutes of Technology (HAG). The noise target for the prototype vehicles has been set at 73 dB(A) and the total funds allocated for the project have been set at DM 210 million of which approximately half is provided by the Federal Government.

Further work on tyre design has also been funded by the BMFT (mainly car tyres). The project comprised two parts, both with 100% governmental funding. The first part (1979–82, DM 6 million) was aimed at understanding the generating mechanisms of tyre/road contact noise with FKFS (Stuttgart research institute on vehicles and engines), technical universities of Berlin, Göttingen and Darmstadt, Messerschmitt company and the Continental tyre company. the second part (1982–84, DM 5 million) concerned the development of a quiet car tyre with four of the previous organizations (FKFS, Berlin and Göttingen TU, and Continental).

8.1.2 France

Research on quietening vehicles was started in 1971 through the ATP Programme (Programmed Thematic Actions).[7] Until the completion of the project in 1982, approximately 40 contracts were placed within the manufacturing industries (Renault, Renault VI, Peugeot, Kléber-Colombes) and research laboratories. The programme was monitored by the Institut de Recherche des Transports (IRT) and the total aid amounted to FF 20 million, representing approximately 65% of the total expense, with the remaining part provided by the industry. Some further contracts have been placed under the sponsorship of the Ministry of Environment, Ministry of Transportation and Ministry of Research. The objectives of the programme concerned identification and assessment of vehicle component noise sources, noise reduction of components including engines, exhaust systems, fans, evaluation of quietened vehicles and the development of sound-proofing materials. The primary aim was to provide industry with general expertise regarding noise reduction, rather than to quieten a particular type of vehicle with a given target. Nevertheless, some demonstration vehicles were evaluated.[1] *Table 8.1* gives details of the vehicle types and the noise quietening achieved.

Two major projects have been initiated by Renault VI and have the objectives of developing a heavy commercial vehicle tractor and a rear-engined diesel autobus. The heavy commercial tractor is being designed to meet different noise targets, the most stringent being 80 dB(A). The autobus project (Autobus 85)[8] has as its objective to attain a target level of 78 dB(A) and involves chassis encapsulation of the engine. These projects are supported by the Ministry of Transportation and the Ministry of Industry.

8.1.3 Japan

The Ministry of International Trade and Industry (MITI) in 1974 placed a contract with four Japanese motor manufacturers with the overall aim of reducing vehicle noise particularly from heavy commercial vehicles and an urban bus.[9] Each manufacturer was asked to tackle certain specific areas of noise generation and to find suitable solutions to be shared with the other manufacturers. This project had a total budget of 600 million yen and ran for a period of 3 years. Using the results of research carried out on individual vehicle components the Japanese industry were able to construct several prototype quiet vehicles.[10] *Table 8.1* gives details of the vehicle types produced and their approximate noise levels before and after treatment.

8.1.4 Netherlands

Several quiet vehicle programmes have been undertaken in the Netherlands under the sponsorship of the Interministerial Committee for noise control (ICG).[11] Research has been concentrated on the development of quiet buses and heavy commercial vehicles. Bus noise has been studied by TNO/TPD of Delft in collaboration with public transport operators (RET-Rotterdam for urban buses and CAB for interurban buses). The results of

Table 8.1 Principal quiet vehicle development projects

Country	Name of programme	Manufacturer or company	Vehicles description	Engine power (kW)	Status[6]	Noise level (ISO R 362) (dB(A))		Date of completion
						Before	After	
FRG	BMFT	Porsche	2 private cars air/water cooled	147	1	82	75–78	1977
	P[1]	Daimler–Benz	Private car	?	1	79	74	1978
	UBA	IVECO Magirus KHD/FKFS	Air-cooled delivery lorry	95	2,3	90	74–77	1981
	UBA	Zündapp	Moped	6	3	80	73	1981
	UBA	VW	3 private cars[3] petrol/diesel	36–51	1	77–80	73–74	1981
	UBA	VW	2 private cars[4] petrol/diesel	36	1	78–80	73	1981
	UBA	Daimler–Benz	5 delivery lorries	48–95	3	83–90	76–81	1983
	UBA	MAN—VW	3 delivery lorries	66–100	2	86–87	79–80	1983
	UBA	IVECO Magirus	Construction work truck	211		Not known		
	AUTO 2000 (BMFT)	Audi, BMW, Daimler–Benz HAG, Porsche VW	Private cars	—	1,3	—	73[2]	1982 to 1984
France	ATP	Peugeot	2 private cars petrol/diesel	48–64	1	81	77	1975
	ATP	Bertin	Private car	44	1	79	73	1975
	ATP	Berliet	Delivery lorry	95	1	89	84	1976
	ATP	Renault V.I.	Urban bus rear engine	132	1,3	90	74–80	1978
	ATP	Renault V.I.	Lorry (tractor)	260	1	91–94[5]	81–87[5]	1982
	ATP	Peugeot	Private car diesel	36	3	77	75	1983
	ME/AFME	Renault V.I.	Delivery lorry	66	2,3	88	80	1984
	VIRAGES	Renault V.I.	Lorry (tractor)	228	3	—	80[2]	Not known
	AUTOBUS 85	Renault V.I.	Urban bus	150	3	—	80[2]	Not known
Japan	MITI	Isuzu	Construction work truck	216	1	89	85	1978
	MITI	Nissan	Lorry (tractor)	207	1	88	85	1978
	MITI	Hino	Lorry (tractor)	223	1	89	85	1978
	MITI	Mitsubishi	Urban bus (?)	195	1	88	85	1978
Netherlands	ICG	TPD–TNO RET	Urban bus	—	2	89	78–82	1979
	ICG	TPD–TNO CAB	Country bus	—	2	87–90	80–84	1980
	ICG	DAF Trucks	Lorry	—		Not known		
United Kingdom	P[1]	Norton-Villiers Manchester Un.	Motor cycle	—	1	98	86	1973
	QHV	T.R.R.L./Foden Rolls-Royce	Lorry (tractor)	255	2,3	92	81	1981
	QHV	T.R.R.L./ Leyland	Lorry (tractor)	156	1	88	80	1978
	P[1]	Ricardo	Lorry	187	1	92	80	1979
	P[1]	British Leyland	Urban bus (double decker)	150	3	Not known		
United States of America	DOT	Freightliner Corporation	Lorry (tractor)	255	1,2	94	78	1976
	DOT	International Harvester	Lorry (tractor)	235	1	94	83–87	1976
	DOT	White Motor C.	Lorry (tractor)	173	1	92	82	1976

Table 8.1 Principal quiet vehicle development projects — *continued*

Country	Name of programme	Manufacturer or company	Vehicles description	Engine power (kW)	Status[6]	Noise level (ISO R 362) (dB(A)) Before	After	Date of completion
United States of America	EPA	Bolt, Beranek and Newman	4 lorries (tractors)	184 to 250	1,2	83–88	79–80	1979–82
	P[1]	Tri Country Met.	Bus	Not known		86–88	81–85	1980
	P[1]	United Parcel Service	2 lorries (tractors)	176	2,3	88	82	1982

Noise levels are adjusted to European test conditions.
[1] Projects carried out by industry without Government sponsorship.
[2] Noise level target.
[3] Chassis encapsulation.
[4] Engine encapsulation.
[5] Maximum noise level on all gears.
[6] 1 = Experimental vehicle only; 2 = in-service testing (with one vehicle or more); 3 = vehicle built to production standards.

these studies have led to the development of an insulation package tested on two prototypes and which has been retrofitted to 200 in-service interurban buses. The average noise reductions achieved with the package amount to 7 dB(A).

Truck noise reduction was studied by Daf-trucks with sponsorship from the Ministries of Health and Environmental Protection. The aim was to develop a heavy vehicle powered by a 11.6 litre diesel engine with 5 dB(A) noise reduction and with lower gaseous emissions. This study was completed in 4 years ending in 1981 with a total cost of HFL 5M. Government support amounted to HFL 2.5M. It was followed in 1981 by a project with the same manufacturer to quieten heavy commercial vehicles.

8.1.5 United Kingdom

The Transport and Road Research Laboratory (TRRL) in 1971 initiated a research and development programme known as the Quiet Heavy Vehicle Project (QHV). The objectives of the programme were (1) to develop a maximum weight heavy commercial vehicle tractor with a noise target of 80 dB(A) under all operating conditions and (2) to evaluate the approximate cost and possible weight penalties involved. A detailed description of this programme, its organization, results and in-service performance of the production vehicle is given in the annexe to this chapter.

Following on from this programme, in 1984, the UK government initiated a new programme of research and development. This programme is intended to provide a range of vehicle components and vehicle types which will meet the new commercial vehicle noise limits required by EEC regulations[12] for the latter part of the 1990s and beyond. The project is known as QHV–90. Funding is provided half by the Department of Transport and the Department of Trade and Industry and half by the commercial motor manufacturing industry. The project is managed by TRRL and by a steering group of officials drawn from within the Departments and from industry. The budget for the total programme has been estimated to be in the region of £10 M.

Further details of the project and its organization is given in a paper by Mitchell.[13]

8.1.6 United States of America

The Department of Transportation (DOT) placed contracts beginning in June 1972 with three American truck manufacturers (Freightliner, International Harvester and White Motors) for the construction of prototype quiet trucks based on series production vehicles with diesel engines. The vehicles studied were all maximum weight commercial vehicle tractors with engine powers in the range 175–261 kW (235–350 bhp). The three programmes have been extensively documented.[14–16] The reports include an evaluation of the initial manufacturing cost, their in-use fuel consumption, maintenance and servicing penalties, etc. Further details of the vehicles developed and the noise levels achieved are given in *Table 8.1*.

In 1978, the Environmental Protection Agency (EPA) financed a programme which was concerned with the reduction of noise from road tractors. A firm of consultants, Bolt, Beranek and Newman (BBN), undertook to design four quietened prototypes of series production vehicles with engine powers ranging from 186 to 254 kW (250–340 bhp).[17] Overall the noise levels achieved were 79–80 dB(A). (Noise levels quoted for American vehicles have been converted to ISO R 362 from levels measured according to S.A.E. noise standard J 366(b), i.e. under accelerating conditions with the microphone at a distance of 15 m from the vehicle axis. This roughly corresponds to a difference of 6 dB(A) less than the noise level according to I.S.O. R. 362.)

8.1.7 Quiet vehicle programmes sponsored by industry

As well as government sponsored programmes, practically all vehicle manufacturers are now involved in research and development projects which are intended to lead to quieter vehicles and their components. For example Volvo, Scania in Sweden, Saurer in Switzerland and Iveco in Italy[18] are working on quiet vehicle development in order to ensure that their products meet any foreseeable changes in the noise regulations. In the United States a programme of in-use testing of production quiet vehicles has been carried out by a haulage contractor (United Parcel Service transportation company UPS). The objective of the programme was to examine the fleet performance of 12 heavy commercial tractors (240 bhp quietened to 82 dB(A) approximately) by gathering information on in-service performance and maintenance problems associated with operating quiet vehicles. *Table 8.1* includes a summary of major industrial projects that will lead or have led to the development of either a research or production prototype vehicle.

8.1.8 Summary of quiet vehicle projects

Various vehicles with reduced noise emission have been developed or are being designed in a number of countries. They include:

1. Research prototypes which enable original design concepts to be developed and evaluated.
2. Production prototypes which determine both production line engineering solutions and in-service performance.
3. Mass production models which take into account the variability introduced by production tolerance.

In principle, the research prototype phase can be used to demonstrate the ultimate degree of noise quietening that can be achieved with current technology. Examples of the acoustic performance of a wide range of prototypes are given in *Figure 8.1*.

Further information on all these projects summarized in this section can be found in the major review carried out for the EEC on this topic[1] and by consulting the references listed in the text.

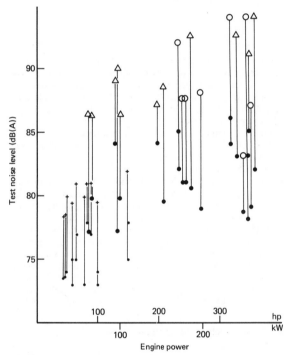

Figure 8.1 Noise level of research prototype vehicles before and after noise quietening. (+): private cars, (△): European lorries, (○): American lorries (noise level adjusted to European test conditions)

8.2 Effects of vehicle quietening on other aspects of vehicle performance

Techniques to reduce vehicle noise emission can interact with other aspects of vehicle performance and design. For example, noise control measures can modify fuel consumption, reduce tare weight, alter dimensions, introduce reliability problems and affect driveability and driver comfort. This section examines some of these design interactions.

8.2.1 Fuel consumption

Fuel consumption may be affected by changes in the weight of the vehicle, its aerodynamics and the efficiency of the power unit. Weight increases, due primarily to the addition of insulation panels and enclosures, can significantly increase fuel consumption. *Table 8.2* gives a summary of the noise level reductions obtained on production prototype vehicles of different types together with the incumbent weight penalty and its average effect on fuel consumption. The figures are only intended to give broad indications as there will be wide variations between vehicles types.

Noise control measures may also result in changes to the vehicle's aerodynamics which could also affect fuel consumption. Internal aerodynamics, i.e. air flow across the radiator, fan and engine compartment, can account for approximately 10% of total vehicle aerodynamic drag. Therefore, changes made to the cooling system and engine compartment can, in principle, produce detectable changes in drag coefficients.[1] External aerodynamics can be affected by changes made to the underbody, suspension and exhaust particularly for a car. This does not necessarily lead to an increase in aerodynamic drag as good underbody designs can improve the vehicle aerodynamics and thus reduce drag coefficients. For example, about 3% reduction in the drag coefficient was obtained with a VW car fitted with an encapsulated engine compartment.[19]

Other aspects that may affect fuel consumption include changes to the combustion system and the use of cylinder scavenging. DI diesel engines offer considerable fuel advantages over IDI and petrol counterparts, but particularly DI engines can be noisy.[20] Turbocharging will tend to improve both fuel consumption and noise.[20-22] Silencer back pressure has a significant effect on engine performance and fuel efficiency particularly for diesel engines.[15,23] However, it is possible to design a silencer having improved acoustic efficiency without impairing energy efficiency (*see* Chapter 7 and Section 8.5) although present designs tend to use large volume expansion chambers and double-walled systems which tend to increase weight.

The use of enclosures to combat noise can reduce the period of running with the engine below normal operating tempera-

Table 8.2 Increase in weight of vehicles as a result of noise quietening, and its marginal effect on fuel consumption

Vehicle type	Reduction in overall noise level* (dB(A))	Approximate noise level attained* (dB(A))	Approximate weight increase (kg)	Percentage of total weight† (%)	Approximate increase in fuel consumption‡ (%)
Private cars	6– 7	74	15– 60	2.5	1.2–3.5
Delivery lorries	8– 9	78	40– 70	0.7–1.5	1.0
Heavy lorries	3– 9	84	15– 40	<0.1	—
	7–12	80	100–300	<1.0	0.2–2.4
Rear-engined buses	9–10	80	100–150	1.0	1.0

*According to ISO R 362 standard.
†Values expressed as a percentage of the maximum permissible laden weight.
‡Range depends on category of vehicle, mode of operation, and load.

tures. This can have a beneficial effect on energy consumption since fuel consumption increases dramatically during the period when the engine temperature is below normal.

Modifications to the power unit and transmission can also affect fuel consumption. For example, de-speeding the engine can reduce both maximum noise and fuel utilization at the expense of some loss in power. Also, introducing an extra gear ratio can reduce both noise and fuel consumption for certain operations although the assessment of the reduction in fuel consumption will depend largely upon the range and frequency of vehicle operation in all gears.

In general, the effects of incorporating various vehicle design changes to reduce noise emission does not greatly affect fuel consumption. In some cases improvements to internal and external aerodynamics or changes to the combustion system can lead to compatible improvements in both noise and fuel utilization. These savings can then be used to offset the increases in fuel consumption caused by increasing the overall weight of the vehicle as a result of engine insulation and enclosure and the use of heavy duty cooling fans and large volume silencers.

8.2.2 Reliability and serviceability

Vehicle noise suppression can lead to reliability and maintenance problems from vehicles in service. Field performance evaluation is therefore needed to determine both whether the vehicle remains in good condition for an acceptable lifetime and whether servicing and repairing the vehicle is impaired by the noise control components. It was found, for example, that early versions of the first 'quiet' city buses operated in Western Germany in 1976–78 could incur cooling and maintenance problems due to a poorly designed engine compartment enclosure.[24] Over a period of several years, the thermal problems were solved and the engine accessibility improved, so that present vehicles are now considered to be satisfactory in these respects.

In general, engine and gearbox encapsulation techniques give rise to cooling problems particularly with engine ancillaries such as alternators or fuel pumps. The presence of an enclosure also makes inspection and maintenance more a problem often leading to increased labour costs when servicing the engine compartment.[17] Improving the airflow over the engine can be made to offset the effects of the enclosure but this generally involves increasing the duty of the fan with associated fuel costs or increasing the fan speed with associated increases in noise level.

Poorly fitting shields or bulky and heavy shields should be avoided as they are often removed from the vehicle during the first service and are not replaced. In keeping with other demonstration heavy duty tractors, the UK Quiet Heavy Vehicle Project reviewed in the Annexe to this chapter incorporates a top engine compartment enclosure. This is attached to the cab of the vehicle so that when the cab is tilted it lifts away from the engine compartment enabling servicing and routine inspection to be carried out without any interference from the shield. This system was found to be totally reliable during a 2-year in-service trial and there was no observable deterioration in the acoustic performance of the shield over its working life. Nevertheless most problems usually arise from the under shields which are in a more severe environment and generally much more difficult to remove.[18]

8.2.3 Driver comfort

The reduction of vehicle noise emission generally ensures that the interior noise at the driver position is also reduced by a roughly equivalent amount. *Figure 8.2* summarizes and compares the noise reductions obtained both externally and internally for a range of quietened production vehicles. The reduction of interior noise levels has, for some time, been a design

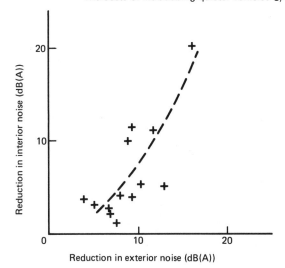

Figure 8.2 Relation between exterior vehicle noise reduction (according to ISO R 362 or similar) and interior (in-cab) vehicle noise reduction

objective for car manufacturers and this has tended to bring forward quiet vehicle technology for the car group. For commercial vehicles, however, the design objectives have not previously included noise as a high priority. With the growing concern over noise and health effects, commercial vehicle designers are now striving to achieve quieter conditions for the operators and this is partly being achieved by vehicle quietening techniques rather than by cab insulation.

8.3 The costs of introducing quieter vehicles

The evaluation of the costs of producing quieter vehicles and studies of the operational performance of production prototypes have enabled estimates to be made of the total cost of introducing quieter vehicles which combines the changes in vehicle first cost with the changes in the costs of maintaining and operating quieter vehicles in-service.

8.3.1 Production costs

Figure 8.3 gives the results of a cost analysis carried out on all available quiet production vehicles expressed as an increase in the cost of production as a function of the noise reduction achieved.[1] As a general guide the increases in first costs for lorries incorporating about 10 dB(A) noise reduction from untreated vehicles with noise levels in the 90–92 dB(A) range, can be broken down as follows:

1. Partial or total encapsulation: 55–75% of total cost increase.
2. Improvements to the exhaust system: 20–35% of total cost increase.
3. Changes to the cooling system: 5–15% of total cost increase.

Buses with rear engines have been quietened from 88–90 dB(A) to 80 dB(A) for an extra cost of between 2.5 and 3.5%. This increased cost is approximately doubled when the noise reduction measures are retro-fitted.

A rule which is sometimes quoted as a rough indicator of vehicle quietening costs is 1% per dB(A). From an analysis of all available vehicle quietening projects this would appear to repre-

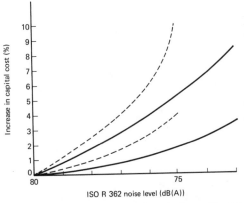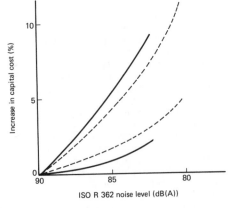

Figure 8.3 Relation between noise reduction and increase of vehicle capital cost. Left, private cars; right, lorries. Taken from (——) Favre and Lambert[1], (– – –) CCMC[25]

sent an upper limit to the cost/noise reduction comparisons observed. Furthermore, it is clear that this simple function cannot be applied outside the range of noise reductions achieved.

8.3.2 Maintenance costs

Data available on the servicing and maintenance costs associated with operating quiet vehicles are rather limited. The Foden lorry operated in the UK for a period of 2 years showed that normal maintenance and servicing costs were increased by 1.5% which represents 0.2% increase in the total cost of operation.[26] The increases were due largely to increased labour costs. The United Parcel Service lorries operated in the United States were reported to require between 350–510 dollars extra in servicing per year, the increases were largely due to labour costs. The second-generation lorries tested as part of this programme incorporated a more efficient engine shield which reduced the maintenance cost increase to 305–312 dollars per vehicle per year.[18]

A profile of maintenance costs for different vehicle types has been produced by the EPA of the United States taking information from the DOT quiet vehicle programmes.[27] These results are summarized in *Figure 8.4*.

As a rough estimate, the extra cost of maintenance can be put at about 1% per dB(A) gained for passenger cars to approximately 0.6–0.7% per dB(A) gained for trucks.

8.3.3 Losses in revenue due to payload reductions

Reductions in payload occur when the overall unladen weight is increased owing to the addition of a variety of noise control components. The lost revenue has been estimated to be as high as 1–2 US dollars per year per kilogram.[15] However, commercial vehicles are generally not operated with a full payload and it is likely, therefore, that the loss in revenue estimates are overstated.

8.3.4 Overall costs of operating quiet vehicles

By combining all the available data on production costs, maintenance, servicing and repair costs, revenue losses and fuel costs, the average increased cost of operating quieter vehicles can be estimated.[1] It is found that:

1. The increased cost for passenger cars quietened from approximately 81 dB(A) to 76 dB(A) amounts to 1.8–2%.

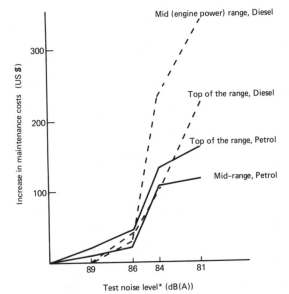

Figure 8.4 Annual average cost of maintaining lorries as a function of noise emission (Data obtained from the results of the US Quiet Vehicle Development Programme[27].)

2. Medium and heavy trucks quietened from approximately 90 dB(A) to 80 dB(A) amounts to 1.1–1.7%.
3. Buses with encapsulated rear-mounted engines reduced from approximately 86 dB(A) to 80 dB(A) amounts to 0.3–0.4%.

8.4 The effect of future vehicle noise legislation on vehicle design

In September 1984 the EEC published its amending Directive stating the maximum permissible noise limits for new vehicles entering service from 1988 to 1989 and well into the next decade.[12] Further details of vehicle noise legislation are given in Chapter 9. The Directive requires noise levels to be reduced from all vehicle categories but particularly from heavy commercial vehicles. This move has resulted in the development of further noise reduction programmes being set up by European Governments and manufacturers.

The basic requirements are for the development of quieter engines to reduce the degree of encapsulation required and improved exhaust and cooling systems. The EEC Directive calls for further examination of noise levels after 1990 and it would seem very likely that a maximum level of 80 dB(A) for heavy commercial vehicles will be the aim.

In mass production it is far more difficult to achieve the noise targets that can be achieved and demonstrated from research and production prototype vehicles and, therefore, in order to achieve these further reductions, particularly for the heaviest vehicles, another order of technological progress will be required.

Engines will have to be designed from scratch with low noise in mind rather than developing existing engines using the same basic structure. If this is not done then the additional degree of enclosure required to lower the external noise level from the engine will be such that severe cooling problems will have to be solved. Cooling systems sited away from the engine may be required so that the restriction in the air flow caused by the enclosure can be avoided. However, the external surfaces of the engine and ancilliary equipment within the enclosure have to be cooled and this would then require a separate fan and duct system.

As engine and exhaust noise levels are reduced still further, items whose noise output was masked before may well become dominant and require treatment; for example, transmission noise from rear axles and reduction gears.

The multiplicity of models and variants which the commercial vehicle manufacturers have to produce makes the quietening process very complicated. The combinations of chassis, cabs, engines, gearboxes and transmissions would have to be matched to provide the required noise levels as well as the normal performance standards. Some current models cannot be quietened and a tightening of the regulatory levels would mean their discontinuation.

It has always been assumed that tyre/road contact noise at the speeds attained during the drive-by test is not contributing significantly to overall vehicle noise. This situation could change if mechanical noise is further reduced, particularly if lugged tyres are used on single drive axles in maximum gross weight vehicles. Consequently, more emphasis must be placed on research into tyre noise and several programmes have been initiated in this direction particularly in the Federal Republic of Germany, Sweden and the United Kingdom, which should help to produce quieter tyres in the future.[28]

These matters are taken into account in discussions aimed at defining the future regulations although due to the interaction between noise reduction requirements and economy, a global approach is necessary requiring all the technical and economic consequences to be assessed before more stringent noise limits are set. This was the philosophy of ERGA-Noise working group in Brussels in 1982, whose report was used to define the further regulatory limits in the European Community.[29]

8.5 Annexe: the development and testing of a prototype quiet lorry (United Kingdom Quiet Heavy Vehicle Project)

8.5.1 Aims and objectives

The Quiet Heavy Vehicle Project (QHV) was initiated by the Transport and Road Research Laboratory (TRRL) in 1971.[30–33]

This followed a recommendation by an independent working group set up by the Minister of Transport to examine and review existing research into traffic noise and to recommend further work.[34] The main aims of the QHV project were to:

1. Demonstrate that practical heavy diesel engined articulated vehicles could be produced with external noise levels some 10 dB(A) lower than the 1971 values (i.e. down to about 80 dB(A)) as measured by the standard drive-by test BS3425:1966 and to indicate the relationship between cost and noise level reduction.
2. To assist the British vehicle industry to meet future legislation on maximum noise levels.
3. To influence the formation of this legislation by demonstrating which levels were technically feasible, having due regard for the likely costs involved.

The principal objective of the QHV Project was to enable British vehicle manufacturers to produce demonstration quiet diesel engined heavy articulated vehicle tractors, one at the weight and power conforming to the then current regulations, i.e. 32.5 tonnes (32 tons) gross vehicle weight and 158 kW (212 bhp), and the other at 44.7 tonnes (44 tons) gvw with an engine of some 262 kW (350 bhp) to match the increase in legislated vehicle weight then thought likely. For both vehicles the following noise targets and general requirements were set:

1. The target level of emitted sound to be at least 10 dB(A) less than current levels with a general target of 80 dB(A). This level was to be achieved not only under the conditions of the standard BS 3425:1966 and ISO 365 drive-by tests but also under any normal operating conditions.
2. In order to achieve the overall target level of 80 dB(A), target levels for the major vehicle components were set as in *Figure 8.5*. Shortly after the commencement of the project the exhaust noise target was extended by setting a maximum value of 90 dB(C) in addition to the 84 dB(A) at 1 m. This change was largely due to the increased interest in controlling low frequency noise. The research was expected to demonstrate whether or not the levels in *Figure 8.5* were reasonable from practical and economic points of view, and a different mix of levels could result in the required 80 dB(A) vehicle.
3. The target level inside the drivers cab to be 75 dB(A).
4. The vehicles would be designed to comply with all current and proposed legislation.
5. All essential features of the vehicles were to be capable of incorporation in practicable production vehicles.
6. An important objective, implicit in the proposals of the Working Group, was the evaluation of the additional costs of quietening the final demonstration vehicles and the establishment of the variation in cost penalty for various degrees of quietening.

British manufacturers of commercial vehicles and engines were approached with proposals for a cooperative research and development programme and British Leyland, Fodens and Rolls Royce Motors Ltd agreed to take part.

The vehicles selected for the project were (1) a standard Leyland Buffalo 4 × 2 tractor unit plated for operation at 32.5 tonnes and powered by a Leyland 510, 158 kW (212 bhp) turbocharged diesel engine, and (2) a Foden 6 × 2 tractor unit designed for a maximum weight of 44.7 tonnes using a Rolls Royce Eagle 261 kW (350 bhp) turbocharged diesel engine. Later in the project the Foden vehicle, which had been chosen to represent what was then thought to be the likely future maximum legislated weight, was replaced by a later design of 4 × 2 tractor with a gross vehicle weight capability of 38/40 tonnes, a figure then thought to be more likely. In the event this was the legislative weight limit agreed upon in the latest regulations.

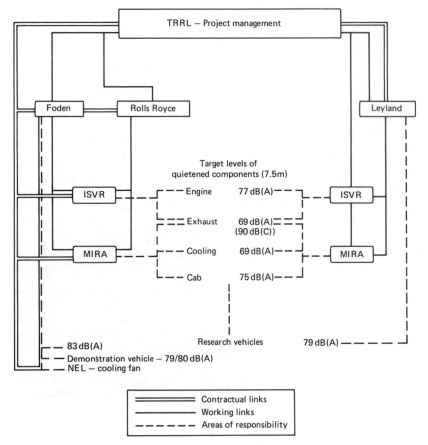

Figure 8.5 Noise targets and organization of UK-QHV project

The replacement Foden vehicle included a new tilt cab with better sound insulation, improved engine mountings and the quietened versions of the exhaust and cooling systems at the stage of development then reached. The research on the basic noise-producing components of the vehicles, i.e. engine, exhaust, cooling fan, which included the design, construction and evaluation of quieter versions of these components, was carried out by the Institute of Sound and Vibration Research (ISVR) at Southampton University, the Motor Industry Research Association (MIRA) and the National Engineering Laboratory (NEL). The TRRL undertook the work on tyre/road surface noise. *Figure 8.5* shows the allocation of work to the research organisations and outlines the contractual and working links between the participating bodies.

For work on the exhaust system design MIRA used the computer based silencer design methods being developed at ISVR. The manufacturers cooperated closely with ISVR, MIRA and TRRL during the research phase and provided specialized facilities and advice to ensure that the outcome was economically viable in production. This industrial involvement assisted a smooth transition from the research phase to the development phase involving the construction of the final demonstration vehicle.

8.5.2 Research on the Foden/Rolls Royce vehicle: engine and gearbox

Since the research activities were similar for both the Leyland and Foden vehicles only the latter will be described here. Also only the Foden vehicle was developed into a demonstration vehicle, Leyland choosing not to proceed via that route but to use the techniques developed during the research phase in future product designs. Baseline noise measurements were made on the Rolls Royce Eagle engine when installed in an anechoic test cell at ISVR (*Figure 8.6*). The engine was loaded by a dynamometer which was mounted outside the test cell so that the noise from the dynamometer was substantially removed. Similar measures were taken to reduce the noise in the cell from air intake, exhaust and engine auxiliaries. With the noise in the test cell coming principally from the engine and gearbox, the whole engine was covered with lead sheeting lined with fibreglass matting. The individual components were then exposed in turn and the noise output measured and compared with the covered engine. Although not permitting the accurate measurement of true noise output from each part of the engine, because even when covered in this way the noise output is only 10–15 dB(A) below that of the uncovered engine, the method did allow the rank order of strengths of the various sources to be established.

The most important sources on the Rolls Royce engine in order of magnitude were (1) block and crankcase, (2) sump, (3) front end, (4) gearbox and (5) air inlet. The noise from the front of the engine emanated largely from the timing gears and oil pump plus its drive gear, although the crankshaft torsional vibration damper, the aluminium gear cover and sump were also efficient noise radiators contributing to front end noise. The latter sources were also important at the sides of the engine. The

Figure 8.6 Rolls-Royce engine installed in the anechoic test cell

experimental replacement of the timing gears by a chain drive reduced the front end noise by 7 dB(A) on average. However the use of chain drive at that power level was not acceptable to Rolls Royce Motors and so a main feature of the research engine designed by ISVR was the placing of the timing gears at the rear of the engine where they were subject to lower excitation forces and their noise was screened by the mass of the engine and gearbox.

Vibration measurements were made at a grid of positions on the engine surface to establish vibration amplitudes. This information indicated where changes in the structural thickness of the block and crankcase were likely to result in reduced surface vibration and hence noise. Together with the noise measurements the vibration data enabled ISVR to design a re-structured and quietened engine. This design used the running gear (pistons, connecting rods, crankshaft etc.) from the standard engine in a strengthened cylinder block/crankcase structure. *Figure 8.7* shows the cross-sections of the original Rolls Royce Eagle and the revised ISVR structure, the basic difference being the provision of a ladder type bedplate to house the lower bearing caps and stiffen the crankcase. The final research engine design, illustrated in *Figure 8.8* contained the following features:

1. A two-piece structured crankcase, split at the crankshaft centreline with a ladder type bedplate incorporating the lower halves of the bearing housings.
2. The walls of the crankcase were designed to accept close-fitted damped panels where possible.
3. Timing gears located at the rear of the engine.
4. Rocker covers incorporating decoupled panels.
5. A quietened fuel injection pump.
6. Sump decoupled from the crankcase by a flexible gasket.

7. A vaneless diffuser turbocharger.

The ISVR research engine emitted noise levels some 6–10 dB(A) less than the standard engine.

The gearbox did not receive any specific noise treatment but was contained in a remote enclosure, provided by an extension of the engine enclosure.

8.5.3 Exhaust system

The open pipe exhaust noise of the engine at the start of the project was 109 dB(A) at 2100 rev/min measured at 7.5 m from the end of the pipe and 60 degrees off the axis. Some initial work on the engine, involving the fitting of a different turbocharger (vaneless diffuser type to reduce blade passing frequency noise) and modifications to the cam profiles using reduced valve clearances, reduced this open pipe exhaust noise by 9 dB(A) thus easing the difficulty of designing a quieter exhaust system.

MIRA provided the following information to ISVR to enable them to produce computer aided designs.

1. One-third octave and overall A-weighted sound levels emitted by the open pipe exhaust.
2. Exhaust gas temperature.
3. Mean exhaust gas velocity at maximum engine power.
4. Data on pipe diameters, position of inlets and outlets relative to the silencer cases, and the space envelope for housing the silencer system.
5. Maximum permissible back-pressure allowed by the engine manufacturers.

MIRA then built practical experimental versions of the designs, tested them and fed back additional information to ISVR for

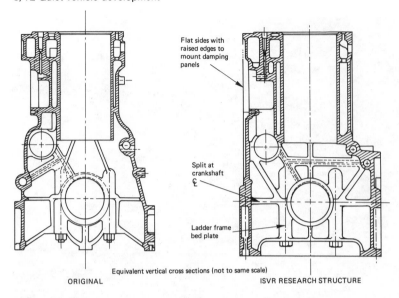

ORIGINAL

Flat sides with raised edges to mount damping panels

Split at crankshaft ℄

Ladder frame bed plate

Equivalent vertical cross sections (not to same scale)

ISVR RESEARCH STRUCTURE

Figure 8.7 Comparison of engine structures

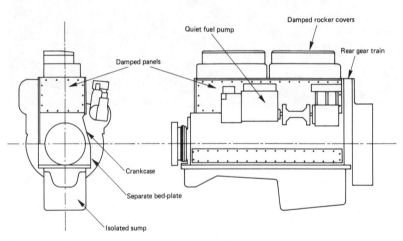

Quiet fuel pump

Damped rocker covers

Rear gear train

Damped panels

Crankcase

Separate bed-plate

Isolated sump

Figure 8.8 Noise reduction features on ISVR/Rolls-Royce engine

further iterations of the design process. The main aims were to achieve greater improvements in overall noise reduction than currently available silencers with particular attention paid to the lower frequencies. The reduction of silencer case noise was also a main aim. The final design (*Figure 8.9*) comprised two separate boxes each containing two extended inlet/outlet expansion chambers employing perforated bridges, and had a total volume of 200 litres, about 60% larger than current designs. The overall target of 69 dB(A) at 7.5 m was met on the basis of a spatial average and the back-pressure to the engine was within specification. The dB(C) target was not fully met by a margin of 2–4 dB(C) which increased with decreasing engine speed owing to the difficulty in silencing the engine firing frequency component. However the dB(C) reduction achieved contributed to the quiet, 'non aggressive', sound of the final vehicle.

8.5.4 Cooling system

The standard cooling system on the Foden vehicle used an axial fan and tests carried out by MIRA showed that fan speed would have to be reduced by about one half to bring the noise level

down to the required 69 dB(A) at 7.5 m. This solution would have resulted in an unacceptable loss in cooling performance and so a new design of cooling system was required.

The fan duty was considerably increased in both the research and final demonstration vehicles by the use of a tunnel enclosure to shield the engine and gearbox. A more elaborate design of fan was therefore needed. MIRA designed a system based on a multivane centrifugal fan which reduced the noise level to that required. It also provided the cooling performance necessary for UK operation and was used for all the testing of the research vehicle. However, since the final cooling system had to provide the cooling performance for operation in a 43°C ambient for southern European conditions, the final demonstration vehicle used a system based on a mixed flow fan designed by the National Engineering Laboratory (NEL) and a new radiator matrix provided by IMI Marston Radiators.

8.5.5 Tyre noise

Some fundamental research on tyre noise was carried out at TRRL. The research concentrated on establishing the sources of

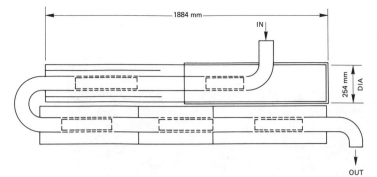

Figure 8.9 Production version of
MIRA/ISVR silencer design

tyre noise and the mechanisms of noise generation. It was found that vibration of the tyre side-walls and tread was mainly responsible for tyre noise for conventional road surfaces and tyre constructions. It was also found that vibration was controlled mainly by the motion of the tyre in the contact with the road surface and the frictional interaction between the tyre polymer and the road base.[35] The research on tyre noise has led to the recommendation that the research and demonstration vehicles be fitted with radial tyres with steel belts having circumferential ribs but no pronounced edge patterns. Further information on tyre noise is given in Chapter 7.

8.5.6 Complete research vehicle

The Foden research vehicle consisted of the ISVR/Rolls Royce research engine fitted in a tunnel enclosure, the MIRA/ISVR exhaust system and the MIRA cooling system with the centrifugal fan. In this condition the external noise level was reduced to $83\frac{1}{2}$ dB(A) when accelerated past the microphone in accordance with the test conditions specified in BS 3425: 1966. The noise level in the driver's cab was reduced from over 90 dB(A) in the original 6 × 2 tractor to 78 dB(A).

8.5.7 Foden/Rolls Royce demonstration vehicle (QHV)

After a 2-year period of development work by Foden and Rolls Royce the final demonstration vehicle was completed and demonstrated publicly in November 1978. The external noise of the vehicle was reduced to 79/81 dB(A) and the cab noise to an overall value of 72 dB(A) under normal operating conditions. This level increased to a maximum of 75 dB(A) under maximum acceleration in the noisiest gear. The cooling fan contributed $\frac{1}{2}$–1 dB(A) to total vehicle noise. *Figure 8.10* compares the one-third octave band spectra of the QHV and a standard, unmodified Foden Fleetmaster. The maximum 'C' weighted noise level recorded during the BS 3425 test was 89 dB(C). The production prototype QHV is shown in *Figure 8.11*. The engine was designed and manufactured to normal production standards by Rolls Royce Motors (Diesel Division) Ltd using the noise reduction features embodied in the ISVR research engine.

The cooling system was developed by Fodens and EMI Marston Radiators Ltd and was based on the NEL fan design. The layout of the cooling package and its position in the vehicle relative to the other components is shown in *Figure 8.12*.

To minimize interference with the normal access and maintenance the engine and gearbox enclosure was designed in two

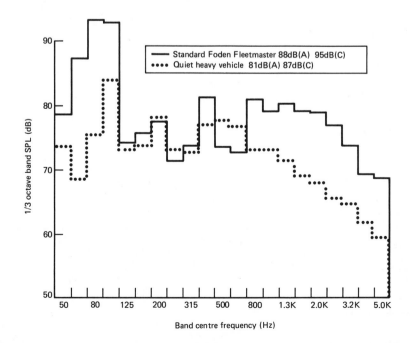

Figure 8.10 Comparison of one-third octave band spectra for QHV and Foden Fleetmaster during standard test condition 81/334/EEC (The spectra were obtained by sampling the total drive by noise in each case and displaying the maximum levels in each $\frac{1}{3}$rd octave band)

Figure 8.11 Demonstration vehicle (QHV)

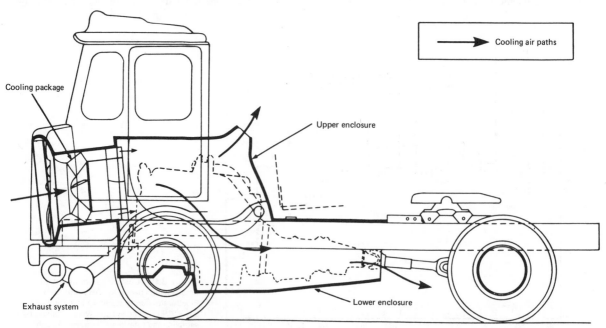

Figure 8.12 Outline of vehicle showing cooling system and enclosure

parts, an upper section which was released and raised automatically when the cab was tilted and a lower section fastened to the chassis frame, the bottom panels of which were held in place by quick-release fasteners. The whole enclosure extended from the front bulkhead to a point about 150 mm to the rear of the gearbox.

The tare weight penalty of the QHV was approximately 4% which represents 0.8% of a fully laden tractor-trailer combination. The increased capital cost for the vehicle was estimated to be about $7\frac{1}{2}$%.

8.5.8 Operational trials

To determine the durability of the QHV's noise reduction features and to find out the effects, if any, on the maintenance and operating costs, the vehicle was placed with a haulage contractor for a trial of 2 years' duration.[36] Data collected during the period showed that the vehicle travelled over 116 000 km and carried over 11 000 tonnes of payload. Maximum payload was carried on approximately 25% of all journeys. The fuel consumption remained fairly constant during the trial period, the monthly average value being 46.45 litres/ 100 km. This compares favourably with fuel consumptions returned for a range of similar but unquietened vehicles (i.e. 40– 45 litres/km).[37,38] A point to note is that the QHV was designed for gross weights up to 38 tonnes and will therefore tend to use more fuel than vehicles designed for 32.2 tonnes. Computer model estimates of fuel consumption obtained for a vehicle of equivalent design gross vehicle weight to the QHV, an average load factor of 53% and average payload of 14 tonnes gave 45.3 litres/km for 36 tonne capability and 48.1 litres/km at 40 tonnes design gross weight. From these and other considerations it can be concluded that the in-service fuel consumption for the QHV is broadly in line with the consumption of conventional, unquietened vehicles of equivalent power and load factor.

The noise emission of the QHV, as measured at regular times throughout the operational trials, increased by 3.5–5 dB(A) from time to time and this was found to be caused by a deterioration of the exhaust system. The perforated sections within the silencer were becoming clogged with soot deposits from the engine. Invariably, either replacing the silencer or steam cleaning the main gas flow pipe returned the noise levels to those achieved at the start of the trials thus proving that there was no significant change in the performance of the other noise reduction measures in the vehicle. Future quiet vehicle designs should take this aspect of silencer performance into account but in the case of the QHV, if this steam cleaning operation were considered to be a routine cleaning operation, it would add only slightly to maintenance costs. However, it should be noted that the QHV engine design did produce more smoke than it needed to because of certain design features and a different engine design could greatly reduce this problem.

Maintenance and servicing costs on the QHV were increased by very small amounts mainly due to the need to remove the undertrays to allow access to the steering linkage and clutch adjustment. All routine maintenance such as oil and oil filter changes could be made without removing enclosure panels. The increase in total maintenance and servicing costs during the operational trials amounted to about $1\frac{1}{2}$%. This represented less than 0.2% of the total operating costs of the vehicle.

References

1 FAVRE, B. and LAMBERT, J. *Prospects for Reducing Road Vehicle Noise by 1985 and 2000 Taking into Account the Technical Possibilities, Energy Consumption and Cost*, EEC Report EUR 8573 EN, FR, Bruxelles-Luxembourg (1983).

2 *Measurement of Noise Emitted by Vehicles*, ISO Recommendation R 362, International Standard Organisation (1964).

3 KEMPER, G. *The Low-noise Vehicle Programme of the Umweltbundesamt*, Inter-Noise 81 Conference proceedings, Amsterdam (1981).

4 FISCHER, J. *Konzepte geräuscharmer Verteilerfahrzeuge (Concepts for Low-noise Spreader Vehicles)*, VDI-Berichte, 499 (1983).

5 HÄRTING, W. and HARTWIG, H. *Geräuschkapseln für Personenkraftwagen: Konzepte und Erfahrungen (Noise Capsules for Private Cars: Concepts and Experience)*, VDI-Berichte 499 (1983).

6 Several articles on the vehicles developed by Mercedes-Benz, VW, Porsche in *ATZ* 83 9 (1981):
STRACKERJAN, B., *Der Mercedes-Benz Forschungs—Personenwagen Auto 2000, ein Zwichenbericht (The Mercedes-Benz research car Auto 2000, current report)*.
SEIFFERT, U. *VW-Auto 2000*.
FREUND, J. and VON SIVERS, R. *Der neue Porsche 944 (The New Porsche 944)*

7 *Actions Thématiques Programmées Energie-Nuisances, Activités du Comité Scientifique (Thematic Actions Energy and Environment, Activities of the Scientific Committee)*, IRT Report (1977).

8 THIRIFAYS, M. *Le projet D'autobus Futur Renault (The Renault Future Bus Project)*, Revue de l'UTPUR, pp. 18–31 (1981).

9 YAMAZAKI, H. Experimental studies on truck and bus noise generation in Japan. In *Inter-Noise 78 Conference Proceedings (1978)*.

10 YAMAGUCHI, J. Government-industry project lowers truck noise. *Automotive Engineering*, **91**, (1983).

11 Project Brombus, Interdepartementale Commissie Geluidhinder. Rapports VL-HR-03-01 to 03-04 (1976–1978).

12 Directive 84/424/CEE concerning road vehicle noise emission limits. *Official Journal of European Community* L238/31, 6th September (1984).

13 MITCHELL, C. G. B. *Quiet heavy vehicles for 1990—The QHV-90 programme*. SAE Technical Paper. Surface Vehicle Noise and Vibration Conference, Michigan, May (1985).

14 *Truck Noise III-A to III-H, Freightliner Quieted Truck Program*, Reports to US-DOT, Office of the Secretary, Office of Noise Abatement, Washington, DC 20590 (1974–1975).

15 *Truck Noise IV-A to IV-M, International Harvester Company Quieted Truck Program*, Reports to US-DOT, Office of the Secretary, Office of Noise Abatement, Washington, DC 20590 (1974–1975).

16 *Truck Noise V, White Motor Quieted Truck Program*, Report to US-DOT, Office of the Secretary, Office of Noise Abatement, Washington, DC 20590 (1975).

17 BENDER, E. K. and REMINGTON, P. J. Controlling the Noise of a Conventional Heavy-Duty Diesel Truck. In *Inter-Noise 81 Conference Proceedings*, Amsterdam (1981).

18 Private communications quoted in reference 1.

19 DANCKERT, H., EBBINGHAUS, W., HARTWIG, H. and STAUDINGER, B. *Geräuschkapseln für Personenkraftwagen*, BMFT-Statusseminar, Entwicklungslinien in Kraftfahrzeugtechnik und Strassenverkehr, S. 579–586 (1980).

20 Diesel engine noise research conference, Loughborough University of Technology, 21–23 September 1980. *The Proceedings, UK Institute of Acoustics* (1980).

21 CHALLEN, B. J. The effect of combustion system on engine noise. Paper presented at *The Diesel Engine Noise Conference* SP 397. SAE 750798 (1975).

22 PRIEDE, T. Design parameters and noise of a diesel engine. *Engineering for Noise Control Symposium*, Xth International Congress on Acoustics, Adelaide-Sydney (1980).

23 ROWLEY, D. W. Truck exhaust noise: challenge for the 1980s. *Automotive Engineering*, December (1977).

24 STEVEN, H. *Vorbeifahrtgeräuschmessungen an Kraftfahrzeugen* (noise levels of passing-by road vehicles). FRG-FIGE Report, February (1980).

25 *Estimation of the Economic and Technical Consequences of a Further Reduction in Permissible Motor Vehicle Noise Levels (Cars and Trucks)*, CCMC Report N/20/80, Bruxelles (1980).

26 NELSON, P. M. and UNDERWOOD, M. C. P. *Operational Performance of the TRRL Quiet Heavy Vehicle*. TRRL Supplementary Report, **746**, 11 (1982).

27 *Background Document for Medium and Heavy Truck Noise*

Emission Regulations, US-EPA Report 550/9-76-008, Washington, D.C. 20590 (1976).

28 *Proceedings of International Tyre Noise Conference*, Stockholm, Sweden, 28–31st August STU Information No. 168 (1980).

29 *Evolution of EEC Noise Regulations; Global Approach (ERGA-Noise)*, Report of ad hoc working group, motor vehicles group, CEC, Bruxelles (1982).

30 TYLER, J. W. *TRRL quiet vehicle programme. Quiet Heavy Vehicle (QHV) Project*. Department of the Environment Department of Transport, TRRL Report SR 521 (Transport and Road Research Laboratory) (1979).

31 TYLER, J. W. The TRRL quiet heavy vehicle project. *Proceedings of The Institution of Mechanical Engineers*, **193** (1979).

32 CAWTHORNE, A. R. and TYLER, J. W. *The Transport and Road Research Laboratory Quiet Heavy Vehicle Project*. SAE Technical Paper, 790452 (1979).

33 TYLER, J. W. and COLLINS, J. F. (Fodens Ltd, now Foden Trucks) *TRRL Quiet Heavy Vehicle Project Development of Foden/Rolls Royce Demonstration Vehicle*. Department of the Environment Department of Transport, TRRL Report LR 1067, (Transport and Road Research Laboratory) (1983).

34 The Working Group on Research Into Traffic Noise. *A Review of Road Traffic Noise*. Ministry of Transport, RRL Report LR 357. Crowthorne (Road Research Laboratory) (1970).

35 UNDERWOOD, M. C. P. *Lorry Tyre Noise*. Department of the Environment Department of Transport, TRRL Report LR 974. Crowthorne (Transport and Road Research Laboratory) (1981).

36 NELSON, P. M. and UNDERWOOD, M. C. P. *Operational Performance of The TRRL Quiet Heavy Vehicle*. Department of the Environment Department of Transport, TRRL Report SR 746. Crowthorne (Transport and Road Research Laboratory) (1982).

37 WILLIAMS, T., SIMMONS, I. C. P. and JACKLIN, D. J. *Fuel Consumption Testing of Heavy Goods Vehicles*. Department of the Environment Department of Transport, TRRL Report SR 687, Crowthorne (Transport and Road Research Laboratory) (1981).

38 GYENES, L. *Fuel Utilisation of Articulated Vehicles: Effect of Gross Vehicle Weight*. Department of the Environment Department of Transport, TRRL Report SR 424, Crowthorne (Transport and Road Research Laboratory) (1978).

9

Road Vehicle Noise Emission Legislation

David Morrison BTech, CEng, MIMechE
Ricardo Consulting Engineers,
Shoreham by Sea, UK

Contents

9.1 Introduction

The legislative constraints on today's automotive industry are considerable. Controls imposed on exhaust emissions, fuel economy and noise are now more restrictive than ever before and will continue to present greater problems to the vehicle and engine manufacturer until an acceptable balance between technical and economic feasibility and environmental/conservation requirements is reached. This chapter highlights one constraint; that of noise regulation and how the various major industrial nations of the world have set about imposing regulatory standards. For simplicity, world-wide automotive noise legislation has been split into three major regions: Europe (including the UK), the USA and Japan. It is proposed to look briefly at the historical events leading up to the legislation as it stands today, to outline current noise limits for the various vehicle categories and to consider the implications of road vehicle noise controls on the community generally. Finally, future trends will be discussed.

At the time of publishing, the procedures and limits described in this chapter were correct but it must be remembered that major changes frequently occur owing to political and economic pressures and the reader is urged to consult the main official journals of the market areas concerned to establish the present situation.

9.2 Road vehicle test methods

9.2.1 Historical review

9.2.1.1 Europe

The various countries constituting Europe, to a greater or lesser extent, have had some form of noise control regulation applying to traffic for many years. For example, the UK has always insisted on motor vehicles having suitable exhaust systems and imposed a degree of control on how the vehicle was driven (so as not to produce 'excessive noise'). It was not until after the publication in 1963 of the Wilson Committee Report on noise, however, that measures were introduced into the UK that stipulated an actual measurement procedure using a sound level meter.[1] At about the same time, the International Standards Organisation was pursuing its own studies and the now well-established ISO R362 Recommendation was issued in 1964.[2] Briefly, the objective of the test procedure was to simulate a driving condition so that the highest noise level to be expected under urban driving conditions could be reproduced. The test entails a 'wide open throttle' acceleration of the vehicle over a 20 m zone from an approach speed (depending on the vehicle gearing) usually of 50 km/h and in second gear. The sound pressure level recorded is the maximum registered on a sound level meter, set to fast response and A-weighting, and with the microphone 7.5 m to the side of the track centre-line. This test method was soon widely adopted by several West European countries. The UK adopted ISO R362 as a basis for BS 3425 in 1966.[3]

Further back, the seeds of harmonization of noise legislation in Europe were sown in 1957, with the formation of the European Economic Community (the EEC) and, in 1958, with the 1958 General Agreement under the United Nations Economic Commission for Europe (the ECE). The latter fundamentally expressed an interest for 'Uniform Conditions of Approval for Motor Vehicle Equipment and Parts'. The standards set by EEC Technical Directives are generally the same as those agreed by the UN/ECE. EEC Article 100 states that member countries are obliged to amend their domestic law and practice to enable the aims of the Directives to be achieved. There is an important difference between the UN/ECE Regulations and the EEC Directives, however. The former are voluntary in application whereas the EEC Directives become mandatory within the member states. If a vehicle satisfies EEC Directives, then it cannot be refused EEC or national approval.

In Europe, therefore, increasing harmonization of vehicle noise legislation (as well as of other vehicle statutory requirements) is clearly indicated and, within the EEC, major vehicle manufacturers are now concerned primarily with meeting EEC noise limits rather than those of individual member countries. The EEC Directive relating to vehicle noise was established in 1970, designated 70/157/EEC[4] and was subsequently amended by 73/350/EEC,[5] 77/212/EEC,[6] 81/334/EEC[7] and recently 84/424/EEC.[8] The test procedure required is essentially similar to ISO R362, previously outlined, and will be discussed in detail in Section 9.2.2.

Some individual member states have their own regulations and procedures for motor-cycle noise, but it was not until December 1975 that an EEC proposal for motor-cycle noise limitation was submitted to the Council.[9] Details of the current procedures are given in Section 9.2.2.

9.2.1.2 USA

Legislative control of vehicle noise in the USA has in the past appeared to have been given less priority than in Europe. The change of relative emphasis for exhaust emission and noise legislation between Europe and the USA is very apparent and, whereas noise regulatory procedures and limits were being formulated in the 1960s in Europe, it was not until 1972 that the US Environmental Protection Agency (EPA) first proposed a set of elementary noise controls, later to be published in the February 1974 *US Federal Register* (Vol. **39** No. 40). The story is very different for exhaust emissions, however, where certain regions of the USA were faced with real pollution problems (attributable partly or wholly to road traffic), out of which emission control measures grew rapidly in the mid-sixties.

The Society of Automotive Engineers (SAE) makes recommendations in the form of standards for the noise testing of a variety of vehicles, for example SAE J986[10] for passenger cars and light trucks. SAE J986 is similar to the ISO R362 procedure, but uses a 15 m track length and a microphone measuring distance of 15 m. There are detailed differences in the use of gears and the interpretation of results but, basically, the test is still a low-gear, wide-open throttle test, measuring the maximum sound pressure level on a sound level meter mid-way along the track.

So far, only the *recommendations* for US automotive noise control have been mentioned. Until 1976, the only noise control regulations applying to road vehicles, as specified in the Federal Register, related to interior noise, general vehicle cruise noise on highways and stationary noise. The interior noise limit was 90 dB(A) for a rated engine speed condition. Basically, the highway limits not to be exceeded were 86 dB(A) where a speed limit of 35 mph (56 km/h) or less was in force and 90 dB(A) where the speed limit was greater than 35 mph, these levels applying to a specified measuring distance of 50 ft (15 m). The stationary test limits varied according to measuring distance and site surface, e.g. 88 dB(A) at 48 ft (14.5 m) for a hard surface and 89 dB(A) at 35 ft (10.5 m) for a soft surface. These control measures were not regarded as making great demands of vehicle manufacturers. In 1976, however, a new statutory test for medium and heavy trucks was introduced which had more significant implications from the manufacturers' viewpoint. *Federal Register* Vol. **41** No. 72[11] set out an accelerative type test basically to SAE J366b (Exterior Sound Level for Heavy Trucks and Buses).[12] The 1978 limit for medium- and heavy-duty trucks, as tested under this procedure, was 83 dB(A) (approximately equivalent to 89 dB(A) under the EEC test procedure). In 1986, the limit is scheduled to be reduced to 80 dB(A) (EEC equivalent approximately 86 dB(A)). These equivalent limits are broadly in line with those applying to truck noise legislation in Europe.

General lobbying by the truck manufacturers has generally deferred the enforcement of noise limits and in general there has been far less activity in developing vehicle noise legislation in the USA than in Europe. In 1981 the most significant change in noise control policy was the reorganization of ONAC, the EPA's Office of Noise Abatement and Control. The former centralized policy on noise control overnight became de-centralized, with individual states responsible for their own controls. With this change came the demise of the EPA research programme into light vehicle noise control test methods.[13] This part-throttle acceleration test was criticized by a number of regulatory authorities, particularly as the EPA had publicly announced in 1980 that the test method was seen as having a world-wide application in the near future. The method was generally thought to be tedious and complex.[14] At present, therefore, in the USA there are no substantive noise controls on light vehicles apart from some nominal highway limits previously referred to (also see Section 9.2.2).

For buses there were also changes of intent. In 1977, *Federal Register* Vol. **42** No. 176 specified test procedures and limits (along the lines of SAE J366b). On 1982, however, it was announced that these were to be dropped, and at the time of writing there is no indication they will be revived in the near future.

The motor-cycle group is still rated as one of the most significant noise sources on the road in the USA along with the heavy trucks, and measures to control such noise nuisance were first introduced in the Federal Register of March 1978.[15] Regulations and limits currently applying to this group are discussed in Sections 9.2.2 and 9.3.2.

9.2.1.3 Japan

In 1968, the Noise Regulation Act was introduced, to be revised in 1970 to include noise limitation of motor vehicles. The Japanese Ministry of Transport later imposed noise regulations on various types in 1975. The five vehicle categories were motor cycles, passenger cars, light van/truck (<3.5 tonne GVW),

medium truck (>3.5 tonne GVW, <200 hp), heavy truck (>3.5 tonne GVW, >200 hp). The noise level limits were then expressed in phons, which, for all practical purposes, may be interpreted as being equivalent to A-weighted sound pressure levels in these cases.

Testing procedures and limits for Japan now generally fall into line with Europe, with one or two exceptions which will be highlighted later.

9.2.2 Current test procedures

It is important to distinguish between a statutory requirement and a national 'standard'. In this chapter which covers *legislation*, only statutory procedures will be covered. There are a great many standards proposed by various bodies throughout the world but relatively few become legislative procedures. As in the main introduction, this section will be divided for convenience into main geographic regions. The procedures will be described concisely and commented on where appropriate. For full details of any regulation the reader is advised to consult the appropriate official journal.

9.2.2.1 Europe

The differentiation between the EEC and ECE regulations has been mentioned previously. The current member states of the EEC (UK, France, West Germany, Luxembourg, Holland, Italy, Belgium, Eire, Denmark, Greece, Spain and Portugal) are adopting or have already adopted the latest EEC Directives, based on 81/334/EEC.[7] Individual member states may still have their own regulations which differ in detail from EEC requirements but these will become less relevant as harmonization within the EEC materializes. It is not intended to deal with individual EEC member state regulations here. The ECE procedures are dealt with later. Also relevant individual European procedures will be covered (e.g. Switzerland).

The Council Directive 81/334/EEC[7] is one of the most significant and widely used current procedures anywhere in the world and is based largely on 70/157/EEC.[4] For full details of these directives the *Official Journal of the European Communities* should be consulted, but the essence of 81/334/EEC is as follows. The test site dimensions are shown in *Figure 9.1* and a photograph of a typical site is given in *Figure 9.2*. This is

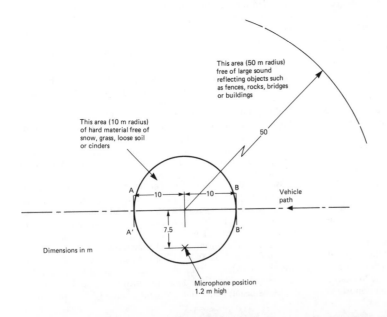

Dimensions in m

Figure 9.1 EEC test site layout and requirements

Figure 9.2 Typical drive-by noise test site to EEC requirements

principally the same as was originally specified in ISO R362. The acoustic specifications of the test site are given in the standard. Briefly, the site must consist of a central acceleration section surrounded by a substantially flat test area. The conditions of a free sound field between the sound source and the microphone must be attained to within 1 dB. This basically means the avoidance of 'large sound reflecting obstacles such as fences, rocks, bridges or buildings within 50 m of the centre of the acceleration section'. The surface of the site must be of hard material such as concrete, asphalt or any other acoustically equivalent material within a minimum radius of 10 m around the centre of the acceleration section and be free of powdery snow, tall grass, loose soil or cinders. As far as weather is concerned measurements must not be made in 'poor atmospheric conditions' and the results must not be affected by gusts of wind. The criterion for this is essentially that any background noise must be at least 10 dB(A) below the sound level produced by the vehicle.

The acoustic instrumentation to be used must be a precision sound level meter as defined in Publication 179, *Precision Sound Level Meter* (2nd edn.) of the International Electrochemical Commission (IEC). The meter should be set to 'A'-weighted and IEC 'fast' response. Appropriate calibration procedures must be carried out. The only other instrumentation specifically called for is a means of measuring the engine and vehicle speed with an accuracy of 3% or better.

The microphone position is 7.5 ± 0.2 m from the centre of the track (*see Figure 9.1*) and 1.2 ± 0.1 m above the ground.

The essence of the test method is to approach the zone at a predetermined steady speed in a pre-determined gear. When the front end of the vehicle has reached line AA' (*see Figure 9.1*) 'the throttle must be fully opened as quickly as practically possible. This throttle position must be maintained until the rear end of the vehicle reaches the line BB'; the throttle must then be returned to the idling position as quickly as possible'. (The general use of the word 'throttle' is also intended to apply to diesel engines which generally operate unthrottled but are instead controlled by a lever which changes the quantity of fuel injected.)

In order to determine the entry speed and gear to be selected it is first necessary to categorize the vehicles for which this Directive applies. The category definitions are given in *Table 9.1*. Goods vehicles are classified as N and passenger vehicles,

M. All vehicles, irrespective of classification, must approach the line AA' at a steady speed equal to the lower of:

1. The speed corresponding to an engine speed equal to $\frac{3}{4}$ of the speed at which the engine develops rated maximum power.
2. 50 km/h.

(There are special important exceptions for certain automatic transmission vehicles, which will be dealt with later.)

For manual transmission vehicles in categories M_1 and N_1 (*see Table 9.1*) fitted with not more than four forward gears, the test is conducted in second gear only. Vehicles in these categories with more than four forward gears must be tested in both second and third gear. (The procedure states that 'only overall gear ratios intended for normal road use must be considered'. This implies that overdrive, for example, is excluded.) The arithmetic mean of the sound levels recorded for each of these two conditions must be calculated. An important exception from this requirement is the high-performance car. 81/334/EEC was adapted in July 1984 by 84/372/EEC[17] to cover special cases of high-performance vehicles and automatic transmission vehicles. (The latter will be discussed later.)

The exception for the high-performance vehicle is that it need only be tested in 3rd gear if it has a gearbox with more than four ratios. (This is effectively to avoid over-speeding of the engine which might occur in the lower gear. There is no limit on the engine speed specified during the test.) The definition of a 'high performance' vehicle in this context is one where the engine power is greater than 140 kW and where the permissible maximum power/maximum mass ratio exceeds 75 kW/t. The final proviso is that the speed of the car at line BB', in third gear, must be greater than 61 km/h.

Returning to 81/334/EEC, the gear ratio selection for vehicles other than M_1 and N_1 is a little more complex. For these vehicles where the total number of forward gear ratios is X (including the ratios obtained by means of an auxiliary gearbox or a multiple-ratio drive axle) tests must be made using, in turn, ratios equal to or higher than $X/2$. If $X/2$ is not a whole number, the nearest higher ratio must be used. The test result is that which is obtained from the ratio producing the maximum sound level. Some results from a typical heavy goods vehicle are shown in *Figure 9.3* and more fully discussed elsewhere.[14] Because of the large number of variants of heavy goods vehicles of a given type

Table 9.1 EEC classification of vehicles

Category M:	Power-driven vehicles having at least four wheels or having three wheels when the maximum weight exceeds 1 tonne and used for the carriage of passengers.
M_1	vehicles with not more than 8 seats (i.e. car)
M_2	vehicles with more than 8 seats and $<5\,t$ (i.e. mini bus)
M_3	vehicles with more than 8 seats and $>5\,t$ (i.e. bus, coach)
Category N:	Power-driven vehicles having at least four wheels or having three wheels when the maximum weight exceeds 1 tonne and used for the carriage of goods.
N_1	vehicles $<3.5\,t$ (i.e. van, pick-up)
N_2	vehicles $>3.5\,t$, $<12\,t$ (i.e. light truck)
N_3	vehicles $>12\,t$ (i.e. medium/heavy truck)

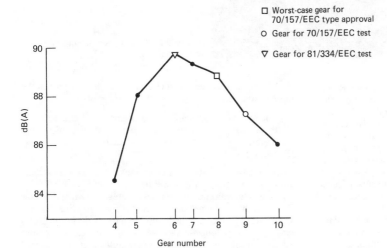

□ Worst-case gear for 70/157/EEC type approval

O Gear for 70/157/EEC test

▽ Gear for 81/334/EEC test

Figure 9.3 Effect of gearing on drive-by noise—81/334/EEC test—heavy duty truck

it is normally only possible to test one vehicle of that type in order to determine conformity for a whole range. This concept of Type Approval is the required procedure for Europe. (This contrasts with the current situation in the USA where self-certification is practised and enforced by severe penalties if spot checks reveal lack of conformity.) However, the vehicle chosen for Type Approval is usually the so-called 'worst case' vehicle with the highest power/mass ratio and the lowest gearing. Also the fan, intake and exhaust systems will also all be 'worst case' components. For this worst case vehicle the procedure above is followed but if a clear 'peak level' is not apparent from the tests made in gears $X/2$ and higher then the next lowest gear will be tested in turn until a clear 'peak' is obtained. This then constitutes the test result.

At least two measurements per side are required and they are considered valid if the difference for consecutive measurements is within 2 dB(A). The highest level is taken as the result, but reduced by a permissible 1 dB(A) 'to take account of inaccuracies in the measuring instruments'. Taking the highest reading and subtracting 1 dB(A) effectively gives a realistic concession to the manufacturer of 3/4 dB(A).[14]

Automatic vehicles deserve special mention as there are further complications with this type of vehicle. Directive 81/334/EEC (or strictly, 70/157/EEC) has been amended by 84/372/EEC[17] to cover automatic vehicles (essentially automatic passenger cars). Basically the selector position to be used is 'Drive'

and the test is conducted essentially as for the manual car, in that wide-open throttle is applied at line AA' and closed at BB'. Although this amendment does not actually specify 'kickdown', it is implied that this is used and not made inoperative as was the case in the past. So far then, this is identical with the original 70/157/EEC procedure but differs from 81/334/EEC which required the highest gear to be used in which change down did not occur and 'kickdown' to be made inoperative. 84/372/EEC now states that if a change down to first gear occurs during the test the manufacturer has the option of either limiting the throttle pedal movement (equivalent to 95% of the fuel supply at that given condition) or progressively increasing the approach speed to a maximum of 60 km/h, such that a change down to first gear is avoided.

If the auto transmission vehicle has no manual selector then it is tested at approach speeds of 30, 40, 50 km/h and the highest noise level taken as the result.

81/334/EEC also requires noise to be measured with the vehicle stationary, 1/2 m from the exhaust outlet and with the engine operating at 3/4 rated speed, no load down to idle (as a result of rapidly closing the 'throttle'). The specified microphone positions are shown in *Figure 9.4*. No noise limits are specified for this, however. Also covered in this Directive are conditions relating to exhaust silencers containing fibrous materials in which the system has to be 'conditioned' either on the road, on a test bed or on a special-purpose rig, and the procedure for Type

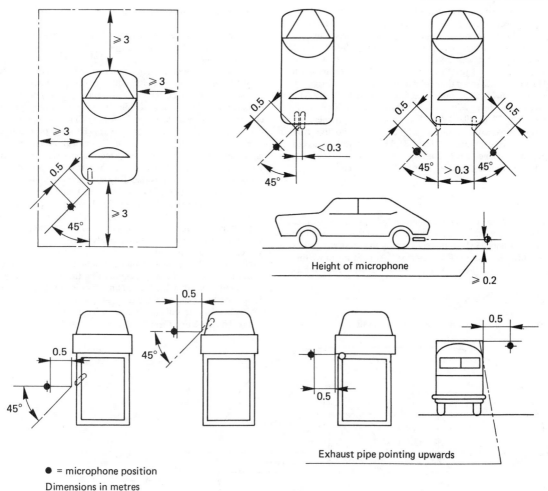

Height of microphone

Exhaust pipe pointing upwards

● = microphone position

Dimensions in metres

Figure 9.4 Test site and microphone positions for the noise measurement of a stationary vehicle—81/334/EEC test. From[7]

Approval of replacement exhaust systems. The Directive should be consulted for full details.

For motor-cycle noise, Directive 78/1015/EEC[18] currently applies (although a proposal to amend the testing methods, to reduce the number of categories of motor cycle and to change the limits was submitted to the Council on 12 September 1984.[19] This proposal, at the time of writing, has yet to be adopted). The same test site as for 81/334/EEC is used. If the motor cycle is fitted with a non-automatic gearbox with not more than four ratios, second gear is used. If there are more than four ratios, third gear is used if the engine swept volume is less than 350 cc and second gear if the swept volume exceeds 350 cc. For automatic motor cycles the selector 'shall be in the position immediately below the position corresponding to the maximum speed of the motor cycle'. The approach speed is 50 km/h if the engine speed is between 50 and 75% of rated, or less than 50 km/h if the engine speed equals 75% of rated, or more than 50 km/h if the engine speed is equal to 50% of rated. The test is similar to that for vehicles tested to other EEC procedures; that is, a wide-open throttle acceleration at the start of the 20 m zone followed by a rapid closing of the throttle at the end. 78/1015/ EEC also calls for a stationary test to assess exhaust noise (similar to 81/334/EEC). The starting engine speed is defined at

1/2 rated if rated > 5000 rev/min or 3/4 rated if rated < 5000 rev/min.

The ECE procedures are essentially similar to those adopted by the EEC. Regulation No. 9[20] corresponds to 70/157/EEC in the test method. Regulation No. 41[21] relates to motor cycles and corresponds to 78/1015/EEC. Regulation No. 51[22] corresponds to 81/334/EEC, both also including an exhaust noise test method with the vehicle stationary.

Special mention should be made of the Swiss noise regulations as for some vehicle categories, notably cars, they currently represent the most severe challenge to the manufacturer in terms of low limits (*see* Section 9.3.1 for values). The Swiss test currently basically follows ECE Regulation No. 9 which is essentially ISO R362. (A stationary test is also called for but only for compressed air equipment exhaust noise and limited categories of vehicles (*see Table 9.5*) and involves a measurement at 7 m from the side of the vehicle. The former ½ m measurement from the exhaust tailpipe is no longer a requirement but may be re-introduced when the Swiss authorities adopt ECE Regulation No. 51.[22]) Full details are given elsewhere.[23] The test method is, however, at present less demanding than 81/334/EEC for certain vehicle categories (principally 5 ratio manual cars and multi-ratio heavy goods vehicles). For 4 ratio cars the procedures are identical and it is for these vehicles that the lower Swiss limits present the most difficulty. In December 1983 a proposed change to the Swiss procedure was highlighted in a letter from the Association of Swiss Vehicle Importers.[24] Here it was stated that the 81/334/EEC was proposed for the future for Switzerland but that for cars up to 3500 kg GVW with more than four forward ratios the originally proposed 1986 75 dB(A) limit would be relaxed to 77 dB(A) in that year. (For light vehicles other than cars the limit would change from 77 to 79 dB(A).) This important statement immediately provided provisional concession to the five ratio manual vehicle, compared with the 81/334/EEC test, by avoiding the high engine speed resulting from additional testing in second gear. This is discussed more fully in reference 14.

9.2.2.2 USA

As with all noise regulations there is always some political influence to a greater or lesser degree. In the USA this has been especially so since 1981. In this sub-section the noise regulations as they currently stand will be described. At the time of writing, noise regulations in the USA exist for the following road vehicle types:

1. Medium and heavy trucks (gross vehicle weight > 10 000 lb (4500 kg)).
2. Motor cycles and motor-cycle exhaust systems.

ation units, once listed as a priority area, have never materialized.

Returning to those regulations that still remain, the test procedure for medium- and heavy-duty trucks will be described. The procedure was originally set out in a 1976 Federal Register.[11] The test site requirements differ considerably from those of the EEC regulations. The site requirements are shown in *Figure 9.5*. Important features are the 50 ft (approx. 15 m) microphone distance from the track centre-line and the 30 m long test area, comprising an end 'test zone' of 12 m. The doubling of the microphone distance compared with all other procedures of Europe, Japan and the rest of the world except Canada, effectively means a noise measurement approximately 6 dB(A) less (assuming a point noise source and true free-field decay of noise with distance[28]). It is therefore important to remember that when comparing limits between the USA and the rest of the world, the equivalent limits in the USA are approximately 6 dB(A) lower. One of the reasons for choosing a 15 m measuring distance was to enable the observer to follow the fluctuating sound level meter needle more easily than when the vehicle passed closer. This had some merit at the time but is now irrelevant in the context of modern digital sound level meters with maximum hold facility, eliminating the earlier vagaries of interpreting exactly what the maximum noise level was. Also the 15 m measuring distance makes a greater demand on the need for ambient noise sufficiently low to have no effect on the test levels. The USA and Canada currently stand alone on maintain-

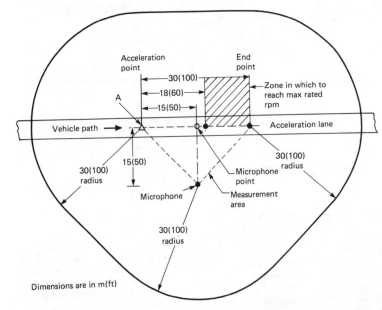

Acceleration point

End point

30(100)

18(60)

15(50)

A

Vehicle path →

Zone in which to reach max rated rpm

Acceleration lane

30(100) radius

30(100) radius

15(50)

Microphone point

Microphone

Measurement area

30(100) radius

Dimensions are in m(ft)

Figure 9.5 Test site dimensions—USA.
Test procedure for medium and heavy trucks

Some individual states have nominal regulations on passenger car and light truck noise (*see Table 9.7* in Section 9.3.2) but these limits have never been considered seriously by the manufacturing industry.

Until recently the EPA imposed noise limits on 'Truck Mounted Solid Waste Compactors' but the regulations were rescinded in August 1983.[25] The reasons given in the Federal Register were '... consideration of the costs this regulation imposes on the compactor manufacturing industry, prevailing conditions of the national economy in general, and the compactor manufacturing industry in particular and the President's policy to reduce the burdens of Federal regulation'. Similarly, the noise regulations for buses proposed in 1977[26] have now been abandoned.[27] Also regulations on truck transport refriger-

ing this distance (although the EPA did recognise the need to conform to a 7.5 m distance in the now abandoned light-vehicle noise test procedure,[13] and Canada now accepts ECE procedures as alternatives).

The usual requirements of site parameters (no reflecting obstacles) are stated in the *Federal Register*[11] which should be referred to for full details. Specifications of the sound level meter are given; also an engine speed tachometer accurate to within 2% is required (not necessarily an *independent* tachometer). The test procedure involves accelerating the truck starting at point A and achieving 'maximum rated or governed engine speed' within the test zone (*see Figure 9.5*). The following conditions apply:

1. The engine speed at point A must not be greater than two-thirds rated engine speed.
2. 35 mph (56 km/h) must not be exceeded before reaching the end-point.
3. The 'highest' gear ratio (lowest numerically) which will permit these criteria to be met is to be used.

The procedure above is for manual transmission trucks. For automatics it is similar except that the engine speed at point A must be two-thirds rated and the gear selected must not cause any up- or down-shifting during the test.

The philosophy behind this test is therefore to assess the truck at the condition at which it produces the most noise in an urban environment (i.e. full load, transient operation, at rated speed). The EEC procedure follows a similar philosophy but with a different approach. Political pressures have dictated many minor amendments to truck noise testing and the reader is advised to consult the latest *Federal Register* for details. Since 1976 many amendments have been issued and these are to be found in Further reading at the end of the chapter.

Turning to motor-cycle test procedures, the original proposals for controlling motor-cycle noise were set out in a *Federal Register* of March 1978[15] and this should be consulted for full details. This procedure covers street motor cycles, mopeds, and off-road motor cycles in various engine size categories. The EPA formally announced in December 1980[16] the issue of these regulations with limits as specified in Section 9.3.2.

The test site requirements are broadly very similar to those for medium and heavy trucks (*see* above) and are shown in *Figure 9.6*. The combined weight of the test rider and equipment must

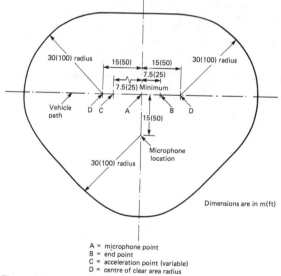

A = microphone point
B = end point
C = acceleration point (variable)
D = centre of clear area radius

Figure 9.6 Test site dimensions—USA. Test procedure for motor cycles

not be greater than 80 kg or less than 75 kg. The measurement procedure is as follows. To establish the acceleration point (*Figure 9.6*), the end-point is approached in second gear from the reverse of the intended test direction at a constant engine speed of 50% rated speed, or closing engine speed less 10% whichever is the lower (*see* below for definition of closing engine speed). When the front of the motor cycle reaches the end-point (in this way) the throttle is fully opened and held open until closing engine speed is reached and the throttle then closed. Closing speed is defined according to engine displacement as follows:

Displacement (cc)	Closing speed (% rated speed)
<175	95
176–675	109–0.08 (displacement in cc)
>675	55

The location of the front of the motor cycle at the time of throttle closure is defined as the acceleration point for the actual test, which is, of course, now carried out in the opposite direction, starting at this acceleration point. There are detailed stipulations regarding the location of the acceleration point, which gears to use if certain conditions cannot be met, and also the procedure for automatic motor cycles. The Federal Register should be consulted for these details. This Register also refers to motor-cycle replacement exhaust systems. Again, political pressures have influenced many changes to these regulations, mainly in the area of record keeping requirements and limit deferment. It is not within the scope of this chapter to detail all these changes. Like the truck regulations, many *Federal Registers* have been issued since the original proposal, these being listed in Further reading. The reader should consult these and the latest *Register* for full details.

9.2.2.3 Japan

The current *Noise Test Procedure for Road Vehicles* was instituted in August 1971.[29] The test site requirements and microphone measurement distance are broadly in line with the European requirements (*see Figure 9.7*). The current Japanese test is in three parts, and given in TRIAS 20-1980.[30]

1. A steady running noise level test.
2. An accelerated running noise level test.
3. A stationary noise level test.

The procedure clearly states that for tractive units these must be coupled to or uncoupled from a trailer according to *Table 9.2*. The vehicle must be fully laden (in contrast to EEC requirements where the vehicle is unladen), except in the case of coupled vehicles where specific provisions apply (*see* reference 30 for details). For both the steady running and accelerating tests the microphone height is 1.2 m. The measuring distance from the vehicle centre-line is 7.0 m for the steady running test but 7.5 m for the accelerating test. For the stationary test the microphone is 20 m behind the exhaust outlet and at a height of 1.2 m. An independent means of measuring vehicle speed is required. This can be obtained using a photoelectric device, fifth wheel or radar types. The test procedures are as follows:

1. *Steady running test*—The vehicle is driven past the microphone at the lowest of the steady speed corresponding to 60% rated engine speed or 35 km/h. The procedure states that 'the gear position or range to be used should be one which is normally used for operating the vehicle at the test speed designated'.
2. *Accelerated running test*—This is essentially the same as the European test procedures, that is, accelerating the vehicle at 'wide open throttle' at the beginning of the zone, with the appropriate gear selected. The gear position and entry speeds are designated in *Table 9.3*.
3. *Stationary noise test*—For this test the engine is run at steady state conditions for approximately 5 seconds at 60% rated speed and the maximum noise level noted. An independent tachometer is required to set the engine speed.

The interpretation of the noise readings is slightly different from the EEC test. The Japanese procedure is to carry out the test twice only. The readings must agree to within 2 dB(A) and the higher level constitutes the result. There is no '1 dB(A) allowance for instrumentation inaccuracy'.

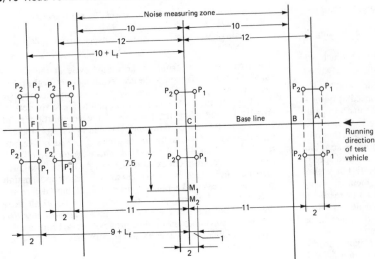

Figure 9.7 Test site requirements—Japanese test procedure

Table 9.2 Test procedures for tractive units, Japan

Test	Tractor with semi-trailer	Others
Steady running	Coupled	Coupled
Accelerating	Coupled	Both
Stationary	Uncoupled	Uncoupled

9.2.2.4 Rest of the world

The three main geographical areas significantly concerned with noise control are Western Europe, Japan and the USA, and it is these three major industrialized areas which the world-wide manufacturer normally treats the most seriously when consider-ing marketing and legislative pressures. However, many other countries in the world have separate noise regulations and a brief summary of these is set out below. It is not an exhaustive list but does cover the most important areas second to the three major ones above. There is an increasing trend towards accept-ing ECE or EEC standards, sometimes as an alternative to a country's own standards. It is not within the scope of this chapter to detail all these, but references are given for further information. The countries are listed in alphabetical order.

Australia Similar to ECE procedure and covers most vehicle categories, including motor cycles.[31,32]

Austria Similar to EEC procedure but with certain qualifica-tions on gear selection. Most vehicle categories covered, includ-ing motor cycles.[33]

Table 9.3 Gear selection and entry speeds for Japanese procedure

Vehicle	Gear	Entry speed
1. All vehicles with manual transmissions	2–4 ratios—use 2nd gear > 5 ratios—use 3rd gear Motor cycles: 2–3 ratios—use 2nd gear 4 ratios—use 3rd gear > 5 ratios—use 4th gear If auxiliary ratios are fitted the 'highest' ratio should be used.	Equivalent to 3/4 rated engine speed or 50 km/h whichever is lower.
2. Vehicles with semi-automatic transmission	Normal position for urban driving (unless has 2 or 3 ratios, when 2nd is used)	Lower of: 3/4 max vehicle speed when driven with gear in required position or 50 km/h.
3. Vehicles with automatic transmission	'Drive'	As above
4. Vehicles with no transmission		As above

Canada   Uses SAE J986[10] for passenger cars, motor cycles and light vehicles, and SAE J366b[12] for heavy vehicles. (Also accepts ECE standards as alternative.)

Czechoslovakia   Specifies ECE 9 and covers most vehicle types.[32]

Finland   Specifies 77/212/EEC or ECE 9 procedures (and ECE Regulation 41 for motor cycles).[32]

Korea   Uses the Japanese test method.[34]

New Zealand   Specifies ISO R362 or BS 3425 and covers most vehicle types, including motor cycles.[32]

Norway   Covers most vehicle types and specifies ECE Regulation 51 or 81/334/EEC.[7,22,32]

Sweden   Generally follows ECE 9 or 77/212/EEC procedures and covers most road vehicles.[6,20,32]

Yugoslavia   Specifies ECE Regulation 9.[20,32]

9.3 Noise limits for road vehicles

In this section the noise limits which currently apply to the major geographic regions covered in Section 9.2 are listed. Also given, where available, are any future proposed limits.

9.3.1 Europe

The current and future proposed EEC limits are given in *Table 9.4*. The limits for Switzerland are given in *Table 9.5*.

9.3.2 USA

The current and future proposed limits for medium and heavy trucks and motor cycles are given in *Table 9.6*. The nominal limits for light vehicles referred to in Section 9.2.2 are given in *Table 9.7*.

9.3.3 Japan

The current and future proposed limits are given in *Table 9.8*.

Table 9.4 Road vehicle noise limits—dB(A), EEC

Vehicle description		*Current* (77/212/EEC)	*Future 1985/86** (81/334/EEC†)		*Future 1988/89** (84/424/EEC)
Passenger car		80	80		77‡
Minibus >9 seats <3.5 t		81	81	<2 t >2 t <3.5 t	78 79
Bus >9 seats >3.5 t		82	82	<150 kW	80
Bus >9 seats >147 kW		85	85		83
Light truck/van <3.5 t		81	81	<2 t >2 t <3.5 t	78 79
Medium truck/van >3.5 t		86	86	<75 kW >75 kW <150 kW	81 83
Heavy trucks >147 kW >12 t		88	88	>150 kW	84
		(78/1015/EEC)	1987 (approx.‖)		1995
Motor cycles	≤80 cc	78			
	≤125 cc	80	≤80 cc	77	75
	≤350 cc	83	>80 cc ≤175 cc	80	78
	<500 cc	85			
	>500 cc	86	>175 cc	82	80

*Precise dates depend on actual vehicle type and when vehicle first enters service. All *new* type approvals for the EEC must be to 81/334/EEC from October 1984.
†Same limits as 77/212/EEC but different test procedure for vehicles with >4 gears.
‡New test method for automatic transmission cars (84/372/EEC).
‖*See* reference 19 for proposed changes to categories, test method and to limits.

Table 9.5 Road vehicle noise limits—dB(A), Switzerland

Vehicle description	Current		October 1986†	
	Drive-by	Stationary	Drive-by	Stationary
Passenger cars	77		75	
			77*	
Light vehicles apart from cars	79		77	
Heavy vehicles				
< 147 kW	84		82	
> 147 kW	86		84	
Motor coaches				
< 147 kW	82		80	
> 147 kW	84		82	
Engine brake noise	86		84	
Motor cycles				
< 50 cc	76		73	
50–125 cc	81		78	
> 125–350 cc	83		80	
> 350–500 cc	85		80	
> 500 cc	85		80	
Vehicles on tracks and metal tyres; work machines mounted on vehicles having a useful power of:				
< 147 kW		80		78
> 147 kW		82		80
Single axle motorized vehicles		82		80
Brake compressor air exhaust noise		80		78

*Proposed for cars with > 4 gears, otherwise 75 dB(A) applies.
†To EEC Regulation No. 51[22]—proposed.

Table 9.6 Road vehicle noise limits—dB(A), USA

Vehicle description	Before 1/1/86	After 1/1/86*
Medium and heavy trucks		
> 10 000 lb (4500 kg) GVW	83	80
Motorcycles		
Street motor cycles	83	80
Moped	70	No change
Off-road motor cycles		
< 170 cc	83	80
> 170 cc	86	82

The above limits apply to new vehicles. The microphone to vehicle distance is 50 ft (15 m); thus to approximately compare with Europe and Japanese limits 6 dB(A) should be added to the USA limits.
*For trucks 80 dB(A) limit row deferred until 2 Jan. 1988.

9.3.4 Rest of world

It is not within the scope of this outline chapter to list noise limits applying to all other countries. The references indicated in Section 9.2.2 should be consulted for details. Broadly speaking, however, the limits are generally in line with the policy of the particular procedure directive. That is, if a country is using an

Table 9.7 USA state and city noise limits for passenger cars/light trucks

Location		Vehicle weight (lb)	1984 limit (dB(A) @ 50 ft)
State:	California	≤ 10 000	80
	Colorado	< 6000	84
	Maryland	≤ 10 000	80
	Nevada	< 6000	84
	Florida	≤ 10 000	80
	Oregon	≤ 10 000	80
	Washington	≤ 10 000	80
County:	Cook County, IL	≤ 10 000	80
City:	Boston, MA	≤ 10 000	80
	Chicago, IL	≤ 10 000	80
	Des Plaines, IL	< 10 000	80
	Urbana, IL	< 8000	80
	Grand Rapids, MI	< 10 000	80
	Madison, WI	≤ 6000	86
	Prairie Village, KS	< 8000	75

General Motors. *Pocket Reference* 1 September 1984 published by GM Environmental Activities Staff, Warren (1984).

Table 9.8 Road vehicle noise limits—dB(A), Japan (only acceleration test limits given)

Vehicle description			Current (1985)	Future
Heavy truck > 3.5 t, > 200 hp			86	83*
Heavy bus 73.9 t, 7200 hp			83	No change announced
Medium truck, bus > 3.5 t GVW < 200 hp			83	No change announced
Light truck < 3.5 t			81	No change announced
Passenger car			78	No change announced
Moped < 50 cc			72	No change announced
Motor cycles	> 50 cc	< 125 cc	75	72†
	> 125 cc	< 250 cc	75	No change announced
	> 250 cc		78	No change announced

* New registrations — December 1986.
  Existing models — November 1987.
  Imported models — April 1988.

† New registrations — October 1986.
  Existing models — September 1987.
  Imported models — April 1988.

EEC type test then to a first approximation the limits will be similar or identical with those specified in the appropriate EEC directive. If a Japanese type test is called for then it is likely the limits will be similar also. (One of the most noteable exceptions is Switzerland, and this is covered separately in Section 9.3.1.)

9.4 Future developments in vehicle noise legislation

At this stage the relationship between reducing noise levels of specific vehicle types and the overall effect on the environment should be examined such that the direction and policy for further noise reductions is then put in perspective. In 1981 the Commission of the European Communities set up a working party[36] with representatives of all member states and the motor industry to examine the scope for further noise reductions. The general objectives are highlighted in a paper presented by the UK Department of Transport in June 1984.[37] The working group met in January 1982 and reported its findings in June of that year. For each category of vehicle a range of noise limits was established spanning the technically feasible and general practice. For each noise level chosen various factors were established, for example the number of vehicle types, increases in cost and effects on fuel consumption. A further and central consideration arising from the global assessments was the likely impact on the environment of introducing stricter noise emission regulations. Future projections were made using traffic noise simulation models assuming that various noise regulations would be implemented. Some of the results obtained are summarized in *Figure 9.8*. The figure shows, for example, that with a long-term limit of 75 dB(A) for cars and 80 dB(A) for trucks and with a 30% truck population the reduction in L_{eq} from 1982 levels would be 4–5 dB(A). The recommendations made for the late 1980s were in fact 77 dB(A) for cars and 84 dB(A) for trucks[37] and these limits were adopted in the Directive 84/424/

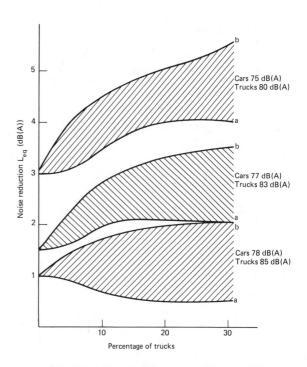

Figure 9.8 Effect on the environment of reductions in regulatory noise levels. *a*=Average reduction obtained, based on the assumption that 90% of trucks comply with Directive 81/334/EEC. *b*=Average reduction obtained, calculated using a distribution curve provided by one of the member states as being representative of the existing fleet. From[37]

EEC[8] published in September 1984. This 84 dB(A) limit for heavy trucks is still far from the 80 dB(A) long-term target mentioned in the 1963 Wilson Report[1] and again stated as a target in the more recent and controversial Armitage Report[38] issued in 1980. The Department of Transport in the UK have also publicly announced that in the longer term even 80 dB(A) may not necessarily represent the final limit.[39]

Nevertheless, despite the clear intention of some Governments to provide stricter noise emission standards, future limit values will only be chosen after careful consideration of all the social and economic benefits and drawbacks following the imposition of such changes. Such assessments will be affected by the delicate nature of world economics, the uncertainty associated with market forces and fuel availability as well as the political imperatives of the Governments concerned.

What is clear is that there will, generally speaking, be a steady reduction in noise limits for most road vehicle categories, as has occurred historically and shown graphically in *Figure 9.9*. In the short term there are likely to be many changes and improvements made to existing noise test procedures. Many still leave much to be desired and more precisely defined, yet practical, procedures need to be developed. Considerable interest has been shown recently[14] in the ISO 7188 test procedure for cars.[40] This test not only sets the vehicle entry speed according to gear ratio (and in the final calculation of the noise level accounts for the power/mass ratio) but also involves a constant speed drive-by. The latter may be more demanding in the context of test site surface variation and tyre noise control. At the time of writing, however, no regulatory authority has adopted ISO 7188.

In the future there may be seen regulations to control tyre noise, brake squeal and possibly low-frequency noise, the latter causing annoyance by exciting resonances in buildings and windows. Although not regulated, one current standard (Australian[41]) specifies a procedure for stimulating body rattle by requiring the vehicle to be driven over a defined block. Interior noise regulation for road vehicles, currently applicable to agricultural tractors, has been discussed in the recent past and strongly resisted by the industry. Such regulation is unlikely to be necessary as this will tend to be controlled by natural competition and the demands of the customer. Developments in stationary noise tests and the ability to enforce regulatory levels by quantifiable spot checks is also a possible subject for future discussion. The current enforcement regulations are generally weak in this area. In the near future refinements and improvements to noise test procedures are likely to be called for, particularly in the areas of specifying the test road surface more precisely, providing an allowance for ambient temperature changes and being more specific about the test fuel.

Traffic noise is one of the most annoying aggravations to the senses and is probably more readily and immediately perceived by most people than say, the effect of exhaust emissions or fuel economy changes on a community. It is therefore in the best interests of regulatory authorities to continue noise reduction policies for road vehicles, while taking account of the need to develop practical and economic means of achieving the quieter vehicles demanded by society.

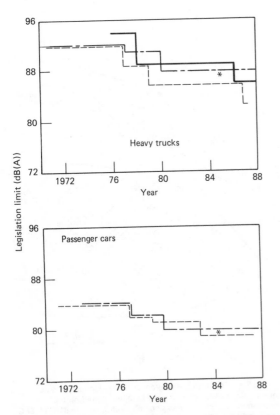

Figure 9.9 International noise limits—past, present and future. — — —=EEC; ——=USA (6 dB(A) added to limits); – – –=Japan.* Change of test procedure for EEC (no rigid control for cars in USA)

References

1 Wilson Committee on the Problem of Noise. *Noise—Final Report*. HMSO, London (1963).
2 *Measurement of Noise Emitted by Vehicles* (1st edn.) ISO Recommendation R362 (1964).
3 *Method for the Measurement of Noise Emitted by Motor Vehicles*. British Standard 3425 (1966).
4 Commission Directive 70/157/EEC. The permissible sound level and the exhaust system of motor vehicles. *Official Journal of the European Communities*, **23 Feb** (1970).
5 Commission Directive 73/350/EEC. Adapting to Technical Progress 70/157/EEC[4]. *Official Journal of the European Communities*, **22** (1973).
6 Commission Directive 77/212/EEC. Directive amending 70/157/EEC[4]. *Official Journal of the European Communities*, **12 March** (1977).
7 Commission Directive 81/334/EEC. Adapting to Technical Progress 70/157/EEC[4]. *Official Journal of the European Communities*, **18 May** (1981).
8 Commission Directive 84/424/EEC. Amending 70/157/EEC[4]. *Official Journal of the European Communities*, **6 Sept** (1984).
9 Commission Proposal COM(74)2177 FINAL. *Official Journal of The European Communities*, **20 Feb** (1975).
10 *Sound Level for Passenger Cars and Light Trucks*. SAE Standard J986.
11 Transportation equipment noise emission controls—medium and heavy trucks. *Federal Register* Vol. 41 No. 72 (1976).
12 *Exterior Sound Level for Heavy Trucks and Buses*. SAE Standard J366b.
13 *Draft Light Vehicle Noise Test Procedure and Industry Comment*. EPA Docket. No. 79–02.
14 MORRISON, D. and WATERS, P. E. *An Evaluation of Test Procedures for Vehicle Exterior Noise*. SAE 820367.
15 Noise emission standards for transportation equipment. Motorcycles and motorcycle replacement exhaust systems. *Federal Register* Vol. 47 No. 51 (1978).
16 Noise emission standards for transportation equipment; motorcycles and motorcycle exhaust systems, final rule. *Federal Register* Vol. 45 No. 252 (1980).

17 Commission Directive 84/372/EEC. Adapting to Technical Progress 70/157/EEC[4]. *Official Journal of the European Communities*, **26 July** (1984).

18 Commission Directive 78/1015/EEC. The permissible sound level and exhaust systems of motorcycles. *Official Journal of the European Communities*, **13 Dec** (1978).

19 Commission Proposal COM(84)438 FINAL. Amendment to Directive 78/1015/EEC[17]. *Official Journal of the European Communities*, **2 Oct** (1984).

20 *Uniform Provisions Concerning the Approval of Vehicles with Regard to Noise.* ECE Addendum 8: Regulation No. 9, 1 June (1980).

21 *Uniform Provisions Concerning the Approval of Motorcycles with Regard to Noise.* ECE Addendum 40: Regulation No. 41, 1 June (1980).

22 *Uniform Provisions Concerning the Approval of Motor Vehicles Having at Least Four Wheels with Regard to their Noise Emissions.* ECE Addendum 50: Regulation No. 51, 15 July 1982.

23 Droit sur la Circulation Routiers. *Ordannance sur la construction et l'équipement des véhicules routiers (OCE).* 27 August 1969. Amended 1 March 1982. (Swiss Regulations.)

24 BRAUNSCHEWEIG, R. and SCHICK, H. P. Letter from the Swiss Automobile Importers Association to the BPICA dated 29 December 1983.

25 Noise emission standards; truck-mounted solid waste compactors. *Federal Register* Vol. **48** No. 137, 15 July (1983).

26 Vehicle noise emission standards; buses. *Federal Register* Vol. **42** No. 176, 12 September (1977).

27 Proposed withdrawal of products from the Agency's reports identifying major noise sources and withdrawal of Rules. *Federal Register* Vol. **47** No. 321, 1 December (1982).

28 HASSAL, J. R. and ZAVERI, K. *Acoustic Noise Measurements* (4th edn.) Bruel & Kjaer (1979).

29 *Automobile Type Approval System in Japan.* Sept. 1977, p. 579. Traffic Safety and Nuisance Research Institute, Ministry of Transport, Japan. TRIAS 20 (1971).

30 Japan Ministry of Transport. Automobile Type Approval Test Division. *Partial Revision of Noise Test Procedure for Road Vehicles.* TRIAS 20 (1980).

31 Australian Transport Advisory Council. *Australian Design Rule 28 for Motor Vehicle Noise.* Last Amendment issued February 1984.

32 *International Automotive Regulations—Vehicle Noise.* Inter Europe Regulations, Wokingham (1986).

33 Canadian Motor Vehicle Safety Test Methods, Section 1106. *Noise Emission Tests for Motor Vehicles*, 15 September 1978.

34 *Legislation of Permissible Noise Level and Legislation of Inspection of Road Vehicles.* Korean Environmental Office, 9 August 1982.

35 *Regulamento do Codigo da Estrada (Highway Code Regulations) Article 16, Codigo da Estrata (Highway Code) Article 29*, September 1983 (Portugal).

36 Report of the Ad-hoc group *Evolution of Regulations—Global Approach (ERGA).* Noise Commission of the European Communities III/540/82—Rev 2EN (unpublished).

37 WOOLFORD, B. V. *Future Trends in Noise Legislation for Road Vehicles.* Institute of Mechanical Engineers, paper C154/84.

38 ARMITAGE, A. *Report of the Inquiry into Lorries, People and the Environment.* HMSO, London (1980).

39 *Seminar—Truck and Bus Noise.* Organised by the Institute of Mechanical Engineers at MIRA on 17 May 1983.

40 *Acoustics—Measurement of Noise Emitted by Passenger Cars under Conditions Representative of Urban Driving.* Draft International Standard ISO/DIS 7188.

41 Australian Standard 2240-1979. *Methods of Measurement of the Sound Emitted by Motor Vehicles.* Standards Association of Australia.

Further reading

MORRISON, D. *A Review of Worldwide Automotive Noise Legislation.* Noise Control Vibration Isolation, Nov/Dec (1978).

PADDY, R. H. *An Evaluation of Light Vehicle Exterior Noise Test Procedures.* SAE 810400.

MUKAI, R. *Legal System of Japan on Motor Vehicles.* JSAE Review July (1981).

SANDBERG, U., STAHL, P., BARRETT, T. J. and MILD, R. *A Comparative Study of Measurement Standards for Regulating Maximum Motorcycle Noise Emission.* National Road and Traffic Research Institute (Sweden) Report 243A (1982).

ALEXANDRE, A. Noise regulations in OECD countries. *Environmental Science and Technology*, **9**, (1975).

FURNESS, J. W. The motor vehicle—a good target for legislation. *Proceedings of The Institute of Mechanical Engineers*, **192** (1978).

BERKOVITCH, I. *Vehicle Noise—Trends in Legislation.* CME July (1974).

CUTHBERT, J. Worldwide Vehicle Diesel Emission and Noise Legislation Trends. *Diesel and Gas Turbine Progress* **July–August** (1973).

ALDEN, J. *The Harmonisation of Truck Technical Regulations Within the European Common Market.* SAE 730635.

WATERS, P. E. *The Effect of Noise Legislation on Vehicle Diesel Engine Design.* SAE 800401.

WATERS, P. E. *Light Vehicle Noise: Origins, Characteristics and Standard Test Procedures.* SAE 801431.

NELSON, P. M. and UNDERWOOD, M. C. P. *Lorry Tyre Noise.* Institute of Mechanical Engineers paper C139/84.

TYLER, J. W. *TRRL Quiet Vehicle Programme. Quiet Heavy Vehicle (QHV) Project.* Department of the Environment, Department of Transport. TRRL Report SR 521 (1979).

BANGHAM, C. J., HEDYEN, B. and FIELD, J. *A National Survey of Lorry Nuisance.* Department of the Environment, Department of Transport, TRRL Report SR 774 (1983).

The Working Group on Research into Road Traffic Noise. A Review of Road Traffic Noise. Department of the Environment, RRL Report LR 357 (1970).

NELSON, P. M. and UNDERWOOD, M. C. P. Operational Performance of the TRRL Quiet Heavy Vehicle. Department of the Environment, Department of Transport, TRRL Report SR 746 (1982).

Revocation of Product Verification Testing, Reporting and Record Keeping Requirements; Corrections. *Federal Register* Vol. **49** No. 127 (1984).

Revocation of Product Verification, Testing, Reporting and Record Keeping Requirements; Correction and Technical Amendments. *Federal Register* Vol. **48** No. 114 June 13 (1983).

Revocation of Product Verification, Testing, Reporting and Record Keeping Requirements. *Federal Register* Vol. **47** No. 249 December 28 (1982).

Noise Emission Standards; Medium and Heavy Trucks. *Federal Register* Vol. **47** No 32 February 17 (1982).

Suspension of Enforcement of Record Keeping and Reporting Requirements. *Federal Register* Vol. **46** No. 157 August 14 (1981).

MORRISON, D. *A Study of Automatic Transmission Vehicle Drive-By Noise Characteristics.* Institute of Mechanical Engineers, paper C152/84.

Noise Emission Standards for Surface Transportation Equipment Light Vehicles. *Federal Register* Vol. **44** No. 99, 21 May (1979).

The future of noise control regulation. *Automotive Engineering*, **89** No. 8 (1981).

HILLQUIST, R. K. *Development of an Exterior Sound Level Measurement Procedure for Light Motor Vehicles.* SAE J986. SAE 800440.

Environmental Control in Japan. JETRO publication—Marketing Series 15, Revised 1983.

IGARASHI, J. *Japanese Experience in Transportation Noise Control.* Internoise 84, Proceedings of International Conference on Noise Control Engineering, Honolulu 3–5 Dec. (1984).

NELSON, P. M. and FANSTONE, J. *Estimates of the Reduction of Traffic Noise Following the Introduction of Quieter Vehicles.* Transport and Road Research Laboratory Report 624. Department of the Environment (1974).

Factors Affecting Traffic Noise, and Methods of Prediction

10

Bernard M. Favre
Ingénieur diplômé ENSPM, ENSMP
Docteur d'Etat ès Sciences,
Renault–Dast
Rueil-Malmaison, France

Contents

10.1 Introduction

The generation of traffic noise varies according to the volume of traffic, the type of vehicles comprising the traffic stream and their mode of operation. Once the noise has been generated, the resulting sound field will depend upon a variety of propagation conditions which are affected by geometrical considerations such as road alignment, land topography as well as screening by obstacles and reflection effects from buildings and other surfaces.

This chapter is concerned with the description of the various factors affecting the generation and propagation of outdoor traffic noise. It is particularly concerned with the mathematical description of these processes and the resulting development of prediction techniques which are now widely used for both the assessment of traffic noise and the planning and design of roads and adjoining land use.

10.2 Some fundamental characteristics of traffic noise

10.2.1 Spectral characteristics

Figure 10.1 compares typical octave band spectra obtained both outside and inside buildings for both urban or interrupted traffic and for traffic freely flowing without interaction. It can be seen that the frequency spectrum characterizing the urban flow traffic (at a speed below 60 km/h) is dominated by the large amount of acoustic energy concentrated in the 63 Hz octave band. This feature of the spectra is related mainly to the high levels of exhaust noise generated by heavy diesel commercial vehicles operating under high load conditions. *See* Chapter 12 for further details of low frequency noise generation. For steady speed operation (i.e. speeds greater than 80 km/h), the external noise spectrum does not contain a substantial peak at these low frequencies since most vehicles are operating at constant speed in top gear and with low load. However, a great deal more energy is present at higher frequencies due mainly to tyre/road surface noise, which is not present at low operating speeds, and

mechanical noise related to the power train components (*see also* Chapter 7).

By 'A' weighting these spectra, the low-frequency components are greatly reduced in both cases and the overall level of external noise is then higher for the freely flowing traffic than for the non-freely flowing traffic. The lower spectra on both graphs show the resulting internal noise spectra in dB(A). Since facade insulation increases with frequency (*see* Chapter 11), the internal noise spectra for the building exposed to interrupted flow traffic again contains a substantial component of low-frequency noise.

This example shows that both the nature of the traffic noise and the variable filtering introduced by the facade can affect the character of noise actually perceived by the listener and can clearly affect the relation between external and internal noise levels. This can also affect the impression of the effectiveness of different noise control measures taken to reduce noise impact since noise reductions achieved by vehicle design, road design or by improved building insulation are all frequency dependent. In particular, this introduces problems for the control of low-frequency noise which is the prime cause of traffic-induced building vibration (*see* also Chapter 12). This type of noise can penetrate the facades of buildings more readily than the higher frequencies and is currently devalued by the use of the dB(A) scale recorded at the external facades of dwellings. For the assessment of low-frequency noise, other scales of measurement such as dB(B), dB(C) may, therefore, be more appropriate.

10.2.2 Level-time characteristics

In addition to the spectral characteristics of traffic noise discussed above, traffic noise is clearly time dependent. This time scale can be both of short duration, i.e. related to rise and fall of sound pressure as individual vehicles pass by, and also long term, i.e. the variation in level over an hour, day, week or longer. Clearly, the physical assessment of traffic noise must take into account both short- and long-term time fluctuations of noise. This aspect together with details of sampling techniques for traffic noise are covered in Chapter 2.

Figure 10.2(a) shows typical noise level-time histories for

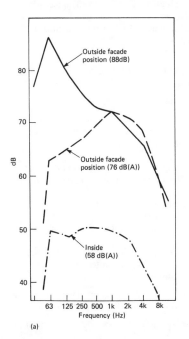

(a)

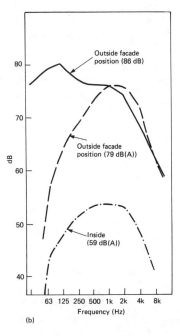

(b)

Figure 10.1 Comparison of traffic noise octave band spectra recorded outside and inside buildings for both interrupted flow (*a*) and freely flowing traffic (*b*)

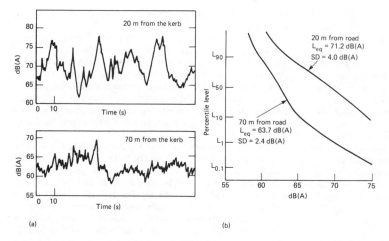

Figure 10.2 Instantaneous time histories for road traffic noise (*a*) and corresponding statistical distributions (*b*)

traffic noise recorded at two different distances from a motorway, and *Figure 10.2(b)* shows the corresponding cumulative distributions with a Gaussian percentile scale. They show that by increasing the distance from a road the overall levels decrease for all percentile levels over the range of interest. Furthermore, the variation in level also decreases with increasing distance. This latter feature is characterized by the change in the standard deviation of the distribution of levels for the two situations. This explains why a distant motorway can appear to emit an almost constant sound level whereas at the kerbside the levels vary considerably as individual vehicles pass by. This feature of traffic noise propagation will be explained further (Section 10.2). A further point to note is that the main parts of the distributions can be approximated by a straight line in compliance with the Gaussian character of traffic noise (*see also* Chapter 2).

Figure 10.3 shows similar time histories and statistical distributions of urban traffic noise measured along a street at two distances, 80 m upstream and 50 m downstream from a set of traffic lights on a one-way street. In this case, the time-level characteristics and the resulting cumulative distributions depend upon the nature of the traffic flow and the resulting noise emission rather than the characteristics of propagation. Upstream the vehicles mainly decelerate or they are stopped by the traffic queue or begin to accelerate from the queue. Downstream, vehicles accelerate at medium speed and noise has regular cycle variations corresponding to traffic light phases (green, yellow, red). Under these conditions the downstream traffic position produces greater noise fluctuations than upstream even though the median percentile levels, L_{eq}s etc., are similar for both situations.

The variation of traffic noise over longer time periods depends mainly upon the volume of traffic and percentage of heavy vehicles. On a week day, the daytime period may be considered to occur between 08.00 and 20.00, and the night-time period may range from midnight to 05.00 with two transition periods from 05.00 to 08.00 and from 20.00 to 24.00, although some countries may have different definitions. On moderate and heavily trafficked roads, during the daytime period, hourly traffic noise scales such as L_{10}, L_{eq}, etc. tend to remain fairly constant, typically fluctuating by 2 dB(A), whereas during the night, noise fluctuations tend to be larger, particularly in areas where traffic flows are very low. *Figure 10.4* shows a typical week-day traffic noise profile of L_l and L_{eq} averaged over each 15 minute period.

Longer term fluctuations may also be important where the road use varies over a year. This is particularly important for

roads which are used as holiday routes which are lightly used during the winter but become heavily trafficked during the summer months particularly at weekends.

In addition to the observed level fluctuations attributed to the change in traffic volume and composition, large fluctuations over long time periods (typically 12 hours) can also occur due to the variable effect of weather conditions. This aspect is discussed further in Section 10.5.

10.3 Theory of traffic noise generation and propagation

The previous section illustrated some of the basic characteristics of traffic noise. They clearly involve factors affecting both the generation of noise and the resulting propagation of that noise to the receiver together with their variations over time. In order to be able to understand and predict these processes, it is first necessary to establish some fundamental theoretical concepts associated with the mathematical description of noise generation and propagation. The reader may consider it useful at this point to consult Chapter 2 which gives an introduction to the theoretical concepts used here.

10.3.1 Free field propagation from a homogeneous road segment (point source)

Consider the following assumptions:

1. Noise from a vehicle is considered to originate from a point located on a hard reflecting plane, source S moving with a speed V, whose location $x(t)$ in space is known (*see Figure 10.5a*).
2. No account is taken of the time of propagation between the source and the reception point and hence of any Doppler effect.
3. The noise level attenuation is assumed to be due to the instantaneous distance between the source and the reception point, with no other attenuating effects being taken into account.
4. It is assumed that there is no constructive or destructive interference resulting from phasor interactions between direct and reflected sound waves.

Given these assumptions, the sound pressure measured at a distance r can be related to the power W of the source by:

$$p^2(t) = \mathrm{DF}(\theta, \varphi)W(t)\rho c/2\pi r^2(t) \qquad (10.1)$$

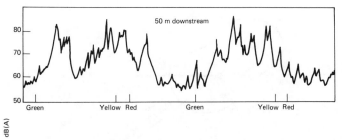

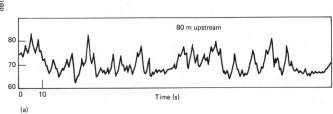

(a)

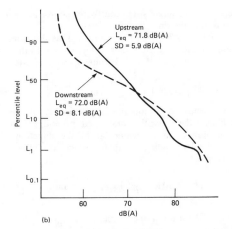

(b)

Figure 10.3 Instantaneous time histories for urban traffic noise measured along a one-way street at 80 m upstream and 50 m downstream from a set of traffic lights (*a*), and corresponding statistical distributions (*b*)

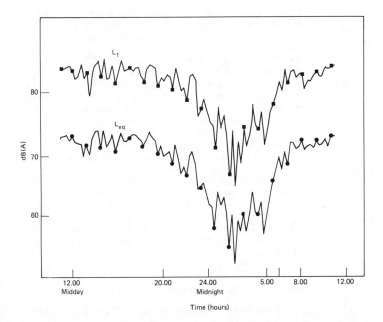

Figure 10.4 Typical 24 hour week-day traffic noise profile taken near to a suburban road

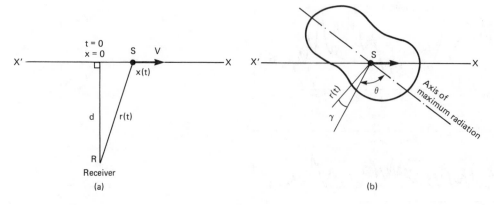

Figure 10.5 Model geometry for a point source. (*a*) Point source geometry. (*b*) Point source radiation directivity (general)

where ρc is the characteristic impedance of air and $DF(\theta, \varphi)$ defines the radiation directivity of the source (*see also* Chapter 2). *Figure 10.5(b)* illustrates this function diagramatically.

In logarithmic form, taking account of the definitions of sound pressure level L_p and sound power level L_W, equation 10.1 can be written:

$$L_p(t) = L_W(t) + 10 \log_{10} DF(\theta, \varphi) - 10 \log_{10} 2\pi r^2(t) \quad (10.2)$$

If it is assumed that the radiation directivity of a vehicle can be represented by a monopole, then $DF(\theta, \varphi) \equiv 1$. However, this assumption may not be appropriate for some road vehicles which have sources with obvious directional characteristics, e.g. cooling fan, exhaust outlet, tunnel encapsulated engines, etc. Consequently, other theoretical directivity patterns could be employed to take better account of vehicle directivity patterns, e.g. for a dipole where $DF(\theta, \varphi) \equiv \cos^2\theta$.

With a *single point source model*, the variations of the instantaneous pressure level can be expressed at a point receiver located at a distance d from the source travelling line X'X. Let p_d be the pressure received at the distance d along the axis of maximum radiation, given by Equation 10.1.

For an omnidirectional source (e.g. monopole), the maximum pressure received as the source passes by the reception point is equal to p_d. Then:

$$p^2(t) = p_d^2 \frac{d^2}{r^2(t)} = p_d^2 \frac{d^2}{x^2(t) + d^2} = p_d^2 \frac{d^2}{V^2 t^2 + d^2} \quad (10.3)$$

where V is the source speed (assumed constant). Converting to the logarithmic form, Equation 10.3 becomes

$$L_p(t) = (L_p)_d - 10 \log_{10}\left(1 + \left(\frac{t}{\tau}\right)^2\right) \quad (10.4)$$

where $\tau = d/V$. By examining the function, it can be seen that points of inflection occur at times $t = \pm\tau$. The slope of the curve is then given by $\pm\left(\frac{-10}{\tau \log_e 10}\right)$. The variation of $L_p(t)$ as a function of τ is shown on *Figure 10.6*.

The equivalent energy level over a period of time $T = t_2 - t_1$ is given by:

$$[\bar{p}^2]_{t_1}^{t_2} = \frac{1}{T}\int_{t_1}^{t_2} p^2(t)\,dt = \frac{1}{T}p_d^2\,\tau\left[\tan^{-1}\frac{t}{\tau}\right]_{t_1}^{t_2} = \frac{1}{T}p_d^2\,\tau a_{12} \quad (10.5)$$

or, in logarithmic form:

$$(L_{eq})_T = (L_p)_d + 10 \log_{10}\frac{\tau}{T} + 10 \log_{10} a_{12} \quad (10.6)$$

where a_{12} is the angle swept out by the source at the reception point during the time T.

The relations between $(L_{eq})_T$ and $(L_p)_d$ as functions of τ for different values of T are shown in *Figure 10.7*. In the particular case where the period T is 1 hour, $a_{12} \simeq \pi$ and equation 10.6 becomes:

$$L_{eq}(\text{1-hour}) = (L_p)_d + 10 \log_{10}\tau - 30 \quad (10.7)$$

If now, instead of a monopole, the source is assumed to be a dipole with the axis either orientated in the direction of travel (in-line dipole) or perpendicular to the direction of travel (perpendicular dipole), it can be shown[1] that Equation 10.6 becomes:

$$(L_{eq})_T = (L_p)_d + 10 \log_{10}\frac{\tau}{T} + 10 \log_{10}\left(\alpha - \tan\frac{T}{2\tau} + \varepsilon\frac{2\tau T}{4\tau^2 + T^2}\right) \quad (10.8)$$

with $\varepsilon = -1$ for an in-line dipole
and $\varepsilon = +1$ for a perpendicular dipole.

Equations 10.6 and 10.8 show that energy mean noise received by near-by observers can be enhanced or diminished for a given total noise strength of a vehicle, depending upon the vehicle noise directivity pattern and its orientation along the travelling axis. For example, according to the last term of Equation 10.8, an in-line dipole type emission reduces the noise exposure compared with a perpendicular dipole of similar power. Such effects have importance when, for example, a vehicle is driven past a stationary receiver. The transverse noise radiated by the vehicle at its nearest point to the receiver may be screened by the body of the vehicle giving rise to an apparently quieter vehicle than indicated by the overall noise power. This directional characteristic of some vehicle sources has cast doubts on the validity of the standard method for testing vehicle noise emissions which, at present, tends to rely solely upon the transverse radiation of noise from the vehicle. (*See* Chapter 9).

For a traffic flow of Q identical vehicles passing the reception point during a time period T, the $(L_{eq})_T$ value obtained for a flow of 1 vehicle is increased by the term $+10 \log_{10} Q$. Consequently, for vehicle sources radiating omnidirectionally it can be shown from Equation 10.7 that:

$$L_{eq}(\text{1-hour}) = (L_p)_d + 10 \log_{10}\tau + 10 \log_{10}Q - 30 \quad (10.9)$$

or, in terms of sound power level, according to equation 10.2,

$$L_{eq}(\text{1-hour}) = L_W - 10 \log_{10}d - 10 \log_{10}V + 10 \log_{10}Q - 38 \quad (10.10)$$

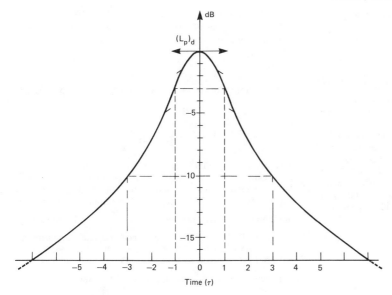

Figure 10.6 Omnidirectional point source time history as function of $\tau = \dfrac{d}{V}$

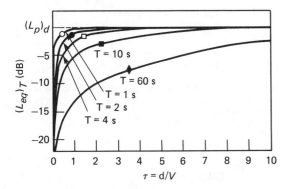

Figure 10.7 Omnidirectional point source: relations between $(L_{eq})_T$ and $(L_p)_d$ as function of $\tau = \dfrac{d}{V}$ for different values of the period of integration time T (after Favre[1])

Equation 10.10 relates the energy-mean sound pressure level at the receiver position to the sound power of the traffic sources. It can be seen that for a given value of sound power level, L_{eq} decreases with distance from the road source line by 3 dB for each doubling of distance from the source line. The term $-10\log_{10}V$ means that when the vehicle moves at a higher speed, it remains a shorter time near the receiver R and consequently the noise energy received by R decreases. At speeds below 60 km/h, $L_W(V)$ is approximated by a constant and therefore L_{eq} decreases by 3 dB per doubling of speed, e.g. when speed increases from 25 km/h to 50 km/h. At higher speeds where the vehicle sound power increases with the third or the fourth power of speed, then $L_W(V)$ varies as $30.\log_{10}V$ or $40.\log_{10}V$ and accordingly L_{eq} increases with speed as $20.\log_{10}V$ or $30.\log_{10}V$ (i.e. 6 or 9 dB per doubling of speed, respectively).

For traffic comprising different classes 1, 2, ... m of identical vehicles with respective power level, speed and flow $((L_W)_1, V_1, (Q_1), \ldots ((L_W)_m, V_m, Q_m)$, L_{eq} is obtained by an energy-combination of $(L_{eq})_1, \ldots (L_{eq})_m$, each component being determined from Equation 10.10.
This can be written as:

$$L_{eq} = 10\log_{10}\left[10^{(L_{eq})_1/10} + \ldots + 10^{(L_{eq})_m/10} \right] \qquad (10.11)$$

Although not mathematically precise, this concept can be usefully adapted to evaluate statistical percentile levels. Such a combination procedure was described and validated by Nelson.[2] In this method, it is first necessary to convert a single vehicle time history into a cumulative time-level distribution which effectively represents the noise distribution from a traffic flow of one vehicle per hour. The assumption is then made that this represents a probability distribution. Distributions for flows of two or more vehicles may then be derived by combining the single vehicle distribution with itself in a statistically correct fashion (independent events). In this way, vehicles are added quite randomly, corresponding to a negative-exponential law for vehicle headways. Since the flow is doubled each time identical distributions are combined, realistic traffic flow situations are achieved after only a few combination calculations. For example, ten combinations are required to generate a flow of 1024 vehicles per hour i.e. 2^{10} vehicles, and of course since any number can be expressed as a binary expansion, the level distribution for any flow can be generated by combining the level distributions associated with the binary powers in the expansion of the flow number.

This technique can also be employed when traffic is considered to comprise m classes of vehicles, each class with a given statistical distribution. Note that one important consequence is the necessity to estimate the whole statistical distribution of every class to be able to obtain any percentile level of the total flow. For example, it is theoretically not possible to estimate the combined L_{10} level of two vehicle categories (or two road sections, etc.), when only the respective L_{10} level of each is known. But in practice, current prediction methods of L_{10} (or L_{50}) are based upon an energy-type combination (i.e. the combined L_{10} or L_{50} levels are obtained by summing levels according to equation 10.11). This approximation produces only small errors for most traffic conditions.

10.3.2 Free field propagation from an homogeneous road segment (line source)

When vehicles are spaced sufficiently close together, the individual point sources can be assumed to combine forming a *continuous line source* such that the total acoustic power can be considered evenly distributed along an equivalent source line representing the trajectory of the traffic stream. Consequently, the source strength is described in terms of constant power per unit length, $\mathcal{W}$. In this case, the expression for the acoustic pressure p_{dx}^2 at the receiver due to an element dx of the line source is:

$$p_{dx}^2 = \frac{\mathcal{W}\rho c}{2\pi d}\,da \qquad (10.12)$$

assuming an omnidirectional radiation of every elementary element of the line source (*see Figure 10.8*). da is the angle subtended at the receiver by the line element dx.

It should be noted from Equation 10.12 that the contribution to the mean-square acoustic pressure from each element of the line source is a linear function of the subtended angle da. Consequently, finite segments of the line source that correspond to equal angles of intercept contribute equally to the total mean-square acoustic pressure. This concept is fundamental to all energy-based traffic noise indices under free-field propagation.

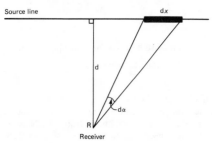

Source line dx

d

da

R
Receiver

Figure 10.8 Model geometry for a line source

Integrating Equation 10.12 between limits of $-\frac{\pi}{2}$ to $+\frac{\pi}{2}$, the acoustic pressure for an infinitely long line source is obtained:

$$p^2 = \frac{\mathcal{W}\rho c}{2d} \qquad (10.13)$$

$\mathcal{W}$ is related to acoustic power of each individual vehicle W, speed V, and traffic flow Q according to $\mathcal{W} = W.Q/3600\,V$. By making the substitution in Equation 10.13 and calculating the L_{eq} it can be seen that both Equations 10.13 and 10.10 are compatible, i.e. both the line source and single point source models lead to the same fundamental relation between vehicle power and L_{eq}.

10.3.3 Modelling the variations of traffic noise over time

If the previous point and line source models lead to general expressions relating the strength of vehicle noise to the resulting equivalent energy level, they do not, however, give any information on the time history of traffic noise (such as represented on *Figures 10.2* or *10.3*). Such information can be obtained by modelling mathematically the movement of individual vehicles and the resulting noise field generated as a function of time and distance from the road.

Johnson and Saunders[3] have derived a simple theoretical model which assumes that all vehicles travel with uniform spacing, the individual sources are incoherent and identical, and are each travelling at the same speed V on a single straight roadway. The mathematical representation of this model is described below.

Johnson & Saunders Model

Let s represent the spacing between consecutive vehicles. The acoustic squared pressure p^2 (t) at the receiver is the summation of an infinite series of terms having the same general form as Equation 10.1, so that:

$$p^2(t) = \frac{W\rho c}{2\pi} \sum_{n=-\infty}^{n=+\infty} \frac{1}{d^2 + (Vt+ns)^2} \qquad (10.14)$$

The summation of the series leads to the general expression:

$$p^2(t) = \frac{W\rho c}{2\pi}\cdot\frac{1}{s}\cdot\left[\frac{\sin h\,\dfrac{2\pi d}{s}}{\cos h\,\dfrac{2\pi d}{s} - \cos\dfrac{2\pi Vt}{s}}\right] \qquad (10.15)$$

This expression defines the variation of sound intensity with time, which clearly depends upon the periodicity of the cyclic terms in the denominator. The actual shape depends on the values of s and d. For a given configuration, maximum and minimum values are obtained when $\cos\dfrac{2\pi Vt}{s} = \pm 1$ respectively. Consequently, when $t = 0$, a vehicle is immediately opposite the receiver and when $t = s/2V$, the nearest vehicles are equidistant on either side of the reception point. The L_{50} percentile value is obtained when $\cos\dfrac{2\pi Vt}{s} = 0$, i.e. for $t = s/4V$. Hence:

$$L_{max} = L_W - 10\log_{10}d + 10\log_{10}\left[\left(\coth\frac{\pi d}{s}\right)/s\right] - 3 \qquad (10.16)$$

and

$$L_{50} = L_W - 10\log_{10}d + 10\log_{10}\left[\left(\tanh\frac{2\pi d}{s}/s\right)\right] - 3 \qquad (10.17)$$

It should be noted that approximations can be made to the hyperbolic tangent and cotangent functions over certain ranges of the arguments.

For example, it can be seen that:

$$L_{max} \simeq \begin{cases} -10\log_{10}d\cdot s & \text{for } d > \dfrac{s}{2} \\[2mm] -10\log_{10}d^2 & \text{for } d < \dfrac{s}{6} \end{cases}$$

and   (10.18)

$$L_{50} \simeq \begin{cases} -10\log_{10}d\cdot s & \text{for } d > \dfrac{s}{4} \\[2mm] -10\log_{10}s^2 & \text{for } d < \dfrac{s}{12} \end{cases}$$

These indices can also be expressed in terms of traffic flow and speed since $s = 3600\,V/Q$. Consequently, at large distances from the traffic stream, both L_{max} and L_{50} values increase by 3 dB per doubling of flow and decrease by -3 dB per doubling of distance. Conversely, at small distances from the traffic stream, doubling the flow increases L_{50} by 6 dB with no effect on L_{max} and doubling the distance reduces L_{max} by 6 dB without affecting L_{50}. According to Rathé,[4] the transition distance between $1/d$ and $1/d^2$ laws for L_{max} is given by the expression $\log_{10} d = \dfrac{s}{\pi}$.

The periodicity introduced by the cosine-term in Equation 10.15 creates a non-Gaussian distribution of percentile levels, which is contrary to field observations of traffic noise which generally exhibit a Gaussian distribution. The principal reason for this is that account must be taken of two intermediate statistical distributions: namely, that of the acoustic power W of the vehicles and of the space (or time) interval s between successive vehicles. The distribution of W is, in turn, a function of the distribution of W at a given speed for each type of vehicle, and the distribution of speeds and types of vehicles. Though such distributions can be obtained from on-site measurements, it will be appreciated that the full mathematical treatment tends to become rather complicated. Some solutions have been given by Weiss[5] or Kurze[6] for random vehicle space distributions and constant acoustic power. Maurin[7] has evaluated solutions for exponential vehicle space distributions and random acoustic power.

A conceptually simpler alternative makes use of Monte Carlo computer simulations such as that developed by Galloway *et al.*[8] Such a simulation consists of summing the noise levels produced at a receiver by a given distribution of headways between successive vehicles having an average flow rate Q. By repeating the process a number of times, each time randomly selecting the vehicle distribution to produce a series of 'snap shots' of the traffic flow, histograms of the noise level as a function of time can be generated according to the equation

$$p^2(t_i) = \frac{\rho c}{2\pi} \sum_{n=-\infty}^{n=+\infty} \frac{W_{ni}}{d^2 + x_{ni}^2} \qquad (10.19)$$

where (W_{ni}, x_{ni}) are acoustic power and position of vehicle n at time t_i. The distributive histograms can then be used to determine the percentile levels of interest. It is important to note that the Monte Carlo computer simulation never describes an infinite array of vehicles, and always considers a finite roadway length.

Headway distributions relevant to modelling traffic flows can be applied equally well for noise modelling purposes. The negative exponential distribution is, perhaps, the most widely known and can be expressed as $P(s \geqslant s_0) = \exp(-s_0/S)$ where P is the probability for the headway s to be greater than s_0, and S is a coefficient depending on the average flow rate Q. However, the use of this distribution results in an artificially high probability regarding short length headways. This deficiency can be remedied by making use of more elaborate headway distributions.

The use of these functions makes it possible to calculate the traffic noise level statistical distribution and the standard deviation which depends essentially on the value of the ratio $d/\bar{s}$ with $\bar{s}$ the average spacing between successive vehicles.

Lamure[9] has pointed out, however, that the results obtained from different calculation methods which employ different headway distributions are, in fact, rather similar. This observation is based on the results given in *Figure 10.9*. For example, for major roads, the value of $d/\bar{s}$ can be considered to range between 0.1 and 4. For this case, both the exponential and random headway models produce essentially identical results. Neverthe-

less, for low traffic flows, the negative exponential distribution is preferred, particularly if higher fractiles such as L_1, which are more sensitive to headways of following vehicles and platoons, are required.

For situations where vehicle interactions occur, such as at road junctions and signal controlled intersections, it may be insufficient to model the traffic stream using a simple point source and headway distribution model. A more precise prediction can then be achieved by computer simulation which aims to reproduce the traffic noise signature $L_p(t)$ by synthesizing the noise emission characteristics of each individual vehicle passing through each road segment. In this way the movement of every single vehicle is simulated as a function of time by taking account of interactions between the vehicles themselves, e.g. car following interactions, and with the road system, such as traffic lights. An example of this type of traffic noise synthesis is described by Favre.[10]

Table 10.1 summarizes the different traffic noise modelling concepts which have been discussed.

10.3.4 Multiple segment roads

Any practical traffic noise problem can be solved by dividing the road network into an array of limited length segments S_1S_2, S_2S_3, ... S_kS_{k+1} .... *Figure 10.10(a)* shows for a practical example how a single road can be simply approximated by four straight line segments with subtending angles a_{12}, a_{23}, a_{34}, a_{45} at the reception point R. Assuming free-field conditions (only geometric attenuation), L_{eq} can be calculated by using Equation 10.12 which states that every road segment k gives a contribution such that:

$$p^2_{S_kS_{k+1}} = \frac{\mathcal{W}\rho c}{2\pi d_k} a_{kk+1} \qquad (10.20)$$

where d_k is the perpendicular distance from R to segment S_kS_{k+1}.

Consequently, the total squared pressure at the receiver position is given by:

$$p^2_{S_1S_{n+1}} = \sum_{k=1}^{n} p^2 s_k s_{k+1} = \frac{\mathcal{W}\rho c}{2\pi} \sum_{k=1}^{n} \frac{a_{kk+1}}{d_k} \qquad (10.21)$$

If the traffic parameters within each segment are not constant, then every road segment k has its own sound power density $\mathcal{W}_k$, and:

$$p^2_{S_1S_{n+1}} = \frac{\rho c}{2\pi} \sum_{k=1}^{n} \frac{\mathcal{W}_k a_{kk+1}}{d_k} \qquad (10.22)$$

In order to calculate statistical percentile levels, for freely-flowing traffic, Nelson's method[2] of distribution combination can be used by considering the single vehicle time history as indicated on *Figure 10.10(b)* for each of the road segments. The total traffic noise percentile levels are obtained by combining the level distribution from every segment. For complex or interactive flow conditions, then Monte Carlo or car following simulation methods can be applied.

10.3.5 Non free field propagation

In most practical cases, it is important to consider propagation phenomena other than purely geometrical spreading of the wavefront.

For a single source, Equation 10.1 becomes

$$p^2(t) = \text{DF}(\theta,\varphi) \cdot W(t)\rho c/2\pi r^2(t) \cdot a(x(t)) \qquad (10.23)$$

where $a(x(t))$ can be regarded as a supplementary attenuation term, which depends upon the propagation conditions existing between the source position S at the abscissa x at time t, and the receiver. Under free field conditions, $a(x(t)) = 1$. When an

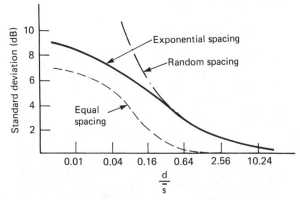

Figure 10.9 Comparison of different vehicle headway distribution models (after Lamure[9])

Table 10.1 Free-field traffic noise models: principal features

Type of model	Output	Noise levels and scales	Mode of approach
Single point source		L_{eq} L_{max} L_i	Analytical model with probability combination
Incoherent line source		L_{eq}	Analytical model
Equally spaced sources		L_{50} L_{max} L_{min}	Analytical model
Unevenly-spaced sources snap shots		L_i	Statistical model Monte Carlo computer simulation
Continuously moving sources		Any	Car following computer simulation

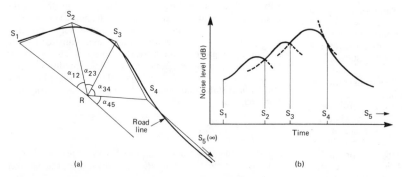

(a)   (b)

Figure 10.10 Method of approximating a road by a series of homogeneous segments (*a*) and corresponding single vehicle time history (*b*)

analytical expression can be found for $a(x(t))$ under non free field conditions, then a computation process such as described in Section 10.3.1 can be applied. Such solutions have been demonstrated by Kutruff[11] or Makarewicz.[12] For most practical situations, however, it is not possible to obtain an analytical solution, and propagation must then be described using either empirical or other non-analytical techniques (*see* Section 10.5).

10.4 Factors affecting the generation of traffic noise

The levels of noise generated by road traffic depend mainly upon the type of vehicle flow, the volume of traffic, the speed and composition of the traffic, the road gradient and the type of road surface.

Equation 10.10 demonstrates how L_{eq} is related to the traffic parameters, speed V and flow Q and to the individual vehicle noise. It is usual, however, to calculate separately the value of L_{eq} for the different categories of vehicles in the total flow and then to combine them together according to Equation 10.11 to obtain the L_{eq} for the combined total flow.

The influence of traffic parameters on statistical percentile levels is more complicated because of their interactive effect on the traffic noise time history as pointed out in Section 10.3.

Therefore, the influence of each parameter on percentile levels cannot be separated in theory since the effect of one depends upon the value of the other parameters (including distance to the road line). However, in practice multilinear regression analysis of wide sets of either measured or computer simulated noise data can be performed and give an accurate evaluation of the separate contribution of each parameter over the whole range of traffic conditions.

10.4.1 Type of traffic flow

When vehicles are driven in traffic, different types of traffic patterns dictate the mode of operation of the vehicle. For example, *Figure 10.11* shows a vehicle speed–distance plot obtained from measurements taken on-board a vehicle travelling over a prescribed 6 km length route in an urban area.[13] Several types of flow pattern can be identified. The points labelled A relate to sections where decelerating/accelerating conditions exist, e.g. stop lines, traffic signals, etc., where local mean speed $\bar{V}$ and standard deviation σ_v are both low. The points labelled B relate to sections where freely-flowing traffic exists and, as a result, $\bar{V}$ is high and σ_v is low. The points labelled C refer to sections with locally stop/go flow under saturated conditions and where $\bar{V}$ is low and σV is high. Such sections often occur in busy commercial streets. The points labelled D refer to road sections which contain vehicles travelling at high speed at

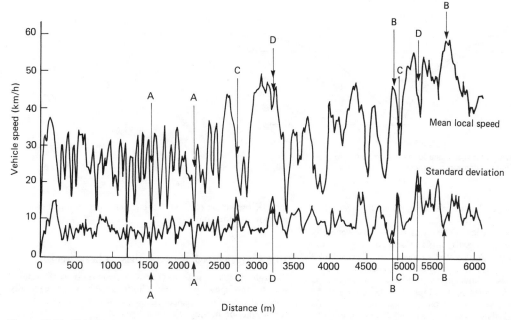

Figure 10.11 Vehicle speed–distance plot for a 6 km urban route. Results obtained from 18 repeat runs with one vehicle[13]

some times, and vehicles travelling at low speed at other times, and where both $\bar{V}$ and σ_V are high. Such situations occur, for example, where there are unsynchronized traffic lights.

The pattern of traffic flowing on different roads can, therefore, be highly space and time dependent and clearly this time dependancy has an effect on both the traffic noise time history and the resulting statistical levels of traffic noise. For this reason, it is usually convenient to refer to the traffic flow pattern as one of two broadly defined categories.

10.4.1.1 Freely flowing traffic

This type of traffic flow refers to the conditions that exist on roads where traffic flow travels without significant interaction, e.g. motorways, urban freeways, etc. Individual vehicles are normally operated in top gear and travel at nearly constant speed. There is then a deterministic traffic flow–speed relationship depending upon speed limit and percentage of heavy vehicles, with the mean speed decreasing when the flow increases up to saturated conditions, as shown on *Figure 10.12(a)*. This relationship governs the effect on traffic noise of both flow rate and traffic speed. As flow rate increases, traffic noise L_{eq} increases up to a maximum, then the effect of the reducing vehicle speed on noise predominates (*Figure 10.12(b)*).

10.4.1.2 Stop–start conditions (interrupted traffic)

This type of flow occurs in most busy commercial streets where vehicles are caused to slow down or stop because of interactions with other vehicles or as a result of an imposed stop line or traffic light control. *Figure 10.13* shows some typical decele-

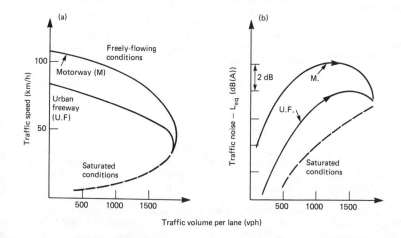

Figure 10.12 Typical speed/flow (*a*) and L_{eq}/flow (*b*) relationships under freely flowing conditions

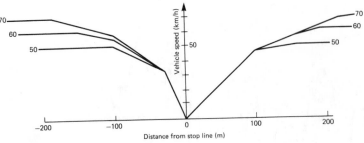

Figure 10.13 Mean traffic speed as a function of distance to the stopping point, for different asymptotic speeds

ration/acceleration profiles for vehicles approaching a stop line at an intersection.

For decelerating vehicles the levels of L_{eq} decrease generally with decreasing vehicle speed as this is governed largely by the fall in power output during the deceleration. For vehicles accelerating from a standing position, the initial acoustic power output is high owing to high engine speed and load conditions and consequently L_{eq} levels are also high at the beginning of the acceleration. These levels may, in fact, drop as the speed of the vehicle increases partly because of the speed dependence of the L_{eq} function (see Equation 10.10) and partly because of the reduced degree of engine loading as the vehicle speed develops. Therefore, for a one-way street there is generally an upstream/downstream contrast on either side of the stopping position, the length and importance of which depends upon the type of vehicles and the asymptotic speed of the traffic stream. For a two-way road, however it is found that by combining the accelerating and decelerating conditions on both sides, the total L_{eq} does not generally change appreciably either side of the stopping point.[10] Similar trends are obtained for mid-range percentile levels.[14]

10.4.2 Flow rate

Whether considering hourly values of L_{eq}, L_{10} etc. as a function of mean hourly flow or longer term averages of these indices, it is generally accepted that over a wide range of traffic flows the variations of these indices with vehicle flow, Q, can be adequately represented by a logarithmic relation of the form:

$$L = C \log_{10} Q$$

There is some evidence from computer simulations that for flows below about 200 vehicles per hour the value C is considerably higher than that for higher flow rates; however, most prediction models currently assume that C remains constant over the range of interest. It has already been shown in Section 10.2 that theoretical models based on point source and line source concepts indicate that the coefficient C should take the value 10 (i.e. noise levels increase by about 3 dB(A) for each doubling of vehicle flow). In practice, provided that speed remains constant over the range of flow conditions considered, this is the measured value for L_{eq}.

However, for the mid-range percentile levels, the value of C has been found to vary quite widely. For example, in the UK a value of 7.5 for freely flowing traffic[15] and values of 8.9–12.0 for urban traffic[16-18] were suggested for L_{10}. Computer simulations of traffic noise tend to give a range of coefficients which depends upon the percentage of heavy vehicles in the traffic stream and the distance to the road.[19,20] However, by taking a value of 10 for the coefficient of the flow rate it is found that the errors of prediction are generally small and this value has been adopted in

the UK prediction method. Further reference to this method is given in Section 10.6.

10.4.3 Mean speed and percentage of heavy vehicles

Though adequate for L_{eq}, attempts to relate traffic noise separately to the speed and composition variables are generally unsatisfactory for statistical scales and it is necessary to allow for interaction between the two variables.

Two speed regions can be identified: above 50–60 km/h where most traffic will be driven under fairly free flow conditions and below 50–60 km/h where interrupted flow conditions can be assumed to exist. Within the low-speed region there is evidence that the average noise level is independent of traffic speed.[17,18,21] In the free flow region most prediction schemes have adopted a relation of the form $L = B \log_{10} V$, where B is a constant. The logarithmic form stems from the fact that nearly all the major sources of noise on a vehicle are logarithmically related to the linear or rotational speed of the engine, although in practice there is little to choose between linear or logarithmic forms to cover the rather narrow range of speeds observed.

Computer simulations have indicated that for L_{10} the value of B should be approximately 17[19] and this has been confirmed by measurements.[16] However, for low flows of commercial vehicles it has been suggested that the value of B would be considerably higher, and also slightly lower for compositions approaching 50%.[19,20]

For the purposes of noise prediction, traffic forecasts are generally limited to two vehicle classes, light and heavy (with the dividing line generally set at 1525 kg unladen weight). Based on multiple regression analysis of field data a linear relation between percentile noise level and composition, $p\%$, has generally been adopted with a coefficient which varies from 0.1 on straight and level roads to nearly 0.2 on gradients. Nevertheless, the effect of varying the composition of traffic depends upon the mean traffic speed. For example, under free flow conditions and a speed of 80 km/h the noise level may increase by 5 dB(A) for a 30% increase in commercial traffic. However, at the lower speed of 30 km/h a similar increase in noise would occur following an increase in commercial vehicles of only 15% of the total flow.

10.4.4 Gradient

It is generally accepted that traffic noise levels are affected by the gradient of a road. Johnson and Saunders[3] concluded that the effect of gradient depends upon the percentage of heavy vehicles and predicted increases of up to 12 dB(A) for a gradient of 1 in 8. However, a later analysis of these data suggested that the initial estimate was much too high and that under normalized conditions the increase was only of the order of 4 dB(A). These later values are in fairly good agreement with the value obtained for motorways.[15,22]

10.4.5 Road surface

Road surface texture affects the noise level generated by traffic because it partially controls the road/tyre interaction noise. Broadly, the noise generated by vehicles travelling on coarse textured surfaces such as newly grooved concrete or surface dressed bituminous materials can emit up to 3 dB(A) more noise than vehicles travelling on a well-worn concrete or asphalt surface.[23] On the other hand, some surfaces which offer the combination of high acoustic absorption properties and good surface texture can be 2–3 dB(A) quieter than a good condition standard surface[24] (*see* also Chapters 7 and 11).

10.5 Factors affecting the propagation of traffic noise

The propagation of traffic noise is influenced by a number of factors. These include the attenuation due to distance, the interaction of the propagating wave with the ground surface, the screening provided by near ground obstacles such as noise barriers, the effect of vegetation, and, for long distance propagation, the effect of varying weather conditions.

10.5.1 Attenuation due to distance

It is shown in Chapter 2 that noise radiated from an omnidirectional point source into a free space attenuates according to the inverse square law, i.e. the acoustic field decreases as $20 \log_{10} d$ decibels. Although road vehicles are neither omnidirectional nor point sources a similar attenuation function can be obtained in the far field for isolated vehicle noise propagating over a hard reflecting ground surface. Consequently, provided these conditions are observed, in practice the peak noise levels from individual vehicles will attenuate by approximately 6 dB(A) per doubling of distance from the source. This attenuation function continues to hold until the distance between successive vehicles on a road segment approaches the distance separating the receiver from the traffic lane. As the flow increases further, the geometric spreading approaches that of a line source such that, theoretically, the acoustic field attenuates as $10 \log_{10} d$ decibels (*see* Equation 10.13).

In practice, the attenuation rate obviously depends on the noise index considered. As shown by the theory (*see* previous sections), the attenuation coefficient approaches 10 for L_{eq} for any traffic condition, and is flow sensitive for the percentile levels. Furthermore, it is extremely difficult to observe unobstructed propagations from a traffic stream where propagation is over a flat, acoustically hard surface. However, the attenuation function for propagation over both concrete slabs[16] and asphalt surfaces[22] has been observed over limited distance ranges together with unpublished data obtained on unobstructed propagation to the upper levels of multi-storey flats. For L_{10}, a value for the coefficient of attenuation between 10.5 and 11 has been obtained. Estimates of the attenuation coefficient based on analysis of computer simulation data relating to hard ground conditions vary from approximately 10.5 to 11.6[25] whilst Monte Carlo simulation for free-space propagation[26] has yielded an attenuation rate of 11.7 dB(A). Therefore, the differences between a theoretical free field line source and a traffic stream propagating over a hard surface are small, and for most practical purposes an attenuation coefficient of 10 for L_{eq} and mid-range percentile levels can be assumed.

Although these relations are inherent to geometry of both point and line source propagation, some additional corrections

may be needed to take account of air absorption. However, generally the distances involved are small, i.e. less than 300 m from the road, and, therefore, this effect is not considered important for traffic noise problems. In contrast, air absorption does affect aircraft noise where a combination of both higher frequencies and longer distances often requires some correction. Chapters 2 and 19 give further information on air absorption of aircraft noise.

The principle of geometrical spreading of sound energy from a traffic noise source has important limitations near to the ground. The basic ground effect for a stationary source and receiver has been investigated experimentally[27,28] and can be readily accounted for theoretically[29] in terms of the established physical basis of the phenomenon: i.e., a complex interference effect between the direct wave and the ground reflected wave (the phase and amplitude of the reflected wave depending critically on angle of incidence). The distance between the source and receiver, their height above the ground, and the complex acoustic impedance and propagation coefficients of the ground surface are the determining factors. For most road and receiver geometrical conditions, ground effect usually gives a destructive interference in the medium frequency range (250–1000 Hz, typical 500 Hz).

Recent analysis carried out by several authors[30–35] using electromagnetic wave theory have attempted to describe mathematically the effect of absorbing ground on wave propagation. This analysis has shown that though different levels of complexity can be used for modelling ground effect, a relatively simple model gives a satisfactory account of road traffic noise propagation, confirming empirical methods based on careful site measurements.[36]

In this model, the ground is treated as a locally reacting surface which means that waves within the ground are not considered. The plane wave coefficient R_p for a wave incident at an angle ψ to the horizontal (*Figure 10.14*) is then given by:

$$R_p = \frac{\sin \psi - Z_1/Z_2}{\sin \psi + Z_1/Z_2} \qquad (10.24)$$

where $Z_1 = \rho c$ is the characteristic impedance of the air and Z_2 is

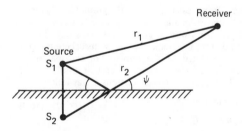

Figure 10.14 Geometry for ground effect calculations

the normal impedance of the ground comprising resistive and reactive terms, i.e. $Z_2 = R_2 + jX_2$. The acoustic pressure amplitude p at the receiver located at distance r_1 from the source may then be written as:

$$\frac{p}{p_0} = \frac{e^{jkr_1}}{r_1} + R_p \frac{e^{jkr_2}}{r_2} + F(w)(1 - R_p) \frac{e^{jkr_2}}{r_2} \qquad (10.25)$$

Here, the time dependence $e^{-j\omega t}$ has been assumed.

k is the propagation coefficient in the air; p_0 is the pressure amplitude at unit distance from the source in the absence of a reflecting plane; w, is called the numerical distance, with modulus $|w|$ and phase b, and is given by:

$$w = |w| e^{jb} = \frac{jkr_2}{2} \frac{(\sin \psi + Z_1/Z_2)}{(1 + \sin \psi Z_1/Z_2)} \qquad (10.26)$$

and $F(w)$, called the amplitude factor, can be written for $|w| > 1$ as follows according to the value of phase b:

$$\text{for } 0 < b < 2\pi, \ F(w) = -\frac{1}{2w} - \frac{1 \times 3}{(2w)^2} - \frac{1 \times 3 \times 5}{(2w)^3} \cdots$$

$$\text{for } -2\pi < b < 0, \ F(w) = -2j(\pi w)^{\frac{1}{2}}e^{-w} - \frac{1}{2w} - \frac{1 \times 3}{(2w)^2} - \frac{1 \times 3 \times 5}{(2w)^3} \cdots$$

$$(10.27)$$

For most traffic noise problems, the angle of incidence ψ is small. Therefore, from *Equation 10.24*, $\sin \psi$ approaches zero, R_p approaches -1, r_1 and r_2 become nearly equal and the first two terms of Equation 10.25 cancel. The sound field is then controlled by the third term of Equation 10.25. *Figure 10.15* shows the variation of the modulus of the amplitude factor $|F|$ as a function of b, the phase of w.

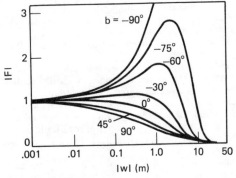

Figure 10.15 Variation of amplitude factor F as a function of $w = |w|e^{jb}$ (reference 33)

The derivation of Equations 10.25–10.27 are given by Chessel.[33] These equations enable the ground attenuation to be calculated as a function of source/receiver geometry and ground impedance Z_2.

In practice, direct measurements of the ground impedance Z_2 are difficult to make. An alternative approach to characterizing the ground properties was suggested by Delany and Bazley.[37] They showed that the impedance of fibrous absorbent materials could be approximated by the porosity of the material as characterized by the flow resistivity per unit thickness. The experimentally determined power relations are as follows:

$$R_2/\rho c = 1 + 9.08(f/\sigma)^{-0.75}$$
$$X_2/\rho c = 11.9(f/\sigma) - 0.73$$
$$(10.28)$$

NB these equations are also given in Chapter 2, where f is the frequency (Hz) and σ the flow resistivity (rayls). The ground impedance is then given by $Z_2 = R_2 + jX_2$.

The model described here has, therefore, the important advantage that the surface impedance depends on σ only. In practice, the value of σ can be determined for a particular ground surface by making several spot measurements over the surface at short ranges. *Table 10.2* gives a range of values of σ for several typical ground conditions.[31] From the table, an appropriate value of σ can be selected for a given ground condition, then Z_2 can be calculated from Equations 10.28 and w from Equation 10.26. $F(w)$ can be found from Equation 10.27, and the ground effect correction compared with free field propagation using Equations 10.24 and 10.25, taking account of r_1, r_2 and ψ according to the geometry given in *Figure 10.14*. *Figure 10.16* shows the results obtained for a practical example.[31]

Table 10.2 Flow resistivities of various ground surfaces[31]

Description of surface	Flow resistivity in rayls (CGS units)
Dry snow, new fallen 10 cm deep	15–30
Sugar snow	25–50
In frost, pine or hemlock	20–80
Grass: rough pasture, airport, public buildings, etc.	150–300
Roadside dirt, ill-defined, small rocks up to 10 cm diameter	300–800
Sandy silt, hard packed by vehicles	600–2500
'Clean' limestone chips, thick layer (12.7–25.4 mm mesh)	1500–4000
Old dirt roadway, fine stones (6.35 mm mesh) interstices filled	2000–4000
Earth, exposed and rain-packed	4000–8000
Quarry dust, fine, very hard-packed by vehicles	5000–20 000
Asphalt, sealed by dust and use	> 20 000

*Values give best fit between measured sound spectrum and that predicted by a one-parameter model.

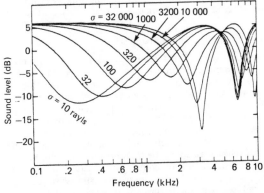

Figure 10.16 Theoretical curves showing interference and ground-wave effects for one configuration of source and receiver heights ($h_s = 0.31$ m, $h_r = 1.22$ m) and distance apart (15.2 m). Zero decibels corresponds to the free field sound level of the same source[31]

Despite the relative simplicity of the approach outlined above in accounting for interference and ground wave effects from traffic sources, many practical ground effect problems remain unsolved, such as propagation over variable ground, interference with atmospheric effects and vegetation, inhomogeneous soils.

Field data on the propagation of traffic noise over different surfaces are fairly numerous.[16,36,38] As the absorption characteristics of different ground surfaces can vary widely, the attenuation rates due to ground effect can also vary over wide limits. It has, therefore, become common practice to categorize broadly all surfaces that are not acoustically hard as 'grassland' (also called porous or soft), which typifies a broad average absorbing surface, and to accept that practical surfaces may vary widely from this broad average. There are several examples of empirically derived attenuation functions for traffic noise propagation over grassland, such as the function given in the UK method *Calculation of Road Traffic Noise* for L_{10}[39] and reproduced in *Figure 10.17*. The figure enables the attenuation in dB(A) over grassland (including geometrical spreading, atmospheric absorption and ground effect) to be estimated for any receiver

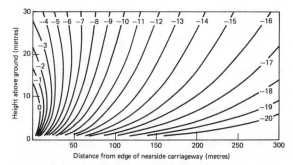

Figure 10.17 Propagation over grassland: correction in dB(A) as a function of distance from edge of nearside carriageway and height above ground[39]

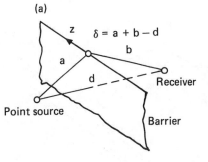

(a)

$\delta = a + b - d$

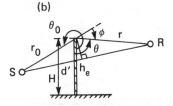

(b)

Figure 10.18 Geometry for thin screen attenuation.
(a) Three-dimensional view (b) Projection in the plane, z=constant

position located within 300 m from the road at ground level. It can be seen, for example, that at 100 m from the road the excess attenuation is $-5\,dB(A)$ at 2 m above the ground plane and $-2\,dB(A)$ at 10 m compared with the attenuation obtained at 30 m high. Note that for reception points located well above the ground such that the angle between the line drawn through the reception point to the source line and the ground plane is greater than about 20 degrees, the excess attenuation becomes small and can be safely ignored for most applications.

10.5.2 Screens and diffraction of traffic noise*

When an obstacle intercepts the line of sight from the source to a receiver, the noise at the receiver is reduced. The amount of screening provided varies according to the amount of sound energy that is diffracted over the top of the barrier and around its ends and to the amount of energy that passes through the barrier. For traffic noise problems, the sound energy transmitted through a roadside screen can generally be neglected since the transmission loss through most barrier materials is much higher than the potential screening performance determined by the barrier geometry. For example, a barrier material with a surface mass of 20 kg/m² will generally provide a transmission loss of more than 20 dB.[40] This, of course, assumes that there are no gaps in the structure.

The most commonly considered type of barrier is a thin screen or wall erected close to the traffic stream. However, there are many types of obstacles with a variety of shapes that also act in a similar way to the thin screen, e.g. buildings, and it has become common practice to approximate complex shaped obstacles to an equivalent or a set of equivalent thin screens.

The theory of screens has been discussed by Kurze.[41] It is stated that Keller's geometrical theory of diffraction leads to relatively simple formulae, the asymptotic solution for a semi-infinite screen being written[42]:

$$\Delta L = -20 \log_{10} \frac{d}{4\pi \sin\beta} \left[\frac{\lambda}{ab(a+b)}\right]^{\frac{1}{2}} \left[\frac{1}{\cos(\theta_0 - \theta)/2}\right.$$

$$\left. + \frac{1}{\cos(\theta_0 + \theta)/2}\right] \tag{10.29}$$

where ΔL is the attenuation in the shadow zone, λ is the wavelength, a, b and d are the path lengths shown on *Figure 10.18(a)*, β is the angle between the incident ray and the barrier edge defined by $\sin\beta = r_0/a = r/b$, and r_0, r, θ_0 and θ are shown in the projection plane $z = $ constant in *Figure 10.18(b)*. According to this equation, the screening ΔL provided by a barrier depends on five parameters and is therefore rather difficult to apply in practice.

* An introduction to this topic is also given in Chapter 2.

On this basis, in order to simplify the method of calculation, a graphical method has been developed which gives an approximation to Keller's theory. Redfearn's chart[43] proposed in 1940 (*Figure 10.19*) gives the attenuation for a point source and a point receiver, as a function of the parameter h_e/λ and angle φ, where h_e is termed the 'effective height' of the screen. This chart is incorrect if the sound incidence is at an oblique angle with the edge of the screen, and if either the source or the receiver are close to the screen (distances less than a wavelength or so).

Maekawa's chart[44] proposed in 1965 (*Figure 10.20*) gives the attenuation for a point source and a point receiver as a function of Fresnel number $N = 2\delta/\lambda$, where δ is the path difference between the diffracted path and direct path and equals $a + b - d$ as defined in *Figure 10.18*.

Figure 10.20 gives a single straight-line function for thin-wall attenuation, with an alternative straight-line for right angle wedge wall attenuation. Note that the abscissa scale is not linear. The method is therefore simple to use and has the added advantage that it is valid for any incidence angle. The equation for thin wall attenuation is set out below:

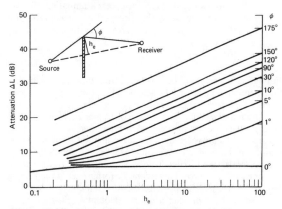

Figure 10.19 Chart giving the attenuation provided by a semi-infinite thin screen (after Redfearn[43])

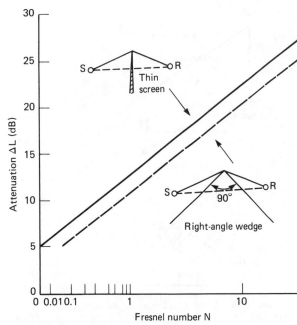

Figure 10.20 Attenuation provided by a semi-infinite screen (after Maekawa[44])

$$\left.\begin{array}{ll} \Delta L = 20 \log_{10} \dfrac{2\pi(N/2)^{\frac{1}{2}}}{\tanh \pi(N/2)^{\frac{1}{2}}} & \text{for } N < 1 \\[3mm] \Delta L = 10 \log_{10}(20N) & \text{for } N \geqslant 1 \end{array}\right\} \quad (10.30)$$

Most current traffic noise prediction methods use Maekawa's chart,[44] as a basis for calculating barrier attenuation and apply the following modifications:

1. The attenuation is given in dB(A) for a typical traffic noise spectrum. NB, A-weighted traffic noise levels behave similarly to 500 Hz octave band levels. Then using this assumption the Fresnel number N becomes equal to $N = 2\delta/0.68$, where 0.68 m is the wavelength at 500 Hz, and the chart is scaled in $\delta = a + b - d$

2. The attenuation is given in terms of L_{eq} or mid-range percentile levels, i.e. for a line source, which is obtained as follows:
   In the presence of a barrier, the intensity of noise from each point source is reduced at the receiver position by the factor $10^{-\Delta L(\alpha)/10}$ dB, where $\Delta L(\alpha)$ is the excess attenuation of a ray from a point source in the direction α. Given Equation 10.12, the excess attenuation $\Delta \bar{L}$ for the entire line source is:

$$\Delta \bar{L} = -10 \log_{10} \frac{2}{\pi} \int_{0}^{\pi/2} 10^{-\Delta L(\alpha)/10} \, d\alpha \tag{10.31}$$

For a long screen, it can be concluded from Equation 10.31 that the attenuation of L_{eq} or L_{10} is less than the attenuation of higher fractile noise levels, since $\Delta L(\alpha)$ reaches a maximum when δ is a maximum and $\alpha = 90°$. This feature of barrier performance has been widely observed in practical installations.[49]

Rapin[60] has proposed an alternative method using a combination of both Redfearn's and Maekawa's methods. Two vertical scales are provided, one for point source attenuation and one for line source. This technique forms part of the French 'Guide du Bruit' traffic noise prediction method.

These methods provide a means of obtaining a reasonably accurate estimation of the acoustic screening provided by simple barriers. They do not permit the accurate calculation of the

screening provided by complex obstacles. For example, noise barrier attenuation depends on barrier cross-section geometries including thin walls, sharp wedges, cylinder-topped wedges, double walls, trapezoids, etc. May and Osman[45] have demonstrated from scale model experiments that higher noise reductions of the order of 2 dB(A) and greater are obtained for wide top barriers, especially with a T-shaped profile. Further improvements were obtained with T-profile absorptive top barriers with cap widths of 0.6 m or more. This measured effect can now be reproduced using computer model techniques which apply the concepts of the geometrical theory of diffraction, as given for example in Hayek[46] or Seznec.[47] It is expected that future advances in these techniques should lead to improved computation schemes in the next few years. In their absence, it is usual to compute the Fresnel number N by taking the upper edge of the obstacle as the top of the barrier. On average, the attenuation predicted in this way is sufficiently accurate for practical purposes, although the values in any particular location can be expected to deviate by a few dB because of the inability to allow for the specific barrier geometry.

Usually, a noise barrier is located on the ground and ground reflections must therefore be included in the analysis. However, the presence of a barrier also tends to increase the mean height of the acoustic path and therefore the ground effect attenuation is reduced. According to Jonasson,[48] four ray paths can be drawn from the source to the receiver when a barrier is present, as illustrated in *Figure 10.21*. The total field at the receiver is given by the pressure summation of the contribution from each path. This can be expressed as:

$$p = p_{SR} + p_{S'R} + p_{SR'} + p_{S'R'} \tag{10.32}$$

where p_{SR} represents the pressure field resulting from the direct path S to R, $p_{S'R}$ and $p_{SR'}$ involve one ground reflection and $p_{S'R'}$ involves two reflections. Each pressure field is affected by barrier diffraction. The previous methods for determining ground and barrier effects can be applied to each term although this is clearly a laborious calculation. Current traffic noise prediction methods generally simplify the computation by separating ground effect and barrier effect. Consequently, in the presence of a barrier, ground effect attenuation is not taken into account, except when the 'barrier' is due to the edge of a cutting in a depressed section of road, the diffracting edge of which is at ground level.

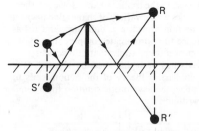

Figure 10.21 Ray path geometry for screen diffraction with ground effect

10.5.3 Effect of atmospheric conditions

For most weather conditions, both wind speed and temperature vary with height above the ground. These vertical gradients cause the speed of sound to vary with height and hence for the sound waves to travel along curved paths from source to receiver: they are concave downwards for downwind propagation or temperature inversion, and upwards for upwind propagation or temperature lapse conditions. For the later situation, the sound ray closest to the ground at any appreciable distance is the one that just grazes the ground tangentially at some small distance from the source. Below this ray near the ground, there is a shadow zone which increases in height with distance from the source. Some sound still penetrates this region because of other processes related to atmospheric turbulence. In effect this limits the reduction of sound levels in the shadow zone to between 10 and 30 dB.[31]

Shadow zones generated by meteorological factors do not generally affect traffic noise propagation over short distances from roads where the most severe community noise problems occur, but wave curvature does modify the mean height of source to receiver path over the ground, and this can then have a significant effect both on ground and on barrier attenuations.[49]

In general, and with a barrier present, the wind gradient has the greatest effect on higher frequencies, at the lower receiver positions and at the greater source-to-barrier and receiver-to-barrier distances. For example, with a positive wind vector of, say, 10 m/sec, i.e. wind blowing in the general direction from the road to the receiver, typically noise barrier attenuations can be reduced by 2–3 dB(A).[49] These effects have been examined under field conditions, but despite attempts to develop empirical[51] or computer-based models[13] of noise propagation, no practical procedure has yet been developed. The main difficulty is in describing the meteorological factors of importance, i.e. wind gradient, temperature, etc. with sufficient precision over a large void space. In practice, methods of traffic noise prediction generally assume that the weather conditions are moderately unfavourable, i.e. positive wind vectors with a speed of 2–3 m/s. It is also usual to standardize measurements to these conditions[50] (*see also* Chapter 2).

10.5.4 Sound attenuation by vegetation

Trees, bushes and plants are of great value in improving the aesthetics of road environment. However, the noise attenuation provided by vegetation is generally overestimated. Kragh[52] has carried out a comprehensive literature survey of the screening provided by vegetation. Though mechanisms are very difficult to isolate because of the complex interaction between the ground, the vegetation and atmosphere, some theoretical explanation for screening by vegetation can be made.

Vegetation may affect the propagation of low-frequency sound by ground absorption which can be enhanced in wooden areas because of the high porosity of the ground resulting from tree roots and fallen leaves, etc. High-frequency propagation is affected by scattering by tree trunks, branches and partly by leaf absorption. It is difficult, however, to provide descriptions of vegetation which can be used to gauge the attenuation of noise. Tree height, depth of planting, and particularly density of planting (for instance in terms of kg/m³) appear to be dominant variables. Though attenuation is not directly proportional to the transmission path length, this may be a useful approximation applicable when a limited frequency band is concerned. Generalizations to dB(A) attenuation values per unit length introduce a greater spread in the observed results. Excess attenuation with respect to grassland of the order of 0.5–1.5 dB(A) per 10 m of dense vegetation depth have been found on average for L_{eq} and L_{10}.[53]

10.5.5 Reflection and scattering

In urban areas, the presence of buildings in close proximity to roads introduce additional complications to the process of traffic noise propagation. Multiple reflections between building facades can occur together with scattering and diffractions. Similar phenomena also occur for some roadway cross sections such as vertical cuttings or parallel vertical noise screens on both

sides of the road. A general review of the processes involved has been prepared by Lyon.[54]

Concerning reflections, the facades of buildings can be considered to act like mirrors on which the incident acoustic wave is reflected with a reflection angle equal to the incidence angle, provided the wavelength is significantly larger than dimensions of the facade texture. The sound energy absorbed depends upon the frequency of the incident wave and the angle of incidence, and has been reported to range between zero and 35% of the incident energy.[55] In most calculations, an absorption coefficient of 0.1 can be assumed to characterize building facades, but it is often approximated by a zero term (i.e. all the energy is reflected). The acoustic mirrors generate image sources symetrically positioned with the primary source, and the image sources can then be considered as additional sources for noise calculation purposes.

Scattering of the incident wave can occur at reflecting boundaries when the wavelength of the incident sound is of the same order as the surface roughness. Then, the reflected energy is spread in all the directions. In densely built-up areas, scattering can be significant because of the large number of scattering elements (facades, parked cars, etc.). Nevertheless, although some attempts have been made to account for the scattering of sound in dense urban environments,[56] for practical purposes scattering is also generally ignored in prediction modelling.

A 'broad brush' technique for assessing the combined effects of diffraction and scattering in urban areas has been suggested by Shaw and Olson.[57] For an idealized homogeneous city, they show that the excess attenuation with respect to hard ground propagation should be a constant value of 15 dB which is independent of the distance.

A commonly occurring situation where the reflection effects are important is a street bounded by vertical facades on either side. Usually, there will be a direct path from the source of noise to the receiver. In addition, if buildings line both sides of the street, there will be a multiplicity of other paths involving reflections and scattering from the faces of the buildings. As long as there is a line of sight from the source to the receiver, the additional paths will serve to enhance the sound received above that obtained in an open terrain situation.

A first theoretical approach of this situation initiated by Wiener *et al.*[58] assumes that the street may be represented by a simple channel between infinite-reflecting planes of known absorption coefficient a as shown on *Figure 10.22*. Then, for source and receiver located on the axis of the street, the total field at R can be approximated by the summation over infinity of two arrays of point sources of sound power $W_i = (1-a)^i W$ and distance to the receiver $r_i = (d^2 + i^2 w^2)^{\frac{1}{2}}$, located on either side of the street of width w. Consequently,

$$p^2 = \frac{W \rho c}{2\pi} \left(\frac{1}{d^2} + 2 \sum_{i=1}^{\infty} \frac{(1-a)^i}{d^2 + i^2 w^2} \right)$$

(10.33)

When the walls are perfect reflectors, $a = 0$ and the asymptotic form of the sound field drops off at 3 dB per doubling of distance instead of 6 dB, because the series of images forms a line source.

An extension of this image source theory has been used by Favre[21] in order to perform traffic noise propagation calculations at street intersections. In this case, the infinite set of image sources over order j is replaced by a single equivalent source, with the same acoustic power as their added power, and with a position at the geometric barycentre of these sources, weighted by their respective power. Thus the equivalent source of $S_{(j)}, \ldots S_{(\infty)}$ image sources has a power equal to $W(1-a)/a$ and a position at the distance $(jW + W(1-a)/a)$ from the axis of the street. This approximation has been used for urban traffic noise prediction and shows good agreement with site and scale model measurements when $a = 0.1$.[13]

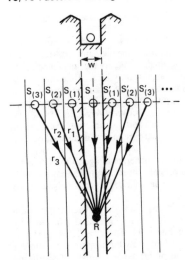

Figure 10.22 Array of image sources for a street bounded by buildings

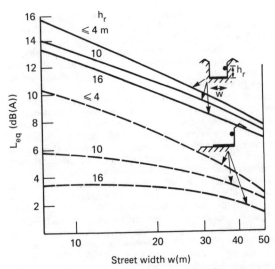

Figure 10.23 Increase in L_{eq} levels at the facades of buildings for different receiver heights (h_r) and street widths (w)[60]

Comparisons of image source theories with field experiments show that an extension to include non-specular reflection is needed for near field propagation because of local scattering effects.[56] In addition, interference effects between direct and/or reflected waves can occur and have been identified as significant for low-frequency noise problems (below 200 Hz).[59]

In a second theoretical approach, it is assumed that a street is a reverberant closed space with a diffuse field and that the general methods of high-frequency room acoustics can be applied. The equivalent absorption surface is estimated from the street dimensions where road surface and buildings facades are reflective ($a = 0$) and the open space above the street is totally absorbent ($a = 1$). For a total surface of ($2w + 2h_b$) per unit length (h_b = height of buildings), the absorption surface is w, and the total equivalent absorption coefficient is $a = w/(2w + 2h_b)$. Kutruff[11] has shown that the squared pressure for a point source then decreases along the street by a constant amount of $4.34/h_b$ (dB/m), and is given at distance d from the source by

$$p^2 = \frac{W\rho c}{2w \cdot h_b} e^{-d/h_b} \tag{10.34}$$

leading to quite different conclusions compared with the previous image source theory. In reality, both theoretical approaches represent extreme situations between which all real situations can be found.

When noise sources are spread over the length of the street, the sum of the whole set of sources along the street for a given receiver position is required. Both methods show that the mean noise level (L_{eq}, L_{10} or similar) then decreases as $-10 \log_{10}w$, where w is the street width. This can be obtained directly from Equation 10.34, or numerically from Equation 10.33. This result has been widely confirmed by field experiments.[61]

Figure 10.23 shows the increase of L_{eq} levels at the facades of buildings in streets flanked by buildings on both sides compared with the same traffic situation with buildings only on one side. The zero dB position relates to free field L_{eq} for the same traffic flow at 30 m from the receiver.

10.6 Methods of prediction

Traffic noise prediction methods have been developed in many countries. In most cases, the methods are used to assess the degree of exposure to traffic noise for a given or projected road scheme but in some countries, they are also used as part of the legal framework to assess entitlement for some form of compensation payment.

The methods can be broadly categorized into one of three groups. First, they take the form of a manual method which permits the calculation of traffic noise levels via the use of a series of simple to use correction charts, tables or formulae. The purpose is to enable prediction to be carried out without the need for a computer. The second type is entirely computer based; it enables the user to carry out a great deal of detailed site-specific calculation and also permits the presentation of area-based noise maps giving a pictorial representation of traffic-noise penetration into a given area. Finally, scale-model techniques are used particularly where the theoretical models fail to deal adequately with a given road layout and land use characteristics. This technique is particularly suited to complex road junctions such as motorway interchanges with complex built form.

This section reviews the main features of these techniques.

10.6.1 Manual methods (formulae or nomograms)

Most manual methods arrive at a predicted noise level through a series of adjustments to a reference noise level. Typically, the steps in this procedure are:

1. Divide the road scheme into one or more homogeneous segments either as a result of variations in the road alignment (*see Figure 10.10*), or as the result of changes to the traffic parameters within the scheme. The objective is to limit the variation of noise within the segment.
2. Calculate for each segment a reference noise level at a given reference distance to the traffic stream as a function of the traffic characteristics (volume, speed, percentage of vehicles in the different classes, type of flow, gradient and road surface).

3. Calculate adjustments to the reference level taking account of distance, ground effect and screening by obstacles, site layout features and size of the source segment.
4. Combine the contributions from all the segments to give the predicted noise level at the receiver for the whole road scheme.

UK In the United Kingdom, a procedure[39] has been developed for predicting traffic noise levels L_{10} (18 − hour). (The 18.00 hour period is 06.00 hrs to midnight.) This method is used in conjunction with the Noise Insulation Regulations (1975) to calculate entitlement for statutory sound insulation of buildings and also for general planning and assessment purposes. In this method, the reference position for each road segment is at 10 m from the edge of the nearside lane and the reference noise level is given by:

$$L_{10} = 10 \log_{10} Q + 33 \log_{10}(V + 40 + \frac{500}{V}) +$$

$$10 \log_{10}\left(1 + \frac{5p}{V}\right) - 27.6 \qquad (10.35)$$

where Q is the traffic volume (vph), V is the mean traffic speed (km/h), and p is the percentage of heavy vehicles. Provision is also given for the effect of gradient and for the unscreened noise generated by traffic running on deeply textured road surfaces.

The prediction method gives correction charts to adjust the reference noise level for distance, ground effect, shielding and reflection effects. Also included is a method to deal with combined screening and reflection problems such as retained cut and dual noise barriers together with procedures to deal with noise from multi-segment road junctions.

The method was originally validated using the results from more than 2000 field measurements. This rigorous test gave an overall mean prediction error (measured-predicted) of − 0.6 dB(A) with a standard deviation of 2.5 dB(A).

This procedure has recently been revised, although at the time of writing the new method has not yet been published. The revision retains the basic philosophy of approach but extends the range of application of the method to take account of a wider range of prediction scenarios and the results of recent research. In particular, significant modifications have been made to the corrections dealing with vehicle flow, taking into account low vehicle flows, as well as road surface corrections, retained cut and both dual and double-barrier configurations.

USA In the USA, the Federal Highway Administration commissioned research to develop a logical and easy-to-use method of calculating L_{eq} for the highway traffic noise specialist. This method, published in 1978,[53] originated from the previous FHWA 72 model.[62]

The model is presented in a logical, step-by-step format, with appendices that cover the theoretical background and identify the assumptions and limitations of the method. The reference level is calculated at a distance of 15 m from the centre-line of a traffic lane, for each class of vehicles considered to comprise the traffic stream. These classes are defined as automobiles, medium trucks (from 4500 to 12 000 kg), and heavy trucks. Because computation of the noise levels on a lane-by-lane basis becomes very tedious for multi-lane roads, the model introduces a notional equivalent single lane located at a distance d_e from the receiver, where $d_e = \sqrt{d_n d_f}$, and d_n and d_f are the perpendicular distances to the near and the far lanes, respectively. When a barrier is present, d_e is then calculated as $d_e = \sqrt{d'_n \cdot d'_f} + X$, where d'_n and d'_f are the perpendicular distances of the barrier to the near and the far lanes, and X is the distance from the barrier to the receiver.

Apart from the usual procedures, the method also takes account of the excess attenuation resulting from 'dense woodland', i.e. a correction of 1 dB(A) every 6 m depth up to a maximum of 10 dB(A). The screening provided by discontinuous rows of buildings is included, i.e. for the first row, 3 dB(A) when the buildings occupy 40–65% of the length of the row, 5 dB(A) if they occupy 65–90% and 1.5 dB(A) attenuation for every additional row up to a maximum of 10 dB(A). In both cases, the excess attenuation provided by ground effects is ignored when calculating the attenuation from woodland or the screening provided by barriers. The model also gives an adjustment factor for converting L_{eq} into L_{10} values, based on the assumption that the vehicles have equal power and are equally spaced.

The method contains nomograms or formulae which can be easily programmed on a small calculator and gives several practical examples illustrating the use of the method.

Scandinavia A manual prediction method has been developed jointly by Denmark, Finland, Norway and Sweden. The so-called NTB computing model for road traffic noise[63] (1979) was prepared by a special working group, including acousticians as well as representatives of relevant authorities within the Nordic countries. The method enables L_{eq} levels to be calculated both for urban as well as for rural areas. This model also includes the calculation of maximum noise levels emitted by isolated passing vehicles.

The reference level is calculated at a distance of 10 m from the centre of the road. Step-by-step corrections are then included to take account of the usual propagation variables.

The method contains a correction to allow for facade insulation when outdoor values have to be converted into indoor values, and a correction to allow for thick barriers (thickness greater than .5 m).

France In France, the traffic noise prediction methods are contained in the *Guide du Bruit des Transports Terrestres (1980)*.[60] This publication replaces the previous *Guide du Bruit (1972)*[64] which was aimed at assessing L_{50} traffic noise levels. The new *Guide* (L_{eq}) covers several volumes and includes advice on noise indices, response assessment, noise barriers, etc. Four methods are given, two of which can be described as step-by-step manual methods. The first manual method is a formulae-based method with graphical presentation to simplify its use. The second is a more detailed method with graphs and additional computation techniques giving vehicle noise levels in terms of vehicle speed, type of vehicle, mode of operation (e.g. freely flowing, accelerating, decelerating, etc.), and propagation attenuations for a wide range of transverse profiles. Using this method, for example, it is possible to calculate manually traffic noise levels near a two-street intersection with parallel facades and accelerating/decelerating lanes. The computer-based program BRUIT and scale-model-based predictions carried out at the CSTB facility in Grenoble complete the range of methods given in the *Guide du Bruit*.

All the prediction procedures described in this section provide reasonably accurate calculations if they are applied as intended. Wesler[65] has pointed out that differences between traffic noise measurements and calculations with available prediction methods can be due to three possible factors. These are atypical sample of vehicles, improper noise measurement techniques or weather conditions (e.g. wind gradients) not considered in the calculation method.

Simple methods of calculation can often be used where a more accurate or more detailed calculation is not required. Some of these methods are listed in the references, e.g. reference[39] for L_{10}, reference[60] for L_{eq}, or reference[66] for L_{10} and L_{eq}. This last reference summarizes several methods in use within the European Economic Community countries.

10.6.2 Computer programs

Computer programs began to be developed in the late 1960s and are now widely used as a tool for predicting traffic noise levels. These programs have been written primarily to ease the burden of calculation when large and sometimes complex schemes need to be evaluated. However, various degrees of sophistication have been incorporated in most programs so that both detailed area based noise maps can be output and site-specific noise predictions can be obtained at the lowest level of sophistication. Computer programs have also been developed for research purposes to gain insight into the complex relations between noise generation and propagation. The different techniques that have been developed are discussed below.

10.6.2.1 Traffic flow synthesis programs

Traffic flow synthesis programs have been devised with the principal objective of obtaining accurate simulations of vehicle flow. In this way, it is possible to evaluate the various flow factors affecting noise level and to determine their complex interaction. In particular, the techniques enable interactive traffic situations occurring in the region of road intersections and at signalized junctions to be studied. Nelson, for example, has used a single vehicle distribution combination method to simulate traffic freely flowing on a 1–6 lane road with up to six separate vehicle categories.[19] This method has been used to evaluate the effects of vehicle flow and composition on noise propagation and to devise appropriate formulae describing these processes. This method has also been used to calculate the effect on traffic noise from individual vehicle categories as a result of current vehicle engineering programmes and assumed legislative action.[67] Monte Carlo vehicle synthesis techniques have been used to model vehicles operating in both free flow and interrupted flow conditions. The technique is particularly useful in modelling flow patterns in the region of junctions and signalized intersections. *Figure 10.24* illustrates a form of output obtained from a Monte Carlo based traffic synthesis program which shows equal L_{Aeq} contours in the vicinity of traffic lights.[10]

10.6.2.2 Noise propagation synthesis programs

Computer techniques are of current use to calculate traffic noise propagation in complex situations. Numerical techniques can be, in principle, operated to solve the Helmholtz equation in a finite element approximation of real space. Even though the method can give an exact solution, provided the boundary conditions relevant to each element can be defined, the method requires a great deal of computing power in order to tackle the extremely large number of elements needed for practical applications. This restriction has so far prevented a wide development of this technique which has been used for complex-shaped screen diffraction calculations.[47]

The random emission of acoustic rays propagating through the urban network and scattered, diffracted or reflected by boundaries has been adapted from room acoustics techniques. However, this method is limited to very specific situations such as two-dimensional spaces[68] or regular geometries[69] in order to reduce the large number of ray segments which have to be generated to fill the space.

More practical methods have been developed using image source theory. The contribution from each image source at the receiver position is calculated taking into account all diffraction and reflection effects in each case. This technique has, for example, been used by Lee and Davies[70] to provide charts accounting for propagation in complex urban streets.

10.6.2.3 Formula based methods

Simple programs have been developed to make use of the manual techniques described in the previous section. These programs operate at various levels of sophistication but in their simplest form they can usually be used with a small desk-top computer or programmable calculator.

At a higher level of sophistication, these methods have been coupled with various ground models that enable detailed site topography to be entered into the computer providing a means of identifying buildings both for display and calculation purposes as well as defining the ground plane for propagation calculations. Such a technique has been developed by Applied Research of Cambridge in the UK (MWAY program), by Rathé in Switzerland[71] (MODEL 77 program) and by Favre[72] (BRUIT program).

The Swiss program provides facilities to input complex ground topography and building layout and height. Different types of ground cover such as asphalt, grass or forest can be included.

Both the Swiss and French programs assume that the source line is a series of point sources. The noise propagated to the receiver from each source is then calculated as a function of the noise power taking into account the traffic, road alignment and sound propagation factors. In the MODEL 77 program, the shortest path between the receiver and the traffic route is determined, and, for this path, a vertical profile through the terrain is defined. The attenuation between the source and the receiver is then calculated.

For unobstructed propagation, the attenuation is calculated according to the distance of the receiver from the source position, the type of ground cover and the height of the acoustic path above the ground section. If the source is screened from the receiver, then an appropriate barrier attenuation is determined. In order to include any side paths around the obstacle, the vertical plane cutting the terrain is then rotated ±80 degrees around a vertical axis at the receiver position, and the minimum barrier attenuation is calculated. This method allows the behaviour of irregular and limited dimension barriers to be determined.

In the BRUIT computer program, the positions of the point sources are defined by drawing a series of lines from the receiver to the source line with a constant 10 degree angular separation. The point sources are defined where these lines intersect the source line. By using a constant angle to define the point source

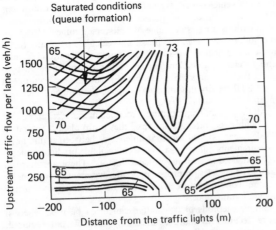

Figure 10.24 Contours of equal values of L_{eq} dB(A) at the roadside with respect to the distance from the traffic lights and the upstream traffic flow per lane ($p=0\%$). Traffic light cycle: 70 s green, 5 s amber, 25 s red[10]

positions, the calculation takes account of the line source property that the energy radiated is proportional to the segment angle (NB Equation 10.12). The contribution from every source along either direct, diffracted or reflected paths is then computed considering the path geometry and the reflection impedances. All possible paths are considered including up to three orders of reflection. Searching for paths is the main mathematical problem, owing to the large number of possibilities in most applications. For example, for n reflectors, there are n first-order reflections possible, $n.(n-1)$ second-order reflections, and $n.(n-1)^2$ third-order reflections. *Figure 10.25* illustrates the number of paths considered by BRUIT for a single point source and for a given building lay-out.

form and road systems increase. This is especially true at urban/suburban sites where multiple reflections and scattering from large numbers of buildings often occur. For these circumstances, the planner is faced with the prospect of establishing designs based on noise data which may be inaccurate or provide only limited guidance.

As an alternative to computer modelling it is also possible to develop a scale model of the scheme and to evaluate by direct measurement how the noise will propagate in the real environment. The primary objective of scale modelling is to establish prior to development of the real scheme the propagation transfer function between the road source (generally a line of point sources) and the receiver positions under scaled conditions

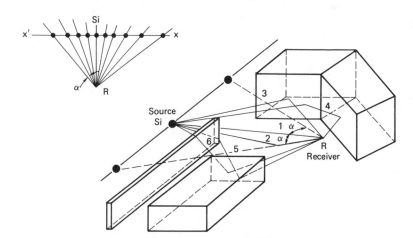

Figure 10.25 Examples of acoustical paths between a point source and a receiver considered by computer program BRUIT. 1, direct path; 2, reflection from the ground; 3, one reflection from one facade; 4, two reflections; 5, lateral diffraction and reflection; 6, vertical diffraction and reflection[72]

In a programme developed by Thomassen,[73] a line is horizontally rotated from the receiver to define homogeneous source segments. These are characterized by the edges of buildings, barriers, etc. The contribution of every segment is then computed as a function of the perpendicular distance to receiver, the angle of view of the segment, the diffraction attenuation if any, and the absorbing characteristics of any reflecting surfaces. The number of reflections taken is not limited in this method.

The different models described above make it possible to reconstitute at the receiver the noise history of the vehicles depending on their position along the line source. A further process, involving an energy—or statistical-based procedure is then carried out to give the noise indices required.

Output from these programs can be in various forms depending upon the user's requirements. If a ground plan is required then considerable detail can be included such as the positions of roads, buildings, ground features and receiver positions, or equal-noise contours. *Figure 10.26* shows typical output formats obtained using MODEL 77 and BRUIT. The first example illustrates an open field propagation lay-out with complex road network and ground geometry. The ground contours are defined by line segments (MODEL 77). The second example concerns a typical urban situation with buildings located alongside the road line (BRUIT). Building facades are either reflective (single lines) or absorbing (double lines).

10.6.3 Scale models

Although computer methods enable ray path and image source methods to be applied to fairly complex road schemes with some success, they require the input of a great deal of information to describe land topography and building geometries. These methods rapidly become unwieldy as the complexity of the ground

and in a carefully controlled acoustic environment. By measuring scale modelled sound pressure levels and estimating source and sound power levels from traffic parameters, traffic noise levels can then be calculated. Acoustic scale modelling is not, however, a commonly used technique and is restricted to specialist organisations mainly because of the special facilities that are required.

A general review of acoustical modelling of road traffic noise has been carried out by Anderson.[74] In order to justify the use of scale models it is usually necessary to consider road sections as long as possible, hence there is a need to create a scale model facility with as large a reduction factor as possible. Since an acoustical scale model is a duplication of a full-size prototype in miniature, this means that all-important acoustical characteristics must be properly scaled so that the model behaves acoustically the same as the prototype. For example, reflecting surfaces on the model must be scaled so that sound energy is reflected, scattered or absorbed, in exactly the same manner as in full scale. This also implies that sound waves themselves have to be scaled, so that the wavelengths are reduced by the scale factor. Consequently in order to estimate accurately traffic noise conditions where most of the energy is in the 500 Hz or 1000 Hz octave bands, it is necessary to reproduce $500 k_s$.Hz or $1000 k_s$.Hz frequencies, where k_s is the scale factor in the model environment. This requires a propagation medium which retains its propagation characteristics together with an adequate apparatus to generate, control, and measure properly such high frequencies.

The choice of propagation medium usually dictates the degree of scaling that can be achieved. It is possible to conceive scale models using water as the propagation medium because of its good transmission characteristics. Scale factors $k_s = 500$ are possible in theory but in practice there are technological prob-

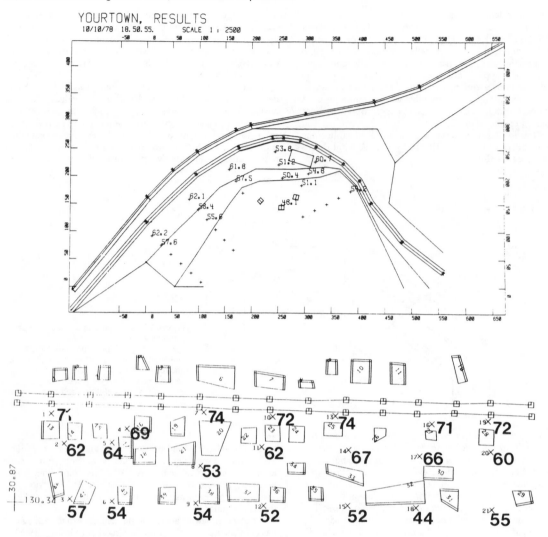

Figure 10.26 Noise maps calculated by computer programs
MODEL 77[71] (top) and BRUIT[13] (bottom)

Figure 10.27 The scale model facility at
CSTB (Grenoble)

lems associated with the design of sources and receivers. It is usual, therefore, to carry out scale model studies in air and, provided the high-frequency components of traffic noise, say above 1 kHz, are not required, a scale factor $k_s = 100$ is possible. It is necessary, however, to control the amount of water vapour in the air to reduce molecular absorption problems. A further problem when dealing with high frequencies is to achieve sufficient detail with the modelled surfaces such as building facades. In addition, surface impedances need to be preserved in the scale model. This is relatively simple for highly reflective surfaces but it presents substantial problems when scaling absorptive materials.

The choice of sound source and receiver also provides difficulties. Although the smallest microphones have a satisfactory acoustic response up to 100 kHz, they have low sensitivity at these frequencies so that high acoustic power sources are needed. For example, 100 dB/octave for a continuous signal, or 110–115 dB for an impulse signal. Impulsive sources such as spark sources emit a very short burst of sound energy which propagates within the model and arrives at the receiving microphone in a succession of pulses with a propagation time which is a direct measure of the length of the path. Each path can generally be studied separately. Continuous sources (air jets, loudspeakers or horns) can be used to collect large quantities of data over an area, whereas impulsive sources are preferably used for path diagnostics.

An example of an acoustic scale model facility developed primarily for roadway modelling is located at the Centre Scientifique et Technique du Bâtiment in Grenoble. A view of the modelling room is shown in *Figure 10.27*. This facility can be used with scale factors of up to 100. The modelling room has a volume of 1350 cubic metres and its walls are covered with mineral wool carpet to minimize wall reflections. The models are built on a 10×10 m test table. They are generally made of high density expanded polystyrene blocks either painted or covered with a hard resin or absorbing material, depending on the absorption coefficients required. Each noise source consists of four air jets which are located in a steel cavity of 2 cm diameter. Air is fed with air under pressure to the jets by a system which can control up to 100 sources at one time. The sources are attached to the table from underneath the road segments so that their top is at the level of the simulated road surface board. A $\frac{1}{8}''$ microphone is automatically moved from an overhead gantry system to each of the selected measurement points. Measurements can be taken at 100 reception points in less than 1 hour. The noise is analysed in third octave bands or directly processed in dB(A) using a computer which controls the operation of sources and receiver, the acquisition and filtering of measurements, and calculates traffic noise levels after weighting the propagation transfer values according to the traffic parameters.

This equipment is run by specialists and is used mainly for problems which require a large amount of data, e.g. construction of new roads, studies of interchanges, the optimization of noise protection devices involving large investments, or the development of architectural details for noise protection where calculation procedures are not suitable. It forms part of the set of methods recommended by the *Guide du Bruit*[60] for French traffic noise evaluation problems.

References

1 FAVRE, B. M. Noise emission of road vehicles: evaluation of some simple models. *J. Sound Vib.*, **91**, 571–582 (1983).
2 NELSON, P. M. The combination of noise from separate time varying sources. *J. Appl. Acoustics*, **6**, 1–21 (1973).
3 JOHNSON, D. R. and SAUNDERS, E. G. The evaluation of noise from freely flowing road traffic. *J. Sound Vib.*, **7**, 287–309 (1968).
4 RATHE, E. J. Note on two common problems of sound propagation. *J. Sound Vib.*, **10**, 472–479 (1969).
5 WEISS, G. On the noise generated by a stream of vehicles. *Transport Res.*, **4**, 229–233 (1970).
6 KURZE, H. J. Frequency curves of road traffic noise. *J. Sound Vib.*, **33**, 171–185 (1974).
7 MAURIN, M. Calcul des niveaux de bruit élevés produits par des véhicules aléatoires dans les trafics faibles. In *11th International Congress on Acoustics*, Paris, Proceedings Vol. 7, pp. 349–352 (1983).
8 GALLOWAY, W. J., CLARK, W. E. and KERRICK, J. S. *Urban Highway Noise: Measurement, Simulation, and Mixed Reactions. NCHRP Report 78*, Highway Research Board (1969).
9 LAMURE, C. The Twelfth Sir Richard Fairey Memorial Lecture: the annoyance due to road traffic noise, the mathematical modelling of such noise and the sound proofing of road vehicles. *J. Sound Vib.*, **79**, 351–386 (1981).
10 FAVRE, B. M. Noise at the approach to traffic lights: results of a simulation program. *J. Sound Vib.*, **58**, 563–578 (1978).
11 KUTRUFF, H. Zur Berechnung von Pegelmittelwerten und Schwankungsgrössen bei Strassenlärm. *Acustica*, **32**, 57–69 (1975).
12 MAKAREWICZ, R. Theoretical foundations of urban noise control. *J. Acoust. Soc. Am.*, **74**, 543–558 (1983).
13 FAVRE, B. M. Méthode pour établir la relation entre le bruit émis par les véhicules routiers et l'impact de ce bruit sur les populations exposées. *Thèse de Doctorat d'Etat, Université de Lyon* (1984).
14 HOTHERSALL, D. C. and JONES, R. R. K. Observed and predicted traffic noise levels around road junctions in the United Kingdom. *ARRB Proceedings*, vol. 8, session 33, pp. 31–36 (1976).
15 Motorway noise and dwellings. *Building Research Establishment Digest*, No. 153 (1973).
16 DELANY, M. E. Prediction of Traffic Noise Levels. National Physical Laboratory Report AC 56 (1972).
17 FISK, D. J., SMITH, G. C. and FILTON, F. Prediction of urban traffic noise. In *Eighth International Congress on Acoustics Proceedings*, Vol. 1, Institute of Acoustics, Edinburgh p. 108 (1974).
18 GILBERT, D., MOORE, L. and SIMPSON, S. *Noise from Urban Traffic under Interrupted Flow Conditions*. TRRL Supplementary Report 620 (1980).
19 NELSON, P. M. *A Computer Model for Determining the Temporal Distribution of Noise from Road Traffic*. TRRL Report LR 611 (1973).
20 DELANY, M. E. Traffic noise prediction techniques for use in environmental planning. In *Models and Systems in Architecture and Building* (ed. Hawkes, D.) The Construction Press Limited, Lancaster (1975).
21 FAVRE, B. M. Urban road traffic noise: characteristics and computation methods. U.K. *Institute of Acoustics, Spring Conference 1984 Proceedings*, Institute of Acoustics, Edinburgh pp. 211–218 (1984).
22 DELANY, M. E., HARLAND, D. G., HOOD, R. A. and SCHOLES, W. E. The prediction of noise levels L10 due to road traffic. *J. Sound Vib.*, **48**, 305–325 (1976).
23 FRANKLIN, R. E., HARLAND, D. G. and NELSON, P. M. *Road Surfaces and Traffic Noise*. TRRL Laboratory Report 896 (1979).
24 NELSON, P. M. and ROSS, N.F. *Noise from Vehicles Running on Open Textured Road Surfaces*. TRRL Supplementary Report 696 (1981).
25 Unpublished data from the Transport and Road Research Laboratory, U.K.
26 FISK, D. J. Attenuation of L_{10} by long barriers. *J. Sound Vib.*, **38**, 305–316 (1975).
27 PARKIN, P. H. and SCHOLES, W. E. The horizontal propagation of sound from a jet engine close to the ground at Radlett. *J. Sound Vib.*, **1**, 1–13 (1964).
28 PARKIN, P. H. and SCHOLES, W. E. The horizontal propagation of sound from a jet engine close to the ground at Hatfield. *J. Sound Vib.*, **2**, 353–374 (1965).
29 DELANY, M. E. and BAZLEY, E. N. A note on the effect of ground absorption in the measurement of aircraft noise. *J. Sound Vib.*, **16**, 315–322 (1971).
30 PIERCY, J. E., EMBLETON, T. F. W. and SUTHERLAND, L. C. Review of noise propagation in the atmosphere. *J. Acoust. Soc. Am.*, **61**, 1403–1418 (1977).
31 EMBLETON, T. F. W. Sound propagation outdoors: improved prediction schemes for the 80s. *Noise Control Eng.*, **18**, 30–39 (1982).

32 CHESSEL, C. I. Propagation of noise along a finite impedance boundary. *J. Acoust. Soc. Am.*, **62,** 825–834 (1977).

33 CHESSEL, C. I. Predicting noise propagation near the earth's surface. In *Tenth International Congress of Acoustics Proceedings*, Australian Acoustical Society, Sydney pp. 43–56, (1980).

34 RASMUSSEN, K. B. Sound propagation over grass-covered ground. *J. Sound Vib.*, **78,** 247–255 (1981).

35 RASMUSSEN, K. B. *Sound Propagation over Non-flat Terrain*. Danish Acoustical Institute. Lydteknisk Institut Technical Report No. 35, Lyngby, Denmark (1982).

36 SCHOLES, W. E., SALVIDGE, A. C. and SARGENT, J. W. Motorway noise propagation and screening. *J. Sound Vib.*, **38,** 281–303 (1975).

37 DELANY, M. E. and BAZLEY, E. N. Acoustical properties of fibrous absorbent materials. *J. Appl. Acoust.* **3,** 105–116 (1970).

38 DELANY, M. E., COPELAND, W. C. and PAYNE, R. C. *Propagation of Traffic Noise in Typical Urban Areas*. National Physical Laboratory Report AC 54 (1971).

39 *Calculation of Road Traffic Noise*. Department of the Environment and Welsh Office joint publication, HMSO, London (1975).

40 *Le Guide du Bruit des Transports Terrestres: Recommendations techniques pour écrans et couvertures*. Ministère de l'Environnement, Ministère des Transports, Paris (1979).

41 KURZE, U. J. Noise reduction by barriers. *J. Acoust. Soc. Am.*, **55,** 504–518 (1974).

42 KELLER, J. B. Geometrical theory of diffraction. *J. Opt. Soc. Am.*, **52,** 116–130 (1962).

43 REDFEARN, S. W. Some acoustical source-observer problems. *Phil. Mag. Ser.*, **7,** 223–236 (1940).

44 MAEKAWA, Z., Noise reduction by screens. *Mem. Fac. Eng., Kobe Univ.* **11,** 29–53 (1965).

45 MAY, D. N. and OSMAN, M. M. Highway noise barriers: new shapes. *J. Sound Vib.*, **71,** 73–102 (1980).

46 HAYEK, S. I., LAWTHER, J. M., KENDIG, R. P. and SIMOWITZ, K. T. *Investigation of Selected Noise Barrier Acoustical Parameters*. National Cooperative Highway Research Program Report, project 3-26, Transportation Research Board, Washington, D.C. 20418 (1978).

47 SEZNEC, R. Diffraction of sound around barriers: use of the boundary element techniques. *J. Sound Vib.*, **73,** 195–209 (1980).

48 JONASSON, H. G. Sound reduction by barriers on the ground. *J. Sound Vib.*, **22,** 113–126 (1972).

49 SCHOLES, W. E., SALVIDGE, A. C. and SARGENT, J. W. Barriers and traffic noise peaks. *Appl. Acoust.*, **5,** 205–222 (1972).

50 MOERKERKEN, A. and VAN WIJK, H. J. L. Meteorological influences on the transmission of traffic noise. *Inter-Noise 79*, pp. 507–510 (1979).

51 MEHRA, S. R. and GERTIS, K. Mittelungspegel beider Ausbreitung von Strassenverkehrslärm in Wohngebiet unter verschiedenen meteorologischen Bedingungen. *Zeitschr. Lärmbekämpfung*, **30,** 127–134 (1983).

52 KRAGH, J. Road traffic noise attenuation by belts of trees and bushes. Danish Acoustical Institute. *Lydteknisk Institut Technical Report* No. 31, Lyngby, Denmark (1982).

53 BARRY, R. P. and REAGAN, J. A. *FHWA Highway Traffic Noise Prediction Model*, FHWA-RD-77-108 Report, Federal Highway Administration, Washington, D.C. 20590 (1978).

54 LYON, R. H. Role of multiple reflections and reverberation in urban noise propagation. *J. Acoust. Soc. Am.*, **55,** 493–503 (1974).

55 STEENACKERS, P., MYNCKE, H. and COPS, A. Reverberation in town streets. *Verkeerlawaai, Nederland akoestisch genootschap, Belgische akoestische vereiniging, Publikatie* No. 38, (1976).

56 DAVIES, H. G. Multiple-reflection diffuse-scattering model for noise propagation in streets. *J. Acoust. Soc. Am.*, **64,** 517–521 (1978).

57 SHAW, E. A. G. and OLSON, N. Theory of steady-state urban noise for an ideal homogeneous city. *J. Acoust. Soc. Am.*, **51,** 1781–1793 (1972).

58 WIENER, F. M., MALME, C. I. and GOGOS, C. M. Sound propagation in urban areas. *J. Acoust. Soc. Am.*, **37,** 738–747 (1965).

59 FAVRE, B. M. Acoustical excitation of buildings by road vehicle low frequency noise. *Inter-Noise 83* (1983).

60 BAR, P., FAVRE, B. M. and RAPIN, J. M. *Guide du Bruit des Transports Terrestres; Prévision des Niveaux Sonores*. Ministère de l'Environnement, Ministère des Transports, Paris (1980).

61 AUBREE, D., AUZOU, M. and RAPIN, J. M. *Etude de la Gêne due au Trafic Automobile Urbain*, Rapport CSTB, Paris (1972).

62 WESLER, J. E. *Manual for Highway Noise Prediction*, Report DOT-TSC-FHWA-72-1, USA (1972).

63 Nordic Council of Ministers' project. *The Computing Model for Road Traffic Noise*, Statens Planverk Report No. 48 (1980).

64 *Le Guide du Bruit*, Ministère de l'Equipement, SETRA Paris (1972.

65 WESLER, J. E. Highway traffic noise prediction: a state-of-the-art review. *Sound Vib.*, **February,** 12–16 (1977).

66 MYNCKE, H., COPS, A. and DE BELDER, P. *Guide Line for the Calculation of Road Traffic Noise*, Final report to the Commission of the European Community, *Laboratorium voor Akoestiek en Warmtegeleiding*, K.U. Leuven, Belgium (1980).

67 NELSON, P. M. and FANSTONE, J. *Estimates of the Reduction of Traffic Noise Following the Introduction of Quieter Vehicles*, TRRL Laboratory Report 624 (1974).

68 HOLMES, D. G. and LYON, R. H. A numerical model of sound propagation in urban areas. Presented at *The Second Interagency Symposium on University Research in Transportation Noise*, North Carolina State University, 5–7 June (1974).

69 LESCHNIK, W. Zur Schallausbreitung in bebauten und bepflanzten Gebieten. *Acustica*, **44,** 14–22 (1980).

70 LEE, K. P. and DAVIES, H. G. Nomogram for estimating noise propagation in urban areas. *J. Acoust. Soc. Am.*, **57,** 1477–1480 (1975).

71 RATHE, E. J. *MODEL 77, Computer Model for Noise*, Swiss Federal Office for Environmental Protection report (1980).

72 FAVRE, B. M. Prévision du bruit routier: quelques développements récents. *Revue d'Acoustique*, **65,** 79–85 (1983).

73 THOMASSEN, H. G. Computer calculation and representation of traffic noise situations in urban areas. *OECD Symposium on Roads and Urban Environment-Proceedings*—Madrid—October (1974).

74 ANDERSON, G. S. *Acoustical Scale Modeling of Roadway Traffic Noise: a literature Review*. Bolt, Beranek and Newman Inc., Report 3630 to Federal Highway Administration (1978).

Methods of Controlling Traffic Noise Impact

11

B. Buna BSc, PhD, MIOA
Institute for Transport Sciences,
Budapest, Hungary

and

M. Burgess BSc, MSc, MAAS
School of Architecture,
University of New South Wales,
Kensington, Australia

Contents

There are two main methods of controlling the impact of traffic noise on communities. One approach is to attempt to reduce noise at its source by the design of quieter vehicles and quieter road surfaces. The second approach involves attempts to limit the spread of noise, once generated, by considering such factors as the traffic flow, the road design and alignment, the use of noise screens and barriers and by planning the land use alongside the road to minimize disturbance to sensitive areas.

A further technique involves the insulation of buildings to minimize the incursion of noise into sensitive areas within the building fabric itself.

This chapter is divided into two parts. The first part deals with control of traffic noise through improvements to the road design, traffic controls and land use and the second part deals with the techniques used to insulate buildings. The control of traffic noise at source by improvements to the design of vehicles is mainly described in Chapters 7 and 8.

11.1 Traffic measures, road design and land use

11.1.1 Traffic measures

The most important factors affecting the noise generated by the traffic stream are the traffic volume and the composition of heavy commercial vehicles in the traffic flow, the traffic speed and whether the flow can be described as free flowing or interrupted as at traffic lights and junctions where vehicle interactions occur.

11.1.1.1 Traffic volume

The most obvious way to reduce traffic noise is to move the traffic away from the noise-sensitive section of the road. Halving the traffic flow, for example, will generally lead to reductions in traffic noise L_{10} and L_{eq} levels of the order of 3 dB(A). However, closing road sections from all traffic can present problems of access. For example, when a general traffic ban was imposed between 10 p.m. and 6 a.m. in the city of Nurnberg, approximately 600 exemptions were issued to allow residents normal access, and the movement of these vehicles reduced substantially the effectiveness of the ban.[1]

The effect of traffic volume controls depends not only on the proportion of traffic removed but also on the volume of traffic both before and after the traffic restrictions. Halving the traffic

flow will reduce L_{eq} provided other parameters do not change. However, traffic volume and speed are generally highly correlated and so a reduction in volume is normally associated with an increase in traffic speed with the result that the optimum benefits expected from the reduced flow are not achieved. Furthermore, removing traffic from one road produces an increase in noise on other roads in the network. However, the fact that traffic noise level and traffic flow are logarithmically related can be used to good effect; for example, taking traffic from a lightly used road and placing it on an already heavily used road will place little additional noise burden on the heavily used road, particularly if it is designed for high flow, but the benefits achieved on the lightly used road can be very substantial. Consequently, by-passes which are specifically designed to take high traffic flows to relieve a network of residential streets from traffic can produce very substantial noise benefits to large numbers of people. For cities and towns where by-passes do not already exist it may be possible to make use of shopping streets by re-routing traffic through these streets during the night. The city of Zurich has introduced such a scheme.[1]

An example of the effectiveness of a by-pass can be seen by examining the data given in *Table 11.1*. The table illustrates the change in flow and resulting noise levels at five sites in the city of Vienna before and after the opening of a new road.[2] The reduction in L_{eq} varied between zero and 4 dB(A).

Methods used to reduce the noise from traffic also include restricting the numbers of heavy trucks using 'sensitive' routes. These techniques generally take the form of bans on heavy vehicles entering a prescribed district either in the form of a total ban on all commercial vehicles above a certain capacity or in the form of restrictions at certain times, usually at night and over the weekend.

In this regard the city of Stockholm has implemented the following regulations specifically to reduce traffic noise:

1. No heavy trucks ($3\frac{1}{2}$ tonnes or over) were allowed at night (10 p.m.–6 a.m.).
2. Long trucks (12 m in length or greater) were restricted to use only designated highways and streets.
3. Heavy trucks were restricted to designated routes.

In West Germany all trucks over 7.5 tonnes are restricted from using a main highway between Bonn and Koblenz during the hours of 10.00 p.m. to 6.00 a.m. In England, the British Government has, through the co-operation of local authorities, introduced a national system of truck routes. In addition, local areas

Table 11.1 Traffic noise levels at five sites before and after the opening of the south-east road tangent in Vienna[2]

Site	Hourly Traffic Flow	0600–1800 hours $L_{eq}/L_1/L_{95}$ (dB(A))	2200–0600 hours $L_{eq}/L_1/Leq_{95}$ (dB(A))	L_{eq} (quietest hour) (dB(A))
		Before opening		
1	4025	75/83/67	70/79/58	66
2	4785	82/89/65	75/85/55	72
3	681	74/85/60	67/79/49	59
4	1491	75/85/58	69/82/47	62
5	2297	75/82/66	68/77/47	63
		After opening		
1	3019	73/80/64	66/75/55	63
2	3772	81/88/65	74/84/55	69
3	297	70/80/56	63/76/47	57
4	743	71/81/52	65/78/49	54
5	1523	75/81/64	68/78/45	63

needing special relief can be protected by banning trucks from entering unless they are needed to collect or deliver goods.[3]

In Switzerland, a dozen streets in Zurich are currently closed to mopeds and motor cycles between 10.00 a.m. and 7.00 p.m. in order to protect the local hospitals and residential areas from noise, and since 1959 vehicles passing through Lausanne have had to go around the city during the night time. In addition, heavy trucks are not allowed to run anywhere in the country during the night with the exception of buses, fire engines and trucks carrying certain perishable goods. In Bonn, public money has been spent on extending trolley bus routes at the expense of bus routes since this form of transport causes less pollution and noise. The Federal Capital of Switzerland probably provides the best example of a combination of traffic measures to combat noise impact, involving a ban on trucks, vehicle-free zones and very quiet public transport.[4]

11.1.1.2 Traffic speed

Theoretically, the reduction of traffic speed is one of the most effective traffic measures controlling traffic noise levels. On high speed roads, halving the average vehicle speed could lead to L_{eq} noise level reductions of between 5 and 6 dB(A). However, reductions of vehicle speed cannot easily be achieved in practice. Speed limits are commonly imposed but, as is shown in *Table 11.2*, where a speed limit of 50 km/h was imposed in four streets in Vienna a large proportion of the motoring population exceed the speed limit.

Table 11.2 Actual vehicle speed values at a limit of 50 km/h (Results are given as percentage of vehicles not exceeding given speed.)

Street No.	Speed (km/h)		
	50	75	100
1	17	90	100
2	15	80	100
3	35	98	100
4	32	96	100

Greater success at achieving speed reductions can be obtained using humps laid across the road surface or by 'striping' the road to give the motorist a greater awareness of speed. Other techniques include road narrowing and road bending. In Berlin a variety of such techniques have been tried at different locations.[5] Road narrowing was established by introducing car parking bays perpendicular to the traffic stream, and road bending was introduced by varying the orientation of parking bays and by introducing coned areas for pedestrian use. A brief description of the measures taken at 5 road sites is given in *Table 11.3*, and *Table 11.4* gives some examples of the results obtained. It can be seen that the speeds were substantially

Table 11.3 Speed reducing measures adopted in five streets in Berlin

Street No.	Road narrowing	Road bending	Perpendicular parking	Parallel parking
1	X	X	X	X
2	X	X	X	X
3	X		X	X
4	X	X	X	
5	X		X	X

reduced at all the sites listed with an average reduction of 12 km/ h. Also the number of noisy events characterized by peak levels greater than 75 dB(A) were in some cases drastically reduced. In most cases the control measures introduced achieved noise reductions of typically 2–3 dB(A) L_{eq}.

Other results, however, do not support the observations made in Berlin.[6] It is clear that the design of the traffic speed restriction method is very important. The measures taken should introduce sufficient restraint on the motorist to introduce speed changes without affecting gear changing which could result in a net increase in noise levels. The methods adopted should also ensure that traffic flows freely through the site to encourage a non-aggressive style of driving. Speed control measures can have other positive advantages. For example, in the UK it was found that striping the road surface on the approach to roundabouts reduced accidents in the vicinity of those junctions by 50%.

11.1.2 Road design

The noise radiated by traffic can be influenced both by the vertical and horizontal alignment of the road and also by designing the type of road surface used. These aspects of the design of the road are often a major consideration at the planning stage.

11.1.2.1 Roadside noise barriers

While the construction and design of roadside barriers may be considered to form part of land use control, in general they are considered to form part of the road design. An acoustic barrier is normally some form of vertical wall although a wide range of designs have been adopted in practice mainly to attempt to improve the aesthetics of the noise screen rather than to improve its screening performance. The design objectives for a successful noise barrier are that it must possess sufficient mass to attenuate the sound, it must be relatively maintenance free once installed and must not result in an increased risk of accident or injury. Other objectives are that it should be economical to erect and have an acceptable visual appearance.

The UK Department of the Environment has given advice on the siting and construction of noise barriers in *Technical Memorandum H14/76*.[7] It states that in order to provide an optimum degree of protection the barrier should be sited near to the noise source or close to the position to be protected and should, if possible, completely obscure the road from view at the buildings or space to be protected. Although the mass of the barrier need not be high because of the limited potential for screening in practice, it is important that all gaps in the barrier are properly sealed. A hole or gap in the barrier fabric may substantially reduce the screening potential of the barrier but also because of resonance effects created by the hole, the character of the transmitted sound can be altered—changing a broad band noise to one with discrete tones. For most practical applications the minimum mass of the barrier material can be determined from the site geometry according to the expression:

$$M = 3 \times \text{antilog}\left(\frac{\Delta L - 10}{14}\right) \text{ kg/m}^2$$

where ΔL (positive) is the potential barrier attenuation and M is the barrier mass (kg/m²). Where the construction consists of more than one panel with an air gap, the minimum mass requirement should be met by each single panel of the construction.

The screening provided by a barrier meeting the above requirements depends upon the path difference between the shortest path over the top of the barrier between noise source and receiver and the length of the direct line between the two.

Table 11.4 Measured result taken before and after the introduction of speed reducing measures

Street No.	L_{eq} level dB(A)		Traffic volume (vehicle/h)		Proportion of heavy vehicles (per cent)		No. of maximum levels ⩾75 (dB(A)/h)		Average speed (km/h)	
	Before	After	Before	After	Before	After	Before	After	Before	After
1	70.3	62.7	430	220	9	8	129	19	38	23
2	65.5	63.2	110	120	17	10	44	39	30	23
3	65.4	63.2	147	138	7	5	56	23	35	27
4	70.0	66.0	760	330	7	8	146	42	45	37
5	69.6	69.9	517	1135	15	17	124	119	57	34

The sound energy generated by traffic can be reflected by a barrier wall effecting receivers located on the source side of the barrier. When there are barriers on both sides of the road a further problem may occur as a result of multiple reflections between the barrier walls. With these configurations the screening potential of each barrier can be significantly reduced as a result of additional noise diffracted over the barrier from the image sources. The mathematical description of noise barrier attenuation including double barrier configurations is given in Chapter 10.

In the UK the height of most roadside barriers is limited to 3 m whereas in Canada, the USA and some European countries, higher barriers are permitted. Higher barriers than 4 m are generally considered to be visually unacceptable to residents. Apart from the height, the shape of the barrier is also important. A simple wall is generally less effective than a berm of similar height. Scale-model investigations have established that T-profile barriers produce greater noise attenuation than equivalent height conventional barriers (*see also* Chapter 10).

Wind loading, snow loading and drifting, and the possibility of road icing in the shadow of a barrier are all important safety considerations. The materials used should also withstand vehicle impacts and not shatter into dangerous fragments. The location of barriers over bridges, viaducts etc., need special considerations because of the need to safeguard roads etc., passing underneath, from falling debris resulting from a vehicle impact. Clearly, an effective barrier must not deteriorate rapidly under the action of sunlight and other weathering effects. The surface mass of wooden barriers should be maintained during installation and not be subject to warping, etc.

Many different types of barrier materials have been used in practice and it is beyond the scope of this chapter to review all these designs. Briefly, barriers can be classified as either reflective or absorptive. The reflective type of barrier is most common and is usually constructed in prefabricated panels. Close-boarded wooden barriers are fairly typical but other materials include vinyl plastic, pre-cast concrete, earth barriers, cellular concrete, aluminium, Devon bank, and caged rock type constructions. Absorbing barriers are intended to reduce the amount of reflected sound from the barrier surface.

Again many designs have been suggested and tried. A typical construction consists of a hollow box type panel which, on the motorway side, has a perforate or open steel face. The box is then filled with an absorbing material such as mineral wool.[8]

11.1.2.2 Elevated and depressed roads

Roads can be elevated above the surrounding land at grade or can be depressed in cuttings. Roads in cuttings are generally well screened by the edge of the screening wall although reflections from the far wall can reduce the screening performance. Elevated roads generally produce greater environmental noise problems but some screening will occur for reception points located below the edge of the embankment or parapet.

An example of an elevated structure is given in *Figure 11.1*. It can be seen that at positions generally below the level of the road surface the noise levels are below 65 dB(A) L_{eq} (1-hour) whereas at distance within 25 m of the structure and above the road height the noise levels range between 70 and 75 dB(A).

An example of the noise field surrounding a section of depressed road is shown in *Figure 11.2*.[9] Various depths of cutting are illustrated ranging from 3 m to 9 m. It can be seen that the noise levels were not greatly affected by the depth of cutting because the improved screening provided by the increased depth of cut is offset by the increase in reflected noise from the opposite wall of the cut area. The separating wall at the centre of the cut screens the direct sound from the second traffic lane causing substantially reduced noise levels in the vicinity of the edge of the cutting. Improvements in the screening provided by this type of configuration can be obtained by reducing the reflectivity of the surface of the reflecting wall or by sloping the reflecting wall away from the vertical. A slope of 15 degrees is usually sufficient to ensure a substantial reduction in reflected noise.

Where the space is not limited, the cutting can be formed by embankments with slopes in excess of 45 degrees. *Figure 11.3* illustrates a typical section.[10] In this case extra screening was required on one side and so the height of the embankment was raised to 8.5 m above the road surface using the soil excavated during the construction of the road. The noise reductions

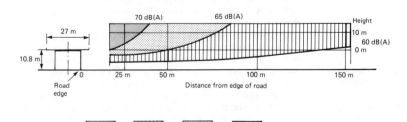

55-60 dB(A)   60-65 dB(A)   65-70 dB(A)   70-75 dB(A)

Figure 11.1 L_{eq} noise levels in vicinity of the Theodor-Heuss bridge, Düsseldorf (1978). Traffic flow=4425 vph, heavy vehicle composition=5%, average traffic speed=75 km/h approximately

(a) Depth 3 m

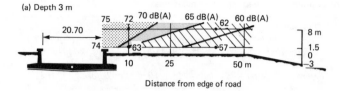

Distance from edge of road

(b) Depth 6 m

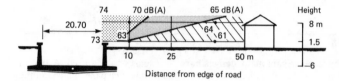

Distance from edge of road

(c) Depth 9 m

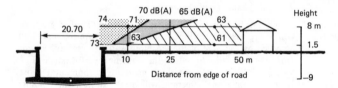

Distance from edge of road

(d) Depth 9 m — with middle wall and one-side louvred

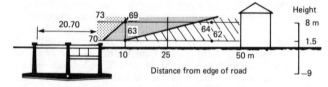

Distance from edge of road

Figure 11.2 L_{eq} noise levels in vicinity of a road in cutting. Traffic flow=3000 vph; heavy vehicle composition ≤4%; average traffic speed=70 km/h

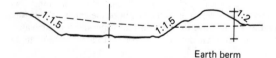

Earth berm

Figure 11.3 Typical cross-section of a cutting, extended by an earth berm

achieved were in the region of 6–8 dB(A) and this was achieved at minimal increased cost due to the more efficient management of the earthworks.

As mentioned previously, the acoustical performance of a cut depends particularly on the form and slope of the reflecting wall and the degree of absorption offered by the surface material.

The design of retained cut structures has been studied using scale models.[9] *Figure 11.4* illustrates the forms of structures investigated. It was found that absorptive lining placed on the retaining walls generally resulted in an additional noise reduction of 3 dB(A) within 25 m from the edge of the cutting and up to 6 dB(A) at greater distances. The greater the ratio between depth and width of the cutting i.e. where h/b increases, the greater was the effectiveness of the absorbing lining. In practice it is not necessary to place absorbing material on the lower parts of the wall up to say, 1.5 m, from the road level. This region of the wall does not contribute greatly to the reflected component and is also the area most likely to deteriorate in use due to water, dirt and chemicals thrown up by the traffic. The additional acoustic performance obtained by a particular cutting fitted with absorptive wall linings is shown in *Figure 11.5* for a range of distances and heights.

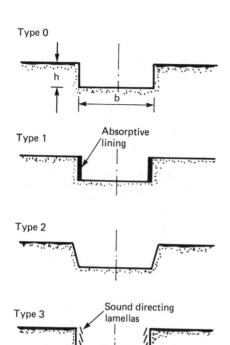

Type 0

Type 1
Absorptive lining

Type 2

Type 3
Sound directing lamellas

Type 4
Absorptive lining

Figure 11.4 Shapes of cuttings used for scale-model investigations

The effect of slope of the reflecting wall has almost the same effect on noise reduction in the lower range of receiver heights as the absorptive lining of the walls, given that the depth–width ratio remains constant. The corresponding noise reduction curves for a retained cut with 15 degree sloping walls is shown in *Figure 11.6*. A similar result was obtained for the vertical retained cut fitted with reflecting lamellas.

The depressed road overhang shown in section as type 4 on *Figure 11.4* gave noise reductions in excess of those obtained with sloping retaining walls. The results are shown on *Figure 11.7*.

A practical design of a road in a cutting with overhang and

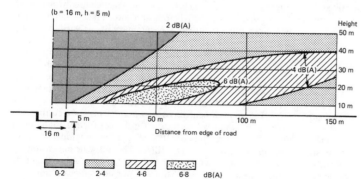

Figure 11.5 Noise reduction curves for a retained cut with absorptive vertical walls in comparison with those without lining

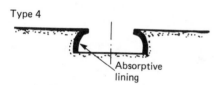

0-2   2-4   4-6   6-8   dB(A)

absorptive barriers is shown in *Figure 11.8*. Four different degrees of sound absorption treatments are indicated. The effectiveness of each case has been calculated for a traffic volume of 780 vph, a traffic speed of 95 km/h and 42% heavy vehicles.[11] These results are listed in *Table 11.5*.

Table 11.5 Computer-simulated traffic noise levels for the depressed road configuration given in *Figure 11.8*

Receiver		L_{eq} noise levels			
Distance (m)	Height (m)	Case 1 (dB(A))	Case 2 (dB(A))	Case 3 (dB(A))	Case 4 (dB(A))
22.5	1.2	52.6	49.3	49.2	47.6
22.5	3.5	54.6	51.0	50.5	48.9
22.5	7.0	58.9	55.4	54.3	51.6
22.5	10.0	62.7	59.4	57.2	54.5
60	1.2	45.6	44.4	43.7	43.7
60	3.5	48.6	46.7	45.7	45.7

The lowest noise levels were obtained for case 4 where a large amount of sound absorption treatment had been applied. In practice the need for lining reflecting surfaces with sound-absorbing material would need to be balanced against the cost of installation and the increased maintenance costs.

The planting of trees and shrubs along the edge of cutting can have an important effect on the screening performance. Generally trees and shrubs, when densely planted, will help to screen noise from a road at grade. Also, planting can help to improve the aesthetics of the road environment (*see also* Section 11.1.5 and Chapter 10). However, trees planted close to the edge of a cutting tend to cause a deterioration in the screening performance provided by the cut alone. The effect is more pronounced for shallow rather than deep retained cut.[12,13]

11.1.2.3 Tunnels and enclosures

Tunnels and enclosures form a natural extension to the retained cut form. The different kinds of retained structures with overhangs and coverings, tunnels enclosures and superstructures (building over the road) are shown diagrammatically in *Figure 11.9*.[14] These structures offer the advantages of very substantial noise screening over conventional retained cut structures, particularly for buildings located close to the road with high-rise accommodation. The disadvantage is the much higher cost involved and the need to provide artificial lighting and good ventilation. A further disadvantage is the fact that the noise levels inside the enclosure or tunnel are generally much higher than for an open road site (e.g. 4–10 dB(A) depending upon the degree of noise absorbing treatments applied to the tunnel walls).

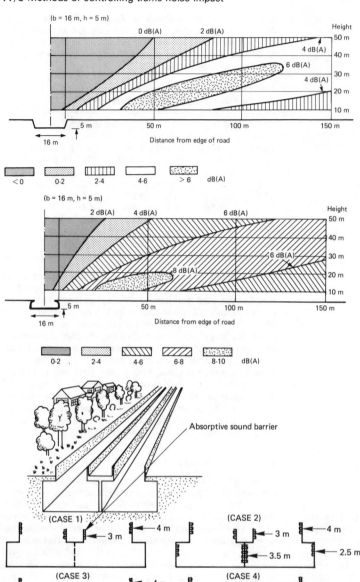

Figure 11.6 Noise reduction curves for a retained cut with sloped walls in comparison with those with vertical walls

Figure 11.7 Noise reduction curves for a cut with vertical wall and overhang both lined with absorptive material in comparison with those without lining and overhang

Figure 11.8 Cross-section of a complex road structure with different absorptive surfaces

A review of the costs involved in constructing tunnels and enclosures was carried out by Krell[14] in 1980. For a road with 2 × 2 lanes the investment costs per km in 1980 were estimated to be:

Tunnels	25–75 million DM
Retained cuts with cover	12–25 million DM
Enclosures	8–15 million DM

In addition, maintenance and servicing costs were estimated to be in the region of 0.8–1.2 million DM per km per year.

The effectiveness of enclosures to sections of retained cut, depends largely upon the design of the covering louvres. In most previous designs, the louvres are arranged in a series of quadri-lateral cells with vertical reflecting blades. However, a range of

alternative louvre designs have been suggested involving sloping blades, 'cornet'-shaped blades and level blade configurations with absorptive treatments. A summary of the various designs suggested is illustrated in *Figure 11.10*.[9]

The noise reduction achieved using a conventional reflective and vertical louvre blade construction is shown in *Figure 11.11*. The results were obtained using scale models.[9] The curves represent the additional noise reduction achieved compared with the retained cut configuration depicted as type 0 in *Figure 11.4*. The greatest benefits occur within 50 m of the cutting and 20 m above the road surface. At distances further than 100 m from the cutting the benefits offered by the louvred cover amount to approximately 2 dB(A). The full-scale dimensions of each cell in the cover were 1 × 1 m and 2 m deep. When the blade depth was increased to 2.5 m there was no significant improve-

Coverings   Enclosures

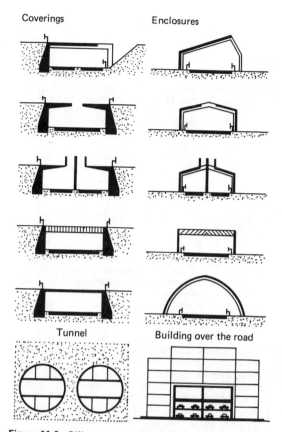

Figure 11.9 Different types of tunnels and enclosures

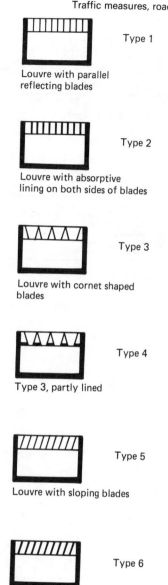

Type 1

Louvre with parallel reflecting blades

Type 2

Louvre with absorptive lining on both sides of blades

Type 3

Louvre with cornet shaped blades

Type 4

Type 3, partly lined

Type 5

Louvre with sloping blades

Type 6

Type 5 with absorptive lining

Figure 11.10 Typical shapes of louvres

ment in the screening effect; however, when the blade dimensions were reduced to 1.5 m, the screening potential was further improved by 1–2 dB(A) over the range of measurement locations studied.

The acoustic performance of the louvre design depends also upon the acoustic properties of the blade surfaces and the shape of the blades. An example of the additional screening provided by a louvre with absorbing material attached to both sides of the blade is illustrated in *Figure 11.12*. The improvement in screening is very dramatic over the whole of the measurement range. Typically reductions of 14 dB(A) were achieved within 75 m of the cutting. When comparing the performance of the different louvre designs depicted in *Figure 11.10* the following ranking was obtained:

type 2 (most effective): type 6: type 4: type 3: type 1 (least effective)

Further studies have examined the noise reductions achieved by louvres as a function of the total blade area treated with absorptive material per square metre of the assembled louvre. The results suggest that for most commonly used louvre designs the optimum surface area that should be treated, bearing in mind the overall cost of treating the louvre blade, is 4 m²/unit area of louvre. By adding further absorptive material the overall improvement of the louvre is not greatly improved and therefore the increased costs are not justified.

One further advantage of using louvres is that they offer greater effective screening for buildings located close to the cutting than conventional barriers. This is particularly relevant for multi-storey accommodation.[15] *Figure 11.13* illustrates this concept.

An example of the integrated design of a tunnel system and building is illustrated in *Figure 11.14*.[16] Examples of similar constructions can be found in other cities (e.g. Zurich). However, this type of structure only really becomes cost effective where land prices are very high and space is restricted. Furthermore, the insulation of the residential parts of the building for structure-borne vibration and noise from the traffic can be very expensive.

11.1.3 Designing road junctions to control noise

It was shown in Chapter 6 that noise from individual vehicles can increase substantially during acceleration, particularly when the initial vehicle speed is low and the subsequent load on the engine is high. Vehicle interactions involving stop–start manoeuvres and vehicle acceleration and deceleration occur at, and

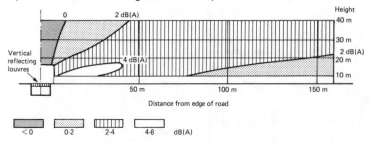

Figure 11.11 Noise reduction curves for a retained cut with a louvred enclosure consisting of reflecting parallel blades compared with a vertical cutting without louvres

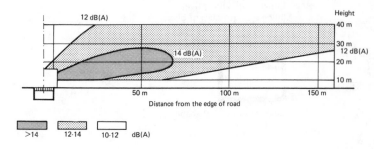

Figure 11.12 Noise reduction curves for a retained cut with louvred enclosure consisting of absorptive parallel blades compared with a vertical cutting without louvres

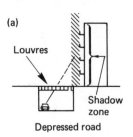

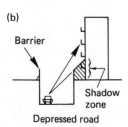

Figure 11.13 Depressed road configurations with (a) a louvred enclosure and (b) roadside barriers

on the approach to junctions. In order to reduce noise, therefore, it is important to consider, in the design of the junction, how best to smooth the flow of traffic to minimize the number of vehicle accelerations. Fortunately, this objective is also the objective of traffic management plans which are designed primarily to reduce journey times and accidents.

Linked or demand-controlled traffic-light systems have been developed and installed in practically every major city in the world. Unfortunately, the effect on traffic noise of these measures is rather less than expected partly because the improvements in flow resulting from these control systems tend to

generate an increase in capacity of the system which is rapidly filled and/or the speed of the traffic is increased. An example of noise changes following the installation of a traffic-light control system where 14 sets of signals were linked to a central computer is given in *Table 11.6*.[17] It can be seen that, although, in most cases the noise levels are reduced the overall benefits are generally small and in most cases are less than 2 dB(A).

Another measure which has been used to smooth the flow through junctions is to switch off the traffic lights at low-density junctions during the night.[18] Such measures, however, have not given rise to any systematic improvement in noise since vehicle speeds are generally increased which offsets the advantages arising from the fewer incidences where vehicles accelerate from rest.

Roundabouts tend to produce rather fewer noise problems than signalized intersections. In general, studies of the noise at roundabouts have indicated that the increased noise from vehicles accelerating is within 1 dB(A) of the free flow level on the approach roads and that noise from the decelerating stream is equal or less than the free flow level. Overall the noise at roundabouts may be increased above the level from an equivalent free flow traffic stream by approximately 1–2 dB(A) and this increase is generally confined to within 50 m of the centre of the roundabout.[19]

11.1.4 Designing the road surface to control noise

The noise generated by the vehicles tyres rolling over the road surface depends primarily on the speed of the vehicle and the design of the tyre and the road surface. Previous studies of tyre noise have established that while some benefits can be obtained by appropriate design of the tyre tread pattern and tyre structure, the design of substantially quieter tyres conflicts with the overriding need to maintain safety, cool running and economy (*see* Chapter 7 for further details of tyre noise research). Consequently, greater scope for reducing tyre/road surface noise lies with the possible alternative designs for the road surface.

The road surface parameters which appear to be important in governing surface noise are the texture applied to the road surface and whether the surface is a bituminous material with a

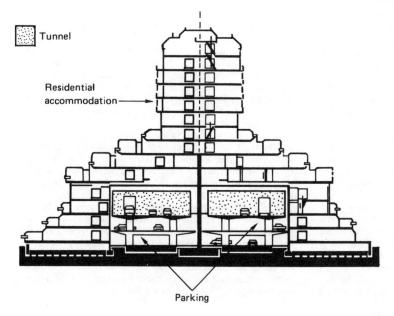

Tunnel

Residential accommodation →

Parking

Figure 11.14 Integrated highway and building design

Table 11.6 Measurements of noise changes following the installation of a computer controlled traffic light system (Urban Traffic Control, UTC)

Site	Before UTC	After UTC	distance from the signal (m)	L_{10} mean (dB(A))	L_{10} difference (dB(A))
	X		0–50	75.6	
		X	0–50	76.0	0.4
1	X		100	74.7	
		X	100	75.0	0.3
	X		270–330	78.0	
		X	270–330	74.9	−3.1
2	X		0–40	78.0	
		X	0–40	77.9	−0.1
3	X		0–50	77.1	
		X	0–50	77.0	−0.1
	X		100	76.8	
		X	100	75.0	−1.8
	X		0–50	74.1	
		X	0–50	73.9	−0.2
4	X		100–130	73.2	
		X	100–130	71.8	−1.4
	X		230–290	76.8	
		X	230–290	75.0	−1.8

random texture pattern or a concrete surface with a predominantly transverse texture. In two independent studies carried out by Sandberg and Descornet it was shown that for car tyres running on different surfaces, the road surface influence was largely dependent upon the macrotexture of the surface.[20] It was also shown that the correlation between noise and texture profile can be divided into two main frequency regions. For frequencies below 1500 Hz, the greatest correlations were obtained with texture wavelengths greater than 10 mm. Higher frequencies in the tyre/surface spectra were correlated with smaller scale texture wavelengths. It is suggested that two

separate mechanisms are involved, with the resulting tyre/surface spectrum being composed of two component or 'partial' spectra. The lower frequency elements of the spectra result from tyre vibration radiation whereas the higher frequencies are probably generated by an air pumping mechanism.

Measurements carried out in the UK have established a simple empirical relation between the skidding resistance afforded by the surface and the total noise generated by vehicles passing over the surface at high speeds.[21] This relation was found to be statistically independent of the type of texture pattern or surface material. Unfortunately, although the result is useful in setting standards for road surface finish which take into account both safety and environmental considerations, it does highlight the conflict that exists between the specifications of low noise surfaces and good high speed safety standards. For example, a smooth road surface can be relatively quiet but is clearly unsafe for the motorist in wet weather.

Fortunately, some road surfaces do not conform to this general pattern and appear to offer the combined advantage of both low noise and good skidding resistance performance. These surfaces generally have an open texture which is pervious to surface water but which also offers good acoustic absorption in the frequency range 400 Hz–2 kHz. *Figure 7.49* illustrates the acoustic absorption characteristics of different surfaces using core samples taken from trial sections of road surfaces. The higher acoustic absorption afforded by the open textured surface is clearly shown.

The benefits achieved in practice can be seen in *Figure 11.15*. The figure compares the peak noise level of cars running on a range of open textured road surfaces laid as part of a full scale trial on various roads in the UK with the generalized regression line obtained for cars running on a wide range of conventional non-pervious surfaces. In both cases the noise levels have been normalized to a steady passing speed of 90 km/h. It can be seen that the noise levels recorded at the open textured sites are all lower than the noise generated on conventional surfaces at equivalent skidding resistance values. The average reduction in peak noise level is 4.0 dB(A) and is highly significant. For heavy vehicles, the reduction in noise obtained was slightly less at approximately 3 dB(A). Consequently, the noise from traffic running on open textured road surfaces can be reduced by between 3 and 4 dB(A) on average depending upon the composition of trucks in the traffic and these benefits are achieved without any need to reduce the safety standards provided by the surface texture.[22]

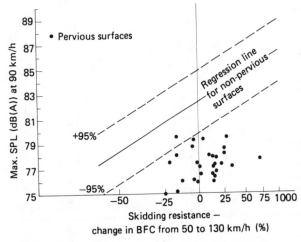

Figure 11.15 Light vehicle peak sound level and change in braking force coefficient (BFC) values for conventional and open textured surfacing

The pervious macadam material was found to retain its noise reduction properties during the effective life of the surface material and, due to its rapid drainage properties, it lessens the incidence of 'splash' noise during wet weather.[22]

In other countries, similar results to that obtained on open textured macadam have been obtained with an open graded covering using a rubberized asphalt as binder.[23] A test surface laid over a grooved concrete section of road on the ring motorway to the east of Brussels reduced the noise levels by about 4 dB(A) at car passing speeds of 70 km/h and 5.5 dB(A) at a speed of 120 km/h. Similarly, in Sweden an open-graded emulsified asphalt mixture[24] and in Canada[25] an open-graded carpet seal were found to reduce traffic noise levels. The latter was found to be 4–5 dB(A) quieter than a random textured asphalt and 3 dB(A) quieter than a worn concrete surface which was far less skid resistant.

In both Norway and Sweden, however, problems with the durability of these surfaces have been found which have been attributed to the action of studded tyres during the winter months. These tyres tend to grind the surface layer to a fine powder which then clogs the pores in the surface texture substantially reducing the absorption characteristics. A new type of surface material is currently being evaluated in Norway and Sweden. This surface has both high acoustic absorption and is highly elastic. The material is termed poro-elastic and it is claimed that the surface is not affected by studded tyres and is also very quiet. The noise reduction is achieved by a combination of acoustical absorption similar to that offered by the pervious macadam and a 'mechanical' reduction of rolling noise due to the reduced stiffness of the surface.

11.1.5 Noise control and land use planning

A major road or motorway generates very high noise levels in its immediate vicinity. When a new traffic route is planned through an existing urban area much of the existing built fabric will remain. Under these circumstances the layout of the road and design of the road itself becomes crucial in minimizing the noise impact resulting from the traffic. However, where a road passes through an area that is, as yet, undeveloped or scheduled for re-development, noise impact control by appropriate management of the adjoining land use can also be considered. Opportunities for successful acoustical site planning are determined by the size of the available space, the terrain and the zoning policy applied. Appropriate techniques include:

1. Placing as much distance as possible between the noise source and the noise-sensitive activity.
2. Placing noise-compatible activities such as parking bays, open spaces and commercial facilities between the noise source and the sensitive activity.
3. Using the built form and plantings as barriers to screen sensitive areas.

11.1.5.1 Zoning and spatial separation

Dwellings can be protected from traffic noise by setting them well back from the source of noise. However, this approach often fails to receive its proper attention from designers because it is assumed to be uneconomic. There is often truth in this assumption since, for example, on a level site next to a motorway the noise will rarely fall below 70 dB(A) at distances less than 100 m from the road. Nevertheless spatial separation should always be considered for in certain circumstances it is the only possible solution. This is especially true in mixed developments which include high-rise blocks, for these cannot be easily screened by barriers and should, therefore, be located as far from the road as the site allows. On such sites the remainder of low-rise dwellings can often be protected by some form of roadside barrier or by reliance on ground attenuation.

One way of ensuring that spatial separation is given full

consideration is for the local administration to impose a zoning policy whereby land adjoining a major road source has development restricted to non-noise sensitive activities (e.g. commerce, agriculture, industry). While such a technique does offer the advantages of clearly defined development policy, unfortunately there is usually not enough demand for such noise-compatible land use to afford adequate protection for every community exposed to noise. Furthermore, this type of strip zoning may not be compatible with other plans for the orderly growth and development of the community, or it could be in direct conflict with the development patterns of adjacent communities. Where areas blighted by traffic noise are not adopted by noise-compatible uses the land involved can become dreary, useless patches of waste land which are often too expensive to maintain.

While there is a need for caution in defining a general zoning policy for an area it is clear also that it can be made to work reasonably well when all sectors of the community combine to form an agreeable plan. For example, in France the towns of Cergy and Pontoise have adopted a system of zoning for land use alongside motorways. In these examples, no housing is allowed within 30 metres from the edge of the carriageway and apartments between 30 and 80 m have to have additional sound insulation. Along other roads, house construction is not permitted within 13 m from the edge of the carriageway.

11.1.5.2 Buildings and plantings as noise shields

Additional noise protection can be achieved by arranging the site plan to use buildings as noise barriers. A long building, or a row of buildings parallel to a highway can shield other more distant structures or open areas from noise. One study shows that a two-storey building can reduce noise levels on the side of the building away from the noise source by about 13 dB(A).[26] Further rows of buildings may only produce a small additional benefit, e.g. 1–2 dB(A) beyond the second row only.

Plants absorb and scatter sound waves and no precise description of their effect has yet been determined (*see also* Chapter 10). However, some general conclusions can be drawn:

1. Plantings which are high, and dense enough to obscure the traffic visually will provide more attenuation than that provided by the mere distance which the buffer strip represents. An attenuation of approximately 1 dB(A) per 10 m depth of planting can be expected. Shrubs or other ground cover are necessary in this respect to provide the required density near the ground.
2. The psychological effect of planting should not be ignored. By removing the noise source from view, plantings can reduce human annoyance to noise. The fact that people cannot see the highway can reduce their awareness of it even though the noise remains.

11.1.5.3 Cluster and mixed use development

A conventional grid subdivision of land affords no real noise protection from the adjacent highway since the first row of houses bears the full impact of the noise. In contrast, cluster developments enable the whole space to be planned as a single entity taking into account the required density of housing depending upon noise exposure and the use of both space and noise-compatible development as buffers.

Figures 11.16 and *11.17* show examples of cluster development concepts in close proximity to a major road.[27] In *Figure 11.16*, the placement of the light industrial units near to the road will provide some measure of screening to the dwellings located closest to the road. The dwellings further from the road are not as well screened but benefit from the increased distance. In this way an acceptable acoustical environment can be achieved for all residents in the estate. Similarly the cluster development concepts established in *Figure 11.17* show how the use of space placed near to the road can provide both protection for residences and both aesthetic appeal and community value.

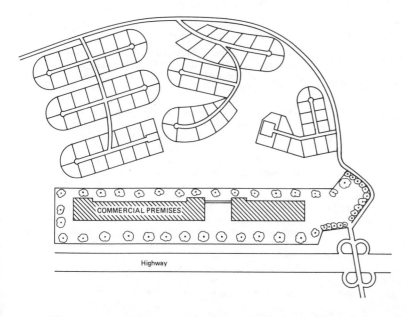

Figure 11.16 Placement of noise compatible land uses near highway

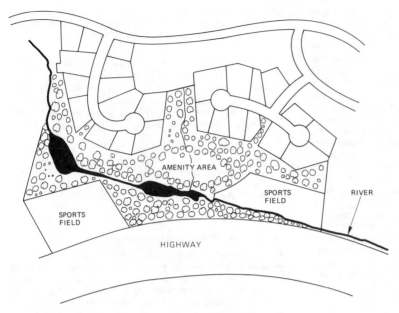

Figure 11.17 Using open space to reduce noise impact on residents

11.2 Insulation of buildings

11.2.1 Introduction

Reduction of the noise from the road traffic by the building itself should only be considered as a last resort; that is when insufficient reduction can be made at the source or between the source and the building. The additional cost of construction for noise-insulated dwellings has been estimated to be about 15% when the external L_{10} value is about 77 dB(A);[28] however by careful design this additional cost can be reduced to only 2 or 3%. At the planning and design stage of a new building the shape, orientation and location of the building and the arrangement of the internal spaces should be chosen to reduce the magnitude of the potential noise problem. In existing buildings there is sometimes scope to make the acoustic environment more acceptable by altering the use of the rooms, but in general it is necessary to improve the noise insulation provided by the building enclosure. When the noise reduction is to be provided by the building fabric it is essential that all possible paths for the transmission of sound are considered. Consequently there may be restrictions and limitations on the lifestyle of the people within the building. For example, windows cannot be opened to provide natural ventilation without reducing the sound insulation. It should also be remembered that while a satisfactory acoustic environment can be provided within the building, the spaces outside the building and near the road will still be subjected to traffic noise.

11.2.2 Guidelines for noise levels in buildings

The noise level within any room is a combination of the noise transmitted into the room and the noise generated within the room itself. The noise transmitted into the room can come from other rooms in the building or from outside the building and is often referred to as the background noise. The acceptable levels for the background noise are related to the activities taking place within the room. For example, there is less need to have a very low background noise level in a machine room where high levels of noise are being produced. The need for speech commu-

nication is also important when considering acceptable background noise levels. Communication over long distances requires much lower background noise levels than if the normal communication distance is only a metre or so. The influence of background noise on different aspects of communication is shown in *Table 11.7*.

Background sound levels which are considered to be acceptable inside buildings for different types of usage and activity are given in *Table 11.8*. These levels were taken from values suggested by the Australian Standards Association[30] and the US National Bureau of Standards.[31] They assume that the background noise is steady and does not contain any prominent tonal components. For each type of space the lower sound level of the range should be considered as the 'goal' level.

11.2.3 Design of buildings

11.2.3.1 Shape and orientation

The need for expensive construction with high sound insulation can be minimized if the shape and orientation of the building is planned with due regard to the noise from the road. The aim should be to avoid reflected sound from any wall surface being directed into the noise-sensitive rooms of the building itself or any nearby building. Some examples of building shapes which can exacerbate noise intrusion are shown on *Figure 11.18(a)*. These same building shapes can be positioned as shown on *Figure 11.18(b)* so that noise is not reflected back into the building. A bonus of the design shown in *Figure 11.18(b)* is that the building itself can be orientated to act as a barrier to the road traffic noise and thereby provide shielding for the spaces behind it.

The shape of the building can be utilized to provide a self-protecting building where some parts, such as wing walls and balconies, provide shielding from road traffic noise. Two examples of self-protecting buildings are shown on *Figure 11.19*. One is a high-rise building set well back on the site so that only the facade of the low-rise podium is exposed directly to the road traffic noise. In the second example the large glass areas, which generally have low sound insulation, are facing away from the

Table 11.7 Speech communication capabilities versus A-weighted sound level of background noise[29]

Communication	Below 50 dB(A)	50–70 dB(A)	70–90 dB(A)
Unamplified Speech	Normal voice at distances up to 6 m	Raised voice at distances up to 6 m	Shouted voice at distances up to 0.5 m
Telephone	Good	Satsifactory to difficult	Difficult to unsatisfactory
Intercom System	Good	Satisfactory to difficult	Unsatisfactory

Table 11.8 Guidelines for acceptable noise levels within buildings[30, 31]

Type of room	Background noise level dB(A))
Residential buildings:	
Work area	35–40
Living room	30–40
Bedroom	30–35
Commercial buildings:	
Office machine area	45–55
Reception and waiting area	40–45
General office	40–45
Private office	35–40
Conference room	30–35
Educational buildings:	
Gymnasia	45–55
Open space teaching area	40–45
Classroom	35–40
Assembly hall, small	30–35
Assembly hall, large	25–30
Auditoria:	
Motion picture theatre	35–40
Lecture theatre	30–35
Concert hall, theatre	25–35
Industrial areas where speech	
communication required	40–60
Restaurants	40–50
Department stores	45–55

road on one side of the building and shielding is provided by the shape of the building. The glass areas on the other side are protected by a solid wing wall which also provides a quiet courtyard.

A thin-walled courtyard between a house and the road has been shown to provide an attenuation in L_{10} of the order of 12 dB(A).[32] Oldham and Mohsen have also developed a design chart[32] for calculation of the reduction which can be obtained when balconies with solid walls are on the facade of a building facing the road. This chart shows that the reduction in L_{10} can range from 5 to 14 dB(A) depending upon the width of the window, the angle between the road and the window, the depth of the balcony and the height of the boundary wall. For balconies located well above the level of the traffic, the underside should be designed so as to reflect sound away from windows at lower levels or it should be covered with a sound absorbing material.

11.2.3.2 Arrangement of rooms

Within any building there will be some rooms in which the

people will be less annoyed by noise from outside than in other rooms, as outlined in Section 11.2.2. As road traffic noise is usually only a problem for the rooms facing directly towards the road, the noise-sensitive rooms should be identified and located on the other side of the building. The less noise-sensitive rooms can then provide a barrier to the penetration of the noise into the other rooms of the building, as illustrated in the examples given in *Figure 11.20*.

For existing buildings a similar approach can be used to minimize the need for expensive alterations to increase the sound insulation of the facade. In large commercial buildings there are usually a number of different types of rooms so a rearrangement of the internal space usage can allow for the noise-sensitive areas to be away from the road facade. Even in residential buildings the relocation of rooms should be considered. Renovations or extensions can often be planned so that the rooms requiring lower ambient noise levels are away from the road and shielded by the other rooms of the house.

11.2.4 Methods for assessing sound insulation

The sound insulation, level difference, noise reduction, sound reduction index and sound transmission loss are all terms relating to the ability of a building element to reduce the sound passing from one space to another via that element. These terms should not be confused with the sound absorption properties of a building component which are related to the ability of the material to reduce the reflection of sound within the space. Thus a solid brick wall has a high sound insulation and poor sound absorption, and a heavy lined curtain has lower sound insulation and higher sound absorption than a brick wall. The commonly used methods for assessing the sound insulation of buildings are described below.

11.2.4.1 Sound reduction index and sound transmission loss

The sound insulation of building elements is determined by the physical properties of the material, the type of construction and the method of installation and so varies with the frequency of the incident sound. The procedures for determining the sound insulation over the range of frequencies from around 100 Hz to around 4000 Hz are specified in National and International Standards.[33-35] The majority of the published data on the sound insulation of building materials is based on laboratory tests where the partition is located in a special frame between two reverberant rooms. One room is used as the source room and the other as the receiving room. The average sound level, in each one-third octave band, is determined for each room and the level differences calculated. When the level difference is corrected for the absorption in the receiving room (A) and the area of the partition (S) by adding the factor $10 \log_{10} \frac{S}{A}$ it is called the *sound reduction index* or the *sound transmission loss*.

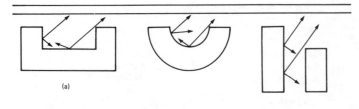

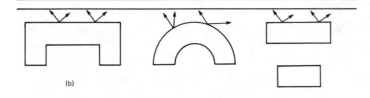

Figure 11.18 Examples of building shapes and orientations which (*a*) produce undesirable reflected sound and (*b*) provide shielding for quiet spaces

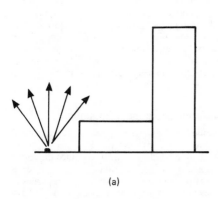

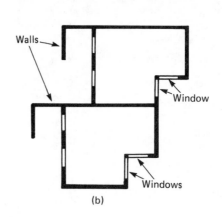

Figure 11.19 Examples of self-protecting buildings; (*a*) the podium provides shielding for most of the tower block and (*b*) the shape of the building provides shielding for the windows and the solid wing wall provides a quiet courtyard

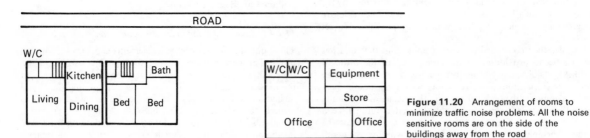

Figure 11.20 Arrangement of rooms to minimize traffic noise problems. All the noise sensitive rooms are on the side of the buildings away from the road

The procedures to be followed when measuring the transmission loss when the elements are installed in a building are also specified in Standards.[33-39] These level differences can be corrected in the same manner as for the laboratory tests or, if the area of the test partition is not clearly defined, they can be standardized to relate to a receiving room having a reverberation time of 0.5 seconds. The reverberation time, T, is the time taken for sound to decay by 60 dB, and the normalizing factor is $10 \log_{10} \frac{T}{0.5}$. Procedures are also specified for the measurement of sound insulation of the building facade with the existing traffic noise as the source in place of the loudspeaker generated noise required for the other tests.

Good agreement is not usually obtained between the laboratory and field measurements of sound transmission loss. The major factors that affect the tests in buildings are the presence of other paths for the transmission of sound, called flanking paths, and the nature of the sound field both on the source and receiving side.[36] Even when the laboratory test procedure is modified to allow for some flanking transmission, the field results have tended to be systematically lower than the laboratory results.[37] However, there is only a limited amount of field data for the sound insulation of facade elements so the laboratory data often have to be used. The fact that the sound insulation provided by the facade is likely to be less than predicted from the laboratory data should, of course, be taken into consideration.

11.2.4.2 Single number rating systems

In order to ensure that the most suitable constructions are chosen to provide acceptable sound levels it is necessary to determine the sound transmission loss at different frequencies within the rooms of a building. This is a complex task and so simple methods have been devised which describe the sound insulation of the construction in terms of a single figure rating. Such methods provide the basis for a coarse selection procedure.

The rating systems in common use are defined in various Standards[38-40] and involve comparison of the measured values of sound reduction index with a series of standard curves. Briefly, the methods require, in each case, the calculation of the sum of the unfavourable deviations, i.e. when the measured value is less than the value for the standard curve, over the frequency range of interest. For the ISO 717 method[38] the appropriate rating curve is the highest for which the sum of the unfavourable deviations between the sixteen one-third octave bands from 100 to 3150 Hz is not greater than 32 dB. The value of the standard rating curve at 500 Hz is then the *sound insulation index rating* (Rw). The rating curves for two examples are shown on *Figure 11.21*. For the masonry construction the unfavourable deviations occur in the mid-frequency range while for the window they occur at higher frequencies.

The *Sound Transmission Class*, or STC, is specified in ASTM E413-73[39] and is determined in a similar manner to that given in ISO 717.[38] The rating curve extends from 125 to 4000 Hz and while the sum of the adverse deviations must not be greater than

32 dB the adverse deviation at any one frequency must not exceed 8 dB.

Two other rating systems are often used to describe the sound insulation of constructions. One method which is rarely used now involves the calculation of the average of the sound transmission loss values over the range 100–3150 Hz.[41] The other method characterizes the sound reduction of building facades in terms of the difference in L_{eq} or L_{10} dB(A) measured simultaneously inside and outside the building.

All single number rating systems have limitations, especially when they are being used to compare the noise attenuation performance of various constructions when traffic noise is the source.[42] For example, the shape of the standard curves used for comparison with the measured values for sound transmission loss have been based on an analysis of domestic and commercial noises which exhibit a wide range of frequency characteristics which can be substantially different from traffic noise. Consequently by using a simple average correction curve, there is a risk that low values of sound transmission loss at some frequencies can be compensated for by high values at other frequencies thereby concealing the true performance of the construction. In addition, the method based on measured dB(A) reductions represents the sound reduction provided for a particular traffic noise spectrum and the same results would not necessarily be obtained for another traffic stream with a different frequency spectrum.

For all the limitations of single number rating systems they are useful for comparing the sound insulation of various constructions and in many cases may provide an adequate basis for selection. However, in circumstances where greater precision is required it will be necessary to compare the sound insulation of the construction over the frequency range with the spectrum of the actual noise source.

11.2.4.3 Sound insulation of composite structures

Few walls are composed of only one type of construction and the sound insulation of a wall comprising doors, windows etc. must be calculated using the sound insulation and area of each component part. For any one component the sound reduction index, R, is related to the transmission coefficient, t, by:

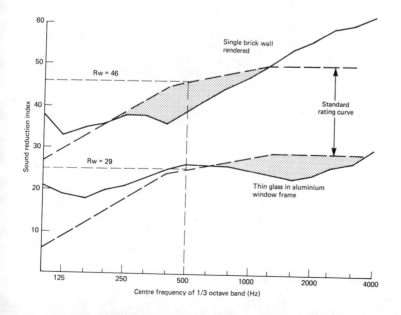

Figure 11.21 Sound insulation for two constructions[40] with the rating curve from ISO 717[38] in the correct position for each

$$R = -10 \log_{10} t \qquad (11.1)$$

The average transmission coefficient, t_{av}, for a wall with n component parts is :

$$t_{av} = \frac{t_1 S_1 + \dots t_n S_n}{S_1 + \dots S_n} \qquad (11.2)$$

where t_n is the transmission coefficient for the nth component and S_n is the area for the nth component. The sound reduction index for the complete wall can then be calculated by using t_{av} in Equation 11.1.

Alternatively the sound reduction index for a composite wall can be determined with the aid of *Figure 11.22* by considering two components at a time. For the first two components the one with the higher sound insulation is called component 1 and the steps are:

1. Determine the difference between the sound reduction indicies for the two components, $R_1 - R_2$.
2. Determine the ratio of the areas of the two components, S_2/S_1 where S_2 is the area of component 2 and S_1 the area of component 1.
3. From the point on the horizontal axis corresponding to $R_1 - R_2$ project a vertical line till it meets the curved line representing the appropriate area ratio.
4. Project horizontally from this intersection point towards the vertical axis to read the value for $R_1 - R_{av}$.
5. Calculate the average sound reduction index for the wall containing these two components by subtracting this value from R_1.

The above procedure is repeated with each additional component in turn and the final value represents the average performance of the complete wall.

The following example shows the use of *Figure 11.22* to determine the sound insulation for a wall, 5 m by 3 m, which is mainly brick but contains one door, 1.8 m by 1.5 m.

$$\text{Area ratio} = \frac{\text{Area of door}}{\text{Area of brick}} = \frac{1.8 \times 1.5}{(5 \times 3) - (1.8 \times 1.5)}$$

$$= 0.22$$

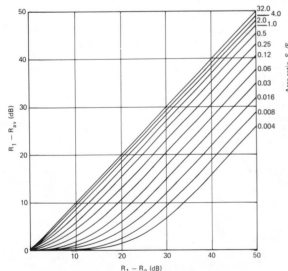

Figure 11.22 Chart for determining the sound insulation for a wall comprising two components of which component 1 has the higher sound insulation

If the sound insulation of the brickwork is 46 and the sound insulation for the door is 14 then:

$$R_1 - R_2 = 46 - 14 = 32$$

Using these data on *Figure 11.22* the value for $R_1 - R_{av}$ is 25 dB. As R_1 is 46 dB, the sound insulation for the brick wall with the door, R_{av}, is 21 dB.

This example highlights the fact that the performance of any composite construction is limited by the sound insulation provided by the weakest component. Even very small areas of one component with low sound insulation can severely reduce the sound insulation of a wall which may have had a potentially high sound insulation. In *Figure 11.23* the effect of various areas of window with sound insulation of only 20 dB in a wall with sound insulation of 50 dB is shown.

11.2.4.4 Installation and attention to detail

The details of a construction must be carefully followed in order to achieve similar sound insulation to that obtained in tests. The components must conform to the manufacturer's specifications and a high standard of workmanship should be achieved. Even a small gap along the length of a wall or around a window can reduce significantly the sound insulation of a facade. For example, it can be calculated using the procedure described in the previous section that a 10 mm gap along the edge of a 5 m by 3 m brick wall would reduce the sound insulation from 46 dB to only 25 dB. Cover strips over joints which allow air to permeate from one side of the wall to the other and consequently provide paths for the transmission of sound should not be used when high sound insulation is required. It is most important that all gaps be sealed, preferably with a flexible sealant which will not crack and split in time and with exposure to the atmosphere.

11.2.5 Sound insulation of building components

As there are often many conflicting requirements for any building it is not always possible to utilize fully the benefits, in terms of noise reduction, which can be obtained by advantageous choice of building shape, orientation and arrangement of the internal spaces. In these cases the building fabric itself must provide the required amount of sound insulation. All components of the building enclosure must be considered as the inclusion of elements with low sound insulation will limit the effective noise reduction achieved (*see* Section 11.2.4).

Methods of construction and the basic materials used in buildings vary both within and between countries and all such changes have an effect on the sound insulation achieved. The data from laboratory or field measurements of the sound insulation of specific constructions should be consulted where precise information is required (for example references 43 and 44 and Further reading); however, the following sections give some guidelines for the general performance of the various elements which form the building enclosure.

11.2.5.1 Walls

The physical characteristics of a wall that lead to high sound insulation are, low stiffness, high damping and high mass. Thus a thick stone wall will have a higher sound insulation than a thin glass panel. For the majority of walls the sound insulation increases with frequency except when resonances occur and in the coincidence region (where there is greater transmission through the wall because the projected wavelength of the incident sound coincides with the bending wave of the wall). *Figures 11.21* and *11.24* show the variations in sound insulation with frequency for some constructions.

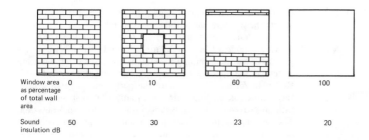

Window area as percentage of total wall area	0	10	60	100
Sound insulation dB	50	30	23	20

Figure 11.23 The effect of having areas of low sound insulation on the overall sound insulation of a composite wall

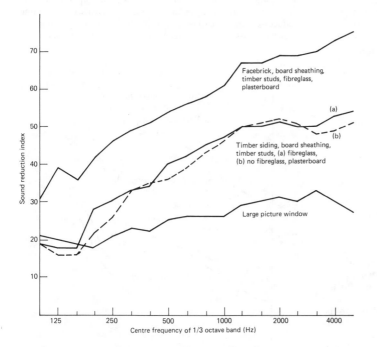

Figure 11.24 Sound insulation for some typical wall constructions from laboratory tests

Road traffic noise often has high sound levels in the low frequency range where the sound insulation of a construction is usually determined by its mass. The so-called 'mass law' relates the sound insulation achieved to the surface mass of a wall structure. This relation is illustrated on *Figure 11.25* as the solid line and can be used to give an indication of the sound insulation likely to be obtained by single leaf constructions such as masonry, concrete and glass. The measured values of sound insulation for some constructions are shown on *Figure 11.25* for comparison with the 'mass law' characteristic.

A double-leaf construction will have a higher sound insulation than a single-leaf construction with the same total mass. For example, a cavity brick wall will have a higher sound insulation than if the same bricks are used to form a solid brick wall. The sound insulation of a double-leaf construction depends on the physical properties of each of the leaves and on the nature of the connections between them. The greater the separation and the less the linkage between the two leaves, the better will be the sound insulation. The transmission of sound via the structural framing can be reduced if a resilient mounting system is used for at least one of the leaves. The inclusion of sound-absorbing material, such as fibreglass, within the cavity of a double-leaf construction can improve the sound insulation but the improvement is not usually great if the two leaves do have rigid connections: *see Figure 11.24*.

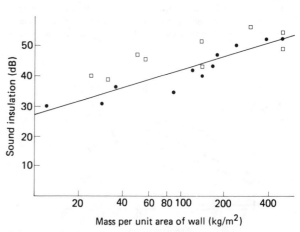

Figure 11.25 Mass law for estimating sound insulation compared with the measured values for some constructions: ● = single-leaf constructions; □ = double-leaf constructions

The typical values of sound insulation for some wall constructions are given in *Table 11.9*; for more details see references 43 and 44 and the Further reading. Note that the values of sound insulation given in the table are based on measurements made in a laboratory (*see* Section 11.2.4).

Table 11.9 Typical values for the sound installation of walls

Description	Approximate mass per unit area (kg/m²)	Sound insulation (dB)
100 mm brickwork or concrete blocks	200	45–50
200 mm brickwork or concrete blocks	400	48–52
Cavity brickwork	400	50–54
100 mm hollow concrete blocks	120	40–42
100 mm brickwork plus 12 mm plasterboard on resilient studs with fibreglass in the cavity	210	50–52
15 mm timber siding plus fibre-board sheathing plus 12 mm plasterboard	30	36–38
As above with fibreglass in the cavity	30	37–39
4 mm glass in fixed frame	10	25–30
Two panes of 4 mm glass with 100 mm cavity in fixed frame	20	35–40

11.2.5.2 Windows

To achieve high sound insulation a wall should not include any light-weight, openable elements such as doors and windows as their poor sound insulation will limit the performance of the facade (*see Figure 11.23*). In practice, buildings are rarely designed in this manner as windows are considered to be important aesthetically, allowing for natural lighting, ventilation as well as visual contact with the external environment.

The sound insulation values for three different thicknesses of glass are shown in *Figure 11.26*.[45] Increasing the thickness of the glass, and hence the mass, improves the performance in the low frequencies but it also leads to the dip, caused by the coincidence effect explained above, occurring at a lower frequency. Thus the reduction of the traffic noise over the whole frequency range is not greatly improved when only the thickness of the glass is increased. The coincidence effect is not as great in the perfor-

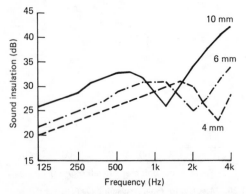

Figure 11.26 Sound insulation for three thicknesses of single glazing[45]

mance of laminated glass because the presence of the interlayer affects the bending wave in the glass panel.

A double-leaf construction, in the form of double glazing, can provide significant improvements in sound insulation. An important factor determining the effectiveness of a double glazing system is the spacing between the component panes. This is shown in *Figure 11.27*[45] where the performance for a typical thermal double glazing system with only 12 mm spacing shows little improvement on the sound insulation for single glazing. The wider spacing of 200 mm results in greater isolation between the component panes and hence the higher sound insulation. To maintain the isolation it is best if a double window system is used where the panes are in separate frames. Absorbent material installed around the reveals of the frame reduces the effects of resonances in the cavity between the two panes of glass and so further improves the sound insulation.

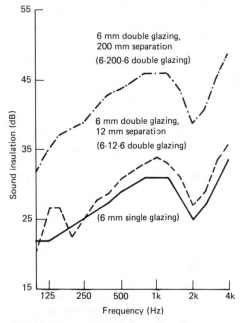

Figure 11.27 The effect of air space width on the sound insulation of double glazing[45]

The sharp dip occurring around 2000 Hz in *Figure 11.27* again results from the coincidence effect. If the double window system comprises glass of different thicknesses the coincidence effect will occur over a wider range of frequencies. As the magnitude of the dip will be reduced the overall noise reduction of the double window system will be improved. If the panes of glass are installed so that they are not parallel, a small improvement can be found in the insulation for both the coincidence region and the region where cavity resonances effect the insulation. However, the improvement in the overall noise reduction obtained by sloping one of the panes rarely justifies the additional construction costs.

The sound insulation of a window depends not just on the sound insulation of the glass but on the complete glazing system. An indication of the typical sound insulation for a range of windows is given in *Table 11.10*.

There is an improvement in sound insulation when the window is sealed because sound can no longer pass through the small gaps which exist even when a window is tightly closed. While the application of weather-stripping around an openable

Table 11.10 Typical values for the sound insulation of windows

Window type	Sound insulation (dB)
Single window open	5–15
Louvre window closed	10–20
Single window closed	20–25
Double window with 100 mm airspace, closed	30–35
Double window with 100 mm airspace, sealed	35

window can produce a similar improvement in the sound insulation, frequent opening of the window can lead to a deterioration in the ability of the weather-stripping to completely seal the gaps.

Once a window is opened for ventilation the sound insulation decreases rapidly as shown in *Figure 11.28*.[46] The staggered opening arrangement shows a higher sound insulation than for the direct opening but it should be remembered that the ventilation rate will be reduced. The sound insulation for louvred windows, which usually cannot be tightly closed, is generally poor.

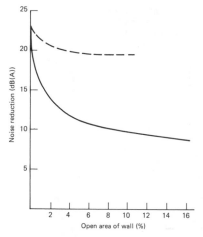

Figure 11.28 The reduction in sound insulation when a horizontal sliding window is opened. ——=single and double windows with a direct air path. – – –=double windows with a staggered opening such that the air pathway is not direct[46]

Tightly closed or sealed windows can no longer be used for natural ventilation and a mechanical ventilation system or air conditioning system must be provided. Such systems should be carefully chosen so that they produce adequate ventilation without unacceptable noise. The associated air vents and inlets should be located away from the roadside facade or should have baffles so that they do not provide paths for the transmission of sound.[47]

Sealed windows, particularly double windows, which are exposed to direct sunshine for long periods of the day can lead to overheating within the room. Some form of sunshading, such as a slatted blind between the two windows[47] or an awning outside, should be used to reduce the thermal gain through the window.

11.2.5.3 Doors

Doors generally provide low sound insulation so it is preferable if they are located on a facade not directly exposed to the source of noise. If a door must be located on the exposed facade its area should be kept as small as possible and it should be fitted with a gasket which provides a good seal all around the door. Ideally, the door should have no openings in it such as letter slots and it should not lead directly into a room which is sensitive to the noise. Some typical values for the sound insulation of doors are listed in *Table 11.11*.

Table 11.11 Typical values for the sound insulation of doors

Door type	Sound insulation (dB)
Light-weight, hollow core door	10–15
Light-weight, hollow core door with well-fitted gasket	15–20
Solid door	15–20
Solid door with well-fitted gasket	25–30
Double door with well-fitted gaskets	35

Door gaskets must provide a good seal so that no cracks exist around the perimeter of the door when it is tightly closed. The gasket should be of good quality so that it is not damaged by the regular opening and closing of the door. If it is not possible for the lower edge of the door to close against a gasketed rebate, a retracting seal or a rag strip should be fitted to the door so that a good seal is obtained when the door is closed.

A double door system, where a second door is installed to form a sound lock, should be used where high sound insulation is required. The sound lock should be large enough that one door is closed before the second is opened and the surfaces should be covered with sound-absorbing material to reduce the reflections of sound between the two doors.

11.2.5.4 Roofs

The roof of a building is usually only an important path for the transmission of traffic noise when the building is below the level of the roadway or when the roof is steeply sloping so that a large area is directly exposed to the noise. Any roof construction usually contains many air gaps which limit the sound insulation that can be provided even by heavyweight tiles. Some typical values for the sound insulation of roof systems, based on tests in a laboratory,[48] are listed in *Table 11.12*.

Any openings in the roof, such as chimneys and pipes, or ventilation openings in the eaves will permit transmission of sound into the roof space. If these openings are not essential

Table 11.12 Typical values for the sound insulation of roof systems including a 9 mm plasterboard ceiling

Roof type	Sound insulation (dB)
Pitched roof, concrete tiles	28
Pitched roof, concrete tiles and 100 mm fibreglass	34
Pitched roof, corrugated steel	26
Flat roof, steel decking	25
Flat roof, steel decking and 50 mm fibreglass	29

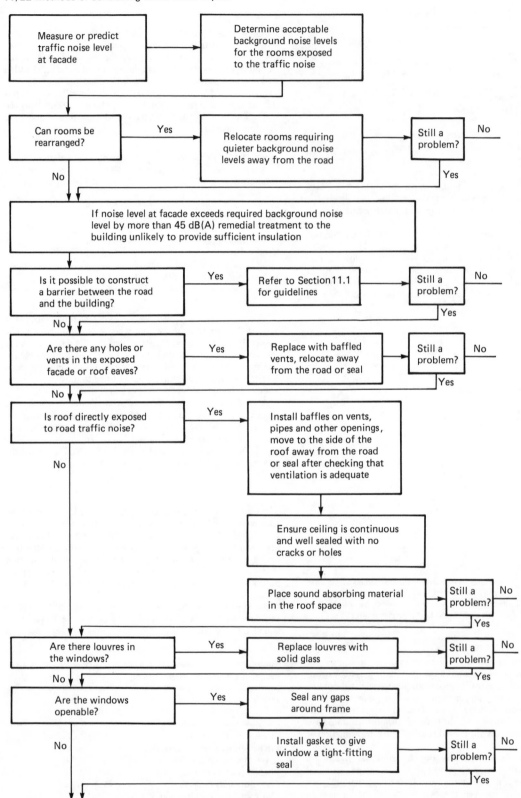

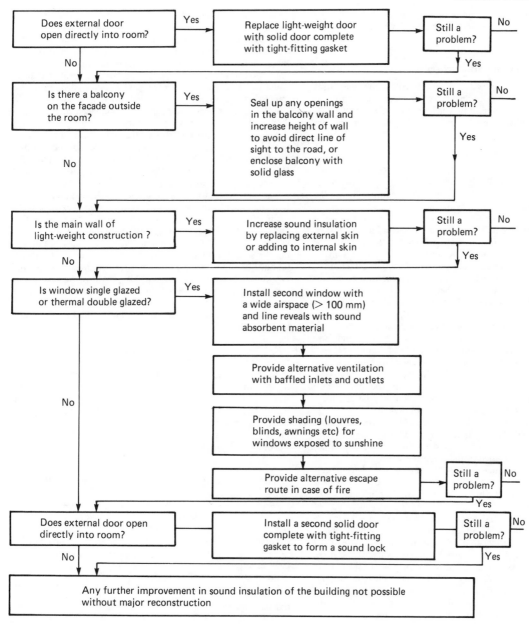

Figure 11.29 Procedure for improving the sound insulation of existing buildings

they should be sealed. However, in the majority of situations ventilation in the roof space is important so the openings should be placed on the side of the building away from the road or fitted with a baffle. An important part of the sound insulation of a roof system is provided by the ceiling. If a light-weight, sound absorbing ceiling is required, as in an office, then a solid ceiling with higher sound insulation should be installed above it.

11.2.6 Treatment of existing buildings

If the traffic noise levels inside a building are considered to be unacceptably high then rearrangement of the rooms inside the building and the construction of a barrier between the building and the road should be considered first. Rearrangement of the rooms involves placing the noise sensitive rooms on the side of the building away from the road (*see* Section 11.2.3).

If it is necessary to increase the sound insulation of the facade of the building, the procedure given by the flow chart in *Figure 11.29* can be followed and the basic principles outlined in the previous section applied. It is important to determine the magnitude of the noise problem because an insulation of greater than 45–50 dB(A) is unlikely to be obtained by remedial treatment to a building of conventional construction. The assessment of the improvement obtained at each stage of the procedure in *Figure 11.29* can be made by measurements. The advantages of continuous assessment are that the amount of treatment and the restrictions on the users of the building produced by the installation of double windows etc., are kept to a minimum.

11.2.7 Statutory insulation schemes

Many countries have introduced legislation on a National, State or City basis which include the requirements for improved sound insulation for buildings which are exposed to high levels of road traffic noise. The schemes adopted in three countries are outlined below.

11.2.7.1 United Kingdom

The Noise Insulation Regulations[49] have been operative in the United Kingdom since 1973 and place the responsibility on the appropriate highway authority to carry out, or make a grant to cover the costs of carrying out, improvements to the noise insulation of eligible buildings. These eligible buildings must be domestic or residential buildings within 300 m of a new or altered road. The calculated noise level at the facade, in terms of L_{10} (18 hour), (the average hourly L_{10} from 0600 to 2400 hours), must increase by at least 1 dB(A) to a value equal to or greater than 68 dB(A). The owners are then offered the noise insulation package for living rooms and bedrooms which have windows and doors exposed to the traffic noise. This package includes the provision of a second window with a wide spacing and with sound-absorbent material in the reveals. Slatted blinds are installed in the double windows exposed to sunlight to provide shading when required. For doors opening directly into the room a sound lock is constructed by fitting a second door some distance from the existing door. If this is not possible then a single door with improved sound insulation may be provided. As the doors and windows must be kept closed to provide the required sound insulation the ventilation for the room must be supplied by a certified ventilation unit and a permanent vent. Specifications on the required sound attenuation for the ventilation systems are included in the regulations.

In 1980 it was estimated that the average cost of insulating three rooms against road traffic noise was £800 and that 50 000 of the 80 000 homes eligible at that time had the noise insulation package installed.[50]

The results of a trial test of the noise insulation package showed clearly that sunshading, in the form of a venetian blind was essential for thermal comfort.[47] From a questionnaire of 882 residents to establish the degree of acceptability of the noise insulation package it was found that only 8% considered the treatment to be unsatisfactory.[51] While the double windows and venetian blinds were considered satisfactory by 88% and 90% of the respondents respectively only 58% thought that the ventilators were satisfactory. Some of the reasons for the dislike of the ventilators were that they were too large and unsightly and let in draughts. From measurements in 154 treated rooms it has been shown that the noise insulation package provides an average noise reduction of 34 dB(A) and the range of noise reduction achieved was 41.5 dB(A) to 25 dB(A).[52] The differences in traffic noise spectrum from site to site account for some of the variation in the measured dB(A) reduction.

11.2.7.2 Norway

Before the Norwegian Traffic Noise Abatement programme was introduced in 1978, the traffic noise levels were surveyed over most of the country and the number of dwellings exposed to various levels of noise were determined.[53] Priority in application of noise reducing measures was given to those dwellings exposed to the higher levels of noise and from 1978 to 1984 approximately 40% of the allocation of NKr 25 million (about £2.3

million) has been spent on building improvements with the remainder spent on noise screens.[53] The building improvements have been directed at increasing the sound insulation of the windows to provide an internal L_{eq} of 35 dB(A), and in Oslo there are two categories of grants.[29] The priority support grant applies when the L_{eq} (24 hour) at the facade is greater than or equal to 74 dB(A) and the owner is offered a 100% grant for improving the sound insulation of existing windows. If the windows are considered to be in need of replacement an offer of 70% of the cost of new windows is made. If the L_{eq} (24 hour) at the facade is at least 68 dB(A) the owner can apply for a 'minimum' support grant which will cover the costs of improvements to existing windows but if the windows need replacing a fixed grant is provided and this covers 20–30% of the cost of replacement windows.

The improvements for existing windows depend on the condition and type of window and include the fitting of extra gaskets, sealing between the frame and wall, installing heavier glazing and installing another window.[54] Although the costs vary greatly because of the different treatments the average cost of improving the sound insulation has been approximately NKr 19 000 (about £1750) and the average improvement has been 9.6 dB.[54] No alternative ventilation system is provided; however, in a survey of treated dwellings only about 10% reported that the ventilation was worse than before.[55] Over 90% considered that overall the improvements in noise insulation had been successful.[56]

11.2.7.3 The Netherlands

In the Netherlands the Noise Abatement Act of 1979 established noise standards for dwellings in zones around major noise sources. The specifications for noise from road traffic are given in terms of the daytime L_{eq}, from 0700 to 1900 hours (day), and the night-time L_{eq}, from 2300 to 0700 hours (night).[56] *Table 11.13* summarizes the noise levels required for both new and existing road systems.

Table 11.13 Noise levels for dwellings required by the Dutch Noise Abatement Act

Location	Outside		Inside	
	Day	Night	Day	Night
New situations:				
Preference	50	40	35	25
Maximum	65	55	35	25
Existing situations:				
Preference	55	45	40	30
Maximum	75	65	45	35

Investigations during the 1970s assessed the effectiveness of various methods for improving the sound insulation of dwellings and the organization between various authorities necessary to implement any large scheme. It has been found that while satisfactory noise reductions can be achieved by improving the sound insulation of windows and any light-weight panels the integration of ventilation and heating systems require further study. For buildings up to 13 m high natural ventilation by means of a baffled opening has been used but a mechanical ventilation system means that the ventilation opening on the facade can be smaller.

The Government funded programmes to achieve the noise standards commenced in 1980 and are considered likely to continue for 15–25 years.[57] Approximately half the money has been spent on sound insulation schemes while the other half has been spent on reducing the noise at source and on noise screens. The cost of improving the sound insulation of each dwelling varies but it has been estimated that the average cost is Hf. 3500 (about £800) and it is planned that 15 000 dwellings be treated each year.[56]

References

1 *Urban Traffic and Noise*, Verband der Automobilindustrie, Frankfurt (1978).
2 LANG, J. Larmbekämpfung durch Verkehrslenkung. In *Proceedings of the 10th International Congress for Noise Abatement*, Baden-Baden, p. 37 (1978).
3 BEHRENS, F. A. and BARRY, T. M. *European Experiences in Highway Noise. Report No FHWA-75-123*. Washington, Federal Highways Administration (1975).
4 ALEXANDRE, A. European efforts to reduce the impact of traffic noise. In *Proceedings: Inter Noise 72*, Washington, DC, p. 208 (1972).
5 GIESLER, H-J. and NOELLE, A. Einfluss von verkehrsberuhigenden Massnahmen auf akustische Kenngrössen. *Zeitschrift für Lärmbekämpfung*, **31**, 31 (1984), and *Proceedings of the 4th FASE Congress*, Sandefjord, Federation of The Acoustical Societies of Europe p. 241 (1984).
6 ULLRICH, S. Der Strassenverkehrslärm bei Fahrzeuggeschwindigkeiten von 30 km/h bis 60 km/h auf Asphalt—und Pflasterdecken. *Zeitschrift für Lärmbekämpfung*, **28**, 137 (1981).
7 *Noise Barriers, Standards and Materials, ODE Engineering Intelligence Division Technical Memorandum No H14/76* (1976).
8 ULLRICH, S. *Experiences with Noise Abatement Measures in the Federal Republic of Germany* (including legislation). In *Proceedings of the PTRC Summer Annual Meeting*, University of Warwick (1975).
9 BEYER, E. *Konstruktiver Lärmschutz*, Forschung und Praxis für Verkehrsbauten, Beton-Verlag, Düsseldorf, p. 65 (1982).
10 KRELL, K. *Schallschutz an Strassen*, Beispiele ausgeführter Massnahmen, Forschungsgesellschaft für das Strassenwesen, Köln, p. 10 (1979).
11 YAMASHITA, M. and YAMAMOTO, K. Prediction of traffic noise exposure based on field experiment. In *Proceedings of The 11th International Congress on Acoustics, Paris*, Vol. **7**, PTRC, p. 309 (1983).
12 KURZE, U. J. Recent developments in Germany regarding noise barriers. *Inter-Noise 80 Conference*, Miami. Vol. II, p. 565 (1980).
13 KURZE, U. J. Shielding of traffic noise by the shoulder of elevated highways, *Inter-Noise 84 Conference*, Honolulu, Proceedings, Vol. I, 325 (1984)
14 KRELL, K. *Handbuch für Lärmschutz an Strassen und Schienenwegen*, Otto Elsner-Verlag, Darmstadt, 134 (1984)
15 YAMAMOTO, K., YOSHIMURA, J. and YAMASHITA, M. Reduction of road traffic noise by louvres, *Inter-Noise 84 Conference*, Honolulu, Proceedings, Vol. II, 751 (1984).
16 KÜRER, R. Neue Möglichkeiten gegen den Strassenverkehrslärm, *Zeitschrift für Lärmbekämpfung*, 29, No 6, 170 (1982).
17 AL-SAMARRAI, H. S. and WATERS, D. M. Urban traffic control systems and noise, *Inter-Noise 80 Conference*, Miami, Proceedings Vol. II. 867 (1980).
18 PIORR, D. and HILLEN, R. Veränderung akustischer Kenngrössen infolge der nachtlichen Abschaltung von Lichtsignalanlagen. *Landesanstalt für Immissionsschutz des Landes Nordrhein-Westfalen*, Essen, Report No 35, 67 (1983).
19 LEWIS, P. T. and JAMES, A. Noise levels in the vicinity of traffic roundabouts, *Journal of Sound and Vibration*, **72**, No 1, 51 (1980).
20 SANDBERG U. and DESCORNET, G. Road surface influence on tyre/road noise—Parts I and II. National Swedish Road and Traffic Research Institute and Belgian Research Centre. International Conference on Noise Control Engineering, INTERNOISE 80, 1980.
21 FRANKLIN, R. E., HARLAND, D. G. and NELSON, P. M. Road surfaces and traffic noise. *TRRL Laboratory Report* 896, Crowthorne (1979).
21 NELSON, P. M. Controlling road traffic noise at source. Presented at *The Noise and Quality Seminar*, Budapest (1984).
22 NELSON, P. M. Low noise road surfaces. In *Proceedings of The 4th FASE Congress*, Sandefjord, Federation of The Acoustical Societies of Europe p. 291 (1984).
23 DE BRABANDER, L. Motorway noise reduction by covering grooved concrete with open graded rubberized asphalt, *Inter-Noise 83 Conference*, Edinburgh, Vol. II, p. 705 (1983).
24 SANDBERG, U. A road surface for reduction of tyre noise emission. *Inter-Noise 79 Conference*, Warszawa, Vol. II, p. 517 (1979).
25 MAY, D. N. and OSMAN, M. M. Noise from retextured and new concrete and asphalt road surfaces, *Inter-Noise 78 Conference*, p. 873 (1978).
26 REICHOW, H. B. Town planning and noise abatement. *Architects Journal*, **137**-7, 357–360 (1963).
27 US Department of Transportation. *The Audible Landscape: A Manual for Highway Noise and Land Use*. (1974).
28 *New Housing and Road Traffic Noise. A Design Guide for Architects. Design Bulletin 26*, Department of the Environment, HMSO, London (1971).
29 HARRIS, C. M. *Handbook of Noise Control* (2nd edn.), McGraw Hill, New York, pp.14–15 (1979).
30 *AS 2107—1977, Ambient Sound Levels for Areas of Occupancy Within Buildings*, Australian Standards Association, Sydney (1977).
31 PALLETT, D. S., WEHRLI, R., KILMER, R. D. and QUINDRY, T. L. *Design Guide for Reducing Transportation Noise in and Around Buildings, Building Science Series 84*, National Bureau of Standards, US Government Printing Office, Washington (1978).
32 OLDHAM, D. J. and MOHSEN, E. A. A technique for predicting the performance of self protecting buildings with respect to traffic noise. *Noise Control Engineering*, **15**, 11–19 (1980).
33 ISO R140/5 *Measurement of Sound Insulation in Buildings and of Building Elements—Part V. Field Measurements of Airborne Sound Insulation of Facade Elements and Facades*. International Standards Organisation, Switzerland (1982).
34 BS 2750 Part 5. *Methods of Measurement of Sound Insulation in Buildings and of Building Elements. Part 5. Field Measurement of Airborne Sound Insulation of Facade Elements and Facades*, British Standards, London (1980).
35 ASTM E90-70. *Standard Recommended Practice for Laboratory Measurement of Airborne Sound Transmission of Building Partitions, Part 18 of Book of ASTM Standards*, ASTM, Philadelphia (1975).
36 JONES, R. The effects of flanking and the test environment on laboratory—field correlations of airborne sound insulation. *Journal of The Acoustical Society of America*, **57**, 1138–1149 (1975).
37 TAIBO, L. and DE DAYAN, H. G. Comparison of laboratory and field measurements of party wall and facade elements. *Journal of The Acoustical Society of America*, **75**, 1522–1531 (1984).
38 ISO 717. *Rating of Sound Insulation in Buildings and Building Elements—Part 3 Airborne Sound Insulation of Facade Elements and Facades*, International Standards Organisation, Switzerland (1982).
39 ASTM E413-73. *Standard Classification for Determination of Sound Transmission Class*, ASTM Standards, Philadelphia (1973).
40 BS 5821. *Methods for Rating Sound Insulation in Buildings and of Building Elements*. British Standards, London (1980).
41 BS 2750. *Measurement of Airborne and Impact Sound Transmission in Buildings*, British Standards, London (1956). (Superseded Standards.)
42 HARMAN, D. and BURGESS, M. A. Single value rating methods. *Applied Acoustics*, **6**, 269–273 (1973).
43 BAZLEY, E. N. *The Airborne Sound Insulation of Partitions*, HMSO, London (1966).
44 SABINE, H. J., LACHER, M. B., FLYNN, D. R. and QUINDRY, T. L. Acoustical and thermal performance of exterior residential walls, doors and windows. *NBS Building Science Series*, 77, National Bureau of Standards, US Government Printing Office, Washington (1975).
45 *Glass and Noise Control*, Pilkington Glass, Merseyside, England (1976).
46 LAWRENCE, A. B. and BURGESS, M. A. Traffic noise and the open window. *Acoustical Society of America*, Meeting 104, Paper XX2 (1982).

47 STACEY, E. F. *et al. An Experimental Investigation of Motorway Noise and Sound Insulation Along the Midlands Link Motorway*, Building Research Station, Current Paper CP 48/74, HMSO, London (1974).

48 COOK, K. R. Sound insulation of domestic roofing systems. *Applied Acoustics*, **13**, 313–329 (1980).

49 *Building and Buildings—The Noise Insulation Regulations*, Statutory Instrument 1975 No. 1763, HMSO, London (1975).

50 Noise Advisory Working Group. *A Study of Government Insulation Policies*, HMSO, London (1980).

51 UTLEY, W. A., KEIGHLEY, E. C. and SARGENT, J. W. Insulating dwellings against road traffic noise'. *Proceedings of The 11th I.C.A.*, Vol. 7, pp. 245–248, Institute of Acoustics, Paris (1983).

52 SARGENT, J. W. Effectiveness of insulation measures against traffic noise. *Proceedings of Institute of Acoustics Spring Conference*, Institute of Acoustics, pp. 318–321 (1984).

53 GRANQUIST, T. E. The development of a national traffic noise abatement program in Norway. *Noise Control Engineering*, **17**, 71–75 (1981).

54 RINGHEIM, M. Reduction of road traffic noise—cost and effect of noise control measures. *Proceedings of Institute of Acoustics Spring Conference*, pp. 245–251 Institute of Acoustics (1984).

55 OSMUNDSEN, E. Facade insulation against road traffic noise in Oslo. *Proceedings of FASE 84* Federation of The Acoustical Societies of Europe (1984).

56 SOLBERG, S., HAGEN, R. and OMMUNDSEN, R. Perceived noise reduction and secondary effects from the use of building insulation and barriers. *Proceedings Internoise 83* Noise Control Foundation, New York (1983).

57 LINGEN, W. VAN DER. A brief history of and topics from experimental projects to 5 year programs for regional planning of house insulation in the Netherlands. *FASE 84*, Invited paper, pp. 47–62 (1984).

Further reading

BERANEK, L. L. *Noise and Vibration Control*, McGraw Hill, New York (1971).

CROOME, D. J. *Noise, Buildings and People*, Pergamon Press, Oxford (1977).

DOELLE, L. L. *Environmental Acoustics*, McGraw Hill, New York (1972).

LAWRENCE, A. B. *Architectural Acoustics*, Elsevier, Amsterdam (1970).

LIM, B. P., RAO, K. R., THARMARATNAM, K. and MATTAR, A. M. *Environmental Factors in the Design of Building Fenestration*, Applied Science Publishers, London (1979).

MOORE, J. E. *Design for Good Acoustics and Noise Control*, MacMillan, London (1978).

PARKIN, P. H., HUMPHREYS, H. R. and COWELL, J. R. *Acoustics, Noise and Buildings*, Faber and Faber, London (1979).

PENN, C. N. *Noise Control*, Shaw and Sons, London (1979).

SCHOLES, E. and SARGENT, J. W. *Designing Against Noise from Road Traffic, Building Research Establishment Current Paper CP 20/71*, Building Research Establishment (1971).

SMITH, B. J., PETERS, R. J. and OWEN, S. *Acoustics and Noise Control*, Longman, UK (1982).

TEMPLETON, D. and LORD, P. *Detailing for Acoustics*, Architectural Press, London (1983).

12

Low-Frequency Traffic Noise and Vibration

H. G. Leventhall MSc, PhD, FINSTP, FIOA
**Atkins Research and Development,
Epsom, UK**

Contents

12.1 Introduction

Simply stated, traffic induced vibration may occur in buildings by two separate processes. Firstly, low frequency sound waves generated by vehicles mainly at the exhaust can couple into the structure via the windows and doors causing different parts of the building to vibrate. Secondly, forces generated by vehicles passing over the road surface profile can generate vibration in the ground which then propagates along the ground surface and

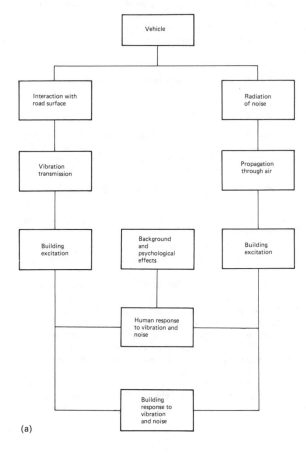

(a)

underlying soil to reach the building foundations. Vibration is then transferred into the building via the foundations and floor supporting walls. *Figure 12.1* illustrates the processes involved.

People experience building vibration in a variety of ways. Perception involves both tactile responses associated with feeling parts of the building vibrate to aural responses such as hearing windows and ornaments rattling. People also find low frequency noise particularly disturbing as at certain levels and frequencies low frequency sound waves can cause body vibration. People are also concerned that traffic vibration can cause damage to property even though the levels involved are generally very low. This attitude can, of course, markedly affect the disturbance caused by vibration.

This chapter considers the generation and propagation of both low frequency noise and ground borne vibration from traffic. The evidence for the probability of structural damage caused by vibration from heavy vehicles is assessed and the validity of complaints of this occurrence are examined. The responses of people to both low frequency noise and vibration are reviewed.

It is worth noting at this point that vibration produced by trains is examined in Chapter 16 and although the sources and generating mechanisms are somewhat different, the propagation paths and receiver environments are similar. Consequently, the two chapters are intended to be complementary and the reader is advised to consult both chapters for a full coverage of this topic.

12.2 The noise source

12.2.1 Vehicle streams

Continuous vehicle flows produce fluctuating noise levels, and statistical analysis of 'A' weighted traffic noise is widely used for assessment purposes. If statistical analysis is carried out in frequency bands at low frequencies the results are typically as in *Figure 12.2*, which shows analysis in octave bands both outside and inside a double-glazed house on a busy urban road.[1] The peak is at 63 Hz with external L_{10} levels of about 90 dB, but the peak may move to the 125 Hz band for rapidly flowing traffic. (NB: A similar result is described in *Figure 10.1*.) The divergence between outside and inside levels increases at higher frequencies, as would be expected from mass law considerations (*see* Chapter

(b)

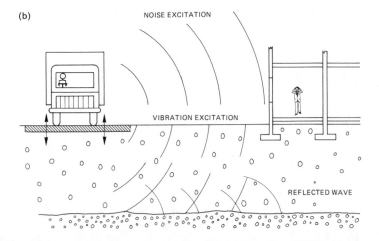

Figure 12.1 Vibration propagation to buildings. (*a*) The vibration and noise chain. (*b*) Diagrammatic representation

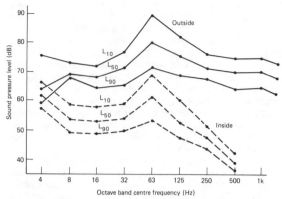

Figure 12.2 Statistical analysis of traffic noise outside and inside a double-glazed house

11). Below 63 Hz there is a general difference of about 20 dB from outside to inside (except at the lowest frequency of 4 Hz) with 10 dB between L_{10} and L_{90} levels. The internal noise is weighted towards low frequencies. More detailed analyses of vehicle streams are given in *Figures 12.3* and *12.4* which illustrate the difference between motorway and urban traffic.[2] *Figure 12.3* is for motorway traffic, 20 m from the nearside kerb with a traffic speed of about 100 km/h, and has peak levels in the 100–125 Hz region. *Figure 12.4* is for urban traffic at about 60 km/h, measured 2 m from the nearside kerb. The peak is in the 63–80 Hz region. It can be concluded that for motorway traffic, there is likely to be a peak at about 125 Hz with an L_{10} level of 85–90 dB near to the carriageway. For urban traffic, the peak will be at about 63 Hz with an L_{10}, close to the carriageway, of about 90 dB. These levels are in one-third octave bands. The peak levels (L_1) are 5–10 dB greater than the L_{10} levels.

12.2.2 Individual vehicles

Typical results are as follows:

1. The spectrum of a bus pull-away noise is given in *Figure 12.5* averaged over nine events.[2] There is a prominent peak at 63 Hz of 90 dB caused by the power surge required to move from rest. The drive-by noise of a similar bus is given

in *Figure 12.6* both outside and inside a house with single windows.[2] Both spectra are weighted towards low frequencies and this effect is further emphasized internally with a general slope of -6 dB/octave.

2. The single event peak sound pressure spectra of *Figure 12.7* show inside and outside noise in one-third octave bands.[3] There is divergence between the spectra at higher frequencies and a difference of about 10 dB at lower frequencies, whilst overlap occurs at the very lowest frequencies. This follows the trends indicated in *Figure 12.2*. An octave band analysis would show the peak at 50 Hz as occurring in the 63 Hz band.

3. Other noise analyses are given in Section 12.5.2 where noise-induced building vibration is considered.

12.2.3 Prediction of vehicle noise at low frequencies

12.2.3.1 Vehicle streams

An initial study aimed at developing predictive equations for low-frequency noise of complex traffic streams[4] resulted in the following equation for a height of 1.2 m and a reference distance of 10 m from the nearside kerb:

$$L_{eq}(40\text{–}125\text{ Hz}) = 53.0 + 9.43 \log_{10}(Q_1 + 10Q_{MCV} + 40Q_{HCV}) \text{ dB} \tag{12.1}$$

where $L_{eq}(40\text{–}125\text{ Hz}) =$ the energy equivalent level over the frequency range stated.

Q_1 = total hourly vehicle flow in vehicles per hour,
Q_{MCV} = flow of medium commercial vehicles in vehicles per hour,
Q_{HCV} = flow of heavy commercial vehicles in vehicles per hour.

The Pearson product moment correlation coefficient was 86.5% and the standard error of the estimate was 1.49 dB.

It is useful at this point to compare Equation 12.1 with the relationships which have been found for general traffic noise. It can be seen, for example, that Equation 10.35 which describes the basic traffic noise prediction formula used in the UK, contains a vehicle flow term which has a much lower dependence on percentage heavy vehicles. This emphasizes the importance of heavy vehicles in low-frequency noise generation.

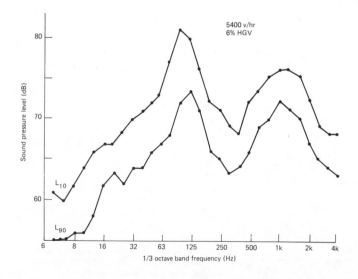

Figure 12.3 Statistical analysis of traffic noise from a motorway

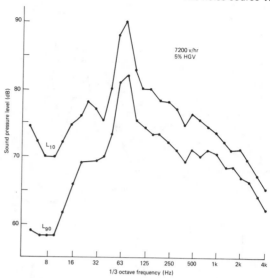

Figure 12.4 Statistical analysis of urban traffic noise

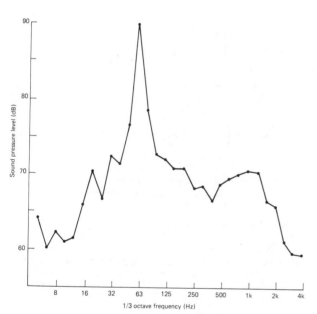

Figure 12.5 Bus pull-away noise (average of nine events)

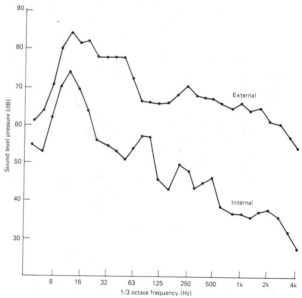

Figure 12.6 Bus drive-by noise outside and inside a house

12.2.3.2 Individual vehicles[5]

Figure 12.8 shows the results of a narrow band (6%) analysis of the noise in a house with partly open window when a 30 tonne lorry passed at a distance of 27 m. The main characteristics of the frequency spectra are peaks at 16 Hz and 64 Hz. The engine speed was approximately 1000 rpm and the engine was a V8, 8 litre, four-stroke diesel. The fundamental frequency is given by:

$$f = \frac{(\text{engine speed}) \times (\text{number of cylinders})}{120} \simeq 67 \text{ Hz}$$

The lower frequency peak (~ 16 Hz) arises from the firing rate

of a pair of cylinders in the V8 configuration. Assuming that the main source of low-frequency noise is the exhaust, which acts as a monopole source, the pressure at a distance r is $p = \frac{\rho}{4\pi r} \frac{\mathrm{d}}{\mathrm{d}t}\left(\frac{\mathrm{dA}}{\mathrm{d}t}\right)$

where $\mathrm{dA}/\mathrm{d}t$ is the rate of volume evolution of the source and ρ the density of the medium. If the pulses at the exhaust outlet are assumed to be of half sine form, occurring 64 times per second, the fundamental component of $\mathrm{dA}/\mathrm{d}t$ can be extracted and the pressure at a distance can be determined. Using the example of *Figure 12.8*, the predicted pressure outside the house was 80 dB, compared with 75 dB measured inside with a partly open window.

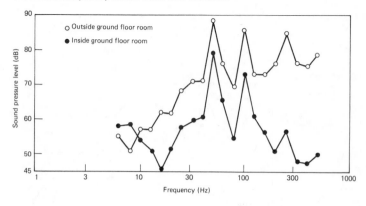

Figure 12.7 Single vehicle peak event sound pressure spectra

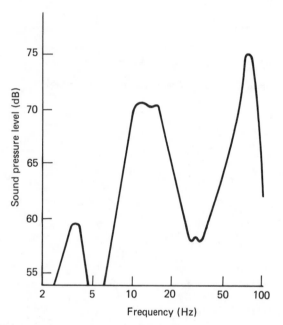

Figure 12.8 Noise in a house as a lorry passes (6% bandwidth analysis)

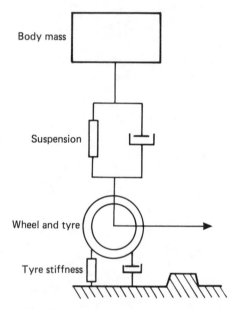

Figure 12.9 Dynamic effect of road discontinuity

12.3 The vibration source

12.3.1 Interaction of vehicle and road

A perfectly balanced mechanical system powering a vehicle on a perfectly smooth road will not produce vibration. Modern vehicles generate low out of balance forces so that it is the tyre/road interaction which produces most vibration. Road surface conditions degenerate with use and irregularities develop, leading to relative motion of the two extremities of the vehicle suspension and variations of the force input to the road. For example, *Figure 12.9* shows a diagrammatic representation of a vehicle wheel passing a discontinuity. If the time to pass over is small compared with the suspension resonant frequency, the force input is impulsive and the resulting effects depend mainly on the suspension and tyre frequencies and damping. The travelling wheel produces oscillatory forces beyond the location of the discontinuity, although the forces became negligible after a few cycles. Assuming a system resonance frequency of, say,

12 Hz decaying in three cycles and vehicle speed of 15 m/s, the effect of the discontinuity is felt up to 3.75 m beyond its location, thus involving a large area of road and possibly causing further damage to the surface.

12.3.2 Dynamic loading

An investigation has been made of the dynamic loading of roads by heavy vehicles of gross weights from 32.5 to 44.7 Mg.[6] The loads were measured by sensors set into the road. Predominant frequencies were in the range 10–16 Hz, corresponding to wheel hop frequencies. The ratio of maximum dynamic axle load to static axle load (impact factor) varied considerably for different vehicles, axles and speeds with a maximum of three, but typically was about 1.5. The level of dynamic force input to the surface may be 10–20 Mg as shown in *Figure 12.10* from reference 6.

12.3.3 Prediction of loading and road response

A detailed study has been carried out by Rudder[7] and his approach is summarized here. There are two main areas of interest:

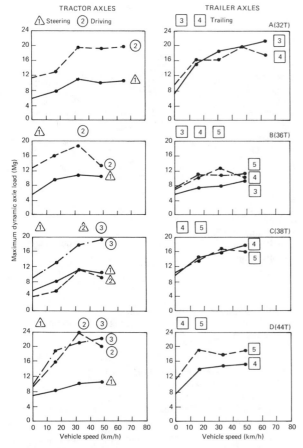

TRACTOR AXLES

⚠ Steering ② Driving

TRAILER AXLES

3 4 Trailing

Figure 12.10 Comparison of maximum dynamic axle load for four vehicles (A, B, C and D) over a 40×250 mm plank. △=steering, ○=driving and □=trailing axles

1. A roadway with random surface roughness.
2. A roadway with bumps or pot holes.

12.3.3.1 Random surface roughness

In the case of random surface roughness the acceleration level is referenced to 2 m from the edge of the roadway and given by:

$$L_0 = -4.155(PSR) + 17.2 \log_{10}(V) + 10 \log_{10}(W_G) - 87.8 \text{ dB}$$
$$\text{re lg} \quad (12.2)$$

where PSR is the Present Serviceability Rating. The PSR is related to the surface roughness power spectral density. For a new surface PSR ~ 4.5, reducing to ~ 2.0 after a design life of 20 years, giving a 10 dB increase in traffic induced ground vibration.[8] V is the vehicle speed in km/h and W_G is the gross weight of the vehicle in tonnes. A 20 tonne vehicle at 55 km/h with a PSR of 3.0 will give an acceleration of -57 dB re lg. For comparison, measurement of traffic induced vibration produced by a laden two-axle lorry along a variety of road types gave acceleration 3.65 m from the edge of the road in the range -60 dB re lg to -48 dB re lg.[9] Rudder[7] considers a PSR range of 1.0–5.0 giving a range of ± 8 dB on the mid-value PSR of 3.0. Doubling vehicle weight gives a change of 3 dB whilst doubling vehicle speed gives a change of 5.2 dB in the acceleration level.

12.3.3.2 Roadway with bumps or holes

When the roadway contains bumps or potholes the dynamic loading and impact factor may be determined from knowledge of the vehicle parameters and geometry of the discontinuity.[7] The quantities involved are:

1. Bump height (h) and length (l).
2. Vehicle speed (V), static tyre load (W_0), tyre stiffness (k_t) and natural frequency of the suspension (f_n).
3. Road/subgrade natural frequency (f_p) and its effective mass $\bar{W}$.

The procedure is to consider the response of a one degree of freedom system to a half-sine displacement equal to the bump height with duration given by the time taken to traverse the bump. The maximum value of load is $P_0 = k_t h$, but this is modified depending on the duration of the excitation in relation to the resonant frequency of the vehicle system. Rudder gives:

$$\left. \begin{array}{l} P_0 = k_t h/(1-v) \quad 0 \leqslant v \leqslant 1/3 \\[2mm] P_0 = k_t h \sin[2\pi v/(1+v)]/(1-v) \quad 1/3 \leqslant v \leqslant 1 \\[2mm] P_0 = 2k_t h \, v \cos[(\pi/(2v)]/(v^2-1) \quad v \geqslant 1 \end{array} \right\} \quad (12.3)$$

where $v = V/\bar{V}$ and $\bar{V} = 2l f_n$ is the speed at which the duration of the excitation is equal to the natural period of the suspension system.

The next step is to consider the response of the road/subgrade system, which is a multi-degree of freedom system. The impulse force from the vehicle is assumed to be rectangular of amplitude P_0 and duration l/V. The maximum acceleration of the road system which results is:

$$Lp_0 = 20 \log_{10}(P_0) - 20 \log_{10}(\bar{W}) + 20 \log_{10}[|\sin(\pi/2\tilde{v})|] + 6 \text{ dB}$$
$$\text{re lg} \quad (12.4)$$

Here P_0 is the peak impulse load (Equation 12.3), $\bar{W}$ is the effective subgrade mass,

$\tilde{v} = \dfrac{V}{\tilde{V}}$, the ratio of vehicle speed to characteristic speed of the subgrade;

$\tilde{V} = 2l f_p$.

The effective subgrade mass is:

$$\bar{W} = 5.5 \, \gamma_f \, bL h_f (1+\mu)/3$$

in which γ_f = density of subgrade material,
b = road width,
$L^4 = E_p \, h_p^3 h_f (1+\gamma_f^2)/12 E_f (1-\gamma p^2)$,
E_p, h_p, v_p and E_f, h_f and v_f are the road (pavement) and subgrade Young's. v_p and v_f are the road and subgrade Poisson's ratio respectively.
μ = ratio of road slab density to subgrade density.

Equation 12.4 shows that knowledge of all parameters involved permits estimation of the impulsively excited road vibration, which may then be considered as a vibration source at the location of the excitation. The following example is given by Rudder:[7]

Suspension natural frequency	12 Hz
Tyre stiffness	840 000 N/m
Tyre static load	23 500 N/m
Vehicle speed	13.4 m/s
Pothole depth	25 mm
Pothole length in direction of travel	900 mm

From these data, the road surface loading is estimated as $P_0 = 37\,700$ N, giving an impact factor of 1.6. The road surface/

subgrade characteristics for a rigid concrete slab and subgrade material assumed by Rudder are shown to be:

$$f_p = 33.2 \text{ Hz}$$
$$\bar{W} = 350\,000 \text{ N}$$

Substituting these values with P_0 into Equation 12.4 leads to a peak acceleration level of -16 dB re lg at the pot-hole, or 1.6 m/s² acceleration. This gives a displacement of about 0.3 mm at 12 Hz.

The method of Rudder, summarized here, shows that it is possible to predict the road surface acceleration as a vibration source. Propagation of vibration from the source is considered in Section 12.4.2.

12.4 Propagation of noise and vibration

12.4.1 Noise

Under circumstances in which low-frequency noise is a problem, the source and receiver are usually close to each other so that excess attenuation due, primarily, to ground absorption is negligible and individual vehicles may be considered as point sources with a direct path from source to receiver. There are occasional complaints of low-frequency 'rumble' from distant traffic, especially at night. Here the greater attenuation of high-frequency noise produces a spectrum weighted towards low frequencies, and this effect is emphasized further by transmission into buildings (see Section 12.5).

12.4.2 Vibration

The complexity of the vibration transmission path is illustrated in Figure 12.1(b). There are several wave types and paths between source and receiver. A general review of wave propagation in the ground is given in Chapter 16, Section 16.3.1, in relation to train vibration. The present Section considers aspects specific to road traffic.[6,7,9–14]

The most important wave motion is surface (Raleigh) waves which decay according to the square root of the distance by geometrical spreading alone, but there are additional dissipating mechanisms in the soil. It has been suggested[13] that a propagation law for peak particle velocity, V, may take the form:

$$V = k/r^x$$

where $x = 1.4$ for clay soils,
   or $x = 0.8$ for silt.
r is the distance from the source in metres.

Typical levels of traffic induced vibration velocity, 3.65 m from the edge of a road, range from 0.06 mm/s to 0.25 mm/s covering a frequency range of 20–30 Hz.[9] Other authors[15] give velocities from 0.025 to 1.4 mm/s for a range of vehicle types at distances up to 50 m. Ground attenuation is such that there is rarely a vibration problem beyond 50–100 m from the source. Comprehensive data on the attenuation of ground vibration with distance have been collected together.[11] The results indicate a considerable spread (± 10 dB), but if one considers the mean of the attenuations, the fall off with distance over the range 2 m to 75 m approximates to:

$$V = \frac{1}{r^{0.5}} \text{ for } 2 < r < 10 \text{ m}$$

$$V = \frac{1}{r^{0.7}} \text{ for } 10 < r < 20 \text{ m}$$

$$V = \frac{1}{r} \text{ for } 20 < r < 75 \text{ m}.$$

Table 12.1 Values of attenuation constant a for different soil types[7]

Soil type	Transverse wave speed (m/s)	α per metre
Moist clay	152	0.025–0.25
Clayey soil		
Silty clay	152	0.019–0.43
Wet clay	152	0.31 –0.50
Loess at natural moisture	259	0.04 –0.13
Dry sand	152–396	0.007–0.070
Dense sand and gravel	250	0.015–0.045
Gravel plus sand and silt	250	0.023–0.053
Fine grained sand:		
Water saturated	110	0.09 –0.30
Water saturated and frozen	110	0.05 –0.17

Rudder[7] considers the two components of the attenuation, geometrical spreading and ground attenuation, combining them to give the level at a receiver as:

$$L(r) = L_0 + 10 \log(d_0/r) - 8.69\alpha(r - d_0) \quad (12.5)$$

where L_0 is the reference level (Equation 12.2),
   d_0 is the reference distance for L_0,
   r is the distance from the source,
   α is the attenuation constant for the earth in the transmission path.

The attenuation term is obtained from the exponential, $e^{-\alpha(r - d_0)}$, which should be compared with Equation 10.4 of Section 16.3.1. Values of a given by Rudder are shown in Table 12.1. These values were obtained from frequency dependent data[16] for a single frequency of 15 Hz, where $\alpha = 2\pi f\zeta/c$. Here f is the frequency, ζ the soil loss factor and c the transverse wave speed.

Referring to Equation 12.5, the distance, r, between source and receiver is time dependent as a vehicle passes by. The equivalent (energy averaged) vibration level is given by integrating over the pass-by period.[7] The result for a single vehicle is:

$$L_e = L_0 + 10_{10} \log(d_0/Vt) - 5 \log_{10}(\alpha d) - 8.69\alpha(d - d_0) + 2.5 \text{ dB} \quad (12.6)$$

where t is the pass-by period (s),
   V is the vehicle speed (m/s),
   d is the distance from receiver to roadway (m).

For N similar vehicles an additional term $10 \log N$ is required, although the heaviest vehicles dominate the flow. Their peak level is given when $r = d$ in Equation 12.4 and L_0 is appropriate to the vehicle concerned.

The summation of Equation 12.6 gives the 'line source' attenuation for the road, whereas Equation 12.5 gives point source attenuation. The frequency content of the excitation from bumps and pot-holes is lower than that from random surface roughness, so that α is smaller. Rudder suggests that the values of α in Table 12.1 should be divided by three to allow for this. Referring to the prediction of the road response in Section 12.3.3 it is now possible to estimate the vibration level at a distance from the pot-hole with the source peak level as -16 dB re lg. For a building 10 m from the source with $\alpha = 0.15$ m, Equation 12.5 gives:

$$L_{(r)} = -16 - 10 \log_{10} 10 - 8.69.(0.15/3).10 \text{ dB re lg}$$
$$= -30 \text{ dB re lg}$$
$$= 0.32 \text{ m/s}^2.$$

The contributions to the attenuation are 10 dB from distance and 4 dB from dissipation. At greater distances the dissipation effects became greater. For example, at 30 m there is 15 dB attenuation from distance and 13 dB from dissipation.

Section 12.3 and 12.4 have shown that it is possible to predict both low-frequency noise and vibration from vehicles and their propagation to a receiving point. The following sections consider the response of buildings and people to the noise and vibration.

12.5 Response of buildings

12.5.1 Response to vibration

The response to ground vibration is independent of the nature of an original, distant, source of vibration and Section 16.4, on the effects of train induced ground vibration is relevant here.

Ground vibrations cause excitation of the building through its foundations.[9–12,16–19] The vibration level of building components may be greater than that of the ground due to resonance effects. Data collected in reference 11 indicate that, for most of the buildings studied, the magnification of velocity was between 0.5 and 2.0, with frequencies in the range 25–30 Hz. However, velocity magnifications as high as 5.0 were also noted. The natural frequencies of building elements are typically[19]:

Beams	5–50 Hz
Floors and slabs	10–30 Hz
Window panes	10–100 Hz
	(depending on size)
Plaster ceilings in houses	10–20 Hz.

These lie in the range of vibration frequencies from traffic. Coupling of the building to the ground vibration depends on the type of foundation. This is discussed in Section 16.4.1. The calculation given in Section 12.4.2 estimated ground vibration at 10 m to be −30 dB re lg for impulse excitation. Assuming a building amplification of 5 dB, the building vibration level is −25 dB re lg. It is shown in Section 12.5.3 that significant damage is unlikely at this level.

12.5.2 Response to noise

The acoustic wave gives a fluctuating force over the building surface, causing vibrations which may be enhanced by resonance. The force is significant at high levels; 94 dB sound pressure level corresponds to 1 N/m², and the total force applied to a building facade is not negligible.

The resonance frequencies of building elements are given in the previous section, although the manner of the energy input from ground vibration is different from that for acoustic excitation. All building elements, but especially windows and lightweight floors, may be excited acoustically.

The importance of low-frequency noise as a source of building vibration has been recognized relatively recently and an early study[20] compared the excitation of a window by vehicle noise and aircraft noise, the latter being entirely airborne. Acceleration was measured by a single accelerometer at the centre of the window, which was approximately 1 m square and had a fundamental resonance frequency of 19 Hz, a coincidence frequency of 2100 Hz, and loss factor 0.1. A microphone measured the incident sound level. The results of a large number of measurements are shown in normalized form in *Figure 12.11* in which the acceleration in g per Pascal is plotted against frequency. The acceleration is about 0.01 g per Pascal over much of the range, but increases at window resonance frequencies. The actual acceleration is clearly dependent on noise spectrum and window response characteristics. However, a compilation of work on building response to peak sound pressure level has been made[21] and is summarized in *Figure 12.12*, which shows averaged window wall and floor accelerations in response to noise excitation. The sources were mainly aircraft (including sonic boom) and wind turbines. Road vehicle noise was not included. The response of windows was approximately 0.015 g/Pa. The walls in *Figure 12.12* were typical North American wooden construction (50 mm by 100 mm studs, doubly sheathed) and more readily excited than masonry walls.

Simultaneous measurements of traffic noise and consequent building vibration clearly show the dependence of vibration on airborne noise.[3,22] In *Figure 12.13* (from reference 3) the vibrations of the window pane follow the external sound pressure. At the peak levels (50 Hz) the acceleration is about −23 dB re lg for 100 dB sound level, or 0.035 g/Pa. The floor vibration follows the internal noise level except for the peak at 12.5–16 Hz in the internal noise, which is not reflected in the floor vibration. This peak could arise from an acoustical effect in the room.

Such an effect would require a Helmholtz resonator type of mechanism, since the lowest mode of the room was about 40 Hz. *Figure 12.14* (from reference 22) shows the effect of a 32 tonne vehicle. There is clear correspondence between the outside and inside sound pressures and between these and the vibration of an upper floor. The peak at 80 Hz is at about −52 dB re lg and results from a sound level of 100 dB. This is close to the value given for floors in *Figure 12.12*. The vibration levels at 16 and 20 Hz are above the ISO 2631 perception threshold.[23]

12.5.3 Damage to buildings

The previous sections have shown that building vibrations result from both groundborne and airborne excitation. There is, however, a wide margin between the occurrence of measurable vibration and the occurrence of damage, unless the vibrations are of a relatively high level and are sustained. The topic is beset with speculations and accusations, but very few hard facts are available despite the obvious interest and importance of the problem.[3,13,14,24–29] Most information on damage to buildings is in relation to blasting and sonic boom, where the vibration levels are much higher than those from traffic, but of a transient nature. (Further information on sonic boom related damaged is given in Chapter 21.) The continuous exposure to traffic noise means that lower limits than for transient excitation may be applicable. Buildings in areas of dense traffic are subject to vibration for much of the 24 hour day. A frequency of, say, 50 Hz maintained for 12 hours, corresponds to about two million cycles a day, so that there is clearly a wide safety margin between traffic induced vibration levels and the onset of fatigue damage.

Damage to buildings has been classified as:

1. Architectural damage: cracks in plaster, loosening or dislodgement of a few roof tiles, etc.
2. Major damage: cracks in walls and lintels, falling ceiling plaster, etc.
3. Severe damage; leading to potential destruction.

Architectural damage normally involves fine cracks up to a few millimetres in width, which can be easily filled and hidden during redecoration. Major damage may result in cracks about 10 mm wide, requiring more extensive (professional) repair, both internally and externally. Severe damage may involve cracks about 25 mm wide. Considerable repair work is then required to maintain habitability and prevent instability developing in the building. The main causes of damage are thermal

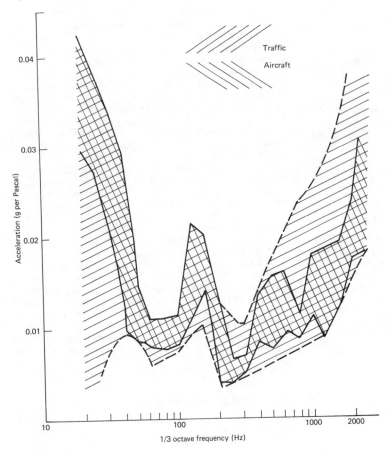

Figure 12.11 Range of window vibration excitations for a variety of road vehicles and aircraft (normalized to g per Pa)

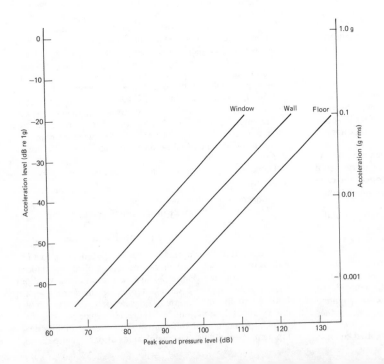

Figure 12.12 Average acceleration responses of building elements for acoustic excitation

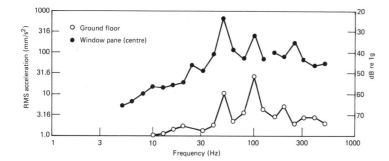

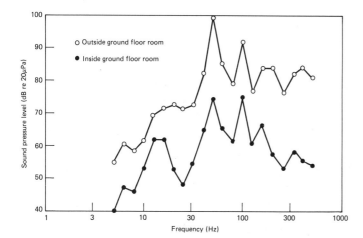

Figure 12.13 Single vehicle peak event acceleration and sound pressure levels

effects, expansion due to moisture, differential settlement of soft ground, 'frost heave' in the soil, clay shrinkage and expansion, chemical attack, adverse effects of nearby trees, etc. Vibration from traffic has a low rating as a general cause of damage, although it may be a significant cause in certain locations.[30,31] It is worth noting at this point that the Transport and Road Research Laboratory in the UK has begun a substantial programme of research on traffic related building damage. At the time of writing an experiment is in progress whereby a dwelling house is being subjected to simulated traffic vibration. It was hoped to gain further information on the long term effects of low level traffic vibration on both buildings and soils.

A study of severe building damage[26] showed that failures in old buildings were often due to a combination of deterioration of strength of elements, coupled with modifications to the building, e.g. opening of apertures in walls. Failures in newer buildings were due to faults, or unauthorized modifications, in construction. Failures in buildings during construction could be caused additionally by inadequate support of incomplete sections.

It is unlikely that vibratory forces produced in buildings by traffic will be a direct cause of more than minor architectural damage. However, compaction of the foundations of buildings close to the road by vibration from heavy vehicles could cause subsidence and differential settlement. This has been postulated as an explanation for the road-wards inclination of cathedrals and other ancient buildings.[28] The settlement of the soil is thought to be related to the product: (total number of cycles) × (amplitude).

Criteria for building damage from vibration have been reviewed.[19] A number of measures have been proposed, but the present tendency is to express limits in terms of velocity or acceleration. Earlier measures include:

1. The Zeller power:

   $$Z = \frac{a^2}{f} = 16\pi A^2 f^3 \text{ (cm}^2\text{s}^{-3})$$

   where a is the acceleration in cm/s²,
   f is the frequency,
   A is the amplitude in cm.

2. The Pal, where:

   Zeller Pal = $10 \log_{10} (Z/Z_1)$
   Z_1 is a threshold Zeller power of 50 mm²/s³ and Z is in mm²/s³.

3. The Vibrar, where the strength in vibrar is:

   Vibrar = $10 \log_{10} Z/10$
   in which Z is the Zeller power (mm²/s³).

4. The DIN Pal, where:
   DIN Pal = $20 \log_{10} V/V_0$
   where V is the RMS vibration velocity and V_0 is 0.316 mm/s.

Limiting values for effects on buildings can be attached to the above measures. For example, in terms of Vibrar, the damage scale is as in *Table 12.2*[19]

As an illustration, a Vibrar strength of 30 at 50 Hz corresponds to an acceleration of −23 dB re 1g or a velocity of 2.25 mm/s, which is associated with the onset of light damage.

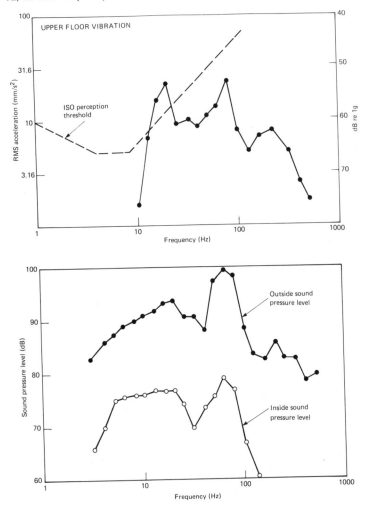

Figure 12.14 Sound pressure and vibration spectra during passage of a 32 tonne commercial vehicle

This compares with DIN 4150 which gives recommendations for transient vibration (sudden shocks) (*Table 12.3*).[32] This standard, originally published in 1938, is generally regarded as being rather cautious and, as a result, difficult to apply in practice. A recent revision of this standard proposes a relaxation of the limits and gives different values for different frequency ranges. In the new standard the criteria for buildings 'sensitive to vibration' is 3–8 mm/s peak particle velocity for frequencies in the range 10–50 Hz and 3 mm/s for frequencies below 10 Hz. For domestic houses the criteria are 5–15 mm/s for 10–50 Hz and 5 mm/s for frequencies below 10 Hz. Higher guide values are allowed for higher frequency ranges.[32]

Threshold levels for potential damage are also considered in reference 7, in terms of constant velocity, and presented in the form of *Figure 12.15*, which includes both human response and

Table 12.3 Recommendations for transient vibration (sudden shocks) according to DIN 4150

Type of building	Maximum velocity (mm/s)
Ruins and buildings of great historical interest	2
Buildings with existing defects, having visible cracks in brickwork	5
Undamaged buildings in good condition	10
Strong buildings, e.g. in reinforced steel or concrete	10–40

building damage criteria. The figure is based on an acceleration 'spectrum level' analysis (i.e. the level in a 1 Hz wide frequency band), but this can be obtained from a wider band analysis by using:

$$L_{spectrum} = L_{band} - 10 \log_{10}(\Delta f)$$

where Δf is the bandwidth.

Rudder[7] suggests a threshold level for building damage of 2.5 mm/s, corresponding to −22 dB re lg at 50 Hz. These are

Table 12.2 Damage scale in terms of Vibrar

Vibrar strength	Damage potential
<30	No structural damage
30–40	Light damage e.g. cracks in plaster
50–60	Destruction of buildings

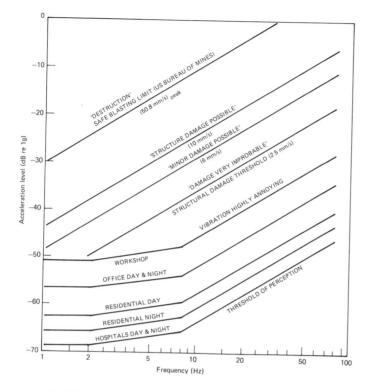

Figure 12.15 Criteria for subjective vibration limits and building damage

close to the Vibrar limit of 30 discussed above. Rudder recommends as an additional safety factor that the maximum permitted acceleration should be -35 dB re lg or 0.18 m/s^2 ($\sim$0.02 g).

The various recommendations and criteria for prevention of damage are in accordance with *Figure 12.16* which is a compilation of:

1. Vibration from various sources which has caused damage to buildings, often slight (from reference 19).
2. Vibration from various sources which has not caused damage (from reference 19).
3. Vibration from pile driving (from reference 13).
4. Vibration from traffic (from reference 9).

In each case the vibrations have been measured on a structural element e.g. foundation, wall or floor. Higher vibration levels have been detected in windows due to traffic, but these are not significant for damage.

From *Figure 12.16*, the borderline for onset of damage is about 0.1 g or 10 mm/s. The traffic-induced vibrations are well below this level and one concludes that damage is unlikely to occur except under the following circumstances:

1. There may be a trigger effect in an already unstable component, leading to failure at an earlier stage than would have occurred in the absence of traffic.
2. Compaction of the earth by heavy vehicles could lead to subsidence in a building close to the road and subsequent damage caused by the distortion produced in the building construction.
3. Long-term fatigue effects which are at present unknown.

Aspects of the above form part of a research programme currently being carried out by the UK Transport and Road Research Laboratory.

12.6 Response of people

12.6.1 Response to vibration[25,33]

Human response to vibration is discussed in Section 16.5.1. In particular, *Figure 16.14* gives limiting criteria for vibration in buildings based on ISO 2631: DAD1. Comparison with the vibration measurements in buildings shown in *Figures 12.13* and *12.14* indicates that feelable vibration from traffic is likely to occur only at the lower end of the vibration spectrum. The subjective effect is experienced mainly through resonance of the lower modes of the building floor and may be erratic in its occurrence, depending on the presence of a suitable exciting vehicle. There are locations close to concentrations of heavy vehicles—e.g. quarries, freight complexes, etc.—where effects are more continuous. Vibration that may escape direct detection sometimes manifests through secondary effects. These include rattling of pictures, ornaments and cupboard doors and movement of glassware on shelves. Rattling effects may also be produced by airborne noise.

12.6.2 Response to noise

Human response to low-frequency noise from traffic includes aspects of (1) audibility and stress; (2) direct effects on the body.

12.6.2.1 Audibility and stress

Whilst low-frequency noise can be masked by high levels at higher frequencies, noise levels in buildings tend to be biased to emphasize the low frequencies, which may become the dominant part of the spectrum (e.g. *see Figure 12.2*). Threshold levels obtained by measurements in a low-frequency chamber are summarized in *Figure 12.17*,[34] from which it is clear that traffic noise at frequencies below about 20 Hz is unlikely to be audible inside buildings (e.g. compare *Figures 12.17* and *12.13*). A

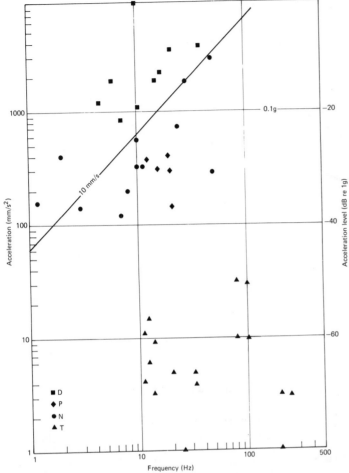

Figure 12.16. Measured building vibrations and damage. D=vibrations which have produced damage; N=vibrations which have not produced damage; P=vibrations from piling; T=vibrations from traffic

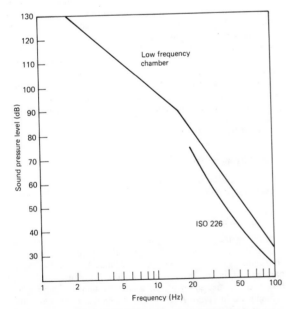

Figure 12.17 Low-frequency hearing thresholds. Chamber measurements (whole body) compared with ISO 226

typical domestic room might have a largest dimension of, say, 5 m, giving a lowest resonant frequency in the 31.5 Hz band. Coincidence of vehicle excitation frequency with a room resonance leads to sound level enhancement, subjectively referred to as 'buzzing' or 'booming'. This effect can be annoying and stressful. Rattling of doors and windows has an onset threshold of 75–80 dB in the lower frequency region where, for a given pressure, particle displacements in the acoustic wave are high.

12.6.2.2 Direct effects

Direct effects on the body arise through excitation of body resonances, the most notable of which is a chest resonance occurring in the frequency range 30–90 Hz, depending on individual characteristics.[35-37] *Figure 12.18* shows chest resonance of two male subjects at excitation levels of 100 and 105 dB, obtained by frequency sweeps.[36] The acceleration peaks at about 0.03 g for 105 dB excitation level. *Figure 12.14* gives a sound level of about 100 dB for external traffic noise in the resonance region and it is to be expected that chest resonances will be felt. (This is confirmed by common experience of pedestrians alongside heavy vehicles, especially in stop/start conditions when engines are used in low gear.) Repeat of the resonance search frequency sweeps when subjects were breathing a helium/oxygen mixture did not change the resonance frequency, indicating a structural effect rather than the involvement of air filled cavities.[35]

A study of 61 subjects (about one-third female, two-thirds

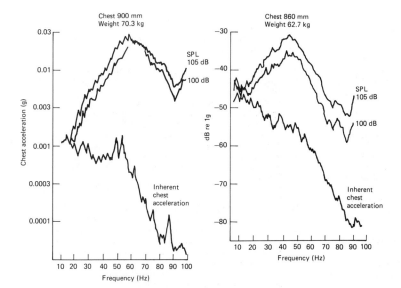

Figure 12.18 Chest resonance of two male subjects

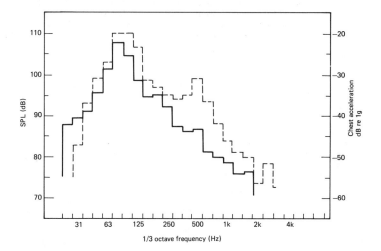

Figure 12.19 Peak levels of chest acceleration and traffic noise. ----=applied sound field, ———=chest acceleration

male) gave a median chest resonance frequency of 74 Hz for males and 64 Hz for females. The first effect to be noted by subjects, as excitation levels were increased, was a voice modulation under chest resonance conditions. The median value of sound pressure for this effect was 98 dB, whilst the lowest recorded value was 84 dB. Tests using recordings of heavy vehicle noise gave the results in *Figure 12.19*.[37] This compares the noise and acceleration spectra obtained in a cumulative 'peak hold' mode of the analyser. The peak level at 80 Hz is about 0.07 g for 110 dB excitation level. An important conclusion of the work was that, although chest resonances could be excited by traffic noise, the subjects generally complained about the level of the noise whilst it was still too low to excite perceptible chest vibrations.

References

1 LEVENTHALL, H. G. The occurrence, measurement and analysis of low frequency noise. In *Proceedings of Conference on Low Frequency Noise and Hearing*, Aalborg, Denmark, Aelborg University Press pp. 15–30 (1980).

2 HASSALL, J. R. A review of low frequency and infrasonic noise affecting London. *M.Sc. Dissertation*, Chelsea College, University of London (1976).

3 MARTIN, D. J., NELSON, P. M. and HILL, R. C. *Measurement and Analysis of Traffic Induced Vibration in Buildings*. TRRL Supplementary Report 402 (1978).

4 HOLLINGSWORTH, G. H. and GILBERT, D. A. M. An exploratory study into the prediction of low frequency traffic noise. *Applied Acoustics*, **15**, 79–95 (1982).

5 LEVENTHALL, H. G. Man-made infrasound. Its occurrence and some subjective effects. In *International Colloquium on Infrasound*, CNRS Paris, pp. 131–152 (1973).

6 LEONARD, D. R., GRAINGER, J. W. and EYRE, R. *Loads and vibrations caused by Eight Commercial Vehicles with Gross Weights Exceeding 32 tons (32.5 Mg)*. TRRL Laboratory Report 582 (1974).

7 RUDDER, F. F. *Engineering Guidelines for the Analysis of Traffic Induced Vibrations*. Report No. FHWA-RD-78-166, US Department of Transportation (1978).

8 RUDDER, F. F. *Determination of Impact from Vibrations Related to Highway Use*. Report No. FHWA-RD-78-167, US Department of Transportation (1978).

9 WHIFFIN, A. C. and LEONARD, D. R. *A Survey of Traffic Induced Vibrations*. Road Research Laboratory Report, LR 418 (1971).

10 BURT, M. E. *Roads and the Environment*. TRRL Report, LR441 (1972).
11 HOUSE, M. E. Traffic induced vibration in buildings. *Highway Engineer*, **February**, 6–16 (1973).
12 MARTIN, D. J. *Ground Vibration Caused by Road Construction Operation*. TRRL Supplementary Report 328 (1977).
13 MARTIN, D. J. *Ground Vibration from Impact Pile Driving During Road Construction*. TRRL Supplementary Report 544 (1980).
14 WATKINS, L. H. *Environmental Impact of Roads and Traffic*. Applied Science Publishers, New York (1981).
15 AMES, W. H., *et al*. *Survey of Earth-borne Vibration due to Highway Construction and Highway Traffic*. Report No. CA-DDT-TL-6391-1-76-20, California Department of Transport (1976).
16 UNGAR, E. E. and BENDER, E. K. Vibration produced in buildings by passage of subway trains; parameter estimation for preliminary design. *Inter-Noise 75*, Institute of Noise Control Engineering (USA) pp. 491–498 (1975).
17 BOSWELL, L. F. Structural response to ground-borne vibration. *Journal of The Society of Environmental Engineering*, **52**, 6–9 (1972).
18 BATA, M. Effects on Buildings of vibrations caused by traffic. *Building Science*, **6**, 221–246 (1971).
19 STEFFENS, R. J. *Structural Vibration and Damage*. HMSO, London (1974).
20 TURNER, C. K. The vibration of windows under acoustic and structural excitation. *MSc Report*, Chelsea College, University of London (1973).
21 HUBBARD, H. H. Noise induced house vibrations and human perception. *Noise Control Engineering*, **19**, 49–55 (1982).
22 MARTIN, D. J. *Low Frequency Traffic Noise and Building Vibration*. TRRL Supplementary Report 429 (1978).
23 ISO 2631 DAD I *Guide for the Evaluation of Human Exposure to Whole Body Vibration* (1978).

24 BRE Digests *Vibration in Buildings—1*, No. 117 (1970) and *Vibration in Buildings—2*, No. 118 (1970).
25 BAUGHAN, C. J. and MARTIN, D. J. *Vibration Nuisance from Road Traffic at Fourteen Residential Sites*. TRRL Laboratory Report 1020 (1981).
26 MCKAIG, T. H. *Building Failures*, McGraw Hill, New York (1962).
27 O'NEIL, D. B. Examples of damage done by noise. *Insulation*, **July**, 228–229 (1959).
28 CROCKETT, J. H. A. Some practical aspects of vibration in civil engineering. In *Vibration in Civil Engineering*, pp. 267–272, Butterworths, London (1966).
29 BOCQUENET, D., *et al*. Les vibrations dues au trafic routier urbain. *Annals Institut Technique et Travaux Public*, **355**, 58–91 (1977).
30 BRE Digest *Cracking in Buildings* No. 75 (1975).
31 BRE Digest *Assessment of Damage in Low-rise Buildings*, No. 251 (1981).
32 DIN 4150 *Vibrations in Building Structures* (1970). Revised April 1984.
33 WATTS, G. R. *Vibration Nuisance from Road Traffic—Results of a 50 Site Survey*. TRRL Laboratory Report 1119 (1984).
34 LEVENTHALL, H. G. Annoyance caused by low frequency/low level noise. *Proceedings of Conference on Low Frequency Noise and Hearing*, Aalborg, Denmark, Aelborg University Press, pp. 113–120 (1980).
35 LEVENTHALL, H. G., BROWN, F. D. and KYRIAKIDES, K. Somatic responses to low frequency noise. *Proceedings of ICA*, Madrid, p. 546 (1977).
36 BROWN, F. D. Acoustically Induced Chest Vibration, *MSc Report*, Chelsea College, University of London, (1976).
37 WALFORD, R. *The Response of the Human Body to Low Frequency Traffic Noise*. TRRL Contract No. 842/275, Chelsea College (1979).

Part 4

Train Noise

13

Introduction to Train Noise

Steven L. Wolfe MS
Wilson, Ihrig & Associates,
Oakland, California, USA

Contents

13.1 Introduction

As the population increases and cities grow larger, new inter-city rail lines and rail transit systems are being built and existing systems are being expanded in order to move both products and people in one of the most efficient and cost effective methods available. Increased train operations coupled with today's concern about the hazards of environmental pollution make the impact of train noise and vibration critically important. The population near new lines have legitimate concerns and those near older facilities are complaining in increasing numbers. Excessive noise can cause annoyance and even hearing loss, as well as other psychological and physiological problems (*see* Chapters 3 and 4). Train 'noise pollution' can result in complaints, lawsuits, government fines and penalties, and in the case of passenger transport, a loss of public support for rail transportation as an alternative to the automobile. The noise and vibration from train operations cannot be ignored. Implementation of available control techniques coupled with appropriate land use planning will decrease adverse noise and vibration impact without sacrificing the ultimate goal of transporting goods and people in a timely and efficient manner.

This chapter presents a general overview of the noise and vibration produced by various types of trains for a variety of conditions. The task is complicated by the wide variety of train types and operating conditions, since trains can operate in subway, at-grade or on an elevated structure over a range of speeds and propulsion types. However, an attempt has been made to characterize these various conditions by wayside and interior noise for both inter-city or mainline railways and transit trains. Systems in the USA and Canada are emphasized, although most of the data presented are applicable to train systems in other parts of the world.

13.2 Wayside noise and vibration

The wayside noise radiated into the community from train operations is, along with the noise created inside the rail vehicles, the most important aspect of train noise. Wayside noise is generally a function of a number of different factors including the interaction of the wheels and rails, the vehicle or locomotive propulsion system, auxiliary equipment, noise radiated from vibrating structures, train speed, train length, and aerodynamics for high-speed operation (i.e. > 250 km/h). Other aspects of wayside noise include warning device or horn noise, ancillary equipment noise, track maintenance noise, and yard and shop noise.

In addition to the airborne noise radiated into the community, there is ground-borne noise and vibration caused by vibration at the wheel/rail interface which travels through the track and support structure and the intervening soil and rock to nearby buildings. This phenomenon is normally experienced as a low-frequency rumbling noise or as a perceptible mechanical vibration. Communities have complained about this problem in areas adjacent to subway, at-grade and elevated structures. For most situations when the track structure is at-grade or elevated, the airborne noise predominates over the ground-borne noise. Details of ground and airborne vibration mechanisms are given in Chapters 10 and 16.

13.2.1 Inter-city or mainline railway

The designation inter-city or mainline railway refers to train operations that generally utilize diesel–electric or electric locomotives which push or pull either freight or passenger rail cars. The noise from such a train pass-by is generally characterized by a high noise level during the locomotive pass-by with lower noise levels or noises of different character during pass-bys of the cars (carriages). The noise from the diesel–electric locomotive is normally dominated by exhaust noise from the generators. This source of noise is independent of the pass-by speed of the train, but dependent on engine load and throttle setting. An electric locomotive usually produces a somewhat lower wayside noise level. The principal source is generally the propulsion system (i.e. electric motors, cooling fans and sometimes gearing) which is dependent on the passing speed. The major noise from the trailing cars is produced by the interaction of the wheels and rails. Rail–wheel interaction is dependent on speed, wheel condition, rail condition and whether the track is jointed or welded. Most mainline railroad operations are on at-grade ballast and tie track with operations in tunnels or over bridges usually comprising only a small percentage of track mileage. This is in contrast to rail transit operations where a greater proportion of the operations occur either in subway or on elevated structure. *Table 13.1* gives a summary of typical maximum A-weighted wayside noise levels taken from mainline freight and passenger train operations. The levels given have been normalized to a distance of 30 m from track centre-line. Similar data on wayside noise levels generated by rolling stock operated by British Rail are shown in *Figure 15.2*. Chapters 14 and 15 also contain further data on locomotive noise generation.

Table 13.1 Typical wayside noise levels from mainline freight and passenger train operations on ballast and tie track — 30 m from track centre-line

Conditions	Speed (km/h)	Noise level (dB(A))
Idling 2000 Hp general-purpose locomotive (4 different locomotives of same model)	0	61–66
Idling 3000 Hp general-purpose locomotive (7 different locomotives of same model)	0	65–68
Passenger train:		
Electric locomotive	132	90
Cars		84–88
Passenger train:		
Electric locomotive	64	92
Cars		88
Passenger electric locomotive — ASEA RC4	160	86
Freight train — 0% grade:		
Diesel locomotive	108	92
Cars		82–89
Freight train — 2% grade:		
Diesel locomotive	45	92
Cars		75–85
Freight train — 1% grade:		
Diesel locomotive	93	91
Cars		82–91

Data taken from references 1–4.

Other wayside noise includes the noise from the locomotive horn or warning device. In the USA a three-chime air horn is generally used for freight locomotives and a five-chime unit is generally used on passenger locomotives. Typical maximum wayside noise levels at 30 m from track centre-line range from 100 to 110 dB(A). If the railway is electrically powered from overhead electrical lines, at-grade substations are usually located at intervals along the line. The noise from the substations varies considerably depending on power requirements and installation details; however, most are not enclosed and in this condition can generate noise levels of 40–45 dB(A) at 30 m from the edge of the substation installation. Although this is a relatively low noise level, substation noise can have significant pure-tone components which can constitute a problem.

Most frequently used mainline rail routes have regularly scheduled track maintenance including ballast cleaning, tamping, and rail grinding. Noise levels from maintenance activities obviously depend on the exact activity occurring; however, the noise levels are typical of diesel, hydraulic, and pneumatic equipment used at heavy construction projects.[5] Some examples of commonly used maintenance equipment and methods used for reducing this noise at British Rail are contained in reference 6.

Yard and shop noise can be a major contributor to wayside noise in community areas adjacent to the yards. Marshalling or classification yards are located at intervals along mainline railroad routes and major repair and maintenance facilities are often located within the yard. These classification and maintenance activities are varied and the noise levels and their duration are dependent on the particular activities, yard layout, and operational patterns.

Yards typically receive incoming trains and redistribute the freight cars into new outgoing trains bound for new destinations. In many yards the cars are shuttled to different tracks by switching locomotives, in which case the major noise sources are the locomotive and the impacts from the cars coupling together. The impact noise is typically 20–30 dB(A) or more above the ambient noise, in the range of 95–100 dB(A) at 30 m from track centre-line. Most large classification yards are 'hump' yards. For this type of yard, cars to be classified are pushed to the top of a hump and are released so that the cars coast through switches and onto one of many classification tracks. The speed of the car is controlled by an active pneumatic or electric retarder which applies pressure to a retarding shoe. The retarding shoe contacts the freight car wheels and, while in contact with the wheels, usually causes a squeal or screech often consisting of multiple pure tones. The maximum level of the squeal noise is in the range of 100–105 dB(A) at 30 m.

Even higher noise levels have been observed near inert retarders. Most inert retarders are normally closed, spring-loaded devices located at the far end of a classification track to restrain 'humped' cars from going out at the end of the classification track and onto other tracks. The major noise arises once the cars on a particular track have been coupled together and are pulled out through the normally closed retarder. Noise levels as high as 126 dB(A) at 3 m lasting for 0.5–8 seconds have been measured. One way of eliminating the squeal is by the use of non-clasp type retarders. Two designs have been used in Europe and by virtue of their non-clasp characteristics are virtually noise free. One design is called an 'oil pressure' retarder and was designed by Dowty of England. The second design is a hydraulic retarder and was designed by ASEA of Sweden. A description of these designs as well as other information on classification yard operations is contained in reference 7. The noise from the retarders and the impact noise from cars coupling together are the major noise sources from a yard and are not only of concern in the wayside community but also to employees in the yard. The levels are sufficient to cause hearing damage when working within close range of the retarders. Typical boundary line noise exposure levels for an active classification yard are 55–70 dB(A) for L_{eq} (24-hour).[8]

13.2.2 Transit trains

The designation transit train refers here to an electric self-propelled train common in large urban areas throughout the world and used mainly to move people. Operations can occur underground, at-grade or on elevated structures. In recent years, a sizable body of data has been established characterizing the noise and vibration characteristics of existing old and new transit systems. The oldest systems, those built during the first half of this century, generally create the highest noise levels. Careful design of modern systems and the rebuilding of older systems with an emphasis on reducing both wayside, station, and vehicle interior noise have created systems with considerably less adverse noise impact on the community.

The primary focus in this chapter is on steel wheel/steel rail transit systems; however, the discussion is also generally applicable to rubber tyre transit systems. Rubber tyre systems differ most from conventional rail transit systems in the generation of rolling noise which results from the rubber tyres rolling on the fixed concrete guideway. Rubber tyre transit systems operate in Mexico City, Montreal,[9] Paris[9] and Sapporo, Japan. General characteristics of rubber-tyred systems are contained in reference 10.

13.2.2.1 Wayside noise from train operations

Noise radiated from train operations and track structures generally constitute the major noise sources from transit systems. The noise and vibration from different transit train operations can take different paths depending on the type of support structure. Airborne noise is radiated from at-grade and elevated operations, while ground-borne noise and vibration is of primary concern for subway operations. However, problems with ground-borne noise and vibration have also occurred with transit trains operating at-grade or on elevated structures.

There are four basic sources of wayside airborne noise:

1. Wheel/rail noise: This is the noise that is radiated directly from the vibrating wheels and rails.
2. Propulsion equipment: this includes noise from traction motors, cooling fans for the traction motors, and reduction gears.
3. Auxiliary equipment: compressors, motor generators, brakes, ventilation systems and any other car-mounted equipment.
4. Elevated structure noise: this is the noise radiated by vibration of the transit structure components that are excited by a train pass-by.

Each of these noise sources can dominate the wayside noise level for specific conditions. At very low speeds (< 15 km/h) auxiliary equipment may predominate. At speeds up to approximately 50 km/h, wheel/rail noise predominates, while at speeds greater than 50 km/h, the propulsion equipment noise predominates, particularly if the traction motor is self-ventilated. For older systems with light-weight steel elevated structures, the structure noise can predominate at all speeds above about 15 km/h.

Aerial structures can be divided into two broad classes—light-weight steel elevated structures and those of higher mass construction. Train operation on light-weight steel structures creates one of the most severe environmental problems facing transit systems. The rail tie and support structure acts as a large sounding board with potentially very high noise levels radiated to the wayside community and into transit cars. The second category of aerial structures are constructed of higher mass materials such as concrete or concrete/steel composites. These structures typically have ballasted trackbeds or concrete decks with resilient rail fasteners. With appropriate noise control treatments, these structures can be placed even in noise-sensitive residential areas without adverse noise impact.

The levels of wayside noise vary significantly between different transit systems. Modern systems with welded rails, resilient rail fasteners, and wheels and rails in good condition are much quieter than many of the older systems—see also Chapters 16 and 17. There can also be significant variations within the same transit system, depending on the wheel and rail condition and on the type of transit car used. In general, trains operating on light-weight steel elevated structures produce the highest levels of wayside noise, while trains on ballast and tie track with smooth rails, the lowest. On ballast and tie track the sound levels can be reduced even further by the use of special noise control features, such as sound barrier walls—*see also* Chapter 17. *Figure 13.1* summarizes typical wayside noise levels as a function of speed.[11–14]

13.2.2.2 Ground-borne noise and vibration

Communities have complained about ground-borne noise and vibration in areas adjacent to subway, at-grade, and elevated structures, which indicates that controls must be considered for all types of track structures. Current technology makes it possible to almost eliminate ground-borne noise and vibration from most types of transit configurations. However, if the distance from the track to the affected buildings is less than 10–15 m, the requisite control methods may be prohibitively expensive.

Ground-borne noise and vibration from rail transit trains transmitted into buildings generally occur in the frequency range of 10–200 Hz and are usually concentrated in only one or two octaves. The octave band rms acceleration levels at the ground surface, at distances of 15–30 m from a subway, are typically 50–70 dB (re 1 micro g) with the peak frequency between 16 and 63 Hz. Various methods have been used to reduce ground-borne noise and vibration, including: reducing the unsprung mass of the vehicle trucks (bogies), use of flexible (i.e. low stiffness) rail fasteners, ballast mats placed beneath the trackbed, and floating slab trackbeds. Each of these methods will reduce ground-borne noise and vibration by varying amounts in different frequency regions when compared with 'rigid' or direct rail fixation. Further information on vibration and ground-borne noise control methods are given in Chapters 16 and 17.

A considerable amount of research is currently in progress regarding the prediction and control of ground-borne vibration[15] and the effects of vibration on people.[16] Recently, research has been concentrated on the development of practical criteria that can be used to assess the acceptability of vibration in buildings. Some suitable criteria are contained in the *Guide to the Evaluation of Human Exposure to Vibration in Buildings*.[17] Further information related to vibration effects on people is given in Chapters 12 and 16.

In the United States research into the prediction and control of ground-borne noise and vibration from transit trains has resulted in a viable method of determining the ground-borne noise and vibration propagated from transit train operations into specific buildings adjacent to proposed new alignments.[15] This prediction method takes into account the train type, train speed, trackbed structure, soil types, building foundation and structure type, and location of nearest critical occupancy within the building. Further details are given in Chapter 16.

13.2.2.3 Station noise

Another aspect of transit train noise is that produced in transit stations. There are five main noise sources in transit stations: (1) trains entering, leaving, and passing through the stations; (2) ancillary equipment, such as heating, ventilation and air conditioning equipment and escalators; (3) crowds; (4) public address systems; and (5) in above-ground stations, street or highway traffic and mainline railroads. The principal means of controlling noise in transit stations are the use of sound absorption treatment, careful design of ancillary equipment to meet sound

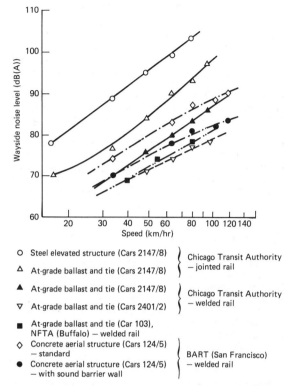

O Steel elevated structure (Cars 2147/8)	Chicago Transit Authority
△ At-grade ballast and tie (Cars 2147/8)	– jointed rail
▲ At-grade ballast and tie (Cars 2147/8)	Chicago Transit Authority
▽ At-grade ballast and tie (Cars 2401/2)	– welded rail
■ At-grade ballast and tie (Car 103), NFTA (Buffalo) – welded rail	
◇ Concrete aerial structure (Cars 124/5) – standard	BART (San Francisco)
● Concrete aerial structure (Cars 124/5) – with sound barrier wall	– welded rail

Figure 13.1 Transit train wayside noise as a function of speed at 15 m from track centre-line

emission criteria, and the use of barriers or buildings to screen noise sources. The noise level at a station platform during a train entrance or exit can be very high if the station lacks sufficient noise control treatment. For example, the maximum noise level in a highly reverberant station can reach 100–105 dB(A).[11] Using effective and properly placed acoustical treatment, these levels can be reduced to about 80–85 dB(A) which is generally considered acceptable by transit patrons.[18] An example of station acoustical treatment is given in Chapter 17.

13.2.2.4 Ancillary equipment noise

An area of transit noise which is not directly related to the movement of the transit vehicles is the noise from ancillary equipment and facilities such as the noise from fan and vent shafts, substations, and chiller plants. The noise from fan and vent shafts can be a problem in areas near subway operations. A vent shaft is not a noise source in itself, but can be a conduit for the transmission of train noise to the surface. A fan shaft is similar to a vent shaft in that it can also be a conduit for the transmission of train noise to the surface. In addition, noise from the operation of the ventilation fans in the shaft can produce noise which is radiated out of the shaft at the surface. The noise that radiates out of a shaft can be controlled with the proper placement of acoustical absorption materials and attaching silencers to the fans. Noise levels from the shafts are dependent on fan size and configuration. Typical noise levels from a 50 000 ft³/min fan without a silencer and no shaft absorption treatment at 15 m from the shaft opening are in the range of 58–64 dB(A). Suitable maximum silencing treatment can reduce this level by about 30 dB(A).[19]

13.2.2.5 Noise from maintenance and storage yards

Noise from maintenance and storage yards is of a different character than the noise of normal transit train operations or from ancillary facilities. This is primarily because of the nature of yard equipment and special trackwork. Major sources of yard and shop noise include: wheel squeal on curves, intermittent noise as wheels pass over joints and through switches, other general train rolling noise, noise from auxiliary equipment operations, coupling and uncoupling of cars, operation of impact tools and machinery, shouting workmen, car washing equipment, telephone or warning buzzers and horns, and with older systems, brakes squealing and air release. The noise from these various activities can be controlled by the supervision of operating procedures, careful design of yard equipment, use of buffer zones (i.e. an area without sensitive uses) and sound barriers, and controls on transit vehicle operations and equipment.

13.3 Interior noise

The noise inside the train vehicles strongly influences the patrons' overall perception of the comfort of the rail system. Generally, the same factors that affect wayside noise also affect interior noise. The primary difference between inter-city or mainline railroad interior noise and transit interior noise is the fact that for mainline railroad operations, the vehicles are generally unpowered and operate at-grade on ballast and tie track, while for transit trains, the vehicle is generally self-propelled and operates in subway, on surface, or elevated structures. Although this is certainly not always the case, it provides a convenient way to categorize the discussion which follows.

There are three major noise sources and paths of car interior noise: (1) external airborne noise transmitted through the car shell; (2) structure-borne noise and vibration; and (3) airborne noise from interior sources. Any of these noise sources or paths can dominate, depending on operating conditions and car design.

13.3.1 Inter-city or mainline railroad

For operations on ballast and tie track, the interior noise levels in passenger cars range from about 55 dB(A) to 80 dB(A), with a typical range of 60–70 dB(A) for a modern air-conditioned (sealed) car at speeds up to 160 km/hr. There are noise level differences at different locations within the car. Noise levels at the ends of the car are usually about 2–5 dB(A) higher than the levels at the centre of the car since the ends are usually nearest the access doors and are over the trucks (bogies). Operations on jointed track result in a noise level increase of approximately 3–6 dB(A) at speeds in the range of 100–160 km/h. Noise levels at low-speed operations or when stationary are usually limited by car auxiliary equipment such as the air-conditioning system, heaters, and generators and generally range from 55 to 65 dB(A) depending on the type and operating conditions of the auxiliary equipment.

13.3.2 Transit trains

In the United States the noise levels inside the rail transit cars range from about 65 to 105 dB(A) during normal operations. This wide range of noise levels is dependent on a number of factors, including:

1. Train speed. Car interior noise levels increase as a function of speed, at rates varying from $15 \log_{10} V$ to $40 \log_{10} V$, where V is the speed of the train.

2. Type of way structure. Noise levels are lowest on at-grade ballast and tie-welded track, and highest for operations on light-weight steel elevated structures and inside subway tunnels with concrete trackbed and no acoustical treatment.

3. Sound insulation provided by the car body. Newer cars provide significantly more sound insulation than older cars which were built without consideration of acoustical design.

4. Type and design of mechanical equipment. This includes the propulsion system and auxiliary equipment, including the air conditioning systems, compressors, and motor generator sets.

5. Wheel and rail condition. Noise levels increase with increasing surface roughness of the wheels and rails. Rail corrugations and wheel flats can increase the noise level by as much as 10–15 dB(A).

Figure 13.2 presents car interior noise levels as a function of speed for representative transit systems in the United States.[11–13,18,20] This figure indicates that there is a wide variation in noise levels even under similar operating conditions. This is particularly evident when comparing different car types on the same system. The figure also indicates that the noise levels are strongly dependent on the type of way structure.

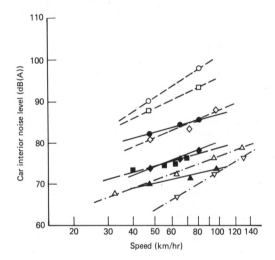

☐ Ballast-and-tie subway (Car 2060)

◆ Ballast-and-tie subway (Car 2534)

○ Concrete trackbed subway (Car 2060)
} Chicago Transit Authority — jointed rail

● Concrete trackbed subway (Car 2534)

◇ At-grade ballast-and-tie (Car 2060)
} Chicago Transit Authority — welded rail

▲ At-grade ballast-and-tie (Car 2601)

■ SLRV, at-grade ballast-and-tie, MBTA (Boston) — welded rail

△ Concrete aerial structure
} Bart (San Francisco) — welded rail

▽ At-grade ballast-and-tie

Figure 13.2. Transit car interior noise as a function of speed

Compared with operations on welded (ballast and tie) track in the open, at speeds of 40–100 km/h, the increases in car interior noise levels on other types of track structures are approximately:

1. Light-weight steel elevated structure $\quad+8-12\,\mathrm{dB(A)}$
2. Subway tunnel with concrete trackbed $\quad+7-12\,\mathrm{dB(A)}$
   without absorptive treatment
3. Subway tunnel with ballast and tie track or $\quad+5-7\,\mathrm{dB(A)}$
   concrete trackbed with absorptive treatment
4. Concrete trackbed (at-grade or aerial) $\quad+2-6\,\mathrm{dB(A)}$

The interior noise levels of new transit cars are considerably lower than those of older cars. Acoustical design considerations have been given increased priority in recent years in order to provide an improved acoustical environment for patrons. Lower noise levels are the result of adherence to acoustical design criteria which are generally included as part of the contract documents for the car construction. Compliance with design criteria have resulted in interior noise levels for steel-wheel/steel-rail systems which are lower than those of current rubber tyre transit systems, generally considered to have low interior noise levels by the general public.

13.4 Design guidelines, criteria and standards used to control noise from trains

The noise and vibration generated by trains are subject to a range of controls as a result of design guidelines or performance criteria and standards.

In the United States, the Environmental Protection Agency (EPA)[21] and more recently the Federal Railroad Administration (FRA)[22] have established noise measurement standards and emission criteria to cover a wide range of mainline rail vehicles and associated equipment. The FRA regulations apply to new and existing locomotives, rail cars, operable retarders, car-coupling operations and locomotive load cell test stands.

The US Department of Transportation (DOT) and the Urban Mass Transportation Agency (UMTA) of DOT do not have any specific noise and vibration guidelines or criteria for rapid transit systems. Their activity in this area is limited to review of environmental impact statements and review of design features to assure compliance with the environmental impact statement requirements and standard practices in industry.

Most new transit systems have included design criteria to control excessive wayside noise and vibration. Older systems have also adopted noise and vibration design criteria for extensions and for both route and station renovations. In the USA and Canada many systems have adopted the format and design goals of the American Public Transit Association.[23] UMTA does have some general guidelines for evaluating the significance of noise impacts.[24] Currently in preparation is the *Guidance Manual for Impacts Analysis of Transit Noise and Vibration* which will provide guidelines to ensure that new transit systems or extensions will be analysed in sufficient detail and that appropriate design features will be included to minimize impact.[25]

In Canada, there are no federal noise standards regulating the line or yard operations of railways. Noise limit standards have been developed by the Central Mortgage and Housing Corporation for new residential construction of public, non-profit and cooperative housing projects funded by the Corporation.[26] Recent noise limit standards and control measures have been proposed for an Ontario provincial policy on the environmental protection of new residential construction adjacent to railways.[27]

There are no standardized criteria for interior noise levels in rail passenger vehicles. However, in the United States AMTRAK (National Rail Passenger Corporation) and most transit authorities have vehicle procurement specifications which limit both the interior and exterior noise produced by the

vehicle. A sample noise and vibration specification from a transit vehicle procurement specification of the Chicago Transit Authority is contained in reference[28]. The practical results achieved by this specification are shown in *Figures 13.1* and *13.2*. Controlling the noise and vibration of new vehicles and facilities is considered an incentive to encourage patronage of the system.

Although most countries have not established specific emission criteria, they have adopted specific measurement procedures to monitor and assess wayside and interior noise.[29,30] Reference 28 also provides useful guidelines for measurement of noise and vibration. Some of the situations requiring the measurement of rail system noise and vibration include: (1) environmental assessment of an existing or proposed rail line; (2) evaluation of noise emission or compliance with purchase specifications; (3) diagnosis of noise and vibration problems or complaints; and (4) evaluation of mitigation measures.

References

1 *Background Document/Environmental Explanation for Proposed Interstate Rail Carrier Noise Emission Regulations*, US Environmental Protection Agency, Report No. 550/9–74–005a, Washington D.C., pp. 4–9 and 10 (1974).
2 RICKLEY, E. J., QUINN, R. W. and SUSSAN, N. R. *Noise Level Measurements of Railroads: Freight Yards and Wayside*, US Department of Transportation, Report No. DOT–TSC–OST–73–46, Washington D.C., pp. 136–137 (1974).
3 HANSON, C. E. Noise from high speed trains in the northeast corridor. *Noise-Con 77 Proceedings*, Noise Control Foundation, New York, p. 135 (1977).
4 SWING, J. W. and PIES, D. B. *Assessment of Noise Environments Around Railroad Operations*, Wyle Laboratories Report No. WCR 73–5, El Segundo, California, pp. 3–61, 3–63, 3–66 (1973).
5 *Noise from Construction Equipment and Operations, Building Equipment and Home Appliances*, US Environmental Protection Agency, Report No. NTID 300.1, Washington, D.C., pp. 10–15 (1971).
6 STANWORTH, C. G. Consideration of some noise sources due to railway operation. *Journal of Sound and Vibration*, **87**, 237–239 (1983).
7 WONG, P. J., *et al. Railroad Classification Yard Technology Manual—Vol. I: Yard Design Methods*, US Department of Transportation, Report No. FRA/ORD–81/20.1, Washington, D.C., pp. 124–127 (1981).
8 WILSON, S. S. *Noise Study in and Around the CP Rail Agincourt Marshalling Yard*, Independent Acoustic Laboratories Ltd., Don Mills, Ontario, (1980).
9 GIORGI, G. *Measures de bruits dans le metro Montreal*, Regie Autonome des Transports Parisiens (RATP), Report No. 71–7123, Paris, France, (1971).
10 SULKIN, M. A. and MILLER, D. R. Rubber-tyred rapid transit. *Mechanical Engineering*, **98**, 26–33, 39–45 (1976).
11 WILSON, G. P. *Noise Levels from Operations of CTA Rail Transit Trains* (prepared for the Chicago Transit Authority), Wilson, Ihrig & Associates, California, pp. 44, 76, 84 (1977).
12 WOLFE, S. L. *Noise and Vibration Test Report—2600 Series Rapid Transit Cars* (prepared for the Chicago Transit Authority), Wilson, Ihrig & Associates, Oakland, California, p. 3 (1982).
13 WILSON, G. P. *Aerial Structure Sound Barrier Walls*, (prepared for Baltimore Region Rapid Transit System) Wilson, Ihrig & Associates, Oakland, California, p. 16 (1973).
14 SAURENMAN, H. J. *Noise and Vibration Tests with Portland Tri-Met Prototype Vehicle at the Transportation Test Center*, Wilson, Ihrig & Associates, Oakland, California, p. 35 (1984).
15 SAURENMAN, H. J. and NELSON, J. T. *Procedures for the Prediction of Ground-Borne Noise and Vibration from Rail Transit Trains*, U.S. Department of Transportation (1985) (In press).
16 NELSON, J. T. and SAURENMAN, H. J. *State-of-the-Art Review: Prediction and Control of Groundborne Noise and Vibration from Rail Transit Trains*, U.S. Department of Transportation, Report No. UMTA–MA–06–0049–83–4, Washington, D.C., pp. 3–1–3–40 (1983).
17 Guide to the Evaluation of Human Exposure to Vibration in

Buildings. *American National Standard S3.29*, American National Standards Institute, New York (1983).

18 WOLFE, S. L. *Noise and Vibration Measurements at the O'Hare Extension Tunnels and Station*, (prepared for the City of Chicago), Wilson, Ihrig & Associates, Oakland, California, pp. 8, 10 (1984).

19 LEE, P. Y. *Modified Air Discharge Plenum (Type A)*, (prepared for Baltimore Region Rapid Transit System), Wilson, Ihrig & Associates, Oakland, California, p. 7 (1976).

20 WOLFE, S. L. *Interior Noise Measurements on the MBTA Green Line*, Wilson, Ihrig & Associates, Inc., Oakland, California, p. 20 (1976).

21 *Environmental Protection Agency Railroad Noise Emission Standards*, Title 40, Code of Federal Regulations, Chapter I, Part 201 (1976, amended 1980 and 1982).

22 *Department of Transportation, Federal Railroad Administration Railroad Noise Emission Compliance Regulations*, Title 49, Code of Federal Regulations, Chapter II, Part 210 (1983, corrected 1984).

23 *Guidelines for Design of Rapid Transit Facilities*, American Public Transit Association, Washington D.C., pp. 96–115 (1979).

24 *Guidelines for Preparing Environmental Assessments*, Urban Mass Transportation Administration (UMTA), Publication No. C5620.1, Washington, D.C. (1979).

25 HANSON, C. E. *Guidance Manual for Impacts Analysis of Transit Noise and Vibration*, U.S. Department of Transportation (1985) (In press).

26 *Road and Rail Noise: Effects on Housing*, Central Mortgage and Housing Corporation Report No. 5156, Ottawa, Ontario (1977).

27 *Proposed Provincial Policy on the Environmental Protection of New Residential Development Adjacent to Railways*, Ministry of Environment, Toronto, Ontario (1982).

28 SAURENMAN, H. J., NELSON, J. T. and WILSON, G. P. *Handbook of Urban Rail Noise and Vibration Control*, U.S. Department of Transportation, Report No. DOT–TSC–UMTA–81–72, Washington D.C. (1982).

29 *Acoustics—Measurement of Noise Emitted by Railbound Vehicles*, ISO Standard 3095–1975, International Standards Organization, Switzerland (1975).

30 *Acoustics—Measurement of Noise Inside Railbound Vehicles*, ISO Standard 3381–1976, International Standards Organization, Switzerland (1976).

14

Sources of Railway Noise

Colin Stanworth BSc
British Railways Board, Research Division,
Railway Technical Centre, Derby, UK

Contents

14.1 Introduction

It is the purpose of this chapter to discuss the noise arising from the principal features of the modern railway, to point out the source or sources responsible, and to indicate what measures need to be taken to reduce the impact. In not all cases is the mechanism of noise generation clear; in these cases it will be appropriate to discuss or speculate on the range of options that appear likely.

Some of the noise sources are the same, whether traffic is moving quickly or moving slowly or stationary, for example the noise from the diesel locomotive engine or the traction motor cooling blowers of some electric stock. This group of sources will be considered first.

Other sources, such as wheel/rail noise and aerodynamic noise, do not come into play until the train is moving over the track. These sources will form the second group treated.

Finally, those sources not directly related to train movement will be discussed (e.g. maintenance machines) together with some other sources which are small in number, but important when they happen.

14.2 Noise sources independent of train movement

14.2.1 Diesel locomotives

The diesel locomotive usually represents the most common, noticeable noise source on the modern railway except for the noise of wheel/rail interaction which is as much a consequence of movement along the track for the locomotive as it is for any other vehicle.

Figure 14.1 shows the peak noise level of a variety of British Railways diesel locomotives on full power, measured 25 m to the wayside.[1] The levels indicated are similar to those given in

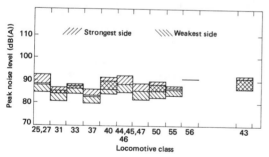

Figure 14.1 Peak noise level, full power, 25 m to the wayside of various BR locomotives[1]

Table 13.1 for freight train operation. The engine powers range from around 1 to 3 MW; some are fitted with silencers and some not, but the range of wayside noise levels is remarkably similar. Like all other vehicles on the railway, the locomotive has to conform to the structure gauge of the system. The structure gauge is the notional smallest cross-section tunnel through which any vehicle will pass at a low speed on straight track, and is a fixed characteristic of any particular railway system. There are a wide variety of gauges in use, the most common structure gauge in Europe being the Berne gauge, but some are larger (Iberian peninsula, Denmark, Russia, North America) and others significantly smaller (Great Britain, Ireland). All of these, however, pose the problem of accommodating a relatively large diesel engine and its auxiliary equipment within a rigidly circumscribed body cross-section. Additional constraints imposed by route availability requirements mean that overall length and all-up weight are also subject to practical limits.

Figure 14.2 shows the principal features of a diesel locomotive, in this case diesel–electric, and demonstrates most of those parts responsible for noise generation. The diesel engine drives a dynamo or alternator, providing direct or alternating current respectively. This current is fed via the electrical control equipment to the traction motors, usually one per wheel pair. Adjacent to the engine is the 'cooling group' in which a fan, driven directly or indirectly by engine power, draws air over heat exchangers to remove the waste heat from the cooling and lubricating fluids of the engine.

The locomotive will also be equipped with compressors and/ or exhausters to provide for various services on the locomotive itself, and to serve the train braking system.

In common with all tractive units, the locomotive will be fitted with a horn or whistle as an emergency warning to people on the track in its path.

Forced cooling may be required for the electrical control gear and will almost certainly be necessary for the traction motors. This may be either cooling air provided by body-mounted fans (traction motor blowers), or it may be provided by fans mounted on the motor shafts themselves (self-ventilated motors). This latter system will usually be restricted to locomotives whose duty is such that they will always be able to accelerate from rest quickly, and the thermal inertia of the motors will control the temperature rise at low speeds, when the air flow is insufficient.

Other diesel locomotives employ hydraulic rather than electrical transmission. In this case the diesel locomotive engine drives a hydraulic pump, and the hydraulic fluid delivered drives motors connected to the wheelsets. The requirements to eliminate waste heat are, however, similar to those of machines with electrical transmission.

14.2.2. The diesel locomotive engine

Most obvious of the noise sources is the diesel locomotive

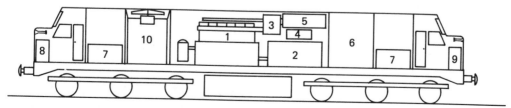

Figure 14.2 Principal features of diesel–electric locomotive.
1 = Engine; 2 = generator; 3 = turbocharger; 4 = air filter; 5 = silencer;
6 = electrical control cubicle; 7 = traction motor blowers;
8 = exhauster; 9 = compressor; 10 = cooling group

engine, of which many different forms are in use. These vary from a few hundred kilowatts power up to several megawatts. They may have from 4 to upwards of 16 cylinders arranged in a variety of configurations: straight in line, dual in line (i.e. two parallel crankshafts geared together), vee engines, and even three crankshafts and opposed pistons in a delta layout. The smaller engines will be naturally aspirated, but the larger engines will be turbocharged or supercharged. Both 4-stroke and 2-stroke engines are in use.

Even with this wide variety of engine sizes and types some common problems of noise emission emerge.

For the naturally aspirated engines the air intake noise is unlikely to be significant compared with other sources on the machine, but on the turbocharged or supercharged engine, noise from the air intake is significant in character though not in level, since it is not the dominant noise source. The whine of the turbocharger(s) is a very familiar feature of the noise from a large diesel locomotive, rising from very low levels when the engine is idling or at low power demand, and passing high into and sometimes beyond the audible spectrum as the power demand increases and the exhaust mass flow and temperature rise. It would be possible to control this noise by the use of an absorption silencer on the intake, but the conflicting demands of a restricted space envelope for the whole locomotive and the need to pass large airflows with as low a pressure drop as possible impose severe restraints.

Similar constraints apply on the exhaust side of the engine. In order for the engine to operate efficiently, a low back pressure from the exhaust system is necessary. On a 4-stroke engine the turbocharger turbine may withstand in the order of 250 Pa (10 in. water gauge) backpressure without apparently affecting the engine performance, but the supercharged 2-stroke is likely to be less tolerant. Silencing the 2-stroke may therefore be much more difficult, even though the fundamental firing cycle frequency is twice that of the 4-stroke.

Maximum engine speeds are typically 750–1500 rev/min. (12–25 rev/s), so that the fundamental firing cycle frequency, even at this maximum engine speed, will only be 6–12 Hz for the 4-stroke engine. This gives rise to the characteristic throbbing note from the locomotive and is particularly noticeable where mechanical and exhaust manifold design results in exhaust 'pulses' which are not uniformly spaced within the engine cycle. An example of a diesel locomotive spectrum at full power is given in *Figure 14.3*.

The low frequencies associated with low engine speeds are no doubt a factor generating complaints about the noise of diesel locomotives standing at signals. It is an unfortunate combination of circumstances that these low frequencies should originate from a source high on the locomotive (i.e. exhaust outlet), which often leads to unrestricted propagation and is virtually unaffected by barrier features. Furthermore, the low frequencies can penetrate most easily into wayside buildings. (*see also* Chapters 16 and 17). Such low fundamental frequencies are obviously very difficult to silence, and would require the use of very large absorption silencers to achieve effective attenuation without imposing unacceptably large backpressures on the engine. Such large silencers could not be accommodated in the space available, although a relatively modest exhaust absorption silencer would be adequate to reduce appreciably that part of turbocharger noise which appears in the exhaust. Even then the silencer would have to cope with the high gas temperatures and with sooting.

Recent work (Halliday[2]) has suggested that it may be feasible to design an effective reactive silencer which is reasonably compatible with both engine performance and space requirements.

Similarly, an experimental installation[3] has shown that useful attenuation of the lower frequencies in the exhaust noise can be achieved with active noise suppression. It is worth noting, at this point, that active techniques offer the additional advantages of zero backpressure and, in principle, small volume units. Similar prototypes are being developed for automotive use. A considerable amount of work needs to be done yet, however, before a practical system that can withstand the rigours of this particular environment can be proved feasible.

In the lower range of locomotive engines, such as shunting locomotives, the silencing problem is less severe, and such machines do not usually pose a problem. The engines are naturally aspirated, so that there is no turbocharger noise, and it is possible to accommodate an adequate conventional silencer with the envelope available.

If the engine exhaust may seem the most obvious source of diesel locomotive noise, there are some instances where it is clearly not the dominant source or may share this role with more insidious sources. Measurements taken 1 m from the exhaust stack (the ORE 'Q' position[4]) cannot always be extrapolated to yield the level at more representative distances from the machine (say 25 m). The most likely other sources are noise radiated directly from the engine carcase, which will probably have the same fundamental frequency as the exhaust noise, but

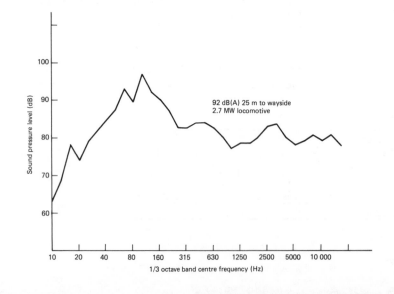

Figure 14.3 Spectrum of diesel locomotive on full power

also be rich in harmonics, and noise radiated from the whole locomotive body, where engine crankcase vibrations have passed into the structure without having been attenuated by the engine mounts. In some instances, the engine is bolted directly to the locomotive chassis. Mount design is complicated by the need to cope with relatively severe longitudinal shunting shocks, whilst providing adequate vertical, lateral and torsional compliance.

Where investigation shows that engine carcase radiation is a significant noise source, the only feasible defence is likely to be in modification of the locomotive casing to provide an adequate barrier. Attention to the locomotive engine itself is unlikely to be a viable possibility: the research and development cost would be very high, and this could not be spread over a large enough market for the cost to be supportable. The alternative of treatment to the locomotive casing seems to be possible[5] but has not been adopted generally. The problems are the ever-present one of space constraints, the need to provide adequate ventilation of oil fumes and access for maintenance. It would, for example, be necessary to install a complete floor pan beneath the diesel engine, leading to the possibility of fire hazard from the retention of spilled and leaked oil.

Excitation of the locomotive structure by engine vibration is best tackled by facing up to the problem of resilient engine mounts. Clearly there are parallel problems in making resilient connections to the engine for air, fuel, coolant, lubricant and possibly exhaust ducting, together with pneumatic hydraulic and electrical services. Electrical, hydraulic or mechanical power take-off will also be affected.

Where the structure-borne vibration problem manifests itself by obvious panel vibration and rattling, simpler *ad hoc* solutions can be used.

It will not usually be possible to mount the engine with a natural frequency of a few hertz, which might be thought necessary due to the low fundamental excitation frequencies involved. Such a mounting would yield an engine which was much too mobile in the chassis in response to the motion of the locomotive over the track, and to cope with the acceleration transients of the engine. Because the natural frequencies of the chassis/body are likely to be much higher, it usually suffices to have a natural frequency of the mounting system in the 10–20 Hz range, but some tuning may be necessary to deal with particular problems of high response at common engine rotational speeds. Locomotive engines usually operate at a restricted number of 'notch' settings, so that mounts can be 'tuned' to have resonant frequencies between notches.

14.2.3 Other noise sources of the diesel locomotive

Most other potential noise sources are associated with cooling, and the problem resolves to one of quiet fan design. The large, low-speed fan of the cooling group does not usually present a noise problem, but the noise of traction motor blowers can be significant.

Although the traction motors are mounted on the locomotive bogies, usually one per axle, for those that need separate cooling, the fans will have to be mounted in the locomotive body for space reasons. The traction motors are also as compact as possible, so that the air passages within them are very tight, and the cooling air has to be provided at a relatively high pressure to yield an adequate cooling flow. Because the connection for the cooling air between the body and the bogie has to cope with the rotation and pitching of the bogie, that air passage too may not be straightforward. Consequently, the traction motor cooling fan is called on to undertake a high flow, high-pressure drop duty, whilst being compact enough to fit in the space available. Modern, quiet fan design should be able to match the constraints imposed, but again, space availability is a significant aspect of the problem.

Self-ventilating motors do not present a problem, since the fan noise increases only as the vehicle speed increases, and does not seem to compete with the wheel/rail noise.

Air compressors and/or exhausters are fitted to all locomotives to service the train's brakes, and these will sometimes be a noticeable noise source. Often the trouble will be that they are bolted direct to the locomotive frame, causing radiation of noise from the structure. This can be cured by the application of resilient mounts in some cases fitted with resilient electrical/hydraulic and delivery connections. Intake/exhaust silencers may sometimes be necessary.

Finally, the loudest single feature of the locomotive is the track warning horn, intended to be audible to men working on the track even about 1 km and more away. With trains now travelling routinely at 200 km/h and more, the warning time at this distance may only be 15 s or less. Even though alternative warning systems should always be in use, the locomotive must be accepted as a warning of last resort.

14.2.4 Summary of diesel locomotive noise

The diesel locomotive presents an array of noise sources. In many instances the diesel engine, with its associated supercharger or turbocharger, will be the dominant noise source. Usually this will be exhaust noise, but engine carcase vibration radiating either directly or via excitation of the locomotive structure may also be possible. Attempts to quieten these sources will always have to cope with constraints imposed by the limited amount of space available.

Other noise sources associated with cooling fans should be amenable to modern design. Compressors and exhausters ought not to give problems if properly mounted. These latter sources will only usually become significant when engine noise has been brought well under control.

In the context of overall train noise, the diesel locomotive is likely to be the dominant noise source on slow freight trains. On passenger trains above (say) 100 km/h, the locomotive noise is of the same order as the wheel/rail noise for traditional iron-block braked rolling stock. With modern disc-braked stock, the locomotive is the dominant source up to the highest speeds likely to be operated by diesel traction (200 km/h).

14.2.5 Electric locomotive noise

Compared with the diesel locomotive, the electric locomotive is very much quieter. Since it carries no prime-mover on board, but derives its power from a third rail or overhead catenary, the worst noise problems do not exist.

The remaining problems are those of cooling fans for the electrical control equipment and for the traction motors, together with compressors for locomotive and train services. These problems are exactly the same as for diesel locomotives, although the generally higher rated traction motors may require a larger cooling supply.

14.2.6 Multiple unit trains

A large class of passenger rolling stock consists of multiple unit trains, which are fixed formation, self-powered trains, which can be coupled and controlled together when traffic demands. Each unit has a driving cab at each end, so that no shunting is required at terminal stations. No locomotives are involved in the operation.

Commonly, both diesel multiple units (d.m.u.s.) and electric multiple units (e.m.u.s.) are in use, but some gas turbine multiple units are also in use, notably in France.

14.2.7 Diesel multiple units

These exist in a variety of forms, some with underfloor engines, some with engines above chassis level. With either engine configuration, mechanical, electrical or hydraulic transmission may be used, and the mechanical transmission may have either driver-controlled or automatic gear change. The train's services are likely to be driven directly from the engine(s), via compressed air or vacuum lines.

The d.m.u.s. with underfloor engines usually employ several engines distributed along the length of the train with a power rating at the upper end of the automotive range using engines mounted on their side adapted from automotive practice. The problems of noise control are closely similar to those found in lorries and buses. Whichever form of transmission is used, the losses are not so great that forced cooling is required, and only a radiator cooling fan is necessary.

d.m.u.s with engines mounted above floor level have fewer, larger engines because of the inroads they make into the load space. These are much more akin to locomotive engines with a power of about 0.5 MW, and with some of the same silencing problems, although they will be naturally aspirated. Again, all types of transmission are possible, but severe cooling, and hence fan noise problems do not usually occur. Only engine coolant and possibly lubricant cooling is necessary.

By comparison with wheel/rail noise, the engine noise of the d.m.u. is not dominant at the top end of its speed range, unless the rolling stock is also fitted with disc brakes. At lower speeds, engine noise dominates. For those units with engines inside the body, the sound is akin in character and level to a lower powered locomotive. It is, therefore, not surprising that the under-floor engined units can sound more like buses.

14.2.8 Electric multiple units

Since these derive their power from a third rail or overhead catenary, they do not offer any prime mover noise. In most cases the traction motors are self-ventilated and so do not cause fan noise which is perceptible above wheel/rail noise. Some units have traction motor blowers, but the noise from these is not dependent on speed and, therefore, is likely to be dominated by wheel/rail noise at speeds above about 30 km/h.

Train services have to be provided by separate motor-driven compressors and/or exhausters, but these rarely prove a significant noise source.

14.3 Noise sources dependent on train movement

There are several noise sources that depend upon the speed of the train. Wheel/rail noise is most common and most often dominant on the railway. It is also the source that is the most abiding problem in railway acoustics. To this problem at its most fundamental level there is not yet an adequate understanding or means of reduction beyond current best practice. Curve squeal is a special case of wheel/rail noise, but one worthy of separate mention. It seems to be distinctly different in some respects from normal rolling noise and proves susceptible to *ad hoc*, but sometimes expensive, remedies.

Although clearly dependent on the wheel/rail input, the noise output of some freight vehicles deserves special consideration. These seem to provide a particularly serious problem for some railway administrations.

Finally, there is the problem of aerodynamic noise generation. At present this is a minor problem which occurs in a few instances and is susceptible to *ad hoc* treatment. It is unlikely that this will be so as train speeds rise substantially, since aerodynamic noise generation, insignificant at present in the general case, will rise much more rapidly with train speed than wheel/rail noise.

14.3.1 Wheel/rail noise generation

Wheel/rail noise arises because the wheel and rail are set into vibration by the action of rolling one over the other. Whatever might be the mechanism by which this vibration is produced, the result is the radiation of noise both to the vehicle and to the wayside.

Examination of the noise spectrum at the wayside of a passing train (*Figure 14.4*) reveals some response peaks emerging from a substantial content of broad-band noise, suggesting that both resonant modes and broad-band response are being excited. Both wheel and rail are capable of being excited into resonant response, but the wheel rings more easily since the rail is more severely damped by its fastening system.

The resonances of the wheel and wheelset (assembly of two wheels rigidly mounted on the axle) fall into three principal categories. The lowest frequencies are associated with the so-called axle-bending modes, whose behaviour is self-explanatory, and which do not radiate significantly into the A-weighted spectrum. The higher frequency modes involve out-of-plane motion of the wheels, and consist of a principal set of modes characterized by diametral node lines, and thus imply bending of the rim out-of-plane (*Figure 14.5*). A third distinct set of modes is characterized by one or more nodal circles and in this case the rim does not bend, although it may rock. In addition there are a host of modes with both nodal circles and diameters.

It is clear that wheel and rail roughness has a profound effect on the noise generated, although it cannot be said for certain that this is an effect on its own, rather than an enhancement and/or modification of more subtle effects.

14.3.2 Overt effects of rail and wheel roughness

The peak noise level measured 25 m to the wayside of many railway lines when a passenger train passes at around 160 km/h (100 mile/h) lies in a narrow range around 91–94 dB(A), and this is true for any country in the world, where this type of traffic commonly circulates. Quite easily described conditions will yield such a noise level. For example, continuously welded rail laid on ballast (type of sleeper-tie immaterial), but free from a

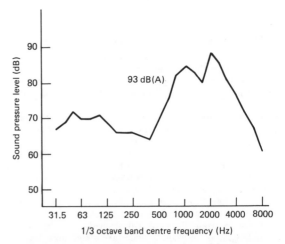

Figure 14.4 Spectrum 25 m to the wayside of a train fitted with iron block brakes passing at 160 km/h on uncorrugated track

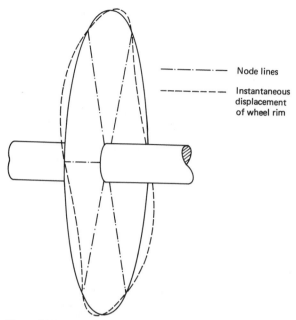

Figure 14.5 Diagram of wheel motion when oscillating with 3 nodal diameter mode

Figure 14.6 Rail corrugation

form of surface wear known as corrugation, traversed by rolling stock with iron block braked wheels. Track laid with continuously welded rail (c.w.r.) is very commonly used on high-speed and heavily used lines. Cast-iron blocks clamped onto diametrically opposite sides of the wheel tyre running surface are by far the most common type of braking system. However, they are not usually used for speeds over 160 km/h (100 mile/h) due to the increased possibility of thermal damage to the wheel treads during braking from the highest speeds.

When the rails show corrugation, the noise level will rise, and may do so by up to 10 dB(A) or more for this type of rolling stock. Corrugation is a form of surface wear which produces longitudinal undulations in the rail-head with a rather irregular pitch, say 50 mm or more, and a depth of several tens of μm, depending on severity (*Figure 14.6*). The mechanism by which corrugations of the rail running surface are formed is a complex subject and no firm conclusions can yet be determined. However, Clarke[6] gives an account of current theories. Suffice it to say that the phenomenon can be reasonably controlled by routine grinding of the rail-head with a specially equipped train, and that use of this remedial train restores the wayside noise level to the previous lower value.

It is, nevertheless, clear that this readily observable phenomenon, with a pitch that is easily measured, and a depth that may be measured with somewhat greater difficulty, promotes a very clearly perceptible increase in wayside noise level. Hence there is an irrevocable link between rail roughness and the wayside noise level, which is further illustrated below.

Modern rolling stock (particularly passenger rolling stock) is being fitted increasingly with disc brakes, invariably so for vehicles with a service speed of greater than 160 km/h (100 mile/h). The use of disc brakes on freight trains is very rare on railways other than British Railways, principally because of cost and of brake compatibility problems on mixed international trains. The use of disc brakes has brought with it a substantial reduction in wayside noise levels as well as sound of a more audibly acceptable character, so that typically, a train of disc-braked passenger rolling stock passing at 160 km/h over track

laid with corrugation-free c.w.r. yield a wayside peak noise level at 25 m of 81–84 dB(A), again an interestingly narrow range. Some care is necessary to maintain this lower noise level, and it is common to fit wheel slide protection equipment to the braking system in order to avoid wheelflats. Wheelflats, when they occur, are clearly audible and of obvious acoustic disbenefit. *Figure 14.7* shows a comparison between the spectra at the wayside due to these two alternative forms of braking.

The alternative method of preventing wheel slips, favoured by some mainland European railways, is to share the braking effort between iron block brakes and disc brakes, with some 75% of the braking effort invested in the latter. The basis for adopting this mixed braking is the belief that tread brakes improve wheel/rail adhesion. The technique of mixed brakes negates the acoustic benefit of disc brakes, however, and the resultant rolling stock is at least as noisy as purely iron block tread-braked stock.

The reason for this, and for the disparity generally between iron-block tread-braked stock and disc-braked stock resides in the effect of the iron blocks on the wheel treads. Close examination of the wheel-tread running surface of tread-braked stock shows a clear alternating pattern of light and dark areas (*Figure 14.8*) which bears a remarkable similarity to the appearance of corrugated rail-heads. The pitch of the effect is also similar to rail corrugation, and similarly erratic. Measurement of this corrugation depth presents much greater difficulty on the wheels, however, than it does on the rails, but as far as can be ascertained the 'corrugation depth' is also a few tens of μm. (NB This concept of 'corrugation' on a curved surface requires some

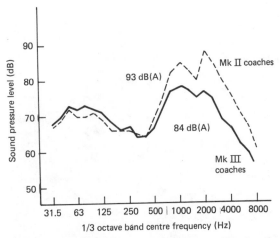

Figure 14.7 Comparison of wayside noise spectra 25 m from the track for vehicles with iron block brakes (Mk 11) and disc brakes Mk 111, both at 160 km/h on uncorrugated track

care in its appreciation. There is never any concavity—merely a variation in degree of convexity.)

By contrast, examination of the wheels of disc-braked stock, free from wheel flats, shows a much smoother running surface, with no sign of a corrugation pattern. Minor pitting of the surface is commonly observed, but does not appear to influence the noise level.

It is clear, therefore, that it is the action of the iron-block brakes on the wheel tyre running surface which causes the

Figure 14.8 Wheel corrugation (The running surface has been acid etched to increase the visibility of the effect.)

corrugation, although there is yet no proven mechanism which causes this. Since rolling stock thus equipped exhibits a very compact range of peak wayside noise levels in standard circumstances, it has to be assumed that the phenomenon is self-limiting by virtue of the brake blocks removing material and re-establishing the corrugation pattern at the same time. Notably, newly turned, unbraked wheels run as quietly as disc-braked wheels. Only a few applications of the iron brakes are necessary to establish the characteristic enhanced wayside noise level.[7] Once the characteristic is established, it never 'runs-out' in the absence of braking; only returning of the wheel tyres removes the effect, until the brakes are applied again.

Consequently, wheel corrugation can raise the wayside noise level by 10 dB(A) from the base case of disc-braked wheels on corrugation-free rails. Rail corrugation can raise the wayside noise level by up to 10 dB(A) and more above the level of iron block-braked wheels on corrugation-free track. What, then, is the effect of corrugated rails on disc braked wheels?

On track that is sufficiently corrugated to increase the peak noise level from tread braked stock by 10 dB(A), the corresponding increase by disc braked stock is 20 dB(A), i.e. the resultant levels are indistinguishable. In addition the trains are not audibly distinguishable either.

It is also true that enhancement of the noise from disc-braked stock starts to occur at lower degrees of corrugation than are required to cause an increase in the already higher level of noise from tread braked stock. The general effect is sketched in *Figure 14.9*, but the horizontal axis is not quantified since the characteristics of corrugation that have acoustic consequence are not sufficiently well defined.

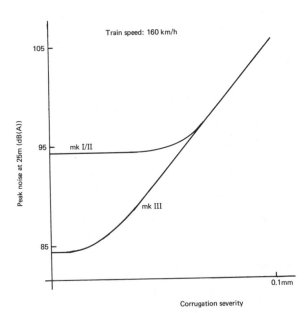

Figure 14.9 General effect of corrugation severity on wayside noise level

It can be deduced, therefore, that either rail or wheel roughness will enhance wayside noise levels, and that the partner with the greater roughness dominates the effect.

When both wheel and rail are as smooth as possible, i.e. uncorrugated continuously welded rail and disc braked stock with no wheelflats, the lowest peak level of current practice is achieved. These levels are typically around 81–84 dB(A) at 25 m to the wayside for 160 km/h (100 mile/h) bogie passenger stock.

14.3.3 Theoretical studies of excitation by roughness

The observations that wheel and rail roughness can produce very noticeable effects on wayside noise levels have been paralleled, largely independently, by the notable theoretical and experimental work of Remington and his colleagues in the USA. The model takes into account the wheel and rail roughness spectra and the effect of the contact area between wheel and rail to produce the excitation forces. These characterize the impedances of both wheel and rail to produce wheel and rail responses and lead to the total radiated noise, taking into account the respective radiation efficiencies and geometrical factors. The processes involved are described in *Figure 14.10*.

These various parts of the model are treated in turn, either by experiment or by theoretical analysis. The prediction accuracy of the model has been applied to a particular railway system in the USA, with very impressive agreement between theory and practice (*Figure 14.11*). However, it can be seen from the figure that rail noise is given a greater importance in the model than wheel noise, and this feature has been challenged by other workers. The objections are based on the observations that the wayside noise is affected by the resonant response of the wheels,[9] and that the measured vibration of the rail could not account for the wayside noise.[10]

At present this discussion of what constitutes the principal noise source remains unresolved, but clearly the model proposed by Remington must be the foundation of its eventual solution. It is possible that the wheel and rail each play dominant roles in different parts of the spectrum, or for different types of excitation.

Remington points out that one part of his model, the 'contact patch' filter, is purely a theoretical construction and does not yet have a direct experimental basis; yet there is some evidence which suggests that such a filter might be in operation.

The load supported by the wheels of a train ranges from a few tons per wheel for bogie passenger vehicles (i.e. 4 axles, 8 wheels; all-up weight 30–50 tonnes) to rather more than 10 tonnes per wheel for heavy freight vehicles and locomotives.

The vehicle weight is supported by elastic deformation of that wheel and rail area in the zone of contact, the so-called contact patch. The patch is of the order of 10 mm wide and 10 mm long, and within this zone, slipping between wheel and rail is assumed not to take place. The size of this contact zone is not a strong function of vertical load.

Roughness of wavelength less than or equal to the contact patch length can be expected to be subject to mechanical averaging and might, therefore, not contribute significantly to vibration generation and consequential noise. Thus it could be expected that high-frequency noise due to these short wavelengths would not be significant. *Figure 14.7* shows the wayside spectrum due to trains passing at 160 km/h (44.4/m/s), and it is clear that the energy content of the spectrum falls steeply at high frequencies. For a train travelling at 44.4 m/s, a 10 mm pitch irregularity, of the same order as the contact patch length, corresponds to a frequency of 4.44 kHz, illustrating that a contact patch filter is consistent with the observed spectrum.

14.3.4 Other mechanisms of wheel/rail noise excitation

It is worth considering, at this point, other possible mechanisms of rail/wheel noise excitation.

Almost without exception, railway wheels are rigidly

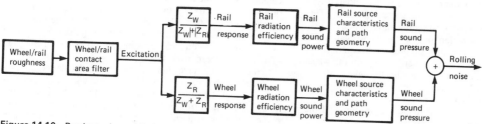

Figure 14.10   Remington's model of wheel/rail noise generation[8]

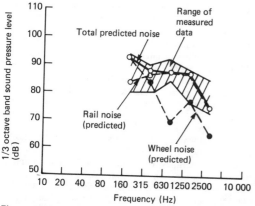

Figure 14.11   Comparison between theory and experiment for one railway system in the USA[8]

mounted to the axle, which rotates with the wheels as an assembly called a wheelset. It follows that both wheels always have the same rotational speed.

In order that the wheelset will run centrally down straight track without invoking flange contact, the wheels are coned, with a semi-angle, of about 1 in 20. The wheels are centralized by the requirement that both wheels must have the same running circle diameter. The majority of curves are followed without 'flanging' because the wheelset can move laterally across the rails to produce the unequal rolling circle diameters necessary to negotiate the curve. The wheelset moves outwards on a curve, i.e. it moves to the left to negotiate a right-hand curve. However, in addition some yaw damping of the wheelset may be necessary to produce stable running.

The question remains as to what might be sources of vibration excitation other than that due to wheel and/or rail roughness. In order to understand what mechanisms could be present it is necessary to consider first the coned wheelset rolling down a straight track.

Since the contact patch has a finite width (about 10 mm) it must encompass a range of rolling circle diameters, and only along a middle line will true rolling take place. Outside that middle line, the resultant contact patch forces will try to slow down the wheel, whilst inside they will try to make it run faster. Since the wheels are constrained by the axle to move parallel to each other, the forces generated produce elastic surface shear deformation of the mating surfaces. In this case, the wheels try to run outwards, resisted by the bending stiffness of the axle. Alternatively expressed, there is a torque about a nearly vertical axis through the contact patch acting on each wheel rim, and an opposite torque on each rail. If these torques are perfectly steady, no excitation results, but if they vary either periodically or randomly, then potentially both wheel and rail might be excited. Such variations might be due to minor changes of contact patch size and/or shape arising, say, from minor changes of rail-head shape, or they might be due to stick–slip relief of the locked torque. Such a mechanism would be particularly effective at exciting resonant modes, akin to the stick–slip action of bowing a violin string, or the ringing of a wine glass when a moist finger is rubbed round the rim.

It is, therefore, tempting to suggest that the reduction or elimination of cone angle would promote quieter running. However, similar effects can be postulated for the rolling of cylindrical wheels.

14.3.5 Reduction of wheel/rail noise

The model of Remington[8] clearly suggests two alternative methods for reducing wheel/rail noise.

The first of these is to reduce the roughness of wheels and/or rails as much as possible, the biggest gain coming from treatment of the roughest member. This has the effect of minimizing the varying component of force between wheel and rail and corresponds to imposing the best of current practice. This means maintaining corrugation-free rails and the use of disc brakes to minimize the formation of wheel tread corrugations. It is also possible that some types of tread brake with composition brake blocks instead of cast iron, but still acting on the wheel tread, also promote quiet running because the wheel surface does not corrugate. Further information on wheel turning and rail grinding is given in Chapters 16 and 17.

Secondly, it is possible to try to reduce the response of the radiating members. The most obvious way to do this is to add damping to the wheels (JNR,[11] Racquet,[12] ORE[13]) or to the rails (JNR,[11] ORE[13]). This has been tried in the context of reducing the squeal from wheels on curves (see Section 14.3.6) but has produced no significant effect for rolling noise on straight or gently curved track. The reason for this lack of success is obscure, but it may imply that the damping present due to the contact patch already exceeds the additional damping imposed. Further details of the effects of using damped wheels is given in Chapters 16 and 17.

Another measure tried has been the use of bogie skirts to provide a physical barrier to the radiated noise: these too have provided very little benefit, 2 dB(A) at most (JNR[11]). The problem with bogie skirts is that they cannot in any case be brought low enough to screen the wheel completely, due to the obvious need that they should not collide with various track features. Also, if Remington's conclusion is correct, and the rail is the principal radiator, screening of the wheels is not likely to provide significant benefit.

A possible alternative is to provide substantial lineside barriers as discussed in Chapters 15 and 17, but it is tempting to consider whether low barriers close to the rails might not work. Unfortunately, barriers are only effective when (roughly) their height exceeds the wavelength of the incident sound. They could

therefore only be expected to have any benefit at the top end of the wheel/rail noise spectrum, and only then if both sides of each rail could be treated.

The remaining possibility for reducing wheel/rail noise would be the very drastic one of reducing the number of wheels per unit length of the train. This appears to show the expected effect.

The 'Talgo' train, operated by the Spanish National Railways, consists of vehicles 10 m long supported at one end by a single pair of wheels, and at the other end by the wheeled end of the adjacent vehicle. This, of course, does not apply for the first or last vehicle of the train. This form of construction where the vehicles cannot stand alone is called articulation.

The train, therefore, has 10 wheel pairs per 100 m of train for most of its length. By comparison, standard bogie coaches have 4 wheel pairs per vehicle, with a length around 25 m, or 16 wheel pairs per 100/m of train. At 25 m to the wayside of a section of corrugation free c.w.r. for a speed of 160 km/h (100 mile/h), the Talgo is about 2 dB(A) quieter at a peak level of 79 dB(A) compared with its competitors. In both cases the brakes do not touch the wheel running surfaces.

It must be mentioned, however, that the Talgo train has other differences as well which might affect noise generation. In particular, the wheels are smaller than standard, they rotate independently instead of being mounted as wheelsets, and the articulation mechanism steers the wheels round bends.

14.3.6 Flange squeal

Flange squeal is the piercing resonant response of wheels as they negotiate sharp curves, although actual flange contact with the gauge face of the rail may not always be necessary.

The simple view of how coned wheels negotiate a curve which is expressed at the beginning of Section 14.3.4 is in practice more complex. When the wheelsets of a vehicle are mounted in bogies, or towards the ends of a two-axle vehicle, they will be mounted parallel to each other, although there may be some yaw compliance incorporated. Therefore, when negotiating a curve, neither axle will lie on a curve radius, and some lateral creepage of the wheel tread over the railhead will take place. In the extreme case this creepage will be forced by flange contact ultimately with both inside and outside rails when the curve is sharp enough (Figure 14.12). Some designs of bogie are now being applied that are capable of steering or being steered round curves, but these will only cope precisely with curves for which the wheel coning provides sufficient curving capability.

The inexact presentation of the wheelset to the curve provokes lateral creepage at both wheel treads because the wheelset is aimed in the wrong direction, and longitudinal creepage of one wheelset or the other occurs because one wheel is trying to turn faster than the other. Stick-slip relief of the creep forces will provide excitation of the resonant modes of the wheel, leading to the characteristic squeal emitted as the vehicle negotiates the curve. The phenomenon of lateral creepage has been analysed by Rudd,[14] who has estimated that squeal will occur when the track radius-of-curvature is less than 100 times the vehicle or bogie wheelbase, for non-steering axles. This estimate accords fairly well with what is observed in practice. Generally, a bogie with 2 m wheelbase will squeal on a curve tighter than 200 m radius, but train speed is also significant.

Attempts to deal with squeal noise by damping of the wheels has been reasonably successful.

The earliest and cheapest technique is the friction damping ring sprung into a groove on the inside of the wheel tyre, and used for many years by London Transport (see also Chapter 17).

Later techniques have included constrained layer damping of the wheel web (ORE[13]), the use of broadly tuned resonant dampers (Racquet[12]) and various types of 'resilient wheel'

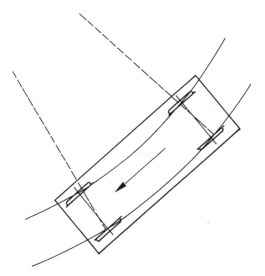

Figure 14.12 Attitude of wheelsets on a bogie or two-axled vehicle during curving

(Bochum, SAB, Acoustaflex) which have also been damped wheels by nature of their construction (Stanworth[15]).

Rudd[14] has deduced that satisfactory control of flange squeal can be achieved by the addition of damping.

Attempts to reduce flange squeal by damping treatment of the rails have been less successful (ORE[13]). Constrained layer damping of the rail web generally does not lead to significant reduction in wayside noise.

Flange lubrication has been used extensively to control flange squeal, but it has not always been successful, and carries with it the risk of rail head and wheel tread contamination leading to reduced levels of adhesion. This can result in 'rail burn' due to locomotive wheelspin and 'wheel flats' due to wheel slide during braking. When carried out correctly, however, flange lubrication seems to work reasonably well. Presumably in these cases, sufficient contamination of the running surfaces occurs to alter the friction characteristics and prevent stick-slip taking place without too much change in limiting adhesion.

Where heavy gradients are combined with sharp curves, the risks associated with flange greasing become much too great. In these circumstances some success has attended the use of water sprays to wet both rails and wheel treads. This seems to modify the friction conditions so that flange squeal does not occur. At the same time, both traction and braking are relatively unaffected.

14.3.7 Freight vehicle noise

In the case of passenger vehicles, the vibration originating at the wheel/rail contact and passing through the suspension up into the body is responsible for part of the vehicle interior noise, notably at low frequencies. The noise radiated outwards by the vehicle body due to this source is, however, quite negligible by comparison with the directly radiated wheel/rail noise. The same is not necessarily the case with freight vehicles.

Passenger vehicles are obviously designed to give an acceptable ride for the occupants, and this very need dictates a suspension that passes vibrations at audible frequencies relatively poorly. In two important respects the suspension requirement of passenger vehicles is simpler than for freight vehicles. It does not have to cater for such a large load/tare ratio, which for freight vehicles may be as high as 4, and the ride standard

required for freight will often be determined only by the need for safe operation of the vehicle, but otherwise the suspension will be as economical in construction as possible, for commercial reasons.

The consequences are easy to see. Vehicles are built relatively crudely, with no particular care taken to see that they do not rattle. Friction damping of the suspension is commonplace, so that vibrations can pass very readily into the body. Freight vehicles enjoy only that minimum maintenance necessary for safe operation.

All of these factors conspire to produce vehicles that may be inherently noisy, often noisier when running empty than when loaded. In the loaded condition the charge will provide the benefits of both mass and damping.

Even the proposed European Community regulations for limitation of railway vehicle noise[16] recognize the commercial reality that freight vehicles may be noisier than passenger vehicles, and allow them to be 3 dB(A) noisier at a given speed. This requirement may set a stiff target for some vehicles.

The means of reducing this noise to the level of passenger vehicles are not difficult to suggest, but may not be affordable. Disc brakes have been shown to be helpful to the extent of 5 dB(A) in one direct comparison. There are, however, usually powerful arguments for the retention of iron block-tread brakes in addition to cost. The varation of brake force with speed is widely different between the two types, and they cannot usually be run in the same train. Hence the operation of international freight trains with the customary mixture of wagon types demands that all wagons, new or old and of any ownership, have the same brake type.

Treatment of the rattles and resonances of the superstructure clearly presents no technical problem, but has to be paid for. Likewise, the application of more favourable suspensions or the use of bogie vehicles rather than long wheelbase 2-axle vehicles which may squeal on otherwise quiet curves, is attended by cost penalties.

14.3.8 Aerodynamic noise sources

In present-day traditional railway practice, obtrusive aerodynamic noise radiated to the wayside is comparatively rare, except for the fans, superchargers and turbochargers of the locomotive mentioned earlier.

The only cases presently recorded are with the Shinkansen trains of the JNR[11] and incipiently with test trains of the German Federal Railways, DB (King et al.[17]).

The JNR experience was associated with the pantograph which collects traction current from overhead catenary. The problem was traced to a particular design of the ceramic insulators on the train roof, which were used to support the pantograph and insulate it from the earthed structure of the train. This produced a howl at the highest train speed (210 km/h), which was noticeable even in the presence of wheel/rail noise. Redesign of the insulator profile cured the problem.

The German experience may turn out to be more indicative of likely problems to come in the future. The discovery was made during tests up to a speed of 250 km/h in which special wayside instrumentation was used in the form of an 'acoustic telescope' to determine, in vertical and horizontal array, the distribution of noise sources from the train above the ground and along its roof line.[17] Although the aerodynamic noise arising from the train's passage was not perceptible at the wayside in the presence of the noise from the wheel/rail system, it could be identified by this particular equipment. It was also possible to estimate the rate of increase of aerodynamic noise with train speed.

By sufficiently sensitive measurement and analysis, it can be proved that aerodynamic sources have a just significant part to play in the acoustic environment within present-day trains at current routine maximum speeds (i.e. 200 km/h, 125 mile/h). As trains are pushed faster to enhance their competitive position, so this problem will increase in significance. It follows that increased train speed will lead eventually to a significant aerodynamic element in the total noise radiated to the wayside.

Wheel/rail noise increases roughly as the cube of speed, whereas aerodynamic noise will increase according to a much higher power. King,[17] when comparing his work with that of Ulrich,[18] concluded that both theoretical and experimental analyses indicated that aerodynamic noise can increase at around the 6th power of speed, which corresponds to an increase of 18 dB per doubling of speed.

At speeds of around 160 km/h (100 mile/h) the aerodynamic noise lies about 10 dB(A) below the wheel/rail noise of current best practice (82 dB(A), 25 m to the wayside for disc-braked stock on corrugation-free c.w.r.). At 350 km/h (220 mile/h) the two sources are about equally significant. Above that speed, the aerodynamic source appears to be dominant, and leads to the interesting conclusion that at such speeds wheel/rail technology will be no noisier than air cushion or magnetic levitation.

14.4 Other railway noise sources

It is, of course, easily possible to catalogue a whole series of other noise sources attributable to the railway and its related operations. Reference to many of them can be found in the reports of the Railway and Tracked Transit System Noise workshops published in the *Journal of Sound and Vibration Research* (*see* Further reading).

In this part of the chapter, reference will be made to two only, the noise from maintenance machines, and the noise due to trains running over bridges.

14.4.1 Railway maintenance machinery

Maintenance of a wide variety of railway structures and equipment is carried out with many different types of tool and machine, large and small. Many are no different to equipment used in other industries, and share exactly the same noise problems. In its maintenance of the track, however, the railway employs a unique range of track-mounted equipment, attended by their own range of noise problems.

The noisiest machine is the ballast cleaner, a machine powered by a diesel engine similar in size to that used in earth moving machinery and which is moved slowly along the track excavating ballast from beneath. Excavation is carried out by a cutting chain which passes continuously beneath the sleepers of the track. Spent ballast is lifted by this chain and dumped onto shaking riddles. Fine stone is rejected by the machine and useable stone is dropped back on top of the sleepers. To reinstate the track for traffic, additional fresh ballast has to be added and the track lifted so that the ballast bed can be tamped back into place below the sleepers. Everything about the operation of such a machine is fundamentally noisy: the cutting of stone from below the sleepers, the chain acting as a conveyor to lift the stone, stone falling onto the riddles and being shaken through or along, and the useable stone being returned to the track. Within the constraints imposed by the structure gauge it is difficult to see what useful work could be done to make the machines quieter. Fortunately, they are used only very rarely on any particular section of track.

Much more common are the tamping machines which are used for the regular adjustment of line and level of the track, although they will also be used (possibly several times) to restore the track in the wake of the ballast cleaner.

The tamping machine works by determining the extent to which the track lies below the desired level, lifting the track by the right amount, and then using tamping tines lowered into the ballast on each side of the rail and at both ends of the sleeper to flow stones below the sleeper. The process is repeated at each sleeper as necessary. The tamping tines are spade-ended arms which are oscillated in the ballast to cause it to flow.

These machines have two principal noise sources, the diesel engine which drives it being the least troublesome. *Figure 14.13* shows a design of engine casing which has made these machines acceptably quiet. It was introduced following cooperation between the manufacture (Messrs. Plasser and Theurer of Austria) and British Railways. Attempts to silence the tamping mechanism have proved to be unsuccessful so far.

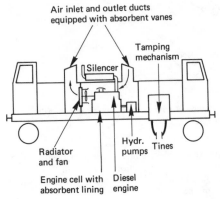

Figure 14.13 Engine silencing arrangement on tamping machine[1]

When the tamping mechanism is new, it will run much more quietly than the diesel engine, but when it has been in service for only a few weeks it will have become rapidly the dominant noise source. The difficulty lies in the oscillating bearings which are an integral part of the mechanism. Oscillating bearings are notoriously difficult to lubricate effectively. In consequence they wear rapidly, no doubt aided by the dust from the tamped ballast, and become very noisy. The problem has been investigated by Herbert[19] who has suggested pumped lubricant bearings. He estimated that elastomeric bearings would rapidly overheat, and would have to be rejected for that reason.

To date, no satisfactory solution has been found, and tamping machines continue to be as noisy as passing express trains. Unfortunately, they pass by at about 1 km/h, leading to complaints that are not levelled at normal passing trains.

14.4.2 Bridge noise

Even as long ago as 1890, the fact that trains passing over bridges could generate perceptibly greater noise was popularly recognized. In that year, the Act of the British parliament authorizing construction of the Tottenham and Forest Gate Railway through northeast London stipulated that 6 foot high parapets should be erected on the bridges carrying the line over roads to shield residents from the noise of trains. The parapets have remained to this day.

That the difficulty has not changed in the intervening years is evidenced by the problems from this source created by the JNR's first Shinkansen line, whose operation provoked loud protest from wayside residents. Much of the line lies on elevated structure and some of those structures are concrete or steel bridges and viaducts, the problem being exacerbated by the close proximity of houses. The steel viaducts and bridges in particular proved to be objectionable, and the JNR[20] has subsequently been involved in considerable expense in providing protection measures. These have included cladding the under-side of the structures with cover plates, resiliently mounted from the structure, extending up the sides to act as a noise screen. In one instance the cladding extended across the top of the bridge as well as to form an enclosing tube the full length of the bridge.

The plain difficulty is that a steel bridge forms a large, relatively lightly damped structure, which in some cases may also rattle when subject to vibration input. It is also fairly common practice to mount the rails on waybeams directly connected to the structure, so that vibration from passing trains is very strongly coupled to the bridge. In such circumstances the wayside noise level may be as much as 20 dB(A) above that which would arise from trains at the same speed on track laid on the ground.

Where, even with steel bridges, conventional sleeper-on-ballast track construction is employed, the result is more favourable, and the increment may only be 10 dB(A).

Concrete bridges are generally more favourable, and concrete bridges carrying ballasted track can sometimes be slightly quieter when trains pass than track in the open. In addition to the bridge being a relatively inert structure, the bridge girders, which also form the parapet wall, provide a barrier against the wheel/rail noise of the train.

Composite bridges, with steel girders and concrete deck usually produce a small enhancement of noise from the open track condition but are, nevertheless, quieter than steel bridges. The ranking of bridge types is discussed by ORE[21] and details of remedial treatments and bridge designs are given in Chapters 16 and 17.

If a bridge is responsible for a noise problem, the economic options available for mitigation are few. Where the rails are laid on waybeams fixed directly to the structure, it may sometimes be possible to rebuild the bridge deck and install ballasted track.

One technique introduced by the JNR has been the installation of elastomeric mats below the ballast on some of its steel-decked bridges. This has the twin effects of reducing the vibration input to the structure, and also providing damping. It is said to have reduced the wayside noise by several dB(A), as well as reducing attrition of the ballast against the steel decking. *See also* Chapters 16 and 17.

The 'solution' ordained for the Tottenham and Forest Gate railway of extending the parapet height will not always work, and may even make matters worse by increasing the radiating area. The sentiment was worthy, however, and apart from the disparity in traffic speed and type, the parallel between this railway and the Shinkansen is interesting. Both are largely elevated and pass through a densely populated region.

Although engineering and operating practices have changed over the years, it is clear that some problems persist, and some lessons remain to be learned.

References

1 STANWORTH, C. G. Consideration of some noise sources due to railway operation. *Journal of Sound and Vibration*, **87** (1983).
2 HALLIDAY, R. Institute of Sound and Vibration Research. Unpublished observations.
3 CHAPLIN, B. The Essex breakthrough. *Chartered Mechanical Engineer*, **January** (1983).
4 Office de Recherche et d'Essais. *Guidelines for Noise Measurements on Railway Vehicles*. Committee E 82, Report No. 4. Paris (1969).
5 LUTZ, R Swedish National Railways. Unpublished observations.
6 CLARK, R. A. P. Stick–slip may hold key to corrugation puzzle. *Railway Gazette International*, **140** (1984).
7 HÖLZL, G. and SCHEINER, K. *Aktive Lärmschutzmassnahmen bei hohen Geschwindichkeiten der Rad/Schien-Technik*. Deutsche Bundesbahn, Munich (1979).
8 REMINGTON, P. Wheel/rail noise: The state-of-the-art. *NOISE—CON 77*. pp. 257–284 (1977).
9 CATO, D. N. Prediction of environmental noise from fast electric trains. *Journal of Sound and Vibration*, **46** (1976).
10 PETERS, S., HEMSWORTH, B. and WOODWARD, B. Noise radiation from a railway rail. *Journal of Sound and Vibration*, **35** (1974).
11 Japanese National Railways. *Shinkansen Noise I*.
12 RAQUET, E. and TACKE, G. Sound Emission of Railway wheels and tests on noise damped wheels for long distance and local rail traffic. Presented at *The 6th International Wheelset Congress* (1978).
13 Office de Recherche et d'essais *Noise Annoyance from Braking and Negotiating Sharp Curves: Fundamental Considerations and First Test Results*, Committee C 137, Report No. 2 Paris (1975).
14 RUDD, M. J. Wheel/rail noise, part II: Wheel squeal. *Journal of Sound and Vibration*, **46** (1976).
15 STANWORTH, C. G. *Railway Noise and the Environment—A Summary* (2nd edn.), British Railways Board. Technical Note TN Phys 4 (1977).
16 Commission of the European Communities. Proposal for a Council directive on the approximation of the laws of the Member States relating to the noise emission of rail-mounted vehicles. *Official Journal of the European Communities*, **C354** (1983).
17 KING, W. F. and BECHERT, D. An experimental study of aerodynamic noise generated by high speed trains. *Noise Control Engineering Journal* (1979).
18 ULRICH, A. and VAN DEN BRULLE, J. *Geräuchmessungen am Transrapid TR–04* MBB Report No TN–BT 22–16/75 (1975).
19 HERBERT, R. G. *Research on Noise of Track Maintenance Machines*. University of Southampton, Department of Mechanical Engineering, Technical Report M.E. 76/2. (1976).
20 Japanese National Railways. *Shinkansen Noise II*.
21 Office de Recherche et d'essais. *Report. Noise from Bridges* Committee C 137.

Further reading

Further information on the generation of railway noise, and the measures that have been introduced for its reduction can be obtained by reading the reports of the first three International Workshops on Railway and Tracked Transit System noise published in the issues of the *Journal of Sound and Vibration* dated 8th April 1977 (Vol. **51**), 8th October 1979 (Vol. **66**) and 22nd March 1983 (Vol. **87**). Further material will be found in the work of Bolt, Beranek and Newman in Vol. **46** (1976) of the same journal.

Many aspects of railway noise are dealt with by the series of reports issued by Committee C137 of the Office de Recherche et d' Essais (ORE) of the Union Internationale des Chemins de Fer. Enquiries about these should be made to their offices at Oudenoord 60, Utrecht, Netherlands.

The North American view of the ways in which urban railway noise might be controlled is given in the US Department of Transportation report No. UMTA–MA–06–0099–80–1 *In-service Performance and Costs of Methods to Control Urban Rail System Noise—Final Report*, December 1979 by Saurenman, Shipley and Wilson.

Finally, a whole range of remedial measures has been tried by the Japanese National Railways, and these are reported (in English) in the two reports *Shinkansen Noise I and II*. There also exists a film about their work with English commentary entitled *Shinkansen Noise*. Enquiries about these should be made to the Japanese National Railways at their Paris office, 24, rue de la Pépinière. A version of the reports has been issued by ORE as *Technical Document DT 52 E* (June 1976) and *Technical Document DT 94 E* (April 1979).

15

Prediction of Train Noise

Brian Hemsworth MRAeS, CEng
**British Railways Board, Research Division,
Railway Technical Centre, Derby, UK**

Contents

15.1 Introduction

Whenever a new railway line is planned or residential development near an existing railway is proposed, an estimate of the relevant noise levels is usually required. For the latter the most accurate results are obtained by carrying out noise measurements at the site in question. In other cases a noise prediction scheme must be employed, where it is generally required to predict the noise levels at the external facade of a building. For this, it is necessary to quantify those parameters that affect train noise levels. Examination is then made of the data available to see whether further source or site specific measurements are needed to provide a sufficiently accurate noise prediction.

The main objectives of this chapter are to:

1. Identify the important parameters which determine train noise levels.
2. Show how noise levels vary with values of these parameters.
3. Suggest how prediction schemes can be developed from that knowledge.

For a noise prediction to be meaningful it must be in terms of a noise scale or rating which can be used to determine the likely subjective response to noise from that source. For railway noise, the scale of L_{eq} is currently accepted for environmental assessment and, therefore, although peak noise level information will also be provided, the aim is to produce a prediction scheme capable of determining the total acoustic energy from a series of train pass-bys within a specified time period.

This does not mean, however, that it is necessary to predict the noise levels associated with each individual pass-by. For prediction purposes it can be assumed that a train service consists of a number of groups of trains, where within a group, the noise level from each train is identical. This is because for a given type of train travelling in a particular direction past a receiver point, variation in train length, expected train speed and locomotive power setting (all factors that affect noise emission levels) would be small enough to assume that each train within an identifiable group produced the same noise. It is therefore only necessary to decide firstly the number of different groups of trains, and secondly to predict the noise levels associated with the pass-by of one train in each group.

Train-noise prediction, therefore, reduces to the ability to predict the noise from a single train pass-by.

15.2 Noise prediction methodology

Prediction methods used today are either empirical or semi-empirical and tend to follow a common pattern. A source-dependent noise level is initially determined and account is then taken of the various propagation features as the noise is radiated to the wayside.

The manner of calculation can be achieved in two ways. Firstly, using computer programs the train can be modelled as a series of discrete sources (i.e. wheels) and the overall level at a receiver point determined by the addition of levels from each of these sources after considering the relevant point source propagation determined by the site geometry.

The second approach is to characterize the train by a single basic noise level for the noise from the trailing vehicles (designated rolling noise) and where necessary an additional one for locomotive noise. Successive, single number, propagation corrections are then made to these noise levels in the determination of the noise level at a particular receiver point.

This latter method, more simplistic in its approach, is likely to appeal to a greater majority of potential users and it is proposed, therefore, to concentrate on that method in this chapter. A general description of some computer programs will, how-

ever, be given in a later section of this chapter. It is worth noting, however, that the sections identifying the important parameters that control the source noise are valid for the computer-based prediction methods and the simplified approach. This prediction method can be described by the following equation:

$$L = L_0 - \Delta_S - \Delta_A - \Delta_G - \Delta_E + \Delta_F \qquad (15.1)$$

where L is the noise from the vehicles (or locomotives) expressed as either peak noise level (L_{max}) or a noise energy equivalent level.

L_0 is the basic noise level and is presented as the noise level for a particular type of rolling stock, or locomotive at a given distance from the track. Implicit in the determination of L_0 is the speed at which the train is travelling and for rolling noise, the track construction.
Δ_S is the attenuation due to geometric spreading and includes for rolling noise any corrections that are required for train length.
Δ_A is the attenuation due to air absorption.
Δ_G is the attenuation due to ground absorption.
Δ_E is the excess attenuation due to features such as track in cutting, track on embankment, lineside noise barriers (including earth banks) and housing development.
Δ_F is the free field to facade correction and is usually 2.5 dB(A) or 3 dB(A) depending on national convention.

The following sections will consider how the various terms in Equation 15.1 can be quantified.

15.3 Basic noise level

15.3.1 Rolling noise

The major parameters that determine the level of rolling noise for distances close to a railway track are:

1. Type of rolling stock.
2. Train speed.
3. Type of track.

For (3) it is normally only necessary to consider whether the track is jointed or is made from continuously welded rail (cwr), and since on most networks the majority of track is cwr the basic noise levels quoted here will be for that situation. It is further assumed that the track is of good quality. The effects of jointed track, deterioration of track quality and other types of construction, including bridges, will be discussed later.

As the speed of a particular train increases, the rolling noise also increases. Noise level prediction data are usually derived from regression analysis of measurements where the regression equation takes the form:

$$L_{max} = k \log_{10} V + C \qquad (15.2)$$

where L_{max} = peak noise level dB(A), V = train speed km/h, and k and C are constants.

Figure 15.1, taken from reference 1, shows a set of measurements, 25 m from the track, for a particular type of train at numerous sites. Each site was judged to have similar track quality. Also shown on this figure is the derived regression equation.

A survey of similar measurements for various types of rolling stock indicates that the constant k varies between 20 and 40. These extreme values correspond to changes of 6 dB(A) and 12 dB(A) for a doubling or halving of train speed.

The factors that cause these differences in speed dependence have not been identified; therefore, in the case where data are

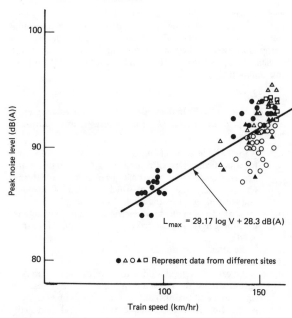

Figure 15.1 Regression analysis for Mk II passenger coaches, 25 m from track

available over only a small speed range (i.e. where the spread of data at one speed is greater than the measured speed effect) it is usual to assume that a value of k = 30 can be used for prediction purposes. Naturally, where reliable measured data exist the relevant value for k should be used.

The need to include 'type of rolling stock' as a variable is demonstrated in *Figure 15.2*, which again is taken from reference 1 and compares the noise level from different vehicles used by British Rail.

The spread of data, at a given speed, is of the order of 10 dB(A), i.e. similar to the change in noise level due to the doubling (halving) of train speed for a given type of rolling stock.

The major factor causing this spread in noise levels appears to be the type of braking employed. This is certainly the case with passenger vehicles where the noisier designs use cast-iron tread brakes and the quieter designs use alternative forms of braking, such as disc brakes.

This can be seen from inspection of *Figure 15.3* which contains data from many railway administrations.[2,3] The type of braking is identified in the figure, and as a general guide it can be assumed that passenger vehicles with cast-iron brakes give rise to noise levels that tend towards the higher noise values shown in *Figure 15.3*. This approximates to:

$$L_{max} = 30 \log_{10} V + 28 \text{ dB(A)} \qquad (15.3)$$

with V expressed in km/h.

Vehicles with alternative forms of braking tend towards the lower levels shown in *Figure 15.3* and this approximates to:

$$L_{max} = 40 \log_{10} V - 4 \text{ dB(A)} \qquad (15.4)$$

Therefore, for passenger vehicles, unless data exist for the particular vehicles under consideration, a knowledge of the braking system will allow an approximate determination of the basic rolling noise using either Equation 15.3 or Equation 15.4.

The simplicity and variety of design of freight vehicles makes it difficult to categorize their noise level characteristics by study of the braking systems alone. It is known, however, that those designs with disc brakes tend to be quieter (*see* Chapter 14). For freight vehicles it is recommended that where no noise data can be found for the type of vehicle in question a measurement programme is initiated to obtain the relevant data. Again if measurements can be obtained only over a limited speed range assume a value for k of 30.

Typical octave band spectra for rolling noise are presented in *Figure 15.4*.[3,4]

It should be noted that although the effect of train length will be discussed later it is not of prime importance in determining L_{max} for a distance of 25 m from the track. Modelling the train as a series of distributed point sources shows that peak noise level is virtually independent of train length at this distance. It only has an effect for very short trains, e.g. single railcars, and here the effect of length will be reflected in the measured basic noise levels.

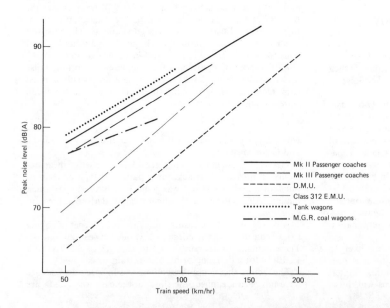

Figure 15.2 Peak noise level at 25 m from track

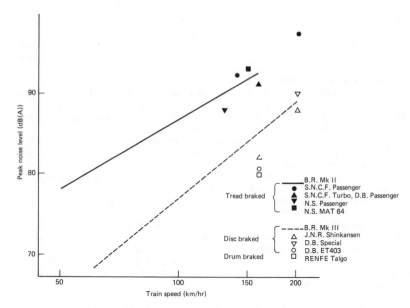

Figure 15.3 Peak noise level for passenger coaches, 25 m from track

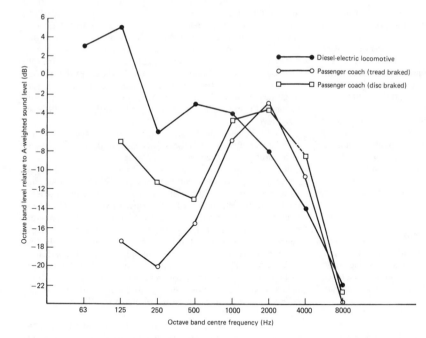

Figure 15.4 Typical train noise spectra

Rolling noise levels are taken to be independent of certain operating factors. These include trains on gradients (uphill or downhill), trains accelerating and trains braking. In all these cases the basic noise level should be derived using the procedure described above by taking the appropriate train speed.

It is accepted that certain vehicles are prone to 'squeal' under emergency brake applications but this is not a normal operating condition and therefore would not require accounting for in a prediction scheme.

15.3.2 Locomotive noise

Naturally there is a rolling noise element in the noise generated by locomotives. The data in *Figure 15.3* are still valid since it appears from measurements that the increased weight of a locomotive relative to a passenger coach does not play a significant part in the level of generated noise. All main-line locomotives in use today have cast-iron tread brakes, therefore rolling noise levels can be found from Equation 15.3.

The mechanical parts of the locomotive are also a source of noise but it has been found that the noise from electric locomotives is no higher than the rolling noise levels. For prediction purposes, therefore, an electric locomotive can be considered as just another vehicle at the head of the train.

Of more importance are the noise levels generated by diesel–electric and diesel–hydraulic locomotives which contain as the main power unit a large diesel engine (up to 3500 hp), many auxiliary fans for cooling etc. and possibly a turbocharger. There is no scheme available at present that allows the noise levels to be calculated for a given design of locomotive; the only recourse is to measured data.

From results, mechanical noise from a diesel locomotive appears to be independent of train speed; the overriding factor is the power setting of the locomotive.[5] This varies from the condition when the locomotive is idling to when maximum power is demanded, as for example when a train with a heavy trailing load is accelerating or traversing an up-hill gradient. The difference between these conditions can be of the order of 20 dB(A). Stanworth[5] gives examples of noise levels for various main-line locomotives used by British Rail when operating at maximum power. The rated horse power of these locomotives varies from 1250 to 2700 hp but there does not appear to be any specific relationship between this and L_{max}.

The data from reference 5 suggest that it is reasonable to use a basic noise level (for British Railways diesel locomotives) of 90 dB(A) at 25 m for the locomotive at maximum power.

Bender et al.[6] summarized measurements taken of the noise levels generated by diesel–electric locomotives in the USA. Based on the passage of 51 locomotives and not accounting for the type of locomotive or the power being demanded, a mean level of 91.7 dB(A) with a standard deviation of 3.2 dB(A) was measured at 100 ft (30.4 m) from the track.

These results are slightly higher than those produced by British Rail. The same report agreed that the position of the power controllers was of paramount importance (the mean noise level for a number of locomotives under idling conditions was 68.6 dB(A) at 100 ft), but it concluded that there was a general trend for the noise at maximum power to increase with rated horse power. For a measurement distance of 100 ft the noise levels were 96.5 dB(A) for 1200 hp to 100 dB(A) for 3000 hp.

The recommendation from inspection of these data is that where possible carry out measurements on the locomotive for which predictions are required. If this is not possible assume a level of 70 dB(A) for a locomotive idling and 90 dB(A) for a locomotive at full power for a measurement distance of 25 m from the track.

A typical octave band spectrum of locomotive noise is given in *Figure 15.4*.[4]

15.3.3 Modifications to basic rolling noise

The noise levels quoted in Section 15.3.1 assume that the train is running on a ballasted track, with sleepers supporting good quality cwr. The following contains information that could be used to determine noise levels for other forms of track construction and rail condition.

An alternative is the use of jointed track, although this is used less on modern railway systems than in the past. Here an increase in noise level relative to normal rolling noise occurs each time a wheel traverses a rail joint. The magnitude of the increase is dependent on many factors including joint geometry, type of rolling stock and train speed. From the results of many measurements it appears that an average increase of about 5 dB(A)[2,5] is likely for peak noise level.

The noise profile consists of a number of 'spikes' superimposed on the normal rolling noise profile and consequently, increases in noise energy will be less than those quoted for peak noise level.

It is known that the quality of the rail-head can deteriorate leading to the formation of short wavelength corrugations.[3] The reasons for this deterioration are discussed in Chapter 14 but they are still a matter of research investigations by many railway administrations. For severe corrugation, increases in noise level

of 10–15 dB(A) have been quoted relative to track of good quality.[2,5] The formation of these corrugations is not, however, a process that occurs throughout the whole of a railway system and where its formation does occur it is gradual over a number of years. Corrugated rails are certainly not installed on a new line.

Thus where predictions for new railway lines are required the assumption of good quality rails (cwr or jointed depending on the proposed design) is a reasonable one and the effect of rail corrugations should not be included.

Also contained in the literature is a comparison of the effect of timber and concrete sleepers on the level of radiated noise. Increases of 2–3 dB(A) for timber sleepered track relative to concrete sleepered track are quoted.[2,7] Site-to-site variation of the noise from a particular type of rolling stock of this magnitude can occur without any change in sleeper material and since the majority of track today includes concrete sleepers it is recommended that the basic noise levels quoted here should be used for all ballasted track irrespective of sleeper material.

A form of track construction that can cause changes in radiated noise levels is 'slab' track. In this design, the ballast is replaced by a massive concrete slab to form the track foundation.

The advantage of this type of track construction is that it requires less maintenance and is often considered as an alternative design for track in tunnel. It is not in common use on open lines but from tests in this situation increases of 2–10 dB(A) have been measured relative to ballasted track.[2,5] The wide spread of results occurred because the tests compared the noise levels from numerous track designs. To date it has not been possible to correlate detail design features with noise increase, to provide a predictable correction factor. In the event that predictions are required for a railway system incorporating a slab track design it will be necessary to obtain measurements from trains on the particular design proposed in order to derive basic noise levels.

Finally, some mention will be made of noise levels from trains on bridges and here again the detail design of the bridge plays an important part in the generated noise levels.

Kurzweil[8] presented data for different designs of bridges, which were generally a combination of steel or concrete construction, with and without ballast. The difference in noise level relative to normal ballasted track varied from + 16 dB(A) for ballastless steel bridges to − 1 dB(A) for ballasted concrete bridges, with parapet. Even then it was not possible to give a definitive correction factor from the knowledge of only two parameters, i.e. steel or concrete combined either with ballast or without ballast. However, it can be concluded that steel bridges tended to be noisier than concrete bridges and those without ballast noisier than those with ballast. Further details on the effects of bridge structures on noise propagation is given in Chapters 16 and 17.

Again it is recommended here that if rolling noise predictions are required for a train traversing a bridge, noise measurements are made for the relevant rolling stock on a bridge of the same design (or as near as possible) as that proposed.

It should be noted that the above discussion is for rolling noise only. The mechanical noise from diesel locomotives will be unaffected by the various changes in track construction.

15.4 Propagation of train noise

15.4.1 Geometric attenuation

Peters[9] concluded that the rolling noise of a train could be modelled assuming the train to be a line of incoherent dipoles. This model fitted the measured attenuation over a flat site, but more importantly provided the best fit to the measured noise profile from a passing train.

The noise level at a section through the centre of and perpendicular to such a line source is given by:

$$L_{max} = 10 \log_{10} \frac{\rho c W}{\pi} + 10 \log_{10}\left[\frac{l}{l^2+d^2} + \frac{1}{2d}\tan^{-1}\frac{l}{2d}\right] \quad (15.5)$$

Where
W = source power/unit length (Watts/m),
ρc = characteristic impedence of air (Ns/m³),
l = length of line source (m),
d = perpendicular distance from line source (m).

The attenuation characteristics are illustrated in *Figure 15.5* for a range of source (train) lengths and distances from the source,

Where
l_0 = train length with known noise level,
l = train length for predicted noise level.

A locomotive is usually modelled as a point source with cosine directivity.[10]

The attenuation from a point source is given by:

$$\Delta_S = 20 \log_{10}\frac{d}{d_0}$$

$$(15.8)$$

15.4.2 Air absorption

Sound propagation over relatively short distances in air involves

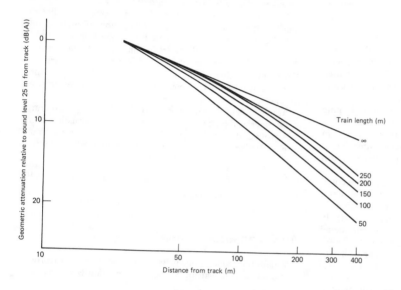

Figure 15.5 Geometric attenuation for rolling noise

with attenuation given relative to the sound level at 25 m. These curves are derived from the equation:

$$\Delta_S = 10 \log_{10}\left[\frac{1}{4D_0^2+1} + \frac{1}{2D_0}\tan^{-1}\frac{1}{2D_0}\right]$$
$$- 10 \log_{10}\left[\frac{1}{4D^2+1} + \frac{1}{2D}\tan^{-1}\frac{1}{2D}\right] \quad (15.6)$$

Where $D_0 = \frac{25}{l}$ (25 m = reference distance d_0)

and $D = \frac{d}{l}$

For an infinite line source the attenuation is 3 dB per distance doubling and this is the asymptote for distances close to the track. At greater distances the decay is closer to that from a point source (6 dB per distance doubling) and this is achieved at distances $d > l$.

Where L_{max} is known at a particular distance and for a given type of rolling stock, but for a train length different from that for which a prediction is required, Equation 15.5 can also be used to determine the relevant correction.

This is given by:

$$\Delta_{\text{TRAIN LENGTH}} = 10 \log_{10}\left[\frac{l_0}{l_0^2+4d^2} + \frac{1}{2d}\tan^{-1}\frac{l_0}{2d}\right]$$
$$- 10 \log_{10}\left[\frac{l}{l^2+4d^2} + \frac{1}{2d}\tan^{-1}\frac{l}{2d}\right] \quad (15.7)$$

slight losses which are frequency, temperature and humidity dependent.

References 11 and 12 give air absorption values which have been used in railway noise prediction schemes. Applying those values to the spectra in *Figure 15.4* gives attenuation of 0.5–1 dB(A) per 100 m for rolling noise and about 0.5 dB(A) per 100 m for locomotive noise.

15.4.3 Ground attenuation

In this section only the absorption by ground cover is considered. The more complex problem of interference and ground impedance effects will be mentioned later.

Rathe[13] suggested attenuation data for grass cover and for ground covered by dense shrubs and those values are given in *Table 15.1*.

It was recommended that for a mean propagation path height of less than 0.8 m above the ground the values of *Table 15.1* should be used, with the values decreasing linearly to zero for a mean path height of 6 m above the ground.

Considering propagation over flat grassland, using the values given in *Table 15.1* and the spectra in *Figure 15.4*, the attenuation of rolling noise would be approximately 4 dB(A) per 100 m. For locomotive noise with a mean path height of 2.5 m (source assumed to be 3 m above rail level) the attenuation is approximately 1.5 dB(A) per 100 m.

Table 15.1 Attenuation by ground absorption (dB/100 m)

Frequency (Hz)	Attenuation for different surfaces	
	Grassland	Dense shrubs
63	0.7	2.5
125	1.0	3.6
250	1.4	5.0
500	2.0	7.0
1000	2.8	10.0
2000	4.0	14.0
4000	5.6	20.0
8000	8.0	28.0

15.4.4 Comparison with measurements

Figure 15.6 gives measurements at various distances for rolling noise from British Railways Inter-City trains (train length 250 m) for propagation over flat grassland.[10] The combined effect of geometric attenuation, air absorption and ground absorption as described above are also shown.

For distances up to 100 m from the track, agreement is quite good, but at greater distances the predicted attenuation is greater than measured. Consequently, even at this early stage in the prediction it can be seen that without noise measurements at the relevant far distances the single number approach can introduce possibly unacceptable errors.

Kurzweil *et al.*[12] showed that rolling noise attenuation could be predicted to a distance of 200 m (the limit of measured data) accurately by using a ground attenuation model which considered sound propagation over a locally reacting surface. In this model the propagation from each wheel is considered separately and the overall level obtained by summation of levels from all wheels for each one-third octave band. The choice of source height above the ground appears to be critical in determining the attenuation.

For the general user, who requires an answer fairly quickly, this approach is probably too detailed and a knowledge of the limitations of the simplified approach is sufficient especially if an opportunity exists for carrying out sample noise measurements. Further information on this topic can be found in references 12, 14 and 15.

An alternative approach has been used in a French prediction scheme[16] where it has been assumed that the total attenuation for propagation over flat grass takes the form:

$$L_{max} = L_{max_0} - k \log_{10}\frac{d}{d_0}$$
(15.9)

The constant k varies between 12 for long trains and 17 for short trains. For the French equivalent of the British Railways Inter-City train k is given a value of 15 and that attenuation characteristic is also shown on *Figure 15.6*. Here again, agreement is good for distances less than 100 m but above that there is a tendency to under-predict the attenuation. It is interesting that a value of k of 17 would fit the data quite well for all distances but there seems to be no justification for using this when considering the various train descriptions in reference 16.

The conclusion from this comparison seems to be that the single-number approach for the attenuation of rolling noise over flat grassland seems adequate for distances up to 100 m. In practice, the vast majority of predictions will be required within this range. If information is required for distances greater than 100 m then either more sophisticated ground attenuation models must be used or measurements taken at the relevant distances.

Application of the same type of analysis for diesel locomotive noise suggests that, notwithstanding the earlier discussion on air and ground absorption, the best estimate for distance attenuation is obtained by considering geometric attenuation only:

$$L_{max} = L_{max_0} - 20 \log_{10}\frac{d}{d_0}$$
(15.10)

This is also recommended in reference 16.

15.5 Excess attenuation

The data presented in this section are considered as corrections to the levels obtained for propagation over flat grassland.

15.5.1 Track in cutting

A railway track in cutting is a common feature, but the amount of data relating to the noise reduction afforded by such cuttings is extremely sparse.

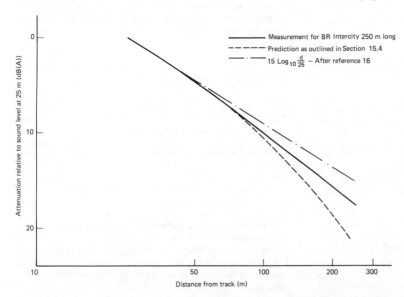

Figure 15.6 Attenuation of rolling noise, comparison of measurement and prediction

Holzl and Hafner[17] present the results from a cutting 6.4 m deep, with slope angles of approximately 26 degrees. From these results and others they derived the following equation for noise reduction of rolling noise:

$$\Delta_{\text{CUTTING}} = 9.4 \log_{10}(2 + 50\delta)\,\text{dB(A)} \qquad (15.11)$$

Where δ is the path difference (in m), as defined in *Figure 15.7* where the geometry is defined at a section through the receiver normal to the railway track and assuming the source to be at the rail-head of the nearest rail. (It should be noted that similar path difference corrections are used for calculating the screening provided by roadside barriers, cuttings, etc. *See* Chapter 10, in particular, Section 10.5.2.)

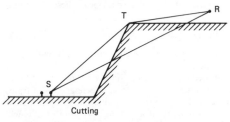

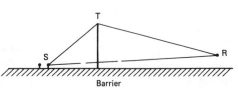

Figure 15.7 Definition of path difference.
S=Source—assumed at rail-head of nearest rail for rolling noise
R=Receiver
Path difference δ=ST+TR−SR

Equation 15.11 is used in a Deutsche Bundesbahn prediction method[18] where it is also stated that for steep-sided cuttings (45–90 degrees) reflections may cause the screening potential to be 3 dB(A) less than the values obtained using Equation 15.11, unless the cutting walls have a sound-absorbent surface. Approximations for rolling noise reduction are also given as a function of cutting depth:

Cutting depth   3 m gives 5 dB(A) reduction
             7 m gives 10 dB(A) reduction
            15 m gives 15 dB(A) reduction

The effect of other cutting depths are obtained by linear interpolation. There appears to be no data for the reduction of diesel locomotive noise by a cutting and as a first approximation it is best to assume that if the roof of the locomotive is visible then there will be no significant reduction. For deep cuttings the reduction could be estimated from one of the barrier theories, e.g. Maekawa[19] using a typical locomotive noise spectrum (unless the relevant one is known) with the source located at roof height on the locomotive.

15.5.2 Track on embankment

For the same conditions described in Section 15.3 (basic noise level) the noise at source from a train on an embankment is the same as the noise from that train at a flat site. Differences in received noise levels occur only because of changed propagation characteristics.

For a receiver close to the base of an embankment a certain amount of shielding may be offered by the embankment shoulder. In this case any corrections should be calculated from barrier attenuation data (*see* Section 15.5.3).

For receiver distances further away, where no shielding occurs, measured levels will be higher than those for the flat site, and this is attributed to reduced ground absorption due to increased height of the propagation path above the ground.

Two methods can be employed for assessing this situation.

First, if data are available at the relevant distance for propagation over flat grassland, these levels can be increased by an amount equivalent to the ground absorption values, e.g. for mean height of propagation above the ground greater than 6 m:

$$\Delta_{\text{EMBANKMENT}} = -4\,\text{dB(A)} \text{ per 100 m}$$

Alternatively, the attenuation due to geometric spreading and air absorption could be calculated and that correction applied to the noise levels at a reference distance of say 25 m from the track. Therefore, depending on train length, the attenuation would be similar to the curves of *Figure 15.5*.

For diesel locomotive noise it can be assumed that the embankment situation is no different to the flat site situation, i.e. attenuation remains at 6 dB(A) per distance doubling.

15.5.3 Barriers

This area of railway noise propagation has received most attention over recent years, probably because it represents the most likely method of reducing noise levels given current knowledge, while still maintaining a workable railway service.

The results of experiments on the reduction of rolling noise are given in references 17 and 20.

From reference 17 a design curve for absorptive barriers was produced:

$$\Delta_{\text{BARRIER}} = 9.4 \log_{10}(2 + 50\delta)\,\text{dB(A)} \qquad (15.12)$$

Where δ is the path difference (in m) as defined in *Figure 15.7*.

Equation 15.12 was determined from regression analysis of results obtained for a variety of trains (passenger, freight) and this includes the effects of change in source spectrum from these different trains.

In reference 20, the investigation was limited to measurements for 161 km/h (100 mph) passenger trains and reflective barriers. The prediction curves derived in this experiment are shown in *Figure 15.8*. The first curve is based on path difference considerations, with the source taken to be at the rail-head of the nearest rail. For $\delta > 0.1$ the equation of the curve is:

$$\Delta_1 = 19.1 + 8.1 \log_{10}\delta \;\text{dB(A)} \qquad (15.13)$$

The second curve is introduced to allow for reflections which would exist between the side of the railway vehicle and the reflecting surface of the barrier.

The equation of this curve is:

$$\Delta_2 = 7.4 - 3.7 \log_{10}D \;\text{dB(A)} \qquad (15.14)$$

Where D is the distance between the nearest rail and the barrier in metres. Total noise reduction is given by:

$$\Delta_{\text{BARRIER}} = \Delta_1 - \Delta_2 \;\text{dB(A)} \qquad (15.15)$$

Although absorptive barriers were not investigated in this experiment, Equation 15.13 would give the noise reduction in

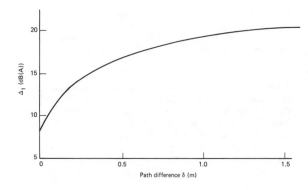

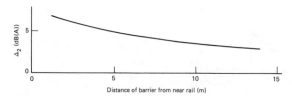

Figure 15.8 Example of barrier attenuation curves. For barrier with absorptive face:
$\Delta \text{Barrier} = \Delta_1$
For barrier with reflective face:
$\Delta \text{Barrier} = \Delta_1 - \Delta_2$

that case. Comparison of Equation 15.12 and 15.13 shows reasonable agreement with Equation 15.12 giving slightly lower values. A possible reason for this is an attempt in that case to use a single curve for the effect of barriers on the noise from trains with a variety of source spectra, with freight vehicles generally containing relatively more low frequency noise than passenger trains.

When considering diesel locomotive noise it will be necessary to use one of the recognized barriers theories, with the locomotive noise spectrum, to obtain the noise reduction. In this case it is generally assumed that the source is at roof level of the locomotive.

15.5.4 Housing development

Data reported thus far give only the noise reduction of rows of houses, and not the effect of reflections within a housing development.

Walker[21] suggests the following:

1. 8 dB(A) reduction for a single row of semi-detached houses with an additional 4 dB(A) for each successive row (this is supported by reference 1).
2. 14.7 dB(A) reduction for a single row of terraced houses 300 m long, increasing to 17.1 dB(A) where two or more rows of similar design are involved.
3. 12.9 dB(A) for two or more rows of terraced houses 150 m long.

Rathe[13] gives the following:

10 dB(A) reduction for a single row of houses close to the track with up to 3 dB(A) additional reduction for each successive row.

The above data relate only to rolling noise. For diesel locomotive noise it is suggested that for rows of houses with large gaps between houses there is no excess attenuation. For terraced houses it is usual to treat the problem in the same way as for a barrier.

15.6 Prediction of L_{eq}

For a specified time period, the total L_{eq}, from M separate noise events, is given by:

$$L_{eq} = 10 \log_{10} \left(\sum_{j=1}^{M} 10^{((L_{eq})_j/10)} \right)$$

(15.16)

Where $(L_{eq})_j = L_{eq}$ of jth event measured over the same time period as L_{eq}.

When assessing the noise from trains passing a particular receiver point it is assumed that all those trains of the same type travelling at or near the same speed and where the locomotive power setting is likely to be the same give rise to the same noise level. Consequently, if there are N_i of these trains during the same time period then the L_{eq} for the passage of these N_i trains is given by:

$$L_{eq} = (L_{eq})_i + 10 \log_{10} N_i$$

(15.17)

Where $(L_{eq})_i = L_{eq}$ for the passage of a single train with those noise characteristics.

It should be noted that this is not simply a grouping of trains by train type as defined in Section 15.3. Where groups of trains of the same type are likely to travel at different speeds, because of, say, the close proximity of a station, then those trains will have to be considered as separate groups. This will also apply where the locomotive power settings vary.

The total L_{eq} for the whole train service is determined by summation of the L_{eq}s of all the different groups of trains. The prediction process can be broken down into the following stages:

1. Define the number of groups of trains whose noise characteristics are different (M).
2. Define the number of trains within each group where the noise characteristics are identical (N_i).
3. Calculate the L_{eq} for the passage of a single train within each group $(L_{eq})_i$.
4. Determine the overall L_{eq} by summation of the various group L_{eq}'s.

$$(L_{eq})_{TOTAL} = 10 \log_{10} \left(\sum_{i=1}^{M} 10^{[((L_{eq})_i + 10 \log_{10} N_i)/10]} \right)$$

(15.18)

$(L_{eq})_i$ is conveniently determined from the relevant value of the Single Event Exposure Level, L_{AX} since:

$$(L_{eq})_i = (L_{AX})_i - 10 \log_{10} T$$

(15.19)

where T is the time period under consideration expressed in seconds.

Mathematically L_{AX} can be expressed as:

$$L_{AX} = 10 \log_{10} \int_{-\infty}^{\infty} 10^{(L_A/10)} \, dt$$

(15.20)

Integration of the theoretical time history for rolling noise[10] gives:

$$L_{AX} = L_{max} + 10 \log_{10} \frac{l}{V} - 10 \log_{10} \left[\frac{4D}{4D^2 + 1} + 2 \tan^{-1} \frac{1}{2D} \right] + 10.5,$$

(15.21)

where L_{max} = peak noise level during a pass-by (dB(A))
l = train length (m)
V = train speed (km/h),
D = $\frac{d}{l}$, and
d = distance from the train in m.

The function $10.5 - 10 \log_{10} \left[\frac{4D}{4D^2 + 1} + 2 \tan^{-1} \frac{1}{2D} \right]$ is shown in *Figure 15.9*.

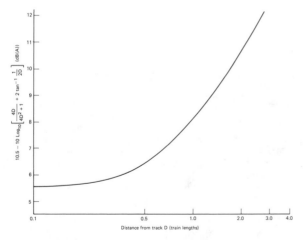

Figure 15.9 Relationship between L_{AX} and L_{max} for rolling noise

$$L_{AX} = L_{max} + 10 \log_{10} \frac{l}{V} + 10.5 - 10 \log_{10} \left[\frac{4D}{4D^2+1} + 2 \tan^{-1} \frac{1}{2D} \right]$$

where l = Train length (m)
V = Train speed (km/h)
d = Distance from track (m)
$D = \dfrac{d}{l}$

Thus one method of calculating $(L_{AX})_i$ (and hence $(L_{eq})_i$) for rolling noise is to determine the basic peak noise level as outlined in Sections 15.3 and 15.4 and convert the result to L_{AX} using Equation 15.21.

Equation 15.21 can also be used to determine correction factors for the effect of train speed, train length or distance, for the noise from a given type of rolling stock should the base data not be available for the required values of those parameters.

Train speed corrections for L_{AX} are given by $(k-10) \log_{10} \frac{V}{V_0}$, where k is the proportional constant for peak noise level for that particular rolling stock, V_0 is the reference speed at which L_{AX} is known and V is the speed at which L_{AX} is required. L_{AX} is therefore less dependent on train speed than peak noise level.

Where L_{AX} has been calculated for a train length of say l_0, but is required for a train consisting of vehicles of the same design but of total length l, then the correction factor is $10_{10} \log \frac{l}{l_0}$, i.e. a 3 dB change for a factor of two change in train length.

For distance corrections only the change due to geometric spreading is given by $10 \log_{10} d/d_0$, i.e. -3 dB for a distance doubling. If there is an appreciable difference between d and d_0 then a further correction due to air and ground absorption (*see* Sections 15.4.2 and 15.4.3) may be needed.

The prediction of L_{AX} can be completed, assuming the excess attenuation values given in 15.5 are also applicable to L_{AX}.

References 12 and 16 suggest alternative corrections for determining L_{AX} from rolling noise peak noise level. Kurzweil[12] uses an approximate form for the duration over which the noise level is within 5 dB of the peak noise level:

$$L_{AX} = L_{max} + 10 \log_{10} \left[3.6 \frac{l}{V} \left(1 + 1.2 \frac{d}{l} \right) \right] \tag{15.22}$$

In reference 16 the duration is taken to be 10 dB down from the peak and can be approximated by:

$$\frac{3.6l}{V} + \frac{6d}{100} \tag{15.23}$$

Therefore,

$$L_{AX} = L_{max} + 10 \log_{10} \left(3.6 \frac{l}{V} + \frac{6d}{100} \right) \tag{15.24}$$

where in both cases l and d are in metres, V is in km/h.

For diesel locomotive noise, integration of a theoretical time history has also been used for determining the relationship between L_{AX} and peak noise level.[10] Assuming a point source with cosine directivity the following expression can be used:

$$L_{AX} = L_{max} + 10 \log_{10} \left(\frac{d}{V} \right) + 8.6 \tag{15.25}$$

This equation implies a decay with distances of 3 dB per distance doubling and reduction of 3 dB per speed doubling, assuming L_{max} is independent of speed. Consequently, when considering the L_{AX} from a whole train with a diesel locomotive on full power, at low speeds, noise from the locomotive will dominate but will reduce with increasing speed. A speed will eventually be reached where the energy contribution from the locomotive and wagons will be equal. At speeds higher than this, noise from the wagons will dominate and the total noise from the train will be less dependent on the power setting of the locomotive. This effect is illustrated in *Figure 15.10*.

Many noise measuring instruments, available today, allow measurement of L_{AX} either directly or from tape recordings. A more satisfactory method of deriving L_{AX} prediction curves would, therefore, be to carry out the regression analysis and corrections described earlier using L_{AX} as the dependent variable instead of peak noise level. Such data probably exist within the records of many researchers but little have, so far, been published. Even from published data it is not always possible to tell whether they are the result of direct measurement or from conversion of peak noise level data.

Two prediction schemes are currently used where energy curves are presented.[16,18] Neither use L_{AX} but prefer to work with the L_{eq} for one train pass-by per hour. In fact this only introduced a constant term difference in the calculations of $(L_{eq})_i$ since:

$$L_{eq} \text{ (1 train per hour)} = L_{AX} - 35.6 \text{ dB(A)}$$
Since $10 \log_{10} 3600 = 35.6$

The methods described in these references follow the same pattern of propagation corrections to a basic noise level as described above and some of the data contained in them have been enumerated in this chapter. Both these references are suggested as further reading for those interested in gaining more information about train noise prediction.

15.7 Computer prediction models

The earlier sections of this chapter have described empirical or semi-empirical methods of predicting train noise, treating the whole train as a single source. For rolling noise each wheel can be considered as a separate source and various computer models have been developed where the received noise level (L_{max} or L_{eq}) is determined by summation of the contribution from each wheel.

It is intended here to present only a general description of those programs and it is suggested that more detailed information is obtained by reading the relevant references or alternatively contacting the program developers.

Rathe[13,22] has adapted a general model of complex traffic noise propagation to deal specifically with railway noise. In this program 'MODEL 77' the computation is carried out in one-third octave bands and each wheel is considered as a point source with cosine directivity in the horizontal and vertical

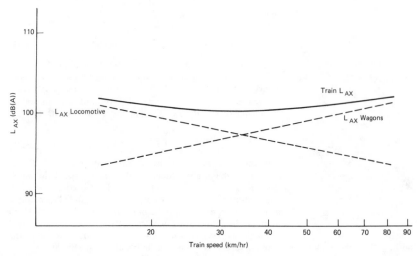

Figure 15.10 Example of train L_{AX} with locomotive on full power

direction. Different types of rolling stock are characterized by a reference one-third octave band spectrum, directivity and wheel spacing.

The propagation from these point sources can be calculated for any specific site geometry, accounting for factors such as cuttings, embankments, barriers and housing development as required. The barrier theory in this program is based on the work of Maekawa.[19] It is also possible to include the effect of different atmospheric conditions.

Summation at the receiver point, over frequency and number of wheels allows the noise level for a specific train position to be calculated. Integration for a number of train positions determines the L_{eq}.

The main advantages of this type of method over the simplified methods described earlier are that it allows calculations to be made for obstacles which vary in height etc., throughout their length, e.g. the transition stage of cuttings. It is also possible to include the effect of ground reflections[12] which are not easily incorporated into the simplified approach. Further, account could be taken of changes in train speed as the train passes the receiver point, if this is relevant.

A second computer-based prediction method, 'SETRAFER', is described in reference 23. It was developed from a program for road traffic noise prediction and although the method of computation differs in detail from that described above it has similar objectives and considers the same propagation parameters. A major difference is that it uses octave band spectra and limits the analysis to 11 fixed positions of the train as it passes the receiver point.

Also included in reference 23 is the description of a simpler program, 'PROPAG', which calculates noise levels in a single vertical plane which intersects the track at right angles. This is essentially a computer-based version of the method described in 15.3–15.6 but with the calculations made for one-third octave bands prior to determination of overall level (L_{max} or L_{eq}).

15.8 Summary

The prediction of train noise can be considered in two separate stages. Initially, from a knowledge of the type of rolling stock, train speed, track condition and, where required, diesel locomotive power setting an estimate can be made of source levels.

Secondly, from site geometry, allowance is made by way of various corrections for the propagation of noise to specific points.

It must be appreciated that data do not exist for every type of railway vehicle in operation and some approximations may need to be made in the calculation of basic noise levels, e.g. categorization of passenger vehicles by type of braking system. If it is felt that such approximations would lead to unacceptable errors then measurements of noise from the relevant design of vehicle must be made.

Care must be taken in choosing the site for these measurements and it is recommended that sites are chosen where vehicles, whose noise levels are already known, are also operating. Using these vehicles as reference, the track can be 'calibrated' to assess its effect on noise level generation, e.g. if predictions are required for track consisting of good quality cwr it would be unwise to use data from a site where noise levels from the 'reference' trains indicate the presence of rail corrugations.

The comment regarding track calibration is valid for all noise measurements where the effect of changing just one parameter is involved, including assessment of the excess attenuation factor. It is essential that all the other parameters are unchanged for the comparisons to be valid.

Concerning the prediction itself, the amount of detailed information on how trains will operate, e.g. speed and locomotive power setting, depend on the length of route for which the information is required. In assessing a new route a first approximation based on locomotives at full power throughout and with trains running at the maximum speed should suffice. From this simplified procedure, potential problem areas can be identified and a separate prediction made for these shorter sections of route using more accurate information relating to the expected operating characteristics of the trains.

References

1   HEMSWORTH, B. Railway noise prediction—data base requirements. *Journal of Sound and Vibration*, **87**, 275 (1983).

2   *Generation and Propagation of Railway Noise*, Report No 5 of ORE Committee C137 (1977).

3   HEMSWORTH, B. Recent developments in wheel/rail noise research. *Journal of Sound and Vibration*, **66**, 297 (1979).

4   LOTZ, R. Railroad and rail transit noise sources. *Journal of Sound and Vibration*, **51**, 319 (1977).

5   STANWORTH, C. G. *Railway Noise and the Environment—A Summary* (2nd Edn.), British Railways Board, Technical Note TNPHYS4 (1977).

6   BENDER, E. K., ELY, R. A., REMINGTON, P. J. and RUDD, M. J. *Railroad Environmental Noise: A State of the Art Assessment* BBN Report, No. 2709 (1974).

7   STUBER, C. Air and structure-borne noise of railways. *Journal of Sound and Vibration*, **43**, 281 (1975).

8   KURZWEIL, L. G. Prediction and control of noise from railway bridges and tracked transit elevated structures. *Journal of Sound and Vibration*, **51**, 419 (1977).

9   PETERS, S. The prediction of railway noise profiles. *Journal of Sound and Vibration*, **32**, 87 (1974).

10 The Noise Advisory Council. *A Guide to the Measurement and Prediction of the Equivalent Noise Level L_{eq}*, HMSO, London (1978).

11 *A Theoretical Model for the Propagation of Railway Noise*. Report No 6 of ORE Committee C137 (1977).

12 KURZWEIL, L. G., COBB, W. N. and KENDIG, R. P. Propagation of noise from rail lines. *Journal of Sound and Vibration*, **66**, 389 (1979).

13 RATHE, E. J. Railway noise propagation. *Journal of Sound and Vibration*, **51**, 371 (1977).

14 PIERCY, J. E., EMBLETON, T. F. W. and SUTHERLAND, L. C. Review of noise propagation in the atmosphere. *Journal of the Acoustic Society of America*, **61**, 1403 (1977).

15 CHESSEL, C. I. Propagation of noise along a finite impedance boundary. *Journal of the Acoustical Society of America*, **62**, 825 (1977).

16 *Guide du Bruit des Transports Terrestres*; Prevision des Niveaux Sonores, Ministere de l'Environnement, Ministere des Transports Paris (1981).

17 HOLZL, G. and HAFNER, P. Untersuchungen der DB und anderer Europaischer Bahnverwaltungen zur Minderung von Eisenbahngerauschen durch Abschirmungen. *Eisenbahn Technische Rundschau*, **29**, 619 (1980).

18 *Neubaustrecken, Information Schall 03*, Deutsche Bundesbahn, Munchen (1980).

19 MAEKAWA, Z. Noise reduction by screens. *Applied Acoustics*, **1**, 157 (1968).

20 HEMSWORTH, B. and WEBB, V. Noise barriers for fast passenger trains. In *Inter-Noise 77*, B465 (1977).

21 WALKER, J. G. Factors affecting railway noise levels in residential areas. *Journal of Sound and Vibration*, **51**, 393 (1977).

22 RATHE, E. J. Computer model for noise propagation studies involving complex noise source and topographical characteristics. In *Inter-Noise 77*, A154 (1977)

23 PARENT DE CURZON, E. Predetermining noise levels in a railway environment. Methods of calculation. *French Railway Review*, **2**, 15 (1984).

16

Low-Frequency Noise and Vibration from Trains

Paul J. Remington BS, MS, PhD
**BBN Laboratories Inc., Cambridge,
Massachusetts, USA**

Leonard G. Kurzweil BS, MS, PhD
**Transportation Systems Center, Cambridge,
Massachusetts, USA**

David A. Towers BS, MS
**Harris Miller Miller and Hanson Inc.,
Lexington, Massachusetts, USA**

Contents

16.1 Introduction

In recent years there has been a resurgence in interest in the environmental impact of ground vibration generated by passing trains. When a train composed of very heavy vehicles (20 000 to 40 000 kg (45 000 to 90 000 lb) for self-powered electric transit cars (carriages), to over 150 000 kg (330 000 lb) for some locomotives) passes by, significant excitation of the ground can occur. The resulting ground vibrations will then propagate through the intervening soil or rock and into buildings in the surrounding community. There the vibration may be felt by occupants or may be radiated into the rooms of the building and heard as a low-frequency rumble. It may also interfere with the operation of vibration-sensitive devices or in severe cases may result in minor structural damage to the building. The purpose of this chapter is to bring together existing analytical and empirical techniques which can be used to:

1. Predict the impact on communities of vibration due to train operations for proposed new alignments.
2. Diagnose the source of vibration problems in existing alignments.
3. Estimate change in community impact due to the use of various vibration control techniques.

The reader is also encouraged to consult Chapter 12, which deals in a similar way with vibration from road traffic. *Figure 16.1* illustrates the source-path-receiver relationship for a train

in a tunnel. Significant levels of ground vibrations can be generated whether the train is in a tunnel, is operating at-grade or is crossing an elevated structure. In general though, the environmental impact of airborne noise from at-grade and elevated operations is more significant than the impact resulting from ground vibration. Consequently, interest in groundborne noise and vibration usually centres on train operations in tunnels.

Figure 16.2 shows the spectrum of the vertical vibration on the floor in the basement of a building near a subway in Toronto.[1] The acceleration is typically dominated by energy in the 10–250 Hz frequency range with a peak in the vicinity of 50 Hz. Although *Figure 16.2* shows a typical response, it can be altered both in level and in frequency content if there are changes in soil conditions, bogie suspension characteristics and rail and wheel conditions.

One of the most difficult problems in assessing the potential impact on the community of vibration from train operations on a proposed alignment is the prediction of vibration levels at distances far removed from the track. The vibrations at track side can often be estimated using measurements of trackbed vibration from similar rail vehicles operating on similar track structures. Prediction of vibration levels at some distance from the track is complicated by a soil and rock structure that varies widely from site to site. That soil structure is usually not well known. Even if information from soil borings is available, the viscoelastic properties of the soil, e.g. shear and compressional

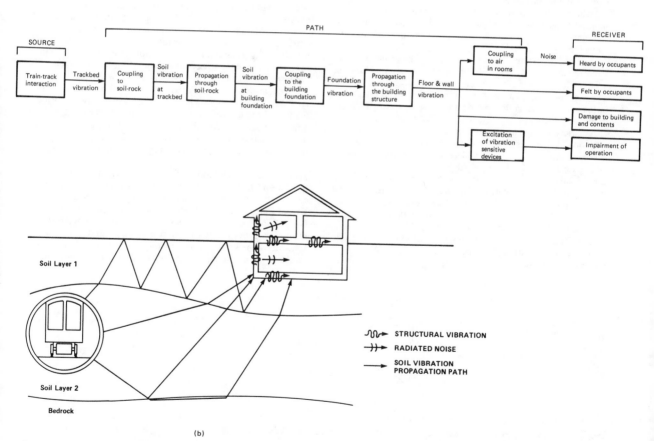

(b)

Figure 16.1 The generation of ground vibration and its transmission to the surrounding community. (*a*) Block diagram. (*b*) Schematic representation

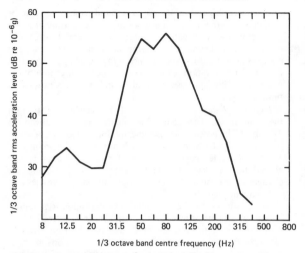

Figure 16.2 Typical floor vibration in the basement of a building near a subway

wave speed and internal damping, crucial to the prediction of vibration propagation, are often not available. Furthermore, even if the soil structure and its mechanical properties are well known, the mathematics for predicting the vibration are very complicated, making it possible to treat analytically only the simplest geometries. Consequently, empirical techniques or a combination of analytical and empirical techniques are used to make these predictions.

Once the vibration reaches a building, the coupling of the vibration in the soil to the building foundation and the resulting propagation through the structure of the building are processes nearly as complicated as the prediction of vibration propagation in the soil. Consequently, empirical techniques are used almost exclusively.

A variety of treatments are available for controlling train vibration in the community. These include treatments at the source, such as wheel truing and reduced primary suspension stiffness; isolation of the trackbed from the soil, such as with floated slabs or resilient rail fasteners; shielding, such as through use of trenches; and isolation of the building itself from the soil through use of neoprene bearing pads, for example.

The structure of this chapter follows closely the source–path–receiver model illustrated in *Figure 16.1(a)*. The chapter begins with a discussion of ground excitation, including both track–train interaction and soil coupling (*see* Section 16.2). Analytical/empirical techniques for predicting the propagation of vibration

through soil and rock are covered in Section 16.3. Similar techniques for predicting building response, including foundation–soil coupling and propagation through the building are discussed in Section 16.4. Criteria for assessing the impact of vibration on the community and techniques for vibration control are discussed in Sections 16.5 and 16.6, respectively.

16.2 Ground excitation

16.2.1 Train/track interaction

At the present time, the mechanism by which the train excites the ground into vibration is not well understood. It is believed that as the train proceeds down the track, dynamic forces arise between the wheel and rail due to irregularities on the surface of the rail and wheel (*see Figure 16.3*) and possibly to irregularities in the support structure beneath the rail.[2]

The rail response velocity, V_R, can be shown to be proportional to the wheel and rail impedances and roughnesses according to the following equation:

$$V_R \propto \frac{Z_W(\omega)}{Z_W(\omega) + Z_R(\omega)}$$

$$\times \text{[combined wheel/rail roughness]} \qquad (16.1)$$

Rail roughness is taken to mean the profile irregularities on the rail such as might be measured by a track geometry car; and wheel roughness refers to the out-of-roundness of the wheel, due to wheel flats, for example. $Z_W(\omega)$ and $Z_R(\omega)$ are the vertical point impedances of the wheel and rail respectively, i.e. the amplitude and phase of the force required to generate a unit velocity at frequency ω. It should be noted that $Z_W(\omega)$ is not just the impedance of the wheel but includes the influence of the axle, the bogie, the car body, and bogie suspension elements.

An equation similar to Equation 16.1 could be written for the lateral forces although such an equation would have to include the lateral friction forces at the wheel/rail interface and, consequently, would involve all the complexities of the lateral dynamics of rail vehicles, e.g. hunting (an instability leading to violent lateral oscillation of a rail vehicle operating at high speed on tangent track). Unfortunately, at present, only the simplest analytical characterizations of the parameters in Equation 16.1 have been utilized and these for the most part have not been compared with measured data.[2-5] Measured data are scarce. Except for the rail vehicle input impedance $Z_W(\omega)$ measured by Nelson[6,7] on a BART bogie, data for the other parameters in the proper frequency or wavelength regime for ground vibration are generally very limited. Consequently, for the present time, we must rely on empirical means for estimating the ground vibra-

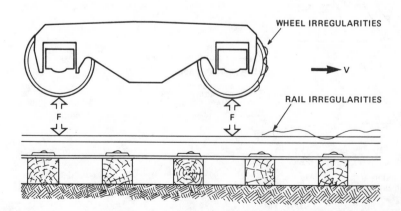

Figure 16.3. Train–track interaction

tion at the trackbed produced by a passing train. A discussion of two such approaches is given in Section 16.2.3. Here we will qualitatively examine with the help of Equation 16.1 how track and bogie parameters may affect ground vibration.

Figure 16.4 shows an order of magnitude representation of Z_W and Z_R for a typical transit car operating on typical tie and ballast rail. Resonances below 10 Hz associated with the secondary suspension (between the car body/bolster and bogie) and first car body bending mode are generally of no interest since ground vibration levels below 10 Hz are usually too small to be of any concern. The reason ground vibration levels are so low at very low frequency is illustrated clearly in *Figure 16.4*. For frequencies less than 5 Hz or so, Z_W is so much less than Z_R that the rail simply does not respond. Consequently, in this frequency region it can be reasonably assumed that when the wheel encounters an irregularity it moves up and over the irregularity and the rail remains essentially stationary.

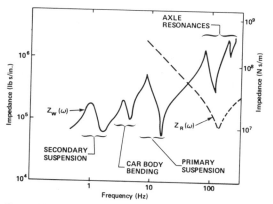

Figure 16.4 Schematic representation of wheel and rail impedance

Between 10 and 30 Hz the vehicle impedance Z_W and rail impedance become more comparable in value although Z_W is still much less than Z_R. The primary suspension resonances that usually occur in this frequency range can have a significant effect on ground vibration.[8,9] To see why, note that below 30 Hz in *Figure 16.4*, $Z_R \gg Z_W$ and, consequently, from Equation 16.1:

$$V_R \propto \frac{Z_W}{Z_R} \tag{16.2}$$

Equation 16.2 shows that if Z_W is made larger due to some design change to the bogie, then the rail and, consequently, the ground will respond more. The rail vehicle impedance Z_W in *Figure 16.4* between the peak below 10 Hz and the trough above 10 Hz is controlled by the primary suspension stiffness. Increasing that stiffness increases Z_W and, as Equation 16.2 shows, increasing Z_W will increase ground vibration. This phenomenon is not speculative and has, in fact, been observed in field tests.[8,9]

Figure 16.4 also explains in part another phenomenon observed in field measurements of train generated ground vibration, i.e., the peak in ground vibration spectra at around 50 Hz (*see Figure 16.2*). Note that in *Figure 16.4* at about 40 Hz where the rail and vehicle impedances are equal that Z_R is spring like and Z_W is mass like. Consequently, Z_W and Z_R are of opposite sign, and the denominator of Equation 16.1, $Z_R \pm Z_W$, is nearly zero. This is essentially a resonant phenomenon in which the equivalent wheel–gearbox–axle–propulsion motor mass, i.e., the unsprung mass, is resonating on the rail foundation at the trackbed produced

tion stiffness, resulting in an amplification of ground vibration.

Above 50 Hz in *Figure 16.4* $Z_W \gg Z_R$ and even though there may be axle resonances in the frequency regime, Equation 16.1 shows that the rail response and ground vibration are independent of either the wheel or rail impedance.

16.2.2 Wheel/rail excitation

As mentioned above, one of the excitation mechanisms for ground vibration is the irregularities on the surface of the wheel and rail. If we are interested in train speeds from 30 to 110 km/h (20–70 mph) and frequencies of 10–250 Hz, then the irregularities with wavelengths of from 35 mm to 3 m (1.5 in to 10 ft) are of primary interest. These wavelengths are longer than those of interest for wheel/rail noise and, consequently, existing techniques for measuring wheel and rail roughness are not applicable here.[10,11] In addition, the technology for measuring rail profile used in track geometry cars by railroads across the world tends to focus on wavelengths somewhat longer than those of interest here.[12,13]

The University of Toronto in studies for the Toronto Transit Commission[2] has attempted to interpolate between these two regimes. An approximate formula has been derived which can be used to estimate the rail roughness spectrum. Unfortunately this formula applies only to rail that is much smoother and well aligned than is found on most railroads and rapid transit systems.

For the wheel the irregularities of greatest importance are flat spots generated when the wheel slides during braking. Analytical estimates of the wheel roughness spectrum due to flat spots at low train speed (< 50 km/h [30 mph]) are available,[2,10] but no field data exist to validate the analyses.

16.2.3 Ground response

As the previous two sections have shown there is a significant shortage of experimentally verified analytical formulae and experimental data for predicting the effects on ground vibration of rail vehicle suspension parameters, rail parameters, train speed, etc. Consequently, it is necessary at the present time to rely on prediction techniques that are at least in part empirical.

In this and subsequent sections in this chapter an examination will be made of an analytical–empirical ground vibration technique developed by Ungar and Bender of Bolt Beranek and Newman. It is not the only technique of its kind. Many others are available.[15–18] However, the approach developed by Ungar and Bender has been in use for about 15 years and has been applied to a wide range of problems. The method yields reasonable agreement with field measurements and is about the most comprehensive of the techniques currently in use. A discussion will also be given of a purely empirical approach currently being developed for the US Department of Transportation by Wilson, Ihrig & Associates.[19–23] This method is based in part on technology developed by London Transport International (LTI).[24]

16.2.3.1 Ungar and Bender[14]

Recognizing the lack of available information on groundborne vibration from trains, Ungar and Bender developed an analytical/empirical technique for predicting an upperbound for the vibration level in a building near a subway during the passage of a train. The discussion given here covers only the characterization of the source, i.e. tunnel wall vibration which is assumed to couple perfectly with the surrounding soil. The propagation of vibration through the soil and into surrounding buildings will be discussed in subsequent sections of this chapter.

As a starting point, Bender and Ungar use the upperbound

tunnel wall octave band vibration spectrum shown in *Figure 16.5*. That spectrum was synthesized from measurements on the New York City, Toronto, and Paris subways. The spectrum is for a train speed of 56 km/h (35 mph) on jointed rail supported on stiff fasteners. For other speeds it is necessary to correct each octave band level by the amount shown in *Figure 16.6*. If resilient rail fasteners are used such that the foundation stiffness beneath the rail is less than 1.4×10^8 N/m² (20 000 lbs/in²), then a further correction of $5 \log_{10} [(K/1.4 \times 10^8)]$ for low-frequency feelable vibration is applied to each octave band where K is the foundation stiffness in N/m². For higher frequencies important for audible noise the correction is $20 \log_{10} (K/1.4 \times 10^8)$. Additional corrections are suggested if the rail is welded rather than jointed and if the tunnel is soil based rather than rock based. Wilson[15,16] provides a somewhat more complete catalogue of corrections for tunnel type, special track work, and type of soil or rock surrounding the tunnel. For the interested reader an excellent review of Wilson's approach can be found in reference 25. For track other than tunnels, i.e. at grade and elevated track, Towers and Kurzweil[26] provide an alternative approach which the interested reader may wish to pursue.

16.2.3.2 WIA/LTI approach[19–24]

Although currently still under development, this approach represents the result of a significant programme funded by the US Department of Transportation. It is entirely empirical with provision for the inclusion of correction factors to allow for

changes in system parameters from those tested. So far there is only a speed correction factor,[22,23] but others may be forthcoming. The approach requires the measurement of two quantities: L_F the force density in dB and L_{TM} the line source transfer mobility in dB. The sum of these two quantities gives the vibration velocity level L_V in dB at the location of interest:

$$L_V = L_F + L_{TM} \qquad (16.3)$$

A detailed discussion of the transfer mobility function L_{TM} is given in Section 16.3.2. For the moment suffice it to say that L_{TM} relates the vertical ground vibration velocity at a location of interest due to an incoherent line force exciting the ground vertically along the track. For a given site L_{TM} is a function both of frequency and of the distance between the line force and the point of interest. The force density is the spectrum of an equivalent incoherent line force that is thought to represent the train. To measure L_F one must have a test site, test track, and test train. L_{TM} is measured at the test site and L_V is measured at the locations of interest as the train passes. The method used to measure both these parameters is discussed later. The force density is then calculated from Equation 16.3. The resulting force density is a function of the wheel condition, the suspension characteristics of the car, the track-bed characteristics, train speed, and rail profile, alignment, roughness, etc. at the test site. Once the force density is known it can be combined with the transfer mobility measured at a site with similar track-bed characteristics and rail condition to estimate the ground vibration that would result from the passage of a rail car with

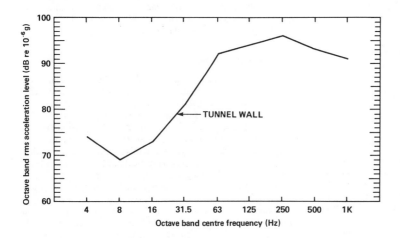

Figure 16.5 Reference upper bound tunnel vibration levels used by Ungar and Bender[14]

characteristics similar to the test car used to obtain the force density. *Figure 16.7* adapted from reference 8 shows force densities for three transit cars measured at the Transportation Test Center of the US Department of Transportation. A catalogue of such data could be obtained for a variety of transit cars or other rail vehicles operating on various types of track beds at various speeds. Such data could then be combined with transfer mobilities measured at a proposed rail site to predict the resulting ground vibration.

Unfortunately, the major drawback of this characterization of the rail vehicle source strength is that the force density will depend on the wheel condition, rail condition (profile, alignment, roughness, etc.) and the type of track structure. Consequently when the force density of a particular rail vehicle is measured that force density cannot be universally applied but can only be used for predictions where wheel and rail condition and track structure type are very similar to those under which the force density measurements were made.

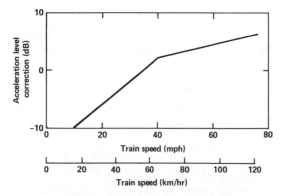

Figure 16.6 Tunnel wall vibration correction used by Ungar and Bender[14] for speeds other than 56 km/h (35 mph)

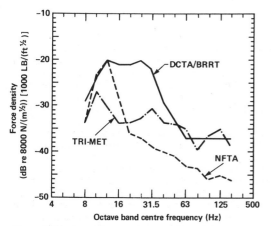

Figure 16.7 Force density tests at the Transportation Test Centre at 80 km/h (50 mph)[8]

16.3 Vibration propagation

16.3.1 Background

Soil and rock are often modelled mathematically as viscoelastic isotropic media. The propagation of vibration in such media when they are of infinite extent is fairly well understood[27–29] and the mathematics are tractable. Two independent wave types exist: shear waves (S-waves) and compressional waves (P-waves). For soil or rock, compressional waves propagate at speeds 2.5–4 times the speed of shear-waves.

Shear wave speeds in soils range from approximately 30–300 m/s (100–1000 ft/s)[29] and in rock are in the order of 1000 m/s (3300 ft/s).[30] Soils of course are not homogeneous isotropic solids but are composed of grains with voids between the grains. If the soil is saturated, the voids will be filled with water and a third wave type may exist that is associated with the coupling of compressional waves in the fluid with compressional waves in the soil.[31]

When boundaries are present, such as a free surface, a tunnel, or a building foundation, and the medium is no longer of infinite extent, the propagation of vibration becomes rapidly more complex and less mathematically tractable. The presence of a free surface, for example, results in an additional wave type, called Rayleigh waves. These surface waves travel at a speed slightly lower than shear waves and tend to be confined to within a wavelength or so of the surface. Because they are confined to the surface, Rayleigh waves are subject to less spreading loss than shear or compressional waves and, consequently, in lightly damped soil or rock can travel greater distances with less attenuation. Finally, when layers of differing elastic properties are present a variety of wave types, too numerous to mention, can exist, further complicating the transmission of vibration.

A serious problem, in addition to mathematical complexity in predicting vibration propagation through the ground, is the lack of information on the geometry and elastic properties of the soil and rock beneath the surface. In the vicinity of a proposed rail alignment, information on the various soil types may be available from borings taken in the soil, but these borings are usually limited in number and the elastic properties of each soil type are often imperfectly known.

Because of the complexity of the mathematics and the lack of knowledge of the soil medium beneath the ground, it is best to rely on on-site measurements to characterize the propagation of vibration from a proposed rail alignment. The WIA approach

which will be discussed in the next section is a technique for acquiring the required data.

If on-site data cannot be obtained, then it makes sense to estimate the propagation loss using only the simplest of analytical models. The Bender and Ungar approach which we will discuss in the next section includes only spreading loss, internal losses in the soil, and transmission losses through layers of differing elastic properties. Spreading losses simply reflect the fact that energy must be conserved when a disturbance spreads out as it propagates through the soil. The spreading loss depends on the geometry of the source and the type of wave, i.e. compressional waves and shear waves, or surface waves such as Rayleigh waves. For locations not too far from the track, trains are best modelled as line sources. Consequently, shear and compressional wave amplitudes would be expected to decay like $R^{-0.5}$ where R is the distance from the track to the location of interest, and Rayleigh waves would be expected to experience little or no spreading loss.

Internal losses in the ground would be expected to cause the vibration amplitude to decay with distance as shown in the following equation:

$$A(R) = A_0 \mathrm{e}^{-\frac{\omega \eta}{2c} R} \tag{16.4}$$

where ω is the frequency in radians/sec, η is the soil or rock loss factor, c the wavespeed and R the distance from the track to the point of interest. Equation 16.4 is derived assuming that the soil or rock is viscoelastic. Although slightly different functional forms have been proposed based on curve fits to field data,[32] Equation 16.4 has a sound basis in physics and provides a reasonable fit to most data, especially if η is allowed to be frequency dependent.

It is interesting to note in Equation 16.4 that if η is not strongly frequency dependent, a situation that appears to be true for rock but is less certain for soil,[29] then ground vibration will decay more quickly for high frequencies. The high decay rate at high frequency accounts in part for the fact that the ground vibration is confined primarily to low frequencies. Equation 16.4 also shows that waves with lower wave speed decay more rapidly. Compressional waves travel at 2.5–4 times the speed of shear and Rayleigh waves in soil and rock. Consequently, if the loss factor is 10% or more, as it is for some soils (particularly clays), at a few wavelengths from the track it is expected that compressional waves would dominate in the transmission of ground vibration, provided the loss factors for the various wave types are about the same. In fact, the loss factors for shear and compressional waves are similar for rock although data for soils are currently lacking. Of course a few compressional wavelengths in rock or stiff soil at low frequency can represent a significant distance from the track. For example, if the compressional wavespeed is 1500 m/s (5000 ft/s) then three wavelengths at 50 Hz is approximately 90 m (300 ft). Beyond 90 m (300 ft) compressional waves might predominate but for distances less than 90 m (300 ft) all wave types are probably significant.

As we will see in the next section, Ungar and Bender assumed that compressional waves predominate in order to simplify the estimation of the attenuation of ground vibration with distance from the source.

16.3.2 Estimation techniques

16.3.2.1 Ungar and Bender approach[14]

As discussed in the previous section it is very difficult to estimate analytically with any accuracy the attenuation of ground vibration with distance from the source. In addition, the lack of accurate knowledge of the geometry and elastic properties of the intervening soil make it difficult to justify anything but the simplest analysis. Ungar and Bender have developed a very simple analysis that neglects all wave types except compressional waves. In effect they have reduced a complex problem in elastodynamics to a simple acoustics problem. The total attenuation of vibration, A_T, from a tunnel to a position, a distance x away, is given by:

$$A_T = A_s + A_d + A_i \qquad (16.5)$$

where:

$$A_s = 10 \log_{10}\left(\frac{r_0 + x}{r_0}\right) , \qquad (16.6)$$

$$A_d = 4.34\frac{\omega\eta x}{c} , \qquad (16.7)$$

$$A_i = 20 \log\left[\frac{1}{2}\left(1 + \frac{\rho_c c_c}{\rho_a c_a}\right)\right] . \qquad (16.8)$$

Equation 16.6 accounts for the spreading loss assuming the train is a line source. The quantity r_0 is the tunnel radius. Equation 16.7 accounts for the attenuation due to internal losses in the soil and rock. Equation 16.8 accounts for changes in soil or rock along the propagation path. It assumes that the compressional wave is travelling from soil a to soil c and is normally incident on the boundary between the two materials. The quantities ρ and c refer to the density and wavespeed in the two soils, respectively. Equation 16.8 is strictly correct only if the two layers are many wavelengths thick. Consequently, Ungar and Bender also provide an additional attenuation term[14] that accounts for an intervening layer between a and c that is on the order of a wavelength or less in thickness.

Finally, to simplify the use of the above formulas Ungar and Bender provide a table of properties for three classes of soil materials. That table is reproduced here as *Table 16.1*. Note that the wavespeed quoted in the table is the longitudinal wavespeed given by:

$$c = \sqrt{\frac{E}{\rho}} . \qquad (16.9)$$

Strictly speaking it is the compressional or dilatational wavespeed, c', that is required in Equations 16.7 and 16.8. The longitudinal wavespeed is related to the compressional wavespeed by:

$$\frac{c'}{c} = \sqrt{\frac{1-v}{(1+v)(1-2v)}} \qquad (16.10)$$

where v is Poisson's ratio. For $v - 0.4$, a typical value for soil, $c'/c = 1.46$. Although it would be simple enough to introduce the correction in Equation 16.10, often v is not known with any certainty and for values of v approaching 0.5, Equation 16.10 changes dramatically with small changes in v. Because the compressional wavespeed is highly dependent on v, Ungar and Bender chose to use the longitudinal wavespeed which is less dependent on v and to accept whatever small error might result.

Table 16.1 Wave propagation properties of typical soils[14]

Soil class (longitudinal wavespeed) c (m/s)	Longitudinal wave speed c (m/s(ft/s))	Loss factor (η)	Density ρ(g/cm³)
Rock	3500 (11500)	0.01	2.65
Sand, silt, gravel, loess	600 (2000)	0.1	1.6
Clay, clayey soil	1500 (4900)	0.5*	1.7

*Although clay-like soils may have this large a loss factor it is important to exercise caution in using so large a value of η since very rapid attenuation of vibration with distance will be predicted. A more conservative value of η would be 0.1–0.2.

16.3.2.2 WIA/LTI[19-24]

As described in Section 16.2.3, Wilson Ihrig and Associates (WIA), under contract to US Department of Transportation, has been developing an empirical technique for the prediction of ground vibration from trains. The characterization of the source by means of the force density has already been discussed. Here the measurement of the transfer mobility, needed in conjunction with the force density to predict wayside ground vibration, is described.

Unfortunately, this approach is still under development and published information is limited. *Figure 16.8*, adapted from reference 8, shows a typical instrumentation set-up for obtaining the transfer mobility for predicting ground vibration from at-grade operations and tunnel operations. The latter requires that a force gauge be lowered into a bore hole, as shown in the figure. Although Saurenman[19] recommends the use of a pneumatic hammer to excite the ground, sledge hammers and the dropping of an automobile tyre have both been used successfully. The excitation force and the vibration at a number of distances from the point of excitation are recorded simultaneously. The data are then analysed as illustrated in *Figure 16.9*, as adapted from reference 8.

First, transfer mobilities are formed by using a standard two-channel spectrum analyser to calculate the transfer functions relating ground velocity to excitation force for each vibration transducer location. These narrow band transfer mobilities are then converted to one-third octave band mobilities. For each one-third octave band the transfer mobility for each transducer is plotted versus its distance from the point of excitation, and a best-fit curve (third-order polynomial) is fitted to the data. These curves are then used to estimate for each one-third octave band the transfer mobility for a uniform incoherent line source. That source characterization is thought to best model a train. The calculation procedure is described, in some detail, in references 22 and 23 and must be carried out for each frequency band and source–receiver distance of interest.

The WIA/LTI approach offers the promise of reasonably accurate predictions of ground vibration. However, it still remains to be proven in extensive comparisons with field measurements.

16.4 Building response

The propagation of vibration through a building structure and the response of walls, floors and ceilings to vibration are complex functions of building design details. Sound radiation due to wall, floor and ceiling vibration inside buildings is dependent on the distribution of vibration on room surfaces as well as on the acoustical and geometrical properties of the room. Further complicating matters in the case of at-grade or elevated train operations is the ambiguity between airborne and ground-borne noise and between groundborne and noise-induced vibration in buildings. As a result of these complexities, existing methods for determining building response to train vibration are largely empirical in nature. These methods are presented in the sections that follow.

16.4.1 Soil-building interaction

The transmission of train vibration from the ground to buildings is dependent on the characteristics of the building foundation. Building foundations can be divided into four basic types:

1. Slab-on-grade.
2. Spread-footings.
3. Piles founded in earth.
4. Piles supported by rock.

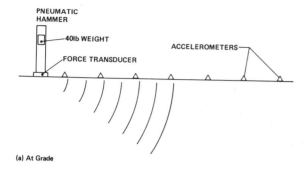

(a) At Grade

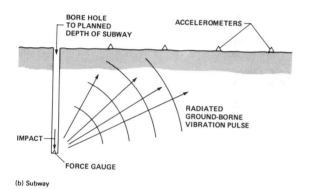

(b) Subway

Figure 16.8 Test geometry for measuring transfer mobilities[8]

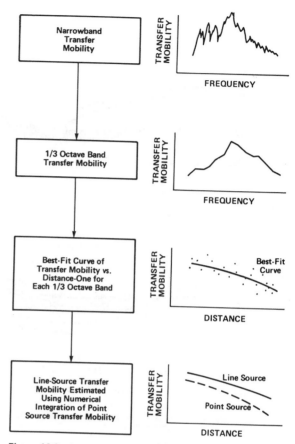

Figure 16.9 Analysis of transfer mobility data[8]

In the case of slab-on-grade floors (and most basement floors) the surface area of the slab is large, and the slab itself is in intimate contact with the underlying soil. Therefore, the vibration of such floor slabs is often similar to that which would exist in the soil without the slab, giving a coupling loss of 0 dB at low frequencies (up to the resonance frequency of the slab on the soil). For the other foundation types, empirical curves for estimating foundation vibration levels from ground surface vibration levels are presented in *Figure 16.10*, as adapted from reference 33.

Building floors, walls, and ceilings are subject to significant amplifications of vibration, relative to the foundation vibration. This effect is most pronounced in residential wood-frame houses. In many cases, the resonance of the floor structure may cause amplification of vibration in the 10–30 Hz frequency range. Problems can result when these floor resonances coincide with peaks in the groundborne vibration spectrum. The amplification of floors, ceilings, and walls is difficult to predict, but it is typically in the range of 5–15 dB in the frequency range of 16–80 Hz. The estimated amplification of vibration by floor slabs supported on columns or sheer walls is given in *Figure 16.11*, based on the work of Nelson and Saurenman.[25]

16.4.2 Vibration propagation within buildings

The propagation of vibration through a building structure and the response of walls, floors, and ceilings to such vibration are very complex in nature. In multi-storey buildings, a common value for the attenuation of vibration from floor-to-floor is approximately 3 dB, as shown in *Figure 16.12*.[25] Data by Ishii and Tachibana[34] show approximately 1 dB floor-to-floor at-

tenuation in the upper floor regions at low frequencies and greater than 3 dB attenuation at lower floors. These data (summarized in *Table 16.2*) result from experiments in floor-to-floor vibration attenuation in a 10-storey, steel-framed, reinforced-concrete building for a point vibration source below the building.

16.4.3 Sound radiation due to groundborne vibration

Groundborne noise is the result of sound waves radiated by the vibrating wall, floor, and ceiling surfaces of a room. The relationship between the vibration of the room surfaces and the noise level is dependent on the amount of sound absorption in the room, the room size and shape, and the distribution of the vibration velocity level over the room surfaces.

The interior sound pressure level arising from groundborne vibration can be estimated approximately by the formula:

$$L_p = L_a - 20 \log_{10} f + 37 \qquad (16.12)$$

where L_a is the floor vertical rms acceleration level in dB re 10^{-6} g, and f the frequency in Hz. This estimate is based on a series of simultaneous noise and vibration measurements conducted in several buildings near the Toronto Subway System.[1]

16.4.4 Low-frequency airborne sound

At locations near at-grade or elevated rail lines, an ambiguity sometimes arises between groundborne and airborne noise inside buildings. For example, in buildings near rail lines where

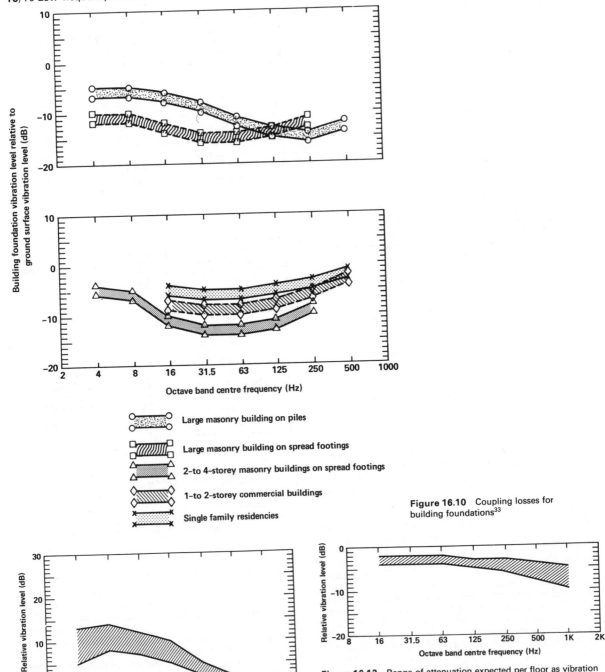

Figure 16.10 Coupling losses for building foundations[33]

Figure 16.11 Range of amplification of vibration due to resonances of floor slabs supported on columns[25]

Figure 16.12 Range of attenuation expected per floor as vibration transmits from floor-to-floor[25]

diesel locomotives are used, it is often the case that airborne noise transmitted through building windows and walls exceeds the noise caused by groundborne vibration. In attempting to evaluate the feasibility of noise control treatments for such a case, it is important to determine the relative contributions of the groundborne and airborne noise components to the total noise inside the building. (*See* Chapters 13 and 15 for methods of estimating airborne noise levels from trains.)

Another complication that arises when evaluating noise and vibration control methods near at-grade or elevated rail lines is that low-frequency airborne sound in the frequency region below 100 Hz can induce building vibration.[35,36] Acoustic coupling of sound waves through openings such as windows can excite walls, floors, ceilings and large windows into vibration,

Table 16.2 Point source below building—attenuation of acceleration level per floor in dB

Frequency (Hz)	Floor level above grade									
	1	2	3	4	5	6	7	8	9	10
Floor-to-floor distance: 3 m (10 ft)										
31	2	2	2	1	1	1	1	1	1	1
63	3	2	2	2	2	1	1	1	1	1
125	3	3	2	2	2	2	2	1	1	1
250	3	3	3	3	3	3	3	2	2	2
500	4	4	3	3	3	3	3	3	3	3
1K	5	5	4	4	4	4	4	3	3	3
Floor-to-floor distance: 3.7 m (12 ft)										
31	2	2	2	2	1	1	1	1	1	1
63	3	2	2	2	2	1	1	1		
125	3	3	3	2	2	2	2	1	1	1
250	4	3	3	3	3	2	2	2	2	2
500	4	4	4	4	4	3	3	3	3	3
1K	5	5	5	4	4	4	4	4	4	4

and resonance may result when the sound-wave frequency corresponds to a natural frequency of the structure being excited. Hubbard[36] has summarized measured house wall, floor and window vibration responses due to noise excitation. These results are presented in *Figure 12.12* in terms of rms acceleration as a function of peak sound pressure level. Using these relationships, it is possible to estimate noise-induced building vibrations based on airborne train noise levels. Comparing the results of such an exercise with estimates of groundborne vibration, the relative contributions of groundborne and noise-induced vibration inside a building may be determined.

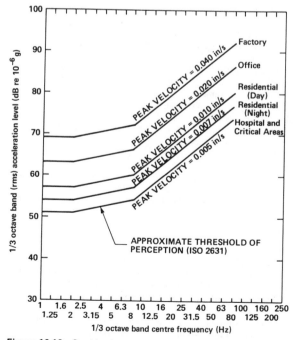

Figure 16.13 Combined response curves for annoyance due to building vibration

16.5 Criteria for impact assessment

Low-frequency noise and vibration from railway trains can have several effects on people and the buildings they occupy. If noticeable to people living or working in the vicinity, such noise and vibration can result in annoyance. The degree of annoyance depends on the magnitude and frequency content of the disturbance as well as the human activity involved. Annoyance can result from a combination of effects involving audible and tactile perception of structure-borne vibrations and airborne noise from trains. For example, vibrations can be generated in buildings either by groundborne vibration (originating from wheel/rail interaction) or by airborne, low-frequency sound from the diesel locomotive exhaust stacks. Noise can be transmitted to people inside buildings via direct paths through walls, windows and openings. In addition, groundborne vibration transmitted to building components can result in the generation of audible, low-frequency rumbling noise, generally referred to as groundborne noise, and in the generation of high-frequency noise due to rattling of loose windows and household accessories.

Besides annoyance, vibration from trains can have other types of effects. For example, even at very low levels, below the threshold of human perception, such vibration can disrupt the operation of sensitive devices such as optical and electron microscopes. At the other extreme, train vibrations may result in damage to nearby buildings or structures if such vibrations are severe enough.

The above discussion suggests four major types of noise and vibration effects that can result from trains: (1) annoyance due to feelable vibrations, (2) annoyance due to audible sound, (3) impairment of sensitive equipment function and (4) structural damage. Criteria for each of these effects are discussed below.

16.5.1 Feelable vibration

In recent years, the principal and most widely quoted human vibration standard has been the International Standards Organization ISO 2631,[37] which is based upon the work of a large number of previous investigators. Although this standard concerns itself with the evaluation of vibration in vehicles and industrial settings, draft addendum ISO 2631/DAD1[38] provides a guide to the evaluation of human exposure to shock and vibration in buildings. More recently, American National Standard ANSI S3.29 1983[39] provides guidelines that are essentially the same as ISO 2631/DAD1. The draft ANSI standard presents limits of vibration acceptability for various building types in the frequency range of 1–80 Hz. Since human sensitivity differs for vibration in the vertical and horizontal directions, a combined standard is included in ANSI Standard S3.29–1983, consisting of a combination of the lowest limits for vertical and horizontal vibration. The combined curves are shown in *Figure 16.13* in terms of the one-third octave band rms (root-mean-square) acceleration level (L_a) defined as follows:

$$L_a = 20 \log_{10} \left(\frac{\text{rms acceleration in } g}{10^{-6}g} \right) \quad (16.12)$$

where g = acceleration due to gravity. Note that for frequencies above 8 Hz, these curves correspond to constant levels of vibration velocity; the corresponding peak velocities are indicated on the curves. Note also that the lowest curve corresponds to the approximate human threshold of perception to whole-body vibration, according to ISO Standard 2631.

In an effort to establish a single-number descriptor for evaluating feelable vibration, the CHABA Working Group 69[40] recommended the use of a weighted acceleration level, based on the proposed ANSI standard. The weighting curve presented in the CHABA report is shown in *Figure 16.14* and is essentially a smooth curve representation of that in the proposed ANSI standard. This weighting curve provides a level proportional to velocity at high frequencies and proportional to acceleration at low frequencies. The weighted acceleration level (L_a) can be obtained from one-third octave band rms acceleration level (L_a) spectra by applying the proposed weighting to each band level, and then by logarithmically summing the results between 1 and 80 Hz.

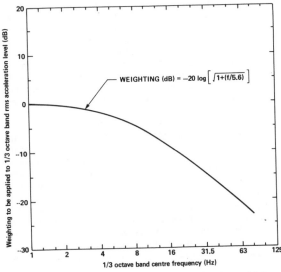

WEIGHTING (dB) $= -20 \log \left[\sqrt{1+(f/5.6)} \right]$

Figure 16.14 CHABA proposed vibration acceleration weighting function[40]

Criteria for annoyance due to feelable vibration (based on the proposed ANSI standard) are summarized in *Table 16.3*, in terms of the weighted acceleration level, (L_a). Note that for residential areas, the most stringent criterion is 54 dB. More recently, Nelson and Saurenman[25] have recommended a maximum acceptable range of 48–53 dB in residential buildings, based on an evaluation of community complaints regarding vibration from transit trains. Although only a few dB lower than the criteria of the ANSI standard, their data indicate that this small difference could be significant. *Figure 16.15* summarizes their recommended range for maximum transit-induced groundborne vibration in residential structures. Above this range complaints are considered likely, below this range complaints should be rare and within this range vibrations are considered marginally acceptable.

There exists only limited data on how the incidence of

Table 16.3 Criteria for annoyance due to groundborne vibration (ANSI-S3.29-1983)

Building use category	Maximum weighted acceleration level (dB re 10^{-6} g)
Hospital & critical areas	51
Residential (night-time)	54
Residential (daytime)	57
Office	63
Factory	69

complaints varies with vibration level. *Figure 16.16* summarizes the results of a survey of about 1000 persons living near factories and near a high-speed railway line in Japan.[41] It is interesting to note that over 50% of the survey respondents reported perceiving vibrations that correspond to the standard threshold of vibration (54 dB). Furthermore, about 35% of the respondents complained of perceiving rattling and nearly 20% complained of having their sleep disturbed by vibrations of that magnitude. In addition, about 15% of the respondents complained of cracks forming in the walls of their dwellings owing to vibration at the standard threshold of perception (experience has shown that people often ascribe structural problems to vibrations or other environmental disturbances, even though the damage may be due to other causes). Therefore, the results indicated in *Figure 16.16* provide an indication that current standards may underestimate the annoyance produced by vibrations.

16.5.2 Audible sound

Audible sound due to train traffic can result in annoyance to people living or working nearby. General outdoor measures of subjective annoyance caused by transportation noise have been discussed in Chapters 2 and 3. This section deals specifically with criteria for evaluating train noise inside buildings.

Criteria for train noise inside buildings have often been presented in terms of Noise Criterion (NC) curves. However, because the NC curves were designed to evaluate steady sources of noise, it is now more common to specify criteria for indoor train noise in terms of maximum A-weighted sound levels. *Figure 16.17* indicates indoor train levels (dB(A)) at which various adverse effects may be expected. The lowest levels shown correspond to those at which moderate complaints may begin to be anticipated. For example, if the train-related noise level in a room exceeds 40 dB(A)), people are likely to complain that the train noise annoys them and interferes with their sleep. *Figure 16.17* also shows the ranges of train-related noise levels that are likely to be acceptable for various building space usages. It is important to keep in mind, however, that noise from sources other than trains generally is also present. The stringent criteria suggested here apply only if the train-related noise exceeds or equals that from all other sources.

A set of criteria for groundborne train noise that has been applied successfully at several transit systems is included in the Guidelines of the American Public Transit Association (APTA).[42] A summary of these guidelines is provided in *Table 16.4*. The general conclusion is that groundborne noise which does not exceed the levels in *Table 16.4* will not be inaudible in all cases, but should be low enough that no significant intrusion or annoyance will occur.[42]

It should be noted that the above criteria for groundborne train noise are most appropriate in cases where there is no significant airborne noise path, such as at locations near subway tunnels. If airborne train noise is dominant, it may be more appropriate to assess annoyance using the general outdoor environmental noise measures described in Chapter 2.

In addition to groundborne noise, building vibration can give rise to audible high frequency rattling sounds due to vibration of wall or floor mounted objects such as pictures, mirrors, plaques, lamps, etc. Such objects are usually in contact with the larger surface at one or more discrete points along a boundary line, and are put into motion because of the vibratory motions of the surface. The rattling of such accessories can be a factor in annoyance.

Criteria for the rattling of wall and floor mounted objects are best expressed in terms of wall or floor vibration. Theoretically, an acceleration of 1.0 g is required to cause rattling in the case of an object resting on a horizontal vibrating surface such as the

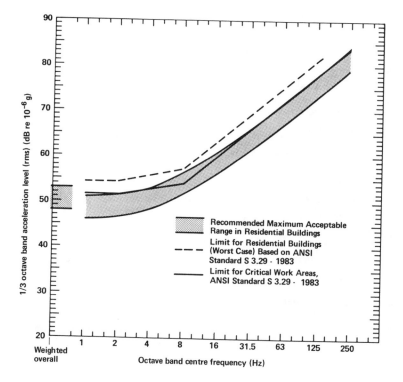

Figure 16.15 Range of maximum acceptable transit induced building vibration in residential areas (acceleration level)[25]

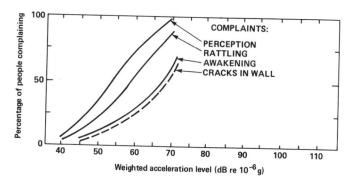

Figure 16.16 Comparison of reported annoyance percentages with vibration level[41]

floor. Data evaluated by Hubbard[36] suggests, however, that in practical cases some rattling might occur at lower levels as a result of small contact areas, local surface imperfections, or misalignments from the vertical. Hubbard recommends a criterion of 0.05 g for cases where objects are suspended in pendulum fashion from the wall. This should apply theoretically to situations where the angle between the wall and hanging flat object is about 3 degrees.

16.5.3 Impairment of equipment function

The continuing trend toward increasing the precision of research instruments and manufacturing equipment has caused these devices to exhibit an increasing sensitivity to vibration. Vibration in buildings may be caused by external sources, such as rail, traffic, or by internal sources, such as people walking and building mechanical equipment.

The operation of sensitive devices such as optical and electron microscopes can be disrupted by vibrations that are below the threshold of human perception. However, the sensitivity of an instrument to floor vibration is highly dependent on the particular characteristics of the instrument's design as well as the manner in which the device is supported. Very sensitive equipment is often supplied with specially designed 'air-spring' tables that can effectively isolate these instruments from floor vibrations down to frequencies as low as a few Hertz.

As suggested by the above discussion, the effects of vibration on sensitive equipment are best evaluated on a case-specific basis. Ideally, vibration-sensitive instruments should be tested by exciting the floor slab in discrete frequency bands and noting the floor vibration levels at which instrument use is affected. The goal of such tests should be the definition of an acceptability threshold for floor vibration near the instrument. However, this approach is often not practical.

In the absence of specific information from the equipment manufacturer or other source, the curves in *Figure 16.18* can be used to assess the effects of vibration on the use of sensitive equipment. These curves, developed by Bolt Beranek and Newman, suggest limits for various types of equipment in terms of vertical rms floor vibration measured in one-third octave bands

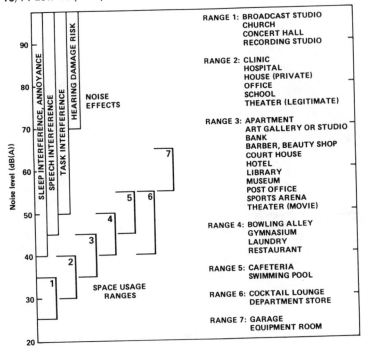

Figure 16.17 Indoor train noise—effects and acceptability criteria

Table 16.4 Criteria and design goals for maximum groundborne noise from train operations[42]

Single family community area category	Maximum groundborne noise level (dB(A))		
	Multi-family dwellings	Hotel/motel dwellings	Buildings
A. Residences and buildings with sleeping areas			
I. Low-density residential	30	35	40
II. Average residential	35	40	45
III. High-density residential	35	40	45
IV. Commercial	40	45	50
V. Industrial/highway	40	45	55

B. Special function buildings

Groundborne pass-by type of building or room	Noise design goal (dB(A))
Concert halls and TV studies	25
Auditoriums and music rooms	30
Churches and theatres	35
Hospital sleeping rooms	35–40
Courtrooms	35
Schools and libraries	40
University buildings	35–40
Offices	35–40
Commercial buildings	45–55

of frequency. Note that the curves in *Figure 16.18* represent the requirements for the most sensitive items of equipment within each category.

16.5.4 Structural damage

Under some circumstances, buildings can be damaged by severe or prolonged vibration. If exposed to extremely high levels of ground vibration, a building may suffer 'major damage', such as serious structural damage, glass breakage, and serious plaster cracking, possibly accompanied by falling plaster. For lower levels of vibration, minor damage may be observed in buildings. This is typically characterized by fine plaster cracking and reopening of old cracks and is generally referred to as 'architectural damage'.

The US Bureau of Mines has identified ground vibration

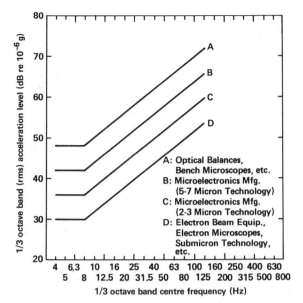

Figure 16.18 Vibration criteria for sensitive equipment in buildings

Graph labels:

- A: Optical Balances, Bench Microscopes, etc.
- B: Microelectronics Mfg. (5-7 Micron Technology)
- C: Microelectronics Mfg. (2-3 Micron Technology)
- D: Electron Beam Equip., Electron Microscopes, Submicron Technology, etc.

levels that may produce damage in residential structures, and recommends a safe limit of 50 mm/s (2.0 in/s) peak particle velocity.[43]

A reassessment of the Bureau of Mines vibration data by Jackson[44] has determined that the threshold of architectural damage to buildings occurs at a peak particle velocity of 5 mm/s (0.2 in/s). For old and historic buildings, German Standard DIN 4150 recommends a maximum velocity of 2 mm/s (0.08 in/s).[45] Although the damage potential of buildings varies widely according to type of construction, age, size, fatigue properties and structural resonances, the above criteria have been found to be reasonable for preventing structural and architectural damage in most circumstances.

As a final note, it should be recognized that vibration levels required to produce damage in buildings are generally much higher than those that would be tolerated by humans. Furthermore, it is rare for vibration produced by trains to even approach the threshold of architectural damage.

In view of the similarity between road traffic vibration and rail traffic, reference is made here to Chapter 12 which gives a further description of damage criteria and risk factors.

16.6 Techniques for control of vibration

It follows from the discussions in previous sections, that the reduction of groundborne noise and vibration from trains is achievable in two conceptually different ways:

1. By reducing the wheel–rail interaction forces.
2. By attenuating the propagation of vibrations.

Some vibration control techniques, particularly those that involve insertion of resilient elements near the rail, affect both the wheel–rail interaction and the propagation of vibrations, thus these two categories are not mutually exclusive. To facilitate the discussion of groundborne vibration control, the treatments are organized below into the following categories:

1. Control at the source.

2. Resilient track support structures.
3. Tunnel construction and vibration barriers.
4. Building isolation.

The principles of each control technique are outlined in this chapter but further information on particular systems that have been installed in practice can be found, in many cases, in the following chapter.

16.6.1 Control at the source

16.6.1.1 Removal of wheel surface irregularities (wheel truing)

Wheel truing serves to reduce discontinuities that may be present on the wheel surface, such as flats, and also reduces wheel roughness. Because the generating mechanism for ground vibration from trains is the interaction of the wheel and the rail, wheel truing produces useful vibration reductions only when the surface roughness on the wheels exceeds that on the rail. This may not be the case when rail corrugation is present. Wheel flats, bad rail joints, or corrugated rail can increase vibration levels by 10–20 dB compared with smooth wheels running on smooth continuous welded rail.[46] In tests on the Southeastern Pennsylvania Transportation Authority's (SEPTA's) Rapid Transit System, truing of wheels in a condition typical of normal service and without noticeable flats resulted in groundborne vibration reductions of 5–10 dB for frequencies above 100 Hz, but little or no reduction (even an occasional increase) for frequencies below 100 Hz.[47]

16.6.1.2 Prevention of wheel surface irregularities

The current approach to preventing or minimizing wheel flat generation is to include slip/slide prevention systems on new cars and in a few instances retrofit existing vehicles with simplified versions of slip/slide control such as the traction fault detector used on some New York City Transit Authority (NYCTA) cars.[48]

Slip/slide control systems are used on most newer transit cars. These systems minimize not only wheel slide during braking, but also wheel spin during acceleration. The NYCTA has reported a 50% reduction in the number of wheel flat occurrences on cars equipped with these systems.[48]

Other approaches to minimizing wheel flat generation include:

1. Implementation of improved methods for lubrication on curves (or improved maintenance of current lubricators) so as to avoid contamination of the running surfaces.
2. Optimization of the wheels' mechanical properties to reduce their susceptibility to wheel flats.
3. Use of composition tread brakes or disc brakes in place of cast-iron tread brakes; tests have shown that cast-iron tread brakes result in significantly increased wheel roughness[49,50] compared with the other brakes mentioned above.

(NB Section 14.3.5 and Chapter 17 also include details of wheel/rail noise and vibration controls.)

16.6.1.3 Detection of wheel surface irregularities

Although wheel flat (or excessive roughness) detection systems are not a vibration control technique *per se*, they are an aid in determining which wheels are in need of maintenance. One such system, developed by the Toronto Transit Commission (TTC), has been in use by them since 1979.[51,52] TTC designed the system specifically to detect rough and flatted wheels which were resulting in complaints of excessive groundborne noise and vibration by people living near the subway. The TTC system employs an accelerometer to measure the vibration on the subway tunnel invert as each train passes. The output from the accelerometer signal is transmitted via telephone lines to a carhouse where it is displayed on a graphic level recorder. Wheels, or at least trucks, that cause high vibration levels are clearly identified. This system is described in more detail in Chapter 17.

One significant advantage to using a wheel flat monitoring system such as that developed by TTC is that the threshold for defining a 'bad' wheel can be varied. This enables automatic identification of only the 'worst' (roughest) wheels and by raising or lowering the threshold for detection, the number of wheels identified as requiring truing can be kept within the truing capacity of the transit system. It may even be possible to use the wheel roughness monitor to indicate what type of truing is necessary; i.e., would a belt grinder suffice or is an underfloor truing machine required.

16.6.1.4 Rail grinding

Rail grinding is used on both rapid transit systems and railways primarily for removing mill and weld imperfections from new rail and for reprofiling and removing corrugations, flaking, head cracks and rail burns (due to wheel slip) from worn rail.

As with wheel truing, the effectiveness of rail grinding in reducing groundborne noise and vibration is highly dependent on both the wheel and rail surface conditions before grinding. In the absence of wheel flats, grinding new rail (with mill scale still present) or normally worn rail (without corrugations) results in 2–10 dB reduction in ground vibration levels.[50] Grinding can result in 10–20 dB(A) reduction in groundborne noise when rail corrugation is present.[46]

Two types of rail grinders are available: abrasive block grinders where abrasive bricks are pulled along at speeds typical of normal service (32–64 km/h (20–40 mph)) while being pressed on the rail surface; and grinding wheels which rotate as they are pulled slowly (3–5 km/h (2–3 mph)) along the track. An abrasive block grinding train, such as that used on the Chicago Transit Authority (which has 14 abrasive bricks on each rail), requires about 110 passes over a rail section to smooth the surface fully.[53] A rotating grinding stone train with 12 grinding wheels over each rail can remove about 0.0038 cm (0.0015 in) of steel per pass and requires about two or three passes to smooth the rail.[53] Further details on rail grinding are given in Section 17.4.3.

16.6.1.5 Rail welding/rail alignment

Any arrangement that reduces the severity of impacts which occur as wheels traverse rail joints also may be expected to contribute to reduction of the associated noise/vibration. Replacement of jointed with continuous welded rail is most beneficial in this regard, since welded joints (if properly ground) eliminate rail joint discontinuities altogether. Careful maintenance and alignment of bolted joints is beneficial where such joints are present, particularly in order to avoid alignments that make the wheels 'step up' at a joint.[11,54] Similarly, noise control benefits may be expected from the use of designs of switches and frogs (e.g., moving point frogs) that reduce impacts and smooth the transition of the wheel load from one rail segment to the next.

16.6.1.6 Reduced primary suspension stiffness

The primary suspension, which supports the truck (bogie) frame on the axles, is perhaps the most significant truck design feature affecting groundborne noise and vibration. Reduction of the primary suspension stiffness on a Metropolitan Atlanta Rapid Transit Authority (MARTA) truck from about 3.1×10^7 N/m (180 000 lb/in) per wheel to 8.7×10^6 N/m (50 000 lb/in) resulted in 1–5 dB of groundborne vibration reduction in the 20–63 Hz frequency range.[9] On the Chicago Transit Authority (CTA) the new 2400 series cars (which have soft primary suspensions) result in 10–20 dB lower ground vibration levels (in the 16–250 Hz range) near at-grade track than the older CTA cars (which have very stiff primary suspensions).[33] Besides the lower primary suspension stiffness, other viscoelastic elements in the CTA 2400 series cars may reduce wheel/rail forces by increasing the structural damping of the truck assembly. Although this is normally only a secondary effect, it can be significant in some circumstances.[33]

16.6.1.7 Resilient wheels

Resilient wheels permit the wheel contact point to deflect more (and the rail less) due to a given wheel–rail asperity, thereby reducing the rail vibrations and the corresponding noise in nearby buildings. Resilient wheels also constitute a part of the suspension system; thus, replacement of standard wheels with resilient ones also leads to changes in the resonance frequencies and damping characteristics of these systems.[55] Resilient wheels have been reported to reduce tunnel vibration levels by 4–10 dB in the frequency range from 40 to 250 Hz.[56,57] Examples of special wheel sets are given in Section 17.5.

16.6.1.8 Reduced train speed

Reducing train speed will reduce groundborne noise and vibration levels on the order of 4–9 dB (typically 6 dB) per halving of speed. That is, in most cases, the changes in vibration levels are proportional to $13–30 \log_{10}$ (speed), typically $20 \log_{10}$ (speed). However, the speed dependence varies both with frequency and vehicle type so the above typical speed relationship should be used with caution, especially at low frequencies (comparable with the wheel rotation rate or the rail fastener (or tie) passage frequency).[8]

16.6.2 Resilient track support structures

16.6.2.1 Resilient rail fasteners

Resilient rail fasteners tend to isolate the vibrating rail from the ties or other components to which the rail is fastened. The rail support modulus K (equal to fastener stiffness divided by fastener spacing) directly affects the vibration transmission to the tunnel structure. For support moduli below about 1.4×10^8 N/m² (20 000 lb/in²), the tunnel vibration levels are proportional to $20 \log_{10} K$ for frequencies above 50 Hz.[56,58,59]

As yet, there is no general consensus on the optimum value of the rail support modulus. A high modulus is desired to minimize rail bending stresses and improve rail stability, while a low modulus is desired for providing vibration isolation. Suggested optimum values are in the order of 1.4×10^7 N/m² (2000 lb/in²)[60] to 2.1×10^7 N/m² (3000 lb/in²),[61] but analysis and testing are needed to determine the best value for specific installations. One guideline for achieving good vibration isolation is to use a fastener whose stiffness is such that the deflection of the rail under the static train load is between 2 mm (0.08 in) and 5 mm (0.2 in).[62] Detailed discussion of resilient fastener design considerations are contained in references 25, 33, 60 and 61 and in Section 17.2 of the next chapter.

16.6.2.2 Resiliently supported ties

In resiliently supported tie systems, a resilient element is placed between the tie and the tunnel invert, whereas with resilient rail fasteners the compliance is introduced between the rail and the tie. The additional mass provided by the floated tie system together with the ability to use softer elements under the tie than can be used in the rail fasteners can result in better vibration isolation performance. Measurements in Paris (RATP)[63] and Atlanta (MARTA)[64] indicated that tunnel vibration levels achieved using a resiliently supported tie system (the RS-STEDEF) were 0–10 dB lower (in the 10–125 Hz range) than the levels resulting from use of direct fixation resilient fasteners with rail support moduli in the range 2.1×10^7 to 4.8×10^7 N/m² (3000–7000 lb/in²). The modulus of the RS-STEDEF tie system was 1.7×10^7 N/m² (2400 lb/in²).

16.6.2.3 Floating slabs

Whereas with resilient rail fasteners and with floated ties the mass atop the resilient supports is dominated by that of the unsprung portion of the car's suspension system, several arrangements exist where the 'floated mass' is significantly greater. These arrangements include floated slabs and floated slablets (also sometimes called floated mini-slabs or double ties). In such floated mass systems, the inertia of the floated mass reduces its vibratory motions at the frequencies of interest. These motions are transmitted to the invert via relatively soft resilient supports, resulting in reduced vibratory forces acting on the invert.

Two designs being used on many of the new transit lines are: the light-weight continuous floating slab and the discontinuous floating slab. The continuous floating slab consists of a resiliently supported slab, 0.2–0.3 m (8–12 in) thick, cast-in-place in a recess in the subway invert. The discontinuous floating slab consists of precast blocks 0.2–0.3 m (8–12 in) thick and 1.5 m (5 ft) long, supported on elastomer pads. Longitudinal and lateral stability is provided by preloaded elastomer blocks located at the side of and between slab sections. The discontinuous floating slab is often referred to as a double-tie floating slab since each precast slab section supports two sets of rail fasteners.

Most floating slabs that are in use on North American transit systems have been designed for resonance frequencies of 14–16 Hz, with a train on the slab. A detailed, theoretical analysis of floating-slab performance, including the effect of rail fastener stiffness and damping,[65] concludes that with reasonable damp-ing, a single-degree-of-freedom model is sufficient for floating-slab design. The vibration reduction for an ideal single-degree-of-freedom isolation system and the reductions that would be predicted for a floating slab are presented in *Figure 16.19*. The broken line indicates that above 125 Hz, 20 dB is the maximum reduction expected for design purposes. Wave motion in slab supports, slab bending modes, and other secondary effects prevent greater vibration reduction at higher frequencies although in some cases, greater reductions (25–30 dB) have been measured for installations now in service. *Figure 16.20* illustrates the vibration reductions achieved by means of various floated mass systems.

For design of floating slabs, the resonance frequency indicated in *Figure 16.19* is typically 12–16 Hz. This figure is determined by the sum of the masses of the slab, the rail, the unsprung mass of the vehicle truck, and by the sum of the support stiffnesses of the slab supports, the perimeter isolation pads, and any entrapped air. There is no entrapped air to consider with discontinuous floating slabs. Detailed discussions of design considerations for floating slabs are contained in references 33 and 68.

16.6.2.4 Ballast mats

Ballast mats are usually thick, resilient layers of elastomer, cork, fibreglass, or rock wool, placed under ballast. Although they are normally used to improve electrical isolation, water drainage, or to reduce pulverization of the ballast, ballast mats also reduce groundborne noise and vibration as indicated in *Figure 16.21*.

16.6.3 Tunnel construction

Tunnel configurations that vibrate less in response to given excitation forces may be expected to transmit less intensive vibrations to their surroundings. Thus, more massive tunnel structures in non-rock soil typically may be expected to result in less noise/vibration in neighbouring buildings. There is limited evidence[25,33] that concrete double box tunnel structures result in less groundborne noise than lighter-weight circular tunnels (whether cast in-place, or made with pre-cast concrete, steel or cast-iron liners). Data from Toronto and Washington, DC indicate that above 63 Hz, ground surface vibration levels for cut-and-cover double box subways are 5–20 dB lower than for

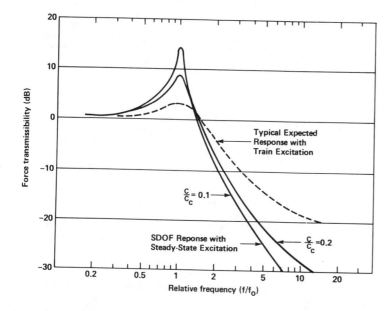

Figure 16.19 The ratio of the force on the invert beneath the slab to the force on top of the floating-slab; f_0 is the slab natural frequency and c/c_c is the critical damping ratio[33]

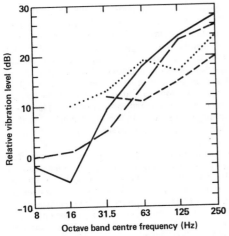

Figure 16.20 Difference in tunnel vibration levels between conventional track and floating slab track (level without floating slab–level with floating slab). ——, New York (NYCTA) continuous concrete slab, support frequency $f_0 \approx 16$ Hz;[65] — —, Washington, DC (WMATA) continuous concrete slab, $f_0 = 16$ Hz[33] – – – –, Cologne continuous concrete trough containing a conventional tie/ballast track, $f_0 \approx 10$ Hz;[66] ....., Frankfurt discontinuous precast concrete 'slablets', $f_0 \approx 10$ Hz[67]

circular tunnels. However, below about 31.5 Hz the levels from the circular tunnel are 0–10 dB lower.

The reported reductions in groundborne noise and vibration resulting from changes in the average tunnel wall thickness ranges from 5 to 18 dB per doubling of the wall thickness.[66,67,69,70,71]

Further research is needed to provide better estimates of the effects of tunnel wall thickness and of tunnel/soil interaction. Although increased tunnel wall thicknesses imply increased construction costs, greater thickness designs may provide the desired noise reduction more inexpensively, more reliably, and with less maintenance requirements than, say, floated slab track in a thinner walled tunnel.

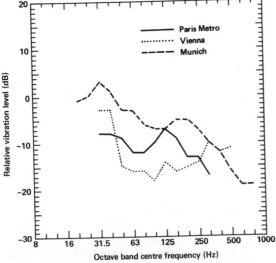

Figure 16.21 Measured change in vibration with ballast mats[33] (Level with mat–level without mat).

16.6.4 Screening

Trenches (either open or backfilled with light-weight water-proof filler) or solid barriers (such as concrete-filled trenches) have seen only limited use as a method for controlling ground-borne noise and vibration from rail systems. Both screening approaches provide an impedance mismatch in the soil so as to interrupt the wave propagation path.

In order to alleviate a groundborne noise problem at a TV studio in a building located about 2.5 m (8.2 ft) from the wall of a rapid transit tunnel, a trench was installed between the tunnel and the building. Measurements were taken before the work began, after excavation of all the soil between the tunnel and the building, to the depth of the bottom of the tunnel and after backfilling the trench to its final width of 20 cm (7.9 in). The basement floor of the building was about 2.3 m (7.5 ft) below the bottom of the tunnel (and trench). Noise reductions in the studio of 8 and 4 dB(A) were obtained before and after the trench was backfilled.[72] The dominant octave band in all cases was 63 Hz.

The results of a test conducted with steel sheet piles (9 m [30 ft] deep and 50 m [165 ft] long) driven in two rows near a Shinkansen aerial structure[73] yielded about 15 dB of reduction in the ground surface vertical acceleration level at 12 m (39 ft), about 4 dB at 20 m (66 ft) and 0 dB at 50 m (164 ft). The reduced effectiveness at larger distances may be due in part to flanking around the ends of the sheet piles.

In another test on the Shinkansen[73] concrete piles (40 cm [16 in] in diameter) were driven in a continuous line about 4 m (13 ft) from an existing (apparently at-grade) track. When driven to a depth of 5 m (16 ft), these piles resulted in a vibration reduction of about 10 dB at 7 m (23 ft). For piles driven to a depth of 3 m (10 ft), the reduction was only about 2 dB.

The Toronto Transit Commission[74] built a 'U'-shaped trench, whose side parallel to the track was 24 m (80 ft) long and whose ends (perpendicular to the track) were 10 m (34 ft) long. The trench was 4.3 m (14 ft) deep and filled with 10 cm (4 in) thick styrofoam. The side parallel to the track was 8 m (26 ft) from the at-grade track centreline. The typical reduction in the ground acceleration level at 9.8 m (32 ft) was 5 dB with reductions at some locations of up to 10 dB.

Some general guidelines for trench and soil barrier design are given by Barkan,[29] Richard et al.,[75] Haupt[76] and Dolling.[77] The primary concern is to provide a trench of sufficient depth to attenuate the primary wave type causing the vibration at the receiver location. Thus, for Rayleigh (surface) waves, the trench depth should be in the order of the Rayleigh wavelength at the dominant frequency. In typical soils, the Rayleigh wavespeed is in the order of 200 m/s (660 ft/s) and the dominant frequency from train vibrations is about 50 Hz. Thus, the Rayleigh wavelength is about 4 m (13 ft).

16.6.5 Building isolation

Insertion of isolation pads in buildings under foundation piles, at column bases or crowns, and at other structural connections can assist in protecting selected buildings or areas within buildings from noise and vibrations. Lead–asbestos pads have found considerable use in isolating large buildings from railroad and subway-induced noise and vibration in New York City since about 1915. More recently (in the 1960s) these pads were used in the construction of Montreal's Queen Elizabeth Hotel and New York's Avery Fisher Hall (formerly the Philharmonic Hall) and appear to result in significant vibration isolation, in the order of 10 dB.[78]

Elastomeric bearing pads have been used in building foundations in the United Kingdom for the purpose of noise and vibration isolation from rail systems since 1964.[79] The general interest in resiliently mounted buildings has led to the development of a recent British Standard on this subject.[80]

Where it is needed to provide a quiet environment in only a few rooms in existing buildings, it may be possible to consider construction of a 'room within a room' for each space of concern. This amounts to providing room floors that 'float' on the structural floors, as well as room walls and ceilings that are isolated dynamically from the structural walls and ceilings.

In all building isolation designs, care must be taken to interrupt all significant vibration transmission paths or to provide them with effective isolation. Otherwise, the vibration will propagate along these paths, largely short circuiting the noise control achieved by the isolation that is used.

References

1 Toronto Transit Commission. *Yonge Subway Northern Extension Noise and Vibration Study*, Book 1, Report RD 115/3 (1976).

2 Toronto Transit Commission. *Yonge Subway Northern Extension Noise and Vibration Study*, Book 2, Report RD 115/3 (1976).

3 PERLMAN, A. B. and DIMASI, F. P. *Frequency Domain Computer Programs for Prediction and Analyses of Rail Vehicle Dynamics*, Vol. 1, Technical Report, U.S. Department of Transportation Report FRA-OR&S-76-135. I (1975).

4 PERLMAN, A. B. and DIMASI, F. P. *Frequency Domain Computer Programs for Prediction and Analyses of Rail Vehicle Dynamics*, Vol. 2, Appendices, U.S. Department of Transportation Report FRA-OR&S-76-135. II (1975).

5 SAURENMAN, H. J. *Modifications to Program Half*, Wilson Ihrig & Associates. Technical memorandum prepared for the U.S. Department of Transportation, Transportation Systems Center, Cambridge, MA. USA (1981).

6 NELSON, J. T. Truck Impedance Measurement of BART Vehicle, Wilson Ihrig & Associates, Technical memorandum prepared for the U.S. Department of Transportation, Transportation Systems Center, Cambridge, MA, USA (1981).

7 NELSON, J. T. Mechanical impedance of a transit car vehicle, *Inter-Noise 82*, San Francisco, CA, USA, 17–19 May, pp. 221–224 (1982).

8 SAURENMAN, H. J., *et al.*, *Ground-borne Vibration Generated by Various Rail Transit Vehicles*, 1984 APTA Rapid Transit Conference, Baltimore, MD (1984).

9 SAURENMAN, H. J. Reduction of ground-borne vibration achieved with reducing primary suspension stiffness, *Inter-Noise 82*, San Francisco, CA, USA, 17–19 May, pp. 225–228 (1982).

10 REMINGTON, P. J., *et al.* Control of Wheel/Rail Noise and Vibration, U.S. Department of Transportation Report DOT-TSC-UMTA-82-57 (1983).

11 REMINGTON, P. J., *et al.* Wheel Rail Noise and Vibration, U.S. Department of Transportation Report UMTA-MA-06-0025-75-10 and 11, in two volumes (1975).

12 BRANDENBURG, E. L. and RUDD, T. J. *Development of an Inertial Profilometer*, U.S. Department of Transportation Report, FRA-ORD&D-75-15 (1974).

13 LEWIS, R. B. Recording track geometry at speed. *Railway Engineer*, **March/April**, 30–38 (1977).

14 UNGAR, E. E. and BENDER, E. K. Vibrations produced in buildings by passage of subway trains: parameter estimation for preliminary design. In *Inter-Noise 75*, Sendai, Japan, 27–29 August, pp. 491–498 (1975).

15 WILSON, G. P. *Noise and Vibration Characteristics of High Speed Transit Vehicles*, U.S. Department of Transportation Report DOT-OS-A9-032 (1971).

16 WILSON, G. P. *Ground-Borne Vibrating Levels from Rock and Earth Based Subways*, Wilson Ihrig & Associates, Oakland, CA (1971).

17 TOKITA, Y., *et al.* On the groundborne noise propagations from a subway. Presented at *The 96th Meeting of the Acoustical Society of America*, Honolulu, HI (1978).

18 LANG, J. Measurement results for structureborne noise control from subways. In *Proceedings of the 7th International Congress on Acoustics*, Budapest, Hungary, pp. 421–424 (1971).

19 SAURENMAN, H. J. *Development and Implementation of an Impact Testing Method for Predicting Ground-Borne Vibration*, Technical Memorandum prepared for the U.S. Department of Transportation, Transportation Systems Center, Cambridge, MA (1983).

20 SAURENMAN, H. J. *Vibration Attenuation with Distance Testing Along BART*, Section B, Technical Memorandum prepared for the U.S. Department of Transportation, Transportation Systems Center, Cambridge, MA, USA (undated).

21 NELSON, J. T. *Transfer Function Measurements at the BART KE Line in Oakland*, Technical Memorandum prepared for the U.S. Department of Transportation, Transportation Systems Center, Cambridge, MA, USA (1982).

22 SAURENMAN, H. J. *Impact Testing to Measure Attenuation of Groundborne Vibration with Distance from At Grade Ballast and Tie Track*, Technical Memorandum prepared for the U.S. Department of Transportation, Transportation Systems Center, Cambridge, MA, (1983).

23 SAURENMAN, H. J. and NELSON, J. T. *Procedures for the Prediction of Groundborne Vibration and Noise from Rail Transit Trains*, U.S. Department of Transportation (1985).

24 BOVEY, E. C. Development of an impact method to determine the vibration transfer charactierstics of railway installations. *Journal of Sound and Vibration*, **87**, 357–370 (1983).

25 NELSON, J. T. and SAURENMAN, H. J., *State of the Art Review Prediction and Control of Groundborne Noise and Vibration from Rail Transit Trains*, U.S. Department of Transportation Report UMTA-06-0049-83-4 (1983).

26 TOWERS, D. A. and KURZWEIL, L. G. *Vibration Impact Assessment for the Proposed Houston High Capacity Transit Corridor Alternative*, Bolt Beranek and Newman Inc. Report No. 5093, (1982).

27 EWING, W. M., JARDETZKY, W. S. and PRESS, F. *Elastic Waves in Layered Media*, McGraw-Hill Book, New York (1975).

28 TIMOSKENKO, S. and GOODIER, J. N. *Theory of Elasticity*, McGraw-Hill Book, New York (1951).

29 BARKAN, D. D. *Dynamics of Bases and Foundations*, McGraw-Hill Book, New York (1962).

30 ROARK, R. J. *Formulas for Stress and Strain*, McGraw-Hill Book. New York (1982).

31 BIOT, M. The theory of propagation of elastic waves on a fluid-saturated porous solid. *Journal of The Acoustics Society of America*, **28**, 168–178 (1956).

32 GUTOWSKI, T. G. and DYM, C. L. Propagation of ground vibration. *Journal of Sound and Vibration*, **49**, 179–193 (1976).

33 SAURENMAN, H. J., NELSON, J. T. and WILSON, G. P. *Handbook of Urban Rail Noise and Vibration Control*, U.S. Department of Transportation, Urban Mass Transportation Administration, Report No. UMTA-MA-06-0099-82-1 (1982).

34 ISHII, K. and TACHIBANA, A. *Field Measurement of Structure-borne Sound in Buildings*, Acoustical Society of America Reprint No. L10, presented at the Joint Meeting of the Acoustical Society of America and the Acoustical Society of Japan, Honolulu, HI (1978).

35 MARTIN, D. J., *Low Frequency Traffic Noise and Building Vibration*, Transport and Road Research Laboratory (U.K. Department of the Environment), Supplementary Report 429 (1978).

36 HUBBARD, H. H. Noise induced house vibrations and human perception. *Noise Control Engineering Journal*, **19**, 49–55 (1982).

37 International Organization for Standardization, *Guide for the Evaluation of Human Exposure to Whole-Body Vibration*, ISO Standard 2631 (1974).

38 International Organization for Standardization. *Guide for the Evaluation of Human Exposure to Vibration and Shock in Buildings; Addendum 1: Acceptable Magnitudes of Vibration*, Standard Addendum ISO-2631:DAD1-1980 (1980).

39 American National Standards Institute. *Guide to the Evaluation of Human Exposure to Vibration in Buildings*, Draft Standard ANSI-53.29 1983 (1983).

40 Committee on Hearing, Bioacoustics, and Biomechanics—Assembly of Behavioral and Social Sciences—National Research Council. *Guidelines for Preparing Environmental Impact Statements on Noise-Report of Working Group 69 on Evaluation of Environmental Impact of Noise*, National Academy of Sciences, Washington, DC (1977).

41 TOKITA, Y. Vibration pollution problems in Japan, In *Inter-Noise 75*, Sendai, Japan, pp. 465–472 (1975).

42 American Public Transit Association. *1981 Guidelines for Design of Rapid Transit Facilities* (1981).

43 NICHOLLS, H. R., JOHNSON, C. F. and DUVALL, W. I. *Blasting Vibrations and Their Effects on Structures*. U.S. Bureau of Mines, Bulletin 656 (1971).

44 JACKSON, M. W. *Threshold of Damage Due to Ground Motion*, International Symposium on Wave Propagation and Dynamic Properties of Earth Materials, University of New Mexico, p. 961 (1967).

45 German Standards Institute, *Vibrations in Building Construction*, Draft Revision of DIN 4150 (1970).

46 KURZWEIL, L. G. Ground-borne noise and vibration from underground rail systems. *Journal of Sound and Vibration*, **66**, 363–370 (1979).

47 SAURENMAN, H. J., SHIPLEY, R. L. and WILSON, G. P. *In-Service Performance and Costs of Methods to Control Urban Rail System Noise—Final Report*, U.S. Department of Transportation Report No. UMTA-MA-06-0099-81-1 (1979).

48 Data compiled Nov. 1976 by T. Paolillo, Environmental Staff Engineer, NYCTA, Private Communication (1980).

49 KURZWEIL, L. G. and WITTIG, L. E. *Wheel/Rail Noise Control—A Critical Evaluation*, U.S. Department of Transportation Report No. UMTA-MA-06-0099-81-1 (1981).

50 KURZWEIL, L. G. Wheel/rail noise—means for control. *Journal of Sound and Vibration*, **87** 197–220 (1983).

51 HUNT, A. D. *Development of Subway Car Flat Wheel Monitoring System*, Toronto Transit Commission, Subway Construction Branch, Engineering Department, Technical Reports (1975).

52 HUNT, A. D. Bloor-Danforth subway vibration monitor system, Toronto Transit Commission presented at *U.S. Department of Transportation Third Urban Rail Noise Abatement Conference*, Cambridge, MA, May 11–12 (1983).

53 SHIPLEY, R. L. and SAURENMAN, H. J. *In-Service Performance and Costs of Methods to Control Urban Rail System Noise—Initial Test Series Report*, U.S. Department of Transportation Report No. UMTA-MA-06-0025-78-7, NTIS-PB-288-838 (1978).

54 VER, I. L., VENTRES, C. S. and MYLES, M. M. Wheel/rail noise, Part III: impact noise generation by wheel and rail discontinuities. *Journal of Sound and Vibration*, **46**, 395–417 (1976).

55 UNGAR, E. E. and KURZWEIL, L. G. Means for the reduction of noise transmitted from subways to nearby buildings. *The Shock and Vibration Digest*, **12**, (1980).

56 Wilson, Ihrig and Associates, *Yonge Subway Northern Extension Noise and Vibration Study—Measurement Program Results*, Report RD 115/3, Toronto Transit Commission (1976).

57 SAURENMAN, H. J. *In-Service Performance and Costs of Methods to Control Urban Rail System Noise—Second Test Series Report*, U.S. Department of Transportation Report No. UMTA-MA-06-0099-79-4 (1979).

58 BENDER, E. K., et al. Predictions of Subway-Induced Noise and Vibrations in Buildings Near WMATA, Phase I, Bolt Beranek and Newman Inc. Report No. 1823 (1969).

59 PAOLILLO, A. W. Control of noise and vibration in buildings adjacent to subways—a case history. *Noise-Conference 73*, pp. 152–157 (1973).

60 BENDER, E. K. *Rail Fastener Design for Noise and Vibration Control*, Bolt Beranek and Newman Inc. Report 2485 (1974).

61 WILSON, G. P. *Acoustical Analysis and Recommendations for Direct Fixation Fastners for the WMATA Metro System*, Wilson, Ihrig and Associates. Report (1970).

62 LANG, J. Measures against airborne and structure-borne noise in the Vienna subway. In *Inter-Noise 76*, pp. 309–314 (1976).

63 COLOMBAUD, J. L. Noise and vibration levels suit ballastless track for underground railways. *Rail Engineering International*, **3**, 235–240 (1973).

64 WILSON, G. P. and WOLFE, S. L. *Vibration and Noise Performance Characteristics of Resilient Track Support Systems used in MARTA Subway*, Wilson Ihrig and Associates (1980).

65 MANNING, J. E., HYLAND, D. C. and TOCCI, G. *Vibration Prediction Model for Floating-Slab Rail Transit Track*, U.S. Department of Transportation Report No. UMTA-MA-06-0025-75-13 (1975).

66 HAUCK, G., WILLENBRINK, K. and STÜBER, C. *Körperschall und Luftschallmessungen an unterirdischen Schienenbahnen, (Measurements of Structure-borne and Airborne Sound in Underground Railways)*, Eisenbahntechnische Rundschau, pp. 289–300 (July/August 1972).

67 HAUCK, G., WILLENBRINK, K. and STÜBER, C. *Körperschall und Luftschallmessungen an unterirdischen Schienenbahnen. Teil 2 (Measurements of Structure-borne and Airborne Sound in Underground Railways, Part 2)*, Eisenbahntechnische Rundschau, pp. 310–321 (1973).

68 UNGAR, E. E., et al., *Reduction of Noise and Vibration in Buildings Near the New York City Subway*, Bolt Beranek and Newman Inc. Report. No. 4481 (1980).

69 STÜBER, C. *Geräusche von Schienenfahrzeugen, (Noise from Rail Vehicles)*, Chapter 15 in *Taschenbuch der technischen Akustik (Pocketbook of Technical Acoustics)*, Edited by M. Heckl and H. A. Müller, Springer-Verlag, Berlin (1975).

70 KOCH, H. W. *Körperschallpegel bei mehrjährig befahrenem Oberbau und bei abgeändertem Schotteroberbau sowie vergleichsfähige Werte, (Levels of Structureborne Sound for Track Support Structures in Multi-Year Use and for Structures with Altered Ballast, as well as Values Applicable for Comparisons)*, VDI-Berichte Nr. 217, pp. 19–20 (1974).

71 KAZAMAKI, T. and WATANABE, T., Reduction of solid-borne sound from a subway. In *Inter-Noise 75*, pp. 85–92 (1975).

72 SHITO, K., OIKAWA, A. and KAZAMAKI, T. Noise and vibration reducing effect of the trench provided in the soil connecting the underground railway tunnel and the building nearby. In *Inter-Noise 75*, Sendai, Japan, pp. 387–390 (1975).

73 MORII, T. Development of Shinkansen vibration–isolation techniques. *Permanent Way*, **18**, 11–37 (1977).

74 LAWRENCE, S. T. *TTC-LRT Trackbed Studies, Groundborne Vibration Testing, Measurement and Evaluation Program*, APTA 1980 Rapid Transit Conference, San Francisco, CA (1980).

75 RICHARD, F. E. (Jr.), HALL, J. R. (Jr.) and WOODS, R. D. *Vibration of Soils and Foundations*, Prentice-Hall, Inc., Englewood Cliffs, NJ (1970).

76 HAUPT, W. *Isolation of Ground Vibrations at Buildings*, (report) Building Research Summaries. Her Majesty's Stationery Office, No 6/73–79. Detailed report in German from Informationsverbundzentrum Raum und Bau, Stuttgart (1979).

77 DOLLING, H. J. *Die Abschirmung von Erschutterungen Durch Bodenschlitz (Shielding Against Vibration by Trenches in the Soil, Part 1)*, (journal article). Die Bautechnik, **5**, 151–158 (in German) (1970).

78 MILLER, L. N. Isolation of railroad/subway noise and vibration. *Progressive Architecture*, **April**, 203–208 (1965).

79 MOSS, P. Noise control for major building projects. *Noise and Vibration Control Worldwide*, **June**, 151–155 (1984).

80 *Guide to the Selection and Use of Elastomeric Bearings for Vibration Isolation of Buildings*, British Standard BS6777-1982, available from British Standards Institute, 2 Park Street, London W1A 2BS.

17

Practical Examples of Train Noise and Vibration Control

Paul J. Remington BS, MS, PhD
BBN Laboratories Inc, Cambridge,
Massachusetts, USA

Leonard G. Kurzweil BS, MS, PhD
Transportation Systems Center, Cambridge,
Massachusetts, USA

David A. Towers BS, MS
Harris Miller Miller and Hanson Inc.
Lexington, Massachusetts, USA

Contents

Previous chapters in this part of the book have described various methods of controlling noise and vibration from trains. This chapter continues this theme by providing several case-study examples of noise and vibration control techniques that have been tested in normal service on rail systems across the world. The techniques include the use of barriers, rail isolation for the control of elevated structure noise and ground vibration, rail welding, wheel condition monitoring systems, wheel truing and rail grinding, resilient wheels, damped wheels and station acoustic treatment. In some cases the treatment was part of the original design of the system. In others, the treatment or technique was applied on a retrofit basis. In all the examples the intent is to show the practical problems that were encountered and the noise and vibration control benefits that resulted.

17.1 Sound barriers

The use of wayside sound barriers is a well-established technique for controlling airborne train noise. This section presents three examples that illustrate the acoustical effectiveness of this technique when applied to elevated sections of track. Both concrete and steel structures are considered, and both absorptive and non-absorptive barriers are illustrated.

17.1.1 Metropolitan Atlanta Rapid Transit Authority (MARTA)[1]

A large portion of the MARTA rapid transit system runs on an elevated structure that consists of a concrete slab deck, supported on a steel box beam as illustrated in *Figure 17.1*. The rail on the structure is continuously welded and is fastened to the concrete deck with resilient fasteners. As *Figure 17.1* shows one side of the concrete slab is provided with a non-absorptive, concrete acoustical barrier. *Figure 17.2* provides a cross-section

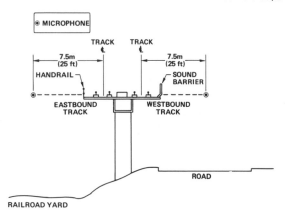

Figure 17.2 Cross-section of the elevated structure showing noise measurement locations

of the elevated structure showing the barrier together with the details of the noise monitoring positions employed to evaluate the acoustical effectiveness of the barrier.

The 1.5 m (5 ft) high barrier is constructed of preformed concrete slabs attached to the concrete deck and is positioned such that there is a gap between the barrier and the side-wall of a transit car of about 0.6 m (2 ft).

The measured acoustical performance of the barrier at the 7.5 m (25 ft) microphone is given in *Figure 17.3*. The results refer to the maximum noise recorded during the passage of a two-car test train. It is shown that the barrier produced a noise reduction of about 9 dB(A) at all passing speeds. Additional tests confirmed that the 5-7.5 cm (2–3 in) gaps that exist where adjacent spans come together (*Figure 17.4*) had no significant effect on the acoustic performance of the barriers.

Figure 17.1 MARTA elevated structure in Atlanta, GA (USA) as seen from the barrier side

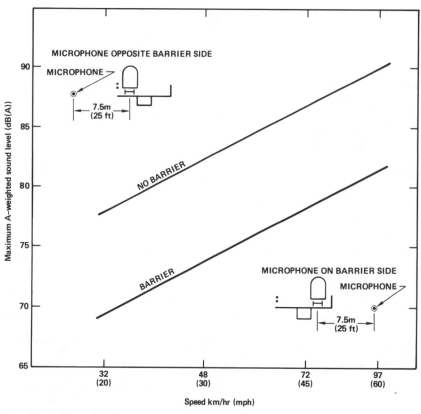

Figure 17.3 Comparison of maximum A-weighted noise levels observed with and without barriers

Figure 17.4 Typical gaps in the MARTA noise barrier at support columns

17.1.2 The Dade County Metrorail System[2]

Figure 17.5 shows a part of the noise barrier erected on an elevated section of the Dade County Metrorail rapid transit system in Miami, Florida. The structure shown is typical of the elevated structures on that system and consists of a concrete slab deck, cast as an integral part of a concrete double-tee girder. The rail on the structure is continuously welded and fastened to the concrete deck by means of resilient rail fasteners. The sound barrier is constructed from 14 gauge sheet metal panels, fastened to the edge of the guideway deck. The gap between the barrier and the side-wall of a transit car is about 0.3 m (1 ft). The top of the barrier extends approximately 1.2 m (4 ft) above the top of the rail. The inner (track-side) face of the panel includes 10 cm (4 in) thick mineral wool contained in 0.017 mm (0.65 mil) polyethylene bags protected by a perforated metal facing; this sound-absorptive treatment extends approximately 0.9 m (3 ft) down from the top of the barrier panels. There is a gap approximately 2.5 cm (1 in) wide between the barrier and the guideway as viewed from below. In addition, there is a 2.5–5 cm (1–2 in) gap between barrier panels at each pier (*Figure 17.5*).

The performance of the barrier was determined from measurements taken at the two microphone locations indicated in *Figure 17.6* during the passage of a two-car test train together with measurements taken at essentially identical locations alongside an unscreened section of track. Of particular interest was the improvement in performance achieved by using the sound absorbing treatment as part of the barrier and the loss of wayside noise reduction incurred as a result of the gaps between adjacent panels and between the barrier and guideway.

The effect of sound absorption was investigated by measuring the change in the noise level following the installation of plywood panels in front of the sound absorbing treatment along a 48 m (160 ft) test section. The effect of the gaps between the barrier and guideway along the test section and between the

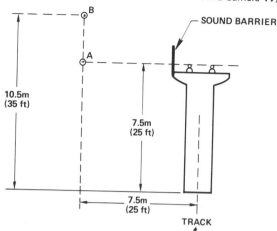

Figure 17.6 Microphone locations at the Dade County (USA) Metrorail test site

barrier panels was investigated by performing measurements after closing off each gap.

Table 17.1 provides a summary of the average sound barrier performance in terms of the reduction in the A-weighted maximum sound level (L_{max}) for various barrier configurations. These results indicate that for the rail height position A, the existing outboard barrier provides a noise reduction of approximately 9 dB(A). Without the sound-absorbing material, the noise reduction drops to about 8 dB(A), but this increases again to 9–10 dB(A) when the gaps are closed off. The best noise-reduction performance was determined to be 11 dB(A), obtained with sealed gaps and sound-absorption included.

Figure 17.5 Existing sound barrier in the Dade County (USA) Metrorail System

Table 17.1 Measured Metrorail sound barrier acoustical performance

Sound barrier configuration	Average reduction in A-weighted maximum sound level (L_{max}) at position A (dB(A))
1. Existing, unmodified barrier	8.9
2. Barrier with no sound absorption	7.8
3. Barrier with no sound absorption, but with barrier/guideway gap sealed	9.4
4. Barrier with no sound absorption, but with barrier/guideway and barrier panel gaps sealed	9.7
5. Barrier with sound absorption and sealed gaps	10.9

Table 17.2 provides a summary of improvements in sound barrier performance due to various treatments. These results indicate that the sound-absorptive treatment provides approximately 1 dB(A) of benefit at the rail height position and approximately 3 dB(A) of benefit at position B which is at a height above the top of the barrier. This suggests that the sound-absorptive treatment is only of significant benefit at sites where noise sensitive receptors are located at heights greater than that of the barrier, and particularly where the noise reduction provided by the barrier is small.

Closing off the gap between the barrier and guideway was shown to provide a 2 dB(A) benefit at rail-height position A and a 1 dB(A) benefit at position B. The gaps between the ends of the barrier panels, on the other hand, were found to have no significant effect on the barrier acoustical performance.

17.1.3 Shinkansen[3,4]

When the Japanese National Railways (JNR) opened the first high-speed railway line between Tokyo and Shin-Osaka in 1964,

Table 17.2 Measured effects of Metrorail noise barrier design features

Sound barrier design feature	Average reduction in A-weighted maximum sound level (L_{max}) due to barrier feature (dB(A))*	
	Position A	Position B
1. Improvement due to including sound-absorptive treatment only	1.1	2.8
2. Improvement due to sealing barrier/guideway gap only	1.6	1.2
3. Improvement due to sealing barrier/guideway and barrier panel gaps only	1.9	1.0
4. Improvement due to including sound-absorptive treatment and sealing all gaps	3.0	3.8

*Relative to a non-absorptive barrier with gaps between barrier and the guideway and gaps between barrier panels.

it became clear quite quickly that the noise generated by Shinkansen would be a serious problem for people living near to the track. To correct the problem the JNR launched an extensive noise abatement programme. Noise from bridges and other elevated structures was soon recognized as one of the more pressing problems. Over 100 locations with a total length of 10 km were identified as requiring extensive noise abatement. At one such location, the Yamashinagawa bridge, an extensive series of barriers was erected in stages and careful measurements made of the resulting noise reduction. This structure is of particular interest because it consists of an open tie deck supported on steel girders with solid plate webs. Such structures are notoriously noisy and are quite common across the world both on railways and urban rail rapid transit systems.

Figure 17.7 shows a cross-section of the bridge in three stages of treatment:

1. Untreated.
2. First level of treatment: side barriers and a barrier under the open tie deck.
3. Second level of treatment: the addition of a barrier between the tracks, an undercover, and absorption applied to the centre barrier and the side barriers.

Although published information on the specific details of the treatments are sketchy, it appears that the barrier panels consisted of two layers of 2.3 mm (0.091 in) thick steel sheets separated by 0.4 mm (0.016 in) synthetic resin for damping and were vibration isolated from the bridge.

Figure 17.8 shows the noise level from the bridge at the wayside at the various levels of treatment. Approximately 7 dB(A) of noise reduction was achieved with the side barriers and the barrier under the tie deck. The addition of the barrier between the tracks, the undercover, and the absorption on the side and centre barriers, resulted in an additional 12 dB(A) of noise reduction. Damping of the main girders (not shown in the figure) was found to provide little additional noise reduction.

Treatments similar to the above have been applied to a number of steel elevated structures on Shinkansen, but for new construction JNR has taken noise abatement into consideration early in the design process. The result has been that in the construction of new rail lines elevated structure designs have been employed that consist of all concrete or are a composite of steel and concrete and are inherently less noisy.[1]

17.2 Rail isolation in elevated structures

Rail isolation in elevated structures has been employed on a number of occasions to control noise. Although somewhat less effective than barriers, rail isolation is usually less costly and much easier to install. In this section two rail isolation techniques are described: an installation of resilient rail fasteners on an open tie deck steel elevated structure in New York City and the use of ballast mats on a number of elevated structures on Shinkansen.

17.2.1 New York City Transit Authority (NYCTA)[1,5]

Within New York City there are over 85 km (52 miles) of steel elevated rail transit structures. Trains operating on these structures tend to be about 10 dB(A) noisier than when they operate on tie and ballast track at grade. In the hope of finding a means of reducing this noise a pilot study was conducted in 1978 to determine the noise reduction effectiveness of replacing the existing rail fastening system (steel tie plates spiked to wood ties) with resilient rail fasteners. The selected site, shown in *Figure*

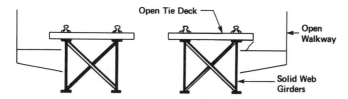

(a) Untreated Structure

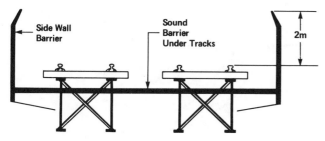

(b) First Level of Treatment

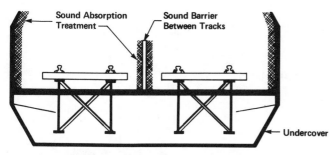

(c) Second Level of Treatment

Figure 17.7 Treatments applied to the Yamashinagawa Bridge on Shinkansen

17.9, is on 10th Avenue in North Manhattan near the intersection of 211th Street. This site was chosen because of complaints at a grammar school located approximately 61 m (200 ft) west of the structure.

At this site, the structure consists of jointed rail on an open tie deck. The wood ties are supported by steel plate girders with their webs directly under the rail axes. The girders are essentially I-beams 15.2 m (50 ft) long and 1.5 m (5 ft) high fabricated from steel plates and angles.

The structure carries three tracks, but only the south-bound track (that is, the one closest to the school) was fitted with the resilient fasteners. The steel tie plate fastener and the resilient fastener are shown in *Figure 17.10*. The resilient fastener is of a type used in tunnels throughout the NYCTA with the exception that the durometer of the rubber pad has been increased from 50 for the tunnel structure to 70 for the elevated structure. The static stiffnesses of the resilient fastener and the asphalt pad under the steel tie plate were obtained from laboratory tests.[5]

Noise measurements were made with microphones 1.5 m (5 ft) above the paved street at 7.5 m (25 ft) and 15 m (50 ft) from the centreline of the treated track. Data were obtained during the passage of regular in-service trains at a variety of speeds before and after installation of the resilient fasteners. Approximately 300 m (1000 ft) of track were treated.

The results of the measurements taken at the 7.5 m (25 ft) microphone location are shown in *Figure 17.11*. It was found that the noise level as characterized by the single event noise

exposure level (SENEL)* was lowered by between 3 and 6 dB(A) at low speeds owing to the resilient fasteners. At speeds greater than about 40 km/h (25 mph) the reductions achieved were negligible due to the intrusion of noise from the traction motor fans which become the dominant source of noise on these transit vehicles at moderate and high passing speeds.[6] Current plans are to install these fasteners on elevated structures in noise critical areas throughout the NYCTA.

17.2.2 Shinkansen[4]

As part of the extensive effort by the JNR to reduce the noise radiated by the railway bridges of Shinkansen, ballast mats were installed on a number of bridges where the noise from train passages was creating a problem in the surrounding communities. A ballast mat is simply an elastomer pad usually of the order of 25 mm (1 in) or more in thickness that is placed between the bridge deck and the ballast to prevent vibration due to the passage of a train from propagating through the ballast to the bridge deck.

For two of those bridges, one steel and one concrete, exten-

---

*For this application the SENEL is the integral of the sound pressure during a time interval that is longer than the train passage time. The integrated sound pressure is normalized to 1 s and expressed in decibels referenced to the standard reference pressure of 20 μPa.

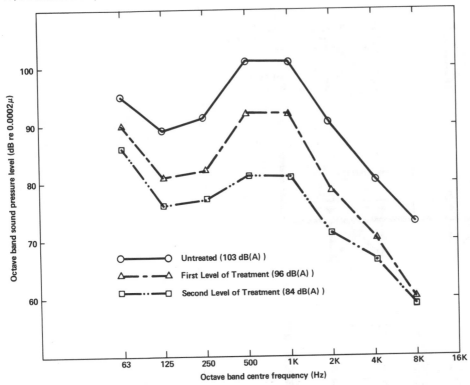

Figure 17.8 Sound levels at various stages of treatment on the Yamashinagawa Bridge; measurements at 25 m (82.5 ft) from the bridge during a train passage at 160 km/h (100 mph)

Figure 17.9 The site of the pilot study on 10th Avenue, New York City

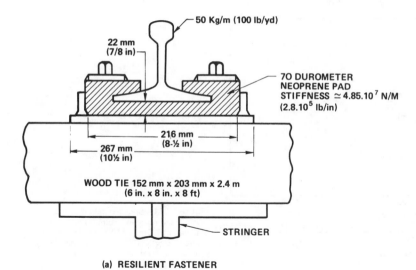

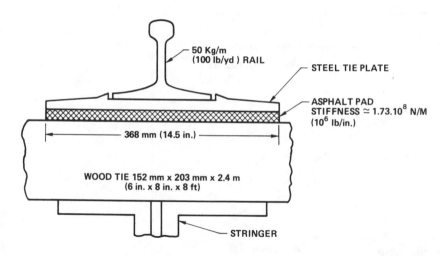

Figure 17.10 Rail fastening systems tested

sive acoustic data were obtained before and after installation of the mats. The Kawabata bridge is a 200 m (660 ft) long concrete viaduct with a side-wall originally equipped with ballasted track. *Figure 17.12* shows a cross-section of the bridge with the ballast mats installed. The noise level during a train passage measured at 25 m (82.5 ft) at ground level before and after installation of the mats is also shown in the figure. (JNR seems to use 1.2 m (4 ft) above the ground as its standard 'ground level' measurement position although for these particular measurements the term ground level is not specified.) The data show only a 4 dB(A) reduction in noise due to the mats. Somewhat larger noise reductions were noted at measurement positions closer to the structure, e.g. 5 dB(A) at 12.5 m (41 ft) and 8 dB(A) directly below the structure.

The Nakamoto-no-uchi Bridge, a 20 m (66 ft) long ballasted steel girder bridge is shown in cross-section in *Figure 17.13*. The figure also shows the noise at 25 m (82.5 ft) at ground level during the passage of a train at 200 km/h (125 mph) before and after the installation of ballast mats. Noise reductions of 7–

8 dB(A) were noted with somewhat higher noise reductions (11–14 dB(A)) underneath the structure.

17.3 Control of ground vibration

Vibration generated by trains as they run through tunnels can propagate through the intervening soil to nearby buildings where it can be felt or heard as a rumbling sound by the residents. In some cases it may also interfere with the operation of vibration-sensitive equipment. Because this vibration is potentially so intrusive, its control has always been a matter of some concern. (*See also* Chapter 16.) In this section two vibration reduction programmes are discussed, one from Vienna and one from Tokyo, in which various techniques to isolate the rail from the tunnel wall were employed.

17.3.1 Vienna Subway[7-10]

The construction of the Vienna Subway was begun in 1969, and

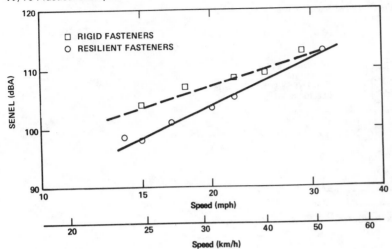

Figure 17.11 Speed variation of the single event noise exposure level obtained at 7.5 m (25 ft) from centre-line of NYCTA elevated track, for standard and resilient rail fasteners

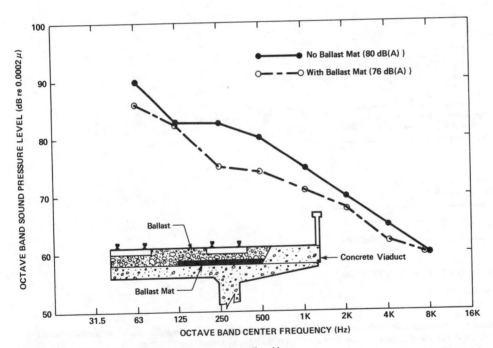

Figure 17.12 The effect of ballast mats on the noise radiated by the Kawabata concrete viaduct; noise measured at ground level 25 m (82.5 ft) from the bridge

the first section was opened in 1978. Since it was to be a totally new system the designers and planners wanted to ensure that noise and vibration from the system would not become a nuisance to the people of Vienna. Consequently considerable efforts were devoted in the early stages of design to ensure that proper noise and vibration control techniques were incorporated.

One of the major noise control issues identified early in the design was the control of structure-borne noise from passing trains. It was estimated that 15 dB of ground vibration attenuation over that achievable with rail on ties and ballast was required to ensure that the rumble of trains passing in tunnels would not exceed a reasonable limit.[7]

Initially 10 m (33 ft) sections of eight different track bed designs were tested using a pneumatic hammer mounted on a track inspection car (stationary tests). Promising results from those tests led to a second series of measurements using 100 m (330 ft) test sections and test trains (running tests). The tests were carried out on the U4 line of the Vienna Subway between Friedensbrucke and Heiligenstadt using four municipal railway cars as a test train. Nine different types of track construction were tested. Rail deflection during train passage and the vibratory velocity on the rail, on the structure and on the ground at 7.5 m (25 ft) and 15 m (50 ft) from the track centre-line were recorded during train passage at 40 km (25 mph).[8] The maximum vibration velocity level during the train passage was

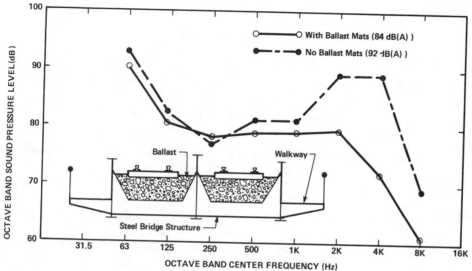

Figure 17.13 The effect of ballast mats on the noise from the Nakamoto-no-uchi Bridge; noise measured at ground level at 25 m (82.5 ft) from the bridge; train speed 200 km/h (125 mph)

determined in the 31.5, 63, and 125 Hz octave bands at each location. The overall level in these three bands with and without A-weighting applied was used as a measure of the performance of the various track support systems. A second set of tests was performed some 2 years after the first with the trains operating at 80 km/h (50 mph). The results of these tests shown in *Table 17.3* indicate that to achieve the required 15 dB of vibration reduction a two-stage isolation system was necessary in which the ties are encased in a rubber boot laid in concrete on a glass fibre slab.

The selected treatment is shown in *Figure 17.14*.[9] It consists of a polyurethane tie encased in a ribbed rubber boot. That assembly is embedded in a 26 cm (10 in) thick concrete slab, and the slab rests on a glass fibre layer (Glasfaserplatte) that in turn rests on the floor of the tunnel. The arrangement shown schematically in *Figure 17.15*[8] was installed in a steel tunnel on the first section of the U1 line of the Vienna Subway. The noise in a residential building some 3 m from the tunnel and in the state opera building was measured during the passage of a transit car. Sound levels of 29 dB(A) were measured in the basement, 24–26 dB(A) at the ground floor and on the second storey, and 20–22 dB(A) on the third storey of the residential building.[7] The sound levels on the stage and in the auditorium of the state opera house nowhere exceeded 22 dB (A) and were considered to be acceptable.

17.3.2 Teito Rapid Transit Authority[11,12]

The urban rail rapid transit system in Tokyo operates six lines comprising 124 km (78 miles) of rail of which 103 km (64 miles) is in tunnel. Prior to 1971 there were few if any complaints from the community concerning ground vibration from passing trains. However, the opening of the Chiyoda line in 1971 resulted in a serious complaint from a theatre and TV studio adjacent to the line. This complaint prompted the Transit Authority to institute a comprehensive study into the control of tunnel vibration. As part of this study three different types of track, designed to reduce the vibration of the tunnel during a train passage, were installed in short sections of the Yurakucho Line, a new line opened in 1974.

Figure 17.16 shows the vibration on the tunnel floor during a train passage at 40 km/h (25 mph) for each of the three track types and for comparison the standard track type in which the rail is directly fastened to the concrete invert with a fastening system having a stiffness of 50 tons/cm (43 000 lb/in) with a fastener spacing of 57 cm (22 in).

The tested track types include the following:

1. 'Vibration damping sleeper' type PL$_4$:
   (a) Rail to tie stiffness—100 tonnes/cm (87 000 lb-in).
   (b) Tie to invert stiffness—30 tonnes/cm (26 000 lb/in).
2. 'Vibration damping sleeper' type PL$_3$:
   (a) Rail to tie stiffness—50 tonnes/cm (43 000 lb/in).
   (b) Tie to invert stiffness—15 tonnes/cm (13 000 lb/in).
3. Ballast mat track:
   (a) Rail to tie stiffness—100 tonnes/cm (87 000 lb/in).
   (b) Ballast/ballast mat stiffness—14 tonnes/cm (12 000 lb/in).

There are few details available on the so-called 'vibration damping sleeper' configurations. They appear to be an arrangement in which there is some resilience introduced between the tie and the concrete invert or floor of the tunnel, possibly similar to the arrangement used in Vienna as described in the previous section. The ballast mat track is similar to that described in Section 17.2.2 in which ordinary crushed stone ballast is laid over an elastomer mat. For all three configurations the tie spacing was 57 cm (22 in).

Figure 17.16 shows that considerable reduction in tunnel floor vibration resulted from the use of any of the three treatments. The ballast mat configuration was especially effective, but that may have been due in part to the fact that the tunnel in which that configuration was tested was 2.8 times as heavy as the tunnels in which the other configurations were tested. Based on these results 2 km of the Yurakucho line was equipped with 'vibration damped sleepers'. The resulting tunnel floor vibration levels were reduced in some instances by only 2 dB over what would have been achieved with the standard track. The precise cause of the reduced performance is not certain but appears to be associated with improper installation.

Table 17.3 Low-frequency-vibration levels measured with passing train for different track support systems

	Sum of vibration levels in the 31.5, 63, 125 Hz octave bands*								Maximum rail deflection (mm)	
	Measured on concrete ground-plate under rail				Measured on pile 7.5 m from track centre-line					
	a†		b‡		a		b		a	b
Track support system	dB(A)	dB	dB(A)	dB	dB(A)	dB	dB(A)	dB		
Wooden sleepers on 20 cm (8 in) ballast	58–62	83–86	56	81	45–48	76–78	41	69	2.0–2.2	2.4
Wooden sleepers on 90 cm (35 in) ballast	58	84	55	83	48	76	48	75	1.4	2.4
Polyurethane sleepers in concrete	57	83	—	—	46	76	—	—	0.5	—
Polyurethane sleepers in concrete on rubber mat	55	81	60	85	44	74	46	77	1.1	1.2
Polyurethane sleepers encased in rubber envelope in concrete	54	81	—	—	45	78	—	—	0.6	—
Polyurethane sleepers encased in rubber envelope in concrete on rubber mat	48	75	—	—	40	73	—	—	1.7	—
Polyurethane sleepers encased in rubber envelope in concrete on mineral wool slab	43	75	46	80	39	72	40	77	2.2	2.8
Wooden sleepers encased in rubber envelope in concrete	55	82	—	—	45	79	—	—	0.7	—
Wooden sleepers encased in rubber envelope in concrete on mineral wool slab	46	76	46	79	36	69	38	75	2.3	2.6

*Vibration velocity levels in dB (re 5×10^{-6} cm/s).[7]
†After construction; Stadtbahn-train, speed 40 km/h (25 mph).
‡Subway-train, speed 80 km/h (50 mph).

17.4 Control of wheel and rail running surface condition

The condition of the running surface of the rail and the tread of the wheel has a significant effect on airborne and groundborne noise from a passing train. Defects in the wheel tread such as flats (due to wheels sliding during braking), spalls (loss of portions of the wheel tread due to thermal fatigue), and shells (loss of portions of the wheel tread due to mechanical fatigue), various rail running surface defects, and rail joints are all major causes of noise and vibration from rail operations (see also Chapter 14). In this section three programmes are described that sought to reduce the noise and vibration from rail operations through the use of wheel and rail smoothing techniques: rail welding on the NYCTA, wheel truing and rail grinding on SEPTA, and a wheel condition monitoring system in Toronto.

17.4.1 Rail welding—NYCTA[13,14]

The New York City Transit Authority (NYCTA) is a large urban rail transit system composed of some 273 route miles, most of which is jointed rail. It had generally been felt by many within the NYCTA that the use of welded rail in noise-sensitive areas such as underground stations would provide significant noise reduction benefits. Unfortunately, no quantitative information existed to allow such judgements to be made. Consequently as part of a larger programme to develop treatments to reduce the noise inside the NYCTA's older transit cars, it was decided to obtain data that would determine just how much quieter welded rail would be than jointed rail.

The test was performed by running a test train through two identical stations, one with welded rail and one with jointed rail. Noise measurements were made at two locations in the car interior, at the centre of the car and over one of the trucks. Two types of transit cars were tested, an older model (R-38) with essentially no noise control and a newer model (R-44/R-46) into which considerable noise control had been incorporated. Both test cars were operated at a variety of speeds through the two stations and both had their wheels trued prior to the tests. The test results are presented in Table 17.4.

For the older transit car, data are presented for three test conditions: end doors and windows open, end doors and windows closed, and all leaks in the car sealed. For the older transit car the data show that the welded rail provides some 1.5 dB(A) of noise reduction while for the newer car the average noise reduction is nearly 3 dB(A). The greater noise reduction

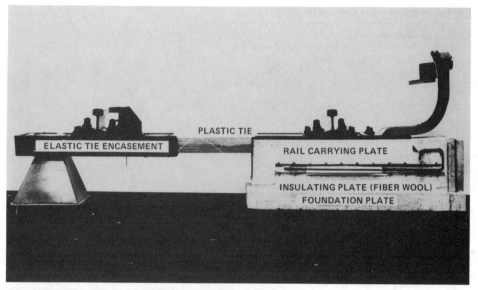

Figure 17.14 Photograph of the Vienna rail support system

CROSSECTION

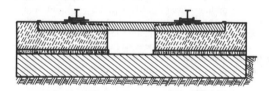

LONGITUDINAL SECTION

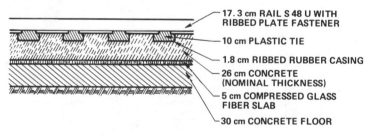

- 17. 3 cm RAIL S 48 U WITH RIBBED PLATE FASTENER
- 10 cm PLASTIC TIE
- 1.8 cm RIBBED RUBBER CASING
- 26 cm CONCRETE (NOMINAL THICKNESS)
- 5 cm COMPRESSED GLASS FIBER SLAB
- 30 cm CONCRETE FLOOR

CUT THROUGH THE PLASTIC TIE WITH RIBBED RUBBER CASING

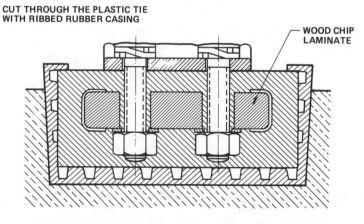

WOOD CHIP LAMINATE

Figure 17.15 Schematic of the Vienna rail support system

Table 17.4 Reduction in transit car interior noise due to welded rail (dB(A))

| Speed (km/h (mph)) | Older transit cars | | | | Newer transit cars |
	Windows open	Windows closed	Car sealed	Average	
32 (20)	1.2	2.0	—	1.6	3.1
48 (30)	2.0	1.7	1.7	1.8	2.2
56 (35)	0.7	1.5	0.7	1.0	—
Average	1.3	1.7	1.2	1.5	2.7

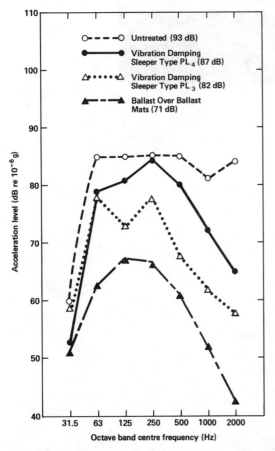

Figure 17.16 Tunnel floor vibration on the Teito Rapid Transit Authority Yurakucho line after various vibration control treatments

with the newer transit car is due at least in part to the quieter propulsion system on the newer NYCTA transit cars.[6] In the older transit car the noise from the cooling fans in the traction motors masks much of the benefit of the rail welding.

Based in part on the results of these tests the NYCTA has continued its programme to weld rail in those noise-sensitive areas where physical and operational constraints allow and has simultaneously begun to establish more stringent specifications on noise from their propulsion systems.

17.4.2 Wheel tread condition monitoring system—Toronto Transit Commission[15-18]

In the course of examining the complaints concerning its rail operations, the Toronto Transit Commission (TTC) found that when wheel defects became sufficiently pronounced, complaints of noise and vibration in buildings adjacent to the subway increased significantly. In an effort to reduce these complaints, the TTC developed a wheel condition monitoring system (now called the TTC Vibration Monitor System). The monitoring system, as currently used, enables the TTC to determine which subway cars have severe wheel defects, so that these cars can be scheduled for maintenance (typically wheel truing), thus avoiding unnecessary annoyance to wayside residents. This procedure has the added benefit of minimizing the time that the vehicles and the track are subjected to the severe impact loads accompanying wheel tread defects.

A block diagram of the Toronto Vibration Monitor System (VMS) is shown in *Figure 17.17*.[17] In each of the tunnel structures (eastbound and westbound) an accelerometer is mounted vertically on the tunnel invert at a position midway between two adjacent rail fasteners and about 15 cm (6 in)

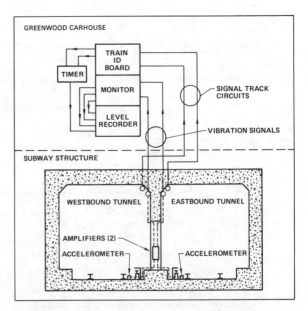

Figure 17.17 Block Diagram of the Toronto vibration monitor system

outside of the inner rail. When a train enters the signal track circuit (block) in the vicinity of the VMS accelerometer, a timer is activated which automatically operates the level recorder for approximately 15 s. This time duration is sufficient to permit monitoring of a complex six-car train operating at normal speed. The vibration signal generated by the passing train is transmitted from one of the amplifiers in the tunnel through existing telephone cables to the monitor and the level recorder, which are located in the carhouse.

The monitor determines if the subway train vibration exceeds a present alarm level. If this level is exceeded, a red light and buzzer are activated to indicate a problem wheel condition on the passing train.

A typical level recorder record for four train passages (two in each direction) is shown in *Figure 17.18*.[17] If the alarm level on the monitor is exceeded, a pen at the top of the record is activated to indicate this.

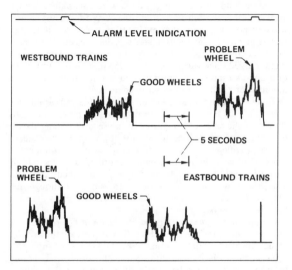

Figure 17.18 Typical level recorder record for four train passages

As currently configured, the train is identified by comparing the time of its passage with the train schedule. If problems occur on the line that cause trains to go off schedule (an infrequent occurrence on the TTC) train identification becomes difficult. An automatic train or car identification system would be a useful improvement to the current system. In 1980, the system cost approximately $28 000 (Canadian).[18]

17.4.3 Wheel truing and rail grinding[19]

The wheel tread condition monitoring system described in the previous section can be very effective in finding wheels with serious tread defects. If those wheels are brought to a wheel truing machine to recondition the tread, then the noise and vibration due to the defects are totally eliminated. The amount of noise and vibration reduction achieved depends on the severity of the defects removed, but can be 10–15 dB for seriously defective wheel treads. Similarly for seriously defective rails, e.g. rails with corrugations, rail grinding can completely remove the defects and provide equally significant reductions in noise and vibration. In the absence of pronounced and noticeable wheel tread or rail running surface defects, wheel truing and rail grinding can still provide reductions in noise and

vibration through reductions in the small-scale roughness on those surfaces. Under these conditions the reductions in noise and vibration are considerably less dramatic but still may be significant.

As part of a larger programme carried out with the Southeastern Pennsylvania Transportation Authority (SEPTA(to examine practical means for the control of urban rail transit noise, the US Department of Transportation instituted a series of tests to explore the reductions in noise and vibration from wheel truing and rail grinding in the absence of severe wheel and rail running surface defects. As part of these tests two-car test trains were operated through a number of test sections. The sections consisted of both jointed and welded rail on ties and ballast on a concrete elevated structure. The trains were equipped with three types of wheels:

1. *Worn wheels* with no obvious tread defects but with one year of normal service wear.
2. *New wheels* with lathe-turned running surfaces to simulate under-car wheel truing machines of the lathe type such as those made by Hegenscheidt.
3. *Trued wheels* recently trued using the SEPTA under-car wheel truing machine which is of the milling machine type.

Tests were run on the welded sections of track before and after grinding the rail with a vertical axis rail grinding train made by Speno, a machine typically used for restoring the profile of worn rail. The jointed rail test sections were tested similarly, but in addition tests were run after realigning the rail joints by installing new joint bars. (The rail had originally been installed some 20 years earlier and the joint bars were no longer effectively aligning the rail ends.)

Test trains were operated through these test sections at 40, 60, and 80 km/h (25, 37.5, and 50 mph). Wayside noise was measured 7.5 m (25 ft) from the track centre-line and 1.5 m (5 ft) above the rail head. Car interior noise was measured at two locations: at the centre of the car and above one bogie pivot. Both microphones were located on the centre-line of the car, 1.2 m (4 ft) above the floor. The noise reduction both at the wayside and inside the car due to rail alignment and rail grinding are shown in *Table 17.5*. In all cases the reduction is relative to unground rail for welded rail and relative to unground, unaligned rail for jointed rail. Noise reductions for wheel truing are shown in *Table 17.6*. There all the reductions are relative to worn wheels.

In general the results show that grinding of welded rail and grinding and alignment of jointed rail can be expected to give 1–2 dB(A) of wayside noise reduction and about 1 dB(A) of interior noise reduction. Wheel truing on the other hand can be expected to provide 1–2 dB(A) of wayside noise reduction and 2–4 dB(A) of car interior noise reduction with the lathe type wheel truing machines providing slightly more noise reduction on the average than the milling type machines. Although these values of noise reduction are modest in themselves, they do show that regular maintenance of wheel and rail running surface condition when used in conjunction with other techniques can help to reduce the noisiness of urban rail transit systems.

17.5 Special wheels

Special wheels, designed to reduce noise and vibration, generally fall into two generic classes, resilient wheels and damped wheels. Resilient wheels were initially developed to reduce the stresses between the wheel and the rail by introducing some resiliency between the tread and the axle. It was found coincidentally that the wheels also reduced squeal noise, ground vibration and car interior noise. Damped wheels are primarily for the suppression

Table 17.5 Noise reduction from grinding and aligning rail with no serious observable running surface defects (dB(A))

Wheel type	Wayside noise				Interior noise			
	Welded rail	Jointed rail			Welded rail	Jointed rail		
		Aligned	Ground	Ground & aligned		Aligned	Ground	Ground & aligned
Worn wheels	1.2	0.3	1.4	1.8	*	1.9	2.0	2.0
New wheels	1.3	1.9	—	—	*	0.9	—	—
Trued wheels	2.6	0.4	2.2	2.2	*	0.5	0.3	0.3
Average	1.7	0.9	1.8	2.0	—	1.1	1.2	1.2

*A slight increase in car interior noise was observed.

Table 17.6 Noise reduction due to truing wheels with no serious observable tread defects (dB(A))

Rail type	Wayside noise		Interior noise	
	New wheels	Trued wheels	New wheels	Trued wheels
Unground, welded rail	2.1	0.9	4.6	2.6
Ground, welded rail	2.1	2.2	3.3	2.7
Unground, jointed rail	1.3	0.9	3.7	1.1
Unground, aligned, jointed rail	2.9	1.0	3.0	0.3
Average	2.1	1.3	3.7	1.7

of squeal noise. In this section two programmes are discussed: one compared several types of resilient wheels on the Philadelphia transit system and the other compared several types of damped wheels on the New York City Transit System.

17.5.1 Southeastern Pennsylvania Transportation Authority[19–23]

A number of different types of resilient wheels are available from commercial sources for reducing the noise and vibration from railways and from urban rail transit systems. Although designs differ considerably, most involve inserting some resilience between the wheel tread and the axle. Here a programme is described in which the ability of these wheels to reduce wayside noise, car interior noise, and ground vibration was examined.

As part of a large study of practical means for controlling rapid transit noise and vibration on the rapid transit system in Philadelphia, PA, USA, the US Department of Transportation installed and tested three types of resilient railroad wheels on three different two-car test trains. Two additional two-car test trains were equipped with standard steel wheels, one with worn wheels and one with recently trued wheels. Each test train was run at a variety of speeds through designated test sections of in-service track.

The three wheel types, the SAB, Acousta Flex, and Penn Cushion (Bochum), are shown in *Figure 17.19*. Each utilizes an elastomeric material between the tread and the hub that is designed to introduce damping into the wheel and to provide vibration isolation between the tread and the hub. The Acousta-Flex wheels consist of a steel rim and aluminium hub threaded together with elasto-elastomeric material injected into the thread space. The Penn Cushion wheels utilize elastomer blocks to isolate the rim from the hub. The SAB wheels achieve the

required vibration isolation and damping through the use of elastomeric discs in shear.

Testing conditions on tangent track were essentially the same as described in Section 17.4.3. The one curved track test section was a turn-around loop of 43 m (142 ft) radius on wood ties and ballast at grade. Car interior and wayside measurement locations were the same as for the tangent test sections. Train speeds on the curved track varied from 15 to 25 km/h (9–16 mph). Tests of ground vibration were also carried out in a tunnel with rail mounted on timber half ties set in concrete.

Table 17.7 summarizes the results for wayside and car interior noise for both tangent and curved track. The noise reductions shown are the result of comparing the noise levels averaged over 6–12 runs and normalized to 60 km/h (37.5 mph). The resilient wheels provide very little reduction in wayside noise on tangent track. However, the internal damping provided by the wheels results in significant reductions in squeal noise on curved track. The results for car interior noise are similar although the reduction in car interior noise levels on curves is less than the reduction in wayside noise.

Ground vibration comparisons are shown in *Figure 17.20* for tangent welded track in the subway. The spectra are the average of six runs with all data normalized to 60 km/h (37.5 mph).

The highest vibration spectra occur with worn wheels. Truing the wheels results in a substantial reduction in ground vibration. Still lower levels are achieved with all three types of resilient wheels in new condition. Although the figure shows some differences between the various resilient wheels, those differences are probably not significant and above 25 Hz it is to be expected that significant reductions in ground vibration through the use of any of the three resilient wheels will occur.

Although the resilient wheels tested showed significant reductions in squeal noise and ground vibration, problems were encountered with all three wheels during the test programme. The Acousta Flex wheels were removed from the programme after a bonding failure occurred between the tread and the elastomeric material. The Penn Cushion and SAB wheels both suffered damage due to overheating. In the case of the SAB wheels the overheating occurred when a hand brake was left on during revenue service. One set of Penn Cushion wheels was damaged when the dynamic braking system failed requiring exclusive use of the tread brakes.

While these results would suggest that resilient wheels may be too fragile for use on rapid transit systems with tread brakes, London Transport by contrast ran SAB and Penn Cushion (Bochum) wheels for several years in revenue service with no failures reported.[23]

17.5.2 New York City Transit Authority[24]

In order to provide the rapid transit community with reliable performance data on a number of damped wheels, the US

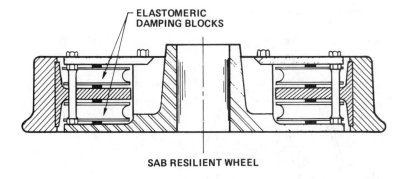

SAB RESILIENT WHEEL

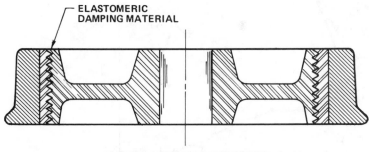

ACOUSTA FLEX RESILIENT WHEEL

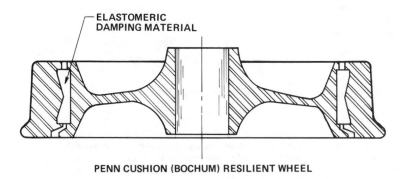

PENN CUSHION (BOCHUM) RESILIENT WHEEL

Figure 17.19 Cross-sections of resilient wheels

Table 17.7 Summary of effectiveness of resilient wheels. The table shows the levels with resilient wheels relative to levels with smooth standard wheels.

Track type	Wheel type	Relative noise level (dB(A))		Relative noise level at squeal frequencies (dB)
		Wayside	Car interior	
All tangent track, welded and jointed	Acousta flex	0 to −1	0 to −2	—
	Penn cushion	0 to −1	0 to −2	—
	SAB	0 to −1	0 to −2	—
Curved	Acousta flex	−8 to −10	−1 to −2	−5 to −30
	Penn cushion	−8 to −10	−1 to −2	−20 to −30
	SAB	−3 to −4	0 to −1	0 to −30

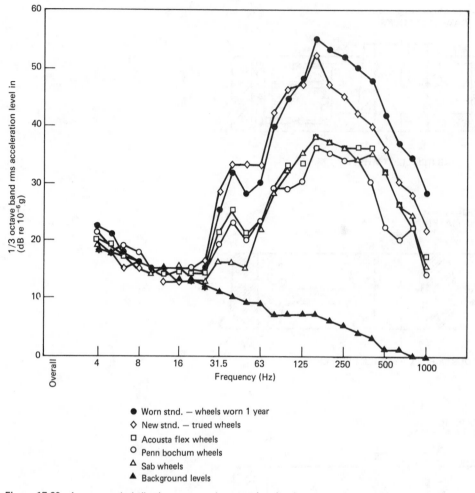

Figure 17.20 Average vertical vibration spectra at basement location (tangent, welded rail, recently ground)

Department of Transportation initiated a programme with the New York City Transit Authority to evaluate five types of damped wheels. The evaluation was to include acoustic testing, long-term performance and cost. The wheels included in the programme were:

1. Standard wheels.
2. Soundcoat Ring Damped Wheels.
3. Soundcoat Constrained Layer Wheels.
4. Sumitomo Ring Damped Wheels.
5. Krupp Tuned Absorber Wheels.
6. Generic ring damped wheels.

The standard wheel on the NYCTA is a 0.86 m (34 in) diameter wrought steel wheel, weighing about 386 kg (850 lb). The Soundcoat Ring Damped Wheel is the standard NYCTA wheel with a semi-circular groove cut into the field side of the rim on the underside. A ring coated with damping material is then inserted in the groove and bonded in place. The ring is rolled from 16 mm (0.625 in) diameter steel rod and is coated with approximately 1 mm (0.05 in) of DYAD damping material.

The Soundcoat Constrained Layer Wheel is also installed on the field side of the standard NYCTA wheel. It consists of a steel angle section rolled into a ring that is bonded to the side of the rim of the wheel with a layer of DYAD damping material

between. Some fairly elaborate and expensive means are provided to attach the angle-ring to the wheel mechanically so as to restrain the ring if the bond to the wheel should fail.

The Sumitomo Ring Damped Wheel consists of a damping ring that is force fit into the circle formed by the inner rim of the wheel. It is installed on the field side of the standard NYCTA wheel. The ring is fabricated from an inner and an outer steel ring separated by a damping layer. Additional mechanical attachments (four screws) are provided should the force fit fail.

The Krupp Tuned Absorber Wheel is the standard NYCTA wheel to which are attached 10 tuned dampers. Each tuned damper consists of five stainless steel blades separated by layers of damping material. The blades can be tuned to the various resonant frequencies of the wheel to enhance the damping performance. In this application the dampers were attached to the gauge (inner) side of the wheel. As with many of the other damped wheels some fairly elaborate and expensive machining is used to attach the dampers mechanically to the wheel.

The Generic Ring Damped Wheel is similar to the Sound Coat Ring Damped Wheel, except that no damping material is used. Instead the ring, rolled from 12.5 mm (0.5 in) diameter steel rod, is simply snapped into the groove in the wheel.

Eighteen wheels of each type were purchased for the programme. Two car trains were fitted with each wheel type and tested on a 75 m (249 ft) radius curve in the Coney Island Yard of the NYCTA. The trains were run around the curve at 14–19 km/h (9–12 mph) and the noise was measured on both sides of the track at 7.5 m (25 ft) from the track centre-line. From five to nine passes were made past the microphones for each wheel type. For four of the wheels the tests were repeated after running the wheels in normal service for 17 months.

Table 17.8 Damped wheel test results

Wheel type	Tests when wheels new		Tests after 17 months of service		Cost ($)
	Average maximum noise (dB(A))	Range of maximum noise (dB(A))	Average noise level (dB(A))	Range of maximum level (dB(A))	
Standard	88	80–104	—	97–100	279
Soundcoat Ring Damped	82	79–82	84	78–86	946*
Soundcoat Constrained Layer	82	80–83	83.5	82–86	1338†
Sumitomo Ring Damped	80	77–81	81	78–84	710
Krupp Tuned Absorber	81	79–82	—	—	629‡
Generic ring damped	83	82–84	—	—	437*

*Includes $279 for the cost of the standard wheel.
†Includes $279 for the standard wheel plus $170 for machining a special T groove in the wheel for mechanical restraints of the angle-ring.
‡Includes the cost of the standard wheel and $350 machining cost for attaching the tuned damper but excludes the cost of the absorbers which were donated to the programme.

The results of the tests are shown in *Table 17.8* along with the cost of the wheels when purchased for the programme in the early 1980s. It should be emphasized that the costs shown are for very small quantity purchases and might change for large quantities.

The noise data shown in the table are the maximum noise level during the passage of a test train past the microphones. Data were taken during 5–9 passes for each wheel type and the table shows both the average and the range of the maximum level during each pass-by. In general all five damped wheels performed about the same. Essentially all of them reduced the tonal noise from the squeal to the point where it no longer was a significant contributor to the A-weighted sound level as the train passed. In addition after 17 months of normal service the three wheels that could be tested showed essentially no degradation or minimal degradation in acoustic performance.

Because squeal can be very intermittent, especially with new standard wheels, the data in the table are somewhat misleading. The average maximum sound level in the table for new standard wheels is shown as 88 dB(A). In fact when the wheels were squealing the level could be as high as 104 dB(A). The low average value in the table reflects the fact that during some of the pass-bys the standard wheels did not squeal at all. Consequently, the apparent noise reduction due to the damped wheels of 5–8 dB(A) from the table should in fact be 21–24 dB(A).

Many of these damped wheels are either currently in service or are planned to be introduced into service in a number of urban rail rapid transit systems across the world. The Soundcoat Constrained Layer Wheel is currently in use on the Paris Metro where it has been found to be effective in reducing squeal.

The Krupp Tuned Absorber wheels have been used extensively in Berlin and Hamburg for nearly 6 years and the generic ring damped wheel has been used in Philadelphia and Chicago and there are plans to introduce it in Miami, New York and possibly Baltimore.

17.6 Station acoustic treatment

Acoustic treatment is an important aspect in the design of subway stations for rail transit systems. Without such treatment, subway stations tend to be highly reverberant, resulting in excessive train and patron activity noise as well as poor speech intelligibility. Acoustic treatment is generally incorporated in stations by adding sound-absorbing material to ceiling, wall, and under-platform surfaces. The main purposes of this treatment are (1) to reduce noise from train arrivals and departures, (2) to prevent focusing of train noise at patron locations, and (3) to reduce reverberation in order to provide good hearing conditions for public address system announcements.

17.6.1 Washington Metropolitan Area Transit Authority (WMATA)[25]

Acoustic treatment was carefully studied during the design of subway stations for the Washington Metropolitan Area Transit Authority (WMATA) rail transit system in Washington, DC (USA). As shown in *Figure 17.21*, the walls and ceilings of the WMATA stations consist of curved coffered vaults made of concrete. The method used for controlling noise in these stations consisted of incorporating acoustic treatment in the coffers of the vaults, in the under-platform overhangs and in the soffits of station mezzanines and bridges.

In order to optimize the design of acoustic treatment in the WMATA stations, acoustic tests were made inside a full-size concrete mock-up of a station (with end walls made of plywood), which was constructed during the design phase of the project (*Figure 17.22* and *17.23*). The sound-absorbing treatment employed consisted of a 24 kg/m³ (1.5 lb/ft³) density glass fibre blanket wrapped in 0.025 mm (1 mil) thick plastic bags, behind a perforated metal facing. *Figure 17.24* provides a view of a perforated metal and glass fibre panel mounted in a coffer of the station mock-up.

Noise measurements were made at several locations inside the station mock-up, using a calibrated noise source. *Figure 17.25* indicates the average noise reduction provided by complete sound-absorbing treatment (coffer panels plus treatment under platform overhangs) compared with no sound-absorbing treatment. As shown, maximum noise reductions occurred in the 500 and 1000 Hz octave bands and amounted to 6.5 dB. Above 1000 Hz, the noise reduction was observed to decrease, going to zero at 8000 Hz. The lower noise reductions at these higher frequencies are believed to result from air absorption effects and from sound absorption provided by the plywood end walls of the mock-up. Thus, greater noise reductions would be expected in an actual station.

Reverberation time measurements were also conducted in the station mock-up. The results of these measurements for the untreated condition and for the fully treated condition are indicated in *Figure 17.26*. Maximum reverberation times measured for the untreated condition were 4.1 seconds at 500 Hz and 4.5 s at 1000 Hz. Below 500 Hz, the reverberation time dropped because of the resonant absorption of the plywood panels on the end walls. Above 1000 Hz, the reverberation time also dropped, probably due to air absorption. For the fully treated condition, the reverberation time was 1.6 s at 1000 Hz and 2000 Hz, and 1.1–1.4 s at other frequencies.

Figure 17.26 also shows the results of reverberation time measurements made in an acoustically treated WMATA

Figure 17.21   Typical WMATA station

Figure 17.22   Concrete mock-up of WMATA station (outside view)

Figure 17.23 Concrete mock-up of WMATA station (inside view)

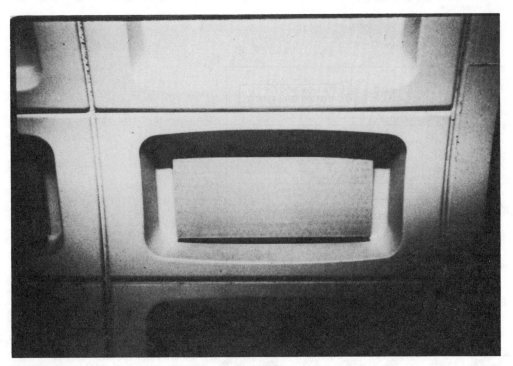

Figure 17.24 Acoustically absorptive panels used in the WMATA
station mock-up

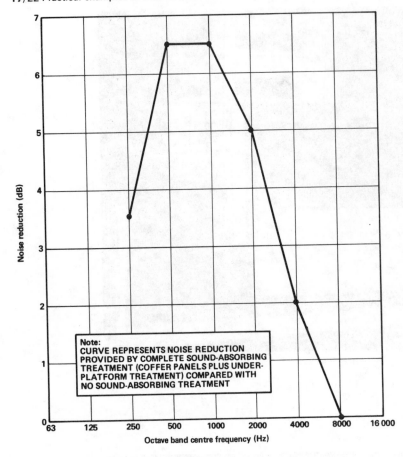

Figure 17.25 The noise reduction measured in the WMATA station mock-up

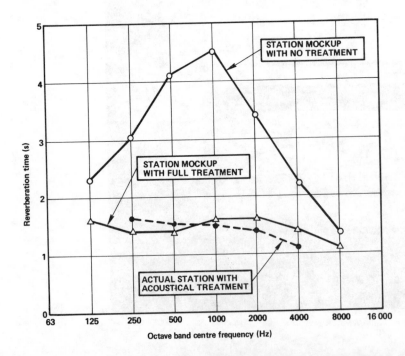

Figure 17.26 Reverberation time measurements in the WMATA station and station mock-up

station, after project completion. This station was treated in a manner representative of the treatment applied to all the stations in the subway. These results indicate reverberation times of 1.1–1.6 s, in good agreement with the mock-up measurements. These values represent an ideal acoustical environment for a subway station.

References

1 UNGAR, E. E. and WITTIG, L. E. *Wayside Noise of Elevated Rail Transit Structures: Analysis of Published Data and Supplementary Measurements*, U.S. Department of Transportation, Urban Mass Transportation Administration, Report No. UMTA-MA-06-0099-80-6 (1980).

2 TOWERS, D. A. *Noise Barrier Study for the Metropolitan Dade County Rapid Transit System—Phase I*, Bolt Beranek and Newman Inc. Report No. 5677 (1984).

3 ABE, H. and ARAI, M. Noise Control Of the Steel Railway Bridges in Shinkansen. In *Internoise 78*, pp. 763–766 (1978).

4 *Shinkansen Noise (II)*, Japanese National Railways (1973).

5 REMINGTON, P. J., WITTIG, L. E. and BRONSDON, R. L., *Prediction of Noise Reduction in Urban Rail Elevated Structures*, Bolt Beranek and Newman Report No. 4347 (1982).

6 REMINGTON, P. J. and DIXON, N. R. Control of rapid transit propulsion system noise. *Transactions of the ASME Journal of Vibration Acoustics Stress and Reliability in Design*, **106**, 270–277 (1984).

7 LANG, J. Measures against airborne and structure-borne noise in the Vienna Subway. In *Inter-Noise 76*, Washington, DC, pp. 309–314 (1976).

8 *Expert Opinion of the Physical–Technical Research Institute for Heat and Sound Technology Concerning the Structureborne Sound Level under Track Emplacements with Various Kinds of Superstructures* (in German). Report of the Physikalisch-Technischen Versuchsanstalt fur Warme und Schalltechnik, Vienna, Austria (1972).

9 *A Subway for Vienna* (in German), Wiener Stadtwerke Verkehrsbetriebe, Vienna (1974).

10 LANG J. *Noise Abatement Measures on the Vienna Underground Railway*, Report of the Physikalisch-Technischen Versuchsanstalt fur Warme und Schalltechnik, Vienna (1980).

11 KAZAMAKI, T. and WATANABE, T. Reduction of solid borne sound from a subway. In *Internoise 75* Sendai August 27–29, pp. 85–92 (1975).

12 KAZAMAKI, T. Subway vibration control. *Permanent Way*, **18**, 38–53 (1977).

13 REMINGTON, P. J. *Measurement and Diagnosis of the Noise from a NYCTA Transit Car, Volume II R-38 Test Car*, Bolt Beranek and Newman Report No. 3885 (1978).

14 REMINGTON, P. J. *Measurement and Diagnosis of the Noise from a NYCTA Transit Car, Volume III R-44/R-46 Test Train*, Bolt Beranek and Newman Report No. 3885 (1978).

15 HUNT, A. D. *Development of Subway Car Flat Wheel Monitoring System*, Toronto Transit Commission, Subway Construction Branch, Engineering Department, Technical Report (1975).

16 *Subway Car Vibration Monitor System*, Toronto Transit Commission Brochure (1979).

17 HUNT, A. D. *Bloor–Danforth Subway Vibration Monitor System*, Toronto Transit Commission Report, presented at *The Third Urban Rail Noise Abatement Conference*, U.S. Department of Transportation, Transportation Systems Center, Cambridge, MA, May 11–12 (1983).

18 LAWRENCE, S. T. *Manager of Engineering Toronto Transit Commission* (unpublished observations) (1980).

19 SHIPLEY, R. L. and SAURENMAN, H. J. *In-Service Performance and Costs of Methods to Control Urban Rail System Noise—Initial Test Series Report*, US Department of Transportation Report UMTA-MA-06-0025-78-7 (1978).

20 HOLOWATY, M. C. and SAURENMAN, H. J. *In-Service Performance and Costs of Methods for Control of Urban Rail System Noise—Experimental Design*, US Department of Transportation Report No. UMTA-MA-06-0025-76-4 (1976).

21 SAURENMAN, H. J. and HOLOWATY, M. C. *In-Service Performance and Costs of Methods to Control Urban Rail System Noise—Test and Evaluation Plan*, US Department of Transportation Report UMTA-MA-06-0025-77-10 (1977).

22 SAURENMAN, H. J. *In-Service Performance and Costs of Methods to Control Urban Rail System Noise—Second Test Series Report*, U.S. Department of Transportation Report UMTA-MA-06-0099-79-4 (1979).

23 SAURENMAN, H. J., SHIPLEY, R. L. and WILSON, G. P. *In-Service Performance and Costs of Methods to Control Urban Rail System Noise*, US Department of Transportation Report UMTA-MA-06-0099-80-1 (1979).

24 MANNING, J. E. *In-Service Evaluation of Four Types of Damped Subway Car Wheels*, US Department of Transportation. In preparation (1985).

25 Personal Communication with Parker Hirtle of BBN Laboratories (1984).

Part 5

Aircraft Noise

18

Subsonic Aircraft Noise

M. J. T. Smith MA
Rolls-Royce Limited,
Derby, UK

and

Professor J. Williams BSc, MSc, PhD,
FRAEeS, CEng
Aeronautics and Astronautics Department,
Southampton University, UK

Contents

18.1 Background

Since the mid-1960s the dominant feature of airport noise has been that from the growing fleet of subsonic commercial and private jet aircraft. There are now around 7000 in the commercial fleet alone, supplemented by a similar number in the business and general aviation sectors. By comparison the propeller powered fleet has remained substantially constant in number for the past 20 years at around 2000, whilst the civil helicopter fleet is in its infancy.

The growth of the jet fleet in the 1960s promoted widespread reaction. Lawsuits in the USA and public action groups in the UK, where in 1920 Winston Churchill removed the right to sue, caused a series of noise control actions to be established. At London's Heathrow and New York's Kennedy Airports noise limits were imposed and monitored. Other major airports followed suit, but such localized action failed to stem the problem and in 1966 the USA, UK and France agreed to introduce Noise Certification into the Airworthiness Type Approval process. Concurrently industry stepped up noise control activities by an order of magnitude in readiness for the legal restrictions that were to appear in the 1970s.

From the work of the subsequent two decades, a wider understanding of aircraft noise sources and control possibilities has been established, and the following sections summarize separately the situation with subsonic fixed wing jet, propeller powered aircraft, and helicopters. Some details on other aircraft types including small business aircraft, microlights and airships can be found in Chapter 19.

18.2 Subsonic jet aircraft noise

Undoubtedly the main source of take-off and landing noise is the aircraft powerplant, although airflow around the airframe and its flap and gear systems can create a recognizable contribution to the overall noise signature during the approach to land.

The engine noise sources can be subdivided conveniently into two categories—those generated internally and those generated externally. The major external source, jet mixing noise, has been obvious since the introduction of the jet engine, but modern turbofan engines now generate most of their noise energy internally. The reason for this is best explained by reference to the types of engine in service (*Figure 18.1*).

The earliest and simplest type is the 'straight' or 'pure' turbojet. Propulsive thrust is generated by the expulsion of hot gas at high velocity through a single exhaust nozzle. In a typical 50 kN thrust engine, around 40 kg airflow per second is drawn into the compression system, mixed with fuel and then burned. Downstream of the combustion section the turbine extracts sufficient energy to drive the compressor, before the hot gas is expelled through the nozzle at around 600–700 m/s.

The acceleration of a small mass of air to high velocity is not the most thermodynamically efficient process, but it was the case with the pioneer breed and is always essential for very high speed flight. It was not until materials and turbine cooling technology advances were made that the by-pass concept established an improvement in efficiency by using up to twice as much air per unit of thrust. In this process only half the airflow is used in a (smaller) gas-producing engine 'core' before being expelled at a fairly high velocity of around 600 m/s, the remainder being retained at a lower pressure to 'by-pass' the primary core flow in a separate duct. It is then expelled through a separate nozzle at around two-thirds of the hot gas velocity; or mixed with the hot core flow, to further improve thermodynamic efficiency, before passing through a single nozzle.

The modern turbofan takes yet another step forward in efficiency by using even higher levels of by-pass flow. Typically, 3–4 times as much air is involved per unit of thrust, only 20–30% being used in the gas producing process. A large single-stage fan provides modest compression (less than 2 : 1) and fan jet velocities of around 300 m/s. The core compression ratio is in the region of 20 : 1 but, with much higher turbine energy extraction to drive the bigger fan and compressors, hot jet velocities are lower than on any other type at around 400–500 m/s.

Since all sources of aerodynamic noise are a function of airflow velocity, as by-pass ratio rises and jet velocity falls, so the external jet mixing noise level falls. Conversely, as *Figure 18.2* shows, the power handling in the turbomachine rises and so do the noise levels from the fan, compressor and turbine. Without the beneficial effects of noise control in the basic design of the turbomachine, and absorption of the internal sources by acoustic lining, the modern turbofan would still be as noisy as the early by-pass engine. To understand this situation it is convenient to work through the engine and consider each major noise-producing area in turn.

18.2.1 Fan and compressor noise

The frequency spectrum of a fan or compressor (*Figure 18.3*) exhibits two main features. On top of a randomly distributed (broad-band) noise source is superimposed a series of single frequency (discrete tone) sources. The two types of sound are generated by quite different mechanisms, which must be considered.

18.2.1.1 Broad-band noise source

The broad-band noise source results from the propagation of the pressure fluctuations associated with turbulent flow. Turbulent flow is an inherent feature of all turbomachines, being induced whenever there is airflow over a solid surface, or a discontinuity in adjacent flow streams. The major areas of turbulence are associated with the multiplicity of blading and the boundary layer on the walls of the compressor ducting. On the first stage, the fan in a turbofan engine, free-stream turbulence levels are low and broad-band noise results largely from interaction of the tips of the rotating blades with the turbulent boundary layer close to the wall of the intake duct. Turbulence in the wakes shed by these blades is a secondary fan noise source, but becomes important in 'downstream' stages of blading. Equally, if the fan has upstream guide vanes or other turbulence-inducing structures, such turbulence then becomes as important as that in the boundary layer.

Early experiments,[1] and independent theoretical analyses,[2-4] have all shown the relationship between turbulence and noise. Published experimental data on aeroengine fans and compressors quantifies the situation. In early multistage compressor tests[5] it was shown that the theoretical 5th power variation of acoustic energy with the velocity of the airflow local to the surface was borne out, and that the mean flow velocity through the compressor dictated the split of radiated energy from the front (inlet) and rear (exhaust nozzle). These findings have subsequently been confirmed on model single-stage fan designs.[6]

Additionally, it is clear that blade incidence is a powerful parameter. Since angle of attack of the bladeform to the oncoming flow will be instrumental in defining the thickness of the trailing edge wake, and hence turbulence levels, it is important that 'off-design' conditions (e.g., low powers for landing) do not produce excessive turbulence levels in the flow-stream. One degree of divergence from optimum incidence angle can increase broad-band noise levels by up to 3 dB.

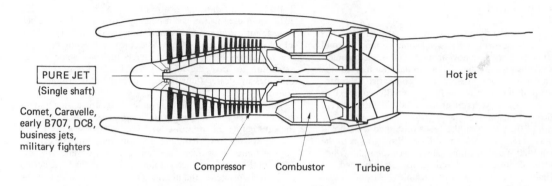

PURE JET
(Single shaft)

Comet, Caravelle,
early B707, DC8,
business jets,
military fighters

Hot jet

Compressor   Combustor   Turbine

BY-PASS
(2 shafts)

Later B707, DC8,
B727, B737,
DC9, BAC 111,
F28, Trident,
VC10, military

Cold bypass jet

Hot core jet

Low and high pressure
compressors

Turbines

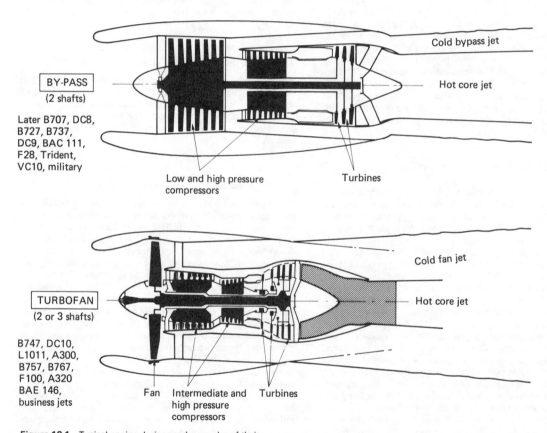

TURBOFAN
(2 or 3 shafts)

B747, DC10,
L1011, A300,
B757, B767,
F100, A320
BAE 146,
business jets

Cold fan jet

Hot core jet

Fan   Intermediate and   Turbines
       high pressure
       compressors

Figure 18.1 Typical engine designs and examples of their application

18.2.1.2 Discrete tones

Discrete tones are most frequently the result of interactions between the pressure fields and/or turbulent wake flows associated with adjacent rotating and stationary blade rows, but there are several other generating mechanisms, and the total subject is complex. Too complex for a full dissertation here, since it would only be of interest to those intimately concerned with turbomachinery design, and further reading is referenced. However, the main features should be summarized.

A rotor in isolation will produce a discrete tone at rotor blade passing frequency, which results from the propagation to the far-field of the almost identical pressure fields associated with each individual rotating blade. The situation is analogous to the unducted propeller (*see Section 18.3*), but, under subsonic tip-speed conditions that prevail at low engine power settings for approach and reduced power flyover operations, the energy involved is low and often masked by other effects. During take-off, where a modern fan is running under supersonic tip-speed conditions, the effect can be marked. With the airflow supersonic in the blade tip region, there is a stand-off shock wave ahead

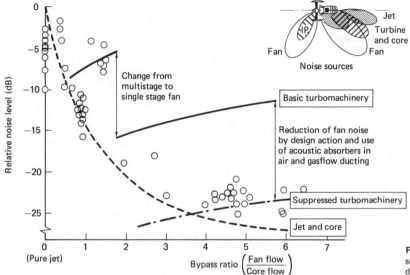

Figure 18.2 Variation of engine noise sources with by-pass ratio at same thrust and distance

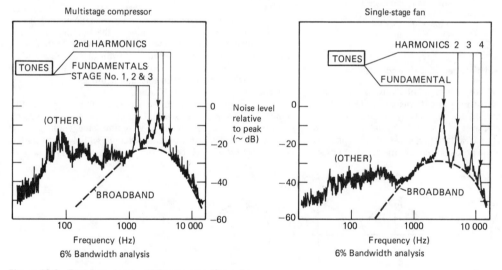

Figure 18.3 Frequency spectrum of compressor/fan noise

of each individual blade, which propagates to the farfield observer (*Figure 18.4*, top).

If the blades are completely regular, such that the shock patterns are identical, then the observer will hear only the fundamental blade passing frequency and its harmonics. However, this is most unusual, for no matter how carefully each blade is manufactured, under the heavily loaded situation of maximum rotational speed the degree of blade untwist varies marginally from blade to blade, and no two shock patterns are identical in either strength or wavefront direction. Under these circumstances each individual blade shock can be heard to a greater or lesser degree in the far-field, as tones from single blade (shaft speed) order through to blade passing order, and as their harmonics above blade passing order. Known most commonly as 'buzzsaw' noise,[7] this phenomenon characterizes the take-off conditions of many modern large transport aircraft. At

large observation distances, where the higher harmonics are absorbed naturally by the atmosphere, the lower shaft orders propagate preferentially and can sound very similar in character to a sawmill or a high-revving motor-cycle exhaust.

At subsonic conditions the shock pattern disappears, and the cyclic pressure field and wake interactions between the rotating and stationary stages are the dominant source. If the rotating and stationary stages are injudiciously placed close to one another there is an intense pressure field interaction and a very strong tone is generated (*Figure 18.4*, centre). For this reason, rotating and stationary rows are generally spaced such that the pressure field interaction intensity is below that of the wake interaction (*Figure 18.4*, bottom). The intensity of generation thus becomes a function of the strength of the velocity/pressure gradients across the wake of each interacting blade, and the frequency at which tones are observed are the function of the

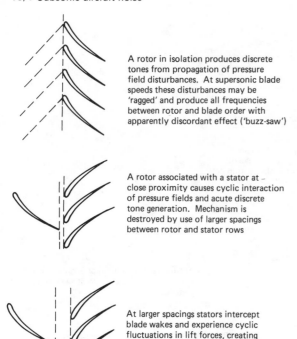

A rotor in isolation produces discrete tones from propagation of pressure field disturbances. At supersonic blade speeds these disturbances may be 'ragged' and produce all frequencies between rotor and blade order with apparently discordant effect ('buzz-saw')

A rotor associated with a stator at close proximity causes cyclic interaction of pressure fields and acute discrete tone generation. Mechanism is destroyed by use of larger spacings between rotor and stator rows

At larger spacings stators intercept blade wakes and experience cyclic fluctuations in lift forces, creating discrete tones. Further increase in spacing improves situation

Figure 18.4 Generation of discrete tones in a compression stage

number of blades on the rotating stage and its speed of rotation. The nearfield pressure (or modal) patterns so produced, their propagation direction and the multiplicity of the wavefront interference effects give rise to a farfield sound distribution which can be likened to the surface of a golf-ball. The elements important in defining the propagation patterns are the number

of blades on the stationary and rotating stages, their relative speeds and the absolute flow velocities of the interacting blade flows. Like broadband noise, intensity is a function of the magnitude of the pressure disturbances, including those caused by any steady distortion pattern in the intake, whereas propagation effects are concerned with the geometry of the situation.

Consider a simple case, i.e. the situation with a four-bladed rotor (*Figure 18.5*). When spinning adjacent to a stator row having only one blade (a most unlikely simplistic situation) there will be an interaction 'pulse' every quarter-revolution, as each rotor blade (R) passes the stator vane (S). This will produce a tone at blade-passing frequency originating at the location of the stator. With two equi-spaced stator blades the process will occur simultaneously in the region of each stator, and with four equi-spaced stators simultaneously four times each quarter-revolution.

However, if the number of stators is an inexact ratio of the number of rotor blades, which is the usual situation in a compressor, the phenomenon becomes more complex. With one stator less than the number of rotors (*Figure 18.6*, top), each quarter-revolution of the four-bladed rotor induces three inter-action pulses, equi-spaced in time but at the position of each successive stator, and occurring in space and time in the direction of rotation. Hence, one full rotation will produce not only a regular interaction at each stator location four times per revolution, but also a superimposed pattern of events that is taking place more rapidly (at three times rotor speed) and occurring in the same direction of rotation as the blading. Even if the rotor is moving subsonically at the tip, the three-fold pattern of events can become supersonic. When there is one more stator blade than the number of rotor blades (*Figure 18.6*, bottom) the pattern of events occurs even more rapidly, at five times the rotor speed, but in this case it moves counter to the direction of rotation of the blading.

This pattern of events can be expressed quite simply. If the number of rotor blades is B and the stator vanes V, a pattern occurring at a harmonic number n times the blade passing frequency can be formed in m circumferential wavelengths, where $m = nB \pm kV$ (k being any integer), and will rotate at

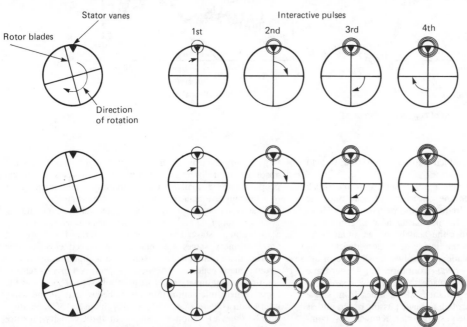

Figure 18.5 Interaction tones—rotor blades an exact multiple of stator vanes

4 rotors,
3 stators

¼ revolution, three successive interactions
12 interactions per complete revolution,
mode rotating *in same direction* as
blades at four times blade speed

4 rotors,
5 stators

20 interactions per revolution, *mode
rotating counter to blades* at four
times blade speed

Figure 18.6 Interaction tones—inexact multiples of rotor and
stator blade numbers

$\frac{nB}{m} = \frac{nB}{nB \pm kV}$ times the rotor speed. In the case of the four-bladed rotor and three bladed stator above, $n = 1$ and for $k = 1$ the speed of the pattern becomes $\frac{4}{4-3}$, or four times the rotor speed.

Most 'real life' fans and compressors have blade numbers in the 20–50 region, and even higher numbers of stators. The analysis is accordingly more complex,[8-10] and has to include consideration of duct propagation criteria. Indeed, in an unconstrained situation, whilst most tones do propagate beyond the confines of the duct, some do not. There is a critical ratio of stator/rotor blade numbers beyond which certain dominant modes can be induced to rotate such that they decay within the duct, and hence do not propagate to a farfield observer. Known as the cut-off condition, it can be simply expressed such that the number of stator vanes (V) has to exceed $1.1 (1 + M_n) nB$, where M_n is the local Mach number. Hence, in order to cut off the fundamental ($n = 1$) tone there need to be just over twice as many stators as rotors, and to cut off the second harmonic ($n = 2$) tone over four times the number of stators as rotors.

The combination of a multiplicity of rotating and blade rows can be seen from the above to produce an extremely complex source. The frequency spectrum of a total 'front end' engine assembly contains discrete tones from both the fan and early stages of the core engine compressor, both at their fundamental blade passing frequencies and higher harmonics; and at intermediate frequencies. The tones at intermediate frequencies, often referred to as 'sum and difference tones' result from the interaction between persistent wakes from early stages of blading with subsequent downstream stages. In the typical engine assembly shown (*Figure 18.7*), whilst tones propagating down the fan duct will normally be a function only of the interaction between the fan blade and its outlet guide vane (OGV), the tones propagating from the inlet are far more numerous and complex in their origin. Wakes from the fan blade will interact not only with the fan OGVs, but with core engine stator vanes (S1, S2, S3, etc.). There will also be basic interactions between the wakes from the core engine stators and rotors (S1-R1-S2, S2-R2-R3, S3-R3-S4, etc.) and, where the fan blade is rotating on a different shaft to the core engine compressor, interactions between the fan blade

wakes and the rotating stages of the compressor (F-R1, R2, R3, etc.). Fortunately, tones generated well into the core engine compressor find it difficult to propagate upstream against both the flow and the physical 'barrier' of the upstream blade rows, which take on the appearance of a series of venetian blinds to the wavefront propagating upstream. The blind may be 'open' or 'shut', depending on the wavefront angle and whether it is propagating with or counter to the direction of rotation of the blading.

The critical issues in the design of a fan can be summarized as follows:

1. Maintenance, under full rotational conditions, of good aero-mechanical similarity between fan blades; to minimize 'buzz' noise at supersonic tipspeeds.
2. Selection of the lowest practical fan and compressor tipspeeds, to minimize airflow velocities over the fan blade, its OGV and early stages of core engine compression, and hence minimize the strength of both tonal and broadband sources.
3. Selection of rotor/stator blade numbers consistent with tone 'cut-off' criteria, in both the fan and early core engine compressor stages, taking advantage of mode rotation direction.
4. Provision of spacing between rotating and stationary blade rows large enough to reduce wake intensity, and hence significant propagating interactions.
5. Elimination of features upstream of the fan which produce flow field disturbances and negate 'cut-off' design action (e.g., inlet guide vanes, divided or non-circular intakes, intake doors, etc.).
6. Maintenance of efficient operating conditions at the 'off-design' conditions associated with low power operations into an airport (e.g., avoiding large changes of blade incidence, and severe changes of aircraft/intake incidence).
7. Additionally, acoustically absorbent material can be incorporated on the walls of the intake and by-pass ducts to reduce tonal and broadband levels close to source (*see* Section 18.2.6).

In all, these control guidelines have resulted in some 20 dB

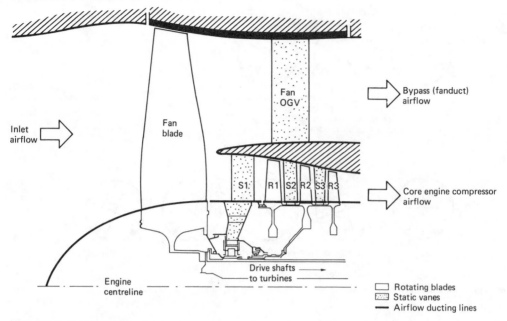

Figure 18.7 Half-section of engine front end assembly, showing relevant blading

reduction in noise from the two-stage turbofan of the 1960s to the modern single-stage fan.

18.2.2 Combustion noise

Following compression in the high pressure compressor, the core engine airflow is mixed with fuel to facilitate the combustion process that provides the energy release to sustain the engine's operation.

By its very nature, the combustion process is turbulent. Not only is the flow turbulent on exit from the compressor, having been agitated in the many stages of compression, but the combustion chamber is designed to mix the air and fuel rapidly in a manner that sustains a stable flame front (*Figure 18.8*). Equally, the burning process itself induces turbulence, and it is hardly surprising that the combustion chamber is the source of an intense broad-band noise signal. Fortunately, it is not so intense that it dominates the engine noise signature, for the burnt gas is then subject to an energy extraction process in the turbine, and the turbulent and noisy exhaust is then expelled from a convergent nozzle to mix violently with the atmosphere and produce jet mixing noise, which frequently masks other sources (*see* Section 18.2.5).

Nevertheless, the combustion noise element of the exhaust noise signature is evident, and needs to be accounted for in the overall noise control process of engine design. More so at low exhaust velocities (where jet noise is low) than at higher velocities. Being random in nature, combustion noise appears as a broadly distributed 'hump' in the low-frequency region of an engine exhaust frequency spectrum and is often difficult to separate from the jet mixing noise. Equally, it is difficult to conduct research work on combustion noise without the presence of jet mixing noise in the experimental arrangement, and therefore quantification of the intensity and spectral character against leading parameters has not yet been established. A recognized method of prediction[11] does exist, but it relies upon

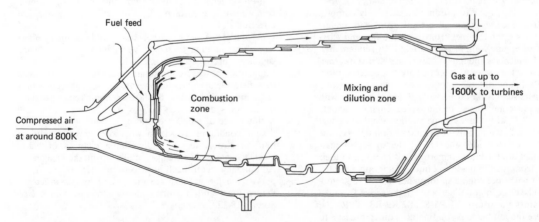

Figure 18.8 Typical combustor section

fairly empirical relationships between combustion mass flow, pressure, temperature rise and turbine energy extraction. It is clear that, in reality, the dimensions of the combustion zones, the type of fuel mixing process incorporated and the effects of the combustor geometry all need to be accounted for,[12,13] but up to now the combustion noise source has not proved to be a limiting feature in the design and operation of engines, and research activity has been of a much smaller magnitude than that related to the turbo-machinery and jet exhaust noise.

Nevertheless, it cannot be discounted, and its presence can often be used as a diagnostic tool in identifying basic aerodynamic problems. Combustion 'rumble, screech and howl' have variously been shown to be associated with flame-front instabilities, or combustion cavity and jetpipe resonances that are not only audible, but can give rise to acoustic fatigue of critical mechanical components. Equally, combustion instabilities can have a powerful effect on the generation of tonal sources in the turbine, which is considered in the next section.

18.2.3 Turbine noise

The engine turbine assembly, which provides the power to drive all the compression stages at the front of the engine, can comprise up to six stages on two or three independently rotating shafts. The noise generating mechanisms are identical with those in the fan and the compressor, but their propagation is different. Firstly, because the flow from the combustion system is directed into the turbine at supersonic speeds, all the turbine noise energy is convected downstream and radiated from the rear of the engine. Secondly, in radiating from the exhaust nozzle, the sound waves have to pass through the turbulent high-speed jet exhaust, which both 'diffuses' the sharpness of discrete tones[14] and refracts all the energy in a preferred direction.

Figure 18.9 shows a typical turbine assembly. Outlet flow from the combustion chamber is directed by a nozzle guide vane (NGV) onto the first high-pressure turbine rotor (HPR1). It is then directed onto the second HP rotor by the interstage nozzle guide vane (NGV2), and similarly then through the LP system (on a different shaft) before passing through the final nozzle.

In the total process the same basic broad-band and tonal noise sources as in a compressor are seen to exist, but the tonal element is more dominant. Whilst it is possible to minimize tones by incorporating large spacings between the early rotating and stationary stages in the fan, it is more difficult to do so in the turbine. Tone energy varies roughly according to the square of

the ratio of stage separation to upstream blade chord, and the introduction of separation ratios of 1 to 2 (as in the fan) in a multistage turbine unit could be achieved only at considerable cost in engine length and weight, and hence overall propulsion system efficiency. Fortunately, several features of a turbine make it less of a problem than the fan. For example, although tipspeeds in the turbine are high, so are the temperatures, and hence the Mach numbers are lower than in a compressor and tone 'cut-off' is easier to exploit. Also, the total mass flow through the turbine on a turbofan is very much less than that into the front of the engine, and even if turbine noise energy/kg of flow were similar to that at compressor inlet, overall levels would be some 5–10 dB lower. Moreover, because the turbine blade numbers are high (up to five times those of the fan), all the tone frequencies are higher and often many are beyond the audible range.

Nevertheless, these tones dominate turbine noise character, as exemplified by the narrowband power spectrum of a cold model three-stage LP turbine in *Figure 18.10* (top). Seen identified are a multitude of blade passing, harmonic and sum and difference tones from all the interacting stages of the turbine. Any broader band analysis will mask the true relevance of the tonal content, as does the diffusing effect of the higher levels of flow stream turbulence in the full-scale engine environment (*Figure 18.10*, bottom). This often erroneously leads to a belief that turbine-produced broadband noise is far more significant than in reality.

As regards radiation from the nozzle (*Figure 18.11*), because of the refraction process that forms part of its propagation path, turbine noise appears to the observer over a comparatively short period of time. Temperature and velocity differences between the primary core gas flow and between the secondary by-pass airflow core gas flow and between the secondary by-pass airflow and the ambient atmosphere all contribute to a fairly sharp refraction boundary,[15] and consequently, a narrow corridor of propagation to the far-field, usually between about 100 and 120 degrees to the intake axis. This compares with the fan noise propagating down the by-pass duct to radiate, after a less complex refraction, up to some 130 degrees. Conversely, fan and compressor noise radiating from the intake is free to range over the whole forward arc, and often into the rear arc up to 110 degrees to the intake axis.

Having regard to the above, and the mechanisms of generation outlined in Section 18.2.1, turbine noise control is usually exercised by a combination of:

1. Taking full advantage of cut-off criteria, which require a

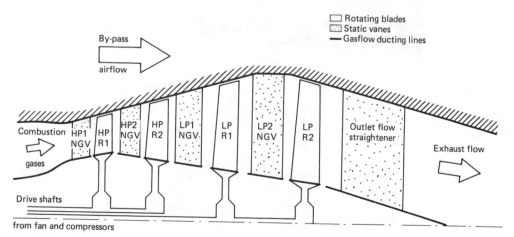

☐ Rotating blades
▨ Static vanes
— Gasflow ducting lines

Figure 18.9 Half-section of turbine assembly, showing relevant blading

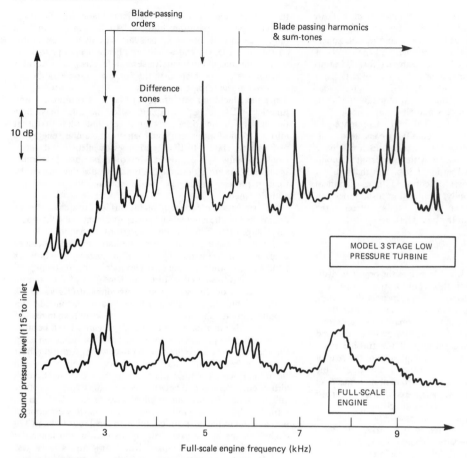

Figure 18.10 Turbine noise spectra from a cold aerodynamic model and a full-scale engine

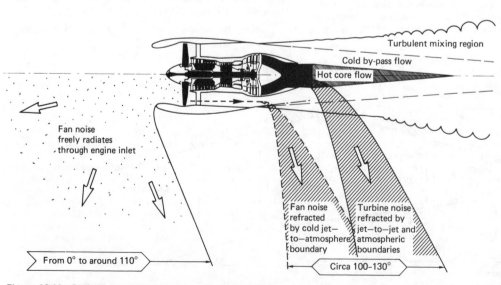

Figure 18.11 Radiation patterns of internal engine sources

lesser ratio of stationary to rotating blades than in the fan, due to the lower Mach numbers in the hot flow.
2. Avoidance of high blade loadings and hence high local velocities.
3. Using as large a spacing between rotating and stationary blade rows as is practicable.
4. Minimizing cyclic pressure field and wake disturbances from the combustion outlet downstream through the turbine.
5. Use of acoustically absorbent liners on the duct walls (*see* Section 18.2.6).

18.2.4 Other internal noise sources

Whilst it is clear that, over and above the turbomachinery and combustor noise sources, there must be a multitude of secondary sources in the engine air and gas flow passages, few have proved to be of great relevance. Some that merit attention in the design of a powerplant are noted below:

Engine variables, which encompass those externally controlled moving parts that maintain efficient engine operation, can 'spike' the otherwise smoothly progressive variation of engine noise with power condition. Variable inlet guide vanes, which control compressor performance over the widely ranging conditions of speed, pressure and temperature in the total mission cycle of an aircraft, can alter sharply local flow velocities, incidences and turbulence levels. Such effects may be beneficial (in providing acoustic blockage) or detrimental (increasing wake disturbances). Similarly, engine bleed valves, which off-load excess core compressor flow at low speeds by dumping air into the by-pass duct, can exhaust at high-pressure ratios and produce internal patches of shock and mixing noise.

Fixed structures, such as those protecting aircraft service offtakes (cabin air, electrical and hydraulic power, fuel lines, etc.) can be substantial and produce both pressure field and wake perturbations in the flow that increase tonal and broadband levels. These can either be in the by-pass or hot core flow, and need to be examined on a case-by-case basis in any particular engine design. Similarly exhaust mixers (introduced to improve the aerodynamic efficiency), bearing support struts, instrumentation sensors, flow straighteners, etc., can all generate sources of turbulence or discontinuity in the flow, and are potential sources, or causes of other sources of noise.

18.2.5 Jet noise

Jet noise is the source of engine noise that has most aggravated the airport noise problem since the late 1950s, and accounted for much research activity over the past 30 years.[16] During this period, nobody has produced a complete engineering 'solution' to the problem, and jet noise reduction has been a process of erosion in the development of each new powerplant. That is, until the introduction of the turbofan really reduced exhaust velocities over earlier engines, and directed an equal degree of research attention at the turbomachine.

The problem with the jet is that, once it is expelled through the final nozzle, it is of little further use in the propulsion process. In fact, it is a distinct embarrassment, causing noise both in the farfield (observer) and nearfield (structural fatigue) regions, and influencing the geometry of the airframe local to the powerplant installation. The only exceptions to the redundancy of the jet plume are where it can be used to augment lift by altering the flow circulation around a wing, or to provide reverse thrust after aircraft landing via impingement on a solid surface. Hence any reduction in the noise from a jet has to be achieved by generally parasitic powerplant features, whether they be mechanical or aerodynamic. However, before consider-

ing jet suppression, it is an advantage to understand the basic sources associated with an exhaust flow.

In gross terms there are only two, one originating in the turbulent mixing process of the jet with the atmosphere, and the other in the shock structure of a supercritical pressure ratio (locally supersonic) jet. These are illustrated in *Figure 18.12* and should be considered separately.

18.2.5.1 Shock-associated noise

This is a characteristic feature of many zero and low by-pass jet engines at full power, where exhaust velocities are in the region of 600–700 m/s and the jet flow is locally supersonic. It radiates almost equally forwards and rearwards of the engine, can be heard well ahead of an aircraft's appearance, and characterizes some powerplants until it is drowned by the jet mixing noise after the aircraft has passed overhead. Audibly it can appear as a harsh 'tearing' noise, and can produce discrete tones locally that are important in structural fatigue considerations. When any convergent circular nozzle is operating at a super-critical pressure ratio, a regular shock structure exists in the jet flow. Early workers[17] identified a feedback mechanism between the shock structure and the nozzle lip to account for the discrete tone source, whilst others[18,19] considered the more broad-band component as a scattering of sound by the interaction of turbulence and the shock structure. These views were subsequently verified by experiment on model jets,[20,21] and a generalized prediction procedure has been defined[11] relating shock intensity and spectral character to the controlling parameters; shock dimensions, flow pressure ratio and temperature.

Since both the discrete and broad-band elements are associated with a regular shock structure, it follows that the destruction of the shock pattern will eliminate the source. This can be accomplished by either using 'mechanical' shock deformation devices, or by close control of the nozzle exit aerodynamics.[22] The problem with shock pattern control, such as with a convergent–divergent nozzle, is that it is normally only really effective at a unique nozzle pressure ratio, and since pressure ratio varies between ground level at take-off (where community noise is important) and high altitude cruise (where performance considerations override) the geometry should vary to satisfy both needs. Geometric variability is not readily accepted, for it introduces additional complexity and control systems.

Fortunately, the conventional 'jet suppressor' (*see* next section) usually provides shock minimization through mechanical means, and where such suppressors are fitted the problem is largely eliminated. With high by-pass ratio powerplants, shock associated noise is not an issue, due to the much lower exhaust velocities.

18.2.5.2 Jet mixing noise

This is the most important source in the exhaust of an engine. At low by-pass ratios it dominates the take-off phase of operation, and can still do so at approach; at high by-pass ratios it is usually significant only during take-off.

The source originates in the turbulent mixing region between the jet and the atmosphere and, in the case of a twin-stream flow, also in the mixing of the hot core and cold by-pass streams. It is heavily dependent upon the shear between the jet and its surrounding environment, and hence (relative) jet velocity. It is broadband in nature, with its frequency spectrum peak being dictated by the dimensions of the jet (nozzle) and the flow Mach number, which also dictates the sound field directivity.

References over the years are voluminous, and range in content from single stream jets,[23–25] through various twin-stream configurations[26,27] to supersonic flows with an 'inverted' velocity profile, where a hot jet surrounds a cold jet.[28] From the point of

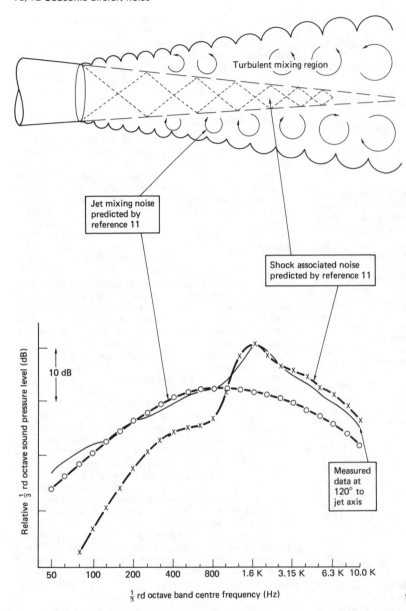

Figure 18.12 Jet mixing and shock noise generation and spectra

view of commercial jet operations, the more normal hot core/cold by-pass flow configuration is now the most important, whereas with pure jets and low by-pass engines the single hot flow condition was afforded the greatest attention and can still be important in the continuing life of older aircraft. The zero/low and high by-pass ratio configurations should be considered separately.

(Mixed) low by-pass or pure jet. Operational exhaust velocities range between 300 and 700 m/s; the lower figure being appropriate to landing and the higher to take-off. At high velocities there may be shock noise present. Over the 300–700 m/s range the acoustic power output varies by over 30 dB, representing a velocity exponent of almost 8 (*Figure 18.13*), and therefore minimization of jet velocity is the most powerful jet noise control tool. This is achieved to a dramatic degree in the change to the high by-pass, or turbofan, engine.

However, with the simplest jet, i.e. that with a single round convergent nozzle, noise control by lowering jet velocity is not normally an available tool, for mission economics dictate the basic engine cycle, and hence jet velocity. Control has to be exercised by secondary means, and the period of the 1950s and 1960s saw an intense effort in this direction. Both engine[29] and airframe manufacturers implemented programmes, and theoretical 'solutions' abounded. Real success was somewhat limited.

Basically, the noise source results from the propagation to the farfield of the pressure fluctuations in the turbulent mixing region between the jet and its surrounding environment.[2,30,31] Small eddies close to the nozzle produce high frequencies, and the larger ones downstream low frequencies. The directivity pattern of the sound field is a function of the eddy convection velocity and the temperature difference between the jet and the atmosphere, but it usually peaks at 30–50 degrees to the jet axis

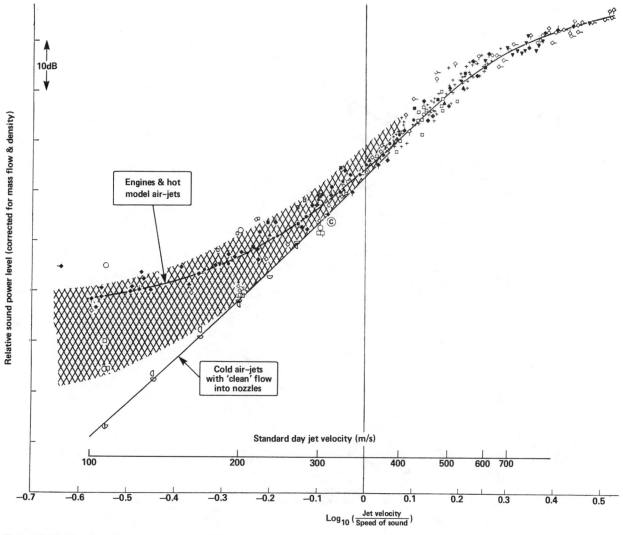

Figure 18.13 Variation of jet mixing noise intensity with jet velocity. Different symbols reflect a wide variety of data sources

(or 130–150 degrees to the flight direction). Temperature appears to have a fundamental influence on spectral character,[32] and is incorporated as a separate function in the most complete published prediction procedure.[11]

Reductions in sound power from the basic level can be achieved only by reducing shear, and hence critical velocities in the mixing process, without altering nozzle pressure ratio. The approach to this has generally been via a subdivision of the jet into smaller elements to 'compact' it and bring it to rest in a shorter distance downstream of the nozzle (*Figure 18.14*). In this way the low-frequency energy is reduced (because the velocity well downstream is much lower) but often the high frequencies are increased (because of an increase in the volume of small-scale turbulence near the nozzle, as nozzle perimeter increases). Fortunately, high frequencies are naturally absorbed by the atmosphere to a greater degree than low frequencies, and at large distances there is a perception of a large decrease in jet noise. It was this principle that led to the chuted, lobed and tubular suppressor nozzles that have been fitted to the B707, DC8, BAC 1-11, F28, etc., over the years.

The degree of suppression achieved with such devices is a function of the efficiency of mixing close to the nozzles, and various attempts at correlating the effects[29] have been published. A simple view, based on nozzle dimensions, is shown in *Figure 18.14* (bottom) for a jet velocity of around 500 m/s. Below this velocity 'suppressors' rapidly lose their effect, and at very low powers and short distances (e.g., on approach to land) they can actually increase perceived noise through the increase of high frequency content.

Additionally, an ejector (*Figure 18.15*), translating to sit just behind the suppressor, can further reduce exit velocities and hence low frequencies and, if treated internally with absorbent lining (*see* Section 18.2.6), can reduce the high frequencies generated close to the nozzle. However, because of their weight, cost, complexity and extra drag, no lined ejector has entered commercial service. One short unlined ejector did on the DC8, but its main function was as a thrust reverser after landing.

Modern turbofan. In the case of the modern turbofan, where there are two major flow streams to be dealt with, the situation

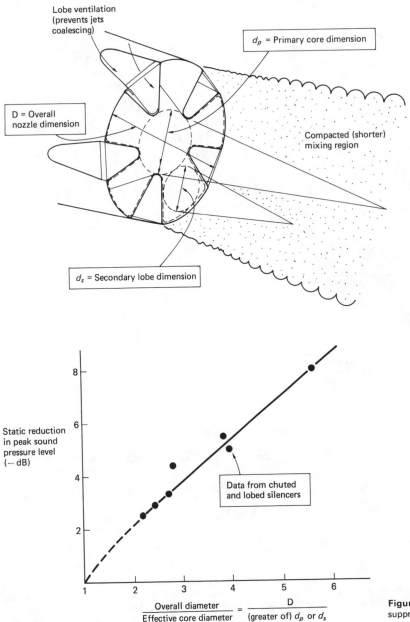

Figure 18.14 Effectiveness of jet suppressors

is much more complex. The mixing pattern (*Figure 18.16*) is composed of various regions, each of which is a noise source in its own right. Initially the fan flow mixes both with the atmosphere and the hot-core jet, and the partially mixed fan and core flows then mix with the atmosphere further downstream. Alternatively, the fan and core flows may be partially or completely mixed within the engine and expelled as a single jet through a single nozzle.

Depending upon the fan/core jet area, temperature and velocity ratios, and nozzle geometry, so the mixing noise energy and spectral character vary. In the case of a fully internally mixed configuration the jet assumes the characteristics of a single uniform flow, and is quieter than most of the unmixed configurations. When unmixed, the spectral shape is different,

often exhibiting separate high- and low-frequency peaks from the major mixing regions close to and downstream of the nozzles respectively.[34] No unique correlation of twin-stream mixing noise has yet emerged, owing to the sensitivity of absolute level to physical details of any particular configuration, but various attempts have been made.[35] Equally, no unique relationship between the noise of a static jet and the same jet under forward speed (flight) conditions has been achieved.

Under forward speed conditions, where it can be argued that a single jet, or fully mixed turbofan jet, will be affected simply by the difference between the absolute jet velocity and the effective environmental flow (i.e. aircraft speed), this is not the case in the more complex twin-stream (unmixed) turbofan flow. Some mixing zones, such as the early regions of fan and core flows, are

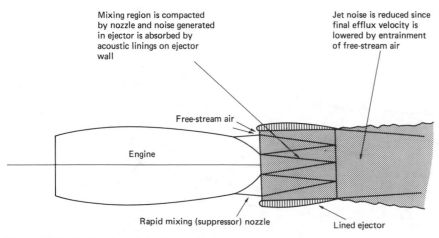

Mixing region is compacted by nozzle and noise generated in ejector is absorbed by acoustic linings on ejector wall

Jet noise is reduced since final efflux velocity is lowered by entrainment of free-stream air

Free-stream air

Engine

Rapid mixing (suppressor) nozzle

Lined ejector

Figure 18.15 Lined ejector philosophy

little affected by the external flow. Moreover, Doppler effects modify the amplitude of the source signal and hence the absolute level, depending on the angle of observation, and also cause progressive frequency changes as the aircraft passes by.

Experimental evidence[36-40] does not universally follow the theory, but it is becoming accepted that the complete effects of flow speed modification need to be accounted for at all angles of propagation in the sound field, from a knowledge of the source structure over the mixing regions, to build a true picture of the situation of a jet in flight. This is not readily available, and for the purposes of prediction more simple published procedures[11,35] can be followed.

18.2.6 Noise control features of aircraft powerplants

18.2.6.1 Sound absorbent linings

From the foregoing sections it is possible to deduce the basic design actions necessary to ensure that engine source noise is kept to a minimum. One general and significant control process, that of utilizing sound absorbent linings, has not been covered.

From airflow entry into the engine, via the inlet duct, through the various air and gas flow ducts upstream of the final nozzle, there is considerable surface area against which internally generated sound waves impinge many times before they radiate to the atmosphere. These duct walls, and other associated large surfaces, have been used to great advantage in the commercial turbofan, and to a lesser degree in lower by-pass ratio engines.

The principle is simple, the implementation less so. If the normally acoustically 'hard' surface of the duct can be made sufficiently 'soft' so as to completely absorb the sound energy incident upon it,[41] then the only internally generated noise that will radiate to the farfield observer will be that unimpeded by a solid surface (*Figure 18.17*). Since most of the propagating wavefronts strike a solid surface at least once, and many on several occasions, before radiating through the inlet or nozzle system, it follows that sound-absorbent linings on these surfaces represent a powerful noise control tool, and the modern engine contains as much as 20 m² of such lining.

These linings are constructed to take benefit from resistive damping in the facesheet (*Figure 18.18*). They consist of a 'porous' facesheet suspended from the engine duct wall by a cellular (typically honeycomb) spacing medium. As the sound waves impinge on the facesheet the resistance to fluctuating velocity exerted by the pores of the facesheet provides a degree of sound absorption by conversion to heat energy. The acoustic velocity through the facing sheet will be a maximum when the

separation between the facing and backing sheets is 1/4, 3/4, 5/4, *et seq.* wavelengths. The most effective broadband absorber comprises a cellular or fibrous interlinked structure, but these 'bulk' absorbers have not been used as yet in engines owing to their propensity for fluid absorption and retention, which degrades their performance and renders them a hazard through icing damage and fuel and oil retention.

The more common liners are simple perforate (metal or composite material) facesheets with an intermediate supporting medium. Some are in service with a woven fibrous facesheet bonded to a perforate to give broader bandwidth attenuation with rigidity. Developments are being made in the field of multi-layer structures, to try to attain the widest possible bandwidth and maximum absorption effects. Even the simplest perforate type is extremely effective, more so in the by-pass duct than elsewhere because of the multi-reflection path of the sound waves, and here they account for a general reduction of around 10 dB on all internally generated sources above 1 kHz.

In detail, their performance is a function of several leading parameters,[43,44] including facesheet hole size and number (porosity)/resistance to flow, cavity dimensions and local environmental effects such as duct width, airflow Mach number, incident wave angle, etc. (*Figure 18.19*). They are normally tuned to suppress dominant features of the engine spectrum, and may vary in type through the engine ducting as source character changes. Structural reliability is of vital importance, and therefore it is usually necessary to ensure drainage of each individual cell to prevent freeze–thaw damage and fuel/oil retention.

18.2.6.2 Low by-pass ratio powerplants

Owing to the dominance of the jet noise source on the early single-stream and low by-pass ratio powerplants, noise control was concentrated on this feature. However, the advances made with the introduction of the high by-pass ratio powerplant has led to a broader base of noise control knowledge which can be applied to lower by-pass ratios. By reference to *Figure 18.20*, the essential actions can be described as follows: the inlet, which in a low by-pass powerplant (LP) usually has a favourable length/diameter ratio, is a prime candidate for acoustic treatment to control landing approach noise. Other sources dominate at the higher powers required during take-off.

Nevertheless, the early stages of the LP compressor are important, and the effect of linings in the inlet can be augmented by attention to the design of the compressor. At low engine

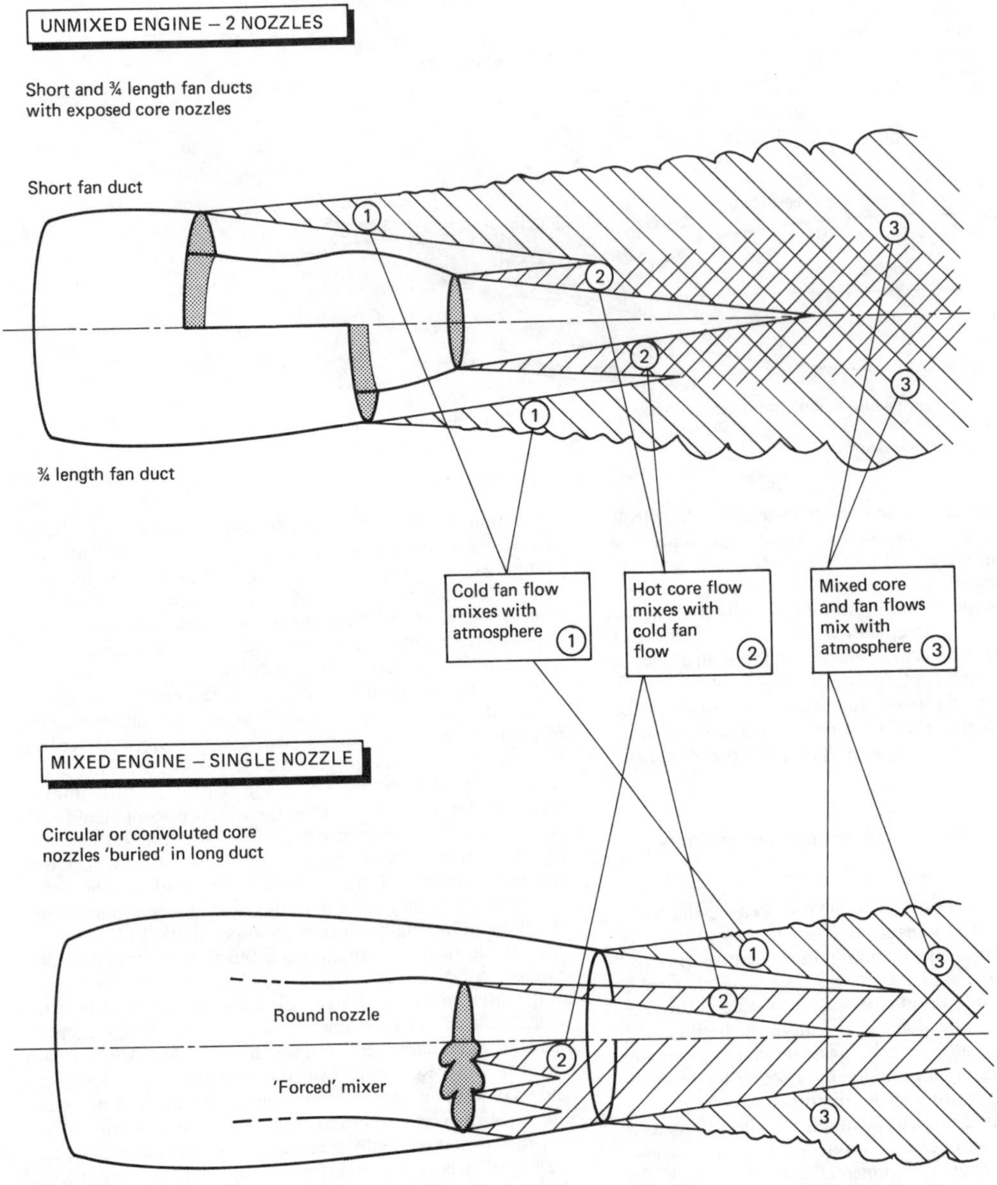

UNMIXED ENGINE – 2 NOZZLES

Short and ¾ length fan ducts
with exposed core nozzles

Short fan duct

¾ length fan duct

Cold fan flow
mixes with
atmosphere ①

Hot core flow
mixes with
cold fan
flow ②

Mixed core
and fan flows
mix with
atmosphere ③

MIXED ENGINE – SINGLE NOZZLE

Circular or convoluted core
nozzles 'buried' in long duct

Round nozzle

'Forced' mixer

Figure 18.16 Turbofan exhaust configurations and their effect on
jet mixing patterns

speeds most of the sound energy generated in the early stages of
compression propagates forwards, but as air velocity in the inlet
increases with engine speed the energy becomes convected
rearwards, and the by-pass duct may also be an area for the
inclusion of absorbent linings. The high-pressure compressor
section of the core engine is not a relevant noise source, but the
latter stages of the turbine are. Basic design action in the turbine
can be augmented by the use of linings in the jetpipe. Prior to the
jetpipe, a forced mixer—rapidly mixing the hot core and bypass
flows—can be beneficial in both performance and in noise
terms. The turbulence induced by the mixer can 'smear' prominent tones originating both in the LP compressor and in the
turbine, and the lowering of mean exhaust velocity will reduce
jet noise.

Depending upon the precise design cycle of the engine,
additional jet noise reduction can be obtained by using a jet
suppressor nozzle. Generally, however, if the jet velocity at
maximum power is less than 500 m/s there is little benefit from
such a nozzle, and it can even be a disbenefit at low powers by
virtue of its augmentation of higher frequencies, which are not
absorbed in the short transmission path from source to observer
on approach to land.

The low by-pass ratio cycle is no longer efficient for general
subsonic transport applications. Nevertheless, it is essential for
very high speed flight (supersonic applications) and often for
high-altitude special-purpose applications (e.g., business jets).
Equally, well-developed low by-pass engines are often an economically preferred alternative to expensive new designs, and they

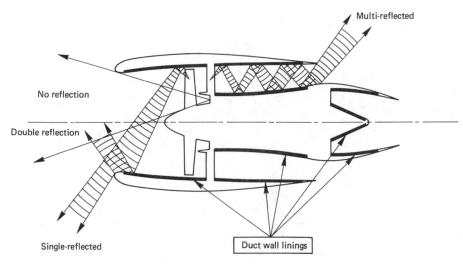

Figure 18.17 Opportunities for noise reduction by sound absorbent lining

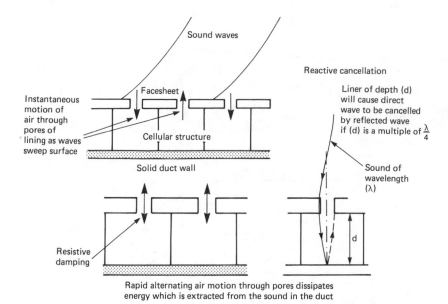

Figure 18.18 Sound absorbent lining mechanisms

have not disappeared completely from the air transport scene. Consequently, the control actions summarized above may still be relevant, and in general will account for a lowering of perceived noise of the order of 3–5 dB.

18.2.6.3 High by-pass ratio powerplants

Since these types of powerplants are now the dominant feature of the manufacturers' production lines, their noise control is of prime concern. Details of such control action are available from earlier sections and the referenced literature. The overall noise control features are summarized in *Figure 18.21*.

For a conventional installation, that having a twin-stream exhaust system, it is necessary to balance noise control action between the engine design and the nacelle treatment. For

example, close adherence to basic design rules in the fan and early stages of core compressor can minimize the amount of noise-absorbent lining necessary in the intake and the by-pass exhaust duct, and hence overall powerplant length. Likewise, design of the turbine can affect both the length and the degree of absorption necessary in the core exhaust duct. The area, velocity and temperature ratios between the core and by-pass jet streams will affect the generation of jet mixing noise.

Beyond these normal control features, it is possible to specify a standard of powerplant and engine which will be some 3–5 dB quieter still, but there is an economic impact (*see* Section 18.2.6). Basic control in the fan section may require a longer installation to allow larger spacings between rotating and stationary components, and the intake may be required to be longer to accommodate a larger area of absorbent lining. For fan noise propagating

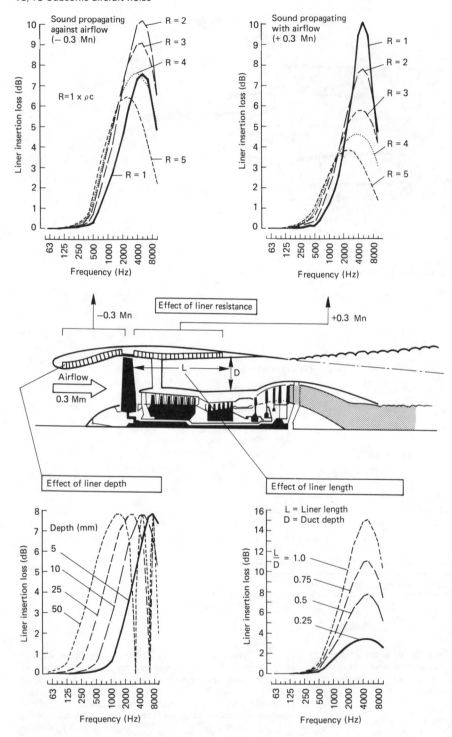

Figure 18.19 Factors influencing liner effectiveness

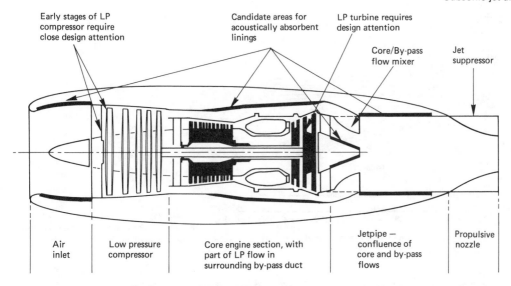

Figure 18.20 Noise control in low by-pass ratio powerplants

rearwards it may be necessary to lengthen the by-pass duct, which could be done in conjunction with conscious mixing of the core and by-pass air flows to promote lower jet velocities, and hence lower jet noise. In this type of installation there is greater opportunity for lining to suppress turbine noise and low-frequency combustor noise. The low frequencies associated with combustion need deeper lining sections, which could be of a double layer construction.

Overall, the multitude of control features in a high by-pass installation will allow for reductions of between 10 and 20 dB compared with the uncontrolled situation.

18.2.6.4 General installation effects

The details of the installation of a powerplant on to an airframe have an important bearing on the overall level of noise perceived by the observer. Two important effects which have to be considered by the aircraft manufacturer relate to the interfer-

ence effects between the exhaust flow and the wing or tailplane structure of the airframe (*Figure 18.22*).[45]

Close to a wing surface there is a jet/surface interaction which can augment low frequency noise by as much as 10 dB. Although this augmentation is frequently below the lower frequency cut-off boundary of the audible range, it does give rise to problems associated with building excitation. Similarly, when the high lift devices at the trailing edge of the wing are deployed there can be a jet/flap interaction of a similar magnitude, but this time within the audible range. It is necessary to optimize the position of the engine on the wing to avoid these effects, which can be as large as the effect of installing an additional engine.

Other effects, some detrimental and some beneficial, can also be important in the overall design. Structural scattering, shielding and reflection, and the propagation of sources through wing tip vortices will all modify the basic engine noise signature when the powerplant is integrated into the aircraft. Many of these effects have not been fully understood or quantified, but they

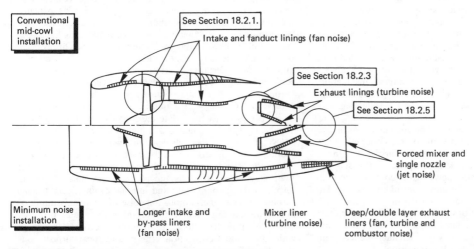

Figure 18.21 Noise control in high by-pass ratio powerplants

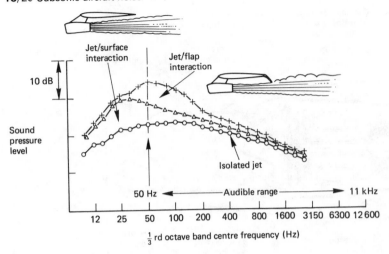

Figure 18.22 Common installation effects (Crown Copyright Reserved/RAE figure.)

will become of increasing importance as the basic powerplant becomes increasingly quieter.

The degree of noise control exercised on a powerplant is always a compromise between the levels of performance and efficiency and the operational needs, or noise requirements, at particular airports.

Basic design action in the turbomachinery areas can add length, weight, cost and degrade performance.[46] The use of acoustically absorbent material will clearly add weight to a powerplant, and depending upon the nacelle definition add length. Choice of the basic engine cycle, is, perhaps, of greatest significance. However, it is often misleadingly assumed that higher by-pass ratios (or more precisely, lower specific thrusts) provide an immediate noise benefit. In fact, higher by-pass ratios imply larger turbomachinery diameters, and this can be a disbenefit in that it becomes increasingly difficult to make the liners, particularly in the inlet, of optimum efficiency. In fact, the selection of engine cycle is a delicate balance between performance and noise requirements.

The choice of engine cycle is usually dictated by the cruise condition, whilst it is low altitude take-off and approach conditions that are vital to noise. The take-off and approach conditions produce a different balance between the internally and externally generated sources (*Figure 18.23* top) whilst the installed efficiency (primarily fuel consumption) produces a different optimum design point. As shown at the bottom of *Figure 18.23*, in going from a 'bare' engine to an aircraft installation there are the effects of power and air offtakes to provide aircraft services, bypass and intake duct losses, overall nacelle drag, and nacelle–airframe interference to be taken into account. The selection of bypass ratio between the competing demands of low and high power noise requirements, and overall cruise efficiency considerations, is fundamental to the overall aircraft design.

It is not possible to provide detailed advice on this subject, but it is true to say that most powerplants contain a weight increment of some 5% or 8% for noise control purposes, and a performance loss which can lead to increases of 3% or so in fuel consumption. The modifications to the engine and powerplant can account for between 10% and 15% of the factory cost, and if increased suppression is necessary the incremental effects can double with every increased 2–3 dB suppression.

18.3 Propeller aircraft noise

The first practical interest in propeller noise probably dates back to World War I, with the feasibility of acoustic detection of aircraft. In 1918, Lanchester showed that he appreciated the mechanism of propeller noise radiation in physical terms. Moreover, he then suggested that a combination of high propulsive thrust and low blade-tip speed (hence low noise) could be achieved by geared propellers operating at high advance ratios, with a relative tip speed only 1.4 times the flight airspeed—a good forecast for the future! The earliest theoretical and experimental research seems to have been published in England and Germany about 1920, relating to the farfield noise of the fixed-pitch propellers. By 1940, the basic groundwork for the prediction of the 'blade-loading' (dipole) and 'blade-thickness' (quasi-monopole) components of the tonal noise had been laid,[47,48] and the importance of broad-band noise recognized. Practical work received American impetus during World War II, directed at improved communications inside long-range bomber aircraft. Both theoretical and experimental research on farfield and nearfield noise then continued apace with propeller aircraft development for about 20 years.[49,50]

Most aeroacoustic research from 1960 to 1975 concentrated on turbojet and turbo-fan engine aircraft. More recently there has been a renewal of interest in efficient propellers.[51,52] Already, for the operation of small short-haul transports, radical advances in wing aerodynamics and in new materials have been successfully applied to the production of light-weight propeller blades of greater propulsive efficiency. With the objective of attaining propeller aircraft cruise speeds competitive with subsonic turbo-fan aircraft, and with better fuel efficiency, the novel 'Propfan' concept combines ideas from modern propeller and turbo-fan technology in a multi-bladed open-disc, with thin swept blades to accommodate the supersonic helical tip Mach numbers ($M_h > 1$) encountered in high-speed cruise.

Overall, the interplay between noise, performance, safety and economics remain strong and complex, as illustrated simply by *Figure 18.24*. For modern turbo-prop aircraft, the propeller itself may be regarded as the predominant noise source in respect of both community and internal-cabin effects, though turbine-engine whine, combustion noise, and transmission/gearbox vibration can become important with quieter propeller installations. Farfield noise requirements are those associated with the Noise Certification criteria and local airport constraints, while nearfield noise requirements are associated with

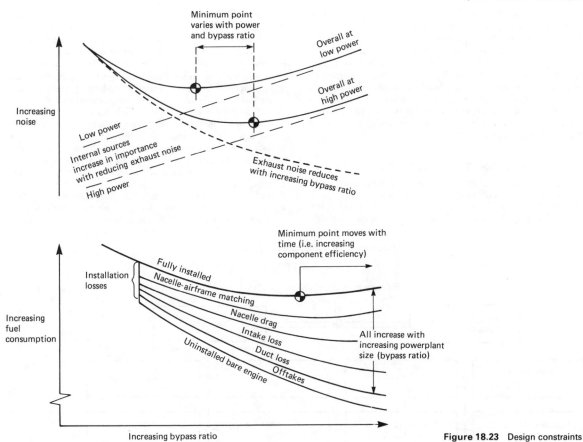

Figure **18.23** Design constraints

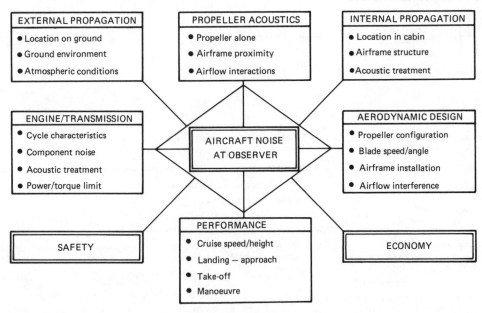

Figure 18.24 Factors influencing the noise of propeller aircraft

providing acceptable cabin-noise levels. To a ground observer, the noise level may peak sometimes just before or even just after the propeller aircraft passes directly overhead. The propeller sound pressure levels measured at the fuselage external surface tend to peak around the plane of the propeller disc, with levels dropping rapidly immediately ahead and behind, then dropping more gradually further away. Internal cabin noise presents further complexities, involving noise propagation and possible amplification/attenuation considerations relating to structure-borne as well as airborne paths, while particular strong tones may aggravate subjective response.

18.3.1 Source and spectrum characteristics

The acoustic emission of propulsive propellers tends not only to grow in intensity I with increases in rotational drive-power P and helical tip-speed V_h, (e.g. $I \propto P \times V_h^3$ as a crude estimate) but also to change in character as the several contributory elements

vary in magnitude. *Figure 18.25* illustrates the various factors that can give rise both to impulsive and to tonal character noises as well as broad-band sources. The spectral characteristics of different aeroplanes or helicopters can be very distinctive, partly because of large differences in blade rotational frequency and size, even while retaining similar tip-speeds. Additionally, the integral acoustic signal reaching the far-field on the ground is dependent on the propagation path characteristics between the aircraft and the observer. *Figure 18.26* illustrates the effect of aircraft relative motion on the propagation path characteristics. In the case of the observer on the ground, Doppler frequency shifts, either upwards or downwards, also influence the spectral character as the aircraft is approaching or receding, while near-field and fuselage-transmission considerations apply in respect of internal cabin noise.

With a well-built isolated propeller under axial airstream flow conditions, sample *time-histories* of the nearfield acoustic pressure exhibit little variation in signal shape as each of the blades

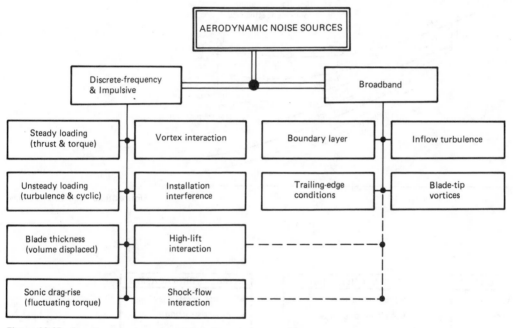

Figure 18.25 Propeller and rotor aerodynamic noise sources

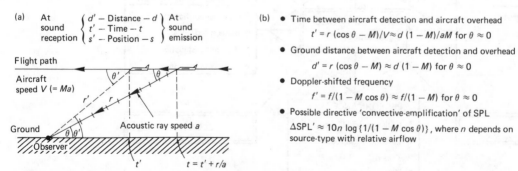

(a) At sound reception $\begin{cases} d' - \text{Distance} - d \\ t' - \text{Time} - t \\ s' - \text{Position} - s \end{cases}$ At sound emission

Flight path

Aircraft speed V (= Ma)

Ground

Observer

Acoustic ray speed a

t'　　$t = t' + r/a$

(b)
- Time between aircraft detection and aircraft overhead
  $$t' = r\,(\cos\theta - M)/V \approx d\,(1 - M)/aM \text{ for } \theta \approx 0$$
- Ground distance between aircraft detection and overhead
  $$d' = r\,(\cos\theta - M) \approx d\,(1 - M) \text{ for } \theta \approx 0$$
- Doppler-shifted frequency
  $$f' = f/(1 - M\cos\theta) \approx f/(1 - M) \text{ for } \theta \approx 0$$
- Possible directive 'convective-amplification' of SPL
  $$\Delta \text{SPL}' \approx 10n\,\log\{1/(1 - M\cos\theta)\}, \text{ where } n \text{ depends on}$$
  source-type with relative airflow

Figure 18.26 Kinematic effects of aircraft motion relative to an observer on the ground. (*a*) Sound emission and reception conditions. (*b*) Changes at observer due to aircraft relative motion

passes the receiver. *Figure 18.27* shows the pressure time histories of a model propeller operating in a wind tunnel. The pressure response at low rotational speeds ($M_h \approx 0.4$) appears to be basically sinusoidal, but the leading-edge of the response curve steepens up as the rotational speed is increased. At high rotational speeds ($M_h \approx 0.8$), there can be a very narrow peak in the response curve, suggesting the possibility of incipient shock formation on the blade surface.

Noise frequency spectra of propeller noise are usually determined in one-third octave frequency bands although narrow, constant percentage bandwidth spectra are sometimes used where a more detailed scientific analysis is required. *Figures 18.28* and *18.29* illustrate both types of spectra for similar propellers tested in a wind-tunnel.

The spectral characteristics can be subdivided according to whether they are 'rotational' type, i.e. comprising both discrete frequency and impulsive elements, or 'broad-band' type which does not correlate directly with the rotational frequency. Normally, the highest value of tonal SPL occurs at the fundamental

blade-passing frequency ($1 \times$ BPF), with other significant tones at harmonics of that frequency ($q \times$ BPF). The SPL of the fundamental tone rises significantly with increases in blade-tip Mach number M_h and in blade-angle β. There are usually complementary rises in the levels and number of the measurable harmonic tones, and corresponding growth in the broad-band (non-periodic) noise levels for moderate to large blade settings.

18.3.1.1 Discrete-frequency components

These can be correlated with contributions from the following blade aerodynamic conditions:

1. Steady loadings on each blade element, from time-averaging torque and thrust distributions, while allowing for changes in the direction of blade-section motion relative to the sound receiver, as the propeller rotates.
2. Unsteady loadings allowing for any periodic changes, from non-uniform inflow fields associated with installation and

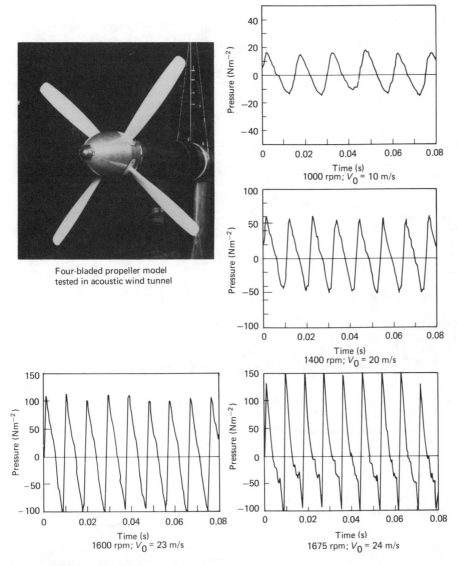

Four-bladed propeller model
tested in acoustic wind tunnel

Figure 18.27 Propeller pressure—time histories: near-field

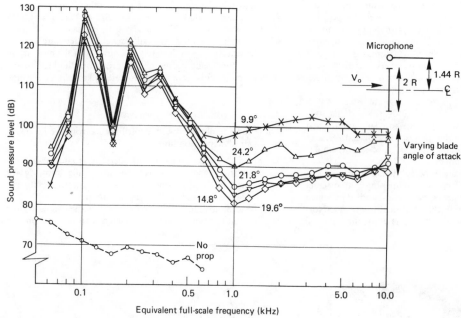

Tunnel wind speed V_0 = 30 m/s; 6400 rev/min; microphone in disc plane

Figure 18.28 One-third octave spectra for $\frac{1}{4}$ scale propeller tested in a wind-tunnel

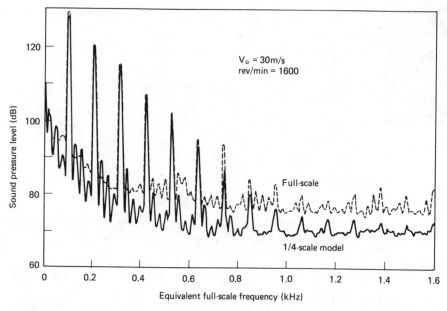

Figure 18.29 Narrowband spectra for $\frac{1}{4}$ and full-scale propellers tested in wind-tunnels

environmental effects, or multi-cyclic pitch control during propeller rotation.

3. Blade-tip thickness influence, producing air-volume displacement effects in rotation, becoming increasingly significant as the blade helical tip Mach number is increased.

4. Blade sonic-flow drag-rise conditions at high rotational tip

speeds and/or high flight speeds, leading to excess loadings (steady and unsteady). *See also Figure 18.25.*

Additional contributions to tone levels can be caused by blade–vortex interactions, airframe installation interference, and blade high-lift or shock–flow interactions. Such effects may appear in the time-domain as sharply *impulsive* signals, especially important and discussed later in relation to helicopter noise. Non-linear aspects in acoustic propagation can further complicate theoretical treatments, particularly where transonic or supersonic blade-tip airflows are present.

18.3.1.2 Broad-band noise

This arises from periodic random pressure fluctuations over a wide frequency range, usually exhibiting a broad peak of sound intensity about a frequency of the order of 10 times the blade-passing-frequency. Fundamentally, broadband noise is associated with turbulent inflow, boundary-layer flows, trailing-edge conditions, or vortex interaction. Theoretical treatments are not well substantiated quantitatively, so practical prediction methods are usually based on empirical derivation of primary one-third octave spectrum features.

Both discrete-frequency and broadband noise components can be affected significantly by kinematic effects (Doppler shift and convective amplification) which are caused essentially by motion of the aircraft noise source relative to a ground observer. These should not be confused with the modified aerodynamic effects which arise from the interaction of the relative mainstream flow past the aircraft during flight through the atmosphere, as well as from propeller rotation.

18.3.2 Empirical parametric analysis

18.3.2.1 Discrete frequency noise

Empirical parametric relations, correlating noise with the propeller geometry and operating conditions, can provide clarification of windtunnel and flight experiments.[53] For example, the near-field sound-pressure-level SPL_1 at the fundamental blade-passing-frequency correlates well at full-scale and $\frac{1}{5}$-scale for two existing four-bladed propellers, and for a full-scale five-bladed propeller, in terms of the aerodynamic power coefficients C_p and of the blade helical tip Mach number M_h. $C_p = \text{Power}/\rho n^3 D_p^5$ where D_p is the propeller disc diameter. An adjustment to allow for the effects of aircraft Mach number M_n is also needed, giving:

$$(L_p)_1 = K + 10 \log_{10}(M_h^8 C_p^2) - 40 M_n \text{dB} \qquad (18.1)$$

where K is a constant for each propeller and noise receiver position, taking a value of about 160 dB for a measurement location in the propeller disc plane at a distance $0.7\,D_p$ from the propeller axis, with an expected reduction of about 6 dB per doubling of distance—omitting atmospheric attenuation.

This illustrates the *significance of C_p and M_h*, and confirms the anticipated reduction in noise level with increasing mainstream speed away from near static conditions. Additionally, the fall-off in the noise level SPL_q of the qth harmonic (frequency $q \times$ BPF) below that of the fundamental tone correlates reasonably, for both full scale and model scale, in the form:

$$(L_p)_q = (L_p)_1 - k(q-1)(0.95 - M_h)\text{dB} \qquad (18.2)$$

where k is a constant for each propeller, taking a value of about 25.

Empirical analysis implies that the different blade shapes have had little effect on the tonal strength for a prescribed aerodynamic performance. In contrast, the much superior aerodynamic 'lift-performance' of modern blade-sections at high speeds allows substantial increase in blade-loading, and thereby decrease of total blade area, relative to conventional sections, for a prescribed propeller performance. Other meaningful correlations of tone noise levels can usefully be attempted in terms of the estimated aerodynamic blade incidence at a convenient reference blade-section (e.g. 0.85 degrees at 85% radius), again

in combination with M_h and with allowance for aircraft Mach number, M_n.

As regards *blade-tip geometry effects*, some simple changes have not led to the envisaged reductions in blade noise levels for a given thrust. These include a five-bladed propeller with the standard tips bent through 90 degrees in the direction of rotation, and a 'Spear-tip' version of a four-bladed propeller with a substantial change in the spanwise distribution of blade-chord and some reduction in blade thickness. This implies that more sophisticated theoretical and experimental models need investigation, as discussed later, in connection with the design of propfan blades.

By increasing the *blade number B*, and retaining the same propeller diameter the solidity of the propeller disc is increased and appreciable reductions in the SPL_1 of the fundamental tone occur for a prescribed propeller power coefficient, Cp and M_h. This benefit is often accompanied by reductions in the number of significant tone harmonics but also in aerodynamic efficiency. Again, model experiments carried out with blade numbers ranging from 3 to 8 have correlated well with full-scale systems.

Naturally, the tone frequencies for the multi-blade propeller rise in proportion to B. This can lead to increases in the far-field frequency spectra at frequencies that subjectively are more annoying, i.e. generally in the 800 Hz to 2 kHz region.

18.3.2.2 Broad-band noise

For practical purposes, broadband noise treatment has largely relied on empirical parametric correlation of far-field propeller noise data. Typically,[54] the spectrum frequency f_b (Hz) corresponding to the broadband peak SPL value of the one-third octave spectrum is derived from a prescribed empirical value for the peak Strouhal number (say 0.28), which is defined as the product of f_b and the blade-section thickness t, divided by the blade-section helical speed V_h at 70% radial distance from the propeller axis. The corresponding peak value for the sound-pressure-level of broad-band noise SPL_b (peak) is expressed algebraically in terms of the sound-ray angle to the axis of the propeller (i.e. a directionality factor), the rotational tip Mach number M_h, the propeller thrust T, the propeller disc or blade areas, and the receiver distance from the disc centre. The broad-band noise spectrum is then completed by the incorporation of a prescribed empirical one-third-octave 'hump' shape about the peak. Unfortunately, past predictions of broad-band noise by this method[53] have been of the order of 10 dB higher than measured values, while the applicability of such analysis in the near-field has not been demonstrated.

18.3.2.3 Overall parametric-graphical prediction methods

Overall noise-level predictions by 'partial-level' summation techniques, employing parametric graphical procedures, are often quoted for rapid practical estimates by Industry. Reference 55 provides estimates of OASPL values, tone-SPL levels and subjectively weighted metrics; reference 56 provides practical estimates for SPL levels of the first ten harmonics at low flight speeds.

18.3.3 Theoretical prediction considerations

18.3.3.1 General background

To ensure reliable clarification of primary noise sources and to predict logically the character of noise variations with changes in propeller running conditions or in propeller geometry, well-defined theoretical frameworks can be employed. Current theoretical prediction frameworks for discrete-frequency noise comprise components generated by rotational blade steady-loading (thrust and torque), by rotational blade-thickness (displaced air-volume), and by blade unsteady-loading (inflow non-uniformities or aerodynamic incidence variation). Non-linear noise, relevant to local transonic flows, can be neglected as insignificant for straight-bladed propellers operating normally at helical tip Mach numbers M_h below 0.85. The non-discrete 'broad-band' noise components from viscous flow effects become significant at the higher frequencies ($>4 \times$ BPF), but in practice still have to be estimated largely from empirical formulae,[54] since more reliable theoretical aerodynamic inputs need to be established, particularly as regards inflow turbulence effects.[57] Finally, propeller axis inclination to the mainstream and airframe installation interference can affect the noise characteristics through changes in the installed propeller aerodynamics and local acoustic propagation conditions. Those various components will now be treated in turn.

18.3.3.2 Steady-loading and thickness noise

Early nearfield prediction methods for discrete-frequency noise produced by rotational steady blade loading expanded the classical Gutin theory to cover forward flight,[58] involving spanwise integration of blade loading effects to evaluate the tone SPL values (BPF and harmonics) at typical fuselage-side positions. The significance of blade-thickness noise contributions, even at moderate subsonic tip-speeds ($M_h > 0.7$), was soon appreciated. The 'FW-H' acoustic analogy,[59] with the quadrupole terms ignored,[60] effectively provides a relation for the time-dependent acoustic pressure produced at a spatial location by a propeller blade source element, comprising a linear sum of pressure contributions generating steady-loading and thickness noise.

Joint predictions of steady-loading and thickness noise may now be based on developments of a subsonic time-domain calculation procedure and allied computer program.[61] A Fourier analysis of the calculated time-dependent signal is performed, to evaluate the noise spectrum values (SPL_q) at the blade-passing frequency and its harmonics. The input data requires a blade-planform mesh definition, the blade geometry, the radial distribution of thrust and torque loadings, and the chordwise distribution of pressure loading. Alternatively, a much simplified spectrum calculation procedure, directly in the frequency domain,[60] is available for propeller applications even at typical nearfield (fuselage) locations,[62] though not providing signal-phase differences. Much more sophisticated theoretical methods exist for both time-domain and frequency-domain calculations with high-speed propellers, particularly those discussed later for propfans.[63-66]

Practical nearfield predictions for isolated subsonic propellers in axial flow imply that the fundamental tone, and usually the second harmonic, are dominated by the steady-loading contribution. This is illustrated in *Figure 18.30*. As harmonic number increases, the thickness contribution becomes increasingly dominant (except at low M_h). Overall, the predicted tone levels at low harmonic number appear to agree reasonably well with measured values, but at higher frequencies parasitic noise sources or inflow interference effects become important. Poor correlation with theory can arise from negative values of the blade lift coefficient C_L, very high values of blade C_L or stalling, aeroelastic modifications of the blade twist distribution, and unknown centrifugal effects.

Early farfield prediction methods for discrete frequency steady-loading noise[54,58] mostly assumed a point-loading approximation (e.g. at 80% radius) to avoid spanwise integration complexities in addition to the absence of nearfield terms. Thereby, the datum sound pressure level (SPL_{qs}) of the resulting steady-loading tone for each qth harmonic of the BPF ($f_q = q$ BN/60) can be expressed algebraically in terms of the following parameters, at unit normalized radial distance:

B the number of blades, N the rev-min; O the acoustic ray angle; M_t the rotational tip Mach number; M_0 the flight

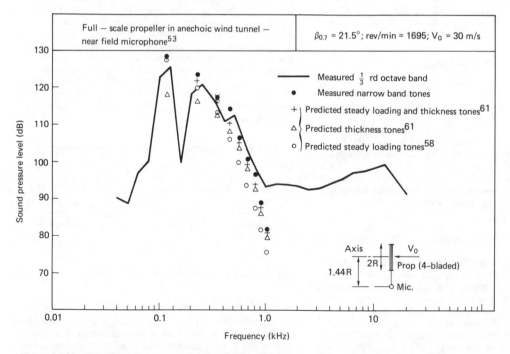

Figure 18.30 Comparison between predicted and measured propeller tones—nearfield[53]

airspeed Mach number; T the propeller thrust; P the aerodynamic power; and D_p the diameter.

Predictions of both steady-loading and thickness noise contributions in the *farfield* can now employ the more recent methods[51,52]—as outlined already for nearfield prediction. Again, the relative magnitudes of these two contributions to the farfield noise levels of an isolated propeller in axial flow also change with harmonic number, in much the same way as discussed for the nearfield (*Figure 18.31*). But, at the higher frequencies, broad-band and unsteady-loading contributions can predominate.

unsteady-loading tone level SPL_{qu}; causing as much as 15 dB reduction for 50 m/s airspeed.[54] The provision of a reliable unsteady-loading input for the estimation of such noise contributions thus still remains of practical concern, particularly with the quieter propeller-design requirements and with subjective-weighting factors taken into account. Usually, unsteady-loading effects have been considered only in relation to farfield noise, as in *Figure 18.31*.

18.3.4 Noise reduction and installation effects

Reduction of propeller noise at source can be achieved by

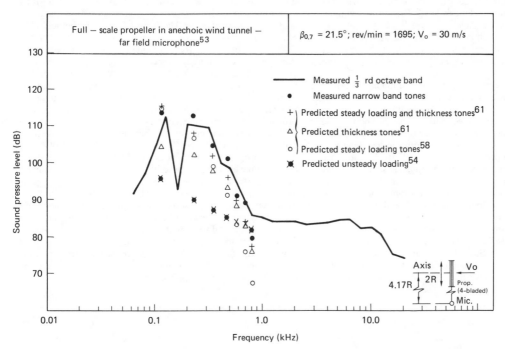

Figure 18.31 Comparison between predicted and measured propeller tones—farfield[53]

Unsteady-loading noise

The unsteady-loading contribution to rotational noise in the farfield can be predicted assuming a point loading, effective at 80% radius; but now with load fluctuations from the average steady load L_0, comprised of rotational components of amplitude L_n for each nth harmonic of the rotational frequency. These random-phased unsteady-loading harmonics are assumed to have amplitudes proportional to L_0 and decaying as n^{-k} so that:

$$L_n = C\, L_0\, n^{-k} \text{ for integral } n > 1, \text{ with C and k prescribed constants.}$$

Then the datum sound pressure level SPL_{qu} of the unsteady-loading tone at each harmonic frequency $(q \times BPF)$ can be expressed again algebraically in terms of the further parameters M, B, O, D_p, T and P, but several unsteady-loading harmonics can contribute to one sound harmonic. Empirical values for C and k have been quoted from correlation of propeller test data under zero forward speed conditions. However, to allow for reduction of propeller inflow-turbulence levels and hence of unsteady loading as flight airspeed is increased, substantial corrections need to be applied to the static prediction for each

minimizing the blade helical tip speed, though the total blade area will need to be increased to maintain propeller thrust for a given standard of blade aerodynamic design. Complementary methods of reducing source noise can include increases in blade number, greater uniformity of blade loading distribution spanwise and chordwise, off-loading the blade tips, reduction of blade tip volume (thickness and chord), and incorporation of blade sweep (as discussed in Section 18.3.5). Such changes have to be compatible and consistent with the particular propeller performance demands, and may compromise weight or aerodynamic efficiency.

The shape and size of a well-designed streamlined-nacelle and spinner are unlikely to have much effect on the free-field acoustic characteristics of an isolated propeller except at high flight Mach numbers. Non-uniform and asymmetric inflows can be important, such as those caused by propeller axis inclination to the mainstream (aircraft incidence) and wing/fuselage mounting interference, or by spurious turbulence and wakes (natural or propeller generated). Moreover, for pusher propeller configurations, the asymmetric flow over the upstream wing and inclined nacelle could further aggravate noise generation.

Propeller-axis inclination upwards from the flight-path direction, associated with the demand for aircraft lift, leads to effective increases in the relative airspeed and aerodynamic incidence of the downgoing blade ('advancing' upstream), along with corresponding decreases for the upgoing 'retreating' blade. Circumferential differences of maximum and minimum loading, on the downgoing and upgoing blades respectively, cause increases or decreases of loading noise accompanied by some local focusing effects. At high M_h and M_n, the then predominant blade-thickness noise component may also be affected by the relative airspeed changes associated with axis incidence. Experiments have shown that, even though 10 degrees inclination of an isolated propeller may cause only some 2 dB rise in the SPL of the first three harmonics measured on the downgoing side, up to 5 dB or even 10 dB rise has occurred in the higher harmonics where the SPL values were relatively low.[53] Theoretical estimates of the noise effects of such propeller-axis inclination, or of other interference, may be attempted by assigning an appropriate upwash influence to the propeller inflow, which then yields the cyclic aerodynamic changes in blade relative airspeed and incidence.[61,62]

For wing-mounted tractor propellers, inclination effects can be aggravated by the accelerated flow upwash over the neighbouring wing nose, arising from wing-lift generation (incidence or lift-flaps) and fuselage blockage, with differing conditions in low-wing or high-wing installations. For twin-engined aircraft, beneficial noise-reduction effects can result from installing propellers rotating in opposite directions, so that all blades are travelling upwards when closest to the fuselage side. From the cabin noise standpoint, benefits can result from a low-wing installation, because the propeller noise propagation may be shielded by the cabin floor, freight-hold and possibly the substantial wing-root area.

Apart from additional broadband noise, extraneous *noise from non-propeller sources* could be caused by the fuselage boundary-layer, wing-fuselage flow distortion, and the power plants. Although these may not influence the measured SPL values at the BPF and lower harmonics of the propeller, they can affect the apparent, i.e. measured, values of broad-band noise or promote spurious peaks at high frequencies (*Figure 18.32*). Present empirical estimates of broad-band noise at higher frequencies have proved much too large under take-off power conditions, while theoretical estimates[57] in terms of trailing-edge noise alone are inadequate.

Propagation of aircraft propeller noise can be influenced by airframe reflection or shielding and by airframe flow-field refraction or scattering. But with large diameter propellers, the far-field effects should be less significant than those encountered previously with compact jet engines. *See* Section 18.2.5.

The concept of a coaxial pair of contra-rotating propellers, matched to minimize wake swirl losses, can provide high thrust with lower tip speeds and smaller diameters than required by single-rotating propellers. The British Fairey Gannet and H.S. Shackleton are well-tried successful examples,[68] along with the Russian Tupolev Bear. Renewed interest has arisen because of the potential reductions in tip speeds and thereby in noise levels. However the aerodynamic interaction between a coaxial pair of propellers, whether contra-rotating or not, can introduce non-uniform and turbulent inflow effects, which in turn can aggravate blade-noise generation. The foundations of contra-rotating propeller noise analysis were laid as early as 1948, with the recognition of the major interference mechanisms. The analytical results have been recently reproduced and extended[69] using modern propeller theories, additionally exploring some of the aerodynamic interference issues that could not be treated analytically nearly 40 years ago. Complementary acoustic experiments on the Fairey Gannet in the USA[70] and the UK, and also on model-scale propellers in acoustic windtunnels,[71] imply that the aerodynamic interaction effects between the two adjacent blade rows can lead to noise increases as high as 10 dB from the fourth harmonic of the blade-passing frequency ($4 \times$ BPF) onwards. But far more detailed aeroacoustic studies are necessary, before practical predictions and assessments can be guaranteed for new aircraft applications.

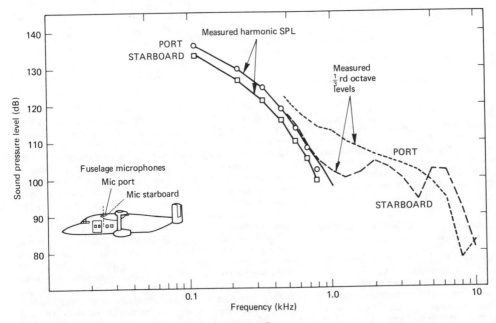

Figure 18.32 Comparison of predicted and measured propeller noise on the fuselage surface—port and starboard on a twin-engined aircraft. Harmonic tone predictions,[61] corrected for installation O——O and fuselage □——□ reflections[53]. SPL = Sound pressure level

18.3.5 Special problems with propfans

Propfan concepts[51,52] now under consideration, for transport aircraft (*Figure 18.33(a)*) at cruise Mach numbers ranging from 0.7 to 0.8, have typically 8–12 swept blades with thin aerofoil sections and wide chords. The blade tip helical Mach number can be supersonic ($M_h > 1$). The spinner and nacelle need to be specially contoured, taking compressibility effects into consideration, in order to retard and control the high velocity flow through the cascade-type root sections of the blades. In addition to introducing supersonic/transonic flow effects, the propfan differs from earlier propellers in that it is very non-compact. The 'Doppler-shifted' source wavelengths become a fraction of the wide blade chord as well as of the span, even for the fundamental blade-passing frequency, because of the high Mach number and large blade number. Moreover, the blades can have considerable twist and out-of-plane sweep, so that sources on the blade surface may not be approximated by sources in the mean disc plane of the propeller. Hence, acoustic signals of comparable strength from different parts of the propeller can arrive at the near-field receiver markedly out-of-phase, thus introducing interference. The inclusion of sufficient blade sweep to minimize transonic flow effects and neglect non-linear (quadrupole) source terms in prediction of the noise signature, allows the

application of linear theory to evaluate the concept of phase cancellation for practical blade designs.

18.3.5.1 Experimental and theoretical analysis

Most experimental data published by late 1984 had been based on American windtunnel and flight tests of isolated small propfan models, of about 0.62 m diameter and incorporating 2–10 blades; the noise reduction potential of sweepback is illustrated in *Figure 18.33(b)*. Flight tests of two model propfans, mounted in turn from a Jetstar aircraft fuselage, with microphones on a boom and the fuselage surface, have confirmed the appreciable noise benefits of blade sweep. These tests also revealed fuselage external noise levels substantially lower ahead of the plane of rotation than originally expected, possibly because the fuselage boundary-layer attenuates the noise propagation to the surface microphone by refraction/scattering/shielding. The effects of installation environment on propfan noise are likely to be significant in respect of the flow-field interactions (steady and unsteady) between the rotating propeller and nearby airframe components (nacelle, wing or tail, and fuselage).

Advanced theoretical methods have been developed to cover

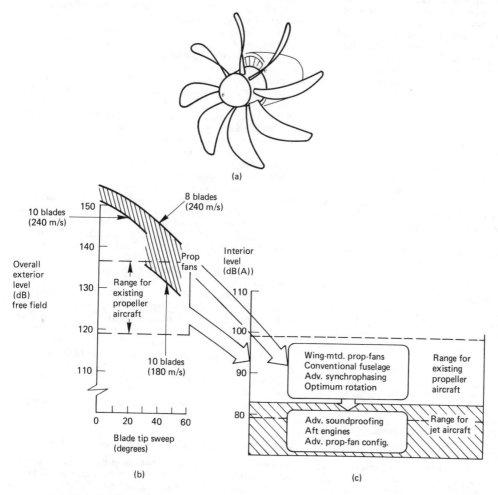

(a)

(b)

(c)

Figure 18.33 Propfan cabin noise—exterior and interior noise at cruise. (*a*) Eight-bladed propfan model. (*b*) Exterior fuselage dB. (*c*) Interior fuselage dB (A) (multi-engine)

supersonic tip-speeds,[63-66] complementary to those discussed in Section 18.8.3 for subsonic propellers. Further developments are especially concerned with more complex frameworks for three-dimensional blade aerodynamics, as regards both steady and unsteady flows, while retaining linearized acoustic propagation theory.[52] Simultaneously, more attention is being devoted to noise predictions for contra-rotating coaxial propfans (Section 18.3.4) because of the feasible reductions in tip speeds,[69-71] towards new unified theories for detailed integrated prediction of propeller acoustic and aerodynamic characteristics,[72,73] and to non-linear acoustic propagation effects.

18.3.5.2 The practical control of propeller aircraft interior noise

This involves both airborne and structure-borne transmission problems, requiring consideration of possible economic reduction of the noise at source, and attenuation of noise and vibration by the design of the fuselage-wall and structure-members. Propfan tone levels at the external surface of the fuselage during high-speed cruise become substantially larger than those for existing turbo-prop aircraft, unless significant rotational tip-speed reductions and blade-tip sweep are incorporated to alleviate the high Mach number effects (*Figure 18.33(c)*). Conventional and novel side-wall treatments, including dynamic absorbers, combined with precise synchro-phasing and opposite-handed rotation of twin propfans, are being explored to provide interior noise levels as low as those of modern turbo-fan aircraft, particularly if combined with aft-engine configurations.[51,70] Nevertheless, much research and development is still needed to guarantee an adequate practical combination of such noise control concepts with tolerable penalties on the aircraft weight, performance and costs.

18.4 Helicopter noise

The first research report specifically directed at helicopter rotor noise was issued in 1960,[74] taking advantage of about 40 years experience in propeller noise. Much of the aeroacoustic research on propeller noise has a direct relevance to both clarification and prediction of helicopter noise characteristics. Consequently, reference will frequently need to be made to the detailed discussion in Section 18.3.

The engineering and operational factors influencing helicopter noise characteristics are again effectively summarized in *Figure 18.24* under the broad block-headings of engine/transmission features, rotor (propeller) acoustics, aerodynamic design and vehicle performance. Nowadays, with the adoption of gas-turbine powerplants incorporating advanced noise-reduction treatments, the contributions to external noise from the engine/transmission/gearbox are usually of secondary importance, in contrast to their relevance for internal noise and vibration.

The noise of helicopter rotors tends to grow in intensity and to change markedly in character with increase in drive power and tip speed, with penetration of blade stalling, or with sonic tip flow developments (*see Figure 18.25*). Main-rotor and tip-rotor noise-spectra characteristics can be very distinctive, partly because of large differences in rotational frequency and size. Moreover, the aerodynamic features and associated acoustic sources of most helicopters are even more complex than those of propeller aircraft. Firstly, each individual rotor axis is aligned almost normal to the flight direction; secondly there are substantial flow interactions between two rotors mounted in close proximity to each other (in-line astern or coaxial); and thirdly there is rotor wake interference with the neighbouring large airframe.

The noise signal reaching the receiver is dependent on the particular propagation path conditions between the helicopter and the receiver (*Figure 18.26*). Consequently, from both sound generation and propagation considerations, the signal characteristics can vary appreciably with the flight conditions of particular interest (cruise, take-off, landing-approach, hover) and with the location of the receiver in the farfield or nearfield. The peak overall noise signal reaching a ground observer from a helicopter in level-cruise flight usually occurs as the helicopter passes overhead. The total duration of acoustic signal audibility (annoyance or detection) is lengthened, as compared with jet aircraft, by the much lower flight speed of the helicopter.

18.4.1 Noise sources

The spectral characteristics are similar to those for propellers (discrete-frequency and broad-band, *Figure 18.25*) but often with strong 'impulsive' elements. Sample sound-pressure-level spectra for narrow constant bandwidths and related pressure-time histories are shown in *Figure 18.34*, for a helicopter in level flyover starting about 1 km from the ground microphone.[75]

Discrete-frequency noise components are subject to Doppler frequency shift and directivity effects as the helicopter is approaching or receding. Blade-passing frequency is of the order of 20 Hz for the main-rotor, R and in the order of 100 Hz for the tail-rotor, T and is dependent on the particular rotor-speed and number of blades. These fundamental tones are accompanied by several main-rotor and tail-rotor harmonics (nR and nT). Such blade-generated tones can be correlated with the blade aerodynamic conditions in a similar manner to propellers (Section 18.3.1); namely, steady-loadings (thrust and torque), unsteady-loadings, blade-tip thickness influence, and fluctuating excess-torque effects from sonic-flow drag-rise conditions. Additionally, even at moderate flight speeds, impulsive noise signals can arise from convective interaction by one blade-tip vortex with another oncoming blade of the same rotor, of a second main-rotor, or of a tail rotor.

Extreme high-lift, strong tip vortices or shock-flow conditions on the rotating blades tend to aggravate discrete-frequency or impulsive noise during take-off, manoeuvres or high-speed cruise. Also, the installation of the lifting-rotor in the airframe can lead to airflow interactions and parasitic noise. Overall, different helicopter types are rich in distinctive acoustic characteristics which extend down to low frequencies and which propagate over large distances. The 'blade-slap' noise of a two-bladed main-rotor contrasts markedly with the 'swish' or 'whine' of some tail-rotors, and with the 'interactive banging' of in-line tandem rotors.

In contrast to propellers, the intensity of the main-rotor broadband noise assumes a practical significance equal to that of the discrete-frequency elements. Again, the broad-band noise components arise from periodic random pressure fluctuations over a wide frequency range, usually exhibiting a broad peak of sound intensity about a frequency of the order of 10 times the blade-passing frequency, though secondary broad-band 'humps' have also been found. Fundamentally, such broad-band noise is associated with blade effects from turbulent inflow, boundary-layer development, trailing-edge conditions or vortex interaction.

18.4.2 Noise characteristics and prediction models

Although the propeller under near-axial flow conditions provides a useful base for the analysis of the helicopter rotor, it can only simulate the flow environment and acoustic signature corresponding to a lifting main rotor and a tail-rotor at negligible forward speed. For a trimmed helicopter in forward flight, typically with cruise speed $V_0 > 70$ m/s and rotational tip-speed

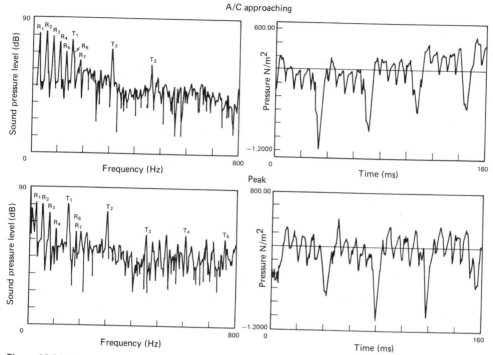

Figure 18.34 Narrowband spectra and pressure time histories for a helicopter flyover

$V_R > 210$ m/s, there is large asymmetry in the local relative airspeed and incidence (cyclic pitch control) between the blades on the advancing side and on the retreating side of the rotor-disc plane. Hence, as each blade rotates, it operates under continually changing flow conditions. Moreover, at higher V_0 or V_R, the helical tip-speed may approach a maximum value ($V_R + V_0$) close to sonic speed on the advancing side—calling for thin transonic blade-section designs. In contrast, the minimum value ($V_R - V_0$) may demand blade incidences approaching the dynamic stall condition on the retreating side—except with thick cambered sections. Considerable asymmetry and downstream distortion of the rotor wake also occurs, so that the blades may operate in very disturbed non-uniform flow conditions. Overall, therefore, the broadband (random loading), unsteady-loading, thickness and impulsive noise contributions tend to become more significant than those from mean steady-loading, especially when subjective factors emphasize the higher frequency and impulsive elements.

Increases in cruise speed much above that for the minimum power condition creates additional problems. Particular account has to be taken of the increase in effective airspeed over the advancing blades (higher tip M_h), of cyclic modifications in the main-rotor blade loadings and pitch control, changes in wake pattern interference, and differences in yaw control power from the tail-rotor. Not only does the acoustic source intensity grow with higher relative airspeed of the advancing-blade tip, but also the acoustic energy may be 'beamed' more directly ahead than rearwards or downwards.

Some useful reviews and historical reference lists on helicopter noise research may be found in references 75–79; together with references 57, 60 and 67 already mentioned for propeller noise. Summaries and evaluations of some semi-empirical treatments for helicopter noise prediction, including graphical para-

metric methods, are given in references 54 (1976) and 79 (1979).

The early prediction methods developed for propellers[58] (Section 18.3.3) have proved useful for predicting helicopter rotor tones at the fundamental BPF and low-order harmonics, from *the mean steady blade-loads* corresponding to lift-force and torque. When *blade-thickness effects* become important ($M_h > 0.7$), joint predictions of mean steady-loading and thickness contributions to the discrete-frequency noise spectrum may employ either an extensive time-domain calculation procedure,[80] or a simpler evaluation directly in the frequency domain[60] if signal-phase correlations at different acoustic receiver allocations are not required. As sonic blade-tip conditions are approached, the thickness noise rises markedly with increasing values of blade-tip volume and of rotational tip Mach number, and also with increases in the component of the forward-speed Mach number resolved in the receiver direction, so introducing an advancing-blade source-directivity bias ahead of the rotor.

Unsteady loadings for rotors tend to be much more severe than for propellers in forward flight, emanating from many mechanisms such as rotor–wake interactions, atmospheric turbulence, blade motion and particular aerofoil characteristics. Quantitative prediction of these unsteady loadings and their detailed measurement is practicable only under limited special conditions.[81] The noise prediction techniques of references 82 and 83 are instructive and applicable for the simultaneous estimation of both steady-loading and unsteady-loading contributions. However, the technique of reference 67 is more widely used, assuming again a point-loading approximation, with random-phased loading harmonics. The unsteady-loading harmonics are taken to have amplitudes L_n expressed in terms of an average steady load L_0, and an exponential decay with increasing order n, so that $L_n = L_0 \, n^{-k}$ for integer $n > 1$. The point-loading location, blade-section lift/drag ratio and decay exponent k are specified empirically.[54] However, the present aerodynamic inputs must be regarded as a provisional expedient, particularly since the loading decay-rate will vary with the type of flight and atmospheric conditions, while very little loading data are available beyond the tenth harmonic.

Special care is needed in spectral analysis to avoid confusion between *broad-band noise* and genuine multiple-tone harmonics or sub-harmonics, further aggravated if ground-reflection effects are present. Theoretical treatments still need development for the reliable prediction of broad-band noise produced by random blade-loading due to inflow turbulence, boundary-layer shedding at the trailing edge and tip-vortex formation.[57] Hence, rotor broad-band noise prediction currently relies on empirical parametric correlation of *farfield* helicopter noise data, as for propellers (*see* Section 18.3.2), but is here of equal significance to the discrete-frequency elements in the noise spectra. A simple normalized hump-shaped spectrum is fitted about a peak SPL-value and its band centre-frequency f_b, again estimated empirically.[54,79,82] The one-third octave broad-band estimates (SPL1/3) fall steadily to some 20 dB below the peak-value, on reaching the band centre frequencies $f_b/32$ and $128 f_b$.

The wake flow of a lifting main-rotor comprises turbulence and helical vortices shed from the blade tips, which can generate *interaction noise* if they impinge either with another main-rotor blade or with tail-rotor blades (*Figure 18.35(a)*). When the core axis of the shed tip-vortex is sensibly parallel to the span of the intersected blade, then a large area of this blade will undergo incidence changes for a short time, resulting in a momentary blade-loading pulse and hence blade impulsive noise. When the vortex-core axis is sensibly normal to the intersected blade span, only a small spanwise extent of the blade is then affected by changes in incidence and possibly local airspeed, but over a longer time-interval. Reliable detailed evaluation of the main rotor wake-vortex strengths and trajectories under helicopter forward-speed conditions can involve complex physical modelling and extensive computer calculations which is still the subject of much research.[84,85] The primary factors with a prescribed rotor geometry are rotational speed, forward-speed, and thrust. The *impulsive noise* from the vortex core impingement on the downstream blade will be dependent on the blade location, relative airspeed and direction of travel at impingement.

The slapping and banging of some main-rotors and of tandem rotors, during low-power descending flight or manoeuvres, are long-standing examples. Possible tail-rotor effects even in level cruise flight are illustrated simply in *Figure 18.35(b)*), where each main rotor tip-vortex is intersected by the four tail-rotor blades as they are moving upstream (anti-clockwise rotation), with the blade-span effectively at right angles to the vortex-core axis. This can give rise to a group of impulses, repeated at regular intervals as the next vortex passes through the tail-rotor disc, manifested as a deep-throated burbling sound, and spectrally exhibiting strong tail-rotor harmonics (*Figure 18.35(c)*) which can be alleviated simply by reversing the rotational direction of the tail-rotor.[86]

The compressible flow field at the blade-tip regions of a transonic or supersonic helicopter rotor can be an important contributor to the radiated noise,[60] even in hover where the blade-loadings are normally steady and axisymmetric. Apart

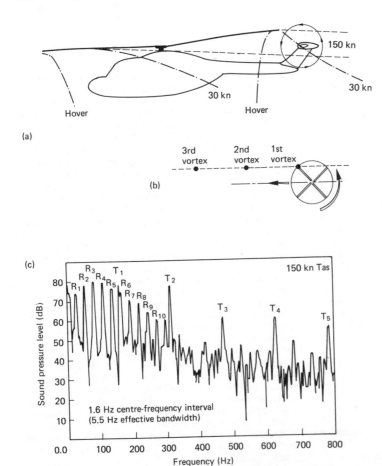

(a)

(b)

(c)

Figure 18.35 Helicopter noise—the effect of main and tail rotor interaction. (*a*) Main-rotor-tip vortex trajectories during hover and forward flight. (*b*) Tail-rotor blade/main-rotor blade intersection points. (*c*) Narrow-band spectra at 1 km approach distance

from aggravated steady-loading and thickness effects at the high tip-speeds, compressibility shocks from the tips of the finite-thickness rotor blades can escape into the acoustic far field, above a tip Mach number which is strongly affected by the tip geometry. Non-linear aerodynamics then play a significant role in the acoustic radiation and should be included in the modelling.[87] For helicopter flight at appreciable forward speeds ($M_n > 0.2$), the resulting unsteady torque-force loadings and unsteady blade-thickness effects under near-sonic blade-tip flow conditions ($M_h > 0.8$) can create significant impulsive noise signatures, again characterized by sharp-slapping or cracking. Such high-speed impulsive noise is very directional, with the acoustic energy propagated predominantly in the disc plane along the direction of forward flight. The advancing tip Mach number M_h appears to be the dominant parameter governing these unsteady compressibility phenomena. As for wake-vortex blade interaction noise, impulsive noise signatures here embrace several important subjective-rating factors, in addition to the peak-to-peak impulse comparison with the background spectrum level; these include impulse rise-time, impulse-group (bang) repetition rate, number of cycles in a 'bang' and main frequency of a 'bang'.

18.4.3 Noise reduction

There is little dispute that decrease of rotor-blade tip-speed represents a powerful method for the reduction of almost all sources in all modes of flight, although the predicted amounts differ widely. The implications of providing a reduced tip-speed are complex, while associated design modifications depend on the particular vehicle performance, and assumed improvements in technology. For a given standard of blade aerodynamic design, the blade area has to be enlarged to maintain rotor aerodynamic performance, either by increasing the blade chord (and perhaps blade span) or by increasing the number of blades, both of which lead directly to a growth in rotor system weight. Additionally, the rise in rotor torque associated with the lower rotor speeds demands greater transmission and gearbox size, thereby increasing weight and cost. At the lower rotor speed, there will be reductions also in helicopter maximum speed, particularly because of retreating blade stall considerations.

Simple generalized analysis has suggested that decreases of 15–20% in rotational tip-speed could lead to reductions in helicopter noise of the order of 5–10 dB. However, the resulting performance penalties could thereby cause drastic reductions in the allowable payload or fuel, and in the attainable forward speed. Fortunately, exploitation of new rotor-blade materials and manufacturing processes has allowed more complex shapes which provide much improved aerodynamic performance. The allied incorporation of thin swept tip shapes can simultaneously alleviate noise generation from near-sonic airspeeds at the advancing blade tip, and from tip vortex flow interactions. More generally, the incorporation of variable-geometry schemes and two-speed rotor concepts in helicopter designs also offers interesting possibilities for noise reduction, at the cost of additional complexity.

18.5 Airframe noise

The passage of air over the airframe structure induces noise of a mainly broad-band character. Until the advent of the high by-pass ratio turbofan it was of little significance from the community noise standpoint, but it has always been of significance in the context of noise in the passenger cabin.

Cabin noise is a specialist arena, bearing intimately upon airframe structural design, engine position and method of attachment, and cabin sound control measures. It is not dealt with herein, other than by directing the reader at primary references[88-94], from which other references may be obtained.

Interest in the community noise aspects of airframe noise heightened in the early to mid-1970s, when the low noise levels of the turbofan engine revealed it as contributing to the approach noise signature. This finding gave rise to a belief at the time that it would be a barrier[95] to further noise reductions, not only on approach to land, but possibly also under take-off conditions. Whilst research work of a largely problem definition nature was put in hand in several countries,[96] the findings did not promote a continuing activity since it was shown that airframe-induced noise is only of real significance during approach, when the engines are operating at low power. In fact, in perceived noise terms, airframe noise is usually no higher in level than one of several individual engine sources.

The cause of the major elements of airframe noise is the temporary deployment of high-lift devices (flaps and slats) on the wings, and the nose and main undercarriage assemblies (*Figure 18.36*). Without these necessary movable structures deployed, it has been shown that the noise from the turbulence induced by the passage of air over the wings, fuselage, tailplane and powerplant nacelles is up to 15 dB lower. In the 'clean' condition, the frequency spectrum generated by the airframe is broad-band in nature, being a function of the eddy sizes in the

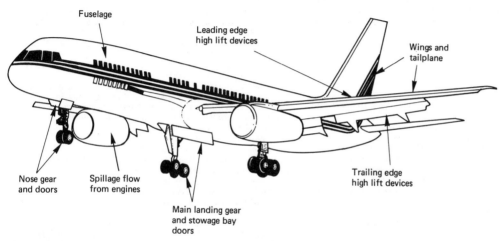

Figure 18.36 Sources of airframe noise

various boundary layer and wake structures. It peaks at around 200 Hz or less, and is reasonably omnidirectional. It varies in intensity according to the mass/volume/linear dimensions of the main structures, and whilst it is also a function of velocity, flight speed is usually held sensibly constant along the final approach flightpath.

The additional and significant effects of the flaps, slats and undercarriage assemblies are again functions of local dimensions, and produce largely broad-band noise. However, tones can be induced by the air flow over cavities (e.g., wheel bays) or struts (undercarriage legs), and the overall directivity pattern can also be altered.

Whilst there is considerable diagnostic information in the literature, little published information is available on practical methods of minimizing the noise from the moving structures. However, it is clear that in the case of the nose and main landing gear structures, improving the 'cleanliness' of the flow would be of great benefit. This could be achieved by, say, modifications to the normal tubular structure of the wheel struts and, where possible, flow control devices around the main wheel assemblies. The problem with slats and flaps is somewhat more difficult, for they are incorporated in the airframe to improve the lift at low flight speeds, and in doing so increase the drag.

Optimum lift/drag ratios are already a basic element in the design of an aircraft, and reductions in noise will go hand-in-hand with generalized improvements. With jet-powered installations, it is probably as important to ensure that the flaps, in particular, do not give rise to additional powerplant/airframe installation effects (*see* Section 18.2.6) as it is to make improvements in the lift/drag ratio. In the case of propeller-powered aircraft the interaction between the propeller wakes and the wing (or wing wake with the propeller, in a 'pusher' configuration) is similarly of equal and probably greater importance (*see* Section 18.3).

Methods of predicting the characteristics of airframe noise are limited. That most frequently referenced[97] is usually taken as an indicator of trends as leading parameters are varied, for the isolation of the individual components is difficult in the presence of the main engine sources and their interaction with the airframe structure. Absolute levels are usually determined from tests where the flight configuration is varied and engine power used in decreasing amounts. Some tests have even involved 'deadstick' landings.

The future importance of airframe noise will be directly related to progress in powerplant noise reduction. Already some local airport requirements are only being satisfied on approach by the utilization of lower flap angles, and longer landing distances. It is possible, therefore, that renewed research interest will emerge in the late 1980s, as the definitive designs for the next century become established.

References

1 SHARLAND, I. J. *Sources of Noise in Axial Flow Fans*. University of Southampton (1963).
2 LIGHTHILL, M. J. On sound generated aerodynamically. General theory (I) and turbulence as a source of sound (II). *Proceedings of The Royal Society* A221, 564–587 (1952), A222, 1–32 (1954).
3 FFOWCS WILLIAMS, J. E. and HAWKINGS, D. L. Sound generation by turbulence and surface in arbitrary motion. *Philosophical Transactions of The Royal Society*, A264, 321–342 (1969).
4 DEAN, L. W. *Broadband Noise Generation by Aerofoils in Turbulent Flow*. AIAA 71-587 (1971).
5 SMITH, M. J. T. and HOUSE, M. E. *Internally Generated Noise from Gas Turbine Engines. Measurement and Prediction*. ASME 66-GT/N-43 (1966).
6 GINDER, R. B. and NEWBY, D. R. *A Study of the Factors Affecting the Broadband Noise of High Speed Fans*. AIAA 76-567 (1976).
7 STRATFORD, B. S. and NEWBY, D. R. *A New Look at the Generation of Buzz-Saw Noise*. AIAA 77-1343 (1977).
8 TYLER, J. M. and SOFRIN, T. G. *Axial Flow Compressor Noise Studies*. SAE 345-D (1961).
9 SCHWALLER, P. J., PARRY, A. B., OLIVER, M. J. and ECCLESTON, A. *Farfield Measurement and Mode Analysis of the Effects of Vane-Blade Ratio on Fan Noise*. AIAA 84-2280 (1984).
10 MOORE, C. J. The measurement of radial and circumferential modes in annular and circular fan ducts. *Journal of Sound and Vibration*, 62, 235–256 (1979).
11 Society of Automotive Engineers. *Gas Turbine Jet Exhaust Noise Prediction*. SAE-ARP 876C (1985).
12 MOTSINGER, R. E. and EMMERLING, J. J. *Review of Theory and Methods for Combustion Noise Prediction*. AIAA 75-541 (1975).
13 MATHEWS, D. C. and REKOS, N. F. Jr. *Direct Combustion Generated Noise in Turbopropulsion Systems—Prediction and Measurement*. AIAA 76-579 (1976).
14 FLETCHER, J. S. and SMITH, P. H. *The Behaviour of Aero Engine Turbine Tones*, AIAA 75-466 (1975).
15 SMITH, M. J. T. *The Problem of Turbine Noise in the Civil Gas Turbine Aero Engine*. ICAS 68-35 (1968).
16 Aeronautical acoustics—in particular jet noise. *Royal Aeronautical Society Journal*, 58, 221–260 (1954).
17 POWELL, A. On the mechanisms of choked jet noise. *Proceedings of The Physics Society*, 866, 1139–1156 (1953).
18 LIGHTHILL, M. J. On the energy scattered from the interaction of turbulence with sound or shock waves. *Proceedings of The Cambridge Philosophical Society*, 49, 531–551 (1953).
19 RIBNER, H. S. *Shock Turbulence Interaction and the Generation of Noise*. NASA Report 1233 (1955).
20 HARPER-BOURNE, M. and FISHER, M. J. *The Noise from Shock Waves in Supersonic Jets*. Proceedings (131) AGARD Paper 11 (1973).
21 TANNA, H. K. An experimental study of jet noise, Part II: shock associated noise. *Journal of Sound and Vibration*, 51, 429–444 (1977).
22 YAMAMOTO, K., BRAUSCH, J. F., BALSA, T. F., JANARDAN, B. A. and KNOTT, R. *Experimental Investigation of Shock Cell Noise Reduction for Single Stream Nozzles in Simulated Flight*. Final Report NASA-CR-3845 (1984). (See also NASA-CR-3846 for Dual Stream Nozzles.)
23 VON GIERKE, H. E., PARRACK, H. O., GANNON, W. J. and HANSEN, R. G. The noise field of a turbo jet engine. *Journal of The Acoustical Society of America*, 24, 169 (1952).
24 HUBBARD, H. H. and LASSITER, L. W. Experimental studies of jet noise. *Journal of The Acoustical Society of America*, 25, 381 (1953).
25 RICHARDS, E. J. Research on aerodynamic noise from jets and associated problems. *Journal of The Royal Aeronautical Society*, 57, 318 (1953).
26 GREATREX, F. B. *Bypass Engine Noise*. SAE National Aeronautic Meeting, New York (1960).
27 CROUCH, R. W., COUGHLIN, C. L. and PAYNTER, G. L. *Nozzle Exit Flow Profile Shaping for Jet Noise Reduction*. AIAA 76–511 (1976).
28 PACKMAN, A. B. and KOZLOWSKI, H. *Jet Noise Characteristics of Unsuppressed Duct Burning Turbofan Exhaust Systems*. AIAA 76-149 (1976).
29 GREATREX, F. B. and BROWN, D. M. *Progress in Jet Engine Noise Reduction* ICAS (1958).
30 LILLEY, G. M. *On the Noise from Air Jets*. Aeronautical Research Council, Vol. 20, 376 (1958).
31 FFOWCS WILLIAMS, J. E. Noise from turbulence convected at high speed. *Transactions of The Royal Society*, A255, 469–503 (1963).
32 HOCH, R. G., DUPONCHEL, J. P., COCKING, B. J. and BRYCE, W. D. Studies of the influence of density on jet noise. *Journal of Sound and Vibration*, 28, 649–668 (1973).
33 BROOKS, J. R., MCKINNON, R. A. and JOHNSON, E. S. *Results from Flight Noise Tests on a Viper Turbojet Fitted with Ejector-Suppressor Nozzle Systems* AIAA 80-1028 (1980).
34 STRANGE, P. J. R., PODMORE, G., FISHER, M. J. and TESTER, B. J. *Coaxial Jet Noise Source Distribution*. AIAA 84-2361 (1984).
35 SAE *Gas Turbine Coaxial Exhaust Flow Noise—Methods of Prediction Considered for Inclusion in SAE ARP 876C*. SAE AIR 1905 (1985).
36 BUSHELL, K. W. A survey of low velocity and coaxial jet noise with application to prediction. *Journal of Sound and Vibration*, 17, 271–282 (1971).
37 HOCH, R. G. and BERTHELOT, M. *Use of the Bertin Aerotrain for the*

Investigation of Flight Effects on Aircraft Engine Exhaust Noise. AIAA 76-534 (1976).

38 GOODYKOONZ, J. H. Experimental Study of Coaxial Nozzle Exhaust Noise. AIAA 79-163 (1979).

39 COCKING, B. J. The Effect of Flight on Subsonic Jet Noise. AIAA 76-555 (1976).

40 BRYCE, W. D. The Prediction of Static to Flight Changes in Jet Noise. AIAA 84-2358 (1984).

41 RICE, E. J. Attenuation of Sound in Soft Walled Ducts. NASA TMX-52442, 1968.

42 LOWRIE, B. W. Simulation of Flight Effects on Aero Engine Fan Noise. AIAA 75-463 (1975).

43 GROENEWEG, J. F. and RICE, E. J. Aircraft Turbofan Noise. ASME 83-GT-197 (1983).

44 KEMPTON, A. J. Ray-Theory Predictions of Intake-Liner Performance: A Comparison with Engine Measurements. AIAA 83-0711 (1983).

45 BRYCE, W. D. Experiments Concerning the Anomalous Behaviour of Aero Engine Exhaust Noise in Flight. AIAA 79-0648 (1979).

46 SMITH, M. J. T. Quietening a Quiet Engine—The RB211 Demonstrator Programme. SAE 760897 (1976).

47 GUTIN, L. On the Sound Field of a Rotating Airscrew. Translation NACA TM 1195, NASA, Washington, DC (1938).

48 DEMING, A. F. Noise from Propellers with Symmetrical Sections at Zero Blade-Angle. NACA TN 605 (1937) and TN 679 (1939).

49 MORFEY, C. L. Rotating blades and aerodynamic sound. Journal of Sound and Vibration, 28, 587–617 (1973).

50 METZGER, F. B. Progress and Trends in Propeller/Prop-fan Noise Technology. AIAA Paper 80-0856 (1980).

51 WILLIAMS, J. (Ed.) Propeller Performance and Noise. Von Karman Institute (Belgium) Lecture Series Publication 1982-08 (1982).

52 AGARD-FDP. Aerodynamics and Acoustics of Propellers. AGARD Conference Proceedings No. 366 (1984).

53 WILLIAMS, J., DONNELLY, R. P. and TREBBLE, W. J. G. Comparative Aeroacoustic Windtunnel Measurements, Theoretical Predictions and Flight Test Correlations on Subsonic Aircraft Propellers. Southampton University AASU Memo 84/13. Short Version—Paper 25 of Reference 42 (1984).

54 MAGLIOZZI, B. V/STOL Rotary Propulsor Noise Prediction and Reduction. USA Reports FAA-RD-76-49 (1976) and FAA-RD-79-107 (1979).

55 Society of Automotive Engineers. Prediction Procedure for Near-Field and Far-Field Propeller Noise. SAE Report Air 1407 (1977).

56 Engineering Sciences Data Unit, Estimation of the Maximum Discrete Frequency Noise from Isolated Rotors and Propellers. ESDU, Item 76020 (1976).

57 GEORGE, A. R. and CHOU, S. T. Comparison of Broadband Noise Mechanisms, Analyses, and Experiments on Helicopters, Propellers and Wind Turbines. AIAA Paper 83-0690 (1983).

58 GARRICK, I. E. and WATKINS, C. E. A Theoretical Study of the Effect of Forward Speed on the Free-Space Sound Pressure Field Around Propellers. NACA Report 1198 (1954). See also Watkins and Durling; NACA TN 3809 (1956).

59 FFOWCS WILLIAMS, J. E. and HAWKINGS, D. L. Sound generated by turbulence and surfaces in arbitrary motion. Philosophical Transactions of The Royal Society A, 264, 321–342 (1969).

60 HAWKINGS, D. L. and LOWSON, M. V. Noise of High Speed Rotors. AIAA Paper 75-450 (1975).

61 SUCCI, G. P. Design of Quiet Efficient Propellers. SAE Paper 790584 (1979).

62 TADGHIGHI, H. and WILLIAMS, J. Some Theoretical Noise Prediction Developments and Complementary Acoustic Windtunnel Measurements for a Subsonic Aircraft Propeller. Southampton University AASU Memo 84/8 (1984).

63 FARASSAT, F. and SUCCI, G. P. A review of propeller discrete frequency technology with emphasis on two current methods for time-domain calculations. Journal of Sound and Vibration, 71, 399–419 (1980).

64 MARTIN, R. M. and FARASSAT, F. Users Manual for Computer Program to Calculate Discrete Frequency Noise of Conventional and Advanced Propellers. NASA TM 83135 (1981).

65 HANSEN, D. B. Near-Field Noise of High Tip Speed Propellers in Forward Flight. AIAA Paper 76–565 (1976).

66 HANSON, D. B. The Influence of Propeller Design Parameters on Far-Field Harmonic Noise in Forward Flight. AIAA Paper 79-0609 (1979).

67 LOWSON, M. V. and OLLERHEAD, J. B. Studies of Helicopter Rotor Noise. USA AVLABS Report 68-80 (1969).

68 BASS, R. M. An Historical Review of Propeller Developments. Royal Aeronautical Society Aeronautics Journal, Paper No. 1089 (1983).

69 HANSON, D. B. Noise of Counter-Rotation Propellers. AIAA Paper 84-2305 (1984).

70 MAGLIOZZI, B. Advanced Turboprop Noise: A Historical Review. AIAA Paper 84-2261 (1984).

71 BLOCK, P. J. W. Installation Noise of Model SR and CR Propellers. NASA TM 8570 (1984).

72 HANSON, D. B. Compressible helicoidal surface theory for propeller aerodynamics and noise. AIAA Journal, 21, 881–889 (1983).

73 FARASSAT, F. The Unified Acoustic and Aerodynamic Prediction of Advanced Propellers in the Time Domain. AIAA Paper 84-2303 (1984).

74 HUBBARD, H. H. and MAGLIERI, D. J. Noise characteristics of helicopter rotors at tip speeds up to 900 feet per second. Journal of The Acoustical Society of America, 32, 1105–1107 (1960).

75 LAW, M. R. P. and WILLIAMS, J. The Influence of Helicopter Operating Conditions on Rotor Noise Characteristics and Measurement Repeatability. R.A.E. T.R. 82030 (1982).

76 LEVERTON, J. W. The sound of rotorcraft. Royal Aeronautical Society Aeronautics Journal, 75, 385–397 (1971).

77 LOWSON, M. V. Helicopter Noise—Analysis, Prediction and Methods of Reduction. AGARD Lecture Series Publication 63, Paper 5 (1973).

78 NASA Helicopter Acoustic Specialists Symposium. NASA Conference Publication 2052 (1978).

79 PEGG, R. J. A Summary and Evaluation of Semi-Empirical Methods for the Prediction of Helicopter Rotor Noise. NASA TM 80200 (1979).

80 FARASSAT, F. and SUCCI, G. P. The prediction of helicopter rotor discrete frequency noise. Vertica, 7, 309–320 (1983).

81 TADGHIGHI, H. and CHEESEMAN, I. C. A study of helicopter rotor noise, with special reference to tail rotors, using an acoustic windtunnel. Vertica, 7, 9–32 (1983).

82 SCHLEGEL, R. G., KING, R. J. and MULL, H. R. Helicopter Rotor Noise Generation and Propagation. USA AVLAABS Technical Report 66-4 (1966).

83 WRIGHT, S. E. Sound radiation from a lifting rotor generated by asymmetric disk loading. Journal of Sound and Vibration, 9, 223–240 (1969).

84 MARTIN, R. M., ELLIOTT, J. W. and HOAD, D. R. Comparison of Experimental and Analytical Predictions of Rotor Blade-Vortex Interactions Using Model Scale Acoustic Data. AIAA Paper 84-2269 (1984).

85 SPLETTSTOESSER, W. R., SCHULTZ, K. J., BOXWELL, D. A. and SCHMITZ, F. H. Helicopter Model Rotor-Blade Vortex Interaction Noise: Scalability and Parametric Variations. Tenth European Rotorcarft Forum, Paper 18 (1984).

86 LEVERTON, J. W., POLLARD, J. S. and WILLS, C. R. Main Rotor Wake/Tail Rotor Interaction. First European Rotorcraft Forum, Paper 25 (1975).

87 SCHMITZ, F. H. and YU, Y. H. Helicopter Impulsive Noise: Theoretical and Experimental Status. NASA TM 84390 (1983).

88 HARRIS, C. M. Handbook of Noise Control. McGraw Hill, New York (1957).

89 BERANEK, L. L. Noise Reduction. McGraw Hill, New York (1960).

90 RICHARDS, E. J. and MEAD, D. J. Noise and Acoustic Fatigue. John Wiley and Sons, New York (1968).

91 LYON, R. H. Lectures in Transportation Noise. Grazier Publishing Co. (1972).

92 DOWEL, E. H. Master Plan for Vehicle Interior Noise. AIAA 79-0582 (1979).

93 PRYDY, R. A., REVELL, J. D., BALENA, F. J. and HAYWARD, J. L. Evaluation of Interior Noise Control Treatments for High Speed Propfan-Powered Aircraft. AIAA 83-0693 (1983).

94 POPE, L. D., WILBY, E. G., WILLIS, C. M. and MAYES, W. H. Aircraft interior noise models: sidewall trim, stiffened structures and cabin acoustics with floor partition. Journal of Sound and Vibration, 89 No. 3, 371–415 (1983).

95 GIBSON, J. S. Recent Developments at the Ultimate Noise Barrier. ICAS 74-59 (1974).

96 FETHNEY, P. and JELLY, A. H. Airframe Self Noise Studies on the Lockheed L1011 TriStar Aircraft. AIAA-80-1061, 1980. Expanded in RAE Technical Report 80056 (1980).

97   FINK, M. R. *Approximate Prediction of Airframe Noise*. AIAA
     76-526 (1976).

Further reading

Most of the above references will direct the reader at further
reading material. Additionally, the reprints from the series of lectures on aerodynamic noise organized by Advisory Group
for Aerospace Research and Development (AGARD), 7 Rue
Ancelle, 92200 Nuilly Sur Senine, France, and the published
papers from the regular conference of the American Institute of
Aeronautics and Astronautics (AIAA), 1633 Broadway, New
York, NY 10019, USA are useful sources of information.

19

Measurement and Prediction of Aircraft Noise

Michael E. House BSc, FIOA
Wolfson Unit, ISVR,
University of Southampton, UK

Contents

19.1 Introduction

This chapter examines the aspects of air transportation noise that affect the community. Noise within aircraft passenger cabins is a separate highly specialist subject which would merit more than its own chapter, hence only brief mention will be made where external noise sources have a direct bearing on cabin noise. Further mention of cabin noise is given in Chapter 18.

The chapter begins by describing the measurement procedures used for external noise with principal reference to the international noise certification schemes operated in both the USA by the Federal Aviation Agency (FAA), and for most other western nations under the International Civil Aviation Organization (ICAO), the chapter then examines the general source noise characteristics of various forms of civil aircraft propulsion before discussing the propagation of aviation noise to the larger distances typical of the community surrounding an airport.

Finally a detailed examination of prediction methods for air to ground noise exposure indices for flight phases with reference to some typical computer-based models is given. The chapter also covers the general philosophy behind the less formally definable prediction of the noise from ground operations close to an airport/community boundary.

19.2 Methods of measurement

There are no international standards for the measurement of airport and aircraft community noise although, at the time of writing, there are several standards technical committees[1,2] active in refining drafts of data provision and noise footprint production. There is an international Standards Organisation (ISO) method[3] for describing aircraft noise as heard on the ground and this refers to method of measurement and data reduction (*see also* Chapter 2).

However, the basis of aircraft noise measurements is well illustrated by reference to the International Aircraft Noise Certification procedures[4,5] which call up international standards for the noise measurement and analysis equipment.[6,7]

19.2.1 Summary of metrics and indices involved

The basic concepts of noise measurement units, scales and rating indices have been covered in Chapter 2. Those commonly used for aircraft noise are also listed in *Table 19.1* which deals with national airport noise exposure metrics and indices and the basic units incorporated into them. The Noise Certification procedures are all based on the effective perceived noise level (EPNL) for the larger aircraft and the maximum 'A' weighted level L_{Amax} for the smaller propeller driven aircraft with maximum certification take-off weight below 5700 kg but take-off distance above 600 m.

19.2.2 General noise measurements and instrument standards

Aircraft flight noise measurements often need to be made for research or development diagnostic purposes. Whilst generally the research organization will be mindful of the airport and noise certification measurement standards, tests will often need to be set up in an *ad hoc* way to explore an effect of particular interest. For example, measurements have been taken using chase aircraft carrying microphones, microphones suspended from balloons, or on high bridge towers to try to gather real data on outside influences of the ground or of near ground level atmospheric gradients and turbulence. Reference 8 summarizes

good practice for such general noise recordings. It also describes noise certification test precedures in some detail. The full requirements for noise instrumentation are far too detailed to cover here. Briefly, the IEC 651 standard for Sound Level Meters[6] specifies categories with overall accuracies as follows:

Type 0	Full laboratory reference instrument	±0.4 dB
Type 1	Laboratory or field precision	±0.7 dB
Type 2	General field use	±1.0 dB
Type 3	Survey meter	±1.5 dB

SLMs should have one or more of the A, B or C weightings and optionally the D weighting and the *Lin* (unweighted) response over a specified frequency range. They should have time characteristics of the indicating meter response of S or slow (1000 ms), F or fast (125 ms) and I or Impulse (not normally relevant for aircraft) and optionally the peak value may be indicated.

Normally, the Type 1 meter or equivalent is used for aircraft or airport work. For this type the microphone directional uniformity should be within limits ranging from 1 dB at 31.5 Hz to 4 dB at the upper 12.5 kHz over 30 degrees to the intended direction of use, which can be normal incidence or grazing incidence for free field microphones. Over 90 degrees the limits are 1.5–16 dB. Other IEC standards lay down precise details of requirements for level and tape recorders and for filters for spectral analysis of noise.[7] Again those appropriate to precision grade are to be preferred for aviation noise measurement. Further information on measuring systems is given in Chapter 2 and for sonic boom measurement in Chapter 21.

19.2.3 Noise certification measurements and analysis

Noise certification has been designed to set a compliance with maximum noise limits on all civil transport aircraft save some special types currently exempted. Western nations have enacted statutory requirements for all relevant types to possess a valid noise certificate in order to continue to be registered with effect from certain declared dates. For example; USA, 1 January 1985; UK, Canada, 1 January 1986; CEC, 1 January 1988. In particular the commission of the European Communities (CEC) has a directive[9] that all member states must comply with similar regulations.

The ICAO noise certification tests for subsonic transports over 5700 kg are illustrated in *Figure 19.1*. The noise is evaluated at three locations designed to represent three typical community noise aspects. The flyover measurement point is chosen at 6500 m from start of take-off roll and along the extended runway centre-line. The aircraft is required to operate to the normal safety certificatable take-off and climb procedure. This procedure has been determined with due regard to the optimum engine power schedule to minimize the noise over the measurement point. There are strict limits to the extent to which the climb gradient, hence engine power, may be reduced as governed by the capability of maintaining at least level flight with one engine inoperative. Consequently, the actual height of this test over the microphone is not directly specified, solely the trackline distance and the safe operating limits for the declared certification aircraft weight.

The noise measurements must be made such that at least six data sets are obtained having a statistical deviation of individual samples falling within ±1.5 dB with 90% confidence.

For the condition closely typical of a landing over a community, the procedure calls for a further minimum of six data sets taken at a point which lies 120 m under the flight path for a standard 3° Instrument Landing System (ILS) glide slope and along the extended centre-line of the approach runway. Here the aircraft height is closely regulated but the power of the engine has to be selected to give a smooth approach along the glide slope under normal safe conditions, i.e. the power may not be

Table 19.1 Metrics and indices for aircraft and airport noise

Country origin	Title (and usual symbol)	Definitive expression	Approx. correction from L_{eq} (12-hour)	Notes
UK	Noise and Number Index – NNI	$L_{PNmax} + 15 \log_{10} N - 80$	-22 at 100/day	1
Federal German Republic	Storindex Q, L_{eq}	$13.3 \log_{10} \sum_i \dfrac{t_i}{T} \times 10^{\left(\frac{L_i}{13.3}\right)}$	-35 (on departure)	2
France	Indice psophique (Isopsophic index) I	$10 \log_{10} \left(\sum_{i=1}^{n} 10^{(N_i/10)} + \sum_{j=1}^{p} 10^{(N_j + 10)/10} \right) - 32$	$+2$ at 100/day and $p = 0$	3
Netherlands	Noise exposure (Kosten unit) B	$\left[20 \log_{10} \sum_i W_i \times 10^{(L_{A\,maxi}/15)} \right] - 157$	–	4
ISO	Aircraft exposure level L_{E}	$\left[10 \log_{10} \sum_i 10^{(L_{EPN}/10)} \right] + 10$	$\approx +20$	
United States	Noise exposure (forecast) – NEF	$L_{EPN} + 10 \log_{10} (n_{\mathrm{D}} + 16.67 n_{\mathrm{N}}) - 88$	≈ -50 at 100/day (no night events)	5
United States	Day night level L_{DNL}	SEL(A) or L_{AX} $+ 10 \log_{10} (n_{\mathrm{D}} + 10 n_{\mathrm{N}}) - 49.4$	-3 for no night events	5
Denmark	Day evening night level DEN	SEL(A) or L_{AX} $+ 10 \log_{10}(n_{\mathrm{D}} + 3.16 n_{\mathrm{E}} + 10 n_{\mathrm{N}}) - 49.4$	-3 for no evening and night events	6
Italy	Weighted equivalent continuous perceived noise level WECPNL(3)	$L_{EPN} + 10 \log_{10} (n_{\mathrm{D}} + 3.16 n_{\mathrm{E}} + 10 n_{\mathrm{N}}) - 39.4 + S$	$+3$ for $S = 0$ and no evening or night events	7
EEC	Equivalent level L_{eq}(A)	SEL(A) or L_{AX} $+ 10 \log_{10}(N)$ $-$ 46.4 or 49.4	Datum (12 hour)	8

1. Evaluated over mid June to mid October, airport movements during 0600–1800 Greenwich Mean Time only.
2. g_i weighting for night (evaluated separately) equivalent to $+5$ dB. Evaluated from 6 am to 10 pm and 10 pm to 6 am respectively for six busiest air traffic months, t_i is duration(s) at 10 dB(A) below maximum, T is total time period per evaluation ($= 15552 \times 10^7$). This is for average movements; for busy-day movements, *see* reference 31.
3. n is the number of daytime flights, 0600–2200, with individual $L_{PNmax} = N_i$. p and N_j similarly refer to night-time operations, 2200–0600.
4. W_i is time of day weighting (23–6 hours = 10, 6–7 hours = 8, 7–8 hours = 4, 8–18 hours = 1, 18–19 hours = 2, 19–20 hours = 3, 20–21 hours = 4, 21–22 hours = 6, 22–23 hours = 8).
5. n_{D} = number of daytime flights, 0700–2200 hours; n_{N} = number of night-time flights, 2200–0700 hours. Formula is for an aircraft type with given average noise descriptor values. Summation for all types and tracks by energy method.
6. As note 5 except n_{E} = number of evening flights, 1900–2200 hours and the daytime flights are for period 0700–1900 hours.
7. S = Seasonal Adjustment; -5 for months with normally less than 100 hours at or above 20°C (68°F); 0 for above this, but less than 100 hours at or above 25.6°C (78°F); $+5$ for above both these conditions. The number (3) following the acronymic abbreviation refers to the division of the 24-hour day into three periods (day, evening and night). Day = 0700–1900, evening = 1900–2200, night = 2200–0700. An alternative form, WECPNL (2), which divides the 24-hour day into two periods, day and night, is given in Section 2.3.15.
8. Alternative constants relate to L_{eq} (12-hour) and L_{eq} (24-hour) respectively, summation across types and events as in (5).

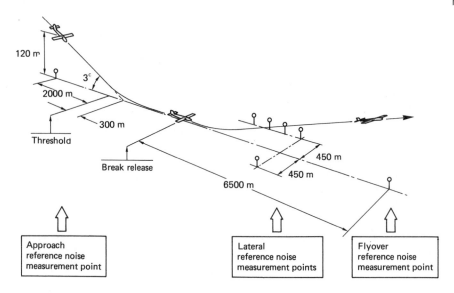

Figure 19.1 Noise certification measurement points (sub-sonic aircraft 5700 kg and over)

deliberately reduced to lower the noise just as the aircraft passes over the microphones.

The third point is a little more difficult to measure. Again the six data sets are needed but this time to represent the maximum noise that could be heard by a community lying a distance 450 m away from the runway line. This means that several trial microphone locations along this line are necessary to determine the maximum. However, the likely range of positions can be judged fairly well since maximum noise occurs as the aircraft elevates above ground attenuation effect (*see* Section 19.4.2). A check must also be made that the noise is reasonably symmetrical about the runway axis.

The terrain used for the tests (usually at an airfield) must be relatively flat and without excessively absorbing ground such as tall grass or woodland surroundings. A conical zone of vertical axis and semi-angle 75 degrees with vertex at the microphone must be free of obstruction.

Atmospheric conditions must be within the envelope shown in *Figure 19.2* and there must be no precipitation and no meteorological evidence of temperature inversion conditions during the measurements.

Aircraft take-off and landing weights must be close enough to those for which a certificate is requested and attendant noise

corrections using approved manufacturers data must be less than 2 and 1 EPNdB respectively. There are limitations to permitted corrections for error to flight over the measuring point, for small intrusion of background noises and small deviations from reference aircraft performance points for the manoeuvres required for the tests and from the datum meteorological condition of 25°C(77°F) and 70% RH. These and other summary conditions are shown in *Table 19.2* taken from reference 8 which also lists the main differences between ICAO and FAR Pt 36.

Detailed requirements are set out in Appendix 1 to reference 5 for calibration procedures, crest factor capacity of indicators, dynamic range for analysers and recorders, sampling rates for one-third octave band filtering and accuracy limits, these being additional to the general equipment standards referred to above.

All recorded data must be analysed according to the process depicted in the flow chart of *Figure 19.3* (*see also* Section 2.3.5) to obtain the averaged EPNL level before considering whether advantage should be taken of permitted trading of levels between the three points (*Table 19.2*). An on-site acoustic level calibration is required before and after each test. In addition, an ambient noise recording is made prior to and after each test event and local meteorological data must be noted.

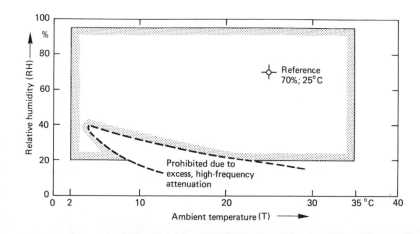

Figure 19.2 Meteorological window for noise certification (subsonic aircraft 5700 kg and over)

Table 19.2 Comparison of aircraft noise certification procedures

Feature	FAR Part 36	ICAO Annex 16	
Applicability	All subsonic aircraft types over 5700 kg weight, excepting supersonic transports (SST) and short take-off and landing aircraft (STOL)	As FAR Part 36	
Future possible applicability	SST and STOL types.	As FAR Part 36	
Measurement points: Take-off (flyover)	3.5 nmi from start of take-off-roll along extended runway centreline	As FAR Part 36 (but defined as 6500 metres from Start of Roll).	
Take-off (sideline)	On a line parallel with runway centreline (extended) and 0.25 or 0.35 nmi to the side for the aircraft with two engines and more than two engines respectively.	As FAR Part 36 0.35 nmi point for all aircraft (but defined as at 650 metres).	
Approach (flyover)	1 nautical mile from threshold on extended runway centreline.	At point on the ground on extended runway line 120 m (394 ft) below glide path of 3° slope originating from a point 300 m (984 ft) beyond threshold – equivalent to 1.08 nmi on level ground.	
Maximum permitted levels (for new aircraft)	Differently formulated but effectively the same results as for the ICAO.	New prototypes	Modified prototypes

Weights in units of 1000 kg. Noise varies linearly with log. weight		Flyover: 2 Engines: $W1 = 48.125$; $W3 = 285$. $N1 = 89$; $N3 = 101$	Flyover: 2 Engines: $W1 = 48.312$; $W3 = 325$. $N1 = 93$; $N3 = 104$.
		3 Engines: $W1 = 28.615$; $W3 = 385$. $N1 = 89$; $N3 = 104$.	3 Engines: $W1 = 34$; $W2 = 66.724$ $W3 = 325$. $N1 = 93$; $N2 = 97.9$ $N3 = 107$.
Maximum permitted levels (see diagram) $LW = 5.7$ $HW = \infty$ $\left.\begin{array}{l} W1 \\ W2 \\ W3 \end{array}\right\}$ See table $\left.\begin{array}{l} N1 \\ N2 \\ N3 \end{array}\right\}$ in EPNdB See table		4 Engines: $W1 = 20.234$; $W3 = 385$. $N1 = 89$; $N3 = 106$.	4 Engines: $W1 = 34$; $W2 = 133.447$ $W3 = 325$. $N1 = 93$; $N2 = 102.9$ $N3 = 108$.
		Sideline: $W1 = 35$; $W3 = 400$. $N1 = 94$; $N3 = 103$.	Sideline: $W1 = 35$; $W3 = 400$. $N1 = 97$; $N2 = 106$.
		Approach: $W1 = 85$; $W3 = 280$. $N1 = 98$; $N3 = 105$.	Approach: $W1 = 35$; $W3 = 280$. $N1 = 101$; $N2 = 108$.
Trade-offs against excesses	Total of excesses not greater than 3 EPNdB. No one excess greater than 2 EPNdB. All excesses are offset by reductions at other points.	Total of excesses not greater than 4 EPNdB. No one excess greater than 3 EPNdB. All excesses are offset by reductions at other points.	
Standard Atmospheric conditions – measurements: Rain or other precipitation Relative humidity Ambient temperature	None Not above 90% or below 30%. Not above ISA + 15°C at 10 metres above ground	As FAR Part 36. As FAR Part 36. Not above 30°C (ISA + 15°C) or below 2°C (ISA − 13°C) at 10 m.	

Table 19.2 (Continued)

Feature	FAR Part 36	ICAO Annex 16
Airport reported wind	Not above 10 kts at 10 m above ground	As FAR Part 36.
Temperature inversions and anomalous wind conditions affecting noise	None	As FAR Part 36.
Terrain	Relatively flat, no excessive absorption characteristics. No obstructions influencing noise within cone 75° half angle of vertical.	As FAR Part 36.
Maximum measurement point altitude difference from nearest runway point without corrections	20 ft.	6 m (20 ft)
Minimum number of noise levels to be averaged to provide certificated levels	6, or sufficient additional to give 90 percent confidence of ±1.5 dB	As FAR Part 36.
Operational:		
Approach	Glide path 3° + 0.5 at reference speed over measurement point and continued to normal touchdown.	As FAR Part 36 but at 1.3 Va + 10 kts, speed stabilized over measurement point at max allowable flap settings.
Take-off	Take-off power to at least 1000′ Alt above runway, at V_2 + 10 kts. After 1000′ Alt, thrust may be cut to climb of at least 6% gradient. Take-off flap to be used throughout.	Take-off power to at least 210 m (700 ft) above runway at V2 + 10 kts. Thrust may be cut to climb gradient of at least 4% Constant take-off configuration except for landing gear.
Reference conditions to which data must be corrected	Max take-off and landing weights for which certification is requested. Approach at 3° glide slope and at 370 ft above approach measuring point. Atmosphere of 70% RH at temperature of ISA + 10°C.	As FAR Part 36. As FAR Part 36 but at 120 m (394 ft) above approach measuring station. Ambient pressure 1013.25 mb Ambient temperature of 25°C (ISA + 10°C) Relative humidity 70% zero wind.
Maximum allowable corrections to noise data		
For weight	2 EPNdB at take-off 1 EPNdB at approach	2 EPNdB 2 EPNdB
To SPL (1/3 octave) for aircraft not above measuring point on take-off, or height and position error on approach	3 dB	—
For noise not 10 dB above background levels	Approved corrections	As FAR Part 36.
Differences between measured EPNL and corrected to reference conditions EPNL	—	Maximum of 15 EPNdB allowed.

For propeller driven aircraft below 5700 kg the process is a little simpler. Only one measurement point is used as illustrated in *Figure 19.4* which also shows the flight path accuracy specified. The meteorological bounds are also different as *Figure 19.5* shows and the noise metric is LAM, the maximum 'A' weighted sound level in dB(A), for level flight under full normal engine revs/min. If level flight at such engine powers is not feasible due to airframe speed limitation the aircraft may be approved to fly a shallow climb path to cross the microphone within the positional error boundary. Again six L_{Amax} values are needed without rejection of data and within confidence

limits. The analysis procedure follows *Figure 19.6*. The take-off performance correction and problems raised by ground attenuation of propeller noise (which can differ between 2, 3, and 4 bladed and multi-engined designs) plus many other factors in avoidance of unfair bias in certification testing are discussed in detail in reference 10.

Noise certification results, despite the intentions that they should be broadly representative of actual airport operations, are not easy if at all possible to translate into data for airport noise predictions although rules of thumb can be determined for use with care (*see* Section 19.5.18).

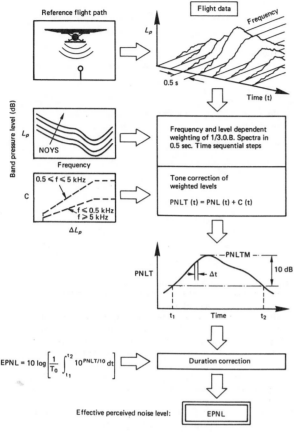

Figure 19.3 Flow chart of noise certification analyses (subsonic aircraft 5700 kg and over)

19.2.4 The ISO 3891 basis

This standard, currently under consideration for revision, provides specifications for a method of measurement and recording, data processing to obtain values on appropriate noise scales, data normalization and reporting conventions. It deals both with full spectral analysis and temporal variation as well as the simpler frequency weighted metrics. It does not deal with noise rating indices such as NNI or L_{DEN}. It is intended to cover all types of aircraft operation including in-flight and ground running although only where basic source data are to be acquired over an almost ideal hard surface with no intervening obstructions. Hence it is inappropriate for measurements of ground noise from airports as received in the community, although the general approach to measurements may be useful to follow. ISO mentions certification of aircraft notwithstanding that these aspects are fully specified in the reference 4 and 5 documents. It briefly refers to measurements of a single event in terms of L_{Amax}, L_{AX} the approximate PNLM or the EPNL and the noise exposure from a succession of events using the approximate EPNL or the L_{AX}.

Microphone location requirements are quite similar to ICAO Annex 16. Both are at 1.2 m above local ground level and over terrain free from tall grass and surrounding shrubs, etc. However, ISO suggests that the effect of the ground should differ less than 0.5 dB from that for an ideal flat reflector plane and uses an 80 degree semi-cone angle to be free of obstruction as against 75 degrees for ICAO. Both set the microphone diaphragm parallel to and in the vertical along the flight path. ISO specifies

instrumentation characteristics according to the same range of IEC standards as are referenced by the Certification methods.

Meteorological conditions for ISO merely limits wind speed to 10 knots (5 m/s) whereas ICAO also limits crosswind component to the flight line to 5 knots (2.5 m/s). Both prohibit precipitation or temperature inversions during measurements. ISO has a different way of excluding certain dry temperature and relative humidity combinations giving high uncertainty over atmosphere attenuation (*Figure 19.7*).

ISO specifically requires background noise to be at least 20 dB below any measured aircraft component of noise. ICAO effects this via its duration correction method for EPNL.

For cases where only the simpler (e.g. A or D weighted) noise level is to be measured, ISO 3891 specifies the slow response setting of SLMs but warns that selection of fast response may be necessary for low fast flying aircraft. If the variability of levels over a period is needed then the recording devices must produce results within 2 dB of those for the equipment used to obtain the full spectral type of data. The temperature/relative humidity envelope is identical with the ICAO for these measurements.

ISO details methods of data reduction for the full spectral method to compute the PNL and Tone Corrected PNL and EPNL much as for ICAO noise certification although nomenclature differs. Reference meteorological data conditions are both identical. For the weighting measurements ISO deals with processing to obtain the L_{eq} and L_{AX}. The equivalent levels are defined both for A weighted and for the PNL based units. It should be noted that its atmospheric attenuation correction data is now superseded.

19.2.5 Noise control monitoring measurements

Many airports operate some form of noise check monitoring. In the UK this is done by the CAA on behalf of the airports authority for the major designated airports such as London Heathrow and Gatwick. Regional and other International airports outside of the London area operate their own systems. Similar monitoring systems operate at most international airports in Europe, the USA and elsewhere. Measurement locations are chosen with two main aims; (1) to determine operational noise on take-off; and (2) to check whether aircraft deviate seriously from minimum noise routes (MNR) designed to avoid the most populated areas. Monitor microphones are set to straddle the nominal Standard Instrument Departure route (SID) at distances along the track which are typical of the community boundary. The microphones used are fitted with de-humidifiers (because accurate condenser microphones do not

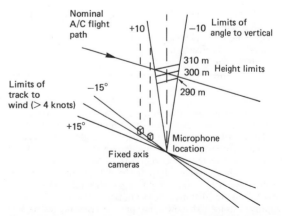

Figure 19.4 Noise certification measurement point and flight-path errors window (propeller-driven aircraft under 5700 kg)

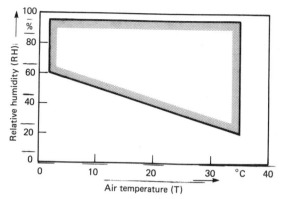

Figure 19.5 Meteorological window for noise certification (propeller aircraft under 5700 kg)

work in very high humidity), combined rain/wind shields, bird roosting deterrents and an in-built means of calibration.

Figure 19.8 illustrates a typical monitoring system concept. State of art electronic microprocessor and communications technology sets almost no bounds on the noise metrics and ancillary information (time reference, wind, temperature, etc.) which can either be data logged locally at the microphone position or else sent some distance to a central computer installation. Microphone and sound analysis techniques follow the same standards as for certification, but the usual metrics are PNLM(or $(L_A)_{max}$, $L_{eq}(A)$, L_{Ax} or SEL(A), $L_{90}(A)$. In countries which use evening and/or night noise sensitivity weightings the systems can be timed to compute the daily noise exposure such as $L_{eq}(A)$, L_{DN} or L_{DEN}.

Reports can be output giving summary or detailed results, or solely infringement results where an operator flight exceeds the set limits (at London Heathrow and Gatwick these are 110 PNdB by day and 102 PNdB by night). Many monitoring systems pass the daily data acquired to a central data base for trends analysis or correlations to identify persistent infringing airlines. Certain airports have facilities to link air traffic control identification data to these records automatically, and this can drive management or sometimes publicly viewable displays of the noise level reached by the flight that has only just departed. Monitoring of approach to land noise is not feasible because of overriding safety considerations, whereas noise reduction techniques for take-off have long been agreed between operators, pilots and air safety authorities.

19.3 Comparison of aircraft noise

The main problem of airport noise is associated with the in-flight phase of operation relatively close to the airport itself. None the less it is important to realize that complaints do arise from other aspects including ground operations, en-route climb to join airways, holding or stacking areas for landing sequence control by Air Traffic Control (ATC), etc. *Figure 19.9* lists most relevant phases with their relative importance indicated. Only those marked * or † will be given further coverage in this chapter. The main distinction is between airside and groundside, which can be considered to be distinguished by the take-off run and the landing deceleration run phases. *Figure 19.10* shows an example airport/community interface is illustrated. Public Safety Zones at the ends of runway strips normally preclude residences extremely close to runways but isolated groups of cottages or farm houses often remain quite close to the runways of airports which have expanded rapidly. In the main it is

feasible for take-offs to avoid communities. Minimum Noise Routes (MNR) have become established with flight tracks deviating to avoid heavily built-up areas within the practicability set by minimum turn radii which aircraft can execute without undue discomfort to passengers. None the less not all pockets of residential development can be avoided and, as illustrated, some villages can be affected by noise routes that are overflown at moderate heights because aircraft necessarily must turn to set course for destinations in the direction opposite to the current runway in use. Occasionally such communities are likely to receive extra noise because flights are held by ATC to a reduced airspeed and height to avoid conflicting air traffic. They can then be subjected to noise due to resumption of climb power at a lower altitude than otherwise would have occurred.

Many airports have residential areas placed to the sides of runways. These grew up during the earlier relatively quiet piston-engined aircraft era but with jet or turbofan operations residents now find that taxiway noise as well as loud take-off noise affects them considerably. Yet other peripheral housing is affected by start-of-roll noise or thrust reverser noise or else noise from apron and passenger terminal stands. All of these activities have distinct noise characteristics involving both different noise versus time traces and spectral compositions. For the airside noise, the main characteristics relate to the aircraft propulsion systems themselves. Chapter 18 deals with the noise sources in origin and Chapter 20 deals with airport noise controls. In this chapter the examination is confined to the general nature of the noise fly-by events as experienced from the different phases of flight for the main classes of aircraft.

The main factors influencing the noise character are:

1. The aircraft category: conventional (CTOL), rotorwing, short take-off and landing (STOL), etc.
2. The powerplant type.
3. The power setting.
4. The aircraft speed (for duration metrics).
5. The installation layout (fuselage or wing shielding).
6. The noise suppression standards fitted.

Figure 19.11 illustrates time dependence, directionality, spectra at time of maximum noise and dependence on engine power for the more usual types of powered aircraft.

19.3.1 Propeller driven aircraft

The sources of propeller noise including helicopter noise are discussed in the previous chapter. Briefly, propeller driven aircraft (*Figure 19.11(a)*) have a distinctive sound caused mainly by the multiplicity of tones that occur at multiples of the blade passing frequency $f_n = n.B.N/60$ where n is harmonic number, B the number of propeller blades per rotor and N the shaft speed in rev/min. Propeller noise is usually dominated by the f_1 component and this peaks just aft of the angle 90 degrees to the forward shaft axis. However, secondary lobes of high noise as well as different angular directions of peaks for other harmonics causes propeller noise to vary in level and pitch during a fly-by. Some high-speed propellers attain sonic flow conditions at the blade tips and this causes a marked buzzing sound from the spinning shock-waves, much like many weak sonic booms at high repetition rate. Propeller noise, being caused mainly by dipole radiation from the rotating loading patterns on the blading, varies with approximately the 6th power of propeller tip speed. New studies of advanced propellers for turbo-prop aircraft use deliberately slowed fans with sweptback blade leading edges to combat this effect which also improves propulsion efficiency (*see also* Section 18.3.5). With piston-engined powerplants exhaust noise can be important particularly at reduced powers. Exhaust harmonics occur at

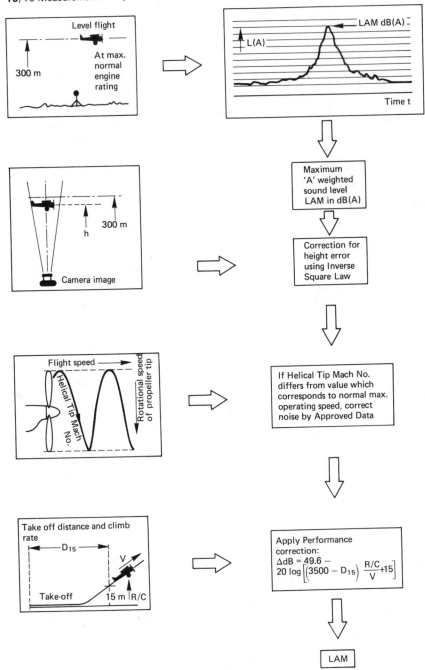

Figure 19.6 Flow chart of noise certification analyses (propeller aircraft under 5700 kg)

firing frequencies depending on the cylinder configuration of the engine as well as shaft speed.

Propeller driven aircraft are generally felt to be noisy inside the passenger cabin and passengers learn to avoid the seats near to the plane of the propeller. The noise arises mainly at low-frequency orders of propeller blade passage close to the fuselage walls and increasing the clearance does a lot to reduce the levels. Also characteristic is the effect of poor synchronization between

several propellers at nominally identical rotation speeds. Propeller aircraft do not cruise at high airspeeds and hence noise due to the fuselage boundary layer pressure fluctuations is not a problem. Low-frequency noise isolation from aircraft cabins is not simple to achieve since acoustic transmission loss depends principally on the superficial mass of the panels and trim materials and weight is usually to be kept minimal for reasons of fuel economy.

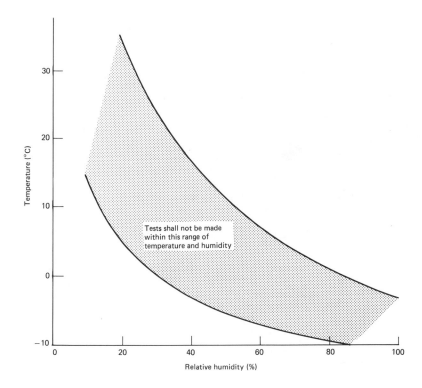

Tests shall not be made within this range of temperature and humidity

Figure 19.7 Meteorological window for ISO 3891 (full analysis)

19.3.2 Turbofan powered aircraft

Chapter 18 gives a detailed review of subsonic jet aircraft noise sources. However, a summary of the principal portions of noise generation from turbofan-powered aircraft is given here. Turbofans can be regarded as encompassing the particular cases of the pure jet, the low by-pass ratio jet, the high by-pass ratio turbine driven ducted fan engine and the geared shaft-driven fan. The jet noise, fan noise and turbine noise elements are usually present and merely change in emphasis with engine design although detailed effects such as special mixer nozzles and fan duct sound absorbent linings alter the spectral composition at peak fly-by noise time (*Figure 19.11(d)*). The jet mixing noise depends on the exhaust velocity to the power of 8 or more, but once the nozzle becomes choked (supercritical flow) there are other sources termed shock-associated noise. This is responsible for the crackle sound well known at take-off power settings from high-performance military aircraft, first-generation SSTs having afterburners (e.g. Concorde) and the older pure and low-by-pass jet aircraft. The mixing noise peaks at about 45 degrees to the rear axis of the engine nozzle whereas the shock associated noise, which only varies with approximately the 4th power of exhaust Mach number, can peak before the aircraft passes by the observer. Usually both types of jet noise have smooth random noise spectral characteristics as shown in *Figure 19.11(c)* although tonal characteristics, sometimes called howl, can occur with military aircraft having afterburners.

The main fan and turbine noise sources are flow interactions with the solid surfaces of the many rotating blades. The noise therefore generally contains discrete tones which, due to the high rotor speeds, fall into the broad frequency range 1000–5000 Hz for fans and compressors and even up to ultrasonic frequencies for turbines. The maximum occurs either at about 60 degrees to the forward axis or 60–70 degrees to the rear axis dependent on the exact design, provision of duct linings and so

forth. Fan and turbine noise levels change with about the 5th or 6th power of blade tipspeed but discrete tones tend to be more protrusive in the spectra at the low speeds used for approach to land especially in the older non-suppressed fan-jets. Modern high by-pass turbofans can also exhibit a buzzing due to supercritical flow over their large single stage fans when at maximum power condition. Fan duct linings have done a lot to minimize this otherwise very noticeable characteristic. Broadly speaking the take-off power noise from a turbofan is a mixture of rearwards directed fan noise with low speed jet mixing noise from the fan duct. For low powers needed at landing approach and even more so for taxiing powers near to ground idle speed the noise levels are dominated by fan inlet and exit radiated noise with perhaps some intrusion of turbine whine. All these factors lead to the noise versus time patterns and spectral distributions shown in *Figure 19.11(d)*.

The cabin noise in jet and turbofan propelled subsonic aircraft is usually dominated by the boundary layer pressure fluctuations which set the fuselage walls into vibration, hence radiating random noise inwards via the thermal insulation and trim materials. Boundary layer noise becomes more prominent towards the rear of the cabin because the boundary layer is thicker and the lower frequency turbulence is less readily isolated. Engine noise is generally not prominent except during the lower speed take-off and landing manoeuvres, but close to wing spars or rear seats on tail installed main engines a low to mid frequency tone caused by vibrations from imperfect engine fan, compressor or turbine balancing can usually be detected. Modern new technology aircraft with high by-pass turbofans have reduced passenger cabin noise considerably.

19.3.3 Turbopropeller driven aircraft

Turbopropeller aircraft have power turbines which extract the

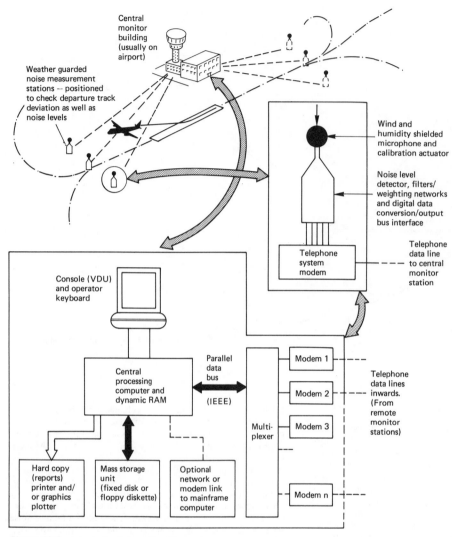

Figure 19.8 A typical noise monitor scheme

Groundside
operations
{
 *Engine ground testing.
 ‡Airport related road traffic.
 ‡Ground services & auxiliary power units
   (APU) at stands and
   in cargo areas.

Airside
operations
{
 ‖Ramp noise (avoided by tug).
 †Taxiing from apron or stands to
   runway hold point.
 *†Start of roll noise.
 *ATC hold procedure noise and re-
   selection of climb power.
 ‡*En route* noise in rural areas.
 ‡Sonic boom (rare, weather sensitive)
   affects land close to routes over sea.
 ‡Inbound routeing.
 ‡Approach hold or stacking.
 ‡Approach sequencing from hold.
 ‡Establishment of landing path.
 *Final appoach.
 *Landing thrust reverse.
 †Taxi into stand or apron.

Figure 19.9 Community noise in relation to airport operations. *Affects community near airport. †Affects individual residences and existing small rural communities near airport boundaries. ‡Only affects communities very distant from airport. ‖Affects airport buildings and terminals.

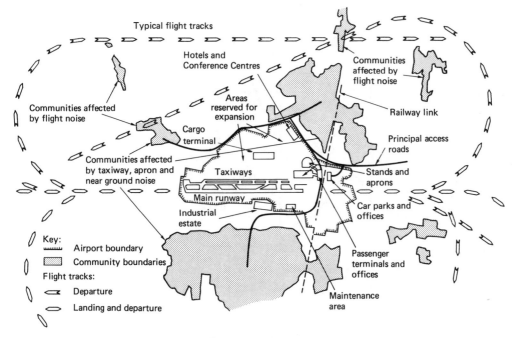

Figure 19.10 The airport and community interface

majority of the exhaust stream energy to drive the propeller shaft, normally via a reduction gear typically of 15:1 ratio. Hence jet mixing noise is almost negligible but compressor and turbine noise influence pre- and post-pass-by noise with the propeller noise (*see* Section 19.3.1) usually being heard distinctly as the aircraft passes abeam. High tip-speed propellers can be heard ahead of pass-by at take-off powers. Consequently, these powerplants exhibit the compounded features of turbofans and propeller as shown in *Figure 19.11(b)*. Some turbopropeller engines have the centrifugal design of compressor which gave the older jet engines their characteristic shrill whine, this dominating the pre-overhead noise spectrum. Modern absorbent liners now offer a retroactive cure for this annoying sound.

Turbopropeller aircraft exhibit the mixed characteristic of propeller and turbofan types except that the boundary layer noise, whilst becoming a factor to contend with for the new technology designs being evolved using high cruise speeds with multi-blade unducted fans, is not important for types currently in service. Advanced ductless fans, especially those concepts with contra-rotating coaxial swept blade rows, are likely to pose considerable design challenges for airframe manufacturers if cabin noise levels are to be kept as low as those set by the advanced turbofan powered aircraft.

In discussing cabin noise there are other noises that occur during the take-off and landing approach flight phases which are not engine related. These include undercarriage and flap operation noises which are very difficult to eliminate.

19.3.4 Flight phase or power relation

The combination of these noise level and spectral characteristics are summarized in *Table 19.3* which gives typical levels for a variety of main classifications of aircraft type. The table includes some comparisons for noise suppressed versions of older aircraft including some types for which retroactive modification to fit sound absorbently lined nacelles will be required for these to continue in service (*see* Section 19.2.3). All noise suppressors,

including the older jet mixing nozzles which could provide about 10 PNdB reduction and the duct liners which can provide 5–15 PNdB lower fan noise, impose operational penalties such as extra weight, powerplant drag or fuel consumption. Hence a sensible trade-off has to be made by the designer. Some duct suppressors have provided a bonus lower nacelle drag where the original short fan duct was not entirely optimum. In general noise suppressors mostly reduce the mid to high frequency spectrum thus, particularly at greater distances from aircraft, the lower frequencies become the dominant feature. Unfortunately low frequencies most readily penetrate building structures.

19.3.5 Short take-off and landing

A vast range of concepts have been proposed or developed as prototypes for this class of aircraft with obvious incentive regarding prospective near city-centre airports or STOLports. Purely Vertical Take-off and Landing (VTOL) concepts were abandoned about a decade ago owing to practical difficulties in achieving low enough noise. Targets were then set at 90 PNdB maximum for 152 m (500 ft) from the aircraft or 80 PNdB peak at the community boundary. The only operational aircraft having STOL performance (in the UK defined as field performance less than 600 m or 2000 ft) at present have straightforward turbopropeller engines which aid high lift wings by making maximum use of the propeller slipstream. Typical data for a few of such types are included in *Table 19.3*, noting that the DHC Dash 7 is strictly speaking not a STOL aircraft as defined in the UK. *Figure 19.12* compares noise footprints (i.e. noise contours for a single flight event take-off and landing along a straight line runway and track) for these and conventional types.

Some of the experimental STOL aircraft use turbofan engines which can augment the lift by increased air entrainment or by blown high lift flaps or by deflected flow using flaps. Generally these types could enable much larger passenger loads to fly out of very short near-city-centre fields but will probably end up a

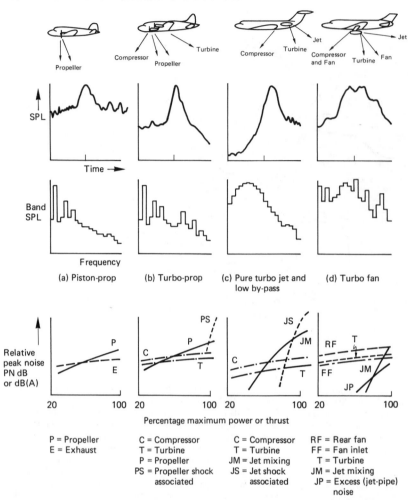

Figure 19.11 Aircraft noise time history and spectral characteristics

degree noisier than current turbopropeller STOL despite the intense efforts to mitigate this by aircraft designers.

From the above it will be appreciated that the noise spectral character of current STOL operational aircraft are very much like ordinary turbo-propeller CTOL types. The turbofan types will sound like turbofan CTOL transports with high-by-pass engines.

19.3.6 Helicopters and tilt rotorcraft

Everyone is aware of the tremendous flexibility of the helicopter which has found increasing applications, from access for workers to offshore oil and gas production platforms to search and rescue and also business/executive flying. The helicopter suffers from a poor reputation over noise character although tremendous strides have recently been made by manufacturers to reduce external and internal noise.[11,12] With care the problem of the sharp pulsating noise, variously called slap, slam or banging, can be avoided but the low-frequency throb of helicopter rotor noise is almost fundamental to the lift production. However, one of the more annoying aspects comes from the increased flight speeds now attainable which causes the advancing side of the rotor combined with the flight speed vector to become transonic, again introducing the familiar shockwave

associated buzz which can be heard well before the helicopter passes by the observer.

Most helicopter designs also have tail rotors for counteraction of the rotor torque and this makes the smaller single-rotor helicopter additionally noisy. Noise character is different to propellers only in the general frequency ranges of the tonal components and the fact that the buzz and high-pitched tail rotor noise propagates well forwards of the craft causing a prolonged pre-flyby noise exposure. Helicopters, by virtue of their manoeuvrability, do not have to abide by well-defined flight tracks and this makes formal estimations of the community noise problematical although there are defined routes for helicopters in the London area and elsewhere for the London Heathrow to Gatwick helicopter link*, as there are for other major cities throughout the world. Further details on helicopter noise sources are given in Chapter 18.

Another concept gaining interest as a spin-off from military prototypes is the tilt-rotor craft. This has large, helicopter-rotor-like propellers which act vertically for lift-off and landing and undergo a gradual transition by swivelling the propeller and engine pod (mounted from the tips of stubby, cruise efficient wings) to provide horizontal thrust for cruise flight. The concept

*This service has ceased with the opening of the motorway link.

Table 19.3 Typical reference noise data for broad classes of civil air transport and private aircraft

Aircraft and Flight Phase			*Noise Metric at 152m range*			
Type category	*Example types*	*Operational condition*	*PNLM(PNdB)*	L_{Amax} *(dB(A))*	L_{AX} *(dB(A))*	*EPNL (EPNdB)*
Old Tech'y Long Range Turbofan	B707 DC–8 VC–10	Take-off Departure Approach	125–133 118–125 112–115	112–120 105–112 99–102	120 107	122 115
Old Tech'y Trijet Low By-pass	Trident 3B	Take-off Departure Approach	128 123 112	115 110 99		
Old Tech'y Trijet Med By-pass	B727 Tu154	Take-off Departure Approach	124 120 107	111 107 94	113 100	115 108
Old Tech'y Twinjet Med By-pass	B737 BAe1–11 DC–9	Take-off Departure Approach	124 121 109	111 108 96	115 113 97	118 116 104
Supersonic Long Range Transport	BAe/SA Concorde	Take-off Departure Approach	139 129 120			
Old Tech'y Large 4 T-Prp	Viscount	Take-off Departure Approach	111 106 100	98 93 87	98 94 91	108 104 97
Old Tech'y Small/Med 4 T-Prp	BAe 748 Fk 27	Take-off Departure Approach	112 106 102	99 93 89		
New Tech'y Long Range Turbofan	B747 DC10–30	Take-off Departure Approach	116–120 112–117 104–109	103–107 99–104 91– 96	110 108 97	118 115 104
New Tech'y Med Range Turbofan	DC10–10 Tristar	Take-off Departure Approach	112–117 110–113 103–105	99–104 97–100 90– 92	116 96	104 101
NT Large Med Range 2 T-Fan	B767–200 A310–200 A300–B4	Take-off Departure Approach	113–114 110–112 103–104	100–101 97– 99 90– 91		
NT Med Med Range 2 T-Fan	B757	Take-off Departure Approach	110 107 100	97 94 87		
NT Short/ Med Range 2 T-Fan	B737–300	Take-off Departure Approach	109 106 98	96 93 85		
NT Feeder -Commuter 4 T-Fan	BAe146– 100/200	Take-off Departure Approach	105 100 98	92 87 85		
Hushed Twinjet Med By-pass	BAe 1–11 /400/500	Take-off Departure Approach	123 119 106	110 106 93		
Re-fanned Twinjet Med/Long R	DC–8–90	Take-off Departure Approach	111 107 100	98 93 87		

Table 19.3 (Continued)

Aircraft and Flight Phase			Noise Metric at 152m range			
Type category	Example types	Operational condition	PNLM (PNdB)	L_{Amax} (dB(A))	L_{AX} (dB(A))	EPNL (EPNdB)
Hushed Trijet Med/Long R	B727–200 refitted	Take-off Departure Approach	121 115 104	108 102 91		
Med/Large STOL 4 T-Prp	DHC–7 (Dash 7)	Take-off Departure Approach	95 92 86– 91	82 79 73– 78	87 85 86– 91	92 90 91– 96
Small STOL 2 T-Prp	DHC–6 (Twin Otter)	Take-off Departure Approach	104 93 89	91 80 76	95 85 81	100 90 86
Private/ Executive Twinjet	BAe 125–600	Take-off Departure Approach	118 112 105	105 99 92		
Private/ Executive Twin T-fan	BAe 125/800 Citation	Take-off Departure Approach	95 95 91	82 82 78		
Private/ Executive Twin T-Prp	BE 90 PA 31T	Take-off Departure Approach	86– 90 86– 90 76– 80	73– 77 73– 77 63– 67		
Private/ Executive Twin Piston	BE 55 C 402 PA 31	Take-off Departure Approach	86–107 86–107 81– 89	73– 94 73– 94 68– 76		
Private/ Executive Sing. T-fan		Take-off Departure Approach	84– 88 84– 88 79– 83	71– 75 71– 75 66– 70		
Private/ Club Sing. Piston	C 150 PA 28 C 182	Take-off Departure Approach	89– 93 89– 93 68– 81	76– 80 76– 80 55– 68		
Microlite Direct Propeller		Take-off Departure Approach		76– 86	88–100	
Microlite Belt Drive Propeller		Take-off Departure Approach		66– 72	78– 86	
Large Twin Rotor Helicopter	Chinook	Level Flt Cruise	102	89		
Large sing. Rotor Helicopter	S61N	Level Flt Cruise	92	79		
Medium Twin Turb Helicopter	S76 Spirit Augusta 109 Bolkow 105	Level Flt 100 to 145 kn	89– 95	76– 84	84– 91	87– 95
Small Sing. Turb Helicopter	Bell 206 Jet Ranger	Level Flt 115 kn	86	75	83	86

NT = New Technology. Sing. = Single. Turb = Turbine. T-fan = Turbofan. T-Prp = Turboprop. Med = Medium. Flt = Flight.
Take-off = Initial Power. Departure = Reduced Power.

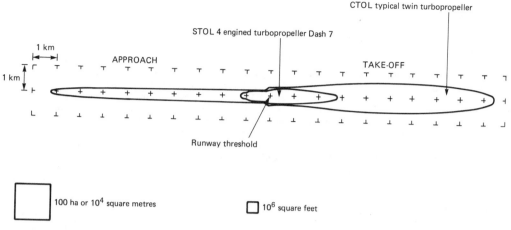

Figure 19.12 Typical 90 PNdB footprints for STOL and CTOL aircraft

was first introduced at the time of the above-mentioned VTOL interest but modern light structures of composite material now enable lower installed power to be used. More efficient rotor performance can be achieved and it is possible that via this concept interest might return to the true VTOLport. Current indications are that the rotor noise from such craft will be only slightly more than the comparable size of turbo-propeller STOL at similar distances to the side of the airfield. The tilt rotorcraft will have a noise character similar to the quieter propeller types rather than the helicopter.

19.3.7 Business and private and training aircraft

These are generally smaller versions of civil passenger transports and can be found in propeller, turbopropeller and jet or turbofan powered types. The smaller and older types of executive jet were particularly noisy but are rapidly being replaced by noise-suppressed turbofan versions capable of meeting the new noise certification limits.

The propeller-driven types tend to have lengthy noise time characteristics and the smaller types used for private flying tuition, or in the UK for newly permitted aerial advertisement banner towing, can cause extra annoyance due to the circuitous flight track or repetitiveness of 'circuits and bumps' for landing and take-off training. There is some evidence that the noise versus distance rules for prediction may be too great to model the noise exposure of these types correctly, at least in terms of the PNLM based NNI. Light propeller-driven aircraft normally can hardly be heard during landing approach except right under the approach path.

19.3.8 Microlight aircraft

Early versions of microlight aircraft used high speed small diameter propellers driven directly from poorly exhaust silenced 'lawn mower' engines. Their noise was therefore particularly annoying due to high-pitched engine and propeller tone buzzing coupled with long fly-by durations owing to the low airspeed (often reduced to near zero groundspeed in strong headwinds). The latest types use pulley and toothed belt driven larger-diameter propellers with very markedly reduced noise output. None the less, the free-roaming nature of the microlight still causes much annoyance to nearby residents and a noise certification scheme has been introduced.[13]

19.3.9 Airships

Civil uses of airships are gaining increased interest now that the light and strong composite materials enable viable designs to be built based on helium-filled semi-rigid envelopes with passenger gondolas again of lightweight and strong honeycomb sandwich panels. The engines tend to be piston (automobile derived) driving ducted and vectorable gear driven fans. The main comment on community noise is on the very long duration due to possible very low groundspeeds. In the USA an experimental compound aircraft of large cargo-carrying potential has aroused interest. It combines the helicopter rotor with a helium-filled envelope and this concept is most unlikely to offer a noise compatible with civil airports close to communities.

19.4 Propagation of aircraft noise

The basic noise emission from an aircraft is usually stated for a standard lineal distance. It is usual to define aircraft source noise at a relatively short distance such that the effects of atmospheric and over-ground attenuation are minimal. In the UK the source noise is quoted as a PNLM (in PNdB) at a reference distance of 152 m (500 ft). This value of PNLM is termed the Reference Noise Level or RNL.

For airport noise predictions it is necessary to extrapolate from the RNL to greater lineal distance making allowance for:

1. *Normal spherical divergence* of the sound waves (inverse square law—ISL). This involves a reduction of $20\log_{10}(D/D_{ref})$ for lineal distance giving 6 dB for each doubling of the distance relative to D_{ref}. However, because distance extrapolation can involve a consequential alteration in the polar angle at which the PNLM occurs, this has a further minor effect on the attenuation rate.

2. *Atmospheric attenuation.* This is mainly from energy dissipation within the molecules of oxygen in the atmosphere when excited by the sound pressure fluctuations. It becomes especially relevant for frequencies close to the relaxation frequency for these molecules which depends on the dry air temperature and the relative humidity. Nitrogen molecule relaxation also occurs but at lower frequencies. Classical viscous absorption usually only assumes importance well above the frequency range of interest to aircraft noise.

Tables are available to determine the combined attenuation.[15] *See also Table 2.2.*

3. *Ground Attenuation* due to interference and absorption of sound as the waves travel close to the ground plane. Naturally this phenomenon is greatest for situations where the observer to aircraft sight-line is at a low elevation angle to the general surface. The major ground attenuation effect occurs at a fairly low frequency of order 200–500 Hz, but is a function of the height above local ground of the receiver, (i.e. a persons ears or microphone for measurement), the height of the source, the horizontal separation between source and receiver and the surface acoustic impedance of the intervening ground.

4. *Wind and temperature gradients* which distort the normal propagation processes compared with the ideal homogeneous atmosphere. With the exception of specialized considerations of the surface wind effect on near to the ground noise (e.g. from thrust reversers) the prediction of airport noise traditionally and consciously avoids these effects by stating noise levels and drawing up contours and footprints for a 'still air' situation. None the less such effects can be important and will be discussed in more detail in Section 19.4.2.

5. *Atmosphere turbulence* can be important in very large distance extrapolations. Even so turbulence has little influence on the long-term average of the received sound level. Instead it causes shorter time-scale fluctuations in the level due to the scattering of the soundwaves causing parts of the waves to travel via distinct paths. This is especially relevant to the longer wavelengths and the separately arriving scattered waves have time-dependent phase differences according to the detailed turbulence structures traversed.

Turbulence causes a fluctuation particularly of the lower frequency sound and it is only in very settled atmospheres, e.g. during very low winds which tend to occur early morning or in the evenings and over night or during clear crisp winter mornings, that the received sound is virtually steady. *Figure 19.13* shows some examples of the turbulence effect on propagation of an artificially produced constant noise to large distance demonstrating that with real aircraft the phenomenon is not a feature of the noise generation at source.

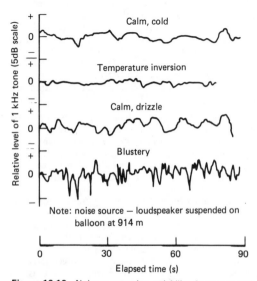

Figure 19.13 Noise propagation variability due to atmospheric disturbance

The attenuation effects in items (2)–(4) above will now be examined in greater depth.

19.4.1 Atmospheric absorption of sound

The principal components of atmospheric attenuation are oxygen molecular relaxation, nitrogen molecular relaxation and classical thermo-viscous rotation damping effects (*see also* Section 2.2.13). The relaxation absorption can be shown to follow a bell-shaped variation with frequency.[14] The bell centres on the molecular relaxation frequency which in turn depends on the percentage of water molecules in the air raised to the power 1.3. It is also directly proportional to the atmospheric pressure. For example, at sea level with 1% water molecules it occurs at about 10 kHz. The value of the maximum molecular absorption at the relaxation frequency depends on the dry temperature of the air and can be empirically approximated by algebraic series.[14]

The nitrogen relaxation follows a similar variation except that the shape is not a symmetrical bell but instead tends to be a shallowly declining plateau above the relaxation frequency (*see Figure 2.7*). The shape is a complicated function of the water percentage as well as atmospheric pressure and the square of frequency. For the same atmospheric parameters as given in *Figure 2.7* the nitrogen effect is less important than for the oxygen relaxation and only dominates at frequencies below about 500 Hz.

The thermo-viscous contribution is dependent on the square of frequency and inversely on the atmospheric pressure. It is also weakly dependent on the dry temperature. For sea level conditions it therefore mainly varies with the frequency and in the example in *Figure 2.7* only starts to dominate the total absorption above the oxygen relaxation frequency.

A detailed account of the theoretical and experimentally determined air absorption characteristics appears in reference 14. *Figure 19.14* is based on a set of experimentally determined data in one-third octave bands from aircraft flights.[15] The combined absorption is in practice relatable to relative humidity and dry temperature for cases where the sound propagates in the atmosphere close to sea level. Such data should not be used directly to estimate air attenuation for airports situated at high altitudes owing to the dependence on atmospheric pressure built into the empirical constants.

For most practical cases the attenuation below 500 Hz is very low unless extrapolation distances are very great. For example at 70% RH and 15°C (59°F) the reduction rate per km for 125 Hz is only 0.7 dB rising to 1.3 for 250 Hz and reaching almost 5 dB at 1 kHz. In the 4 kHz octave band there is over 25 dB per km attributable to atmospheric attenuation. In view of the dominance of the frequencies in the range 1–4 kHz in subjective units of noise it can be appreciated that air humidity and dry temperature can greatly influence the distance attenuation. Because of this, noise contours are usually predicted for a sea level 70% RH and ISA reference (or ISA + 10°C equivalent to 25°C for hotter airports). Hence the day to day reality of noise reception can be quite different to that taken into account on average in the predictions.

These complex variations due to air absorption can be accounted for fairly accurately by the engine manufacturer when assessing noise performance and developing noise emission data. The matter is not practically feasible to apply to the airport noise environment assessment by those not in possession of all the detailed engine noise and performance parameters which are necessary for a proper extrapolation using, say, one-third octave band data as a basis. The airport noise prediction expert therefore relies on more global trends which have been found from measurements of in-flight noise at various distances from the observer.

At its most refined the observed distance effect on the PNLM

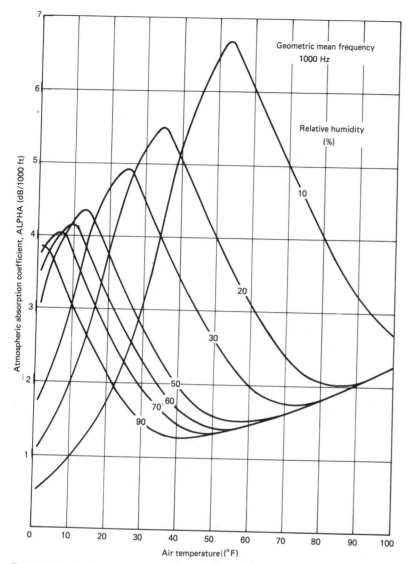

Figure 19.14 Typical noise absorption chart (SAE ARP 866)

or the EPNL or the SEL(A) are available from data bases as a tabulation against one-third octave intervals of the lineal distance from 100 ft (30.48 m) to 10 000 ft (3048 m). The reduction rate for scales such as PNLM is greater than the SEL(A) because the latter includes an inverse effect due to the duration of the sound which tends to be almost linearly related with distance.

At its simplest, the distance effect can be expressed as a number of PNdB's reduction per doubling of the distance over the D_{ref}. This is the basis of extrapolation used in the UK for NNI prediction purposes. An empirically determined rule originally determined from first-generation civil jet aircraft established this as an 8 PNdB reduction per doubling at elevation angles well above the onset of ground attenuation (i.e. above 15 degrees to the horizontal). Thus for the PNLM there is about an extra 2 dB reduction per doubling of distance compared with the ISL value of 6 dB.

19.4.2 Ground attenuation of aircraft noise

Figure 19.15 illustrates the process of ground absorption for a source at height h_s above a ground plane having acoustical impedance Z_G as received at a point distance s away at a height h_r above the ground. The difference in sound level at the reception point in the presence of the ground, compared with that in total absence of it, is controlled largely by the change in the noise propagation path between the direct line from source to receiver and the line from source to receiver via the intervening ground. The ground impedance modifies this for situations of a relatively high source/receiver in comparison with the horizontal separation. The form of this expression is as shown in *Figure 19.16* when evaluated for a typical ground impedance over grassland and for the case of a standard 1.5 m height microphone when the source is at a low elevation. In the figure the expression has been integrated by one-third octave bands

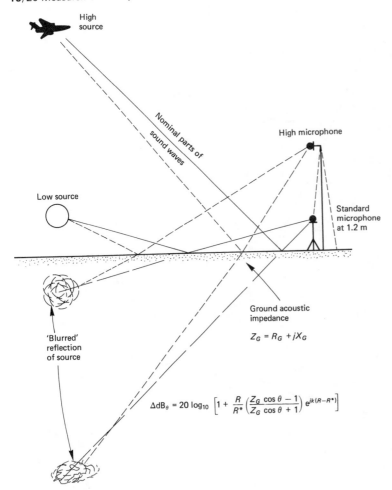

High
source

Nominal parts of
sound waves

Low source

High microphone

Standard
microphone
at 1.2 m

'Blurred'
reflection
of source

Ground acoustic
impedance

$$Z_G = R_G + jX_G$$

$$\Delta dB_\theta = 20 \log_{10} \left[1 + \frac{R}{R^*} \left(\frac{Z_G \cos \theta - 1}{Z_G \cos \theta + 1} \right) e^{jk(R-R^*)} \right]$$

Figure 19.15 The basic mechanism of ground absorption. Subscript G denotes ground. *Complex conjugate; θ=angle between source to ground line and the vertical; k=wave number; R= radial path from source to receiver; Z, R, X=complex, real and imaginary ground impedance.

with random phase so that at low frequency the trend is to an increase of 3 dB compared with no ground. This corresponds to classical reflection close to a rigid boundary wherein the sound pressure doubles. The function falls to a deep trough as frequency increases to about 300 Hz and then rises fairly quickly to waver about an asymptotic line at zero, i.e. the free field value.

For a case where the microphone is elevated to over 4 m above ground the frequency of the ground absorption trough decreases.[16] Hence a procedure has been suggested to enable engine and airframe manufacturers to ascertain the true field noise spectrum from tests conducted close to a rigid ground (e.g. concrete or asphalt) by combining the lower frequencies of a high microphone sampled spectrum with the high frequency portion from a low microphone sample.

Such potentially effective experimental methods require a great deal of knowledge of the source and ground acoustic characteristics and are usually beyond the scope of airport operators to predict. The global influence of the ground on the overall metrics such as PNLM, EPNL or SEL(A) is preferred since this requires no knowledge of the one-third octave band spectrum of the source nor the time variation of this spectrum during the fly-by event. At its simplest this has been expressed in the method used for NNI prediction in the UK. Below a certain elevation angle the rate of attenuation for the PNLM is increased from 8 to 10 PNdB per doubling of distance. The progression has been arranged to be a smooth function between

the onset at about 15 degrees to the horizon down to 0 degrees where the full extra 2 PNdB is reached. The exact curve and algebraic expression involved are given in *Figure 19.17* from reference 23 which outlines the method of calculating NNI.

A slightly more involved but essentially straightforward way of allowing for ground effect on the EPNL or SEL(A) scales has been published.[17] It has been formulated after extensive comparisons of actual aircraft noise data by assuming that noise propagated to a distance directly under the flight-path (observer to aircraft elevation angle, 90 degrees) contains no extra ground attenuation. In contrast, data samples for lower elevation angles arranged to have identical slant ranges from the source differ from the under flight-path data by the required ground attenuation correction. This method of calculation is illustrated in *Figure 19.18* with the governing empirical equations.

These can be split into the distance effect for elevations as low as 3 degrees and the elevation angle effect for large distance. The resulting combined curves are shown in *Figure 19.19*. Note that the analysed data for various classes of aircraft type and for landings versus take-off did differ but was not so scattered as to prevent a good prediction to be made using the mean trend for all civil aircraft types examined. The results were based on the duration dependent metrics PNLM and SEL(A), but the reference states that the method is expected to apply also for the PNLM.

It is of interest to compare the global method for UK ground

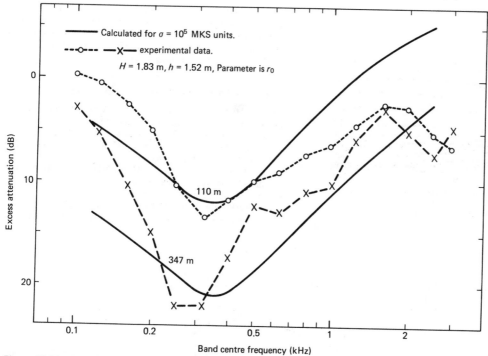

Figure 19.16 An example ground attenuation characteristic.
H=source height (m); h=receiver height (m); r_o=horizontal
separation between source and receiver along the ground (m);
σ=ground surface effective resistance (Rayls/m).

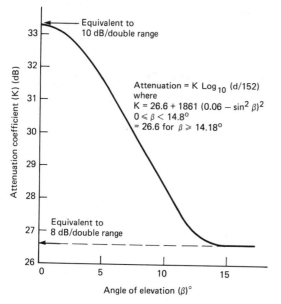

Figure 19.17 Allowance for ground attenuation in NNI
predictions

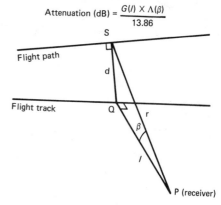

$G(l) = 15.09\ [1-e^{-2.74 \times 10^{-3}l}]$
  for $0 \leqslant l \leqslant 914$ m (3000 ft)
$G(l) = 13.86$ for $l > 914$ m (3000 ft)

$A(\beta) = 3.96 - 0.066\beta + 9.9e^{-0.13\beta}$
  for $0° \leqslant \beta \leqslant 60°$
$A(\beta) = 0$ for $60° < \beta \leqslant 90°$

$$\text{Attenuation (dB)} = \frac{G(l) \times \Lambda(\beta)}{13.86}$$

Figure 19.18 Basis for SAE ground attenuation date
comparisons

attenuation in NNI with the SAE method. *Figure 19.20* shows
that for the almost zero elevation case the NNI rule underestimates ground attenuation given by the SAE method by up to
3.5 dB at distances around 900 m from the source, but then
reverts to equality with the SAE method at 3200 m. For much
larger distances the NNI rule provides the greater attenuation
due to the ground. Above 5 km from the source, the NNI
method gives approximately 2 dB more attenuation.

Another empirical method was formerly used extensively in
aircraft noise prediction models both in the USA and some
European countries.[18-20] The expression and the distance trend is
shown in *Figure 19.21* where it is noted that the onset elevation
angle is 10 degrees. The onset angle for the UK method is 14.18
degrees, nominally 15.0 degrees, and for the SAE method it is

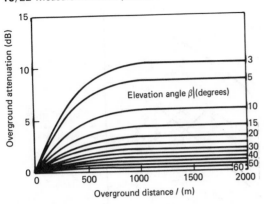

Figure 19.19 SAE ARP 1751 ground attenuation versus distance and elevation angle

about 60 degrees for the larger distances over the ground. The SAE method would seem to be based on the more thorough methodology and greater data base and it could become almost universally embodied in future prediction methods for both footprints and exposure index contours.

19.4.3 Wind and temperature gradient effects

Relatively few practical studies have been conducted leading to prediction of surface wind or temperature gradients on aircraft noise propagation. *Ad hoc* examples have been reported on effects of temperature inversions and it is well known that atmospheric sounding techniques employing frequencies of about 2 kHz can show up temperature inversions and other thermal or turbulence patterns in the lower atmosphere for interpretation by meteorologists.

Temperature inversion effects on aviation noise can be particularly marked causing a sound funnelling effect between

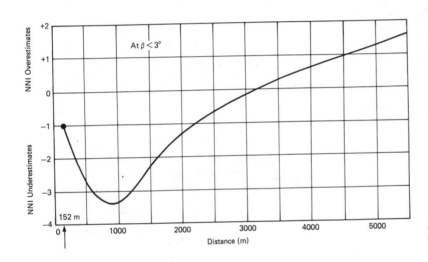

Figure 19.20 Difference between UK NNI and SAE 1751 ground attenuation at low elevation angle

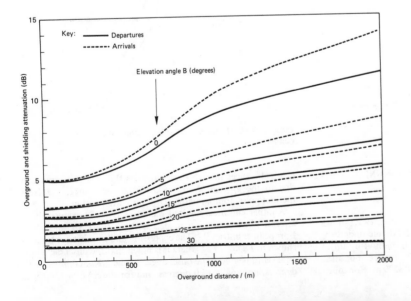

Figure 19.21 Other prediction schemes for ground attenuation and shielding effects

inversion layer and ground which effectively turns the usual ISL spreading into two-dimensional propagation with consequently a much lower attenuation rate. In the UK temperature inversions, albeit often only partial ones, occur on a very large proportion of the days of the year. In aircraft noise certification tests it has already been noted that checks must be made to ensure that inversion conditions do not exist. Noise prediction techniques are invariably drawn up for non-inversion conditions, hence in real day-to-day cases the noise propagation can be stronger over the longer distances than predictions allow for. The author knows of no systematic aircraft noise prediction method allowing for temperature gradient effects.

The effects of temperature and wind gradients are also described in Chapter 2 and the effects on noise propagation from an elevated source are illustrated in *Figures 2.11* and *2.12*. For the wind gradient case it is seen that the sound wave propagation paths curve asymmetrically in the upwind and downwind senses. The downwind effect causes rather more sound energy to reach ground level than for a homogeneous still atmosphere, whereas upwind there is a mechanism for a sound shadow zone to exist. The latter effect can produce a sudden marked attenuation amounting to tens of decibels but for large distances the effect appears to be almost progressive versus ground distance traversed. This is illustrated in *Figure 19.22* and is taken from a study performed on the effect of wind on noise propagation for near ground aircraft noises using thrust reversers as sound sources.[21] Although the data showed considerable scatter the mean trend was clearly for a correction of about 0.7 dB per knot of vector wind component (from source to receiver position, i.e. positive noise algebraic addition for receivers downwind and negative for upwind) at a rate of about one-third dB per m/s of vector wind. This is broadly in line with experience from near to the ground industrial and road traffic noise over flat terrain.

Although such wind effects are undoubtedly valid the formal prediction of noise contours excludes them by referring to still atmosphere datum conditions. It is left to specialists to argue for such effects to be considered in special and relevant circumstances during planning inquiries and similar forums.

19.5 Prediction of aircraft noise—flight operations

In this section the techniques for computer modelling of aircraft noise footprints and airport noise exposure indices are discussed. Wherever possible the subject will be treated generally,

but it will frequently be necessary to refer to specific computer models currently widely used. The main points can be illustrated by reference to two principal methods. The first is that developed by the FAA and used in the USA for contour predictions in NEF and other indices. The second method of interest is the NNI model used within the UK and Eire. Most other national prediction methods available use various combinations of the technique and features contained in these two models.

The FAA method is known as the Integrated Noise Model or INM. Several updates have been issued, the last to date being Version 3.[22] The FAA has made tapes of the model with its associated comprehensive and well-validated data base available widely to computer bureau and consultancy firms as a means of achieving uniformity over environmental noise impact determinations for airport developments in the USA.

The UK method is documented as a guideline to calculation of the NNI.[23] There is no universally published or supplied computer program made available by the responsible authority, but there are sufficient details published or understood by prediction practitioners to enable competent authorities to arrive at virtually identical answers for the same input data.

The INM mainly predicts exposure indices based on duration dependent noise scales EPNL and SEL(A). It therefore has to include the means of correcting for changes of duration due to flight speed and to curvature in the flight tracks where ground positions of interest lie close to the centres of circular track segments. In contrast the NNI method only uses the peak noise metric PNLM and in particular the very maximum value which occurs for a given aircraft movement. Consequently, there could be, say, three maxima of PNL arising at a ground position like that in *Figure 19.23*. The first arises from the portion of the take-off where the aircraft is still in contact with the runway, including the generally noisier start-of-roll. The second can arise after the aircraft has climbed sufficiently for the ground attenuation to become negligible (*see* Section 19.4.2). The third can arise where a curved flight track causes in effect another pass-by event.

Not all ground points will have three maxima and computer implementations of the NNI model can be made to skip cases which clearly do not apply. In general each value of maximum PNL has to be evaluated and the absolute maximum retained for inclusion in the NNI, but only if this value does not fall below 80 PNdB. It is over the precise algorithms used for these and other complications in the NNI formulation and current assessment practice that slight variations between one or other firm's computer output can and do arise.

Despite this there are some common points between the NNI and the NEF predictions which will now be discussed.

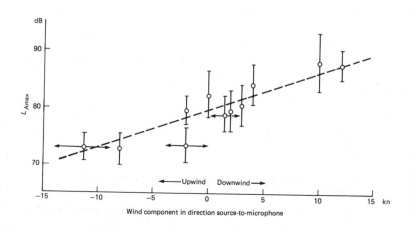

Figure 19.22 Effect of wind vector on noise propagation from near ground aircraft sources. Values are given as means with 90% confidence limits. Arrows indicate variable winds during measurements.

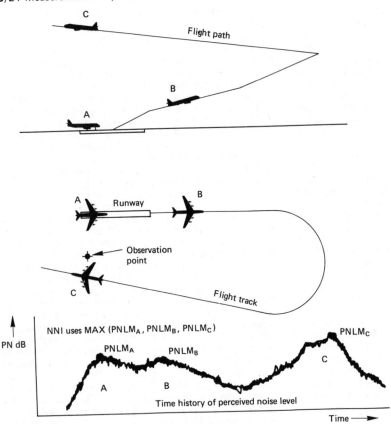

Figure 19.23 Multiple PNLM situations in NNI prediction. A=start of roll. B=out of ground effect. C=closest approach to observation point.

19.5.1 Basic framework for prediction process

Figure 19.24 illustrates the elements of the flight events for which noise must be determined by reference to the phase of the flight profile (i.e. the attendant power setting needed for the powerplant), the attenuation from aircraft to ground point, and the summation for the number of movement per relevant time period and (if valid) the time of day weightings. The procedure must be repeated for all combinations of flight track influencing the ground point and then repeated for all ground points reasonably close to the airport to enable contours of equal noise exposure to be inferred. The outline algorithm is shown in block diagram form in *Figure 19.25*.

Before discussing the detail it is necessary to organize certain data to deal with ground positions, flight tracks and so forth.

19.5.2 Coordinates system for computer modelling

Almost all computer models use a cartesian coordinate grid for the ground map over which the noise contours are required. In general all that is necessary is to use the coordinate system consistently to specify the locations of runways and the ground tracks in suitably sized segments. When choosing the origin and axes orientation it is often simplest to align one axis along the centre-line of the principal or perhaps only airstrip. This can ease the determination of many segments of landing and initial take-off coordinates. Also some programs are arranged to reduce the ground grid points to be covered by a process of working outwards from close to the runways from a high to lower noise exposure results. Once the result falls well below the lowest value of the noise index of interest the program switches to visit another column or row of the ground point grid. Choice of one axis to align with a runway simplifies this type of contour search algorithm.

Alternatively there can be merit in aligning the grid with the national map grid. In the UK this is the Ordnance Survey National Grid Reference framework use for all cartographic work. Use of the 100 km square Easting and Northing parameters as direct coordinates for the airports features becomes naturally advantageous when it comes to the plotting of the output noise contours to overlay standard-scale topographical maps. Also, since it is rarely the case that an airport region straddles a 100 km square boundary the coordinates origin becomes automatically outside the ground area of interest. This again saves coordination transposition necessary for popular contour determining packages which cannot handle negative grid values. The local definition of tracks and runways needs to be accurate to about 1 m, but this is usually not a problem since relevant positional data are very accurately specified on air navigation charts.

19.5.3 Data representation for runways and flight tracks

Whatever the chosen coordinates system the model requires as

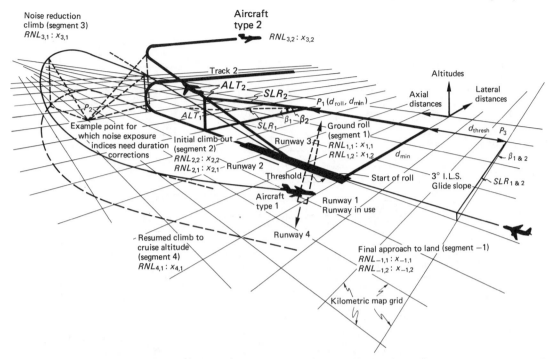

Figure 19.24 Noise contributions from multiple flight tracks. $\overline{L_{P_i}}=\overline{\Sigma}\Sigma$ (RNL—distance and ground correction). $\overline{\Sigma}$=Logarithmic summation; L=noise level; X=thrust setting; RNL=reference noise level; ALT=altitude; SLR=slant range; β=elevation angle; P=ground point; d_{roll}=axial distance (or track curve distance) from start of roll; d_{min}=minimum distance to track; d_{thresh}=axial distance to threshold.

input the ground line projections of aircraft flight paths (tracks) and the start-of-roll reference point on the runway for departure movements or the landing threshold reference point for arrival movements. This is accomplished by assigning a unique track number to each departure or arrival path carrying a significant portion of the airports movements in the period of interest. In some models the departure and arrival tracks are signalled to the computer by reserving, e.g. track numbers 31 and above for arrivals and 1 to 30 for departures. In other models the signalling is via the altitude profile numbering (see Section 19.5.5).

The SOR or Threshold references for a chosen track are achieved by making these the first specified point in its definition coordinates list. Incidentally arrival events are regarded in computer models as 'flying backwards' from threshold towards intermediate approach phase of the ATC procedure. Obviously this makes no difference at all to the calculated noise exposure and simplifies the computer program.

Tracks are usually defined by fairly short segments (*Figure 19.26*). A convenient way of segmenting is by marking the straight line and curved sections of the track. The curved segments can be represented by a pair of values the first being the turn radius and the second the angular change of course achieved at the end of the turn. A positive radius denotes an anticlockwise turn looking down on the map, a negative radius being for a clockwise turn. This definition fits the x axis to y axis convention for positive angle rotations in the cartesian reference frame. Turns must all be presumed to be circular arcs, or else effectively made to be so by splitting up variable radius tracks into shorter approximately circular segments.

By the same rationale the straight sections can be specified by

length value followed by a zero value for the turn angle. The successive segments are deemed to follow an initial direction according to the final direction of the previous segment. An obvious shortcoming of this system is that the radii of curves and the angles of turn must be very accurately specified in order that the ground coordinates 'flown over' at the larger distances from the airport remain accurate. It might be argued that aircraft navigational procedures followed on the flight-deck also rely on distances and (magnetic) course settings. However, aircraft are required by ATC to pass closely over certain navigation beacons at fixed ground locations at various points along the track. Consequently, a system of track coordinates liable to increasing positional area at large track-run distances is not ideal.

Another track segment system preferred in the UK for NNI modelling is to specify a list of the coordinates for straight-line equivalents to the curved sections (also shown in *Figure 19.26*). For straight segments this system still needs only two input values for the x and y coordinate component at the end of the line (the other end being specified by the previous segment and the first point of all being the SOR or Threshold reference point coordinate pair). For curves some 8–12 short lines are fitted to straddle the real track curve so that errors are minimized. This practice has the merit that it can be used to fit non-circular arcs. Additionally, the computer model has no need for algorithms to deal with two types of track segment for computing shortest distances from aircraft to a ground point.

19.5.4 Specification of lateral scatter of flown tracks

Because studies using radar and other techniques show that

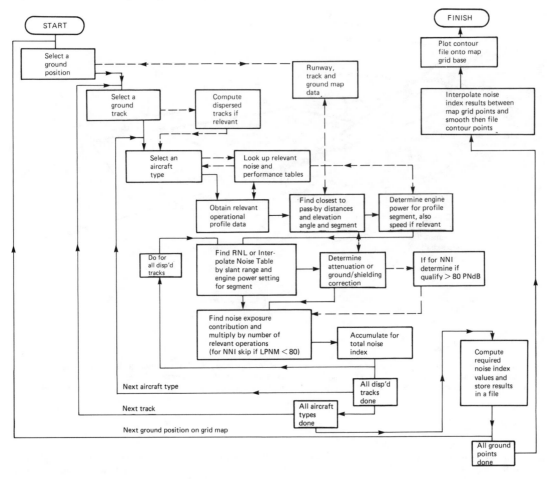

Figure 19.25 A general airport noise prediction architecture

aircraft follow paths which can deviate considerably from the tracks specified (e.g. as Standard Instrument Departures or SIDs laid down as ATC procedures to be pursued by all transport aircraft departure movements from a given airport), it is preferable to allow for this in the model. Not all national aircraft noise exposure calculation methods do so, but the UK NNI model is fairly typical of those that do.

Again from the radar or other observations over a relevant time period, the standard deviation (SD) of the lateral error of actual tracks from the standard track is determined and plotted versus trackline distance (*Figure 19.27*). Where the mean deviation is much different from the nominal SID then a new nominal trackline can be specified as the coordinates of the track to the computer model. A parallel exercise has to be done to define the SD versus track-run distance for the landing approach and although naturally enough the values are found to be only about 60% of the departure dispersion close to the airfield there can be difficulty over very diffuse arrival tracks in the approach phases well away from the final approach paths.

It has been found that by allocating fractions of the actual movements for the nominal track (as shown in the table below) the overall NNI calculated is acceptably close to the value which would be computed for the actual tracks found from the radar study:

Sub-track No.	1	2	3	4	5
Later track offset from nominal in SD multiples	+2.857	+1.355	0	−1.355	−2.857
Percentage of nominal air movements assigned	1.125	22.21	53.33	22.21	1.125

As indicated in *Figure 19.25* it is a simple matter to get the model to loop around noise calculations for these extra 'dummy' tracks, making appropriate modifications to the slant distances and elevation angles concerned, and using the appropriate factor for the number of aircraft movements to be included in the noise index contribution summation. For the NNI there is the added complication that each sub-track must be tested to see if the PNL computed for the current aircraft type and operational engine power falls below the value 80 PNdB. If it does so then the attendant number of events assigned to that sub-track is ignored in the exposure summation.

INM does not contain specific provision for dealing with dispersed tracks although the user can specify extra defined tracks and associated movements data within the capacity allowed by the program. In a model called CANAR[24] (using the

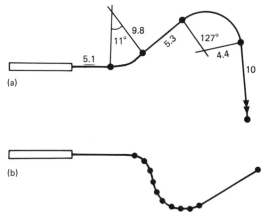

Figure 19.26 Track segments representation (INM/CANAR and NNI models). (a) for INM or CANAR. (b) for NNI model (ISVR).

basic structure of a pre-cursor to INM and developed by the Commission of the European Communities' Directorate General for the Environment, Consumer Protection and Nuclear Safety) the ability to handle track lateral dispersion has been incorporated together with several other useful facilities.

A discrete sub-track lateral dispersion model can pose difficulties over contour plotting which are discussed in Section 19.5.14.

19.5.5 Profile data for aircraft height and speeds

Figure 19.28 shows typical profiles of altitude and also the attendant engine power and flightspeed for the departure procedure and arrival landing approach adopted by civil transports. Usually the departure profile includes some form of reduced power, and hence reduced climb gradient, intended to abate noise over critical along-track positions near residential communities. Landing profiles may likewise incorporate power settings and appropriate airspeed and gradient data for a noise

reducing steep approach or a continuous descent approach rate (CDA) or low power/low drag (LPLD) technique.

In the computer model, the flight path is approximated by straight-line sections for which values of distance along track and height above initial start-of-roll reference are specified in a data array. In the NNI model this is accompanied by the attendant values of RNL (*see also* Sections 19.5.4 and 19.5.8), whereas in INM the values of necessary engine power for the profile section and the aircraft speed for correction of the duration-dependent noise index are stored within the array. The computer algorithm uses the convention that the RNL, power and airspeed data relate to the section of the altitude profile up to the associated trackline distance. The first point of the profile is matched to the appropriate current track reference point for start-of-roll or threshold. Profiles are assigned numbers in INM which can be associated with a given aircraft type. The take-off profiles are numbered less than 100 and those for landings greater than 100. In the NNI model the profiles are only specified for take-offs because a common profile for a standard 3 degree ILS approach plus the intermediate approach phase can be used for all arrival moments.

In INM the same commonality of standard approach profiles can be achieved in a slightly more involved but effective way. Engine power, airspeed and other details can be read by the computer from sets of approach data for the specific aircraft type and yet input via an approach altitude profile by a pre-arranged set of negative integer numeric codes. For example placing -3 as the engine power and -6 in the airspeed row of the array for a section of the descent slope means 'use the final approach airspeed and the engine power for a 3 degree glide slope with landing flap setting for this approach phase'.

INM (also CANAR) contain permanent profile and approach data sets for most commonly encountered aircraft types of interest for western nation civil airport noise studies. However, provision is made to substitute specific additional or alternative data to suit particular user cases.

19.5.6 Allowances for ATC override of take-off profile

In the case of some international airports situated in very busy

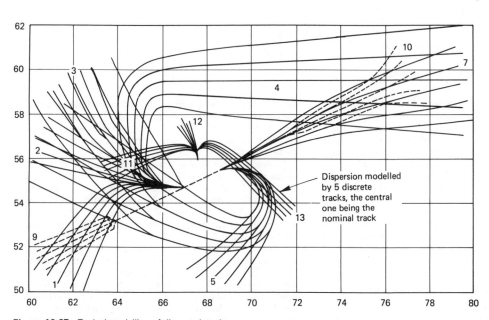

Figure 19.27 Typical modelling of dispersed tracks

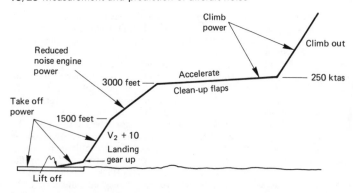

Examples of input data—departures

Profile — NR: 32

INM
CANAR

Distance (ft)	0.00	6000.00	9580.00	19500.00	36450.00	66200.00	94950.00
Height (ft)	0.00	0.00	260.00	1500.00	3000.00	4350.00	7000.00
Airspeed (kn)	332.00	165.00	165.00	165.00	165.00	165.00	250.00
Power (lbf)	15200.00	15200.00	15200.00	12600.00	12600.00	12300.00	0.00

Plane No. 1

NNI
(ISVR
MODEL)

Distance (m)	500	1000	4000	6000	20000
Heights (m)	0	15	450	914	2600
Noise	132.0	126.0	119.0	119.0	119.0

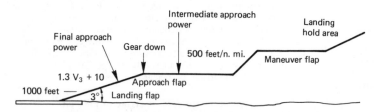

Examples of input data—approach for CANAR or INM

Profile — NR: 101

Distance (ft)	−1.00	−954.00	21950.00	67760.00	126000.00	135500.00	184100.00
Height (ft)	0.00	0.00	1000.00	3000.00	3000.00	3000.00	7000.00
Airspeed (kn)	32.00	−2.00	−2.00	−2.00	160.00	160.00	200.00
Power (lbf)	−10.00	−3.00	−6.00	−5.00	−7.00	−8.00	0.00

(Note NNI model presumes 3° ILS approach profile)

Figure 19.28 Take-off and landing profiles
(INM/CANAR and NNI models)

ATC zones there is a need to prevent departing flights from climbing freely at the aircrafts' normal *en-route* climb power and flight path gradient in order to avoid conflicting air traffic patterns, e.g. on approach or on other SIDs with tracks looping back to cross others. In such cases the flight is required to hold to a speed, usually 250 kts EAS, and height of typically 2000 ft above airfield level (a.a.l). Comprehensive noise models enable the current profile to be overridden by these 'hold' constraints on altitude and speed, substituting an attendant engine power setting or RNL for the level flight condition and maintaining this until a distance along track for which 'release from hold' is specified (*Figure 19.29*). Beyond this latter trackline distance the normal *en-route* climb-out section of the profile is adopted with its attendant power, RNL and speed data.

19.5.7 Representation of aircraft movements data

This to an extent depends on the index being modelled, but usually the time period concerned is all or part of the 24 hour day. For NNI it is a 12-hour daytime period and the movements data is specified as the average over the three peak summer months. For the NEF the day is split into two periods and it is necessary to apply noise sensitivity weightings to the night portions of the movements.

In the NNI model it is thus only necessary to supply the model with a data array file of average daily movements for all tracks and for all aircraft types with distinct noise or profile characteristics within these track divisions of the total movements. Track numbers signalled as being for arrivals carry similar data for the (roughly) half of the total daily movement for the airport.

Because the INM model computes indices such as NEF requiring movements in various periods of the day to be treated separately, the movements mix is specified as a list against each track number in groups of four parameters. These are for the noise data set to be used relevant to the aircraft's engines (*see* Section 19.5.8), the profile data set for the aircraft take-off or approach (*see* Section 19.5.5), the day period movements, and

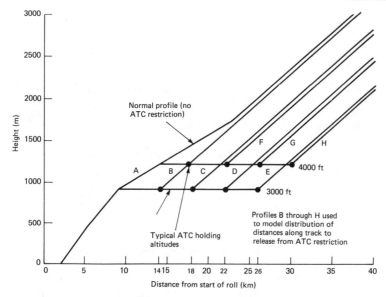

Figure 19.29 ATC override of take-off profile

finally the night movements. The latter is preceded by an extra parameter for evening movements in models such as CANAR for use in computing indices like L_{DEN}.

It should be noted that non-integer movements can be valid because of the average basis over the period of the year or choice of busiest weekday, as distinct from the real airport day where whole numbers of movements must essentially take place. In forecasting the movements it often transpires from examination of past movements logs that there is an imbalance between the total arrivals and the total departures within a single daytime window. Obviously this state of affairs cannot continue over longer time scales without either manufacturing or stockpiling aircraft! None the less an unequal number of movements for the NNI time window frequently is valid and justifiable since quite usually the departures from UK airports to Europe and the USA occur in the NNI period and very many of the return flights from Europe arrive in the early evening.

19.5.8 Representation of aircraft reference noise data

In the NNI model the departure mode RNLs are specified along with the relevant height profile data (*see* Section 19.5.5). It will be recalled that the RNL for NNI is the PNLM for a lineal distance of 152 m (500 ft) from the flightline. A value is supplied as a row of the array corresponding to each section of the profile, reducing in value from that appropriate to maximum take-off power for the engines, to that for initial climb with flaps retracted, then a reduced power noise abatement phase, then back to a higher power for *en-route* climb (*see Figure 19.28*).

For the landing approach the same height profile is used for all aircraft types so a separate data list is input for association with each type number. In the special version of the NNI model run at ISVR, University of Southampton, this list contains two or more RNL values which can be used by the model to assign noise data either to several phases of the approach (e.g. intermediate and then final) or can be used to set noise levels for a level flight segment of the take-off subjected to an ATC override on any chosen tracks.

For the INM the noise data is stored as a two-dimensional array against 8 standard lineal distances and up to six engine power settings. Two array sub-blocks are provided for each distinct engine type one for EPNL values and the other for SEL(A). Because of the temporal variations of these data they

are all standardized to an aircraft flight speed of 250 kts EAS and the speed data in the profiles or approach data sets (*see* Section 19.5.5) are used to correct the values to other required conditions. Note that INM provides for noise data to be associated with an engine type so that different performance aircraft having the same powerplant types can share noise data. INM (and CANAR) has its own comprehensive noise data base for most civil transport and executive aircraft which are encountered at western nation airports. User specified data can always be input, however. In CANAR sufficient basic noise metrics are stored to enable all European national as well as the $L_{eq}(A)$, L_{DN} and NEF to be selected for computation. This entails storage of four sub-blocks per powerplant type having the PNLM and $(L_A)_{MAX}$ metrics as well as those in INM.

19.5.9 Modelling start of roll

This is a very specialized topic not always properly understood and seldom modelled in other than noise footprint calculations. The possible extra noise lobes behind and to the side of the aircraft as it starts its take-off roll can have a marked effect on the local shape of airport noise contours. In the UK additional noise has been introduced into the standard NNI model for certain older technology aircraft types by assigning a higher RNL, applicable only to the initial 200 m of the runway roll, whilst modelling the rearwards lobe of start-of-roll noise by a simple semi-circular arc contour shape of radius determined by the RNL for this initial segment. For specialized exercises more sophisticated adaptations of the model have been made[25] but at the time of writing the procedures for computing the effect more accurately are under revue internationally.[1,2] The extra noise for the relevant types of aircraft principally arises because the data base accumulated for the initial take-off climb flight-phase from actual operational surveys at UK airports had been taken to apply unmodified to the runway-ground roll phase.

Measurement studies[26] show that the almost static condition at initial take-off elevates the RNL above that found for the initial climb. Furthermore, the peak is directed approximately 45 degrees to the rear axis (whereas for the in-flight noise the PNLM is taken to occur at some unspecified position along the lineal distant line from the aircraft path). The increase is confined largely to the older narrow-bodied aircraft but all types exhibit the rearwards lobe. The measurement exercise encountered the surface wind effect on propagation (*see* Section 19.4.2) and inferences were made after the best available corrections were applied to the raw data.

Based on this work the (ISVR) NNI model now incorporates a procedure to check for a start-of-roll noise situation for each ground position and take-off flight track combination where the ground distance in a lobe at 45 degrees to the rear is short enough to be significantly affected. The model stores incremental values for the initial take-off climb RNLs of each aircraft type for the purpose and synthesizes the lobe shape using a function of the azimuth angle to the rear axis which fits typical static jet and rear radiated fan noise directivity data.

The official NNI model does not include the thrust reverser noise which typically occurs about halfway along the landing runway for those aircraft types using this form of additional speed brake. The ISVR model can allow for this as a special exercise by using a similar technique to that described above for the start-of-roll noise, although in this case the noise is taken as omnidirectional since reverser jets spread via cascades of vanes in the jet pipe or fan duct walls or via deflectors which move into place behind the normal exhaust nozzles.

19.5.10 Modelling distance effects

In INM or CANAR there is no need to model specific effects of distance extrapolation of the noise unless the elevation angle from flight path to ground falls below the ground attenuation limit (*see* Section 19.4.2). Distance effect from air to ground is automatically found by interpolating the noise data array for the engine power and slant range determined in the model from the profile data and the track geometry. For ground attenuation, former versions of INM and CANAR used the corrections of *Figure 19.21* but the latest versions have provision for using the SAE corrections of *Figure 19.19* from reference 17. The corrections are straightforward functions of the elevation angle and the shortest ground level path from the ground position to the flight track (i.e., the slant range times the cosine of the elevation angle).

In the NNI model the distance effect for ground effect is built into the coefficient K which is a function of the elevation angle. K is used as a factor on the logarithm of the lineal distance ratio to the reference value of 152 m. K becomes 26.6 above 14.18 degree elevation angle and this makes the distance attenuation of PNLM equivalent to 8PNdB per doubling of the lineal distance. At 0 degree elevation K becomes 33.3 equivalent to 10 PNdB per doubling of the slant range.

19.5.11 Modelling duration effects for curved track segments

Whereas the duration changes in the EPNL or SEL(A) due to distance are found from the noise table interpolations in the INM and CANAR programs, extra duration effects can be encountered at certain ground positions lying close to the ground track projections of circular arc flight path segments. This arises because the noise table is derived from straight flight path test measurements. A procedure in the model is invoked automatically to test for such cases and extra noise exposure of up to 3 EPNdB or dB(A) to all duration related indices over relevant ground localities.

19.5.12 Summing contributions from tracks and movements

Accumulation of contributions for the various indices selected for calculation by the model is performed at the end of the routine for each selected aircraft type within the program loops for ground location and flight track. At this stage the exposure

contribution, which has been converted into an exponent to the base 10 for normal decibel summation rules, is factored by the number of movements assigned to the current track for the aircraft type. This is done for the night (and evening if relevant) movements using the weighting for subjective sensitivity relevant to the index concerned.

At the close of all loops for aircraft types and tracks the total accumulated exposure contribution is re-converted to logarithm base ten form and hence into the total noise index for the current ground position.

19.5.13 Application of weightings for time of day indices

This has been covered in part under Section 19.5.12 above. However, in the CANAR model many national indices are selectable including NNI, L_{eq}(A), I, Q, B, WECPNL(2), WECPNL(3), L_{DEN} and L_{DN}.

19.5.14 Noise contour coordinates determination and mapping

A noise contour map (for example, *Figure 19.30*) can be regarded as a topographical map with the noise level being analogous with ground contour height. The earlier versions of the USA prediction models used a method of tracing along a line of least slope around a 'hill' by testing the local gradient of a small group of grid points. Then by moving on round the contour in the indicated direction, with some trial and error either side, the next point was determined and this process was continued until a closed contour was reached. The procedure which is explained in detail in reference 27 had the aim of avoiding the need to scan all points of a grid around the airport if a single NEF contour was all that was required. However, if several contours are needed, say NEF 20–50 in steps of 5, it transpires that this method actually scans far more points (with up to 50 tries per interval 'around the hill') than needed for a simple calculation of a whole rectangular grid followed by a two-dimensional contour interpolation process.

The latter process is now followed by most multi-value noise contour prediction programs including the NNI and the CANAR models. The contour search algorithm is similar to that employed in standard graphics plotting package implemented on many mainframe systems.

The contour algorithm usually incorporates some form of smoothing routine, necessary because of the limited resolution of the map grid, aircraft profile, noise data tabulation and where relevant lateral track dispersion within the modelling. This can lead to asymmetry in contours or footprints where a theoretical axis of symmetry is known to exist. Plotting algorithms, therefore, incorporate a procedure whereby a group of successive coordinates from a contour search are 'fitted' with the best 3rd order or spline function and the exact smoothed valued stored. The group is then successively advanced by two points along the contour file, the process of smoothing repeated and the overlapping smoothed values averaged. Any reasonable order for the smoothing function could have been chosen but the 3rd order seems to give good results. Too much smoothing effect needs to be avoided otherwise the sharper ends of contours become distorted. For some contours even 3rd order smoothing leads to incorrect exhibition of symmetry where none is to be expected and for critical cases (such as a single aircraft event footprint) the smoothing process should be performed by taking the coordinate pairs in the closed contour points file firstly in the order as filed, then again smoothly in the reverse order of the file, and finally averaging the resulting two sets of smoothed x,y values.

Especial care should be taken over low valued noise exposure

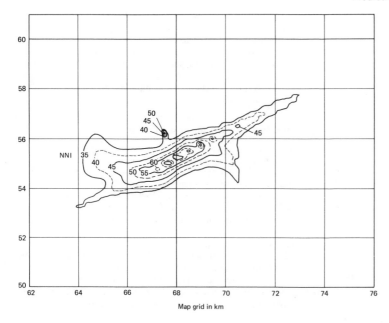

Figure 19.30 An example set of contours for NNI using the dispersed track data of *Figure 19.27*

contours for an airport where the five dummy track dispersion model is employed, since unless optimum smoothing is used the contours can display individual distortions due to the positions of the dummy tracks on the map. This is an artefact of the discrete track modelling technique employed instead of a totally random distributed model for aircraft positioning errors, and hence such distortions are not really expected in practice.

19.5.15 Areas within contours, populations included

It is useful to know the area of terrain that is enclosed between successive contours or the total area lying within a contour. A contour mapping routine developed at ISVR can automatically generate a list of these, making due allowances for areas of a given noise value lying outside a main contour or conversely embedded within a main contour where the local noise field falls into a 'hollow'. Given a population density matrix from Census data the included population estimate can also be output. These features are also offered by the latest version of INM and CANAR. The ISVR model permits accurate lists of the smoothed coordinates to be produced so that cartographers and planners can define statutory noise insulation compensation scheme zones etc.

19.5.16 Other interpretation aids

Besides evaluations based on area or population within contours, maps may be drawn up showing the land classes which would become impacted by airport developments. Special considerations naturally apply to schools, hospitals and places of worship as well as leisure/recreation areas, wildlife sanctuaries and similar noise sensitive zones. Reference 28 gives detailed procedures for such assessments as practised in the USA in connection with its environment protection policies. *See* Chapters 20 and 22 for further details on airport noise planning and assessment procedures.

19.5.17 Additional reports generation

The INM model contains many additional reports generation features to aid detailed diagnosis of the effectiveness of noise

control or basic airport design/development options. For example, a report can be output listing the flight tracks and aircraft types most contributory to a particular ground location's noise exposure. INM also allows a user to review the data base for noise, profiles, input tracks and movements as required to verify the correct noise contour analysis for any application.

19.5.18 Sources of data for input to models

Where noise or profile data are not provided within the model or are not suitable the user has to input the best available alternatives. The INM data base has recently been updated following extensive validation exercises at real airports.[29] It is understood to be the CEC Directorate General's intention to update CANAR to be compatible with future releases of the INM data base.

In the UK none of the Government Departments nor the CAA department responsible for generated NNI maps for civil airports publishes a general data base. Each year samples of movements numbers and operational noise recordings in the vicinity of the major London Heathrow and Gatwick airports are collected and used as the basis for the official NNI maps. For public planning inquiries and other prediction situations the authorities are helpful on an *ad-hoc* basis supplying summary data for appropriate aircraft types, or statistics for flight tracks and movements distributions or arriving at a consensus view over consultants' data where this conflicts.

Naturally the vast and unified body of data with INM provide a useful source for users who do not have direct access to the unpublished reference noise levels and profiles. Also the FAA has published a series of advisory documents[30] with the results of FAR Part 36 aircraft noise certification levels and a rank order list of aircraft loudness in dB(A) units derived from the basic test data for certification. Such data can be used with caution to derive reasonably good estimates for non-duration dependent indices like NNI. *Table 19.4* gives some general guidance for this, but it is emphasized that the results reflect the strictly controlled meteorological and flight procedures used for the aircraft type certification programme at its declared maximum operating weights. Also, the best guess has to be made as to how the 'trading' of the 3 point levels have been agreed and

Table 19.4 Approximation for obtaining RNL for NNI starting from noise certification results

Aircraft category	Sideline	Approach
From ICAO or FAR Pt. 36 Three Point Aircraft Noise Certification Results (not requirement levels) in EPNdB		
Old-technology long-range jets	+10.5	+9.5
Old-technology medium-range jets	+6.5	+20.0
Old-technology Short-range jets	−1.0	+19.0
Older wide-bodied long-range turbofan	+11.0	+16.0
New-technology Short/medium-range airbus	+0.0	+18.0

From ICAO or FAR Pt. 36 Single Point Aircraft Noise Certification Results (not requirement levels) in dB(A).
All types, to obtain take-off PNLM at 150m distance, add +5.0 to the LAM numerical result. Due to the possible performance correction in the certification process this may lead to a value up to 5.0 PNdB too high for types with inferior sea level rate of climb performance.

Sideline gives take-off PNLM and Approach gives Arrival PNLM in PNdB at 152m distance ±2 PNdB. Certification trade-off effects not included and must be allowed for if relevant.

made within the trading rules permitted, and these were noted earlier to be different between the USA and the ICAO rules. Finally the detailed profiles for noise abatement flown by an operator at a given airport might not be the same as optimized to gain the best certification at the three standard locations.

Where suitable data cannot be found in existing data bases or by adjusting official certification results it is preferable to make direct measurements for representative operations at the existing or another similar airport. For most airports of interest the flight tracks to be used are set out in air navigation instructions for flight-deck crew. *Figure 19.31* shows an example SID track instruction and from the longitude and latitude and bearings given for the various navigation beacons the nominal track to be flown, the initial portion of which is usually aligned with official UK airports minimum noise routes or MNRs, can be mapped quite accurately. However, most major airports can supply ready-made topographical map overlays of these SID tracks as well as the arrival tracks, landing approach hold areas (stacks) and so forth.

Lateral dispersion statistics are not so easy to determine but some general results can be stated in terms of airports without complicated curve SIDs (e.g. the track dispersion in the model used by the French Civil Aviation Authority is stated in terms of a splay angle which differs from 12 degrees for major airports departure tracks to 6 degrees for smaller local airfields).

All civil airports keep detailed runway control logs of all departures, arrivals and training circuits with data as to the event time, runway used, aircraft type and registration, whether flight is under Visual or Instrument rules, and usually the navigational departure route for which clearance was given by ATC. Analysis of such log data for existing airports can be used to predict movements allocations amongst relevant noise classifications of aircraft type and amongst relevant tracks for any period of the day or for a given season. Of course noise contours for future scenarios require suitable forecast movements mix data, a complex business requiring specialist knowledge of the air transport market.

19.5.19 Comparisons of prediction models

There is not space in this chapter to make comparisons of prediction validity as between the various models mentioned, nor for other national methods (e.g. the very specific procedure used in the Federal German Republic, reference 31). Some guidance is given in reference 32 which compares the INM and NOISEMAP models and indicates that significant differences can occur for essentially the same input to different prediction programs. The international working parties are actively drawing up schemes which, by using performance and noise data which originates or is recognized as valid by the airframe and engine manufacturers, will enable single event footprints of noise to be generated. These footprints could then be used to produce noise exposure index contours in a way that could be replicated by all concerned with their application.

19.6 Prediction of aircraft noise—ground operations

Generally, the prediction of aircraft noise is determined taking into account the various phases of in-flight operation described previously in Section 19.5. In the case of the NNI this necessarily excludes the noise produced from the moment of touchdown on landing up to the end of the taxi to the commencement of the departure runway start-of-roll point. None the less these ground operation phases can often cause noise annoyance to the community close to the airport and has to be predicted to aid the planning decision process. In this section the questions that need to be addressed are reviewed. In total these are complex and fall into two groupings:

1. Those to do with ground operations of aircraft within the airport complex (taxi in, apron servicing and aircraft systems support, ground testing of engines, taxi out).
2. Those on the landside (vehicle transportation for passengers, airport workers and cargo activities).

Noise impact studies for these activities are necessary where airport developments are planned (e.g. new or expanded passenger terminals, runway or taxiway extensions or surface access improvements), or else for a proposed completely new airport and its infrastructure. In each instance the first approach is to measure the existing noise environment. Subsequent analysis must then provide an estimation of the additional intrusion of the proposed development. The relative importance of near ground noise compared with that from overflying aircraft is highly dependent on the relationship to the airport and the surrounding communities. The communities affected by near-ground operation are potentially subject to a greater variety of aircraft related noise sources than those affected mainly by overflying aircraft and therefore a detailed analysis of the problem is essential in order to identify those sources contributing to the overall noise exposure. A similar problem also occurs when analysing the problem of noise control within the airport boundary. To establish noise exposure baseline measurements are preferable to analytical estimates, providing insight to local operation effects and environmental parameters.[33] Measurement locations should sample the noise from taxiways, start-of-take-

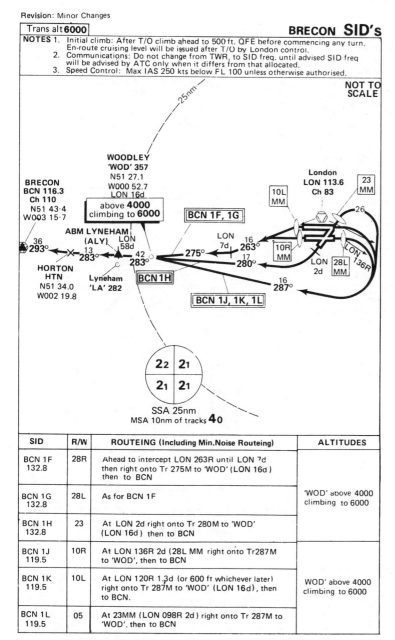

Trans alt **6000**		**BRECON SID's**

NOTES 1. Initial climb: After T/O climb ahead to 500 ft. QFE before commencing any turn. En-route cruising level will be issued after T/O by London control.
2. Communications: Do not change from TWR, to SID freq. until advised SID freq will be advised by ATC only when it differs from that allocated.
3. Speed Control: Max IAS 250 kts below FL 100 unless otherwise authorised.

NOT TO SCALE

SID	R/W	ROUTEING (Including Min.Noise Routeing)	ALTITUDES
BCN 1F 132.8	28R	Ahead to intercept LON 263R until LON 7d then right onto Tr 275M to 'WOD' (LON 16d) then to BCN	'WOD' above 4000 climbing to 6000
BCN 1G 132.8	28L	As for BCN 1F	
BCN 1H 132.8	23	At LON 2d right onto Tr 280M to 'WOD' (LON 16d) then to BCN	
BCN 1J 119.5	10R	At LON 136R 2d (28L MM right onto Tr 287M to 'WOD', then to BCN	
BCN 1K 119.5	10L	At LON 120R 1.3d (or 600 ft whichever later) right onto Tr 287M to 'WOD' (LON 16d), then to BCN.	WOD' above 4000 climbing to 6000
BCN 1L 119.5	05	At 23MM (LON 098R 2d) right onto Tr 287M to 'WOD'. then to BCN	

Figure 19.31 Example of minimum noise route/standard instrument departure navigational instructions

off-roll, thrust reversal, engine ground testing, cargo and maintenance areas and road traffic.

Measurement locations must represent areas within the airport complex and adjacent community where noise appears to present a serious problem. The type of measurement conducted depends on the sensitivity of the problem of each location and recorded data must establish an accurate noise environment representation. Sample times might vary from 10 minutes per site up to 24 hours for a really accurate baseline. Weather and airport operation characteristics can greatly affect the noise environment and variations of 10 dB(A) between similar aircraft types for equivalent ground manoeuvres dictates sufficient measurements per location to estimate the standard deviation of the noise level in terms of L_{90} and $L_{eq}(A)$. These are the descriptions necessary to characterize general environment and background noise. The attenuation of ground noise did not fit any of the hitherto published procedures for estimation and it has been necessary to collect fresh experimental evidence on this.[34]

19.6.1 Taxiway noise

The taxiways of modern airports often form a complex network of paths via which aircraft proceed from stands to the take-off runway start or from the landing run turn-off to the stands, also between maintenance and cargo areas. At any moment aircraft may need to manoeuvre or queue depending on ground traffic density and clearance for take-off via ATC. Taxiing involves low engine thrusts, indeed often so low on the larger turbofan powered types that taxiing takes place entirely at minimum ground idle power. For other types it is necessary to increase power somewhat to get the aircraft rolling and then reduce power to minimal. This action tends to produce noise highly variable in level and character. The source directivity alters a lot at these powers and also the alignment of the aircraft axis varies to the observer as taxiway curves are negotiated. Again it is preferable to measure representative taxi-by events for each relevant type and to use these results as a basis for synthesis of the hourly or daily schedule. Measurements are taken if possible at a standard short lineal distance and the attributes of the time history (e.g. L_{Amax} and SEL(A)) used for the synthesis by using the aforementioned collected attenuation data.

Allowances ideally include shielding due to airport buildings and other large noise screening features, but the recent evidence of *Figure 19.32* would indicate that at large distances the screening effect becomes swamped by the general variance of

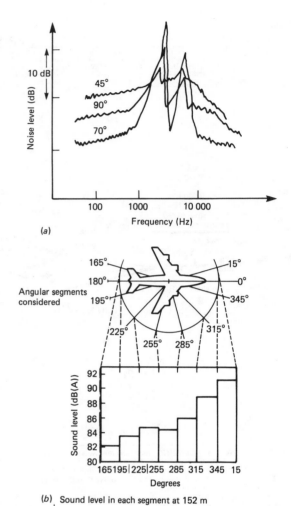

Figure 19.33 Example ground running directivity and spectra. (*a*) Typical engine noise spectra at taxiing powers. (*b*) Typical noise levels in angular segments from taxiing wide-bodied aircraft

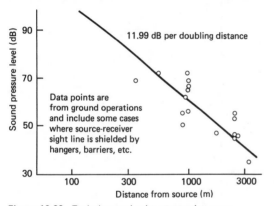

Figure 19.32 Typical ground noise attentuation curve

distance attenuation which averages some 12 dB(A) reduction per doubling of range over the ground.[34] Without specific taxiway measured data it is possible to employ the limited availability data taken around aircraft running their engines statically[33] (*Figure 19.33*). However, this brings in certain problems. The aircraft static data are often contaminated due to fuselage shielding effects which are more noticeable at close range and this is the more so if only one engine can be run at a time. Also it then becomes necessary to synthesize the taxiway noise from this polar noise data with allowances for the timings taken over taxiing and direction changes and periods of waiting at runway intersections, etc. None the less such estimates can be reasonably made given realistic surveys for these events and good distance attenuation data for the location.[35–37] This work tends to be conducted in an *ad hoc* fashion rather than using a formal prediction model as for flight noise. The author knows of no formal model equivalent to INM or CANAR for the taxiway noise process, but specialized unpublished microcomputer programs have been set up in ISVR to ease parts of the calculation. The problem lies in the large degree of manual interpretation and selection of the relevant measured data that have to be made and which makes formal models unworkable to date.

None the less the same detailed analysis of movements by type and runway mode as is needed for the flight noise is essential as input as the various paths of the taxiway network are utilized differently according to size of aircraft and runway in use. This means that certain community areas close to the aircraft boundary can receive several days of noise followed by periods of almost no noise. Clearly, the average movements situation usually taken for flight noise becomes misleading for ground noise when dealing with hourly or 24-hour noise exposure metrics.

19.6.2 Apron and terminal stands noise

Taxiing takes place right onto the apron areas adjacent to passenger terminals or cargo/maintenance areas. Some quick-turn around short-haul or commuter flights load passengers without stopping engines so this forms one possible source of extended low engine power noise exposure for residential areas close to terminals. Mainly, however, the aircraft engines are shut down but larger aircraft can continue to run auxiliary power units (APU), which are small gas turbine units driving generators, in order to maintain essential on-board air conditioning and power for electrical equipment. APU noise data have preferably to be sample measured for relevant types (*Figure 19.34*) and used with appropriate distance and shielding attentuation rules to predict exposure at the residences. Although manufacturers now fit suppressors to APU exhausts the duration of APU noise activity often leads to high noise exposure compared with local background noise (in the absence of the airport related noise) because several stands affecting the dwellings are occupied more or less continuously for any sizeable and economically viable airport offering plentiful air transport services. APU noise tends to have fairly high frequency components which attenuate rapidly with distance and yet leaves a distinctive noise highly varied by atmospheric and ground attenuation short-term fluctuations. Hence choice of noise statistical descriptors such as the L_{10}, L_{eq}(A) and the sampling or estimating period (1/4 hour, 1 hour?) is important.

More recently there has been a development in the procedure used by some types of older technology turbofan powered aircraft to move back from the passenger loading 'airbridges' at terminals. Push-back using special tugs operating on the nose wheel is rapidly being disfavoured by operators of B727, DC9 and B737 aircraft at airports in the USA, and push-back is being achieved by using the thrust reversers (at lower than normal maximum engine reverse thrust ratings). The process is said to prove economic and safe. No studies yet of the additional noise exposure have been noted in the literature to date.

19.6.3 Cargo terminal and maintenance area noise

Cargo area noise is rarely dominated by the aircraft themselves once taxiing has been completed. Sometimes aircraft are towed to and from the area by tractor. Where complaints are received these are usually due to loading/unloading equipment and maintenance tools or hydraulic test equipment operated in or near hangers with opened doors, especially during hot summer weather. This is virtually impossible to estimate and sample measurements plus judicious scaling for activity escalation and

revised working procedures have to be employed in a similar way to assessment of industrial noise activity affecting residential areas.

In the special case of ground testing of engines there is a problem that essential work is rarely forecastable via a work schedule. Mostly such engine tests are only conducted on airports without regular main overhaul bases where some unscheduled engine fault has occurred requiring a short functional check-out before the aircraft returns to service. This nearly always happens during the more critical night period because this is the time when aircraft have to be checked over after a day's operation. Nowadays all airports involved with ground runs of engines insist on appropriate mufflers and increasingly complete noise testing pens or hush houses to reduce turbofan intake as well as exhaust noise. The prediction of ground running exposure calls for specialized knowledge not only of the engine types but also of muffler acoustic performance together with statistics of occurrence and reliable ground attenuation data, perhaps for night-time. An increasing number of airports are now banning night ground running altogether.

19.6.4 Infrastructural noise

This is mainly the extra noise caused by passenger, airport worker and cargo and supplies surface access. Obviously, roads and parking areas feature predominantly and for certain airports there are rail links and automatic local rail or magnetically levitated and guided people conveyors operating between terminals and external transportation interfaces. The assessment and prediction of these noise elements follows the same practice as for normal road and rail noise problems (*see* Parts 3 and 4).

References

1 Society of Automotive Engineers, A-21 Aircraft Noise Measurement Committee (and Sub-Committees). This U.S.A. committee has in particular sub-committees which deal with noise

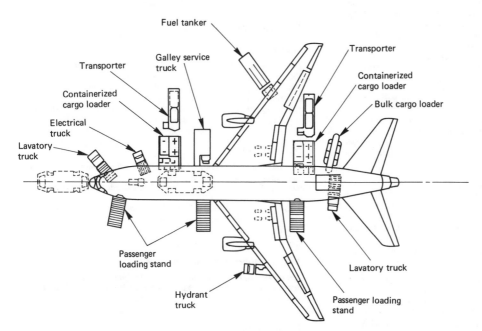

Figure 19.34 Noise from ground services and auxiliary power unit operations

measurement procedures, data normalization techniques and airport noise monitoring and prediction. Others deal with source noise and subjective acoustics. The airport noise contours sub-committee is evolving an ARP (Aerospace Recommended Practice) on the procedure for calculation of aircraft noise in the vicinity of airports, including single aircraft footprint contours. SAE also publishes *Aerospace Information Reports (AIR)*

2 Abatement of Nuisance Caused by Air Transport (ANCAT), a working group of the Technical Committee of the European Civil Aviation Conference (ECAC) with headquarters in Paris. ECAC has representation from 22 European nations via their civil aviation authorities. In particular ANCAT has been actively evolving a footprint-based method for more accurate prediction of single aircraft noise based on approved manufacturers noise and aircraft performance data, seeking proposals from AECMA (Association Europeene des Constructeurs de Materiel Aerospatial) for the detailed framework for the method.

3 International Standards Organisation ISO 3891: 1978, *Acoustics—Procedure for Describing Aircraft Noise Heard on the Ground*. This standard has an identical equivalent British Standard BS5727: 1979. ISO 3891 replaced two former ISO Recommendations R507: 1970 and R1761: 1970 which covered broadly equivalent areas.

4 *United States of America—Public Law 90–411*. Part 36 of the Federal Aviation Regulations.

5 International Civil Aviation Organisation. *International Standards and Recommended Practices—Aircraft Noise*, Annex 16 to the Convention on International Civil Aviation (1971 and subsequent revised editions).

6 International Electrotechnical Commission. *Sound Level Meters*. Standard Publication 651 (1979)

7 International Electrotechnical Commission. *Octave, Half-Octave and Third-Octave Band Filters intended for the Analysis of Sounds and Vibrations*. 225 (1966)

8 HOUSE, M. E. *Aircraft Flyover Measurements*, AGARD Lecture Series No. 80 on Aerodynamic Noise, AGARD-LSP-80 (1976)

9 The Council of the European Communities. *Council Directive of 20 December 1979 (80/51/eec)* on the limitation of noise emissions from subsonic aircraft (1979)

10 HELLER, H. *Propeller Aircraft Noise-Certification and Flight Testing*, Deutsche Forschungs- und Versuchsanstalt fur Luft- und Raumfahrt Report DFVLR-Mitt.82.16 (1982)

11 National Aeronautics and Space Administration, NASA Conference Publication 2052 (in 2 parts). *Helicoper Acoustics. Proceedings of The International Specialists Symposium*, NASA Langley Research Center Hampton, Virginia (1978)

12 LEVERTON, J. W. *The Airport and the Environment as Affected by the Helicopter*, Westland Helicopters Research Paper 449 (1973)

13 WHATMORE, A. R. University of Southampton, WUNVC ISVR Consultation Report 2619A, *Noise Measurement on Microlight Aircraft* (1984)

14 BAZLEY, E. N. *Sound Absorption in Air at Frequencies up to 100 kHz* National Physical Laboratory (NPL) Acoustics Report Ac74, (1976)

15 SAE ARP 866A. *Standard Values of Atmospheric Absorption as a Function of Temperature and Humidity* (1975)

16 SUTHERLAND, L. C. *Sound Propagation over Open Terrain from a Source Near the Ground—A Brief Review*, 84th Acoustical Society of America Meeting (1972)

17 SAE AIR 1751. *Prediction Method for Lateral Attenuation of Airplane Noise during Take-off and Landing* (1981)

18 Federal Aviation Administration. *FAA Integrated Noise Model, Version 1, Basic Users Guide*. Report FAA-EQ-78-01 (1978)

19 DICKENSON, P. J. *Mathematical Model to Determine the Economic Impact of Achieving Reduced Community Noise from Aircraft*, University of Southampton ISVR Contract Report (1971)

20 O.A.C.I. Circulaire 116 AN/86 *Descriptive de la Methode I_P (France)*.

21 HIGGINSON, R. F. and RENNIE, R. J. *Noise from Engine Thrust Reversal of Landing Aircraft*, National Physical Laboratory (NPL) Acoustics Report Ac83 (1977)

22 Federal Aviation Administration, *FAA Integrated Noise Model, Version 3, Users Guide* Report FAA-Ee-81-17 (1982)

23 DAVIES, L. I. C. *A Guide to the Calculation of NNI*, DORA Communication 7908 (2nd edn.), Civil Aviation Authority, London (1981)

24 Commission of the European Communities (CEC), Directorate General for the Environment, Consumer Protection and Nuclear Safety, Brussels, *The Consequences of Aircraft Noise Abatement Regulations (CANAR), [Airport Noise Contour and Single Event Footprint prediction system]* (1982).

25 HOUSE, M. E. *Gatwick Second Terminal Inquiry—Proof of Evidence* Ref. S.C.C. 3,3A (1980) and S.C.C. 3(S),3(S)A (1980)

26 DAVIES, L. I. C. *Ground-Roll Noise Modelling in the DORA Noise and Number Index Computer Model and Measurements at Heathrow and Gatwick*, DORA Communication 8204, Civil Aviation London, (1982)

27 BARTEL, C., COUGHLIN, C., MORAN, J. and WATKINS, L. *Airport Noise Reduction Forecast (Volume II)*, U.S. Department of Transportation Report DOT-TST-75-4 (1974)

28 U.S. Department of Transport, *Environmental Assessment Notebook Series: Airports* (in 3 parts plus user guide), DOT P 5600.5 (1978)

29 FLATHERS, G. W. *FAA Integrated Noise Model Validation: An Analysis of Carrier Flyovers at Seattle-Tacoma Airport*, FAA-EE-82-19 (1982).

30 Federal Aviation Administration, U.S. Department of Transportation, *Estimated Airplane Noise Levels in A-Weighting Decibels*, Advisory Circular Ac 36 (updated editions).

31 Federal Republic of Germany *Durchfuhrung des Gesetzes zum Schutz gegan Fluglarm* (BGB1, I S. 282) (1971)

32 CHAPKIS, R. L., BLANKENSHIP, G. L. and MARSH, A. H., Comparison of aircraft noise-contour prediction programs. *Journal of Aircraft*, **18**, 926–933 (1981)

33 LARGE, J. B. and HOUSE, M. E. The status of airport noise prediction, with special reference to the United Kingdom and Europe. *Noise Control Engineering*, **17** (1981)

34 WALKER, J. G. and FLINDELL, I. H. *Long Range Prediction of Airport Ground Noise, Proceedings of Internoise 83*, Edinburgh U.K. (1983)

35 LARGE, J. B. *Public Inquiry into the Proposed Development of Birmingham Airport—Proof of Evidence on Noise from Airport Operations*, Ref Report 2217 (plus Annexes A–D) (1979)

36 LARGE, J. B. *An Assessment of Ground Noise Associated with BAA Proposals for the Development of Gatwick Airport—London*, British Airports Authority Report (in 2 vols.) (1979)

37 LARGE, J. B. *Stansted Airport—London, Future Development, Ground Noise Assessment*, British Airports Authority Report (in 2 vols.) (1981)

Further reading

General

LYON, R. H. *Lectures in Transportation Noise*, Grozier Publishing (1973)
Proceedings of Internoise Conferences (Annual)
Proceedings of Noise-Con 77, NASA Langley Research Centre, Hampton, Virginia, USA (1977)
Proceedings of International Congresses of Acoustics (ICA), held every 3 years, 1953 ... 1974 et seq.

Measurement

HASSALL, J. R. and ZAVERI, K. *Acoustic Noise Measurements*, Bruel and Kjaer (1978)
BRUEL, P. Sound level meters—The Atlantic divide. *Noise Control Engineering*, **20**, 64–75
TANIGUCHI, H. H. and RASMUSSEN, G. Selection and use of microphones for engine and aircraft noise measurements. *Sound and Vibration*, **13**, 12–20 (1979)

Aircraft noise sources/comparisons

VON GIERKE, H. E. Aircraft noise sources. In *Handbook of Noise Control* (Ed. Harris, C. M.), Chapter 23 McGraw-Hill, New York (1957)

Propagation

DELANEY, M. E. *Sound Propagation in the Atmosphere: A Historical*

Review. Institute of Acoustics Tyndall Lecture 1975, Proc. IoA, I, Medal Lectures (1974–77)

Group of Aeronautical Research and Technology in Europe (Garteur), Section 5: Aircraft Noise. Third Specialist Meeting on Atmospheric and Ground Effects on Sound Propagation, Royal Aircraft Establishment, Farnborough, UK, June 1978.

DELOACH, R. *On the Excess Attenuation of Sound in the Atmosphere*, NASA Technical Note TN D-7823, March (1975)

Acoustic Effects Produced by a Reflecting Plane, SAE AIR 1327 (1976)

Predictions—flight

CANAR—Information Bulletin No. 1, Commission of the European Communities, Ref. XI/791/82-FR, ANTEWG 5—INF 2 (1982)

CONNOR, T. L. and FORTESCUE, D. N. *Area Equivalent Method on Visicalc*, FAA Report EE-84-8 (1984)

SPEAKMAN, J. D. NOISEMAP—The USAF's computer program for predicting noise exposure around an airport. *Proceedings. Internoise 80*, (1980)

GALLOWAY, W. J. Airport noise contour predictions—improving their accuracy. *Internoise 80* (1980)

MONK, R. R. and BUTLER, M. C. *Survey of Track Keeping of Aircraft Departures from Gatwick Airport*. CAA Paper 78014, Civil Aviation Authority, London (1978)

Airport Strategy for Great Britain (in 2 parts), HMSO, London (1975/1976)

Criteria/ratings

BERANEK, L. L. *Noise and Vibration Control*, Chapters 7, 18, McGraw-Hill, New York (1971)

Environmental Health Criteria 12—Noise, World Health Organisation (1980)

SCHULTZ, J. Community noise ratings. *Applied Acoustics* Suppl. 1 (1972)

20

Control of Airport Noise Impact

Clifford R. Bragdon PhD, AICP
**Georgia Institute of Technology, Atlanta,
Georgia, USA**

Contents

20.1 Introduction

Airports are an increasingly important component of the total transportation network. Civil aircraft in 1982 flew world-wide over 9 billion km, carrying 649 870 000 passengers.[1] *Table 20.1* gives a list of the busiest airports and the passengers carried in 1985.[2] During the past decade the number of passengers carried by the civil fleet has more than doubled and the number of annual operations involving civilian and military movements at airports is rapidly growing. These operations include both fixed- and rotary-wing (helicopter) aircraft that use civilian (public and private) and military facilities.

While the control of noise impact generated by aircraft can be considered to be primarily the concern of the aircraft engineer to develop quieter aircraft, clearly this can only be considered to be part of the solution, and noise control has to be extended to the management of the complex interactions of airports and their surrounding communities.

This chapter addresses the two basic approaches to controlling aircraft noise impact. They include operational controls for the aircraft and land use controls for the surrounding land area. Operational controls can be further divided into the air- and ground-related activity, while land use in this chapter addresses regulations and economic incentives. (Chapter 19 also gives

Table 20.1 World's 50 busiest airports in 1985

Airport	Passengers*	Airport	Passengers*
1 O'Hare International: Chicago	45 725 939	26 Sea-Tac International: Seattle	10 477 166
2 Hartsfield Atlanta International: Atlanta	38 989 314	27 International: Philadelphia	10 286 281
3 International: Los Angeles	34 361 715	28 Sky Harbor International: Phoenix	10 239 690
4 Dallas/Ft. Worth Airport	32 267 444	29 Madrid–Barajas Airport: Madrid	10 225 303
5 Kennedy International: New York	29 934 779	30 McCarran International: Las Vegas	9 944 967
6 Heathrow Airport: London	29 147 200	31 International: Minneapolis-St. Paul	9 653 170
7 Stapleton International: Denver	28 806 349	32 Simon Bolivar International: Caracas	9 561 254
8 International: San Francisco	24 192 895	33 International: Hong Kong	9 538 900
9 International: Newark	23 654 163	34 Malaga International: Japan	8 942 824
10 La Guardia: New York	20 302 511	35 New Tokyo International: Japan	8 942 824
11 Boston-Logan International	19 417 972	36 Copenhagen Airport Kastrup	8 872 595
12 International: Miami	19 328 057	37 International: Orlando	8 726 645
13 Frankfurt/Main: West Germany	18 319 305	38 Zurich Airport	8 673 183
14 International: Osaka	17 669 899	39 Stockholm Arlanda Airport	8 638 220
15 Orly Airport: Paris	17 174 397	40 Charlotte/Douglas International	8 615 347
16 Lambert-St. Louis International	16 628 584	41 Changi Airport: Rep. of Singapore	8 379 528
17 International: Honolulu	16 559 673	42 International: Tampa	8 341 783
18 International: Toronto	14 752 499	43 King Abdulaziz International: Saudi Arabia	8 278 447
19 National Airport: Washington, DC	14 573 558	44 Kingsford Smith International: Australia	7 900 047
20 Gatwick Airport: London	13 953 600	45 Duesseldorf Airport	7 535 706
21 Charles de Gaulle: Paris	13 628 105	46 International: San Diego	7 173 272
22 International: Pittsburgh	13 414 626	47 William P. Hobby: Houston	7 134 794
23 Intercontinental: Houston	12 807 085	48 International: Salt Lake City	7 128 332
24 Metropolitan: Detroit	11 685 189	49 Vancouver International	6 895 059
25 International: Mexico City	11 481 024	50 Munich-Riem Airport	6 890 384

*Enplaned, deplaned, and transfer, in millions.
Source: Airport Operators Council International.

In the USA, for example, there are nearly 17 000 civil and military airports.[3] The majority of airports are privately operated (69%) and handle general aviation operations exclusively (88%).[4] There are no national statistics compiled for the number of operations since logs are kept only at towered airports during certain periods of the day. However, it is estimated that, where records are maintained, the fleet generates over 100 000 000 flight operations a year.

These airports contribute to the economic base of the community. Often, they influence the location of new business and industry, enhance economic development and stimulate employment opportunities. Nevertheless, despite the many positive airport impacts, there are certain undesirable by-products or negative impacts, of which noise is a leading concern. For example, the data collected annually by the US Bureau of Census for the Department of Housing and Urban Development show that approximately 5 000 000 US residents are affected by civil aircraft noise in excess of an annual 65 Day–Night Average Sound Level (DNL);[5] and that noise, in a general sense, is consistently ranked the most undesirable neighbourhood condition.[5]

information on aircraft operation, mainly in relation to source identification and prediction modelling.)

The methods of controlling airport noise and community impact within the USA are presented in *Tables 20.2* and *20.3*. The tables summarize the number and variety of methods currently in place based on surveys conducted at a total of 402 airport locations.[7,8] The techniques listed form the basis of the structure of this chapter, and although the methods listed here have direct relevance to US practice, the methods are generally applicable and have been implemented in other countries.

20.2 Control of noise impact (air controls)

The regulation of navigable airspace in most countries is a federal or national responsibility, which permits interstate commerce to occur uninterrupted. Legal questions continue to arise, especially when actions are taken by local authorities or an airport proprietor. Important in the testing of any proposed or

Table 20.2 Airport noise control methods: operational

Rank order	Operational controls	Airport communities	
		Number	Per cent[a]
1	Preferential runway	139	34.5
2	Ground run-up restrictions	94	23.3
3	Flight training restrictions	81	20.1
4	Noise abatement flight tracks	68	16.9
5	Noise abatement profiles	55	13.6
6	Aircraft bans	42	10.4
7	Partial curfew/ban	41	10.1
8	Noise monitoring	36	8.9
9	Slots (number of operations)	35	8.7
10	Noise emission levels	26	6.4
11	Displaced landing thresholds & take-off points	24	5.9
12	Capacity limits	6	1.4
13	Aircraft towing	5	1.2
14	Curfews	4	0.9
15	Operational fees	3	0.7

[a] Per cent of sample (402 airports).

Table 20.3 Airport noise control methods: land use

Rank order	Land use controls	Airport communities	
		Number	Per cent[a]
1	Zoning	133	33.0
2	Comprehensive plan	108	26.8
3	Land acquisition	77	19.1
4	Avigational easement	49	12.1
5	Noise disclosure	34	8.4
6	Environmental impact review	33	8.2
7	Building code	32	7.9
8	Capital improvements	18	4.4
9	Sound insulation	16	3.9
10	Development rights	10	2.4
11	Site design	9	2.2
12	Land banking	7	1.7
13	Subdivision regulations	6	1.4
14	Purchase assurance	4	0.9
15	Tax incentives	3	0.7

[a] Per cent of sample (402 airports).

enacted airport control is whether it might be discriminatory or place an undue burden on commerce. These legal, administrative, and political questions will continue to be discussed with case law and administrative policy being reviewed and re-examined.

20.2.1 Curfews

Air controls of this type generally apply to the time aircraft are permitted to operate. These time-use restrictions are referred to as curfews and they typically limit the hours in which an airport may permit flight operations to occur. Switzerland's International Airport at Geneva, with approval from the Federal Office of Civil Aviation, imposes a night-time operational curfew between 2200 and 0600, for all traffic.[9] Air carrier operations are restricted at Washington, DC, National Airport between 2200 and 0659.[10]

A partial curfew is also common where the airport proprietor permits certain operations at night, based upon the type or class of aircraft. For example, Palm Beach Florida International Airport prohibits scheduled departures of noisier aircraft between 2200 and 0700, specifically Stage 1 and Stage 2 aircraft defined using FAA, Part 36, Noise Certification.[11,12] Boston Logan International Airport adopted a similar provision using a slightly different time period (2230–0630) in early 1986.[13] Many international airports are adopting such rules referencing Annex 16 (Aircraft Noise and Engine Emissions) to the Convention of International Civil Aviation Organization (ICAO).[14]

Some airports place a restriction on the total number of operations over a selected time period. London's Heathrow International Airport permits 3650 aircraft operations at night (2230–0630) during the summer, while Gatwick allows 4300 for the comparable period. The Civil Aviation Authority, Department of Transport, would like to relax this requirement but there is considerable opposition.[15]

Restrictions in many countries are not limited to only civil aircraft. Tromsø Airfield in Norway uses a night-time restriction between 2200 and 0700 for all aircraft, including Harrier aircraft that use this facility for military exercises.[16] NATO countries use noise restrictions as part of military training, where feasible, particularly at night and during weekends.[17]

In rare instances complete curfews are in effect restricting any aircraft, usually at night. There are only four US airports known to have this restrictive a curfew (i.e., Santa Rosa Air Center, California; Austin Lakeway, Texas; Jackson Hole, Wyoming; San Martin, California).[7]

Curfews are considered by the aircraft industry to be the most severe form of noise control. They can have significant economic consequences for the industry, particularly when air transportation involves multiple time zones. Nevertheless, many airport communities throughout the world have instituted some type of partial or limited curfew.

20.2.2 Landing/take-off restrictions

The manner in which an aircraft must operate during take-off (departure) or landing (arrival) is heavily influenced by noise abatement procedures. *Table 20.2* shows that noise abatement profiles are used at 55 different US airports.

Figure 20.1 illustrates a departure profile consisting of three distinct phases. The first phase represents take-off, i.e. high initial thrust and small-to-moderate flap settings, initial climb-out and gear retraction. Maximum climb-out is desirable if there are sensitive land uses at some distance from the airport, but not immediately adjacent to the operational runways. Some US airports use this as a standard procedure.[7] Depending upon take-off procedure, the aircraft will retract flaps or clean-up and reduce the thrust to a specified setting. This is phase 2 of the take-off flight profile and is often referred to as take-off thrust reduction or cut-back. This procedure is currently standard practice at 10 major airports in the USA.[7] The overall objective is to limit the noise exposure during take-off until sufficient altitude has been obtained. However, the reduction in rate of climb can worsen the situation for people living slightly further away from the airport who would naturally prefer that the aircraft reached a good height before overflying their area. Clearly, the pattern of housing under the route has to be studied before a fair balance can be struck between these conflicting interests and the control is, in fact, unsuited to some airports. An additional factor which is of paramount importance is ensuring the safety of the aircraft. *Figure 20.1* shows the effect of reduced take-off thrust on the ground noise levels.

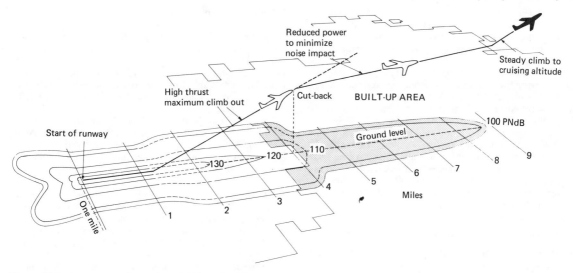

Figure 20.1 Departure profile used to minimize noise impact

Aircraft on final approach have certain noise abatement techniques that can also reduce the overall noise level. The Federal Aviation Administration has a recommended profile for landing aircraft using a 3° glide slope.[18] A similar glide slope is used for aircraft landing at Heathrow, London (see *Figure 20.2*). A reverse thrust is used when landing as soon as practicable to reduce aircraft speed at many airports. However, at airports with limited land, it can create a high peak noise level off the airport. Currently, five US airports apply thrust reversal controls as part of their noise abatement plan and several European airports do not permit reverse thrust procedures due to high noise impact.[21]

Both landing and take-off restrictions have been demonstrated to reduce the size of an airport noise contour. Most air carriers have adopted a noise abatement procedure as a policy wherever they operate. Northwest Orient Airlines developed the first corporate-wide noise abatement profile and their pilots are given training in operating this procedure.

20.2.3 Perimeter rule

This rule is used to limit the stage length of flights departing from and arriving at the airport. The stage length of a flight can influence noise in several different ways.

First, it can impact the capacity of a given airport. In general, the fewer number of operations will limit the overall noise on a time-integrated basis. With restricted stage lengths the aircraft's overall weight (i.e., maximum gross take-off weight), which is

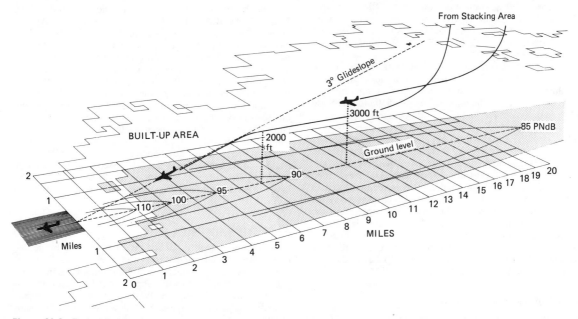

Figure 20.2 Typical flight profiles used as approach to a major airport

heavily influenced by fuel, is less. A lesser weight on take-off permits more lift which, in turn, can reduce the ground noise contour of the aircraft. Lastly, the type of aircraft needed for a reduced stage length may be quieter in comparison with aircraft used for longer flights.

This procedure has certain appeal, particularly when there are nearby airports that can operate without such restrictions. For example, Washington National Airport places a 1000 mile non-stop limit on commercial air carriers,[10,19] but this airport is paired with Dulles International Airport which does not have these restrictions, nor does Baltimore Friendship Airport. John Wayne Airport in California also had a policy on stage lengths permitting them to be no longer than 500 miles.[19] Again, there are other airports in the Los Angeles metropolitan area that can provide needed services. The application of this procedure has, however, been very limited, and the legal viability of technique may be questionable.

20.2.4 Noise abatement flight tracks

Unique flight tracks are prescribed for departures and/or arrivals to avoid overflight of noise-sensitive areas.

The flight track is the projection onto the ground plane of the three-dimensional flight path of aircraft. There is a flight track for both approach and departure activities. For noise abatement purposes, the flight track can be useful in positioning the aircraft in space relative to ground and land uses.

Many airports assign headings that place aircraft over non-populated land masses including water; agricultural land, forested and wilderness areas; or open space. This is a common feature in the location of airports in the United States. For example, 28 airports have been deliberately located near to stretches of water in order to minimize noise impact on communities.[7] Washington National uses the Potomac River, Los Angeles the Pacific Ocean, Philadelphia International the Delaware River, and Norfolk International the Atlantic Ocean as part of their operational noise control programme. The specific daytime flight tracks for Washington National are shown in *Figure 20.3*. Note that within the District of Columbia these tracks generally follow the Potomac River corridor.[20] This avoids considerable population exposure. Other airports, including 26 in Europe, have specific operational noise measures, based on an International Civil Airports Association study conducted by the European Region Working Group on Environmental Matters.[21]

At Norfolk Virginia International Airport, operations on both Runway 5 and 23, as stated in their noise abatement procedure, require arrivals over water. For example, for an arrival on Runway 23, the pilot maintains a 2500 foot altitude until the coastline is reached. The final approach is then made over the water.[22]

Flight-track procedures are a popular technique found at 68 of the 402 US airports sampled.[7,8] Owing to existing population densities surrounding many airports, particularly in older airport communities, a flight track method such as this has limited value. For these situations a rotation of operating runways may be of benefit. Such a system is used at 11 US airports where the objective is to attempt to spread the noise geographically more equitably to affected communities.[7] Therefore, the flight tracks are distributed in a more or less equal pattern. Palm Beach Florida International Airport uses this procedure for Runway 27R where three rotational headings (60°, 90°, and 120°) are used on departure.[23]

20.2.5 Noise emission standards

In general, noise emissions from every aircraft operation must stay within limits measured at one or more positions. These limits may be expressed in terms of single events and/or integrated over time (day/yearly). This Section deals with the actual noise levels that a political jurisdiction may impose upon aircraft. Such a level can be applicable to a single event or individual flyover, or alternatively may apply to an aggregate number of aircraft over time. Typically this involves a peak noise level applicable to any individual aircraft operating beyond the airport boundaries, usually as part of a take-off or landing procedure.

In most of Europe the noise limits for aircraft are based on the International Civil Aviation Organization (ICAO) Annex 16.[14] This Annex contains noise certification criteria for various aircraft categories. A reference of three measuring points has been established:

1. *Lateral reference noise measurement point*—The point on a line parallel to and 450 m from the runway centreline, where the noise level is a maximum during take-off.
2. *Flyover reference noise measurement point*—The point on the extended centreline of the runway and at a distance of 6.5 km from the start of roll.
3. *Approach reference noise measurement point*—The point on the ground, on the extended centreline of the runway, 2000 m from the threshold. On level ground this corresponds to a position 120 m (395 ft) vertically below the 3° descent path originating from a point 300 m beyond the threshold. (Chapter 19 gives further details of noise certification measurements and monitoring procedures.)

In order to obtain a certificate of airworthiness on or after 6 October 1977, aircraft have to meet the maximum noise level criteria established for the three reference measurement points described above. The limit values are specified in terms of the Effective Perceived Noise Level (EPNL) in decibels and they depend on weight of the aircraft and number of engines (*see* also Chapter 19). At 25 European airports ICAO Annex 16 noise levels are cited as the acceptable limits of noise emission. A similar practice is followed in the USA. However, these airports generally reference the FAA, Federal Aviation Regulation, Part 36, Noise Certification document.[12]

Some airports have established aircraft noise levels that differ from either the ICAO or FAA noise certification levels. At John Wayne Orange County airport, an 89.5 Single Event Noise Exposure Level has been established during 2200–0700 hours. San Francisco International Airport uses 102 dB for all departing aircraft as a maximum, New York's John F. Kennedy International Airport applies a maximum of 112 PNdB while Washington National at night on take-off specifies 72 dB(A).[24] In certain situations, communities not responsible for the operation of an airport have tried to enact and enforce laws with noise limits. Often these have not been legally upheld by the courts.

Penalties for failure to comply range considerably. Often warnings are given to the offending airline without any legal penalty. More commonly, a fine is assessed since the violation frequently constitutes a misdemeanour. At some airports this information is published in the newspapers, citing the offending airline.

20.2.6 Noise monitoring

Noise monitoring on a continuous 24-hour basis by permanently installed equipment has been a possibility for some considerable time, and interest by airport authorities in acquiring these facilities is growing. Presently there are at least 56 systems located in 16 countries throughout the world. Over half of these are located in the United States and West Germany (*Table 20.4*).[20,25]

Such noise monitoring systems serve a variety of purposes,

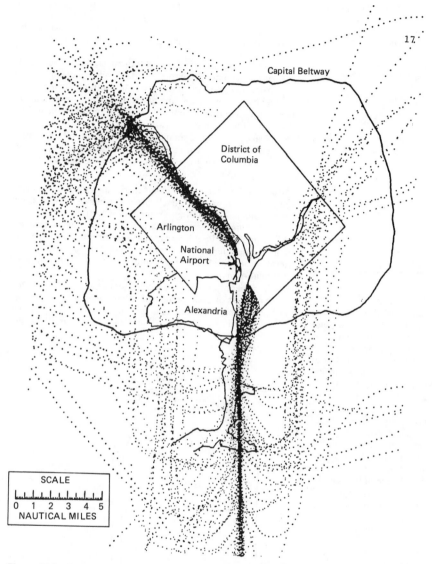

Figure 20.3 Daytime flight tracks for Washington National Airport

depending upon the needs of the airport proprietor. These include:

1. The assessment of alternative flight procedures for noise control.
2. Assistance in the investigation of specific public inquiries and complaints.
3. Instil public confidence that airport-related noise is being monitored to protect the public's interest.
4. Validation of noise modelling methods at the airport over an extended period of time (e.g., 1 year).
5. Assistance in addressing land-use planning and noise-impact issues.
6. Indicate official concern for airport noise by the jurisdiction and its governing body.
7. Detection of unusual flight events.
8. Education of aircraft pilots, airlines, the airport proprie-

tor, and the public about airport noise and its characteristics.
9. Determination of valid statistical data using an objective and scientific resource.
10. Application of research tools to assist the airport in performing certain tasks, as required or mandated.
11. Assessment of compliance with some voluntary or mandatory noise level.

It appears that enforcement is the leading reason for the use of these systems in Europe, while in the USA there does not appear to be a central theme. However, wherever they are used, the airport operators have come to rely upon them for a variety of reasons.

Airport noise monitoring consists basically of four components, which include a series of remote monitoring stations, a central processing station, computer software, and graphic map

Table 20.4 Number of civil airports with noise monitoring systems

Country	Number of airports
USA	23
West Germany	8
England	3
Canada	3
France	3
Spain	3
Austria	2
Japan	2
Switzerland	2
Denmark	1
Greece	1
Hungary	1
Indonesia	1
Israel	1
Italy	1
Netherlands	1
Total	56

terminal(s). *Figure 19.8* illustrates these concepts.

Many airports maintain an electronic map at the terminal building, which gives a graphic display of the monitored noise levels, often in real time. At certain airports, these monitored aircraft operations are shown with coloured lights indicating the degree of compliance. For example, a flashing red light indicates exceedance of level of permissible take-off noise and a flashing green light indicates compliance. Such maps are situated in various locations, ranging from public access areas to worker or airport employee areas.

Although these systems have a short history, less than 20 years, they are becoming increasingly popular. With time, many modifications have occurred, making them more useful to airport noise abatement staff. They are now into their second and third generation at several different airports. Contributing to their popularity is the fact that in the US federal funds under FAA, FAR Part 150, can be used to acquire such systems.[26] Such funding is available on a matching federal/local basis.

20.2.7 Training restrictions

Aircraft training activities are a major source of regulation by airport managers. This applies both to civilian and military flight operations. This is the third most common type of operational noise control method, found at 81 US airports (*see Table 20.1*).[7,8]

There are several reasons for these flight training restrictions, including:

1. *Safety*—Accident potential is elevated, particularly when training flights are interspersed with normal flight operations. This type of integrated flight activity has also been demonstrated to be a major reason for increased noise complaints. Noise and safety are inextricably associated with human response in airport environments. In 1985 a US Air Force KC135 practising landing and take-off crashed in northern California killing all seven crew members, 1 mile from the end of the runway.
2. *Occurrence*—Training flights, particularly among the military, occur at random times over a 24-hour period. Both early morning, late evening, and night-time events generate more complaints and higher levels of annoyance than do normal daytime events.
3. *Numbers*—Owing to the requirements such flight activity is

generally repetitive. For example, practising touch-down etc., is a continuous process with patterned flyovers occurring over the same population on an extended basis. This activity can rapidly increase the total number of airport operations.

4. *Flight operation*—The type of training heavily influences the airport community impact. Certain military operations, in particular, require high-speed, low-altitude flying on a repetitive basis, including at night. Altitude, speed, thrust, and flap setting, among other factors, influence the overall impact in communities surrounding airports.
5. *Sound level*—Since training operations tend to be repetitive and generally occur in sizeable numbers at night after 2200 and before 0700 they can contribute significantly to the integrated noise level at an airport.

Based on these factors, many air carrier airports do not permit flight training, or alternatively place restrictions on such training. *Figure 20.4* shows an example of a restricted flight track used to minimize areas impacted by noise during training. Minneapolis-St. Paul International Airport prohibits any training. A violation of this training ban legally constitutes a misdemeanour.[26] Similar prohibitions exist at Palm Beach International Airport.

Air carrier airports which have military flight activities often place controls on training-related military operations. The Port of Portland has established an agreement with the Oregon Air National Guard at Portland International Airport. Basically,

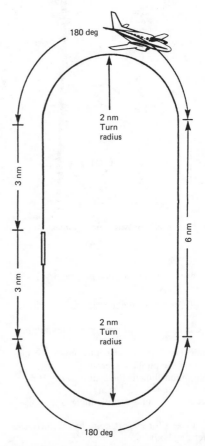

Figure 20.4 Flight track concept used to minimize noise impact during training exercises

military training flight departures are restricted to 0800–1930 (Monday to Saturday) and 0900–1600 on Sundays while arrivals are restricted to 0800–2200 throughout the week.[28] NATO member countries operating military airfields are very sensitive to the issue of community noise impact. A wide range of controls are being implemented to limit the extent of impact. They recently sponsored an international meeting on this subject and have agreed to study this problem and develop solutions over a one-year period.[29]

20.3 Control of noise impact (ground controls)

The management of the airport can have a significant influence on controlling noise. Airport design and its operational runways, run-up areas, buildings, and noise shields and barriers can influence community impact. Administrative controls and remedies, such as operationally based charges for noise, are increasingly common. The legal questions of interference with interstate commerce, discrimination, and legal authority are questions that continually need to be evaluated.[30]

20.3.1 Slots

Slot controls place a limit on the number of operations that can be conducted within a specified time period at an airport. This can involve restrictions on how many air carrier movements are allowed during a 24-hour period. For example, only 37 daytime (0700–2159) air carrier operations are allowed at Washington National.[10] Similarly, Islip, Long Island MacArthur Airport has established a procedure whereby aircraft are permitted to operate based on a total noise level. The number of slots is related to aircraft performance, with the airport having an over noise budget maximum or quota.[31]

Similar stipulations have recently been agreed for John Wayne Airport, Orange County, California. The City of Newport Beach, California, passed a resolution approving a joint powers agreement with Orange County promoting air transportation improvements and limiting the expansion of this Airport.[32] Final approval was given in late 1985 by the US District Court of the Central District of California.[33] Slots have been assigned to airlines and they in turn are permitted a limited number of operations per day, based on a noise level class.

The trend is to assign slots to airlines that use noise abated or quieter aircraft types in order to encourage the concept of noise control by the air carrier. It should be noted, however, that slot allocations using performance criteria such as noise level indirectly have an impact on the carrying capacity of the aircraft and airport.

20.3.2 Capacity

Airport capacity generally refers to the number of flights and/or passengers permitted over a defined period, frequently one year. A major reason for such a capacity threshold is to limit aircraft noise impacting airport communities.

Currently, John Wayne Airport has a passenger capacity limit of 4 750 000 annual passengers. This passenger limit will be increased to 8 400 000 by the year 2005. Actual aircraft operations is more flexible, and it is based upon noise emission. Three categories of operations are permitted at this airport and these are described in *Table 20.5*. It can be seen that only 55 daily operations are allowed for those Class A and Class AA aircraft that generate a maximum of greater than 86 on the Single Event Noise Exposure Level. Any other aircraft below 86 (SENEL) are not restricted at all.

Boston Logan International Airport is considering a similar

Table 20.5 John Wayne Orange County Airport capacity limitations

Category	Sound level maximum (SENEL) (dB(A))[a]	Operation	Flights per day
Class A	100	Departure or landing	39
Class AA	89.5	Departure or landing	16
Class AAA	86	Departure	Unrestricted[b]

[a] Single Event Noise Equivalent Level (SENEL).
[b] Passenger capacity 4.75 million annually (1985–1989).

scheme. In this case, airlines would not be permitted to expand their future aircraft capacity unless they introduced quieter, Stage 3, aircraft. Capacity could only be considered if 43.9% or more of present operations are classified as quiet or whether they meet the airport noise per seat index.[13] This somewhat controversial policy is being reviewed by the FAA. US courts have held that local airport proprietors can establish noise limits as a means for achieving reasonable goals. However, they must not pose an undue burden on interstate or foreign commerce nor may that be unjustly discriminatory or unreasonable.

Local airport incentives to deal with noise are having an influence on the airline operators to modernize their commercial fleets. Currently, in the USA there appears to be strong congressional interest to accelerate the acquisition of quieter Stage 3 aircraft. The US House of Representatives and the Appropriations Committee have asked the FAA to report on alternatives available to accomplish fleet modernization for noise control purposes.[5]

20.3.3 Preferential runways

More than one-third (34.5%) or 139 US airports have a preferential runway procedure for noise abatement purposes (*see Table 20.2*). This is the most common operational technique in use. European airports also find this to be an important procedure. Currently 26 different airports throughout Europe are using a preferred runway system, including the major airports located in the cities of Berlin, Budapest, Liverpool, Marseilles, Warsaw, Salzburg, Torino, and Madrid.

One of the world's busiest airports, McCarran International Airport, Las Vegas, Nevada (*see Table 20.1*) restricts the use of Runway 1R-19L by commercial jets.[34] At McCarran International they assign aircraft, when feasible, to the cross-wind Runway 25. This reduces the exposure over the more populated runway 1R-19L corridor, northeast of the airport. They have raised the permitted cross-wind maximum from 6 to 15 knots on Runway 25, along with a runway scheduling strategy which increases the Runway 25 traffic capacity.

At smaller airports which have a single runway system this technique is not possible. A parallel runway or cross-wind preferential system is used. However, cross-wind runway limitations may be constraining due to windspeed, runway length, load, and capacity.

20.3.4 Displaced threshold

There is a geographical point along the runway which is used as a landing threshold for arriving aircraft or a take-off point for departing aircraft. Some airports displace this point so that the approach or departure trajectory will place the aircraft at a higher altitude above the ground. By increasing this altitude the noise exposure contour is reduced, thereby affecting fewer people. Consequently, the land area beneath these aircraft becomes more compatible.

Today, 24 different US airports have developed a displaced threshold technique for noise control purposes. Several large airports have adopted this, including San Francisco International, New York's John F. Kennedy, and Newark International. Assuming a three degree glide slope for landing aircraft, the increase in altitude is only 50 feet for every 1000 feet displacement, as indicated by *Figure 20.5.*[20]

This technique appears to have very limited noise value unless the runway is considerably longer than necessary. The displacement has to be rather large to provide the corresponding increase in altitude. Any runway extension represents a major capital expenditure. One possible justification in construction cost is the benefit from a safety perspective. Greater runway capacity (length) improves safety for equivalent-type aircraft.

4. *Site design*—An outdoor run-up location is usually acoustically buffered. This buffer may consist of vacant land, vegetation cover (e.g. forested area), earth berm, and/or noise walls (i.e. barrier).
5. *Abatement equipment*—Portable silencers or mufflers are used for testing aircraft at many installations, particularly military. In situations where the problem is extremely critical, in-door test facilities are installed.

The Air Traffic Noise Act of the Federal Republic of Germany enacted a law in April 1971 which regulates run-up noise at both civilian and military airports.[35] Under the Act all military airfields of the German Bundeswehr have been equipped with engine test cells, while at commercial airfields engine test cells, walls, or mufflers are now in place when a noise impact problem is identified.[36]

Local political subdivisions, outside the jurisdiction of the airport, often have developed noise run-up ordinances. In the US, the courts have upheld the constitutional right for a local

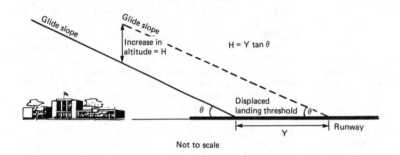

Figure 20.5 Effect of displaced landing threshold on altitude of glide slope

20.3.5 Ground run-up

Many airports maintain facilities for the maintenance and repair of aircraft. As part of this process, aircraft must undergo static tests requiring a certain thrust or engine power setting. Auxiliary power units (APUs), generator sets, and other accessory equipment that are not part of an in-place apron grid system may be other contributing sources of noise. Such run-ups—depending upon location, time of day, aircraft type, and facility—can generate an off-airport noise impact. (NB Chapter 19 considers the prediction of ground operating noise at airports.)

Since most run-up activity occurs during a low utilization period, the off-peak hour maintenance frequently is at night or early in the morning. This can create a possible community impact because it is the most noise sensitive time of day. Nearly a quarter (23.3%) or 94 US airport operators have established run-up noise control techniques.[7] In these circumstances, enforcement is usually achieved by enacting a local ordinance containing the following features:

1. *Noise emission limit*—Typically, an overall noise limit is established for the closest residential property boundary or zoning district. Historically, these limits were expressed as a peak single event level (i.e., dB(A)). Now, more frequently, the permissible levels are based on the scales of L_{eq}, L_{10} and L_{50}.
2. *Time of day*—Restrictions are usually applied to evening and night-time periods of the day, typically from 2200–0700. During these hours no run-ups are permitted.
3. *Location*—Most designated outdoor run-up areas are delineated on an airport layout plan. This is normally in the most geographically isolated part of the airport, furthest from noise-sensitive land uses.

government to enact noise laws even though the airport is beyond their legal and administrative authority.

20.3.6 Aircraft towing

The towing of aircraft for noise control purposes is not common, and it is usually done only as a part of engine maintenance and repair. Aircraft are towed to a designated run-up area with all systems shut down, prior to conducting a test. This action also provides a saving in fuel costs.

During the peak of the energy crisis some airports experimentally began towing aircraft, from the apron area, to the operational runway. Tests were conducted to determine whether there were noise and energy benefits that would offset the increased time and cost of equipment. However, questions were raised about possible damage to the airplane's mechanical wheel assembly and support system, and within the US this noise abatement method is no longer practised. Nevertheless, this technique may reappear, depending upon safety, energy, and noise cost-benefits in the future.

20.3.7 Noise based charges

European airports have provided the leadership in establishing noise-based charges. The basic philosophy is that the aircraft operators should pay a fee proportionate to the noise they generate. The operators of noisier aircraft are financially penalized while the operators of quieter aircraft are rewarded by reduced landing charges. At present, there are at least 27 European airports with some noise-based charge system in operation.[9,20] (*See also* Chapter 24.)

The airports at Geneva and Zurich have established five classes of aircraft with surcharge tax for noise levied on a graduated scale (*Table 20.6*). The noisiest aircraft, which include the DC-8 Series 20 to 40, currently pay 400 Swiss francs per operation.[8] Widebodied (e.g., Airbus A-300, Boeing 757–767) current technology aircraft, in contrast, are not required to pay any noise surcharge. The Aeroports de Paris Company (ADP) manages the noise landing fee fund at both the Orly and Charles De Gaulle airports in France. They also use a sliding percentage, based on noise. Approximately 15 500 000 francs were collected during 1985.[37] At 20 airports in Europe, quiet aircraft actually received a financial rebate. This represented a financial incentive for being quiet in comparison with the remaining aircraft fleet.

Table 20.6 Aircraft noise surcharge tax: Geneva and Zurich, Switzerland

Aircraft classification	Aircraft description (examples)	Amount (Swiss Francs)
I	DC-8 Series 20–40	400
II	Boeing 707 Series 100–400	265
III	Boeing 707 Series 100B/300B/300C BAC 1–11 Boeing 727 Series 200 Adv (JT8D-15/17)	200
IV	Boeing 737 Series 100/200 Boeing 720B Boeing 727 Series 100–200	135
V	Airbus A-300 Boeing 737 Series 300 Boeing 747, 757, 767	0

Source: *Switzerland—AIC 120/84*, June 28, 1984.

These experiences are beginning to be noticed across the Atlantic. Palm Beach International Airport has become the first US airport to enact a specific operational fee for noise. This occurred in 1985, with the provision becoming effective on June 1, 1986.[11] It applies only to scheduled departures after 2200 and before 0700. The goal of the airport authority is to encourage quiet aircraft and to maximize operations during less sensitive daytime hours. To accelerate this goal, a variable operating fee policy is used. The structure of the fee policy is to provide an incentive for airlines to operate with quieter aircraft and to minimize their night-time operations. In developing the policy, aircraft were grouped into three categories: non-FAR Part 36 aircraft, FAR Part 36 certified aircraft, and Stage 3 certified aircraft. In addition, two time periods were involved: daytime (7 am to 10 pm) and night-time (10 pm to 7 am).

This fee schedule is shown in *Table 20.7*. Although the airlines

Table 20.7 Commercial jet 1986 noise-related operating fee schedule Palm Beach International Airport

Aircraft category	Time of day	Noise level fee factor
Non FAR Part 36	Night	16.0 × base
Non FAR Part 36	Day	1.6 × base
FAR Part 36 Certified	Night	13.0 × base
FAR Part 36 Certified	Day	1.3 × base
Stage III Certified	Night	1.0 × base
Stage III Certified	Day	Credit

initially resisted this ordinance, they have complied with the noise level fee schedule. The airport authority expects to collect approximately $1 000 000 a year which will be set aside for their noise abatement and mitigation programme.[38]

Other US airports are also considering implementing a similar-type programme. The State of Rhode Island passed a bill in their General Assembly applicable to all state-operated airports.[39] It specifies that all airport leases, concessions, licences, and landing fee schedules provisions are to be included requiring a graduated scale of payments designed to discourage take-offs and landings after midnight and before 6.30 am, and that all aircraft be equipped with pertinent noise and emission abatement devices.

The Boston and Minneapolis-St. Paul airports, among others, are also studying this particular method. The FAA in their Report to Congress believes that this is less desirable than accelerated fleet modernization.[5] Noise-based charges at local airports will act as a stimulant for modernization in the long run.

20.4 Land use control regulations

Land use control can be an effective way to minimize population exposure around airports. Aircraft technology, although an important component in abating noise, will not be sufficient alone to eliminate or adequately control aircraft noise. Incompatible land development is an undesirable by-product of improper planning, especially when it adversely affects the health, safety, and welfare of the population.[40]

There are many land use control related methods available to encourage and ensure that noise compatible land planning occurs in the vicinity of airports. The diversity and number of methods varies considerably throughout the United States as is shown in *Table 20.3*. Zoning, comprehensive planning, land acquisition, and avigational easements are the four leading measures found in a sample of 402 US airports.[7,8] This call for compatible land use planning around airports in the USA is not new, and concern about this problem can be related back to 1952 when President Truman received the report, *Airport and Its Neighbors*, from the Doolittle Commission.[41]

The application of these land use measures is international. European countries generally have been more successful in applying these land use controls on a large-scale basis (i.e., country, state, region). Within the USA their application is not as comprehensive, and they are usually applied at a more local governmental level (i.e., municipality, township, borough). As a rule, the European nations also have more aggressively implemented these provisions, while within the US implementation of enacted land regulations varies widely.

20.4.1 Comprehensive plan

A comprehensive plan, often referred to as a structure or master plan, usually is an official public document adopted by a local government. This plan is a policy guide to decisions about physical development of an area. Consequently, it is concerned with land use management practices. To be useful in guiding the future growth of an area, these plans are long range, covering a period from 10 to 20 years.

Basic elements of the comprehensive plan include the private uses of land, community facilities, and circulation or transportation. All three of these elements involve decisions influencing land use compatibility and potential environmental impact. The recognition of community-generated noise, among other environmental factors, is an important ingredient to a successful comprehensive plan.

The use of a comprehensive plan for municipal development

must reflect existing and future airport-related needs. The airport master plan should be an integral part of a community master plan. Historically, they have often been separate and isolated processes. Both military and civilian facilities are now developing airport noise-based land-use compatibility studies in the United States.[42-44] First initiated by the US Air Force, all branches of the service are preparing either *Airport Installation Compatible Use Zone (AICUZ)* or *Installation Compatible Use Zone (ICUZ)* plans. On the civilian side, the FAA is supporting *Airport Noise Compatibility Plans* for any federally certified airports, and to date 124 have been funded.[45] These studies are important input to comprehensive plans adopted by local jurisdictions. Nearly 90% of all incorporated US cities (2205) have some type of master plan, and the majority discuss noise and land use compatibility.[46]

Canada has developed governmental regulations for airport noise planning, implemented at the provincial level. For example, the Province of Alberta adopted *The Planning Act— Airport Vicinity Protection Area* in 1975.[47] To protect airport environs, a schedule of permitted, conditionally permitted or prohibited uses of land, based on noise criteria, is in the Act. The Federal Interagency Committee on Urban Noise established similar US noise land use planning guidelines in 1980.[48] For each basic category of land use (e.g., residential), there are noise zones based on Day Night Average Levels (DNL). *Table 20.8* gives further details. ICAO has also published a Land Use Planning Manual, using noise compatibility criteria.[49]

Consistent and continuous enforcement is essential. As a practical matter, several European countries are strictly enforcing the land use noise provisions. In Germany, the Air Traffic Noise Act at the federal level and the town and country planning laws within each state integrate planning for airports and land compatibility. The State of North Rhine-Westphalia has prepared a Regional Development Plan (IV), applicable to all 16 civil airports and 7 military airfields. *Table 20.9* presents the applicable planning restrictions.[50]

20.4.2 Zoning

To be effective, the comprehensive plan must be implemented, and the zoning ordinance or code is the most popular method. One-third of all US airports sampled (133) use some type of zoning, and it ranks as the leading method for controlling environmental noise at the municipal level.[7,8,46] As a legal tool it can regulate various aspects of land use development, including:

1. Height, bulk, and density of buildings.
2. Area of land which may be occupied, and the size of required open spaces.
3. Density of population.
4. Permitted uses of structures and land use development.

A zoning ordinance usually classifies or subdivides land into use districts. Permitted uses are usually specified for each district, including various physical requirements. Ordinances containing acoustical criteria are generally designed to regulate fixed (stationary) noise sources.

There are at least three ways in which zoning can be applied to airport community environments as a means of protecting the airport from incompatible land use development, restricting litigation, and protecting the public in terms of public health, safety, and welfare:[51]

1. *Airport overlay zone*—This is a zone intended to place additional land use conditions on land impacted by the airport while retaining the existing underlying zone. The components should include the clear zone (when not owned by the airport sponsor), approach safety zone and noise corridor zones.
2. *Airport impact zone*—A separate zone used to place land use

Table 20.8 FAA Part 150 land use compatibility guidelines

Land uses	Yearly day–night average sound level (L_{DN}) in decibels					
	Below 65	65–70	70–75	75–80	80–85	Over 85
Residential						
Residential, other than mobile homes and transient lodgings:	Y	N[a]	N[c]	N	N	N
Household units						
Single units, detached						
Single units, semidetached						
Single units, attached row						
Two units, side-by-side						
Two units, one above the other						
Apartments, walk up						
Apartments, elevator						
Group quarters						
Residential hotel						
Other residential						
Mobile home parks	Y	N	N	N	N	N
Transient lodgings	Y	N[a]	N[b]	N[c]	N	N

Y = yes; land use and related structures compatible without restrictions. N = no; land use and related structures are not compatible and should be prohibited.
[a] Where the community determines that residential uses must be allowed, measures to achieve outdoor to indoor Noise Level Reduction (NLR) of at least 25 dB and 30 dB should be incorporated into building codes and be considered in individual approvals. Normal construction can be expected to provide a NLR of 20 dB, thus the reduction requirements are often stated as 5, 10, or 15 dB over standard construction and normally assume mechanical ventilation and closed windows for all ambient conditions. However, the use of NLR criteria will not eliminate outdoor noise problems.
[b] Compatible where measures to achieve NLR of 25 are incorporated into the design and construction of portions of these buildings where the public is received, office areas, noise-sensitive areas where the normal noise level is low.
[c] Compatible where measures to achieve NLR of 30 are incorporated into the design and construction of portions of these buildings where the public is received, office areas, noise-sensitive areas or where the normal noise level is low.

Table 20.9 Regional development plan no. IV for the State of North Rhine–Westphalia

Noise Protection Area A [L_{eq} exceeding 75 dB(A)]	General ban on making up new development plans containing settlement structures which are sensitive to noise. They include: All kinds of residential areas Especially institutions in need of protection such as hospitals, homes for the aged, and convalescent homes Central school locations, university institutes, as well as leisure-time and recreational centres
Noise Protection Area B [L_{eq} from 67 to 75 dB(A)]	General ban on making up new development plans containing settlement structures which are sensitive to noise, except the rounding off of existing residential areas, including such institutions as form part of a residential infrastructure (as e.g., kindergartens, schools); sound-absorbing constructional measures will have to be taken, if necessary.
Noise Protection Area C [L_{eq} from 62 to 67 dB(A)]	Requirement of balancing for both regional and land use planning when making up new development plans to consider long-term annoyance to be expected due to aircraft noise, and also to provide sound-absorbing constructional measures, if necessary.

conditions on land impacted by airport operations. Unlike the airport overlay zone, this establishes a new zone which replaces an existing zone designation and standards. The components include the clear zone (not owned by the airport sponsor), approach safety zone and noise corridor zones.

3. *Airport development zone*—A separate zone classification used for the airport property and proposed property acquisition.

These three techniques are proposed for implementation by the Texas Aeronautics Commission for all airports within their state.[52] They have established controlled areas where noise compatibility zoning may take place, covering an area 1.5 statute miles from the centreline of a runway and 5 miles from each end of the paved surface of a runway.[53]

Norway's Department of the Environment, in 1984, established noise zone districts and permitted uses for all airports in their country.[54] Based on an Equivalent Aircraft Noise level, they are now implementing these requirements with various degrees of success. Netherlands appears to be implementing these zoning requirements more rigorously under their Aviation Act as amended in 1978.[55] By law, they must be adopted into the local development plan, with prescribed noise levels for each zone.

There are a variety of noise units used in each of these countries for describing permitted or recommended noise zone limits. No one universal noise index is used, although the Day/Night level (DNL) is well recognized. Efforts are being made to establish comparability, if not consensus.[56]

20.4.3 Building code

A building code prescribes the minimum standards for the construction of structures. Typically, a code is legally adopted by a local governing body and is designed to guarantee the health, safety, and welfare of the community. The building code, for example, can require that all residential structures constructed within the areas impacted by aircraft noise be insulated to meet a certain sound transmission class (STC).

Codes of this type have not been widely applied in the United States since only 65 are known to be used by local governments[46] and just 32 airport communities.[7,8] Factors other than noise (i.e., health, safety, and energy) have been adopted in the model

building codes as well. There are exceptions among some cities and counties. Oklahoma City amended their building code to include a new article (Article 22) specifically for airport environments.[57] Building requirements are specified for a minimum noise level reduction (NLR), ranging from 25 to 35 dB reduction. The state of California has adopted a law applicable to all public buildings (e.g. schools) exposed to highway noise.[58]

Most European cities and particularly those around airports do have ordinances with noise provisions. Many of these have been enacted at the national level. All Dutch airports (civilian and military) have noise zone boundaries, expressed in Kostenunits (B) (*see* Section 2.3.13).[59] Depending upon the noise contour boundary, noise abatement must be in compliance with specific attenuation. As shown in *Table 20.10*, a noise load of 40–55 Kostenunits will require an attenuation of 30–40 dB(A) for those structures. Similar zones are established at all German airfields.[36] To date, over 135 million Deutsche Marks have been spent on implementing the sound insulation requirements at 47 airfields in the Federal Republic of Germany.

Clearly the efforts of implementing regulations in Europe are further advanced than in the USA. Even in Europe, building codes with noise provisions are not universally enacted.

20.4.4 Site design

It is important that potentially noise impacted sites be sensitively designed. This requires that a review procedure is established through a public agency so that the environmental factors, among others, are properly considered and integrated into the land use planning process. This procedure must consider building placement and the need to use natural or man-made barriers. The formal process by a government that may require noise to be specifically identified is not too common.

Architects, town planners, and developers usually go through this process, particularly when they are trying to obtain governmental approval. For example, the Central Mortgage and Housing Corporation of Canada has developed a site planning handbook to assist those trying to obtain a government-backed mortgage.[60] There are minimum requirements for the financing and construction of residences under the Canadian National Housing Act, using the Noise Exposure Forecast (NEF). US Housing and Urban Development (HUD) has had a major influence on site design for noise when Federal funds are being considered as part of a development proposal. This agency uses

Table 20.10 Dutch airfield zoning and insulation requirements

Noise load (Kostenunits)	Required attenuation (dB(A))
40–50	30–35
50–55	35–40
55+	40

specific noise standards.[61] Unfortunately, noise is not always considered when the financing for the residential development involves private investment dollars as opposed to public funds.

20.4.5 Environmental impact review

The review of possible environmental impacts can be a direct part of the site process. In many instances such a review process is an extension of site design, but goes much farther. This process is frequently modelled after the US National Environmental Policy Act (NEPA).[62]

Any project that has possible noise impacts is examined under an environmental review process. Noise issues are generally dealt with in a larger perspective on the environment as a whole. Sometimes there is a 'balancing' of noise issues in relationship with other possible impacts (e.g., air quality, solid waste management, asbestos, etc.). Most states and over 300 cities have such environmental review procedures.

The FAA submit airport master plans and Part 150 studies to the Environmental Impact Review process. Noise impact issues are identified and methods for abating noise are addressed in a review procedure when federal financial support is involved. This process requires the review by other federal, state, and local governments, as well as interested public groups. Generally, public hearings are also held to receive public input before a final decision is rendered.

Many large-scale corporations are now using this similar procedure, but adopting it to the needs of private enterprise. An environmental impact document establishes a baseline for developing preventive-type long-range solutions, including those for business. A comprehensive review of the methods of environmental appraisal when applied to transport plans is given in Chapter 22.

20.4.6 Capital improvements

A function usually delegated to a planning agency is the establishing of a programme of capital improvements for a municipality. Determining the priority and location for improvements such as utilities, roads, schools, and libraries relate directly to land use compatibility. Many of these capital improvements are either noise generators themselves or are sensitive to noise. A thoughtfully prepared improvement programme can be used to encourage compatible development with a concern about noise, among other environmental problems.

Capital improvement projects provide the infrastructure for future development. In order for subsequent compatible land development to occur, properly planned streets, utilities, etc., are required. Residential development cannot happen without the necessary infrastructure of capital improvements. Many cities perform this important review, even though only 4.4% of the US airports use this as a noise abatement strategy.[7,8] Capital improvements are not a substitute for other noise abatement strategies, but should be regarded as a complementary method to zoning and comprehensive planning. In the USA, Arlington County, Virginia, and Inglewood, California, have very active capital improvement related procedures.

20.4.7 Noise disclosure

It is becoming increasingly common for people to consider environmental land use impact questions when they are negotiating the sale or lease of property. In some cases, such information is made available by a real estate firm as part of a property profile in a deed or lease.

Noise-related disclosures are found among 34 US airports (8.4%) sampled. In California this is a state requirement for the initial transaction of residential property from the developer to the purchaser. Attached to the mortgage is a statement of the annual Community Noise Equivalent Level (CNEL) expected on this property in question. The purchaser must sign this declaration statement, confirming they are aware of the possible noise impact.

Portland, Oregon, has developed a noise disclosure ordinance with respect to their airport environment.[27] It states:

No person shall sell or offer to sell any residential structure or land within the L_{DN} 65 airport noise zone unless the prospective buyer has been given the following notice in writing:

Disclosure Statement

The tract of land situation at (——) lies within the Airport Zone as depicted on the official zoning map. The purchaser is hereby notified that this land is affected by noise resulting from aircraft on the approach and departure routes to and from Portland International Airport and is subject to noise levels that may be objectionable.

The undersigned purchaser(s) of said land hereby certify(ies) that (he/she/they) (has/have) read and understand(s) the above disclosure statement and acknowledge(s) the pre-existence of the above named airport and the potential for objectionable noise.

(signed) Buyer

The undersigned seller(s) of said land hereby certifies(y) that this disclosure statement has been presented to the prospective purchaser; and that (he/she/they) (has/have) read and understand(s) the above disclosure statement.

(signed) Seller

Such a statement is designed to protect both buyer and seller of property. Disclosures of this type are related to the truth in advertising and sales that has evolved out of consumer protection and product liability. With the development of noise contour maps for airport environments which delineate geographical, political, and land use features, the public is becoming more aware of the noise and its relationship to real property. Under the provisions of FAA Part 150, such contours are not to be used in a court of law, but rather for planning purposes only.[26] Furthermore, the publishing of such contours for an airport relieves the airport proprietor of any possible litigation under this legislation. The interpretation of these provisions will have to wait the test of time and any legal challenges.

20.4.8 Subdivision regulations

Land subdivision regulations refer to the guidance of land subdivision development by a public authority, usually a planning agency. A subdivision review procedure can check site design features of a proposed development. Typically, these include the location and width of streets; width and depth of housing plots; location, type, and size of open space; and planned buffer zones. During the preliminary phases of the site plan review process, a planning agency can indicate possible areas of noise sensitivity and can suggest design alternatives. Certainly the location and type of open space can be extremely important to residential comfort. Many cities have adopted noise analysis as part of the sub-division review procedure.

Such regulations can complement the zoning ordinance and can be tied to specific noise impact standards.[63] However, this technique is not frequently used in airport communities in the USA as *Table 20.3* shows. Only six airports are quoted out of a sample of 402.[6,7] Subdivision regulations are relied upon by cities to regulate land development[64] using design requirements; however, noise is not often incorporated.

20.4.9 Land acquisition

Airports frequently purchase property to avoid or minimize any incompatible use from occurring. Fee title acquisition is the most secure way to manage land in noise-sensitive areas. It may be necessary to condemn land using eminent domain if it is for a public purpose. A major problem is the capital investment necessary to acquire land by title. SEA-TAC International Airport, operated by the Port of Seattle, initiated a programme in 1972 to acquire noise-sensitive properties as part of a noise remedy program.[65] Some 1369 parcels of land have been identified at an acquisition cost of approximately $50 000 000. Atlanta Hartsfield International Airport has already programmed nearly $75 000 000 for acquisition and relocation in high-impact noise areas.[66]

Based on the fact that nationally there are between 6000 and 10 000 residences being impacted by civilian aircraft noise, the acquisition of all these properties within the USA would be prohibitively expensive. A programme of this type has limited application due to the financial requirements.

In the USA, it is the third leading land use noise control method involving 77 airports (19.1%), as indicated in *Table 20.3*.[7,8] Acquiring land in noise-impacted areas is also common in Europe. Presently, 23% of the 52 major airports sampled are purchasing land by fee title.[21]

Normally, governmental support is required for such purchases at this scale. In the USA the FAA provides funding for acquiring land on a percentage basis, 75% federal with the remaining 25% contributed by local and state government. Most acquisition programmes include noise impacted residential areas where the annual DNL (L_{DN}) exceeds 75. In the USA eligible candidate structures for such programmes are generally owner occupied and single-family. For those dwellings in the programme, it is common to purchase, acoustically treat, and then lease them back for either residential or commercial purposes. Any subsequent renter or leasee must sign a conditional release form based on noise disclosure (*see* Section 20.4.7).

20.4.10 Avigation easement

An avigated easement involves the purchase, lease, agreement, or condemnation of airspace for a period of time and the legal right to trespass. In terms of an airport environment, the property owner may sell the rights to a prescribed air space at a fixed price, thereby permitting aircraft to fly over a particular land area.

Avigational easements for noise control are becoming more popular at many airports owing to tighter controls on finances available for land use planning. Such easements are designed to notify the owner legally that the property is subject to aircraft noise which may infringe upon a resident's enjoyment of their property. As a rule, these easements do run with the land. In the USA there are 49 airports employing this technique for noise control purposes (*see Table 20.3*).[6,7]

A typical easement cost represents a rather low percentage of the fair market value of the property. Although this figure varies, it usually averages 10% of the residential fair market value. Most airports that do acquire easements attach other restrictions including building height or development restrictions. Avigational easements have been obtained as part of the development plans of all subdivisions in Sedgwick County, Kansas, near the airport. Since 1970 land in the vicinity of the Wichita Mid-Continent Airport must be continued for all subdivisions being developed within the navigable airspace.[67]

The Oregon Department of Transportation, Aeronautics Division, has prepared an Airport Noise Easement and Model Avigation and Hazard Easement as part of the state aviation system planning programme.[51] Such easements must be properly drafted for them to have legal standing.

Both SEA-TAC[68] and Atlanta[69] have established avigational easement procedures and agreements for their respective noise programmes. In both cases the easements run with the land and are binding and enforceable against all successors to the real property. Noise is among several burdens mentioned, and these include noise, vibration, fumes, and deposits of dust or other particulate matter. The Port of Seattle does not specify building heights; however, Atlanta restricts heights of structures to no more than 100 feet above ground level.

These easements have no time limit and are held in perpetuity, unless specified otherwise. There is recourse in the event aircraft noise increases above a defined noise level. The property owner can seek additional compensation from the airport proprietor. Although less expensive than land acquisition costs, easements provide limited protection from noise exposure and the compensation received for the easement may not be used to abate noise acoustically.

20.4.11 Housing code

Housing codes are established to protect the health, safety, and welfare of community residents.[70,71] They deal with potential physical problems such as sanitary conditions, plumbing, water supply, light access, and air, but they can encompass noise.

Similar to the building code, the health code does not actually prevent development around airports. The codes, however, can protect people from the noise impact of the nearby airport. A noise standard can be built into the code that would apply to noise-sensitive uses, such as a residence. The developer could then be required to exhibit excessive noise levels properly in the development under consideration or find an alternative that is less noise sensitive.

Many health departments have taken an active role in the development and initiation of noise control regulations at the local governmental level. Modern noise laws by health organizations have had a notable influence on noise ordinance development in California and Ohio, among other states.

20.4.12 Sound insulation

Programmes for reducing the amount of noise transmitted into buildings in airport communities are increasing. Generally referred to as sound insulation measures, their primary goal is to provide acoustical treatments of the building against aircraft and other external noise. This involves treatments to the exterior walls, windows, doors, and roof systems, i.e. essentially the outer shell of a structure (*see Figure 20.6*). The principle and effects of insulating buildings against noise is reviewed in detail in Chapter 11.

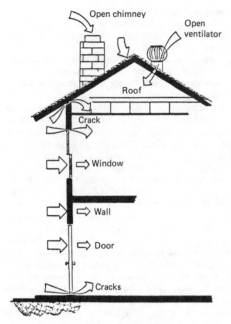

Figure 20.6 Building features requiring sound insulation treatment

The USA is engaged in pilot and demonstration programmes at 16 airports.[7,8] Most of these structures are single-family, owner-occupied dwellings although schools are also included. However, no multi-family dwellings have yet undergone sound insulation.[72] Based on seven active programmes reviewed, by Bragdon, nearly 1600 single-family and multi-family dwellings will be insulated against noise over the next 24 months, including 16 schools. Over $26 000 000 will be spent on both insulation and land acquisition at these airports, which include Los Angeles, Boston, Atlanta, Minneapolis, Seattle, St. Louis, and San Jose. The majority of these structures (75%) are located in the 75 DNL annual noise contour.

European airports are considerably more active in introducing sound insulation prgrammes, with nearly 70 schemes being implemented, including both military and civilian facilities. In England, for example, 10 public airport authorities are implementing plans to insulate over 50 000 public and private dwellings.[73] *Table 20.11* gives some further details of the numbers of buildings and the costs. Approximately £34.6 million are projected to be spent at these 10 airports by 1990, with the government contributing 65–100%, depending upon the dwelling location and noise exposure.

While the insulation programme is considered an important step in reducing impacts, preference is given to planning so that communities are not located near to the centres of noise production as far as possible. In England, guidance on land planning with regard to noise control is given in a Department of Environment Circular.[74]

The Netherlands Ministry of Defence has attempted to estimate the cost of noise insulation around their military installations. Depending upon the insulation required, the cost of implementation has been estimated to range from NFl 35 000 to NFl 120 000 for each dwelling (*Table 20.12*)[75] Based on 6800 dwellings in the three Kostenunits, these total costs are estimated to be NFl 421 000 000. In the highest zone (55+ Ke), this would average nearly 80% of the fair market value of the dwelling to comply.

Clearly, realistic implementation criteria need to be estab-

Table 20.11 Civil airport sound insulation programme in England

Category	Response
Airports	10
Dwellings involved	
Public	46 606
Private	3885
Total	50 491
Cost	
Current (1983)	14.7 million (pounds)
Projected (1990)	34.6 million (pounds)
Government contribution	65–100%
Dates covered by the Programme	1972–1990

Source: John Ollerhead.

lished, including acceptable cost factors. An important fact to keep in mind is that insulation represents only a partial solution to protecting property from noise exposure since the outdoor environment is still unaffected.

20.5 Land use controls: economic

The basic philosophy for implementing land use controls has been regulation; enacting laws is prescriptive or regulatory in nature. Many of these laws are in response to the need to provide effective enforcement and are public-sector oriented. Another approach is aimed at introducing controls that emphasize economic well-being that combine a public- and private-sector perspective. Economic incentives are associated with the solution rather than absolute penalties. It may also mean that they have an environmental equity component whereby there are economic benefits for those affected.

These techniques have not been widely applied to airport environments. In many ways they may offer new and fresh insights to the problem of noise control.

20.5.1 Tax incentives

The use of a tax reduction is an increasingly common method for encouraging land management practices. This concept is often applied to agricultural lands in metropolitan areas as an incentive to maintain open space. Such an incentive can be a positive inducement for noise reduction on an equitable basis. An associated technique is a differential property tax assessment for property owners in a particular geographic area where a high noise exposure condition exists.

Differential property assessment for noise-impacted properties and therefore a lower property tax rate is being used at a few airports. At the Frankfurt and Nuremberg airports, residents are compensated for the depreciation of their property due to noise. SEA-TAC International Airport developed a purchase assurance programme for residents in particular high noise areas around the airport. Palm Beach County, Florida, historically used a lower property assessment for homeowners living adjacent to Palm Beach International Airport.

20.5.2 Sales agreement

An essential ingredient in transferring real estate into a valuable commodity is the written agreement.[76] A contract is a legally binding agreement in which certain parties agree to do or refrain from doing some lawful thing. The sales agreement is a legal

Table 20.12 Insulation costs and environmental standards around military airports in the Netherlands

Noise load (Ke)	Insulation standard (dB)	Average cost per dwelling (NFl)	Number of dwellings	Total costs (NFl) $\times 10^6$
40–45	30–32.5	35 000	3000	105
45–55	32.5–40	80 000	3500	280
55+	40	120 000	300	36

contract which may be enforced by legal process by either of the parties if the other party does not willingly comply with contract terms.

A sales agreement is needed for the establishment of the terms agreed upon by the seller and buyer.[77] The buyer usually accepts the terms in the purchase agreement. Final acceptance of the purchase or sales agreement may be conditional upon proof of a clear title, re-zoning to fit the land use plans of the buyer, or adequate financing from lenders.[78] The minimum requirements for a sales contract are the parties agreeing to the conditional sales agreement, description of the property, and signatures of the agreeing parties.

An airport or air installation, through sales agreements, may restrict the use of surrounding lands if they own or control them. Of course, the buyer must accept the terms of the sales agreement. After signature, the agreement becomes a legally binding contract. Conditions placed upon the sale can stipulate noise compatible land uses thereby avoiding later incompatible encroachment.

20.5.3 Loans and mortgages

In order for land developers to fund their projects, they often need to borrow funds from lending institutions. If these funds could not be obtained, then development would be curtailed. Restricting or prohibiting mortgage and/or other type loans that do not meet certain noise requirements could be an effective tool.[79]

· Most restrictions on noise for loan approval are associated with public funds (government supported). This includes both the US Department of Housing and Urban Development and the Canadian Mortgage and Housing Corporation.[60,61]

This land control technique would be extended to private lending institutions, including banks, savings and loans, credit unions, and insurance companies. There are examples where these private financial institutions do rely on environmental performance standards, similar to a public agency, before a loan application is approved. Such performance standards would improve the financial risk, while also minimizing future incompatible land development near airports.

20.5.4 Purchase option

An option is an agreement between the buyer and seller of a piece of property. In the agreement, the seller will hold the property for a specified time. In turn, the buyer agrees to pay a sum of money as consideration for the offer, or as a first right of refusal.[80]

At the time the option is granted, no real property ownership rights pass. Instead, the buyer is purchasing the right to buy at a fixed price within a specified period of time.[81] The seller of the option retains the money paid regardless of whether the option is exercised. Option costs vary, but they usually include the property taxes and a standard interest charge.

The option can be used when funds cannot be acquired to purchase the property outright. During the time of the option, funds can be obtained to make the purchase. The time during an option can also be used to examine re-zoning possibilities or

other factors that would affect ownership of the property. This provides leverage, and in the event there is pressure to develop in an incompatible manner, the airport proprietor as a buyer can exercise this option.

20.5.5 Public private leaseback

A leaseback is a financial arrangement in which land is acquired and controlled, but not necessarily occupied by the owner. This method can be used both by the public and by private sectors.

The leaseback arrangement in the private sector requires two simultaneous steps.[82] First, an investor purchases real estate owned and used by a business firm or government. Second, the property is leased back to the firm or government by the purchaser. In the public sector, a public agency can acquire lands and lease them to private persons for specific uses, in accordance with the approved plan for the area. Customarily, the terms of the lease ranges from 20 to 40 years.

Leaseback can be used as an alternative to restrictive sales. An airport or installation may purchase a parcel of land and lease it with restrictions on permitted uses. Agricultural, industrial, open space, and commercial facilities are possible permitted uses.

Leasebacks offer a way for public agencies to acquire land, yet provide for the continued use of the land. Public agencies can limit the permitted use of the land, while acquiring some income from the property. The leaseback method is popular in the private sector because it provides equity capital from outside sources, and it is a flexible form of financing.

Los Angeles International Airport purchased homes in a high noise area, sound insulated them, and then leased them back with a set of conditions. Other airports are using this technique to avoid real estate holdings that do not provide income. It is very common to lease land, without structures, to farmers in order that they may produce a crop. This provides a lease income to the airport and maintains the land as open space or agricultural land, therefore avoiding the possibility of incompatible development.

20.5.6 Land banking

The term land banking can be defined as a system in which a government acquires a substantial fraction of land in a region that is available for future development for the purpose of implementing a public land use policy.[82] Such a policy may be restricting residential development from occurring in a specific airport noise zone.

Land banking requires that the land being acquired does not become committed to specific use at the time of acquisition and that the land is sufficiently large enough to have a substantial effect on urban growth patterns.[83] Also, land banking differs from permanent acquisition in that it places the land in a temporary holding status to be turned over for development at a future date.

Land banking can be used when development of a future installation is known. Additional land in excess of that required for the installation can be purchased and held for future use.[84]

The two primary arguments in favour of land banking are: (1)

it will have an anti-inflationary effect on land prices, thus preventing land speculation; and (2) it will permit more rational patterns of development, rather than urban sprawl. There may be legal restrictions that do not permit public land banking on constitutional grounds.

20.5.7 Special districts

Special districts are organized governmental entities that have a structure, official name, perpetual succession, the power to perform certain functions, the right to sue and be sued, the right to make contracts, and the right to acquire and dispose of property. Special district officials are chosen by local government officials. Despite this, special district governments possess considerable fiscal and economic independence.

Higher governments may be empowered to create and allocate powers to special purpose governments within their boundaries. Special districts can be created for areas surrounding airports for financial, land control, and noise abatement purposes.

A district is empowered to render services, even though the area lies within the jurisdiction of general purpose governments (i.e., counties, municipalities). There is no limit to the size of the special district. Most districts established to date are only zoning districts and are, therefore, not empowered to render services.

20.5.8 Transfer development rights

The transfer of development rights (TDR) involves a purchase of the development rights in a property and the transferring of those rights to another piece of property. Thus, development of the original property is prevented.

The rights that are transferred do not necessarily have a monetary value attached to them. Rather, they can be floor areas, bulk or dwelling units.

The effect of TDR is that development is prevented in areas like airports, but yet, because the rights of development are purchased, they can be transferred to an area where the municipality wishes to encourage development.

There are several steps involved in creating a transferable development right. First, the area to be preserved must be specifically identified and conform to the community's master plan. Second, the local government must determine the development capacity of the property, and then convert that value into development rights. Finally, the community must designate other districts in which higher density development caused by the TDR will be permitted.

Preserving open space around airports would be one goal in the use of TDR. For example, the state of New Jersey has proposed using TDR to preserve open space. Their proposal attempts to create a market for the TDR by following the steps to create a TDR. Similarly, all municipalities could create a market for development rights of land around airports by designating these areas as open space. The property owner whose rights had been sold could receive a property tax break as incentive.

The programme would be inexpensive or cost-free to the airfield since the local government would administer it. The programme could also stimulate growth and development of the property to which the development rights were transferred. Despite these arguments, TDRs have been under used, and, at present, few airports have applied this technique for noise abatement purposes.

References

1 Department of International Economic and Social Affairs, *Statistical Yearbook*, 33rd Issue, United Nations, New York (1985).

2 *Information Please Almanac: 1986*, 39th edn., Houghton Mifflin, Boston, Massachusetts (1986).

3 BRAGDON, C. R., Status of airport noise control in the US. In *Inter-noise 1983*, Edinburgh, Scotland (May 1983).

4 *Statistical Abstract of the United States: 1986*, 106th edn., US Department of Commerce, Bureau of Census, Washington, DC (1986).

5 *Alternatives Available to Accelerate Commercial Aircraft Fleet Modernization*, Report to Congress, US Department of Transportation, FAA (April 11, 1986).

6 *Annual Housing Survey*, US Department of Housing and Urban Development, Prepared by US Department of Commerce, Bureau of Census, Washington, DC (Each year since 1973).

7 CLINE, P. A., *Airport Noise Control Strategies*, FAA, Office of Energy and Environment, Washington, DC, FAA-EE-86-02 (May 1986).

8 BRAGDON, C. R. Airport/aircraft related noise control in the United States. *NATO Proceedings*, Committee on the Challenge of Modern Society, Mittenwald, Germany (September 1986).

9 *Instruction Concernant L'Applicant Des Limites Imposees Au Trafic De Nuit* (de 22 a 06 h. loc.), Aeroport De Geneve, Direction Generale (January 1985).

10 BRAGDON, C. R., *Part 150: Airport Noise and Land Use Planning Manual*, Vol. 1–2, Prepared Under Contract with the FAA, Washington, DC (March 1984); Metropolitan Airports Policy: Environmental Impact Statement, US Department of Transportation, FAA (September 1981).

11 Ordinance 85-35, Prohibit Scheduled Departures of Certain Noisier Aircraft, Palm Beach International Airport (October 10, 1986—Effective Date June 1, 1986).

12 *Noise Standards: Aircraft Type and Airworthiness Certification*, Federal Aviation Administration Regulation, Part 36, US Department of Transportation (June 1974 as amended).

13 Noise Abatement Rule, Boston Logan Airport Commission, Massachusetts Airport Authority (February 12, 1986).

14 ICAO. *Annex 16, International Standards and Recommended Practices, Environmental Protection*, 1st edn., Volumes I—II, Aircraft Noise, Aircraft Engine Emissions, ICAO, Montreal, Canada (1981).

15 Proposal to Increase Night Flights at Gatwick, Heathrow Draws Criticism. *Noise Regulation Reporter*, Bureau of National Affairs, Washington, DC (August 15, 1986).

16 *Planutvalget for Tromsø Lufthavn-Langnes: Aircraft Reduction Plan* (in Norwegian), Asplan A/S (1984).

17 *Aircraft Noise in a Modern Society: Proceedings*, NATO, Committee on the Challenge of Modern Society, Mittenwald, Federal Republic of Germany (September 1986).

18 Noise Abatement Departure Profile, Advisory Circular 91–53, US Department of Transportation, FAA, Washington DC.

19 *Report and Recommendations of the Airport Access Task Force*, Pursuant to Public Law 97-248, Airport Access Task Force, Presented to Congress (March 10, 1983).

20 SELLMAN, E. W. Noise restriction alternatives and considerations: An FAA perspective. In *Airport Noise and Land Use Planning*, Clifford R. Bragdon (Ed.), Georgia Institute of Technology, Atlanta, Georgia (January 28–30, 1986).

21 *Measures Dealing with Aircraft Noise*, International Civil Airports Association, European Region Working Group, France (November 1985).

22 Noise Abatement Procedures, Norfolk International Airport, Norfolk Port and Industrial Authority, Norfolk, Virginia (1984).

23 *Noise Abatement and Mitigation Study, Noise exposure Map and Noise Compatibility Program Submittal*, Prepared for the FAA, Palm Beach County Department of Airports (December 1985).

24 BRAGDON, C. R. *Noise Pollution: The Unquiet Crisis*, University of Pennsylvania Press, Philadelphia (1971).

25 BRAGDON, C. R. Airport Noise Monitoring Systems in North America, *Issues in Transportation Related Environmental Quality*, Transportation Research Record 1033, Transportation Research Board, National Research Council, Washington, DC (1985).

26 *Airport Noise Compatibility Planning*, Federal Aviation Regulation Part 150, US Department of Transportation, FAA (January 1981).

27 *Aircraft Training Activities*: Noise Restrictions, Ordinance 67, Minneapolis-St. Paul Airports Commission (July 1986).

28   *Noise Abatement Plan: Technical Report*, Portland International Airport (June 1983).

29   *Aircraft Noise in a Modern Society: Proceedings*, NATO, Committee on the Challenge of Modern Society, Mittenwald, Federal Republic of Germany (September 1986).

30   DANFORTH, R. Legal Aspects of Airport Noise Control FAA Perspective. In *Airport Noise and Land Use Planning*, Clifford R. Bragdon (Ed.), Georgia Institute of Technology, Atlanta, Georgia (January 28–30, 1986).

31   Skystar Wins Allocation of Noise Slots. *Noise Regulation Reporter*, The Bureau of National Affairs, Inc., Washington, DC (August 8, 1986).

32   Agreement Between the County of Orange and the City of Newport Beach, Resolution Number 84-10 (January 23, 1984).

33   Judge Gives Final Approval to John Wayne Airport Agreement. *Noise Regulation Reporter*, The Bureau of National Affairs, Washington, DC (January 6, 1986).

34   *Airport Environs Comprehensive Plan: Clark County, Nevada*, Clark County Planning Commission (December 1985).

35   *Air Traffic Noise Act*, The Minister of the Interior, Federal Republic of Germany (February 1981).

36   GUMMLICH, H. J. Noise zoning and sound insulation near airports: ten years' implementation of the German Air Traffic Noise Act. *Airport Noise Abatement*, Number 137, Proceedings of a Seminar, NATO, Soesterberg, The Netherlands (November 1982).

37   Landing fees provide over $2 million in aid to Paris airport neighbors in 1985. *Noise Regulation Reporter*, The Bureau of National Affairs (September 12, 1986).

38   WESLEY, P. Airlines accommodate late-night flight ban. *Palm Beach Post* (August 25, 1986).

39   *Act Relating to Airports, Senate Bill 85-S287, Substitute A*, General Assembly, State of Rhode Island (January 1985).

40   NEWMAN, J. S. and BEATTIE, K. R. *Aviation Noise Effects*, US Department of Transportation, Federal Aviation Administration, Washington, DC (March 1985); *Noise Control and Land Compatibility Planning for Airports*, Advisory Circular, A/C 150/5020–1, US Department of Transportation, FAA (August 5, 1983).

41   *The Airport and Its Neighbors*, The Report of the President's Commission, US Government Printing Office, Washington, DC (1952).

42   *Air Installation Compatible Use Zones*, Instruction No. 4165.57, US Department of Defense (July 30, 1973).

43   *Environmental Protection and Enhancement, Installation Compatible Use Zone Program (ICUZ)*, US Department of the Army, AR200–1 (June 15, 1982).

44   *Airport Noise Compatibility Planning*, Federal Aviation Regulations (FAR) Part 150, US Department of Transportation, FAA (January 1981).

45   FAR Part 150, *Airport Noise Compatibility Planning Program: Status of Maps and Programs*, FAA, Office of Energy and Environment, Washington, DC (September 1986).

46   BRAGDON, C. R. The status of noise regulatory controls: state and local. In *Proceedings: International Workshop on Noise and the Built Environment*, Sponsored by the National Science Foundation, UCLA, Los Angeles, California (May 1986).

47   *The Planning Act: Airport Vicinity Protection Area*, Regulation 291/75, Government of the Province of Alberta, Canada (October 30, 1975).

48   *Guidelines for Considering Noise in Land Use Planning and Control*, Federal Interagency Committee on urban Noise, US Department of Transportation, Washington, DC (June 1980).

49   *Airport Planning Manual: Land Use and Environmental Control*, 2nd ed., International Civil Aviation Organization (ICAO), Montreal, Canada (1985).

50   HUNERMAN, K. Land use planning around airfields with noise protection areas. In *Aircraft Noise in a Modern Society: Proceedings*. NATO, Committee on the Challenge of Modern Society, Mittenwald, Federal Republic of Germany (September 1986).

51   *Airport Compatibility Guidelines*, Volume IV, Oregon Aviation System Plan, Oregon Department of Transportation—Aeronautics Division (1981).

52   *Airport Compatibility Guidelines*, Texas Aeronautics Commission, Texas Transportation Institute (January 1986).

53   Creating an Airport Zoning Ordinance for General Law Cities, Home Rule Cities, and Counties, State of Texas.

54   BUGGE, J. J., *et al.* Norwegian Aircraft Noise Units—Experiences on Regulations on Land Use Planning.

55   The Netherlands Aviation Act, Bulletin of Acts, Orders and Decrees 354 (June 7, 1978).

56   MATSCHAT, K. and MULLER, E. A. *Comparison of National and International Methods for Assessing Aircraft Noise—Establishment of Approximate Relations Between the Noise Indices*, Max Planck-Institut fur Stromungsforschung, Federal Minister of the Interior, Germany (March 1984).

57   Airport Environs Zone Sound Attenuation Construction Methods, Article 22, Ordinance 16 072, Oklahoma City, Oklahoma (December 1980).

58   California Regulation on Freeway Noise Affecting Classrooms, Chapter 54, Section 216, Streets and Highways Code, California Department of Transportation, California (September 17, 1973).

59   Bulletin of Acts, Orders and Decrees of the Kingdom of the Netherlands, Noise at Large Aerodomes Decree, Article 25 (July 15, 1981).

60   *New Housing and Airport Noise: A Supplement to the Site Planning Handbook*, Central Mortgage and Housing Corporation, Ottawa, Canada (1975).

61   *Regulations for Determining Acceptibility of Housing Projects in Terms of Noise Exposure*, 24 CFR, Part 51, Department of Housing and Urban Development (December 27, 1978).

62   National Environmental Policy Act (NEPA) of 1969, Public Law 91–190, US Environmental Protection Agency (December 30, 1969).

63   MAGAN, A. *Quiet Communities: Minimising the Effects of Noise Through Land Use Controls*, National Association of Counties Research, Washington, DC (March 1979).

64   PATTERSON, T. W. *Land Use Planning Techniques of Implementation*, Van Nostrand, New York (1979).

65   *Noise Remedy Program for SEA-TAC International Airport and Environs*, Port of Seattle, Seattle Washington (January 8, 1985).

66   MINTON, K. William B. Hartsfield Atlanta International Airport Noise Abatement Program. *Airport Noise and Land Use Planning*, Clifford R. Bragdon, Ed., Georgia Institute of Technology, Atlanta, Georgia (January 28–30, 1986).

67   *Airport Master Plan*, Wichita Mid-Continent Airport, Sedgwick County, Kansas (1984).

68   *Avigation Easement*, Port of Seattle, SEA-TAC International Airport, Seattle, Washington.

69   *Property Interest Agreement*, William B. Hartsfield Atlanta International Airport, Fulton County, Georgia.

70   HAGMAN, D. G. *Public Planning and Control of Urban Land Development*, 2nd edn., West Publishing, St. Paul, Minnesota (1981).

71   Procedures for Noise Reduction and Control, Technical Report N-143, Construction Engineering Research Laboratory (January 1983).

72   BRAGDON, C. R. *Airport Noise Control Methods*, Consultation Report, Palm Beach International Airport, Department of Airports, Palm Beach County, Florida (September 1986).

73   OLLERHEAD, J. B. *Noise Abatement Procedures*, Airport Management and Planning Courses, Department of Transport Technology, Loughborough University of Technology (1985).

74   *Planning and Noise*, Circular 10/73, Department of the Environment, United Kingdom (January 1973).

75   SONS, J. Experience with Implementation of Insulation Projects, Their Costs and Effectiveness, *Aircraft Noise in a Modern Society: Proceedings*, NATO, Committee on the Challenge of Modern Society, Mittenwald, Federal Republic of Germany (September 1986).

76   BROWN, R. K. *Real Estate Economics: An Introduction to Urban Land Use*, Houghton Mifflin Company, Boston, Massachusetts (1965).

77   HAGMAN, D. G. *Urban Planning and Land Development Control Law*, West Publishing, St. Paul, Minneapolis (1981).

78   HINES, M. A. *Principles and Practices of Real Estate*, R. D. Irwin, Inc., Homewood, Illinois (1976).

79   ENGLEMAN, L. A. and RASPET, R. *Construction Engineering Research Laboratory Technical Report N-143*, US Army Corps of Engineers (January 1983).

80   SELDIN, M. and SWESNIK, R. H. *Real Estate Investment Strategy*, 2nd edn. John Wiley & Sons (1979).

81   SMITH, H. C., TSCHAPPAT, D. J. and RACSTER, R. *Real Estate and*

Urban Development, Richard D. Irwin, Homewood, Illinois (1981).

82 HAGMAN, D. G. *Public Planning and Control of Urban and Land Development*, Cases and Materials, 2nd edn. West Publishing, St. Paul, Minnesota (1980).

83 STRONG, A. L. *Land Banking*, The Johns Hopkins University Press, Baltimore Press, Baltimore and London (1979).

84 WRIGHT, R. B. and GITELMAN, M. *Land Use*, 3rd edn., West Publishing, St. Paul, Minnesota (1982).

Further reading

American National Standard. *Sound Level Descriptors for Determination of Compatible Land Use*. Acoustical Society of America (1980).

American Society of Planning Officials. *Planning the Airport Environment*, Chicago, 1968, (PAS 231).

Arde, Inc., and Town and City, Inc., *Study of Optimum Use of Land Exposed to Aircraft Landing and Takeoff Noise*, Washington, US National Aeronautics and Space Administration, 1966. (NASA Contractor Report CR 410)

BISHOP, D. E. and CLARK, W. E. *Analysis of Community and Airport Relationships*, Prepared for the Federal Aviation Agency by Bold Beranek and Newman, Inc., Springfield, Virginia, Clearinghouse for Federal Scientific and Technical Information, 1964, 3 vols. (FA-RD-64-148).

BIXLER, O. C., Jr. Community Noise Survey: Its Purpose, Techniques, and Results as Related to Land Use Planning. *Journal of the Acoustical Society of America*, 58(1) (1975).

BOHANNON, M. T. Airport Easements. *Virginia Law Review*, 54, 355–381 (1968).

BRAGDON, C. R. Environmental Noise Control Programs in the United States. *Journal of Sound and Vibration*, 11(12), 12–16 December (1977).

BRAGDON, C. R. Municipal Noise Ordinances. *Sound and Vibration*, 8(12), December (1974).

BRAGDON, C. R. *Noise Pollution: A Guide to Information Sources*, Gale Research Corporation, Detroit (1979).

BRAGDON, C. R. *The Status of Noise Control in the United States: 1978*, Washington, D.C., Environmental Protection Agency (1978).

BRAGDON, C. R. Urban planning and noise control. *Sound and Vibration* (1973).

BRANCH, M. C. Outdoor Noise, Transportation, and City Planning. *Traffic Quarterly*, April, 167–168 (1971).

BRANCH, M. C. Urban air traffic and city planning: A case study of Los Angeles County. *Traffic Quarterly*, July, 377–397 (1973).

Council of State Government. *Model State Noise Control Act*, 1973.

ENGELMAN, L. A. and RASPET, R. *Analysis of Legal Precedents and Land-Use Controls As Applied to the Installation Compatible Use Zone (ICUZ) Program*, Construction Engineering Research Laboratory, U.S. Army Corps of Engineers, Technical Report N-143, January (1983).

Federal Aviation Administration, *Airport Environmental Handbook* Department of Transportation, March 21, 1980.

FINK, L. S. Canadian Law and Aircraft Noise Disturbance: A Comparative Study of American, British, and Canadian Law. *McGill Law Journal*, n:55–69 (1966).

FOSTER, C. R. and DANFORTH, RICHARD W. *Regulation of Aircraft Noise, Handbook of Noise Control* (Harris, Cyril, M. Ed.), Chapter 39, McGraw-Hill (1980).

GALLOWAY, W. J. *Community Noise Exposure Resulting from Aircraft Operations: Technical Review*, United States Air Force, AMRL, TR-73-106, November (1974).

GOODWIN, J. R. Environmental Airport Regulations, American Society of Civil Engineers Air Transportation Division, *Special Conference Proceedings*, pp. 105–118, April (1977).

HAAR, C. M. Airport noise and the urban dweller: a proposed solution. *New York Law Journal*, 159:4, May 24 (1968).

HABERCOM, G. A. *Airport Noise: A Bibliography With Extracts*, Springfield, Va., National Technical Information Service, August (1978).

HARRIS, A. S. Designing For Noise Control At Air Carrier Airports: Runway Layout and Use. *Noise Control Engineers*, November–December (1980).

HARRIS, A. S. Noise abatement at general aviation airport. *Noise Control Engineering*, 10(2), 82–84, March–April (1978).

HARRISON, O. C. Use and Enjoyment of Land—Compensation for Noise Damage. *Natural Resources Lawyer*, 4(2): 429–52, April (1971).

HILDEBRAND, J. L. (ed.) *Noise Pollution and the Law*, Buffalo, W.S., Hein (1970).

HOLGER, D. K. Prediction of Changes in Aircraft Noise Exposure. *Noise Control Engineers*, May–June (1980).

KENTON, E. *Urban Noise Pollution: A Bibliography With Extracts*, Springfield, Va., National Technical Information Service, July (1978).

KING, R. L. *Airport Noise Pollution*, Metuchen, N.J.: Scarecrow Press (1972).

LARGE, J. B. Status of Airport Noise Prediction with Special Reference to the United Kingdom and Europe. *Noise Control Engineers*, July–August (1981).

LARGE, J. B., SINCHIRMS, A. GARCIA, DE ANDES, J. A. Strategies for land use planning around Spanish airports. In *Proceedings, International Conference on Noise Control Engineering*, San Francisco, May 8–10, 1978, pp. 717–722.

MCDONALD, J. A. Airport noise. *Town and Country Planning*, 31, 297–300, July (1963).

MCGRATH, D. C. Jr. Aircraft noise: fugitive factor in land use planning. *Journal of Urban Planning and Development*, Proceedings of the American Society of Civil Engineers 95 (UPI): 73–80, April 1969, A.S.C.E. Paper (no. 6520).

MEYER, A. F. E.P.A.'s Implementation of the Noise Control Act. *Sound and Vibration*, 9(2), December 1975.

MILLER, J. D. *Effects of Noise on People*, Washington Office of Noise Abatement and Control, U.S. Environmental Protection Agency, 1971. (NTID 300.7) EPI. 2:N69/10.

MILLER, R. J., et al. *Procedures for Determining Needs, Methods, and Costs for Insulating Existing Homes Near Airports Against Aircraft Noise*, Washington, U.S. Department of Housing and Urban Development, 1966. (NTIS-N6-25625).

Model Ordinance to Control Urban Noise through Zoning Performance Standards. *Harvard Journal of Legislation*, 8, 608 (1971).

OLLERHEAD, J. B. *Scales for Measuring Helicopter Noise*. Loughborough University, England.

OLLERHEAD, J. B. *Subjective Evaluation of General Aircraft Noise*, Washington, U.S. Federal Aviation Administration, 1968, Technical Report No. 68–35.

POWERS, J. O. Airborne transportation noise—its origin and abatement. *Journal of Acoustical Society of America*, 42, 1176 (1967).

RICHARDS, E. J. and CAPLAN, H. Control of Aircraft Noise Perceived at Ground Level: Technical Aspects; Legal Aspects. *Royal Aeronautical Society Journal*, 68, 45–53 (1964).

ROBINSON, D. W. Towards a unified system of noise assessment. *Journal of Sound and Vibration*, 14(3), 279–98 (1971).

SCHULZ, THEODORE. Some sources of error in community noise measurement. *Sound and Vibration*, February 18–27, (1972).

SEAGO, E. The airport noise problem and airport zoning. *Maryland Law Review*, 28, 120–135 (1968).

Tracor, Inc., *Community Reactions to Airport Noise*, Vol. 1, Washington, U.S. National Aeronautics and Space Administration, 1971. (NASA Contractor Report CR 1761).

US Department of Defense. *Tri-Service Manual for Land Use Planning Related to Aircraft Noise* (1977).

US Department of Housing and Urban Development. *Siting of HUD Assisted Projects in Designated Clear Zones and Accident Potential Zones at Civil Airports and Military Airfields*, January (1983).

US Department of Transportation. *Planning for the Airport and Its Environs: The Sea-Tac Success Story*, April (1978).

US Environmental Protection Agency. Airport Noise Land-Use Compatibility by the Year 2000. *Noise*, Office of Noise Abatement and Control, August, (1982).

US Environmental Protection Agency. *Information on Levels of Environmental Noise Requisite to Protect Public Health and Welfare with an Adequate Margin of Safety*, March (1974).

US Environmental Protection Agency. *Model Noise Ordinance*, March (1975).

US Environmental Protection Agency, Office of Noise Abatement and Control, *Conference on General Aviation Airport Noise and Land Use Planning*, October 3–5, 1979. Georgia Institute of Technology, Atlanta, Georgia.

US Federal Aviation Administration, *Model Airport Zoning Ordinance*, Washington, 1967. (Advisory Circular AC 150/5190-3)

US National Bureau of Standards, *The Economic Impact of Noise*,

Washington, Office of Noise Abatement and Control, US Environmental Protection Agency, (NTID 300.14) (EP 1.2:N69/17), 1971.

US National Library of Medicine, *Effects of Noise on Man*, Bethesda, Maryland (1968).

WESLER, J. Airport Noise Abatement: How Effective Can It Be? *Sound and Vibration*, **9(2)**, February (1975).

21

Supersonic Travel and Sonic Boom

C. H. Warren MA, FRAeS, FIMA, FCASI
Formerly of Royal Aircraft Establishment, Farnborough, UK

Contents

21.1 General description of the sonic boom phenomenon

21.1.1 Introduction

The sonic boom is a phenomenon peculiar to supersonic flight. It is not an event that an aircraft creates just when it 'breaks the sound barrier'. It exists throughout an aircraft's supersonic flight, and is caused by the Mach waves that an aircraft inevitably generates aerodynamically when it flies at a speed greater than that of sound. Roughly speaking these waves take the form of compression waves from the bow and the stern, separated by expansion waves. The compression waves coalesce and form steep rises in pressure which are called shockwaves. These waves extend from the aircraft as an audible pattern of roughly conical shape, much as the water waves from a boat extend from it as a visible pattern of roughly V-shape. Similarly, as the water waves from a boat cause a disturbance that often extends to and travels along a neighbouring shore as the boat passes by, so do these shockwaves from an aircraft cause a disturbance that normally extends to and travels along the ground as the aircraft flies over. The passage of these shockwaves is perceived as a sonic boom by all recipients upon whom the shockwaves actually impinge. Such recipients on the ground are said to be on the *sonic boom carpet*, which extends in length roughly from the place where the aircraft accelerates to supersonic speed to the place where it decelerates back to subsonic speed, as illustrated in *Figure 21.1*. The edge of the sonic boom carpet is called a *cut-off line*. A glossary of the most significant technical terms appropriate to the sonic boom is given in *Table 21.1*.

21.1.2 Propagation

The propagation of the sonic boom is an acoustic event which is well described by the theory of quasilinear geometric acoustics.[1] This theory states that a sonic boom may be considered to be propagated along rays.[2] Accordingly, the sonic boom will be subject to the well-known phenomenon of refraction due to temperature and wind speed gradients in the atmosphere. The effects of refraction can be quite complicated. One usually important effect is that the down-going rays are curved such that some may only just graze the ground, along a line on the ground called a *graze line*. Most of the cut-off line that is the edge of the sonic boom carpet is a graze line. *Figure 21.2* illustrates that, generally, the higher and faster an aircraft cruises the further out will be the graze lines, and hence the wider will be the sonic boom carpet.

If the aircraft's speed over the ground is less than the speed of sound propagation in that direction at ground level, then, owing to the effects of refraction, none of the rays from an aircraft flying level in the stratosphere will reach the ground, and hence it will not create any sonic booms, even on the track. In the absence of winds this situation will occur if the flight Mach number is less than about 1.15.

Another important effect of refraction is that up-going rays, either initially up-going or after reflection from the ground, can be refracted back towards the ground by the high temperatures and winds that can exist at certain times of year in the vicinity of the stratopause and in the thermosphere. Such sonic booms, when they reach the ground, are called *secondary booms* (the usual booms now being called *primary booms*). The generation of secondary booms is shown schematically in *Figure 21.3*. The region on the ground where the secondary booms are received is called the *secondary boom carpet*.

21.1.3 Waveform

In the immediate vicinity of the aircraft the aerodynamic wave pattern, and hence the sonic boom waveform, is relatively complicated, but, as the waveform propagates it 'ages' and becomes progressively simpler, until, at very large distances from the aircraft, providing the ageing process is complete, the *pressure signature* has very closely an *N-wave* form. Accordingly, at very large distances, the outdoor sonic boom event is experienced in less than half a second, and consists of an initial sudden rise in pressure, followed by a gradual fall, and then by a sudden rise again to bring the pressure back to ambient. It is the two sudden rises in pressure which, when they occur with a separation greater than about 100 ms, give the sonic boom its characteristic 'double-bang' sound.

When the waves reach the ground they are subject to reflection and diffraction by the ground itself, by buildings, and by any object which they meet. Accordingly, the wave pattern becomes complicated again. It is common, therefore, to describe a sonic boom in terms of its relatively simple waveform just before it reaches the ground, in *free-field conditions*. A second, and more common, way is to describe a sonic boom in terms of its waveform in an idealized situation called *datum ground conditions*. These conditions—perfectly flat, hard ground—are admittedly idealized, but they can be closely approximated in practice, thereby enabling a sonic boom in these conditions to be measured.

A composite of a sonic boom waveform in either free-field or ground conditions is illustrated in *Figure 21.4*. For reasons that

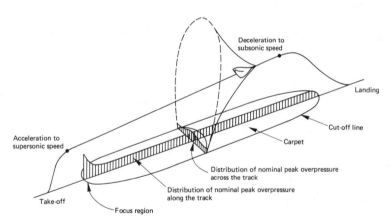

Figure 21.1 Schematic distributions of nominal peak overpressure on the sonic boom carpet for the flight of a supersonic aircraft

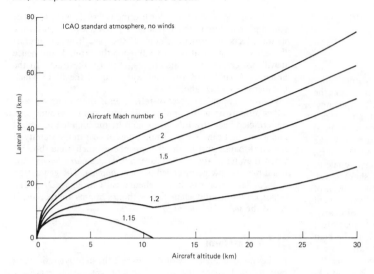

Figure 21.2 Lateral spread from the flight track of the graze lines produced by an aircraft in steady level flight

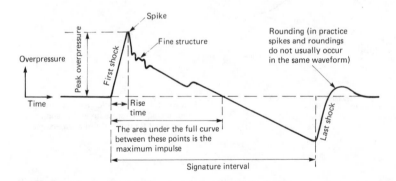

Figure 21.3 Schematic showing the generation of secondary booms

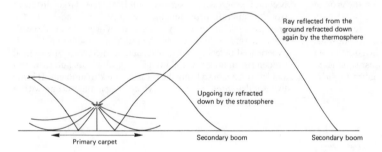

Figure 21.4 Composite of pressure signature characteristics

will be given in Section 21.1.5, there is frequently some 'fine structure' to the waveform, consisting often of either spikes or roundings, or superimposed 'noise'. The presence of such fine structure makes it difficult to pick upon a precise quantity that is a sufficiently representative characteristic of the sonic boom. Nevertheless, the concept of the so-called *characteristic over-pressure* has been introduced, which, for a signature having closely an N-waveform, would be the highest value of the *overpressure* that would have been observed were it not for the fine structure.

A spectral curve showing the distribution of boom energy in terms of frequency is shown schematically in *Figure 21.5*. The spectral energy is a maximum at a relatively low frequency which is inversely proportional to the *signature interval* (Δt).

This low frequency energy is important in regard to the effects on structures and terrain, especially when the low frequency is well-matched to a resonant frequency of the structure. The spectral energy at high frequencies is determined mainly by the *rise times* (τ) of the shocks and by the fine structure of the waveform. This high-frequency energy is important with regard to the effects on human beings and animals because it is closely related to the subjective loudness and startle effect of the boom.

21.1.4 Focusing

A complicated situation arises if the aircraft manoeuvres in any way, such as if it accelerates, if it turns, or if it pushes over into a

Table 21.1 Glossary of terms

Title	Definition
Characteristic over-pressure	The characteristic overpressure ΔP_c is defined by the formula $$\Delta P_c = \frac{4I}{\Delta t},$$ where I is the maximum impulse and Δt is the signature interval. For an N-wave the characteristic overpressure is the same as the peak overpressure.
Cut-off line	A cut-off line is a line which separates the region where sonic booms are experienced from the region where they are not.
Datum ground conditions	Datum ground conditions exist when reflecting objects other than the perfectly flat hard ground itself are sufficiently remote that their effects on the wave system are negligible at the place considered.
Focused boom	A focused boom is the sonic boom experienced on a focus line.
Focus line	A focus line is a line where the surface on which the rays have an envelope intersects the ground.
Free-field conditions	Free-field conditions exist when the ground and other reflecting objects are sufficiently remote that their effects on the wave system are negligible at the place considered.
Graze line	A graze line is a line where the rays just graze the ground.
Maximum impulse	The maximum impulse I is the maximum value of the running integral of the overpressure with respect to time.
Nominal	Nominal is an adjective used to denote the boom characteristics and carpet details which would occur if the atmosphere were the ICAO standard atmosphere,[11] if there were no winds or turbulence, and if the sonic booms were received on a flat ground having a reflection factor of 2.
N-wave	An N-wave is a pressure signature which resembles the letter N.
Overpressure	The overpressure ΔP is the difference between the pressure at a point at any instant and the ambient atmospheric pressure, positive when the pressure is greater than the ambient atmospheric pressure and negative when it is less.
Peak overpressure	The peak overpressure ΔP_{max} is the highest positive value of the overpressure.
Pressure signature	The pressure signature is a graph of the variation of the overpressure with time.
Primary boom	A primary boom is a sonic boom which reaches the ground directly, and not through being refracted from high altitude.
Reflection factor	A reflection factor K_r is the ratio of the pressure rise across a wave at a point of impingement with a reflecting object to the pressure rise across the incident wave.
Rise time	The rise time τ of a shock is the time interval between the onset of the shock and its specified termination.
Secondary boom	A secondary boom is a sonic boom which reaches the ground through being refracted from high altitude.
Signature interval	The signature interval Δt is the time interval between the onset of the first shock and the onset of the last shock in the signature.
Sonic boom	A sonic boom is the acoustic event which is a manifestation, notably on the ground, of the wave system generated by an aircraft when it flies at a speed greater than the speed of sound.
Sonic boom carpet	The sonic boom carpet is the region on the ground where sonic booms are experienced.

dive. This is because all manoeuvres can lead to the phenomenon of focusing. Focusing occurs when the rays, along which the sonic boom waveform is propagated, converge. The effect of this is that the usual decrease of the overpressures as the waveform propagates, which is associated with divergence of the rays, can be reduced or even reversed, thereby leading to a magnification of the overpressures.

Although all the manoeuvres mentioned could in principle

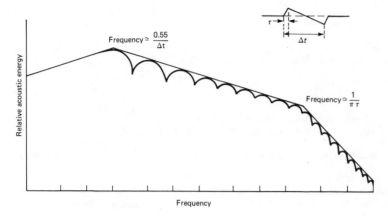

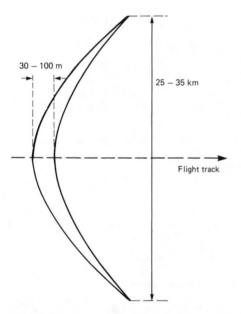

Figure 21.5 Schematic energy spectrum of an N-wave having a finite rise time

Figure 21.6 Crescent zone of the focused boom associated with transonic acceleration

lead to boom magnification by focusing, for the rates of turn or push-over likely to be made in normal circumstances by civil transport aircraft, noticeable focusing is unlikely, except for the manoeuvre when the aircraft accelerates from subsonic to supersonic speeds. The effect of this manoeuvre is to make the initial rounded end of the sonic boom carpet a *focus line*, in the form of a crescent which has been colloquially called a 'horse-shoe' (*see Figures 21.1* and *21.6*). The value of the magnified characteristic overpressure along the focus line is believed to be, typically, several times the more or less constant value subsequently attained some 10 km along on the carpet (reference 3, Section 1.4.3).

21.1.5 Effects of atmospheric turbulence

The atmosphere introduces an element of considerable variability in the signature of a sonic boom. The smaller scale atmospheric effects, which are the source of this variability, are random in nature, and hence cannot be treated as deterministic phenomena. The main effect can be described as a scattering,

which leads to the fine structure in the waveform illustrated in *Figure 21.4*. Spikes caused by the superimposed fine structure can lead to observed *peak overpressures* of two or three times the *nominal* level, while rounding can lead to decreased peak overpressures. The effects of atmospheric turbulence appear to be correlated only over small localized areas of the sonic boom carpet (reference 3, Section 1.5.3). Thus, considerable variations in fine structure can occur over relatively short distances, of the order of 100 m. Consequently, the sonic boom carpet can have a highly non-uniform distribution of, in particular, peak overpressure and rise time.

21.1.6 Effects of the ground environment

Near the ground the wave pattern becomes complicated owing to reflection and diffraction by the ground itself, by buildings and by other objects. The effect of the ground, when it is flat and open, leads to an approximate doubling of the overpressures on the ground due to reflection, with no change in the signature interval, compared with local free-field conditions. Greater magnifications can occur when there are, additionally, reflections from buildings. These magnifications can be large—up to a further factor of four in the vicinity of corners under special conditions—but they are very localized in their extent (reference 3, Section 1.6.1).

The acoustic event that is observed indoors when a sonic boom impinges upon the building concerned depends both upon the outdoor sonic boom and upon the transmission and resonance characteristics of the building, the dimensions of and furnishings in the room, and whether or not the windows or doors are open. The indoor boom is very different in waveform and character from the outdoor boom (reference 3, Section 1.6.2).

Because the speed of sound in water is about four times that in air, there is appreciable transmission of the sonic boom into water only if the rays strike the water at less than about 13 degrees to the normal to the surface. Generally, at larger angles, there will be total reflection of sonic booms at a water surface, with little penetration of sound from sonic booms.[4]

21.2 Measurement of physical properties of the sonic boom

21.2.1 Introduction

In this section is detailed a method that provides the basis for the measurement and description of sonic boom signatures. The conditions of measurement envisaged include those in which the direction and the time of arrival of the pressure disturbance and even its approximate intensity are not necessarily known in advance.

21.2.2 Measuring system

21.2.2.1 General performance requirements

The measuring system of microphone, amplifier and recorder shall have an overall frequency response, over the range of at least from 0.1 Hz to 5 kHz, which shall be flat within 2 dB.

However, if, for example, sonic booms of very fast rise rates need to be analysed very carefully, then the high frequency end of the range should be increased to 10 kHz. Similarly, if sonic boom events of very long duration need to be studied, then the low frequency end should be extended to 0.01 Hz.

21.2.2.2 Microphone

For events where high frequency fidelity is required, care should be taken to ensure that the microphone is adequately damped so as to avoid overshoot distortion.

The dimension of the sensitive surface of the microphone determines the degree of fineness with which the overpressure at a location can be measured. For most applications a dimension not exceeding 20 mm is recommended.

If the microphone has a fully sealed capsule, then appropriate calibration corrections shall be applied to cater for ambient pressure variations, but temperature and wind effects will often preclude their use, and a very slowly vented microphone is usually more satisfactory.

A shield may be necessary in order to reduce the effects of wind on the microphone, or to protect it from rain and dirt. Such a shield shall be designed so that the response of the microphone is not significantly affected.

The microphone shall be adequately shock-mounted in order to reduce vibration transmitted through the mountings.

Normally the calibration of the microphone shall be in terms of the free-field sensitivity appropriate to the angle of incidence of the signal. However, for ground conditions the calibration shall be in terms of pressure sensitivity. Accurate calibration is not so important for frequencies below about 5 kHz, but becomes increasingly significant above 5 kHz. The variations of the sensitivity of the microphone to environmental conditions shall be corrected in such a way that the resulting sensitivity is within 0.3 dB of the calibration value.

The calibration at low frequencies can be checked with a pistonphone operating into a volume in which the microphone is placed.

21.2.2.3 Amplifier

Modern tape recorders can tolerate an input of, typically, 0.2–1 V. So, if reasonable prediction of the overpressure is difficult, the optimum amplifier gain setting cannot be predetermined. In these circumstances it is recommended that more than one channel be recorded simultaneously with different gain settings at 5 or 10 dB intervals. This will ensure recordings of the sonic boom with adequate signal-to-noise ratio by utilizing the full dynamic range of at least one channel of the recording system.

The total harmonic distortion of the amplifier and its associated microphone shall not exceed 3% at the maximum overpressure to be measured.

21.2.2.4 Recorder

The dynamic range of the recorder shall be at the very least

45 dB, under the condition that the total harmonic distortion is less than 1% measured at 1 kHz.

The specified minimum dynamic range of the recorder may be insufficient to permit full-range frequency analysis of a sonic boom. For such measurements it may be desirable to include pre-emphasis in one channel of the recording system in order to improve signal-to-noise ratio at the higher frequencies: the inverse de-emphasis has to be applied to the playback system during frequency analysis. Such equalization should not be used for the recording and reproduction of the pressure signature, except where necessary to meet the overall frequency response requirement of the measuring system.

21.2.3 Environmental conditions

21.2.3.1 Ground conditions

In ground conditions the microphone shall be mounted with its axis perpendicular to the ground with its sensitive surface facing upwards and flush with a hard surface at ground level.

Provided that measurements are required only at frequencies up to about 5 kHz, then, in circumstances where flush mounting is impracticable, the microphone should be mounted with its axis either perpendicular or parallel to the ground and with its sensitive surface as close to the ground as possible, avoiding a face-down condition. The microphone body and associated equipment shall be sufficiently remote that their presence does not influence the measurements.

Datum ground conditions are those of open ground in which undulations and obstructions in total subtend a solid angle of less than 0.004 steradians.

21.2.3.2 Free-field conditions

Datum free-field conditions are those above ground where obstructions in total subtend a solid angle of less than 0.004 steradians, and where the microphone can be mounted at a sufficient height above the ground that reflections from the ground do not interfere with the relevant part of the signal.

The determination of the whole pressure signature from an aircraft in level flight in free-field conditions may necessitate a height of more than 100 km. For this reason datum ground conditions will usually be preferred. However, to resolve rise times, a height of 5 m may be sufficient.

21.2.3.3 Other conditions

On board ships or in mountainous or built-up areas, where the purpose is to approximate to results that would be obtained in datum conditions, the requirements stated earlier should be followed as far as possible. The special conditions e.g. sea state, should be reported. Measurements made for the purpose of relating human or structural response in specific environments shall be made with the microphone placed at a position appropriate for the receiver. For a seated human observer, for example, the microphone should be placed at approximate ear level—1.2 m above ground—and in an appropriate representative acoustical environment.

21.3 Effects on human beings

21.3.1 Physiological and physical effects

Apart from the effects of startle, no adverse physiological effects of exposure to sonic booms appear to have been observed, even when the overpressures have been many times greater than those associated with contemporary supersonic transport aircraft. The probability of direct injury is very low. However, some indirect injuries have been reported, resulting from persons being struck by falling objects or injured as a result of startle (reference 3, Section 3.2.1.3).

21.3.2 Startle

Sonic booms undoubtedly have a startling effect. At the intensity of sonic booms associated with contemporary supersonic transport aircraft, there is evidence that sleeping persons can be awakened, although there is evidence of adaptation of sleep patterns to regular exposure[5] (*see also* Chapter 5). Sonic booms can also cause arm–hand startle responses which could have adverse effects on occupational tasks in which arm–hand steadiness is the principal skill required.[6] However, there is little evidence that these responses significantly impair performance on less sensitive psychomotor tasks.

21.3.3 Annoyance

The results of many studies have shown that some persons can be seriously disturbed and annoyed by the sonic booms generated by contemporary supersonic transport aircraft. The degree of annoyance varies widely from person to person, depending upon such factors as the type of activity being disturbed, the quality of the environment, how the person earns his living, and also upon his political beliefs and attitudes to supersonic flight generally. The causes of annoyance are cited, typically, as 'house rattles', 'startles', 'interrupts sleep', 'interrupts rest', 'interrupts conversation', 'interrupts radio-TV'. House rattles are cited most frequently, and the annoyance seems to be associated with a concern about possible damage to the person's property (reference 3, Section 3.2.3.1).

Many studies have suggested that annoyance increases markedly as the rise time of the sonic boom shocks decreases, as well as with the degree of 'spikiness' in the signature.

21.4 Effects on structures

21.4.1 Nature of the problem

It is known that sonic booms impinging on a structure will induce transient vibrations which will depend markedly upon the resonance characteristics of the structure. If the strains associated with these vibrations at any point in the structure exceed the local elastic limit, then irreversible changes, or damage, will occur. Because the occurrence of damage depends upon so very many factors, it is impossible to comment upon the damage problem other than in statistical terms. The nature of the problem is illustrated diagrammatically in *Figure 21.7*. The abscissa is a measure of the 'intensity' of a sonic boom which is considered to be relevant to the structure considered. The broken curve shows how damage in its broadest sense may be expected to increase with increase in sonic boom intensity. The full curve shows how the frequency of occurrence of different intensities can be expected to vary, even for a given nominal overflight, owing to atmospheric effects, etc. The figure shows that, up to a certain threshold of sonic boom intensity, no damage would be expected to occur. Sonic booms of intensity greater than the threshold value would be expected to occur with decreasing frequency, as illustrated by the full curve, but would be expected to have progressively greater extents of damage associated with them, as illustrated by the broken curve.

The curves in *Figure 21.7* are very generalized. Extent of damage (broken curve) for nominally identical structures could be expected to vary depending upon such things as the amount of prestressing accidentally built into a structure, the age of a structure and the degree and quality of maintenance carried out, etc. Furthermore, frequency of occurrence (full curve) will vary with different aircraft and flight plans, etc. Accordingly, it can be seen that the problem is very complex, and only comments of a broad, statistical nature can be given. It is with this limitation that the observations in the following two sections are made.

21.4.2 Buildings

Buildings are the structures most susceptible to sonic boom damage, mainly because of the presence of much brittle secondary structure such as glass and plaster. This is illustrated by the following distribution by category of the frequency of occurrence of adjudged valid damage claims for a series of controlled overflights over the Saint Louis area of the USA in 1961–62,[7] in which the average peak overpressure was about 100 N/m² (2 lb/ft²).

Glass only	37 %
Plaster only	22 %
Glass and plaster	11 %
Bric-a-brac	$18\frac{1}{2}$%
Tiles and fixtures	$7\frac{1}{2}$%
Other structural damage	4 %

However, in monitored structures in controlled overflight experiments, residential-type windows of up to 1 × 1 m showed no observable damage for peak overpressures up to 1000 N/m² (20 lb/ft²) (reference 3, Section 4.2.3.2). Also, in laboratory

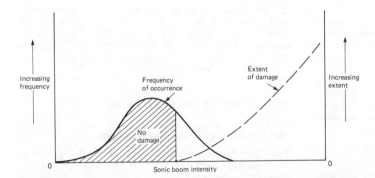

Figure 21.7 The problem of damage induced by sonic booms

studies commercially mounted plate-glass windows of dimensions $4\,m \times 2\,m \times 6\,mm$ have successfully withstood repeated simulated sonic boom loadings of up to about $1000\,N/m^2$ $(20\,lb/ft^2)$ peak overpressure (reference 3, Section 4.2.2.1). Nevertheless, in some controlled overflight experiments in Sweden in 1970,[8] it was found that movement of 1 mm in a prefabricated house occurred as indicated in the following:

Movement of an external wall away from an internal wall	$400\,N/m^2$ $(8\,lb/ft^2)$
Movement between two external wall sections	$1000\,N/m^2$ $(20\,lb/ft^2)$

It was conjectured that these differential movements of different parts of a built-up structure could have caused wallpaper cracks had the walls been papered. However, other measurements have shown that the movements associated with a sonic boom of $400\,N/m^2$ $(8\,lb/ft^2)$ are of the same order as those that can occur due to door slamming, and other such shock occurrences to which a building is subject from time to time, as well as being of the same order as those associated with seasonal movements owing to variations in moisture content.

21.4.3 Vehicles of various forms

Controlled tests made on many types of aircraft, including light aircraft and gliders, indicate that sonic-boom-induced motions are of an order of magnitude lower than those associated with routine flight and ground operations (reference 3, Section 4.2.7.1). This is not surprising since aircraft are designed, constructed and maintained to withstand loads far in excess of those associated with the sonic booms from supersonic transport aircraft.

Road vehicles and ships are even more robust than aircraft, and accordingly are even less likely to suffer sonic boom damage.

21.5 Effects on animals

Animals, like humans, are undoubtedly startled by the sonic boom. In most cases the response is mild, but there have been cases in which more serious reactions have occurred, particularly in regard to domestic animals. For example, there is evidence that, on occasions, cattle have stampeded, and chickens have crowded and reacted with pandemonium (reference 3, Section 5.2.2, 5.2.1). There is, however, evidence that animals do, with time, adapt to sonic booms (reference 3, Section 5.2.3). There is little evidence of any marked effect on animal wildlife, either terrestrial or aquatic.

21.6 Effects on terrain

Although sonic booms cause only very slight excitation of the ground, there does exist the possibility that avalanches might be triggered by sonic booms incident upon unstable snow accumulations. However, no direct evidence of cause and effect has become available, either in regard to avalanches, or other unstable terrain features.

21.7 Factors that help to reduce sonic boom levels

21.7.1 The formula for sonic boom intensity

A simple, but reasonably approximate, formula[9] for the nom-

$$\Delta P = \sqrt{(\Delta P_v)^2 + (\Delta P_L)^2} \qquad (21.1)$$

where ΔP_v is the peak overpressure associated with the aircraft's volume, given by:

$$\Delta P_v \simeq 1.34 K_f (M^2-1)^{\frac{1}{8}} P_g^{\frac{1}{2}} P_a^{\frac{1}{2}} \frac{S_{max}^{\frac{3}{4}}}{h^{\frac{3}{4}} l^{\frac{3}{4}}} \qquad (21.2)$$

and ΔP_L is the peak overpressure associated with the aircraft's lift, given by:

$$\Delta P_L \simeq 1.09 K_f \frac{(M_n^2-1)^{\frac{3}{8}}}{M_n} P_g \frac{W^{\frac{1}{2}}}{h^{\frac{3}{4}} c^{\frac{1}{4}}} \qquad (21.3)$$

where M_n is Mach number,
h is altitude,
P_g is ambient air pressure at ground level,
P_a is ambient air pressure at altitude h,
S_{max} is maximum cross-sectional area of the aircraft,
l is length of the aircraft,
W is weight of the aircraft,
c is fore-and-aft length over which the lift is borne,
K_f is a focus factor.

21.7.2 Aircraft design

Equations (21.2) and (21.3) indicate that, for aircraft of the same slenderness ratio (roughly the same value of S_{max}/l^2) and of the same wing loading (roughly the same value of W/c^2), the nominal peak overpressure will vary as the size of the aircraft to the power $\frac{3}{4}$ of the linear dimensions. However, the nominal peak overpressure can be reduced by making the aircraft more slender, and by reducing the wing loading.

The Mach number of flight, if above about 1.5, is not, directly, an important factor. Increasing the Mach number increases the nominal peak overpressure associated with the aircraft's volume, and decreases that associated with the aircraft's lift, in each case roughly to the power $\frac{1}{4}$ only.

By far the most important design factor affecting peak overpressure, as might be intuitively presumed, is the altitude of flight. In addition to the inverse $\frac{3}{4}$-power term in both Equations (21.2) and (21.3), there is the $(P_a)^{\frac{1}{2}}$ term in equation (21.2), which has a very large effect owing to the rapid decrease of ambient air pressure with altitude.

Finally there could be designs of aircraft,[10] having reduced sonic booms, for which the simple formulae given in Section 21.7.1 do not apply. However, none of the theoretical proposals so far made has been developed to a stage where they can be considered practical design possibilities.[2]

21.7.3 Aircraft operation

There are three matters to be borne in mind when considering how a supersonic aircraft should be operated in order to keep down sonic boom levels.

First, the relevant factors mentioned in Section 21.7.2 should be observed. Principally this means endeavouring to fly the aircraft at as high an altitude as possible.

Second, it is a natural consequence of the necessary acceleration to supersonic speed that the aircraft will create a 'focused boom' during this transitional phase. The strength of this focused boom does not lend itself to detailed calculation, and its effect is represented in Equations (21.2) and (21.3) by the factor K_f. It is generally accepted that K_f could have a value in the range $2\frac{1}{2}$–5, which makes it an extremely dominant factor.

Although it can probably be reduced by keeping down the transonic acceleration, its effect is usually alleviated in operations by routing the aircraft so that the focused boom is 'planted' on less sensitive terrain, such as at sea.

Third, the formulae given in Section 21.7.1 are for nominal peak overpressure. This is the peak overpressure that would occur in the ICAO standard atmosphere[11] in the absence of both winds and turbulence. However, in the real atmosphere there are winds, which can be very great at very high altitudes, and these can lead to the propagation of sonic booms to points well outside the nominal sonic boom carpet, for the reasons given in Section 21.1.2. Meteorological information and operational experience can indicate the times of year when such conditions are likely to prevail, and alterations to the route planning can then be made to mitigate the effects. For example, following detailed analysis of the operational experience obtained during the winter of 1976–77, the inbound track of the Concorde to Paris was significantly revised, which produced immediate beneficial effects—the primary booms previously experienced in south-western England and islands in the Channel were eliminated and the secondary booms heard over southern England were drastically reduced.

References

1 PIERCE, A. D. *Acoustics An Introduction to Its Physical Principles and Applications*, Chapter 8, McGraw-Hill, New York, pp. 371–423 (1981).
2 HAYES, W. D. Sonic boom. *Annual Review of Fluid Mechanics*, **3**, 269–290 (1971).
3 *Report of Sonic Boom Panel Second Meeting Montreal 12–21 October 1970*, International Civil Aviation Organization (1970).
4 WATERS, J. F. and GLASS, R. E. *Penetration of Sonic Boom Energy into the Ocean: An Experimental Simulation*, Hydrospace Research Corporation, Rockville Maryland Technical Report 288 (1970).
5 LUKAS, J. S. and KRYTER, K. D. *Awakening Effects of Simulated Sonic Booms and Subsonic Aircraft Noise on Six Subjects, 7 to 72 Years of Age*, National Aeronautics and Space Administration, Report CR-1599 (1970).
6 THACKRAY, R. I., TOUCHSTONE, R. M. and BAILEY, J. P. A comparison of the startle effects resulting from exposure to two levels of simulated sonic booms. *Journal of Sound and Vibration*, **33**, 379–389 (1974).
7 NIXON, C. W. and HUBBARD, H. H. *Results of USAF-NASA-FAA Flight Program to Study Community Responses to Sonic Booms in the Greater St Louis Area*, National Aeronautics and Space Administration, Technical Note D-2705 (1965).
8 WILHELMSEN, A. M. and LARSSON, B. *Sonic Booms and Structural Damage*, National Swedish Building Research, Document D3 (1973).
9 WARREN, C. H. E. The propagation of sonic bangs in a nonhomogeneous still atmosphere. *Proceedings of the 4th Congress of the International Council of the Aeronautical Sciences*, pp. 177–206 (1964).
10 SEEBASS, R. and GEORGE, A. R. Sonic boom minimization. *Journal of the Acoustical Society of America*, **51**, 686–694 (1972).
11 International Civil Aviation Organization, Montreal Canada and Langley Aeronautical Laboratory, Langley Field Va, *Standard Atmosphere Tables and Data for Altitudes up to 65800 ft*, National Advisory Committee for Aeronautics, Report 1235 (1955).

Further reading

HAYES, W. D., HAEFELI, R. C. and KULSRUD, H. E. *Sonic Boom Propagation in a Stratified Atmosphere, with Computer Program*, National Aeronautics and Space Administration, Report CR-1299 (1969).

Part 6

Decision-Making Methods for Transport Noise Control: Environmental Appraisal and Economic Instruments

22

The Environmental Appraisal of Transport Plans

C. J. Baughan BSc, MSc, MEngs
**Transport and Road Research Laboratory,
Crowthorne, UK**

Contents

22.1 Introduction

Other sections of this book deal with the generation, consequences and control of noise from transport systems. However, the fact that transport systems do generate noise, and that this has undesirable consequences, does not necessarily mean that noise controls should be applied at any price. Resources are limited, and therefore decisions have to be made about what resources to devote to noise control.

Consider, for example, a new road being planned. The road will produce benefits to those who use it, and indirectly to others. It will consume resources in construction and maintenance, and noise from its traffic will be heard by people living nearby. The road may also relieve traffic elsewhere, thus improving the noise environment of other people.

In this example, decisions are needed on:

1. Which route to use,
2. The design of the road, and the noise control measures to incorporate in the design,
3. Whether people who have their noise environment made worse should be compensated,
4. Whether the road is justified at all, in the light of the disadvantages it brings.

Similar problems occur in planning the siting and pattern of use of airports and air routes, in managing road traffic, and in deciding what noise control measures to include in the design of aircraft and surface vehicles.

One of the difficulties with such decisions is that the costs and benefits tend to fall upon different groups of people. This means that the producer of the impacts may not feel all the consequences of his decisions as costs or benefits to himself, i.e. they may impinge only or mainly on other people. In consequence, the producer may, knowingly or unknowingly, fail to take proper account of these 'externalities' when he makes decisions.

There are several ways in which society can act in order to combat this problem:

1. Constrain the producer's decisions by imposing standards for noise and other emissions. If the producer intends to keep within the law, he must act as though violation of a standard has infinite cost. If he is willing to break the law, violation of the standard has the cost associated with fines and bad publicity.
2. Leave the decision to the producer of the impacts, but make him see his externalities as costs by imposing on him taxes based on the cost to society of the noise and other impacts that he produces. Given certain rather important assumptions, this should in theory result in decisions that are optimal to society. It also can be seen as compensating society for the pollution that is produced.
3. Leave decision making to the producer, but impose a decision making framework that requires him to take account of the consequences to society of his actions. This forces the producer at least to be aware of such consequences. In a sense, it makes him see them as real costs or benefits, since his decisions are exposed to public scrutiny and because society retains the sanction of refusing to ratify decisions that do not comply with the framework it has imposed.
4. Remove decision making power from the producer, and operate the decision making framework at society level.

In the field of noise and other environmental impacts, activities associated with the decision making framework at (3) and (4) above have become known as environmental appraisal, and form the subject matter of the present chapter.

One appraisal method discussed is cost benefit analysis, which requires the importance of impacts to be expressed in money units. Approaches to obtaining money values for environmental impacts are briefly reviewed in this chapter, while Chapter 23 gives a more detailed description of methods for deriving money values for noise. As well as being required for cost benefit analysis, money values are also needed for deciding the levels of pollution taxes—a subject covered in Chapter 24.

The first stage in an environmental appraisal is to identify all the important impacts, such as noise, and forecast their magnitudes. Following this analytical phase, the information has to be brought together in some way and an overall view taken, based on judgements about the importance of the impacts. The more detailed and wide ranging the output of the analytical phase, the more difficult becomes the task of synthesizing it—a conflict that has been called the 'evaluation dilemma'.[1]

A variety of methods have been used for environmental appraisal. The most informal give little or no guidance on what impacts to take into account, how to assess their magnitudes, or how to interpret the information. At the other extreme are methods that list the impacts to be considered and give techniques for assessing their magnitudes. They then attempt to cope with the difficulties that detailed information poses for decision making, by specifying a weighting system for combining impacts into an index of environmental performance.

Such 'grand index' methods remove at least some of the scope for judgement from the decision maker and transfer it, embodied in the weighting system, to the appraisal method itself. This raises important issues that have proved difficult to solve. For example, there is the question of who decides the weights.

To avoid these problems, intermediate approaches have been proposed. These use a detailed and formal analytical phase but do not specify a method of calculating a grand index. Instead they leave the decision, with its inherent value judgements, to the decision maker.

This chapter aims to give an introduction to the various tasks of environmental appraisal, the ways in which these tasks have been tackled and the issues raised by the different approaches. Criteria for a 'good' method are discussed, so as to enable readers to judge for themselves the advantages and disadvantages of any appraisal method. To illustrate some of these points in more detail, several environmental appraisal methods are described and criticized, and the procedural background to environmental appraisal is briefly discussed.

22.2 Terminology

The literature on environmental appraisal shows some variation in terminology, and it is therefore necessary to define terms as they are used in this chapter.

Plans, policies, schemes and actions: A discussion of environmental appraisal needs a general term for 'that which is to have its environmental consequences appraised'. The word 'scheme' has particular connotations for road builders, whilst 'policies' and 'actions', either of which may be the subject of an environmental appraisal, exclude each other. In this chapter, the term 'plan' will be used to denote anything that requires an environmental appraisal.

Environmental: This applies most obviously to effects on the natural environment, but potentially it describes any effect of a plan on its surroundings. It is certainly used to cover perceived nuisance, community severance, health changes and other effects on people, although terms such as social impact are sometimes used to distinguish these from effects on the natural environment.[2] In this chapter the term 'environmental' will be used in its broadest sense.

Environmental performance: Describes the 'goodness' of a plan from the point of view of its environmental consequences.

Assessment, evaluation, appraisal: A distinction similar to that suggested by Catlow and Thirlwall[3] will be followed, 'assessment' being used to denote the production of a detailed factual, objective description of impacts. 'Evaluation' will be reserved for a process that involves the making of value judgements about the importance or significance of impacts. 'Appraisal' will be used as a general term covering the whole sequence of collecting and processing information on the environmental consequences of plans, and the reaching of judgements and decisions on these consequences.

Effects and impacts: A plan will generally have chains of environmental consequences. For instance, physical effects, such as changes in noise level, may lead to further changes in health or perceived nuisance. Although the terms 'effect' and 'impact' are often used synonymously, it has been suggested[3] that 'effect' should refer to the physical changes, whilst 'impact' is reserved for consequences of these changes. The dividing line between effects and impacts is not always very clear but, in so far as it can be made, the distinction is useful since it is often easier to judge the importance of the impacts than that of the immediate effects.

Appraisal team, decision maker: The tasks of environmental appraisal include: (1) identifying impacts and collecting data, (2) forecasting the magnitudes of impacts, (3) judging the importance of impacts and (4) reaching decisions on the environmental performance of the plans being appraised. The literature commonly allocates tasks (1) and (2) to an appraisal team and task (4) to a decision maker, responsibility for task (3) being less clearly specified and depending on the type of appraisal method being discussed. This convenient simplification will be followed here as well. However, in practice, the distinction between appraisal team and decision maker is often blurred. This is particularly so with appraisals at early stages in the design of plans, or where formal procedures are used for combining impacts into indices of environmental performance. In the latter case, the role of the decision maker may be reduced to ratifying decisions that have already been taken by the appraisal method itself; although it could be argued that a 'grand decision'—that the appraisal method gives good results—has already been made.

22.3 Approaches to the tasks of environmental appraisal

The different approaches to environmental appraisal can most easily be examined by looking at the ways of tackling its constituent tasks.

Figure 22.1 illustrates how the analysis and synthesis phases[4] may be broken into sub-tasks; a classification similar to that used by Warner and Preston[5] and others.[6,7]

22.3.1 Identifying the impacts

The first task is to decide what impacts should be included in the

appraisal, the objective being to ensure that all important impacts are covered without wasting effort on unimportant ones.

Methods here range from the largely unguided application of common sense on the one hand,[8] to the use of comprehensive and detailed checklists on the other.[9–19] Two-dimensional checklists or matrices are a feature of some methods—with impacts as one dimension, and type of project activity, or groups of people on whom the impacts may fall, as the other.[20–28] Some procedures make special attempts to identify interactions between impacts.[29–33]

Detailed checklists help to ensure that impacts are not overlooked; but they may cause resources to be wasted on unimportant impacts and emphasize wide coverage at the expense of quality of assessment.[6] Attention has therefore been given to ways of restricting the scope of appraisal to the important impacts only.[34–37]

A technique[38,39] using map overlays has been employed for selecting highway routes. Each overlay is marked with data on a particular type of environmental factor or human concern. When superimposed, either manually or by computer, the overlays can help to identify the impacts of the alternative routes.

Consulting people likely to be affected by the plan is another way of identifying impacts. It can range from interviewing representatives of the affected groups,[19] to inviting public comment on proposed plans.[20]

22.3.2 Forecasting the magnitude of impacts

Once it has been decided what impacts should be included in the appraisal, the next task is to forecast the level of each impact in descriptive or quantitative terms. Generally, this will be needed for all the alternative plans being considered (one of which may be a 'do nothing' or 'do minimum' plan).

Forecasting techniques are available for many of the impacts of transport plans and research to add to and improve on these is continuing.[20,40–48] Chapters 10, 15 and 19 discuss some of the techniques appropriate to transportation noise. Different forecasting techniques are required for different levels of appraisal. Techniques that are suitable for the appraisal of a detailed project may be unusable at the early stages of design or for the general appraisal of transport policies.

Sometimes it is not possible to use a scientifically developed and validated forecasting method. A suitable method may not exist, or the input data or resources it requires may not be available. An alternative in such cases is to use the judgements of experts to obtain the required forecasts.[49,50]

22.3.3 Attaching importances to impacts

The synthesis task starts by attaching an importance to each of the forecast impacts. Appraisal methods tackle this in a variety

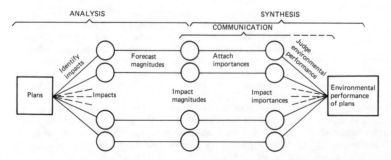

Figure 22.1 The tasks of environmental appraisal

of ways, differing in terms of the formal complexity of the process, the source of the importance judgements, and the way that the outcome is expressed.

22.3.3.1 Complexity

Judging the importance of impacts has several components:

1. Impacts may have been expressed on a scale such that equal increments along the scale are not equally important. For example, it may be judged that the difference between noise levels of 55 and 60 dB(A) is more (or less) important than that between 75 and 80 dB(A).
2. An impact is unlikely to be distributed uniformly: different geographical areas, periods of time, or groups of people, will experience different magnitudes of the impact.
3. Coping with (1) and (2) above would enable comparisons to be made within a given type of impact. For example, it would enable one plan to be compared with another in terms of noise nuisance. To allow comparisons to be made across impacts, a third component is needed, which takes account of the relative importance of the different types of impact.

Some appraisal methods tackle these components by incorporating formal procedures to transform measurement scales and apply importance weights[13,16,33,51,52]; others use only a simple scoring system.[10,18,25] A further approach is to rely on the individual components being taken into account informally by the decision maker.[20]

22.3.3.2 Source of judgements

Possible sources of information on importance are:

1. The judgements of the appraisal team, the designers of the appraisal method or other 'experts'.
2. The judgements of the decision maker.
3. The views of the public expressed through:
   (a) Market prices.
   (b) Travelling or other behaviour, from which it is sometimes possible to estimate willingness to pay for unmarketed goods.
   (c) Other attempts to obtain money valuations, such as direct questioning.
   (d) Consultation with the public or their representatives.
   (e) Political lobbying.

In (1) or (2) above, the appraisal team or decision maker may be assisted by giving them experience of the various impacts, describing the impact magnitudes in terms that are as meaningful as possible, or by summarizing the views of the public.

22.3.3.3 Expressing the outcome

There are several ways of expressing the importance of impacts; and a given appraisal method may employ more than one of them. Some methods[10,13,16,18,25,50,51,52] yield numerical scores in units that have no particular significance except in that they allow the environmental impacts to be expressed on the same scale, and then combined to form an overall index. However, there has been a great deal of interest in being able to obtain impact scores in money units, so that they may easily be used in an overall appraisal, alongside construction costs and other economic factors.[53-62] Further information on these methods is given in Section 22.5.1 and in Chapter 23. Another possibility is the use of verbal descriptions of importance instead of numerical indices.

Some methods do not require the importance of all individual impacts to be stated explicitly, but ask the decision maker to make judgements of impact importance while reaching an overall view on environmental performance.[20,63]

22.3.4 Judging environmental performance

The purpose of an environmental appraisal is to help people make decisions on:

1. Which of a set of alternative plans has the best environmental performance.
2. Whether a plan satisfies stated environmental criteria.
3. How a plan's environmental performance might be improved.
4. How good (in an absolute sense) is a plan's environmental performance—so that this can be compared with the other consequences of the plan in an overall appraisal.

The way that this is achieved is largely determined by the method used to attach importances to impacts. Grand index methods require the numerical importance scores to be summed to give an index of environmental performance. Methods that rely on the decision maker to judge the importance of impacts also ask him to reach a view on overall environmental performance, although they may assist him by:

1. Using sub-indices to combine some impacts when this can be done without the value judgements inherent in producing a single grand index.[64]
2. Suggesting other strategies for simplifying the decision making task. For example, eliminating impacts that are below some threshold value for all the alternative plans being considered; comparing plans impact by impact; eliminating plans that such comparisons show to be inferior on all counts[6]; comparing plans in pairs instead of attempting to evaluate all the alternatives simultaneously.[65]

22.3.5 Communication

A task of environmental appraisal that is often identified in the literature, but which may appear not to fit neatly into the analysis/synthesis model, is that of communication. However, the objective of the analysis phase is really to communicate the impacts to the decision maker (or, in the case of the grand index methods, to the equations and weighting procedures of the formal synthesis stage).

There may be other needs for communication. One of the objectives of an appraisal might be to describe the environmental advantages and disadvantages of the plans to the public—perhaps as part of a consultation exercise designed to elicit opinions, preferences and values.

Lee[6] describes two views of the role of communication in environmental appraisal, and points out that the choice between them influences each of the other appraisal tasks. One view confines communication with the public to a late stage in the proceedings, where it takes place in an adversarial atmosphere. According to Lee, this encourages 'defendable' appraisals in which little explanation of methods is given and too much effort is devoted to covering unimportant impacts. Lee's alternative view has communication starting at an early stage in the planning process, where it assists in identifying impacts and alternative plans, and helps to assess the importance of impacts. The later stages of communication then take place in a less confrontational atmosphere and cover a more useful agenda.

22.4 Criteria for environmental appraisal methods

22.4.1 Value judgements

Environmental appraisal involves judgements that depend on

human values. Views must be taken on the importance of various impacts, the desirability of particular distributions of impacts over groups of people, and the way in which future impacts should be weighed against those that act immediately. An important characteristic of these value judgements is that they are not susceptible to objective testing.

If the results of an environmental appraisal cannot be said to be objectively correct or incorrect, but depend on value judgements, questions arise as to what and, more particularly, whose values should be used. Answering these questions itself involves value judgements, so that no precise rules can be specified. However, it is possible to suggest criteria based on the idea that an appraisal should be consistent with widely accepted values, especially those on which society is based. This implies that in a democracy, the values incorporated in an appraisal method ought to be those of the public. Some methods seem intrinsically more likely than others to satisfy this criterion, but the procedural context in which the method is applied is often the determining factor. Section 22.6 covers this topic in more detail.

A fuller discussion of values and value judgements in environmental appraisal, together with many of the other issues touched upon in this chapter, is given in the book by McAllister (*see* reference 1).

22.4.2 Distribution of impacts

A public project such as a transport plan affects different groups of people in different ways, and the interests of the various groups have to be weighed against each other in reaching a decision. Judgements may be needed as to whether it is better to have a few people very annoyed or many people slightly annoyed; or as to whether minor benefits to a large number of people should be allowed to outweigh severe losses to a few people. There is therefore plenty of opportunity for the interests of one group of people to be overridden by those of another—a problem that has long been recognized as a serious threat to the satisfactory operation of democracies.[66-69]

Two partial solutions to this difficulty are: (1) to ensure that attention is given to impacts on minority groups,[70] and (2) to preserve information on the distribution of impacts, rather than use some method of aggregation that incorporates, and might disguise, important value judgements.[20,63]

22.4.3 Treatment of time

Transport plans, particularly those that involve building new roads or other long-lived facilities, have impacts that extend well into the future, and an appraisal method needs to be able to take account of this.

The issue is a very difficult one. No attempt will be made to prescribe definite criteria here, except to say that an appraisal method should recognize the problem and attempt to cope with it. As far as possible this should be done in a way that reflects the values held by society—with attention being given to the fact that unborn generations do not have the opportunity of expressing their opinions at all.

Further discussion will be reserved until specific environmental appraisal methods are considered in more detail.

22.4.4 Qualitative values

A crucial requirement for environmental appraisal methods is they should allow full expression to be given to the importance of impacts. It has been argued[71] that numerical ratings of importance do not satisfy this criterion because they cannot adequately capture the qualitative nature of human values such as deep moral feelings. Such a point of view might be challenged, especially if a rating system allows very high or infinite

ratings to be given. Nevertheless, a belief that appraisal methods are not taking account of deeply held qualitative values could well reduce public faith in their operation.

22.4.5 Unquantified impacts

In comparison with other consequences of plans, some environmental impacts are difficult to quantify. This poses problems for grand index methods that need quantified impacts for their weighting factors to operate on. Even when appraisal methods do allow them to be included, unquantified impacts may tend to be overlooked if quantified impacts are competing for the decision maker's attention. It is highly desirable for an appraisal method to be able to give proper weight to all impacts, quantified or unquantified, although any unquantified impacts will need to be described well enough to allow judgements to be made about their importance.

22.4.6 Uncertainty

Forecasts of environmental impacts, as well as being difficult to express quantitatively, are subject to uncertainty. Likewise, there will be uncertainties over the relative importances of the impacts and over the other value judgements being made.

An appraisal method needs to be able to cope with such uncertainties. This has been attempted by testing the outcome's sensitivity to uncertainty, avoiding uncertainty by assuming the worst, or by using expected values (in the statistical sense) of the uncertain variables.[6,72] An alternative is to make the whole appraisal and environmental management process adaptable, so that there is a continual cycle of appraisal and modification during the life of the project.[73]

22.4.7 Practical criteria

The criteria discussed so far have stemmed mainly from the philosophical issues underlying environmental appraisal. Several other criteria, associated more with the practicalities of conducting an appraisal, may also be stated.

1. The need for communication at various stages of the appraisal has implications for the types of impact descriptions used, and for the desirability of using complicated forecasting and weighting procedures. Descriptions and procedures that are difficult for the public or decision maker to comprehend are likely to reduce the credibility of the appraisal method and lead to poor decisions.[74]
2. The method must be able to cope with the planning system in which it is required to operate. If it is to be exposed to a public inquiry, an appraisal method will need to have a robust and justifiable logic that can be explained to and understood by the layman.[40,75]
3. The method must operate within available resources, although the resources that are made available ought to depend on the importance of the plans being appraised.
4. Repeated applications of the method to the same plans (but using different appraisal personnel) should lead to similar outcomes. This poses problems for methods that require arbitrary scores or choices from the appraisal team, or where the decision maker uses his own judgements without reference to the views of the public.
5. The method should ensure that all important impacts are considered, while avoiding wastage of resources on unimportant ones.
6. A good appraisal should include a description of the assumptions and limitations associated with it, so as to enable the decision maker (and the public) to interpret it properly.

Table 22.1 Criteria for environmental appraisal methods

1.	*Good decisions*	Appraisal method should lead to 'good' decisions.
2.	*Value judgements*	Should be consistent with society's values. In a democracy, therefore, values should be those of the public.
3.	*Distribution of impacts*	The appraisal method should take proper account of the way that impacts are distributed over groups of people.
4.	*Time*	Distribution of impacts over time should be dealt with in a way that satisfies the other criteria, especially (2) and (3).
5.	*Qualitative values*	Method should allow full expression to be given to qualitative values concerning the importance of impacts.
6.	*Unquantified impacts*	Proper weight should be given to all impacts, quantified or unquantified.
7.	*Uncertainty*	Method should cope with uncertainties in forecasting impacts etc.
8.	*Comprehensible*	Procedures and descriptions should be comprehensible to public and decision maker.
9.	*Planning system*	Method needs to be able to cope with the planning system in which it is required to operate.
10.	*Resources*	Method must operate within available resources.
11.	*Reliability*	Repeated applications of the method to the same plans (but using different appraisal personnel) should lead to similar outcomes.
12.	*Coverage*	Method should ensure that all important impacts are covered without wastage of resources on unimportant ones.
13.	*Limitations*	Assumptions and limitations should be clearly described.

Criteria for a good appraisal method are summarized in *Table 22.1*

22.5 Review of some environmental appraisal methods

22.5.1 Cost–Benefit Analysis

Cost–Benefit Analysis (CBA) is really a technique for overall appraisal, in that it is not restricted to environmental effects. It was developed to deal with the economic effects of water schemes[76] but has since been applied to the environmental effects of airports, railways and highways.[56,62,77-80]

A brief review of CBA is given here, since it raises some of the issues that have been touched upon earlier, and because several of the other methods to be discussed are attempts to improve upon it. The following chapter gives a more detailed coverage of some aspects of the technique and the studies that have attempted to establish money values for noise impacts.

In its simplest form CBA values, in money units, all the consequences of a plan. It then sums the positive and negative values (benefits and costs) to arrive at a net value. Potentially, it is an attractive solution to the appraisal problem, offering a way of expressing all impacts in a familiar unit and combining them into a single index of performance. However, there are theoretical and practical difficulties concerning (1) combining the values to produce an overall index and (2) obtaining the money values in the first place.

22.5.1.1 Combining impact values

(a) Distribution of costs and benefits

Different groups of people will experience different levels of impacts. If the impacts are to be combined to give an index of the effects of the plan on public welfare, the question arises as to what rule should be used to decide whether one distribution of impacts is better than another.

Once again the answer to this question is a value judgement, not susceptible to objective testing. This value judgement can be avoided only by adopting an extremely restrictive decision rule about whether welfare has increased or decreased. Such a rule was advanced by Pareto,[81] who argued that it is possible to be sure that public welfare has increased only if at least one person is made better off, and no-one is made worse off.

The Pareto criterion is not very useful for practical decision making since few, if any, projects would satisfy it. However, a relaxation proposed by Kaldor[82] and Hicks[83] stated that a project is worth while if at least one person would benefit even when the gainers had fully compensated the losers. It is important to notice here that compensation does not actually have to be paid. A project is judged worth while if it has the *potential* to satisfy the Pareto criterion by the payment of compensation. Adopting this 'potential Pareto criterion' as a basis for decision making is equivalent to accepting the value judgement that the effect of a project on public welfare is independent of the distribution of costs and benefits.

What is not always understood about CBA is that the apparently innocuous operation of summing all the individual costs and benefits incorporates the potential Pareto criterion together with its implied value judgement. So long as the net gainers could fully compensate the net losers and there still remain at least one net gainer, a plan is judged to have a positive value. This is irrespective of whether the losers actually are compensated.

Whether this value judgement is acceptable to the public and, therefore, whether CBA in its simplest form satisfies the criterion that a good appraisal method should incorporate the values of the public, might be questioned. The need to protect minority interests is also relevant here. The indifference of the potential Pareto criterion to the distribution of impacts means that it is possible for the interests of a majority of people, each gaining a small benefit, to outweigh the interests of a minority, each suffering a severe cost.

(b) Treatment of time

Given the choice between receiving a benefit now or waiting until some time in the future, the tendency is to choose now. This is often a rational response to uncertainty about the future and to the opportunity to use the benefit immediately. To make people indifferent to timing, the size of the benefit has to be reduced as it is brought nearer to the present. For example, £5 now is generally preferred to £5 in a year's time, but if the choice was between £4 now and £5 in a year there might not be a preference. That is, £5 to be received in a year's time might have a present value of only £4.

In CBA the usual treatment is to apply a discount rate to

reduce the value of future impacts to their present value. This can be expressed as:

$$V_0 = V_t/(1+r)^t$$

where: V_0 is present value of year t's impact,
V_t is value of impact in year t,
r is discount rate (expressed as a proportion).

Choosing a discount rate is not a straightforward task, and there is no unequivocally 'correct' rate, as the extensive literature on the subject makes clear.[84-90] This is unfortunate, because the choice of discount rate can affect whether a plan is seen to have a beneficial or a deleterious effect (positive or negative present value). Where alternative plans are being evaluated, the final order of preference can similarly be affected by the discount rate.

Another characteristic of discounting is that it virtually ignores long and even medium term future impacts. At the unusually low discount rate of 4%, a £100 impact occurring in 50 years time has a present value of only about £14, and this reduces to £0.85 if a rate of 10% is used. Perhaps even more striking is Nash's[87] example: at a discount rate of 10%, an impact that commenced in year 51 with a value of a million pounds for that year, and continued unchanged forever at a million pounds per year, would have a present value of only £85 000. In fact, discounting yields such small present values for long-term future impacts that it is conventional for CBA to adopt a cut-off point (say 30 or 50 years into the future) beyond which impacts are ignored.

Whether this treatment of time is a good one is again largely a value judgement. But if there is doubt about what discount rate to use, and if the results of an appraisal are sensitive to which rate is used, the method plainly has difficulties. The very small weight given to medium- and long-term future impacts is also a potential problem. It does ensure an early return on investment, but may lead to decisions that impose unacceptable costs on future generations.[87,91,92]

22.5.1.2 Obtaining money values for environmental impacts

The foregoing discussion is concerned with how CBA turns impacts, valued in money terms, into an index of performance. However, many of the problems of CBA, and many of the objections that arise, have to do with attaching money values to the impacts in the first place.

Chapter 23 gives a detailed account of the techniques that have been used to attempt to find approximate money values for noise: a brief outline only is given here.

A benefit may be defined as an increase of something desired, or a decrease of something not desired. A cost, conversely, is a decrease of something desired or an increase of something not desired. (The term 'disbenefit' is often used for components of cost that are by-products of the project, leaving 'cost' to refer to actual money spent by the promoter of the project. In what follows, the wider definition of cost will be used.)

In the absence of a way of measuring directly the utility of costs and benefits, CBA attempts to value them by estimating the maximum amount that people are willing to pay to receive the benefit or avoid the cost. Willingness to pay is normally expressed in money units, but there is nothing fundamental about this. The idea is to value a benefit or cost by finding what quantity of some other good or service has equivalent value, i.e. by finding what quantity of this other good or service an individual is willing to sacrifice in order to obtain the benefit or avoid the cost. Money simply provides a convenient common unit for expressing these valuations.

The actual method used to estimate willingness to pay depends on which type of cost or benefit is being considered. In

some cases it is possible to use market information: a demand curve or even just a market price. However, this means assuming that a 'perfect market' exists.[93] For many environmental and other impacts there is no market to provide prices or demand curves, and indirect methods must be used to estimate willingness to pay, often with rather unsatisfactory results:

1. Willingness to pay for amenities like public parks has been estimated from the expenditure that people incur on travelling to visit them. This is a method originated by Clawson.[94]
2. Attempts have been made to estimate willingness to pay for quiet from house price changes or noise insulation costs[54] (described in more detail as 'surrogate market' approaches in Chapter 23) and by asking people directly about their willingness to pay[55,58] (Chapter 23's 'hypothetical markets' approach). District valuers' estimates of property depreciation, as used to determine payments under the Land Compensation Act,[96] have also been suggested as a partial valuation of noise and other environmental effects of road traffic.[59]
3. Air pollution has been treated by identifying individual effects, such as health changes, and then attempting to value them. (This is the non-monetary damage function approach described in Chapter 23.) Direct questioning and house price techniques have also been tried for this type of environmental impact[97,98].

The willingness to pay method has a great asset in that it seeks to use the values of the public in attaching importances to impacts. However, it is not without its problems, as described below.

(a) Inaccuracies in estimating maximum willingness to pay

1. Markets, especially markets for the effects of public plans, are not 'perfect' in the economist's sense. This means that, even when available, market data give an imperfect estimate of willingness to pay.
2. Indirect methods of finding willingness to pay often yield partial (lower limit) estimates. It is sometimes said[99] that a partial valuation is better than none at all, since it does at least allow the impact to be considered in an appraisal from which it would otherwise be excluded. This is a powerful argument, but there is a danger that the appraisal will lose sight of the partial nature of the valuation. It might be better to use an appraisal method designed to cope with unmonetized impacts.
3. Studies of house price differentials are beset with statistical and other difficulties (*see* Chapter 23).

(b) Shortcomings of willingness to pay as an indicator of welfare

1. In circumstances where people are considered to have a right to something that is being denied them, willingness to accept compensation may be more appropriate than willingness to pay.[100] No proven techniques are available to estimate willingness to accept compensation, although novel approaches have been tried. One involved the idea of paying people to accept a noise-generating machine in their home.[60]
2. Willingness to pay is influenced by ability to pay, so that it tends to give more weight to impacts falling on people with high incomes than it does to impacts affecting the less well off. Using willingness to pay therefore entails the value judgement that the existing distribution of income is a good one. Attempts are sometimes made to support this judgement by arguing that the distribution of income in a democracy must be good, otherwise society would change it. Reference [101] discusses this point.

3. Willingness to pay is sometimes a poor indicator of welfare because people are not always good at deciding what is best for themselves. For example, we tend to provide insufficiently for the future and find it difficult to make judgements in situations where there is a very low probability of something very important happening. Also, it has been argued that complex, long-term social issues can probably not be dealt with adequately by aggregating the uncoordinated willingnesses to pay of individuals.[102]

(c) General problems

1. It is sometimes said[103] that certain things are more fundamental than money and that attempting to value them in money terms is at best useless (making them less rather than more meaningful) and at worst actively harmful, bringing them down to an inferior, material level. Against this is the fact that decisions do have to be made about how much of one type of impact is worth a given amount of another, whether this is done explicitly, as in CBA, or implicitly by a decision maker. It is not so much the principle of using money values, but the adequacy of the values actually obtained, that really needs questioning.
2. The procedures for estimating willingness to pay are not easy for decision makers and members of the public to understand. This may mean that the money values obtained have to be accepted on faith with no appreciation of their limitations.
3. Impacts that partially or completely elude money valuation may suffer by being excluded from the appraisal. Even if they are described in the supporting documents, there is still a danger of insufficient emphasis being placed on them by the decision maker.

22.5.1.3 Improvements to CBA

In view of the problems identified above, it is most important that decision makers are made aware of the assumptions, value judgements and incomplete valuations that are inherent in CBA. Apart from this, several improvements to the basic CBA method have been suggested.

The insensitivity of CBA to the distribution of impacts can be tackled by reporting separately the costs and benefits falling to different groups of people. Distributional effects, as well as the net present value of the plan, can then be considered by the decision maker.[63,104,105] Another possibility for reducing distributional inequities is to attempt to ensure that losers actually are compensated. Hicks[83] recommended this as a way of rendering projects 'approximately innocuous' from the distributive point of view. It would, in satisfying the Pareto criterion, ensure that a project did actually increase public welfare. However, it is possible that a greater increase in welfare would be obtained by not paying compensation.[101] This is because the Pareto criterion is a rule for ensuring that welfare is increased, not that it is maximized. Some other distribution of costs and benefits—for example, that produced by leaving losers uncompensated—may yield a greater increase in welfare. To decide whether this is true in any given case requires value judgements.

A further approach to the distribution issue is to argue that inequities arising from individual projects are likely to cancel each other out when the consequences of a set of projects are taken together. Someone who loses from one project will gain from another. So long as the individual projects satisfy the potential Pareto criterion (the argument runs) the overall effect will be a net gain for everyone. This view helps to set the issue in perspective, but does not resolve it. Impacts of a project may be such that it is unacceptable to rely on losers being compensated in the long run by benefits from other projects. First, losers may not be prepared to accept such diffuse, uncertain and long-term

compensation as an adequate justification for the project. Secondly, there may be people who tend to lose consistently. People with low incomes, and hence low willingness to pay, will tend to fall into this category.[106]

It has been suggested[87] that using different discount rates for short- and long-term projects might improve the treatment of time by CBA. Calculating the net value of the project to future generations and adding this to the net present value has also been proposed.[92] Another possibility[107] is to restrict discounting to impacts occurring in the lifetime of the current generation, and to report separately impacts to future generations. Testing the sensitivity of the outcome of an appraisal to choice of discount rate, or calculating the rate that would result in a zero net present value, have also been suggested as ways of helping to interpret the results of a CBA.

One approach to the problem of impacts for which it is difficult to obtain money values is to calculate the value that these impacts would have to have if the plan were to break even (i.e. achieve zero net present value).[108] The decision maker then has to judge whether the impacts are actually worth more or less than this break even value—a task that may be considerably easier than judging the absolute value of the impacts.

The problem of willingness to pay being affected by ability to pay may in theory be tackled by applying weights based on tax rates (on the grounds that these represent society's judgement of of the different values of money to people at different income levels),[109] other estimates of the marginal utility of income,[89] or some system of equity weights to reflect considerations of fairness and justice.[88] However, it is probably true to say that doubts about the actual weights to use mean that these are theoretical rather than practical improvements.

Several of the above modifications entail a broadening of the decision criterion away from the simple use of net present value. A further broadening is often needed. For instance, to rank alternative plans, it is desirable to take into account not only net present value but also the amount of gross benefit, and perhaps the ratio of benefits to costs. Choice of indices here is once again a value judgement.

22.5.1.4 CBA and design

The above discussion assumes that what is being evaluated is either a single plan, or a set of competing plans. That is, we wish to be able to say whether a plan is acceptable, or which of a number of plans is the best one to adopt. A further possibility is the use of CBA in the designing of plans—for example, in setting a standard or deciding how much to spend on alleviating environmental nuisance. Here, the emphasis is on optimization—i.e. using CBA to determine the point at which the net cost of the impact and the alleviation measure is at a minimum. This is discussed in more detail in Chapter 23.

22.5.2 Cost effectiveness analysis

The principle of cost effectiveness analysis (CEA) is that the money costs of a plan are compared with its outputs.[110] The plan that maximizes a desired output for a given cost may be chosen, or the one that minimizes the cost of obtaining a given level of output. CEA is sometimes thought to avoid the problems of getting money values for impacts. However, a decision to adopt the best plan implies that the benefits are worth at least as much as the costs and is therefore equivalent to putting a lower limit value on the benefits.

CEA is such a broad method that it is not easy to criticize. However, the method is best suited to cases where a single 'output' is to be considered. There is also the question of whose value judgements should be used in the decision to go ahead with a plan. Other criticisms have concerned the fact that, although optimization procedures are often used in CEA, it is not always made clear that the results tend to be optimal only in a very restricted sense.[111]

22.5.3 The Planning Balance Sheet (PBS)

The planning balance sheet (Lichfield[63,112]) is an adaptation of CBA that attempts to provide a better way of dealing with un-monetized impacts than simply describing them 'in the prose accompanying the cost–benefit arithmetic'. It also records details of the distribution of costs and benefits so that the decision may take account of them. The motivation for these developments was the requirement to evaluate urban and regional plans, where unquantified and un-monetized impacts, and the distribution of costs and benefits, were felt to be particularly important.

Attention is focused on the distribution of costs and benefits by making the analysis in terms of 'sectors', i.e. convenient groupings of 'consumers' or 'producers' of impacts. For each sector the costs and benefits are tabulated, and a view taken by the appraisal team as to which of the competing plans has the net advantage for that sector.

A framework or grid is provided for setting out the information at various stages of the appraisal process. Costs and benefits are measured in money units when possible. However, other types of quantification are accepted, and symbols are specified for use where the magnitude of an impact has not been estimated. Numerical subscripts against these symbols refer to descriptions accompanying the tables. Future quantities are discounted to their present value. The PBS does not produce a grand index. In deciding which plan has the advantage within a sector and overall, judgements are needed as to the relative importance of the sectors and the trade-off between the impacts.

The PBS goes some way towards solving the problems that it was designed to solve; but unquantified impacts may still be at a disadvantage because they are not described in detail in the tabular presentation. It is also possible that impacts, or groups of people, that happen to be scattered across sectors, will not be given due weight.

An important point concerning the PBS and other methods using the judgement of a decision maker or appraisal team is that to a large extent it is the procedural context of the appraisal that determines whether or not the values of the public are incorporated. This subject is returned to in Section 22.6.

22.5.4 The Goals Achievement Matrix

The goals achievement matrix (GAM) is a method of overall appraisal developed by Hill[51,113] based on the proposition that costs and benefits have meaning only in relation to a defined objective or goal. Hill argued that neither conventional CBA nor PBS require such goals to be stated, and could therefore lead to wrong decisions based on effects that were unrelated to the original purposes of the plans: the best plan in terms of net present value might not solve the problem it was meant to solve. In fact, as Lichfield et al.[63] have pointed out, the idea of goals has also been introduced into the PBS.

The GAM also attempts to improve on CBA by allowing a formal treatment of unquantified impacts and distributional effects, and by avoiding the need for theoretical assumptions that are seldom satisfied.

A GAM appraisal starts with the identification of a set of community goals such as noise reduction, increase in accessibility and reduction of air pollution; and a set of groups of people (incidence groups). Goals and incidence groups form the axes of a two-dimensional matrix. For each cell in the matrix, benefits and costs (defined as movements towards or away from goals) are listed. These are quantified where possible although unquan-

tified impacts are included. Measurement units are those thought to be most suited to indicating the degree of achievement of the relevant goal. Time is treated by conventional discounting, applied to all the quantified impacts. A grand index of goals achievement (excluding the unquantified impacts) is calculated by applying a system of weights.

The distinguishing feature of the GAM is its concentration on goals, but there is some uncertainty in the literature as to exactly what is meant by goals and how they should be identified. Hill's writings concentrate on the construction and analysis of a GAM after the goals have been identified. He does suggest, however,[113] that identifying and valuing goals should be approached from a particular theory of government. Thus in a constitutional democratic state, elected representatives should have ultimate responsibility; although he argues that in practice a complex iterative process may have to be used, involving consultation with elected representatives, officials, and interest groups. Alternatively, he suggests indirect approaches such as examining previous planning decisions to identify the goal priorities implicit in them.

Perhaps the most controversial aspect of the GAM is the idea that once the goals have been identified, only impacts that are related to them should be allowed to influence the appraisal. Not surprisingly, this has met with objections: it seems unjustifiable to exclude important impacts from the appraisal just because they are unrelated to a pre-specified goal.

However, saying that an impact is important is really equivalent to saying that it is related to some goal. The fact that the goal does not appear in a pre-specified list is really a reason for adding to the list rather than for excluding the impact. Interpreted like this, the GAM's emphasis on goals would seem to be a useful way of ensuring that the central purposes of a plan are borne in mind during an appraisal. It also allows the effects of a plan on wider community goals to figure in the appraisal— effects that might otherwise not be considered.

Although the GAM leads to the calculation of a grand index, the usefulness of this is diminished by the exclusion of unquantified impacts, and by the lack of a proven method for obtaining the importance weights.

The extent to which GAM satisfies the 'public's values' criterion depends on how the goals are established, how the importance weights are obtained, and how the decision maker takes account of the unquantified impacts excluded from the grand index. The GAM does not specify the methods to be used for these tasks, although possibilities are discussed.

A further criticism that has been made of GAM[114] is that it encourages the quantifying of impacts in obscure and complicated ways that are meaningless to decison makers and the public, and reduce the likelihood of obtaining sensible importance weights. This is a telling point, although the problem does not appear to be inherent in the method, but rather is a feature of the examples given by Hill.

22.5.5 The Environmental Evaluation System

The Environmental Evaluation System[13,115] was designed to assess water projects, but the approach could be adapted for use in other fields, including transport plans. Unlike the three methods considered so far, the EES is not a system for overall appraisal but restricts itself to environmental effects.

The main characteristic of the EES is its use of expert judgements to derive the importance weights necessary to allow an overall index of environmental performance to be calculated.

The method specifies a set of environmental impacts to be considered in the appraisal. The impacts of the plan are first estimated, using scientifically developed procedures where possible. All impacts, quantified or unquantified, are then converted into ratings on a scale of environmental quality. This is done by means of pre-specified 'value functions' that show the relation between the size of the impact and the environmental quality scale rating. The value functions are derived using a mixture of expert judgement and scientific information.

Each environmental quality score is multiplied by a weight denoting the relative importance of that impact type, and the results are summed to give a composite score. In addition, red flags are used to indicate the serious environmental effects of the plan, so as to direct attention to adverse impacts and reduce the chances of their being submerged in the overall environmental index.

The EES is an interesting attempt at a full 'grand index' appraisal method, and illustrates well some of the factors that need to be considered in producing a weighting system for such a method. However, the value functions and weights may not adequately represent the public's views. Distribution of impacts is not taken into account, and impacts are measured in units that are not easily understood except by technical experts. The composite index is in units that have no particular meaning and it is difficult to see how it could be used to weigh environmental effects against the other costs and benefits of the plan. The obvious thing to do would be to ignore the composite score and try to use the detailed impact information.[116]

22.5.6 The Judgemental Impact Matrix

The judgemental impact matrix (JIM)[50] was developed to assess alternative plans for wastewater management, but is included here because its rationale could be of interest in the environmental appraisal of transport plans.

The method was designed to compare large numbers of alternative plans for which it would be too expensive to forecast impact magnitudes using technical procedures. Instead, the JIM uses the judgements of experts. It has an unusual way of subdividing the appraisal procedure—estimating separately the impacts of each component of the plan. Given some sweeping assumptions about the way the impacts of the various components combine, this makes it easy to deal with components that appear in more than one of the competing plans. The method also emphasizes the need to consider results of an impact on society as well as immediate physical impacts: both are specifically included in the appraisal procedure. Expert judgements are also used to specify weights that allow a grand index to be computed, although the originators do not consider the grand index to be a necessary feature.

The JIM is a relatively cheap way of screening a large number of plans, but does not address many of the issues of environmental appraisal. Distributional aspects and treatment of time are omitted, and there is no assurance that the weights used in the grand index represent the values of the public.

The use of experts to forecast impact magnitudes is of particular interest but has its limitations since the results lack the tested validity of scientifically developed forecasting methods. Also, as the originators point out, there are difficulties in communicating to the experts what is to be judged, aggregating their views, and explaining the results. The originators also recognize that the JIM greatly oversimplifies the impact process.

22.5.7 Multiple criteria analysis

The synthesis phase of environmental appraisal involves a decision about how good a plan is at simultaneously satisfying multiple objectives such as minimizing adverse impacts and maximizing beneficial ones. During the last decade there has been much interest in the application of systematic decision making methods to this type of problem—a field known as multiple criteria analysis (MCA).[117-120]

The MCA literature abounds with mathematical language,

but many of the underlying principles and issues are those discussed earlier in this chapter. Indeed, all the appraisal methods described here are really MCA methods, although the MCA literature tends to see CBA as an attempt to reduce all the impacts to a single criterion, rather than as an attempt to cope with multiple criteria.

Some types of MCA use scoring and weighting schemes to produce an index of success for each of the alternative plans being appraised. Other variants compare alternative plans in pairs, impact by impact, and judge the relative performance of the plans by the extent to which one 'dominates' another in these comparisons. The strategies for decision making referred to in Section 22.3.4 contain similar ideas. Some MCA methods use only the ordinal properties of the input data (impact magnitudes and importance weights), and so are more suitable for situations where quantification is difficult.

MCA methods are subject to the same criteria for a good appraisal method as discussed earlier. For example, the issue of where importance weights ought to come from, and the danger that important value judgements may be concealed within the method, should not be overlooked. There may also be difficulties in making some MCA methods comprehensible and justifiable to the public.

22.5.8 Trunk Road Appraisal in England: the Department of Transport's Framework Approach

Environmental effects of trunk road schemes in England are assessed using a method[20] developed by the Department of Transport following suggestions by the Leitch Committee[121] and its successor, the Standing Advisory Committee on Trunk Road Assessment.[122]

The method, known as the 'framework approach', allows the 'economic' aspects of plans to be considered alongside environmental effects. It is used at all stages of trunk road route selection. Its purposes are: to assist highway designers to produce plans that are likely to be environmentally acceptable, to inform the public about the feasible alternative plans and about the appraisal method itself, to guide in the selection of a preferred route from these alternatives, to show at public inquiry the reasons for the Department's preferred option, and to assist in the final decision on the route to be built.

The method uses a matrix or framework with rows denoting impacts and columns the alternatives being appraised. At least two alternatives are included, i.e. a plan and the 'do nothing' or 'do minimum' alternative.

Impacts are considered for six 'appraisal groups'. Three of these—travellers, occupiers of property, users of facilities—allow distributional aspects of the impacts to be shown. Two other groups cover more general and indirect effects, such as changes in the natural environment or the pattern of land use. This is done by examining the way the plan relates to environmental, development and transport policies—an approach reminiscent of the GAM. The sixth appraisal group deals with financial effects.

The general approach in the framework is to indicate the numbers of people affected, the way in which they will be affected, and the degree of change expected. The degree of change may be expressed (depending on the impact) in quantified or unquantified terms, methods of doing this being described in the manual. Impacts on travel time, vehicle operating costs, and accidents are expressed in money units (accompanied, in the case of accidents, by estimated changes in the numbers of casualties). As well as appearing in the 'travellers' appraisal group, these monetized impacts also appear in the financial effects group, along with expenditure on design, construction, land, compensation and maintenance. All monetized impacts are discounted over a 30-year period from a stated date, using a discount rate fixed by the Government.[123]

Effects of noise on occupiers of property are dealt with in one of two ways. At the early stages of planning, before a particular route has been picked as the Department's preference, the distance of properties from the roads, together with changes in traffic flows, are used as a rough guide to noise exposure. At the public inquiry stage, when a preferred route has been chosen and detailed design work done, the framework shows the numbers of properties expected to experience a change in noise of more than 3 dB(A), and the size of the maximum change expected during the first 15 years after opening. Noise levels are expressed as dB(A) L_{10} *18 hour*, and are calculated using a specified method.[124]

The need for flexibility is emphasized. Assessors are not restricted to the impact categories described in the manual but are free to add or delete categories as appropriate. The degree of detail presented in the framework varies according to the size and complexity of the scheme being assessed and the particular stage that has been reached in the planning process. The way is left open for improved methods of forecasting and describing impacts to be used as they become available.

The method does not seek to calculate a grand index or to attach importance weights to the impacts, but is seen as a way of compiling and presenting information so as to assist planners, the public and decision makers to reach informed judgements. However, advice is given on a paired comparisons strategy for deciding between the alternative plans.[65]

To understand the extent to which the values of the public are incorporated, it is necessary to know something of the planning and decision making process of which the appraisal forms a part. This is described in the following section.

22.6 The procedural background to environmental appraisal

The bulk of this chapter is concerned with environmental appraisal methods—that is, with ways of collecting, compiling and presenting information on, and making decisions about, the environmental performance of plans. However, the adequacy of most appraisal methods can be ascertained only if the procedural background within which they operate is taken into account. For example, it is often the procedural background that largely determines whether an appraisal incorporates the values of the public. If the formal appraisal is preceded or accompanied by effective public consultation, and if the judgements of the decision maker are subject to some form of democratic control, the chances of the appraisal reflecting the values of the public are improved.

A comprehensive review of the environmental appraisal procedures of even one country is outside the scope of this chapter, but an overview is given here for the USA and Great Britain. The European Economic Community directive on environmental assessment, adopted in June 1985,[125] is also mentioned. Reviews of the position in other countries may be found in the Further Reading section.

22.6.1 Great Britain

In Great Britain a statutory system of land use planning applies over the whole country and to almost every kind of development.[126] This is in addition to laws dealing specifically with environmental health and with control of pollution.[127] Nearly all development requires planning permission to be obtained from the planning authority.

There is at present no general legislative requirement to incorporate a formal environmental appraisal into this system,

but environmental effects are considered when decisions on planning permission are being made. There are various procedures designed to ensure that the public know about planning applications and have an opportunity to influence decisions on planning permission.

Much of this system of development control operates at local authority level, although central government may be involved in certain circumstances. These include settling appeals against refusal of planning permission, and deciding on planning applications that raise issues of national or regional importance.

Development carried out by government departments does not require planning permission, but there are usually equivalent authorization procedures. In England, trunk roads and motorways are the responsibility of the Department of Transport. Procedures and guidelines adopted by the Department[20,65,128,129] specify both the environmental appraisal method to be used (the 'framework approach', described in the previous section) and the procedures to be followed in planning the road and consulting the public.

There are seven identifiable phases to the planning and decision making process for trunk roads:

1. Department of Transport regional staff consider whether a problem could be solved by a new or improved trunk road.
2. The Department considers possible routes, with a view to selecting a shortlist of options on which to seek the public's opinions.
3. A public consultation is held to inform the public that a road scheme is being considered; to indicate some possible options and their likely consequences; and to discover the public's views on the options, the comprehensiveness of the appraisal data, and the relative importance of the expected consequences.
4. After further investigation, the Department of Transport chooses its preferred route.
5. A detailed design is drawn up for the preferred route.
6. If there are unresolved statutory objections a public inquiry is normally held, chaired by an independent inspector, at which the Department's preferred route is open to challenge.
7. Secretaries of State for Transport and for the Environment jointly make the final decision, taking into account the Inspector's report of the Public Inquiry, and all other relevant information.

Thus to ensure that the value judgements made during the appraisal reflect those of the public, the procedure relies on the exposure of the plans to public scrutiny at consultation and inquiry, and on the fact that the final decision is made by Ministers responsible to the public's elected representatives in Parliament. This approach, combined as it is with the presentation of information in a way that enables the public to form views and preferences and to understand the reasons for the decisions made, would seem to offer a reasonable degree of assurance that public values will be respected.

22.6.2 The USA

At Federal level in the USA, environmental appraisal is governed by the National Environmental Policy Act (NEPA) of 1969.[130] An environmental impact statement (EIS) must be prepared in advance of every 'recommendation or report on proposals for legislation and other major Federal actions significantly affecting the quality of the human environment'. As well as ensuring that information about environmental impacts is available to the decision maker, the EIS is used for public consultation.

A draft EIS is made available to the public, and relevant agencies and officials, at least 90 days before a final decision is made on the proposed action. After a review period of at least 45 days, a final EIS is drawn up. This incorporates comments made during consultation, and shows how significant issues have been resolved. The final EIS is then filed with the Council on Environmental Quality (CEQ) at least 30 days before a final decision is reached. These timings may under certain circumstances be varied in the interests of national policy. The final EIS is used as the basis for a decision by the appropriate agency, which must prepare a concise public record of what the decision was, stating whether the environmentally preferred option was selected. Arrangements for monitoring and enforcing any mitigating measures must also be summarized. If any practicable mitigating measures have not been adopted the agency must say why.

The particular appraisal method to be used is not specified, and many of the methods referred to in this chapter were devised to assist in the compiling and use of EISs. However, the legislation and guidelines do require an EIS to have certain characteristics. Summarized, the current regulations[34] require an EIS to:

1. Describe the purpose of and need for the plans.
2. Describe the environment to be affected by the plans.
3. Describe the environmental consequences of the plans under consideration. Topics to be discussed include: direct and indirect effects and their significance; possible conflicts with land use policies; the implications for energy and other natural or depletable resources; implications for urban quality, historical and cultural resources, and the design of the built environment; mitigation of adverse environmental impacts.
4. Present the environmental impacts of the proposal and all reasonable alternatives (including the no action alternative) in comparative form, so as to enable the reader to evaluate the merits of the alternatives being considered.
5. Identify the agency's preferred alternative (unless doing so is prohibited by law, or unless, at the draft EIS stage, no preferred alternative yet exists).
6. Describe mitigation measures not already included in the proposed action or alternatives.
7. Discuss the relation between any CBA that has been prepared, and unquantified environmental impacts.
8. The regulations and subsequent guidelines[37] make provision for determining the range of impacts and alternative plans to be considered in the EIS ('scoping'). Guidance on avoiding repetition at the different stages of policy and plan formulation ('tiering') is also given.

The NEPA requirements apply to Federal plans. At State and local level, the situation is complex and variable, but many states have introduced legislation that requires EISs to be produced.[131]

22.6.3 The EEC

The European Community has recently adopted a directive 'on the assessment of the effects of certain public and private projects on the environment'.[125] Under it, an environmental assessment must be made of certain major types of public project before development consent is given. The projects concerned include the construction of motorways and express roads, airports, long-distance railways and certain ports and inland waterways.

The directive requires the developer to provide a description of the project and its environmental effects, and of measures designed to mitigate adverse effects. Public authorities with relevant information in their possession are required to make that information available to the developer. Public authorities with relevant environmental responsibilities are to be consulted, and the public are to be given an opportunity to comment on the application for development consent, and the environmental assessment, before development consent is given. When deciding whether to consent to the development, the authority responsible is required to take into account the information gathered and comments received.

Member states have until July 1988 to take the measures necessary to comply with the directive. It is beyond the scope of this chapter to examine the changes that might be needed to accomplish this, but at the time of writing the intention in Great Britain is to accommodate the new requirements within existing planning systems, rather than adopt the US approach of bringing into force completely new legislation and environmental authorities to operate alongside existing planning procedures.[132] In fact, the appraisal of trunk road schemes in England would seem largely to satisfy the requirements already.

2.2.7 Conclusions

The various approaches to environmental appraisal have advantages and disadvantages, and it is unlikely that any single method can be fully satisfactory for all situations. However, certain trends are apparent.

The opinion is still heard that environmental impacts cannot be incorporated into decision making unless they have already been expressed in money units. The opposite view—that valuation in money units should be rejected as bringing environmental effects down to an inferior, material level—also has some adherents. However, a less extreme position now seems to be more common. This accepts that the making of a decision by any method requires some type of valuation of the impacts, but recognizes that this valuation may be done by the decision maker instead of being derived in advance. In this view, the problems of CBA lie more with the adequacy of the actual money values obtained, and with the danger that important and controversial value judgements will be concealed, than with some fundamental inappropriateness of money valuation itself.

Many of the difficulties experienced by CBA apply to the other grand index methods, and it is fair to say that the weaknesses of these methods are now widely understood.

The result of all this has been to heighten interest in 'intermediate' appraisal methods that leave the value judgements to the decision maker while assisting him as much as possible by providing the relevant information in a useful form. There are implications here for the forecasting of impacts. Instead of being seen as vague and unusable, descriptions of effects on people become of central importance to the appraisal process. The need for improved methods of forecasting these effects is well demonstrated by the amount of active research in this area.

Most appraisals have been done for specific projects, but there is a move towards conducting appraisals at the stage of broad formulation of policy.[6,34] This offers some obvious benefits, but does require methods that can cope with the type of impact data available at these early stages. The intermediate type of appraisal method would again seem to have much to offer here. Indeed, the Department of Transport's framework approach, while not being directed towards policy formulation, is intended for use at all stages of road planning and design, and illustrates the flexibility of this type of method.

Environmental appraisal involves making difficult judgements about complicated phenomena. The methods most likely to lead to good decisions commanding the respect of the public seem to be those that recognize the complexity of the problem and the futility of searching for an objectively correct, value-free solution. They are methods that avoid the more extreme approaches to the environmental appraisal problem. Money valuations are not rejected on philosophical grounds, but are not insisted upon either; planning goals are recognized as important, but not to the exclusion of impacts that happen to be unrelated to pre-specified goals; decision makers are assisted in their task without having their scope for judgement curtailed. Perhaps most important of all, value judgements are not concealed within the appraisal method but are recognized as essential ingredients that need to be dealt with overtly and with some assurance that they reflect the views of the public.

References

1 MCALLISTER, D. M. *Evaluation in Environmental Planning*, MIT Press, Cambridge, Ma., p. 68 (1980).

2 FINSTERBUSCH, K., LLEWELLYN, L. G. and WOLF, C. P. (eds) *Social Impact Assessment Methods*, Sage Publications, London (1983).

3 CATLOW, J. and THIRLWALL, C. G. *Environmental Impact Analysis*, Department of the Environment, London, Research Report 11 (1976).

4 MCALLISTER, D. M. *Evaluation in Environmental Planning*, MIT Press, Cambridge, Ma., p. 6 (1980).

5 WARNER, M. L. and PRESTON, E. H. *Review of Environmental Impact Assessment Methodologies*, Batelle Columbus Labs, Columbus, Ohio (1974).

6 LEE, N. The future development of environmental impact assessment. *Journal of Environmental Management*, **14**, 71–90 (1982).

7 CLARK, B. D., CHAPMAN, K., BISSET, R. and WATHERN, P. *Environmental Impact Assessment in the USA: A Critical Review*, Research Report 26, Departments of the Environment and Transport, London (1978).

8 US Water Resources Council. Principles and standards for planning water related land use resources. *Federal Register*, **38**, 24778–24867 (1973).

9 Multiagency Task Force. *Guidelines for Implementing Principles and Standards for Multiobjective Planning of Water Resources, Review Draft*, United States Bureau of Reclamation, Washington, D.C. (1972).

10 ADKINS, W. G. and BURKE, D. *Social, Economic and Environmental Factors in Highway Decision Making*, Texas Transportation Institute, Texas A and M University, Austin, Texas, Research Report No. 148–4 (1974).

11 LEE E. Y. S., JAIN, R. K., LEE, E. K. C. and GOETTEL, B. *Environmental Impact Computer System*, United States Army Construction Engineering Research Laboratory, AD-787 295, Champaign, Illinois (1974).

12 BALBACH, H. E. and NOVAK, E. W. Field investigation of an environmental computer system. In Hutchings, B., Forrester, A., Jain, R. K. and Balbach, H. (eds) *Environmental Impact Analysis: Current Methodologies and Future Directions*, Department of Architecture, University of Illinois at Urbana-Champaign, Urbana, Illinois, pp. 131–136 (1975).

13 DEE, N., BAKER, J., DROBNY, N., DUKE, K., WHITMAN, I. and FAHRINGER, D. An Environmental Evaluation System for Water Resource Planning. *Water Resources Research*, **9**, 523–535 (1973).

14 DEE, N. *et al. Environmental Evaluation System for Water Resources Planning*, Report to the US Bureau of Reclamation, Battelle Memorial Institute, Columbus, Ohio (1972).

15 DEE, N. *et al. Planning Methodology for Water Quality Management: Environmental Evaluation System*, Battelle Memorial Institute, Columbus, Ohio (1973).

16 Institute of Ecology, University of Georgia. *Optimum Pathway Matrix Analysis Approach to the Environmental Decision Making Process: Test Case: Relative Impact of Proposed Highway Alternatives*, University of Georgia, Institute of Ecology, Athens, Georgia (1971).

17 SMITH, W. L. *Quantifying the Environmental Impact of Transportation Systems*, Van Doren-Hazard-Stallings-Schnacke, Topeka, Kansas (undated), cited in reference 5.

18 STOVER, L. V. *Environmental Impact Assessment: A Procedure*, Environment and Technology Assessments Inc., Pottstown, Pensylvania (1972) (cited in reference 5).

19 WALTON, L. E. and LEWIS, J. E. *A Manual for Conducting Environmental Impact Studies*, Virginia Highway Research Council, Charlottesville, Virginia (1971).

20 Department of Transport, *Manual of Environmental Appraisal*, Assessment Policy and Methods Division, Department of Transport, London (1983).

21 LEOPOLD, L. B., CLARKE, F. E., HANSHAW, B. B. and BALSLEY, J. R. *A Procedure for Evaluating Environmental Impact*, US Geological Survey Circular 645, United States Geological Survey, Washington (1971).

22 PARKER, B. C. and HOWARD, R. V. The first environmental monitoring and assessment in Antarctica: The Dry Valley Drilling Project. *Biological Conservation*, **12**, 163–177 (1977).

23 Central New York Regional Planning and Development Board, *Environmental Resources Management*, Central New York Regional Planning and Development Board, New York (1972).

24 Sphere Environmental Consultants. *Loch Carron Area: Comparative Analysis of Platform Construction Sites*, Sphere Environmental Consultants, London (1974).

25 HYDE, L. W. *Environmental Impact Assessment by Use of Matrix Diagram*, Alabama Development Office, Montgomery, Alabama (1974).

26 WELCH, H. W. and LEWIS, G. D. Assessing environmental impacts of multiple use land management. *Journal of Environmental Management*, **4**, 197–209 (1976).

27 FISCHER, D. W. and DAVIES, G. S. An approach to assessing environmental impacts. *Journal of Environmental Management*, **1**, 207–227 (1973).

28 TOFTNER, R. O. A balance sheet for the environment. *Planning*, **39**, 22–25 (1973).

29 Environment Canada. *An Environmental Assessment of Nanaimo Port Alternatives*, Environment Canada, Ottawa (1974).

30 SORENSEN, J. C. Some procedures and programs for environmental impact assessment. In Ditton, R. B. and Goodale, T. L. (eds) *Environmental Impact Analysis: Philosophy and Methods*, Madison, Wisconsin: University of Wisconsin Sea Grant Program, 97–106 (1972).

31 GILLILAND, M. W. and RISSER, P. G. The use of systems diagrams for environmental impact assessment: procedures and an application. *Ecological Modelling*, **3**, 188–209 (1977).

32 ROSS, J. H. *Quantitative Aids to Environmental Impact Assessment*, Occasional Paper Number 3, Lands Directorate, Environment Canada, Ottawa (1974).

33 ROSS, J. H. *The Numeric Weighting of Environmental Interactions*, Occasional Paper Number 10, Lands Directorate, Environment Canada, Ottawa (1976).

34 Regulations for Implementing the Procedural Provisions of NEPA. *Code of Federal Regulations*, 40, parts 1500–1508 (1978/9). Reproduced as Appendix E of: Council on Environmental Quality, *Environmental Quality 1980*, 11th Annual Report of the CEQ, CEQ, Washington, D.C. (1980).

35 Federal Environmental Assessment Review Office. *Guide for Environmental Screening*, FEARO, Ottawa (1978).

36 Council on Environmental Quality. *Memorandum for General Councils, NEPA Liaisons and Participants in Scoping*, CEQ, Washington, D.C., April (1981).

37 Council on Environmental Quality. CEQ guidance regarding six topics in the NEPA process. *Federal Register*, **48**, 34263 (1983). Reproduced as Appendix B of: Council on Environmental Quality, *Environmental Quality 1983*, 14th Annual Report of the CEQ, CEQ, Washington, D.C. (1983).

38 MCHARG, I. *A Comprehensive Highway Route-Selection Method*, Highway Research Record No. 246, Highway Research Board, Washington, D.C., pp. 1–15 (1968).

39 KRAUSKOPF, T. M. and BUNDE, D. C. Evaluation of environmental impact through a computer modelling process. In Ditton, R. B. and Goodale, T. L. (eds) *Environmental Impact Analysis: Philosophy and Methods*, Madison, Wisconsin, University of Wisconsin Sea Grant Program, pp. 107–125 (1972).

40 LASSIERE, A. *The Environmental Evaluation of Transport Plans*, Department of the Environment, London, Research Report 8 (1976).

41 WATKINS, L. H. *Environmental Impact of Roads and Traffic*, Applied Science Publishers, Barking, Essex (1981).

42 MSJ Keys Young Planners, *Environmental Evaluation* (Report prepared for the Department of Main Roads NSW), MSJ Keys Young Planners, New South Wales (1976).

43 Transport and Road Research Laboratory, *Roads and the*

Environment, Department of the Environment, Department of Transport, Transport and Road Research Laboratory, Crowthorne, TRRL Supplementary Report SR536 (1980).

44 CANTER, L. W. *Environmental Impact Assessment*, Chapters 4–9, McGraw-Hill, New York (1977).

45 NELSON, P. M. *Computer Model for Determining the Temporal Distribution of Noise from Road Traffic*, Department of the Environment, Transport and Road Research Laboratory, Crowthorne, TRRL Laboratory Report LR611 (1973).

46 BAUGHAN, C. J. and MARTIN, D. J. *Vibration Nuisance from Road Traffic at Fourteen Residential Sites*, Department of the Environment Department of Transport, Transport and Road Research Laboratory, Crowthorne, TRRL Laboratory Report LR 1020 (1981).

47 WATTS, G. R. *Vibration Nuisance from Road Traffic—Results of a 50 Site Survey*, Department of Transport, Transport and Road Research Laboratory, Crowthorne, TRRL Laboratory Report LR 1119 (1984).

48 HICKMAN, A. J. and WATERFIELD, V. H. *A Users' Guide to the Computer Programs for Predicting Air Pollution from Road Traffic*, Department of Transport, Transport and Road Research Laboratory, Crowthorne, TRRL Supplementary Report SR 806 (1984).

49 PILL, J. The Delphi method: substance, context, a critique and annotated bibliography. *Socio Economic Planning and Science*, **5**, 57–71 (1971).

50 PETERSON, G. L., GEMMEL, R. S. and SCHOFER, J. L. Assessment of environmental impacts: multidisciplinary judgements of large scale projects. *Ekistics*, **37**, 23–30 (1974).

51 HILL, M. A method for the evaluation of transport plans. *Highway Research Record*, **180**, 21–34 (1967).

52 SONDHEIM, M. W. A comprehensive methodology for assessing environmental impact. *Journal of Environmental Management*, **6**, 27–42 (1978).

53 WALTERS, A. A. *Noise and Prices*, Clarendon Press, London (1976).

54 STARKIE, D. N. M. and JOHNSON, D. M. *The Economic Value of Peace and Quiet*, Lexington Books, Farnborough (1975).

55 HEDGES, B. *Attaching Money Values to Environmental Disturbance: A Review Paper*, Social and Community Planning Research, London (1972).

56 Commission on the Third London Airport (Chairman: The Hon. Mr. Justice Roskill), Report, HMSO, London (1971).

57 NELSON, J. P. Highway noise and property values. *Journal of Transport Economics and Policy*, **16**, 117–138 (1982).

58 LANGDON, F. J. Monetary evaluation of nuisance from road traffic noise: an exploratory study. *Environment and Planning A*, **10**, 1015–1034 (1978).

59 BRIDLE, R. J., BROOME, M. R. and HOLMES, R. W. Environmental appraisal of trunk roads. *Proceedings of The Institute of Civil Engineers, Part 2*, **71**, 287–304 (1981).

60 PLOWDEN, S. P. C. and SINNOTT, P. R. J. (Metra Consulting Group Ltd), *Evaluation of Noise Nuisance: a Study of Willingness to Receive Payment for Noise Introduced into the Home*, Department of the Environment Department of Transport, Transport and Road Research Laboratory, Crowthorne, TRRL Supplementary Report SR261 (1977).

61 FLOWERDEW, A. D. J. The cost of airport noise. *The Statistician*, **21**, 31–46 (1972).

62 FOSTER, C. D. and BEESLEY, M. E. Estimating the social benefit of constructing an underground railway in London. *Journal of the Royal Statistical Society, Series A, General Volume*, **126**, 46–93 (1963).

63 LICHFIELD, N., KETTLE, P. and WHITBREAD, M. *Evaluation in the Planning Process*, Urban and Regional Planning Series, Vol. 10, Pergamon Press, Oxford (1975).

64 MCALLISTER, D. M. *Evaluation in Environmental Planning*, MIT Press, Cambridge, Ma., p. 269 (1980).

65 Department of Transport. *Choice Between Options for Trunk Road Schemes*, Department of Transport, London, Departmental Advice Note TA 30/82 (1982).

66 DE TOQUEVILLE, A. *Democracy in America*, Vol. 1, edited by P. Bradley, A. A. Knopf, New York, pp. 268–269 (1948).

67 MADISON, J. Checks and balances. In Hamilton, A., Madison, J. and Jay, J. *The Federalist* (edited by B. F. Wright), The Belknap Press of Harvard University Press, Cambridge, Ma., p. 358 (1961).

68 MILL, J. S. *Considerations on Representative Government*. Chapters 6 and 7, Longman, London (1865).

69 POPKIN, R. H., STROLL, A. and KELLY, A. V. *Philosophy Made Simple*, W. H. Allen, London, pp. 73–80 (1969).

70 MCALLISTER, D. M. *Evaluation in Environmental Planning*, MIT Press, Cambridge, Ma., p. 39 (1980).

71 MCALLISTER, D. M. *Evaluation in Environmental Planning*, MIT Press, Cambridge, Ma., p. 61 (1980).

72 ABELSON, P. *Cost Benefit Analysis and Environmental Problems*, Saxon House, Farnborough, pp. 47–49 (1979).

73 HOLLING, C. S. (ed.) *Adaptive Environmental Assessment and Management*, John Wiley and Sons, Chichester (1978).

74 LEITCH, SIR GEORGE (Chairman) *Report of the Advisory Committee on Trunk Road Assessment*, HMSO, London, p. 91 (1977).

75 WATKINS, L. H. *Environmental Impact of Roads and Traffic*, Applied Science Publishers, Barking, Essex, p. 8 (1981).

76 ECKSTEIN, O. *Water Resource Development: the Economics of Project Evaluation*, Harvard University Press, Cambridge, Ma. (1958).

77 MOHRING, H. *The Nature and Measurement of Highway Benefits*, Transportation Center Report, Evanston, Il. (1960).

78 Cost Benefit Analysis and Accessibility and Environment, *Traffic in Towns*, Reports of the Steering Group and Working Group appointed by the Minister of Transport, HMSO, London, Appendix 2 (1963).

79 ABELSON, P. *Cost Benefit Analysis and Environmental Problems*, Chapter 6. Saxon House, Farnborough (1979).

80 BEESLEY, M. E., GIST, P. and GLAISTER, S. *Cost Benefit Analysis and London's Transport Policies*, Progress in Planning, Vol. 19 Part 3, Pergamon Press, Oxford (1983).

81 PARETO, V. *Manual of Political Economy* (Translated by A. S. Schweir from the French edition of 1927) Augustus M. Kelly, New York, p. 451 (1971).

82 KALDOR, N. Welfare propositions of economics and interpersonal comparisons of utility. *The Economic Journal*, **49**, 549–552 (1939).

83 HICKS, J. R. The foundations of welfare economics. *The Economic Journal*, **49**, 696–712 (1939).

84 BAUMOL, W. J. On the discount rate for public projects. In Haveman, R. H. and Margolis, J. (eds) *Public Expenditure and Policy Analysis*, Chapter 10, Markham Publishing Company, Chicago (1970).

85 ABELSON, P. *Cost Benefit Analysis and Environmental Problems*, Saxon House, Farnborough, p. 44 (1979).

86 PEARCE, D. W. *Environmental Economics*, Longman, London (1976).

87 NASH, C. A. Future generations and the social rate of discount. *Environment and Planning*, **5**, 611–617 (1973).

88 DASGUPTA, A. and PEARCE, D. W. *Cost-Benefit Analysis: Theory and Practice*, Macmillan, London (1972).

89 PEARCE, D. W. *Cost Benefit Analysis*, Macmillan, London (1971).

90 KULA, E. An Empirical Investigation on the Social Time Preference Rate for the United Kingdom. *Environment and Planning A*, **17**, 199–212 (1985).

91 PEARCE, D. W. *Environmental Economics*, Longman, London, p. 30 (1976).

92 KULA, E. Future generations and discounting rules in public sector investment appraisal. *Environment and Planning A*, **13**, 899–910 (1981).

93 MCALLISTER, D. M. *Evaluation in Environmental Planning*, MIT Press, Cambridge, Ma., p. 289 (1980).

94 CLAWSON, M. *Methods of Measuring the Demand for and Value of Outdoor Recreation*, Resources for the Future, Washington DC, RFF reprint no. 10 (1959).

95 ABELSON, P. *Cost Benefit Analysis and Environmental Problems*, Saxon House, Farnborough, Chapter 8 (1979).

96 Land Compensation Act. Ch. 26. HMSO, London (1973).

97 RIDKER, R. G. *The Economic Costs of Air Pollution*, Praeger, New York (1967).

98 ROWE, R. D. and CHESTNUT, L. G. *The Value of Visibility: Economic Theory and Applications for Pollution Control*, Abt Books, Cambridge, Ma. (1982).

99 PEARCE, D. W. *Environmental Economics*, Longman, London, p. 108 (1976).

100 MCALLISTER, D. M. *Evaluation in Environmental Planning*, MIT Press, Cambridge, Ma., p. 134 (1980).

101 KRUTILLA, J. V. Welfare aspects of benefit-cost analysis. *Journal of Political Economy*, **69**, 226–235 (1961).

102   MCALLISTER, D. M. *Evaluation in Environmental Planning*, MIT Press, Cambridge, Ma., p. 143 (1980).

103   MCALLISTER, D. M. *Evaluation in Environmental Planning*, Chapter 8, MIT Press, Cambridge, Ma. (1980).

104   MCKEAN, R. N. *Efficiency in Government Through Systems Analysis*, John Wiley and Sons, New York (1958).

105   ABELSON, P. *Cost Benefit Analysis and Environmental Problems*, Saxon House, Farnborough, p. 50 (1979).

106   MCALLISTER, D. M. *Evaluation in Environmental Planning*, MIT Press, Cambridge, Ma., p. 102 (1980).

107   MCALLISTER, D. M. *Evaluation in Environmental Planning*, MIT Press, Cambridge, Ma., p. 112 (1980).

108   MCALLISTER, D. M. *Evaluation in Environmental Planning*, MIT Press, Cambridge, Ma., p. 122 (1980).

109   ECKSTEIN, O. A survey of the theory of public expenditure criteria. In *Public Finances: Needs, Sources and Utilisation*, Princeton University Press, Princeton (1961).

110   CHESLOW, M. D. Issues in the evaluation of metropolitan transport alternatives. *Transportation Research Record*, **751**, 1–8 (1980).

111   MCALLISTER, D. M. *Evaluation in Environmental Planning*, MIT Press, Cambridge, Ma., p. 121 (1980).

112   LICHFIELD, N. Cost benefit analysis in plan evaluation. *Town Planning Review*, **35**, 160–169 (1964).

113   HILL, M. A goals achievement matrix for evaluating alternative plans. *Journal of the American Institute of Planners*, **34**, 19–29 (1968).

114   MCALLISTER, D. M. *Evaluation in Environmental Planning*, MIT Press, Cambridge, Ma., p. 167 (1980).

115   BAKER, J. K., DEE, N. and FINLEY, J. R. Measuring impacts of water resource developments on the human environment. *Water Resources Bulletin*, **10**, 10–21 (1974).

116   MCALLISTER, D. M. *Evaluation in Environmental Planning*, MIT Press, Cambridge, Ma., p. 226 (1980).

117   NIJKAMP, P. and SPRONK, J. (eds) *Multiple Criteria Analysis*, Gower, Aldershot (1981).

118   NIJKAMP, P. Stochastic quantitative and qualitative multicriteria analysis for environmental design. *Papers of the Regional Science Association*, **39**, 175–199 (1977).

119   FREIZ, T. L., TOURREILLES, F. A., FU-WHA HAN, A. and FERNANDEZ, J. E. Comparison of multicriteria optimisation methods in transport project evaluation. *Transportation Research Record*, **751**, 38–41 (1980).

120   PERL, J. Goal-programming approach to multiobjective highway network design model. *Transportation Research Record*, **751**, 41–44 (1980).

121   LEITCH, SIR GEORGE (Chairman) *Report of the Advisory Committee on Trunk Road Assessment*, HMSO, London (1977).

122   Standing Advisory Committee on Trunk Road Assessment, *Trunk Road Proposals—A Comprehensive Framework for Appraisal*, HMSO, London (1979).

123   H.M. Treasury, *The Nationalised Industries*, Cmnd 7131, HMSO, London (1978).

124   Department of the Environment, Welsh Office, *Calculation of Road Traffic Noise*, HMSO, London (1975).

125   European Economic Community, Council Directive of the 27th June 1985 on the Assessment of the Effects of Certain Public and Private Projects on the Environment (85/337/EEC), Official Journal No L.175, Page 40–48 (1985).

126   Central Office of Information, *Planning and the Environment in Britain*, No. 87/83, Reference Series, Central Office of Information, London (1983).

127   *Control of Pollution Act*, Chapter 40, HMSO, London (1974).

128   Department of Transport. *Traffic Appraisal Manual*, Assessment Policy and Methods Division, Department of Transport, London (1984).

129   Department of Transport. *COBA 9 Manual*, Assessment Policy and Methods Division, Department of Transport, London (1981).

130   United States Congress. National Environmental Policy Act of 1969, *Public Law 91–190*, 91st Congress, 2nd Session, pp. 1–5, December (1969).

131   CLARK, B. D., CHAPMAN, K., BISSET, R. and WATHERN, P. *Environmental Impact Assessment in The USA: A Critical Review*, Research Report 26, Chapter 2, Departments of the Environment and Transport, London (1978).

132   LEE, N. and WOOD, C. EIA—a European perspective. *Built Environment*, **4**, No. 2, 101–109 (1978).

Further reading

ALLETT, E. J. Environmental Impact Assessment and Decision Analysis. *Journal of The Operational Research Society*, **37**, 901–910 (1986).

BLACKWELL, J. and CONVERY, F. J. *Promise and Performance: Irish Environmental Policies Analysed*, The Resource and Environmental Policy Centre, Dublin (1983).

BUGLIARELLO, G., ALEXANDRE, A., BARNES, J. and WAKSTEIN, C. *The Impact of Noise Pollution: a Socio-Technological Introduction*, Pergamon Press, New York (1976).

CUMMINGS, R. G., BROOKSHIRE, D. S. and SCHULTZ, W. D. (eds) *Valuing Environmental Goods: An Assessment of The Contingent Valuation Method*, Rowan and Allanheld, Totowa, New Jersey (1986).

Environmental Resources Limited, *Milieu-Effectrapportage 17 Prediction in Environmental Impact Assessment*, Ministry of Public Housing, Physical Planning and Environmental Affairs, and Ministry of Agriculture and Fisheries, Netherlands (1984).

FOWLER, R. J. *Environmental Impact Assessment, Planning and Pollution Measures in Australia*, Australian Government Publishing Service, Canberra (1982).

HAU, T. D. Distributional Cost-Benefit Analysis in Discrete Choice. *Journal of Transport Economics and Policy*, **20**, 313–338 (1986).

Highway Research Board, *Environmental Considerations in Planning, Design and Construction*, Special Report 138, Highway Research Board, Washington, D.C. (1973).

JEFFERSON, J. R. (Chairman), *Route Location With Regard to Environmental Issues: Report of a Working Party*, Department of Transport, London (1977).

LAKSHMANAN, T. R. and NIJKAMP, P. *Systems and Models for Energy and Environmental Analysis*, Gower, Aldershot (1983).

LAMBERT, C. M. *Environmental Impact Assessment: a select list of references based on the DOE/DTp Library*, Bibliography no. 204, Departments of the Environment and Transport, London (1981).

LAMBERT, C. M. *Road Traffic Pollution: A Select List of Material Based on the DOE/DTp Library*, Library Bibliography 17H, Departments of the Environment and Transport, London (1982).

LAMBERT, C. M. *Stockholm Commemoration Part A*, Library Bibliography 205A, Departments of the Environment and Transport, London (1982).

LAMBERT, C. M. *Stockholm Commemoration Part B: a select list of material on the environment 1971–1981*, Library Bibliography 205B, Departments of the Environment and Transport, London (1982).

LEE, N. and WOOD, C. Environmental Impact Assessment of Projects in EEC Countries. *Journal of Environmental Management*, **6**, 57–71 (1978).

LEE, N. and WOOD, C. *Methods of Environmental Impact assessment for use in Project Appraisal Physical Planning*, Occasional Paper Number 7, Department of Town and Country Planning, University of Manchester, Manchester (1980).

MILLSAP, W. (ed.), *Applied Social Science for Environmental Planning*, Westview Press, Boulder, CO (1984).

NWANERI, V. C. Equity in Cost-Benefit Analysis: Third London Airport. *Journal of Transport Economics and Policy*, **4**, 235–254 (1970).

PRASARTSEREE, M. A Conceptual Development of Quantitative Environmental Impact Assessment Methodology for Decision Makers. *Journal of Environmental Planning*, **14**, 301–307 (1982).

The Environmental Protection Law of the People's Republic of China. *Journal of Environmental Management*, **15**, 279–285 (1982).

WILLIAMS, R. H. (ed.), *Planning in Europe*, George Allen and Unwin, Hemel Hempstead, Urban and Regional Studies 11 (1984).

WOOD, C. and LEE, N. *Physical Planning in the Member States of the EEC*, Occasional Paper Number 2, Department of Town and Country Planning, University of Manchester, Manchester (1978).

SHARP, C. and JENNINGS, T. *Transport and the Environment*, Leicester University Press, Leicester (1976).

23

The Valuation of Noise

Ariel Alexandre PhD **and**
Jean-Phillippe Barde PhD
Organisation for Economic Cooperation and Development, Paris, France

Contents

23.1 Introduction

The previous chapter describes how different techniques can be used to allow judgements to be reached about the environmental consequences of transport plans. One of the methods discussed was the technique known as cost–benefit analysis (CBA). This technique attempts to attribute money values to environmental factors such as noise impact in order to provide a common method of accounting for all the consequences of a plan. For example, cost–benefit analysis can be used to assess the noise cost to a community following the opening of a motorway and this could then be offset against the benefits obtained from the road itself.

Although, in principle, this technique offers an attractive solution to an intractable problem, the method is totally dependent on the ability and acceptability of placing appropriate valuation to environmental factors such as noise impact.

This chapter is primarily concerned with the methods that have been developed to attribute an appropriate social cost to noise and the problems and assumptions that are needed to achieve this goal. Further information on the role of cost–benefit analysis in environmental appraisal and decision taking with regard to transport planning can be found in Chapter 22.

23.2 Some definitions and concepts

'Benefit' is defined here as the *damage avoided* as a result of the control measures, however, this concept of benefit encompasses a number of different types of avoided damages often poorly quantified and in different units of measurement. Hence, the first requirement of a benefit assessment is to use a common yardstick to measure, quantify and aggregate the various constituent parts of the benefits (e.g., reduced sleep disturbance and annoyance, reduced hearing loss, better communication, etc.).

Noise abatement measures generally have an associated cost, and how much money should be spent on noise abatement is often a key issue in developing transport plans. Economics is the science of managing scarce resources and society cannot afford to abate noise at any cost, nor to reduce noise to a 'zero level' (i.e. a 'zero disturbance' level such as 20–30 dB(A)) at prohibitive cost even if it were technologically feasible. Noise emission limits or emission standards can be arbitrarily fixed but this does not indicate whether the associated benefits are worth the costs of achieving these standards.

In economic terms, the 'optimum level' of noise is the level where an extra unit of benefit equals the extra unit of cost of achieving this benefit (an extra unit of benefit (or cost) is also termed as 'marginal' benefit (or cost)); that is, noise should be reduced to the level where the *total cost* of noise, including both abatement and damage cost, is a minimum. This can be determined only if the benefits are expressed in the same unit as the cost, i.e. in *money* terms. This implies that money must be used as the common yardstick to measure benefits.

This economic rationale is illustrated in *Figure 23.1*. Curve C is total abatement cost curve and D is the total damage cost curve. The total cost of noise $(C+D)$ is represented by curve T. The optimum level of noise corresponds to the point N_0 where the total cost is a minimum. If curves C and D are translated into marginal units $(C_m$ and $D_m)$, the optimum level of noise corresponds to the intersection of C_m and D_m. More noise abatement, say to N_1, would imply that the cost of abatement from N_0 to N_1, exceeds the benefit of that extra abatement. Less abatement at say, N_2, means that society is not getting an overall maximum of net benefits: it is foregoing the net benefits of the move from N_2 to N_0.

The methodology used to determine this optimum level of

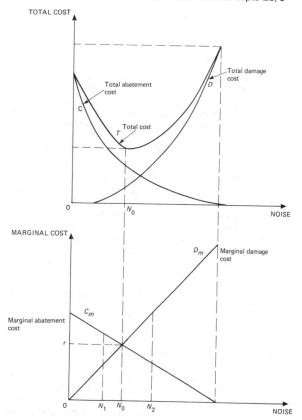

Figure 23.1   Determining the optimal level of noise

pollution (in this case noise) is *cost–benefit analysis*, defined as a procedure for:

1.   Measuring the gains and losses to individuals, using money as the measuring rod of these gains and losses.
2.   Aggregating the money valuations of the gains and losses of individuals and expressing them as net social gains or losses (Pearce[1]).

Once we have assessed the usefulness of conducting cost–benefit analysis there remains the problem of how to measure benefits in monetary terms. For tradeable goods and services individuals express their preferences in the market place in the form of their *willingness to pay* (WTP) for these goods and services. This willingness to pay can equal the price paid. If it is less, individuals will not purchase the good on offer but it can also be more if people would be willing to pay more than the market price. In this case, they get a *net benefit* also defined as the *consumer surplus*, i.e. the difference between the maximum WTP and what is actually paid by the consumer.

But in the case of noise, there is no market where people can express their preferences for the level of 'peace and quiet' they want. Indeed, noise is only a particular case of the general problem of public goods (and bads) that are not traded on a market (examples of 'public goods' are: clean air or water, quiet, wildlife, public parks. Pollution, noise, insecurity are 'public bads'). No market means no price; but it does not imply that the WTP is zero. If we want people's preferences expressed in monetary terms (i.e. their WTP for peace and quiet) we have to find *surrogate means* to have this WTP revealed. Consequently, the net benefit of any noise abatement measure will be the difference between what people are willing to pay to obtain a quiet environment and what is or has to be paid to abate noise (the cost), i.e.:

Net Benefit = WTP − cost

Where WTP = the money valuation of benefits. In other words, cost benefit analysis (CBA) aims at calculating the net social benefit (or net present value of benefits discounted over time (on discounting *see* Chapter 22)) or cost to society of a given course of action. The criterion for the economist is to maximize net benefits.

In the case of noise, CBA can be used for three main purposes:

1. To determine noise abatement policy by identifying the optimum economic level (point N_o in *Figure 23.1*) and hence maximize the net social benefit of noise control measures.
2. To calculate the level of a charge on noise that would ensure the achievement of this objective if it is decided to use this policy tool (*see* Chapter 24). (In this case the unit rate of the charge should be fixed at the level r in *Figure 23.1*.)
3. To decide which of a set of alternative plans to put into action (*see* Chapter 22).

Having established the need for and the rationale of CBA, there remains the delicate conceptual and methodological issue of how to put a money value on noise.

23.3 The social cost of noise

Noise has a cost to society; the cost of the damage caused to people and the cost of measures taken to reduce noise. The sum of these two categories of cost is sometimes defined as 'total social cost'. One purpose of CBA is to determine the minimum level of this total social cost. The *damage* cost of noise is often referred to as 'social cost'.

The previous section elucidated the rationale for CBA. Before explaining the techniques for putting a money value on noise, it is necessary to underline that CBA is based on two value judgements. The first is that people's preferences should count. In other words, consumers' sovereignty constitutes the basic hypothesis. The second arises from the fact that in CBA, peoples' preferences are expressed as a willingness to pay. This means that the more people are willing to pay for a commodity the more their preferences count. In most cases, the larger the income, the greater the ability and the willingness to pay. Therefore, it is explicitly accepted that the prevailing income distribution between members of society is optimal. This is the second value judgement.

These value judgements may be disputed but they constitute the basic assumptions of CBA. Both can be modified—i.e. by giving different 'social weights' to different social groups, and by adopting 'expert'; 'political' or consensus valuations rather than individual judgements (*see also* Chapter 22).

In estimating social costs or so-called 'damage functions', it is necessary to make a distinction between 'non-monetary damage functions' and 'monetary damage functions'. The former refers to establishing 'physical' relationships between exposure to a pollutant and the environmental effects caused. In the case of noise, one non-monetary damage function would be the relationship between noise exposure levels and the number of people highly annoyed.[2,3] The problem here is that a number of such 'physical' functions need to be assessed. For example, the physiological effects of noise, the effects of noise on children at school, productivity losses at work, etc. If all such damage functions could be assessed, it is then possible to put a money value on each, and then aggregate the whole set, thus obtaining a 'monetary damage function' suitable for CBA.

There are two main difficulties associated with this approach. First, reliable damage functions for each type of damage caused by noise are lacking, except perhaps for the relationship between noise levels and percentage of people highly annoyed. Second, putting a money value on some of these damages is extremely difficult, e.g. how can annoyance be attributed to a 'cost'?

This is why economists prefer to calculate *directly* monetary damage functions. Since there is no market for peace and quiet, it is necessary to create 'surrogate markets' or 'hypothetical markets'. These concepts will be dealt with in turn in the following sections.

23.3.1 Surrogate markets

There is no specific market for peace and quiet but other markets may indirectly reflect the willingness of individuals to pay for peace and quiet. Two such markets have been identified. One is the market in equipment and facilities used to protect individuals against noise (this can be termed the exclusion facilities approach). The other is the housing market (hedonic prices approach).

23.3.1.1 The exclusion facilities approach

This approach was originally developed by Starkie and Johnson.[4] The method relies on the observation that people exposed to noise or some other public 'bad', freely incur expenses to protect themselves against these disbenefits. A typical example is the installation of double glazing by householders. Starkie and Johnson suggests this action reflects a willingness to pay for quiet.

In this example it can be assumed that the householder will choose to purchase noise protection facilities if:

$G < N - N'$

where G = cost of the window insulation, N = the subjective valuation of the total noise without insulation, and N' = the subjective valuation of the noise left after insulation. Householders will purchase exclusion facilities when the *benefit* of noise reduction, $N - N'$, exceeds the *cost* of protection G, and they will continue to be motivated to purchase sound insulation until,

$\Delta N - \Delta N' = \Delta G$

Where 'Δ' means a small or marginal change. This is a direct application of the marginal principles introduced earlier.

The cost G is, therefore, an expression of the willingness to pay for noise reduction. If it is possible to derive a demand curve for noise insulation, i.e. a curve that relates the quantity of exclusion facility demanded to the price of this facility, the area under this curve would represent the consumer's surplus, i.e. the benefit provided by noise insulation.

Empirical results obtained by Starkie and Johnson using surveys and regression analysis on the case of Heathrow airport[4] indicate a willingness to pay for insulating a five-room house (providing an average 14 dB(A) reduction) of about 5% of income.

Although willingness to pay for window insulation provides an indicator of benefit, other behavioural patterns may also require consideration. For example, people exposed to noise may not insulate their houses, they may instead choose to move to another, quieter, area. In this case, the cost of moving, the financial loss incurred by selling a house which may have a reduced value because of noise and the loss of consumer's surplus must be taken into account. In other words, provided insulation serves no other purpose, the model operates only for those who stay in the noisy area and provides a *minimum* estimate of the social cost of noise, excluding the social cost incurred by those who move to another area.

Starkie and Johnson argue that this bias had little effect on benefit because very few of the households in their study area actually moved. This was attributed to a number of constraints such as the financial costs, access to credit, finding a new job or having to endure longer journeys to and from work etc. The demographic, socio-economic and geographical characteristics of each area affected by noise are bound to differ from site to site. It is not surprising, therefore, that other studies have found higher movement rates in noisy areas.[5]

There is, however, another reason why the willingness-to-pay for noise insulation may underestimate the social cost of noise. Insulation does not affect the noise exposure of balconies and gardens and does not remove indoor noise altogether. Willingness to pay for insulation ignores the social cost of this 'residual noise'.

On the other hand, there is a joint benefit or cost aspect of noise insulation because insulation devices such as double glazing provide additional benefits in terms of thermal insulation and security. This gives an element of *over-estimate* of the social cost of noise which act in opposition to the other elements which implicitly underestimate social cost. Furthermore, installing window insulation will tend to raise property prices, thus securing a capital gain to the householder.

In summary, Starkie and Johnson's approach appears to be an interesting one. It has the merit of being relatively simple although, as noted by Pearce,[6] it provides only an *average* valuation of noise for a specific range of noise reduction so that there is no marginal valuation (i.e. valuation for given noise increases) applicable to other ranges.

23.3.1.2 The hedonic prices approach

(a) Background

The 'hedonic prices' approach or 'house price differentials' methodology is the most widely used for evaluating the social cost of noise. The basic idea underlying this method is a simple one: the value of a house depends not only on its intrinsic characteristics such as the number of rooms, facilities such as garages, gardens, etc., but is also a function of a number of other 'environmental attributes' such as accessibility, proximity to schools, shops and parks, and pollution including noise. Therefore, if the value of a house is, amongst other factors, a function of noise, this means that when individuals buy or rent a house (noise can be reflected in rents as well as in prices; the price is the capitalized value of the rent) they have the possibility, within their price range of buying a property in a quiet location rather than a similar property in a noisy location. It is reasonable to expect that houses located in noisy areas are of less value (other factors being equal) than those located in quiet areas. Hence the housing market constitutes a 'surrogate market' for noise.

For a house having n attributes $C_1 \ldots C_n$, the value, V, of the house can be expressed as:

$$V = f(C_1, C_2 \ldots C_n) \tag{23.1}$$

The marginal valuation of any attribute C_i is given by:

$$\frac{\delta V}{\delta C_i} a_i$$

where a_i is the 'hedonic price' of attribute c_i. Most studies take a_i as a measure of the marginal willingness to pay.

In practice, a_i is found by regressing observations of V on observations of $C_1, C_2 \ldots C_n$, i.e. the regression equation has the form:

$$V = a_1 C_1 + a_2 C_2 + a_3 C_3 \ldots + a_n C_n \tag{23.2}$$

Note that the 'noise attribute' is expected to have a *negative price* since it decreases the value f for the house.[5-8]

(b) Example

In a study of the influence of aircraft noise on house prices, in Washington DC, Nelson[7] built up the following equation for the value of property ($R^2 = 0.863$):

$$\text{Log}_{10} \ V = 1.564 + 0.027(\log_{10} X_1) + 0.196(\log_{10} X_3) + 1.350(\log_{10} X^3) + \ldots + 0.019(\log_{10} X_4) + 0.073(X_5 - 0.332(\log_{10} X_6) - 0.010 \ (\text{NEF})$$

V = median property value, X_1 = percentage of housing built before 1930 (an 'age' characteristic); X_2 = percentage with air conditioning; X_3 = number of rooms per house; X_4 = the average size of the plot in which the house stands; X_5 = a dummy variable (i.e. entered as 0 to 1) according to whether houses were located in a 'desirable' neighbourhood, or not; X_6 = travel time to work; and NEF = aircraft noise in NEF units.

In this equation the noise coefficient (-0.010) indicates that an increase of one unit in NEF will depreciate the house price by 1%.

It is worth noting that the use of a log–linear equation implies that the marginal (damage) cost of noise is constant irrespective of the noise level. That is, the depreciation of the house is the same whether the noise changes from 35 to 36 NEF or from 45 to 46 NEF. This may be valid, but it is more likely that the rate of depreciation will increase with the noise level, starting from a zero depreciation at a low noise threshold where noise does not affect property prices, e.g. 20 NEF or about 52 dB(A) (L_{eq}).

The various estimates of hedonic noise prices can be expressed as elasticities—i.e. percentage depreciation in V due to a one percentage change in some agreed measure of noise. Take, for example, a hypothetical airport where the operation of an additional runway increases the noise level of a given area from 40 to 50 NNI (an increase of ΔNNI = 10). Consider also that 15 000 dwellings (T = 15 000) are impacted and the average value of each house is £50 000 (V = 50 000). If the estimated elasticity, e, is 0.5, then the social cost of noise C is:

$$C = \Delta \text{NNI}. \ e. \ \overline{V}. \ T$$

Therefore,

$$C = 10 \times \frac{0.5}{100} \times 50\,000 \times 15\,000 = £37.50 \text{ million}$$

(c) Comparison of hedonic price studies

A significant number of hedonic price studies have been carried out in various countries over the last 15 years. Pearce[6] has attempted to compare the results obtained from studies of aircraft noise by examining the percentage depreciation for a standard house priced at $28 000 in 1970. These results are summarized in *Table 23.1*. This brings together an earlier synthesis by Nelson[7,10] and Walters[5] with extra material obtained by the OECD. Note that the comparisons drawn in *Table 23.1* can only be approximate since the various studies reported are not entirely comparable. Different noise measures have been transformed to equivalent scales and some studies comprise valuations which are increasing functions of house prices, i.e. the percentage depreciation increases with the level of house price.

Although the depreciation elasticity varies widely (between 0.18 and 2), most of the results are in the range of 0.5 to 1.0. In the 1980 survey, carried out by Nelson, it was suggested that the index converges to a value of 0.5, i.e. a 0.5% depreciation per unit of noise.

A similar comparison of studies carried out on traffic noise (*Table 23.2* taken from Nelson[31]), similarly indicated elasticities covering a wide range from 0.08 to 0.88, but the majority of results are within the range 0.4–0.5, giving a mean of 0.4. Based

Table 23.1 Aircraft noise and house price depreciation elasticities[a]

Study	Nelson (NEF)[b]	Walters (NNI)[c,d]	Walters (NNI+ adjusted price)[e]	Airport
McClure[12]	—[f]	0.7	0.78	Los Angeles
Colman[13]	—	0.7	0.78	Englewood, California
Paik[14,15g]	1.6–2.0	0.7	0.78	Kennedy
Emerson[16]	0.4	0.55	0.62	Minneapolis
[17]	0.58			
Dygert and Sanders[18]	[h]	0.4–0.8	0.45–0.90	San Francisco
Dygert[19]	0.5	—	—	San Francisco
Price[20]	0.4	—	—	Boston
Nelson[21,22]	1.0	—	—	Washington
Mieskowski and Saper[23i]	(CNR converted to NNI)		(NNI adj)	Toronto
(1976) (i)	0.2–0.34	—	0.18–0.31	
(1976) (ii)	0.5–0.7		0.49–0.60	
CTLA[24]		1.0	1.12	Heathrow
		1.3	1.46	Gatwick
Abelson[25j]	NEF			
(i)	0.4			Sydney
(ii)	0			
McMillan et al.[26k]	0.5			Edmonton
Nelson[26,27]	0.5			[e]
de Vany[28m]	0.58–0.80			Dallas
Gautrin[29]	0.56–0.68			Heathrow
Maser[30n]	0.55–0.68			Rochester

[a] Source: Pearce.[6]
[b] Nelson's original results per unit NEF (Noise Exposure Forecast) with house price of $28 000.
[c] Walter's original results per unit NNI (Noise and Number Index) with house price of $25 000.
[d] No attempt has been made to place the Nelson and Walters' surveys on a comparable noise measure basis since there is no straightforward transformation of NEF into NNI.
[e] Walter's original results converted to a $28 000 'standard' house. In Emerson's study depreciation is an increasing function of house price so that the result here may understate the 'true' value. However, Walters (1975) doubts the validity of the assumed increasing function in Emerson's study.
[f] A dash means that the study in question was not considered by the relevant author in the columns (i.e. Nelson or Walters).
[g] The figure of 1.6 is obtained from Paik's study but Nelson reports an adjusted figure of 2.0. In fact the Paik study has a range of 1.85–2.46 for 20–40 NEF.
[h] The Dygert and Dygert and Sanders' studies report the same results.
[i] The Mieskowski/Super study was not considered by either Nelson or Walters. Noise units used were CNR and the conversion used for *Table 23.1* is CNR = 1.5 NNI. Study (i) relates to Etobicoke for CNR = 95–105, house price of $35 000 and an apartment price of $25 000. Study (ii) relates to Missisuaga for the same noise and price levels. Houses and apartments are in the approximate ratio of 60:40 so we have used a weighted average of $31 000 asm, the price to be converted to $28 000 to secure comparison with other studies: i.e. a conversion factor of 0.9.
[j] Area (i) is Marrickville and area (ii) is Rockdale. Abelson (1979) suggests the Marrickville results indicate a non-linear relationship between NEF and house prices. No relationship was found for Rockdale. Holsman and Aleksandric (1977) consider the time series of house prices in the same area and suggest that airport noise has short-term impacts only on property prices, with price trends returning to 'non-externality' levels over longer periods.
[k] Using a linear function with 60-NEF exponential form.
[l] An average for San Francisco, St. Louis, Cleveland, New Orleans, San Diego, Buffalo, with a range of 0.29–0.74%.
[m] de Vany (1976). The lower value relates to a partitioned sample of properties 2–3 miles from the airport.
[n] As reported by Nelson (1980).

on available evidence it would seem that a depreciation index of 0.4–0.5% per unit of noise could be taken as a reasonable estimate for this form of transportation noise.

In a recent study, Pearce, Barde and Lambert[41] have attempted to calculate the value of the social cost of traffic noise impact for the housing stock in France in 1980. Taking a depreciation in property value of 0.4% per unit of noise and applying this factor to the number of dwellings exposed to noise levels between 55 and 80 dB(A) on the L_{eq} scale, for each 5 dB(A) class of noise, it was found that the total depreciation obtained was 61.424 billion French Francs. *Table 23.3* gives further details of the property value depreciation for each 5 dB(A) band. If annualized over a period of 20 years at a 5% discount rate, this gives an annual depreciation value of 1.85 billion French Francs. Annual expenditure on traffic noise abatement in France amounts to 0.5 billion francs, which means that the estimated damage cost of noise is almost four times higher than the direct level of expenditure.

Clearly, if hedonic price theory is even approximately reliable,

it would constitute a convenient and acceptable guide for planning transport to optimize noise abatement investment. However, a number of criticisms of this approach have been made and these are briefly summarized below.

(d) Criticisms levied against hedonic price theory
Among the great number of criticisms made of the hedonic prices approach, some relate to the underlying assumptions or hypotheses, while others to the practicality of the method.

Hedonic price theory is based on *three basic hypotheses* each of which are subject to controversy. The first hypothesis is *consumers' sovereignty*. It is assumed that individuals are supposed to have the possibility of buying more or less quiet on the housing market. In other words, individuals are free to move to another quieter area if they deem it worth while. The counter-argument suggests that this freedom of movement does not exist.

As mentioned earlier many financial, social and cultural

Table 23.2 Traffic noise and house depreciation elasticities[10]

Study, noise index and area	Unadjusted elasticity (%)	Adjusted L_{eq} (%)
Allen[32] — L_{10}		
Northern Virginia	0.15	0.15
Tidewater	0.14	0.14
Anderson and Wise[33] — NPL		
North Springfield	0.14	0.18
Towson	0.43	0.54
Four areas	0.25	0.31
Bailey[34]		
North Springfield	0.30	0.38
Gamble et al.[35] — NPL		
North Springfield	0.21	0.26
Towson	0.43	0.54
Four areas	0.26	0.32
Hall et al.[36] — L_{eq}		
Toronto suburbs	1.05	1.05
Langley[37]		
North Springfield	0.32	0.40
Langley[38]		
North Springfield	0.40	0.50
Nelson[8] — L_{DN}		
Washington, D.C.	0.87	0.88
Palmquist[39] — L_{10}		
Kingsgate	0.48	0.48
N. King County	0.30	0.30
Spokane	0.08	0.08
Vaughan and Huckins[40] — L_{eq}		
Chicago	0.65	0.85
Average — all studies	—	0.40 (0.26)‡
Average — excluding Spokane and Toronto	—	0.40 (0.20)‡
Average-weighted†	—	0.40 (0.23)‡

Source: Nelson[8] and Pearce.[6]
* Since original studies use different measures of noise, adjustment has been made to make these measurements comparable (in DNL units).
† Includes an average of the elasticities for Anderson and Wise, and Gamble et al., and an average of the elasticities for Bailey and Langley, Spokane and Toronto are excluded.
‡ Figures in parentheses are standard deviations.

constraints prevent people from changing houses and location. Also, it is not known how far people are aware of the effects of noise. They may feel annoyance and suffer sleep disturbance but remain unaware of possible cumulative effects on their health. Their behaviour on the housing market may, therefore, not fully reflect the effects of noise. House price differentials can be identified only if noise is a localized phenomenon. People must have a real opportunity of finding and buying houses in quiet areas. Pearce[6] has stressed that, in many instances, noise is so widespread (e.g. in large conurbations), that mobility may be constrained and no price differentials can be identified. In fact, the assumption of perfectly competitive housing markets with full information is far from being fulfilled.

The second hypothesis is the *similarity of utility functions*. This assumes that each individual attaches the same value to the various 'attributes' which determine the value of their house. In the case of noise, this means that hedonic—negative—price of noise is the same for everyone. There are many reasons to believe that this is not the case. Not only will the *perception* of noise differ between individuals but also their valuations (their 'utility functions') will vary. Consequently, what is measured is a mixture of different functions with a number of unknown biases. The consequence is that the exact meaning of the hedonic price as measured by house prices differentials is not known.

The third hypothesis is the *homogeneity of utility functions* (Pearce and Edward[42]). This implies that the individual's valuation of noise is independent of his overall level of 'utility' (or welfare). This also may not be the case; for example, the higher the level of welfare, the higher might be the valuation of 'intangibles' such as quiet relative to other components of the utility function. If utility functions are not homogeneous, again the real meaning of hedonic prices is indeterminate.

Putting aside the restrictive hypothesis mentioned above, the calculation of hedonic prices also presents difficulties in practice.

Firstly, the statistical analysis is delicate, the various attributes must be precisely and separately identified. The inclusion of too many explanatory variables in a regression analysis raises the difficult problem of multicollinearity. This problem, which is not properly discriminated in a regression analysis, is particularly acute when (1) human estimates, evaluations, judgements are included in the analysis; (2) environmental problems are being dealt with, some of which may simply be repetitive of others (e.g. poor environment and low land value, excessive outdoor noise and poor housing, etc.). In many cases, regression and correlation analysis cannot simply prove that there is a causality of events or a simple ordered sequence of such events.

Secondly, either by assumption or because of the specification of models, the unit price of noise is taken as independent of its level. This means that the negative price of one additional dB(A) will be the same between, say, 55 and 60 dB(A) as between 65 and 70 dB(A). As mentioned earlier in this chapter, this linearity is probably not supported in reality. The cost of noise is likely to be small or nil at low levels and increases as noise levels become higher. This also raises the question of a threshold below which no depreciation of house values takes place. To overcome this a more complex model is required to describe the valuation procedure.

Finally, as hedonic prices measure the *willingness to pay* for quiet, they rest on the implicit assumption that the initial right of making noise has been conferred on or appropriated by the noise makers. Consequently, the willingness to pay off 'victims' is evaluated. Conversely, if the opposite assumption is made, i.e. that quiet is a 'right', individuals should not have to pay because the cost of noise would correspond to the sum of money individuals would demand in *compensation* for the damage they suffer. This compensation will obviously be higher than the willingness to pay, which might therefore, *undervalue* noise.

(e) Conclusion on hedonic prices
Despite the many theoretical and practical pitfalls attributed to hedonic prices, this approach has been the most widely used for obtaining a money value to put on noise. Also, some convergence of results can be identified.

Two opposite standpoints can be taken: the first suggests that the theoretical pitfalls of hedonic prices are such that no confidence should be put in this approach whatsoever. The second is that, despite all their shortcomings, the surrogate market values derived for noise are better than no evaluations at all. Yet great uncertainties remain about the actual meaning of these values. For example, what types of effects of noise do they capture? What biases are introduced by the non-similarity and

Table 23.3 Traffic noise exposure and depreciation of property prices: France 1980[41]

(a) Noise level dB(A) (L_{eq} scale) (daytime)	(b) Number of dwellings*	(c) Mean 'excess' dB per household †	(d) Value of housing stock (Francs $\times 10^9$)‡	(e) (c) × 0.4% House price (e) × (d)	(f) Depreciation at 0.4% of (Francs $\times 10^9$)
55–60	3 442 128	2.5	860.5	1.0	8.605
60–65	2 214 265	7.5	553.6	3.0	16.608
65–70	1 765 117	12.5	441.3	5.0	22.065
70–75	709 709	17.5	177.4	7.0	12.418
75+	76 939	22.5	19.2	9.0	1.728
Total	8 208 158		2052.0		61.424

*IRT (1982) p. IV.11. This comprises 44.2% of all dwellings.
†Taking 55 dB(A) as the origin and 80 dB(A) as the maximum.
‡At an average of 250 000 1980 French Francs per dwelling.

non-homogeneity of utility functions? Do hedonic prices tend to over- or underestimate the price of noise?

No valuation technique is perfect and there are pros and cons for each. However, the rather wide body of experience and the convergence of many studies towards a 0.4–0.5% depreciation index would indicate that this value can be taken as a useful guide for action.

23.3.2 Hypothetical markets

23.3.2.1 Background

Instead of using 'surrogate markets', as defined in the previous section, it is possible to create so-called 'hypothetical markets' that attempt to put individuals in a hypothetical situation where they could purchase quiet. In fact, this approach amounts to having individuals reveal in money terms their preference for more or less noise or quiet. Hence, they are *asked* to state either their *willingness to pay* for quiet (e.g. for getting rid of noise) or the sum of money they demand *in compensation* for the noise they suffer.

These two types of question will give different valuations since the sum of money requested in compensation for noise nuisance is likely to be greater than the willingness to pay for reducing noise, even if this willingness to pay does not imply *actual* payment. It has already been mentioned that people consider that quiet is a 'natural right' for which they should not have to pay, and that they should get compensation if they cannot fully benefit from this 'right'.

23.3.2.2 Practical application

In practice, hypothetical markets are approached through direct questionnaires; this is also known as the 'bidding games' approach. Different types of questions can be put to the interviewees, such as: 'How much money would you be willing to pay to have noise reduced to a given level?' (To make the question explicit, various noise levels are often simulated.[43,44].) 'If you had to sell your house and buy another in a quieter area, what financial benefit would you require to feel compensated for this removal?'[43] 'What do you think it is "worth" to reduce traffic noise?'[44]

Quantitative results of questionnaire surveys will not be presented here, because it would be of little value since they vary widely between studies. Further details of individual studies can be obtained by consulting the references. The main difficulties

associated with this approach are briefly mentioned below.

First, interviewees are put in hypothetical situations which they find particularly difficult to grasp: they have few ideas about the means and costs of reducing noise, and, as already mentioned, they are not fully aware of the real damage they have to suffer, and hence are ignorant of what a suitable compensation would be.

Second, a significant proportion of interviewees refuse to 'play the game'. In other words, they refuse to put a money value on an 'intangible commodity' like noise, or to reveal any willingness to pay for what they deem a 'natural right'. For example, in the Third London Airport study,[43] 47% of those asked stated that they were not prepared to pay anything to reduce noise. In a study on the social cost of noise around Paris-Orly airport,[45] 77% of respondents stated that they would accept any compensation for noise.

Third, bidding games are subject to a number of biases such as[18]:

1. Strategic bias.
2. Information bias.
3. Hypothetical bias.
4. Vehicle bias.
5. Starting point bias.

Strategic bias occurs when interviewees purposely mis-state preference since they know that, in reality they will not have to pay. *Informational bias* implies that the nature of the question and the type of information provided will influence the response; *hypothetical bias* is due to the lack of knowledge and experience of the real situation; *vehicle bias* is introduced by the method of payment (taxation, profit on selling house, etc.); *starting-point bias* relates to the amounts or ranges of valuations presented in the questionnaire to suggest 'reasonable' ranges of value to the respondent.

Brookshire *et al.*[46-47] claim that it is possible to overcome or control these biases, and although some successes are claimed these difficulties remain, giving rise to conjecture regarding the use of hypothetical markets to establish noise valuations.[48]

23.4 Conclusions

It is tempting to conclude that applying cost–benefit analysis to noise is extremely complex and subject to so many shortcomings that this decision-making tool should be abandoned. Yet many decisions made regarding noise abatement policies are significant in terms of cost and in terms of the number of people affected. Noise is a major environmental and social concern and therefore economic calculus, though imperfect, should not be avoided merely because of complexities. A significant amount of data have been collected and assimilated regarding hedonic valuations against noise exposure and as a result many economists are beginning to accept that, despite its limitations, hedonic modelling does represent an adequate method of approximating noise benefits.

Of course, there are still major uncertainties regarding the real meaning of hedonic prices, i.e. what effects of noise they actually capture. Even if this issue is not satisfactorily resolved the fact remains that hedonic prices do capture some of the effects of noise. When using hedonic values, however, it should be remembered that the valuations obtained are not precise and that margins of safety should be allowed.

As a rule of thumb, a 0.5% house value depreciation per decibel constitutes a reasonable guide and is based upon a substantial number of different studies. However, it is probable that this depreciation rate is valid only above a certain noise threshold, say 50 dB(A) L_{eq}, since most surveys show a very low level of annoyance below this level. It might also be that the unit percentage of depreciation increases both with the noise level and with the value of the house. These points merit further investigation.

Acknowledgements

We are grateful for the comments made on an earlier draft by Professor D. W. Pearce from University College in London. We bear full responsibility for any error or omission in this chapter.

References

1 PEARCE, D. W. *Cost Benefit Analysis* (2nd edn.), MacMillan, London (1983).
2 SCHULTZ, T. J. A synthesis of social surveys on noise annoyance. *Journal of the Acoustical Society of America*, **64**, 377–405 (1978).
3 ALEXANDRE, A. and BARDE, J. ph. Noise charges: an international assessment. *Noise Control Engineering*, **10**, March, (1974).
4 STARKIE, D. N. M. and JOHNSON, D. M. *The Economic Value of Peace and Quiet*, Saxon House, Lexington (1975).
5 WALTERS, A. *Noise and Prices*, Oxford University Press, London (1975).
6 PEARCE, D. W. The price of environmental quality. In *Essays in Honour of Clifford Sharp*, Leicester University Press (1985).
7 NELSON, J. P. *Aircraft Noise, Residential Property values and Public Policy*. Paper prepared for 1977 Annual Convention of the Easter Economic Association.
8 NELSON, J. P. *Economic Analysis of Transportation Noise Abatement*. Ballinger, Cambridge, Ma., p. 264 (1978).
9 NELSON, J. P. *An Analysis of Jet Aircraft Noise and Residential Property Values*, Pennsylvania State University, Mimeo (1976).
10 NELSON, J. P. Airports and property values: a survey of recent evidence. *Journal of Transport Economics and Policy*, **XIV**, 37–52 (1980).
11 OECD *Noise Abatement Policies*, Paris (1980).
12 MCLURE, P. *Indication of the Effect of Jet Noise on the Value of Real Estate*, RAND Corporation Paper 4–1117, California (1969).
13 COLMAN, A. H. *Aircraft Noise Effects on Property Values*, Environmental Standards Circular, Inglewood, California (1972).
14 PAIK, I. K. *Impact of Transportation Noise on Urban Residential Property Values with Special Reference to Aircraft Noise*, Consortium of Universities, Washington D.C. (1970).
15 PAIK, I. K. *Measurement of Environmental Externality in Particular Reference to Noise*, PhD Dissertation, Georgetown University (1972).
16 EMERSON, F. C. *The Determinants of Residential Value with Specified Reference to the Effects of Aircraft Nuisance and Other Environmental Features*, PhD Dissertation, University of Minnesota (1969).
17 EMERSON, F. Valuation of residential amenities: an econometric approach. *Appraisal Journal*, **40**, 268–278 (1972).
18 DYGERT, P. K. and SANDERS, D. *On Measuring the Cost of Noise from Subsonic Aircraft*, Institute of Transportation and Traffic Engineering, Berkeley, California (1972).
19 DYGERT, P. K. *Estimation of the Cost of Aircraft Noise to Residential Activities*, PhD Dissertation, University of Michigan (1973).
20 PRICE, I. *The Social Cost of Airport Noise as Measured by Rental Changes: The Case of Logan Airport*, PhD Dissertation, Boston University (1974).
21 NELSON, J. P. *The Effects of Mobile Source Air and Noise Pollution on Residential Property Values*, Report DOT-TST-75-6 United States Department of Transportation, Washington, D.C. (1975).
22 NELSON, J. *An Analysis of Jet Aircraft Noise and Residential Property Values*, Pennsylvania State University (1976).
23 MEISKOWSKI, P. and SAPER, A. An Estimate of the Effects of Noise on Property Values. *Journal of Urban Economics*, **5**, 425–40 (1978).
24 Commission of the Third London Airport (CTLA). *Report*, HMSO, London (1971).
25 ABELSON, P. W. Property prices and the value of amenities. *Journal of Environmental Economics and Management*, **6**, 11–28 (1971).
26 MACMILLAN, M., REID, 8., GILLEN, D. *An Approach Towards Improved Estimates of Willingness to Pay for Public Goods from Hedonic Price Functions: A Case of Aircraft Noise*, University of Alberta (1978).
27 NELSON, J. Measuring benefits of environmental improvements: aircraft noise and hedonic prices. In V. K. Smith (ed.) *Advances in Applied Microeconomics*, Vol. 1, JAI Press, Greenwich, Connecticut (1981).
28 DE VANY, A. An economic model of airport noise pollution in an urban environment. In S. Lin (ed.) *Theory and Measurement of Economic Externalities*, Academic Press, New York, pp. 205–14 (1976).
29 GAUTRIN, J. F. An evaluation of the impact of aircraft noise on property values with a simple model of urban land rent. *Law Economics*, **51**, 80 (1975).
30 MASER, S. M., RIKER, W. H. and ROSETT, W. The effects of zoning and externalities on the price of land: an empirical analysis of Monroe County, New York. *Journal of Law and Economics*, **20**, 111–132 (1977).
31 NELSON, J. P. Highway noise and property values: a survey of recent evidence. *Journal of Transport Economics and Policy*, **16**, 117–138, (1982).
32 ALLEN, G. R. *Highway Noise, Noise Mitigation, and Residential Housing Values*, Virginia Highway and Transportation Research Council (1980).
33 ANDERSON, R. and WISE, D. *The Effects of Highway Noise and Accessibility on Residential Property Values, DOT-FH-11-8841, NTIS, March* (1977).
34 BAILEY, M. J. *Report on Pilot Study: Highway Noise and Property Values*, University of Maryland (1977).
35 GAMBLE, H. B., *et al. Community Effects of Highways Reflected by Property Values*, United States Department of Transportation, Washington, D.C. (1973).
36 HALL, F., *et al.* Effects of highway noise on residential property values. In *Transportation Research Record 686*, NAS, Washington (1978).
37 LANGLEY, C. J. Adverse impacts of the Washington beltway on residential property values. *Land Economics* (1976).
38 LANGLEY, C. J. *Highways and Property Values: The Washington Beltway Revisited*. University of Tennessee (1980).
39 PALMGUIST, R. *Impact of Highway Improvements on Property Values in Washington*, WA-RD-37.1, NTIS, March (1980).
40 VAUGHAN, R. J. and HUCKINGS, L. *The Economics of Expressway Noise Pollution Abatement*, RAND Corporation, California (1975).
41 PEARCE, D. W., BARDE, J. Ph. and LAMBERT, J. Estimating the cost of noise pollution in France. *Ambio*, **XIII**, 27–28 (1984).
42 PEARCE, D. W. and EDWARDS, R. *The Monetary Valuation of Noise Nuisance: Implications for Noise Abatement Policy. Progress in Environmental Management and Resource Planning*, Vol. 1, John Wiley and Sons (1978).
43 This was the type of question used for the study on the third London airport. (Commission of the Third London Airport. *Report*, HMSO, London (1971).)

44 LANGDON, F. J. Monetary evaluation of noise nuisance from road traffic noise: an exploratory study'. *Environment and Planning*, **10** (1978).

45 SEDES. *Le coût social de bruit* French Ministry of Environment, Paris (1980).

46 BROOKSHIRE, D. S., *et al*. The valuation of aesthetic preferences. *Journal of Environmental Economics and Management*, **3**, 325–346 (1976).

47 BROOKSHIRE, D., D'ARGE, R., SCHULZE, W. and THAYER, M. *Methods Development for Assessing Tradeoffs in Environmental Management*. US EPA-600/6-79-991b, Vol. II of *Methods Development for Assessing Air Pollution Control Benefits*, Washington (1979).

48 ROWE, R. D. and CHESTNUT, L. G. Valuing environmental commodities: Revisited. *Land Economics*, **59**, 404–410 (1983).

24

Economic Instruments for Transport Noise Abatement

Ariel Alexandre PhD and
Jean-Phillippe Barde PhD
**Organisation for Economic Cooperation
and Development, Paris, France**

Contents

24.1 Introduction

Government actions to control transportation noise have generally resulted in the specification of regulations and standards. This approach has led, in many countries, to the development of a complex legal framework to deal with noise problems with inherent administration and enforcement problems. Furthermore, the setting of standards cannot be achieved arbitrarily. There may be many social and economic factors and the administrator who has the responsibility for setting an effective standard will need to be aware of their complex interaction.

Such 'fine tuning' can seldom be achieved in practice and, as a result, noise standards are often set at a level which provides little initial incentive to technological progress. Indeed, many regulations merely reflect the state of existing technology and do not, by themselves, promote innovation.

The success of regulatory actions depends largely on the organization of the regulation and on the choice of the regulatory authority. Where the imposition of standards is entrusted to an agency who has a vested interest in the promotion of that industry then the noise control measures are likely to be weakly upheld. In the past it is generally acknowledged that the balance of advantage has tended to favour the noise producer rather than the noise recipient. Furthermore, governments can be very reluctant to support standards based on regulations which industry cannot easily meet or claims it cannot. The process of standardization is, therefore, stifled by the natural caution adopted by industry when confronted with the need to provide new technology without obvious economic benefits.

The introduction of a noise tax or some other form of fiscal incentive can, in principle, offer advantages over the rigid legal process. For example, a tax levied on the polluting output would, if the tax were set high enough, tend to encourage the polluter to reduce his tax burden by improving his product in this respect. In addition the revenue gathered in by the tax can be used to finance a variety of noise control measures such as building insulation.

While the case for regulatory standards to control noise does continue to have considerable force, the above considerations make it necessary to doubt the absolute efficacy of the legal approach and to examine more closely the possibility of using less interventionist policies, either as an alternative or as an adjunct to regulated standards.

This chapter examines the various economic instruments applicable to noise abatement. Noise charges are the most commonly cited but other incentives such as damage compensation or market promotion of quieter products can also be implemented. The chapter looks at the principles behind noise charges and their implementation to aircraft and motor vehicle sources. Also discussed are the other types of economic instruments, and the possible future for economic incentives.

24.1.1 Definition of noise charges

In economic terms, noise produces uncompensated 'externalities' or 'social costs' (*see also* Chapter 22). In other words, people exposed to noise are unilaterally subjected to the effects of an activity that occurs outside the market (without any voluntary transaction). If this noise-producing activity was given a price which would have to be paid by the agent responsible for the activity, market decisions would reflect the social cost of noise. Giving a price to noise would induce noise producers either to reduce noise or to pay for the noise they produce through charges. What is called the neoclassical tradition in environmental economics favours the use of a 'tax' or 'charge' on polluters in order to correct for the misallocation of resources brought about by the existence of uncompensated externalities.[1]

Noise charges can be defined as a payment to the appropriate authority for each unit of noise above a certain level emitted into the environment, or on each unit of disamenity imposed on the community because of this noise (*see* OECD[2]). Noise and disamenity are expressed in 'assessment units' and the charge levied is then calculated by multiplying the unit rate of charge by the number of assessment units emitted per unit of time. Charges put a price on noise. Their effectiveness in achieving noise abatement depends on whether the relevant markets operate in such a way that the response of noise makers is as required.

Charges are intended to induce noise makers to abate noise to reduce the burden imposed by the charge. In addition, the funds collected may be redistributed for noise control purposes. The redistributive function can take various forms, such as the total or partial financing of collective noise control facilities, noise control investments by the noise maker, and the payment of compensation to victims. Experience shows that, up to now, the redistributive function is prevailing. But, set at an appropriate level, noise charges can, in principle, provide a lasting inducement for polluters to abate noise and consequently act as a constant stimulus to technical progress. In addition, they could enable noise to be abated at minimum cost to the community.[2] Clearly, therefore, noise charges can have both an incentive and a financing function. The charge is an incentive up to the level where the marginal cost of noise abatement equals the unit rate of the charge. The money collected through charges can be used to finance noise abatement measures but not necessarily if an optimum level of noise is achieved (*see* Baumol and Oates[3]).

The degree of incentive involved by noise charges depends not only on their rate, but also on the assessment basis. Charges should relate as closely as possible to the noise emission and impact created. For example, noise charges such as a flat tax per aircraft passenger are not likely to have any incentive effect. Charges are not intended to be substituted for direct controls and regulations. Experience has shown that charges and direct controls, far from being incompatible, must be used in combination as complementary instruments.

24.1.2 The cases for and against charges

Pollution charges are by no means a new approach to pollution control. They have been in existence for a long time for the control of water and solid waste pollution in many countries. However, pollution charges and noise charges in particular still encounter opposition. It is, therefore, important to look into the arguments for and against charges, as opposed to regulations.

It was pointed out in the introduction to this chapter that in certain cases, regulations, which often take the form of emission standards, can be static and provide little incentive for innovation. They are often formulated only after lengthy negotiation and frequently reflect the 'line of least resistance', e.g. they reflect the needs of the least efficient (noisiest) operator. The updating of standards is also slow and infrequent. In contrast, noise charges are, in principle, more dynamic and they provide a permanent incentive to abate noise.

It is argued, however, that a charge is only a way of paying for the right to pollute and that excessive noise should simply be prohibited instead of compensated. This argument has some force as long as the charge is set at too low a level so that it is cheaper for the noise producer to pay the charge than to abate noise. If noise charges are set at a 'price' that is high enough to act as an incentive for the reduction of noise the argument disappears. It can also be argued that the absence of charges gives unrestricted permission to pollute and that noise regulations (standards) can be interpreted as giving permission to emit noise at a stated level.

Another major argument against charges is that the results

remain uncertain, whereas a properly administered standard fixes a compulsory and precise ceiling. Some of the uncertainty associated with charges can be removed if the charges are set high enough to ensure the achievement of objectives. Furthermore, charges can be combined with regulations thus providing additional incentive and finance for the achievement of the objectives set by regulations.

One of the most frequently cited objections against noise charges stems from the assertion that regulations are well known, familiar and a proven means of controlling noise, whereas charges are new and not well known to administrators, the industry and the public. However, some transportation noise problems have continued to increase almost unchecked over the past 20 years. The familiar methods based on regulation may be proving to be too rigid, costly and ineffective when used alone. The potential offered by economic instruments then used in association with regulations could, therefore, be viewed as an alternative and possibly more effective means of noise control.

24.2 Aircraft noise charges

Aircraft are already subject to landing fees at airports. A noise charge can therefore be applied as an additional landing fee. Such a charge acts as a *complement* to existing ICAO (International Civil Aviation Organisation) standards which limit aircraft noise emissions and to existing local anti-noise procedures (take-off and landing procedures, restrictions on airport and aircraft use, etc.; *see* also Chapter 26). An aircraft noise charge has three main functions:

1. To encourage airlines to retrofit or replace their noisiest aircraft, and to assign their noisiest aircraft to long-haul journeys (minimizing therefore the landings giving rise to a noise charge) and/or to locations where no noise charges are collected.
2. To encourage manufacturers to produce quieter aircraft.
3. To allow the financing of soundproofing, rehousing and execution of various measures aimed at protecting airport neighbours from excessive noise.

The first two functions are incentive functions. The third one is a financing function.

Aircraft noise charge schemes exist now in the Netherlands, in France, in Switzerland, in Japan, in the United Kingdom and in Germany[4,7] and some pilot schemes have begun to appear in the US. The European schemes are summarized below and are also mentioned in Chapter 20, where they appear as an aspect of the airport noise control procedures.

France In France, a charge of one franc per passenger on domestic flights and of three francs for international flights has been levied since 1973 at Orly and Charles de Gaulle airports, Paris.

This charge has provided financial assistance for the soundproofing of buildings used for education or medical-welfare purposes in the noisiest vicinities of the Orly and Charles de Gaulle airports, and also of housing in the vicinity of the Charles de Gaulle airport. The charge, which is still independent of the level of noise emitted by different aircraft, is therefore, not an incentive to reduce noise. (To give an extreme example, a quiet 300-seat Airbus flying from Paris to Moscow pays nine times more than a noisy Caravelle flying from Paris to Lyons in France.) The low level of the charge also limits its financing potential. The scheme has raised a yearly average of 2.5–3.7 million dollars since it was first introduced. The funds for the noise abatement measures undertaken have been allocated in the following manner:

1. Acoustic insulation of educational and health-care establishments: one-third.
2. Acquisition and demolition of dwellings: two-thirds.

It was decided in 1983 to link the landing fee with the noise levels emitted by aircraft, and to extend the aid programme for people living around airports to all French airports. For the purpose of calculating the noise charge, as of the January 1, 1987, aircraft will be classified in one of five noise groups, the quietest (Group 5) paying the nominal landing fee minus 10%, Group 4 paying the nominal landing fee, Group 3 paying the landing fee +5%, Group 2 paying the landing fee +10% and Group 1 paying the landing fee +20%.

Switzerland In Switzerland, the airports of Zurich and Geneva implemented an aircraft noise charging scheme in 1980 which established a close link between the charge levied and the impact of noise on people. This charge, determined by a classification of aircraft in five categories, is levied in addition to the standard landing fee. The airlines operating the quietest aircraft pay no noise charge, whereas operators using the noisiest aircraft pay 400 Swiss francs for each landing. (NB: *Table 20.6* gives further details of the scale of charges.) The total revenue expected from the noise charge, and therefore the rates of the noise charge, are calculated in such a way that the charges collected will entirely cover the anticipated expenditures needed at both airports for sound insulation and compensation.

Japan In Japan a special landing fee designed to finance noise abatement has been charged since September 1975. It is based on the weight of the aircraft and its sound level on landing and at take-off. The noise charge in Yen is calculated by the following formula:

$$\left[\begin{array}{c} \text{Maximum weight in} \\ \text{tonnes at take-off} \end{array} \right] \times 290$$

$$+ \left[\left(\frac{\text{EPNL at take-off} + \text{EPNL on landing}}{2} \right) - 83 \times 3260 \right]$$

For example, a Boeing 747 with an average noise level of 106 EPNdB at take-off and landing, would incur an additional charge amounting to approximately 26% of the total landing fee. In 1983, this tax was:

1200 dollars for a Boeing 747.
700 dollars for a Lockheed 1011.
280 dollars for a DC9.

The fee, paid by the airlines, is partly recovered in the form of a flat rate added on to the price of the ticket (about $3.80 for adults).

Netherlands In the Netherlands, a charge scheme on aircraft noise was put into force in 1983. The charge for acoustically certified aircraft, i.e. those that comply with ICAO standards, of a maximum weight exceeding 20 tonnes, is computed as follows:

$$T = f \times n \times 10^{\frac{(L_r - 270)}{45}}$$

where:

F = the charging rate.

n = an equalization factor to make the noise levels as measured according to ICAO and FAA (USA) procedures comparable.

L_r = the sum of the noise levels at the three ICAO measuring points.

The charge for uncertified aircraft, i.e. those that do not comply with ICAO standards, is computed as follows:

$$T = F \times k \times W^{2/3}$$

where:
k = a constant depending on the noise category of the aircraft (e.g. 0.15 for the quietest aircraft and 0.9 for the noisiest).
W = maximum permitted weight.

The noise charges for some aircraft in common use in 1985 are:

	US dollars
Boeing 707	192
Boeing 727	85
DC10	56
Airbus 300	15
Boeing 747	15

The proceeds are being used to finance noise abatement programmes in the vicinity of airports. This includes soundproofing and purchasing buildings located in high exposure areas.

The rates have been calculated to yield enough income for a 10-year plan starting in 1983, with an annual expenditure of around 4 million dollars.

UK In the United Kingdom the airports of London Heathrow, Gatwick and Stansted, as well as the airport of Manchester, apply a 10–15% reduction of the landing fee for aircraft complying with ICAO standards. Although this is not, strictly speaking, a charge, rather a *rebate*, the objectives and the results of the scheme are similar to the charging schemes.

Germany In Germany, a rebate system has also been introduced amounting to an 18–21% reduction of the landing fee at all commercial airports for aircraft complying with ICAO standards.

As demonstrated by the above examples, aircraft noise charges are now implemented in at least six different countries. At the charge levels set they mainly fulfil a financing function. However, it is likely that as more airports levy discriminating charges for noisy aircraft, the greater will be the incentive effect on operators and on manufacturers who have to satisfy the operators demands. Alternatively, noise charges could be increased further, although this action is likely to be strongly resisted.

The extension of such charging schemes will obviously have to take into account various constraints such as enforcement problems while avoiding complexity and excessive cost of implementation. The schemes would also need to be developed taking care to preserve links with international agreements, and in particular ICAO standards and regulations.[4]

24.3 Motor vehicle noise charges

As with aircraft, it is possible to impose some form of noise tax on road vehicles. The fundamental question is, who will provide the payments, e.g. the manufacturers, the road authority or, of course, the owner or driver of the vehicle? In other words, should the incentive effect be directed towards the manufacturer, the user or both?

An incentive to the manufacturer would appear to offer two main advantages. Firstly, it would influence the design of new quieter vehicles since it is in the manufacturer's interest to reduce the component costs. Secondly, the charge would be imposed on 'stationary' transactors who could be easily identified and controlled. In the case of aircraft noise, the stationary transactors are the airlines. The main disadvantage to this approach is that there is no direct link between the scale of taxation and the scale of noise impact. This arises because although vehicle noise potential depends largely upon the power output capability of the vehicle, the noise impact also depends upon the driving style adopted by the user. Consequently, a quiet vehicle can cause considerable noise impact if driven noisily along a quiet street at night. However, by applying an impact related tax on the user no real advantage in this respect can be gained since, clearly, the implementation of an appropriate noise charge to each individual driver and vehicle type is an impossible proposition. Therefore, if a charge were to be imposed on the user this would have to be based on a much simpler model than the past notion of tax directly related to noise impact. A simpler alternative is to apply a discriminatory scale of taxation according to the maximum noise characteristics of the vehicle and at the same time to promote the concept of enforcement action to deal with drivers who deliberately drive their vehicles noisily.

A discriminatory noise tax levied annually could help to ensure that vehicles are properly maintained in use. This could be combined with a sliding scale tax applied to new vehicles, penalizing the noisier types. This type of tax system therefore inciting both the manufacturer and the owner of a vehicle would influence both the user/consumer and the manufacturer. The consumer would be attracted to use quieter vehicles because they are cheaper and the manufacturer would be encouraged to produce quieter vehicles in order to remain competitive and attract customers.

Several methods of assessing the level of taxation have been considered. One method defines for each category of vehicles a threshold value below which vehicles would not be taxed, while each decibel in excess of this threshold value would be charged at the same rate.[5] Such a system would, in principle, be simple to conceive and to operate. The threshold value would be determined in order to encourage users not to buy the noisiest vehicles. An alternative method employs an exponential growth curve to determine the tax levels at each dB above the threshold. The amount levied is doubled for each 10 dB increase above the threshold.[5] Further correction could be made to allow for the average annual mileage covered by the vehicle type and for the type of environmental zone in which it operates (e.g. urban, rural).

Clearly, the above considerations are still theoretical and as a result there remains a great deal of opposition to charge schemes for road vehicles. At present no charge system for road vehicle noise emission has been put into practice.

In the *Netherlands*, a noise charge or tax on vehicle fuel has been in force since December 1980, the purpose of which is to help finance the comprehensive Dutch noise abatement programme.[2] This form of taxation represents a charge on the actual use of the vehicle and is not really linked to the intrinsic noise output of each vehicle type. Hence the user of a large-capacity saloon car with high fuel consumption will be taxed at a higher rate per km than the user of a small car with low fuel consumption. This does not necessarily reflect the noise impact of the two vehicles as it could be argued that the larger vehicle in traffic will emit less noise due to the lower engine speed and better quality of noise insulation. This type of tax does, however, relate to the total mileage travelled which implicitly places a higher tax burden on the users of vehicles which impact, environmentally, most people.

The rate of the charge is currently set at approximately 0.50 dollars per hectolitre of petrol or diesel fuel. The total revenue amounts to around 40 million dollars per year. This charge is now equivalent to 0.9% of the cost of petrol and 1.2% of the cost of diesel fuel. This charge on vehicle fuel is a typical case of a non incentive charge, the only purpose being to raise funds to finance noise abatement measures such as noise barriers, insulation of buildings, administrative cost, etc.

To summarize, the present experience with charging schemes on motor vehicle noise is much more limited than that of aircraft. Potential difficulties in the design and implementation of such schemes, as well as political difficulties, have so far prevented their adoption.

24.4 Other economic incentives

As a complement to regulations and noise charges, some countries have adopted other economic incentives, such as the promotion of low noise equipment, financial subsidy to carry out research and compensation for damages due to noise.

24.4.1 Promotion of quiet vehicles and subsidies

Restriction on the use of noisy vehicles at certain times and/or at certain locations have been put into operation in different countries following the introduction of new regulations. However, when exemptions from restrictions are granted for very quiet vehicles, such a decision acts as an economic incentive because it promotes the production and purchase of quiet vehicles.

In Germany, there are plans to introduce in a supplement to the highway code the notion of 'low noise vehicles'. The town of Bad Reichenhal (a commune in Bavaria with a population of 15000) has introduced a local ordinance which permits quieter vehicles to enter areas otherwise restricted to traffic.[6] The extension of this local action to the national road network requires a precise definition of what is meant by quiet vehicles and how they can be identified. Discussions have been held with the motor vehicle industry, which is now able to supply a limited range of vehicles complying with the noise emission limits laid down by the authorities. The aim is that heavy goods vehicles should not be substantially noisier than the average private car. It is proposed that vehicles of a total permitted laden weight exceeding 2800 kg be regarded as 'quiet vehicles' if they comply with the following sound levels.

Engine power ⩽ 75 kW:	77 dB(A);
Engine power 76–150 kW:	78 dB(A);
Engine power > 150 kW:	80 dB(A).

Manufacturers who sell heavy goods vehicles which comply with these sound levels will be authorized to affix a special plate to their vehicles worded '*Larmarmes Kraftfahrzeug*' (low-noise lorry). An official plate of this kind will indicate clearly to local authorities whether the vehicle is permitted to enter a protected area covered by traffic restrictions. At present it is not regarded to be economically possible for all trucks to be replaced by quiet vehicles and so traffic will be restricted to low noise vehicles alone only in those areas that need to be protected and only at particularly sensitive times during the day. These limitations of time and place will be decided at the local level. It is intended that the relevant noise abatement regulations will be published in the highway code and supplied to the relevant departments of all land governments.

Another type of economic incentive is the financial assistance granted by public authorities to research institutes developing low-noise equipment.

In Germany, a full-scale research programme was launched in 1978, sponsored by the Environment Agency and aimed at developing and producing industrial prototype vehicles with low-noise emission. Total aid contributed was in the neighbour-

*Levels obtained according to the test conditions defined in 81/EEC/334.

hood of 1 million dollars spread over 5 years. Some very quiet vehicles were developed (73 dB(A) for a car, 77 dB(A) for a heavy goods vehicle). In France, more than 2 million dollars have been given to motor vehicle manufacturers and to consulting firms and university laboratories since 1972. The impact of these schemes is important since the results obtained are likely to be applied in the medium term to production vehicles, either following a change in the regulations or, possibly on the basis of these results, through noise charges. Further details of individual vehicle noise quietening programmes is given in Chapter 10.

Another type of incentive is the granting of subsidies stimulating investments in favour of the environment. Tax relief or subsidies to enterprises which invest in quiet vehicles (buses and lorries) have been granted in the Netherlands since 1980. Subsidies for the purchase of quiet heavy lorries or buses can reach 7.5% of the cost if their noise level is below 79 dB(A), 3% if their noise level is below 87 dB(A).

24.4.2 Compensation

It could be argued that noise compensation is not an incentive as such but rather a kind of financial penalty on those responsible for the noise, and a legitimate redress in favour of those suffering from noise. It has, however, the characteristics of an economic incentive by the simple fact that if the noise producers (highway administration, airports, municipalities, etc.) know that they may be subject to the payment of compensation, they will act in such a way as to minimize this payment, either by not producing a noise which may generate a request for compensation or by including the costs of compensation in their investment calculations. In this way compensation can be considered as an economic incentive.

Compensation is defined as a payment, in cash, and/or in kind, designed to restore as far as possible a person to his state of welfare before the damage occurred. The need to compensate for noise is particularly acute in existing built-up areas around airports and along highways. Intolerable situations may occur because no satisfactory preventive or curative measure can be adopted. In such cases, the only solution may be to provide compensation in the form of sound insulation of property and in cash. This does not mean that prevention should not remain the priority. It simply means that compensation is a last resort when all other means have been tried.

The general principles of law recognize already that victims of damage have a right to redress, but redress implies court proceedings, which generally means a slow, costly and uncertain process. There is, therefore, a need for the creation of specific mechanisms of compensation for environmental damage and especially noise damage. These mechanisms should, of course, be simple to operate.

Some countries have adopted special provisions in their legislation allowing for compensation to be granted mainly in kind, such as soundproofing (Germany, the Netherlands, Japan, France), but only one country (the United Kingdom) has established a specific law—the Land Compensation Act—granting not only compensation in kind, but also for compensation for loss of value of property or loss of amenity value. Further information on this legislation is given elsewhere in this book, principally Chapter 11.

24.4.2.1 Compensation in kind[4,7]

In the *United Kingdom*, the Noise Insulation Regulations made under the Land Compensation Act of 1973 provide that where dwellings are or will within 15 years be subjected to increased traffic noise from a new or improved highway of at least 1 dB(A), resulting in an end noise level of 68 dB(A) or above on the L_{10} (18 hour) index, a duty arises for the highway authority to provide insulation at its expense. It has been estimated that some 30 000 dwellings along major roads are eligible.

In *Germany*, the Air Traffic Noise Control Act of 1971 and the 1974 Pollution Act provide for the payment of insulation expenses for buildings exposed to sound levels exceeding the prescribed limits. Several municipalities have undertaken soundproofing programmes. For example, from 1974 to 1979 the City of Munich spent 9 million dollars on insulating buildings from traffic noise. This cost represents 50% of the total cost, the other 50% was borne by the owners.

In the *Netherlands*, the Noise Nuisance Act of March 1979 provides that above a noise level of 50 dB(A) (L_{eq}) at the front of dwellings, protective measures must be taken to ensure that the sound level within dwellings does not exceed 35 or 55 dB(A), the level depending on whether the buildings are to be constructed or already exist. The cost of these soundproofing measures is borne by the municipalities and financed by means of charges on motor-vehicle noise.

In *France*, there is no Act expressly providing for the sound-proofing of dwellings exposed to excessive sound levels. However, provision is often made for sound insulation measures by the public authorities where frontage levels exceed 65 dB(A) L_{eq} over the working day.

In the *United States*, under specific conditions, individual states are permitted to use Federal Highways funds for acoustical treatment of severely affected buildings. The practice of providing compensation in the form of soundproofing is also extensively used in the vicinity of major airports. *See* also Chapter 20.

In the *United Kingdom*, a system of financing the insulation of dwellings around London's Heathrow Airport operated from 1966 to 1972. The British Airport Authority was required to pay 50% of insulation expenses for dwellings situated within the 55 NNI (Noise and Number Index) zone, i.e. about 77 dB(A) L_{eq} (24 hour). Since 1972 a new system introduced for Heathrow established zones entitled to 100% payment of costs incurred.

In *Germany*, the Air Traffic Noise Control Act of 1971 provides for measures to soundproof dwellings in the vicinity of more than 40 civil and military airports. More than 8 million dollars has now been spent on sound insulation treatment up to 1984.

In the *Netherlands*, aircraft noise charges are used to pay for the soundproofing of the most exposed dwellings. Some 20 000 dwellings close to Amsterdam-Schiphol Airport have been treated.

24.4.2.2 Compensation in cash[3,7]

In addition to a compensation of kind, e.g. soundproofing, which, as the above examples show, is the most widely used, a cash compensation regulation is also provided in the United Kingdom. This second type of compensation involves a cash payment to the 'victim' to compensate wholly or in part for the damage suffered. The payment is therefore the monetary equivalent of the damage and may cover:

1. The fall in the value of property situated within the area affected by noise.
2. The fact that housing has been rendered totally unsuitable for use as accommodation.
3. The loss of amenity.

In the *United Kingdom*, the Land Compensation Act referred to above provides that any dwelling whose value falls due to noise from public works such as roads and airports, has a right to compensation. The depreciation in value is calculated with reference to the market price 1 year after the works are put into service. Where dwellings are soundproofed, the corresponding increase in value is taken into account.

It is clear from this overview that several compensation schemes exist already. Most of these schemes are limited to compensation in the form of insulation grants but they do offer the opportunity to alleviate the problem of noise when other control procedures fail to achieve an acceptable solution and without the need to involve protracted court proceedings. Currently, the most comprehensive and 'preventative' scheme is the British Land Compensation Act which provides both loss of value compensation as well as procedures for the sound insulation of property.

24.5 Conclusions

Various kinds of economic incentives which include noise charges, subsidies, and compensation schemes have been developed to supplement direct regulations such as noise emission standards. Their implementation is still, however, restricted but their definition and, as yet, limited implementation marks a definite step forward in the adoption of economic instruments to abate transportation noise impact.

For *aircraft noise* the use of noise charges has grown in recent years and has now been adopted in six countries. Some systems introduced a strong measure of discrimination between the noisiest aircraft and those which are acoustically most advanced. There is still room for progress in the planning and implementation of these schemes, but it has been shown that this type of economic incentive is feasible and useful, particularly for financing local noise abatement policies.

The use of *motor vehicle noise charges* is not considered, at present, to be technically and politically feasible. Such systems need to remain relatively simple if their application is not to be made too cumbersome. While their redistributive role is readily apparent, there appears to be greater difficulty in making their incentive role effective. For this reason some countries have considered promoting the *marketing of low-noise vehicles* through incentives such as the introduction of the quiet vehicle design principle enabling municipalities to introduce traffic restrictions in 'sensitive' areas that only quiet vehicles would be authorized to enter. If combined with a noise charge system, which would enable financial resources to be gathered, such a scheme would be attractive, since it provides the incentive to motor vehicle manufacturers to produce quieter vehicles and affords protection for areas which had previously been particularly exposed.

Finally, schemes have been introduced which provide *compensation* to people badly impacted by transport noise. These schemes generally take the form of building insulation grants, but can also include compensation in direct monetary terms for loss of value of property or enjoyment of land. These schemes ensure that there is some redress by those people suffering excess noise when other forms of control are insufficient to create an acceptable noise environment. They also provide an incentive to the planning authorities who have to consider the costs of compensation as part of the overall economic evaluation of the transport development plan.

References

1 ALEXANDRE, A., BARDE, J. ph. and PEARCE, D. W. The practical determination of a charge for noise pollution. *Journal of Transport Economics and Policy*, 205–220 (1980).
2 OECD (Organisation for Economic Co-operation and Development). *Pollution Charges in Practice*, Paris (1980).
3 BAUMOL, W. J. and OATES, W. E. *The Theory of Environmental Policy*. Prentice Hall, Englewood Cliffs (1975).

4 OECD. *Reducing Noise in OECD Countries*, Paris (1978).

5 ALEXANDRE, A. and BARDE, J. Ph. The economics of traffic noise abatement. *Traffic Quarterly* **April,** No. 2, (1976).

6 DENNERL, J. *Ein Neuer Weg der Verkehrslarmminderung—Modell Bad Reichenhall.* Mimeograph Bad Reichenhall City Hall (1982).

7 OECD. *Conference on Noise Abatement Policies*, Paris (1980).

Appendix 1

Units, Symbols and Conversion Factors

Contents

Units, Symbols and Conversion Factors

A brief statement of the symbology convention adopted in this book is given on page vii preceding the contents summary. This appendix provides further information on the metrication system adopted, more general statements about preferred symbology and, for convenience, it gives a summary of commonly used multiplying factors to allow conversion between the International Metric System of Units and their imperial equivalents.

A1.1 The SI System

The International System of Units (SI) is the modern form of the metric system agreed at an international conference in 1960. It has been adopted by the ISO and the IEC and its use is recommended wherever the metric system is applied. It is likely to remain the primary world system of units of measurement for a very long time. SI units are used throughout this reference book although reference to imperial measures are sometimes given for comparison.

SI units and rules for their application are contained in ISO Resolution R1000 (1969 updated 1973) and an informatory document *SI–Le Système International d'Unités*, published by the Bureau International de Poids et Mesures (BIPM). An abridged version is given in the British Standards Institution (BSI) publication PD 5686 *The Use of SI Units* (1969, updated 1973), and BS3763 *International System (SI) Units*: BSI (1964) incorporates information from the BIPM document.

In constructing a coherent unit system, the starting point is the selection and definition of a minimum set of independent 'base' units. From these, 'derived' units are obtained by forming products or quotients in various combinations, again without numerical factors. Thus the base units of length (metre), time (second) and mass (kilogram) yield the SI units of velocity (metre/second), force (kilogram-metre/second-squared) etc. As a result there is, for any given physical quantity, only one SI unit with no alternatives and with no numerical conversion factors.

For example, a single SI unit (joule = kilogram metre-squared/second-squared) serves for energy of any kind, whether it be kinetic, potential, thermal, electrical, etc., thereby unifying the usage in all branches of science and technology.

The SI has seven base units, and two supplementary units of angle. Each physical quantity has a preferred symbol (e.g. m for mass) that represents it in equations, and a unit (e.g. kg for kilogram) to indicate its SI unit of measure. The seven basic units are given in *Table A1.1*. The supplementary angular units are given in *Table A1.2* and the commonly used derived units are listed in *Table A1.3*.

To express magnitudes of a unit, decimal multiples and submultiples are formed using the prefixes given in *Table A1.4*.

Table A1.1 Basic SI units

Base unit	Quantity symbol	Unit name	Unit symbol
Length	l	metre	m
Mass	m	kilogram	kg
Time	t	second	s
Electric current	i	ampere	A
Thermodynamic temperature	T	kelvin	K
Luminous intensity	I	candela	cd
Amount of substance	Q	mole	mol

Table A1.2 Supplementary angular SI units

Supplementary units	Quantity symbol	Unit name	Unit symbol
Plane angle	α, β	radian	(rad)
Solid angle	Ω	steradion	(sr)

Table A1.3 Commonly used derived SI units

Quantity	Unit name	Unit symbol	Derivation
Area	square metre	m^2	—
Volume	cubic metre	m^3	—
Mass density	kilogramme per cubic metre	kg/m^3	—
Linear velocity	metre per second	m/s	—
Linear acceleration	metre per second squared	m/s^2	—
Angular velocity	radian per second	rad/s	—
Angular acceleration	radian per second squared	rad/s^2	—
Force	newton	N	$kg.m/s^2$
Pressure	pascal	Pa	N/m^2
Power	watt	W	J/s
Energy	joule	J	N.m
Electric charge/flux	coulomb	C	A.s
Electrical potential	volt	V	J/C, W/A
Frequency	hertz	Hz	l/s
Resistance	ohm	Ω	V/A
Power density	watt per square metre	w/m^2	—
Energy density	joule per cubic metre	J/m^3	—

NB. Units for which a statement in base units would be lengthy or complicated are often given special names, e.g. Newton instead of kilogram metre per second squared. In the above table all such entries are named from scientists and engineers and as such are symbolized by an initial capital letter: all other named derived units use lower case letters.

Table A1.4 Magnitudes for SI units

Multiplication factor	Prefix	Symbol
One million million (10^{12})	tera	T
One thousand million (10^9)	giga	G
One million (10^6)	mega	M
One thousand (10^3)	kilo	k
One hundred (10^2)	hecto*	h
Ten (10^1)	deca*	da
Unit (1)		
One tenth (10^{-1})	deci*	d
One hundredth (10^{-1})	centi*	c
One thousandth (10^{-3})	milli	m
One millionth (10^{-6})	micro	
One thousandth millionth (10^{-9})	nano	n
One million millionth (10^{-12})	pico	p
One thousand million millionth (10^{-15})	fento	f

*To be avoided where possible.

A1.2 Metric to Imperial conversion factors

Table A1.5 gives a list of commonly used SI units and their imperial equivalents.

Table A1.5 Metric to Imperial conversion

Name	SI units	Imperial units
Length	1 μm	$39.37.10^{-6}$ in
	1 mm	0·039 370 in
	1 cm	0·393 701 in
	1 m	3·280 84 ft
	1 m	1·093 61 yd
	1 km	0·621 371 mile
Area	1 mm²	$1·550.10^{-3}$ in²
	1 cm²	0·155 0 in²
	1 m²	10·763 9 ft²
	1 m²	1·195 99 yd²
	1 ha (10^4 m²)	2·471 05 acre
Volume	1 mm³	$61·023\ 7\ 10^{-6}$ in³
	1 cm³	$61·023\ 7\ 10^{-3}$ in³
	1 m³	35·314 7 ft³
	1 m³	1·307 95 yd³
Capacity	1 litre	0·219 969 gal*
		1·759 80 pint
	1 m³	219.969 gal
	10^6m³	$219.969.10^6$ gal
Velocity	1 m/s	3·280 84 ft/s
		2·236 94 mile/h
	1 km/h	0·621 371 mile/h
Acceleration	1 m/s²	3·280 84 ft/s²
Mass	1 g	0·0352 74 oz
	1 kg	2·204 62 lb
	1 t	0·984 207 ton
		19·684 1 cwt
Mass per unit length	1 kg/m	0·671 969 lb/ft
		2·015 91 lb/yd
Mass per unit area	1 kg/m²	0·204 816 lb/ft²
Force	1 N	0·224 809 lbf
Moment of force (torque)	1 Nm	0·737 562 lbf ft
Pressure	1 N/m²	$1·450\ 38.10^{-4}$ lbf/in²
	1 bar (10^5 N/m²)	14·5034 8 lbf/in²
		0·986 923 atmosphere
	1 mbar (10^2 N/m²)	0·401 463 in H₂O
		0·029 53 in Hg
Stress	1 N/mm²	$6·47490.10^{-2}$ tonf/in²
Energy	1 J	0·737 562 ft lbf
	1 MJ	0·277 78 kWh
Power	1 W	0·727 562 ft lbf-s
	1 kW	1·341 Hp
Temperature (preferred)	°K + °C + 273.15	
Temperature (acceptable)	°C	$°C = \dfrac{°F - 32}{1.8}$
Road fuel consumption	litre/100 km	0·003 540 gal/mile

*1 gallon US = 0·832 68 gallon (Imperial).

Appendix 2

Definition of Terms Relating to Environmental Acoustics

Definition of Terms Relating to Environmental Acoustics

Throughout this book, definitions of terms used in transportation noise control are given in various chapters. In particular, Chapter 2 contains some basic definitions of commonly used units, scales and indices, and Chapters 21 and 22 contain short glossaries which deal specifically with terms used in the field of supersonic travel and sonic boom and environmental appraisal respectively.

For convenience, the definitions of terms that are used frequently in the fields of acoustics and audiology are also listed here. Although many of the definitions are taken from appropriate standards (*see* Appendix 3) the wording used reflects the preference of the editor.

Acoustics (a) The science of sound including its generation, propagation and effects.
    (b) Those factors that determine the character of a room with respect to the quality of the received sound.

Acoustical material Any material considered in terms of its acoustical properties. Commonly a material designed to absorb sound.

Acoustic impedance $Z = R + jX$ (Pa. s/m^3) of a surface for a given frequency, the complex quotient obtained when the sound pressure averaged over the surface is divided by the volume velocity throughout the surface. The real and imaginary components are called, respectively, *acoustic resistance* and *acoustic reactance*.

Acoustic reactance See Acoustic impedance.

Acoustic refraction The proces by which the direction of sound propagation is changed because of spatial variation of the wave velocity of the medium.

Acoustic resistance See Acoustic impedance.

Acoustic scattering The irregular and diffuse reflection, refraction, or diffraction of sound in many directions.

Ambient noise The composite of airborne sound from many sources near and far associated with a given environment.

Amplitude of a periodic quantity The maximum value of the quantity.

Anechoic room A room designed to simulate free-field conditions.

Angular frequency ω(rad/sec), 2π times the frequency of a periodic quantity.

Antinode A point, line or surface of an interference pattern at which the amplitude of the sound pressure or particle velocity is a maximum.

Audibility threshold The minimum root mean square value of the sound pressure which excites the sensation of hearing.

Audio frequency Any frequency corresponding to a normally audible sound wave, roughly from 15 Hz to 20 kHz.

Audiogram A graph showing hearing loss, per cent hearing loss, or per cent hearing as a function of frequency.

Background noise Noise from all sources unrelated to a particular sound that is the object of interest, eg. when traffic noise is of interest, background noise would ideally comprise all audible sounds from, other than traffic, sources.

Band pressure level The sound pressure level of the sound energy within a specified frequency band. The width of the band may also be indicated, e.g. *octave* band pressure level, $\frac{1}{3}$rd octave band pressure level.

Beats Periodic variations that result from the superposition of two simple harmonic motions of different frequencies, F_1 and F_2. They involve the periodic increase and decrease of the amplitude at the beat frequency ($F_1 - F_2$).

Characteristic impedance ρc (Pa. s/m), the specific normal acoustic impedance at a point in a plane wave in a free field. The particle velocity and the sound pressure are in phase and it is equal in magnitude to the product of the density ρ and the speed of sound in the medium, c. (NB. The characteristic impedance of air at 20°C and 101 325 kPa is 413 rayl (Pa. s/m).

Coincidence effect An effect manifested as an increase of the sound transmission coefficient of a partition, which occurs when the wavelength of bending waves along the partition approaches equality with the projection, in the direction of propagation of the bending waves, of the wavelength of the incident sound waves.

Compliance Reciprocal of stiffness.

Compressional wave A wave in an elastic medium which causes an element of the medium to change the volume without undergoing rotation.

Continuous spectrum The spectrum of a wave, the components of which are continuously distributed over the frequency region.

Damp To cause a loss or dissipation of the oscillatory or vibrational energy of an electrical or mechanical system.

Decay rate d (dB/sec), for airborne sound, the rate of decrease of sound pressure level after the source of sound has stopped; for vibration, the rate of decrease of vibratory acceleration, velocity or displacement level after the excitation has stopped.

Decibel (dB), the term used to identify ten times the common logarithm of the ratio of two like quantities proportional to power or energy.

The powers P_1 and P_2 are said to be separated by an interval of n bels (or 10 n decibels) when $n = \log_{10} (P_1/P_2)$. When the conditions are such that the ratios of sound particle velocities and ratios of sound pressures are the square roots of the corresponding power ratios the number of decibels by which the corresponding powers differ is expressed by the following formulae:

$$n = 20 \log_{10} (u_1/u_2) \text{ dB}$$
$$n = 20 \log_{10} (p_1/p_2) \text{ dB}$$

where u_1/u_2 and p_1/p_2 are the given ratios of sound particle velocity and sound pressure respectively.

Diffraction A change in the direction of propagation of sound energy in the neighbourhood of a boundary discontinuity such as the edge of a reflective or absorptive surface. Reflection and refraction are special cases of diffraction; *reflection* occurs when the wave front impinging on a boundary between two medias is changed in direction within the first medium. *Refraction* occurs when the wave front passes into the second medium. *Scattering* is the combined effects of diffraction from an irregular array of objects, and is generally expressed in terms of its average effect at a large distance from the objects.

Diffuse sound field A sound field such that the sound pressure level is everywhere the same, and all directions of energy flux are equally probable.

Direct sound field The sound that arrives directly from a source without reflection.

Direction of propagation The direction in which the energy associated with a wave is flowing.

Directivity factor (source) The ratio of the intensity of the radiated sound, at any remote point on a reference axis, to the average for all directions in space, of the intensity of the sound at the same distance from the effective centre of the source.

Directivity factor (microphone) The square of the ratio of the free-field sensitivity in a reference direction to the random incidence sensitivity.

Directivity index Ten times the logarithm to the base 10 of the directivity factor.

Doppler effect The change in the observed frequency of a wave caused by the time rate of change in the length of the path between the source and the observer.

Excess attenuation That part of the attenuation of the sound propagated which is not accounted for by energy spreading along the expanding wavefront. For surface mix propagation this generally relates to the attenuation affected by the absorbing properties of the ground and, at high frequencies, by the atmosphere.

Far field That part of the field of a source radiating sound in *free-field* conditions, wherein the sound pressure and the particle velocity are substantially in-phase or in which the particle velocity is inversely proportional to the distance from the source.

For practical purposes the far field can be assumed to exist at a distance from the source of $2a^2/\lambda$ or $2a$ whichever is the larger, where λ is the wavelength and a is the typical linear dimension of the radiating surface.

Flanking transmission The tranmission of sound from one room to an adjacent room, via common walls, floors or ceilings, flanking a partition between the rooms, when air-borne sound is generated in the first room.

Free-field A soundfield in a medium of such extent that the effects of the boundaries are negligible throughout the region of interest.

Free-field room *See Anechoic room.*

Free progressive wave A wave in a medium free from boundary effects. A free wave in a steady state can only be approximated in practice.

Free vibration The oscillation of some physical quantity of the system when there are no externally applied driving forces. Such oscillation is maintained by the transfer of energy between elastic restoring forces and inertia forces. The oscillation may arise from initial displacements, velocities, or a force suddenly applied and withdrawn.

Fundamental mode The mode of vibration of a system having the lowest frequency. The fundamental frequency of a periodic quantity is equal to the reciprocal of the shortest period during which the quantity repeats itself.

Harmonic A sinusoidal quantity having a frequency that is an integral multiple of the fundamental frequency of a periodic quantity to which it is related.

Hearing loss The amount in decibels at a specified frequency, by which the *threshold of audibility* for an ear exceeds the normal threshold. Also used, in a general sense, to describe the process of losing auditory sensitivity.

Helmholtz resonator A resonator consisting of a cavity in a rigid structure communicating by a narrow neck or slit to the outside air. The frequency of resonance is determined by the mass of air in the neck resonating in conjunction with the compliance of the air in the cavity.

Impedance An impedance is the complex ratio of a force-like quantity (force, pressure, voltage) to a related velocity-like quantity (velocity, volume velocity, or current). *See Acoustic impedance.*

Impedance ratio $Z/c \equiv r/\rho c + jx/c$: the ratio of the specific normal acoustic impedance at a surface to the characteristic impedance of the medium. The real and imaginary components are called, respectively, *resistance ratio* and *reactance ratio*.

Infrasonic frequency A frequency lying below the audio-frequency range.

Insertion loss The decrease in *sound power level* at a given frequency measured at the receiver when a sound insulator or sound attenuator is inserted in the transmission path between the source and the receiver.

Level *See Sound pressure level* and *Sound power level.* The level of a quantity is the logarithm of the ratio of that quantity to a reference quantity of the same kind.

Longitudinal wave *See Compressional wave.*

Loudness An observer's auditory impression of the strength of a sound. *Loudness level* of a sound is measured by the sound pressure level of a standard pure tone of specified frequency which is assessed by observers as being equally as loud as the sound being measured. The level is expressed in phons when the standard pure tone is produced as a plane progressive wave coming from directly in front of the observer and having a frequency of 1 kHz.

Masking The process by which the threshold of hearing of one sound is raised due to the presence of another.

Mass law The approximately linear relationship between the sound insulation of a partition, expressed in decibels, and the logarithm of its weight per unit area.

Mechanical impedance The impedance obtained from the ratio of force to either velocity or displacement during simple harmonic motion. The ratio of force to velocity is designated *velocity impedance*; the ratio force to displacement is designated *displacement impedance.*

Modal number A vibratory system can be analysed in terms of its *normal modes*. The modes may be arranged in a discrete sequence associated with a set of integers which are called modal numbers.

Monopole A source that radiates sound in an isotropic medium uniformly in all directions under free-field conditions.

Natural frequency The frequency of free vibration of a system. For a multi degree of freedom system, the natural frequencies are the frequencies of vibration in *normal modes*.

Near field That part of the field of a source radiating sound in free-field conditions, wherein the sound pressure and particle velocity are not in phase. The extent of the near field will depend upon the wavelength of the radiating sound, the type and complexity of the source and on the linear dimensions of the source. Points that lie close to the source in relation to its dimensions are sometimes said to lie in the near field but it should be noted that in certain cases, when the wavelength is very short, the sound pressure and particle velocity may then be in phase. In such cases the term 'close field' may be used to distinguish this region from the true near field.

Node A point, line or surface of an interference pattern at which the amplitude of the sound pressure or particle velocity is zero or a minimum.

Noise Sound that is undesired by the recipient.

Noise induced permanent threshold shift *See Permanent threshold shift.*

Noise rating curves An agreed set of empirical curves relating octave band pressure level to the centre frequency of the octave bands, each of which is characterized by a 'noise rating' (NR), which is numerically equal to the sound pressure level at the intersection with the ordinate at 1000 Hz. The noise rating of a given noise is found by plotting the octave band spectrum on the same diagram and selecting the highest noise rating curves to which the spectrum is tangent.

Normal modes A pattern of motion assumed by a system in which the motion of every particle is simple harmonic with the same period and phase. Vibration in a normal mode thus occurs at a natural frequency of the system. In general, any composite motion of a system can be expressed as a summation of normal modes.

Octave A *pitch* interval of 2:1.

Octave band pressure level The octave-band pressure level of a sound is the *band pressure level* for a frequency band corresponding to a specified octave. The frequency of each octave band is usually specified as the geometric mean of the upper and lower frequencies of the octave-band. *See* Chapter 2 for details of both octave and $\frac{1}{3}$rd octave band frequencies used in acoustics.

Particle velocity At a point in a sound field. The alternating component of the total velocity of movement of the medium at the point. The term 'particle velocity' may be qualified by the terms 'instantaneous', 'maximum', 'rms' etc. the unqualified term is usually taken to imply the rms value.

Peak sound pressure The maximum absolute value of the instantaneous sound pressure for a specified time interval.

Peak to peak amplitude The algebraic difference between the extremes of an oscillating quantity.

Period For a periodic quantity, the smallest value of the independent variable for which the quantity repeats itself.

Permanent threshold shift The component of threshold shift which shows no progressive reduction with the passage of time when the apparent cause has been removed.

Phase of a periodic quantity The fractional part of a period through which the independent variable has advanced, measured from an arbitrary origin. For a sinusoidal quantity, the origin is usually taken as the last previous passage through zero from the negative to positive direction.

Phase difference between two instantaneous values of the same sinusoidal quantity is the fraction of a whole period which elapses between these occurrences.

NB. A phase difference is usually expressed as an angle on the basis that one period represents 2π radians or 360°. The unit is the radian or degree.

Phase velocity Of a sinusoidal plane progressive wave. The velocity of a point of constant phase in the direction of propagation to the wave normal.

Phon The unit of *loudness level.*

Pitch That attribute to auditory sensation in terms of which sound may be ordered on a scale related primarily to frequency.

Plane wave A wave in which the wavefronts are everywhere parallel planes normal to the direction of propagation.

Power spectrum The spectrum of the sound as expressed in terms of the *spectral density.*

Presbycusis Hearing loss mainly for high tones due to advancing age.

Pure tone A sound wave where the instantaneous sound pressure is a simple sinusoidal function of time.

Random-incidence sound-field See *Diffuse sound field.*

Rayleigh wave A type of wave which may be propagated over the free surface of a solid and is characterized by elliptical motion of the particles and an exponential decay rate of amplitude from the surface.

Reflection coefficient Of a surface or material at a given frequency. The ratio which the reflected sound pressure from a surface or material bears to the incident sound pressure.

Resonance A condition whereby the response of a system to a sinusoidal stimulus of constant magnitude reaches a maximum at a particular frequency (resonance frequency).

Resonant absorber An absorber operating by virtue of the physical resonance of some part of its structure or the air associated with it, e.g. a panel or flexible membrane which vibrates and absorbs sound.

Reverberant field A sound field resulting from the superposition of many sound waves due to reflections at the boundaries. May be approximated to a diffuse *sound field.*

Reverberation In an enclosure. The persistance of sound due to repeated reflections at the boundaries. A *reverberation chamber* is an enclosure in which all the surfaces have been made as sound-reflective as possible. Usually a room designed for specific acoustical measurements.

Reverberation time The time required for the average sound pressure level, originally in a steady state, to decrease by 60 dB after the source has stopped. The rate at which the sound pressure decreases is termed the *reverberation decay rate.*

Root mean square value The square root of the mean value of the squares of the instantaneous values of the quantity. In the case of a periodic variation the mean is taken over one period.

Shadow zone A zone where ray theory predicts zero energy. In practice the sound level is not zero. In the case of a noise barrier, the term may be used to describe the space behind a barrier that is not in a direct line of sight with the source position. In such circumstances the sound pressure level in the shadow zone may only be a few decibels below the unobstructed sound pressure field.

Shear wave A sound wave in which the particle displacement at each point in the medium is perpendicular to the wave normal. The term *transverse wave* or *rotational wave* may also be used to describe this type of particle motion.

Simple source See *Monopole.*

Sound absorption coefficient The complement of the *sound energy reflection coefficient*, i.e. it is equal to 1 minus the sound energy reflection coefficient of the surface or material. The normal incidence sound absorption coefficient is a frequently used measure and refers to the fraction of the perpendicularly incident sound energy absorbed or otherwise not reflected.

Sound energy E (Joules), the energy added to an elastic medium by the presence of sound, consisting of potential energy in the form of deviations from static pressure and of kinetic energy in the form of particle velocity.

Sound energy density D (Joules/m³) the quotient obtained when the sound energy in a region is divided by the volume of the region. The sound energy density at a point is the limit of that quotient as the volume tends to zero.

Sound energy/pressure reflection coefficient The ratio which the sound energy/pressure reflected from the surface or material bears to the incident sound energy/pressure. NB. The term 'sound reflection coefficient' usually refers to the pressure reflection coefficient.

Sound insulation The capacity of a structure to prevent sound from reaching a receiving location. Sound energy is not necessarily absorbed; impedance mismatch, or reflection back toward the source, is often the principal mechanism.

Sound intensity I(W/m³), the quotient obtained when the average rate of energy flow in a specified direction is divided by the area through which it flows. The intensity at a point is the limit of that quotient as the area tends to zero.

Sound isolation The degree of lack of acoustical connection. There are, in general, two ways to achieve a degree of sound isolation: by preventing the sound reaching the receiver, and by attenuation, reducing the intensity of sound as it travels towards a receiving location.

Sound power W(Watts), the rate at which acoustic energy, in a specified frequency band, is radiated from a source.

Sound power level L_w, ten times the common logarithm of the ratio of the sound power under consideration to the standard reference power of 1 pW (pico). The quantity obtained is expressed in decibels.

Sound pressure p (Pa), a fluctuating pressure superimposed on the static pressure by the presence of sound. In air the static pressure is barometric pressure. The term is analogous to alternating voltage and, similarly, can be expressed in several ways, such as instantaneous sound pressure, or peak sound pressure. The unqualified term generally means root-mean-square sound pressure.

Sound pressure level L_p, ten times the common logarithm of the ratio of the square of the sound pressure under consideration to the square of the standard reference pressure of 20 μPa (micro). The quantity so obtained is expressed in decibels.

NB. The pressures are squared because pressure squared rather than pressure is proportional to power or energy. In this book, where the reference pressure is omitted, a value of 20 µPa can be assumed.

Sound pressure spectrum The spectrum of a sound expressed in terms of the root-mean square pressure per unit bandwidth. This is the sound spectrum obtained from an analysis of the output from a pressure actuated microphone. It is usually plotted in terms of the rms pressure divided by the bandwidth used for the analysis which is often an *octave* or $\frac{1}{3}$*rd octave* wide.

Sound transmission coefficient The fraction of the airborne sound power, in a specified frequency band, incident on a partition that is transmitted by the partition and radiated on the other side.

Sound transmission loss TL, ten times the common logarithm of the ratio of the airborne sound power in a specified frequency band incident on a partition to the sound power transmitted by the partition and radiated on the other side. The quantity to obtained is expressed in decibels.

Specific normal acoustic impedance $Z = r + jx$, rayl (Pa. s/m), the complex quotient obtained when the sound pressure averaged over the surface is divided by the component of the particle velocity normal to the surface. The real and imaginary components of the specific normal acoustic impedance are called, respectively, *specific normal acoustic resistance* and *specific normal acoustic reactance. The specific normal acoustic admittance*, $y = g - jh$ (reciprocal rayl (m/Pa.s)), is the reciprocal of the specific normal acoustic impedance. The real and imaginary components are called the specific normal acoustic conductance and the specific normal acoustic susceptance, respectively.

Spherical wave A wave where the wavefronts are concentric spheres.

Standing waves Periodic waves having a fixed distribution in space which is the result of interference of progressive waves of the same frequency and kind. Such waves are characterized by the existence of *nodes* and *antinodes* which are fixed in space.

Temporary threshold shift The component of threshold shift which shows progressive reduction with time when the apparent cause has been removed.

Threshold of hearing Of a continuous sound, the minimum RMS value of the sound pressure which excites the sensation of hearing.

Transducer A device to receive oscillatory energy from one system and to supply related oscillatory energy to another. In acoustics the process of transduction is used to convert acoustical or mechanical energy into electrical energy.

Ultrasonic frequency A frequency lying above the audio-frequency range.

Waveform The shape of the graph representing the successive values of a varying quantity.

Wavefront The locus of parts on a progressive wave which has the same phase at a given instant.

White noise Noise of a statistically random nature having equal energy per unit frequency bandwidth over a specified frequency band.

Appendix 3

Standards Relating to Transportation Noise and its Control

A3.1 Introduction

The various chapters in this book refer to standards, regulations, recommendations and codes of practice which apply to noise and vibration measurement and transport noise and vibration control. Many international standards have been developed on these topics which have subsequently been used by different countries for their own domestic programmes. While it would be possible to list all such national and international standards which exist at the present time this would necessarily mean considerable duplication, with particular standards cited several times at different points in the list. In addition, the standards of different countries are constantly being added to

and updated and so a comprehensive coverage at any particular moment in time is not a feasible proposition. Instead this Appendix provides a summary of the standards, regulations etc., which are commonly referred to in the fields of acoustics and transportation noise and its control. Many but not all listed here also appear in the reference lists in the various chapters of this book.

Although it is intended that the list will provide a reasonably comprehensive reference to standards in different branches of the subject, and in different countries, it may well be necessary to check with the relevant standards authorities to ensure that the latest versions are being referred to. For this purpose, the appendix also contains a list of Standards Authorities and their addresses.

A3.2 List of Standards

Subject area	Standards Authority	Title	
General: Acoustical measurement and noise rating	ISO	Quantities and units of acoustics	ISO R31 Part VII:1965
	BSI	Glossary of acoustical terms	BS 661:1969
	IEC ANSI	Specification of sound level meters	IEC 651:1979 S1.4:1971
	ISO	Preferred reference quantities for acoustical levels	ISO 1683:1983
	BSI	Sound level meters (industrial grade)	BS 3489:1962
	BSI	Sound level meters for the measurement of noise emitted by motor vehicles	BS 3539:1962
	ANSI	Calibration of microphones	S1.10:1966
	IEC	Precision method for free-field calibration of one-inch standard condenser microphones by the reciprocity technique	IEC 486 (1974)
	BS	Preferred frequencies for acoustical measurement	BS 3593:1963
	ISO		ISO R266:1975
	IEC	Octave, half-octave and $\frac{1}{3}$rd octave band filters intended for the analysis of sounds and vibrations	IEC 225:1966
	ANSI	Specification for octave-band and fractional-octave-band analog and digital filters	S1.11:1986
	IEC	Definition of dynamic ranges at the input of digital signal processing equipment for acoustical measurement	Draft
	ISO	Digital processing of acoustical signals	Draft
	BSI ISO	Normal equal loudness contours for pure tones and normal threshold of hearing under free field listening conditions	BS 3383:1961 ISO R226:1961
	ISO	Expression of the power and intensity levels of a sound or noise	R357:1963
	ISO	Method for calculating loudness level	ISO R532:1975
	ISO	Relation between sound pressure levels or narrow bands of noise in a diffuse field and in a frontally incident free field for equal loudness	ISO R454:1965
	BSI	The relation between the sone scale of loudness and the phon scale of loudness level	BS 3045:1958

Subject area	Standards Authority	Title	
	ISO	Determination of sound power levels of noise sources—Guidelines for the use of basic standards and for the preparation of noise test codes	ISO 3740:1980
	ISO	Determination of sound power level of noise sources—precision methods for discrete-frequency and narrow-band sources in reverberation rooms	ISO 3742:1975
	ISO	Determination of sound power levels of noise sources—engineering methods for special reverberation test rooms	ISO 3743:1976
	ISO	Determination of sound power levels of noise sources—engineering methods for free field conditions over a reflecting plane	ISO 3744:1981
	ISO	Determination of sound power levels of noise sources—precision methods for anechoic and semi-anechoic rooms	ISO 3745:1977
	ISO	Determination of sound power levels of noise sources. Survey methods	ISO 3746:1979
	BSI	Method of measurement of attenuation of hearing protectors at threshold	BS 5108:1974
	ISO	Standard reference zero for the calibration of pure tone air conduction audiometers	ISO 389:1985
	ANSI	Criteria for background noise in audiometer rooms	S3.1:1960
	ISO	Assessment of occupational noise for hearing conservation purposes	ISO 1999:1982
	UK Department of Environment	Code of practice for reducing the exposure of employed persons to noise	1972
	UK HM Government	Control of Pollution Act	1974
	ANSI	American national standard methods for the calculation of the articulation index	ANSI S3.5:1969
	ANSI	American national standard for rating noise with respect to speech interference	ANSI S3.14:1977
	ISO	Assessment of noise with respect to its effect on the intelligibility of speech	R 3352:1974
	ISO	Recommended methods for measuring the intelligibility of speech	Draft
	ISO	Guide to the measurement of acoustical noise and the evaluation of its effect on man	ISO R2204:1973
	ANSI	Methods for the Evaluation of the potential effect on human hearing of sounds with peak A-weighted sound pressure levels above 120 dB and peak C-weighted sound pressure levels below 140 dB	S3.28:1986 (Draft)
	EEC	Proposal for a Council Directive on the protection of workers from the risks related to exposure to chemical/physical and biological agents at work	C289/1–6:1982

Subject area	Standards Authority	Title	
Building acoustics and materials	SAA	Ambient sound levels for areas of occupancy within buildings	AS 2107:1977
	UK, HM Government	Building and buildings—The noise insulation regulations (Statutory Instrument)	1763:1975
	BSI	Part 2: sound insulation and noise reduction (in buildings)	BS CP3:1972
	BSI	Measurement of airborne and impact sound transmission in buildings	BS 2750:1956
	ISO BSI	Measurement of sound insulation in buildings and of building elements—Part V field measurements of airborne sound insulation of facade elements and facades	ISO R140/5:1982 BS 2750:1980
	BSI ISO	Method for the measurement of sound absorption in a reverberation room	BS 3683:1963 ISO 354:1985
	ANSI	Sound absorption of acoustical materials in reverberation rooms	S1.7:1970
	ASTM	Standard recommended practice for laboratory measurement of airborne sound transmission of building partitions	ASTM E90–75:1975
	ASTM	Standard classification for determination of sound transmission class	ASTM E413–73:1973
	BSI	Methods for rating sound insulation in buildings and of building elements	BS 5821:1980
	ISO	Rating of sound insulation in buildings and building elements—Part 1: airborne sound insulation in buildings and of interior building elements	ISO 717/1:1982
	ISO	Rating of sound insulation in buildings and building elements—Part 2: impact sound insulation	ISO 717/2:1982
	ISO	Rating sound insulation in buildings and building elcments—Part 3: airborne sound insulation of facade elements and facades	ISO 717/3:1982
	ISO	Measurement of sound insulation in buildings and of building elements—Part 9	ISO 140/9:1985
	ASTM	Standard method of test for impedance and absorption of acoustical materials by the tube method	C 384–58:1972
	ASTM	Standard definitions of terms relating to acoustical tests of building construction and materials	ASTM C634–73:1973
	UK Department of Environment	Noise barriers, standards and materials (Technical Memorandum)	H14/76:1976
	BSI	Part 15: Specification for barriers for the attenuation of noise	BS 1722:Draft
Vibration measurements and control	ISO	Vibration and shock—vocabulary	ISO 2041:1975
	ISO	Mechanical vibration and shock affecting man. Vocabulary	ISO 5805:1981
	ISO	Guide for the evaluation of human exposure to whole body vibration	ISO 2631:1978

Subject area	Standards Authority	Title	
	ANSI	Guide to the evaluation of human exposure to vibration in buildings	S3.29:1983
	ISO	Guide for the evaluation of human exposure to vibration and shock in buildings; Addendum 1: Acceptable magnitude of vibration	ISO 2631, DAD1:1980
	DIN	Vibrations in buildings—effects on structure	DIN 4150:1984
	BSI	Guide to the selection and use of elastomeric bearings for vibration isolation of buildings	BS 6777:1982
	ISO	Vibration and shock—isolators—specifying characteristics for mechanical isolation (guide for selecting and applying resilient devices)	ISO R2017:1972 :1982
	ISO	Guidelines for the evaluation of the response of occupants of fixed structures to low frequency horizontal motion (0.063–1 Hz)	ISO 6897:1984
Vehicle and Road Traffic Noise	UK Department of Environment	Calculation of Road Traffic Noise (Technical Memorandum)	Welsh Office:1975
	ISO	Measurement of noise emitted by accelerating road vehicles	ISO R362:1981
	BSI	Method for the measurement of noise emitted by motor vehicles	BS 3425:1966
	EEC (Directive)	The permissible sound level and the exhaust system of motor vehicles (Official Journal of the European Communities)	70/157/EEC:1970
	EEC	Adapting to technical progress 70/157/EEC	73/350/EEC:1973
	EEC	Directive amending 70/157/EEC	77/212/EEC:1977
	EEC	Adapting to technical progress 70/157/EEC	81/334/EEC:1981
	EEC	Adapting to technical progress 70/157/EEC	84/372/EEC:1984
	EEC	Directive amending 70/157/EEC	84/424/EEC:1984
	EEC (Directive)	The permissible sound level and exhaust systems of motorcycles (Official Journal)	78/1015/EEC:1978
	ISO	Measurement of noise emitted by passenger cars under conditions representative of urban driving	ISO/DIS 7188:1985
	SAE	Methods of measurement of the sound emitted by motor vehicles	AS 2240:1979
	SAE	Sound level for passenger cars and light trucks	SAE J986:1972
	SAE	Exterior sound level for heavy trucks and buses	SAE J366b:1973
	ANSI	Sound level for passenger cars and light trucks	S6.3:1973
	SAE	SAE recommended practice, maximum sound level potential for motorcycles	SAE J47:1975 SAE J331a:1973

Subject area	Standards Authority	Title	
	SAE	SAE recommended practice, sound level of highway truck tires	SAE J57:1973
	SAE	SAE standard, sound level for truck cab interior	SAE J336:1973
	SAE	Exterior loudness evaluation of heavy trucks and buses	SAE J672a:Draft
	SAE	SAE recommended practice, subjective rating scale for evaluation of noise and ride comfort characteristics related to motor vehicle tyres	SAE J1060:1973
	SAE	SAE standard, performance of vehicle traffic horns	SAE J377:1969
	ISO	Road vehicles—sound signalling devices on motor vehicles, acoustic standards and specifications	ISO R512:1974
	ISO	Measurements of noise emitted by stationary road vehicles	ISO 5130:1982
	ISO	Measurements of noise inside motor vehicles	ISO 5128:1980
Railway noise	ISO	Measurement of noise emitted by railbound vehicles	ISO 3095:1975
	ISO	Measurement of noise inside railbound vehicles	ISO 3381:1976
	EPA	Railroad noise emission standards (Code of Federal Regulations)	Part 201:1976 1980 1982
	EEC	Proposal for a Council Directive on the approximation of the laws of the Member States relating to the noise emission of rail mounted vehicles (*Official Journal of the European Communities*)	C354:1983
Aircraft noise	SAE	SAE aerospace information report, jet noise prediction	SAE AIR 876:1965
	BSI IEC	Specification for frequency weighting for the measurement of aircraft noise	BS 5721:1979 IEC 537:1976
	SAE	SAE aerospace recommended practice, frequency weighting network for approximation of perceived noise level for aircraft noise	SAE ARP 1080:1969
	SAE	SAE aerospace recommended practice, definitions and procedures for computing the effective perceived noise level for flyover aircraft noise	SAE ARP 1071:1973
	ANSI	Definitions and procedures for computing the effective perceived noise level for flyover aircraft noise	S6.4:1973
	FAA	Noise standards—Aircraft type and air worthiness certification	Part 36, DOT:1974
	SAE	SAE aerospace information report, determination of minimum distance from ground observer to aircraft for acoustic tests	SAE AIR 902:1966
	ISO	Procedure for describing aircraft noise around an airport	ISO R 1761:1970

Subject area	Standards Authority	Title	
	ISO	Monitoring aircraft noise around an airport	ISO R 1761:1970
	SAE	SAE aerospace information report, methods of comparing aircraft take-off and approach noise	SAE AIR 852:1965
	ISO BS	Procedure for describing aircraft noise heard on the ground	ISO 2881:1978 BS 5727:1979
	EEC (Directive)	Limitation of noise emissions from subsonic aircraft	80/51/EEC:1980
	SAE	SAE aerospace information report, comparison of ground moving and flyover noise levels	SAE AIR 1216:1972
	SAE	SAE aerospace recommended practice standard values of absorption as a function of temperature and humidity for use in evaluating aircraft flyover noise	SAE ARP 866A:1975
	ISO	Measurement of noise inside aircraft	ISO 5129:1981
	ISO	Description and measurement of physical properties of sonic booms	ISO 2249:1973
Environmental impact appraisal and planning	UK Department of Transport	Manual of Environmental Appraisal	DTp:1983
	US Congress	National Environmental Policy Act	91st Congress:1969
	EEC (Directive)	The assessment of certain public and private projects on the environment (Official Journal)	85/337/EEC:1985
	ISO	Description and measurement of environmental noise—Part 1: basic quantities and procedures	ISO 1996/1:1982

A3.3   List of Addresses of Standards Authorities

International Organizations

International Bureau of Weights and Measures/Bureau International des Poids et Mesures (BIPM)
Pavillion de Breteuil,
92310 Sevres, France

International Commission for Conformity Certification of Electrical Equipment/Commission Internationale de Certification de Conformite de L'equipement 'Electrique (CEE, IEC)
Utrechtesecrey 310,
6812 AR Arnhem,
Netherlands

International Civil Aviation Organisation (ICAO)
Place de l'Aviation Internationale
1000 Sherbrooke Street West,
Suite 400
Montreal,
(Quebec)
Canada H3A 2RZ

International Electrotechnical Commission (IEC)
3, Rue de Varembe,
1211 Geneve 20,
Switzerland

International Organisation for Standardisation (ISO)
1, Rue de Varembe,
1211 Geneve 20,
Switzerland

Member Bodies of ISO and National Standards Authorities

Albania (BSA)
*Komiteti i Cmimeve dhe Standarteve
Prane Keshillit te Ministrave
Tirana

Algeria (INAPI)
*Institut algérien de normalisation et de propriété industrielle
5, rue Abou Hamou Moussa
B.P. 1021—Centre de tri
Alger

Argentina (IRAM)
Instituto Argentino de Racionalización de Materiales
Chile 1192
C. Postal 1098
Buenos Aires

*Agent for ISO publications.

Australia (SAA)
*Standards Association of Australia
Standards House
80–86 Arthur Street
North Sydney–N.S.W.2060

Austria (ON)
*Österreichisches Normungsinstitut
Heinestrasse 38
Postfach 130
A–1021 Wien

Bangladesh (BDSI)
*Bangladesh Standards Institution
3-DIT (Extension) Avenue
Motijheel Commercial Area
Dhaka 2

Belgium (IBN)
*Institut Belge de Normalisation
Av. de la Brabanconne, 29
B-1040 Bruxelles

Brazil (ABNT)
*Associação Brasileira de Normas Técnicas
Av. 13 de Maio, nº 13–28º andar
Caixa Postal 1680
CEP:20.003—Rio de Janeiro-RJ

Bulgaria (BDS)
*State Committee for Science and Technical Progress
Standards Office
21, 6th September Str.
1000 Sofia

Canada (SCC)
*Standards Council of Canada
International Standardization Branch
2000 Argentia Road, Suite 2-401
Mississauga, Ontario

Chile (INN)
Instituto Nacional de Normalización
Matias Cousino 64—6º piso
Casilla 995—Correo 1
Santiago

China (CAS)
China Association for Standardization
PO Box 820
Beijing

Colombia (CONTEC)
*3 Instituto Colombiano de Normas Técnicas
Carrera 37 No. 52–95
PO Box 14237
Bogota

Cuba (NC)
*Comité Estatal de Normalización
Egido 602 entre Gloria y Apodaca
Zona postal 2
La Habana

Cyprus (CYS)
Cyprus Organization for Standards and Control of Quality
Ministry of Commerce and Industry
Nicosia

Czechoslovakia (CSN)
*Uřad pro normalizaci a měřeni
Václavské náměsti 19
113 47 Praha 1

Denmark (DS)
*Dansk Standardiseringsraad
Aurehøjvej 12
Postbox 77
DK-2900 Hellerup

Egypt, Arab Rep. (EOS)
*Egyptian Organization for Standardization
2 Latin America Street
Garden City
Cairo–Egypt

Ethiopia (ESI)
*Ethiopian Standards Institution
PO Box 2310
Addis Ababa

Finland (SFS)
*Suomen Standardisoimisliitto r.y.
PO Box 205
SF–00121 Helsinki 12

France (AFNOR)
*Association Française de Normalisation
Tour Europe
Cedex 7
92080 Paris La Defense

Germany, Federal Republic (DIN)
*DIN Deutsches Institut für Normung
Burggrafenstrasse 4–10
Postfach 1107
D–1000 Berlin 30

Ghana (GSB)
*Ghana Standards Board
PO Box M.245
Accra

Greece (ELOT)
*Hellenic Organization for Standardization
Didotou 15
106 80 Athens

Hungary (MSZH)
*Magyar Szabványügyi Hivatal
Budapest
PF24
1450

India (ISI)
*India Standards Institution
Manak Bhavan
9 Bahadur Shah Zafar Marg
New Delhi 110002

Indonesia (YDNI)
*Badan Kerjasama Standardisasi LIPI–YDNI
(LIPI–YDNI Joint Standardization Committee)
Jln. Teuku Chik Ditiro 43
PO Box 250
Jakarta

Iran (ISIRI)
*Institute of Standards and Industrial Research of Iran
Ministry of Industries
PO Box 2937
Tehran

*Agent for ISO publications.

Iraq (COSQC)
Central Organization for Standardization and Quality Control
Planning Board
PO Box 13032
Aljadiria
Baghdad

Ireland (IIRS)
*Institute for Industrial Research and Standards
Ballymun Road
Dublin–9

Israel (SII)
*Standards Institution of Israel
42 University Street
Tel Aviv 69977

Italy (UNI)
*Ente Nazionale Italiano di Unificazione
Piazza Armando Diaz 2
1–20123 Milano

Ivory Coast (DINT)
Direction de la Normalisation et de la Technologie
Ministere du Plan et de l'Industrie
B.P. V65
Abidjan

Jamaica (JBS)
*Jamaica Bureau of Standards
6 Winchester Road
PO Box 113
Kingston 10

Japan (JISC)
*Japanese Industrial Standards Committee
c/o Standards Department
Agency of Industrial Science and Technology
Ministry of International Trade and Industry
1-3-1, Kasumigaseki
Chiyoda-ku
Tokyo 100

Kenya (KEBS)
*Kenya Bureau of Standards
Off Mombasa Road
Behind Belle Vue Cinema
PO Box 54974
Nairobi

Korea Democratic People's Republic of (CSK)
Committee for Standardization of the Democratic People's
Republic of Korea
Committee of the Science and Technology of the State
Sosong guyok Ryonmod dong
Pyongyang

Korea, Republic of (KBS)
*Bureau of Standards
Industrial Advancement Administration
Yongdeungpo-Dong
Seoul

Libyan Arab Jamahiriya (LYSSO)
Libyan Standards and Patent Section
Department of Industrial Organization and Services
Secretariat of Light Industries
Tripoli

Malaysia (SIRIM)
Standards and Industrial Research Institute of Malaysia
Lot 10810, Phase 3, Federal Highway
PO Box 35, Shah Alam
Selangor

Mexico (DGN)
*Dirección General de Normas
Calle Puente de Tecamachalco N°. 6
Lomas de Tecamachalco
Sección Fuentes
Naucalpan de Juárez
53 950 Mexico

Mongolia (MSC)
State Committee for Prices and Standards of the Mongolian
People's Republic
Marshal Zhukov Avenue, 51
Ulan Bator

Morocco (SNIMA)
Service de normalisation industrielle marocaine
Direction de l'industrie
Ministere du Commerce et de l'industrie
5, rue Arrich
Rabat

Netherlands (NNI)
*Nederlands Normalisatie-instituut
Kalfjeslaan 2
PO Box 5059
2600 GB Delft

New Zealand (SANZ)
*Standards Association of New Zealand
Private Bag
Wellington

Nigeria (NSO)
*Nigerian Standards Organisation
Federal Ministry of Industries
No. 4, Club Road
P.M.B. 01323
Enugu

Norway (NSF)
*Norges Standardiseringsforbund
Postboks 7020 Homansbyen
N–Oslo 3

Pakistan (PSI)
*Pakistan Standards Institution
39 Garden Road
Saddar
Karachi–3

Peru (ITINTEC)
Instituto de Investigacion Tecnologica Industrial y de Normas
Tecnicas
Jr. Morelli—2da. cuadra
Urbanizacion San Borja—Surquillo
Lima 34

Philippines (PSA)
*Product Standards Agency
Ministry of Trade and Industry
361 Sen. Gil J Puyat Avenue
Makati, Metro Manila 3117
Manila

*Agent for ISO publications.

Poland (PKNMiJ)
*Polish Committee for Standardization Measures and Quality Control
Ul. Elektoralna 2
00-139 Warszawa

Portugal (DGQ)
*Direcção-Geral da Qualidade
Rua José Estêvão, 83–A
1199 Lisboa Codex

Romania (IRS)
°Institutul Român de Standardizare
Căsuţa Poştală 63–87
Bucarest 1

Saudi Arabia (SASO)
*Saudi Arabian Standards Organization
PO Box 3437
Riyadh

Singapore (SISIR)
*Singapore Institute of Standards and Industrial Research
Maxwell Road
PO Box 2611
Singapore 9046

South Africa, Republic of
*South African Bureau of Standards
Private Bag X191
Pretoria
0001

Spain (IRANOR)
*Instituto Español de Normalización
Calle Fernandez de la Hoz, 52
Madrid 10

Sri Lanka (BCS)
*Bureau of Ceylon Standards
53 Dharmapala Mawatha
PO Box 17
Colombo 3

Sudan (SSD)
*Standards and Quality Control Department
Ministry of Industry
PO Box 2184
Khartoum

Sweden (SIS)
*SIS—Standardiseringskommissionen i Sverige
Tegnergatan 11
Box 3 295
S-103 66 Stockholm

Switzerland (SNV)
*Association suisse de normalisation
Kirchenweg 4
Postfach
8032 Zurich

Syria (SASMO)
Syrian Arab Organization for Standardization and Metrology
PO Box 11836
Damascus

Tanzania (TBS)
*Tanzania Bureau of Standards
PO Box 9524
Dar es Salaam

Thailand (TISI)
*Thai Industrial Standards Institute
Ministry of Industry
Rama VI Street
Bangkok 10400

Trinidad and Tobago (TTBS)
Trinidad and Tobago Bureau of Standards
Century Drive
Trincity Industrial Estate
Tunapuna
PO Box 467
Trinidad and Tobago

Tunisia (INNORPI)
Institut national de la normalisation et de la propriété industrielle
BP 23
1012 Tunis–Belvedere

Turkey (TSE)
*Türk Standardlari Enstitüsü
Necatibey Cad. 112
Bakanliklar
Ankara

United Kingdom (BSI)
*British Standards Institution
2 Park Street
London W1A 2BS

Department of the Environment (DOE)
Department of Transport (DTp)
2 Marsham Street
London SW1P 3PY

USA (ANSI)
*American National Standards Institute
1430 Broadway
New York, NY 10018

American Society for Testing and Materials (ASTM)
1916 Race Street
Philadelphia
PA 19103

Society of Automotive Engineers (SAE)
400 Commonwealth Drive
Warrendale
PA 15096

Federal Aviation Administration (FAA)
Washington DC
20591

USSR (GOST)
USSR State Committee for Standards
Leninsky Prospekt 9
Moskva 117049

Venezuela (COVENIN)
*Comisión Venezolana de Normas Industriales
Avda. Andrés Bello-Edf. Torre Fondo Común
Piso 11
Caracas 1050

Vietnam, Socialist Republic of (TCVN)
Direction generale de standardisation de metrologie et de controle de la qualite
70 rue Tran Hung Dao
Hanoi

*Agent for ISO publications.

Yugoslavia (SZS)
*Savezni zavod za Standardizaciju
Slobodana Penezica-Krcuna br.35
Pošt Pregr 933
11000 Beograd

Zambia (ZABS)
Zambia Bureau of Standards
National Housing Authority Building PO Box 50259
Lusaka

*Agent for ISO publications.

Appendix 4

List of Addresses

A4.1   Acoustical Societies

Australia
Australian Acoustical Society
c/o Science Centre
35 Clarence Street
Sydney N.S.W. 2000

Austria
Osterreichischer Arbeitsring fur Larmbekampfung
Wextrasse 19–23
A-1200 Wien

Belgium
Association Belge des Acousticiens
Belgische Akoestische Vereniging (ABAV)
Celestijnenlaan 200 D
B-3030 Heverles

Brazil
Sociedade Brasileira de Acustica (SOBRA)
Azevedo Baring
Caixa Postal 24085
05091 Sao Paulo SP

Canada
The Canadian Acoustical Association
PO Box 3651 Station C
Ottawa, Ontario KIY 4J7

China
Acoustical Society of China
No. 5 Zhongguancun Street
Beijing

Denmark
Danish Acoustical Society
Lundtoftevej 100
DK 2800 Lyngby

Finland
The Acoustical Society of Finland
Institutet for Arbetshygien
Bredanga Vagen 1
SF-01620 Vantaa 62

France
Groupe Acoustique Industrielle et Environment
Groupement des Acousticiens de Langue Francaise
Conservatoire National des Arts et Metiers
292 Rue St. Martin,
F-75141 Paris Cedex O3

Germany
Verein Deutscher Ingenieure
VDI-Kommission Larmminderung
4 Dusseldorf 1
Postfach 1139

Hungary
The Acoustical Commission of the Hungarian Academy of Sciences
Acoustics Research Laboratory
PO Box 132
H-1502 Budapest 112

Italy
Associazione Italiana di Acoustica
Via Cassia 1216
00189 Roma

Japan
Acoustical Society of Japan
Ikeda Building
2-7-7 Yoyogi, Shibuya-ku
Tokyo 151

The Institute of Noise Control Engineering of Japan
Kobayasi Institute of Physical Research
Kokubunji, Tokyo 185

Korea
Acoustical Society of Korea
Department of Electronics
Yonsei University
134 Shinchun-Dong
Seudamun-Ku, Seoul

Netherlands
Nederlands Akoestisch Genootschap
Postbus 162
NL-2600 AD Delft

Norway
The Acoustical Society of Norway
Acoustics Laboratory—ELAB
N-7034 Trondheim-NTH

Poland
The Committee on Acoustics of Polish Academy of Sciences
Palac Kurluty i Nauki
Skrytka pocztowa 24
00-901 Warszawa

Portugal
Sociedade Portuguesa de Acoustica
Avenida do Brasil 101
1799 Lisboa

Romania
Academia Republicii Romania
Commission d'Acoustique
125 Calea Victoriei
71 102 Bucarest

Singapore
Noise Section, Environmental Engineering Society of Singapore
National University of Singapore
Kent Ridge 0511

South Africa
The South African Acoustics Institute
National Physical Research Laboratory
PO Box 395
Pretoria

Sweden
The Swedish Acoustical Society
Institution for Taleoverforing
Kungl. Tekniska Hogskolan
104 44 Stockholm

Switzerland
Schweizerische Gesellschaft fur Akustik
Postfach 251
CH-8600 Dubendorf

United Kingdom
The Institute of Acoustics
25 Chambers Street
Edinburgh
EH1 1HU

USA
Acoustical Society of America
335 East 45th Street
New York
NY 10017

Institute of Noise Control Engineering USA
PO Box 3206
Arlington Branch
Poughkeepsie
NY 12603

A4.2   General

(AGARD) Advisory Group for Aerospace Research and Development
7 Rue Ancelle, 92200, Nuilly Sur Seine, France.

(AIAA) American Institute of Aeronautics and Astronautics
1633 Broadway, New York, NY 10019, USA.

(APTA) American Public Transit Authority
1225 Connecticut Avenue N.W., Suite 200,
Washington DC, 20036, USA.

(AECMA) Association Europeane des Constructeurs de Materiel Aerospatial
88 Boulevarde Male Sherbes, F-75008, Paris, France.

(ASME) American Society of Mechanical Engineers
345 East 47th Street, New York, NY 10017, USA.

(CEC) Co-ordinating European Council
61, New Cavendish Street, London W1M 8AR, UK.

(CSTB) Centre Scientifique and Technique du Batiment
4, Avenue du Recteur, Poincarè, 75782, Paris, France.

Establissement de Grenoble
24, Rue Joseph, Fouries, 38400, St. Martin—D'heres, France.

(DOE, DTp) Department of the Environment and Transport
Marsham Street, London SW1P 3EB, UK.

(DOT) US Department of Transport
400 Seventh Street, SW, Washington DC, 20590, USA.

(ECAC) European Civil Aviation Conference
3 Bis Villa, Emile Bergerat, F 92522, Neuilly Sur Seine, France.

(EEC) Commission of European Communities
Rue de la Loi, B-1049, Brussels, Belgium.

(EIA) Electronic Industries Association
2001 Eye Street, NW, Washington DC, 20006, USA.

(EPA) Environmental Protection Agency
Office of Noise Abatement and Control, 401 Main St SW, Washington DC, 20460, USA.

(ICAO) International Civil Aviation Organisation
1000, Sherbrooke Street West, STE. 400, Montreal H3A 2R2, Canada.

(ISVR) Institute of Sound and Vibration Research
University of Southampton, Highfield, Southampton SO9 5NH, UK.

(IEEE) Institute of Electrical and Electronic Engineers
345 East 47th Street, New York NY 10017, USA.

(IMechE) Institution of Mechanical Engineers
1, Birdcage Walk, Westminster, London SW1H 9JS, UK.

(INRETS) Institut Nationale de Recherche sur les Transport et le Securite
109 Avenue Salvador Allende, BP 75, 69672 Bron, France.

(MIRA) Motor Industry Research Association
Watling Street, Nuneaton, Warwickshire CV10 0TU, UK.

(NASA) National Aeronautics and Space Administration
Lewis Research Center, Cleveland, Ohio 44135, USA.

(NCF) Noise Control Foundaton
PO Box 2469, Arlington Branch, Poughkeepsie, NY 12603, USA.

(NPL) National Physical Laboratory
Queens Road, Teddington, Middlesex TW11 0LW, UK.

(OECD) Organisation for Economic Co-operation and Development
2 Rue Andre Pascal, Paris16, France.

(OREUIC) Office for Research and Experiments of the International Union of Railways/ Office de Recherche et d'Essais, Union Internationale des Chemins de Fer
Oudenoord 60, 3513 EV, Utrecht, Netherlands.

(SAE) Society of Automotive Engineers
400 Commonwealth Drive, Warrendale PA 15096, USA.

(UNESCO) United Nations Educational, Scientific and Cultural Organisation
7, Place de Fontenoy, 75700, Paris, France.

(WHO) World Health Organisation
Avenue Appia, 1211 Geneve 27, Switzerland.

Index